Buckley: The Law of Negligence

BUTTERWORTHS COMMON LAW SERIES

Buckley: The Law of Negligence

Fourth Edition

SERIES EDITOR

Andrew Grubb MA (Cantab), LLD (Lond), FMedSci
Professor of Medical Law and Head of Cardiff Law School, Cardiff University

AUTHOR

Richard A Buckley MA, D Phil
of Lincoln's Inn, Barrister
Professor of Law in The University of Reading
Formerly Fellow of Mansfield College, Oxford

LexisNexis®
Butterworths

Members of the LexisNexis Group worldwide

United Kingdom	LexisNexis Butterworths, a Division of Reed Elsevier (UK) Ltd, Halsbury House, 35 Chancery Lane, LONDON, WC2A 1EL, and RSH, 1–3 Baxter's Place, Leith Walk EDINBURGH EH1 3AF
Argentina	LexisNexis Argentina, BUENOS AIRES
Australia	LexisNexis Butterworths, CHATSWOOD, New South Wales
Austria	LexisNexis Verlag ARD Orac GmbH & Co KG, VIENNA
Canada	LexisNexis Butterworths, MARKHAM, Ontario
Chile	LexisNexis Chile Ltda, SANTIAGO DE CHILE
Czech Republic	Nakladatelství Orac sro, PRAGUE
France	Editions du Juris-Classeur SA, PARIS
Germany	LexisNexis Deutschland GmbH, FRANKFURT and MUNSTER
Hong Kong	LexisNexis Butterworths, HONG KONG
Hungary	HVG-Orac, BUDAPEST
India	LexisNexis Butterworths, NEW DELHI
Italy	Giuffrè Editore, MILAN
Malaysia	Malayan Law Journal Sdn Bhd, KUALA LUMPUR
New Zealand	LexisNexis Butterworths, WELLINGTON
Poland	Wydawnictwo Prawnicze LexisNexis, WARSAW
Singapore	LexisNexis Butterworths, SINGAPORE
South Africa	LexisNexis Butterworths, Durban
Switzerland	Stämpfli Verlag AG, BERNE
USA	LexisNexis, DAYTON, Ohio

First edition published in 1988
© Reed Elsevier (UK) Ltd 2005
Published by LexisNexis Butterworths

A CIP Catalogue record for this book is available from the British Library.

ISBN 0 406 95941 2

Typeset by Kerrypress Ltd, Luton, Beds, http://www.kerrypress.co.uk
Printed and bound in Great Britain by William Clowes Limited, Beccles, Suffolk
Visit LexisNexis Butterworths at www.lexisnexis.co.uk

Dedication

For Olivia

Series Preface

The common law is justifiably seen as a jewel in the crown of English law. The common law has travelled far afield to many other countries where it has been adopted and developed by the local courts. No longer the sole preserve of the judges in London (or Edinburgh and Cardiff), its durability and richness has been due in no small way to the diversity of approach that exists between the common law countries throughout the world. Many of the great judges in England, such as Coke, Mansfield, Blackburn, Atkin, Devlin, Reid and Denning, and those from overseas such as Oliver Wendell Holmes, Benjamin Cardozo and Owen Dixon, have been masters of the common law. As we enter the new Millennium, the common law continues to influence the development of law elsewhere. It will remain a major export, but now also an import, of this country.

Butterworths Common Law Series conceives of the common law in broad terms, providing analyses of the principles informing the frameworks of the law derived from judicial decisions and legislation. The *Series* seeks to provide authoritative accounts of the common law for legal practitioners, judges and academics. While providing a clear and authoritative exposition of the existing law, the *Series* also aims to identify and examine potential developments in the common law drawing on important and significant jurisprudence from other common law jurisdictions. Judges have increasingly looked to academic works for guidance on the accepted view of the law but also when contemplating a reformulation or change of direction in the law. The *Series* may, it is hoped, provide some assistance such that the law is less likely to be left undeveloped 'marching ... in the rear limping a little', to quote a famous judicial aphorism (*Mount Isa Mines v Pusey* (1970) per Windeyer J).

Andrew Grubb

Preface

The law of negligence has seen some extraordinary changes in recent times. On a doctrinal level incrementalism has replaced the confidence of a generation or so ago that a strong presumption in favour of a duty of care was appropriate whenever harm to another could be foreseen. This change of emphasis has not, however, impeded the expansion of the concepts of reasonableness and foreseeability into areas of liability formerly regarded as discrete. The most conspicuous of these is nuisance, which can no longer sensibly be regarded as separate from that of negligence. As Lord Cooke of Thorndon put it in *Delaware Mansions v Westminster City Council*, in both areas 'the concern of the common law lies in working out the fair and just content and incidents of a neighbour's duty rather than affixing a label and inferring the extent of the duty from it'. Although differences clearly exist, the degree of similarity between nuisance and negligence is such that it no longer makes sense for an account of the latter not to include treatment of the former. I have therefore sought to integrate the two areas in the present work.

This book draws upon my previously published works, *The Law of Nuisance* and *The Modern Law of Negligence,* but it contains a substantial volume of additional material and includes new chapters on professional negligence. All the pre-existing material has also been restructured and extensively rewritten. In accordance with the aims of the *Butterworths Common Law Series*, I have tried to provide an exposition of the law which combines detail with analysis, and also takes some account of the leading developments in other Commonwealth jurisdictions, as well as noting the increasing volume of academic writing in the area.

I am grateful to Reading Law School for the grant of study leave, without which the book could not have been written, and to the publishers for their professionalism and tolerance of delay. The text was completed by the end of November 2004, but a number of subsequent appellate decisions were added in brief at the proof stage.

R A Buckley
Reading, April 2005

Contents

Contents

Contents

Contents

Table of Statutes

References at the right-hand side of the column are to paragraph number. Where a paragraph number is in **bold** this indicates that the Act is set out in part or in full.

Table of Statutes

Table of Statutory Instruments

References at the right-hand side of the column are to paragraph number. Where a paragraph number is in **bold** this indicates that the Statutory Instrument is set out in part or in full.

Table of EU Legislation

Directives

Table of Cases

Table of Cases

Table of Cases

Part one

The structure of the modern law

Chapter 1

Liability for carelessness

A The changing fortunes of foreseeability

Generalisation: its rise and fall

[1.01] In the 1987 case of *Smith v Littlewoods Organisation*[1], Lord Goff of Chieveley said in the House of Lords:

> 'It is very tempting to try to solve all problems of negligence by reference to an all-embracing criterion of foreseeability, thereby effectively reducing all decisions in this field to questions of fact. But this comfortable solution is, alas, not open to us. The law has to accommodate all the untidy complexity of life; and there are circumstances where considerations of practical justice impel us to reject a general imposition of liability for foreseeable damage.'

Ten or more years before this statement was made, it seemed as though the courts *were* leaning in favour of an approach which could potentially have elevated foreseeability into an all-embracing test for negligence liability. It is true that if one goes back even further, to the years immediately following the decision in *Donoghue v Stevenson*[2], Lord Atkin's famous attempt in that case to state the law of negligence in general terms by reference to the concept of foreseeability[3] long met with a rather cautious response. It was rarely allowed to displace established rules of law which were inconsistent with it (see *Travers v Gloucester Corpn*[4] (builder's immunity)), and in some cases the courts continued to approach claims in a manner fundamentally at variance with the underlying logic of the principles propounded in it. (See *Ball v LCC*[5] ('dangerous things').) But in 1970, it seemed as though a turning point in favour of a more far-reaching application of the foreseeability principle might have been reached. In that year Lord Reid, in *Home Office v Dorset Yacht Co Ltd*[6], said in reference to Lord Atkin's speech in *Donoghue v Stevenson* that: 'the time has come when we can and should say that it ought to apply unless there is some justification or valid explanation for its exclusion.'

[1] *[1987] AC 241 at 280, [1987] 1 All ER 710 at 736.*
[2] *[1932] AC 562, [1932] All ER Rep 1.*
[3] *[1932] AC 562* at 580: 'You must take reasonable care to avoid acts or omissions which you can reasonably foresee should be likely to injure your neighbour.'
[4] *[1947] KB 71, [1946] 2 All ER 506.*
[5] *[1949] 2 KB 159, [1949] 1 All ER 1056, CA.*
[6] *[1970] AC 1004 at 1027, [1970] 2 All ER 294 at 297, HL.* In *Anns v Merton London Borough Council [1978] AC 728, [1977] 2 All ER 492, HL,* Lord Wilberforce observed that: '... it may well be that full recognition of the impact of *Donoghue v Stevenson* ... only came with the decision of this house in *Home Office v Dorset Yacht Co.*'

Anns v Merton London Borough Council and its demise

[1.02]   Lord Reid's approach was subsequently given greater emphasis in the very well-known case of *Anns v Merton London Borough Council*[1]. In that case Lord Wilberforce said that 'reasonable contemplation' that 'carelessness ... may be likely to cause damage' was sufficient to generate 'a prima facie duty of care'[2] in favour of the person likely to suffer that damage. Although Lord Wilberforce's approach was subsequently referred to in the Court of Appeal as marking 'the coming of age of the law of negligence'[3], per Goff LJ (the case was decided in 1982)), it soon became the subject of hostile judicial criticism. Lord Keith of Kinkel, in particular, was in the forefront of the criticism. In one case he observed that any tendency to treat the Wilberforce formula as being 'of a definitive character' was 'a temptation which should be resisted'[4], and in another case, when delivering the judgment of the Judicial Committee of the Privy Council, he intimated that the 'test formulated by Lord Wilberforce for determining the existence of a duty of care in negligence had been elevated to a degree of importance greater than it merits, and perhaps greater than its author intended'.[5] Other Law Lords were content to follow the lead thus given and to reject the Wilberforce approach,[6] including those who had once been among its supporters.[7] Finally, the actual decision of the House of Lords in the *Anns* case was itself overruled by a seven-member House in the 1990 case of *Murphy v Brentwood District Council*.[8]

[1]   *[1978] AC 728, [1977] 2 All ER 492, HL.*
[2]   See *[1978] AC 728 at 751–752, [1977] 2 All ER 492 at 498, HL.*
[3]   See *Paterson Zochonis & Co Ltd v Merfarken Packaging Ltd [1986] 3 All ER 522 at 539, CA.*
[4]   See *Peabody Donation Fund (Governors) v Sir Lindsay Parkinson & Co Ltd [1985] AC 210 at 240, [1984] 3 All ER 529 at 534, HL.*
[5]   See *Yuen Kun Yeu v A-G of Hong Kong [1988] AC 175 at 191, [1987] 2 All ER 705 at 710*. See also *Rowling v Takaro Properties Ltd [1988] AC 473, [1988] 1 All ER 163, PC.*
[6]   See Lord Oliver in *Murphy v Brentwood District Council [1991] 1 AC 398 at 487, [1990] 2 All ER 908 at 934–935, HL.*
[7]   Compare, for example, the observations of Lord Roskill in *Caparo Industries plc v Dickman [1990] 2 AC 605 at 628, [1990] 1 All ER 568 at 582* with those of the same Law Lord in the earlier case of *Junior Books Ltd v Veitchi Co Ltd [1983] 1 AC 520 at 541–542, [1982] 3 All ER 201 at 210–211, HL.*
[8]   *[1991] 1 AC 398, [1990] 2 All ER 908, HL.* See D Howarth 'Negligence after Murphy: Time to Re-think' [1991] 50 CLJ 58. A modified version of the *Anns* approach has, however, survived in Canada: see the decision of the Supreme Court in *Cooper v Hobart 2001 SCC 79*, discussed by Jason Neyers in 'Distilling Duty: The Supreme Court of Canada amends *Anns*' (2002) 118 LQR 221.

Generalisation gives way to 'incrementalism'

[1.03]   In *Yuen Kun Yeu v A-G of Hong Kong*[1], Lord Keith of Kinkel quoted with approval a statement by Brennan J in the High Court of Australia in *Sutherland Shire Council v Heyman*[2] as follows:

> 'It is preferable, in my view, that the law should develop novel categories of negligence incrementally and by analogy with established categories, rather than by a massive extension of a prima facie duty of care ...'

The central objection to the *Anns* concept of a 'prima facie duty of care' appears to have been rooted in a fear that, in situations not precisely covered by existing authority, such a concept would point too readily in favour of liability at the expense of important factors which might indicate the opposite conclusion. In the now leading case of *Caparo Industries v Dickman*[3] Lord Roskill said:

'Phrases such as "foreseeability", "proximity", "neighbourhood", "just and reasonable", "fairness", "voluntary acceptance of risk" or "voluntary assumption of responsibility" will be found used from to time in the different cases. But ... such phrases are not precise definitions. At best they are but labels or phrases descriptive of the very different factual situations which can exist in particular cases and which must be carefully examined in each case before it can be pragmatically determined whether a duty of care exists and, if so, what is the scope and extent of this duty. If this conclusion involves a return to the traditional categorisation of cases as pointing to the existence and scope of any duty of care ... I think this is infinitely preferable to recourse to somewhat wide generalisations which leave their practical application matters of difficulty and uncertainty.'

This statement encapsulates the approach which has found favour with the higher judiciary in preference to Lord Wilberforce's much more general formula in *Anns v Merton London Borough Council*. The new approach now appears to be of general application, and the vague notions of 'proximity' and 'justice and reasonableness' have become as central to the modern law of negligence as the longer established concept of 'assumption of responsibility'. The way in which these notions are deployed must now be examined[4].

1   *[1988] AC 175 at 191, [1987] 2 All ER 705 at 710.*
2   *(1985) 60 ALR 1 at 43–44.*
3   *[1990] 2 AC 605 at 628, [1990] 1 All ER 568 at 581–582.*
4   See also per Brooke LJ in *Parkinson v St James and Seacroft University Hospital NHS Trust [2001] EWCA Civ 530, [2001] 3 All ER 97* at para 17, (referring to *Clerk and Lindsell on Torts* (18th edn, 2000) pp346–347 and cases there cited).

B The language of the modern law

'Proximity'

[1.04]   The word 'proximity' had been used by Lord Wilberforce himself in his formula in the *Anns* case,[1] but without overmuch significance seemingly being attached to it. The approach which has been adopted in preference to that of Lord Wilberforce, however, seeks to place increased emphasis upon the notion – apparently in order to import considerations of 'policy' into the initial primary determination of whether the situation in question is one apt to create liability. Under the Wilberforce approach, such matters were to be considered openly at a later stage of the negligence inquiry as 'considerations which ought to negative, or to reduce or limit'[2] the scope of the prima facie duty of care. Since the word 'proximity' is only an empty metaphor, however, it is difficult to see its invocation for this purpose as anything other than an unfortunate step backwards to an earlier age of judicial reticence[3]. It is submitted that the restrictions on the application of the foreseeability principle, and the valid reasons for them in some cases, should be considered openly rather than be obscured by the use of opaque language.[4] In situations in which no special policy factors are involved the notion of 'proximity' appears to add nothing to the 'foreseeability' requirement itself, and therefore to be unnecessary[5].

1   See *[1978] AC 728* at 751–752, *[1977] 2 All ER 492* at 498, HL.
2   See *[1978] AC 728* at 751–752, *[1977] 2 All ER 492* at 498, per Lord Wilberforce.
3   See criticism of the proximity concept by the High Court of Australia in *Sullivan v Moody (2001) 75 ALJR 1570* (discussed by Christian Witting in 'The Three-Stage Abandoned in Australia – or not?' (2002) 118 LQR 214).

4 Cf J Steele 'Scepticism and the Law of Negligence' [1993] 52 CLJ 437 at 466, who writes that 'current decision-making techniques in the law of negligence have come to represent a partnership between exhausted principle and obscured pragmatism'.
5 See *per* Lord Oliver in *Caparo Industries v Dickman [1990] 2 AC 605* at 633, *[1990] 1 All ER 568* at 583: '… in some cases the degree of foreseeability is such that it is from that alone that the requisite degree of proximity can be deduced …'. See also *Kent v Griffiths [2000] 2 All ER 474* at paras 48–49 *per* Lord Woolf MR.

'Just and reasonable'

[1.05]   In *Peabody Donation Fund (Governors) v Sir Lindsay Parkinson & Co Ltd*[1] Lord Keith said that 'in determining whether or not a duty of care of particular scope was incumbent on a defendant it is material to take into consideration whether it is just and reasonable that it should be so'. The expression 'just and reasonable' has been adopted in later cases[2] and become part of the familiar vocabulary of the contemporary law of negligence. Like 'proximity', however, it is conspicuous for its vagueness. Perhaps the expression is best regarded as a frank admission of the fact that there is an irreducible element of intuition in the judicial process. In *Rich (Marc) & Co AG v Bishop Rock Marine*[3] the plaintiffs were the owners of cargo which was lost when the vessel in which it was being carried sank. The defendants were a classification society, one of the bodies responsible for inspecting vessels for insurance purposes, whose servant had carelessly passed the vessel as seaworthy and thereby enabled the ill-fated voyage to take place. In the House of Lords the plaintiffs contended that, as the case involved physical damage as distinct from pure economic loss, liability was not dependent upon satisfaction of the 'just and reasonableness' test but followed from the fact that what had occurred had been foreseeable. One dissentient member of the House accepted this argument, and would have found for the plaintiffs,[4] but the other members of the House rejected it and the claim failed.[5] Lord Steyn, speaking for the majority, said[6] that it was 'settled law that the elements of foreseeability and proximity as well as considerations of fairness, justice and reasonableness are relevant to all cases whatever the nature of the harm sustained by the plaintiff'.[7] In the circumstances of the instant case his Lordship considered that it was not 'just and reasonable' to impose liability in favour of the cargo-owners: to do so might render classification societies unduly defensive in carrying out their functions and would be an inappropriate use of resources when cargo-owners already enjoyed contractual claims for loss against the ship-owners[8].

1 *[1985] AC 210* at 241, *[1984] 3 All ER 529* at 534, HL.
2 See eg the passage quoted above from the speech of Lord Roskill in *Caparo Industries plc v Dickman [1990] 2 AC 605* at 628, *[1990] 1 All ER 568* at 581–582, HL and the observations of Lord Bridge in the same case: *[1990] 2 AC 605* at 618, *[1990] 1 All ER 568* at 574.
3 *[1996] AC 211*, *[1995] 3 All ER 307*, HL.
4 Lord Lloyd of Berwick.
5 Cf *Perrett v Collins [1998] 2 Lloyd's Rep 255, CA*, in which the Court of Appeal distinguished *Rich (Marc) & Co AG v Bishop Rock Marine* and held that a passenger in a light aircraft, which had crashed, was owed a duty of care by those statutorily responsible for certifying airworthiness.
6 See *[1996] AC 211* at 235, *[1995] 3 All ER 307* at 326.
7 See also *Mulcahy v Ministry of Defence [1996] QB 732*, *[1996] 2 All ER 758, CA*. The plaintiff was a soldier during the 1991 Gulf war against Iraq, who suffered personal injuries when a gun was negligently fired. Neill LJ said (at 771) that: 'The issue to be determined is whether it is fair, just and reasonable that a duty of care should be imposed on one soldier in his conduct towards another when engaging the enemy during hostilities.' (The court answered the question in the negative and the plaintiff's claim was struck out.)
8 In other contexts the nature of related contractual arrangements might point in *favour* of the imposition of negligence liability: see *British Telecommunications plc v James Thomson & Sons (Engineers) Ltd [1999] 2 All ER 241, HL*.

Flexibility and statutory powers

[1.06] The phrase 'just and reasonable' has proved particularly popular where statutory powers are concerned, often in order to emphasise that a wide variety of factors, including the purpose of the statutory provision in question,[1] may be relevant in such cases.[2] It has, for example, been invoked in a continuing debate about the extent to which, if at all, a common law duty of care should be superimposed on the statutory responsibilities of local authorities for child protection. The recent cases in this particular area have indicated that the test had been interpreted in such a way as to render the scope for liability unduly limited[3]. Nevertheless the Court of Appeal confirmed, in one of the cases, that the test itself remains a legitimate and integral part of the law of negligence[4].

1   See *Peabody Donation Fund (Governors) v Sir Lindsay Parkinson & Co Ltd [1985] AC 210, [1984] 3 All ER 529, HL.* Cf *Caparo Industries plc v Dickman [1990] 2 AC 605, [1990] 1 All ER 568, HL.*
2   For further discussion see CHAPTER 15 below.
3   See *D v East Berkshire NHS Trust [2003] 4 All ER 796.* See also *Barrett v Enfield London BC [1999] 3 All ER 193, HL.* Cf *X v Bedfordshire County Council [1995] 2 AC 633, [1995] 3 All ER 353, HL.*
4   See *D v East Berkshire NHS Trust [2003] 4 All ER 796, CA* at para 22.

Distributive justice[1]

[1.07] The language of 'fairness, justice and reasonableness' has proved particularly apposite to encapsulate reasoning based on the Aristotelian notion of 'distributive justice'[2]. This expression has recently been invoked in support of denial of recovery, when allowing it could be perceived as unfair if viewed from a wider perspective[3]: even though it would have been appropriate as between the parties themselves under the more usually applied principles of 'corrective justice'[4].

1   See Lord Steyn 'Perspectives of Corrrective and Distributive Justice in Tort Law' (John Maurice Kelly Memorial Lecture, Dublin, 2002); Richard Mullender 'Corrective Justice, Distributive Justice, and the Law of Negligence' (2001) 17 Professional Negligence 35.
2   See *Parkinson v St James Hospital [2001] 3 All ER 97,* at para [38] *per* Brooke LJ. See also *per* Hale LJ at para [82].
3   See *White v Chief Constable of South Yorkshire [1999] 1 All ER 1, HL* at 48 *per* Lord Hoffman; *McFarlane v Tayside Health Board [1999] 4 All ER 961, HL* at 977–978 *per* Lord Steyn. For trenchant criticism see Laura CH Hoyano 'Misconceptions About Wrongful Conception' (2002) 65 MLR 883 at 905: 'Distributive justice …permits the judiciary to abdicate its responsibility to identify and explain intellectually rigorous and coherent principles as the basis for decisions, in favour of an empirically untested appeal to public opinion, yielding unpredictable results …'.
4   See *McFarlane v Tayside Health Board [1999] 4 All ER 961, HL* at 990 *per* Lord Hope.

'Assumption of responsibility'

[1.08] In *White v Jones*[1] Lord Nolan said:

'It was argued that the failure by the appellants in the present case was a fault of omission, and that omission is not as a rule a ground upon which liability in negligence can be based. That argument cannot, to my mind, have any force where the omission occurs after the duty of care has been assumed by the defendant. Once the duty exists, it can make no difference whether its breach occurs by way of omission or of positive act.'

In *White v Jones* the defendant solicitors omitted to prepare changes to a client's will, when they had been instructed to do so, with the result that, on his death, his intended beneficiaries did not receive the gifts which he had sought to make. The defendants argued, inter alia, that they could not be liable for a mere omission; and that the concept of assumption of responsibility could be invoked only by a solicitor's own client and not by third parties. By a bare majority the House of Lords rejected the defendant's argument and found for the plaintiffs. In so holding they approved the decision, although not the reasoning, of Megarry V-C 15 years before in *Ross v Caunters*,[2] in which solicitors had been held liable to a beneficiary when a will failed because, due to the solicitors' carelessness, it had not been duly attested. In *White v Jones* the House of Lords chose to base liability upon the notion of assumption of responsibility, and in so doing significantly to expand the scope of the concept. Lord Browne-Wilkinson and Lord Nolan redefined it in terms of responsibility for the *work undertaken* itself rather than in terms of legal accountability to the individual who commissioned that work. Thus, Lord Browne-Wilkinson both expanded the concept to include third parties, and countered earlier criticism of the concept, in the following words:[3]

> 'Just as in the case of fiduciary duties, the assumption of responsibility referred to is the defendants' assumption of responsibility for the task, not the assumption of legal liability. Even in cases of ad hoc relationships, it is the undertaking to answer the question posed which creates the relationship. If the responsibility for the task is assumed by the defendant he thereby creates a special relationship between himself and the plaintiff in relation to which the law (not the defendant) attaches a duty to carry out carefully the task so assumed. If this be the right view, it does much to allay the doubts about the utility of the concept of assumption of responsibility ... As I read those judicial criticisms they proceed on the footing that the phrase "assumption of responsibility" refers to the defendant having assumed legal responsibility. I doubt whether the same criticisms would have been directed at the phrase if the words had been understood, as I think they should be, as referring to a conscious assumption of responsibility for the task rather than a conscious assumption of legal liability to the plaintiff for its careful performance.'

1 *[1995] 2 AC 207 at 295, [1995] 1 All ER 691 at 736, HL.*
2 *[1980] Ch 297, [1979] 3 All ER 580.*
3 See *[1995] 1 All ER 691 at 715–716, HL.*

Intuitive appeal

[1.09]   The concept of 'assumption of responsibility' has been subjected to powerful criticism.[1] It is undeniably heavily infected with both fiction and circularity. Nevertheless, the law of negligence itself is pervaded by an uneasy and unstable relationship between intuitive notions of responsibility on the one hand and broader questions of social policy on the other.[2] As long as this tension persists, the search for an appropriate conceptual structure will be as inevitable as its discovery will be elusive.[3] Despite the logical difficulties, the concept of 'assumption of responsibility' clearly retains a degree of intuitive appeal. It was applied in novel circumstances in *Watson v British Boxing Board of Control*[4]. The Board, a non-statutory organisation, took it upon itself to regulate professional boxing and to stipulate the level of medical support which should be available at the ringside. The Court of Appeal held that the stipulated requirements were inadequate and imposed liability upon the Board in favour of a boxer who suffered brain damage. Lord Phillips MR said[5]:

> 'It seems to me that the authorities support a principle that, where A places himself in a relationship to B in which B's physical safety becomes dependent

upon the acts or omissions of A, A's conduct can suffice to impose on A a duty to exercise reasonable care for B's safety. In such circumstances A's conduct can accurately be described as the assumption of responsibility for B, whether "responsibility" is given its lay or legal meaning.'

[1] See especially K Barker 'Unreliable Assumptions in the Modern Law of Negligence' (1993) 109 LQR 461.
[2] Cf B Hepple 'Negligence: The Search for Coherence' (1997) 50 CLP 69.
[3] See, generally, the papers collected in D Owen (ed) *Philosophical Foundations of Tort Law* (1995).
[4] *[2001] QB 1134, CA.* See also *Perrett v Collins [1998] 2 Lloyd's Rep 255, CA.*
[5] See *[2001] QB 1134* at para. 49. The decision of the Court of Appeal in *Watson's* case is criticised by James George in (2002) 65 MLR 106.

Overcoming immunity

[1.10] If a claimant is seeking to impose liability in a context in which a degree of policy-based immunity has been held to exist, the presence of a *specific* undertaking given by the defendant to the claimant may enable the immunity to be overcome on the basis that responsibility had been assumed in the circumstances. Thus, in *W v Essex County Council*[1] the House of Lords, affirming a majority decision of the Court of Appeal, refused to strike out a claim alleging negligence by social workers; a situation in which, at that time, the courts were reluctant to impose liability[2]. One of the distinguishing features in *W*'s case, which was considered arguably to justify the imposition of liability, was that one of the social workers involved had provided specific assurances which were 'integral'[3] to the plaintiff's case.[4]

[1] *[2000] 2 All ER 237, HL.*
[2] See *X v Bedfordshire County Council [1995] 2 AC 633, [1995] 3 All ER 353, HL.* Cf *D v East Berkshire NHS Trust [2003] 4 All ER 796.*
[3] See *per* Judge LJ in the Court of Appeal: *[1998] 3 All ER 111* at 136.
[4] Cf *Welton v North Cornwall District Council [1997] 1 WLR 570, [1997] PNLR 108, CA.* See also *Swinney v Chief Constable of the Northumbria Police [1997] QB 464, [1996] 3 All ER 449, CA*, discussed at para [1.34] below.

Justiciability of 'policy'

[1.11] An even more extreme view than that which favours the shielding of what are loosely termed 'policy' factors behind expressions such as 'proximity' and 'justice and reasonableness' is the thesis that such factors are not justiciable at all. In *McLoughlin v O'Brian*,[1] in which the House of Lords had to consider the extent of liability for psychiatric damage, Lord Scarman expressed the view that consideration of the well-known 'floodgates' argument, the fear of uncontrollably large numbers of plaintiffs in certain situations, was outside the proper scope of the judicial function. He said:

'… the policy issue where to draw the line is not justiciable. The considerations relevant to a decision are not such as to be capable of being handled within the limits of the forensic process.'[2]

This statement provoked a sharp response from Lord Edmund-Davies in the same case, who referred to explicit judicial statements to the contrary.[3] 'My Lords', he asserted, 'in accordance with such a line of authorities I hold that public policy issues are "justiciable" '.[4]

[1] *[1983] 1 AC 410, [1982] 2 All ER 298, HL.*

2   *[1983] 1 AC 410 at 431, [1982] 2 All ER 298* at 311. See also, per Lord Roskill in *Junior Books v Veitchi [1983] 1 AC 520* at 539, *[1982] 3 All ER 201* at 209: 'My Lords, although it cannot be denied that policy considerations have from time to time been allowed to play their part in the last century and the present either in limiting or in extending in the scope of the tort of negligence since it first developed as it were in its own right in the course of the last century, yet today I think its scope is best determined by considerations of principle rather than of policy.'
3   *Rondel v Worsley [1969] 1 AC 191* at 228, *[1967] 3 All ER 993* at 998 (Lord Reid); *Home Office v Dorset Yacht Co [1970] AC 1004* at 1058, *[1970] 2 All ER 294* at 324 (Lord Diplock); *British Railways Board v Herrington [1972] AC 877 at 897, [1972] 1 All ER 749* at 756–757 (Lord Reid).
4   *[1983] 1 AC 410* at 428, *[1982] 2 All ER 298* at 309 (emphasis is that of Lord Edmund-Davies).

Ambiguity

[1.12]   Part of the difficulty here is perhaps an ambiguity in the notion of 'policy' itself. Lord Scarman was apparently concerned, on constitutional grounds, that the courts should not interfere in areas properly belonging solely to the legislature.[1] Clearly, the courts should not attempt to involve themselves in broad social and political questions such as, for example, the delineation of the boundaries of the welfare state or the desirability of retaining nuclear weapons.[2] There are also situations in which the judges appropriately defer to Parliament, not for constitutional reasons, but simply because the higher degree of generality which legislation can achieve makes it a more appropriate form of law-making for the particular area in question.[3] Difficult questions can arise when Parliament has already legislated in the general area, but omitted to deal with the particular point in issue. Was the limited scope of the legislation a clear decision in favour of the status quo, or did it reflect an acceptance that room should be left for further development by the common law itself?[4]. Furthermore, special principles apply to cases involving negligence claims based upon alleged carelessness in the exercise of statutory powers, in order to ensure that the various activities of public bodies are not unduly fettered.[5] But it is simply not accurate to categorise *any* judicial concern for the likely *consequences* of deciding a particular case one way or the other, for example, whether it will give rise to many more claims or generate anomaly in analogous situations, as raising constitutional or other issues of this kind. Indeed, consideration of such matters seems to be inherent in the common law process itself. The decision whether to extend or limit the applicability of principles laid down in previous cases cannot be made in a total vacuum. It is therefore submitted that the objections of Lord Scarman were misconceived and that the views of Lord Edmund-Davies are to be preferred

1   Ie '… the courts' function is to adjudicate according to principle, leaving policy curtailment to the judgment of Parliament … If principle leads to results which are thought to be socially unacceptable Parliament can legislate to draw a line or map out a new path': *[1983] 1 AC 410* at 430, *[1982] 2 All ER 298* at 310, HL.
2   Cf *Chandler v DPP [1964] AC 763, [1962] 3 WLR 694.*
3   See *Morgans v Launchbury [1973] AC 127, [1972] 2 All ER 606, HL.* See also *Southwark London BC v Mills [1999] 4 All ER 449* at 454, HL *per* Lord Hoffman.
4   See eg *per* Lord Hoffman in *Arthur J S Hall v Simons [2000] 3 All ER 673* at 704, HL. See also para [1.46] below.
5   See generally CHAPTER 15 below.

C Omissions

Crucial distinction

[1.13]   The question of the extent of liability for inaction raises fundamental issues for the nature of civil liability which emphasis upon 'foreseeability' alone cannot resolve. In *Stovin v Wise*[1] Lord Hoffmann said:

'There are sound reasons why omissions require different treatment from positive conduct. It is one thing for the law to say that a person who undertakes some activity shall take reasonable care not to cause damage to others. It is another thing for the law to require that a person who is doing nothing in particular shall take steps to prevent another from suffering harm from the acts of third parties ... or natural causes.'

Although in borderline cases the distinction between acts and omissions may obviously be difficult to draw, that does not derogate from its crucial importance to any system of civil liability based upon intuitive notions of responsibility[2] or, indeed, upon any conception of human action which is geared to the notion of freedom to make choices.[3]

[1]   *[1996] AC 923 at 943, [1996] 3 All ER 801* at 819, HL.
[2]   Cf *Barrett v Ministry of Defence [1995] 3 All ER 87*, in which a naval rating died as a result of excessive drinking. The Court of Appeal declined to hold the defendants liable for failing to discourage such activities. Beldam LJ considered that: 'To dilute self-responsibility and to blame one adult for another's lack of self-control is neither just nor reasonable and in the development of the law of negligence an increment too far' ([1995] 3 All ER 87 at 95). But see also *Jebson v Ministry of Defence [2000] 1 WLR 2055, CA*, in which *Barrett's* case was distinguished and a soldier succeeded in a claim for injuries sustained while drunk (subject to a 75% deduction for contributory negligence).
[3]   See T Honore 'Are Omissions Less Culpable?' in Cane and Stapleton (eds) *Essays for Patrick Atiyah* (1991).

Dangers where the distinction is overlooked

[1.14]   It has been persuasively argued that many of the apparent difficulties in the contemporary law of negligence can be attributed to a tendency to lose sight of the distinction between acts and omissions,[1] and to treat foreseeability as a sufficient justification for imposing liability even in cases of nonfeasance.[2] Thus, in *Anns v Merton London Borough Council*[3] the House of Lords held that liability could exist where the defendant local authority had allegedly failed to exercise powers of housing inspection which might, if an inspection had actually taken place, have prevented a careless builder from inflicting loss on the plaintiffs. In effect, the existence of the statutory power to inspect, contained in the *Public Health Act 1936*, was held to create a relationship between the plaintiffs and the defendant local authority, whereby the latter were exceptionally under a positive duty to take measures to protect the former from harm inflicted by third parties. In view, however, of the great emphasis placed in the case on foreseeability as a criterion of liability, the legitimacy of using the legislation in question as a basis for creating an exception to the general principle of no liability for mere omissions did not receive the attention which it might have done. This in turn may have led to the making, albeit unsuccessfully, of claims which would more readily have been perceived to be doomed if foreseeability had not been wrongly regarded as a universal panacea which had obliterated the distinction between acts and omissions. It is significant that many of the cases in which the general formula developed by Lord Wilberforce in *Anns v Merton London Borough Council* was criticised involved, as had *Anns* itself, attempts to impose liability in negligence upon a defendant for *omitting* to prevent a third party from inflicting harm upon a plaintiff. It is perhaps unfortunate that the strictures on the Wilberforce formula contained in those cases were not confined to that context, so that the generalising tendency of the formula could continue to have been regarded as useful in the rather more straightforward situation of harm caused by positive action.[4]

¹ See Smith and Burns '*Donoghue v Stevenson*: the Not So Golden Anniversary' (1983) 46 MLR 147 (cited by Lord Bridge in *Curran v Northern Ireland Co-ownership Housing Association [1987] AC 718 at 724, [1987] 2 All ER 13* at 17, HL).

² There can, of course, be liability for nonfeasance provided further conditions are satisfied: eg for situations involving failure to exercise control over a third party (see below) and situations involving an assumption of responsibility by the defendant.

³ *[1978] AC 728, [1977] 2 All ER 492*, HL.

⁴ It is noteworthy that in *Yuen Kun Yeu v A-G of Hong Kong* Lord Keith sought to reinforce his argument for reducing the emphasis upon foreseeability which the *Anns* formula had promoted by observing that '... otherwise there would be liability in negligence on the part of one who sees another about to walk over a cliff with his head in the air and forbears to shout a warning'. But this is an example of an omission and is therefore beside the point as far as liability for misfeasance is concerned.

Distinction applied

[1.15] In *P Perl (Exporters) v Camden London Borough Council*¹ the plaintiffs and defendants owned adjoining basement flats. The plaintiffs ran a clothing business and used their flat for the purpose of storage. The defendants' flat was unoccupied and, despite the fact that they received complaints about lack of security, and were aware that their premises were accessible to vagrants, the defendants took no action even to ensure that their flat was adequately locked. One day thieves broke onto the defendants' premises, drilled a hole through the wall which separated the two flats, and stole a substantial number of the plaintiffs' garments. The plaintiffs sued the defendants for negligence, and although they succeeded at first instance, they failed before a unanimous Court of Appeal.² Waller LJ observed that: 'It is not sought here to make the appellants liable for any act, it is sought to make the appellants liable for an omission to act'.³ His Lordship went on to conclude that, despite the 'very considerable carelessness on the part of the appellants', he was satisfied that there was 'no breach of duty by the appellants to the respondents'.⁴ This decision was clearly correct. To have upheld the trial judge would have had far-reaching and unacceptably harsh potential consequences for very many occupiers.⁵ The decision in *Perl* was subsequently followed, by the Court of Appeal itself, in *King v Liverpool City Council*.⁶ In this case a local authority's failure to prevent vandals from so damaging an empty council flat, that water flooded from it into the plaintiff's flat, was held not to give rise to liability.

¹ *[1984] QB 342, [1983] 3 All ER 161, CA*. For discussion see M A Jones (1984) 47 MLR 223.

² See also *Lamb v Camden London BC [1981] QB 625, [1981] 2 All ER 408, CA*, but cf *Ward v Cannock Chase District Council [1986] Ch 546, [1985] 3 All ER 537* (a special case in which the defendants had assumed responsibility to take measures to protect the plaintiff).

³ *[1984] QB 342 at 352*. See also per Oliver LJ at 352: '... the case is one, not of an act, but of an omission.'

⁴ *[1984] QB 342 at 352*. A duty in not dissimilar circumstances might, however, be impliedly created by a contract between the parties: see *Stansbie v Troman [1948] 2 KB 48, [1948] 1 All ER 599, CA*.

⁵ 'Is every occupier of a terraced house under a duty to his neighbours to shut his windows or lock his door when he goes out, or to keep access to his cellars secure, or even to remove his fire escape, at the risk of being held liable in damages if thieves thereby obtain access to his own house and thence to his neighbours house? I cannot think that the law imposes any such duty', per Robert Goff LJ (*[1984] QB 342 at 360*). See also per Oliver LJ at 357–358.

⁶ *[1986] 3 All ER 544, [1986] 1 WLR 890, CA*.

Smith v Littlewood's Organisation

[1.16] The whole matter received the attention of the House of Lords in *Smith v Littlewood's Organisation*,¹ in which vandals set fire to an empty cinema owned by the defendants. The fire spread to the plaintiff's adjoining property. Again, the claim failed[2]. Although the decision was unanimous, it is interesting that their Lordships revealed differing approaches to the solution of the problem. Two members of the House delivered full speeches. Lord Mackay of Clashfern insisted that foreseeability should be the determining factor even in cases involving omissions to prevent harm being caused by third parties; but the difficulty of predicting the activities of such parties would mean that liability would rarely be imposed. Lord Goff of Chieveley, on the other hand, consistently with his earlier judgment in *P Perl (Exporters) v Camden London Borough Council*,[3] rejected this view. 'I wish to emphasise', he said, 'that I do not think that the problem in these cases can be solved simply through the mechanism of foreseeability'. Earlier in his speech he stated simply: 'Why does the law not recognise a general duty to prevent others from suffering loss or damage caused by the deliberate wrongdoing of third parties? The fundamental reason is that the common law does not impose liability for what are called pure omissions.' It is respectfully submitted that the approach of Lord Goff is the correct one.[4] It was applied by the Court of Appeal in *Banque Financiere v Westgate Insurance*[5] to deny liability where one of the parties to a negotiation omitted to pass on to the other party information, of which it had happened to become aware, to the effect that that party had been defrauded by one of its own agents.

[1]   *[1987] AC 241, [1987] 1 All ER 710*, HL. See Professor B S Markesinis 'Negligence, Nuisance and Affirmative Duties of Action' (1989) 105 LQR 104.
[2]   See also the decision of the High Court of Australia in *Modbury Triangle Shopping Centre Pty v Anzil (2000) 75 ALJR 164* (no liability for leaving shopping centre car park unlit after dark enabling criminals to attack the claimant). For comment see Margaret Fordham 'Liability for the criminal acts of third parties' (2001) 117 LQR 178.
[3]   *[1984] QB 342, [1983] 3 All ER 161*.
[4]   But for a powerful argument in support of Lord Mackay's approach see D Howarth 'My Brother's Keeper? Liability for Acts of Third Parties' (1994) 14 LS 88.
[5]   *[1989] 2 All ER 952*; affd on other grounds in *[1990] 2 All ER 947, HL*. See also *Bank of Nova Scotia v Hellenic Mutual Ltd [1990] 1 QB 818, [1989] 3 All ER 628, CA*.

Failure to exercise control

[1.17]   One situation in which an exception is made to the general proposition that failure to prevent third parties from causing harm does not give rise to liability is where the defendant is in a position actually to *control* their activities. Thus, in the leading case of *Home Office v Dorset Yacht Co*[1] the House of Lords held that borstal officers, and hence the Home Office as their employer, could in principle be liable for negligence if, owing to neglect of their duties, inmates of a borstal institution escaped and did damage.[2] Even here, however, it is significant that the foreseeability test is not applied *simpliciter*. Lord Reid observed that:

> 'where human action forms one of the links between the original wrongdoing of the defendant and the loss suffered by the plaintiff, that action must at least have been something very likely to happen if it is not to be regarded as novus actus interveniens breaking the chain of causation. I do not think that a mere foreseeable possibility is or should be sufficient ...'[3]

The ordinary test of foreseeability is, however, likely to be appropriate where failure to control animals[4] or young children[5] is the basis of complaint. But where intentional adult activity is concerned, and the degree of control over that activity enjoyed by the defendant is either non-existent or very low, the claimant will fail even if the likelihood of harm occurring is very high. This is because the case will fall within the general rule of non-liability for mere omissions. *Home Office v Dorset Yacht Co* was, therefore, distinguished by the House of Lords itself in *Hill v Chief Constable of West Yorkshire*.[6] In this case it was held that, even assuming that the police had been at fault in failing to apprehend a murderer as quickly as they should have done, making it very probable that he would strike again, this was not sufficient to render them liable in negligence in respect of the murderer's activities.[7] On the other hand, allowing a recent, and potentially unstable, recruit to the police service to have access to a firearm, which he used in a personal dispute, has been held to be negligent[8].

---

1   *[1970] AC 1004, [1970] 2 All ER 294*. See also *Vicar of Writtle v Essex CC (1979) 77 LGR 656*. Cf *Smith v Scott [1973] Ch 314, [1972] 3 All ER 645*.
2   If there is a substantial gap in terms of time and space between the initial escape, and the damage done by the escapee, the claim is likely to fail on general grounds of remoteness: see *O'Reilly v C [1978] 3 WWR 145 (Can)*.
3   *[1970] AC 1004* at 1030, *[1970] 2 All ER 294* at 300. It is noteworthy that, in a subsequent case, Lord Reid's dictum was actually criticised on the ground that *it did not go far enough* in emphasising the need for an exceptionally high degree of probability where intervening human acts are concerned: see *Lamb v Camden London, CA [1981] QB 625* at 635, *[1981] 2 All ER 408* at 412–413, per Lord Denning MR. See also per Oliver LJ at 642–643. This was, however, a case in which the defendants were strangers over whom the defendants had no control.
4   See *Draper v Hodder [1972] 2 QB 556, [1972] 2 All ER 210, CA.*
5   See *Camarthenshire CC v Lewis [1955] AC 549, [1955] 1 All ER 568, HL*. A school can therefore be liable for failure to prevent bullying: see *Bradford-Smart v West Sussex County Council (2001) 3 LGLR 28, CA* (no liability on the facts).
6   *[1989] AC 53, [1988] 2 All ER 238, HL* (affg *[1988] QB 60, [1987] 1 All ER 1173, CA*).
7   See also *Palmer v Tees Health Authority (2000) 2 LGLR 69, CA.*
8   See *Attorney-General of the British Virgin Islands v Hartwell [2004] 1 WLR 1273, PC.*

Failure to rescue

[1.18]   The distinction between acts and omissions has been applied in favour of other emergency services, as well as the police. Thus the fire-brigade and the coastguard have successfully defeated claims against them on the basis that the failure of the former to extinguish a fire[1], and of the latter to effect a rescue at sea[2], constituted mere omissions. In other cases, however, notions such as that of 'assumption of responsibility' have been invoked to warrant the imposition of liability on the emergency services[3]. The position of such services is therefore considered at greater length below.

---

1   See *Capital and Counties plc v Hampshire CC [1997] QB 1004, [1997] 2 All ER 865, CA.*
2   See *OLL v Secretary of State for Transport [1997] 3 All ER 897.*
3   See *Kent v Griffiths [2000] 2 All ER 474, CA* (ambulance service).

D The erosion of traditional immunities

[1.19]   A marked feature of the expansion of the tort of negligence in recent decades has been the progressive erosion of a number of earlier immunities from liability which had managed to survive the decision in *Donoghue v Stevenson* itself.

Negligent misstatement and economic loss

[1.20]   In 1990, the House of Lords emphatically re-stated the long-standing judicial hostility to the recovery of pure economic loss.[1] Nevertheless, the much earlier decision of the House in *Hedley Byrne & Co v Heller & Partners Ltd*[2] remains a landmark which shattered the assumption that the tort of negligence did not extend in any circumstances to the protection of purely economic interests. And its continuing influence is apparent in a trio of relatively recent decisions in which the House of Lords significantly extended the scope of liability for pure economic loss, in negligent misstatement or analogous situations.[3] These issues are dealt with in subsequent chapters.[4]

[1]   See especially *Murphy v Brentwood District Council [1991] 1 AC 398, [1990] 2 All ER 908, HL*.
[2]   *[1964] AC 465, [1963] 2 All ER 575, HL*.
[3]   See *Spring v Guardian Assurance [1995] 2 AC 296, [1994] 3 All ER 129, HL*; *White v Jones [1995] 2 AC 207, [1995] 1 All ER 691, HL*; *Henderson v Merrett Syndicates [1995] 2 AC 145, [1994] 3 All ER 506, HL*.
[4]   See CHAPTERS 4 and 5 below.

Advocates

[1.21]   In *Arthur J S Hall v Simons*[1], decided in the year 2000, a seven-member House of Lords swept away the limited immunity from liability for negligence enjoyed by advocates[2]. In so holding the House consigned to history its own decision, thirty years before, in *Rondel v Worsley*[3]. The position of advocates is considered in detail in a later chapter[4].

[1]   *[2000] 3 All ER 673*.
[2]   See *Kelley v Corston [1998] QB 686, [1997] 4 All ER 466, CA*. Cf *Saif Ali v Sydney Mitchell [1980] AC 198, [1978] 3 All ER 1033, HL*.
[3]   *[1969] 1 AC 191, [1967] 3 All ER 993, HL*.
[4]   See below CHAPTER 8.

Buildings

[1.22]   It has long been the law that the vendor or lessor of real property owes no duty of care in negligence to purchasers or lessees, or to third parties,[1] with respect to the state of the premises.[2] This is so even if the vendor or lessor is actually aware that the premises are in a dangerous or dilapidated condition.[3] In *Bottomley v Bannister*[4] the Court of Appeal held that this so-called owner's immunity even protected *builders* from a negligence action when they had built on their own land, and subsequently sold, a house so defectively constructed as to cause the deaths of two inhabitants. This case was decided shortly before *Donoghue v Stevenson*, but in a subsequent case it was expressly held that the immunity of builder-owners had survived the decision of the House of Lords in that case.[5] More recently, however, the expansion of the tort of negligence resulted in this immunity being regarded with judicial hostility. It was first made clear that the immunity did not extend automatically to all situations involving realty, so that builders who had not also been owners of the land were unable to invoke it.[6] Finally, in *Anns v Merton London Borough Council*,[7] *Bottomley v Bannister* was overruled.

[1]   There may, however, be liability to third parties in nuisance: see *Brew Bros v Snax [1970] 1 QB 612, [1970] 1 All ER 587, CA*. See below CHAPTER 11.
[2]   'Fraud apart, there is no law against letting a tumble-down house': *Robbins v Jones (1863) 15 CB (NS) 221* at 240. See also *Baxter v Camden London BC [1999] 1 All ER 237, CA*, affmd sub. nom *Southwark BC v Mills [1999] 4 All ER 449, HL*.
[3]   See *Cavalier v Pope [1906] AC 428, HL*: a case which 'must be kept in close confinement', per Stephenson LJ in *Rimmer v Liverpool City Council [1985] QB 1* at 9, *[1984] 1 All ER 930* at 935, CA, echoing Denning LJ in *Greene v Chelsea BC [1954] 2 QB 127* at 138, *[1954] 2 All ER 318* at 324, CA.

⁴   *[1932] 1 KB 458, CA.*
⁵   See *Otto v Bolton and Norris [1936] 2 KB 46, [1936] 1 All ER 960.* See also *Davis v Foots [1940] 1 KB 116, [1939] 4 All ER 4, CA; Travers v Gloucester Corpn [1947] KB 71, [1946] 2 All ER 506.*
⁶   See *Sharpe v Sweeting [1963] 2 All ER 455, [1963] 1 WLR 665; Gallagher v McDowell [1961] NI 26.* Cf *Green v Chelsea BC [1954] 2 QB 127, [1954] 2 All ER 318, CA.* See also the *Defective Premises Act 1972, s 1.*
⁷   *[1978] AC 728, [1977] 2 All ER 492, HL.* See also *Batty v Metropolitan Property Realisations Ltd [1978] QB 554, [1978] 2 All ER 445, CA.*

Limited scope of surviving immunity

[1.23]   The overruling of *Anns* itself in order to disallow the recovery of pure economic loss,¹ has not had the effect of re-instating *Bottomley v Bannister* as far as physical injury or damage is concerned.² Thus, although two recent decisions of the House of Lords have held expressly that pure economic losses, such as the cost of repair, cannot be recovered in negligence actions against builders with whom the plaintiffs were not in contractual relationships,³ both builders and builder-owners whose carelessness causes physical injury or damage to subsequent owners or occupiers will remain liable in tort.⁴ Moreover, architects can also be liable on the same principle to subsequent owners with whom they had no contract⁵. Nevertheless, the immunity of a 'bare' landlord or vendor (ie one who was not also the builder) still survives. 'It may be', said Stephenson LJ in *Rimmer v Liverpool City Council*,⁶ 'that to impose a duty on all landowners who let or sell their land and dwellings, whether or not they are their own designers or builders, would be so great a change in the law as to require legislation'. But it should not be overlooked that lessors may be liable in public nuisance to third parties not actually on the premises, and that such liability extends to damages for personal injury.⁷ This being the case, it must be doubted whether the immunity would survive a thorough examination of the area by the House of Lords. Moreover, a limited statutory liability for failure to repair is imposed upon landlords by the *Defective Premises Act 1972, s 4.*⁸

¹   See *Murphy v Brentwood District Council [1991] 1 AC 398, [1990] 2 All ER 908, HL.*
²   See *Targett v Torfaen Borough Council [1992] 3 All ER 27, CA.*
³   See *D & F Estates Ltd v Church Comrs for England [1989] AC 177, [1988] 2 All ER 992, HL* and *Department of the Environment v Thomas Bates & Son [1991] 1 AC 499, [1990] 2 All ER 943, HL.* For further discussion see CHAPTER 5 below.
⁴   See *Rimmer v Liverpool City Council [1985] QB 1, [1984] 1 All ER 930, CA.* See also *Targett v Torfaen Borough Council [1992] 3 All ER 27, CA.*
⁵   See *Baxall Securities v Sheard Walshaw Partnership [2001] Lloyd's Rep PN 85* (revsd. on other grounds in *[2002] Lloyd's Rep P.N. 231, CA*). See also *Tesco Stores v The Norman Hitchcox Partnership [1998] 56 Con LR 42.*
⁶   *[1984] QB 1 at 16, [1984] 1 All ER 930 at 939.*
⁷   See CHAPTER 14 below.
⁸   See CHAPTER 10 below

Effect of the European Convention on Human Rights

[1.24]   A factor which may now destabilise immunities from liability is Article 6(1) of the European Convention on Human Rights, which provides that 'everyone is entitled to a fair and public hearing' for 'the determination of his civil rights and obligations'. In one case this provision was controversially interpreted by the European Court of Human Rights in such a way as to call into question the validity of any principles which have the effect of negating liability without detailed scrutiny of the facts of the individual claim¹. Subsequently, however, the European Court modified the position which it had earlier adopted in relation to the application of the Article to the way in which English courts resolve disputes². Moreover, the House of Lords has confirmed that immunities conferred by the substantive (as distinct from the procedural) law of a member state are beyond the reach of Article 6(1), provided no fundamental right conferred by the Convention is contravened³. Nevertheless the Article, and the jurisprudence associated with it, should have the effect of ensuring that surviving 'immunities' are no wider than necessary for the achievement of their purpose. Thus, Lord Woolf MR has observed that a 'positive consequence' of the approach based upon the Convention is that it 'does draw attention to the fact that in this area of the law there is a danger that statements made in judgments will be applied more widely and rigidly than was in fact intended'⁴. In the light of these developments, the courts are now particularly reluctant to accede to striking out applications which are based on the argument that it would not be 'just and reasonable' to impose a duty of care: the balancing exercise implicit in that stage of the negligence inquiry is usually best carried out at trial rather than on the basis of assumed facts⁵. That balancing exercise does, however, remain an integral and legitimate part of the law of negligence and does not, in itself, involve any violation of Article 6⁶.

¹ See *Osman v UK (1998) 5 BHRC 293, ECtHR*, and discussion by Lord Browne-Wilkinson in *Barrett v Enfield London BC [1999] 3 All ER 193* at 198–200, HL.
² See *Z v UK (2001) 10 BHRC 384, ECtHR*. See Conor A Gearty 'Osman Unravels' (2002) 65 MLR 87.
³ See *Matthews v Ministry of Defence [2003] 1 All ER 689.*
⁴ See *Kent v Griffiths [2000] 2 All ER 474* at 484, CA.
⁵ See *L v Reading Borough Council [2001] 1 WLR 1575, CA.*
⁶ See *D v East Berkshire NHS Trust [2003] 4 All ER 796, CA* at para 22 per Lord Phillips MR.

E Factors which can limit liability

[1.25]   A court faced with a negligence claim in a novel situation is now obliged to consider whether liability should be extended incrementally by analogy with previous decisions. Whether the court chooses to make its reasoning explicit, or instead to adopt the more reticent stance on the open discussion of 'policy' issues facilitated by the 'just and reasonable' approach, several factors can be identified as being among those which may be relevant to resolution of the issue for or against expansion.¹

¹ See J Stapleton 'Duty of Care: Peripheral Parties and Alternative Opportunities for Deterrence' (1995) 111 LQR 301, for a theoretical analysis of the 'need to develop countervailing principles to restrain the explosive potential of negligence liability' (at 341).

'Floodgates' argument

[1.26]   Probably the most familiar 'policy' argument is that it would be wrong to allow the claimant to succeed because so many other people have suffered, or could suffer, loss or damage in similar situations, in a manner indistinguishable in principle from that of the claimant, that the field of liability thus opened up could be uncontrollable and potentially oppressive on defendants. This argument still exerts a powerful influence in restricting liability for economic loss, a matter which is considered at length in a later chapter.¹

¹   See CHAPTER 5 below.

Conflicting interests

[1.27]   An argument which has sometimes prevailed is that the imposition of liability for negligence would be inappropriate because the defendant filled a role which obliged him to be conscious of other, and potentially conflicting, interests in addition to those of the claimant. Thus, one of the reasons which used to be given for the now defunct advocate's immunity was that the advocate owes a duty to the court which may conflict with that owed to his client.[1] Before its demise in the field of litigation itself, however, this type of argument had already begun, in recent times, to fall into disfavour in other contexts. It was advanced both by architects seeking to avoid liability for negligence in evaluating and certifying work done by builders under a building contract,[2] and by accountants attempting to do so for carelessness in valuing shares at the request of vendor and purchaser.[3] In both cases the House of Lords unanimously rejected the argument and imposed liability.[4] The fundamental proposition that victims of carelessness should normally be allowed to seek reparation from those responsible, with inroads into that principle for reasons of public policy being kept to a minimum, was robustly reasserted.

[1] See *Rondel v Worsley [1969] 1 AC 191, [1967] 3 All ER 993, HL*. See now *Arthur J S Hall & Co v Simons [2000] 3 All ER 673, HL*, discussed in Chapter 8 of the handbook.
[2] See *Sutcliffe v Thackrah [1974] AC 727, [1974] 1 All ER 859, HL*.
[3] See *Arenson v Casson, Beckman, Rutley & Co [1977] AC 405, [1975] 3 All ER 901, HL*. For further discussion see Chapter 5 below.
[4] See also *Berry Taylor v Coleman [1997] PNLR 1, CA*.

Need for caution

[1.28] The underlying logic of the proposition that liability should be negated because of the involvement of conflicting interests is not attractive. If the defendant's role requires him to exercise difficult functions with regard to the balancing of such interests, then negligence may be very difficult actually to *prove*.[1] But the suggestion that sheer carelessness as such should go unremedied for *a priori* reasons is one which must always be treated with caution.[2] Nevertheless, even if arguments specifically in favour of general immunities based on conflicting interests have relatively recently attracted a degree of healthy scepticism, analogous arguments putting similar ideas under umbrellas such as 'justice and reasonableness' have enjoyed a more favourable reception. They have been upheld in cases involving public servants, who may be faced with situations of particular complexity when balancing a variety of conflicting interests in the exercise of statutory discretions,[3] and whose judgment may supposedly be affected adversely by the possibility of litigation.[4]

[1] Cf per Lord Diplock in *Saif Ali v Sydney Mitchell [1980] AC 198* at 220, *[1978] 3 All ER 1033* at 1043, HL. In *Thorne v University of London [1966] 2 QB 237, [1966] 2 All ER 338, CA*, it was held that university examiners owe no duty of care: sed quaere.
[2] '… the public policy consideration which has first claim on the loyalty of the law is that wrongs should be remedied and … very potent counter-considerations are required to override that policy': per Lord Browne-Wilkinson in *X v Bedfordshire County Council [1995] 2 AC 633* at 749, *[1995] 3 All ER 353* at 380. (His Lordship did, however, identify such considerations in the case before him.)
[3] See *Yuen Kun-yeu v A-G of Hong Kong [1988] AC 175, [1987] 2 All ER 705, PC; Davis v Radcliffe [1990] 2 All ER 536, [1990] 1 WLR 821, PC*.
[4] See *Rowling v Takaro Properties [1988] AC 473, [1988] 1 All ER 163, PC*. On negligence and the exercise of statutory powers, see generally Chapter 12 below.

Social work: the retreat from Bedfordshire

[1.29] In *X v Bedfordshire County Council*[1] the House of Lords declined to impose liability upon a local authority in respect of alleged negligence by social workers and a psychiatrist working in the field of child protection. Lord Browne-Wilkinson observed[2] that 'the task of the local authority and its servants in dealing with children at risk is extraordinarily delicate' since the 'relationship between the social worker and the child's parents is frequently one of conflict, the parent wishing to retain care of the child, the social worker having to consider whether to remove it'. In those circumstances his Lordship considered that 'if a liability in damages were to be imposed, it might well be that local authorities would adopt a more cautious and defensive approach to their duties', and he therefore thought that it would be wrong to sanction litigation 'the cost of which both in terms of money and human resources [would] be diverted from the performance of the social service for which they were provided'.[3] Cases decided in more recent years have, however, had the effect of significantly eroding the scope and authority of *Bedfordshire*.

1   *[1995] 2 AC 633, [1995] 3 All ER 353, HL.*
2   See *[1995] 2 AC 633* at 750, *[1995] 3 All ER 353* at 381.
3   *[1995] 2 AC 633* at 750, *[1995] 3 All ER 353* at 381.

Barrett v Enfield London BC

[1.30]   It is noteworthy that the decision in *X v Bedfordshire County Council* was distinguished rather narrowly, by the House of Lords itself, in the subsequent case of *Barrett v Enfield London BC*[1]. The plaintiff in this case had been in the care of the defendant authority from the age of ten months until he was 17. He alleged that the authority had negligently failed to provide him with proper social workers, had made placements for him with inappropriate foster parents, and had moved him too frequently between different residential homes; leaving his personal development adversely affected. The Court of Appeal struck out the claim, relying on *X v Bedfordshire County Council*, but the House of Lords reinstated it. *Bedfordshire* was distinguishable in as much it had been concerned with the processes involved in deciding whether or not to take someone into care, as distinct from decisions taken during the period of care itself. Nevertheless, it is striking how the various policy factors considered under the 'just and reasonable' umbrella in the former case, including the problem of conflicting interests, were considered in the latter *not* to 'have the same force separately or cumulatively'[2] so as to outweigh the plaintiff's right to have his case substantively determined. The decision in *Barrett* demonstrated that, notwithstanding the acutely difficult and sensitive nature of the issues sometimes involved, a common law duty of care may be imposed in respect of negligence by social workers[3].

1   *[1999] 3 All ER 193, HL.*
2   See *[1999] 3 All ER 193* at 208 *per* Lord Slynn.
3   See also *W v Essex CC [2000] 2 All ER 237, HL*; *S v Gloucestershire CC [2000] 3 All ER 346, CA.*

D v East Berkshire NHS Trust

[1.31]   In this case, in which the Court of Appeal heard three appeals together in 2003, the Court reviewed the subsequent developments, and declared that 'in so far as the position of a child is concerned, we have reached the firm conclusion that the decision in *Bedfordshire* cannot survive'[1]. They continued[2]:

'It follows that it will no longer be legitimate to rule that, as a matter of law, no common law duty is owed to a child in relation to the investigation of suspected child abuse and the initiation and pursuit of care proceedings. It is possible that there will be factual situations where it is not fair, just or reasonable to impose a duty of care, but each case will fall to be determined on its individual facts'.

The court did, however, draw a sharp distinction between the interests of children and their parents in such cases and held, consistently with *Bedfordshire*, that no duty would be owed to the latter. They said[3]:

> 'It will always be in the parents' interests that the child should not be removed. Thus the child's interests are in potential conflict with the interests of the parents. In view of this we consider that there are cogent reasons of public policy for concluding that, where child care decisions are being taken, no common law duty of care should be owed to the parents'[4].

D's case was referred to by the Court of Appeal itself in the subsequent case of *A v Essex CC*[5], in which adoptive parents complained that they had been given insufficient information about the children they subsequently adopted. The court held that 'there is in general no duty of care owed by an adoption agency or the staff whom it employs in relation to deciding what information is to be conveyed to prospective adopters'[6]. Nevertheless, the claimants succeeded on the facts since the defendant agency had been negligent administratively in failing to convey information which it had itself earlier decided *should* be conveyed.

1   See *[2003] 4 All ER 796* at para 83 *per* Lord Phillips MR delivering the judgment of the court.
2   See *[2003] 4 All ER 796* at para 84.
3   See *[2003] 4 All ER 796* at para 86.
4   See also *B v Attorney-General of New Zealand [2003] 4 All ER 833, PC*.
5   *[2003] EWCA Civ 1848, [2003] All ER (D) 321 (Dec)*.
6   See *[2003] All ER (D) 321 (Dec)* at para 59 *per* Hale LJ delivering the judgment of the court.

The police[1]

[1.32]   A specific area of public service in which the notion of conflicting and overriding interests of public policy has sometimes been invoked to justify the negation of negligence liability is that of police activity. In view of the increasing influence of human rights jurisprudence in this field[2], however, the reasoning in some of the decisions may now have to be treated with a degree of scepticism in so far as immunity could be said to have been conferred without full consideration of the merits. A case which is nevertheless still important is *Hill v Chief Constable for West Yorkshire*,[3] in which it was alleged that the police had been culpable in failing to catch a murderer.[4] The public policy argument was adopted by the House of Lords as a subordinate ground of decision. Lord Templeman observed:[5]

> '... if this action lies, every citizen will be able ... to investigate the performance of every policeman. If the policeman concentrates on one crime, he may be accused of neglecting others. If the policeman does not arrest on suspicion a suspect with previous convictions, the police force may be held liable for subsequent crimes. The threat of litigation against a police force would not make a policeman more efficient. The necessity for defending proceedings, successfully or unsuccessfully, would distract the policeman from his duties.'[6]

In several subsequent reported decisions, police authorities successfully relied on *Hill*'s case to get personal injury actions against them dismissed as disclosing no reasonable cause of action even though the facts were very different from those in *Hill*.

1   See generally R Clayton and H Tomlinson *Civil Actions Against the Police*.
2   See R Clayton and H Tomlinson above.

3   *[1989] AC 53, [1988] 2 All ER 238, HL.* Cf *Doe v Metropolitan Toronto (Municipality) Comrs of Police (1989) 58 DLR (4th) 396 (Can).*
4   See also *Osman v Ferguson [1993] 4 All ER 344, CA.* In subsequent proceedings in this case before the European Court of Human Rights, however, that court held that a blanket immunity for the police could constitute a violation of art 6.1 of the European Convention on Human Rights in so far as it operated as a disproportionate restriction on the right of access to a court. The applicants in *Osman's* case were accordingly awarded £10,000 for loss of the opportunity to have their case against the police fully adjudicated: see *Osman v United Kingdom [1999] 1 FLR 193.* Cf *Z v UK (2001) 10 BHRC 384, ECtHR.*
5   *[1989] AC 53* at 65, *[1988] 2 All ER 238* at 245.
6   See also *Elguzouli-Daf v Metropolitan Police Comr [1995] QB 335, [1995] 1 All ER 833, CA* (Crown Prosecution Service).

Immunity applied

[1.33]   In *Clough v Bussan*[1] Kennedy J struck out a claim based upon alleged failure to respond sufficiently quickly when traffic lights became defective, and in *Hughes v National Union of Mineworkers*[2] May J struck out one based upon alleged negligence during a riot control operation. In *Ancell v McDermott*[3] the Court of Appeal struck out a claim based upon alleged failure by the police to deal adequately with a traffic hazard resulting from a spillage of diesel oil, which led to a fatal accident when a vehicle skidded on the oil. The principle in *Hill's* case has therefore not been confined to the context in which it was enunciated, which concerned the detection of crime.[4] Decisions such as that in *Ancell's* case indicated a readiness to extend the principle to protect what might be described as 'routine' carelessness in the discharge of duties such as traffic control.[5] The Court of Appeal has also held that police officers present at an eviction, to prevent a breach of the peace, did not owe a duty of care to the tenant to prevent the eviction itself even though it was in fact illegal[6]. In other cases, however, the courts have declined to extend the immunity.

1   *[1990] 1 All ER 431.*
2   *[1991] 4 All ER 278.*
3   *[1993] 4 All ER 355, CA.*
4   Cf *Alexandrou v Oxford [1993] 4 All ER 328, CA* (decided in 1990).
5   Cf C Brennan 'Police negligence defined' (1992) NLJ 1118.
6   See *Cowan v Chief Constable for Avon and Somerset* (2001) Times, 11 December.

Liability contemplated

[1.34]   A potentially important exception to the scope of police immunity is suggested by *Swinney v Chief Constable of Northumbria.*[1] In this case the plaintiff gave information in confidence to the police but, owing to the carelessness of officers involved, her identity was revealed to the person whom she had reported when a document was left unattended and fell into the hands of criminals. As a result the plaintiff was subjected to threats of violence and suffered psychiatric damage. The Court of Appeal refused to strike out her negligence claim.[2] They distinguished *Hill's* case and held that, in the circumstances, it was arguable that a special relationship had existed between the plaintiff and the police.[3] In the words of Ward LJ:[4]

'Proximity is shown by the police assuming responsibility, and the plaintiffs relying on that assumption of responsibility, for preserving the confidentiality of the information which, if it fell into the wrong hands, was likely to expose the first plaintiff and members of her family to a special risk of damage from the criminal acts of others, greater than the general risk which ordinary members of the public must endure ...'

[1.35] *Liability for carelessness*

The decision in *Swinney's* case was referred to with approval by the House of Lords in *Waters v Commissioner of Police of the Metropolis*[5]. The appellant, an officer in the Metropolitan Police, claimed that she had been raped by another officer, and that the respondent had been negligent in failing adequately to investigate her complaint. Although the Court of Appeal struck out the claim[6], applying *Hill's* case, the House of Lords reinstated it. The House emphasised that the existence, in effect, of an employment relationship between appellant and respondent was a significant distinguishing feature of the case. Nevertheless the speeches of the majority[7] are notable for their assertion of the weight which may be attached generally to countervailing policy considerations in limiting the sphere of application of the principle in *Hill v Chief Constable for West Yorkshire*.

[1]   *[1996] 3 All ER 449*, CA. Cf *W v Essex CC [1998] 3 All ER 111, CA*.
[2]   Cf *Leach v Chief Constable of Gloucestershire Constabulary [1999] 1 All ER 215, CA*, in which a claim for psychiatric damage (by an 'appropriate adult' present at the questioning of notorious mass-murderer Frederick West) *was* partially struck out on the basis of police immunity.
[3]   See also the unusual case of *Costello v Chief Constable of the Northumbria Police [1999] 1 All ER 550, CA*, in which a police officer who had assumed responsibility for assisting a fellow officer was held liable for failing to come to her aid when she was attacked by a violent suspect in her police station.
[4]   *[1996] 3 All ER 449* at 467.
[5]   *[2000] 4 All ER 934, HL*.
[6]   See *[1997] ICR 1073, CA*.
[7]   See especially *per* Lord Hutton in *[2000] 4 All ER* at 945–946. See also *per* Lord Slynn *[2000] 4 All ER* at 940. Cf *per* Lord Jauncey in *[2000] 4 All ER* at 941 (effectively dissenting on the point).

Emergency services

[1.35]   An immunity similar to that sometimes accorded to the police has been extended in two decisions to other emergency services. In *Capital and Counties plc v Hampshire CC*[1] the Court of Appeal held that the fire-brigade does not owe a common law duty of care to victims of fire unless it chooses to intervene and, through its carelessness, actually makes matters worse[2]. In *OLL v Secretary of State for Transport*[3] the same principles were held to be applicable in a case involving the coastguard service. These cases were, however, distinguished in *Kent v Griffiths*[4] in which a substantial delay by an ambulance service, in responding to an emergency call, had disastrous consequences. The Court of Appeal upheld a substantial award of damages in favour of the claimant holding that, once a call had been accepted, the ambulance service owed a duty of care to respond in a timely fashion. Lord Woolf MR acknowledged that 'situations could arise where there is a conflict between the interests of a particular individual and the public at large'[5], but there was no question of that in the instant case. Moreover, as a part of the health service, there was no reason why 'the position of ambulance staff [should] be different from that of doctors or nurses' who conventionally owe a duty of care. Lord Woolf concluded that:[6]

> '... the arguments based on public policy are much weaker in the case of the ambulance service than they are in the case of the police or the fire service. The police and fire services' primary obligation is to the public at large ...It is ...appropriate to regard the London Ambulance Service as providing services of the category provided by hospitals and not as providing services equivalent to those rendered by the police or the fire service'.

[1]   *[1997] QB 1004, [1997] 2 All ER 865*.
[2]   For discussion based upon empirical research into the consequences of *Capital and Counties* see Hartshorne, Smith and Everton, 'Effects of Negligence Liability Upon the Fire Service' (2000) 63 MLR 502.
[3]   *[1997] 3 All ER 897*.

4   *[2000] 2 All ER 474, CA.* See also the interlocutory decision of the Court of Appeal in the same case: *[1999] PIQR P192.*
5   See *[2000] 2 All ER 474* at para 45.
6   See *[2000] 2 All ER 474* at para 45.

Public policy and the sanctity of life

[1.36]   In *McKay v Essex Area Health Authority*[1] the plaintiff's mother contracted german measles during pregnancy. The defendant doctor negligently failed to diagnose or treat the illness, and consequently failed to advise the mother of the desirability of considering an abortion in such circumstances. The plaintiff was born disabled and claimed damages from the defendant for 'entry into a life in which her injuries are highly debilitating'. The Court of Appeal struck out the claim as disclosing no cause of action. The court held that while a doctor might in such cases owe a duty to the *mother* to afford an opportunity for termination of the pregnancy, 'to impose such a duty towards the child would ... make [an] ... inroad on the sanctity of human life which would be contrary to public policy'.[2] Although decided in 1982, the birth in this case occurred before the coming into effect of the *Congenital Disabilities (Civil Liability) Act 1976*, in which the legislature itself ruled out such claims in future. The Act provides that a child may have a cause of action where the defendant's negligent breach of duty to his mother during pregnancy caused him to be born disabled.[3] It is, however, 'so worded as to import the assumption that, but for the occurrence giving rise to a disabled birth, the child would have been born normal and healthy, not that it would not have been born at all'.[4] This reflected the view of the Law Commission, which originally drafted the Act, that there should be no so-called right of action for 'wrongful life'.[5]

1   *[1982] QB 1166, [1982] 2 All ER 771, CA.*
2   *[1982] QB 1166* at 1180, *[1982] 2 All ER 771* at 781, per Stephenson LJ.
3   See *s 1.* The Act resolved uncertainty which existed at common law as to whether such a cause of action existed (see now *Burton v Islington Health Authority [1993] QB 204, [1992] 3 All ER 833, CA,* holding in respect of a pre-Act birth that it did). The mother herself cannot be liable to her child except in cases arising out of her own negligent driving (when the claim will in effect be against an insurance company): see *s 2* of the 1976 Act.
4   Per Ackner LJ in *McKay v Essex Area Health Authority [1982] QB 1166* at 1186–1187, *[1982] 2 All ER 771* at 786, referring to *ss 1(2)(b)* and *4(5)* of the 1976 Act.
5   See the Law Commission's Report on *Injuries to Unborn Children* (Law Com no 60, Cmnd 5709), para 89. See also the Report of the *Royal Commission on Civil Liability and Compensation for Personal Injury* (Pearson) vol 1 (Cmnd 7054–I) para 1485.

'Wrongful birth'

[1.37]   A different type of claim from that for 'wrongful life' is one brought 'by parents of an unwanted child for damage resulting *to them* from the birth of the child'[1].These are sometimes called actions for 'wrongful birth'. The issue was recently considered by the House of Lords in two cases decided within four years of each other: *McFarlane v Tayside Health Board*[2], decided in 1999, and *Rees v Darlington Memorial Hospital NHS Trust*[3], in which a seven-member House was invited in 2003 to reconsider the earlier decision. In *McFarlane v Tayside Health Board* a surgeon employed by the defendants negligently reported to Mr McFarlane that his vasectomy operation had been successful. In consequence Mr McFarlane and his wife, who already had four children, had a fifth as a result of their ceasing to take contraceptive measures. By a majority[4] the House of Lords held that Mrs McFarlane could recover for the pain of her pregnancy itself, and financial losses associated with it. The House was, however, unanimous in concluding that the much more substantial costs involved in actually bringing up the child were *not* recoverable[5]. Although their Lordships were unanimous in their conclusion, they were divided in their reasoning. The majority[6] based the decision on the proposition that the claim was for pure economic loss and, as such, was subject to the restrictive approach adopted by the law of negligence generally to the recovery of such losses[7]. The minority[8], by contrast, openly held that it would be 'morally offensive'[9] to permit recovery. It is submitted that of the two the latter approach is to be preferred; in as much as to decide the case on 'technical' grounds would, in the words of Lord Steyn, be in effect 'to mask the real reasons'[10] for the decision. The broader approach was favoured by the Court of Appeal in *Greenfield v Irwin*[11], in which *McFarlane's* case was applied. In *Greenfield's* case the claimant sought unsuccessfully to distinguish *McFarlane* by basing her claim not on the cost of bringing up her child but instead upon her own lost earnings as a result of giving up work to look after the child: a distinction which the Court of Appeal had no hesitation in rejecting.

[1] *Per* Lord Steyn in *McFarlane v Tayside Health Board [1999] 4 All ER 961* at 972, HL.
[2] *[1999] 4 All ER 961, HL*. For criticism see Laura C H Hoyano 'Misconceptions about Wrongful Conception' (2002) 65 MLR 883.
[3] *[2003] 4 All ER 987, HL*.
[4] Lord Millett dissenting.
[5] The High Court of Australia, by a bare majority, has taken the opposite view and awarded the cost of bringing up a healthy child as damages: see *Cattanach v Melchior [2003] HCA 38*, discussed by Peter Cane in (2004) 120 LQR 23. See also the decision of the Court of Appeal in *Thake v Maurice [1986] QB 644, [1986] 1 All ER 497, CA*, now no longer law, in which damages were awarded for the upkeep of a healthy child.
[6] Lord Slynn, Lord Hope, and Lord Clyde.
[7] See below CHAPTER 5.
[8] Lord Steyn and Lord Millett.
[9] See *per* Lord Millett in *[1999] 4 All ER 961* at 1003.
[10] See *[1999] 4 All ER 961* at 977.
[11] *[2001] 1 WLR 1279*. See also *AD v East Kent NHS Trust [2003] 3 All ER 1167*.

Conventional sum now awarded

[1.38]   *McFarlane's* case was distinguished by the Court of Appeal in *Parkinson v St James and Seacroft University Hospital NHS Trust*[1], in which a child born following a negligently conducted sterilisation operation was disabled. The Court of Appeal held that the parents could recover the *additional* costs, over and above those involved in bringing up a healthy child, which they would incur as a result of the disability. The precise status of this decision is now open to doubt, however, following the bare majority decision of a seven-member House of Lords in *Rees v Darlington Memorial Hospital NHS Trust*[2]. In this case a mother who had sought to avoid pregnancy because of her *own* disability sought to recover the additional childcare costs to which that disability would give rise, even though the child to which she gave birth, following a negligent sterilisation, was himself normal and healthy. The House held unanimously that the decision in *McFarlane's* case, that substantial damages for the cost of bringing up a healthy child should not be awarded, would not be departed from. A bare majority[3] also went on to hold, however, that all 'wrongful birth' cases involving a healthy baby would in future result in the award of a conventional sum of £15,000 to the parents; to reflect the wrong that had been done to them in negligently depriving them of their freedom to choose not to have a baby. The dissentients[4] condemned this result in strong terms, as being unprincipled, ill-considered, and quasi-legislative. But it is submitted that it can be supported as a bold and courageous attempt to achieve justice and certainty, in the midst of profoundly difficult and conflicting moral and social considerations. Lord Bingham of Cornhill said[5]:

> 'This solution is in my opinion consistent with the ruling and rationale of *McFarlane's* case. The conventional award would not be, and would not be intended to be, compensatory. It would not be the product of calculation. But it would not be nominal, let alone a derisory, award. It would afford a more ample measure of justice than the pure *McFarlane's* case rule'.

[1]   *[2001] 3 All ER 97.* Brooke, Hale LJJ and Sir Martin Nourse. Cf *Emeh v Kensington and Chelsea and Westminster Area Health Authority [1985] QB 1012, CA.*
[2]   *[2003] 4 All ER 987.* See Peter Cane 'Another Failed Sterilisation' (2004) 120 LQR 189.
[3]   Lord Bingham, Lord Nicholls, Lord Millett and Lord Scott.
[4]   Lord Steyn, Lord Hope and Lord Hutton.
[5]   See *[2003] 4 All ER 987* at page 993.

Position uncertain where child is disabled

[1.39]   It is not entirely clear, following the decision in *Rees v Darlington Memorial Hospital NHS Trust*, whether parents in 'wrongful birth' cases, whose child is born disabled, will henceforth be limited to the conventional sum or will still be able, following the decision of the Court of Appeal in *Parkinson v St James and Seacroft University Hospital NHS Trust,* to recover the costs of upbringing in so far as those would exceed the costs of bringing up a healthy child. The majority in *Rees'* case did not speak with one voice on the point. Lord Bingham and Lord Nicholls would have confined such claimants to the conventional sum, thereby effectively overruling *Parkinson.* Lord Millett and Lord Scott, however, preferred to leave the point open; although even they seemed to lean in favour of the view that such claimants should also be limited to the conventional sum[1].

[1]   See *[2003] 4 All ER 987* at paras 112–122 (Lord Millett) and paras 144–147 (Lord Scott).

Illegality and public policy

Criminal activity

[1.40]   In *Pitts v Hunt*[1] the 18-year-old plaintiff was a passenger on a motor cycle owned and driven by a 16-year-old friend who, to the plaintiff's knowledge, was unlicensed and uninsured. After both had been on a heavy drinking session the owner, aided and abetted by the plaintiff, drove his motor cycle at high speed in, as Beldam LJ put it, a 'reckless, irresponsible and idiotic way'. The two 'were clearly showing no concern for other users of the road' and it appeared 'that they were deliberately riding in a way calculated to frighten others'.[2] They were involved in a collision in which the driver was killed. The plaintiff sued his estate for the serious injuries which he suffered in the accident but the Court of Appeal, upholding the decision of the trial judge, rejected his claim. Beldam LJ held that it would be contrary to public policy to allow it to succeed[3]. Balcombe and Dillon LJ, although agreeing as to the result, preferred to base their conclusion on the proposition that, as it was put in an Australian case, 'the plaintiff must fail when the character of the enterprise in which the plaintiffs are engaged is such that it is impossible for the court to determine the standard of care which is appropriate to be observed'.[4] It is submitted that the approach of Beldam LJ is to be preferred. Indeed, as he pointed out, the 'duty of care approach' seemed itself to be based upon public policy and would therefore appear to be question-begging.[5]

Moreover, his Lordship persuasively observed that he was 'not convinced of the wisdom of a policy which might encourage a belief that the duty to behave responsibly in driving motor vehicles is diminished even to the limited extent that they may in some circumstances not owe a duty to each other, particularly when those circumstances involve conduct which is highly dangerous to others'.[6]

1   *[1991] 1 QB 24, [1990] 3 All ER 344*, CA.
2   *[1991] 1 QB 24* at 36, *[1990] 3 All ER 344* at 347.
3   The principle is sometimes encapsulated in the Latin maxim *ex turpi causa oritur non actio*.
4   *Per* Mason J in *Jackson v Harrison (1978) 138 CLR 438* at 455, quoted by Balcombe LJ in *[1991] 1 QB 24* at 49–50, *[1990] 3 All ER 344* at 358.
5   Cf *per* Sedley LJ, dissenting, in *Vellino v Chief Constable of Greater Manchester [2002] 3 All ER 78* at para [58].
6   *[1991] 1 QB 24* at 46–47, *[1990] 3 All ER 344* at 355–356.

Vellino v Chief Constable of Greater Manchester

[1.41]   The contrast between the 'no duty' approach to cases involving criminal activity, and overt acceptance of illegality as an independent doctrine based on public policy, is also reflected in the judgments delivered in the Court of Appeal in *Vellino v Chief Constable of Greater Manchester*[1]. In this case the claimant suffered serious injuries by jumping from a window in an attempt to escape from police custody. It was found as a fact that his conduct had been foreseeable, and he sought damages for the failure by the police to prevent his escape. Escaping from custody is itself a criminal offence, and the court held, by a majority, that the claim would fail. Schiemann LJ considered that there was an 'overlap between the considerations which go to the question "is there a duty?" and those which attend the defence of ex turpi causa'[2]. He preferred, however, to base his decision on 'absence of duty'[3]. Although expressing his agreement with Schiemann LJ, Sir Murray Stuart-Smith examined 'the maxim ex turpi causa' at some length. He summarised the position as he saw it in the form of four propositions as follows[4]:

'(1) The operation of the principle arises where the claimant's claim is founded upon his own criminal or immoral act. The facts which give rise to the claim must be inextricably linked with the criminal activity. It is not sufficient if the criminal activity merely gives occasion for tortious conduct of the defendant. (2) The principle is one of public policy; it is not for the benefit of the defendant. Since if the principle applies, the cause of action does not arise, the defendant's conduct is irrelevant. There is no question of proportionality between the conduct of the claimant and defendant. (3) In the case of criminal conduct this has to be sufficiently serious to merit the application of the principle. Generally speaking a crime punishable with imprisonment could be expected to qualify. If the offence is criminal, but relatively trivial, it is in any event difficult to see how it could be integral to the claim. (4) The 1945 Act is not applicable where the claimant's action amounts to a common law crime which does not give rise to liability in tort'.[5]

1   *[2002] 3 All ER 78*.
2   See *[2002] 3 All ER 78* at para [28].
3   Sed quaere.
4   See *[2002] 3 All ER 78* at para [70].
5   Cf the powerful dissenting judgment of Sedley LJ, who would have allowed the claim to succeed subject to a reduction of the damages by two-thirds for the claimant's contributory negligence.

Pragmatic approach

[1.42]   The question whether the tortious conduct and the criminal activity were 'inextricably linked', and that of whether the criminality was 'sufficiently serious', will need to be resolved in relation to the facts of each case. In truth, a degree of uncertainty in the law is unavoidable in situations involving illegality, as the more numerous cases on the topic in the law of contract[1] amply demonstrate. Precise tests for the operation of public policy are illusory and the adoption of a pragmatic approach based on the gravity of the case is inevitable.[2] Questions arising out of deliberate criminal activity involving violence or dishonesty will be relatively easy to answer. Thus, in *Ashton v Turner*[3] Ewbank J denied recovery where the plaintiff suffered serious personal injuries when involved in a collision while passenger in a get-away car. The vehicle was being driven by the defendant to escape at speed from the scene of a burglary in which both parties had participated. In so holding, his Lordship followed an earlier decision of the High Court of Australia.[4]

[1]   On the applicability of the defence in the law of contract: see, generally, R A Buckley, *Illegality and Public Policy* (London, 2002). See also *Hewison v Meridian Shipping Services [2003] PIQR P252*, in which the defence of illegality succeeded, and both the contractual and tortious authorities were reviewed by the Court of Appeal (especially in the dissenting judgment of Ward LJ).
[2]   See per Bingham LJ in *Saunders v Edwards [1987] 2 All ER 651* at 666, *[1987] 1 WLR 1116* at 1134.
[3]   *[1981] QB 137, [1980] 3 All ER 870*.
[4]   See *Smith v Jenkins (1969) 119 CLR 397, 44 ALJR 78, Aust HC* (Barwick LJ, Kitto, Windeyer, Owen and Walsh JJ). See also *Gala v Preston (1991) 172 CLR 243*. Cf *Burns v Edman [1970] 2 QB 541, [1970] 1 All ER 886* (widow of burglar unable to recover damages under the Fatal Accidents Acts).

[1.43]   The defence of illegality was also upheld in rather different circumstances in *Clunis v Camden and Islington Health Authority*.[1] The plaintiff in that case had stabbed a stranger to death in an unprovoked attack, and had subsequently been convicted of manslaughter when his plea of diminished responsibility to a murder charge was accepted. He sued the defendant health authority for their allegedly negligent management of the mental health disorder from which he suffered, claiming that appropriate measures, which the defendants should have taken, would have prevented the tragic killing and his own resulting detention in a secure hospital. The Court of Appeal struck out his claim.[2] Beldam LJ said[3] that the plaintiff 'must be taken to have known what he was doing and that it was wrong, notwithstanding that the degree of his culpability was reduced by reason of mental disorder'. In those circumstances his Lordship considered that the 'court ought not to allow itself to be made an instrument to enforce obligations alleged to arise out of the plaintiff's own criminal act'.[4]

[1]   *[1998] QB 978, [1998] 3 All ER 180, CA*. See also *Wilson v Coulson [2002] PIQR P22*.
[2]   Cf *Meah v McCreamer [1985] 1 All ER 367*, in which a plaintiff who became a rapist as a result of personality changes resulting from injuries in a road accident caused by the defendant's negligence, received damages which included compensation for the fact that the behavioural changes had led to his imprisonment. The correctness of this decision was doubted by the Court of Appeal in *Clunis v Camden and Islington Health Authority [1998] QB 978, [1998] 3 All ER 180* at 189.
[3]   See *[1998] 3 All ER 180* at 189 (judgment of the court).
[4]   See also *Meah v McCreamer (No 2) [1986] 1 All ER 943*.

Burglar succeeds

[1.44]   A case in which the 'defence' of illegality was unsuccessful is *Revill v Newberry*.[1] The plaintiff was a burglar who had been injured while trying to enter the defendant's premises. The latter had used a shotgun to fire through a small hole in the door as the plaintiff tried to break in. The Court of Appeal held that denial of any liability in favour of the plaintiff in such circumstances would entail 'that the trespasser who was also a criminal was effectively an outlaw'.[2] Such a conclusion was felt to be inconsistent with the existence of statutory duties in favour of trespassers[3] and would have meant that 'any claim by the assailant or trespasser would be barred no matter how excessive or unreasonable the force used against him'.[4] The plaintiff therefore recovered damages in respect of conduct by the defendant which had been 'clearly dangerous and bordered on reckless'.[5] The damages were, however, reduced by two-thirds on the ground of contributory negligence.

[1]   *[1996] QB 567, [1996] 1 All ER 291, CA.*
[2]   See *[1996] QB 567* at 579, *[1996] 1 All ER 291* at 301, *per* Evans LJ.
[3]   See the *Occupiers' Liability Act 1984*, and CHAPTER 16 of the handbook.
[4]   See *[1996] QB 567* at 580, *[1996] 1 All ER 291* at 302, *per* Millett LJ.
[5]   *[1996] QB 567* at 580, *[1996] 1 All ER 291* at 302, *per* Millett LJ.

Suicide

[1.45]   Negation of liability on the ground of illegality will clearly often be appropriate where serious criminal offences are concerned. At least in theory, however, the principles of public policy are not necessarily confined to cases involving criminality. For example, Lord Denning MR once expressed the view, obiter, that public policy should operate to prevent persons who injured themselves in unsuccessful suicide attempts, or their personal representatives if the attempt was successful, from suing for negligence those allegedly at fault in failing to prevent what had occurred.[1] Although suicide was formerly a crime, it ceased to be so with the passing of the *Suicide Act 1961*[2]. Lord Denning's view has, however, been emphatically rejected by the Court of Appeal and, in effect, also by the House of Lords. In *Kirkham v Chief Constable of Greater Manchester*,[3] the Court of Appeal disapproved of his dictum in so far as it applied to suicide attempts by persons suffering from mental illness, and the personal representatives of the deceased succeeded in obtaining damages for the negligent failure of prison authorities to follow correctly their own procedures for handling known potential suicides.[4] More recently, in *Reeves v Metropolitan Police Comr*,[5] the House of Lords reached the same result in a case in which the deceased had been of sound mind at the time when he took his own life, thereby effectively rejecting a defence suggestion that the non-applicability of the public policy defence in this context should be limited to the mentally ill.[6] Although the plaintiffs in the *Kirkham* and *Reeves* cases therefore succeeded, it will often be difficult to establish carelessness on the facts in such situations. In *Knight v Home Office*,[7] which also concerned the suicide in prison of a person known to be at risk, Pill J examined exhaustively the procedures which had been adopted to monitor the deceased, before dismissing on the facts the allegation that the medical staff had been negligent. Similarly, in *Orange v Chief Constable of West Yorkshire*[8] the Court of Appeal emphasised that the extent of the precautions required in any given case were related to the degree of risk presented by the individual prisoner. The court rejected a submission that the fact that there is a higher level of suicide among prisoners generally, when compared with the community as a whole, necessitated the taking of specific precautions in every case regardless of their apparent irrelevance.

[1]   'By his act, in self-inflicting this serious injury, [the plaintiff] has made himself a burden on the whole community … The policy of [the] law should be to discourage these actions': *Hyde v Tameside Area Health Authority [1981] CLY 1854, [1981] CA Transcript 130*, quoted in *Kirkham v Chief Constable of Greater Manchester [1990] 2 QB 283* at 292, *[1990] 3 All ER 246* at 252.

2   *s 1*. Cf *per* Morritt LJ in the Court of Appeal in *Reeves v Metropolitan Police Comr [1998] 2 All ER 381*
      at 403, CA: 'I would not think it appropriate in those circumstances for a court to brand as contrary to
      public policy or offensive to the public conscience an act which Parliament has so recently legalised'.
      See also *per* Lord Bingham CJ in the Court of Appeal in the same case: *[1998] 2 All ER* at 404–405.
      Even before the 1961 Act it was held that if the deceased committed suicide as a result of depression
      directly induced by injuries caused by the negligence of the defendants, his dependants could recover
      under the Fatal Accidents Acts: *Pigney v Pointers Transport Services Ltd [1957] 2 All ER 807, [1957]
      1 WLR 1121.*
3   *[1990] 2 QB 283* at 291, *[1990] 3 All ER 246* at 251.
4   See also *Selfe v Ilford and District Hospital Management Committee (1970) 114 Sol Jo 935.*
5   *[1999] 3 All ER 897.*
6   The argument was, in fact, abandoned in the House of Lords, where the argument turned solely on
      questions of causation: see *per* Lord Hoffman in *[1993] 3 All ER 897* at 902 ('The question of public
      policy or *ex turpi causa*, which had not found favour with any member of the Court of Appeal, was not
      pursued'.)
7   *[1990] 3 All ER 237.*
8   *[2002] QB 347.* Cf *Funk v Clapp (1986) 68 DLR (4th) 229 (Can)*; see also *Funk Estate v Clapp (1988)
      54 DLR (4th) 512.*

Existing law

[1.46]   In *Home Office v Dorset Yacht Co Ltd*[1] Lord Reid observed that a 'justification or valid explanation' for exclusion of the ordinary principles of negligence might
be found in 'cases ... where the law was settled long ago and neither Parliament nor
the House sitting judicially has made any move to alter it'. Accordingly, one of the
more difficult questions to gain prominence when the law of negligence was going
through a period of relative expansion, concerned those situations in which detailed
rules of law already existed; having developed before the full ripening of negligence
concepts. Rules which could readily be perceived as being anomalous and out-dated
yielded relatively easily to the advancing tide.[2] Elsewhere, the position was often
more difficult, and in a number of cases traditional formulations of doctrine remained
resistant to change.[3] One conservative argument, which arguably combines excessive
caution with an undue preoccupation with symmetry, concerns the relationship
between the common law and the legislature. It amounts to a presumption against
expanding the former if the latter has by its enactments intervened in a particular area,
but done so in a limited fashion: the questionable assumption being that Parliament
must thereby have intended to ossify the law and discourage further development.
Thus, the limited existing scope of statutory protection for employees has been
invoked as a justification for not expanding the duties resting at common law upon
employers,[4] and legislation regarding defective premises[5] has been similarly treated
as a justification for not increasing the tortious liability of builders.[6]

1   *[1970] AC 1004* at 1027, *[1970] 2 All ER 294* at 297, HL.
2   See above paras [1.19] to [1.24], 'Erosion of traditional immunities'.
3   See *Smith v Scott [1973] Ch 314, [1972] 3 All ER 645; Stephens v Anglian Water Authority [1987]
      3 All ER 379, [1987] 1 WLR 1381, CA.* See also *per* Lord Templeman in *Downsview Nominees v First
      City Corpn Ltd [1993] AC 295* at 316, *[1993] 3 All ER 626* at 638, PC, referring to 'the danger of
      extending the ambit of negligence so as to supplant or supplement other torts, contractual obligations,
      statutory duties or equitable rules in relation to every kind of damage ...'
4   See *Reid v Rush & Tompkins Group plc [1989] 3 All ER 228, [1990] 1 WLR 212, CA.* On employers'
      liability to their employees, see generally CHAPTER 14 below.
5   Ie the *Defective Premises Act 1972.*
6   See *D & F Estates v Church Comrs for England [1989] AC 177, [1988] 2 All ER 992 HL.* See also
      Murphy v Brentwood District Council [1991] 1 AC 378, [1990] 2 All ER 908, HL.

Exaggerated fear of uncertainty

[1.47]   In some areas the overriding need for certainty, and the need not to upset
long-term transactions entered into on the basis of the existing law, will make the

resolution of the matter in favour of the status quo relatively straightforward. It is nevertheless submitted that the courts should not be too eager to rule on *a priori* grounds against the entry of negligence into unfamiliar areas. The fear that merely contemplating putting old rules to the test of relevance to contemporary circumstances will cause de-stabilising uncertainty is probably exaggerated. Indeed, in two important decisions the House of Lords has fairly recently indicated a striking readiness to allow negligence liability to expand in the face of conservative arguments to the contrary. In *Spring v Guardian Assurance plc*[1] the House held, by a majority, that the writer of a reference could be liable in negligence to the job applicant about whom it was written. This was notwithstanding the contention that such liability would outflank the protection accorded to referees by the doctrine of qualified privilege in the law of defamation, which imposes liability only in the event of malice. And in *Henderson v Merrett Syndicates*[2] the House held that, in a situation potentially involving concurrent remedies in contract and tort, the plaintiff was entitled to choose the more advantageous: he was not obliged to proceed in contract. In so holding, their Lordships went against the balance of pre-existing authority, which appeared to favour according priority to contractual principles in such circumstances and to regard tort as supplementary. But, as Lord Goff asserted in *Henderson's* case: '… the law of tort is the general law, out of which the parties can, if they wish, contract.'[3] It is submitted that both of these decisions are to be welcomed.

[1]   *[1995] 2 AC 296, [1994] 3 All ER 129.*
[2]   *[1995] 2 AC 145, [1994] 3 All ER 506.*
[3]   See *[1995] 2 AC 145* at 193, *[1994] 3 All ER 506* at 532.

Legislative or administrative solution more suitable?

[1.48]   In some cases the imposition of liability may have such far-reaching consequences that legislation, or administrative action initiated by local or national government, may be perceived as more likely to provide an acceptable framework for the delineation of rights and duties in the particular sphere.[1] For example, a suggestion that a particular method of road planning or construction was negligent, and the cause of an accident, might involve a wide-ranging inquiry with substantial resource implications.[2] In *Budden v BP Oil*[3] it was alleged that the defendants had been negligent in marketing petrol which contained dangerously high levels of lead, but the Court of Appeal struck the claim out. The lead levels had not exceeded the maximum laid down in regulations made by the Secretary of State, and any change in the permitted level, which would necessarily apply to all manufacturers and suppliers of petrol throughout the country, should be made by Parliament and not by the courts.[4] In some cases, especially those involving government, the existence of statutory powers may be relevant to a potential negligence claim; in which event special factors apply and the need not to fetter administrative discretion has to be taken into account.[5] But to allow foreseeably harm-causing activities to continue unremedied in other contexts for, in effect, economic or political reasons or considerations of administrative convenience, is a course which should surely only be adopted in rare cases.[6] An important part of the function of tort, along with law generally in a free society, is to ensure that powerful bodies, public or private, are subject to its constraints.[7] Of course, many activities, of which transport is the prime example, necessarily involve risk and will predictably continue to result in death and injury. An irreducible degree of evaluation will therefore be involved in determining whether, say, certain methods of road-building, or the construction techniques of particular car mmanufacturers, have appreciably *added* unnecessarily to risks which we all accept as part of day to day life. But the courts should not be too eager to invoke the existence of this need for evaluation as an excuse for wholly abrogating the application, on its own common-sense basis, of the law of negligence.

¹ In *Morgans v Launchbury [1973] AC 127, [1972] 2 All ER 606*, the House of Lords refused to extend the scope of vicarious liability on the ground that only the legislature could consider adequately the far-reaching implications for the insurance market.
² Cf *Stovin v Wise [1996] AC 923, [1996] 3 All ER 801, HL.* See also *Knight v Home Office [1990] 3 All ER 237* at 243, per Pill J: '... the court must ... bear in mind as one factor that resources available for the public service are limited and that the allocation of resources is a matter for Parliament.'
³ *(1980) 124 Sol Jo 376, [1980] JPL 586, CA.*
⁴ See *[1980] JPL 586* at 587, per Megaw LJ.
⁵ See generally CHAPTER 15 below.
⁶ Cf per Sir Thomas Bingham MR, dissenting, in the Court of Appeal in *M (a minor) v Newham London Borough Council [1995] 2 AC 633, [1994] 4 All ER 602* at 619: '... it would require very potent considerations of public policy ... to override the rule of public policy which has first claim on the loyalty of the law: that wrongs should be remedied.'
⁷ '... lack of funds would not excuse a public body which operated its vehicles on the public roads without any system of maintenance for the vehicles if an accident occurred because of lack of maintenance. The law would require a higher standard of care towards other road users': per Pill J in *Knight v Home Office [1990] 3 All ER 237* at 243.

Alternative remedy more appropriate?

[1.49] If the possibility exists of actual compensation being available, by a route different from the common law of negligence, the court may occasionally consider that to be a particularly persuasive argument against the imposition of liability. Thus, at the Court of Appeal stage in *Hill v Chief Constable of West Yorkshire*,[1] in which the mother of a murder victim sought unsuccessfully to sue the police for failing to apprehend the mass-murderer involved soon enough to prevent her daughter's death, Fox LJ referred to the existence of the Criminal Injuries Compensation Scheme[2] and said:[3]

'The scheme ... make[s] quite wide provision for compensation for such persons as are likely to suffer financial loss as a result of a crime of violence. It is not desirable that inequalities should be produced by providing additional remedies for negligence. Either such remedies will merely duplicate the scheme, or they may give rise to inequalities which may be offensive to the families of other victims of crimes of violence in cases where no negligence by the police was involved ... I think that the problems of compensation for injury from crimes of violence are best dealt with in the framework of the scheme ...'

Similar remarks were made by Lord Denning MR in an earlier case,[4] in which a plaintiff unsuccessfully sought to sue his employer for failing adequately to protect him from the risk of robbery when collecting the firm's wages, a risk which materialised resulting in his incurring serious personal injuries.[5]

¹ *[1988] QB 60, [1987] 1 All ER 1173, CA*; affd *[1989] AC 53, [1988] 2 All ER 238, HL.*
² Now the Criminal Injuries Compensation Authority.
³ *[1988] QB 60* at 73, *[1987] 1 All ER 1173* at 1182.
⁴ *Charlton v Forrest Printing Ink [1980] IRLR 331, CA.*
⁵ 'I hope that the compensation board for the victims of crime will realise the plight which [the plaintiff] has been left in by these robbers, and will award him full and adequate compensation for the distressing injury he has received. So I would leave it to the compensation board – and not to the employers': *[1980] IRLR 331* at 333, per Lord Denning MR.

Remedy should rarely be denied

[1.50] Like the previous argument based on the feasibility of legislative or adminis-trative solutions, however, the existence of the Criminal Injuries Compensation

Authority,[1] or similar arrangements, should not be allowed to become a general justification for denying a negligence remedy. Whatever arguments may be advanced about the efficient administration of such special funds, public or private, as exist to compensate the victims of misfortune,[2] reliance upon the existence of those funds as a reason *in itself* for denying recovery would undermine the structure and coherence of the common law.[3] Where the alternative 'remedy' would not provide for the possibility of compensation, the case for negating negligence liability is even weaker. In *Barrett v Enfield London Borough Council*[4] the House of Lords was concerned with the statutory responsibilities of local authorities with respect to children at risk. In the earlier case of *X v Bedfordshire County Council* the existence of statutory complaints mechanisms, and the possibility of investigation by the local authorities' ombudsman, had been contemplated as a reason for denying negligence liability in such cases[5]. The *Bedfordshire* case was distinguished in *Barrett,* however, and Lord Hutton said[6]:

> '… if the plaintiff suffered …injury by reason of carelessness amounting to negligence at common law, I consider that the jurisdiction of the court should not be excluded because of the existence of other avenues of complaint'.

[1]   On the Criminal Injuries Compensation Authority, see CHAPTER 31 of the handbook.
[2]   See generally CHAPTER 31 and CHAPTER 32 below.
[3]   Cf per Sir Thomas Bingham MR, dissenting, in the Court of Appeal in *M (a minor) v Newham London Borough Council [1995] 2 AC 633* at 667, *[1994] 4 All ER 602* at 623: 'Save in clear cases, it is not for the courts to decide how public money is best spent nor to balance the risk that money will be wasted on litigation against the hope that the possibility of suit may contribute towards the maintenance of the highest standards.'
[4]   *[1999] 3 All ER 193.*
[5]   See *[1995] 2 AC 633* at 751, *[1995] 3 All ER 353* at 381–382 per Lord Browne-Wilkinson. See also *Elguzouli-Daf v Metropolitan Police Comr [1995] QB 335, [1995] 1 All ER 833* at 840, per Steyn LJ.
[6]   See *[1999] 3 All ER 193* at 228.

F Psychiatric damage[1]

Frontiers of liability

[1.51]   The question of whether, and in what circumstances, claimants who suffer psychiatric damage, or nervous shock[2] as it was formerly known, can sue in negligence has traditionally been seen as raising a problem on the frontiers of liability in the tort.[3] It was for long unclear whether the ordinary test of reasonable foreseeability applied to such cases, or whether some narrower principle was applied out of a fear of opening up what might prove to be an unduly wide area of liability.[4] Until recently the cases were usually confined to situations in which the claimant suffered psychiatric disorder either as a result of the sudden infliction of death or serious injury upon a third party, or as a result of fear by the claimant for his own safety. In recent years, however, claims for psychiatric disorder resulting from causes other than sudden trauma have also been considered by the courts. In the traditional type of case, typically involving a sudden catastrophe to a third party, it was possible to discern a pattern in the actual decisions: the courts would rarely impose liability where the victim who suffered injury was a stranger, unknown to the plaintiff,[5] or where the plaintiff merely learnt of the injury second-hand and was not present at the scene.[6] This tended to suggest that control devices to limit liability were being applied and that foreseeability was merely a necessary, and not a sufficient, condition. On the other hand, the judges tended obstinately, if somewhat implausibly, to stick to the ordinary language of foreseeability in such cases; implying that what might have appeared to be policy limitations on liability in fact simply reflected the situations in which nervous shock happened to be foreseeable.[7] All earlier cases on psychiatric damage now have to be read in the light of five decisions of the House of Lords: *McLoughlin v O'Brian*,[8] *Alcock v Chief Constable of South Yorkshire Police*,[9] *Page v Smith*[10], *White v Chief Constable of South Yorkshire Police*[11] and *W v Essex County Council*[12].

[1] See the Law Commission Report on *Liability for Psychiatric Illness* (Law Com no 249) (1998). See also N J Mullany and P R Handford *Tort Liability for Psychiatric Damage: The Law of 'Nervous Shock'* (1993).

[2] In *Attia v British Gas [1988] QB 304* at 317, *[1987] 3 All ER 455* at 462, CA, Bingham LJ said: '[The] claim is … one for what have in the authorities and the literature been called damages for nervous shock. Judges have in recent years become increasingly restive at the use of this misleading and inaccurate expression, and I shall use the general expression "psychiatric damage", intending to comprehend within it all relevant forms of mental illness, neurosis and personality change.'

[3] For recent academic discussion see also N J Mullany and P R Handford 'Hillsborough Replayed' (1997) 113 LQR 410. See also Chris Hilson 'Liability for Psychiatric Injury: Primary and Secondary Victims Revisited' (2002) 18 Professional Negligence 167; H Teff 'Liability for Negligently Inflicted Psychiatric Harm: Justifications and Boundaries' [1998] 57 CLJ 91; A Sprince 'Negligently Inflicted Psychiatric Damage: a Medical Diagnosis and Prognosis' (1998) 18 LS 59; J Murphy 'Negligently Inflicted Psychiatric Harm: A Re-appraisal' (1995) 15 LS 415.

[4] See *Chester v Waverley Municipal Council (1939) 62 CLR 1* at 7–8, per Latham CJ.

[5] See *Bourhill v Young [1943] AC 92, [1942] 2 All ER 396, HL*. For an exception see *Chadwick v British Transport Commission [1967] 2 All ER 945, [1967] 1 WLR 912* (rescuer). Cf *Dooley v Cammell Laird [1951] 1 Lloyd's Rep 271* (discussed at para [1.62] below).

[6] See *per* Bankes LJ *Hambrook v Stokes Bros [1925] 1 KB 141* at 152, CA.

[7] See especially *Bourhill v Young [1943] AC 92, [1942] 2 All ER 396, HL* and *King v Phillips [1953] 1 QB 429, [1953] 1 All ER 617, CA*.

[8] *[1983] 1 AC 410, [1982] 2 All ER 298, HL*.

[9] *[1992] 1 AC 310, [1991] 4 All ER 907, HL*.

[10] *[1996] AC 155, [1995] 2 All ER 736*.

[11] *[1999] 1 All ER 1, HL*.

[12] *[2000] 2 All ER 237*.

The issues

[1.52] As a result of *Page v Smith*, it has become clear that a distinction must be drawn between situations in which the claimant suffers psychiatric damage as a result of his having been himself exposed to a foreseeable risk of physical injury ('primary victims'); and situations in which he witnessed, or became aware of, death or injury to someone else ('secondary victims'). The familiar problem of determining the precise limits of liability, and ascertaining the relevance of 'policy' considerations, is now seen to be largely confined to the *latter* category – ie those actually involving third parties. Those situations in which the claimant was himself in danger, as in *Page v Smith* itself, are considered to be more straightforward and not to require the invocation of different principles from those ordinarily applied in personal injury cases. Until *White v Chief Constable of South Yorkshire Police*, a source of complication was that cases in which the plaintiff had been himself in danger were perceived not to be the *only* ones in which the 'policy' constraints, normally imposed upon liability, were removed. There were also some 'three-party' situations in which those requirements were thought not to be insisted upon. Thus, cases involving 'rescue' were long considered to provide appropriate examples of the constraints on liability being relaxed in the plaintiff's favour.[1] But the controversial, and subsequently reversed, decision of the Court of Appeal in *White's* case[2] seemed to suggest that cases involving an employer's duty of care to his employees might warrant similar generous treatment. As a result of the decision of the House of Lords in *White's* case, however, the proposition that rescue and employment situations are governed in this area by distinct, and especially favourable, principles is apparently no longer tenable. But a

33

third possible exceptional category, the possible existence of which was left open by the House of Lords in *White*'s case, is that of involuntary participation or 'survivor's guilt'. These are cases in which the negligence of the defendant created a situation in which the claimant, although blameless, considered himself to have been responsible for death or injury to another. It is therefore necessary, in order to present a clear picture, to examine various types of situation in the light of the authorities: both those still considered to constitute separate legal categories and those no longer considered to do so.

¹   See eg *Chadwick v British Transport Commission [1967] 2 All ER 945, [1967] 1 WLR 912.*
²   See *Frost v Chief Constable of the South Yorkshire Police [1998] QB 254, [1997] 1 All ER 540*, revsd sub nom *White v Chief Constable of South Yorkshire Police [1999] 1 All ER 1, HL.*

Situations involving third parties

[1.53]   In *McLoughlin v O'Brian*¹ the plaintiff was at home, two miles from the scene, when her husband and their three children were involved in a road accident caused by the negligence of the defendant. One of the children was killed, and the other children and the husband were seriously injured. Very shortly after the accident, the plaintiff visited the hospital to which the victims had been taken, and witnessed their condition for herself. Her claim for psychiatric damage failed at first instance and in the Court of Appeal, but succeeded in the House of Lords². Lords Edmund-Davies, Russell, Scarman and Bridge all found for the plaintiff by applying the reasonable foreseeability test. Only Lord Wilberforce expressly admitted that the traditional limitations on the extent of recovery for psychiatric damage did in fact reflect policy considerations. He also made clear his sympathy for those considerations and decided the case on the narrow ground that, although the plaintiff's claim was 'upon the margin', her attendance at the hospital meant that her situation was not different in principle from what it would have been if she had actually been at the scene of the accident herself.³ The fact that the situation in *McLoughlin v O'Brian* could thus be seen as justifying recovery even on the traditional criteria makes the significance of the wide-ranging views expressed in the other speeches difficult to assess.

¹   *[1983] 1 AC 410, [1982] 2 All ER 298, HL.* See also the decision of the *High Court of Australia in Jaensch v Coffey (1984) 54 ALR 417*, noted by P A Trindade in (1985) 5 OJLS 305.
²   See also *Galli-Atkinson v Seghal [2003] EWCA Civ 697, [2003] Lloyd's Rep Med 285, CA.*
³   See *[1983] AC 410 at 419, [1982] 2 All ER 298 at 302.* See also *Vernon v Bosley [1997] 1 All ER 577, CA*, in which the plaintiff arrived at the scene of the accident in time to witness the unsuccessful rescue attempts to save his two young children from drowning. But for cases on the other side of the line from *McLoughlin v O'Brian*, in which the arrival of relatives at hospital was considered to be too late to enable them to benefit from the 'aftermath' doctrine see *Taylorson v Shieldness Produce Ltd [1994] PIQR P329* and *Taylor v Somerset Health Authority [1993] 4 Med LR 34*, sed quaere.

Alcock v Chief Constable of South Yorkshire Police

Hillsborough disaster

[1.54]   The speeches in the important and difficult case of *Alcock v Chief Constable of South Yorkshire Police*,¹ which arose out of the 1989 Hillsborough football stadium disaster in Sheffield, were also expressed in rather general terms. But their basic tenor is in contrast with the approach in *McLoughlin*'s case in that they indicate reluctance to contemplate any general expansion of liability in this area: the attitude of their

Lordships in the earlier case being, if anything, more liberal. Of the four Law Lords who delivered speeches, Lord Keith and Lord Jauncey seemed to prefer the language of 'foreseeability' and 'proximity', while Lord Ackner and Lord Oliver seemed to favour a more overtly policy-based approach. But all reached the same result and indicated that since psychiatric damage cases would depend largely on their own circumstances, it was vain to seek clear guidelines. In *Alcock*'s case itself 95 lives were lost in a football stadium when a failure of crowd control by the police caused large numbers of people to be crushed together. Of the particular plaintiffs with whose claims for psychiatric damage the House of Lords was concerned, one who was actually at the ground himself lost two brothers, while another lost his brother-in-law, whose body he subsequently identified in the mortuary. Other plaintiffs were not present at the ground but watched the event, a televised cup semi-final, on live television, including one woman who lost her fiancé and a couple who lost their son. All the claims were rejected. In brief, those who had been present at the ground were not proved to have had a sufficiently close relationship with the particular victim in question, whereas those who would have succeeded on this basis were disqualified by their absence from the scene of the tragedy: the television broadcasts not being regarded in the circumstances as equivalent to actual presence.

---

[1] *[1992] 1 AC 310, [1991] 4 All ER 907, HL.* See H Teff 'Liability for Psychiatric Illness after Hillsborough' (1992) 12 OJLS 440; K J Nasir 'Nervous Shock and *Alcock*: The Judicial Buck Stops Here' (1992) 55 MLR 705.

Relationship, time and space

[1.55]   Their Lordships held that a close relationship would normally be necessary for a successful claim (although the possibility of bystanders recovering in exceptionally horrific circumstances was not altogether ruled out[1]), and that the existence of such a relationship would have to be proved to have existed on the facts of each case, albeit effectively being presumed in cases such as loss of a child. But the relationship remains only a necessary condition: 'proximity to the accident must be close both in time and space.'[2] The television pictures in the Hillsborough case itself did not satisfy this requirement, not least because, as broadcasting guidelines required, they had not involved transmission of images of identifiable individual victims.[3] Their Lordships indicated that merely being told of the death, or identifying the body, would not satisfy the time and space requirement from which it followed that two decisions at first instance, shortly before the Hillsborough case, appeared insupportable.[4] Nevertheless, the Law Commission has recommended that the law should be changed as far as the time and space requirements are concerned[5], and it is significant that the High Court of Australia has also departed from the view favoured by the House of Lords with respect to these two requirements. In *Annetts v Australian Stations Pty*[6] the plaintiff's son went missing, as a result of the defendants' negligence, and his skeleton was discovered several months later. The High Court, reversing the courts below, imposed liability for psychiatric illness suffered by the plaintiffs. Gummow and Kirby JJ observed that 'neither the lack of the applicants' direct perception of their son's death or its immediate aftermath nor the circumstances that the applicants may not have sustained a "sudden shock", is fatal to the applicants' claims'[7].

---

[1] Eg, if a petrol tanker were to career out of control into a school in session and burst into flames: *[1992] 1 AC 310* at 403, *[1991] 4 All ER 907* at 919 (Lord Ackner). But cf per Stuart-Smith LJ in *McFarlane v EE Caledonia Ltd [1994] 2 All ER 1* at 14: 'In my judgment both as a matter of principle and policy the court should not extend the duty to those who are mere bystanders or witnesses of horrific events unless there is a sufficient degree of proximity, which requires both nearness in time and place and a close relationship of love and affection between plaintiff and victim.' It is submitted that the approach of Lord Ackner is to be preferred.

2   *[1992] 1 AC 310* at 404, *[1991] 4 All ER 907* at 920 (Lord Ackner).
3   But cf per Nolan LJ in the Court of Appeal, sub nom *Jones v Wright [1991] 3 All ER 88* at 122, *[1992] 1 AC 310* at 386–387: 'I would not exclude the possibility in principle of a duty of care extending to the watchers of a television programme. For example, if a publicity-seeking organisation made arrangements for a party of children to go up in a balloon, and for the event to be televised so that their parents could watch, it would be hard to deny that the organisers were under a duty to avoid mental injury to the parents as well as physical injury to the children, and that there would be a breach of that duty if through some careless act or omission the balloon crashed. But that would be a very different case.' Lord Ackner in the House of Lords agreed with this dictum: see *[1991] 4 All ER 907* at 921.
4   See *Hevican v Ruane [1991] 3 All ER 65* and *Ravenscroft v Rederiaktiebolaget Transatlantic [1991] 3 All ER 73*. In the light of the observations of the House of Lords in the Hillsborough case the Court of Appeal subsequently reversed the decision in *Ravenscroft*, finding in favour of the defendants without finding it necessary to hear argument on their behalf: see *[1992] 2 All ER 470n*.
5   See below.
6   *[2002] HCA 35, 76 ALJR 1348*. See F A Trindade 'Reformulation of the Nervous Shock Rules' (119) 2003 LQR 204.
7   Quoted in Trindade (as above).

Fire and foreseeability

[1.56]   The general tenor of the views of their Lordships in *Alcock v Chief Constable of South Yorkshire Police* therefore appears to have been that the approach of the courts as to the proper limits of liability for psychiatric damage should change, if at all, marginally in the direction of greater scrutiny and caution before admitting claims.[1] But it is noteworthy that in a 1987 case, which was not considered by the House of Lords in either of the two psychiatric injury cases arising out of the Hillsborough disaster,[2] the Court of Appeal held, on trial of a preliminary issue, that a claim for psychiatric damage might be sustainable where the plaintiff had witnessed her house and its contents being damaged by a fire caused by the defendants' negligence, even though there was no threat to anyone's personal safety.[3] This attractive decision illustrates the great variety of potential psychiatric damage situations which makes generalisation about them hazardous. Nevertheless, the negative proposition that this is a sphere in which the foreseeability test is subject to a substantial degree of qualification on policy grounds is now clearly established.[4]

1   Cf per Lord Steyn in *White v Chief Constable of South Yorkshire Police* [1999] 1 All ER 1 at 39: 'In my view the only sensible general strategy for the courts is to say thus far and no further. The only prudent course is to treat the pragmatic categories as reflected in authoritative decisions such as *Alcock*'s case and *Page v Smith* as settled for the time being but by and large to leave any expansion or development in this corner of the law to Parliament.'
2   Ie *Alcock v Chief Constable of South Yorkshire Police* [1992] 1 AC 310, [1991] 4 All ER 907 and *White v Chief Constable of South Yorkshire Police* [1999] 1 All ER 1.
3   See *Attia v British Gas* [1988] QB 304, [1987] 3 All ER 455, CA. Cf *Owens v Liverpool Corpn* [1939] 1 KB 394, [1938] 4 All ER 727, CA.
4   The relevant policy factors are clearly set out in the speech of Lord Steyn in *White v Chief Constable of South Yorkshire Police* [1999] 1 All ER 1 at 32–33. See also the Law Commission Report on *Liability for Psychiatric Illness* (Law Com no 249) (1998), paras 6.5–6.9.

Injuries self-inflicted by the defendant

[1.57]   Another type of situation in which policy considerations, rather than the absence of foreseeability, were held to negate liability for psychiatric harm, arose in *Greatorex v Greatorex*[1]. The defendant suffered injury in a road-accident caused by his own negligent driving. His father was a fire officer who attended the scene in his professional capacity, and subsequently developed post-traumatic stress disorder as a result of witnessing his son's plight. The father brought an action against his son for damages. Cazalet J held, however, that the claim would fail. Although the claimant obviously fulfilled the 'relationship' requirement for liability, it was the very fact that he did so which was considered to raise policy objections to his succeeding. His Lordship held that it could exacerbate tensions within the family unit for one member to be able to sue another for causing him psychiatric illness. Litigation between family members can, of course, already exist in respect of physical injuries arising out of road accidents. Nevertheless, it did not follow that the special cause of action normally *only* open to family members, by virtue of the 'relationship' requirement, should also give rise to liability.

1   *[2000] 4 All ER 769.* See Basil Markesinis 'Foreign Law Inspiring National Law. Lessons from *Greatorex v Greatorex' [2002] 61 CLJ 386;* Peter Handford 'Psychiatric Damage Where the Defendant is the Immediate Victim' (2001) 117 LQR 397.

Claimant in danger

[1.58]   If the claimant suffered psychiatric damage as a result of his involvement in an accident in which he himself, as distinct from any third parties, was at risk of injury, the test for liability *does* appear to be based upon foreseeability alone. Moreover, foreseeability of any injury to the claimant will suffice – ie foreseeability of physical injury (whether or not it occurred) will suffice, whereas in 'three-party' cases foreseeability of psychiatric damage itself is insisted upon. In *Page v Smith*[1] the car which the plaintiff was driving was involved in a collision with the defendant's car, for which the latter was to blame. Neither party suffered any physical injury and the plaintiff was able to drive his car home after the collision. Nevertheless, the incident unfortunately led to the recurrence of a psychiatric illness, ME, from which the plaintiff had formally suffered. As a result of this disability the plaintiff became permanently incapable of working and he was awarded over £162,000 in damages at first instance. Although the Court of Appeal reversed the trial judge, on the ground that psychiatric damage had not been foreseeable, a bare majority of the House of Lords[2] reversed the Court of Appeal and reinstated the award. The majority saw the situation as an ordinary personal injury case. Lord Lloyd of Berwick said:[3]

> 'Foreseeability of psychiatric injury remains a crucial ingredient when the plaintiff is the secondary victim, for the very reason that the secondary victim is almost always outside the area of physical impact, and therefore outside the range of foreseeable physical injury. But where the plaintiff is the primary victim of the defendant's negligence, the nervous shock cases ... are not in point. Since the defendant was admittedly under a duty of care not to cause the plaintiff foreseeable physical injury, it was unnecessary to ask whether he was under a separate duty of care not to cause foreseeable psychiatric injury.'

Accordingly, since the general principles relating to remoteness of damage in personal injury cases require a defendant to 'take the plaintiff as he finds him',[4] the latter's predisposition in the present case to ME afforded no defence. Lord Lloyd observed[5] that the need for 'control mechanisms' to limit the number of potential claimants, including the requirement that 'the defendant will not be liable unless psychiatric injury is foreseeable in a person of normal fortitude', does not arise 'where the plaintiff is the primary victim'.

1   *[1996] AC 155, [1995] 2 All ER 736, HL.* See also *Simmons v British Steel [2004] UKHL 20 (Scot), [2004] ICR 585.*
2   Lord Ackner, Lord Browne-Wilkinson and Lord Lloyd of Berwick, Lord Keith of Kinkel and Lord Jauncey of Tullichettle dissenting.

Danger as a condition of liability

White v Chief Constable of South Yorkshire

Rescuers

[1.59]   In situations in which the claimant suffers psychiatric damage as a result of going to the rescue of the person put in danger by the defendant's negligence the 'control mechanisms' normally required in 'third-party' cases such as a relationship with the victim, and perhaps also the requirement that the claimant himself should have been a person of 'normal fortitude', do not appear to be insisted upon. Thus, in *Chadwick v British Transport Commission*[1] the plaintiff suffered psychiatric damage after helping to rescue victims of a major train disaster, and his claim succeeded notwithstanding his having suffered from mental illness earlier in his life.[2] Since the decision of the House of Lords in *White v Chief Constable of South Yorkshire*,[3] however, claims for psychiatric injury caused during rescue attempts are now subject to the major limitation that recovery will be dependent upon the claimant having actually been in personal danger during the rescue. In *White*'s case the plaintiffs were police officers who had been on duty in the football stadium at the time of the Hillsborough disaster and who had developed post-traumatic stress disorder as a result. They based their claims for damages partly on their activities as rescuers but, by a bare majority, the House held that they would fail.[4] Lord Steyn said:[5]

> 'I … accept that *Chadwick*'s case was correctly decided. But it is not authority for the proposition that a person who never exposed himself to any personal danger and never thought that he was in personal danger can recover pure psychiatric injury as a rescuer. In order to recover compensation for pure psychiatric harm as a rescuer it is not necessary to establish that his psychiatric condition was caused by the perception of personal danger … But in order to contain the concept of rescuer in reasonable bounds for the purposes of the recovery of compensation for pure psychiatric harm the plaintiff must at least satisfy the threshold requirement that he objectively exposed himself to danger or reasonably believed that he was doing so.'

This new limitation was subjected to trenchant criticism in the two dissenting speeches[6] and would appear to be a potential source of anomaly.[7] But it is submitted that the majority were at least correct in their anxiety, in view of the earlier Hillsborough decision in *Alcock v Chief Constable of South Yorkshire*,[8] to reject the plaintiffs' claims because 'most people would regard it as wrong to award compensation for psychiatric injury to the professionals and deny compensation for similar injury to the relatives.'[9]

1   *[1967] 2 All ER 945, [1967] 1 WLR 912.*
2   Cf *McFarlane v EE Caledonia Ltd [1994] 2 All ER 1, CA*, in which the unsuccessful plaintiff, who had been present on a rescue boat at the 'Piper Alpha' oil-rig disaster in 1988 but whose attempt to have himself classified as an actual rescuer was rejected by the court, was described as 'not a person of average fortitude or customary phlegm and … probably more susceptible to psychiatric injury than the average man' (see per Stuart-Smith LJ in *[1994] 2 All ER 1* at 5).
3   *[1999] 1 All ER 1.*

⁴   Lord Browne-Wilkinson, Lord Steyn and Lord Hoffmann; Lord Griffiths and Lord Goff of Chieveley dissented.

⁵   See *[1999] 1 All ER 1* at 38 (the italics are those of Lord Steyn). See also per Lord Hoffmann at 47: 'The concept of a rescuer as someone who puts himself in danger of physical injury is easy to understand. But once this notion is extended to include others who give assistance, the line between them and bystanders becomes difficult to draw with any precision.'

⁶   'What rescuer ever thinks of his own safety? It seems to me that it would be a very artificial and unnecessary control, to say a rescuer can only recover if he was in fact in physical danger. A danger to which he probably never gave thought, and which in the event might not cause physical injury': per Lord Griffiths, *[1999] 1 All ER 1* at 7.

⁷   See the hypothetical example given by Lord Goff in *[1999] 1 All ER 1* at 27.

⁸   *[1992] 1 AC 310, [1991] 4 All ER 907, HL.*

⁹   *Per* Lord Hoffmann in *White v Chief Constable of South Yorkshire Police [1999] 1 All ER 1* at 48.

Threshold requirement

[1.60]   Lord Steyn's observations quoted above were applied in favour of *claimants* in *Cullin v London Fire Authority*[1]. In that case the Court of Appeal emphasised, when rejecting a strike out application by defendants, that providing the threshold requirement of danger is satisfied, it is not necessary for the rescuer's psychiatric harm to have been caused by fear for his own safety; nor for the dangerous situation to have been precisely the same as that which caused the deaths of the victims, as long as both situations were part of the same general event.

¹   *[1999] PIQR P314.*

Employees

[1.61]   In *White v Chief Constable of South Yorkshire Police*[1] the plaintiffs based their claims not only on their activities as 'rescuers', but also on the contention that, as 'employees' of the Chief Constable, they were owed a duty of care to protect them from injury in the course of their work. The submission was that psychiatric damage constituted 'injury' for this purpose and thereby obviated any need for employees to satisfy the 'control mechanisms', such as a close relationship with someone killed or injured, which other plaintiffs in 'three party' situations normally have to satisfy. The House of Lords rejected this argument, which had apparently been found persuasive by two members of the Court of Appeal, and it is submitted that they were right to do so. Lord Hoffmann put it as follows:[2]

> 'The liability of an employer to his employees for negligence, either direct or vicarious, is not a separate tort with its own rules. It is an aspect of the general law of negligence. The relationship of employer and employee establishes the employee as a person to whom the employer owes a duty of care. But this tells us nothing about the circumstances in which he will be liable for a particular type of injury. For this one must look to the general law concerning the type of injury which has been suffered.'[3]

Clearly, there can be situations in which a Chief Constable as employer will owe a duty of care to his officers different from that which he owes to members of the public, eg to supply protective armour to those expected to confront violent criminals.[4] But in a situation like Hillsborough, which concerned crowd control, it is far from obvious that their employment contracts should have impliedly conferred upon police officers a greater entitlement to sue for psychiatric damage than the members of the public whom the police officers were themselves there to protect. It is true that the police officers were, in a sense, present under compulsion whereas the members of the public were not, but neither group expected to be in a situation in which they might suffer psychiatric damage.[5] As a result of the decision in *White* it is therefore now clear that employees, simply *qua* employees and without more,[6] do not fall into any specially favoured category for the purpose of recovering damages for psychiatric injury.

[1]   *[1999] 1 All ER 1, HL.*
[2]   *[1991] 1 All ER 1* at 43–44.
[3]   See also *per* Lord Griffiths, *[1991] 1 All ER 1* at 6: 'The law of master and servant is not a discrete branch of the law of tort, but is to be considered in relation to actions in tort generally'; and *per* Lord Steyn, *[1991] 1 All ER 1* at 36: 'The rules to be applied when an employer brings an action against his employer for harm suffered at the workplace are the rules of tort. One is therefore thrown back to the ordinary rules of the law of tort which contain restrictions on the recovery of compensation for psychiatric harm.'
[4]   Cf *Schofield v Chief Constable of West Yorkshire* (1998) Times, 15 May, CA.
[5]   This is not to suggest that the plaintiffs in *White* were inherently undeserving, but rather that the decision of the House of Lords in *Alcock* was too restrictive. See N J Mullany and P R Handford 'Hillsborough Replayed' (1997) 113 LQR 410 (contending, inter alia, that the plaintiffs in *White* should have recovered as 'bystanders' within Lord Ackner's hypothetical horrific situation example in *Alcock*: *[1992] 1 AC 310* at 403, *[1991] 4 All ER 907* at 919). Cf per Lord Hoffmann in *White v Chief Constable of South Yorkshire Police [1999] 1 All ER 1* at 48: 'It seems to me that in this area of the law, the search for principle was called off in *Alcock v Chief Constable of South Yorkshire Police*.'
[6]   An employer may owe a duty to protect an employee from a nervous breakdown where such a breakdown is reasonably foreseeable from work-related stress: see *Walker v Northumberland County Council [1995] 1 All ER 737* (social worker). See also CHAPTER 14 below.

Involuntary participants

[1.62]   In certain circumstances a claimant may suffer psychiatric damage due to the belief that he was involved in, or responsible for, the death or injury of someone else. If the situation out of which the perceived fatality or injury occurred was caused by the defendant's negligence, the latter may be liable to the claimant even though no rescue of the victim or close relationship of love and affection with him was involved. Thus, in *Young v Charles Church (Southern) Ltd*[1] the plaintiff succeeded when a colleague working only feet away from him was killed and set alight by electrocution through contact with an overhead power line.[2] In the earlier case of *Dooley v Cammell Laird & Co Ltd*[3] the plaintiff was a crane driver from whose crane the load fell away, due to a defective rope, leading the plaintiff to believe that it had killed or injured people working in the hold of the ship below. The plaintiff recovered for psychiatric damage against his employers and also those responsible for fitting the defective rope. In both the *Young* and *Dooley* cases the plaintiff was very close to the accident himself and perceived it immediately with his own senses.

[1]   *(1997) 33 BMLR 101, CA.*
[2]   See also *Wigg v British Railways Board [1986] NLJ Rep 446n* (death of train passenger: claim by driver).
[3]   *[1951] 1 Lloyd's Rep 271.*

Hunter v British Coal Corporation

[1.63]   In the most recent case of this type, *Hunter v British Coal Corpn*,[1] the Court of Appeal has held, by a majority, that literal proximity of that kind is, in fact, a requirement for success. The plaintiff in *Hunter*'s case was the driver of a truck in the defendant's coal mine. Due to the defendant's negligence, the truck collided with an exposed fire hydrant. The plaintiff left the scene in pursuit of remedial measures, and when he was 30 metres away he heard a loud bang as the hydrant exploded and killed his colleague. The plaintiff was told of the death 15 minutes later and subsequently suffered from a depressive illness, but his claim for damages was dismissed. Brooke LJ said that 'the law requires a greater degree of physical and temporal proximity than was present in this case'.[2] Hobhouse LJ dissented and referred to a hypothetical case[3] involving a signalman, who believes that defective equipment operated by him has caused a train crash some miles away. His Lordship considered that the signalman should be able to recover and that that situation was analogous to the case before him. It is submitted that the reasoning of Hobhouse LJ is to be preferred to that of the majority. *Hunter*'s case was not considered by the House of Lords in *White v Chief Constable of South Yorkshire Police*, but Lord Hoffmann did refer to situations in which 'the plaintiff had been put in a position in which he was, or thought he was about to be or had been, the immediate instrument of death or injury to another'[4] and his Lordship conceded that 'there may be grounds for treating such a rare category of cases as exceptional and exempt from the *Alcock* control mechanisms'. It is not clear whether such claimants would also be exempt from the new *White* test of having been themselves in personal danger, but it is submitted that they *should* be thus exempt. The illogicality of subjecting such claims to that requirement would be even greater than in the case of rescue – a context in which its arbitrariness was emphasised by the dissentients in *White v Chief Constable of South Yorkshire Police* itself.

[1] *[1998] 2 All ER 97, CA.*
[2] See *[1998] 2 All ER 97* at 109. See also per Sir John Vinelott in *[1998] 2 All ER 97* at 114, who considered that where a plaintiff 'learns of the accident after it has happened, psychiatric injury suffered by him by reason of his feelings of guilt or otherwise is too remote to found an action for damages'.
[3] Originally mooted by the Law Commission in their Consultation Paper on *Liability for Psychiatric Illness*: see Law Com no 137 (1995), para 5.37.
[4] See *[1999] 1 All ER 1* at 45–46.

Situations not involving sudden catastrophe

[1.64]   Sudden catastrophes are not the only situations which have given rise to negligence claims for psychiatric harm[1]. In recent years, such harm induced by stress suffered over time in the course of the claimant's employment has become accepted as a basis for liability in appropriate circumstances[2]. It has also been held to be arguable that the police owe a duty to provide *counselling* to persons who attend police interviews in a voluntary capacity, as 'appropriate adults' to assist suspects, if such persons could be at risk of psychiatric harm as a result of hearing details of exceptionally gruesome crimes[3].

[1] For a suggestion that the requirement that the claimant should have suffered a recognisable psychiatric illness should itself be abandoned, see the dissenting judgment of Thomas J in the New Zealand Court of Appeal in *van Soest v Residual Health Management Unit [2001] 1 NZLR 179*, discussed by Nicholas J Mullany in 'Distress, disorder and duty of care: the New Zealand front' (2001) 117 LQR 182.
[2] See *Hatton v Sutherland [2002] 2 All ER 1*. See, generally, CHAPTER 17 below.
[3] See *Leach v Chief Constable of Gloucestershire Constabulary [1999] 1 All ER 215, CA*. See also *McLoughlin v Jones [2002] 2 WLR 1279*, in which a solicitor's negligence was claimed foreseeably to have resulted in his client's wrongful imprisonment and consequent psychiatric illness.

W v Essex County Council

[1.65]   Another type of situation was considered in *W v Essex County Council*[1]. The claimants were foster parents who themselves suffered psychiatric damage when it emerged that their own children had been seriously sexually abused by a boy whom they had fostered. The abuser was already under suspicion for sexual offences before he was placed by the defendant local authority with the claimants, and the making of the placement had been contrary to an express stipulation by the claimants that they were not willing to foster any child who was suspected to have committed sexual abuse. Although the parents' claim for psychiatric harm had been struck out below, the House of Lords unanimously reinstated it and allowed it to proceed. The House appeared to contemplate a degree of flexibility in the application of existing concepts in the area. Lord Slynn said[2]:

'... the categorisation of those claiming to be included as primary or secondary victims is not as I read the cases finally closed. It is a concept still to be developed in different factual situations'.

In the circumstances of the instant case it was not beyond argument that the claimant's could not qualify as 'secondary'[3], or even as 'primary'[4] victims. Too much should not be read into a decision on a striking out application. Nevertheless, the recognition by the House of Lords that liability for psychiatric damage may extend into novel types of situation is clearly not without considerable potential significance.

[1]   *[2000] 2 All ER 237, HL.*
[2]   See *[2000] 2 All ER 237* at 243.
[3]   See *[2000] 2 All ER 237* at 244.
[4]   See *[2000] 2 All ER 237* at 243.

Reform?

[1.66]   As part of its Sixth Programme of Law Reform, the Law Commission undertook a major study of liability for psychiatric illness and it produced its final report in 1998.[1] The Commission's central recommendation is that, in 'three-party' situations, the only control device, or policy limitation on liability, which should be retained is the requirement that the claimant should have had a close tie of love and affection for the victim. The requirement that the claimant should have suffered 'shock' by virtue of his own immediate sensual perception of the accident or its aftermath was considered to be unnecessary and to make little sense in medical terms, and the Commission therefore recommends its abandonment. The central recommendation is put as follows:[2]

'there should be legislation laying down that a plaintiff, who suffers a reasonably foreseeable recognisable psychiatric illness as a result of the death, injury or imperilment of a person with whom he or she has a close tie of love and affection, should be entitled to recover damages from the negligent defendant in respect of that illness, regardless of the plaintiff's closeness (in time and space) to the accident or its aftermath or the means by which the plaintiff learns of it.'

The Commission also proposes[3] that there should be 'a fixed list of relationships where a close tie of love and affection shall be deemed to exist,[4] while allowing a plaintiff outside the list to prove that a close tie of affection existed between him or herself and the immediate victim'. In other respects the Commission is broadly in favour of allowing the common law to develop in this area and it therefore does not recommend the introduction of a general statutory code.

[1]   See *Liability for Psychiatric Illness*, Law Com no 249 (1998).
[2]   See the Report, para 6.16.

3   See the Report, para 6.26.

4   The list would include spouses, parents, children, siblings and couples who had cohabited for at least two years: see the Report, para 6.27.

Chapter 2

Evaluation of conduct

A Foreseeability and objectivity

Incapacity normally disregarded

[2.01]   The concept of negligence in the law of tort represents an uneasy compromise between, on the one hand, the supposed principle of 'no liability without fault' and, on the other, the desire to see those who have suffered injury compensated. The former principle has retarded the development of strict liability in this branch of the law; while the latter has prevented a subjective or 'genuine' concept of blameworthiness being adopted, since that would inevitably reduce the number of defendants who would succeed in recovering damages. The law therefore adopts the artificial objective standard of the 'reasonable man', which involves ignoring the realities of the defendant's situation in so far as his capacities differ from that standard.[1]

---

[1]   'The standard of foresight of the reasonable man is ... an impersonal one. It eliminates the personal equation and is independent of the idiosyncrasies of the particular person whose conduct is in question': *per* Lord Macmillan in *Glasgow Corpn v Muir [1943] AC 448* at 457, *[1943] 2 All ER 44* at 48, HL.

Reasonable level of competence

[2.02]   This requirement of a reasonable level of competence applies to skills which can only be acquired by training and effort, as well as to basic attributes which most people can be expected to possess.[1] Thus, drivers of motor cars owe the same duty to drive with the degree of skill and care to be expected of a competent and experienced driver. The fact that the defendant was incapable of attaining that standard because he was a learner,[2] or had suffered a stroke minutes before the accident,[3] is irrelevant. This insistence upon an objective test, to the benefit of the plaintiff, is not confined to situations in which liability insurance is compulsory or usual, such as those involving motor cars. Thus, in a case involving ordinary domestic repairs to his property carried out by a householder, it was held that:

> 'the degree of care and skill required of him must be measured not by reference to the degree of competence in such matters which he personally happened to possess, but by reference to the degree of care and skill which a reasonably competent carpenter might be expected to apply to the work in question.'[4]

---

[1]   For the negligence of professional people, see CHAPTER 6 to CHAPTER 9 below.
[2]   *Nettleship v Weston [1971] 2 QB 691, [1971] 3 All ER 581, CA.* But cf *Cook v Cook (1986) 68 ALR 353* (also involving a learner driver), in which the High Court of Australia rejected the reasoning in *Nettleship*'s case.

3   *Roberts v Ramsbottom [1980] 1 All ER 7, [1980] 1 WLR 823*. The driver must, however, have had *some* awareness of his condition, otherwise he cannot, even on an objective assessment, be said to have been at 'fault'. Moreover, it is not only sudden disabling events which can thereby preclude liability; even *gradual* ones may do so provided the driver is wholly *unaware* of his incapacity: see the decision of the Court of Appeal in *Mansfield v Weetabix [1998] 1 WLR 1263*.
4   *Wells v Cooper [1958] 2 QB 265* at 271, *[1958] 2 All ER 527* at 530, *per* Jenkins LJ (no liability on the facts).

Nature of the duty

[2.03]   It is important to remember, however, that the standard of care to be expected will depend upon the nature of the duty owed by the defendant in the overall context of the case. Thus a police force which provides a decompression facility for divers is not assuming the same degree of responsibility towards users, or potential users, of the facility as might be owed by qualified members of the medical profession[1]. Similarly, the duty of care owed by a practitioner of 'alternative medicine' will not be the same as that owed by a qualified medical practitioner[2].

1   See *Hardaker v Newcastle HA [2001] Lloyd's Rep Med 512*.
2   See *Shakoor v Situ [2000] 4 All ER 181*. For further discussion of this case see CHAPTER 7 below.

Duty owed by children

[2.04]   The general rule of a uniform standard of care is modified in cases involving injuries caused by children, in that the duty of care is limited to what is normally to be expected of a child of the defendant's age and experience. In *Mullin v Richards*[1] the 15-year-old plaintiff lost an eye when a fragment snapped from a plastic ruler while she and the defendant, who was the same age, were 'fencing' with their rulers at school. The Court of Appeal, reversing the trial judge, held that the claim failed on the facts, since there was no evidence that the rulers were liable to snap and hence no proof of negligence. The court did, however, clarify the law relating to the liability of children on which there was little previous English authority.[2] Thus, Hutchison LJ said:[3]

> 'The test of foreseeability is an objective one; but the fact that the first defendant was at the time a 15-year-old schoolgirl is not irrelevant. The question for the judge is not whether the actions of the defendant were such as an ordinarily prudent and reasonable adult in the defendant's situation would have realised gave rise to a risk of injury, it is whether an ordinarily prudent and reasonable 15-year-old schoolgirl in the defendant's situation would have realised as much.'

In so holding, the Court of Appeal expressly adopted *McHale v Watson*,[4] in which a full court[5] of the High Court of Australia gave extensive consideration to the liability of children. In that case a 12-year-old boy escaped liability when a piece of steel rod thrown by him accidentally hit another child and caused serious injury to one of her eyes. Kitto J said:[6]

> 'The standard of care being objective, it is no answer for him [ie the defendant child], any more than it is for an adult, to say that the harm he caused was due to his being abnormally slow-witted, quick-tempered, absent-minded or inexperienced. But it does not follow that he cannot rely in his defence upon a limitation upon the capacity for foresight or prudence, not as being personal to himself, but

as being characteristic of humanity at his stage of development and in that sense normal. By doing so he appeals to a standard of ordinariness, to an objective and not a subjective standard.'[7]

1 *[1998] 1 All ER 920, [1998] 1 WLR 1305, CA* (Hutchison and Butler-Sloss LJJ and Sir John Vinelott).
2 Although there had been isolated English cases in which persons below full age have been held liable in negligence (see *Gorely v Codd [1966] 3 All ER 891, [1967] 1 WLR 19*: mentally retarded 16-year-old), the question of the nature of liability had never previously been fully explored. For discussion see P Rowe 'Negligent Children' (1976) 126 NLJ 354. In the unreported case of *Staley v Suffolk County Council and Dean Mason (1985)*, Staughton J held a 12-year-old boy liable for injuries caused when a tennis ball hurled by him, with the intention of hitting another boy, hit and injured a member of the school's catering staff: see *Clerk and Lindsell on Torts* (18th edn, 2000) para 7–169.
3 See *[1998] 1 All ER 920* at 924, *[1998] 1 WLR 1305* at 1308.
4 *(1966) 115 CLR 199*.
5 McTiernan ACJ, Kitto and Owen JJ (Menzies J dissenting).
6 See *(1966) 115 CLR 199* at 213–214, quoted by Hutchison J in *Mullin v Richards [1998] 1 All ER 920* at 924, *[1998] 1 WLR 1305* at 1308.
7 See also the American Law Institute's *Restatement of the Law of Torts* (2nd) para 238A: 'If the actor is a child, the standard of conduct to which he must conform to avoid being negligent is that of a reasonable person of like age, intelligence, and experience under like circumstances.'

Reluctance to stigmatise children

[2.05]   Despite what might be seen as unfairness to the claimant, the courts are understandably reluctant to stigmatise a child as a tortfeasor as long as the fault principle still retains a foothold in this branch of the law.[1] Both *Mullin v Richards* and *McHale v Watson* were applied in *Etheridge v K (A Minor)*[2]; in which a claim for head injuries suffered by a teacher, when struck by a basketball thrown downstairs by a thirteen year old pupil while playing with other pupils between classes, was unsuccessful[3]. A similar approach is adopted in cases in which it is alleged that an infant claimant has been contributorily negligent;[4] even though the underlying issue in such cases, in which the courts are understandably reluctant to deprive a child of damages on this ground, is rather different.

1 In practice, claims of this kind are rare, since a child is rarely worth suing; it is more common to go primarily against the parent or guardian alleging negligently inadequate supervision: see eg *Donaldson v McNiven [1952] 1 All ER 1213*; affd *[1952] 2 All ER 691, CA* (claim failed on the facts); *Floyd v Bowers (1978) 21 OR (2d) 204*; affd *(1979) 106 DLR (3d) 702* (parent held liable along with child).
2 *[1999] Ed CR 550*.
3 The school itself was also acquitted of liability.
4 See *Gough v Thorne [1966] 3 All ER 398, [1966] 1 WLR 1387, CA*. See also *Yachuk v Oliver Blais Co Ltd [1949] AC 386, [1949] 2 All ER 150, PC* and CHAPTER 4 below.

B The measurement of risk

Degree of probability

[2.06]   The concept of reasonable foreseeability does not mean that liability will be imposed whenever it might conceivably have crossed the mind of a normal person that the occurrence of damage was a possibility.[1] The law also takes into account the degree of *probability*[2] of its doing so.[3] Thus, in the well-known case of *Bolton v Stone*[4] the defendant cricket club was exonerated from liability when a cricket ball was hit out of the ground on to the highway, where it injured the plaintiff. The possibility of such an event occurring was clearly foreseeable, because balls had escaped from the ground before. But the fact that they had done so only on some six occasions over a period of 30 years meant that the risk, in the circumstances, was one which the reasonable man could legitimately choose not to guard against.[5] The actual degree of probability required is not fixed but necessarily varies from case to case.[6] This is because three other factors are taken into account in assessing the overall risk. These are: the seriousness of the harm if it does actually occur; the overall utility or value of the activity upon which the defendant is engaged; and the extent and cost of effective precautions[7].

[1]   '... people must guard against reasonable probabilities, but they are not bound to guard against fantastic possibilities', *per* Lord Dundedin in *Fardon v Harcourt-Rivington (1932) 146 LT 391, HL.*

[2]   This does not, of course, mean that the occurrence itself has to have been 'probable' in order to give rise to liability. Obviously, there will very frequently be a duty to take precautions even though the odds in favour of an accident are a very long way below an evens chance. Cf *Koufos v c Czarnikow, The Heron II [1969] 1 AC 350, [1967] 3 All ER 686, HL.*

[3]   'The standard of care in the law of negligence is the standard of an ordinarily careful man, but, in my opinion, an ordinarily careful man does not take precautions against every foreseeable risk. He can, of course, foresee the possibility of many risks, but life would be almost impossible if he were to attempt to take precautions against every risk which he can foresee. He takes precautions against risks which are reasonably likely to happen. Many foreseeable risks are extremely unlikely to happen and cannot be guarded against except by almost complete isolation': *Bolton v Stone [1951] AC 850* at 863, *[1951] 1 All ER 1078* at 1083, HL, *per* Lord Oaksey.

[4]   *[1951] AC 850, [1951] 1 All ER 1078, HL.* See also *Mullin v Richards [1998] 1 All ER 920* at 925–926, *[1998] 1 WLR 1305* at 1309–1310, CA, *per* Hutchison LJ.

[5]   But note the warning of Lord Reid: 'I think ... that this case is not far from the border-line. If this appeal is allowed, that does not, in my judgment, mean that in every case where cricket has been played on a ground for a number of years without accident or complaint, those who organise matches there are safe to go on in reliance on past immunity. I would have reached a different conclusion if I had thought that the risk here had been other than extremely small because I do not think that a reasonable man, considering the matter from the point of view of safety, would or should disregard any risk unless it is extremely small ...' *[1951] AC 850* at 867–868, *[1951] 1 All ER 1078* at 1086. Cf *Miller v Jackson [1977] QB 966, [1977] 3 All ER 338, CA.*

[6]   See *Orange v Chief Constable of West Yorkshire [2002] QB 347*: precautions against suicide by prisoners can be lower for those not considered to be especially at risk. Cf *Pearson v Lightning [1998] 20 LS Gaz R 33, CA,* in which a golfer was held liable to the plaintiff who was hit by a ball which bounced off a tree: the risk was not so remote that it would not have been anticipated by a reasonable person.

[7]   For a stimulating discussion of the cases and their implications see Professor Stephen G Gillies 'The Emergence of Cost-Benefit Balancing in English Negligence Law' (2002) 77 Chicago-Kent LR 489.

Gravity of harm

[2.07]   If the harm, should it take place, would be particularly serious, it may be necessary to take precautions to prevent it even if the possibility of its occurring is very low. Thus, an employer may be negligent in failing to supply goggles to a workman with one good eye, when injury to that eye could deprive him of sight altogether, even where the risk of any injury occurring is sufficiently small to justify ignoring it where fully sighted workmen are concerned.[1] The good sense of this is apparent: the precautions needed when organising a boxing match, for example, are of a different order of magnitude from those required when playing cricket. The gravity of the harm which can readily be anticipated in the former, brain damage, requires elaborate resuscitation facilities to be provided at the ringside in order to minimise the risk.[2]

[1]   *Paris v Stepney Borough Council [1951] AC 367, [1951] 1 All ER 42, HL.* See also *Buchan v Ortho Pharmaceutical (Canada) Ltd (1984) 46 OR (2d) 113* (duty to warn unusually susceptible users of contraceptive pill of danger of stroke occurring even though risk small).

[2]   See *Watson v British Boxing Board of Control [2001] QB 1134, CA* in which liability was imposed for failing to provide such facilities.

Utility of the defendant's conduct

[2.08] In *Watt v Hertfordshire County Council*[1] the defendants' fire station received a call to an emergency which could only be dealt with by transporting a heavy jack to the scene of a road accident, in which someone was trapped under a bus. Unfortunately, the only vehicle equipped to carry the jack was out dealing with another matter. The jack was therefore loaded on to a different vehicle upon which it could not, in fact, be properly secured. During the journey to the scene of the accident the jack moved, and in so doing it trapped the plaintiff fire officer and injured him. The Court of Appeal held that the defendants had not been negligent. Denning LJ observed:

> '… you must balance the risk against the end to be achieved. If this accident had occurred in a commercial enterprise without any emergency, there could be no doubt that the servant would succeed. But the commercial end to make profit is very different from the human end to save life or limb. The saving of life justifies taking considerable risk …'[2]

In effect, therefore, the law operates a kind of sliding scale. At one extreme are positively laudable activities, such as that involved in *Watt v Hertfordshire County Council*[3]. In the middle are acts such a playing cricket, which are legitimate or even desirable. At the other extreme are activities which are undesirable or even unlawful. The degree of probability, necessary to create a duty to take precautions, falls as the latter end of the spectrum is approached.[4]

1   *[1954] 2 All ER 368, [1954] 1 WLR 835.*
2   *[1954] 2 All ER 368* at 371, *[1954] 1 WLR 835* at 838. In cases where negligent driving is alleged, however, the courts are not prepared to sanction the adoption of lower standards of care by police or other emergency vehicles: *Gaynor v Allen [1959] 2 QB 403, [1959] 2 All ER 644*; *Wardell-Yerburgh v Surrey County Council [1973] RTR 462*. Cf *Marshall v Osmond [1983] QB 1034, [1983] 2 All ER 225, CA*.
3   But note the doubts expressed by Buxton LJ in *King v Sussex Ambulance NHS Trust [2002] ICR 1413* as to the correctness of the principle in *Watt's* case: '… why should those men of courage, who are the persons who run the risk on behalf of the public, suffer if the risk eventuates?' His Lordship suggested that the principle might one day require reconsideration.
4   'If the activity which caused the injury to Miss Stone had been an unlawful activity there can be little doubt but that *Bolton v Stone* would have been decided differently': *Overseas Tankship (UK) v Miller SS Co Pty, The Wagon Mound (No 2) [1967] 1 AC 617* at 242, *[1966] 2 All ER 709* at 718, PC, *per* Lord Reid.

Extent of the precautions necessary for protection

[2.09] Once it is established that the degree of risk was such that the defendant should in principle have taken precautions, the next step in determining whether the imposition of liability for negligence would be appropriate is to measure the precautions in fact taken (if any) against those which might reasonably have been expected. The defendant may succeed in avoiding liability at this stage of the inquiry, even in the face of an established risk. In *Latimer v AEC Ltd*[1] the defendants' factory was badly affected by a flood, during which rain-water became mixed with an oily liquid used in the manufacturing process. After the water had drained away, the floor of the factory remained slippery. Although the defendants spread sawdust on the floor, the amount available was insufficient to cover the total area. The plaintiff workman subsequently slipped on the floor and injured himself. The trial judge held the defendants liable on the ground that, in the circumstances, they ought to have closed the factory, but this view was rejected by both the Court of Appeal and the House of Lords. Lord Porter

considered that it had not been established 'that a reasonably careful employer …
ought to have taken the drastic step of closing the factory'.[2] It should be noted that the
question of probability still remains relevant at this stage of the inquiry.[3]

---

[1]   *[1953] AC 643, [1953] 2 All ER 449, HL.*
[2]   *[1953] AC 643* at 653, *[1953] 2 All ER 449* at 451, HL.
[3]   '… the degree of risk was too small to justify, let alone require, closing down': *[1953] AC 643* at 662,
    [1953] 2 All ER 449 at 457, *per* Lord Asquith.

C Care and its quality

Protection of minorities

[2.10]   Although the basic test for the existence of a duty of care is the foreseeability
of a reasonable or average person, it does not of course at all follow that only such
persons are themselves foreseeable as persons to whom the duty of care is *owed*.
Depending upon the circumstances, minorities, or people in relatively unusual categories, may well be foreseeable and a duty of care may be owed to them.[1] Thus, in *Haley
v London Electricity Board*[2] the House of Lords held that the plaintiff, who was blind,
could recover damages from the defendants when he fell into a trench created by the
defendants' road excavations. Although the precautions the defendants had taken
were adequate to protect sighted pedestrians, they were not sufficient to protect the
blind.[3] The evidence in the case was that about one in 500 members of the population
were blind, and that many of them habitually went out alone. Lord Reid observed that
it was therefore 'quite impossible to say that it is not reasonably foreseeable that a
blind person may pass along a particular pavement on a particular day'. His Lordship
concluded that since, on the facts, there was 'no question … of any great difficulty in
affording adequate protection for the blind', liability would be imposed.[4] It is to be
noted, that in so holding, the House of Lords unanimously reversed both the trial
judge[5] and a unanimous Court of Appeal.[6]

---

[1]   '… a measure of care appropriate to the inability or disability of those who are immature or feeble in
    mind or body is due from others who know of, or ought to anticipate, the presence of such persons
    within the scope and hazard of their own operations': *Glasgow Corpn v Taylor [1922] 1 AC 44* at
    67, HL, *per* Lord Sumner.
[2]   *[1965] AC 778, [1964] 3 All ER 185.*
[3]   See also *Morrell v Owen* (1993) Times, 14 December (organisers of sporting events must take greater
    precautions where the participants are disabled than where they are able-bodied).
[4]   *[1965] AC 778* at 791, *[1964] 3 All ER 185* at 188. Cf the *Disabled Persons Act 1981, s 1.*
[5]   Marshall J.
[6]   Lord Denning MR, Donovan and Danckwerts LJJ: see *[1964] 2 QB 121, [1963] 3 All ER 1030.*

Duty owed to children

Duty owed by parents

[2.11]   '[T]he court should be wary', observed Sir Nicolas Browne-Wilkinson V-C
in *Surtees v Kingston-upon-Thames Borough* Council,[1] 'in its approach to holding
parents in breach of a duty of care owed to their children'. It is clear that in appropriate
cases liability may be imposed[2] but, as Sir Nicolas Browne-Wilkinson V-C continued:

> 'There are very real policy considerations to take into account if the conflicts
> inherent in legal proceedings are to be brought into family relationships.

Moreover, the responsibilities of a parent (which in contemporary society normally means the mother) looking after one or more children, in addition to the myriad other duties which fall on the parent at home, far exceed those of other members of society. The studied calm of the Royal Courts of Justice, concentrating on one point at a time, is light years away from the circumstances prevailing in the average home. The mother is looking after a fast-moving toddler at the same time as cooking the meal, doing the housework, looking after the other children and doing all the other things that the average mother has to cope with simultaneously, or in quick succession, in the normal household. We should be slow to characterise as negligent the care which ordinary loving and careful mothers are able to give to individual children, given the rough-and-tumble of home life.'

Thus, in the *Surtees* case itself a majority[3] of the Court of Appeal dismissed a claim in respect of a scalding injury which occurred to a two-year-old girl, while in the care of a foster-parent.

[1] *[1991] 2 FLR 559* at 583–584, CA.
[2] See *McCallion v Dodd [1966] NZLR 710, NZCA.* Cf *Hahn v Conley (1971) 45 ALJR 631 (High Court of Australia).*
[3] Sir Nicolas Browne-Wilkinson V-C and Stocker LJ; Beldam LJ dissenting.

Older children

[2.12] As children get older other factors also become relevant. In *Porter v Barking and Dagenham London Borough Council*[1] the defendant father allowed his own son, who was 14, and the plaintiff, another boy of the same age, to practise putting the shot. An accident occurred, injuring the plaintiff, but Simon Brown J dismissed a claim against the defendant. It was desirable to encourage initiative and independence in children of the plaintiff's age and not to be over-protective of them. With that in mind, the defendant's conduct had not fallen short of the standard to be expected of a reasonably prudent parent.

[1] (1990) Times, 9 April.

In loco parentis

[2.13] The test of what a 'reasonably careful parent' would have done can apply to those *in loco parentis* as well as to parents themselves. In *Chittock v Woodbridge School*[1] the seventeen-year-old claimant was left disabled after an accident during a school skiing trip. Reversing the trial judge, the Court of Appeal rejected the submission on behalf of the claimant that he should have been banned from skiing as a punishment for earlier misbehaviour during the trip. The defendant teacher's decision merely to administer a severe reprimand, which left the claimant free to continue skiing, was 'within a range of reasonable responses for a teacher in his position, acting as a reasonably careful parent'.[2]

[1] *[2002] PIQR P13.*
[2] *[2002] PIQR P13* at para 27 *per* Auld LJ.

Schools

[2.14] In *Gower v London Borough of Bromley*[1] Auld LJ summarised the duties of teachers as follows:[2]

'The duty is to exercise the skill and care of a reasonable headteacher and/or teachers, applying the *Bolam* test, namely, whether the teaching and other provision for a pupil's educational needs accords with that which might have been acceptable at the time by reasonable members of the teaching profession …'[3]

The teachers' employers may be held vicariously liable for breaches of that duty but, as Lord Slynn said when confirming this in *Phelps v London Borough of Hillingdon*[4], the 'professionalism, dedication and standards of those engaged in the provision of educational services are such that cases of liability for negligence will be exceptional'[5]. These passages were quoted by the Court of Appeal in *Bradford-Smart v West Sussex CC*[6], in which a school was held not have been in breach of duty in circumstances involving alleged bullying. The court emphasised, however, that a duty of care existed in such circumstances; and that its use might require the use of disciplinary powers in respect of behaviour outside school[7]. In *Kearn-Price v Kent CC*[8] the Court of Appeal imposed liability for inadequate playground supervision in the period just before the start of the school day, as a result of which the claimant suffered a serious eye injury. Schools will necessarily also owe duties to their pupils in respect of the state of their premises.[9]

[1] [1999] ELR 356, CA, affmd in *Phelps v London Borough of Hillingdon [2000] 4 All ER 504, HL.*
[2] See *[1999] ELR 356* at 359.
[3] For the *Bolam* test see below, CHAPTER 6.
[4] See *[2000] 4 All ER 504* at p 519, HL.
[5] See also *Liennard v Slough BC [2002] EWHC 398, [2002] ELR 527.*
[6] *[2002] 1 FCR 425.*
[7] See *[2002] 1 FCR 425* at para 34. See also *R v London Borough of Newham ex parte X [1995] ELR 303* at 306 *per* Brooke J.
[8] *[2003] PIQR P167.*
[9] See *B v Cardiff CC [2002] ELR 1* (child tripped on raised surface in playground: no liability on the facts).

Infinite range of possible cases

[2.15] Obviously parents and teachers are not the only defendants who may find themselves liable to children as a result of a negligent failure to take special precautions in situations in which they are involved. Motorists no doubt form the largest category, but the range of possible cases is infinite. Thus the unlawful sale of petrol to a thirteen-year-old child recently resulted in a garage-owner incurring common law liability for burning injuries, suffered by the purchaser when the petrol caught fire[1]. Of course in some cases defendants will be able to refute allegations of negligence by pointing to the responsibility of parents, particularly of small children, to protect them from situations of possible danger.[2]

[1] See *E (A Child) v Souls Garages* (2001) Times, 23 January. See also *Yachuk v Oliver Blais [1949] A C 386, PC.*
[2] See *B (A Child) v Camden LBC [2001] PIQR P9* (baby coming into contact with central heating pipes).

Relevance of common practice[1]

[2.16] The defendant may sometimes be able to show that the practices or methods of working he followed, at the time when the incident occurred, accorded with what was common or usual in the particular activity or profession.[2] Such evidence may be of value to the defendant in tending to negative or limit liability.[3] Nevertheless, it will not be conclusive since the court may be prepared to infer that the usual practice was itself negligent.[4] The courts are, however, rather more reluctant to draw this conclusion where the activity in question is a highly skilled profession, such as medicine, than where it is not.[5]

[1]   See J Holyoak 'Raising the standard of care' (1990) 10 LS 201.
[2]   See *Bolam v Friern Hospital Management Committee [1957] 2 All ER 118, [1957] 1 WLR 582*; *Maynard v West Midlands Regional Health Authority [1985] 1 All ER 635, [1984] 1 WLR 634, HL*; *Knight v Home Office [1990] 3 All ER 237.*
[3]   See *Thompson v Smiths Shiprepairers (North Shields) Ltd [1984] QB 405, [1984] 1 All ER 881.* See also *Gray v Stead [1999] 2 Lloyd's Rep 559, CA.*
[4]   See *Morris v West Hartlepool Steam Navigation Co [1956] AC 552, [1956] 1 All ER 385, HL*; *Cavanagh v Ulster Weaving Co [1960] AC 145, [1959] 2 All ER 745, HL*;
[5]   But cf *Greaves & Co (Contractors) v Baynham, Meikle and Partners [1974] 3 All ER 666, [1974] 1 WLR 1261, CA* (engineer). See generally CHAPTER 6 to CHAPTER 9 below for discussion of negligence in situations involving special skill.

Carelessness not to be inferred from subsequent adoption of protective measures

[2.17]   It has often been judicially emphasised that the defendant's conduct should be considered in the light of knowledge reasonably to have been expected of him at the time of the incident itself.[1] In *Glasgow Corpn v Muir*[2] Lord Thankerton said:

> 'The court must be careful to place itself in the position of the person charged with the duty and to consider what he or she should have reasonably anticipated as a natural and probable consequence of neglect, and not to give undue weight to the fact that a distressing accident has happened, or that witnesses, in the witness box, are prone to express regret, ex post facto, that they did not take some step, which it is now realised would definitely have prevented the accident.'

It follows that the fact that changes in practice have been introduced since the incident, possibly as a direct result of it, should not be taken into account.[3]

[1]   See *per* Thesiger J in *Philpot v British Rlys Board [1968] 2 Lloyd's Rep 495* at 502 and in *McAlpine & Sons Ltd v Minimax Ltd [1970] 1 Lloyd's Rep 397* at 416. See also *per* Webster J in *Wimpey Construction v Poole [1984] 2 Lloyd's Rep 499* at 507.
[2]   *[1943] AC 448* at 454–455, *[1943] 2 All ER 44* at 47, HL.
[3]   See *Roe v Minister of Health [1954] 2 QB 66* at 86, *[1954] 2 All ER 131* at 139, CA, *per* Denning LJ: 'If the hospitals were to continue the practice after this warning, they could not complain if they were found guilty of negligence. Indeed, it was the extraordinary accident to these two men which first disclosed the danger. Nowadays it would be negligence not to realise the danger, but it was not then.' See also *Worlock v Saws (1981) 20 BLR 94* at 116, *per* Woolf J.

'Errors of judgment'

[2.18]   A mere error of judgment, especially in a situation in which rapid action or decision-making is required, does not necessarily constitute actionable negligence. In *Wooldridge v Summer*[1] the defendant, who was competing in a horse show, misjudged a bend. As a result he fell off his horse which, out of control, left the track and collided with the plaintiff spectator, severely injuring him. The Court of Appeal, finding for the defendant, held that 'he was guilty of an error or errors of judgment or a lapse of skill' but that that was 'not enough to constitute a breach of the duty of reasonable care which a participant owes to a spectator'.[2] On the other hand, in *Smoldon v Whitworth*[3] the referee of an under-19s rugby football match was held liable to a player whose neck was broken when a scrum collapsed; his refereeing had fallen below an acceptable standard, notwithstanding that he had had to take split-second decisions during a fast-moving game.[4] This case was considered in *Caldwell v Maguire*[5] in which a jockey who had been seriously injured in a horse race sued two other jockeys alleging that their negligence had caused the accident. Although the conduct of the defendants had been in breach of Jockey Club rules, it was held to have consisted merely of 'errors or lapses of judgment' falling short of actionable negligence.[6]

[1]   *[1963] 2 QB 43, [1962] 2 All ER 978.*
[2]   *[1963] 2 QB 43* at 72, *[1962] 2 All ER 978* at 989–990, *per* Diplock LJ. Cf *Condon v Basi [1985] 2 All ER 453, [1985] 1 WLR 866, CA.*
[3]   *[1997] ELR 249, CA.*
[4]   See also *Vowles v Evans [2003] 1 WLR 1607* in which the Court of Appeal held an amateur rugby referee liable to a paralysed player for negligently failing to comply with the laws of the game. Cf *McCord v Swansea City AFC* (1997) Times, 11 February (football player liable in negligence for injury suffered by another player).
[5]   *[2002] PIQR P6.*
[6]   See *[2002] PIQR P6* at para. 33 *per* Judge LJ referring to the judgment of Holland J at first instance.

Questionable terminology

[2.19]   The *principle* reflected in these cases is evidently applicable beyond the special situation of sporting events. It has been applied by the Court of Appeal, in the defendant's favour, in a case involving 'horseplay' by fifteen-year-old boys.[1] Nevertheless, it should be noted that use of the *terminology* of 'error of judgment', by way of deliberate contrast with the concept of actionable negligence, has been criticised by the House of Lords as question-begging and as being unlikely, at least in medical negligence cases, to be of assistance.[2]

[1]   See *Blake v Galloway [2004] 3 All ER 315.*
[2]   See *Whitehouse v Jordan [1981] 1 All ER 267* at 281, *[1981] 1 WLR 246* at 263, *per* Lord Fraser (quoted in CHAPTER 7 below). See also *[1981] 1 All ER 267* at 276, 284, *[1981] 1 WLR 246* at 257–258, 268, *per* Lord Edmund-Davies and Lord Russell.

D Proof of negligence

Causation[1]

[2.20]   The plaintiff must show, on the balance of probabilities, not only that the defendant was careless, but also that that carelessness caused, or helped to cause, the injury or damage for which he claims.[2] In *Barnett v Chelsea and Kensington Hospital Management Committee*[3] a doctor for whom the defendants were responsible negligently failed to treat the deceased, who subsequently died from arsenic poisoning. The defendants escaped liability on the ground that even if the doctor had not been negligent, and treatment had been given to the deceased, the probability was that he would have died anyway.

[1]   See also CHAPTER 3 below.
[2]   See *Page v Smith (No 2) [1996] 3 All ER 272, [1996] 1 WLR 855, CA* (burden discharged on the facts).
[3]   *[1969] 1 QB 428, [1968] 1 All ER 1068.*

Probability not relevant to historical fact

[2.21]   Nor are the courts prepared in cases broadly similar to *Barnett* to assess the matter on the basis of degrees of probability, and to award the claimant a percentage of his loss on the basis that the defendant's negligence had deprived the plaintiff of some chance of recovery.[1] In *Hotson v East Berkshire Area Health Authority*[2] the plaintiff injured his hip in a fall from a tree. Unfortunately, the medical treatment which he received included a negligent delay in the proper diagnosis of the extent of his injuries. He subsequently developed a permanent disability, which he argued that prompt treatment would have averted. The defendants, however, contended that the disability had been inevitable from the moment of the fall. The trial judge, who was upheld by the Court of Appeal, awarded the plaintiff 25% of his loss on the ground that although the risk of his developing the disability after the fall had been as high as 75%, there had been a chance, albeit a relatively small one, that prompt treatment would have brought about a complete recovery. The House of Lords, reversing the courts below, held that the plaintiff failed altogether. It was implicit in the trial judge's finding of fact that, on the balance of probabilities, the fall and not the negligent treatment had caused the disability. Accordingly, it would appear that, in personal injury cases, the question of whether a defendant's carelessness had had any causative effect must be determined one way or the other as a matter of historical fact.[3]

[1]   See CHAPTER 3 below for the differing approach adopted in cases where the outcome would have depended upon the hypothetical future action of an independent third party.

[2]   *[1987] AC 750, [1987] 2 All ER 909, HL*. See T Hill 'A Lost Chance for Compensation in the Tort of Negligence by the House of Lords' (1991) 54 MLR 511. Cf W Scott 'Causation in Medico-Legal Practice: A Doctor's Approach to the "Lost Opportunity" Cases' (1992) 55 MLR 521.

[3]   For criticism of the approach of the House of Lords, see J Stapleton 'The Gist of Negligence' (1988) 104 LQR 213 and 389, who argues that it side-steps the question as to the nature of the 'damage' which the defendant needs to be shown to have caused. If that damage were to be perceived as the loss of the chance itself, rather than the actual disability, the not unattractive solution reached by the courts below would be seen to be justified. 'It cannot be over-emphasised that the formulation of the "damage" forming the gist of the action defines the causation question. Logically, one can only deal with causation after one knows what the damage forming the gist of the action is': J Stapleton (1988) 104 LQR 213 at 393. Cf M Lunney 'What price a chance' (1995) 15 LS 1.

Gregg v Scott

[2.22]   In *Gregg v Scott*[1] a bare majority of the House of Lords[2] applied the *Hotson* principle to a case in which there had been a negligent delay in diagnosing that the claimant had cancer. Since the prospect of cure, in the event of timely diagnosis, had been less than 50% the claim was dismissed notwithstanding that the claimant had in practice been deprived of a not insubstantial chance of cure. The decision of the majority appears to have been based, at least in part, on policy considerations: the need for certainty and the need to protect the National Health Service from increased litigation[3].

[1]   *[2005] UKHL 2*.

[2]   Lord Hoffman, Lord Phillips and Lady Hale, Lord Nicholls and Lord Hope dissenting.

[3]   See eg per Lord Phillips at para 170.

Where causative factor impossible to isolate

[2.23]   If the situation was such that more than one cause *materially contributed* thereto, the claimant does not have to prove that the cause for which the defendant was responsible would have been sufficient to produce injury *by itself*.[1] Special difficulty arises, however, if the situation is such that it is impossible, because of the current limits of science, for the claimant to prove which of several possible causes was the actual one. Assuming that breach of duty with respect to the possible causes has already been established against the defendant, or against all the defendants if there were more than one, to insist also upon proof of causation in the usual way would, *ex hypothesi*, be to insist upon the impossible and to condemn the claimant to failure despite the defendant's proven breaches of duty. The injustice of such a result to the claimant has led the House of Lords, in two leading cases decided thirty years apart, to modify for some cases of this type the usual rule relating to the need for proof of actual causation.

¹ See *Bonnington Castings Ltd v Wardlaw [1956] AC 613, [1956] 1 All ER 615, HL.*

Limits of science

[2.24]   The first case, *McGhee v National Coal Board*¹, which was decided in 1972, concerned more than one possible cause but only one possible defendant. The plaintiff contracted dermatitis through contact with brick dust at his place of work. It was not alleged that this exposure in itself constituted negligence on the part of his employers, but that their failure to provide shower facilities did so, since it obliged him to keep the dust on his skin until he arrived home. As it happened, however, it was impossible for the plaintiff to prove scientifically that the absence of washing facilities had contributed to his contraction of dermatitis; the initial non-negligent contact during his work might have caused it in any event. The House of Lords nevertheless allowed him to recover, asserting that where a defendant's negligence could be taken, in the existing state of knowledge, to have materially increased the risk of the plaintiff's developing a certain disease, this was sufficient to justify the imposition of liability²; even though medical science was simply too uncertain to explain how the particular disease came to develop.³

¹ *[1972] 3 All ER 1008, [1973] 1 WLR 1, HL.*
² See also *Brown v Corus (UK) [2004] PIQR P30, CA.*
³ Jane Stapleton 'The Gist of Negligence' (1988) 104 LQR 213 and 389 argued (at 401ff) that in holding the defendants liable for the *entire* loss, the result in this case was too harsh, and that a more sophisticated definition of the plaintiff's 'damage' in such situations (ie in terms of the increased *chance* of contracting the disease rather than in terms of the disease itself) could lead to a more satisfactory outcome.

Several defendants

[2.25]   The second case, *Fairchild v Glenhaven Funeral Services and others*¹, decided in 2002, was more complicated in that there were several possible defendants. The claimants had all developed a rare form of cancer for which exposure to asbestos was nearly always responsible. They had all also, during their working lives, been employed by more than one employer. But each of the employers had exposed them to asbestos, and been in proven breach of duty in so doing. Unfortunately, however, because science has not yet established the precise mechanism whereby asbestos triggers the cancer, the claimants could not establish which of the employers had been the one for whom they had been working at the time when the disease was actually contracted. The Court of Appeal accordingly held that since the claimants could not show which employer was the one whose breach of duty had caused their illness they could not recover from any of them. The House of Lords unanimously reversed this decision, and decided in favour of the claimants. 'Any other outcome', said Lord Nicholls of Birkenhead, 'would be deeply offensive to instinctive notions of what justice requires and fairness demands'².

1   *[2002] 3 All ER 305.* See Jane Stapleton 'Lords A'Leaping Evidentiary Gaps' (2002) 10 Torts Law
    Journal 276; Jonathan Morgan 'Lost Causes in the House of Lords' (2003) 66 MLR 277.
2   See *[2002] 3 All ER 305* at para. 36.

McGhee confirmed and extended

[2.26]   After an exhaustive review of the approach adopted in other jurisdictions as
well as of the English cases, the House in *Fairchild* concluded that the underlying
principle in *McGhee v National Coal Board* was not only valid, which had sometimes
been doubted[1], but that it was also capable of extension to cases involving more than
one defendant. Lord Bingham of Cornhill said:[2]

> '… there is a strong policy argument in favour of compensating those who have
> suffered grave harm, at the expense of their employers who owed them a duty to
> protect them against that very harm and failed to do so, when the harm can only
> have been caused by breach of that duty and when science does not permit the
> victim accurately to attribute, as between several employers, the precise respon-
> sibility for the harm he has suffered. I am of opinion that such injustice as may
> be involved in imposing liability on a duty-breaking employer in these circum-
> stances is heavily outweighed by the injustice of denying redress to a victim'.

Thus, employers who neglect straightforward and commonsense precautions cannot
expect to rely upon the impossibility of proving causation to escape liability. Moreover, it appears that the claimant will be able to recover in full against any of the
relevant employers[3], leaving them to resolve between themselves any question of
apportionment on the usual rules relating to contribution between tortfeasors.[4]

1   Cf the observations of Lord Bridge in *Wilsher v Essex Area Health Authority [1988] AC 1074* at 1090,
    [1988] 1 All ER 871 at 881–882, which sought to confine *McGhee's* case to its own facts, and which
    were disapproved by the House in *Fairchild.*
2   See *[2002] 3 All ER 305* at para 33.
3   Cf *Holtby v Brigham & Cowan (Hull) Ltd [2000] 3 All ER 421, CA,* discussed by Louise Gulllifer in
    'One Cause After Another' (2001) 117 LQR 403. See also *Allen v British Rail Engineering [2001]
    PIQR Q10.*
4   See below, CHAPTER 22.

Outer limits of the Fairchild principle

[2.27]   The precise outer limits of the principle in *McGhee v National Coal Board*
and *Fairchild v Glenhaven Funeral Services and others* are not altogether clear. In
both cases all the possible causes had the same basic source of danger in common:
brick dust in one and asbestos in the other. If that is not the case, it appears that the
claimant will not normally be able to invoke the principle. Thus in the *Fairchild* case
the House of Lords emphasised that its own earlier decision in *Wilsher v Essex Area
Health Authority*[1] had been correct. In that case a premature baby developed a
disorder which *might* have been caused by a slip for which the defendants were
responsible. But the disorder *could* have had several other causes *unrelated* to the slip,
and was one to which premature babies are prone in any event. The trial judge, relying
on what was subsequently held to have been a misreading of *McGhee v National Coal
Board*, nevertheless imposed liability on the ground that, given that the slip had been a
possible cause, the burden of proving that it had not been an *actual* one lay on the
defendants. Although a majority of the Court of Appeal felt able to uphold his
decision,[2] the House of Lords ordered a retrial on the causation issue. In *Fairchild,*

Lord Rodgers of Earlsferry said *Wilsher's* case was different because 'the principle does not apply where the claimant has merely proved that his injury could have been caused by a number of different events, only one of which is the *eventuation of the risk* created by the defendant's wrongful act or omission'.[3]

¹   *[1988] AC 1074, [1988] 1 All ER 871.*
²   See *[1987] QB 730, [1986] 3 All ER 801.*
³   See *[2002] 3 All ER 305* at para 170, italics supplied. See also *per* Lord Bingham at para 22 ('single noxious agent'). But cf *per* Lord Hoffman at para 70 onwards, who doubted whether *Wilsher* could satisfactorily be distinguished in this way, even though he agreed that it had been correctly decided.

No liability after penicillin overdose

[2.28]   Thus, in the earlier case of *Kay v Ayrshire and Arran Health Board*[1] the House of Lords refused to regard *McGhee* as relevant in a case in which the plaintiff was found to be deaf after an attack of meningitis, in the course of the treatment for which he had received a massive overdose of penicillin. Since deafness is a common after-effect of meningitis, but there is no recorded case of a penicillin overdose having caused deafness, the House of Lords held that there was simply no factual basis for the contention that the overdose had materially increased the risk that the plaintiff would suffer from this particular after-effect.

¹   *[1987] 2 All ER 417, HL.*

Res ipsa loquitur

The initial presumption

[2.29]   If the claimant suffers injury or damage through contact with some mechanical or other agency, he may experience difficulty in gathering evidence to prove negligence if that agency was throughout under the control or management of the defendant. The presumption embodied in the maxim *res ipsa loquitur*, or 'the thing speaks for itself'[1], may assist the claimant in such a situation. If, but only if,[2] what occurred was something which would not normally be expected to occur in the absence of carelessness on the part of those who have control or management of the operation, then a presumption of negligence will be raised in the claimant's favour.[3] It follows that in such a case the defendant cannot succeed on a submission of no case to answer.[4] The defendant must offer evidence if he is to succeed in defeating the claimant's claim.[5] If the defendant is able to explain fully and in detail how the accident occurred it will be for the court to decide, applying in the usual way the ordinary principles relating to the evaluation of conduct, whether or not negligence liability should be imposed.[6] The initial presumption in the claimant's favour will have no part to play at this conclusive stage of the inquiry in such a relatively straightforward case. Difficult questions arise, however, if even the *defendant* is unable to explain the full sequence of events leading up to the accident. Logically, all that a defendant can do in such a case, in an attempt to rebut the presumption of negligence, is to show two things. First, that his system of working complied with what was usual in the particular activity, and secondly that a reasonably plausible hypothesis exists as to how the accident *might* have been caused which would be consistent with him or his servants not having been careless on the particular occasion.

¹   See *Fryer v Pearson* (2000) Times, April 4, CA at para 9 *per* Waller LJ. Cf *per* May LJ at para 18: 'It troubles me that we still tend to fall into the habit of talking about maxims or doctrines which go under

labels in Latin whose meaning does not express a defined principle'. See also Christian Witting, 'Res ipsa loquitur: some last words?' (2001) 117 LQR 392.

2   Cf *Stafford v Conti Commodity Services Ltd [1981] 1 All ER 691.*

3   The classic statement is to be found in the judgment of Erle CJ in *Scott v London and St Katherine Docks Co (1865) 3 H&C 596* at 601: '… where the thing is shown to be under the management of the defendant or his servants, and the accident is such as in the ordinary course of things does not happen if those who have the management use proper care, it affords reasonable evidence, in the absence of explanation by the defendants that the accident arose from want of care.'

4   See *Widdowson v Newgate Meat Corp [1997] 47 LS Gaz R 31, CA.*

5   See *Lloyde v West Midlands Gas Board [1971] 2 All ER 1240* at 1246–1247, *[1971] 1 WLR 749* at 755, CA, *per* Megaw LJ.

6   See *Barkway v South Wales Transport Co [1950] AC 185, [1950] 1 All ER 392, HL.* See also *Ng Chun Pui v Lee Chuen Tat [1988] RTR 298, PC.*

Covert strict liability?

[2.30]   In two cases in which causation remained a mystery, *Moore v R Fox & Sons*[1] and *Colvilles Ltd v Devine*,[2] the defendants failed, despite advancing causation hypotheses consistent with the absence of fault. At first glance, these decisions might be taken to suggest that *res ipsa loquitur* had been converted from a mere rule of evidence into a rule of law covertly imposing strict liability. This is because evidence of the kind indicated towards the end of the last paragraph is the only kind which a defendant unable to explain the cause of the accident *can* give. Accordingly, if such evidence were to be denied any probative value simply on *a priori* grounds that would effectively turn *res ipsa loquitur* into an *irrebuttable* presumption. If strict liability is indeed being imposed in this way, it would be objectionable. Although it can be argued that a general regime of strict liability would be preferable, at least in personal injury cases, to the operation of the law of negligence, it would hardly be appropriate to introduce it arbitrarily depending upon whether or not the facts happened to entitle the claimant to reply on the maxim *res ipsa loquitur.* Nevertheless, it has indeed been suggested that the courts have used the presumption in this way so as to expand the scope of strict liability.[3]

1   *[1956] 1 QB 596, [1956] 1 All ER 182, CA.*

2   *[1969] 2 All ER 53, [1969] 1 WLR 475, HL.*

3   See P Atiyah 'Res Ipsa Loquitur in England and Australia' (1972) 35 MLR 337; J Millner *Negligence in Modern Law* (1967) pp 89ff. See also C Manchester 'Yoghurt Spillage and Res Ipsa Loquitur' (1977) 93 LQR 13.

Better view is that fault principle survives

[2.31]   It is submitted that the strict liability thesis is not correct. It is important to remember that, in order to rebut the presumption, the defendant must show *both* that his system was the usual one adopted *and* that a causation hypothesis consistent with the absence of fault existed. Merely to prove one without the other clearly cannot be enough.[1] Thus, a defendant who shows that his system is the usual and accepted one cannot, if the case is one to which the presumption applies, succeed on proof of this *alone* (ie without advancing a hypothetical cause for the accident consistent with the absence of fault). The court would still be entitled to conclude that it was more likely than not that the system broke down on the particular occasion, for example because of an isolated act of carelessness on the part of his servants for which he would be vicariously liable.[2] Equally, a defendant who does not even attempt to show that the usual precautions were taken obviously cannot expect to succeed, given the initial presumption, however many hypotheses consistent with the absence of fault he is able to devise. The failure of the defendants in both *Moore v R Fox & Sons*[3] and *Colvilles Ltd v Devine*,[4] despite advancing causation hypotheses consistent with the absence of fault, is explicable simply because they had not shown in addition that the usual precautions were taken.[5]

[1]   See *Colvilles Ltd v Devine [1969] 2 All ER 53* at 57, *[1969] 1 WLR 475* at 477–478, *per* Lord Guest.
[2]   See *Hill v James Crowe (Cases) Ltd [1978] 1 All ER 812, [1978] ICR 298* (not following *Daniels and Daniels v R White & Sons and Tarbard [1938] 4 All ER 258*).
[3]   *[1956] 1 QB 596, [1956] 1 All ER 182, CA.*
[4]   *[1969] 2 All ER 53, [1969] 1 WLR 475.*
[5]   '... it was the duty of the maintenance man to inspect the apparatus weekly and the duty of the foreman to supervise the deceased ... There was, however, no evidence that either of these duties had been performed. There was, therefore, no evidence of conduct which, whatever the actual cause of the accident, was in accordance with a proper performance of the duty of care': *per* Evershed MR in *Moore v R Fox & Sons [1956] 1 QB 596 at 609, [1956] 1 All ER 182* at 187. Similarly, in *Colvilles v Devine* 'No evidence was forthcoming from the appellants as to any inspection of the filters being made by them ... They led no evidence to suggest that any inspection of the filters was ever made to see if they were working properly': *[1969] 1 WLR 475* at 478, *per* Lord Guest. See also *per* Lord Donovan at 479.

Defendant's evidence must not be avoidably incomplete or inadequate

[2.32]   Even if the defendant *does* furnish evidence relating both to hypothetical causation and the taking of the usual precautions, the court might still legitimately conclude, without in effect imposing strict liability, that his evidence overall was not satisfactory. There might, for example, be good grounds for supposing that the evidence included significant gaps which the defendants could have filled had they chosen to do so. In *Henderson v Jenkins*[1] the brakes on the defendants' lorry suddenly failed, and a fatal accident resulted. The defendants showed that the generally accepted procedures for inspection and servicing of the lorry had been adopted, and postulated that the failure, which had occurred when a hole developed in a pipe carrying brake fluid, might have been due to a latent defect causing the pipe to corrode much more rapidly than was usual. But it was also possible that the corrosion might have been the result of the lorry being put to an unusual use, perhaps involving contact with acid or salt-water, in which case more elaborate procedures for inspection and servicing than those used generally, would have been appropriate. The defendants did not disclose, however, the uses to which the lorry had been put. They might perhaps, in the words of Lord Pearson:

> 'have been able to show by evidence that the lorry had not been used in any way, or involved in any accident, that would cause abnormal corrosion or require special inspection or treatment, or at any rate that they neither knew nor ought to have known of any such use or incident. But they did not call any such evidence. Their answer was incomplete'.[2]

[1]   *[1970] AC 282, [1969] 3 All ER 756, HL.* See also *J (A Child) v North Lincolnshire CC [2000] PIQR P84. CA.*
[2]   *[1970] AC 282* at 303, *[1969] 3 All ER 756* at 768. See also *[1970] AC 282* at 291, 299, *per* Lord Reid and Lord Donovan. Cf *Worsley v Hollins [1991] RTR 252, CA.*

Ward v Tesco Stores

[2.33]   Another case in which the evidence taken as a whole, combined with the operation of the presumption, justified the imposition of liability for negligence notwithstanding the efforts of the defence, was *Ward v Tesco Stores*.[1] The plaintiff slipped on a pool of yoghurt which had been spilt on the floor of the defendants' supermarket. The defendants stated that they had a system for dealing with spillages, which involved each member of staff being instructed to watch out for them and take immediate action when one was noticed; that was in addition to periodical brushing of the floor throughout the day. Moreover, it was possible that the particular spillage had been caused by a customer only seconds before the plaintiff slipped on it, in which case the defendants could not have been regarded as careless. Neither the plaintiff nor the defendants were in fact able, however, to prove how long the spillage had been on the floor and therefore whether it had, in fact, occurred very recently or not. The Court of Appeal held, by a majority,[2] that the maxim *res ipsa loquitur* applied, and upheld the decision of the county court judge in favour of the plaintiff. The judge had found as a fact that the defendants had not taken reasonable care. This might have been because he felt that although they had a system for spotting and dealing with the spillages, it was simply not quite rigorous enough. Alternatively, he might have considered that the defendants' servants had not been as zealous as they should have been in putting an otherwise sound system into effect, a proposition for which there was some evidential support.[3]

---

[1] *[1976] 1 All ER 219, [1976] 1 WLR 810, CA*. Cf *Dulhunty v J B Young (1975) 7 ALR 409 (High Court of Australia)*, noted in *(1977) 93 LQR 486*.
[2] Lawton and Megaw LJJ, Ormrod LJ dissenting.
[3] On a subsequent visit to the same supermarket, the plaintiff herself noticed that some orange juice which had been spilt was left on the floor for about a quarter of an hour with no one coming to clear it up: see *[1976] 1 All ER 219* at 223, *[1976] 1 WLR 810* at 812E.

Presumption can be rebutted

[2.34]   Accordingly, although the presumption embodied in the maxim *res ipsa loquitur* is capable of giving genuine assistance to claimants, it is probably not true to say that it amounts to a rule of law covertly imposing strict liability in an unprincipled fashion. A defendant who can show that all the usual precautions were taken, and can also adduce an explanation for the incident consistent with the absence of fault, should still succeed in rebutting the presumption provided his evidence is perceived to be frank, thorough and plausible.

Chapter 3

Causation and remoteness

A Introduction

Causation and quantification

[3.01] It is important to distinguish the causation of damage from the quantification of damages.[1] Questions of quantification clearly cannot arise until it is established that the defendant's carelessness has caused damage to the claimant of a kind which is recoverable in law. For legal purposes the relevant 'causal' relationships will usually be those perceived on a practical, or day-to-day basis rather than those identified by some kind of rigorous scientific analysis.[2] In the majority of cases such relationships will either be self-evident or easily established. Of course, this 'common sense' approach begs underlying questions of a fundamental nature, and it is sometimes contended that the supposed 'practical' assumptions of the law are themselves evaluative and are influenced by the content of the existing rules for the ascription of legal responsibility, or views as to what such rules ought to contain.[3] But it would not be appropriate in a book of this kind to attempt an investigation of the philosophical issues relating to causation.[4] As a result, rather than collect together in this chapter all the cases which touch upon problems of a causal nature, reference is made to some of them elsewhere according to the overall context in which they arose.[5]

[1]   See below.
[2]   Cf *Galoo Ltd v Bright Grahame Murray [1995] 1 All ER 16* at 29, CA, *per* Glidewell LJ.
[3]   But for the better view, see H Hart and T Honoré *Causation in the Law* (2nd edn, 1985).
[4]   For discussion see section IIIB of D Owen (ed) *Philosophical Foundations of Tort Law* (1995), especially T Honoré 'Necessary and Sufficient Conditions in Tort Law'.
[5]   See especially chapters 2,7,21,22 and 24 of the above publication.

'But for' test

[3.02]   The traditional question to ask is whether the loss would have occurred 'but for' the defendant's negligence. Although the application of this test will usually be straightforward, this will not always be the case. It will sometimes be necessary for the court intuitively to select, from more than one possible candidate, which factor is to be elevated to the status of 'cause'. In one such case, *Casey v Morane Ltd*[1], Mance LJ put it as follows:

' ... a "but for" test is only one customary (although itself not absolutely invariable) aspect of causation. Where a number of factors combine to lead to a situation in which a claimant incurs loss, a more sophisticated approach is required. It may become appropriate to select the "predominant" or "real" or "effective" cause ... '

The 'but for' test notoriously breaks down in rare but much-debated cases where two persons simultaneously carry out acts, either of which would have caused the damage. The test would seem to produce the unsatisfactory result that neither person can be liable. To meet such difficulties Professor Richard Wright has argued that 'a comprehensive test of causal condition' can be formulated known as the 'NESS' test (acronym of 'necessary element of a sufficient set') which 'states that a condition contributed to some consequence if and only if it was necessary for the sufficiency of a set of existing antecedent conditions that was sufficient for the occurrence of the consequence'[2]. This sophisticated test can, in carefully defined circumstances, treat acts as 'causes' even if the outcome would have been the same if they had not occurred; and thereby produce more satisfactory results in the case of simultaneous negligent acts[3].

[1]   See *[2001] ICR 316* at para 23, CA.
[2]   See 'Once More into the Bramble Bush: Duty, Causal Contribution, and the Extent of Legal Responsibility' (2001) 53 Vanderbilt LR 1071, at pp 1101 onwards.
[3]   Professor Jane Stapleton has put forward an alternative test known as the 'Targeted But-For Test': see 'Cause-in-Fact and the Scope of Liability for Consequences' (2003) 119 LQR 388, at 393–394 (and references there cited); see also Wright, at p 1109 onwards.

'Remoteness of damage'

[3.03]   The expression 'remoteness of damage' is most appropriately used to denote the problem of whether or not to ascribe legal responsibility to the defendant when it is clear that he 'caused' the claimant's harm, but the causal chain happened to involve a particularly freakish concatenation of circumstances.[1] In practice, however, the phrase 'too remote' is sometimes used rather more widely, to refer to situations which are not in themselves factually uncommon but which happen for *other* reasons to raise controversial questions relating to the ascription of legal responsibility. This usage is unfortunate[2], since it is often associated with the temptation to evade substantive issues of principle by pretending that they are largely questions of fact.[3] Thus, many of the cases on intervening human action, especially those on 'rescue', raise normative or policy questions rather than illustrate freakish events.[4]

[1]   See also M A Jones *Textbook on Torts* (8th edn, 2002) pp 257–258: ' … it … seems sensible to maintain a distinction between cases of multiple cause, where the question is which cause is to be treated as having legal significance, and cases where on any view the defendant's negligence was the cause of the harm, but it is thought to be unfair to hold him responsible because it occurred in some unusual or bizarre fashion.'
[2]   On the importance of separating normative from factual issues in the causation context see Stapleton 'Cause-in-Fact and the Scope of Liability for Consequences' (2003) 119 LQR 388, and also in (2001) 54 Vanderbilt LR 941.
[3]   For an example of such unfortunate usage, see *SCM (UK) Ltd v Whittall & Son Ltd [1971] 1 QB 337* at 344–346, *[1970] 3 All ER 245* at 251, *per* Lord Denning MR (economic loss).
[4]   'We should explicitly focus directly on the substantive normative arguments about responsibility under the relevant cause of action … rather than be distracted by some alleged free-standing characterisation of the intervening factor': J Stapleton 'Cause-in-Fact and the Scope of Liability for Consequences' (2003) 119 LQR 388 at 421–422.

B Nature of loss and measure of damages

Loss and damages

[3.04]   'Before one can consider the principle on which one should calculate the damages to which a plaintiff is entitled as compensation for loss', said Lord Hoffmann in *South Australia Asset Management Corpn v York Montague Ltd*,[1] 'it is necessary to decide for what kind of loss he is entitled to compensation'. It may not always be self-evident whether the issue before the court is to determine whether what occurred was the defendant's responsibility at all, or whether it is merely to quantify the claimant's loss on the basis that recoverability in principle could be taken as established. Nevertheless, the distinction is obviously fundamental. Questions relating to the assessment, in pecuniary terms, of a claimant's loss are separate from the rules, including those on remoteness, which determine what types of damage are remediable. Thus, although 'foreseeability' is the fashionable criterion for determining remoteness,[2] a motorist who runs over an apparent vagrant remains liable for his victim's loss of earnings even when the latter turns out, unforeseeably, to be a prosperous member of the Bar Theatrical Society on the way to a performance of some avant-garde drama.

[1]   *[1997] AC 191* at 211, *[1996] 3 All ER 365* at 369.
[2]   See below.

Relationship between duty and loss

[3.05]   Conversely, merely because the loss suffered by the claimant was foreseeable, and would not have occurred if the defendant had not been careless, it does not necessarily follow that the defendant will be liable, since he may not have owed any duty to the claimant in respect of the particular kind of loss which materialised.[1] In *South Australia Asset Management Corpn v York Montague Ltd*[2] Lord Hoffmann gives the following hypothetical example:

> 'A mountaineer about to undertake a difficult climb is concerned about the fitness of his knee. He goes to a doctor who negligently makes a superficial examination and pronounces the knee fit. The climber goes on the expedition, which he would not have undertaken if the doctor had told him the true state of his knee. He suffers an injury which is an entirely foreseeable consequence of mountaineering, but has nothing to do with his knee.'

Although the injury is a foreseeable consequence of the doctor's carelessness, in the sense that he would not have embarked upon the expedition if he had been told about the true state of his knee, Lord Hoffmann concludes that the doctor is not liable: 'The injury has not been caused by the doctor's bad advice, because it would have occurred even if the advice had been correct.'[3]

[1]   Cf *Bristol and West Building Society v Mothew [1996] 4 All ER 698, CA.*
[2]   *[1997] AC 191* at 213, *[1996] 3 All ER 365* at 371, HL; revsg sub nom *Banque Bruxelles Lambert SA v Eagle Star Insurance Co Ltd [1995] QB 375, [1995] 2 All ER 769, CA.*
[3]   *[1997] AC 191* at 214, *[1996] 3 All ER 365* at 371.

Need for careful analysis

[3.06]   The causal approach reflected in this example highlights the need for a careful analysis of the precise *duty* owed to the claimant by the defendant[1]. The *South Australia Asset Management Corpn* cases[2] involved the lending of money against the security of property following negligent over-valuations. After the loans had been made, the property market fell, and the lenders contended that the valuers should be liable for the additional losses suffered as a result of this fall, on the ground that the market movement was foreseeable and that they would not have entered into the transactions if they had been given accurate valuations. The House of Lords, reversing the Court of Appeal, rejected the lenders' claims and held that the damages would be assessed on the difference between the careless valuations, and the correct figures, at the date of the valuations themselves.[3] Lord Hoffmann[4] did, however, emphasise that this decision was predicated on the limited nature of the duty normally undertaken by a valuer as compared, for example, with someone whose role is to provide actual *advice*. His Lordship put it as follows:[5]

> 'The principle thus stated distinguishes between a duty to *provide information* for the purpose of enabling someone else to decide upon a course of action and a duty to *advise* someone as to what course of action he should take. If the duty is to advise whether or not a course of action should be taken, the adviser must take reasonable care to consider all the potential consequences of that course of action. If he is negligent, he will therefore be responsible for all the foreseeable loss which is a consequence of that course of action having been taken. If his duty is only to supply information, he must take reasonable care to ensure that the information is correct and if he is negligent, will be responsible for all the foreseeable consequences of the information being wrong.'

[1] See *Petersen v Personal Representatives of Rivlin (Deceased) [2002] Lloyd's Rep P N 386, CA*. Cf *Michael Gerson (Investments) v Haines Watts [2002] Lloyd's Rep P N 493*.
[2] Three cases were heard together raising the same point.
[3] See J Stapleton 'Negligent Valuers and Falls in the Property Market' (1997) 113 LQR 1.
[4] His Lordship delivered the only substantive speech, with which the other Lords agreed.
[5] *[1997] AC 191* at 214, *[1996] 3 All ER 365* at 372–373 (the emphasis is Lord Hoffmann's).

Loss of a chance

[3.07] The importance of distinguishing between the existence of a recoverable head of damage, and the assessment of the extent of the claimant's loss, is also illustrated by situations in which the defendant's carelessness deprives the claimant of the chance of avoiding a loss or of making a gain; but where the actual outcome, if the claimant had not been deprived of the chance, would have been dependent upon the actions of persons or events over whom neither party had control. As Stuart-Smith LJ put it in *Allied Maples Group Ltd v Simmons & Simmons:*[1] 'where the plaintiffs' loss depends upon the actions of an independent third party, it is necessary to consider as a matter of law what it is necessary to establish as a matter of causation, and where causation ends and quantification of damage begins.'

[1] *[1995] 4 All ER 907* at 914, *[1995] 1 WLR 1602* at 1609, CA.

Allied Maples

[3.08] In the *Allied Maples* case a solicitor omitted to advise the plaintiffs, who were negotiating the acquisition of certain businesses, to seek to obtain from the vendors protection against certain potential liabilities. When the liabilities unfortunately materialised, and the solicitor was sued for negligence, he argued that since the vendors might well have refused to grant the protection even if they had been asked to do so, the plaintiffs were unable to prove that they had suffered any loss and therefore had no cause of action. Stuart-Smith LJ formulated the issue as follows:[1]

> ' ... does the plaintiff have to prove on the balance of probability, as [the defence] submits, that the third party would have acted so as to confer the benefit

or avoid the risk to the plaintiff, or can the plaintiff succeed provided he shows that he had a substantial chance rather than a speculative one, the evaluation of the substantial chance being a question of quantification of damages?'

The court[2] had no doubt that the plaintiff's argument was correct, and the case was therefore remitted for the lost chance to be evaluated and the damages assessed.[3]

[1] See *[1995] 4 All ER 907* at 915–916, *[1995] 1 WLR 1602* at 1611.
[2] Stuart-Smith, Hobhouse and Millett LJJ. (Millett LJJ differed from his brethren but only as to the facts: he considered that the plaintiffs had failed to cross the threshold of establishing that the lost chance was substantial rather than purely speculative, see *[1995] 4 All ER 907* at 928–930.)
[3] See also *Davies v Taylor [1974] AC 207, [1972] 3 All ER 836, HL* (CHAPTER 9 below). Cf *Chaplin v Hicks [1911] 2 KB 786, CA.*

The principle applied

[3.09]   *Allied Maples v Simmons & Simmons* was applied in *Doyle v Wallace*[1] in which the plaintiff contended that an accident for which the defendants were responsible had deprived her of a 50% chance, which she had had formerly, of obtaining a certain type of employment. The Court of Appeal again rejected a defence submission that, on the balance of probability, the plaintiff had failed to prove the relevant loss, and upheld an award reflecting the possibility that the desired employment might have been secured.[2] In *Motor Crown Petroleum v SJ Berwin*[3] the Court of Appeal upheld a decision to apply the *Allied Maples* principle to a claim against solicitors for negligent failure to advise appealing against a refusal of planning permission. It was held that an appeal would have had a 40% chance of success, and the claimants were therefore awarded 40% of the value of the site in question if planning permission had been granted.

[1] *[1998] 30 LS Gaz R 25, CA.*
[2] See also *Stovold v Barlows [1996] PNLR 91, CA.*
[3] *[2000] Lloyd's Rep PN 438.*

Crucial distinction

[3.10]   Since damages for 'loss of a chance' are only recoverable when the stage of assessing damages is reached, it is apparent that the distinction between causation and quantification will be crucial; since if causation is not established on the balance of probability no question of recovery can arise. Accordingly, if a given situation is analysed as involving an issue on causation rather than quantification, and the relevant probability is, say, 40%, the claimant will recover nothing. On the other hand, if causation is taken to have been established the claimant will recover 40% of his loss. It will not, however, always be easy to classify the issue as one of causation or quantification. The leading case is the decision of the House of Lords in *Hotson v East Berkshire AHA*[1] in which, as a result of clinical negligence, a claimant who lost a 25% chance of making a full recovery after an accident was awarded nothing: the issue was categorised as one of causation rather than quantification even though it was accepted that the case 'hover[ed] on the border' between the two categories[2]. The issue is often critical in clinical negligence claims, and in *Gregg v Scott*[3] a bare majority of the House of Lords confirmed, in 2005, that in such cases there can be no damages for a reduction in a patient's chances of recovery, caused by negligence, if the chance of recovery would have been less that 50% in the absence of negligence. This matter is also discussed in CHAPTER 2 above.

1   *[1987] AC 750, [1987] 2 All ER 909.*
2   See *[1987] AC 750* at 792, *[1987] 2 All ER 909* at 921.
3   *[2005] UKHL 2.*

C The foreseeability test

Background

[3.11]   In the famous case of *Overseas Tankship UK (Ltd) v Morts Dock and Engineering Co Ltd, The Wagon Mound*[1], the Judicial Committee of the Privy Council held that the concept of 'foreseeability' should be used to determine the extent of the ensuing harm for which a defendant, who had been careless, should be held liable. The Board accordingly refused to impose liability on the defendant shipowners when oil, carelessly discharged from one of their ships, was ignited in a manner taken to be unforeseeable and a conflagration resulted in which the plaintiffs suffered damage. In so holding, the Board disapproved the well-known decision of the Court of Appeal, 40 years earlier, in *Re Polemis, Furniss Withy & Co.*[2] In that case the careless dropping of a plank led, due to an accumulation of petrol vapour, to a fire which, like that in *The Wagon Mound*, was on the facts unforeseeable. But liability was imposed on the ground that, once the damage was 'directly traceable to the negligent act', the fact that the precise outcome 'was not foreseen [was] immaterial'.[3] In *The Wagon Mound*, however, the proposition that 'for an act of negligence which results in some trivial foreseeable damage, the actor should be liable for all consequences, however unforeseeable and however grave, so long as they can be said to be 'direct', was castigated as not 'consonant with current ideas of justice or morality'.[4]

1   *[1961] AC 388, [1961] 1 All ER 404.*
2   *[1921] 3 KB 560, CA.*
3   *[1921] 3 KB 560* at 577, *per* Scrutton LJ.
4   *[1961] AC 388* at 422, *[1961] 1 All ER 404* at 413, *per* Lord Simonds, delivering the judgment of the Board.

Foreseeability not a universal panacea

[3.12]   Although the Privy Council decision has been accepted by the courts in subsequent cases, as being the governing authority for the purposes of English law, theoretical controversy still takes place as to whether the earlier decision of the Court of Appeal did not, in fact, embody the better approach. Those who favour *The Wagon Mound* test believe that its use follows logically from the fact that foreseeability is used to determine whether the defendant's act was negligent in the first place, and that it would be inconsistent and unfair to hold the defendant liable for harm which was not part of the reason for stigmatising his act as culpable initially.[1] But it is submitted that this argument is misleading in that the concept of 'foreseeability' is really being used in a different sense, when remoteness of damage is in issue, from when the earlier question of duty of care is being addressed.[2] Using it to determine the normative question of how the defendant ought to have behaved before the event is different from using it to determine how far the consequences of an accident might normally be expected to extend after it has occurred.[3] Moreover, given that some damage to the claimant must have been foreseen (and *Re Polemis* is no authority for the proposition that a wholly unforeseeable claimant can recover), it is not obvious that justice requires the innocent claimant rather than the negligent defendant to bear the loss.[4]

1   See G Williams 'The Risk Principle' (1961) 77 LQR 179. For a recent discussion see Marc Stauch 'Risk and Remoteness of Damage in Negligence' (2001) 64 MLR 191.
2   See R Kidner 'Remoteness of Damage: The Duty-Interest Theory and the Re-interpretation of the *Wagon Mound*' (1989) 9 LS 1.
3   For discussion see, generally, H Hart and T Honoré *Causation in the Law* (2nd edn, 1985) ch 9. See also J Stapleton 'Cause-in-Fact and the Scope of Liability for Consequences' (2003) 119 LQR 388 at 390–391.
4   See J Jolowicz [1961] CLJ 30.

Wagon Mound a source of uncertainty

[3.13]   Although the Privy Council criticised the *Polemis* rule as supposedly leading 'to nowhere but the never-ending and insoluble problems of causation',[1] it is not without significance that decisions since 1961 have shown the *Wagon Mound* principle itself to be a source of considerable uncertainty in practice. A line of cases difficult to reconcile, some of which seem to be closer in spirit to the earlier approach, have been subsequently handed down. The problem of loss which was clearly foreseeable but which arose indirectly through, for example, intervening human acts, is one of the situations which has given rise to difficulty.[2] Paradoxically, this is an area in which unqualified application of the foreseeability test yields results which seem intuitively too *generous* to claimants rather than the reverse. More generally, however, the vagueness inherent in the concept of foreseeability itself, and the covert discretion which *The Wagon Mound* test consequently confers on the court, has been a marked feature of the subsequent decisions. The attempt, in *The Wagon Mound*, elegantly to unify virtually the entire law of negligence around the concept of foreseeability, has led to greater uncertainty than the supposedly more theoretically vulnerable approach of *Re Polemis*.

1   *[1961] AC 388* at 423, *[1961] 1 All ER 404* at 413.
2   See *Lamb v Camden London Borough Council [1981] QB 625, [1981] 2 All ER 408*, CA, discussed below at para [3.37].

The present state of the law

[3.14]   In *Hughes v Lord Advocate*,[1] decided two years after *The Wagon Mound* by the House of Lords, the House proceeded on the basis that the general principle enunciated by the Privy Council represented the law. Their Lordships went on to interpret that principle, however, in a manner which extended the scope of liability beyond that which might have been considered appropriate if the *Wagon Mound* test had been adhered to closely or literally. Thus, Lord Pearce observed that when 'an accident is of a different type and kind from anything that [a defendant] could have foreseen he is not liable for it', but his Lordship added that 'to demand too great precision in the test of foreseeability would be unfair to [plaintiffs] since the facets of misadventure are innumerable'.[2] In *Hughes*'s case employees of the Post Office negligently left some paraffin lamps unattended near an open manhole. An eight-year-old boy began to play on the deserted site. He tripped over one of the lamps, which then dropped into the manhole; an escape of paraffin vapour was ignited by the flame of the lamp causing an explosion which threw the boy himself into the manhole, where he suffered severe burns. The House of Lords accepted that this precise concatenation of circumstances, and in particular an explosion, could not have been foreseen. Liability was nevertheless imposed on the ground that some injury by burning to children at play could have been foreseen from leaving the lamps unattended, and the fact that this foreseeable type of harm came about in an unforeseeable manner was immaterial.[3] In a later case, Lord Reid, who had been a party to both of them, summed up the effect of the decisions of the Privy Council and the House of Lords as follows:

> 'It has now been established by *The Wagon Mound* and by *Hughes v Lord Advocate* that ... damages can only be recovered if the injury complained of not only was caused by the alleged negligence but also was an injury of a class or character foreseeable as a possible result of it.'[4]

[1] *[1963] AC 837, [1963] 1 All ER 705, HL.*
[2] *[1963] AC 837* at 853, *[1963] 1 All ER 705* at 715, HL.
[3] 'This accident was caused by a known source of danger, but caused in a way which could not have been foreseen, and in my judgment that affords no defence': per Lord Reid *[1963] AC 837* at 847, *[1963] 1 All ER 705* at 708.
[4] See *Overseas Tankship (UK) Ltd v Miller SS Co Pty Ltd, The Wagon Mound (No 2) [1967] 1 AC 617* at 636, *[1966] 2 All ER 709* at 714. (This case arose out of the same fire as *The Wagon Mound* and the conclusion was reached that it had been foreseeable after all! But a different plaintiff was involved and different considerations applied.)

Decisions difficult to predict

[3.15] Unfortunately, the even greater than usual degree of artificiality and hindsight in the foreseeability principle caused by using it in the post-accident situation as a test for remoteness, combined with the vagueness inherent in the concept of 'class or character' itself, has had the effect of making the attitudes of the courts to particular situations far from easy to predict. Indeed, shortly after it was decided *Hughes v Lord Advocate* itself was narrowly distinguished in the Court of Appeal. In *Doughty v Turner Manufacturing Co Ltd*[1] the defendants carelessly dropped an asbestos cement cover into a cauldron of molten liquid. It was accepted that if the plaintiff workman, who was nearby, had been splashed by the molten liquid, and burnt as a result, this would have been a foreseeable consequence of the accident for which the defendants would have been liable. As it happened, however, no such splash apparently occurred but a violent chemical reaction, unknown to science at that time, happened instead. This caused the molten liquid to erupt from the cauldron with the result that the plaintiff suffered injury by burning. His claim failed. Harman LJ said that 'the damage ... was of an entirely different kind from the foreseeable splash', and added that it would have been 'wrong on these facts to make another inroad on the doctrine of foreseeability'.[2] But the nature of the injuries was the same as those which could have been foreseen from a splash, and the act which the defendants ought to have prevented in order to protect the plaintiff from splashing (ie the dropping of the asbestos into the cauldron) was the same as that which occurred and caused the explosion. These facts do, to say the least, render the decision in sharp contrast with that in the *Hughes* case. *Doughty* seems to require precise foresight of causation[3]; whereas the House of Lords in *Hughes* might be taken to have held that providing normal precautions had been carelessly neglected, and harm similar to that which could have been foreseen had occurred as a result, the plaintiff should still recover even if the method of causation itself could not have been foreseen.

[1] *[1964] 1 QB 518, [1964] 1 All ER 98, CA.*
[2] *[1964] 1 QB 518* at 529, *[1964] 1 All ER 98* at 102, CA.
[3] In *Attorney-General of the British Virgin Islands v Hartwell [2004] 1 WLR 1273*, PC at para 29 Lord Nicholls of Birkenhead observed, in relation to *Doughty's* case, that 'it must be questionable whether a distinction of this character would commend itself to the courts today'.

Spectrum of liability

Room to manoeuvre

[3.16] In the aftermath of *Hughes* and *Doughty,* a series of cases were reported which seem to indicate that those two decisions represent opposite ends of a spectrum, within which courts have considerable room to manoeuvre to determine whether or not a particular claim can be regarded as fulfilling the requirements of the foreseeability test. Thus, injury from frost-bite, so rare in England as to be in itself unforeseeable, was nevertheless held in one case to be within the general class of injury to health from severe cold, to the risk of which the defendant had carelessly exposed the plaintiff, and liability was imposed accordingly.[1] But in another case the court chose to draw a fine distinction between different types of illness caused by rats. On the assumption that the defendant farmer had carelessly exposed one of his employees to the risk of illness, by allowing the farm to become infested with rats, the employee's claim still failed on the ground that the particular illness in fact contracted was extremely rare, and therefore to be distinguished from the foreseeable risk of injury by biting or by food-poisoning.[2]

[1] *Bradford v Robinson Rentals [1967] 1 All ER 267, [1967] 1 WLR 337.* See also *Robinson v Post Office [1974] 2 All ER 737, [1974] 1 WLR 1176; Wieland v Cyril Lord Carpets [1969] 3 All ER 1006; Vacwell Engineering v BDH Chemicals [1971] 1 QB 88, [1969] 3 All ER 1681;* varied *[1971] 1 QB 111n, [1970] 3 All ER 553n, CA.*
[2] *Tremain v Pike [1969] 3 All ER 1303, [1969] 1 WLR 1556.*

Jolley v Sutton London BC

[3.17] The application of the foreseeability test for remoteness of damage in tort was recently considered by the House of Lords in *Jolley v Sutton London BC*[1]. The defendant Council admitted negligence in failing to remove an abandoned boat which had been left near a housing estate. The claimant, a 14-year-old boy, sought, with his friends, to *repair* the boat as part of a fantasy in which they planned to take it from London to Cornwall to sail it. Unfortunately, the boat fell on top of him causing very serious spinal injuries. The Council relied upon *The Wagon Mound (No 1),* contending that, although minor injuries to playing children caused by falling through the rotten planks of the boat would have been a foreseeable consequence of its negligence, the particular accident which occurred was not. The claimant, by contrast, relied upon *Hughes v Lord Advocate* arguing that the accident had not been too remote. The continuing uncertainty in this area is reflected by the fact that the trial judge decided in favour of the claimant, but his decision was unanimously reversed by the Court of Appeal, only to be restored when a unanimous House of Lords reversed the Court of Appeal. Lord Hoffman, in the House of Lords, said[2]:

> ' ... what must have been foreseen is not the precise injury which occurred but injury of a given description. The foreseeability is not as to the particulars but the genus. And the description is formulated by reference to the nature of the risk which ought to have been foreseen ... The short point in the present appeal is therefore whether the judge was right in saying in general terms that the risk was that children would "meddle with the boat at the risk of some physical injury" or whether the Court of Appeal were right in saying that the only foreseeable risk was of "children who were drawn to the boat climbing upon it and being injured by the rotten planking giving way beneath them". Was the wider risk, which

would include within its description the accident which actually happened, reasonably foreseeable? ... I think that the judge's broad description of the risk ... was the correct one'.

Jolley's case was subsequently considered by the Court of Appeal in *Jebson v Ministry of Defence*[3], in which a group of drunken off-duty soldiers had been transported in a lorry without adequate supervision. It was held to be within the risk created by the negligent lack of supervision that one of the soldiers would attempt to climb on to the roof of the moving lorry, and suffer injury as a result[4].

[1]   *[2000] 3 All ER 409.* See Robert Williams 'Remoteness: Some Unexpected Mischief' (2001) 117 LQR 30.
[2]   See *[2000] 3 All ER 409* at 418–420.
[3]   *[2000] PIQR P21.*
[4]   For a case in which a claimant's attempt to rely on *Jolley* was unsuccessful see *Pratley v Surrey CC [2004] ICR 159, CA.*

Nature of precautions relevant

[3.18]   In *Jolley v Sutton London BC* Lord Hoffman also emphasised[1], that no greater precautions would have been necessary in order to prevent the wider risk from materialising than would have been necessary to prevent the risk accepted as foreseeable even by the defendants, ie the boat should simply have been removed. It would thus appear that if, in a borderline case, a risk materialises which would have been prevented by exactly the same precautions as those which the defendants should have taken anyway, the court is unlikely to show particular enthusiasm for adopting a definition of the nature of the risk sufficiently narrow to enable the defendants to escape from liability.

[1]   See *[2000] 3 All ER 409* at 418–419: '"Reasonably foreseeable" is not a fixed point on the scale of probability ... [O]ther factors have to be considered in deciding whether a given probability of injury generates a duty to take steps to eliminate the risk'. See also *per* Lord Reid in *The Wagon Mound (No 2), Overseas Tankship (UK) Ltd v Miller Steamship Co Pty Ltd, [1967] 1 AC 617* at 642, *[1966] 2 All ER 709* at 718.

Effect of extraneous circumstances

The 'egg-shell skull' rule

[3.19]   The operation of the foreseeability principle as a test for remoteness of damage is subject to an important modification or exception in a certain special type of personal injury case. The situation in question is that in which the claimant suffers from some unusual, and unforeseeable, latent disease or disability. An accident, arising out of the defendant's negligence and for which he is responsible, foreseeably causes some injury to the claimant. As a result of his latent condition, however, the claimant suffers harmful consequences which, although in a sense triggered by the defendant's negligence, are far more serious or extensive than could have been foreseen as a result of it. In such cases the defendant remains liable for the full extent of the claimant's injuries. In *Smith v Leech Brain & Co Ltd,*[1] which was decided very shortly after *The Wagon Mound,*[2] it was declared that this long-established rule, often known as the 'egg-shell skull' principle, had survived the decision of the Privy Council. The plaintiff suffered burns to his lip when, due to his employer's negligence, molten liquid was spattered upon it. The burn unfortunately activated a pre-malignant condition and the plaintiff subsequently died of cancer. Lord Parker CJ held the defendant employers liable for his death, observing that it had 'always been the law of this country that a tortfeasor takes his victim as he finds him'.[3]

[1]   *[1962] 2 QB 405, [1961] 3 All ER 1159.*
[2]   *[1961] AC 388, [1961] 1 All ER 404.*
[3]   *[1962] 2 QB 405 at 414, [1961] 3 All ER 1159 at 1161. See also Warren v Scruttons Ltd [1962] 1 Lloyd's Rep 497.*

Principle applied

[3.20]   In a later case the Court of Appeal even applied the principle in circumstances involving a longer and more complicated chain of causation. In *Robinson v Post Office*[1] the defendants were held fully liable when the medical treatment which the plaintiff received for a minor injury, caused by their negligence, reacted with a pre-existing allergy to cause brain damage, which could not have been foreseen. The principle has also been applied to situations in which the unforeseeable severity of the claimant's suffering takes the form of exacerbation of pre-existing nervous or neurotic conditions, as well as those involving physical disabilities in the narrow sense.[2] 'There is no difference in principle', Geoffrey Lane J observed in one case, 'between an egg-shell skull and an egg-shell personality'.[3]

[1]   *[1974] 2 All ER 737, [1974] 1 WLR 1176, CA. See also Wieland v Cyril Lord Carpets Ltd [1969] 3 All ER 1006.*
[2]   Cf *Page v Smith [1996] AC 155, [1995] 2 All ER 736, HL. See also Simmons v British Steel [2004] UKHL 20 (Scot), [2004] ICR 585.*
[3]   *Malcolm v Broadhurst [1970] 3 All ER 508 at 511. See also Cotic v Gray (1981) 33 OR (2d) 356 Ont CA; Brice v Brown [1984] 1 All ER 997.*

Not applicable in property cases

[3.21]   Notwithstanding the importance of the rule that the defendant takes the claimant as he finds him, it is important not to lose sight of its limitations. It appears to be confined to personal injury cases, presumably on grounds of policy,[1] and does not extend to cases of damage to property. Thus, it is generally accepted that if the facts of *Re Polemis*[2] were now to recur, the decision would, after *The Wagon Mound*, be different and the defendants would escape liability on the ground that the damage had been unforeseeable. But if a principle analogous to the 'egg-shell skull' rule applied the accumulation of petrol vapour in the hold of the ship could plausibly be seen as a pre-existing condition, and the same decision reached as in the case itself.

[1]   But for criticism of the rule, even in personal injury cases, see P Atiyah *Accidents, Compensation and the Law* (6th edn, 1999, Cane ed) p 106 onwards.
[2]   *[1921] 3 KB 560, CA.*

Relationship with the foreseeability principle

[3.22]   Moreover, even within the personal injuries field, the rule does not in itself constitute a general abrogation of the foreseeability principle, but only an exception applicable in special circumstances. Thus, if no part at all of the claimant's injuries are held to have been foreseeable, his claim will fail, notwithstanding that he may have suffered very seriously as a consequence of the defendant's carelessness.[1] But it is arguable that the courts are becoming discernibly more ready, in personal injury cases, to define the kind of injury, which ought to have been foreseen, very broadly in the claimant's favour.[2] To the extent that this is true, the 'egg-shell skull' principle should become progressively less significant; and personal injury litigation generally perceived as attracting a distinctive approach as far as remoteness of damage is concerned.[3]

[1]   See *Doughty v Turner Manufacturing Co [1964] 1 QB 518, [1964] 1 All ER 98, CA; Tremain v Pike [1969] 3 All ER 1303, [1969] 1 WLR 1556.*
[2]   See above, paras [3.16]–[3.17] and cases there cited. See also *Page v Smith [1996] AC 155, [1995] 2 All ER 736, HL.* Cf Smith *Liability in Negligence* (1984) ch 8.
[3]   See P J Rowe 'The Demise of the Thin Skull Rule?' (1977) 40 MLR 377.

Demise of the rule in The Edison

The Edison

[3.23]   There was formerly said to be a principle, derived from the 1933 decision of the House of Lords In *Liesbosch Dredger v SS Edison*[1], that additional losses suffered by the claimant due to his impecuniosity would not be recoverable even if foreseeable. In *The Edison* the plaintiffs' losses, when their ship was negligently sunk by the defendants, were more extensive than they might have been due to their own financial position. Lack of funds prevented the plaintiffs from purchasing a replacement ship straight away, and they had to incur hiring charges instead. This additional loss was held to be too remote to be recoverable. Lord Wright observed that the plaintiffs' 'financial disability' was not 'to be compared with that physical delicacy or weakness which may aggravate the damage in the case of personal injuries'.[2] Subsequently, however, the rule in *The Edison* came in for criticism as being too harsh on plaintiffs.[3] Moreover, it was said in *Clippens Oil Co v Edinburgh & District Water Trustees Ltd*,[4] which was decided by the House of Lords more than 20 years before *The Edison* itself, that a defendant could not argue that the plaintiff had failed to take sufficient steps to *mitigate* his loss if impecuniosity had prevented him from doing so.

[1]   *[1933] AC 449.*
[2]   *[1933] AC 449* at 461.
[3]   See Brian Coote 'Damages, The Liesbosch, and Impecuniosity' [2001] 60 CLJ 511; Vanessa Kodilinye 'Property Damage and the Impecuniosity Factor in Commonwealth Jurisdictions' (2000) 10 Caribbean LR 75. See also *Perry v Sidney Phillips & Son [1982] 3 All ER 705, [1982] 1 WLR 1297, CA* discussed below at para [3.24].
[4]   *[1907] AC 291* at 303, *per* Lord Collins.

'Rule' construed narrowly

[3.24]   The Court of Appeal decisions manifested an inclination to construe the rule in *The Edison* narrowly.[1] In *Dodd Properties v Canterbury City Council*[2] the plaintiffs' building was damaged by the defendants' building activities. The plaintiffs nevertheless chose not to repair their building straight away. They happened to be going through a period of financial stringency but considered in any event that it would have been commercially imprudent to repair the building in the absence of acceptance of liability for the damage, and the cost of making it good, from the defendants – which was not forthcoming. As a result, several years went by during which the cost of the repairs increased substantially and the defendants ultimately contended, relying on *The Edison*, that only the much smaller sum which the repairs would have cost if they had been carried out earlier could be recovered. The Court of

Appeal rejected this contention. In all the circumstances it had been reasonable for the repairs to be postponed.[3] In the later case of *Perry v Sidney Phillips*[4] a plaintiff again failed to repair at the outset a defective building, one which he would not have acquired but for the negligence of the defendant surveyors. The plaintiff lacked the means to carry out the repairs but was nevertheless able to recover damages for the vexation and distress caused to him by having to live in a defective house. Reliance by the defendants on *The Edison* was again to no avail. Oliver LJ observed that the 'real question' was 'was it reasonable in all the circumstances for the plaintiff not to mitigate his damage by carrying out the repairs which were required?'[5] Noting that, as in the *Dodd* case, the defendants' refusal to accept liability had contributed to the plaintiff's financial difficulties, his Lordship answered the question in the latter's favour.

[1]   See also *Burns v M A N Automotive (1987) 61 ALJR 81.*
[2]   *[1980] 1 All ER 928, [1980] 1 WLR 433.*
[3]   See also *Martindale v Duncan [1973] 2 All ER 355, [1973] 1 WLR 574, CA.*
[4]   *[1982] 3 All ER 705, [1982] 1 WLR 1297, CA.*
[5]   *[1982] 3 All ER 705 at 711, [1982] 1 WLR 1297 at 1305.*

Lagden v O'Connor

[3.25]   Finally, in 2003, the House of Lords held that the rule associated with *The Edison* is not law. In *Lagden v O'Connor*[1] The House held that the claimant's impecuniosity could be taken into account where it would have prevented him from hiring a substitute car, when his own was off the road for repairs, following an accident for which the defendant was responsible. The claimant was held to be entitled to take advantage of the credit hire package provided by a specialist firm, and to charge the full cost of that package to the defendant, even though it exceeded the cost of ordinary hire[2]. Lord Slynn of Hadley said[3]:

'In the light inter alia of the criticisms and qualifications of [*The Edison*]... it seems to me with great respect that your Lordships should now say that observations that a claimant's lack of means should not be taken into account when assessing his loss should no longer be followed'.

[1]   *[2004] 1 All ER 277.*
[2]   For further discussion see CHAPTER 27 below.
[3]   See *[2004] 1 All ER 277* at para 12. See also para 8 (Lord Nicholls), 61 (Lord Hope), 82 (Lord Scott) and 102 (Lord Walker).

D Intervening act by the claimant

Remoteness occasionally relevant

[3.26]   In some cases the acts of persons other than the defendant, which have become interposed between the original negligence and the injury suffered by the claimant, may be treated by the court as rendering that injury too remote from the negligence and hence as absolving the defendant from liability[1]. If the act in question is one of the claimant's own, the matter will usually be treated, if it is regarded as affecting the outcome at all, as one merely of contributory negligence or, occasionally, as giving rise to the defence of assumption of risk; the concept of remoteness of damage will seldom be invoked. Indeed, in view of the flexible apportionment machinery available when a case is held to fall within the *Law Reform* (*Contributory*

Negligence) Act 1945, the use of that machinery, as distinct from the 'all or nothing' concept of remoteness, would seem to be the preferable approach.[2] Nevertheless, in one case decided by the House of Lords, *McKew v Holland & Hannen & Cubitts (Scotland) Ltd*,[3] their Lordships wholly rejected the pursuer's claim by holding, in effect, that his own act rendered his injury too remote from the defendant's negligence. That negligence had caused an accident at his place of work as a result of which the plaintiff suffered injuries which included a tendency, on occasions, for his left leg to go numb. Some days later, when visiting a block of flats, he chose to descend by himself, without waiting for assistance which was available, a steep flight of stairs which had no handrail. His leg suddenly went numb and he fell, suffering much more serious injuries. The House of Lords held that the plaintiff's conduct in attempting to descend the stairs was so unreasonable that it constituted a novus actus interveniens rendering the defendants immune from liability for the injuries caused by the fall, even though it would not have occurred but for their initial negligence.

[1]   See below.
[2]   See M Millner 'Novus Actus Interveniens: The Present Effect of *Wagon Mound*' (1971) 22 NILQ 168.
[3]   *[1969] 3 All ER 1621, HL.*

Foreseeability not a sufficient condition

[3.27]   The speech of Lord Reid in *McKew's* cases is particularly striking for its refusal to treat the foreseeability test as the sole determinant of liability. His Lordship was prepared to accept that what had happened to the plaintiff may well have been foreseeable as a result of the defendants' original negligence, but that did not of itself mean that his claim should succeed:

> 'A defender is not liable for a consequence of a kind which is not foreseeable. But it does not follow that he is liable for every consequence which a reasonable man could foresee. What can be foreseen depends almost entirely on the facts of the case, and it is often easy to foresee unreasonable conduct or some other *novus actus interveniens* as being quite likely. But that does not mean that the defender must pay for damage caused by the *novus actus* ... For it is not at all unlikely or unforeseeable that an active man who has suffered such a disability will take some quite unreasonable risk. But if he does he cannot hold the defender liable for the consequences.'[1]

Notwithstanding dicta apparently to the contrary by Lord Simonds in *The Wagon Mound*[2] itself, this statement by Lord Reid clearly affirms that foreseeability is merely a necessary test for recovery and not a sufficient one. It is submitted that this affirmation is in itself welcome, even if the actual decision in *McKew*'s case seems rather harsh on its facts.

[1]   *[1969] 3 All ER 1621* at 1623.
[2]   See *[1961] AC 388 at 426, [1961] 1 All ER 404* at 416.

McKew distinguished

[3.28]   It is perhaps significant that three weeks elapsed between the dates of the two accidents in *McKew v Holland & Hannen & Cubitts (Scotland) Ltd*. The narrower the interval between the initial negligence and the subsequent injury, the less likely it is that the claimant's claim will fail altogether on grounds of remoteness. In *Wieland v*

Cyril Lord Carpets Ltd[1] the plaintiff had to have a surgical collar fitted to her neck due to injuries received in a motor accident caused by the defendants' negligence. This device made it more difficult for her to move her neck, and hence adjust her sight in the manner required by the bi-focal spectacles which she had worn for many years. As a result, later in the same day on which the collar was fitted, she fell down stairs and suffered further injuries. Eveleigh J held the defendant fully liable for these as well as for those suffered in the original accident.[2]

[1] *[1969] 3 All ER 1006.*
[2] See also *Pyne v Wilkenfeld (1981) 26 SASR 441.*

'Dilemma' situations

[3.29] If the act by the claimant, which is alleged to have broken the chain of causation, actually occurred in the immediate aftermath of the defendant's negligence the court is particularly unlikely to be sympathetic towards the latter.[1] A claimant whose actions in an emergency might, with hindsight, be subjected to criticism will therefore rarely wholly fail on causal grounds[2], although a reduction in the damages might sometimes be made for contributory negligence.[3]

[1] Cf *The Oropesa [1943] P 32, [1943] 1 All ER 211, CA*, especially, *per* Lord Wright *[1943] P 32* at 39:
    'The question is not whether there was new negligence, but whether there was a new cause.'
[2] See the recent (contract) case of *Vinmar International v Theresa Navigation [2001] 2 All ER (Comm) 243.*
[3] See *Sayers v Harlow UDC [1958] 2 All ER 342, [1958] 1 WLR 623, CA.*

Suicide cases

[3.30] In *Reeves v Metropolitan Police Comr*,[1] in which a prisoner had committed suicide while in the defendant's custody, it was contended that the deceased's own act had broken the chain of causation. By a 4–1 majority the House of Lords rejected this argument. Lord Jauncey of Tullichettle said[2]:

> 'Where ... a duty is specifically directed at the prevention of the occurrence of a certain event I cannot see how it can be said that the occurrence of the event amounts to an independent act breaking the chain of causation from the breach of duty, even although it may be unusual for one person to come under a duty to prevent another person deliberately inflicting harm on himself. It is the very thing at which the duty was directed ... The deceased's suicide was the precise event to which the duty was directed and as an *actus* it was accordingly neither *novus* nor *interveniens*'.

[1] *[1999] 3 All ER 897.*
[2] See *[1999] 3 All ER 897* at 908–909.

Where duty not directed at suicide

[3.31] Although causal arguments against liability will clearly be more powerful if the defendant's duty of care did not relate to the prevention of suicide as such, the chain of causation will not necessarily be broken even in those cases. In *Pigney v Pointer's Transport Services Ltd*[1] the deceased committed suicide as a result of depression brought about by head injuries caused by the defendants' negligence. His widow was able to recover damages from them under the Fatal Accidents Acts. Although *Re Polemis* was referred to in the judgment in this case, which was decided before *The Wagon Mound*, it is submitted that it would be decided the same way today. Suicidal depression can presumably be taken to be a foreseeable consequence of serious personal injuries.[2] Nevertheless, the task of proving the causal link by medical evidence may sometimes be difficult.[3] But if the deceased had a history of depression the 'egg-shell skull' principle may be prayed in aid; as in a successful claim in Canada, on facts similar to *Pigney*, in which the problem received extensive consideration in the Ontario Court of Appeal.[4]

[1]   *[1957] 2 All ER 807, [1957] 1 WLR 1121.*
[2]   Cf *Meah v McCreamer [1985] 1 All ER 367.*
[3]   Cf *Farmer v Rash [1969] 1 All ER 705, [1969] 1 WLR 160.*
[4]   See *Cotic v Gray (1981) 33 OR (2d) 356.*

Rescue

[3.32]   It is well known that the law is naturally reluctant to deny claims brought by claimants who have suffered injury while engaged in rescue activities necessitated by the negligence of defendants. Nor is this reluctance confined to situations in which the lives and safety of human beings are at risk; in appropriate circumstances it may extend to cases merely involving damage to property.[1] It will only very rarely, therefore, be possible for the maxim *volenti non fit injuria* to be invoked successfully against a rescuer.[2] Nor will remoteness defences usually fare any better: rescue being regarded as pre-eminently likely to occur if an emergency is created.[3] Occasionally, however, claimants in rescue situations might find themselves defeated by remoteness arguments. In *Crossley v Rawlinson*[4] the plaintiff tripped and fell while running with a fire extinguisher towards the scene of a fire caused by the defendant's negligence. His claim for the injury he suffered in the fall was unsuccessful, even though the defendant abandoned assumption of risk as a defence in the course of the trial. The judge held that what had occurred was not reasonably foreseeable and was therefore too remote.[5] Such cases are, however, likely to be rare.

[1]   See *Hyett v Great Western Rly Co [1948] 1 KB 345, [1947] 2 All ER 264, CA.*
[2]   For a case in which the defence succeeded see *Cutler v United Dairies (London) Ltd [1933] 2 KB 297,*
[3]   See generally *Baker v T E Hopkins [1959] 3 All ER 225, [1959] 1 WLR 966, CA.*
[4]   *[1981] 3 All ER 674, [1981] 1 WLR 369.*
[5]   Quaere whether this decision is consistent with *Hughes v Lord Advocate [1963] AC 837, [1963] 1 All ER 705.* See criticism of *Crossley v Rawlinson* by M A Jones in (1982) 45 MLR 342.

High regard

[3.33]   The high regard in which the law rightly holds rescuers is further illustrated by resolution in their favour of the question of whether they can sue in cases where the victim carelessly placed *himself* in the situation of danger requiring rescue;[1] a point formerly sometimes doubted on largely unfounded conceptual grounds. Recovery is therefore not limited to the more usual type of case in which the peril has been created by the negligence of a third party. It is also important to note that the House of Lords has confirmed that 'professional' rescuers are not in principle to be treated differently from others. Thus, unlike the position apparently prevailing in some American jurisdictions, firemen injured in the course of their duties can sue those whose negligence started the fire.[2] But if rescuers, professional or otherwise, suffer *psychiatric* damage, they will not normally be able to recover unless they were also at risk of physical injury[3].

[1] See *Harrison v British Rlys Board [1981] 3 All ER 679* (Boreham J).
[2] See *Ogwo v Taylor [1988] AC 431, [1987] 3 All ER 961, HL.*
[3] See *White v Chief Constable of South Yorkshire [1999] 1 All ER 1, HL*, discussed in CHAPTER 1 above.

E Intervention by third parties

'Deliberate and mischievous' acts[1]

[3.34] 'It is tempting to conclude', observed Robert Goff LJ in *Paterson Zochonis v Merfarken Packaging*,[2] 'that, in the absence of some special relationship, there can be no liability for damage caused to the plaintiff by the deliberate wrongdoing of a third party'.[3] It is true that he went on to point out that this proposition was too wide as it stood; not least because liability in tort would presumably be imposed on a defendant who had himself committed a deliberate act, for example by handing the third party a gun knowing that the latter intended to shoot the claimant.[4] Nevertheless, it remains true that, where the defendant has merely been careless, the deliberate and wrongful acts of third parties will only exceptionally, in so far as the issue is seen as one of remoteness, give rise to liability.[5]

[1] The phrase is taken from *Prosser & Son Ltd v Levy [1955] 3 All ER 577 at 587, [1955] 1 WLR 1224* at 1230.
[2] *[1983] FSR 273.*
[3] See also the same judge, as Lord Goff of Chieveley, in *Smith v Littlewoods Organisation Ltd [1987] AC 241 at 271ff, [1987] 1 All ER 710, HL.*
[4] Cf *Setchell v Snowdon [1974] RTR 389, CA.*
[5] Thus, owners of stolen motor-cars, who had left their vehicles unlocked, have been held not liable for death or damage caused by the driving of the thieves: see *Topp v London Country Bus (South West) Ltd [1993] 3 All ER 448, [1993] 1 WLR 976, CA.* For criticism of this decision see D Howarth 'My brother's keeper? Liability for acts of third parties' (1994) 14 LS 88.

Where duty is based on risk of intervention

[3.35] The picture is rather different if the underlying issue in the case is perceived, not as one of remoteness, but as one concerning the criteria for predicating that the defendant's carelessness was capable of constituting negligence in law in the first place. Thus, those in charge of children may sometimes be liable if, through their failure to keep them under proper control, injury is inflicted on the claimant.[1] Similarly, in the well-known case of *Home Office v Dorset Yacht Co Ltd*,[2] the House of Lords held that those entrusted with the custody of offenders could in principle be liable for failing to prevent them from escaping and causing damage. These are situations in which the defendants' conduct is evaluated in terms of a foreseeable risk of injury to the claimants through the medium of deliberate human action by others.[3] But the courts do not readily evaluate conduct in terms of this particular risk.[4] Indeed, this is an area in which, despite the difficulties sometimes associated with it, the distinction between acts and omissions remains important.[5]

[1] See *Carmarthenshire County Council v Lewis [1955] AC 549, [1955] 1 All ER 565; Vicar of Writtle v Essex County Council (1979) 77 LGR 656.*
[2] *[1970] AC 1004, [1970] 2 All ER 294, HL.* See also CHAPTER 1 above.

3   Of course, such situations may themselves give rise to questions of remoteness: see *O'Reilly v C [1978] 3 WWR 145 (Can.)*.

4   'The general rule is that one man is under no duty of controlling another man to prevent his doing damage to a third': *Smith v Leurs (1945) 70 CLR 256* at 262, *per* Dixon J: cited with approval in *Home Office v Dorset Yacht Co Ltd [1970] AC 1004, [1970] 2 All ER 294, HL*. See also *Hill v Chief Constable of West Yorkshire [1989] AC 53, [1988] 2 All ER 238, HL*.

5   See *P Perl Exporters Ltd v Camden London Borough Council [1984] QB 342, [1983] 3 All ER 161, CA* (especially *per* Waller LJ *[1984] QB 342* at 352, *[1983] 3 All ER 161* at 166). See generally chapter 1 above.

High degree of probability required

[3.36]   The question whether the defendant ought to be held liable for loss caused by the independent acts of others becomes one of remoteness in situations where the defendant has admittedly been careless, but not in a way usually associated with a risk of damage through the medium of third parties. Nevertheless, as a consequence of that carelessness harm is occasioned to the claimant, the immediate cause of which is intervening human action. This is an area in which the foreseeability approach propounded in *The Wagon Mound*[1] has proved to be particularly unsatisfactory.[2] The judicial intuition that losses suffered in this way will normally be too remote seems to be unchanged as a result of that decision. But it has made giving effect to that intuition unnecessarily difficult and complicated, simply because it may often be unrealistic to deny that the intervening events were foreseeable. Under the *Re Polemis*[3] test, however, claims of the type in question could plausibly have been dismissed simply as being for losses suffered in a manner too 'indirect'[4] to be recoverable.

1   *[1961] AC 388, [1961] 1 All ER 404, PC*.
2   Cf M A Jones 'Paying for the Crimes of Others' (1984) 47 MLR 223.
3   *[1921] 3 KB 560, CA*.
4   Cf *Weld-Blundell v Stephens [1920] AC 956 at 986, HL per* Lord Sumner.

Lamb v Camden London Borough Council

[3.37]   The difficulties are well illustrated by *Lamb v Camden London Borough Council*.[1] The defendant council, while replacing a sewer, carelessly broke a water main. The escaping water undermined the foundations of the plaintiff's house and made it dangerous to live in. In consequence, the house was left empty, but squatters moved in and caused considerable further damage for which the plaintiff sought to hold the defendant council liable. The Court of Appeal was unanimous that the claim should fail. At first instance, however, it had been found as a fact that at that time, in that part of London, the entry of squatters was a clearly foreseeable consequence of a property being left vacant for any length of time; nor was the Court of Appeal itself really disposed to disagree with that finding. In resolving the issue of liability in favour of the defendants, the members of the Court of Appeal adopted different reasoning. Lord Denning MR said that the question of remoteness was ultimately one of policy, and that the plaintiff should have protected herself against the losses which had occurred by taking out insurance rather than by looking to the defendants. Watkins LJ held expressly that foreseeability was merely a necessary, and not a sufficient, condition for damage not being too remote, and that policy and judicial intuition had a part to play. Oliver LJ held that, where intervening human action was concerned, a very high degree of probability was required if the loss was not to be held to be too remote, and that that requirement was not satisfied in the instant case. He attempted to reconcile his approach with the foreseeability test by putting special emphasis upon the adjective 'reasonable' in the phrase 'reasonably foreseeable'. Although this attempted reconciliation seems strained, the reasoning of Oliver LJ perhaps gets closest to the heart of the problem of deliberate intervening human action. His Lordship suggested that:[2] 'There may ... be circumstances in which the court would require a degree of likelihood amounting almost to inevitability before it fixes a defendant with responsibility for the act of a third party over whom he has and can have no control.'

[1]   *[1981] QB 625, [1981] 2 All ER 408, CA.*
[2]   *[1981] QB 625* at 644, *[1981] 2 All ER 408* at 419.

Varying degrees of probability

[3.38]   Accordingly, it is submitted that it can be taken as established that foreseeability alone, at any rate in the sense in which that concept is normally used, will be insufficient to prevent damage caused by the deliberate acts of third parties from being too remote, and that a high degree of probability will usually be required in addition if liability is to be imposed. Just how probable the intervention was will obviously be a question of fact in each case. The precise degree of probability that will need to be established may also vary according to the circumstances of each case, including the nature of the defendant's carelessness or other breach of duty. In *Ward v Cannock Chase District Council*[1] the defendants expressly undertook to repair the plaintiff's house, which had been rendered uninhabitable by their own earlier negligence. They failed to honour their undertaking and, in consequence, vandals entered the empty house and caused further damage. Scott J imposed liability on the defendants and distinguished *Lamb v Camden London Borough Council*. He held, in effect, that a duty actually to repair an empty house warranted requiring a lower degree of probability of illegal entry, for the purposes of remoteness of damage, than did a duty not carelessly to burst a water main.[2] His Lordship also held that, in any event, 'the likelihood of unoccupied property receiving the attention of vandals was very much higher'[3] in the locality in question in the case before him, even than it had been in the *Lamb* case.

[1]   *[1986] Ch 546, [1985] 3 All ER 537.*
[2]   Cf *Stansbie v Troman [1948] 2 KB 48, [1948] 1 All ER 599, CA.*
[3]   *[1986] Ch 546* at 570, *[1985] 3 All ER 537* at 553.

Negligence

[3.39]   If the intervening act was merely careless or negligent, as distinct from deliberate and mischievous, it is less likely to render the damage ultimately suffered by the claimant too remote from the defendant's own initial negligence. It is particularly unlikely to do so if the intervening act was itself a reaction, albeit perhaps with hindsight an unfortunate one, to the situation which the defendant had created. Theoretically questionable decisions taken in a dangerous and uncertain situation produced by a collision at sea, for example, will not readily be treated as depriving of causal force the carelessness responsible for the initial collision.[1]

[1]   See *The Oropesa [1943] P 32, [1943] 1 All ER 211, CA.*

Unexpected acts

[3.40]   Nevertheless, each case necessarily depends upon its own facts and, in *Knightley v Johns*,[1] in which the whole subject was considered at length by the Court of Appeal, an intervening act of negligence *was* held to have broken the chain of causation. The defendant's negligence caused a serious accident near the exit of a tunnel carrying one-way traffic. Unfortunately, the police inspector who arrived at the scene forgot to close the tunnel to traffic and subsequently ordered the plaintiff, one of his subordinates, to do so belatedly by riding his motor cycle through the tunnel against the oncoming traffic. In so doing the plaintiff met with an accident for which the trial judge held the defendant liable. The Court of Appeal, however, reversed this decision holding that 'the inspector's negligence was not a concurrent cause running with [the defendant's] negligence, but a new cause disturbing the sequence of events'.[2] But Stephenson LJ, who delivered the judgment of the court, emphasised that the test was one of reasonable foreseeability in all the circumstances.[3] *Knightly v Johns* is therefore a rather unusual case and, as a general principle, an unusually high degree of probability will *not* be required before the defendant can be held liable for all that occurred if the intervening act was merely negligent as distinct from intentional. On the contrary, only relatively *unexpected* acts of subsequent negligence will suffice to discharge the defendant in such cases.

1 *[1982] 1 All ER 851, [1982] 1 WLR 349, CA.*
2 *[1982] 1 All ER 851* at 866, *[1982] 1 WLR 349* at 367, CA.
3 See *[1982] 1 All ER 851* at 866, *[1981] 1 WLR 349* at 366.

Inadequate medical treatment

[3.41] A particular context in which the defendant sometimes contends that the chain of causation has been broken is where the victim of an accident, for which his negligence was responsible, subsequently receives medical treatment which is alleged to have been inadequate or negligent. The courts have, on the whole, been reluctant to absolve defendants in such cases. Nevertheless, until the decision of the Court of Appeal in *Webb v Barclay's Bank*, which is discussed below, there was no clear English decision to the effect that negligent medical treatment will not sever the chain of causation.[1] On the contrary in *Hogan v Bentinck West Hartley Collieries*[2] the House of Lords apparently held, albeit by a bare majority in a case decided under the old Workmen's Compensation Acts, that it *would* do so.[3] But in practice claimants have usually succeeded in full against those responsible for the initial accident, because the courts are reluctant to hold that intervening medical treatment was actually negligent. The usual technique is to hold that it involved a mere error of judgment, falling short of negligence,[4] or that in any event it ultimately had no causative effect on the outcome.[5]

1 But see *Thompson v Toorenburgh (1973) 29 DLR (3d) 608*; affd *50 DLR (3d) 717 (Can)*.
2 *[1949] 1 All ER 588.*
3 See also *David v Toronto Transit Commission (1977) 77 DLR (3d) 717 (Can)*. Sed quaere.
4 See *Liston v Liston and Sleep (1983) 31 SASR 245 (Aus)*. See also *per* Lord Reid, dissenting, in *Hogan v Bentinck Collieries [1949] 1 All ER 588* at 607–608.
5 See *Robinson v Post Office [1974] 2 All ER 737, [1974] 1 WLR 1176; Conley v Strain [1988] IR 628*. Cf *Barnett v Chelsea and Kensington Hospital Management Committee [1969] 1 QB 428, [1968] 1 All ER 1068*.

Original defendant should remain liable

[3.42] There is, however, much to be said for holding overtly that the possibility of negligently induced misadventure can be foreseen as a result of emergency hospital treatment, for example, and that those whose carelessness creates a need for such treatment should therefore as a general rule be liable for its consequences notwith-standing inadequacies in its administration.[1] The recent decision of the Court of Appeal in *Webb v Barclay's Bank*[2] suggests that this may now in fact be the law. The claimant injured her leg in a fall at work. The leg was then amputated unnecessarily as a result of medical negligence. The Court of Appeal held that that negligence had not broken the chain of causation from the original fall[3]. The Court cited with approval a passage from *Clerk and Lindsell on Torts*[4] to the effect 'that only medical treatment so grossly negligent as to be a completely inappropriate response to the injury inflicted by the defendant should operate to break the chain of causation'.

[1]   See J Smith *Liability in Negligence* (1984) pp 151–153.
[2]   *[2002] PIQR P8.*
[3]   See also *Mahoney v Kruschick Demolitions Pty Ltd (1985) 156 CLR 522 (Aust HC).*
[4]   18th edn, paras 2–55.

Part two

Negligence and economic interests

Chapter 4

Liability for negligent misstatement

A The impact of Hedley Byrne[1]

The concept of the 'special relationship'

[4.01]   Prior to the decision in *Hedley Byrne & Co v Heller & Partners Ltd*,[2] the law of tort did not impose liability for careless words which had caused the plaintiff to suffer financial loss, unless there was a fiduciary relationship between the parties,[3] or unless fraud was proved.[4] Liability for careless words causing physical injury was, however, recognised.[5] In *Hedley Byrne* itself, the House of Lords held that bankers who carelessly gave a favourable reference, about one of their customers, to another bank could in principle be liable in negligence to a customer of the inquiring bank for losses thereby suffered. The defendant bank in fact escaped liability, however, because they had issued a disclaimer with their advice declaring it to be given 'without responsibility'. The precise effect of the change in the law brought about by this decision was a source of considerable uncertainty, some of which remains four decades later. This uncertainty was caused partly by the fact that the members of the House interwove in their speeches the two separate questions of the legal principles relating to a certain type of *conduct*, ie the making of negligent statements, with those relating to liability for a certain kind of *harm*, ie pure economic loss (as distinct from physical injury and losses consequent thereupon).[6]

[1]   See generally P Cane *Tort Law and Economic Interests*, O.U.P.
[2]   *[1964] AC 465, [1963] 2 All ER 575, HL.*
[3]   *Nocton v Lord Ashburton [1914] AC 932, HL.* Cf N J McBride and A Hughes '*Hedley Byrne* in the House of Lords: An Interpretation' (1995) 15 LS 376, who conclude (at 389) that 'Liability under the principle in *Hedley Byrne* should ... be expelled from the category of "obligations arising from *negligence*" and brought under the category of "obligations arising from breach of a *fiduciary duty*" ... or put into its own category' (emphasis in the original).
[4]   *Derry v Peek (1889) 14 App Cas 337, HL.* Cf *Commercial Banking Co of Sydney v Brown & Co [1972] 2 Lloyd's Rep 360 (Aust HC).*
[5]   See *Clayton v Woodman & Son (Builders) Ltd [1962] 2 QB 533, [1963] 3 All ER 249*: advice by an architect (claim failed on the facts). For a case, in which liability for physical injury was imposed applying *Hedley Byrne* itself, see *T (a minor) v Surrey County Council [1994] 4 All ER 577* (misleading statement by local authority causing mother to place child with a registered child-minder who was already suspected of injuring children).
[6]   See *[1964] AC 465* at 509 (Lord Hodson); 517 (Lord Devlin); 538 (Lord Pearce).

Reliance

[4.02]   It so happened in *Hedley Byrne* itself that both questions arose, but in other situations they can obviously arise independently (ie a negligent misstatement may give rise to physical injury and negligent action may give rise to economic loss). One thing which did emerge clearly from the speeches, however, was that the House of Lords was anxious to limit the extent of the newly created liability for misstatement by requiring a 'special relationship' between the parties before it could arise.[1] This would involve 'reliance' upon the defendant by the plaintiff, with the former being aware that that reliance existed.[2] This was, of course, a narrower approach than that adopted to the problem of careless acts in *Donoghue v Stevenson*,[3] where, in general, the objective concept of the foreseeability of the reasonable man is the most important influence upon the imposition of liability. The nature of the 'special relationship' concept was expounded and further developed by the House of Lords in *Caparo Industries plc v Dickman*.[4] This case, which is of great importance in determining the contemporary scope of liability for negligent misstatement and, indeed, the scope of the modern law of negligence in general, is discussed later in this chapter at para [4.21].

1 See *[1964] AC 465* at 483, 486 (Lord Reid); 502–503 (Lord Morris); 511 (Lord Hodson); 528–529 (Lord Devlin: 'circumstances in which, but for the absence of consideration, there would be a contract'); 539 (Lord Pearce).
2 See *[1964] AC 465 at 486* (Lord Reid); 497 (Lord Morris); 514 (Lord Hodson).
3 *[1932] AC 562.*
4 *[1990] 2 AC 605, [1990] 1 All ER 568.*

Broader concept

[4.03] In some cases, however, the *Hedley Byrne* principle has been used as a springboard for imposing liability in cases in which the plaintiff cannot meaningfully be said to have 'relied' on the defendant, and to do so even in situations going beyond the sphere of 'misstatement' as such. Thus, in *White v Jones*[1] the House of Lords used the principle in order to impose liability, in favour of plaintiff beneficiaries, upon a solicitor whose negligent failure to prepare a will before his client's death had deprived the plaintiffs of the gifts which the deceased had intended to make.[2] In this case, and in another relatively recent decision of the House,[3] their Lordships appeared to favour the notion that a defendant's 'assuming responsibility' for a particular task, where the adverse effect upon the plaintiff if it were not discharged was foreseeable, could provide an adequate foundation for liability.[4] This concept is broader than that adopted in *Hedley Byrne* itself, where the fact that 'reliance' existed made it unnecessary to consider whether that requirement was in truth a necessary condition for the imposition of liability in all analogous situations.[5] But since the notion of 'reliance' cannot meaningfully be applied to situations such as that in *White v Jones*,[6] in which third parties seek to sue for pure economic loss arising out of interactions to which they were not themselves parties,[7] the existence of liability in cases of that type clearly cannot be predicated on that being a requirement.

1 *[1995] 2 AC 207, [1995] 1 All ER 691.* For further discussion, see paras [5.38] to [5.41] below.
2 See also *Ross v Caunters [1980] Ch 297, [1979] 3 All ER 580* (the correctness of which was confirmed by the decision in *White*'s case).
3 *Henderson v Merrett Syndicates Ltd [1995] 2 AC 145, [1994] 3 All ER 506.*
4 See especially *per* Lord Browne-Wilkinson and Lord Nolan in *White v Jones [1995] 1 All ER 691* at 714–716 and 735 respectively, and *per* Lord Goff and Lord Browne-Wilkinson in *Henderson v Merrett Syndicates Ltd [1994] 3 All ER 506* at 520–521 and 543–544 respectively. For further discussion, see below.
5 See *White v Jones [1995] 2 AC 207* at 272, *[1995] 1 All ER 691* at 714, *per* Lord Browne-Wilkinson.
6 *[1995] 2 AC 207, [1995] 1 All ER 691.*
7 See *Ministry of Housing and Local Government v Sharp [1970] 2 QB 223, [1970] 1 All ER 1009, CA.*

Difference and overlap

[4.04] It is therefore appropriate to distinguish, as Buxton LJ put it in *Andrew v Kounnis Freeman*[1], between 'two different, but interrelated, types of case. The first, closely following *Hedley Byrne & Co v Heller & Partners Ltd*, is where, in limited circumstances, advice is given by an adviser to an "advisee" … The second case is where, more generally, the defendant's conduct can be objectively analysed as involving an assumption of responsibility for the performance of a task in the course of performing or omitting to perform which he foreseeably causes economic loss to the plaintiff'. In some respects the requirements for the two types of case will overlap, particularly in respect of the degree of care to be expected of the defendant. In what follows the requirements for establishing liability will be dealt with first, much of which will be relevant to both types of case. Claims by third parties, of which some, but not all[2], will be based upon the more general 'assumption of responsibility' doctrine, will be dealt with subsequently. The next section focuses upon situations in which an *omission* by the defendant serves to highlight the question of whether or not a duty was owed to the claimant at all. The chapter will conclude by considering the respects in which issues of public policy have arisen in this area, and by examining the topic of disclaimers of liability.

---

[1] See *[2000] Lloyd's Rep PN 263*.
[2] In some cases a third party may have foreseeably 'relied' on the statement, and thus be able to invoke the narrower doctrine.

B Establishing liability

Types of misstatement

[4.05] Negligent misstatement can take many different forms. The most obvious type of case is a careless response to a request for a specific piece of information, as in *Hedley Byrne* itself.[1] But it also includes careless advice and evaluation in situations requiring special skill, such as underwriting,[2] and extends to professional activities of a more positive nature, such as the carrying out of an audit on a company[3] or the preparation of maps[4] and charts[5] and the like.[6] It might also be taken to include cases of negligent design, for example, of buildings,[7] or of cranes[8] and other complex pieces of machinery.[9]

---

[1] See also *Spring v Guardian Assurance plc [1995] 2 AC 296, [1994] 3 All ER 129*, HL (reference for job applicant).
[2] See *Henderson v Merrett Syndicates Ltd [1995] 2 AC 145, [1994] 3 All ER 506, HL*. Cf *Williams v Natural Life Health Foods Ltd [1998] 2 All ER 577, [1998] 1 WLR 830, HL* (advice and assistance to franchisees setting up a new business).
[3] See *Caparo Industries plc v Dickman [1990] 2 AC 605, [1990] 1 All ER 568, HL*.
[4] Cf *Post Office v Mears Construction Ltd [1979] 2 All ER 813*.
[5] See *Caltex Oil (Australia) Pty Ltd v Dredge Willemstad (1976–77) 136 CLR 529*.
[6] See *per* Lord Steyn in *Williams v Natural Life Health Foods Ltd [1998] 2 All ER 577* at 581, *[1998] 1 WLR 830* at 834, HL: '*Hedley Byrne* … is not confined to statements but may apply to any assumption of responsibility for the provision of services.'
[7] See *Rimmer v Liverpool City Council [1985] QB 1, [1984] 1 All ER 930, CA*.
[8] See *Rivtow Marine Ltd v Washington Ironworks (1973) 40 DLR (3d) 530*.
[9] See *Hindustan Steam Shipping Co Ltd v Siemens Bros & Co [1955] 1 Lloyd's Rep 167* at 177, *per* Willmer J (design of ship's engine-room telegraph). Cf *Lexmead (Basingstoke) Ltd v Lewis [1982] AC 225* (defective coupling mechanism for towing vehicles on the road).

Special skills?

[4.06]   In one case the 'special relationship' requirement was used as a device sharply to limit the scope of liability for negligent misstatement.[1] In *Mutual Life and Citizens' Insurance Co Ltd v Evatt*[2] the plaintiff sought advice from the defendant company about the safety of investments in another company, which was a subsidiary company of the same organisation as that to which the defendant company itself belonged. By a bare majority[3] the Judicial Committee of the Privy Council held that the plaintiff would fail since the defendant company did not hold itself out as having any special skill and competence in giving advice on investments, and that possession by the defendant of a special skill was a general, though not exclusive,[4] condition for the existence of a 'special relationship'.[5] If it had been followed, the decision would have severely limited the impact of *Hedley Byrne*. Significantly, however, two of the three members of the Board in *Evatt* who had also been members of the House of Lords which decided *Hedley Byrne* itself,[6] dissented asserting that a limitation of the new liability to persons possessing special skills had not been envisaged when the earlier case was decided. Subsequently, there were judicial expressions of dislike in the Court of Appeal for the principle in *Evatt*'s case,[7] and the better view would therefore seem to be that the case does not now represent English law. Nevertheless, in so far as the court is no doubt more likely to view the prospect of liability with favour if the defendant possesses special skill (or knowledge[8]) than if he or she does not do so,[9] the views of the majority in *Evatt* may perhaps still be said to embody a limited and partial degree of validity.[10]

[1]   See *Mutual Life and Citizens' Assurance Co Ltd v Evatt [1971] AC 793, [1971] 1 All ER 150, PC* (discussed at para [4.06]).
[2]   *[1971] AC 793, [1971] 1 All ER 150.*
[3]   Lord Hodson, Lord Guest and Lord Diplock (Lord Reid and Lord Morris dissenting).
[4]   See the treatment, discussed below, by the majority (*[1971] AC 793* at 809, *[1971] 1 All ER 150* at 161) in the case of *WB Anderson & Sons Ltd v Rhodes (Liverpool) Ltd [1967] 2 All ER 850.*
[5]   'The carrying on of a business or profession which involves the giving of advice of a kind which calls for special skill and competence is the normal way in which a person lets it be known to the recipient of the advice that he claims to possess that degree of skill and competence and is willing to exercise that degree of diligence which is generally possessed and exercised by persons who carry on the business or profession of giving advice of the kind sought': *[1971] AC 793* at 805, *per* Lord Diplock delivering the judgment of the majority.
[6]   Ie Lord Reid and Lord Morris.
[7]   See *Esso Petroleum Co Ltd v Mardon [1976] QB 801* at 827, *[1976] 2 All ER 5* at 22, *per* Ormrod LJ; *Howard Marine and Dredging Co Ltd v Ogden & Sons (Excavations) Ltd [1978] QB 574* at 591 (Lord Denning MR) and 600 (Shaw LJ). See also *L Shaddock & Associates v Parramatta City Council [1979] 1 NSWLR 566* at 586, *per* Hutley J A: 'The judgment of the majority has given almost universal dissatisfaction both to courts and to the learned.'
[8]   See below.
[9]   But cf *Chaudhry v Prabhakar [1988] 3 All ER 718, [1989] 1 WLR 29, CA*, discussed at para [4.12].
[10]   In *Caparo Industries plc v Dickman [1990] 2 AC 605* at 637, *[1990] 1 All ER 568* at 588 Lord Oliver observed that it was unnecessary in that case to express a view as to the correctness of *Mutual Life v Evatt* since *Caparo* involved something done in the ordinary course of the defendants' business (ie the certification of accounts by auditors).

Delicate judgments

[4.07]   Where the alleged misstatement takes the form of professional advice[1] a distinctive feature is that the giving of such advice will frequently have involved the exercise of judgment and evaluation. For this reason claims based upon it may give rise to special difficulties of proof. Advice which eventually turns out to have been 'wrong' was not necessarily given negligently. In *Stafford v Conti Commodity Serv-*

ices Ltd[2] an investor who had incurred large losses on the commodities market unsuccessfully sought to sue his broker for negligent advice. It was held that 'a broker cannot always be right in the advice that he gives in relation to so wayward and rapidly changing a market'.[3] Where advice takes the form of prediction (as it often does), much will therefore depend in practice upon the degree of accuracy generally to be expected in the particular field.[4] The clearest example of liability being imposed in such a case is *Esso Petroleum Co Ltd v Mardon.*[5] An employee of the defendant[6] oil company told a tenant of one of the company's new garages that his throughput of petrol would be in the order of 200,000 to 250,000 gallons per year. In fact, the garage subsequently turned out to be capable of little more than a quarter of this figure. The Court of Appeal held the company liable. They had great experience in judging the capacity of retail outlets for their product, which the plaintiff did not have. In the words of Lord Denning MR:[7]

> 'It seems to me that *Hedley Byrne*, properly understood, covers this particular proposition: if a man, who has or professes to have special knowledge or skill, makes a representation by virtue thereof to another – be it advice, information or opinion – with the intention of inducing him to enter into a contract with him, he is under a duty to use reasonable care to see that the representation is correct, and that the information or opinion is reliable. If he negligently gives unsound advice or misleading information or expresses an erroneous opinion, and thereby induces the other side into a contract with him, he is liable in damages.'

[1] In such cases the parties will obviously frequently be in a contractual relationship, but (except in very rare cases where the defendant expressly undertakes otherwise) it is well established that even the contractual duty is not absolute but is limited to the taking of reasonable care.

[2] *[1981] 1 All ER 691.* Cf *Elderkin v Merrill Lynch Royal Securities Ltd (1977) 80 DLR (3d) 313* (liability imposed upon stockbroker for negligent investment advice).

[3] *[1981] 1 All ER 691* at 697a, *per* Mocatta J.

[4] See *Ormindale Holdings v Ray, Wolfe, Connel, Lightbody & Reynolds (1980) 116 DLR (3d) 346* (lawyer's advice not necessarily negligent merely because his opinion as to the law is ultimately rejected by the court). The narrowness of the line which may separate negligence from a view subsequently rejected is, however, illustrated by cases involving the valuation of property in which liability has been imposed: see *Singer and Friedlander Ltd v John D Wood & Co [1977] 2 EGLR 84.* For further discussion, see, generally, PART THREE (PROFESSIONAL NEGLIGENCE).

[5] *[1976] QB 801, [1976] 2 All ER 5, CA.* Cf *Intervention Board for Agricultural Produce v Leidig [2000] Lloyd's Rep PN 144, CA.*

[6] Ie on a counter-claim: the oil company had itself brought the action which their tenant (as plaintiff in the counter-claim) resisted.

[7] *[1976] QB 801* at 820, *[1976] 2 All ER 5* at 16.

Knowledge or skill

[4.08]   It is to be noted that in this passage Lord Denning refers to '*knowledge or skill*' (italics supplied). Clearly, one can exist without the other.[1] Indeed, *Esso Petroleum Co Ltd v Mardon* was one of those cases in which the opportunity was taken to make clear that the restrictive approach favoured by the Privy Council in *Mutual Life & Citizens' Assurance Co Ltd v Evatt,*[2] which would have required the possession of skill of a professional nature as a prerequisite to liability in most cases, would not be adopted. In the pre-*Evatt* case of *Anderson & Sons Ltd v Rhodes (Liverpool) Ltd,*[3] Cairns J, sitting at Liverpool Assizes, held expressly that the duty of care under *Hedley Byrne* was not limited to professional people. In *Anderson*'s case fruit and vegetables dealers, who sometimes also acted as commission agents, were held liable to other traders for a negligent misstatement as to the creditworthiness of certain potato merchants with whom they had had business dealings. In *Mutual Life v Citizens*

Assurance Co Ltd v Evatt Lord Diplock apparently suggested that the decision in *Anderson v Rhodes* should be regarded as correct, and distinguishable from *Evatt*, on the narrow basis that, in the absence of a professional skill, liability would only be imposed when the 'advisor has a financial interest in the transaction on which he gives his advice'.[4] However, this limited interpretation of the case, of which there is no suggestion in the actual judgment, can probably be regarded as incorrect in view of the predominantly hostile reception which the decision in *Evatt* itself received.[5]

[1] Cf *Henderson v Merrett Syndicates Ltd [1995] 2 AC 145* at 180, *[1994] 3 All ER 506* at 520, *per* Lord Goff: '… the concept of a 'special skill' must be understood broadly, certainly broadly enough to include special knowledge.'
[2] *[1971] AC 793, [1971] 1 All ER 150*.
[3] *[1967] 2 All ER 850*.
[4] *[1971] AC 793* at 809, *[1971] 1 All ER 150* at 161. Quaere, however, whether such a financial interest did not exist in *Evatt*'s case itself, since the advice led the plaintiff to invest a company belonging to the same group as the defendants: cf *per* Lord Reid, delivering the judgment of the minority *[1971] AC 793* at 811.
[5] See above.

Degree of care

[4.09] In any type of misstatement case difficult questions may arise as to the precise degree of care which a defendant ought to have shown. An interesting example is provided by *Howard Marine and Dredging Co Ltd v Ogden & Sons (Excavations) Ltd*.[1] In this case, which concerned pre-contractual negotiations, the defendant[2] was asked to give the carrying capacity of certain of his firm's barges, which the plaintiffs were thinking of hiring. He gave an immediate answer in reliance on the figure given in Lloyd's Register, which unfortunately turned out to be inaccurate, instead of taking the trouble to consult the ships's documents, which would have given the true figure. The plaintiffs took the barges in reliance on the statement, but the error as to carrying capacity rendered them useless for the purpose for which they had been hired. The trial judge, Bristow J, exonerated the defendant on the ground that it was reasonable for him to have relied on Lloyd's Register, an error in that publication being most unusual. By a majority, Lord Denning MR dissenting, the Court of Appeal reversed that decision.

[1] *[1978] QB 574, [1978] 2 All ER 1134, CA*.
[2] Ie on a counterclaim. The parties referred to in the text as plaintiff and defendant, for the sake of convenience, in fact had their roles reversed in the main action.

'Off the cuff' advice

[4.10] The case turned mainly on the *Misrepresentation Act 1967, s 2*, but the position as to liability under the principle in *Hedley Byrne v Heller* was also considered. Lord Denning MR felt that the statement was an 'impromptu opinion given offhand'[1] and that the plaintiffs had been aware of that. In those circumstances the defendant's only duty was to be 'honest', which he had been. Bridge LJ, who based his decision in favour of the plaintiffs solely on the 1967 Act, was sympathetic to Lord Denning's approach on the common law point. Shaw LJ, however, expressed a clear view in favour of liability under *Hedley Byrne*. The fact that the only reliable source of knowledge, ie the ships' documents, were exclusively in the defendant's possession, and that the question of carrying capacity was crucial to the outcome of the negotiations, was sufficient to enable the plaintiffs to succeed. Shaw LJ said[2] that, in those circumstances, the fact that the defendant 'chose to answer an important question from mere recollection "off the cuff" does not in my view diminish, if I may adopt the language of Lord Pearce,[3] the "gravity of the inquiry or the importance and influence attached to the answer" '. The judgment of Shaw LJ is a salutary warning to those who make statements which are obviously central to the matter under consideration, and of which the maker of the statement is in a particularly strong position, by contrast with the person to whom it is made, to know whether it is true or false. In these circumstances the relatively informal manner in which the inquiry might happen to be made, should not mislead the person giving the answer into skimping his inspection of the relevant sources.

[1] *[1978] QB 574 at 591, [1978] 2 All ER 1134 at 1141.*
[2] *[1978] QB 574 at 601, [1978] 2 All ER 1134 at 1148.*
[3] Ie in *Hedley Byrne & Co Ltd v Heller & Partners [1964] AC 465 at 539, [1963] 2 All ER 575 at 617,* HL.

Informal planning advice

[4.11] The giving of informal advice by planning officials to enquirers will rarely give rise to liability for negligent misstatement in the event of the advice proving inaccurate[1]. Thus casual telephone calls to a local authority's planning department, without subsequent written confirmation being sought, are unlikely to provide an appropriate basis for 'reliance' on the part of the caller[2]. In *Haddow v Secretary of State for the Environment* Kennedy LJ said[3]:

> 'The ordinary process of giving routine advice to an applicant for planning permission and answering such questions as he or she may raise, especially when the applicant is one known to have her own professional advisers, does not give rise to any duty of care'.

Of course each case will depend on its own factual context, and if formal searches are carelessly carried out, liability can arise[4]. It appears, however, that the requirement that the *purpose* for which the information was sought should have been known to the person providing the information[5], if liability is to arise, will be construed fairly strictly in favour of the local authority in such cases[6].

[1] See *per* Buxton J in *Tidman v Reading Borough Council [1994] PLR 72.*
[2] See *Fashion Brokers v Clarke Hayes [2000] Lloyd's Rep PN 398, CA.*
[3] See *[2000] Env LR 212, CA.*
[4] Cf *Ministry of Housing and Local Government v Sharp [1970] 2 QB 223, [1970] 1 All ER 1009, CA.*
[5] See below.
[6] See *Gooden v Northamptonshire CC [2002] PNLR 18.*

Social occasions

An exceptional case

[4.12] In *Chaudhry v Prabhakar*[1] the defendant acted as unpaid adviser for the plaintiff, a friend of his who was seeking to buy a second-hand motor car. When the car turned out to be unroadworthy and quite valueless the plaintiff sued him for negligent misstatement – and the Court of Appeal, albeit with some reluctance on the part of one member of the court, who felt that the imposition of liability in such cases could 'make social regulations and responsibilities between friends unnecessarily hazardous'[2] – held him liable. The case is complicated by the fact that counsel for the defendant had *conceded* the existence of a duty of care[3], and fought the case on the basis of what standard of care that admitted duty imposed. The decision is therefore a somewhat uncertain guide for future cases. Indeed, Stocker LJ emphasised that 'in the absence of other factors giving rise to such a duty, the giving of advice sought in the context of family, domestic or social relationships will not in itself give rise to any duty in respect of such advice'.[4] If one single factor can be identified as having tipped the scales against the defendant, it is probably that his advice was sought in a very specific situation leading to the actual purchase of the vehicle which he sought out and recommended. Thus, Stuart-Smith LJ said:

' ... where, as in this case, the relationship of principal and agent exists, such that a contract comes into existence between the principal and the third party, it seems to me that, at the very least, this relationship is powerful evidence that the occasion is not a purely social one, but ... is in a business connection.'[5]

[1] *[1988] 3 All ER 718, [1989] 1 WLR 29, CA.*
[2] *[1988] 3 All ER 718* at 725, *[1989] 1 WLR 29* at 39, *per* May LJ.
[3] May LJ doubted whether this concession had been rightly made: see *[1988] 3 All ER 718* at 725, *[1989] 1 WLR 29* at 38.
[4] *[1988] 3 All ER 718* at 723, *[1989] 1 WLR 29* at 36.
[5] *[1988] 3 All ER 718* at 722, *[1989] 1 WLR 29* at 35.

Risk minimal

[4.13] Professional people who happen casually to express opinions on matters within their sphere at social gatherings are therefore probably safe in assuming that they are at no greater risk of incurring *Hedley Byrne* liability after *Chaudhry v Prabhakar* than they were before. This risk would still seem to be minimal. Apart from *Chaudhry v Prabhakar*, the only decision which touches on the point is the old case of *Fish v Kelly*.[1] The defendant was a solicitor who had drawn up, and who kept in his possession, a deed relating to the terms of employment for workers at a company for which he acted. When he happened to be on the company's premises, one of the employees took the opportunity to ask him whether the deed provided for certain moneys to be paid to him if he left the company's service. The defendant honestly replied in the affirmative, having unfortunately forgotten that the detailed provisions of the deed meant that the moneys would only be payable to the plaintiff's executor after his death. The plaintiff left the company in consequence of the answer which he received, and subsequently sued the solicitor. The action failed. Erle CJ was 'unable to perceive any duty arising out of the casual conversation here',[2] and Byles J said that 'If this sort of action could be maintained, it would be extremely hazardous for an attorney to venture to give an opinion upon any point of law in the course of a journey by railway'.[3]

[1] *(1864) 17 CBNS 194.*
[2] *(1864) 17 CBNS 194*, at 206.
[3] *(1864) 17 CBNS 194* at 207.

Reluctance to impose liability

[4.14] Of course, the *Fish v Kelly* case was decided long before *Hedley Byrne* and was based in part (though not, interestingly enough, wholly) on the absence of a contract between plaintiff and defendant. On its facts the decision seems rather harsh.

The defendant was the person best qualified to answer the plaintiff's query, and to expect the latter to cross-examine the company's solicitor to ensure that the advice given had been fully considered, or to request confirmation from him in writing, was surely expecting rather a lot of an ordinary employee. Perhaps, however, this criticism would be less valid today, when employees are better educated and informed, than in the middle of the nineteenth century when the case was actually decided. Nevertheless, *Fish v Kelly* would still seem to be a decision very close to the borderline, and the specific context of the question posed to the defendant might possibly have led to liability if the approach subsequently adopted in *Chaudhry v Prabhakar* had been applied. There can be little doubt, however, that the courts will remain reluctant to hold liable those who are, in a sense, generous in choosing to respond to chance inquiries made in informal circumstances.[1]

---

[1]   Cf The American Law Institute's *Second Restatement of the Law of Torts* (1977) p 130 (comment in para 552), denying liability 'when an attorney gives a casual and offhand opinion on a point of law to a friend whom he meets on the street'.

C Claims by third parties

Fear of indeterminate liability

[4.15]   The development of liability for negligent misstatement has long been influenced by a belief which was encapsulated in a famous dictum of Cardozo CJ in *Ultramares Corpn v Touche*,[1] in which he expressed fear of the danger of 'liability in an indeterminate amount for an indeterminate time to an indeterminate class'. In the *Ultramares* case itself the Court of Appeals of New York refused to hold accountants, who had carelessly audited the accounts of a company, liable to an investor who lost heavily in reliance on the bill of health given to the company by the defendants. This was despite the fact that they had been fully aware that the balance sheet, when certified by them, would be exhibited to 'banks, creditors, stockholders, purchasers, or sellers, according to the needs of the occasion'.[2]

---

[1]   *174 NE 441* at 450 (1931). But see also the reference to this dictum by Woodhouse J in *Scott Group v McFarlane [1978] 1 NZLR 553* at 571–572: 'those ... words have been repeated in some judgments almost as though they reveal a self-evident truth; and not unnaturally they were referred to by counsel for the auditors in the present case. But the attraction and force of the language ought not to lead to uncritical acceptance of that sort of argument.'

[2]   *174 NE 441* at 442.

Three devices

[4.16]   The same result was reached, on similar facts, in the case of *Candler v Crane Christmas & Co*,[1] which provoked the famous dissenting judgment of Denning LJ,[1] later to be vindicated in *Hedley Byrne v Heller*. In cases decided since *Hedley Byrne* three devices have been developed in an attempt to avoid the danger of indeterminate liability while nevertheless allowing some claims by third parties to succeed. The three devices are, first 'assumption of responsibility', secondly, the concept of 'purpose', and thirdly, the notion of a 'class' of possible claimants.

---

[1]   *[1951] 2 KB 164, [1951] 1 All ER 426, CA.*

Assumption of responsibility

[4.17] In *Henderson v Merrett Syndicates Ltd*[1] Lord Goff pointed out that, in *Hedley Byrne*, 'all of their Lordships spoke in terms of one party having assumed or undertaken a responsibility towards the other'. Although the concept of 'assumption of responsibility' was criticised in the House of Lords in two cases subsequent to *Hedley Byrne*[2], its validity was emphatically reaffirmed by the House itself in *Henderson v Merrett Syndicates Ltd*[3] and *White v Jones*.[4] Of these two, only the latter really concerned liability to a third party; *Henderson's* case was a rather more straightforward situation concerning the relationship between Lloyd's 'names' and their underwriting agents. In both cases, however, the concept of assumption of responsibility was redefined as revolving around the *task* which the defendant undertook to carry out rather than the notion of an assumption of *legal* responsibility towards a specific individual. The earlier approach had been open to criticism on grounds of artificiality, not least where liability was imposed under the *Hedley Byrne* principle despite the defendant's having sought to *disclaim* responsibility.[5] By focusing upon the work undertaken, rather than the person who originally commissioned it, the new approach sought not only to avoid that artificiality but also to provide a coherent basis for the imposition of liability in favour of third parties.

[1]   See *[1995] 2 AC 145* at 180, *[1994] 3 All ER 506* at 520.
[2]   See *per* Lord Griffiths in *Smith v Eric S Bush [1990] 1 AC 831* at 862, *[1989] 2 All ER 514* at 534 (not 'a realistic or helpful test for liability'), and *per* Lord Roskill in *Caparo Industries plc v Dickman [1990] 2 AC 605* at 626, *[1990] 1 All ER 568* at 582.
[3]   *[1995] 2 AC 145*, *[1994] 3 All ER 506*.
[4]   *[1995] 2 AC 207*, *[1995] 1 All ER 691*.
[5]   Eg as in *Smith v Eric S Bush [1990] 1 AC 831*, *[1989] 2 All ER 514* itself. On disclaimers see further from para [4.46] below.

Responsibility for the task

[4.18] In *White v Jones*[1] a solicitor who accepted instructions to draw up a will, but who negligently failed to so before his client died, was sued by the disappointed potential beneficiaries. By a bare majority[2] the House of Lords held that the claim would succeed. The majority held that the principle underlying *Hedley Byrne v Heller* was wide enough to embrace the situation. This was notwithstanding that the plaintiffs were obviously not parties to the contract between the defendant and his client; the claim being, in effect, one for failure to make a financial gain due to the defendant's negligent omission rather than for loss resulting from 'reliance' on any misstatement by him. The dissentients considered that allowing the claim to succeed could lead to a wide and unprincipled expansion of liability for financial 'losses',[3] but the majority considered that the concept of 'assumption of responsibility', if understood as being *for* the task in hand rather than *towards* any specific individual, created an adequate foundation for the decision.[4] Lord Browne-Wilkinson said:[5]

> '… the assumption of responsibility referred to is the defendants' assumption of responsibility for the task, not the assumption of legal liability … The solicitor … by accepting the instructions has entered upon, and therefore assumed responsibility for, the task of procuring the execution of a skilfully drawn will knowing that the beneficiary is wholly dependent upon his skilfully carrying out his function … It is not to the point that the solicitor only entered on the task pursuant to a contract with the third party (ie the testator).'[6]

[1]   *[1995] 2 AC 207*, *[1995] 1 All ER 691*, HL.

2   Lord Goff, Lord Browne-Wilkinson and Lord Nolan; Lord Keith and Lord Mustill dissenting.
3   See especially *per* Lord Mustill *[1995] 2 AC 207* at 291, *[1995] 1 All ER 691* at 733.
4   See especially *per* Lord Browne-Wilkinson and Lord Nolan *[1995] 2 AC 207* at 272–274 and 293–294,
     [1995] 1 All ER 691 at 714–716 and 735 respectively.
5   *[1995] 2 AC 207* at 273 and 275, *[1995] 1 All ER 691* at 715–16 and 717–718.
6   Cf *per* Lord Nolan in the same case: 'If the defendant drives his car on the highway, he implicitly
     assumes a responsibility towards other road users, and they in turn implicitly rely on him to discharge
     that responsibility.' *[1995] 2 AC 207* at 293, *[1995] 1 All ER 691* at 735.

Not an isolated case

[4.19]   In *White v Jones* itself the House of Lords was content to leave any difficulties to be dealt with if and when they arose.[1] They were fortified by the fact that in the well-known case of *Ross v Caunters*,[2] decided 16 years earlier, Sir Robert Megarry V-C had reached the same result on not dissimiliar facts without any adverse consequences for the development of the law.[3] The Court of Appeal was willing to contemplate the application of *White v Jones* to a very different factual situation in *Farah v British Airways*[4]. In this case the court refused to strike out a claim against the Home Office based on the alleged negligence of an immigration officer in advising British Airways wrongly about the entry status of the claimants, who consequently suffered loss when the airline refused to fly them to the UK. In permitting the claim to proceed, Chadwick LJ stated that the relevant question was whether the Home Office could be said to have 'assumed responsibility' towards the claimants for the accuracy of the information given to the airline; a way of putting the question which his Lordship observed that he preferred to that of asking simply whether there was 'a sufficient degree of proximity' between the claimants and the Home Office. Counsel for the Home Office contended unsuccessfully that *White v Jones* was an unusual decision which should be confined to its own facts. Lord Woolf MR responded as follows:

'Although I recognise that *White v Jones* is dealing with a situation which is out of the ordinary, I do not regard the approach of the House of Lords either in *White v Jones* itself, or in the cases by which it has been followed, as indicating that the case cannot be applied to appropriate analogous situations'.

1   'If by any chance a more complicated case should arise to test the precise boundaries of the principle in
     cases of this kind, that problem can await solution when such a case comes forward for discussion': *per*
     Lord Goff *[1995] 1 All ER 691* at 712. Cf *Carr-Glynn v Frearsons (a firm) [1997] 2 All ER 614.*
2   *[1980] Ch 297, [1979] 3 All ER 580.*
3   ' … with the benefit of experience during the 15 years in which *Ross v Caunters* has been regularly
     applied, we can say with some confidence that a direct remedy by the intended beneficiary against the
     solicitor appears to create no problems in practice': *per* Lord Goff in *[1995] 1 All ER 691* at 710. See
     also *per* Lord Nolan at 735: 'To reverse the decision in *Ross v Caunters* at this stage would be, in my
     judgment, a disservice to the law.'
4   (2000) Times, 26 January. Quotations from the judgments are via LEXIS.

Relationship with the 'just and reasonable' test?

[4.20]   The concept of 'assumption of responsibility', as now understood, is not without its intuitive attractions.[1] Nevertheless, it is questionable how widely certain observations of Lord Goff in *Henderson v Merrett Syndicates Ltd*[2] should be interpreted. His Lordship considered that 'if a person assumes responsibility to another in respect of certain services, there is no reason why he should not be liable in damages for that other in respect of economic loss which flows from the performance of those services'. He therefore suggested that 'once the case is identified as falling within the *Hedley Byrne* principle, there should be no need to embark upon any further inquiry whether it is 'fair, just and reasonable' to impose liability for economic loss'. While this proposition would seem to be appropriate in straightforward cases of direct reliance by one person upon another, such as happened broadly to be the situation in *Henderson v Merrett Syndicates Ltd* itself, it would not appear to be applicable where claims by third parties are concerned[3]. Indeed, it would be surprising if the courts were prepared wholly to forego possible use of the 'just and reasonable' control device in such cases, since situations could arise where the scale of potential liability upon defendants might be perceived as oppressive[4]. However unattractive invocation of that device might be when used to render judicial reasoning avoidably opaque in less complex situations,[5] it is probably unavoidable when dealing with exceptional cases.[6]

[1]   But for criticism see S Whitaker 'The application of the "broad principle of *Hedley Byrne*" as between parties to a contract' (1997) 17 LS 169. See also K Barker 'Unreliable Assumptions in the Modern Law of Negligence' (1993) 109 LQR 461; and CHAPTER 1 above. Cf the response of Lord Steyn in *Williams v Natural Life Foods Ltd [1998] 2 All ER 577* at 584, *[1998] 1 WLR 830* at 831, HL: 'In my view the general criticism is overstated. Coherence must sometimes yield to practical justice.'
[2]   See *[1994] 3 All ER 506* at 521. See also *Williams v Natural Life Foods Ltd [1998] 2 All ER 577* at 581, *[1998] 1 WLR 830* at 834, HL, *per* Lord Steyn.
[3]   See *Andrew v Kounnis Freeman [2000] Lloyd's Rep PN 263 per* Buxton LJ.
[4]   Cf *Marc Rich & Co AG v Bishop Rock Marine Co, The Nicholas H [1996] AC 211, [1995] 3 All ER 307, HL.*
[5]   See generally CHAPTER 1 above.
[6]   Eg the famous hypothetical case of the marine hydographer whose carelessness causes the loss of an ocean liner: see *per* Asquith LJ in *Candler v Crane, Christmas & Co [1951] 2 KB 164* at 194–195, *[1951] 1 All ER 426* at 442; Winfield was apparently the first to raise this possible fact-situation: see his *Textbook of the Law of Tort* (1st edn, 1937) p 414. Cf *Marc Rich & Co AG v Bishop Rock Marine Co Ltd [1996] AC 211, [1995] 3 All ER 307, HL.*

Purpose

[4.21]   In *Caparo Industries plc v Dickman*[1] the plaintiff shareholders in a public company, having received the company's audited accounts, purchased further shares. When the shares underwent a dramatic fall in value, due to profits being well below their predicted level, the plaintiffs sued the company's auditors, alleging that they had been negligent in auditing the accounts. The action ultimately failed in the House of Lords, having also failed at first instance but having succeeded by a majority in the Court of Appeal. The House considered that to hold auditors liable to the investing public generally, notwithstanding the foreseeable possibility of their reliance on the accounts, 'would be to create a liability wholly indefinite in area, duration and amount and would open up a limitless vista of uninsurable risk for the professional man'.[2] The mere fact that the plaintiffs were existing shareholders did not distinguish them from investors generally, at least as far as the purchase of additional shares was concerned.[3] Their Lordships focused upon the legislative policy underlying the requirement for annual audited accounts, which was considered to be to enable shareholders to exercise their powers of control over the company.[4] 'In my judgment', said Lord Oliver, 'the *purpose* for which the auditor's certificate is made and published is that of providing those entitled to receive the report with information to enable them to exercise in conjunction those powers which their respective proprietary interests confer on them and not for the purposes of individual speculation with a view to profit'.[5]

[1]   *[1990] 2 AC 605, [1990] 1 All ER 568*; revsg *[1989] QB 653, [1989] 1 All ER 798.*

2 *[1990] 2 AC 605* at 643, *[1990] 1 All ER 568* at 593, *per* Lord Oliver. See also *per* Lord Roskill: 'The submission that there is a virtually unlimited and unrestricted duty of care in relation to the performance of an auditor's statutory duty to certify a company's accounts, a duty extending to anyone who may use those accounts for any purpose such as investing in the company or lending the company money, seems to me untenable': *[1990] 2 AC 605* at 628, *[1990] 1 All ER 568* at 582.

3 The House appears to have left open the question, upon which the Court of Appeal had been divided, of whether shareholders who *sold* their *existing* shares, in reliance upon negligently audited accounts, would be able to claim. Lord Bridge and Lord Oliver do not rule out the possibility of such liability (see *[1990] 2 AC 605* at 627, 653, *[1990] 1 All ER 568* at 581, 601, respectively) but the reasoning of Lord Jauncey (see *[1990] 2 AC 605* at 621, *[1990] 1 All ER 568* at 607–608: 'no duty to an individual shareholder') would appear to do so.

4 See the *Companies Act 1985, Pt VII.*

5 *[1990] 2 AC 605* at 654, *[1990] 1 All ER 568* at 601, italics supplied. See also *per* Lord Jauncey *[1990] 2 AC 605* at 658, *[1990] 1 All ER 568* at 605.

Utility of the concept

[4.22] It is therefore clear from *Caparo Industries plc v Dickman*[1] that the *purpose* with which the statement was made will often be a factor of great importance in determining the extent of liability for negligent misstatement, and one which will often be related closely to the notion of assumption of responsibility. Of course, the statement in *Caparo's* case had been made pursuant to a statutory duty, which itself provided the context in which the statement was made, and the notion was in consequence somewhat easier to apply than it might otherwise have been.[2] But the concept does appear to have wider utility. It can be seen at work in cases in which lower courts have either applied or distinguished the decision of the House of Lords in *Caparo Industries plc v Dickman* itself.

1 *[1990] 2 AC 605, [1990] 1 All ER 568, HL.*

2 See also *West Wiltshire District Council v Pugh [1993] NLJR 546* (Morritt J). But even against a statutory background the application of the notion will often be far from automatic. Cf *Smith v Eric S Bush [1990] 1 AC 831, [1989] 2 All ER 514*, discussed below at para [4.25].

After Caparo

[4.23] In *Al-Nakib Investments (Jersey) Ltd v Longcroft*[1] Mervyn Davies J held that alleged misstatements in a prospectus issued to shareholders for the particular purpose of inviting a *subscription* for further shares did not avail a plaintiff shareholder who chose, albeit in reliance on the prospectus, to buy his shares in the stock market instead. But in the contrasting case of *Possfund Custodian Trustee Ltd v Diamond*[2] Lightman J held that it is now arguable that there is 'an additional perceived intention on the part of the issuer and other parties to a prospectus, namely to inform and encourage after-market purchasers', and that there might therefore be a duty of care 'owed to those investors who (as intended) rely on the contents of the prospectus in making such purchases'.[3] And in *Morgan Crucible plc v Hill Samuel Bank*[4] the Court of Appeal held that directors and financial advisers of a target company in a contested take-over bid situation risk liability if they choose to make express representations for the *purpose* of influencing the conduct of the bidder.[5]

1 *[1990] 3 All ER 321, [1990] 1 WLR 1390.*

2 *[1996] 2 All ER 774, [1996] 1 WLR 1351.*

3 See *[1996] 2 All ER 774* at 788, *[1996] 1 WLR 1351* at 1366.

4 *[1991] Ch 295, [1991] 1 All ER 148.*

5 See also *Galoo Ltd v Bright Grahame Murray [1995] 1 All ER 16, [1994] 1 WLR 1360, CA*, especially, *per* Glidewell LJ at 37, *[1994] 1 WLR 1360* at 1382: 'Mere foreseeability that a potential bidder may rely on the audited accounts does not impose on the auditor a duty of care to the bidder, but if the auditor

is expressly made aware that a particular identified bidder will rely on the audited accounts or other statements approved by the auditor, and intends that the bidder should so rely, the auditor will be under a duty of care to the bidder for the breach of which he may be liable.'

Caparo distinguished

[4.24]   *Caparo* was also distinguished in *Andrew v Kounnis Freeman*[1], in which the defendant auditors submitted the unqualified accounts of a travel company to the Civil Aviation Authority the day before expiry of a deadline on which the company had been due to have its licence revoked due to concerns about its financial stability. The licence was renewed, but the company subsequently collapsed involving the claimants in substantial compensation payments. The Court of Appeal refused to strike out a claim, on behalf of the Civil Aviation Authority, against the auditors for negligence. Beldam LJ observed that it was at least arguable 'that in certifying [the company's] accounts the defendants were doing so not merely to the company and its shareholders but also to the authority with the intention that the authority should act on them in deciding whether or not to renew the licence'[2].

[1]   *[2000] Lloyd's Rep PN 641, CA.*
[2]   See above.

The purpose of surveys

[4.25]   On one view the application of the notion of 'purpose' by the House of Lords in *Caparo Industries plc v Dickman* is not easy to reconcile with the slightly earlier decision of the House in *Smith v Eric S Bush (a firm)*[1]. In this case the defendant firm of surveyors prepared a survey report for a building society, on the basis of which the plaintiff was able to obtain a mortgage advance from the society in order to buy the property surveyed. Unfortunately, the defendants failed to exercise reasonable care and skill and defects, which should have been detected, materialised subsequently causing considerable damage. The House of Lords held the surveyor, whose only contract had been with the building society, liable to the plaintiff. In so holding, the House approved a first instance decision some years earlier,[2] and confirmed a significant stage in the development of liability to third parties for negligent misstatement.[3] 'The valuer', said Lord Templeman, 'is liable in tort if he receives instructions from and is paid by the mortgagor but knows that the valuation is for the purpose of a mortgage and will be relied on by the mortgagee'.[4] But although the valuation was, in a sense, for the purpose of the plaintiff's mortgage, it was commissioned pursuant to a statutory duty which is imposed upon building societies to protect their investments[5]; and is hence arguably analogous to the statutory duty upon companies in the *Caparo* case to provide shareholders with audited annual accounts.

[1]   *[1990] 1 AC 831, [1989] 2 All ER 514*; affg *[1988] QB 743, [1987] 3 All ER 179, CA*. The case was decided jointly with another appeal which raised the same point: *Harris v Wyre Forest District Council [1988] QB 835, [1988] 1 All ER 691*, CA; revsd *[1990] 1 AC 831, [1989] 2 All ER 514.*
[2]   *Yianni v Edwin Evans & Sons (a firm) [1982] QB 438, [1981] 3 All ER 592.*
[3]   ' ... no decision of this House has gone further than *Smith v Eric S Bush*': *per* Lord Oliver in *Caparo Industries plc v Dickman [1990] 2 AC 605* at 642, *[1990] 1 All ER 568* at 592.
[4]   *[1990] 1 AC 831* at 844, *[1989] 2 All ER 514* at 520.
[5]   See the *Building Societies Act 1986, s 13.*

Different situations

[4.26]   The fact situations in *Caparo* and *Smith* were, however, very different[1]. Moreover, in *Smith's* case the House emphasised, in the words of Lord Griffiths,[2] that the case before it concerned 'a dwelling house of modest value in which it is widely recognised by surveyors that purchasers are in fact relying on their care and skill'.[3] While the decision would 'obviously be of general application in broadly similar circumstances', it could not be taken to apply 'in respect of valuations of quite different types of property for mortgage purposes, such as industrial property, large blocks of flats or very expensive houses'. Purchasers of such properties would normally be expected to obtain their own survey rather than rely on that commissioned by the mortgagor.[4]

[1] See the observations of Hoffmann J in his (reversed) judgment in *Morgan Crucible Co Ltd v Hill Samuel Bank plc [1990] 3 All ER 330* at 334–335 (revsd *[1991] 1 Ch 295, [1991] 1 All ER 148*).
[2] *[1990] 1 AC 831* at 859, *[1989] 2 All ER 514* at 532.
[3] In *Halifax Building Society v Edell [1992] Ch 436, [1992] 3 All ER 389* Morritt J held that the Building Societies Ombudsman Scheme gave jurisdiction to the ombudsman to investigate claims by house-buyers that surveys carried out on behalf of the societies had been negligent, rejecting the argument by the societies that such claims fell outside the scope of the scheme.
[4] For further discussion of the liability of surveyors see CHAPTER 9 below.

Notion of a class

[4.27]   In the search for a workable test to limit liability to third parties for negligent misstatement a device sometimes invoked is the notion that a duty will be owed only to an 'ascertainable *class*'[1] of potential claimants. But in the absence of criteria to determine how the 'class' is to be identified, this notion is ambiguous.[2] If it merely encapsulates what a reasonable man, in the position of the defendant, ought to have foreseen, it adds nothing to the foreseeability test and remains unacceptably wide.[3] Alternatively, and more probably, it reflects the opposing narrow view that the defendant needs to have had a specific *type* of transaction in mind, and simply emphasises that it is not a requirement that the defendant should have known the precise *identity* of the particular claimant.[4] In *Hedley Byrne v Heller* itself the defendants did not know the identity of the plaintiffs (Hedley Byrne), the request for advice having come from the plaintiffs' bankers (National Provincial). Nevertheless, this was not regarded as an obstacle to liability. Lord Morris expressly stated that this fact was not material, since the defendants 'must have known that the inquiry was being made by someone who was contemplating doing business with Easipower Ltd and that their answer or the substance of it would in fact be passed on to such person'.[5]

[1] Per Lord Oliver in *Caparo Industries plc v Dickman [1990] 2 AC 605* at 638, *[1990] 1 All ER 568* at 589 (emphasis supplied). Lord Bridge, in the same case, speaks of an 'identifiable class' (*[1990] 2 AC 605* at 621, *[1989] 1 All ER 568* at 576). See also *Haigh v Bamford [1976] 3 WWR 331*.
[2] Cf *Candlewood Navigation Corpn Ltd v Mitsui OSK Lines Ltd [1986] AC 1* at 24, *[1985] 2 All ER 935* at 945, PC, *per* Lord Fraser.
[3] See *Esanda Finance Corpn Ltd v Peat Marwick Hungerfords (1995–1997) 188 CLR 241* at 249 (Aus), *per* Brennan CJ: 'In actions for negligence occasioning economic loss suffered in consequence of a statement made or advice given by a defendant, foresight or reasonable foreseeability that a member of a class including the plaintiff might rely on the statement or advice and thereby suffer loss has never been held sufficient to support recovery. Something more is needed.'
[4] Cf the American Law Institute's *Restatement of the Law of Torts* (2nd edn) para 552, and see the commentary on it which includes the following (at pp 132–133): 'It is enough that the maker of the representation intends it to reach and influence either a particular person or persons, known to him, or a group or class of persons, distinct from the much larger class who might reasonably be expected sooner or later to have access to the information, and foreseeably to take some action in reliance upon it.' See also *Prosser and Keeton on Torts* (5th edn, 1984) pp 746–747.
[5] *[1964] AC 465* at 493–494, *[1963] 2 All ER 575* at 580. See also *per* Lord Reid at 482 ('It seems to me quite immaterial that they did not know who these contractors were … ').

References

[4.28]   A familiar situation in which a statement addressed by one person to another may cause loss to a third party is that of the giving of references, for employment or for other purposes. This situation was formerly governed solely by the principles of the tort of defamation, which provide that such references are protected by qualified privilege, whereby a referee is not liable for errors in his reference to the person *about whom* it was written,[1] provided only that he had not been malicious. The law was, however, decisively altered by the decision of the House of Lords in *Spring v Guardian Assurance plc*.[2] In this case an employee sued his former employer in negligence for writing, carelessly but without malice, an inaccurate reference about him to a prospective employer. Their Lordships[3] held that, in principle, liability could exist in such circumstances.[4] 'I can see no justification', said Lord Woolf, 'for erecting a fence around the whole of the field to which defamation can apply and treating any other tort, which can beneficially from the point of view of justice enter into part of that field, as a trespasser if it does so'.[5] He concluded that to hold careless employers liable for inaccurate references would be 'wholly fair' and 'would amount to a development of the law of negligence which accords with the principles which should control its development'.[6] Any fear that employers would be discouraged from providing frank references was discounted. 'Even if it is right', observed Lord Slynn, 'that the number of references given will be reduced, the quality and value will be greater and it is by no means certain that to have more references is more in the public interest than to have more careful references'.[7] Notwithstanding the far-reaching significance of *Spring*'s case in refusing to allow defamation principles to defeat the plaintiff's claim, it should be noted that their Lordships still remained cautious about how ready in practice the courts would be to find negligence proved in circumstances not involving the key relationship of employer and employee.[8]

1   The possibility of liability in negligence to the person *to whom* a carelessly *favourable* reference is addressed would seem to be established by *Hedley Byrne v Heller* itself: see *Spring v Guardian Assurance plc [1995] 2 AC 296* at 335, *[1994] 3 All ER 129* at 161, *per* Lord Slynn, and at 352, 177, *per* Lord Woolf. But cf *per* Lord Goff at 320, 147.

2   *[1995] 2 AC 296, [1994] 3 All ER 129*. See C Hilson 'Liability for Employment References: The Possible Effects of *Spring v Guardian Assurance*' (1996) Anglo-Am LR 441.

3   Lord Goff, Lord Lowry, Lord Slynn and Lord Woolf; Lord Keith dissenting.

4   There appears to have been some difference of emphasis among the members of the majority as to the precise basis of recovery. Lord Goff founded his decision exclusively on *Hedley Byrne* (see *[1994] 3 All ER 129* at 143, 144), whereas the others seemed to have been prepared to contemplate the application of somewhat wider principles relating to the recovery of damages for pure economic loss in situations of high 'proximity' (see eg *per* Lord Woolf *[1994] 3 All ER 129* at 168). On liability for pure economic loss see generally CHAPTER 6 below.

5   *[1995] 2 AC 296* at 351, *[1994] 3 All ER 129* at 176.

6   *[1995] 2 AC 296* at 346, *[1994] 3 All ER 129* at 172.

7   *[1995] 2 AC 296* at 336, *[1994] 3 All ER 129* at 162. See also *per* Lord Goff at 344, 151 and *per* Lord Woolf at 352, 177.

8   'It seems to me that for the purposes of deciding whether the law recognises the duty as being fair, just and reasonable there may be a difference between the situation where it is an employer or ex-employer who gives a reference and the situation where a reference is given by someone who has only a social acquaintance with the person the subject of the reference. There may be difficult situations in between but these will, as is the common practice, have to be worked out in particular situations': *per* Lord Slynn *[1995] 2 AC 296* at 336, *[1994] 3 All ER 129* at 162–163. Cf *per* Lord Goff at 322, 149.

Disciplinary proceedings

[4.29]   The giving of references in situations in which an ex-employee had been involved in unresolved disciplinary proceedings at the time of his departure is a particularly sensitive area, in which special care needs to be taken not to give an unfair impression about the former employee[1].

¹   See *Cox v Sun Alliance [2001] IRLR 448*. Cf *Bartholomew v Hackney LBC [1999] IRLR 246, CA*.

Third party in negotiation with recipient of advice

[4.30]   In certain circumstances a plaintiff may claim to have relied to his detriment on advice which had been specifically addressed to another person, with whom the claimant was negotiating. In *McInerny v Lloyds Bank*¹ a manager of the defendant bank wrote to a customer of his about certain guarantees to be given to the plaintiff, McInerny, in connection with a complex transaction involving him and the customer. In his letter the manager used the words 'I think … Mr McInerny ought to be satisfied with this'. As was intended by all the parties, this letter was copied to McInerny himself who, on the strength of it, went ahead with the transaction. When things subsequently went wrong, he attempted to sue the bank for negligent misstatement. His claim failed, both before Kerr J at first instance and in the Court of Appeal. On the facts all the judges who heard the case were unanimous that the plaintiff had misinterpreted the letter and, by choosing to rely upon it, had attached a degree of importance to its contents which they did not warrant. There was, however, a significant difference between the way in which Lord Denning MR analysed the case, in the Court of Appeal, and the way in which Kerr J, along with the other two members of the Court of Appeal, Megaw and James LJJ, did so.

¹   *[1973] 2 Lloyd's Rep 389*; affd *[1974] 1 Lloyd's Rep 246, CA*.

Duty of care?

[4.31]   The majority of the judges in *McInerny* felt that the bank manager did not even owe the plaintiff a duty of care in the first place. Kerr J felt that it was not appropriate to impose a duty in favour of a third party 'where the statement has been addressed to a particular person concerning his affairs, so that it was made that person's interests primarily in mind', and that this was so 'even if it was liable to be shown by him to another person for information or confirmation of its contents'.¹ Lord Denning, however, took a different view:

> 'When [the defendant] sent his reply to the customer, he knew that it was likely that the customer would show it to the other party … He must have known that both would study his reply, and, if it was satisfactory, would sign the contract on the faith of it. Such conduct seems to me to put him in a position such that he must be regarded as accepting responsibility for what he said – *not only to the customer to whom he said it – but also to the other party to whom it was to be passed.*'²

¹   *[1973] 2 Lloyd's Rep 389* at 401. Cf *Abbott v Strong [1998] 2 BCLC 420*.
²   *[1974] 1 Lloyd's Rep 246* at 254 (emphasis supplied).

Denning view preferred

[4.32]   It would now seem clear that Lord Denning's view represents the law.¹ Advice is normally given in circumstances in which it is confidential to the recipient, and the person giving it will have no reason to suppose that the latter, even though he is free to do so, will disclose it to a third party.² In such cases there can be no question of liability. But if the adviser is aware that the advice is to be shown to a third party, particularly if to his knowledge it is actually sought with this in mind, there is no reason why he should escape liability for negligence merely because of the relationship between himself and the original recipient of his advice.[3] Parties who have formed differing views on the application of the law to a particular situation about which they are negotiating, for example, sometimes agree that counsel's opinion should be sought by one of them and that they will both accept the result. If counsel is aware of this there seems to be no reason why he should not owe to both parties a duty to take care in giving his advice.

[1]   Cf *Smith v Eric S Bush [1990] 1 AC 831, [1989] 2 All ER 514, HL.* See also *per* Lord Oliver in *Caparo Industries plc v Dickman [1990] 2 AC 605* at 638, *[1990] 1 All ER 568* at 589, HL.

[2]   See *per* Neill LJ in *McNaughton Papers Group v Hicks Anderson [1991] 2 QB 113, [1991] 1 All ER 134* at 144, CA: 'In many cases ... the statement will have been prepared or made, or primarily prepared or made ... for the benefit of someone other than the advisee. In such cases it will be necessary to look carefully at the precise purpose for which the statement was communicated to the advisee.' Cf *Machin v Adams (1997) 59 Con LR 14, CA.*

[3]   Cf *Punjab National Bank v de Boinville [1992] 3 All ER 104* at 118, *[1992] 1 WLR 1138* at 1153–1154, *per* Staughton LJ: ' ... an insurance broker owes a duty of care to the specific person who he knows is to become an assignee of the policy, at all events if ... that person actively participates in giving instructions for the insurance to the broker's knowledge.'

D Omissions

Focus upon question of law

[4.33]   In many cases the distinction between making a statement and failing to do so, in effect the same as that between misfeasance and nonfeasance, will be artificial. If a statement is made, but owing to carelessness it is incomplete, seldom will anything be gained by attempting to classify the situation in those terms.[1] But if the complaint is that the defendant remained wholly silent, or failed to take a specific step which it is alleged he ought to have taken, the distinction does have utility. Just as in the rare cases of *inaction* where it is alleged that the defendant had been under a positive duty, the distinction facilitates clarification of the fundamental issue involved.[2] The investigation is less likely to be a factual one into whether or not the defendant was careless, as an inquiry into whether or not, as a matter of law, the defendant owed a duty of care to the claimant requiring the taking of positive steps.[3] Thus, in *White v Jones*[4] the plaintiff's claim failed at trial partly on the ground that the defendant solicitor had been guilty of a mere failure to draw up a will as distinct from any specific act of carelessness.[5] But the Court of Appeal and House of Lords reversed the trial judge. 'That argument cannot', said Lord Nolan,[6] 'have any force where the omission occurs after the duty of care has been assumed by the defendant. Once the duty exists, it can make no difference whether its breach occurs by way of omission or of positive act'.

[1]   Insurance brokers have often been held liable for omissions of this kind: see *Cherry Ltd v Allied Insurance Brokers Ltd [1978] 1 Lloyd's Rep 274; Reardon v King's Mutual Insurance Co (1981) 120 DLR (3d) 196.* Cf *McNealy v Pennine Insurance Co Ltd [1978] 2 Lloyd's Rep 18, CA* (failure to ask a relevant question).

[2]   Cf J Smith and P Burn '*Donoghue v Stevenson* – The Not So Golden Anniversary' (1983) 46 MLR 147.

[3]   See *Paterson Zochonis v Merfarken Packaging Ltd [1986] 3 All ER 522, CA* (printers under no duty to check that material printed involves breach of copyright).

[4]   *[1995] 2 AC 207, [1995] 1 All ER 691, HL;* affg *[1995] 2 AC 207, [1993] 3 All ER 481, CA.*

[5]   See *[1995] 2 AC 207* at 254, *[1995] 1 All ER 691* at 697 (per Lord Goff summarising the reasoning of Turner J).

[6]   *[1995] 2 AC 207* at 295, *[1995] 1 All ER 691* at 736. See also *per* Lord Goff in *[1995] 2 AC 207* at 268, *[1995] 1 All ER 691* at 711 ('Since the *Hedley Byrne* principle is founded upon an assumption of

responsibility, the solicitor may be liable for negligent omissions as well as negligent acts of commission'), and the same Law Lord in *Henderson v Merrett Syndicates Ltd [1995] 2 AC 145* at 181, *[1994] 3 All ER 506* at 521.

No duty

[4.34]   Conversely, if there is no duty then a claim based on a mere omission will necessarily fail. Thus, in *Argy Trading Co Ltd v Lapid Developments Co Ltd*,[1] landlords of business premises who had previously relieved their tenants of the obligation to insure the premises, by doing so themselves, suddenly decided not to renew the relevant policies but omitted to inform the tenants of this. The tenants were unable to sue for losses incurred when the premises were gutted by fire because it was held, after argument, that the defendants simply owed no duty to notify the plaintiffs of their decision: the responsibility for checking annually that their premises were adequately insured lay with the plaintiffs.[2] Similarly, in *Banque Keyser Ullman SA v Skandia (UK) Insurance Co Ltd*[3] the Court of Appeal held that liability for misstatement by *omission*[4] in a pre-contractual situation could not be imposed in circumstances in which that liability would upset the rule, long-established in the law of misrepresentation, that there is no general duty of disclosure in such situations.[5] It has also been held that, in the absence of a contractual provision, an employer which is trustee of its own pension scheme owes no duty in tort to give advice to members of the scheme.[6]

[1]   *[1977] 3 All ER 785, [1977] 1 WLR 444.*
[2]   *[1977] 3 All ER 785* at 800, *[1977] 1 WLR 444* at 461.
[3]   *[1990] 1 QB 665, [1989] 2 All ER 952*, sub nom *Banque Financiere de la Cite SA v Westgate Insurance Co Ltd [1989] 2 All ER 952, CA*; affd on other grounds: *[1991] 2 AC 249, [1990] 2 All ER 947 HL.*
[4]   It was established by the Court of Appeal in *Esso Petroleum Co Ltd v Marden [1976] QB 801, [1976] 2 All ER 5* that *Hedley Byrne* liability can attach to *positive statements* made in pre-contractual negotiations.
[5]   See especially *[1990] 1 QB 665* at 802, *[1989] 2 All ER 952* at 1013, *per* Slade LJ (delivering the judgment of the court).
[6]   See *Outram v Academy Plastics [2001] ICR 367, CA.*

Relevance of contract

[4.35]   As the cases cited in the previous paragraphs (paras [4.33]–[4.34]) illustrate, the extent of liability for omissions is one of those questions which can highlight the need to identify the appropriate relationship between tortious and contractual principles. This issue was clarified by the decision of the House of Lords, albeit not concerned with omissions as such, in *Henderson v Merrett Syndicates Ltd*.[1] In this case certain Lloyd's 'names', who had incurred large losses, sought to sue their underwriting agents in tort for negligence. Although the plaintiffs and defendants were in contractual relationships, the former needed to establish liability in tort to take advantage of the differing principles governing limitation; their contractual claims being out of time. The House of Lords held unanimously that the plaintiffs could succeed, and rejected the contention that the existence of the contracts had had the effect of creating an exclusive zone of liability which precluded the possibility of an action in tort.[2] Emphasising that 'the law of tort is the general law', Lord Goff stated that 'the common law is not antipathetic to concurrent liability' and concluded as follows:[3]

'... in the present case liability can, and in my opinion should, be founded squarely on the principle established in *Hedley Byrne* itself, from which it follows that an assumption of responsibility coupled with the concomitant reliance may give rise to a tortious duty irrespective of whether there is a contractual relationship between the parties, and in consequence, unless his contract precludes him from doing so, the plaintiff, who has available to him concurrent remedies in contract and tort, may choose that remedy which appears to him to be the most advantageous.'

1 *[1995] 2 AC 145, [1994] 3 All ER 506, HL.*
2 See also *Holt v Payne Skillington (a firm) [1996] PNLR 179, CA.*
3 See *[1995] 2 AC 145 at 194, [1994] 3 All ER 506 at 533.*

Shaping tortious duties

[4.36] The emphasis in the speeches in *Henderson*'s case is in sharp contrast to that of Lord Scarman a decade earlier in *Tai Hing Cotton Mill Ltd v Liu Chong Hing Bank Ltd*,[1] in which his Lordship had asserted[2] that there was nothing to be gained to the law's development by 'searching for a liability in tort where the parties are in a contractual relationship'. In effectively reversing any trend *against* concurrent liability, which had been reflected in the *Tai Hing* case,[3] their Lordships in *Henderson v Merrett Syndicates Ltd* were nevertheless at pains to emphasise that the terms of the particular contract in any given case might well be effective to prevent the imposition of tortious liability.[4] Thus, Lord Browne-Wilkinson explained that recognition of the possibility of concurrent liability must be accompanied by an understanding 'that the agreement of the parties evidenced by the contract can modify and shape the tortious duties which, in the absence of contract, would be applicable'.[5] Accordingly, the actual decision in *Tai Hing Cotton Mill Ltd v Liu Chong Hing Bank Ltd* is probably still correct. In that case the plaintiff bank sought unsuccessfully to use the law of tort to impose a novel positive duty upon the defendants to check their bank statements: a duty which was above and beyond the limited contractual duty owed to them by their customers under well-established principles of banking law.[6] Moreover, even in cases in which the contractual relationship is not between the plaintiff and defendant themselves, but between the defendant and a third party, 'the existence and terms of the agreement', as Lord Nolan observed in *White v Jones*,[7] 'may be relevant in determining what the law of tort may reasonably require of the defendant in all the circumstances'.

1 *[1986] AC 80, [1985] 2 All ER 947, PC.*
2 See *[1986] AC 80 at 107, [1985] 2 All ER 947 at 957.*
3 It was evident from the outset that Lord Scarman's dictum had been too wide if taken literally, since concurrent liability in both contract and tort had long been a well-recognised feature of a number of situations, eg employers' liability to their employees. See also *Punjab National Bank v de Boinville [1992] 3 All ER 104, [1992] 1 WLR 1138, CA*; *Midland Bank Trust Co v Hett, Stubbs & Kemp [1979] Ch 384, [1978] 3 All ER 571.*
4 Lord Goff considered that the situation in *Henderson's* case itself, which was such as to enable tortious liability to be imposed was 'most unusual' and continued: ' ... in many cases in which a contractual chain comparable to that in the present case is constructed it may well prove to be inconsistent with an assumption of responsibility which has the effect of, so to speak, short-circuiting the contractual structure so put in place by the parties'. See also *Simaan General Contracting Co v Pilkington Glass Ltd (No2) [1988] QB 758, [1988] 1 All ER 791, CA* and *Greater Nottingham Co-operative Society Ltd v Cementation Piling and Foundations Ltd [1989] QB 71, [1988] 2 All ER 971, CA*. But cf *Junior Books Ltd v Veitchi Co Ltd [1983] 1 AC 520, [1982] 3 All ER 201, HL* (considered in CHAPTER 5).
5 *[1995] 2 AC 145 at 206, [1994] 3 All ER 506 at 544.* See also the majority decision of the New Zealand Court of Appeal in *R M Turton & Co v Kerslake & Partners [2000] Lloyd's Rep PN 967.*

6   See *Henderson v Merrett Syndicates Ltd [1995] 2 AC 145* at 186, *[1994] 3 All ER 506* at 526, *per* Lord Goff.

7   *[1995] 2 AC 207* at 294, *[1995] 1 All ER 691* at 736. Cf *Voli v Inglewood Shire Council (1963) 110 CLR 74* at 85, *per* Windeyer J.

Tort and property

The Moorgate Mercantile case

[4.37]   A case in which what was, in effect, an omission to make a statement led to a sharp difference of judicial opinion as to whether on the facts a duty of care existed was *Moorgate Mercantile Co Ltd v Twitchings*.[1] Finance houses set up a voluntary clearing house to receive notice of cars let on hire purchase, so as to provide a register against which any car offered for sale could be checked. Moorgate Mercantile, a finance company, became a member of the clearing house but carelessly omitted to register a car, the letting of which on hire purchase it had financed. Prior to absconding, the person who was purchasing the car offered it for sale to a dealer who, having checked the register, assumed that the title to the vehicle was clear and bought it. Moorgate Mercantile subsequently sought to assert their title against the dealer, who resisted the claim by alleging that they were liable to him under *Hedley Byrne* for the loss caused by their failure to register the car with the clearing house. The Court of Appeal, by a majority,[2] found for the dealer but were reversed by a bare majority[3] of the House of Lords which found for Moorgate. The majority felt that, since finance houses were not compelled to become members of the clearing house, and even if they did so, were not actually compelled by the rules of the scheme to register their transactions, those which joined should not be put in a worse position with respect to the assertion of their title than those which had not bothered to join at all. The dissentients were not impressed by this supposed paradox; they felt that membership of the clearing house was mutually advantageous to its members and that they owed a duty of care to register their transactions once they had joined. It is submitted that the minority view is to be preferred. The case involved a conflict between the protection of title under the law of personal property, and the more fluid approach of tort which seek to compensate victims of carelessness. There can be valid grounds for resisting the encroachments of tort into areas where existing rules are clear, and where undesirable uncertainty would be caused by upsetting them, particularly in the real property field where the rules may have formed the background to long-term transactions.[4] But it is not easy to see why justice to the victim of carelessness should have been subordinated in the *Moorgate Mercantile* situation.[5]

1   *[1977] AC 890, [1976] 2 All ER 641*; revsg *[1976] QB 225, [1975] 3 All ER 314*.

2   Lord Denning MR and Browne LJ, Geoffrey Lane LJ dissenting.

3   Lord Edmund Davies, Lord Fraser and Lord Russell; Lord Wilberforce and Lord Salmon dissenting.

4   Cf R J Smith 'The Economic Torts: Their Impact on Real Property' (1977) 41 Cov (NS) 318.

5   After the facts which gave rise to the litigation had arisen, the rules of the clearing house scheme were themselves amended so as to impose a duty to register upon members: *[1977] AC 890* at 910, *[1976] 2 All ER 641* at 651, *per* Lord Salmon.

E Public policy

Only to be invoked in clear cases

[4.38]   A question that may arise, in certain types of case involving negligent advice, is whether the defendant should be immune from liability on grounds of public policy.

In *Spring v Guardian Assurance plc*[1], discussed above at para [4.28], the House of Lords held that a person about whom an inaccurate reference had been written by his employer could sue the writer under *Hedley Byrne*. The defendant strenuously, but unsuccessfully, argued that the imposition of liability would be against public policy in that it would tend to discourage frankness and candour in the writing of references. Lord Lowry responded as follows:[2]

> 'I ... believe that the courts in general and your Lordships' House in particular ought to think very carefully before resorting to public policy considerations which will defeat a claim that *ex hypothesi* is a good cause of action. It has been said that public policy should be invoked only in clear cases in which the potential harm to the public is incontestable, that whether the anticipated harm to the public will be likely to occur must be determined on tangible grounds instead of on mere generalities and that the burden of proof lies on those who assert that the court should not enforce a liability which prima facie exists. Even if one should put the matter in a more neutral way, I would say that public policy ought not to be invoked if the arguments are evenly balanced: in such a situation the ordinary rule of law, once established, should prevail.'

[1]   *[1995] 2 AC 296, [1994] 3 All ER 129, HL.*
[2]   *[1995] 2 AC 296 at 326, [1994] 3 All ER 129 at 153.*

No immunity for advocates

[4.39]   Formerly advocates were accorded immunity from suit, on grounds of public policy. In the well-known case of *Rondel v Worsley*[1] the House of Lords held that counsel could not be sued for alleged negligence in the conduct of a case in court or in work preparatory to it. The reasons for the immunity included recognition of the fact that counsel owes a duty to the court as well as to his client, and a desire to prevent unsuccessful litigants from indirectly seeking retrials by taking proceedings against their legal advisors. Advocates were not protected from suit, however, for negligence in drafting documents or other work unconnected with litigation. The sometimes difficult distinctions which had to be drawn in consequence are, however, no longer of any relevance. This is because the immunity itself now belongs to history. It was swept away by a seven-member House of Lords in 2000 in the case of *Arthur J S Hall (a firm) v Simons*[2], which effectively set aside the doctrine in *Rondel v Worsley*. The implications of this for professional negligence actions against advocates are considered in a later chapter[3].

[1]   *[1969] 1 AC 191, [1967] 3 All ER 993, HL.*
[2]   *[2000] 3 All ER 673.*
[3]   See below CHAPTER 8.

Abuse of process

[4.40]   In *Somasundaram v Melchior & Co*[1] the plaintiff sued his solicitors for negligence, alleging that he had been wrongly pressurised to plead guilty to an offence in criminal proceedings. The Court of Appeal struck out the claim as an abuse of process on the ground that it involved a collateral attack on a court of competent jurisdiction. The need to protect the decisions of criminal courts from collateral attack is thus perceived to be an important principle.[2] It was confirmed by the House of Lords in *Arthur J S Hall (a firm) v Simons*, which treated the existence of the principle as part of the reasoning underpinning the conclusion that immunity from liability in negligence was not necessary to prevent collateral attacks on criminal convictions[3]. Nevertheless, the mere fact that the claimant has been convicted by a criminal court will not in itself render it an abuse of process for him to allege that that conviction resulted from negligence on the part of his lawyers. Thus, if the claimant was acquitted on appeal,[4] or an appeal which might have succeeded was not proceeded with,[5] a negligence claim will not necessarily constitute an abuse of process.

1   *[1989] 1 All ER 129, [1988] 1 WLR 1934, CA.*
2   See also *Smith v Linskills [1996] 2 All ER 353, [1996] 1 WLR 763, CA*; *Hunter v Chief Constable of West Midlands [1982] AC 529, [1981] 3 All ER 727, HL.*
3   Lord Hoffman considered, however, that the protection thereby accorded to criminal convictions should not extend to the decisions of *civil* courts: see *[2000] 3 All ER 673* at 705–706.
4   See *Acton v Graham Pearce & Co (a firm) [1997] 3 All ER 909*. But cf *Bateman v Owen White [1996] PNLR 1, CA.*
5   See *Walpole v Partridge & Wilson (a firm) [1994] QB 106, [1994] 1 All ER 385, CA.*

Witnesses

[4.41]   In *L v Reading Borough Council*[1] Otton LJ said:

'It has long been considered that those participating in legal proceedings must be given a degree of immunity to ensure that priority is given to the independence and proper functioning of those proceedings. Witnesses have immunity both in relation to evidence given in court and work on the evidence which is preliminary to its presentation in court'.

In *Evans v London Hospital Medical College,*[2] the defendants were pathologists whose alleged negligence in carrying out a post-mortem investigation, and producing a report containing their findings, led to the plaintiff being charged with murder (she was subsequently acquitted when the prosecution offered no evidence). The plaintiff conceded that the defendants would have been immune from liability for anything said in court, but contended that there was no immunity in respect of negligent acts or omissions prior to the prosecution even being commenced. Drake J held that this argument would fail and that the action would be struck out[3]. The police frequently collected statements from large numbers of witnesses, sometimes even before it was known whether any criminal offence had been committed at all. Public policy required that these should be protected from liability, otherwise 'the immunity attaching to the giving of evidence in court ... could easily be outflanked and rendered of little use'.[4]

1   See *[2001] 1 FCR 673.*
2   *[1981] 1 All ER 715, [1981] 1 WLR 184.*
3   In *Darke v Chief Constable of West Midlands [2000] 4 All ER 193, HL* (see below at para [4.42]) the House of Lords emphasised that the decision in *Taylor's* case had been correct even though the reasoning of Drake J was considered to have been too widely drawn.
4   *[1981] 1 All ER 715* at 721, *[1981] 1 WLR 184* at 191. See also *Taylor v Serious Fraud Office [1999] 2 AC 177, HL* (employees of the Serious Fraud Office enjoy immunity in respect of documents prepared in the course of criminal investigations).

Limitations on the doctrine

[4.42]   In *Darke v Chief Constable of the West Midlands Police*[1], decided in 2000, the House of Lords subjected the doctrine of witness immunity to a fundamental examination. Lord Hope emphasised that 'the public interest in matters relating to the administration of justice' had to be balanced against 'the principle that a wrong ought not to be without a remedy' and that the 'immunity is a derogation from a person's right of access to the court which requires to be justified'[2]. The actual decision in *Darke's* case was to the effect that the immunity would not extend to the *fabrication* of evidence. Furthermore, if no judicial proceedings are contemplated, immunity clearly cannot be invoked merely because the statement in question is made by a professional person employed by a local authority with respect to that authority's responsibilities for the welfare of a child.[3] The immunity given to expert witnesses, especially in civil litigation, is also far from being unlimited. In *Palmer v Durnford Ford (a firm)*[4] it was held that since 'the immunity should only be given where to deny it would mean that expert witnesses would be inhibited from giving truthful and fair evidence in court' there was 'no good reason why an expert should not be liable for the advice which he gives to his client as to the merits of the claim, particularly if proceedings have not been started, and a fortiori as to whether he is qualified to advise at all'.[5]

¹   *[2000] 4 All ER 193, HL.*
²   See above at p 195. See also *D v East Berkshire NHS Trust [2003] 4 All ER 796* at paras 113–117 *per* Lord Phillips MR delivering the judgment of the court. Cf *per* Lord Browne-Wilkinson in *X v Bedfordshire County Council [1995] 2 AC 633* at 755, *[1995] 3 All ER 353* at 385–386 (apparently doubted in *D v East Berkshire NHS Trust [2003] 4 All ER 796*, at para 116).
³   See *Waple v Surrey County Council [1998] 1 All ER 624, CA* (statement by solicitor).
⁴   *[1992] QB 483, [1992] 2 All ER 122* (doubted, but not on this point, in *Walpole v Partridge & Wilson (a firm) [1994] QB 106, [1994] 1 All ER 385, CA*).
⁵   *[1992] QB 483* at 488, *[1992] 2 All ER 122* at 127, *per* Simon Tuckey QC sitting as a deputy judge of the High Court. See also *Hughes v Lloyds Bank plc [1998] PIQR P98*, CA. But cf *Stanton v Callaghan [1998] 4 All ER 961, CA* (immunity in respect of a report prepared for exchange between experts prior to trial).

Unsuccessful claims to immunity

Architects as arbitrators

[4.43]   Another area in which liability for negligent misstatement has prevailed over a suggested immunity based upon public policy is indicated by the decision of the House of Lords in *Sutcliffe v Thackrah*[1]. In this case the House held that the issuing of interim certificates by an architect, which create an obligation upon his client to pay the builder involved in the construction, is not a function which attracts an immunity from liability for negligence, analogous to that enjoyed by judges, merely because the architect is under a duty to act fairly and impartially as between the two parties involved. In so holding, their Lordships overruled a decision of the Court of Appeal which had stood for over 70 years.[2] Lord Salmon suspected that the contrary argument rested 'on the fallacy that since all judges and arbitrators must be impartial and fair, anyone who has to be impartial and fair must be treated as a judge or an arbitrator'.[3]

¹   *[1974] AC 727, [1974] 1 All ER 859, HL.*
²   Ie *Chambers v Goldthorpe [1901] 1 KB 624, CA.*
³   *[1974] AC 727* at 759, *[1974] 1 All ER 859* at 882. See also *per* Lord Reid *[1974] AC 727* at 737, *[1974] 1 All ER 859* at 863.

Mutual valuers

[4.44]   In *Arenson v Casson Beckman Rutley & Co*,[1] a case which came soon after *Sutcliffe v Thackrah*, the hostility to the existence of immunity from liability, beyond the narrowest conception of necessity dictated by policy, was again demonstrated, if not increased. The defendant was the auditor of a private company who was asked to value a parcel of shares in the company when one member decided to sell them to another member. Shortly afterwards, the company went public and the purchaser sold the shares for six times the valuation price at which he had purchased them from the plaintiff. The latter claimed that the valuation had been negligent, but the auditors claimed that, in valuing the shares, they had been acting in a quasi-arbitral capacity which rendered them immune from suit. This argument, which was supported by earlier authority, prevailed in the Court of Appeal. The House of Lords reversed that decision, however, on the ground that an arbitrator was someone called upon to resolve a specific dispute, and that a mutual valuer was not in this position. Moreover, two members of the House, Lord Kilbrandon and Lord Fraser, cast doubt upon the proposition that even an actual arbitrator, formally appointed to settle a dispute, would enjoy immunity, while a third, Lord Salmon, also admitted that this question may have to be examined in the future. Lord Kilbrandon considered that immunity should be limited to judges,[2] tribunal chairmen and the like, appointed by the state as distinct from persons appointed by parties to a dispute: 'Immunity is judged by the origin and character of the appointment, not by the duties which the appointee has to perform, or his methods of performing them.'[3]

[1]   *[1977] AC 405, [1975] 3 All ER 901, HL.* See also *Killick v Price Waterhouse Coopers [2001] Lloyd's Rep PN 17.*
[2]   See *Sirros v Moore [1975] QB 118, [1974] 3 All ER 776, CA.* Cf *Jones v Department of Employment [1989] QB 1, [1988] 1 All ER 725, CA* (no private law duty of care owed by adjudicating officer considering claims for unemployment benefit).
[3]   *[1977] AC 405* at 432, *[1975] 3 All ER 901* at 919.

Immunity now rare

[4.45]   It would thus appear that attempts to defend claims for negligent misstatement by seeking to invoke an immunity based upon public policy will nowadays rarely succeed.[1] Such a defence was nevertheless upheld in one relatively recent case in which the Court of Appeal decided that a district auditor, when making an urgent report under *s 15(3)* of the *Local Government Finance Act 1982,* 'must be free to criticise an officer of the local authority without fear of exposing himself to an action for negligence at the suit of that officer'.[2] Where attempts to invoke immunity are unsuccessful, however, it does not follow that claimants will find actions alleging negligent advice easy to win. Especially where difficult questions of judgment are involved, there is no indication that courts are any more prepared that heretofore to infer that a prognosis invalidated by hindsight was careless when it was made.

[1]   In *IRC v Hoogstraten [1985] QB 1077, [1984] 3 All ER 25* the Court of Appeal rejected a suggestion that the public interest in the administration of justice required that sequestrators appointed by the court should be immune from actions for negligence.
[2]   See *West Wiltshire District Council v Garland [1995] 2 All ER 17* at 27, *per* Balcombe LJ.

F Disclaimers of liability[1]

When possible

[4.46]   The circumstances in which potential liability for negligent misstatement can be made the subject of an effective 'disclaimer' is an important question, the significance of which has been increased by the expansion of liability to include claims by third parties. The use of a disclaimer was, of course, the basis of the actual decision in *Hedley Byrne & Co v Heller & Partners Ltd* itself, in favour of the defendants.[2] But if the way in which the claimant suffers as a result of the statement is indirect (especially where the negligence is by omission),[3] it will often be impossible for any disclaimer, even if one had been made, to have been brought to the claimant's attention. Of course, the mere fact that the situation is one involving a third party will not *necessarily* make it impracticable for liability to be disclaimed. If, as will often be the case, a written document is involved, an appropriate clause can be included in it. But if the situation *is* one in which the third party will normally be unaware of the disclaimer, or be powerless in any event to take any special steps to protect himself in consequence of it, it is unlikely to be effective unless it can be argued that the disclaimer defined the scope of the duty which the defendant initially assumed.[4]

[1]   See also CHAPTER 4 below.
[2]   See *[1964] AC 465* at 492–493 (Lord Reid); 504 (Lord Morris); 553 (Lord Devlin); 540 (Lord Pearce).
[3]   Cf *White v Jones [1995] 2 AC 207*, *[1995] 1 All ER 691, HL*, discussed above at para [4.18].
[4]   For this issue see below, CHAPTER 5 and CHAPTER 22. The *Unfair Contract Terms Act 1977* can apply to such disclaimers: see below.

Ineffective disclaimer

[4.47]   An early case in which the ineffectiveness of a disclaimer against a third party appears to have been assumed is *Ministry of Housing and Local Government v Sharp*[1]. The plaintiffs, the Ministry of Housing, were entitled by statute to receive payment, from the developer involved, should planning permission to develop a certain piece of land ever be granted by the relevant authority. This was because the Ministry had earlier paid compensation to the then owner of the land in respect of a refusal of planning permission. The Ministry's entitlement, known as a 'compensation notice', was entered on the local land charges register. Planning permission was subsequently granted and solicitors acting for the new owner sent a requisition for an official search of the register. Unfortunately, an employee of the registry carried out the search carelessly and issued the owner with a clear certificate which omitted the compensation notice. As a result, the Ministry lost their right, and successfully sued the registry for negligent misstatement to recover their loss. In fact, the registry's reply to the owner's requisition had contained a disclaimer of legal responsibility in respect of the replies to the inquiries.[2] But it was never suggested that this could have any effect on the claim since by the Ministry, which was not the recipient of the search.[3]

[1]   *[1970] 2 QB 223*, *[1970] 1 All ER 1009*. (This report contains the reversed judgment of Fisher J at first instance as well as the judgments delivered in the Court of Appeal).
[2]   See *[1970] 2 QB 223* at 243, *per* Fisher J.
[3]   An analogous situation occurred in *Moorgate Mercantile v Twitchings* where the clearing-house disclaimed liability but this was not relevant since they were not the defendants: see *[1976] QB 225* at 239, *[1975] 3 All ER 314* at 321, *per* Lord Denning MR.

Requirements

[4.48]   If the situation is one in which disclaiming liability is possible, it is important that any statement to this effect should be express and unambiguous: the court will not be prepared to identify a disclaimer as a matter of inference.[1] It should also be noted, however, that even an express provision that a statement is made 'without responsibility' will not protect a defendant who is fraudulent.[2]

1   See *Box v Midland Bank Ltd [1979] 2 Lloyd's Rep 391* at 399, *per* Lloyd J.
2   See *Commercial Banking Co of Sydney v R H Brown & Co [1972] 2 Lloyd's Rep 360 (High Ct of Australia)*.

Effect of the Unfair Contract Terms Act[1]

[4.49]   It is important to remember that if the negligent misstatement was made in the course of a business, its enforceability may depend upon its satisfying the 'requirement of reasonableness' under the *Unfair Contract Terms Act 1977*.[2] Despite the title of the Act, its provisions extend to disclaimers of tort liability outside contract. In *Smith v Eric S Bush*[3] a surveyor who surveyed a house for a building society, but whose report, in accordance with widespread practice, was supplied to the purchaser, sought unsuccessfully to rely on a general disclaimer of responsibility contained in the report when sued by the purchaser for negligence. The House of Lords held that the disclaimer was invalidated by the Act and that the claim would succeed. 'It is not fair and reasonable', said Lord Templeman, 'for building societies and valuers to agree together to impose on purchasers the risk of loss arising as a result of incompetence or carelessness on the part of valuers'.[4]

1   See also CHAPTER 22 below.
2   See *ss 1(3)*, *2(2)* and *11(3)* of the *Unfair Contract Terms Act 1977*. If the statement actually gave rise to death or personal injury the reasonableness requirement will not be relevant and the disclaimer will automatically be ineffective: *s 2(1)*.
3   *[1990] 1 AC 831*, *[1989] 2 All ER 514*.
4   *[1990] 1 AC 831* at 854, *[1989] 2 All ER 514* at 528. In the unusual case of *Stevenson v Nationwide Building Society [1984] 2 EGLR 165*, in which the plaintiff was himself an estate agent, a disclaimer *was* held to be effective to protect against a surveyor's negligence. For criticism see, generally, M Harwood 'A Structural Survey of Negligent Reports' (1987) 50 MLR 588.

Reasonableness

[4.50]   The House of Lords was anxious to emphasise in *Smith v Eric S Bush* that nullification of disclaimers by the statutory 'reasonableness' test necessarily depends upon the particular circumstances in question.[1] The instant case concerned domestic purchasers of small houses.[2] Other situations might be very different. Lord Griffiths said:[3]

> 'I would not ... wish it to be thought that I would consider it unreasonable for professional men in all circumstances to seek to exclude or limit their liability for negligence. Sometimes breathtaking sums of money may turn on professional advice against which it would be impossible for the adviser to obtain adequate insurance cover and which would ruin him if he were to be held personally liable. In these circumstances it may indeed be reasonable to give the advice on a basis of no liability or possibly of liability limited to the extent of the adviser's insurance cover.'

His Lordship outlined some of the factors relevant to determining 'reasonableness'.[4] These included equality of bargaining power, the practicability of obtaining advice from an alternative source, the difficulty of the task being undertaken, and the consequences to the parties of upholding the disclaimer. In *McCullagh v Lane Fox and Partners*[5] the Court of Appeal held that the defendant estate agents had established that it was reasonable for them to rely on a disclaimer against the plaintiff house purchaser, who was 'a sophisticated and experienced member of the public' and had had 'ample opportunity to regulate his conduct having regard to the disclaimer'.[6]

1   Cf *First National Commercial Bank plc v Loxleys (a firm) [1997] PNLR 211, CA.*
2   'We are dealing … with a loss which will be limited to the value of a modest house and against which it can be expected that the surveyor will be insured. Bearing the loss will be unlikely to cause significant hardship if it has to be borne by the surveyor but it is, on the other hand, quite possible that it will be a financial catastrophe for the purchaser who may be left with a valueless house and no money to buy another': *[1990] 1 AC 831 at 859, [1989] 2 All ER 514* at 531, *per* Lord Griffiths.
3   See *[1990] 1 AC 831* at 859, *[1989] 2 All ER 514* at 531–532. See also the Limited Liability Partnerships Act 2000 (on the possibility of limiting the consequences of large damages awards for professional negligence).
4   See *[1990] 1 AC 831* at 858, *[1989] 2 All ER 514* at 531.
5   *[1996] PNLR 205, CA.*
6   See *[1996] PNLR 205, per* Hobhouse LJ. Cf *Duncan Investments Ltd v Underwoods [1998] EGCS 98, CA,* in which the defendant estate agents were *unable* to rely on a disclaimer similar to that in *McCullagh's* case, even though the plaintiffs were property developers, because, as a matter of construction, it was not applicable on the facts.

Denial of duty

[4.51]   In *Harris v Wyre Forest District Council*[1] the House of Lords rejected an argument, which had found favour with the Court of Appeal in that case, that a disclaimer of tort liability for negligent misstatement could be drafted which would escape the provisions of the *Unfair Contract Terms Act 1977* by denying the existence of a duty of care in the first place instead of seeking to exclude an admitted existing liability.[2] The House preferred the view that a provision in the Act which 'also prevents … excluding or restricting liability by reference to terms or notices which exclude or restrict the relevant obligation or duty'[3] was, in the words of Lord Jauncey, 'entirely appropriate to cover a disclaimer which prevents a duty coming into existence'.[4]

1   *[1990] 1 AC 831, [1989] 2 All ER 514, HL*; revsg *[1988] QB 835, [1988] 1 All ER 691, CA.* The appeal was decided by the House simultaneously with that in *Smith v Eric S Bush.*
2   See B Coote 'Unfair Contract Terms Act 1977' (1978) 41 MLR 312. Cf *Overbrooke Estates Ltd v Glencombe Properties Ltd [1974] 3 All ER 511, [1974] 1 WLR 1335.*
3   *Section 13(1).* See E McDonald 'Exclusion clauses: the ambit of s 13(1) of the Unfair Contract Terms Act 1977' (1992) 12 LS 277.
4   *[1990] 1 AC 831 at 873, [1989] 2 All ER 514* at 543. The proposition that *Hedley Byrne* disclaimers precluded the existence of a duty was based on the idea that the notion of 'voluntary assumption of responsibility' depended upon the defendant's undertaking *legal responsibility* to a particular claimant rather than upon his agreeing to carry out a specific *task*, but the latter interpretation is now preferred: see *Henderson v Merrett Syndicates Ltd [1995] 2 AC 145, [1994] 3 All ER 506, HL* and *White v Jones [1995] 2 AC 207, [1995] 1 All ER 691, HL*, discussed above.

G Contributory negligence[1]

Relevance of the defence

[4.52]   The original development of liability for negligent misstatement via such concepts as 'special relationship' and 'reliance' probably accounts for the relative dearth of reported English appellate authority on the role of contributory negligence in this sphere in the early years.[2] There is no intrinsic reason, however, why contributory negligence should not, on the facts of a particular case, be established in this area. A person might legitimately have been heavily influenced by the defendant's misstatement, while also being himself blameworthy for having failed to seek appropriate further advice.[3] In practice, the availability both of the defence itself in negligent misstatement cases,[4] and of the apportionment provisions of the *Law Reform (Contributory Negligence) Act 1945*,[5] are now taken for granted.[6]

1 See generally CHAPTER 22 below.
2 Cf B Bishop in 'Negligent Misrepresentation through Economists' Eyes (1980) 96 LQR 360 at 373: 'Reasonable reliance subtracts out contribution before the negligence sums are computed. In effect it functions in exactly the way that contributory negligence did before the enactment of apportionment statutes – it functions as an all-or-nothing bar.'
3 Cf *McCullagh v Lane Fox and Partners [1996] PNLR 205, CA*.
4 See *Credit Agricole Personal Finance v Murray (a firm) [1995] EGCS 32*.
5 In *Drinkwater v Kimber [1951] 2 All ER 713* at 715 Devlin J suggested a peculiarly narrow construction of the Act which would have led to the opposite conclusion, but his view was expressly rejected by Woolf J in *JEB Fasteners v Marks, Bloom & Co [1981] 3 All ER 289* at 297: a case which actually dealt with negligent misstatement (the point was not considered on appeal in *[1983] 1 All ER 583, CA*).
6 In *Gran Gelato Ltd v Richcliff (Group) Ltd [1992] Ch 560, [1992] 1 All ER 865* the availability of the apportionment provisions to common law negligent misstatement claims was assumed to be self-evident.

Not to be established easily

[4.53] Of course, the existence of the possibility of apportionment does not imply that the courts should strain to make findings of contributory negligence against claimants in negligent misstatement cases. In the particular context of house purchasers relying on their building societies' survey reports, for example, it has been forcefully argued that there are cogent policy reasons for refusing to categorise as contributory negligence the purchasers' failure to commission their own separate surveys.[1] Such an allegation of contributory negligence failed on the facts in one important early case.[2]

1 See M Harwood 'A Structural Survey of Negligent Reports' (1987) 50 MLR 588.
2 See *Yianni v Edwin Evans & Sons [1982] QB 438* at 457, *[1981] 3 All ER 592* at 606, *per* Park J. But cf *Perry v Tendring District Council (1984) 1 Const LJ 152*, where the view was expressed obiter that if liability had been established against the defendants they could have invoked contributory negligence.

Chapter 5

Financial loss caused by careless acts

A The background to the modern law

Fear of multiplicity of claims

[5.01]   In the well-known case of *Cattle v Stockton Waterworks Co*[1] the Court of Queen's Bench held that economic losses consequential upon damage to property not owned by the plaintiff were not recoverable. The plaintiff was a contractor who had undertaken to do certain work on the land of a third party. It transpired, however, that the defendant's negligence, or other breach of duty, had caused damage to the land such as to render the plaintiff's task more expensive to carry out, with the result that his contract became less profitable. If the plaintiff's claim for this loss were to succeed, it would follow, said Blackburn J delivering the judgment of the court, that in, for example, a case where a mine was flooded the person responsible:

> 'would be liable, not only to an action by the owner of the drowned mine, and by such of his workmen as had their tools or clothes destroyed, but also to an action by every workman and person employed in the mine, who in consequence of its stoppage made less wages than he otherwise would have done.'[2]

[1]   *(1875) LR 10 QB 453.*
[2]   *(1875) LR 10 QB 453* at 457. See also *La Société Anonyme de Remorquage à Hélice v Bennetts [1911] 1 KB 243.*

Consequential loss recoverable

[5.02]   Infliction of actual physical damage upon the property of a third party is obviously not the only way in which careless deeds may cause pure economic loss. Nevertheless, *Cattle v Stockton Waterworks & Co*, and the fear of very extensive liability which it adumbrated, continues to exert a major influence upon the approach of the common law to the general question of the recovery of such losses. It is important to distinguish 'pure' economic loss from economic loss consequential upon physical damage to the claimant's own person or property. It has, of course, always been clear that a plaintiff who himself suffered personal injury, or whose property was damaged, could recover financial losses consequential upon this injury or damage. The most common example is a claim for lost income by a person incapacitated through the defendant's negligence.

Pragmatic approach

[5.03]   The distinction thus drawn, for the pragmatic reason of protecting defendants from a possible avalanche of claims, between 'pure' economic loss and financial loss consequential upon injury or damage to the claimant or his property, is apt to appear arbitrary from the point of view of principle.[1] It also has the paradoxical effect of enabling a defendant who has caused havoc, in the form of widespread economic loss, to avoid liability while at the same time holding liable with full rigour a defendant who has merely damaged the property of one claimant. Nevertheless, apart from one House of Lords' decision in 1947,[2] which was arguably inconsistent with the orthodox view in that it allowed recovery for pure economic loss, but the significance of which was obscured by its somewhat esoteric context,[3] it was not until *Hedley Byrne & Co Ltd v Heller & Partners Ltd*[4] was decided in 1963 that there appeared any serious possibility of the law in this area undergoing any change or modification.

[1]   See the criticisms by Edmund Davies LJ in his dissenting judgment in *Spartan Steel and Alloys Ltd v Martin & Co (Contractors) Ltd [1973] QB 27* at 39ff, *[1972] 3 All ER 557* at 564ff. But for an attempt at a principled defence of the denial of liability see P Benson 'The Basis for Excluding Liability for Economic Loss in Tort Law' in D Owen (ed) *Philosophical Foundations of Tort Law* (1995). See also Christian Witting 'Distinguishing Between Property Damage and Pure Economic Loss in Negligence: A Personality Thesis' (2001) 21 LS 481.

[2]   See *Morrison SS Co v SS Greystoke Castle (Cargo Owners) [1947] AC 265, [1946] 2 All ER 696, HL*.

[3]   Ie the law of general average.

[4]   *[1964] AC 465, [1963] 2 All ER 575, HL*.

Effect of Hedley Byrne[1]

[5.04]   In *Hedley Byrne* Lord Hodson observed that it was 'difficult to see why liability as such should depend on the nature of the damage'.[2] Lord Devlin, similarly, could 'find neither logic nor commonsense' in the proposition that it should be crucial 'whether financial loss is caused through physical injury or whether it is caused directly'.[3] Since, however, the primary focus of *Hedley Byrne* was upon financial loss caused by negligent misstatement, which could be regarded as a special case,[4] the precise effect of the decision upon the more general question of liability for pure economic loss consequential upon negligent deeds, rather than words, was equivocal. The first major case on the point to be decided, after *Hedley Byrne*, adopted a conservative approach. In *Weller & Co v Foot and Mouth Disease Research Institute,*[5] a virus escaped, due to the negligence of the defendants, causing an outbreak of foot and mouth disease among cattle in the vicinity. The plaintiffs were auctioneers, who lost business due to the closure of the cattle markets. Widgery J held that they could not recover for their losses; only the owners of the cattle affected could have had a claim against the defendants. *Hedley Byrne* had not altered the rule 'that in an action of negligence founded on failure to take care to avoid damage to the property of another, only those whose property is injured, or is at least indirectly threatened with injury, can recover'.[6]

[1]   See generally P Cane *Tort Law and Economic Interests*. O.U.P.

[2]   *[1964] AC 465* at 509, *[1963] 2 All ER 575* at 598.

[3]   *[1964] AC 465* at 517, *[1963] 2 All ER 575* at 602.

[4]   See generally P Atiyah 'Negligence and Economic Loss' (1967) 83 LQR 248. See also J Dwyer 'Negligence and Economic Loss' in P Cane and J Stapleton (eds) *Essays for Patrick Atiyah* (1991), who reviews developments in this area since the publication of Atiyah's influential 1967 paper.

[5]   *[1966] 1 QB 569, [1965] 3 All ER 560*.

[6]   *[1966] 1 QB 569* at 583, *[1965] 3 All ER 560* at 567.

Orthodoxy challenged

[5.05]   Although the traditional hostility to allowing recovery for economic loss subsequently came under some strain, and decisions which apparently created exceptions to the general rule were handed down by appellate courts both in England[1] and the Commonwealth,[2] this liberal trend was more recently put into reverse. Accordingly, the older orthodoxy, and the authoritative status of the *Cattle* case itself,[3] were reasserted at the highest level. This followed a period of about a decade, starting around the middle of the 1970s, when it looked as though two factors were combining to destabilise the long-standing hostility to liability for pecuniary loss. The first was a series of decisions in which plaintiffs recovered in tort for the cost of repairs to buildings which, owing to various kinds of negligence, had been, or would become, unsafe due to defective construction.[4] The various fact situations involved in these cases served to highlight the narrowness, in practice, of any line purporting to separate a claim based upon the alleged dangerousness of a building from one which simply alleged that it was less valuable than it ought to have been.[5] The other factor favouring a change in the law was that some judges began to manifest a degree of hostility towards arguments based upon 'policy', particularly the so-called 'floodgates', or avalanche of claims, argument used in *Cattle v Stockton Waterworks Co* and succeeding economic loss cases.[6] There was, for a time, a degree of judicial awareness that the history of other branches of the law, in which this fear has been used to resist change, has subsequently shown it to have been exaggerated.[7]

[1]   See especially *Junior Books Ltd v Veitchi Co Ltd [1983] 1 AC 520, [1983] 3 All ER 201, HL.*
[2]   See *Caltex (Australia) Pty Ltd Oil v Dredge Willemstad (1976) 136 CLR 529.*
[3]   See *Candlewood Navigation Corpn Ltd v Mitsui OSK Lines Ltd [1986] AC 1* at 17, *[1985] 2 All ER 935* at 944, PC, *per* Lord Fraser. See also *Esso Petroleum Co Ltd v Hall Russell & Co Ltd [1989] AC 643, [1989] 1 All ER 37, HL.*
[4]   See *Dutton v Bognor Regis Urban District Council [1972] 1 QB 373, [1972] 1 All ER 462, CA*; *Bowen v Paramount Builders (Hamilton) Ltd [1977] 1 NZLR 394, NZ CA*; *Anns v Merton London Borough Council [1978] AC 728, [1977] 2 All ER 492, HL*; *Batty v Metropolitan Property Realisations Ltd [1978] QB 554, [1978] 2 All ER 445, CA*; *Dennis v Charnwood Borough Council [1983] QB 409, [1982] 3 All ER 486, CA.*
[5]   See generally A Grubb 'A Case for Recognising Economic Loss in Defective Building Cases' [1984] CLJ 111.
[6]   See especially *per* Lord Roskill in *Junior Books Ltd v Veitchi Co Ltd [1983] 1 AC 520* at 539. See also *Bowen v Paramount Builders (Hamilton) Ltd [1977] 1 NZLR 394* at 422, *per* Cooke J ('floodgates' argument described as 'specious'). Cf *McLoughlin v O'Brian [1983] 1 AC 410, [1982] 2 All ER 298, HL.*
[7]   See the notorious dissenting speech of Lord Buckmaster in *Donoghue v Stevenson [1932] AC 562* at 566ff.

Traditional learning restored

[5.06]   But despite these doubts, the House of Lords and Privy Council subsequently made it clear, in a number of decisions culminating in the 1990 case of *Murphy v Brentwood District Council,*[1] that at least in the two most prominent categories of economic loss case the older learning which rejected liability would be restored in full vigour. These two categories are as follows: first, those cases in which the claimant complains that his *own* property, *while undamaged*, has nevertheless given rise to economic loss as a result of the defendant's negligence; and, secondly, those in which, as in *Cattle v Stockton Waterworks Co* itself, the claimant suffers pure economic loss as a result of damage to *someone else's* property[2].

[1]   *[1991] 1 AC 398, [1990] 2 All ER 908, HL.*
[2]   These categories are merely those generated by the case law: they are arbitrary in the sense that they do not reflect any distinct underlying theories of responsibility.

Continuing development

[5.07]   The law does not, however, stand still and in a number of cases decided by the House of Lords even more recently, in the mid-1990s, economic loss claims falling *outside* those two established categories did not suffer the same fate of *a priori* dismissal.[1] This more liberal approach reflects a degree of renewal in the fertility of the principle underlying *Hedley Byrne v Heller* itself, especially in cases in which the defendant's carelessness is not readily classifiable as either an 'act' or a 'statement'. It also appears to reflect a marked change of emphasis in the attitude of the law towards the relationship between contract and tort. Conceptual orthodoxy had seemed increasingly to favour confining the recovery of pure economic loss to the law of contract as far as possible,[2] but the position has undergone a significant change as a result of the decision of the House of Lords in *Henderson v Merrett Syndicates Ltd.*[3] In that case concurrent liability for such loss in both tort and contract was permitted, and Lord Goff observed that, far from being merely supplementary to the law of contract, 'the law of tort is the general law'.[4]

[1] See *White v Jones [1995] 2 AC 207, [1995] 1 All ER 691, HL; Henderson v Merrett Syndicates Ltd [1995] 2 AC 145, [1994] 3 All ER 506, HL; Spring v Guardian Assurance [1995] 2 AC 296, [1994] 3 All ER 129, HL.*

[2] See *Tai Hing Cotton Mill Ltd v Liu Chong Hing Bank Ltd [1986] AC 80, [1985] 2 All ER 947, PC,* especially *[1986] AC 80 at 107, [1985] 2 All ER 947 at 957* (Lord Scarman).

[3] *[1995] 2 AC 145, [1994] 3 All ER 506.*

[4] *[1995] 2 AC 145 at 193, [1994] 3 All ER 506 at 532.*

Four categories

[5.08] The effect of the foregoing is that any attempt to provide a coherent exposition of the law relating to the recovery of pure economic loss, in situations other than the 'straightforward' cases of negligent misstatement dealt with in the CHAPTER 4, must be divided into four categories. The two 'established' categories referred to above need to be followed by a third dealing with claims based upon the notion of 'assumption of responsibility', which is growing in importance. Finally, if untidily, a brief residual category is necessary in order to mention situations such as statutory powers and public nuisance, which are also dealt with in other chapters.

B Economic loss resulting from undamaged products

Older approach still valid

[5.09] In *Murphy v Brentwood District Council*[1] Lord Bridge said:

' … if a manufacturer produces and sells a chattel which is merely defective in quality, even to the extent that it is valueless for the purpose for which it is intended, the manufacturer's liability at common law arises only under and by reference to the terms of any contract to which he is a party in relation to the chattel; the common law does not impose on him any liability in tort to persons to whom he owes no duty in contract but who, having acquired the chattel, suffer economic loss because the chattel is defective in quality.'

His Lordship added that if 'a dangerous defect is discovered before it causes any personal injury or damage to property, because the danger is now known and the chattel cannot be safely used unless the defect is repaired, the defect becomes merely a defect in quality'. Moreover, he made clear his belief that 'these principles' are not confined to chattels but 'are equally applicable to buildings'. In *Murphy*'s case the House of Lords held that in exercising its statutory powers of building control a local authority owes no duty of care to building owners, to protect them from expenditure on repairs, should the authority carelessly permit defective construction to take place. In so holding, the House, which consisted of seven members on this occasion, overruled its own earlier decision in *Anns v London Borough of Merton*,[2] which had held that such a duty did exist if the relevant defect was a source of imminent danger to the health and safety of the occupants of the building.

1   *[1991] 1 AC 398* at 475, *[1990] 2 All ER 908* at 925.
2   *[1978] AC 728, [1977] 2 All ER 492, HL.*

Strands of reasoning in Anns

[5.10]   The emphasis in *Anns* upon health and safety reflected three interwoven strands in the reasoning in that case. First, the legislation which formed the basis of the negligence claim against the local authority was itself concerned with public health.[1] Secondly, liability ostensibly based upon safety could seem, in a sense, to be closer to liability for actual personal injury than to the much more doubtful area of pure economic loss.[2] Thirdly, assuming that liability would have been imposed if the building in question had actually collapsed and caused personal injury, it would be illogical to deny recovery for the cost of a pre-emptive strike by an occupier who averted disaster by repairing in advance.[3]

1   Ie the *Public Health Act 1936.*
2   'To allow recovery for ... damage to the house follows, in my opinion, from normal principle. If classification is required, the relevant damage is in my opinion material, physical damage, and what is recoverable is the amount of expenditure necessary to restore the dwelling to a condition in which it is no longer a danger to the health or safety of persons occupying': *Anns v London Borough of Merton [1978] AC 728* at 759, *[1977] 2 All ER 492* at 505, *per* Lord Wilberforce.
3   This point was made more emphatically in the earlier Court of Appeal decision of *Dutton v Bognor Regis Urban District Council [1972] 1 QB 373, [1972] 1 All ER 462*, which was upheld in *Anns v Merton London Borough Council* (and subsequently overruled in *Murphy* along with *Anns* itself). See especially *per* Lord Denning MR in *Dutton [1972] 1 QB 373* at 369, *[1972] 1 All ER 462* at 474.

Rejection of Anns

[5.11]   In *Murphy v Brentwood District Council*[1] the reasoning in *Anns* was compre-hensively rejected.[2] The House of Lords in the later case refused to accept that the health and safety idea rendered the situation analogous to one involving actual property damage or personal injury. It was 'incontestable on analysis', said Lord Oliver, 'that what the plaintiffs [ie in *Anns*] suffered was pure pecuniary loss and nothing more'.[3] There was 'equally nothing in the statutory provisions', his Lordship continued, 'which even suggest that the purpose of the statute was to protect owners of buildings from pure economic loss'.[4] The House also undermined the argument in favour of allowing occupiers to recover from allegedly negligent local authorities the cost of repairs in advance of collapse by expressly reserving its opinion on the question of whether a local authority, as distinct from a negligent building owner, could be held liable on the basis of its statutory powers even if a badly constructed building *did* collapse and cause injury.[5] Finally, the House considered that to impose liability in favour of occupiers on the *Anns* basis would outflank the limited scope of the statutory protection afforded to them by the *Defective Premises Act 1972*.[6] Lord Keith robustly summarised the views of the House in *Murphy* thus:

'In my opinion it is clear that *Anns* did not proceed on any basis of established principle, but introduced a new species of liability governed by a principle indeterminate in character but having the potentiality of covering a wide range of situations, involving chattels as well as real property, in which it had never hitherto been thought that the law of negligence had any proper place.'[7]

---

[1]   *[1991] 1 AC 398, [1990] 2 All ER 908 HL.* See R O'Dair *'Murphy v Brentwood District Council*: A House With Firm Foundations?' (1991) 54 MLR 561. See also Sir Robin Cooke 'An Impossible Distinction' (1991) 107 LQR 46.

[2]   See I N Duncan Wallace QC *'Anns* Beyond Repair' (1991) 107 LQR 228. See also B S Markesinis and S Deakin 'The Random Element of their Lordships' Infallible Judgment: An Economic and Comparative Analysis of the Tort of Negligence from *Anns* to *Murphy*' (1992) 55 MLR 619.

[3]   *[1991] 1 AC 398* at 484, *[1990] 2 All ER 908* at 932.

[4]   *[1991] 1 AC 398* at 490, *[1990] 2 All ER 908* at 937.

[5]   See *[1991] 1 AC 398* at 457, 463, 492, *[1990] 2 All ER 908* at 912, 917, 938, *per* Lord Mackay LC, Lord Keith and Lord Jauncey, respectively.

[6]   See *[1991] 1 AC 398* at 457, 472, 480, 491, 498, *[1992] 2 All ER 908* at 912, 923, 930, 938, 942–943, *per* Lord Mackay, Lord Keith, Lord Bridge, Lord Oliver and Lord Jauncey, respectively. On the *Defective Premises Act 1972* see CHAPTER 10 below.

[7]   *[1991] 1 AC 398* at 471, *[1990] 2 All ER 908* at 922.

'Complex structures'?

D & F Estates

[5.12]   In the 1988 case of *D & F Estates Ltd v Church Comrs For England*,[1] decided by the House of Lords two years before its decision in *Murphy*, the House addressed directly the liability in tort for pure economic loss of a *builder*; as distinct from that of a local authority which was the focus of both the *Anns* and *Murphy* cases. In the *D & F Estates* case the plaintiffs, who were the lessees and occupiers of a flat, sought to claim from the defendant builders, with whom they were not in a contractual relationship, the cost of repairing allegedly defective plastering work which had been carried out when the block of flats in question had been constructed. The claim failed.[2] 'It seems to me clear that the cost of replacing the defective plaster', said Lord Bridge,[3] 'was not an item of damage for which the builder … could possibly be made liable in negligence under the principle of *Donoghue v Stevenson* or any legitimate development of that principle. To make him so liable would be to impose on him for the benefit of those with whom he had no contractual relationship the obligation of one who warranted the quality of the plaster as regards materials, workmanship and fitness for purpose'. The House criticised the *Anns* case, which had not then been overruled, but distinguished it by emphasising its focus upon local authority liability and health and safety concepts. Moreover, the argument that, since the builder would be liable if his defective structure caused personal injury or damage to property other than the structure itself, he should also be liable in tort for the cost of repairs made pre-emptively by the owner, was rejected.[4] In the words, again, of Lord Bridge:[5]

'If the defect is discovered before any damage is done, the loss sustained by the owner of the structure, who has to repair or demolish it to avoid a potential source of danger to third parties, would seem to be purely economic. Thus, if I acquire a property with a dangerously defective garden wall which is attributable to the bad workmanship of the original builder, it is difficult to see any basis in principle on which I can sustain an action in tort against the builder for the cost of either repairing or demolishing the wall. No physical damage has been caused. All that has happened is that the defect in the wall has been discovered in time to prevent damage occurring.'

¹ *[1989] AC 177, [1988] 2 All ER 992, HL*. See I N Duncan Wallace QC 'Negligence and Defective Buildings: Confusion Confounded?' (1989) 105 LQR 46.

² See also *Department of the Environment v Thomas Bates & Son Ltd [1991] 1 AC 499, [1990] 2 All ER 943, HL* (decided by the House of Lords on the same day as *Murphy v Brentwood District Council*).

³ *[1989] AC 177* at 207, *[1988] 2 All ER 992* at 1007.

⁴ Lord Bridge did, however, subsequently suggest in *Murphy v Brentwood District Council* that recovery of pre-emptive costs might be possible in one situation: ' ... if a building stands so close to the boundary of the building owner's land that after discovery of the dangerous defect it remains a potential source of injury to persons or property on neighbouring land or on the highway, the building owner ought, in principle, to be entitled to recover in tort from the negligent builder the cost of obviating the danger, whether by repair or demolition, so far as that cost is necessarily incurred in order to protect himself from potential liability to third parties': *[1991] 1 AC 398* at 489, *[1990] 2 All ER 908* at 926. This suggestion, which perhaps reflects the influence of the law of nuisance was, however, doubted by Lord Oliver in his own speech in *Murphy*'s case: see *[1991] 1 AC 398* at 489, *[1990] 2 All ER 908* at 936.

⁵ *[1989] AC 177* at 206, *[1988] 2 All ER 992* at 1006.

Attempting to identify distinct elements

[5.13] Unfortunately, in an attempt to limit the scope of his own dictum, Lord Bridge continued in a manner which was to cause a degree of confusion, which had to be clarified when *Murphy v Brentwood District Council* was decided. He stated that, while the principle operated to negate liability on the facts of *D & F Estates* itself, he could 'see that it may well be arguable that in the case of complex structures, as indeed possibly in the case of complex chattels, one element of the structure should be regarded for the purpose of the application of the principles under discussion as distinct from another element, so that damage to one part of the structure caused by a hidden defect in another part may qualify to be treated as damage to "other property" ' so as to give rise to liability in tort on orthodox general principles.¹ This 'complex structure' theory, motivated in part by a desire to provide a possible rationalisation for the description by Lord Wilberforce in *Anns* of the damage in that case as 'material, physical damage',² caused concern to critics who feared that it would lead to much sterile litigation in which plaintiffs would seek to distinguish between the component parts of what were, in essence, single unified buildings or products.

¹ See also *per* Lord Oliver, *[1989] AC 177* at 212, *[1988] 2 All ER 992* at 1010.

² See *[1978] AC 728* at 759, *[1977] 2 All ER 492* at 505.

Where parts interdependent

[5.14] In *Murphy v Brentwood District Council* Lord Bridge clarified his earlier judgment as follows:¹

> 'The reality is that the structural elements in any building form a single indivisible unit of which the different parts are essentially interdependent. To the extent that there is any defect in one part of the structure it must to a greater or lesser degree necessarily affect all other parts of the structure. Therefore any defect in the structure is a defect in the quality of the whole and it is quite artificial, in order to impose a legal liability which the law would not otherwise impose, to treat a defect in an integral structure, so far as it weakens the structure, as a dangerous defect liable to cause damage to "other property".'

Accordingly, no distinction would be drawn between the foundations of a house and its superstructure². This reasoning was applied by the Court of Appeal in *Bellefield Computer Services v E Turner & Sons*³. A building contractor constructed negligently a commercial building divided into several different compartments. When, as a result of the defective constuction, a fire was able to spread from one compartment to another, the contractor was held liable in tort to the subsequent owner for the contents of the building which had been damaged by the fire, but not for the damage to the building itself. On the other hand, 'if a defective central heating boiler explodes and damages a house or a defective electrical installation malfunctions and sets the house on fire', Lord Bridge in *Murphy's* case saw 'no reason to doubt that the owner of the house, if he can prove that the damage was due to the negligence of the boiler manufacturer in the one case or the electrical contractor in the other, can recover damages in tort on *Donoghue v Stevenson* principles'.[4]

[1]   *[1991] 1 AC 398* at 478, *[1990] 2 All ER 908* at 928.
[2]   See *Payne v John Setchell [2002] PNLR 7,* especially at para 39 *per* Judge Humphrey Lloyd QC. See also *Hamble Fisheries v L Gardner & Sons [1999] 2 Lloyd's Rep 1, CA* (no attempt to distinguish between an engine and its pistons).
[3]   *[2000] BLR 97*. See I N Duncan Wallace '*Donoghue v Stevenson* and "complex structures": *Anns* revisited?' (2000) 116 LQR 530.
[4]   *[1991] 1 AC 398* at 478, *[1990] 2 All ER 908* at 928. See also *per* Lord Keith, *[1991] 1 AC 398* at 470, *[1990] 2 All ER 908* at 922.

Borderline cases

[5.15]   Although there may be difficult borderline cases, it is therefore now clear that the courts will not encourage the analysis of the components of buildings and chattels into separate parts in order to facilitate liability by concluding that one part had damaged another. In *Bacardi Martini Beverages v Thomas Hardy Packaging*[1] a drinks manufacturer had to recall its product when the carbon dioxide used in the manufacturing process turned out to have been contaminated. In an action in tort for the economic loss arising out of the recall, the question arose whether the carbon dioxide had 'damaged' the other ingredients of the final product with which it had been mixed. The Court of Appeal held that it could not be said to have done so. Although the case was 'close to the border' the drink was a single product which had been 'merely defective from the moment of its creation'[2]. The tort claim was therefore one for 'pure' economic loss and could not succeed. Accordingly, as the law now stands, the traditional position has been re-established that a claimant unable to rely on a contract will normally have no redress for a defect which reduces the value of any building or chattel acquired by him, unless he is afforded protection by a statute such as the *Defective Premises Act 1972*.[3]

[1]   *[2002] 2 All ER (Comm) 335*.
[2]   See above, *per* Mance LJ at para 18.
[3]   See CHAPTER 16 below. See also, for discussion of possible reform of this area of the law, J A Hayes 'After Murphy: Building on the Consumer Protection Principle' (1992) 12 OJLS 112.

Commonwealth divergence

[5.16]   The refusal of the House of Lords in *Murphy v Brentwood District Council* and *D & F Estates Ltd v Church Comrs for England* to countenance liability in tort for economic loss arising out of defective construction has produced a significant divergence between the law in England and that in other leading Commonwealth jurisdictions. In *Bryan v Maloney*[1] the High Court of Australia held that a subsequent purchaser could sue the negligent builder for such loss. Mason CJ[2] said that the approach in *Murphy* and *D & F Estates* 'rested upon a narrower view of the scope of the modern law of negligence' than was acceptable in Australia. Similarly, in *Winnipeg Condominium Corp No 36 v Bird Construction Co Ltd*[3] the Supreme Court of Canada held that there could be liability for economic loss if the defects in the building were dangerous. Moreover, in *Invercargill City Council v Hamlin*,[4] on facts resembling those in *Murphy v Brentwood District Council*, the Privy Council itself sanctioned the refusal by the New Zealand Court of Appeal to follow that decision. Differing social circumstances in New Zealand made it appropriate for municipalities to shoulder a greater degree of responsibility for the integrity of construction in their areas. 'The particular branch of the law of negligence with which the present appeal is concerned', said Lord Lloyd, delivering the opinion of the Board,[5] 'is especially unsuited for the imposition of a single monolithic solution'.

[1]   *(1995) 128 ALR 163*. See I N Duncan-Wallace (1997) 113 LQR 355.
[2]   See *(1995) 128 ALR 163* at 173.
[3]   *[1995] 1 SCR 85, 121 DLR (4th) 193*.
[4]   *[1996] AC 624, [1996] 1 All ER 756*.
[5]   See *[1996] AC 624 at 640, [1996] 1 All ER 756* at 765.

An exception?

[5.17]   A possible exception to the general rule in English law of non-liability in tort for defective products is based upon the controversial majority decision of the House of Lords in *Junior Books Ltd v Veitchi Co Ltd*.[1] In this case the plaintiffs contracted with a building company to construct a factory. Specialist sub-contractors were appointed by the building company to carry out flooring work in the factory. Unfortunately, this work was done carelessly and the floor was seriously defective: although it posed no threat to persons, or to other property of the plaintiffs', keeping it properly maintained would have been vastly more expensive than if the work had been done properly. For some reason which was never explained, the plaintiffs chose not to proceed in contract against the building company, but instead sued the careless sub-contractors, with whom they were not in a contractual relationship, in tort. By a majority the House of Lords held that the claim succeeded. Lord Roskill and Lord Fraser, with whom Lord Russell agreed, asserted that, *in the particular circumstances of the case*, pure economic loss resulting from a product being, in effect, less valuable than it ought to have been, was recoverable in tort.

[1]   *[1983] 1 AC 520, [1982] 3 All ER 201, HL*.

Dissenting speeches

[5.18]   Lord Brandon disagreed with the view of the majority and delivered a dissenting speech. He broadly favoured the traditional view that the proper sphere of such liability was contract.[1] Similarly, Lord Keith, although he somehow felt able to agree with the majority as to the actual result,[2] in effect dissented. He felt that it would 'necessarily follow', from the approach of the majority, 'that any manufacturer of products would become liable to the ultimate purchaser if the product, owing to negligence in manufacture, was, without being harmful in any way, useless or worthless or defective in quality so that the purchaser wasted the money he spent on it'.[3] His Lordship expressly associated himself with Lord Brandon in rejecting this proposition.

[1]   This particular *a priori objection* to the decision of the majority in *Junior Books*, predicated on the existence of an exclusive contractual zone of liability, is now less compelling in view of the decision of

the House of Lords in *Henderson v Merrett Syndicates Ltd [1995] 2 AC 145, [1994] 3 All ER 506*. Nevertheless, it is remains possible to contend that the imposition of tortious liability was inappropriate on the facts of *Junior Books* given the nature of the actual contractual structure in the case: cf *per* Lord Goff in *Henderson v Merrett Syndicates Ltd [1995] 2 AC 145* at 196, *[1994] 3 All ER 506* at 535.

² His Lordship's reasoning is far from easy to follow and seems to be internally contradictory: it apparently contemplated recovery for pure pecuniary loss on an extraordinarily wide basis where a plaintiff's general economic prospects had been adversely affected while expressly denying it in the much narrower specific situation of a defective product.

³ *[1983] 1 AC 520* at 536, *[1982] 3 All ER 201* at 207, HL.

Close proximity

[5.19] Of course, if the wide proposition which Lord Brandon denounced *had* accurately stated the ratio decidendi of the majority, *Junior Books* would clearly now no longer be good law after *D & F Estates v Church Comrs* and *Murphy v Brentwood District Council*. But the majority did *not* accept that the wide general proposition of liability for forseeable economic loss caused by products defective in quality, was implicit in their reasoning in the way that Lord Brandon and Lord Keith alleged that it was. Such liability was appropriate in the instant case, the majority argued, because of the very close relationship between plaintiffs and defendants; it did not follow that other cases, in which the relationship was not so close, would be decided the same way merely because the loss suffered by the plaintiff was in some sense foreseeable. In the instant case the plaintiffs had actually nominated the defendants as specialist sub-contractors and, in the words of Lord Fraser, the 'proximity' between them was 'extremely close, falling only just short of a direct contractual relationship'.¹

¹ *[1983] 1 AC 520* at 533, *[1982] 3 All ER 201* at 204, HL. See also *per* Lord Roskill, *[1983] 1 AC 520* at 546, *[1982] 3 All ER 201* at 214: 'The relationship between the parties was as close as it could be short of actual privity of contract.' *Actual* privity, however, in a situation similar to that in *Junior Books* may paradoxically put the plaintiff at a disadvantage: see *Greater Nottingham Co-operative Society v Cementation Piling and Foundations Ltd [1989] QB 71, [1988] 2 All ER 971, CA*.

Not an everyday transaction

[5.20] Lord Roskill considered that the language and concepts used in the negligent misstatement cases, particularly *Hedley Byrne v Heller* itself, were applicable in the present context. He said that 'The concept of proximity must always involve, at least in most cases, some degree of reliance'. This requirement 'would not easily be found to exist', he continued, 'as between an ultimate consumer and a manufacturer … in the ordinary everyday transaction of purchasing chattels when it is obvious that in truth the real reliance was on the immediate vendor and not on the manufacturer'.¹ In both *D & F Estates v Church Comrs for England*² and *Murphy v Brentwood District Council*³ the House of Lords appears to have accepted the correctness of the decision in *Junior Books* on the basis that it did indeed concern the application of *Hedley Byrne* principles to a 'uniquely proximate relationship'.⁴ Thus, when facts similar to those in *Junior Books Ltd v Veitchi Co Ltd* occur, the decision still stands as an authority for the imposition of liability. On this view the case is probably best seen as an application of the concept of 'assumption of responsibility'.⁵

¹ See *Muirhead v Industrial Tank Specialities Ltd [1986] QB 507, [1985] 3 All ER 705, CA*; *Simaan General Contracting Co v Pilkington Glass Ltd (No 2) [1988] QB 758, [1988] 1 All ER 791, CA*.

² See *[1989] AC 177* at 202, 215, *[1988] 2 All ER 992* at 1003, 1013, *per* Lord Bridge and Lord Oliver.

³ See *[1991] 1 AC 398* at 466, 481, *[1990] 2 All ER 908* at 919, 930, *per* Lord Keith and Lord Bridge.

⁴ Per Lord Bridge in *D & F Estates Ltd v Church Comrs for England [1989] AC 177* at 202, *[1988] 2 All ER 992* at 1003.

Relevance of the contract

[5.21]   Although the number of cases in which the *Junior Books* principle will actually be applicable is likely to be few, a difficulty which may arise in them concerns the evaluation of the *allegedly* defective chattel or building. What if, for example, the quality of the product was lower than the contract which provided for its construction intended, but the agreement incorporated a clause which purported to restrict or exclude the manufacturer's contractual liability? In *Junior Books* itself Lord Roskill suggested that, in principle, a contractual provision could be relevant to the particular type of tort claim there in issue, notwithstanding that the plaintiff was not a party to the contract.[1] It is true that in the later case of *Leigh and Sillivan Ltd v Aliakmon Shipping Co Ltd*[2] Lord Brandon reiterated his own opposition to this proposal, and expressed specifically his continued disagreement with Lord Roskill's views in *Junior Books*. The facts of the *Aliakmon* case were, however, far removed from those of *Junior Books* and the relationship between the parties was nowhere near as close.

[1]   See 1 *[1983] AC 520* at 546, *[1982] 3 All ER 201* at 214.
[2]   *[1986] AC 785* at 817, *[1986] 2 All ER 145* at 155.

Exemption clauses

[5.22]   It is submitted that, at least within the peculiarly narrow sphere of a true *Junior Books* type of claim, which presupposes a very high degree of reliance by the plaintiff on the defendant, usually involving knowledge on the part of the former of the terms of the contract, the views of Lord Roskill are to be preferred.[1] Accordingly, even an exemption clause could in principle be effective, 'according to the manner in which it was worded',[2] to limit the defendant's duty of care in tort as well as in contract. Such a disclaimer would not be effective against a third party suing for personal injury,[3] but in appropriate cases it probably should be against a claim for economic loss. The clause might have been incorporated, conceivably even at the suggestion of the original purchaser, in order to relieve the manufacturer of the burden of carrying liability insurance and thereby enable a lower price to be charged for the product. In such circumstances it would not be appropriate to impose upon the defendant a liability to which, at the outset, it was not intended he should be subjected.[4]

[1]   See also *per* Lord Nolan in *White v Jones [1995] 2 AC 207* at 294, *[1995] 1 All ER 691* at 736, HL: ' ... the existence and terms of the contract may be relevant in determining what the law of tort may reasonably require of the defendant in all the circumstances.' Cf *Voli v Inglewood Shire Council (1963) 110 CLR 74* at 85.
[2]   *[1983] AC 520* at 546, *[1982] 3 All ER 201* at 214, *per* Lord Roskill. See also *Southern Water Authority v Carey [1985] 2 All ER 1077* at 1086 and *Norwich City Council v Harvey [1989] 1 All ER 1180, [1989] 1 WLR 828*, CA. But Cf *British Telecommunications plc v James Thompson & Sons [1999] 1 WLR 9, HL*.
[3]   Cf *Mint v Good [1951] 1 KB 517* at 528, *[1950] 2 All ER 1159* at 1166, CA, *per* Denning LJ. See also the *Unfair Contract Terms Act 1977, s 2(1)*.
[4]   Cf *New Zealand Shipping Co v Satterthwaite [1975] AC 154, [1974] 1 All ER 1015, PC*. But note that the *Unfair Contract Terms Act 1977*, which applies to common law liability for negligence (ie is not confined to actions in contract) subjects all attempts to exclude liability outside the personal injury sphere (where any exclusion is normally prohibited) to the 'reasonableness' test: see *ss 2(2)* and *11*. The relevant part of the Act only applies to things 'done or to be done by a person in the course of a business' (*s 1(3)(a)*), but most defective products cases will obviously fall within this definition.

C Where the claimant suffers economic loss which is consequential upon injury or damage to a third party

Traditional approach reasserted

[5.23]   The House of Lords, in *Leigh and Sillivan Ltd v Aliakmon Shipping Co Ltd*,[1] and the Judicial Committee of the Privy Council, in *Candlewood Navigation Corpn Ltd v Mitsui OSK Lines Ltd*,[2] both reasserted in the 1980s the traditional position, that the law of tort does not provide a remedy for those who suffer financial losses due to the infliction of damage to property in which they do not have an interest. These cases affirmed the authority of the two best-known pre-existing decisions on the point handed down in recent times: the decision of Widgery J in *Weller & Co v Foot & Mouth Disease Research Institute*,[3] which was set out earlier in this chapter at para [5.04] above, and *Spartan Steel and Alloys Ltd v Martin & Co (Contractors) Ltd*.[4]

---

[1]   *[1986] AC 785, [1986] 2 All ER 145, HL*, see below. See also *Esso Petroleum Co Ltd v Hall Russell & Co Ltd [1989] AC 643, [1989] 1 All ER 37, HL.*
[2]   *[1986] AC 1, [1985] 2 All ER 935, PC*, see below.
[3]   *[1966] 1 QB 569, [1965] 3 All ER 560.*
[4]   *[1973] QB 27, [1972] 3 All ER 557, CA.*

Spartan Steel

[5.24]   This case was a majority decision of the Court of Appeal. It concerned the negligent severing, by the defendants' employees, of an electricity cable while they were doing excavating work on a road near to a factory at which the plaintiffs manufactured stainless steel alloys. The damage to the cable, which was the property of the electricity board, led to the electricity supply to the factory being cut off for many hours. As a result, the plaintiffs suffered physical damage when molten metal began to solidify in their furnaces and they also suffered pure economic loss through the cessation of production. The defendants denied liability for the latter, a contention which Lord Denning MR and Lawton LJ accepted.[1] Lawton LJ stressed the authorities, in particular *Cattle v Stockton Waterworks Co*,[2] while Lord Denning MR frankly based the decision upon policy: 'If claims for economic loss were permitted for this particular hazard, there would be no end of claims.'[3] Edmund Davies LJ dissented. He favoured the wide proposition 'that an action lies in negligence for damages in respect of purely economic loss, provided that it was a reasonably foreseeable and direct consequence of failure in the duty of care';[4] and found these conditions satisfied in the instant case. The court was, however, unanimous in rejecting the proposition that the plaintiffs could recover for their lost production simply because they happened fortuitously to have a valid, but independent, claim arising out of the same incident for physical damage. A so-called doctrine of 'parasitic damages', for which some support could be found in the authorities,[5] enabling a plaintiff to attach a claim for economic loss to one for physical damage, even if the former was unconnected with the latter, was repudiated. In the result, therefore, although the plaintiffs were in fact awarded a modest sum for economic loss, the calculation of it was strictly limited to losses flowing directly from the physical damage which had occurred in the furnaces.[6]

---

[1]   See also *Electrochrome Ltd v Welsh Plastics Ltd [1968] 2 All ER 205.*
[2]   *(1875) LR 10 QB 453.*
[3]   *[1973] QB 27 at 38.*
[4]   *[1973] QB 27 at 45.*
[5]   See *Horton v Colwyn Bay and Colwyn Urban District Council [1908] 1 KB 327* at 341, CA, *per* Buckley LJ, and *per* counsel, *arguendo*, in *Spartan Steel [1973] QB 27* at 32.

6   See also *British Celanese v A H Hunt (Capacitors) Ltd [1969] 2 All ER 1252, [1969] 1 WLR 959; SCM (UK) Ltd v Whittall & Son Ltd [1971] 1 QB 337, [1970] 3 All ER 245, CA.*

Avalanche of claims

[5.25]   The underlying reason for denying liability in cases of this general type remains the fear that some of them could generate a wholly oppressive avalanche of claims against the defendant. The following example was given in an Australian case:[1]

' ... if, through the momentary inattention of an officer, a ship collided with a bridge, and as a result a large suburban area, which included shops and factories, was deprived of its means of access to a city, great loss might be suffered by tens of thousands of persons, but to require the wrongdoer to compensate all those who had suffered pecuniary loss would impose upon him a burden out of all proportion to his wrong.'[2]

It has been argued by one commentator that this position has validity when subjected to economic analysis.[3] It would be both inefficient and impracticable to expect those whose isolated acts of carelessness in, for example, excavating near underground cables, could deprive a whole town of electricity to insure against all economic losses resulting therefrom. It is much more sensible, it is said, for individual businesses to insure against interruption of production from such causes if they wish.[4] This highly pragmatic reason for denying liability is often reinforced in the cases by two further ones. First, there is the contention that to make exceptions to the general rule in situations in which, on the facts, there would be no danger of an avalanche of claims would be potentially anomalous and a cause of uncertainty. Secondly, there is the conceptual argument that economic losses should be the prerogative of the law of contract. Such losses are frequently inflicted through the operation of the *market*, which is an intrinsic function of a capitalist society: even *intentional* losses thus inflicted having to be accepted if they were suffered in the ordinary course of business competition.[5] The doctrinal objection to liability has been reinforced by the decisions of the House of Lords in *D & F Estates Ltd v Church Comrs For England*[6] and *Murphy v Brentwood District Council*,[7] discussed above. The *a priori* hostility to the recovery of pure economic loss in tort demonstrated by these cases is not confined to their own context of defective buildings or products reduced in value by the tortfeasor.

1   *Caltex Oil (Australia) Pty Ltd v Dredge Willemstad (1976) 136 CLR 529* at 551–552, *per* Gibbs J. Cf *Weller & Co v Foot and Mouth Disease Research Institute [1966] 1 QB 569, [1965] 3 All ER 560.*
2   Cf the Canadian case *Gypsum Carrier Inc v R (1977) 78 DLR (3d) 175* (ship collided with railway bridge owned by third party: railway company unable to claim for cost of re-routing trains). But see also *Canadian National Rly Co v Norsk Pacific Steamship Co (1992) 91 DLR (4th) 289* discussed below at para [5.35], in which the Supreme Court of Canada *imposed* liability in similar circumstances to those in the *Gypsum* case.
3   See W Bishop 'Economic Loss in Tort' (1982) 2 OJLS 1, especially pp 14–17.
4   See P Atiyah *Accidents, Compensation and the Law* (4th edn, 1987, Cane ed) p 75 (omitted from the 5th edition).
5   See J Smith Liability in Negligence (1984) p 77: 'It would indeed be strange if one were to be held liable for doing negligently that for which there would be no liability if done intentionally.'
6   *[1989] AC 177, [1988] 2 All ER 992, HL.*
7   *[1991] 1 AC 398, [1990] 2 All ER 908, HL.*

Confirmation of orthodox view

[5.26]   In *Candlewood Navigation Corpn Ltd v Mitsui OSK Lines Ltd*[1] the plaintiffs, who were time charterers of a vessel which was damaged in a collision caused by the negligent navigation of the defendants' vessel, sought to recover the profits they lost due to the ship being unable to trade while it was undergoing repair. The Privy Council rejected the claim. In their capacity as time charterers the plaintiffs did not own the damaged vessel[2] so that their loss was purely economic. Lord Fraser, delivering the judgment of the Board, referred to the fact that *Cattle v Stockton Waterworks* had 'stood for over a hundred years' and asserted that 'the justification for denying a right of action to a person who has suffered economic damage through injury to the property of another is that for reasons of practical policy it is considered to be inexpedient to admit his claim'.[3] Although the Board had been pressed by counsel for the plaintiffs with the argument that the policy justification for denying liability based upon an avalanche of claims was not applicable on the facts of the case, in that no such avalanche was conceivable, their Lordships remained unimpressed. To distinguish on that factual basis between economic loss cases which in principle were considered to be similar would undermine the certainty important in commercial relationships, nor were attempts to draw more principled distinctions by attempting to *classify* various groups of potential plaintiffs likely to prove successful.[4]

[1]   *[1986] AC 1, [1985] 2 All ER 935.* The case is criticised in (1986) 102 LQR 13 (M A Jones), and defended in [1986] 45 CLJ 10 (A Tettenborn).
[2]   As it happened, the plaintiffs *were* the owners of the vessel, but due to the peculiar facts of the case they were unable to sue for the relevant loss in that capacity.
[3]   *[1986] AC 1* at 17.
[4]   See *[1986] AC 1 at 24.*

Possibility of exceptions to the general rule rejected

[5.27]   Towards the end of his judgment in the *Candlewood* case,[1] Lord Fraser conceded that there might be 'exceptional cases', unlike the one before him, in which liability for pure economic loss caused by a negligent act would, contrary to the general rule, be imposed. In the subsequent case of *Leigh and Sillivan Ltd v Aliakmon Shipping Co Ltd*,[2] however, the House of Lords apparently set its face against the possibility of such exceptions, notwithstanding that a persistent and not unpersuasive line of earlier authorities favoured them.

[1]   See *[1986] AC 1* at 25.
[2]   *[1986] AC 785, [1986] 2 All ER 145, HL.* See also *Esso Petroleum Co Ltd v Hall Russell & Co Ltd [1989] AC 643, [1989] 1 All ER 37, HL.*

The pre-Aliakmon cases

[5.28]   In a number of these cases the recovery in tort of pure economic loss, consequential upon physical damage to a third party's property, was either anticipated obiter or even actually allowed. The underlying reasoning appears to have been that such a claim should be permitted if the commercial relationship between the plaintiff and the owner of the damaged property was so close that it would be artificial to allow the incidence of liability to depend upon the ownership of that property, especially since such particular facts are unlikely to give rise to the 'floodgates' problem. A hypothetical example of the application of this approach was given by Lord Roche, in the House of Lords, in *Morrison Steamship Co Ltd v Greystoke Castle (Cargo Owners)*.[1] His Lordship said:[2]

' ... if two lorries A and B are meeting one another on the road, I cannot bring myself to doubt that the driver of lorry A owes a duty to both the owner of lorry

B and to the owner of goods then carried in lorry B. Those owners are engaged in a common adventure with or by means of lorry B, and if lorry A is negligently driven and damages lorry B so severely that, while no damage is done to the goods in it, the goods have to be unloaded for the repair of the lorry and then reloaded or carried forward in some other way and the consequent expense is (by reason of his contract or otherwise) the expense of the owner of the goods, then, in my judgment, the owner of the goods has a direct cause of action to recover such expense.'

This dictum was subsequently referred to with approval by Lord Denning MR.[3]

1   *[1947] AC 265, [1946] 2 All ER 696, HL.*
2   *[1947] AC 265 at 280.*
3   See *SCM (UK) Ltd v Whittall & Son Ltd [1971] 1 QB 337* at 346, *[1970] 3 All ER 245* at 252, CA.

Caltex Oil

[5.29]   A decision of the High Court of Australia in the 1970s which appeared in effect to provide an example of this principle in operation, is *Caltex Oil (Australia) Pty Ltd v Dredge Willemstad.*[1] A pipeline laid across a bay, which belonged to an oil refinery, was fractured when a dredging vessel collided with it due to the negligence of the defendants. The pipeline connected the refinery to an oil terminal, on the opposite shore of the bay, operated by the plaintiffs. There was an arrangement whereby the plaintiffs supplied the oil refinery with crude oil through the pipeline and received back refined oil by the same method. The plaintiffs successfully sued the defendants for the economic loss which they suffered while the pipeline, which they did not own, could not be used. It is not easy to extract a single ratio decidendi from the five judgments delivered.[2] The members of the court do, however, appear to have been in general agreement that policy factors precluded the imposition of liability for pure economic loss on the same general basis as for physical damage.[3] But they were also unanimous that the present case was nevertheless one of those in which recovery could be permitted. The fact that the pipeline served only the plaintiffs and its owners, so that there was no danger of an avalanche of claims, was regarded as relevant. Moreover, it was a case in which 'the plaintiff, and the person whose property was injured, were engaged in a common adventure'.[4]

1   *(1976) 136 CLR 529.*
2   For a note on the case see P F Cane in (1977) 93 LQR 333.
3   See the particularly clear statement in *(1976) 135 CLR 529* at 555, *per* Gibbs J: 'In my opinion it is still right to say that as a general rule damages are not recoverable for economic loss which is not consequential upon injury to the plaintiff's person or property. The fact that the loss was foreseeable is not enough to make it recoverable.'
4   *(1976) 135 CLR 529* at 555, *per* Gibbs J. See also *per* Stephen J at 579–580. But cf *per* Jacobs J at 602: 'I do not think that Lord Roche's reference [ie in the *Greystoke Castle* case] to "common adventure" was more than a statement of commercial reality. It introduced no special qualification of law.' Cf *Bow Valley Husky (Bermuda) Ltd v St John Shipbuilding Ltd [1997] 3 SCR 1210, 153 DLR (4th) 385 (Can SC).*

The Aliakmon case

[5.30]   *Leigh and Sillivan Ltd v Aliakmon Shipping Co Ltd*[1] concerned a situation involving the carriage of goods by sea. The plaintiffs had agreed to buy the goods in question but, owing to the peculiar facts of the case, they were not holders of the bill of lading and so did not have title to them at the time when the goods were unfortunately damaged in transit. The question arose whether the plaintiffs could nevertheless sue the defendant shipowners in negligence. A majority of the Court of Appeal, and a unanimous House of Lords, held that they could not. Lord Brandon, who delivered the only speech in the House of Lords, re-asserted the 'floodgates' doctrine as a general proposition, and responded as follows to the suggestion that it was not appropriate to apply that doctrine to the facts of the particular case:[2]

'If an exception to the general rule were to be made in the field of carriage by sea, it would no doubt have to be extended to the field of carriage by land, and I do not think that it is possible to say that no undue increase in the scope of a person's liability for want of care would follow. In any event, where a general rule, which is simple to understand and easy to apply, has been established by a long line of authority over many years, I do not think that the law should allow special pleading in a particular case within the general rule to detract from its application. If such detraction were to be permitted in one particular case, it would lead to attempts to have it permitted in a variety of other particular cases, and the result would be that the certainty, which the application of the general rule presently provides, would be seriously undermined. Yet certainty of the law is of the utmost importance, especially but by no means only, in commercial matters.'

[1]   *[1986] AC 785, [1986] 2 All ER 145, HL.*See also *Homburg Houtimport BV v Agrosin Private Ltd [1999] 2 All ER (Comm) 591.*
[2]   *[1986] AC 785* at 816–817, *[1986] 2 All ER 145* at 154–155. See also *Esso Petroleum Co Ltd v Hall Russell & Co Ltd [1989] AC 643, [1989] 1 All ER 37, HL.*

Just result?

[5.31]   Lord Brandon also denied that the result was inherently unjust, by arguing that, with proper advice, the plaintiffs could have taken precautions in advance to ensure that they would have had a right to sue in the circumstances which ultimately transpired.[1] The plausibility of this particular point is, however, open to question. Even assuming that such a move had been a realistic and practical,[2] as distinct from theoretical[3] possibility, it is hardly convincing in itself as a justification for shifting responsibility from an actual wrongdoer. A victim's failure to lock his house does not exonerate a burglar.

[1]   See *[1986] AC 785* at 818–819, *[1986] 2 All ER 145* at 156.
[2]   See the doubts expressed in Todd 'Actions by Banks Against Carriers – An Update of the Tort Position' (1986) 2 J Int Banking L 127 at 130 (cited in B S Markesinis 'An Expanding Tort Law – The Price of a Rigid Contract Law' (1987) 103 LQR 354 at 386, n 92.
[3]   See the doubts expressed by M Clarke in 'Buyer Fails to Recover Economic Loss from the Negligent Carrier' [1986] 45 CLJ 382 at 384.

Goff LJ and the 'principle of transferred loss'

[5.32]   When the *Aliakmon* case was before the Court of Appeal, Goff LJ (as he then was) found himself in the minority on the point of principle and favoured recovery on the basis of what he described as 'the principle of transferred loss'. He expounded this principle as follows:[1]

'Where A owes a duty of care in tort not to cause physical damage to B's property, and commits a breach of that duty in circumstances in which the loss of or physical damage to the property will ordinarily fall on B but (as is reasonably foreseeable by A) such loss or damage, by reason of a contractual relationship between B and C, falls on C, then C will be entitled, subject to the terms of the contract restricting A's liability to B, to bring an action in tort against A in respect of such loss or damage to the extent that it falls on him, C.'

Lord Brandon flatly rejected this proposition and overruled an English decision at first instance which had been consistent with it.[2] In principle, however, the theory of Goff LJ has much to commend it. If, as Lord Brandon asserted, the ultimate reason for the denial of liability is the purely pragmatic 'floodgates' argument, that argument should surely not be applied outside situations in which a real danger of an avalanche of claims exists: *unless* refusal to do so would indeed lead to the drawing of arbitrary factual distinctions between claims on the basis of hindsight and hence to injustice and uncertainty. The approach of Goff LJ could perhaps have facilitated the develop-ment of rules which might have succeeded in avoiding these difficulties, while at the same time ensuring that the application of the 'floodgates' argument was not need-lessly extended. Indeed, more recently, as Lord Goff of Chieveley, his Lordship revisited the notion of transferred loss, albeit in a different context, in his speech as one of the majority of the House of Lords in *White v Jones*.[3]

[1]   *[1985] QB 350 at 399, [1985] 2 All ER 44 at 77.*
[2]   See *Schiffahrt und Kohlen GmbH v Chelsea Maritime Ltd, The Irene's Success [1982] QB 481, [1982] 1 All ER 218.*
[3]   See *[1995] 2 AC 207 at 264–265, [1995] 1 All ER 691* at 707–708. For further discussion of this case see below at para [5.38].

Tort and contract

[5.33]   Part of the reasoning which underpinned the judicial reluctance to embrace the notion of transferred loss, or to make any other exception to the general rule of non-liability for economic loss consequential upon damage suffered by a third party, has itself been undermined by subsequent developments in other contexts involving economic loss. The hostility to recovery in the *Aliakmon* case was based in part upon a conceptual preference for confining the recovery of pure economic loss to the law of contract as far as possible. But in *Henderson v Merrett Syndicates Ltd*[1] the House of Lords rejected the notion of an exclusive contractual zone of liability[2]. Their Lord-ships affirmed the possibility of concurrent liability in both tort and contract in situations falling within the *Hedley Byrne* principle and emphasised, in the words of Lord Goff,[3] that 'the law of tort is the general law, out of which parties can, if they wish, contract'. And in *White v Jones*[4] the House confirmed that a solicitor can be liable to a third party in negligence for pure economic loss arising out of the careless performance of his contract with his client. It is submitted that the rejection, in these two decisions, of any rigid and inflexible distinction between contract and tort is in tune with the deeply pragmatic nature of the common law itself. In the light of these developments it is open to question how long the blanket rule of non-liability in tort for pure economic loss consequential upon damage suffered by a third party will remain intact.[5]

[1]   *[1995] 2 AC 145, [1994] 3 All ER 506.*
[2]   See also *Weldon v GRE Linked Life Assurance [2000] 2 All ER (Comm) 914* (possibility of tortious duty coexisting with contract of insurance).
[3]   See *[1995] 2 AC 145 at 193, [1994] 3 All ER 506 at 532.*
[4]   *[1995] 2 AC 207, [1995] 1 All ER 691.*
[5]   Cf B S Markesinis 'An Expanding Tort Law – The Price of a Rigid Contract Law' (1987) 103 LQR 354 at 389, who says of the *Aliakmon* case that its 'reasoning, which aims at re-establishing the authority of

a rule that has clearly broken down in practice ... makes [him] doubt the longevity of the judgment'. See also J Stapleton 'Duty of Care and Economic Loss: a Wider Agenda' (1991) 107 LQR 249.

Liability imposed in Canada

[5.34]   Just as other common law jurisdictions have chosen not to follow the English refusal to permit tort claims for pure economic loss in cases where the plaintiff's property was reduced in *value* by the defendant's negligence,[1] so also the refusal to allow recovery for such loss when consequential upon injury or damage to a *third party* has not commended itself to other Commonwealth courts as an unqualified general proposition.

[1]   See above.

Norsk

[5.35]   In *Canadian National Rly Co v Norsk Pacific Steamship Co*,[1] in which *Murphy v Brentwood District Council* was considered along with most of the other leading English cases, the Supreme Court of Canada chose by a bare majority not to adopt the exclusionary approach to the recovery of pure economic loss. In *Norsk* a barge which was being towed down a river by the defendants' tug collided with a bridge, due to the defendants' negligence, and caused extensive damage to it. The bridge was owned by a third party but the plaintiffs, who had no legal interest in the bridge itself, had a contractual right to run trains across it and suffered pure economic loss when it was closed for several weeks for repairs. By a four to three majority the Supreme Court held that the plaintiffs could recover their losses from the defendants. The majority[2] considered that there was sufficient 'proximity' between plaintiffs and defendants and, on the facts of the case, no danger of a 'floodgates' situation: the close relationship which in practice existed between the plaintiffs and the actual owners of the bridge being treated as an important factor in this respect. The dissentients[3] considered that the nature of the plaintiffs' loss was in principle indistinguishable from the economic loss suffered by many people in the 'ripple' effect following a major disruption of the kind in question, and that the case therefore did raise the spectre of indeterminate liability.

[1]   *(1992) 91 DLR (4th) 289*. See B S Markesinis 'Compensation for Negligently Inflicted Pure Economic Loss: Some Canadian Views' (1993) 109 LQR 5.
[2]   L'Heureux-Dubé, Cory, McLachlin and Stevenson JJ.
[3]   La Forest, Sopinka and Iacobucci JJ.

Proceeding with caution

[5.36]   More recently, in *Bow Valley Husky (Bermuda) Ltd v St John Shipbuilding Ltd*,[1] the Supreme Court has adopted a rather more restrictive and cautious approach to the recovery of economic loss and emphasised that such recovery will only be permitted in exceptional circumstances. It nevertheless remains clear, however, that the Canadian courts are ready, in a way in which the English courts at present are not, to consider claims for pure economic loss caused by injury to a third party in particular circumstances.

[1]   *[1997] 3 SCR 1210, 153 DLR (4th) 385*. See B Feldthusen (1998) 6 TLR 164.

D Assumption of responsibility

Need for 'something more'

[5.37]   Even in England it would be a major over-simplification to assume that recent decisions have put into reverse all earlier developments in the direction of expanding liability for economic loss. In *Murphy v Brentwood District Council*[1] Lord Oliver of Aylmerton said:

> 'It does not ... follow as a matter of necessity from the mere fact that the only damage suffered by a plaintiff in an action for the tort of negligence is pecuniary or "economic" that his claim is bound to fail ... The critical question ... is not the nature of the damage in itself, whether physical or pecuniary, but whether the scope of the duty of care in the circumstances of the case is such as to embrace damage of the kind which the plaintiff claims to have sustained ... The infliction of physical injury to the person or property of another universally requires to be justified. The causing of economic loss does not. If it is to be categorised as wrongful it is necessary to find some factor beyond the mere occurrence of the loss and the fact that its occurrence could be foreseen. Thus, the categorisation of damage as economic serves at least the useful purpose of indicating that something more is required ... '

The challenge facing the law is to achieve greater clarity in identification of the factors, outside the established special area of liability for negligent misstatement,[2] which are capable of constituting 'something more'.

[1]   *[1991] 1 AC 398* at 458–487, *[1990] 2 All ER 908* at 933–934.
[2]   See CHAPTER 4 above.

Significance of White v Jones

[5.38]   'Assumption of responsibility' is a concept which has gained increased prominence as a basis for widening the range of situations in which economic loss can be recovered. In *White v Jones*[1] the defendant solicitors were instructed by a client to draw up a new will. The defendants carelessly omitted to carry out their instructions with appropriate despatch and, as a result, their client died before the will had been prepared. The disappointed beneficiaries of the proposed will sued the solicitors for negligence seeking damages equivalent in amount to the intended bequests. The case did not fall within the existing parameters of the area of liability for economic loss established by *Hedley Byrne*: the plaintiffs had not 'relied' in any meaningful sense upon any 'statement' by the defendants, the latter having been instructed solely by their client to draw up a will for him. Nevertheless, the House of Lords held by a bare majority[2] that the claim would succeed.[3] Lord Goff took the view that the benefit of the undertaking by the defendants to the testator could be deemed, as a matter of law, to have been *transferred* to the plaintiffs.[4] Lord Browne-Wilkinson and Lord Nolan, however, decided the case on the broader ground that the notion of 'assumption of responsibility' extended to assuming responsibility for carrying out a specific *task*, and was not be confined to situations within the *Hedley Byrne* paradigm of an implied assumption of *legal* responsibility by the defendant for statements made directly to the plaintiff. In the words of Lord Browne-Wilkinson:[5]

> ' ... the solicitor by accepting the instructions ... entered upon, and therefore assumed responsibility for, the task of procuring the execution of a skilfully

drawn will knowing that the beneficiary [was] wholly dependent upon his carefully carrying out his function … It is not to the point that the solicitor only entered on the task pursuant to a contract with the third party (ie the testator).'

1   *[1995] 2 AC 207, [1995] 1 All ER 691, HL.*
2   Lord Goff, Lord Browne-Wilkinson and Lord Nolan; Lord Keith and Lord Mustill dissenting.
3   The decision of the House therefore confirmed the correctness of the much-debated decision of Megarry V-C, 15 years earlier in *Ross v Caunters [1980] Ch 297, [1979] 3 All ER 580*, in which a solicitor was held liable in negligence to a disappointed beneficiary when a will became invalid due to its not having been correctly witnessed.
4   See *[1995] 2 AC 207* at 264–269, *[1995] 1 All ER 691* at 707–711. Cf *Linden Gardens Trust Ltd v Lenesta Sludge Disposals Ltd [1994] 1 AC 85, [1993] 3 All ER 417, HL.*
5   *[1995] 2 AC 207* at 275, *[1995] 1 All ER 691* at 717–718. See also *per* Lord Nolan at 293, 735.

Far-reaching potential

[5.39]   Since the defendants had 'assumed responsibility' for a task which was intended to benefit the plaintiffs, it was considered by the majority to be no objection to liability in tort that the defendants had merely 'omitted' to confer a 'gain' upon the plaintiffs as distinct from actually inflicting a 'loss' upon them.[1] While the actual decision in *White v Jones* is, it is submitted, an attractive one,[2] it is still not yet entirely clear how far the principle which it embodies extends. The wide interpretation of 'assumption of responsibility', upon which it is based, is potentially capable of expanding liability for pure economic loss to a point at which it could begin to de-stabilise the recently reaffirmed general rule of non-liability for such loss where careless action or inaction is concerned. Indeed, Lord Mustill observed, in a trenchant dissenting speech, that he could see nothing 'sufficiently special about the calling of a solicitor to distinguish him from others in a much broader category'[3] and posed the following question: 'If A promises B to perform a service for B which B intends, and A knows, will confer a benefit on C if it is performed, does A owe to C in tort a duty to perform that service?'[4]

1   'Since the *Hedley Byrne* principle is founded upon an assumption of responsibility, the solicitor may be liable for negligent omissions as well as negligent acts of commission … I do not consider that damages for loss of an expectation are excluded in cases of negligence arising under the principle … simply because the cause of action is classified as tortious': *per* Lord Goff, *[1995] 1 All ER 691* at 711. See also *per* Brennan CJ in *Hill v Van Erp (1997) 188 CLR 159 (Aus)*: 'The objection that no claim for damages for economic loss lies in negligence unless it is in respect of damage to an existing right or interest is, in my opinion, erroneous … A benefit that the plaintiff would have received but for the negligence of the defendant is a loss, whether or not the benefit would have been gratuitous.' Cf J Stapleton 'The Normal Expectancies Measure in Tort Damages' (1997) 113 LQR 257 at 282.
2   It is significant that the High Court of Australia subsequently reached the same result (with one dissentient) in a case involving failure of a bequest due to improper attestation: see *Hill v Van Erp (1997) 188 CLR 159.*
3   *[1995] 2 AC 207* at 291, *[1995] 1 All ER 691* at 733.
4   *[1995] 2 AC 207* at 283, *[1995] 1 All ER 691* at 725. See also *per* McHugh J, also dissenting, in the similar case of *Hill v Van Erp (1997) 188 CLR 159* at 214: 'Consider, for example, the case of the accountant who is paid a fee by a client to investigate the prospects of a business knowing that the client intends to purchase the business as a gift for the relative. Does the accountant owe the relative a duty of care? Is the accountant liable for the profits that the relative would have earned if, but for the accountant's negligence in assessing its viability, the business had been purchased?'

A manageable principle?

[5.40]   Although the ratio decidendi of *White v Jones* is not confined exclusively to solicitors, it is submitted that a coherent and manageable principle can be derived from the case if a positive answer is given to Lord Mustill's question but one which is qualified in three important respects. First, the service which A promises to perform must involve some special *knowledge or skill* as distinct from a merely routine task which anyone could perform. Secondly, the nature of the benefit, and the *context* in which it is to be conferred, must be *financial*. Thirdly, it must be *just and reasonable* for liability to be imposed upon A. The actual decision in *White v Jones* itself clearly satisfies all three conditions, and the first two reflect the fact that the new development has its origins in the *Hedley Byrne* principle.[1]

[1]   Cf *Spring v Guardian Assurance plc [1995] 2 AC 296, [1994] 3 All ER 129*, in which the House of Lords held that writing a reference about the plaintiff to his prospective employer can give rise to a duty of care upon the writer.

Conditions confined to benefit cases

[5.41]   It should be emphasised that these conditions are confined to cases involving the conferring of a *benefit*[1]. If the defendant assumes responsibility for protection of the claimant from loss or harm a more relaxed attitude to the conditions for the imposition of liability is appropriate, and no special knowledge or skill is required. Thus in *Weldon v GRE Linked Life Assurance*[2] the court refused to strike out a claim in tort for negligently failing to implement the claimant's direct debit mandate for the payment of insurance premiums, thereby leaving him uninsured. It was held that responsibility for implementing the mandate had been voluntarily assumed by the defendants. Similarly, in *Lennon v Metropolitan Police Commissioner*[3] the defendant was held vicariously liable for failing to ensure that the claimant's conditions of service were appropriately protected when he transferred to another employer, one of the defendant's employees having told the claimant 'to leave everything to her'[4]. Mummery LJ rejected a contention that the claim was novel, and said[5]:

'It is now well-established that liability in tort for pure economic loss can arise from the negligent carrying out of a task undertaken pursuant to an express voluntary assumption of responsibility, on which the claimant has relied'.

[1]   Cf the *Contracts (Rights of Third Parties) Act 1999*, which in certain circumstances now enables third parties to enforce contracts made for their 'benefit'. (The Act itself will not usually be applicable to situations of the particular kind under consideration here, since the negligent defendant's failure will normally relate merely to the *service* which he agreed to provide: eg in *White v Jones* the actual *benefit* was to be conferred by the deceased client, not by the defendant solicitor.)
[2]   *[2000] 2 All ER (Comm) 914.*
[3]   *[2004] 2 All ER 266.*
[4]   See *[2004] 2 All ER 266* at para 14.
[5]   See *[2004] 2 All ER 266* at para 24.

Relevance of 'just and reasonable'?

[5.42]   A possible difficulty with the proposition that the 'just and reasonable' test can be relevant to cases brought by third parties under the *White v Jones* principle lies in a dictum of Lord Goff in *Henderson v Merrett Syndicates Ltd*.[1] His Lordship said that 'if a person assumes responsibility to another in respect of certain services, there is no reason why he should not be liable in damages for that other in respect of economic loss which flows from the negligent performance of those services'. He then concluded:[2] 'It follows that, once the case is identified as falling within the *Hedley Byrne* principle, there should be no need to embark upon any further inquiry whether it is "fair, just and reasonable" to impose liability for economic loss.' A careful reading of Lord Goff's words, however, would seem to confine his suggestion of the irrelevance of the 'just and reasonable' requirement to cases in which the assumption of responsibility was by one person *to* another and in respect of a statement; ie cases truly within the *Hedley Byrne* negligent misstatement principle in its original bilateral form. There is no reason to suppose that Lord Goff had in mind cases such as *White v Jones*, in which the existence of liability to third parties for careless action or inaction is in issue, and it is submitted that application of the 'just and reasonable' requirement to such cases is appropriate.

1   *[1995] 2 AC 145* at 181, *[1994] 3 All ER 506* at 521.
2   *[1995] 2 AC 145* at 181, *[1994] 3 All ER 506* at 521.

Losses due to failure to insure

[5.43]   In two cases decided at the end of the 1980s, before the more recent developments surrounding the doctrine of assumption of responsibility, plaintiffs in existing contractual relationships with defendants suffered economic loss due to their being uninsured when they suffered serious personal injury. In *Reid v Rush & Tompkins Group plc*[1] the plaintiff, while working abroad for the defendant employer, was injured by an uninsured driver in a road accident in a country which had no scheme similar to the Motor Insurers' Bureau which compensates victims in Britain in such circumstances.[2] The plaintiff alleged that his employers should have insured him against such injuries themselves or should have advised him to insure himself, but the Court of Appeal rejected his claim. Similarly, in *Van Oppen v Bedford Charity Trustees*[3] the Court of Appeal denied that a school owed a duty to pupils to insure them against the risk of injury while playing rugby football or to advise their parents to take out such insurance. 'An existing relationship between the parties', said Balcombe LJ,[4] 'which may give rise to a duty of care by one party for the physical well-being and safety of the other (eg master and servant), does not of itself mean that there is sufficient proximity between the parties to justify finding the existence of a duty of care not to cause economic loss'.

1   *[1989] 3 All ER 228, [1990] 1 WLR 212, CA*.
2   See CHAPTER 31 below.
3   *[1989] 3 All ER 389, [1990] 1 WLR 235, CA*; affg *[1989] 1 All ER 273*.
4   *[1989] 3 All ER 389* at 409, *[1990] 1 WLR 235* at 260.

Open to question

[5.44]   It is submitted that the correctness of these decisions is open to question. Both of them seem to have been based in part upon the view, prevalent at the time when they were decided, that the law of tort was subordinate to the law of contract.[1] It was apparently considered to follow from this view that, in the absence of a specific undertaking, the court would not allow the law of tort to supplement the strictly limited rules governing the implication of terms into contracts. But since the marked change in the relationship between tort and contract, brought about by the decision of the House of Lords in *Henderson v Merrett Syndicates Ltd*,[2] it would seem that the test for the exclusion of tortious liability should be actual inconsistency with the terms of the agreement; ie the mere fact that the law of contract would not itself have been prepared to imply a term equivalent to liability in tort should not in itself be fatal to the imposition of such liability. Once the contractual objection is removed, both of the cases could be brought within the scope of the 'assumption of responsibility' concept.

The relationships between the parties, as employer and employee and school and pupil respectively, were close; and it was taken for granted in the cases themselves that the defendants could easily have foreseen the situations which occurred and easily have taken appropriate precautions to protect the plaintiffs from financial loss.

[1]   See *Tai Hing Cotton Mill Ltd v Liu Chong Hing Bank Ltd [1986] AC 80, [1985] 2 All ER 947*, PC.
[2]   *[1995] 2 AC 145, [1994] 3 All ER 506*, especially at 193, 532, *per* Lord Goff: ' ... the law of tort is the general law.' See also *per* Lord Browne-Wilkinson at 206, 544: 'I can see no good reason for holding that the existence of a contractual right is in all circumstances inconsistent with the co-existence of another tortious right ... '

Failure to warn

[5.45]   In *Hamble Fisheries v L Gardner & Sons*[1] the Court of Appeal considered a question formulated by Tuckey LJ as follows[2]:

'In what circumstances is there a common law duty of care to warn where it is foreseeable that the failure to do so will cause economic loss?'

The plaintiffs owned a fishing vessel, the building of which they had themselves commissioned some years earlier. The defendants owned the business which had supplied the engines for the vessel to the boatbuilders as contractors to the latter, but there was no contractual relationship between the plaintiffs and the defendants. The defendants became aware that one of the components in the type of engine which had been fitted in the plaintiff's vessel was proving defective, and causing the engines to fail. They nevertheless decided not to pass this knowledge on to the owners of vessels fitted with the engines, even though they could have done so by using lists of known purchasers or by advertising through trade channels. The engine in the plaintiff's vessel subsequently failed causing economic loss, for which the plaintiffs sued the defendants. The Court of Appeal decided that their claim would fail[3]. The defendants were held not to have assumed responsibility to pass on any warnings to persons in the position of the plaintiffs. In particular, statements in the instruction manuals delivered with the engines, indicating how long they could be expected to last, did not constitute such an assumption of responsibility.

[1]   *[1999] 2 Lloyd's Rep 1*.
[2]   See above at p ?
[3]   Cf the decision apparently to the opposite effect of the Supreme Court of Canada in *Rivtow Marine v Washington Iron Works (1973) 40 DLR (3d) 530*, which the Court of Appeal did not follow.

Only economic loss irrecoverable

[5.46]   The Court of Appeal reached its decision with some regret, in view of the unattractive conduct of the defendants, and observed that the latter's deliberate decision not to pass on the warnings might well have sufficed to make them liable for any damage to person or property, if such had occurred.[1] The decision was therefore based squarely upon the continuing perceived need to keep the recoverability of pure economic loss within narrow confines for policy reasons. Mummery LJ said that this approach was 'explicable by rational and pragmatic considerations', which he summarised as follows[2]:

' ... the disproportionate burden of imposing indeterminate liability ...; the evidential difficulties in establishing causation and delimiting remoteness; the relative cost and practicability of obtaining insurance cover for risks of pure financial loss suffered to an unlimited degree by an amorphous class of claimants; the apprehension of a deluge, in an already overstretched legal system, of litigation by an indefinite number of claimants with multiple claims arising out of a single incident: (eg the businessman driver losing a profitable deal as a result of a breakdown of his car caused by a defective engine part or as a result of delays in a traffic tailback caused by the breakdown of another's car for a similar reason); the dubious and lethal colonization by the tort of negligence of the conceptual territory of contract; the perception that financial loss occupies a significantly lower place than physical injury to person and property in the scale of contemporary social and ethical values; and the inevitability (and acceptability) of widespread and uncompensatable financial loss in a free market economy … '.

1 See *[1999] 2 Lloyd's Rep 1* at p 9 *per* Mummery LJ, and at p 10 *per* Nourse LJ.
2 See *[1999] 2 Lloyd's Rep 1* at p 8.

E Other cases of economic loss

Statutory powers

[5.47] Another factor which may indicate, in the words of Lord Oliver quoted above from *Murphy v Brentwood District Council*, that 'the scope of the duty of care in the circumstances of the case [was] such as to embrace damage of the kind which the plaintiff claims to have sustained' is the existence of a statute creating the context in which the defendant acted or failed to act. Thus, in *Lonrho plc v Tebbit*[1] the Court of Appeal in 1992 refused to strike out a negligence action against a Secretary of State, in which the plaintiffs alleged that the defendant's supposedly careless failure to release them from a redundant and superseded undertaking had caused them economic loss. This aspect is dealt with in a later chapter.[2]

1 *[1992] 4 All ER 280, CA*; affg *[1991] 4 All ER 973*.
2 See CHAPTER 15 below.

Recovery of economic loss in nuisance

Public nuisance

[5.48] The law relating to public nuisance is an area of the law of tort which is unusual in that it has long allowed the recovery of pure economic loss.[1] In *Tate & Lyle Industries Ltd v Greater London Council*[2] the plaintiffs sought to recover for foreseeable economic loss caused to them through the defendants' having carelessly allowed a river to become silted up. The House of Lords allowed the claim to succeed in public nuisance, for interference with the right of passage along a public navigable river, but disallowed the claim as framed in negligence.

1 See CHAPTER 14 below.
2 *[1983] 2 AC 509, [1983] 1 All ER 1159, HL*.

Private nuisance

[5.49] There is little explicit authority on the scope of liability for economic loss in private nuisance. In *Dunton v Dover District Council*[1], however, Griffiths J anticipated that clear evidence of a falling-off in bookings could enable a hotel proprietor to recover for a drop in takings caused by a nuisance. Thus provided the claimant has a cause of action in nuisance irrespective of the economic loss, eg because fumes or noise from an adjacent factory render his business premises unpleasant, it is submitted that he can recover for pecuniary loss resulting from the deterrent effect of the nuisance upon his customers. The need to prove the existence of a good cause of action in nuisance, before the loss can be recovered, should help to ensure that defendants in such cases are not embarrassed by a multiplicity of claims, and reduce the plausibility of any attempt to invoke the 'floodgates' argument.

[1]   *(1977) 76 LGR 87* at 93.

Abolition of actions for loss of services

[5.50]   Consistent with the principle that normally disallows the recovery of pure economic loss in negligence, the infliction of injury upon one person does not at common law provide another with a cause of action. Formerly, however, there were two ancient exceptions to this rule.[1] These were the master's right to sue for the loss of the services of his servant,[2] and the husband's right to sue for the loss of the services of his wife. As specific actions these were long seen to be anomalous,[3] and they were finally abolished by the *Administration of Justice Act 1982, s 2*.

[1]   See *Salmond and Heuston on Torts* (18th edn, 1981) pp 326–336.
[2]   The person injured had to be a 'menial' servant, eg injury to an established civil servant did not give rise to the action: *IRC v Hambrook [1956] 2 QB 641, [1956] 1 All ER 807.*
[3]   Eg the wife enjoyed no corresponding right to the services of her husband: *Best v Samuel Fox & Co Ltd [1952] AC 716, [1952] 2 All ER 394, HL.*

Part three

Professional negligence

Chapter 6

General principles[1]

A The Bolam test

Standard of care

[6.01]   The classic statement of the test for liability in professional negligence cases is that of McNair J in *Bolam v Friern Hospital Management Committee*[2], as follows:

> ' ... where you get a situation which involves the use of some special skill or competence, then the test as to whether there has been negligence or not is not the test of the man on the top of a Clapham omnibus, because he has not got this special skill. The test is the standard of the ordinary skilled man exercising and professing to have that special skill. A man need not possess the highest expert skill; it is well established law that it is sufficient if he exercises the ordinary skill of an ordinary competent man exercising that particular art ... he is not guilty of negligence if he has acted in accordance with a practice accepted as proper by a responsible body of ... men skilled in that particular art ... Putting it the other way round, a man is not negligent, if he is acting in accordance with such a practice, merely because there is a body of opinion who would take a contrary view.'

---

[1]   See R Jackson and J Powell *Professional Negligence* (5th edn, 2001); A Dugdale and K Stanton *Professional Negligence* (3rd edn, 1998); R Hodgin (ed) *Professional Liability: Law and Insurance* (1996).

[2]   *[1957] 2 All ER 118* at 121, *[1957] 1 WLR 582* at 586. See also *Chin Keow v Government of Malaysia [1967] 1 WLR 813, PC*; *Wimpey Construction (UK) Ltd v Poole [1984] 2 Lloyd's Rep 499.*

Qualifications to the test

[6.02]   The area is clearly a sensitive one because in resolving disputes concerning specialist expertise, by using the test set out in this passage, there is a danger that the court may inadvertently surrender the ultimate power of decision, which is its responsibility alone, to the profession in question. It is apparent that the way in which any expert evidence presented is assessed by the court will often be of fundamental importance if this pitfall is to be avoided. Accordingly, in the Court of Appeal in *JD Williams & Co v Michael Hyde Associates*[1], Ward LJ identified three 'qualifications' to the *Bolam* test. These were later summarised by Judge Richard Seymour QC in *Royal Brompton Hospital NHS Trust v Hammond (No 6)*[2] as follows:

> ' ... the test ...[does] not apply in three situations, namely:

[6.03] *General principles[1]*

i. where some professional opinion expressed is not capable of logical analysis;

ii where the evidence of professional opinion adduced in the case did not constitute evidence that the particular opinion in question was one to which a responsible body of the particular profession subscribed;

iii where no special skill was required to determine whether there had been negligence.

In such cases, it would appear, the court can supply any lack of expert evidence by the application of its own judgment and common sense'.

It is convenient to adopt these three headings for further exposition.

[1]   See *[2001] BLR 99* at 107.
[2]   See *(2000) 76 Con LR 131* at para 26.

(i) Where professional opinion is not logically supportable

[6.03]   It is noteworthy that in the passage from *Bolam's* case, quoted above, McNair J referred to a *'responsible'* body of expert opinion. This was subsequently emphasised by Lord Browne-Wilkinson in the House of Lords in *Bolitho v City and Hackney Health Authority*[1], who said:

' … the court has to be satisfied that the exponents of the body of opinion relied on can demonstrate that such opinion has a logical basis. In particular, in cases involving, as they often do, the weighing of risks against benefits, the judge before accepting a body of opinion as being responsible, reasonable or respect-able, will need to be satisfied that, in forming their views, the experts have directed their minds to the question of comparative risks and benefits and have reached a defensible conclusion on the matter … if, in a rare case, it can be demonstrated that the professional opinion is not capable of withstanding logical analysis, the judge is entitled to hold that the body of opinion is not reasonable or responsible'.

Thus the court will occasionally be willing to hold that a widely accepted method of professional practice was itself negligent[2].

[1]   See *[1998] AC 232* at 243, *[1997] 4 All ER 771* at 778–9.
[2]   See *Edward Wong Finance Co v Johnson Stokes & Master (a firm) [1984] AC 296 PC.* Cf *Patel v Daybells [2002] PNLR 6.* See also *Hucks v Cole (1968) [1993] 4 Med LR 393.*

Difficult to establish

[6.04]   The situations in which the court will be willing to condemn established professional practice in this way, however, will necessarily be rare. One case in which such an attempt was made unsuccessfully is that of *Calver v Westwood Veterinary Group*[1]. The claimant's mare died as a result of a rare infection following equine abortion. It was alleged that the defendant veterinary surgeon had been negligent in not administering antibiotics. The expert evidence called for the defence, which supported the decision not to administer antibiotics, was attacked as being illogical. The attack succeeded at trial, but the decision in the claimant's favour was reversed in the Court of Appeal. Simon Brown LJ said[2]:

' … the judge's findings … based on his assessment of the risk/benefit analysis … really came down to this: antibiotics are cheap and easy to administer. Unless, therefore, in respect of any given abortion the vet can be 100 per cent sure that there is no risk whatever of infection (which would hardly ever be the case) he is bound to administer prophylactic antibiotics. If that, indeed, were regarded as the only logical approach and this judgment were to stand, then, it is plain … there will have to be a great deal more prophylactic use of antibiotics in future than in the past'.

In reaching its conclusion the court noted that official bodies had sought to discourage the widespread prophylactic use of antibiotics[3]. That this was taken to be a relevant factor highlights the range of considerations which may legitimately be taken into account by a profession in weighing 'risks and benefits', without the conclusion reached being condemned as 'illogical'; it would appear that they can include policy issues which might go beyond the immediate interests of the particular claimant.

[1]   *[2001] Lloyd's Rep PN 102.*
[2]   See above at para 32.
[3]   See *[2001] Lloyd's Rep PN 102* at para 28.

(ii) Opinion not representative

[6.05]   In *Merivale Moore plc v Strutt & Parker*[1] Buxton LJ said in relation to professional negligence cases that:

> 'The judge … can only determine such disputes on the basis of evidence about professional practice: albeit evidence that he will approach critically, and with due regard to how representative it can be shown to be'.

Clearly the court must be satisfied that the evidence adduced, on behalf of either claimant or defendant, is genuinely representative of a 'responsible body' of professional opinion, and does not consist simply of a statement of what the individual witness would himself have done if confronted with the situation in question.

[1]   See *[1999] 2 EGLR 171, CA* at p 178.

Standards differing from those of average practitioner

[6.06]   While no doubt usually striving to be impartial, there is a danger that defence experts may be subconsciously influenced by sympathy for a colleague. And on the claimant's side there is a danger that the particular witness may be a paragon whose practice is of a higher standard than that reasonably to be expected of the average practitioner[1]. In *Royal Brompton Hospital NHS Trust v Hammond (No 6)*[2], in which the expert evidence for the claimant was rejected as inadequate, Judge Richard Seymour QC put it as follows[3]:

> 'It is, in my judgment, essential for an expert witness in the trial of a professional negligence action to perform what is actually a very difficult task, at least unless one is experienced in doing it, and that is to put on one side his own personal professional standards and to concentrate on the standards of the ordinarily competent member of his profession. There is a natural temptation to regard one's own standards as those which should be shared by all member's of one's profession, but as those who are approached to act as expert witnesses are often

approached just because they are especially prominent members of their profession or particularly experienced it is a temptation which must be resisted'.

[1] See *Hammersmith Hospitals NHS Trust v Troup Bystanders and Anders (a firm) [2001] EWCA Civ 793*.
[2] *(2000) 76 Con LR 131*. See also *76 Con LR 148* (Court of Appeal rejected an application for permission to appeal).
[3] See *(2000) 76 Con LR 131* at para 21

Limited precautions may be acceptable

[6.07] In *Bradford-Smart v West Sussex CC[1]* the Court of Appeal was concerned with the extent to which a school might be under an obligation to take measures to prevent bullying which occurred off the premises outside school hours. Although expert evidence for the claimant was to the effect that some schools had instituted patrols to address the problem, the court considered that this was a 'matter of discretion rather than duty' and, applying the *Bolam* test, concluded that 'enough had been done'[2].

[1] *[2002] 1 FCR 425*.
[2] See above at paras 32 and 36 *per* Judge LJ delivering the judgment of the court.

(iii) No special skill required

[6.08] In *Royal Brompton Hospital NHS Trust v Hammond (No 6)[1]* Judge Richard Seymour QC said:

'In a case such as the present, if I am satisfied on the evidence that an obvious mistake was made which would not have been made by any careful person of whatever profession, or, indeed, of none, then I can find that the person who made that mistake was negligent'.

Thus in the earlier case of *JD Williams & Co v Michael Hyde & Associates[2]* the Court of Appeal agreed with the trial judge who had held that an architect's decision not to make further investigations into a matter of concern, and instead simply to accept at face value assurances received after the making of initial inquiries, was not a matter for the application of special professional skill. The *Bolam* test was therefore inapplicable, and a finding that the architect had been negligent was upheld.

[1] See *(2000) 76 Con LR 131* at para 26.
[2] See *[2000] Lloyd's Rep PN 823* at para 30.

The court and the expert

[6.09] A judge who rejects expert evidence will normally be expected to give detailed reasons for so doing. In *Eckersley v Binnie*, Bingham LJ said[1]:

'In resolving conflicts of expert evidence, the judge remains the judge; he is not obliged to accept evidence simply because it comes from an illustrious source; he can take account of demonstrated partisanship and lack of objectivity. But, save where an expert is guilty of a deliberate attempt to mislead (as happens only very rarely), a coherent reasoned opinion expressed by a suitably qualified expert should be the subject of a coherent reasoned rebuttal, unless it can be discounted for other good reasons'.

Failure by the judge to provide appropriate reasons will, in itself, constitute a ground of appeal since, without them, the parties will not be in a position to evaluate their own chances of seeking a reversal of the decision². Expert witnesses, for their part, and those commissioning them, should ensure that their evidence is focussed on the appropriate issues, and that irrelevance and excessive length are avoided. Failure to do so is to invite adverse judicial comment and, potentially, penalties in costs³.

¹　See *(1988) 18 Con LR 1* at 77–78 (a dissenting judgment, but that is not material to the passage quoted).
²　See *Flannery v Halifax Estate Agencies Ltd [2000] 1 All ER 373, [2000] 1 WLR 377*, CA. See also *English v Emery Reimbold & Strick [2002] 3 All ER 385*.
³　See *per* Dyson J in *Pozzolanic v Bryan Hobson Associates [1999] Lloyd's Rep PN 125* ('Postcript on experts' reports').

Defendants who never addressed the issues

[6.10]　What if a defendant in a professional negligence action never consciously thought the matter through, but is nevertheless able to adduce a responsible body of opinion in support of what he actually *did*? Can such a defendant successfully invoke the *Bolam* principle to avoid liability? In *Adams v Rhymney Valley DC¹* the defendant council fitted, without significant deliberation upon the matter, a certain type of window lock in its council houses. In a tragic fire, the windows could not be opened and three children perished. When the council was sued for negligence it established that a respectable body of opinion could legitimately have decided, after a careful balancing of the risks involved, to install the same kind of lock. The relevant risks were ease of escape during fire as against small children opening the windows and falling out. Sedley LJ, in a vigorous dissent in the Court of Appeal, argued that since the council had never balanced the risks it could not invoke the *Bolam* principle in its defence. But the majority, Morritt LJ and Sir Christopher Staughton, rejected this view and held that the council could successfully invoke the principle so as to avoid liability.

¹　*(2001) 3 LGLR 9*, CA.

Advice cases

[6.11]　It is to be noted that *Adams v Rhymney Valley DC* concerned specific *action* which the defendants had carried out; it might be more difficult for defendants who had given *advice* to escape liability by reliance upon the *Bolam* principle, if they had never addressed the issues. This is because the quality of advice will often be inseparably dependent upon the reasoning underlying it. Nevertheless, reliance upon the *Bolam* principle will not automatically be precluded in advice cases. In one case Chadwick LJ said, obiter, the following¹:

> 'If the advice is correct, it may well be irrelevant whether the adviser hit upon it as the result of careful and detailed thought, or as a result of experience which overrode the need for detailed analysis of the reasoning process, or purely by luck. I would not endorse the view that, in every case, a professional adviser will be held negligent because he does not spell out in detail the reasons which led him to the advice which he gives'.

¹　See *Green v Hancocks (a firm) [2001] Lloyd's Rep PN 212*, CA

145

B State of knowledge

[6.12] Speaking very broadly, professional expertise may be divided into two component parts: possession of the relevant *knowledge* on the one hand, and the application of *skill* on the other. The body of professional knowledge in any field increases in size as time goes by, and the court will endeavour to avoid hindsight in determining whether the defendant's state of knowledge was such as could reasonably have been expected of him prior to the accident. Thus, in *Roe v Minister of Health[1]* the plaintiffs were paralysed after being injected, for minor operations, with an anaesthetic solution which had been contaminated. The possibility of such contamination, through invisible cracks in the containers in which the solution had been kept, was not known to the medical profession before this tragic case brought it to light; and an appropriate warning was then inserted in to the textbooks. The defendants were acquitted of negligence but, as Denning LJ pointed out, 'nowadays it would be negligence not to realise the danger, but it was not then'.[2]

[1] *[1954] 2 QB 66, [1954] 2 All ER 131, CA.* See also *McLean v Weir and Goff [1980] 4 WWR 330 (Can).*
[2] *[1954] 2 QB 66 at 86, [1954] 2 All ER 131 at 139, CA.*

Obscure professional literature

[6.13] If the knowledge which would have prevented the accident which occurred to the claimant did exist, but only buried in relatively obscure professional literature, difficult questions of fact may arise as to the extent of the professional person's duty to delve into such literature before giving advice or embarking on a course of action. In *Vacwell Engineering Co Ltd v BDH Chemicals Ltd[1]* an explosion occurred which could have been avoided if the defendants' chemists had consulted pre-war textbooks which contained a warning of the particular risk, based on experiments carried out by a nineteenth-century French chemist. Unfortunately, the leading modern textbooks, which were consulted, omitted any reference to the risk. The trial judge nevertheless held the defendants liable for negligence for failing to 'carry out an adequate research into the scientific literature'.[2] On the other hand a phenomenon may be so obscure that, *even if* reasonable attempts *had* been made to investigate it, the probability is that the appropriate scientific information would not have been unearthed. In that event, a defendant who negligently failed to do sufficient research will nevertheless succeed in avoiding liability on the ground that causation had not been proved[3].

[1] *[1971] 1 QB 88, [1969] 3 All ER 1681.*
[2] *[1971] 1 QB 88 at 109, [1969] 3 All ER 1681* at 1698. An appeal by the defendants was subsequently settled on terms broadly favourable to the plaintiffs: see *[1971] 1 QB 111n.*
[3] See *JD Williams & Co v Maxwell Hyde & Associates [2000] Lloyd's Rep PN 823, CA* ('phenolic yellowing').

C Errors of judgment

[6.14] In most professions, part of the 'skill' component of expertise will include a capacity for the making of fine judgments. Merely because such a judgment subsequently turns out to have been 'wrong', in the sense that, with hindsight, it can be seen that adopting a different course would have produced a better result, does not of itself constitute negligence. In attempting to express this with clarity, Lord Denning MR in *Whitehouse v Jordan[1]* drew a sharp distinction between mere 'errors of judgment' on the one hand and 'negligence' on the other. When the case reached the House of Lords, however, the distinction was condemned as a 'false antithesis'.² Lord Fraser expressed himself as follows:³

'Merely to describe something as an error of judgment tells us nothing about whether it is negligent or not; it depends on the nature of the error. If it is one that would not have been made by a reasonably competent professional man professing to have the standard and type of skill that the defendant held himself out as having, and acting with ordinary care, then it is negligent. If, on the other hand, it is an error that a man, acting with ordinary care, might have made, then it is not negligence.'

But whether or not the concept of an 'error of judgment' as a term of art is regarded with disfavour, the practical importance of the approach which that expression was used to denote remains unchanged. The court will not attempt to 'second-guess', nor will it lightly condemn, a competent professional person doing his best to exercise his judgment in an uncertain situation.⁴

¹   See *[1980] 1 All ER 650* at 658, CA.
²   See *[1981] 1 All ER 267* at 276, *[1981] 1 WLR 246* at 257–258. See also *per* Donaldson LJ in the Court of Appeal: *[1980] 1 All ER 650* at 662.
³   *[1981] 1 All ER 267* at 281, *[1981] 1 WLR 246* at 263.
⁴   See *Watts v Savills [1998] 25 LS Gaz R 34, CA*. Cf *Stafford v Conti Commodity Services Ltd [1981] 1 All ER 691, [1981] 1 Lloyd's Rep 466*.

D Denial of duty

[6.15]   If the defendant did not owe a duty of care to the claimant, the application of the *Bolam* test for evaluation of conduct will necessarily be pre-empted. In some cases judicial reluctance for policy reasons to expose professional people to negligence litigation has indeed led the court to deny the existence of a duty of care, usually by asserting that the imposition of such a duty would not be 'just and reasonable'. Thus, social workers and psychiatrists working in the 'extraordinarily delicate' field of child abuse were once held not to 'assume any general professional duty of care' to the children involved.¹ And in another local government context it has been held that a district auditor 'must be free to criticise an officer of the local authority without fear of exposing himself to an action for negligence at the suit of that officer'.² More recently, however, that the tide in favour of denial of duty in this way has receded significantly, partly due to the influence of the European Convention on Human Rights³. The end of the advocate's immunity is a powerful example of how blanket protection of professional people from negligence liability is no longer considered appropriate⁴.

¹   See *X v Bedfordshire County Council [1995] 2 AC 633* at 750, 753, *[1995] 3 All ER 353* at 381, 384, HL, *per* Lord Browne-Wilkinson (but cf *per* Lord Nolan, *[1995] 2 AC 633* at 772, *[1995] 3 All ER 353* at 400).
²   See *West Wiltshire District Council v Garland [1995] Ch 297* at 312, *[1995] 2 All ER 17* at 27, CA, *per* Balcombe LJ. Cf *Rich (Marc) & Co AG v Bishop Rock Marine Co Ltd [1996] AC 211, [1995] 3 All ER 307, HL* (marine surveyor).

[6.15]   *General principles[1]*

[3]   See *Barrett v Enfield London BC [1999] 3 All ER 193, HL.* See also *Phelps v Hillingdon London Borough Council [2000] 4 All ER 504.* See, generally CHAPTER 1.
[4]   See below CHAPTER 8.

Chapter 7

Clinical negligence

A Difficulties of proof

[7.01]   The cost of clinical negligence claims to the National Health Service has increased dramatically in recent years[1]. A major factor has been a significant change in the method of assessing damages[2]; but an increase in the overall number of claims resulting from a greater readiness to sue, assisted by the introduction of conditional fee agreements, would also appear to have played a part[3]. It is unlikely that the figures reflect any change in the general attitude of the courts towards such cases, in the sense of their being more ready than formerly to find them proved. Although the standard of proof to be applied in cases of alleged clinical negligence is in theory no different from that applicable elsewhere, there does in the past appear to have been a degree of reluctance on the part of the courts to hold that a doctor had been careless unless the evidence was particularly clear.[4] This attitude may have undergone a degree of change in recent years, but not to an extent that could itself have led to the dramatic increase in the overall cost of liability to the National Health Service.

1   In 2003, the National Audit Office reported that in 2001–2002 the National Health Service paid out £446 million, which was £31 million more than the previous year. The overall anticipated liability for current or expected claims then stood at £5.25 billion, which was more than double the figure for 1998.
2   See especially *Wells v Wells [1999] 1 AC 345, [1998] 3 All ER 481, HL*, discussed in CHAPTER 25 below.
3   See the report of the Public Accounts Committee on clinical negligence (2002).
4   In 1978 the Report of the *Royal Commission on Civil Liability and Compensation for Personal Injury* (Pearson) (Cmnd 7054–I) reported that: 'The proportion of successful claims for damages in tort is much lower for medical negligence than for all negligence cases. Some payment is made in 30–40% of claims compared with 86% of all personal injury claims.' (para 284). See also M A Jones 'Medical Negligence – The Burden of Proof' (1984) 134 NLJ 7.

Difficulties faced by claimants

[7.02]   Where obvious blunders have been made, such as the administration of wrong drugs or dosages with fatal results,[1] compensation will invariably be forthcoming without resort to litigation.[2] But if a case is sufficiently uncertain to be remotely worth fighting, it appears that the claimant will often face considerable difficulty in establishing his claim.[3] The deference frequently shown towards expert witnesses called for the defence is one factor[4]. It is in contrast to the approach adopted in cases of alleged negligence by lawyers, where even the introduction of such evidence is discouraged[5]. And even if the trial judge can be persuaded to find a case proved, there is some indication from decisions in the relatively recent past that the appellate courts will be more generous, than they usually are to defendants, in allowing what are

149

essentially questions of fact to be ventilated afresh on appeal.[6] Nor will the maxim *res ipsa loquitur* readily be invoked to assist the claimant.[7] There would appear to have been three reasons for this judicial reluctance to find negligence proved in medical cases. The first was a recognition of the fact that the response of the human body to treatment can rarely be predicted beyond all doubt, and that 'medical science has not yet reached the stage where the law ought to presume that a patient must come out of an operation as well or better than he went into it'.[8] The second reason was one of policy: anxiety to discourage the development of excessive 'medical malpractice' litigation along the lines perceived to exist in America, with its supposed disadvantages including causing doctors to practise 'defensive medicine' through constant fear of lawsuits.[9] The third reason was a particular solicitude for the standing of individual doctors who are alleged to have transgressed.[10] It is possible, however, that the contemporary judiciary is disposed to subject defence evidence in clinical negligence cases to closer scrutiny than was the practice in the past, so that claimants may no longer face quite the same uphill struggle as that experienced by their predecessors.

[1]   See *Strangeways-Lesmere v Clayton [1936] 2 KB 11, [1936] 1 All ER 484; Collins v Hertfordshire County Council [1947] KB 598, [1947] 1 All ER 633, Bovenzi v Kettering Health Authority [1991] 2 Med LR 293*; See also *Kralj v McGrath [1986] 1 All ER 54* (' … horrific treatment, completely unacceptable, breaking all the rules … '). Cf *Prendergast v Sam and Dee Ltd [1989] 1 Med LR 36, CA* (doctor liable, along with pharmacist, where bad handwriting on a prescription caused pharmacist to supply wrong drug).

[2]   Nevertheless, proving *causation* of harm may still be an insurmountable obstacle even if breach of duty is established (see below).

[3]   Cf Lord Ackner 'The Doctor in Court – Victim or Protected Species?' (1992) 8 PN 54.

[4]   See *Maynard v West Midlands Health Authority [1985] 1 All ER 635, [1984] 1 WLR 634, HL* (discussed below at para [7.13]).

[5]   See CHAPTER 8 below.

[6]   See the majority decision of the Court of Appeal in *Whitehouse v Jordan [1980] 1 All ER 650, CA* and its affirmation by the House of Lords: *[1981] 1 All ER 267, [1981] 1 WLR 246*. See also *Maynard v West Midlands Regional Health Authority [1985] 1 All ER 635, [1984] 1 WLR 634, HL*. For criticism of *Whitehouse v Jordan* see G Robertson in (1981) 44 MLR 457.

[7]   See *Girard v Royal Columbian Hospital (1976) 66 DLR (3d) 676 (Can)*. But cf *Cassidy v Ministry of Health [1951] 2 KB 343, [1951] 1 All ER 574, CA*.

[8]   *Girard v Royal Columbian Hospital (1976) 66 DLR (3d) 676* at 691 (Can). See also *per* Lawton LJ in *Whitehouse v Jordan [1980] 1 All ER 650* at 659, CA: 'Medical practice these days consists of the harmonious union of science with skill. Medicine has not yet got to the stage, and maybe it never will, when the adoption of a particular procedure will produce a certain result.'

[9]   See eg *per* Lord Denning MR in *Whitehouse v Jordan [1980] 1 All ER 650* at 658, CA. See also *per* Lawton LJ (at 659).

[10]   'In my opinion allegations of negligence against medical practitioners should be considered as serious … the defendant's professional reputation is under attack. A finding of negligence against him may jeopardise his career and cause him substantial financial loss over many years': *per* Lawton LJ in *Whitehouse v Jordan [1980] 1 All ER 650* at 659, CA.

Proposals for change

[7.03]   The question whether a different way could be found of dealing with medical mishaps, instead of the law of tort, has often been debated. In 2003 the Chief Medical Officer published a consultation paper called *Making Amends*. The proposals include a special redress scheme to speed up the claims process, with powers to award up to £30,000; and special provisions for the families of babies brain-damaged at birth. Of particular significance is a suggestion to introduce a concept of 'sub-standard care', easier to establish than common law negligence, as a basis for the award of compensation under the proposed scheme. Even if the scheme were to be implemented, however, at least some patients could be expected to continue to seek redress through the courts; not least because the damages obtainable in successful negligence claims would be greater than the level of awards available under the scheme.

B Standard of care

General duty

[7.04] Reported instances of successful negligence claims in recent years have included failure to detect a pulmonary embolus[1], an error during a sterilisation operation[2], inadequate post-operative care following spinal surgery[3], and failure to diagnose deep vein thrombosis[4]. A doctor must always show the degree of skill appropriate to his post and the duties required of him, even though the tradition of 'learning on the job' may mean that an unrealistically high level of competence is thereby required of junior medical staff. This tradition has therefore not resulted in any qualification being made to the principle that the care taken must be evaluated against a generally established standard of reasonableness. 'To my mind', observed Mustill LJ in *Wilsher v Essex Area Health Authority*,[5] 'it would be a false step to subordinate the legitimate expectation of the patient that he will receive from each person concerned with his care a degree of skill appropriate to the task which he undertakes to an understandable wish to minimise the psychological and financial pressures on hard-pressed young doctors'.[6]

[1] See *Hutton v East Dyfed HA [1998] Lloyd's Rep Med 335*.
[2] See *Taylor v Shropshire HA [1998] Lloyd's Rep Med 395*.
[3] See *Newbury v Bath DHA (1998) 47 BMLR 138*.
[4] See *Starcevic West Hertfordshire HA (2001) 60 BMLR 221*.
[5] *[1987] QB 730* at 751, *[1986] 3 All ER 801* at 813, CA.
[6] See also *per* Glidewell LJ, *[1986] 3 All ER 801* at 831. Sir Nicolas Browne-Wilkinson V-C dissented on this point: see *[1986] 3 All ER 801* at 833. *Wilsher*'s case subsequently went to the House of Lords (*[1988] AC 1074, [1988] 1 All ER 871*), but this aspect of the opinions expressed in the Court of Appeal was not considered.

Context

[7.05] In *Knight v Home Office*,[1] Pill J said that 'the standard of care required will vary with the context. The facilities available to deal with an emergency in a general practitioner's surgery cannot be expected to be as ample as those available in the casualty department of a general hospital, for example'. In *Knight*'s case itself, which involved an unsuccessful claim with respect to a suicide by a mentally ill prisoner, Pill J was 'unable to accept that the practices in a prison hospital are to be judged in all respects by the standard appropriate to a psychiatric hospital outside prison. There may be circumstances in which the standard of care in a prison falls below that which would be expected in a psychiatric hospital without the prison authority being negligent'.[2] *Knight*'s case should not, however, be regarded as an authority to justify any general *reduction* in the level of health care in particular situations. In the case itself Pill J emphasised that the Home Office could not have sought to justify inadequate medical facilities in prisons on the ground of lack of resources[3]. Moreover, in the later case of *Brooks v Home Office*[4], which was concerned with the allegedly negligent treatment in prison of an expectant mother[5], Garland J said:

'I cannot regard *Knight* as authority for the proposition that the plaintiff should not, while detained in Holloway, be entitled to expect the same level of antenatal care, both for herself and her unborn infants, as if she were at liberty, subject of course to the constraints of having to be escorted and, to some extent, movement being retarded by those requirements'.

1 *[1990] 3 All ER 237* at 243.
2 *[1990] 3 All ER 237* at 243.
3 See above, at the same page.
4 See *[1999] 2 FLR 33*.
5 The claim ultimately failed on the facts.

Resources

[7.06] At the same time, however, the courts are not oblivious to the realities of financial constraint faced by health providers. Thus, in *Knight's* case Pill J also observed that 'in making the decision as to the standard to be demanded the court must … bear in mind as one factor that resources available for the public service are limited and that the allocation of resources is a matter for Parliament'[1]. In *Hardaker v Newcastle HA*[2] Stanley Burnton J similarly observed that he was 'in no position to criticise the Authority's allocation of its doubtlessly limited resources' when it decided not to devote substantial sums to the treatment of divers' 'bends', of which there were only about four cases per year in its area.

1 See *[1990] 3 All ER 237* at 243.
2 See *[2001] Lloyd's Rep Med 512* at para 57.

Practitioners of alternative medicine

[7.07] In *Shakoor v Situ*[1] the question arose as to the standard of care to be expected of a practitioner of non-orthodox medicine, in this case traditional Chinese herbal medicine. The defendant, who was not qualified to register as an orthodox medical practitioner in Britain, recommended a herbal remedy for a skin condition for which the only recognised orthodox treatment was elective surgery. The patient unfortunately suffered an idiosyncratic reaction to the drug and died from liver failure. Bernard Livesey QC, sitting as a deputy High Court judge, held that the application of the *Bolam*[2] test in such a situation could not be based on the standard to be expected of orthodox medical practitioners, but nor could it be based exclusively on the practices of those engaged in traditional Chinese herbal medicine. The requisite standard would have regard to the fact that the alternative medicine was being practised in a society in which health care is monitored, and practitioners of alternative medicine would be expected to keep up to date with developments in orthodox medicine in so far as they reported adverse reactions to the drugs he was using. Although the defendant succeeded in avoiding liability on the ground that he had not fallen below the standard thus identified, the judge outlined the position as follows[3]:

'First of all, the practitioner has to recognise that he is holding himself out as competent to practise within a system of law which will review the standard of care he has given to a patient. Secondly, where he prescribes a remedy which is taken by a patient it is not enough to say that the remedy is traditional and believed not to be harmful, he has a duty to ensure that the remedy is not actually or potentially harmful. Thirdly, he must recognise the probability that any person suffering an adverse reaction to such a remedy is quite likely to find his way into an orthodox hospital and the incident may well be "written up" in one or other of the orthodox medical journals. An alternative practitioner who prescribes a remedy must take steps to satisfy himself that there has not been any adverse report in such journals on the remedy which ought to affect the use he makes of it'.

¹   *[2000] 4 All ER 181.*
²   See below and also CHAPTER 6 above.
³   See *[2000] 4 All ER 181* at 189.

C Relevance of common practice

[7.08]   The courts will very rarely be persuaded to condemn as careless methods of treatment which the defendant is able, with the assistance of expert witnesses, to show was not unusual. 'A doctor is not guilty of negligence', said McNair J in *Bolam v Friern Hospital Management Committee*,¹ 'if he has acted in accordance with a practice accepted as proper by a responsible body of medical men skilled in that particular art'.² The House of Lords has emphasised, however, the importance of the word 'responsible' in this classic passage.³ The court does not wholly abdicate in the face of medical evidence: it needs to be satisfied that that evidence 'has a logical basis'.⁴ Nevertheless, attempts to convince the court that a generally accepted practice was itself negligent, which may occasionally succeed in other contexts,⁵ will be a particularly daunting forensic task in the medical area.

¹   *[1957] 2 All ER 118* at 122, *[1957] 1 WLR 582* at 587. See also *Sidaway v Bethlem Royal Hospital Governors [1985] AC 871, [1985] 1 All ER 643, HL.*
²   The *Bolam* test is also applicable to situations involving mental patients not competent to give consent to treatment: *F v West Berkshire Health Authority [1990] 2 AC 1, [1989] 2 All ER 545, HL* (see, especially, *per* Lord Brandon, *[1990] 2 AC 1* at 68, *[1989] 2 All ER 545* at 560, disagreeing with the Court of Appeal, which had favoured a special, more stringent, test for such cases).
³   See *Bolitho v City and Hackney Health Authority [1998] AC 232* at 241–242, *[1997] 4 All ER 771* at 778, HL, *per* Lord Browne-Wilkinson.
⁴   *[1997] 4 All ER 771* at 778. See further below.
⁵   See *Morris v West Hartlepool Steam Navigation Co [1956] AC 552, [1956] 1 All ER 385, HL; Cavanagh v Ulster Weaving Co [1960] AC 145, [1959] 2 All ER 745, HL.*

Changes in practice

[7.09]   Nor will *deviation* from a generally accepted practice apparently be in itself enough even to shift the burden of proof on to the defendant doctor.¹ In *Newbury v Bath AHA*² the defendant accepted that he was 'probably the only mainline surgeon' still using a particular method of spinal surgery in 1991. Although one of the claimant's experts considered that the use of the method, 'Harrington's rods' was, in the circumstances, 'an accident waiting to happen' there was no evidence that the technique had been generally condemned, and the court held that the defendant had been entitled to use a method with which he was familiar even if it had become unusual³. Moreover, even if developments in practice mean that particular treatment would in fact no longer be considered appropriate, the court will be scrupulous not to use hindsight when applying the *Bolam* test, and will endeavour to ensure that the treatment is judged by the standards prevailing at the time when it was administered⁴.

¹   See *Wilsher v Essex Area Health Authority [1987] QB 730, [1986] 3 All ER 801, CA*, overruling a dictum of Peter Pain J in *Clark v MacLennan [1983] 1 All ER 416.*
²   *(1998) 47 BMLR 138.*
³   The claim nevertheless succeeded on the ground that the post-operative care had been negligent in failing to detect the need to remove the rods before damage resulting from them had become irreversible.

⁴   See *Nawoor v Barking Havering and Brentwood HA [1998] Lloyd's Rep Med 313.*

Administrative practices

[7.10]   Where the alleged negligence relates not to clinical practices as such, but rather to the *administrative system* within which those practices were carried out, the position is slightly different and 'expert' evidence is potentially less compelling. Claims have, for example, succeeded on the basis of inadequate supervision by senior medical staff of their juniors.¹ It has been suggested, obiter, by two members of the Court of Appeal,² that the overall management position of a hospital might be made the basis of negligence liability towards individual patients. It is submitted that this suggestion is an attractive one, notwithstanding the need to persuade the court in each case that the matter is within the province of the law of negligence and does not raise non-justiciable policy questions³ relating to the allocation of scarce resources.⁴

¹   See *Jones v Manchester Corpn [1952] 2 QB 852, [1952] 2 All ER 125; Drake v Pontefract HA [1998] Lloyd's Rep Med 425.* See also *Collins v Hertfordshire County Council [1947] KB 598, [1947] 1 All ER 633.*
²   Sir Nicolas Browne-Wilkinson V-C and Glidewell LJ in *Wilsher v Essex Area Health Authority [1987] QB 730, [1986] 3 All ER 801, CA.* For discussion see J Montgomery *Suing Hospitals Direct: What Tort?* (1987) NLJ 703. See also CHAPTER 18 below.
³   Cf *Department of Health and Social Security v Kinnear (1984) 134 NLJ 886.* See, generally, Newdick *Whom Should We Treat?,* O.U.P., 2nd edn, 2005.
⁴   For discussion of the negligence liability of public bodies see generally CHAPTER 15 below.

D Questions of fact

Factual issues distinct from judgements

[7.11]   It is important to bear in mind that the *Bolam* test is confined to questions of professional *judgment,* and does not apply to questions of *fact.* This was emphasised by the Court of Appeal in *Penney v East Kent HA*¹, in which negligence was held to have been established in several claims concerning cervical smear tests. The court was required to determine, on the facts, what slides taken from the claimants actually revealed. Even though the assistance of experts was needed to make the determination, and their evidence conflicted, the question remained one of fact which the court was obliged conclusively to determine.

¹   *[2000] Lloyd's Rep Med 41.*

Causation

[7.12]   It is important to note that the *Bolam* test similarly has no place in determining questions of *causation,* which is also a question of fact to be determined ultimately by the court, albeit with the assistance of expert witnesses. Proving causation can prove a formidable obstacle in medical cases, even if carelessness is undoubted.¹ In *Bolitho v City and Hackney Health Authority*² a two-year-old boy suffered catastrophic brain damage as a result of respiratory failure while he was in hospital for treatment for croup. Although the doctor responsible failed to attend the patient when summoned by a nurse, which was conceded in the circumstances to have been a breach of duty, it was nevertheless held that, even if the doctor had attended, the tragedy would not have been prevented.[3] The claim therefore failed. Other recent cases in which claims have failed on the ground of lack of proof of causation, notwithstanding proven or admitted breaches of duty, have concerned situations such as delays in treatment[4], failure promptly to diagnose pre-eclampsia in an expectant mother[5], and failure to keep a student under proper observation in a college sick-bay[6].

[1]   See *Kay v Ayrshire and Arran Health Board [1987] 2 All ER 417, HL*: no liability for administration of dose of penicillin 30 times greater than that prescribed to patient suffering from meningitis; causal link with subsequent brain damage not proved. See also *Wilsher v Essex Area Health Authority [1988] AC 1074, [1988] 1 All ER 871, HL.*

[2]   *[1998] AC 232, [1997] 4 All ER 771, HL.*

[3]   Although there was an effective measure which could have been taken to prevent what occurred, the defendant doctor satisfied the court that she would not have chosen to adopt it even if she *had* attended. The court was also satisfied that in making that choice the defendant would have been acting in accordance with a responsible body of medical opinion: the *Bolam* test *was* relevant to *that* aspect of the case (see below).

[4]   See *Brooks v Home Office [1999] 2 FLR 33.*

[5]   See *R v Tilsey (2001) 60 BMLR 202.*

[6]   See *Morera-Loftus v Wray Castle Ltd [1999] Lloyd's Rep Med 159.*

E Where there are differing professional schools of thought

[7.13]   It may sometimes be the case that professional opinion is divided as to the most appropriate procedure to adopt in a particular situation. In such a case the court will not see its function as being to decide which of the rival contentions is the better. On the contrary, a doctor will normally succeed in negating liability if he shows that his approach is regarded as proper by one well-established school of thought, notwithstanding that there exists an equally well-established school of thought to the opposite effect. The leading case is *Maynard v West Midlands Regional Health Authority*.[1] The defendants carried out an operation for diagnostic purposes which, although properly conducted, carried the inherent risk of permanent impairment of the patient's power of speech. The risk unfortunately materialised and the plaintiff alleged that the operation had been unnecessary, in that ample evidence on which to make a diagnosis had existed without it. This contention was supported by a powerful expert witness, whose evidence the trial judge preferred to that of the defendants' expert witnesses. He accordingly found for the plaintiff, but his decision was reversed by the Court of Appeal and this reversal was upheld by the House of Lords. The House held, in effect, that the judge had been wrong to seek to make a choice between the views expressed by the expert witnesses on the two sides.[2] Lord Scarman put it as follows:[3]

> 'A case which is based on an allegation that a fully considered decision of two consultants in the field of their special skill was negligent clearly presents certain difficulties of proof. It is not enough to show that there is a body of competent professional opinion which considers that theirs was a wrong decision, if there also exists a body of professional opinion, equally competent, which supports that decision as reasonable in the circumstances ... [A] judge's "preference" for one body of distinguished professional opinion to another also professionally distinguished is not sufficient to establish negligence in a practitioner whose actions have received the seal of approval of those whose opinions, truthfully expressed, honestly held, were not preferred.'[4]

[1]   *[1985] 1 All ER 635, [1984] 1 WLR 634 HL.* See also *Bolam v Friern Hospital Management Committee [1957] 2 All ER 118, [1957] 1 WLR 582; Newbury v Bath DHA (1999) 47 B M L R 138.*

[2]   See also *Hughes v Waltham Forest Health Authority [1991] 2 Med LR 155, CA.*

[3]   *[1985] 1 All ER 635* at 638–639, *[1984] 1 WLR 634* at 638–639.

4 See also *per* Slade LJ in the non-medical case of *Luxmoore-May v Messenger May Baverstock [1990] 1 All ER 1067* at 1076: 'The valuation of pictures of which the artist is unknown, pre-eminently involves an exercise of opinion and judgment, most particularly in deciding whether an attribution to any particular artist should be made. Since it is not an exact science, the judgment in the very nature of things may be fallible, and may turn out to be wrong. Accordingly, provided that the valuer has done his job honestly and with due diligence, I think that the court should be cautious before convicting him of professional negligence.'

Professional opinion must have a logical basis

[7.14] The law relating to cases in which there is a conflict of medical evidence was reviewed by the House of Lords in *Bolitho v City and Hackney Health Authority*.[1] In this case it was accepted that a particular course of action, which had not been adopted, could have prevented the occurrence of cardiac arrest leading to brain damage. There was, however, a sharp conflict between the plaintiff's experts, who claimed that they *would* have administered the relevant treatment, and those of the defendant who claimed that, without the benefit of hindsight, they would *not* have done so: the treatment itself not being risk free. Although the House of Lords upheld a decision in the defendant's favour, applying the test in *Bolam v Friern Hospital Management Committee*, the House also emphasised that the court still had to be satisfied, which very occasionally it might not be,[2] that the expert evidence represented, in the words of Lord Browne-Wilkinson, a 'defensible conclusion' following a focused comparison of 'risks and benefits'.[3] His Lordship concluded as follows:[4]

> ' ... the court is not bound to hold that a defendant doctor escapes liability for negligent treatment or diagnosis just because he leads evidence from a number of medical experts who are genuinely of opinion that the defendant's treatment or diagnosis accorded with sound medical practice ... if, in a rare case, it can be demonstrated that the professional opinion is not capable of withstanding logical analysis, the judge is entitled to hold that the body of opinion is not reasonable or responsible.'

1 *[1998] AC 232, [1997] 4 All ER 771*.
2 See the 1968 decision of the Court of Appeal in *Hucks v Cole* (reported in *[1993] 4 Med LR 393*) in which liability was imposed; Sachs LJ observing that the 'court must be vigilant' to ensure that professional opinion does not 'stem from a residual adherence to out of date ideas'. Cf *Newbury v Bath DHA (1999) 47 DMLR 138* (discussed above at para [7.09]).
3 *[1998] AC 232* at 242, *[1997] 4 All ER 771* at 778.
4 *[1998] AC 232* at 241–243, *[1997] 4 All ER 771* at 778–779.

Rejecting expert opinion

[7.15] In *Marriott v West Midlands RHA*[1] the *Bolitho* test was applied by the judge who, after scrutiny, rejected the expert opinion advanced for the defence. The plaintiff was discharged from hospital following a head injury, but continued to feel unwell. His GP declined, however, to refer him back to hospital. A few days later his condition deteriorated, leaving him permanently disabled. Finding for the plaintiff, the judge held that if a body of expert opinion supported the defendant's failure to seek readmission of the plaintiff to hospital it was imprudent; and the contrary view of the plaintiff's expert was chosen in preference. The judge's decision was upheld by the Court of Appeal, which held that she had been entitled to make her own assessment of the risks and to reject the defence opinion as unreasonable. A judge who rejects an expert opinion is, however, obliged to provide a coherent and fully reasoned justification for so doing[2]. But provided he does so, he is not obliged to state in detail precisely why he considered the evidence of particular experts to have been unhelpful or partial[3].

---

[1] See *[1999] Lloyd's Rep Med 23.*
[2] See *Glicksman v Redbridge NHS Trust (2002) 63 BMLR 109* (retrial ordered).
[3] See *Lakey v Merton Sutton and Wandsworth HA [1999] Lloyd's Rep Med 119, CA.*

F The duty to warn

Absence of warning

[7.16]   In *Sidaway v Governors of Bethlem Royal Hospital*[1] a risk of paralysis, which was attendant upon an operation properly conducted upon the plaintiff in the vicinity of her spinal cord, unfortunately materialised. This particular risk had not been explained to her prior to the operation, and she contended that she would not have gone ahead if it had been. She sued the surgeon alleging that the absence of such a warning constituted negligence.[2] It was accepted that, in omitting the warning, the defendant had been 'following a practice accepted as proper by a responsible body of competent neurosurgeons'.[3] But the plaintiff argued that the test in *Bolam v Friern Hospital Management Committee*[4] should be confined to cases involving criticism of a doctor's *treatment*, as distinct from his explanation and discussion with the patient beforehand. She sought to introduce into English law the doctrine of 'informed consent', with its special emphasis upon a person's autonomy of decision over his own body,[5] which has found favour in north America, including the Supreme Court of Canada.[6] By a majority, Lord Scarman dissenting, the House of Lords rejected the plaintiff's argument and her claim failed. Their Lordships considered that it would be undesirable and unrealistic to draw the suggested distinction in the context of the doctor's overall duty to care for his patient, and expressly affirmed the applicability of the *Bolam* test to allegations of negligence in the context of the doctor-patient relationship generally.[7]

---

[1]   *[1985] AC 871, [1985] 1 All ER 643, HL.*
[2]   Attempts to base claims against doctors in *trespass*, alleging that inadequate disclosure vitiated consent, have met with strong judicial disapproval in England: see *Chatterton v Gerson [1981] QB 432, [1981] 1 All ER 257; Hills v Potter [1983] 3 All ER 716, [1984] 1 WLR 641*n. For discussion of the relationship between trespass and negligence in this context see Tan Keng Feng 'Failure of Medical Advice: Trespass or Negligence?' (1987) 7 LS 149.
[3]   *[1985] 1 AC 871* at 896, *[1985] 1 All ER 643* at 660, *per* Lord Bridge.
[4]   *[1957] 2 All ER 118, [1957] 1 WLR 582.*
[5]   For discussion, see generally G Robertson 'Informed Consent to Medical Treatment' (1981) 97 LQR 102; M Brazier 'Patient Autonomy and Consent to Treatment: the Role of the Law?' (1987) 7 LS 169. See also I Kennedy 'The Patient on the Clapham Omnibus' (1984) 47 MLR 454.
[6]   See *Reibl v Hughes (1980) 114 DLR (3d) 1*, and especially at 13, *per* Laskin CJC.
[7]   See also *Gold v Haringey Health Authority [1988] QB 481, [1987] 2 All ER 888*, in which the Court of Appeal held that the *Bolam* test applied to contraceptive advice, and rejected a suggestion that a distinction should be drawn between 'therapeutic' and 'non-therapeutic' medical advice so as to exclude the *Bolam* test from the latter.

Fuller disclosure sometimes required

[7.17]   The *Sidaway* decision has been criticised on the ground that it is paternalistic in its approach,[1] but it should be noted that there are important indications in the speeches that in two respects fuller disclosure of risks may be required of doctors than an unqualified application of the *Bolam* test might have indicated. First, a patient who asks specific questions must be given full and accurate answers to them:[2] the 'common practice' approach is only relevant as to the appropriateness of *volunteering* information.[3] Secondly, the court reserves the overriding power to hold that the common practice with respect to disclosure in a given situation may be inadequate. In theory, of course, this power always exists, but as far as actual treatment is concerned it is in practice rarely exercised. But there is reason to suppose that in the case of disclosure of risk, where ethical considerations are obviously prominent and the issue itself is not so immediately technical, the court may be rather more ready to exercise the power. Thus, Lord Bridge was 'of opinion that the judge might in certain circumstances come to the conclusion that disclosure of a particular risk was so obviously necessary to an informed choice on the part of the patient that no reasonably prudent medical man would fail to make it'.[4] Both Lord Bridge and Lord Templeman approved of the decision (though not the reasoning) of the Canadian Supreme Court in *Reibl v Hughes*,[5] in which a neurosurgeon who failed to warn his patient of a 10% risk of a stroke, which materialised, was held liable.

[1]   See H Teff 'Consent to Medical Procedures: Paternalism, Self-Determination or Therapeutic Alliance?' (1985) 101 LQR 432.
[2]   But cf *Blyth v Bloomsbury Area Health Authority [1993] 4 Med LR 151, CA*, decided in 1987, (unsuccessful claim by patient who had sought further information before administration of a drug which subsequently caused her harm: no obligation on the hospital to give the patient all the information at its disposal in response to such an inquiry.)
[3]   ' ... when questioned specifically by a patient of apparently sound mind about risks involved in a particular treatment proposed, the doctor's duty must, in my opinion, be to answer both truthfully and as fully as the questioner requires': *per* Lord Bridge in *[1985] AC 871* at 898, *[1985] 1 All ER 643* at 661; see also *[1985] 1 AC 871* at 895, 902, *[1985] All ER 643* at 659, 664, *per* Lord Diplock and Lord Templeman. See also S Lee 'Operating under Informed Consent' (1985) 101 LQR 316.
[4]   *[1985] AC 871* at 900, *[1985] 1 All ER 643* at 663. See also *[1985] AC 871* at 904–905, *[1985] 1 All ER 643* at 665, *per* Lord Templeman. It has also been suggested that the *Sidaway* principles imply the existence of a 'duty of candour' requiring doctors to be frank about what occurred *after* treatment has been given and a mishap has taken place: see *Naylor v Preston Area Health Authority [1987] 2 All ER 353* at 360, *[1987] 1 WLR 958* at 967, CA, *per* Sir John Donaldson MR, re-iterating the views expressed by himself and Mustill LJ in *Lee v South West Thames Regional Health Authority [1985] 2 All ER 385* at 389–390, *[1985] 1 WLR 845* at 850, CA.
[5]   *(1980) 114 DLR (3d) 1.*

Successful claims

[7.18]   In view of the drastic consequences which can result from unsuccessful spinal surgery, as in *Sidaway v Governors of Bethlem Royal Hospital* itself, it is perhaps inevitable that such cases feature prominently among those in which patients have successfully sought to establish that, even under the unqualified *Bolam* test, they were not given an adequate warning[1]. It is clearly important that the risks are not deceptively minimised, even if only to avoid alarming anxious patients[2]. If there are any alternatives to surgery these must be clearly explained. On the other hand, it has been held that it is not essential to volunteer the information that the technique which the surgeon proposes to adopt is unusual[2].

[1]   See *Chester v Afshar [2002] 3 All ER 552*; *Chinchen v University Hospital of Wales [2002] CLY 3251*.
[2]   See *Newbury v Bath DHA (1999) 47 BMLR 138*, sed quaere.

Warning and causation

[7.19]   If a claimant does succeed in proving that a proper warning was not given, his claim will then succeed providing he is able to show that treatment would in fact have been declined if one had been given. The question is a subjective one related to the patient's individual situation.[1] Thus, Lord Scarman in *Sidaway v Governors of Bethlem Royal Hospital*[2] referred to the patient's need 'to consider and balance the medical advantages and risks alongside other relevant matters, such as, for example, his family, business or social responsibilities of which the doctor may be only partially, if at all, informed'. Although his Lordship was dissenting, there is no reason to suppose that the majority would have disagreed with him on this point. In the Australian case of *Chappel v Hart*[3] the plaintiff, whose voice was essential to her employment in the field of education, succeeded in establishing that she would have postponed elective surgery on her throat had she known of the risk of damage to her vocal chords, which unfortunately materialised.

[1]   See the decision of the High Court of Australia in *Rosenberg v Percival [2001] HCA 18, 75 ALJR 734*. For discussion see Kumaralingam Amirthalingam 'A New Dawn for Patients' Rights?' (2001) 117 LQR 532. See also *Videto v Kennedy (1981) 125 DLR (3d) 127* (patient anxious to avoid scarring after sterilization operation which she had wished to keep secret from her Catholic parents). Cf *Reibl v Hughes (1981) 114 DLR (3d) 1* at 6.
[2]   *[1985] AC 871* at 886, *[1985] 1 All ER 643* at 652.
[3]   See *(1998) 72 ALJR 1344, [1999] Lloyd's Rep Med 223 (High Court of Australia)*. For discussion see Peter Cane 'A Warning About Causation' (1999) 115 LQR 21; Marc Stauch 'Taking the Consequences for Failure to Warn of Medical Risks' (2000) 63 MLR 261.

Where operation would have been postponed

[7.20]   What if the patient is unable, or does not seek, to contend that he would *never* have had the operation; but *does* establish that, if a proper warning had been given, the operation would have been postponed and further advice sought? In the important recent case of *Chester v Afshar*[1] the defendant succeeded in establishing that a proper warning had not been given prior to her undergoing spinal surgery, and that if it had been she would have postponed the surgery. As it was the operation went ahead with drastic, albeit non-negligent, consequences. The defendant nevertheless contended that since the operation would eventually have become inevitable, and might have had the same adverse result, causation was not proved. By a bare majority the House of Lords[2], affirming the Court of Appeal, rejected this contention. Since the risk of adverse consequences was very small, being of the order of 2% or less, the probability was that they would not have occurred at any other given time. Lord Bingham and Lord Hoffman, who dissented, would nevertheless have rejected the claim on causal grounds. But the majority held that broader considerations of justice, and the need to vindicate the duty to warn, required a modified approach to causation in the circumstances, enabling the claim to succeed. It is submitted that they were right to do so. Lord Hope of Craighead said[3]:

'To leave the patient ... without a remedy, as the normal approach to causation would indicate, would render the duty [ie to warn] useless in the cases where it may be needed most. This would discriminate against those who cannot honestly say that they would have declined the operation once and for all if they had been warned. I would find that result unacceptable. The function of the law is to enable rights to be vindicated and to provide remedies when duties have been breached. Unless this is done the duty is a hollow one, stripped of all practical force and devoid of content. It will have lost its ability to protect the patient and thus to fulfil the only purpose which brought it into existence. On policy grounds therefore I would hold that the test of causation is satisfied in this case. The injury was intimately involved with the duty to warn'.

In reaching its conclusion the House followed the decision (also by a majority) of the High Court of Australia in *Chappel v Hart*[4], which was to the same effect. It follows from the reasoning adopted in the *Chester* and *Chappel* cases that the result would have been different, and causation would not have been established, if disaster had occurred during the operation as a result of an event unconnected with the duty to warn, such as an anaesthetic accident[5].

[1]   *[2004] 4 All ER 587.*
[2]   Lord Steyn, Lord Hope of Craighead, and Lord Walker of Gestingthorpe. Lord Bingham of Cornhill and Lord Hoffman dissenting.
[3]   See *[2004] 4 All ER 587* at para 87.
[4]   *(1998) 72 ALJR 1344, [1999] Lloyd's Rep Med 223.*
[5]   See *[2004] 4 All ER 587* at para 94 *per* Lord Walker of Gestingthorpe.

G Contractual negligence

[7.21]   If the patient was treated privately, so that he entered into a contractual relationship with his doctor, the question may arise as to whether his chances of success are higher in contract than in tort. In theory, this could be so if the contract was a most unusual one in which the doctor guaranteed that his treatment would succeed. In practice, however, such guarantees are seldom, if ever, given and the court will lean strongly against implying any term to that effect. In *Thake v Maurice*[1] the plaintiff had a sterilisation operation which was properly carried out. Subsequently, however, he regained his fertility and his wife became pregnant. Although his contention that the surgeon had, albeit inadvertently, contractually guaranteed sterility was upheld by the trial judge,[2] that decision was reversed by the Court of Appeal.[3] In the similar case of *Eyre v Measday*,[4] in which the Court of Appeal reached the same result, Slade LJ put it as follows:[5]

> ' ... in my opinion, in the absence of any express warranty, the court should be slow to imply against a medical man an unqualified warranty as to the results of an intended operation, for the very simple reason that, objectively speaking, it is most unlikely that a responsible medical man would intend to give a warranty of this nature. Of course, objectively speaking, it is likely that he would give a guarantee that he would do what he had undertaken to do with reasonable care and skill; but it is quite another matter to say that he has committed himself to the extent suggested in the present case.'

As this quotation illustrates, the term usually to be implied in medical contracts is that the doctor will act with reasonable care and skill,[6] and hence the result on any given set of facts should normally be the same irrespective of whether or not there was a contractual relationship between doctor and patient.

[1]   *[1986] QB 644, [1984] 2 All ER 513.*
[2]   See *[1986] QB 644, [1984] 2 All ER 513.* For discussion, see generally W Rogers 'Legal Implications of Ineffective Sterilization' (1985) 5 LS 296. See also A Grubb 'Failed Sterilisation: Is a Claim in Contract or Negligence a Guarantee of Success?' [1986] 45 CLJ 197.
[3]   It should be noted, however, that the defendant's appeal itself was dismissed and the plaintiff retained the judgment in his favour. This was because, on the facts, the doctor had failed to give an adequate *warning* of the possibility of the return of fertility.
[4]   *[1986] 1 All ER 488, CA.*
[5]   *[1986] 1 All ER 488* at 495.
[6]   See also *Thake v Maurice [1986] QB 644* at 684–685, *[1986] 1 All ER 497* at 510, CA, *per* Neill LJ.

Chapter 8

Lawyers

A End of the advocate's immunity

Arthur J S Hall v Simons

[8.01]   In the landmark case of *Arthur J S Hall & Co (a firm) v Simons*[1], decided in 2000, a seven-member House of Lords reviewed the public policy based immunity from suit, then enjoyed by advocates, for any alleged negligence in the conduct of a case in court.[2] The House held unanimously that, in respect of civil litigation, the immunity would be abolished. It had applied irrespective of whether the advocate had been a solicitor or a barrister,[3] but had been progressively narrowed over the years[4], and long perceived as vulnerable to criticism[5]. Lord Hoffman observed that 'in general English law provides a remedy in damages for a person who has suffered injury as a result of professional negligence', and that accordingly 'any exception which denies such a remedy requires a sound justification'[6]. The House reviewed at length the arguments in favour of immunity, including the fact that an advocate owes a duty to the court as well as to his client,[7] and comprehensively rejected them.

[1]   *[2000] 3 All ER 673.* Lord Steyn, Lord Browne-Wilkinson, Lord Hoffman, Lord Hope, Lord Hutton, Lord Hobhouse, and Lord Millett.
[2]   See *Rondel v Worsley [1969] 1 AC 191, [1967] 3 All ER 993, HL.*
[3]   See the *Courts and Legal Services Act 1990, s 62.*
[4]   See *Saif Ali v Sydney Mitchell & Co [1980] AC 198, [1978] 3 All ER 1033, HL* in which the House of Lords held, albeit by a bare majority, that a barrister could be liable for negligence in advising the plaintiff on the selection of defendants in anticipated litigation arising out of a motor accident.
[5]   Cf *Kelley v Corston [1998] QB 686, [1997] 4 All ER 466, CA.*
[6]   See *[2000] 3 All ER 673* at 689.
[7]   'This factor is the pivot on which in 1967 the existence of the immunity hanged. But for it the case (ie *Rondel v Worsley*) would probably have been decided differently': per Lord Steyn in *[2000] 3 All ER 673* at 678.

Striking out vexatious claims

[8.02]   In response to the argument that immunity was necessary to prevent advocates from being harassed by vexatious claims, the House emphasised that the new Civil Procedure Rules make summary dismissal of bad claims easier than in the past[1]. A claim can now be struck out if the court considers that 'the claimant has no real prospect of succeeding on the claim'. The Court of Appeal drew attention to the observations of the House in *Simon's* case, in relation to the new Rules, when striking out a claim against a barrister in *Hussain v Cuddy Woods & Cochrane*[2]. The defendant in that case was alleged to have negligently advised his client, the claimant, to accept an inappropriately low settlement in litigation in which he had been engaged on the client's behalf. Buxton LJ observed that 'the suggestion that the estimate of value of the claim was wrong to the extent of being negligent' was 'entirely hopeless'[3]. Buxton LJ had earlier quoted the following passage from the speech of Lord Hobhouse in *Simon's* case[4]:

'The standard of care to be applied in negligence actions against an advocate is the same as that applicable to any other skilled professional who has to work in an environment where decisions and exercises of judgment have to be made on often difficult and time constrained circumstances. It requires a plaintiff to show that the error was one which no reasonably competent member of the relevant profession would have made. This is an important element of protection against unjustified liabilities. Similarly, there now exist improved procedures to enable obviously unsustainable claims to be brought to a conclusion at any early stage of any litigation'.

Moreover, the subjective nature of advocacy will make it very difficult to base a claim purely on the perception that an advocate's performance in court was lack-lustre, and that a more determined approach would have produced a different result. In striking out one such claim, it was judicially observed that the 'lack of robustness in any cross-examination ... cannot normally hope to found an allegation of negligence if only because differences in style make it difficult to set a universal standard'[5].

[1]   See CPR 1999, rule 24.2. See also *per* Lord Steyn in *[2000] 3 All ER 673* at 681 and *per* Lord Hoffman at 691–692.
[2]   *[2001] Lloyd's Rep PN 134*. Cf *Green v Hancocks (a firm) [2001] Lloyd's Rep PN 212* (in which the Court of Appeal *refused* to strike out a claim against a barrister under the new rules.)
[3]   See *[2001] Lloyd's Rep PN 134*.
[4]   See *[2000] 3 All ER 673* at 736.
[5]   *Per* Judge Playford QC sitting as a Deputy High Court Judge in *Prettys v Carter [2002] PNLR 11* at para 11.

Criminal cases

[8.03]   Unlike their ruling in relation to civil litigation, the House of Lords in *Simon's* case was not unanimous on the question whether the advocate's immunity should also be removed in criminal cases. But, by a bare majority of four to three[1], the House decided that it should be. The dissentients felt that the public interest in the operation of the criminal justice system, including the need to prevent collateral challenges to the validity of convictions and any undermining of the independence of advocates by fear of vexatious litigation, merited a different approach from that adopted towards civil cases. The majority, however, felt that other mechanisms, in particular the power to strike out a claim as an abuse of process[2], provided sufficient safeguards making it unnecessary to preserve the immunity even in the criminal sphere. Since the only claims before the House of Lords in *Simon's* case were civil, the decision of the majority in favour of abolishing the negligence immunity even in criminal cases was technically obiter. In particular Lord Hobhouse, one of the dissentients, was insistent that final resolution of the issue would 'have to await a case in which it does arise for decision'[3]. Nevertheless, it is submitted that the views of the four members of the House who favoured abolition will in practice be regarded as having settled the matter.

[1]   Lord Hope, Lord Hutton and Lord Hobhouse dissenting.
[2]   See *Hunter v Chief Constable of West Midlands [1982] AC 529, [1981] 3 All ER 727*, HL. See also *Somasundaram v M Julius Melchior & Co (a firm) [1989] 1 All ER 129, [1988] 1 WLR 1394, CA.*

Negligence not to be readily inferred

[8.04]   In *Moy v Pettman Smith (a firm)*[1] it was alleged that a barrister had been negligent in failing to give realistic advice as to the prospects of success if a settlement offered by a defendant health authority in clinical negligence litigation was rejected. As a result of the rejection the barrister's client was subsequently obliged to accept a much lower figure in settlement of the claim. The optimistic advice which had led to the rejection of the settlement was based on the assumption that the judge would permit further evidence to be admitted at a late stage in the proceedings, which he declined to do.

1   *[2005] 1 All ER 903.*
2   See above at para 66.

Door of the court

[8.05]   The trial judge in *Moy's* case had held that the barrister had not been negligent, but his decision was reversed by the Court of Appeal which took the view that the risks attendant upon rejection of the offer of settlement had not been adequately explained to the client[1]. The House of Lords, however, reinstated the decision of the judge and acquitted the barrister of negligence both in relation to the rejection of the settlement and the adequacy of her explanation. The advice had been given at the door of the court, with the inevitable accompanying pressure and time-constraints, and there was no evidence that a reasonably competent barrister would not have adopted the same course as the defendant. Lord Carswell said[2]:

> '... the difficulties faced by an advocate who is advising on acceptance or rejection of a settlement are manifold and the pressures, especially if the advice has to be given at the door of the court, can be heavy. In such circumstances it would be surprising if every such piece of advice were reasoned with as much comprehensive precision as may be applied in hindsight by an appellate tribunal which has had the benefit of extensive argument and leisurely reflection'.

1   See *[2002] Lloyd's Rep PN 513.*
2   See *[2005] 1 All ER 903* at para 60.

B Types of claim

Infinite variety

[8.06]   Because the facts of each of the cases and matters with which they deal are themselves unique, the circumstances in which solicitors or barristers might find themselves facing allegations of negligence admit of infinite variety. Obviously, legal advice cannot be deemed 'negligent' merely because a court eventually adopts a different view of the law from that which the legal adviser originally propounded to his client.[1] In one case a leading counsel was held not to have been negligent when he actively discouraged his clients from taking a point which they wished to take[2], and on which they ultimately succeeded when it was taken by the Court of Appeal of its own motion. The clients argued, in a subsequent professional negligence claim against their former counsel that substantial costs would have been saved if the point had been taken at the outset as they had wished. But their claim failed: the counsel was held to have had good reasons for handling the case in the way in which he had done, notwithstanding the unexpected turn of events in the Court of Appeal. On the other hand, if, for instance, counsel's opinion carelessly omitted a crucial statute the imposition of liability in negligence would be appropriate[3]. The same could be said if a recent decision of the House of Lords or Court of Appeal, which any practitioner in the relevant speciality would without question have regarded as being directly in point, was overlooked. In one recent case a junior chancery barrister was held to have been negligent in the drafting of a settlement which resulted in unnecessary exposure to tax[4].

[1]   See *Ormindale Holdings v Ray, Wolfe, Connel, Lightbody & Reynolds (1980) 116 DLR (3d) 346*. See also *per* Lord Salmon in *Saif Ali v Sydney Mitchell (a firm) [1980] AC 198* at 231, *[1978] 3 All ER 1033* at 1051: 'Lawyers are often faced with finely balanced problems. Diametrically opposite views may and not infrequently are taken by barristers and indeed by judges, each of whom has exercised reasonable, and sometimes far more than reasonable, care and competence. The fact that one of them turns out to be wrong certainly does not mean that he has been negligent.' See also *[1980] AC 198* at 214, 214–221, *[1978] 3 All ER 1033* at 1038, 1043, *per* Lord Wilberforce and Lord Diplock.

[2]   See *First City Insurance Group v Orchard [2002] Lloyd's Rep PN 543*.

[3]   See *Green v Collyer-Bristow [1999] Lloyd's Rep PN 798* in which *section 2* of the *Law Reform (Miscellaneous Provisions) Act 1989* (need for contracts for the sale of land to be in writing) was overlooked.

[4]   See *Estill v Cowling Swift & Kitchin [2000] Lloyd's Rep PN 378*.

Establishing negligence

[8.07]   The most straightforward cases are those in which obvious slips have been made, such as failing to register a land charge,[1] or failing to start proceedings in time so that they become statute-barred. The existence of liability, on the part of the solicitor responsible, will normally be virtually self-evident in cases of this kind. Rather more difficult to decide, depending upon the facts, will be cases in which it is alleged that a solicitor failed adequately to investigate the factual circumstances surrounding a particular matter. At the easier end of the spectrum of this type of case will be situations in which complex documents, such as commercial leases,[2] have been perused (or drafted) with insufficient care[3] and some aspect vital to the client's interest has simply been overlooked.[4] In one case in which a complicated agreement was held to have been negligently drawn up it appeared that two departments of the defendant solicitors' firm had been involved in the drafting, but without any single individual taking responsibility to oversee the process and ensure that the various parts fitted together coherently[5]. It may also be negligent, even in an apparently simple conveyancing transaction,[6] to accept the word of the other party on some crucial question of fact without making further checks.[7] Thus where vendors misrepresented that building consent had been obtained for renovations when it had not, the purchasers successfully sued their own solicitors for failing to check with the local authority whether the requisite consent had been obtained[8].

[1]   See *Midland Bank Trust Co Ltd v Hett, Stubbs & Kemp [1979] Ch 384, [1978] 3 All ER 571; Bell v Peter Browne & Co [1990] 2 QB 495, [1990] 3 All ER 124, CA*. Cf *Griffiths v Dawson & Co [1993] 2 FCR 515*.

[2]   For a case in which negligence liability was established against a solicitor with respect to an unusual clause in a commercial lease see *County Personnel (Employment Agency) Ltd v Alan R Pulver & Co [1987] 1 All ER 289, [1987] 1 WLR 916, CA*.

[3]   See *Allied Maples Group Ltd v Simmons & Simmons [1995] 4 All ER 907* at 913, CA ('the defendants ... never gave any thought to the matter').

4   See *Sykes v Midland Bank Executor & Trustee Co Ltd [1971] 1 QB 113, [1970] 2 All ER 471, CA*. See
    also *Hill v Harris [1965] 2 QB 601, [1965] 2 All ER 358, CA*. Cf *Ford v White & Co [1964] 2 All ER
    755, [1964] 1 WLR 885*.
5   See *Summit Financial Group v Slaughter & May* (1999) Times, 2 April.
6   On which see generally H W Wilkinson 'Negligent Conveyancing, One Thousand Ways of Erring'
    (1986) NLJ 887 at 911.
7   See *Goody v Baring [1956] 2 All ER 11, [1956] 1 WLR 448*.
8   See *Cottingham v Attey Bower & Jones [2000] Lloyd's Rep PN 591*.

Common practice and expert evidence

[8.08]   Less straightforward will be situations in which some precaution has been
omitted which with hindsight it would have been prudent to take, but expert witnesses
differ as to whether they would in fact have taken the precaution in the circumstances.[1]
If the defendant can establish that he followed common practice[2], this will clearly be
of assistance to him. In *Patel v Daybells*[3] the Court of Appeal upheld, 'after some
initial scepticism'[4], a decision in favour of solicitors who had been sued by their
clients for losses occurring when a small risk, which was inherent in conventionally
accepted conveyancing practice, in fact materialised. Nevertheless, the court will be
likely, for obvious reasons, to scrutinise the legitimacy of existing practice with
particular thoroughness when it is invoked in cases of alleged negligence by lawyers[5].
Indeed, in one case Oliver J even cast doubt upon the propriety of expert evidence in
cases of this kind. In *Midland Bank Trust Co Ltd v Hett, Stubbs & Kemp*[6] he said:

> 'I have heard the evidence of a number of practising solicitors ... I must say that
> I doubt the value, or even the admissibility, of this sort of evidence, which seems
> to be becoming customary in cases of this type. Clearly, if there is some practice
> in a particular profession, some accepted standard of conduct which is laid down
> by a professional institute or sanctioned by common usage, evidence of that can
> and ought to be received. But evidence which really amounts to no more than an
> expression of opinion by a particular practitioner of what he thinks he would
> have done had he been placed, hypothetically and without the benefit of
> hindsight, in the position of the defendants is of little assistance to the court,
> whilst evidence of the witnesses' view of what, as a matter of law, the solicitor's
> duty was in the particular circumstances of the case is, I should have thought,
> inadmissible, for that is the very question which it is the court's function to
> decide.'

In another case Arden J observed that 'there are limits on the extent to which expert
evidence, whether of solicitors or counsel, can assist the court on a question of
professional negligence'; and she 'placed specific limits on the expert evidence that
could be adduced' in a complex action alleging that advice had been negligent in
relation to the taxation implications of a trust[7]. Where proper investigation of title is in
issue the Court of Appeal has suggested that evidence of conveyancers as to proper
practice should not be admitted[8]. On the other hand, evidence as to proper practice has
been held to be appropriate in cases alleging negligence by conveyancers in relation to
unusual problems concerning highways,[9] and mortgages[10]. And judges have occasionally criticised the *failure* to submit expert evidence of the practice of solicitors[11].

1   See *G & K Ladenbau (UK) Ltd v Crawley and de Reya [1978] 1 All ER 682, [1978] 1 WLR 266*.
2   See *Simmons v Pennington & Son [1955] 1 All ER 240, [1955] 1 WLR 183, CA*.
3   *[2002] PNLR 6*.
4   See above at para 64.
5   See *Edward Wong Finance Co Ltd v Johnson Stokes & Master [1984] AC 296, [1984] 2 WLR 1, PC*.

6   *[1979] Ch 384* at 402, *[1978] 3 All ER 571* at 582, referred to with approval by the Court of Appeal in *Pretty v Daybells [2002] PNLR 6* at para 44.
7   See *Estill v Cowling Swift & Kitchin [2000] Lloyd' Rep PN 378*.
8   See *Bown v Gould & Swayne [1996] PNLR 130*.
9   See *May v Woollcombe Beer & Watts [1999] PNLR 283*.
10 See *Archer v Hickmotts [1997] PNLR 318*.
11 See *per* Jacob J in *Guild (Claims) Ltd v Eversheds [2000] Lloyd's Rep PN 910* at para 33; see also *per* Brooke LJ in *Balamoan v Holden & Co 1999 WL 477470, CA (LEXIS)*.

Delay

[8.09]   While establishing that there was negligent failure to act on instructions with reasonable promptness can inevitably raise questions of degree, the court will not hesitate to impose liability in clear cases. In *Hunter v Earnshaw*[1] a personal injuries claim had been struck out for want of prosecution. When sued for negligence the claimant's solicitor relied unsuccessfully on his client's failure to keep in touch with him. In view of the serious head injuries which he had suffered in the accident, however, the client was prone to memory loss and concentration difficulties. Garland J found that if the solicitor had himself adopted a more active and conscientious approach to the litigation he could have obtained adequate instructions from his client, and his Lordship had 'no hesitation' in concluding that 'the defendant's conduct fell far short of that to be expected of a solicitor of reasonable competence in the conduct of a personal injuries claim'[2]. In *LR v Witherspoon*[3] a solicitor was instructed by the mother of a very young child, who had been placed in foster care, to seek the return of the child. The solicitor did nothing for well over a year and, as a result, the mother lost any effective chance of preventing a subsequent court order to terminate her contact with the child. Although her negligence claim against the solicitor was struck out the Court of Appeal reinstated it. Brooke LJ expressed himself as follows[4]:

> 'In my judgment, it is the passage of time which makes all the difference in this case. In many cases (including some family cases where the children are much older) the passage of time may not make a significant difference, or indeed any difference at all, but in some cases it may be a relevant factor, and in this case it was a most important factor'.

1   *[2001] PNLR 42*.
2   See above.
3   *[2000] 1 FLR 82*.
4   See above at para 29.

Reliance by solicitors upon counsel

[8.10]   In *Ridehalgh v Horsefield*[1] Sir Thomas Bingham MR said:

> 'A solicitor does not abdicate his professional responsibility when he seeks the advice of counsel. He must apply his mind to the advice received. But the more specialist the nature of the advice, the more reasonable is it likely to be for a solicitor to accept it and act upon it'[2].

Moreover, even if the context is in some sense specialist in nature 'a reasonably competent solicitor' should normally take 'steps to give himself some general knowledge of the subject'[3], so as to enable him to ensure that counsel's opinion had addressed all the relevant issues. Thus failure to do so, in a case in which the defendant solicitor had omitted to seek clarification of the taxation consequences of inappropriate advice by counsel in an estate planning matter, resulted in the imposition of liability[4]. In another case a solicitor was held to have been negligent for failing to appreciate that counsel's opinion contained a fundamental error relating to the enforceability of agreements for the transfer of interests in land[5].

1 See *[1994] Ch 205* at 237, *[1994] 3 All ER 848* at 866, endorsing views in *Locke v Camberwell Health Authority [1991] 2 Med LR 249*.
2 See *First City Insurance Group v Orchard [2002] Lloyd's Rep PN 543* at paras 82–83 *per* Forbes J, in which a solicitor was held entitled to have acted on the advice of counsel.
3 See *per* Arden J in *Estill v Cowling Swift & Kitchin [2000] Lloyd's Rep PN 378*.
4 See *Estill v Cowling Swift & Kitchin [2000] Lloyd's Rep PN 378*.
5 See *Green v Collyer-Bristow [1999] Lloyd's Rep PN 798*.

Use of foreign lawyers

[8.11] In transactions involving the use of foreign lawyers, an English solicitor may, in certain circumstances, find himself liable to his client for losses arising out of failure on the part of the foreign lawyers to discharge their own responsibilities competently. In *Gregory v Shepherds*[1] the defendant firm, which offered a 'Spanish Property Conveyancing Service', acted for the claimants in relation to the purchase of a Spanish property. When it transpired that there were defects in the title, which the Spanish lawyer appointed by the defendants should have discovered, the claimant sued his English solicitors. The Court of Appeal emphasised that no subcontractor or agency relationship existed, so as to render the solicitors vicariously liable for the Spanish lawyer's failures as such. Nevertheless the court went on to hold that the English solicitors owed a duty to obtain specific and unequivocal confirmation from the Spanish lawyer that all the relevant searches had been properly carried out, before parting with their clients' money; and that their failure to do so rendered them liable.

1 *[2000] Lloyd's Rep PN 724*.

Adequacy of explanation

[8.12] Perhaps the most difficult kind of negligence claim against a solicitor to resolve, because it involves subjective personal interaction, is one in which it is alleged that he failed adequately to *explain* to his client the legal implications of a particular document or situation.[1] In such cases much will necessarily depend upon the level of education and expertise of the client himself[2]. 'An inexperienced client', Donaldson LJ once observed,[3] 'will need and will be entitled to expect the solicitor to take a much broader view of the scope of the retainer and of his duties than will be the case with an experienced client'. Thus a solicitor will normally owe a duty to an inexperienced lay client to be alert to the danger of misapprehension, and should be willing to clarify with the client the nature of the advice which is required as well as the advice itself[4]. On the other hand, it is hardly likely to be necessary to spell out to an experienced property developer the obvious fact that he could be sued if he did not comply with the clear terms of a proposed contract.[5] Nor is a barrister always obliged to ensure that his lay client fully understands the implications of his advice; depending upon the circumstances counsel may well be entitled to leave that task to the solicitor involved.[6]

1 Cf *County Personnel (Employment Agency) Ltd v Alan R Pulver & Co [1987] 1 All ER 289, [1987] 1 WLR 916, CA*. See also *Allied Maples Group Ltd v Simmons & Simmons [1995] 4 All ER 907, CA; Petersen v Personal Representatives of Rivlin (Deceased) [2002] Lloyd's Rep PN 346.*

2   See *Harwood v Taylor Vintners (a firm) [2003] EWHC 471*, (2003) Times, 1 April, at para 84. A solicitor is not obliged to put his advice in writing: see above at the same paragraph *per* Judge Richard Seymour QC, sitting as a High Court Judge.

3   See *Carradine Properties Ltd v D J Freeman & Co (1982) 126 Sol Jo 157, CA* (the passage in the text was quoted from the transcript by Staughton J in *R P Howard v Woodman Matthews & Co [1983] BCLC 117* at 121–122).

4   See *Gray v Buss Murton [1999] PNLR 882*.

5   See *Aslan v Clintons (1984) 134 NLJ 584*. Cf *Sykes v Midland Bank Executor and Trustee Co [1971] 1 QB 113, [1970] 2 All ER 471, CA*.

6   See *Mathew v Maughold Life Assurance Co (1987) 3 PN 98, CA*.

Uncertainty

[8.13]   A difficulty often faced by those giving legal advice is to what extent they should communicate to the client the presence of an element of doubt or uncertainty as to the possible outcome of a given situation. In *Queen Elizabeth's Grammar School Blackburn v Banks Wilson*[1], Sedley LJ said:

'Clients, 1 know, want two inconsistent things. They want confident advice on which they can act, and they want cautionary advice about the risks of doing so. It is a solicitor's unhappy lot to have to try to satisfy both requirements simultaneously'.

In the case from which these words are taken the Court of Appeal held that the claimants' solicitors had been negligent in failing to advise that a restrictive covenant was ambiguous and could give rise to dispute.

1   See *[2002] PNLR 14* at para 51.

Charging the family home

[8.14]   It will normally be necessary for a solicitor advising someone providing security for loans to a relative to explain clearly the exact nature and extent of the commitment being undertaken.[1] The situation often arises in which one partner wishes to use a jointly owned family home as security for a loan in connection with that partner's business interests. If it should become necessary for the security to be enforced the other partner may sometimes contend that he or she was a victim of undue influence by the other partner, and that the creditor had constructive notice of this thereby rendering the security unenforceable. The approach to be adopted by the court in cases of this kind was considered and developed by the House of Lords in eight appeals heard together in 2001[2]. This approach takes the form of a code of practice directed primarily towards lenders, and is rooted in equitable principles which fall outside the scope of this book. Nevertheless the quality of the legal advice received by the partner who alleges undue influence will often be an issue in these cases, and practitioners will need to be familiar with the relevant law.

1   Cf *Forster v Outred & Co [1982] 2 All ER 753, [1982] 1 WLR 86, CA*. See also *Fox v Everingham (1983) 50 ALR 337 (Federal Court of Australia)*.

2   See *Royal Bank of Scotland v Etridge (No 2) [2002] 2 AC 773, [2001] 4 All ER 449*.

Nature and effect of the documents to be signed

[8.15]   Although claims usually take the form of attempts by lenders to enforce their security, one of the eight appeals heard by the House of Lords in 2001, *Kenyon-Brown* *v Desmond Banks & Co*, concerned a claim against a solicitor for negligently failing to advise the partner, who had reluctantly agreed to the loan transaction, as to its full implications. The House reversed a majority decision of the Court of Appeal in favour of the debtor, and restored the decision of the trial judge in favour of the solicitor. Lord Scott said:[1]

'The normal duty of a solicitor instructed to advise a would-be surety, whether a wife of the principal debtor or anyone else, about the document or documents the surety is being asked to sign, is to explain the nature and effect of the document in order to try and make sure that the surety knows what he or she is doing. The particular circumstances of a particular case may add to or reduce the extent of the duty owed by the solicitor'.

In the instant case there was 'nothing in the circumstances' to 'add to the normal duty'. The Court of Appeal had considered that the defendant solicitor should have asked the claimant about the stability of her marriage, but Lord Scott considered that such inquiries 'would have been an unpardonable impertinence'[2]. He said that the defendant had been entitled to treat the claimant 'as a mature lady able to make up her own mind as to whether to allow her share in [the property] to become security for her husband's debts'. On the facts, the solicitor had discharged his obligation 'to try and make sure that she understood the nature and effect of the document she was being asked to sign'[3].

[1] See *[2002] 2 AC 773* at para 373.
[2] See *[2002] 2 AC 773* at para 374.
[3] See above.

C Tort and contract

Coexistence of tort duty

[8.16] In *Midland Bank Trust Co Ltd v Hett, Stubbs & Kemp*[1] Oliver J held that, alongside the contractual relationship existing between them, a solicitor owes to his client a duty of care in tort. This marked a radical departure from the position as previously understood, based upon a well-known decision of the Court of Appeal in 1938 that a solicitor's duty to his client was in contract only.[2] In the *Hett* case itself the effect of the decision of Oliver J was that the plaintiff client was able to take advantage of a more favourable limitation period than he would otherwise have been able to do, in an action against his solicitor for loss caused by the latter's carelessness. The proposition that professional people may owe duties to their clients concurrently in both contract and tort was subsequently expressly confirmed, after full consideration, by a unanimous House of Lords in *Henderson v Merrett Syndicates Ltd*.[3] In that case the decision of Oliver J in *Hett* was expressly approved and his judgment was praised for the thoroughness of its analysis.[4]

[1] *[1979] Ch 384, [1978] 3 All ER 571*. See also *Aluminium Products Pty Ltd v Hill [1981] Qd R 33 (Qld Full Ct SC)*.
[2] See *Groom v Crocker [1939] 1 KB 194, [1938] 2 All ER 394, CA*.
[3] *[1995] 2 AC 145, [1994] 3 All ER 506*.
[4] See *[1995] 2 AC 145* at 188, *[1994] 3 All ER 506* at 527 onwards (Lord Goff).

D Liability to third parties

Wills and beneficiaries

Background

[8.17]   Shortly after the decision in *Midland Bank Trust Co Ltd v Hett, Stubbs & Kemp* came the famous case of *Ross v Caunters*,[1] in which Sir Robert Megarry V-C held that a solicitor owed a duty of care in tort not only to his own client but also, in certain circumstances, to third parties who might be adversely affected by his negligence in advising or acting on behalf of his client. In that case a solicitor was held liable to the proposed beneficiary under a will whose gift was rendered void due to the failure of the testator, as a result of the solicitor's negligence when advising and acting for him, to comply with the formalities of the *Wills Act 1837*.[2] Although a controversial decision for many years, the correctness of *Ross v Caunters* was subsequently, like *Hett*'s case, confirmed by the House of Lords.

[1]   *[1980] Ch 297, [1979] 3 All ER 580*. See also *Smith v Claremont Haynes & Co* (1991) Times, 3 September.
[2]   See also the decision of the New Zealand Court of Appeal in *Gartside v Sheffield, Young & Ellis [1983] NZLR 37* in which many of the Commonwealth cases on this point, some of them conflicting, are referred to.

White v Jones

[8.18]   In *White v Jones*[1] the defendant solicitors had, due to their negligence, wholly failed to comply, before his death, with the request of the testator that a will should be drawn up to benefit the plaintiffs. Imposing liability, the House of Lords, by a majority, approved the decision (although not the reasoning) in *Ross v Caunters* and applied it.[2] Moreover, in *Hill v Van Erp*,[3] which was decided after *White v Jones*, the High Court of Australia reached the same result in a case involving very similar facts to *Ross v Caunters*.[4] Observing that it was 'fair, just and reasonable to impose liability on the solicitor', Lord Browne-Wilkinson said in *White v Jones*:[5]

> 'Save in the case of those rash testators who make their own wills, the proper transmission of property from one generation to the next is dependent upon the due discharge by solicitors of their duties. Although in any particular case it may not be possible to demonstrate that the intended beneficiary relied upon the solicitor, society as a whole does rely on solicitors to carry out their will-making functions carefully. To my mind it would be unacceptable if, because of some technical rules of law, the wishes and expectations of testators and beneficiaries generally could be defeated by the negligent actions of solicitors without their being any redress. It is only just that the intended beneficiary should be able to recover the benefits which he would otherwise have received.'

[1]   *[1995] 2 AC 207, [1995] 1 All ER 691, HL*.
[2]   See also *Carr-Glyn v Frearsons [1999] Ch 326, [1998] 4 All ER 225, CA*.
[3]   *(1997) 188 CLR 159*.
[4]   Ie solicitor's negligence with respect to attestation.
[5]   See *[1995] 2 AC 207* at p 276, *[1995] 1 All ER 691* at 718.

Scope of the principle in White v Jones

[8.19]   The decision in *White v Jones* does not imply that disappointed beneficiaries will enjoy a remedy against the testator's solicitors in a wide range of cases. They will clearly not do so when the testator, during his lifetime, entered with the assistance of the solicitor into transactions which adversely affected the subject matter of the devise.[1] Nor will the solicitor be liable to someone whom he is unaware the testator intended to benefit[2]. Although difficult questions may sometimes arise as to the extent of the solicitor's duty to assist the client in clarifying his own intentions[3], any claim by disappointed 'beneficiaries' necessarily requires convincing evidence that the testator in fact intended to benefit them[4]. On the other hand the principle is not necessarily precluded merely because the situation is one in which, unlike *White v Jones* itself, the solicitor's negligence resulted in a loss not only to the intended beneficiary but also to the *estate* itself, for which it would have a claim against the solicitor[5]. In such cases the law will endeavour to 'impose complementary duties' to avoid 'double recovery and double liability'[6].

[1] See *Clarke v Bruce Lance & Co [1988] 1 All ER 364, [1988] 1 WLR 881, CA*. See also *per* Lord Goff in *White v Jones [1995] 2 AC 207* at 262, *[1995] 1 All ER 691* at 704. Cf *Hemmens v Wilson Browne [1995] Ch 223, [1993] 4 All ER 826*.
[2] See *Gibbons v Nelsons [2000] Lloyd's Rep PN 603*.
[3] See *Gibbons v Nelsons [2000] Lloyd's Rep PN 603*. Cf *Kecskemeti v Rubens Rabin & Co* (1992) Times, 31 December.
[4] See *Walker v Geo H Medlicott & Son [1999] 1 All ER 685, CA*. See also *Trusted v Clifford Chance [2000] WTLR 1219*.
[5] See *Carr-Glyn v Frearsons [1999] Ch 326, [1998] 4 All ER 225, CA*. Cf *Chappell v Somers & Blake [2003] 3 All ER 1076* (claim by executrix for damage suffered by beneficiaries due to delay by solicitors in progressing the administration of the estate).
[6] See *Carr-Glyn v Frearsons [1999] Ch 326, [1998] 4 All ER 225* at 235 *per* Chadwick LJ. Cf *Corbett v Bond Pearce [2001] 3 All ER 769; Worby v Rosser [1999] Lloyd's Rep PN 972, CA*.

What constitutes delay?

[8.20] Where, as in *White v Jones* itself, the testator dies before the will is drawn up, and allegedly negligent delay by the solicitor is the basis of the claim, determining the scope of the defendant's duty on the particular facts can be difficult, especially if the case is near the borderline. Two decisions may be contrasted. In *Hooper v Fynmores*[1] the defendant solicitor cancelled, for personal reasons, an appointment made by his client to execute the latter's will on 13 October. The client was eighty-three-years-old, and seriously ill in hospital. Although a subsequent appointment was made for 28 October, his client unfortunately died on 21 October without having executed his will. The defendant was held liable to the claimant, a disappointed beneficiary. Pumfrey J said[2]:

> 'In my judgment, when dealing with an elderly client in hospital an appointment for the execution of a will is to be kept unless it is clear that the client is content for the appointment to be missed'.

On the other hand in *X (A Child) v Woollcombe Yonge*[3] a solicitor who took instructions from a terminally ill client in hospital on 26 June, with a view to having the will ready for signature on 3 July, was held not to have been negligent when his client died on 1 July.

[1] *[2002] Lloyd's Rep PN 18*.
[2] See above at para 17.
[3] *[2001] Lloyd's Rep PN 274*.

Rectification?

[8.21] In cases in which a will was actually drawn up and executed, but it is alleged that due to negligent drafting by the solicitor it failed to represent the true intentions of the testator, a disappointed beneficiary will be able to seek rectification of the will as well as a remedy in negligence[1]. In *Walker v Geo H Medlicott*[2] the Court of Appeal held that in cases of this type the beneficiary should normally be expected to seek rectification of the will in order to mitigate the damage caused to him by the solicitor's negligence, and any tort damages would then be confined to the costs of the rectification proceedings. The requirement to mitigate is, however, subject to an overall test of reasonableness[3]. In a subsequent case the Court of Appeal distinguished *Walker's* case on the facts and held that in a complicated situation, which included an interested party living in Canada, the plaintiffs had not failed to mitigate by omitting to seek rectification of the will within the six month time-limit allowed for bringing such proceedings[4].

[1]   See the *Administration of Justice Act 1982, s 20*.
[2]   *[1999] 1 WLR 727, [1999] 1 All ER 685*. See Eoin O'Dell 'Restitution, Rectification, and Mitigation: Negligent Solicitors and Wills, Again' (2002) 65 MLR 360.
[3]   See *Pilkington v Wood [1953] Ch 770, [1953] 2 All ER 810*.
[4]   See *Horsefall v Haywards [1999] 1 FLR 1182, [1999] Lloyd's Rep PN 332*.

Where interests of third party and client do not coincide

[8.22]   In general the potential for a lawyer to be liable to a third party will usually be limited by the need, of which the 'will' cases are the paradigm, for both client and third party to have been, as Sir Robert Megarry put it in *Ross v Caunters*, 'on the same side'.[1] But the case of *Al-Kandari v J R Brown & Co*[2] indicates that those words should not be taken too literally. In that case the defendant firm of solicitors, who were acting for the husband in a matrimonial matter, undertook to retain their client's passport. He nevertheless managed to get it back and to take the children of the marriage out of the country[3]. The Court of Appeal held the solicitors liable in negligence to the plaintiff wife for failing to alert her to the fact that the passport had left their possession.[4] On the other hand, in *Connolly-Martin v Davis*[5] the defendant barrister incorrectly advised his client that he was no longer bound by an earlier undertaking given to the court on the latter's behalf. The opposing party suffered loss as a result and sued the defendant, but without success. The Court of Appeal held that a barrister handling litigation will normally owe no duty of care to his client's opponents.

[1]   See *[1980] Ch 297* at 310, *[1979] 3 All ER 580* at 598.
[2]   *[1988] QB 665, [1988] 1 All ER 833, CA*. Cf *Welsh v Chief Constable of Merseyside [1993] 1 All ER 692*.
[3]   See also *Hamilton Jones v David & Snape [2004] 1 All ER 657*.
[4]   The court reversed the decision of French J at first instance (reported in *[1987] QB 514*) who, while holding that a duty of care had existed, had rejected the plaintiff's claim essentially on grounds of remoteness.
[5]   *[1999] Lloyd's Rep PN 790*.

Liability exceptional

[8.23]   On the whole, therefore, situations in which lawyers will be liable to parties whose interests are not coincident with those of their own clients are likely to continue to be rare.[1] In *Ross v Caunters* itself Sir Robert Megarry said:[2]

'In broad terms, a solicitor's duty to his client is to do for him all that he properly can, with, of course, proper care and attention … The solicitor owes no such duty to those who are not his clients. He is no guardian of their interests. What he does for his client may be hostile and injurious to their interests; and sometimes the greater the injuries the better he will have served his client. The duty owed by a solicitor to a third party is entirely different. There is no trace of a wide and general duty to do all that properly can be done for him. Instead, in a case such as the present, there is merely a duty, owed to him as well as the client, to use proper care in carrying out the client's instructions for conferring the benefit on the third party.'[3]

Of course, these remarks were directed at cases in which the plaintiff never relied on the solicitor's advice. If a third party *did* actually rely on that advice, to the solicitor's knowledge, and did so to his detriment, then he should be able to claim against the solicitor simply on the principle in *Hedley Byrne & Co v Heller & Partners Ltd*[4], without invoking the rule in *White v Jones*. Thus, where the client is a company, for example, the solicitor might also owe a duty in tort to the principal shareholder, if the latter was relying on him to protect his interests.[5] But experienced businessmen will usually be regarded as capable of protecting their own interests, especially in straightforward transactions[6].

[1] Cf B Markesinis 'Fixing Acceptable Boundaries to the Liability of Solicitors' (1987) 103 LQR 346.
[2] See *[1980] Ch 297 at 322, [1979] 3 All ER 580* at 599.
[3] See also *per* Brennan CJ in *Hill v Van Erp (1997) 188 CLR 159*: ' … the solicitor's duty is to exercise professional skill and knowledge in the lawful protection and advancement of the client's interests in the transaction in which the solicitor is retained and that duty cannot be tempered by the existence of a duty to any third person whose interests in the transaction are not coincident with the interests of the client. But the interests of a client who retains a solicitor to carry out the client's testamentary instructions and the interests of an intended beneficiary are coincident.'
[4] *[1964] AC 465, [1963] 2 All ER 575, HL*. See generally CHAPTER 4 above.
[5] See *R P Howard Ltd v Woodman Mathews & Co [1983] BCLC 117*. Cf *Woodward v Wolferstans [1997] NPC 51*.
[6] See *Brownie Mills v Shrimpton [1999] Lloyd's Rep PN 39 (NZ CA)*.

Conveyancing

[8.24] If a solicitor is merely acting as agent for his own client in the latter's dealings with a third party, it has been held, in *Gran Gelato Ltd v Richcliff (Group) Ltd*,[1] that liability for negligent misstatement will rarely be imposed on the solicitor. 'In normal conveyancing transactions', observed Sir Donald Nicholls V-C,[2] 'solicitors who are acting for a seller do not in general owe to the would-be buyer a duty of care when answering inquiries before contract or the like'. The decision in the *Gran Gelato* case, has however, been the subject of considerable criticism,[3] and may be vulnerable to re-examination in a suitable future case.[4] In so far as it constitutes an exception to liability for negligent misstatement, which would otherwise be expected to arise upon general *Hedley Byrne* principles, it may be based upon a specific policy immunity relating to conveyancing transactions.[5]

[1] *[1992] Ch 560, [1992] 1 All ER 865*.
[2] *[1992] Ch 560 at 570, [1992] 1 All ER 865 at 872*.
[3] See especially *per* Hobhouse LJ in *McCullagh v Lane Fox & Partners [1996] 1 EGLR 35, CA*. See also P Cane 'Negligent Solicitor Escapes Liability' (1992) 109 LQR 539 and A Tettenborn 'Enquiries Before Contract – The Wrong Answer?' [1992] 51 CLJ 415.
[4] Cf C Passmore 'When do Solicitors Owe Third Party Duties of Care' (1996) NLJ 409.
[5] See *per* Hobhouse LJ *McCullagh v Lane Fox & Partners [1996] 1 EGLR 35, CA*.

E Nature of a solicitor's contractual duty

[8.25] As far as a solicitor's relationship with his *own* client is concerned, the co-existence, since the decisions in *Midland Bank Trust Co v Hett, Stubbs & Kemp* and *Henderson v Merrett Syndicates Ltd*, of duties in contract and tort, has had an incidental effect on limitation and also, possibly, upon issues such as remoteness.[1] In certain circumstances it can significantly increase the scope of recoverable damage[2]. It has not, however, altered the scope of the solicitor's duty to his client nor the standard of care which he must show to him. 'A solicitor's retainer', as Chadwick LJ observed in *UCB Bank v Hepherd Winstanley v Pugh*[3], 'is defined by the instructions which he receives'[4]. But there may, of course, be disputes as to the scope of the retainer, particularly if it is unwritten.[5] Difficult questions can therefore arise as to exactly what the solicitor's obligations were on the facts of a particular case. Three issues may perhaps be identified. First, how should the instructions given to a solicitor be interpreted? Secondly, when, if at all, should a solicitor go beyond his instructions as literally interpreted? Thirdly, does the standard of care to be expected of a solicitor vary with his own level of expertise or specialisation?

[1] Cf *H Parsons (Livestock) Ltd v Uttley Ingham & Co Ltd [1978] QB 791, [1978] 1 All ER 525, CA.*
[2] See *Hamilton Jones v David & Snape [2004] 1 All ER 657* (mental distress).
[3] See *[1999] Lloyd's Rep PN 963*, CA.
[4] See also *per* Oliver J in *Midland Bank Trust Co v Hett, Stubbs & Kemp [1979] Ch 384* at 403.
[5] See *Griffiths v Evans [1953] 2 All ER 1364, [1953] 1 WLR 1424, CA.* Cf *Hall v Meyrick [1957] 2 QB 455, [1957] 2 All ER 722, CA.*

Interpreting the instructions

[8.26]   In *Credit Lyonnais v Russell Jones & Walker* [1] Laddie J said:

'In deciding what are the duties shouldered by a solicitor, the first step is to construe the instructions given by the client and accepted by the lawyer. In doing this, it must be borne in mind that in most cases the client is not a lawyer. He will ask the lawyer to carry out certain tasks for him, although the formulation of those tasks may not be expressed with the precision one would expect of a lawyer. The lawyer accepts the instructions on that basis. If there is a bona fide obscurity as to the terms of the instructions, the lawyer should clarify them'.[2]

The approach which should be adopted by a solicitor, towards the interpretation and clarification of his instructions, will therefore depend to some extent upon the degree of sophistication to be expected of the client. In *Lloyds Bank v Burd Pearse*[3], Evans-Lombe J, acquitting solicitors of an allegation that they had been negligent by merely confirming a transfer of title to land instead of carrying out an investigation of it, said that the defendants 'were being instructed by a well-established and experienced mortgage lender and were entitled to construe the document evidencing their retainer narrowly'[4].

[1] See *[2003] Lloyd's Rep PN 7* at para 21.
[2] Cf *Gray v Buss Murton [1999] PNLR 882* (presumption in favour of client's view where terms of retainer are in dispute).
[3] See *[2000] PNLR 71*.
[4] See also *National Home Loans Corpn plc v Giffen, Couch & Archer (a firm) [1997] 3 All ER 808, [1998] 1 WLR 207, CA; Riley v Pickersgill [2004] UKPC 14, [2004] PNLR 31.*

Going beyond literal interpretation?

[8.27]   In *Clark Boyce v Mouat*[1] Lord Jauncey, delivering the Opinion of the Judicial Committee of the Privy Council, said:

'When a client in full command of his faculties and apparently aware of what he is doing seeks the assistance of a solicitor in the carrying out of a particular transaction, that solicitor is under no duty whether before or after accepting instructions to go beyond those instructions by proffering unsought advice on the wisdom of the transaction. To hold otherwise could impose intolerable burdens on solicitors.'

This passage was applied by Jacob J when acquitting defendant solicitors of negligence in *Guild (Claims) Ltd v Eversheds*[2] for not advising specifically that material should be included in a circular to be distributed to the shareholders of a company, in circumstances in which the material and the question of inclusion were familiar to the directors and had been considered by them. On the other hand, as Jacob J himself emphasised, although 'commercial matters are for the client ... things are not so simple that one can say the solicitor's duty simply stops at questions of law'; this is not least because 'solicitors concerned with assisting parties in relation to commercial transactions are often faced with commercial considerations'[3].

[1] See *[1994] 1 AC 428* at 437.
[2] See *[2000] Lloyd's Rep PN 910* at para 21.
[3] See above at para 22.

Scope of the 'retainer'

[8.28] In practice the question of how the instructions should have been construed, and that of whether the solicitor should have regarded his duties as going beyond those indicated by a literal interpretation, will often not be separated but instead subsumed under the general process of determining the scope of the 'retainer'. In *Credit Lyonnais v Rusell Jones & Walker*[1] Laddie J said:

' ... If, in the course of doing that for which he is retained, [a solicitor] becomes aware of a risk or a potential risk to the client, it is his duty to inform the client. In doing that he is neither going beyond the scope of his instructions nor is he doing "extra" work for which he is not going to be paid. He is simply reporting back to the client on issues of concern which he learns of as a result of, and in the course of, carrying out his instructions'[2].

In the *Credit Lyonnais* case a firm of solicitors was held to have been negligent in failing to warn of the consequences of a specific clause in a commercial lease; notwithstanding their contention that their instructions, literally interpreted, merely required them to find out whether the landlord was prepared to extend the notice period. On the other hand a solicitor acting for a claimant is not, as a matter of course, expected to investigate the solvency of the defendant[3]. Nor should he disclose confidential information obtained while acting for someone else[4].

[1] See *[2003] Lloyd's Rep PN 7* at para 28.
[2] See also *Mortgage Express Ltd v Bowerman & Partners [1996] 2 All ER 836* at 842 *per* Bingham LJ; *Boyce v Rendells (1983) 268 EG 268* at 272 *per* Lawton LJ.
[3] See *Thomas Snell & Passmore v Rose [2000] PNLR 378, CA*. See also *Riley v Pickersgill [2004] UKPC 14, [2004] PNLR 31*.
[4] See *Hilton v Barker Booth & Eastwood [2005] 1 All ER 651*.

Standard of care

[8.29] As far as the *standard* of care is concerned, it has long been accepted that it is to use reasonable care and skill. The question whether a defendant solicitor complied with that standard can obviously be a fertile source of disputes, but the principle involved will normally be clear. Megarry J once questioned whether the contractual standard of care owed by a solicitor to his client might not in fact be *higher*, at least in some cases, than the approach adopted by the law of tort[1]. But the proposition that the duty of care owed by a solicitor to his client, and normally implied into the contract between them, might vary depending upon such factors as the reputation, expertise and cost of the particular firm, would be replete with difficulty; and it has never been adopted. Nevertheless, the standard of care is, of course, itself related to the expertise professed by the lawyer in question.[2] A specialist will therefore be judged by the standard reasonably to be expected of specialists in that branch of the law[3], and general practitioners by the standard of the reasonably competent general practitioner[4]. In assessing the standard reasonably to be expected of local solicitors, the Court of Appeal will apparently 'place great weight' on the opinion of the local circuit judge, if he was the judge below[5].

[1]   See *Duchess of Argyll v Beuselinck [1972] 2 Lloyd's Rep 172* at 183 wondering if the client who 'engages an expert, and doubtless expects to pay commensurate fees, is … not entitled to expect something more than the standard of the reasonably competent?'
[2]   See *Yates Property Corp v Boland [1999] Lloyd's Rep PN 459 (Aus)*.
[3]   See *Matrix-Securities Ltd v Theodore Goddard (a firm) [1997] NLJR 1847*, in which a firm of solicitors and a QC were both unsuccessfully sued for negligence in respect of a tax matter. Lloyd J observed that the solicitors' duty was 'to exercise all such skill and care as reasonably competent solicitors professing specialist tax expertise' would exercise, and that the QC was similarly 'under a duty to exercise all such skill and care as a reasonably competent tax specialist silk would devote' to the tasks in question: both duties were held to have been discharged. See also *Green v Collyer-Bristow [1999] Lloyd's Rep P N 798* (liability imposed).
[4]   See *Balamoan v Holden & Co (1999) WL 477470 (LEXIS), CA*. Cf *Estill v Cowling Swift & Kitchin [2000] Lloyd's Rep PN 378*.
[5]   See *per* Brooke LJ in *Balamoan v Holden & Co (1999) WL 477470 (LEXIS), CA*.

F Acting for separate parties

Conveyancing

[8.30]   It is common in conveyancing transactions for the same solicitor to act both for the purchaser of the property and for the mortgagee providing part of the finance. In recent years institutional lenders have been disposed to increase the scope of their standing instructions to solicitors, thereby potentially increasing the number of cases in which the latter may be liable in the event of default by the borrower. This practice has become a matter of concern to conveyancers, and has generated a considerable volume of litigation.[1] In *Mortgage Express Ltd v Bowerman & Partners*[2] the Court of Appeal had occasion to consider the scope of a defendant solicitor's liability in such a case. The defendant happened to discover, while investigating title, that the property in question had very recently changed hands for a very much smaller sum than the figure at which it had been valued for the purpose of the current transaction, and much smaller than the size of the mortgage. The defendant drew this discrepancy to the attention of the purchaser, who nevertheless proceeded, but not to the plaintiff mortgagees. The purchaser defaulted, and when their security proved to be inadequate, the plaintiffs sued the solicitor for failing to advise them of the discrepancy. Their claim succeeded. There was no conflict of interest between purchaser and mortgagee rendering the information confidential to the former, and the instructions issued to the defendant by the plaintiff 'did not suggest that the solicitor's duty began and ended with the report on title'[3] as the defendant had originally suggested. Sir Thomas Bingham MR concluded that:

'A client cannot expect a solicitor to undertake work he has not asked him to do, and will not wish to pay him for such work. But if in the course of doing the work he is instructed to do the solicitor comes into possession of information which is not confidential and which is clearly of potential significance to the client, I think that the client would reasonably expect the solicitor to pass it on and feel understandably aggrieved if he did not ... if, in the course of investigating title, a solicitor discovers facts which a reasonably competent solicitor would realise might have a material bearing on the valuation of the lender's security or some other ingredient of the lending decision, then it is his duty to point this out.'

1 See D Halpern and T Rosen Peacocke 'What is the Extent of a Solicitor's Duty of Disclosure to a Mortgagee?' (1997) NLJ 97.
2 *[1996] 2 All ER 836, CA.* Sir Thomas Bingham MR, Millett and Schiemann LJJ.
3 See *per* Sir Thomas Bingham MR, *[1996] 2 All ER 836* at 841. The instructions referred to the 'normal duties of a solicitor when acting for a mortgagee'.

Absence of specific instructions

[8.31]   *Bowerman*'s case was distinguished by the Court of Appeal itself in *National Home Loans Corp plc v Giffen Couch & Archer*.[1] In this case the instructions issued by the lenders to the defendant solicitors were construed strictly, and the defendants were held to have been under no duty to pass on information which put in doubt the capacity of the borrowers to repay the loan, since they had not been given a specific instruction to do so. *Bowerman*'s case was said to have turned on its 'particular circumstances', including the wider instructions issued to the solicitors and the fact that the information which they failed to pass on had been discovered directly in the process of investigating title.[2]

1 *[1997] 3 All ER 808, [1998] 1 WLR 207, CA,* Peter Gibson, Hobhouse and Leggatt LJJ.
2 See *per* Peter Gibson LJ (with whom Hobhouse and Leggatt LJJ agreed) in *[1997] 3 All ER 808* at 815, *[1998] 1 WLR 207* at 215–216.

Nationwide cases

[8.32]   In 1999 Blackburne J heard a substantial number of cases brought by the Nationwide Building Society against various solicitors, many of which were claims for professional negligence. The solicitors had all acted for both the Society and the mortgagors in situations in which the latter had subsequently defaulted. In many of the cases the claims succeeded, typically on the ground of non-disclosure, but sometimes with a substantial reduction for the Society's own contributory negligence in the manner of its lending. Although each of the cases turned largely upon its own facts, the decisions do collectively represent an important body of material illustrating the application of the principles governing claims by lending institutions against solicitors in such situations[1]. They are all conveniently reported in the 1999 volume of Lloyd's Reports on Professional Negligence.

1 See also the decisions of Chadwick J reported sub nom *Bristol and West Building Society v Fancy & Jackson (a firm) [1997] 4 All ER 582.*

Other situations

[8.33]   Cases in which solicitors may find themselves acting for more than one party to a transaction are not confined to conveyancing. In any such situation the solicitor should be aware of the danger of a conflict of interest, and should decline to act if necessary[1]. The House of Lords has, however, recently confirmed that solicitors may continue to act for both husband and wife when the husband proposes that the family home should be used as security for a loan for his own business purposes. In *Royal Bank of Scotland v Etridge (No 2)*[2], Lord Nicholls said:[3]

'A requirement that a wife should receive advice from a solicitor acting solely for her will frequently add significantly to the legal costs. Sometimes a wife will be happier to be advised by a family solicitor known to her than by a complete stranger. Sometimes a solicitor who knows both husband and wife and their histories will be better placed to advise than a solicitor who is a complete stranger ... When accepting instructions to advise the wife the solicitor assumes responsibilities directly to her, both at law and professionally. These duties ... are owed to the wife alone. He is concerned only with her interests. I emphasise, therefore, that in every case the solicitor must consider carefully whether there is any conflict of duty or interest and, more widely, whether it would be in the best interests of the wife for him to accept instructions from her ... If at any stage the solicitor becomes concerned that there is a real risk that other interests or duties may inhibit his advice to the wife he must cease to act for her'.

[1]   See *Hilton v Barker Booth & Eastwood [2005] 1 All ER 651*.
[2]   *[2002] 2 AC 773, [2001] 4 All ER 449*.
[3]   See above at paras 73 and 74.

G Counting the cost

Lost claims

'Loss of chance'

[8.34]   If a solicitor's negligence has resulted in a possible claim being struck out or becoming statute-barred, the judge trying the negligence claim should not attempt to 'try' the lost claim himself, in order to determine whether or not it would have succeeded[1]. Instead damages should be assessed on a 'loss of chance' basis[2], with any discount, if appropriate in the circumstances, for the hazards of litigation[3], and any other factors relevant in the particular situation[4]. In a well-known passage in his judgment in *Mount v Barker Austin (a firm)*[5] Simon Brown LJ set out the principles to be adopted in cases of this type, and in the later case of *Sharif v Garrett & Co* he summarised his own earlier exposition as follows[6]:

'First, the court has to decide whether the claimant has lost something of value or whether on the contrary his prospects of success in the original action were negligible. Secondly, assuming the claimant surmounts this initial hurdle, the court must then 'make a realistic assessment of what would have been the plaintiff's prospects of success had the original litigation been fought out'. With regard to the first stage, the evidential burden rests on the negligent solicitors: they, after all, in the great majority of these cases will have been charging the claimant for their services and failing to advise him that in reality his claim was worthless so that he would be better off simply discontinuing it. The claimant, therefore, should be given the benefit of any doubts as to whether or not his original claim was doomed to inevitable failure. With regard to the second stage ... the court will tend to assess the claimant's prospects generously given that it was the defendant's negligence which has lost him the chance of succeeding in full or fuller measure'.

1 See *Sharif v Garrett & Co [2002] 3 All ER 195.*
2 See *Channon v Lindley Johnstone [2002] Lloyd's Rep PN 342.* For the very different approach adopted in clinical negligence cases see *Gregg v Scott [2005] UKHL 2*, discussed above in CHAPTER 2 at para [2.22] and CHAPTER 3 at para [3.10].
3 Such a discount should not be made automatically. See *per* Swinton Thomas LJ in *Charles v Hugh James Jones & Jenkins (a firm) [2000] 1 All ER 289* at 305–306: ' ... there must be facts and evidence which support such a deduction being made'.
4 See *Harrison v Bloom Camillin (No 2) [2000] Lloyd's Rep PN 89.*
5 See *[1998] PNLR 493* at 510–511. See also *Kitchen v Royal Air Forces Association [1958] 2 All ER 241, [1958] 1 WLR 563* and *Allied Maples Group Ltd v Simmons and Simmons (a firm) [1995] 4 All ER 907, [1995] 1 WLR 1602, CA.*
6 See *[2002] 3 All ER 195* at page 206.

Negotiations

[8.35] The 'loss of chance' approach is not confined to litigation, it may also be applied where the claimant contends that, but for the solicitor's negligence, he might have been able to secure a more favourable outcome in negotiations with a third party[1].

1 See *Allied Maples Group Ltd v Simmons and Simmons (a firm) [1995] 4 All ER 907, [1995] 1 WLR 1602, CA.* See also *Lloyds Bank v Parker Bullen [2000] Lloyd's Rep PN 51; Brinn v Russell Jones & Walker (a firm) [2003] Lloyd's Rep PN 70.* Cf *Motor Crown Petroleum v SJ Berwin & Co [2000] Lloyd's Rep PN 438, CA.*

Date for assessment

[8.36] The date for the assessment of damages will be the date on which the notional trial of the 'lost' claim would notionally have taken place. Consideration of developments since to that date will normally be inappropriate[1]. In certain circumstances, however, subsequent developments may be taken into account if relevant to quantification of an already established head of damage[2]. In *Charles v Hugh James Jones & Jenkins* Swinton Thomas LJ said[3]:

> '[I]t would be absurd ... if ... at the notional trial date the medical evidence indicated that there was a strong probability that the claimant would in future suffer some adverse medical consequence as a result of the injuries sustained in the accident, but it was shown as at the date of the actual hearing that there was no such risk, that the claimant should recover damages in respect of it. Similarly, if there was evidence as at the notional trial date that that the probability was that the claimant would never work again, but at the actual trial date he or she had obtained remunerative employment, it would be wrong not to take that fact into account. Equally if the evidence was less certain as to the claimant's prospects of obtaining employment at the notional trial date, but it was quite certain as at he actual trial date that she would be unable to go back to work again, that is a fact which can properly be considered by the judge. In my judgment, it would be absurd and wrong in principle to disregard such evidence'.

1 See *Hunter v Earnshaw [2001] PNLR 42.*
2 See *Charles v Hugh James Jones & Jenkins [2000] 1 All ER 289, CA.*
3 See above at p 301. But cf *per* Sir Richard Scott V-C at p 306, who appeared to reserve his opinion on the point.

Insolvency

[8.37]   A solicitor will not normally, however, however, have a duty to guard against a claim becoming worthless as a result of person against whom it is made becoming insolvent, even if timely prosecution of the claim would have resulted in a judgment being obtained before the insolvency occurred[1].

[1]   See *Pearson v Sanders Witherspoon [2000] Lloyd's Rep PN 151, CA.*

Negligent advice

Action or omission?

[8.38]   Where a solicitor has negligently given inadequate advice, or incorrect information, to his client, a number of issues may arise. In *Bristol and West Building Society v Mothew*[1] the defendant solicitor, while acting in a mortgage transaction for both the plaintiff lenders and the borrower, negligently provided incorrect information to the plaintiffs as to other indebtedness of the borrower. When the latter defaulted, the question arose as to the nature and extent of the defendant's liability to the plaintiffs. In the Court of Appeal Millett LJ distinguished as follows between positive action and mere omission:[2]

> 'Where a client sues his solicitor for having negligently failed to give him proper advice, he must show what advice should have been given and (on a balance of probabilities) that if such advice had been given he would not have entered into the relevant transaction or would not have entered into it on the terms he did. The same applies where the client's complaint is that the solicitor failed in his duty to give him material information ... Where, however, a client sues his solicitor for having negligently given him incorrect advice or for having negligently given him incorrect information, the position appears to be different. In such a case it is sufficient for the plaintiff to prove that he *relied* on the advice or information, that is to say that he would not have acted as he did if he had not been given such advice or information. It is not necessary for him to prove that he would not have acted as he did if he had been given the proper advice or the correct information.'[3]

[1]   *[1998] Ch 1, [1996] 4 All ER 698, CA*; Millett, Otton and Staughton LJJ.
[2]   See *[1998] Ch 1* at 11, *[1996] 4 All ER 698* at 705–706 (emphasis supplied).
[3]   See also *Downs v Chappell [1996] 3 All ER 344, [1997] 1 WLR 426, CA*, on which Millett LJ relied.

Application of SAAMCO principles

[8.39]   In *Mothew*'s case itself the defendant had positively misrepresented the position to the plaintiffs, the case therefore came within the second category and 'the necessary causal link between the defendant's negligence and the mortgage advance was proved'.[1] Although liability was therefore established, the damages recoverable (if any) remained to be assessed. On this point Millett LJ referred to the speech of Lord Hoffmann in the House of Lords in *South Australia Asset Management Corp v York Montague Ltd*[2] and drew a distinction 'between a duty to advise someone as to what cause of action he should take and a duty to provide information for the purpose of enabling someone else to decide upon his course of action'.[3] The instant case was of the latter type. Millett LJ then continued as follows:[4]

'In the former case, the defendant is liable for all the foreseeable consequences of the action being taken. In the latter case, however, he is responsible only for the consequences of the information being wrong. The measure of damages is not necessarily the full amount of the loss which the plaintiff has suffered by having entered into the transaction but only that part, if any, of such loss as is properly attributable to the inaccuracy of the information. If the plaintiff would have suffered the same loss even if the facts had actually been as represented the defendant is not liable.'[5]

In *Mothew's* case the borrowers had defaulted soon after taking out the mortgage even though their other borrowing, with respect to which the defendant had been in beach of duty to the plaintiffs, had actually been trivial. It was therefore possible that they would have defaulted *even if* there had been no other borrowing and hence no breach of duty by the defendant; any loss suffered in consequence of the default could then have been due to a fall in property values at the time when the plaintiff realised the security, for which they would have been remediless. The case was therefore remitted for this issue to be determined and damages assessed in consequence.

¹   See *[1998] Ch 1* at 11, *[1996] 4 All ER 698* at 706. Cf *Boateng v Hughmans [2002] Lloyd's Rep PN 449*.
²   See *[1997] AC 191*, *[1996] 3 All ER 365* and CHAPTER 3 above.
³   See *[1998] Ch 1* at 12, *[1996] 4 All ER 698* at 706.
⁴   See *[1998] Ch 1* at 12, *[1996] 4 All ER 698* at 707.
⁵   See also *Bristol and West Building Society v Fancy & Jackson (a firm) [1997] 4 All ER 582*.

Chapter 9

Property and finance

A Land, valuation, and construction

The 'property' professions

[9.01]   A number of related professions deal with various aspects of real property, including the valuation of land and buildings and the design and construction of the latter. Architects, civil engineers and surveyors are the main groups involved; but the important function of valuation is often carried out by estate agents, who will often, but not necessarily, also be qualified surveyors.

Valuation

[9.01A] In *Singer & Friedlander Ltd v John D Wood & Co*[1] Watkins J said:[2]

'The valuation of land by trained, competent and careful professional men is a task which rarely, if ever, admits of precise conclusion. Often beyond certain well-founded facts so many imponderables confront the valuer that he is obliged to proceed on the basis of assumptions. Therefore, he cannot be faulted for achieving a result which does not admit of some degree of error.'

His Lordship went on to accept, on the basis of expert evidence, that the 'permissible margin of error' is 10 to 15% above or below the figure which at the time of valuation 'a competent careful and experienced valuer' would have arrived at 'after making all the necessary inquiries and paying proper regard to the then state of the market'. He concluded that any valuation falling outside this 'bracket' brought 'into question the competence of the valuer and the sort of care he gave to the task of valuation'.[3] In *Singer & Friedlander Ltd v John D Wood* itself the defendant firm of surveyors and valuers was found to have been negligent, after the application of these criteria, and was held liable to the plaintiff bankers for losses suffered as a result of an excessive valuation.[4] A valuer clearly does need to take care adequately to research the market in the area of the property in question[5]. In situations involving unusual properties, for which no market comparables are readily available, a valuer may be under a duty to *qualify* his valuation so as to indicate to the client the degree of uncertainty involved[6]. Moreover, he should also report any changes in the market to his client, such as a similar neighbouring property being sold for an unexpectedly high price[7]. A qualified surveyor is also expected to keep abreast of changes in the law affecting land valuation.[8]

[1]   *(1977) 243 EG 212, [1977] EGD 569.*

2   *(1977) 243 EG 212* at 213, *[1977] EGD 569* at 574.
3   Cf *per* Buxton LJ in *Merivale Moore plc v Strutt & Parker [1999] 2 EGLR 171* at 177: 'To find that his valuation fell outside the bracket is … a necessary condition of liability, but it cannot in itself be sufficient'. But failure to provide any *explanation* for the figure falling outside the bracket could establish negligence: see *Lloyd's TSB Bank v Edward Symmons & Partners [2003] 2 EGLR 95* at para 107 *per* Judge Richard Seymour QC.
4   For further discussion see two articles by H W Wilkinson: 'Valuing Within the "Bracket" ' (1995) NLJ 1267, and 'The Permissible Margin of Error' (1998) NLJ 481. See also J Murdoch 'The Margin of Error Approach to Negligence in Valuations' (1997) 13 PN 81.
5   See *Baxter v F W Gapp & Co Ltd [1939] 2 KB 271, [1939] 2 All ER 752, CA* (overruled in *Swingcastle Ltd v Alastair Gibson [1991] 2 AC 223, [1991] 2 All ER 353, HL*, but not on this point). For a detailed analysis of valuation procedures on particular facts see *Halifax Mortgage Services Ltd v Simpson (1998) 64 Con LR 117* (negligence claim failed). See also *UCB Corporate Services v Halifax [2000] EGLR 87, CA*.
6   See *Merivale Moore plc v Strutt & Parker [1999] Lloyd's Rep PN 734, CA*.
7   See *John D Wood (Residential & Agricultural v Knatchbull [2003] PNLR 17*.
8   See *Weedon v Hindwood, Clarke & Esplin (1975) 234 EG 121, [1975] EGD 750*.

Structural defects

[9.02]   Of course, in a case in which a surveyor simply overlooks obvious structural defects in a property he is asked to value[1], negligence will be easier to prove than in one in which the more abstract aspects of the process by which he arrived at his figure are called into question.[2] On the other hand, it has been held that a valuation is not to be confused with a structural survey, so that an estate agent asked to value a property for purchase as a retirement home was held not to have been negligent in failing to warn that the house had been built on peat and that settlement problems could lead to difficulties on resale.[3]

1   See *Philips v Ward [1956] 1 All ER 874, [1956] 1 WLR 471, CA*; *Hodder v Countrywide Surveyors Ltd [2003] PNLR 3*. See also *Yianni v Edwin Evans & Sons [1982] QB 438, [1981] 3 All ER 592*; *Perry v Sidney Phillips & Son [1982] 3 All ER 705, [1982] 1 WLR 1297, CA*; *London and South of England Building Society v Stone [1983] 3 All ER 105, [1983] 1 WLR 1242, CA*; *Morgan v Perry (1973) 229 EG 1737*.
2   See *Roberts v J Hampson & Co [1989] 2 All ER 504*, in which a surveyor was held liable for failing to spot dry-rot when carrying out a building society inspection of a home to be purchased by a couple of modest means. The judgment of Ian Kennedy J considers in some detail the extent of a surveyor's duty with respect to such matters as moving furniture and lifting carpets. See also *Baxall Securities Ltd v Sheard Walshaw Partnership [2002] Lloyd's Rep PN 231* (failure to detect defects in drainage system).
3   See *Sutcliffe v Sayer [1987] 1 EGLR 155, (1987) 281 Estates Gazette 1452, CA*. For criticism of this case on the ground that the distinction between a survey and a valuation is not tenable, see M Harwood, 'A Structural Survey of Negligent Reports' (1987) 50 MLR 588 at 594: 'Whether a house is bought to let, to live in or to die in, its valuation can only be related to its saleability.' But the defendant in *Sayer's* case was not a qualified surveyor, and this could limit the applicability of the decision in other cases.

Extent of compensateable loss

Prima facie rule

[9.03]   The prima facie rule for the measure of damages where a house has been negligently surveyed in a case involving a private purchaser is the diminution in value[1]. In addition 'the purchaser is entitled … to the reasonable costs of extricating himself from the purchase'[2].

1   See *Patel v Hooper & Jackson (a firm) [1999] 1 All ER 992, CA*.
2   See *Patel v Hooper & Jackson (a firm) [1999] 1 All ER 992* at 1001b *per* Nourse LJ. For further discussion of the measure of damages in property cases see, generally, CHAPTER 27 below.

The South Australia Asset Management case

[9.04]   It is now established, following the decision of the House of Lords in *South Australia Asset Management Corpn v York Montague Ltd*,[1] that where a valuer is negligent in assessing the value of property which is to be used as security for a loan, he will normally only be liable for the difference between his negligently assessed figure, and the 'true' figure, with the comparison being made *at the date of the valuation*. This means that the valuer will not be liable for any additional losses suffered by the lender, which are caused by subsequent falls in the property market, since these are considered to fall outside the scope of the vendor's duty[2]. If, however, the market *rises*, the valuer can take advantage of this as having partially or totally extinguished the claimant's loss.[3] The underlying principle applied in the *South Australia Asset Management* case is that the precise scope of the duty undertaken must be defined prior to the determination of the sum to be awarded as damages[4]. This principle is not confined to losses caused by falls in the market. In *Duncan Investments v Underwoods*[5] it was applied by the Court of Appeal to limit the liability of a negligent valuer in circumstances in which he had been asked to value a porfolio of properties on their individual residential resale value, but had been held liable to damages in the court below calculated with reference to their portfolio value.

[1]   *[1997] AC 191, [1996] 3 All ER 365, HL*. See CHAPTER 3 above.
[2]   In *Kenny & Good Pty Ltd v MGICA (1992) Ltd [2000] Lloyd's Rep PN 25* the High Court of Australia declined to follow the *South Australia Asset Management* case holding, in similar circumstances, that the valuer *would* be liable for losses resulting from a fall in the property market. See also criticism of the *South Australia Asset Management* case by Jane Stapleton in 'Negligent Valuers and Falls in the Property Market' (1997) 113 LQR 1.
[3]   See *per* Lord Hoffmann, *[1997] AC 191* at 218, *[1996] 3 All ER 365* at 376.
[4]   See *per* Lord Hoffmann, *[1997] AC 191* at 212–213, *[1996] 3 All ER 365* at 371–372.
[5]   *[1998] PN LR 754*.

Contributory negligence by lender

[9.05]   In *Platform Home Loans Ltd v Oyston Shipways*[1] Ltd the House of Lords had to consider a situation in which the lender's loss had exceeded the amount by which the negligent valuation had been excessive, but in which the lender had also been contributorily negligent. The House held that the deduction in respect of contributory negligence should be made to the basic loss i.e. the difference between the true value of the property at the date of the negligent over-valuation and the amount which the lenders had actually realised on a subsequent sale. The House reversed the Court of Appeal which had argued that, since the figure representing the extent of the over-valuation was the maximum which the lenders could have been awarded in any event, the deduction should have been applied to *that* (lower) figure. The property in the case itself had originally been worth £1 million, but had been negligently over-valued at £1.5 million on the strength of which the claimants had advanced a loan of £1 million. When they subsequently sold the property, however, the lenders realised only £430,000, thus making a basic loss of £570,000. Nevertheless, in lending such a high proportion of the figure at which the property had been valued the claimants were held to have been guilty of contributory negligence, assessed at 20%. The House of Lords awarded them £456,000[2] (ie 80% of the basic loss), whereas the Court of Appeal would have limited the award to £400,000 (ie 80% of the extent of the £500,000 over-valuation). The House emphasised, however, that the contributory negligence of the lender's had not contributed to the over-valuation itself and that, had it done so, the approach adopted by the Court of Appeal might have been appropriate[3].

1 *[1999] 1 All ER 833*. See Jane Stapleton 'Risk-Taking by Commercial Lenders' (1999) 115 LQR 527.
2 The actual figures in the case itself differ slightly from those in the text, which have been simplified for the sake of example.
3 See *per* Lord Millett in *[1999] 1 All ER 833* at 853.

Liability to third parties

The principle in Smith v Eric S Bush

[9.06]   In addition to his contractual duty to his own client to use reasonable care and skill, it is established that a surveyor valuing property may also find himself liable in tort to third parties.[1] In *Smith v Eric S Bush*[2] the plaintiff bought a house on mortgage and, in common with the widespread practice of such purchasers, particularly at the lower end of the market, did not commission her own independent survey but relied on that carried out for the building society. Unfortunately, the building society's surveyor negligently failed to notice major defects in the property. The House of Lords held that he was liable to the plaintiff in tort. He should have known that the purchaser, as well as the building society, was likely to rely on his valuation.[3] The status of the decision in *Smith v Eric S Bush*, in the light of developments in the law of negligence since it was decided, was reviewed by the Court of Appeal in *Merrett v Babb*[4]; a case considered by a majority of the Court of Appeal to have been indistinguishable on its facts from *Smith v Eric S Bush* itself. May LJ, with whom Wilson J agreed, observed that *Smith's* case was 'influenced by particular public policy considerations'[5] relating to the protection of purchasers of modest houses, and that its authority had not been diminished by later decisions of the House of Lords dealing with different situations[6].

1 On the important question of the extent to which *disclaimers* of liability can be effective in such cases, see CHAPTER 4 above and CHAPTER 27 below. See also paras [9.09] and [9.10] below.
2 *[1990] 1 AC 831, [1989] 2 All ER 514, HL.*
3 Approving the decision of Park J in *Yianni v Edwin Evans & Sons [1982] QB 438, [1981] 3 All ER 592.*
4 *[2001] QB 1174.* May LJ and Wilson J, Aldous LJ dissenting.
5 See *[2001] QB 1174* at para 30.
6 Eg *Caparo Industries v Dickman [1990] 2 AC 605, [1990] 1 All ER 568.* On 25 July 2001 the Appeal Committee of the House of Lords dismissed a petition by the defendant in *Merrett v Babb* for leave to appeal.

Qualifying as a 'third party'[1]

[9.07]   Nor is a surveyor's liability to third parties necessarily restricted to those who themselves act in reliance on his valuation. Thus, a surveyor who values a property on behalf of a mortgagee who is exercising his power of sale may also owe a duty to the mortgagor if, as will often be the case, it can be foreseen that his interests will suffer if the property is sold on the basis of an under-valuation.[2] On the other hand a valuer's liability to a 'lender' is confined to the party who *formally* made the loan; not to the party who in reality provided the funds – if that happened to be different[3].

1 See *Raja v Austin Gray (a firm) [2003] Lloyd's Rep PN 126.*
2 See *Garland v Ralph Pay & Ransom (1984) 271 EG 106, [1984] EGD 867.* Cf *Cuckmere Brick Co Ltd v Mutual Finance Ltd [1971] Ch 949, [1971] 2 All ER 633, CA* (see also *Tse Kwong Lam v Wong Chit Sen [1983] 3 All ER 54, [1983] 1 WLR 1349, PC*).
3 See *Barex Brokers Ltd v Morris Dean & Co [1999] PNLR 344, CA*: ' … the duty cannot attach to anyone who subsequently acquires by assignment the rights of the original lender': *per* Hutchison LJ.

Personal liability of surveyor

[9.08]   A surveyor's liability rests upon him or her as a professional person. An attempt in *Merrett v Babb*[1] to contend that, in the case of an employed surveyor, the liability rested solely with his firm to the exclusion of himself was rejected by a majority of the Court of Appeal. It is therefore incumbent upon each surveyor to ensure that sufficient professional indemnity cover is in place[2]. In *Merrett v Babb* itself the insolvency of his employer, without adequate insurance, left the defendant surveyor personally liable to meet a substantial claim without cover.

1   *[2001] QB 1174.*
2   See *[2001] QB 1174* at para 46 *per* May LJ.

Estate agents' particulars

[9.09]   In *McCullagh v Lane Fox & Partners*[1] the purchaser of a property sued the vendor's estate agent for misrepresentation in the particulars. Unusually, the plaintiff had decided to dispense with an independent survey and the defendants had become aware of this. The Court of Appeal was unanimous in holding that the defendants' standard disclaimer, printed in the particulars, had been effective to exclude any duty of care. The court was, however, divided on the question whether a duty of care would have arisen in the absence of the disclaimer. Sir Christopher Slade and Nourse LJ were of the opinion that, on the facts of the case, no duty would have arisen. Hobhouse LJ, in a long and detailed judgment, was, however, of the opinion that liability for negligent misstatement would have arisen under ordinary *Hedley Byrne* principles once the defendants knew that no independent survey was intended by the purchaser. It is submitted that the reasoning of Hobhouse LJ is to be preferred.

1   *[1996] 1 EGLR 35, CA.*

Inapplicable disclaimer

[9.10]   In *Duncan Investments Ltd v Underwoods*[1] estate agents sued in respect of a negligent valuation sought unsuccessfully to rely on a standard disclaimer, which had been printed in the particulars of the properties in question. The disclaimer stated that the vendor of the properties gave no representation or warranty, and that the estate agents had no authority so to do. On the facts of the case, however, the surveyor employed by the defendant estate agents had been asked by the claimant purchasers to advise separately on the resale value of the properties in particular circumstances, and the Court of Appeal held 'unhesitatingly' that the disclaimer had no application in respect of *that* advice – which was unrelated to the vendor and to the absence of authorisation from him to give representations or warranties.

1   *[1998] PNLR 754.*

Design and construction

[9.11]   It is beyond question that, on appropriate facts, an architect or engineer who is negligent in designing a structure, or in otherwise giving advice in the context of building operations, can be liable in tort to third parties, as well as in contract to his clients, for any loss or damage so caused. This was clearly established and illustrated by the 1963 case of *Clay v A J Crump & Sons Ltd*,[1] in which architects were held liable when their carelessness in the performance of their duties under a demolition contract was partly responsible for the collapse of a wall which killed two workmen on the site and injured a third. More recently, in *Rimmer v Liverpool City Council*[2] the defendants were held liable when a panel of excessively thin glass, which had been negligently incorporated by their architects into the design of a council flat, broke and injured the plaintiff[3].

1   *[1964] 1 QB 533, [1963] 3 All ER 687, CA.*
2   *[1985] QB 1, [1984] 1 All ER 930, CA.* Cf *Kelly v City of Edinburgh District Council (1983) SLT 593.*
3   See also *Baxall Securities v Sheard Walshaw Partnership [2002] Lloyd's Rep PN 231* (negligent design of drainage facilities: liability only negated by surveyors' negligence in failing to spot the defect, which broke the chain of causation).

Relevance of contract

[9.12]   Although it is obviously not in itself a defence to a claim by an injured third party that the defendant was acting under a contract with someone else, that contract may be *relevant* to tortious liability by determining the overall scope of the defendant's responsibilities in the operation. Thus, in *Clayton v Woodman & Sons (Builders) Ltd*[1] and *Oldschool v Gleeson (Contractors) Ltd*,[2] which involved claims against architects and consulting engineers respectively, the defendants were absolved from liability on the ground that their alleged carelessness amounted to no more than a legitimate refusal to interfere with responsibilities which had been allocated not to them but to the building contractors themselves. In similarly rejecting a claim against an architect in *Bellefield Computer Services v E Turner & Sons*[3], Potter LJ said:

' ... the question whether a particular defect in a building comes within the scope of an architect's duty of care to a subsequent occupier will depend upon the original design and/or supervisory obligations of the architect in question. The architect will not owe a duty of care in respect of defects for which he never had any design or supervisory responsibility in the first place'.

1   *[1962] 2 QB 533, [1962] 2 All ER 33, CA.*
2   *(1976) 4 BMLR 103.*
3   See *[2003] Lloyd's Rep PN 53, CA* at para 47.

Contractual liability without negligence?

[9.13]   Where professional people are sued by their own clients for breach of contract the usual implied term relating to the nature of the obligation undertaken is merely that reasonable skill and care will be used. But where the contract is for the production of a specific chattel, or perhaps even a building, albeit by the use of professional skill, there is some authority for the proposition that a term familiar in contracts for the sale of goods, namely that the object will be reasonably fit for its purpose, may be implied. If so, this will obviously put the professional person under a much more onerous obligation, since he will be liable even if he was not careless. The Court of Appeal held in the 1943 case of *Samuels v Davis*[1] that this higher contractual duty applied to a contract between a dentist and his patient for the supply of dentures. The proposition by counsel for the dentist that the obligation was merely the usual professional one of reasonable skill and care was expressly rejected. Du Parcq LJ distinguished situations involving surgery, such as the extraction of a tooth, where that would indeed be the standard, and observed that 'the case is entirely different where a chattel is ultimately to be delivered'.[2] This view subsequently received powerful support, albeit obiter, in the House of Lords. In *Independent Broadcasting Authority v BICC Construction Ltd*[3] a television aerial mast, which had been designed by the defendant structural engineers, collapsed. Three members of the House[4] inclined to the view that the designers, who were held liable for negligence, would still have been liable even if they had not been negligent. The clearest statement to this effect was made by Lord Scarman. He referred with approval to *Samuels v Davis* and expressed himself as follows:[5]

> 'The extent of the obligation is, of course, to be determined as a matter of construction of the contract. But, in the absence of a clear, contractual indication to the contrary, I see no reason why one who in the course of his business contracts to design, supply, and erect a television aerial mast is not under an obligation to ensure that it is reasonably fit for the purpose which he knows it is intended to be. The Court of Appeal held that this was the contractual obligation in this case, and I agree with them ... Counsel for the appellants, however, submitted that, where a design, as in this case, requires the exercise of professional skill, the obligation is no more than to exercise the care and skill of the ordinarily competent member of the profession ... However, I do not accept that the design obligation of the supplier of an article is to be equated with the obligation of a professional man in the practice of his profession ... In the absence of any terms (express or to be implied) negativing the obligation, one who contracts to design an article for a purpose made known to him undertakes that the design is reasonably fit for the purpose.'

[1]   *[1943] KB 526, [1943] 2 All ER 3, CA.*
[2]   *[1943] KB 526* at 530, *[1943] 2 All ER 3* at 6. See also *Young & Marten Ltd v McManus Childs Ltd [1969] 1 AC 454, [1968] 2 All ER 1169, HL* (especially *per* Lord Upjohn *[1969] 1 AC 454* at 473, *[1968] 2 All ER 1169* at 1176).
[3]   *(1980) 14 BLR 9.* See also the decision of the Court of Appeal: *(1978) 11 BLR 38.*
[4]   See *(1980) 14 BLR 9* at 26, 44–45, *per* Viscount Dilhorne and Lord Fraser of Tullybelton. For Lord Scarman's speech see n 5 below.
[5]   *(1980) 14 BLR 9* at 47–48. See also *per* Roskill LJ in the Court of Appeal: (1978). *11 BLR 38* at 51–52.

B Financial services

Accountants[1]

Standard of care

[9.14]   Accountants and auditors owe the usual professional duty of reasonable care and skill to their contractual clients. As in other professions the standard required to satisfy this test is not static. In *Re Thomas Gerrard & Son Ltd*,[2] decided in 1967, Pennycuick J held auditors liable for negligence for accepting too readily explanations from the managing director of a company, relating to altered invoices, when they should have investigated further and might then have discovered a fraud being perpetrated on the company. His Lordship distinguished an 1896 decision of the Court of Appeal,[3] in which auditors had been held not liable on similar facts, on the ground that 'the standards of reasonable care and skill are, on the expert evidence, more exacting today than those which prevailed in 1896'.[4] Moreover, while it will obviously sometimes be appropriate to recommend the taking of specialist advice, for example in relation to taxation, such a recommendation will not absolve from liability for negligence if the matter should have been within the defendant's competence in any event[5].

[1]   See generally *Law and Accountancy* (MLR Special Issue, November 1991).
[2]   *[1968] Ch 455, [1967] 2 All ER 525.*

3   See *Re Kingston Cotton Mill Co (No 2) [1896] 2 Ch 279, CA.*
4   *[1968] Ch 455* at 475, *[1967] 2 All ER 525* at 536.
5   See *Sayers v Clarke Walker [2002] EWCA Civ 910.*

Relevance of circumstances

[9.15]   The degree of care which should be taken will necessarily depend upon the circumstances of the particular case[1]. Thus a letter in which an accountant passes on information supplied to him, which subsequently turns out to have been inaccurate, will not necessarily constitute negligence, in the same way as it might do if the accountant had undertaken to provide independent verification of the information[2].

1   See *University of Keele v Price Waterhouse [2003] EWHC 1595, [2004] PNLR 8* (negligent misinterpretation of legislation).
2   See *HIT Finance v Cohen Arnold & Co [2000] Lloyd's Rep PN 135, CA.*

Applicability of general law on negligent misstatement

[9.16]   The most far-reaching change in the law relating to the liability of accountants has been the development of liability in tort as a result of expansion of the general law relating to negligent misstatement. This aspect of the law is of particular importance to accountants, not least because their work will often foreseeably be relied on by other persons as well as their clients.[1] It is also, however, of wider importance and is therefore considered at length in CHAPTER 4 above, to which reference should be made for further discussion of the applicable general principles. Nevertheless, recent cases involving negligence claims against accountants have highlighted issues which it is appropriate to consider here.

1   Cf *Caparo Industries plc v Dickman [1990] 2 AC 605, [1990] 1 All ER 568, HL.*

Alleging negligent tax advice

[9.17]   Clients who become embroiled in disputes with the Inland Revenue, which they feel obliged to compromise, may seek to allege that the tax advice given to them by their accountants was negligent. Those acting for such claimants should ensure that they plead their cases with sufficient particularity to make clear whether their allegation is that unqualified advice was negligently given in an area where the law was uncertain, and the risk of a dispute with the Revenue was high, or whether they are alleging that the advice was actually 'wrong'. Failure to make clear that the former was intended may result in the case being lost if the court decides that the advice was correct even if, in practice, the claimant would never have acted upon it if he had been properly advised as to the extent of the attendant uncertainty[1].

1   See *Grimm v Newman [2003] 1 All ER 67, CA.*

Duties to regulatory bodies

Solicitors' accounts

[9.18]   In *Law Society v KPMG Peat Marwick*[1] the defendant accountants were retained by a firm of solicitors to prepare the annual report to the Law Society required of solicitors by statute[2]. The form of the report, and the requisite accountancy qualifications of those preparing it, are prescribed by delegated legislation. The firm in question subsequently ceased to practice in circumstances which involved the commission of substantial frauds against its clients. As a result the solicitors' compensation fund paid out over £8 million. The Law Society sued the defendants alleging that they had been negligent in failing to qualify their report, and that had they not been the Law Society could have intervened earlier to prevent some of the losses. The defendants denied that they owed a duty of care to the Law Society, and this matter was tried as a preliminary issue. The Court of Appeal, unanimously upholding Sir Richard Scott V-C, decided in favour of the Law Society. The defendants argued, inter alia, that the claimants' regulatory function belonged to public law and that it was not an appropriate basis for a private law negligence action. The Court of Appeal had no hesitation in rejecting this argument, and in holding that the claim satisfied the criteria for the recovery of economic loss in tort.

[1]   *[2000] 4 All ER 540 CA*, affirming *[2000] 1 All ER 515*.
[2]   *Solicitors Act 1974, s 34*.

Aviation

[9.19]   In the earlier case of *Andrew v Kounnis Freeman*[1] the Court of Appeal declined to strike out a negligence claim by the Civil Aviation Authority against the auditors of a travel company which had collapsed, resulting in substantial expenditure by the fund which repatriates stranded passengers in such circumstances. The court below had been persuaded to strike out the claim applying *Caparo Industries v Dickman*[2], but the Court of Appeal held that it was at least arguable that that case was distinguishable on the facts. In the instant case the Authority had indicated that it would refuse to renew the travel company's licence unless it received audited accounts before a certain date. The defendant sent the accounts to the Authority, along with assurances about the company's finances. In these circumstances, the Court of Appeal indicated that the case would need to be tried to determine whether the accountants had assumed responsibility to the Authority for the accounts, thereby taking the case outside the *Caparo* principle that an auditor's duty is primarily to the company alone and not third parties.

[1]   *[2000] Lloyd's Rep PN 263*. See also *Independents Advantage Insurance Co v Personal Representatives of Cook (Deceased) [2003] Lloyd's Rep PN 109*.
[2]   *[1990] 2 AC 605, [1990] 1 All ER 568, HL*, see above CHAPTER 4.

Assuming responsibility

Distinguishing Caparo

[9.20]   The general principle in *Caparo Industries v Dickman* has been held to be arguably distinguishable in a number of other cases in which attempts to strike out negligence claims brought by third parties against auditors have been unsuccessful. In one of them, *Electra Private Equity Partners v KPMG Peat Marwick*[1], Auld LJ said:

'Actions of negligence against auditors ... are a notable example of facts-sensitive cases where the law is still in a state of transition and in which courts should normally take particular care before determining the matter against the plaintiff before the full facts are known'[2].

It is clear that the courts will not allow the *Caparo* decision to be used as a ritual incantation to prevent thorough exploration of cases in which it is alleged that defendant auditors had, on the facts, assumed responsibility to third parties in addition to the company itself[3]. Auditors who detect serious fraud on the part of a company's management may also be under an obligation to act as 'whistle blowers' by informing a third party, such as a regulator, at the earliest opportunity[4].

[1] See *[2001] 1 BCLC 589* at 614.
[2] See also *per* Chadwick LJ in *Coulthard v Neville Russell [1998] PNLR 276* at 289, CA.
[3] See also *Siddell v Smith Cooper & Partners [1999] Lloyd's Rep PN 79*, CA.
[4] See *Sasea Finance Ltd v KPMG [2000] 1 All ER 676*, CA.

Investment advice

Speculative transactions

[9.21]   Since their professional duties are usually relatively well defined, accountants are, in a sense, at one end of the spectrum of those whose work involves giving advice and information in a financial context. At the other end are stockbrokers and others who advise generally on investment. Clearly, the more speculative the field in question the more difficult it will be to establish that advice which led to losses was in fact given negligently. In *Stafford v Conti Commodity Services Ltd*[1] Mocatta J refused to hold a broker liable for advice given in respect of the commodities futures market, observing that 'in such an unpredictable market as this, it would require exceedingly strong evidence from expert brokers in relation to individual transactions to establish negligence on the part of the defendants'.[2] This decision was subsequently applied by the Court of Appeal in *Merrill Lynch Futures Inc v York House Trading Ltd*.[3] In this case the court struck out a counterclaim by the defendant investors who alleged negligent advice, relying solely on the fact that they had incurred losses, when sued by the plaintiff commodity brokers for unpaid commission.

[1] *[1981] 1 All ER 691*.
[2] *[1981] 1 All ER 691* at 698.
[3] *[1984] LS Gaz R 2544*, CA.

Factual and procedural errors

[9.22]   On the other hand, liability will be easier to establish if a broker carelessly gives advice based upon misleading factual information.[1] Liability will also be imposed if a stockbroker fails adequately to monitor investments when he had undertaken to do so[2].

[1] See *Elderkin v Merrill Lynch, Royal Securities Ltd (1977) 80 DLR (3d) 313*.
[2] See *Voisin v Matheson Securities (1999–2000) 2 ITELR 907 (Jersey Court of Appeal)*.

Personal financial planning

[9.23]   Although a degree of uncertainty necessarily accompanies all financial planning, not all financial advice involves investment of a highly speculative nature. It is clear, for example, that financial advisers involved in selling products such as pensions and mortgages can be shown to have been negligent in appropriate cases[1].

¹   See *Investors Compensation Scheme Ltd v West Bromwich Building Society (No2) [1999] Lloyd's Rep P N 496*; *Martin v Britannia Life Ltd [2000] Lloyd's Rep PN 412* (negligence proved but claim statute-barred). See also See G McMeel 'The liability of financial advisers in the wake of the pension mis-selling scandal' (1997) 13 PN 97.

Insurance

Brokers and the law of negligence

[9.24]   Whereas the rights and duties of underwriters are typically governed by the law of contract, specifically the rules of construction and the principles relating to such matters as disclosure and misrepresentation, the position of insurance *brokers* in the law of negligence has not infrequently been examined by the courts¹. Brokers must exercise professional skill and care in determining whether the wording of the cover they effect is appropriate to their client's requirements², and in ensuring that any limiting conditions are promptly and clearly explained to the client³.

¹   See *Alexander Forbes Europe v SBJ [2003] Lloyd's Rep PN 137* (Successful claim by insurance brokers against their own professional indemnity brokers for failing to provide notification of claims).
²   See *National Insurance & Guarantee Corpn v Imperio Reinsurance Co (UK) Ltd [1999] Lloyd's Rep IR 249*.
³   Cf *Pangood v Barclay Brown [1999] 1 All ER (Comm) 460, CA*.

Duty to protect client from avoidable uncertainty

[9.25]   In *FNCB v Barnet Devaney*¹ the claimant bank was mortgagee of a property which had been destroyed by fire. The claimants sued the defendant brokers for failing to effect valid insurance, the cover having been rejected by the insurers. The question whether the cover had in fact been valid involved a point of law which, at the time, had been unresolved. Although the defendants contended that the cover had been valid, the Court of Appeal held that they had been negligent in failing to effect readily available cover which would unquestionably have been valid, and which would have involved any necessity for the resolution of a disputed point of law in order to ascertain its validity².

¹   *[1999] 2 All ER (Comm) 233, CA*.
²   Cf *Grimm v Newman [2003] 1 All ER 67* at para 89 (Carnwath LJ).

Need to determine width of duty

[9.26]   A case of particular significance, decided by the House of Lords in 2001, is *Aneco Reinsurance Underwriting v Johnson & Higgs*¹. The claimants instructed the defendant brokers in the course of entering into a complex transaction for which the claimants required reinsurance cover. The defendants effected such cover but it subsequently proved to be invalid and unenforceable, involving the claimants in disastrous losses. The claimants sued the defendants for negligence, and the question arose whether the defendants owed a duty not merely to effect valid reinsurance cover but also to advise on the availability, in the particular circumstances, of appropriate cover in the market. The Court of Appeal held that the defendants owed the wider duty and, moreover, that appropriate valid cover would not, in fact, have been available at all. The latter finding, which differed from that of the judge at first instance, was significant because if the claimants had known that effective reinsurance was unavailable they would not have entered into the transaction at all. The case proceeded to the House of Lords on the appropriate measure of damages. The defendants contended that, on the principle applied in *South Australia Management Corpn v York Montague Ltd*, their liability was limited to the losses resulting from the reinsurance having been ineffective, and did not extend to all the losses which the claimants had incurred as a result of entering into the transaction in the first place – which was a much larger sum.

1   *[2001] 2 All ER (Comm) 929.*

South Australia distinguished

[9.27]   The House of Lords, by a majority[1], distinguished the *South Australia* case and resolved the damages issue in the *Aneco* case favour of the claimants. Unlike the case of the valuers in the *South Australia* case, the brokers had owed a wide duty to advise on the situation in the reinsurance market as it affected the claimants' proposed transaction, and not merely to carry out a specific task such as a valuation. There was no doubt that the larger loss was a foreseeable consequence of the claimants entering into the transaction, and in view of the width of the defendants' duty the general principle that foreseeability is the relevant criterion for determining recoverable loss applied[2].

1   Lord Slynn, Lord Browne-Wilkinson, Lord Lloyd and Lord Steyn, Lord Millett dissenting.
2   See also *Youell v Bland Welch & Co Ltd (No 2) [1990] 2 Lloyd's Rep 431.*

Part four

Liability arising from land use

Chapter 10

Liability of occupiers

A The scope of 'occupation'

What can be 'occupied'?

[10.01]   The majority of situations which give rise to questions concerning occupiers' liability inevitably concern land and premises. Nevertheless, it is important to realise that the scope of the two relevant statutes, the *Occupiers' Liability Acts* of *1957* and *1984*, is not confined to such situations. The Acts also apply to 'any fixed or moveable structure, including any vessel, vehicle or aircraft'.[1] Thus, ships,[2] lorries,[3] ladders[4] and scaffolding,[5] for example, come within the legislation, as do empty houses which are no longer inhabited.[6]

[1]   *Occupiers' Liability Act 1957, s 1(3)(a)*. See also the *Occupiers' Liability Act 1984, s 1(2) and (9)*.
[2]   See *Ellis v Scruttons Maltby Ltd and Cunard Steamship Co Ltd [1975] 1 Lloyd's Rep 564*.
[3]   Cf *Lewys v Burnett and Dunbar [1945] 2 All ER 555*.
[4]   See *Wheeler v Copas [1981] 3 All ER 405*.
[5]   See *Kearney v Eric Waller Ltd [1967] 1 QB 29, [1965] 3 All ER 352*.
[6]   *Harris v Birkenhead Corpn [1976] 1 All ER 341, [1976] 1 WLR 279, CA*.

Who is an 'occupier'?

[10.02]   The *Occupiers' Liability Acts* provide that the question of who is an 'occupier', for their purposes, is to be answered by recourse to the common law.[1] In the leading case of *Wheat v E Lacon & Co Ltd*,[2] Lord Denning, in the House of Lords, said[3]:

> 'In order to be an 'occupier' it is not necessary for a person to have active control over the premises. He need not have exclusive occupation. Suffice it that he has some degree of control. He may share control with others. Two or more may be 'occupiers'. And whenever this happens, each is under a duty to use care towards persons coming lawfully on to the premises, dependent on his degree of control. If each fails in his duty, each is liable to a visitor who is injured in consequence of his failure, but each may have a claim to contribution from the other.'

In *Wheat v Lacon* itself a brewery company owned a public house which was run on their behalf by a resident manager who had living accommodation on the first floor. When a fatal accident occurred to a visitor in this accommodation, which was to all intents and purposes treated by the manager as his private dwelling, the House of Lords held that, on the facts, the brewery company retained sufficient control over the accommodation to qualify as an 'occupier' of it, in addition to the manager and his wife themselves.[4] The concept of dual occupation is also seen in cases in which even contractors, working only temporarily on premises, have been held to have sufficient control to qualify, along with others, as occupiers.[5] One consequence of the concept of dual occupation is that it is possible for a person to be a visitor in relation to one occupier but a trespasser in relation to another.[6]

[1] See the *Occupiers' Liability Act 1957, s 1(2)* and the *Occupiers' Liability Act 1984, s 1(2)(a)*.
[2] *[1966] AC 552, [1966] 1 All ER 582, HL.*
[3] *[1966] AC 552* at 578, *[1966] 1 All ER 582* at 594. See also *Bailey v Armes [1999] EGCS 21, CA.*
[4] The claim in respect of the accident ultimately failed due to lack of proof of any breach of the duty of care.
[5] See *Fisher v CHT Ltd* [1965] 2 All ER 601, [1965] 1 WLR 1093. See also *AMF International Ltd v Magnet Bowling Ltd* [1968] 2 All ER 789, [1968] 1 WLR 1028.
[6] See *Ferguson v Welsh [1987] 3 All ER 777* at 785, *[1987] 1 WLR 1553* at 1562–1563, *per* Lord Goff.

[10.03] The fact that *control*, rather than physical presence on the premises, is the key to the concept of 'occupation' was strikingly illustrated in *Harris v Birkenhead Corpn.*[1] In that case the defendant corporation was held to have been the 'occupier' of a house which it owned, but which had been left empty when the tenant vacated it. The Court of Appeal held the corporation liable for failing to take steps to board up the premises and prevent them from becoming a hazard to child trespassers.[2]

[1] *[1976] 1 All ER 341, [1976] 1 WLR 279, CA.* See, especially, *per* Megaw LJ *[1976] 1 All ER 341* at 349, *[1976] 1 WLR 279* at 288: '[It is] clear that in law the quality of being in physical possession, or having been in actual physical possession, is not in all cases – and is not in this case – a necessary ingredient of the legal status of occupier for the purposes with which we are concerned.'
[2] See also *Collier v Anglian Water Authority* (1983) Times, 26 March, CA (water authority 'occupier' of sea wall). Cf *Jordan v Achara (1988) 20 HLR 607, CA.*

B Liability to visitors

Persons qualifying as 'visitors'

[10.04] The common law, prior to the passing of the *Occupiers' Liability Act 1957*, imposed a two-tier standard of care upon occupiers (except to trespassers and to persons who contracted with the occupier for a right of entry) corresponding to a distinction which was drawn between two types of entrant: invitees and licensees. Broadly speaking, the occupier had to take reasonable care for the safety of his invitees, with whom he had a shared interest in their entry on to his property, but a lower duty, merely to warn of concealed dangers of which the occupier was actually aware, to his licensees; the latter being those who had his permission to enter but shared no common purpose with him.

Unified category

[10.05] One of the major changes in the law made by the 1957 Act was to abolish the distinction between invitees and licensees, and the separate duties of care associated with it, and to provide that entrants who would formerly have been members of either category would henceforth belong to a single, unified, category of 'visitors'.[1] It follows that, as far as the scope of the new category is concerned, the common law only remains relevant in determining its outer frontier so as to exclude those, such as trespassers, who were neither invitees nor licensees. Prior to the passing of the Act, there was a not inconsiderable body of case law in which the somewhat uncertain frontier *between* the two superseded categories was of importance.[2] But since the Act relatively little space has been taken up in the law reports, within the occupiers' liability context, by judicial consideration of which persons qualify as 'visitors' and most, but not all,[3] of it has been concerned with the question of whether or not the entrant was in fact a trespasser.[4] At the same time, the number of reported decisions in which the *standard* of care imposed by the Act has been considered has also been fairly small.

[1]   See the *Occupiers' Liability Act 1957, s 1(2)*.
[2]   For discussion and criticism of the previous law see, generally, the Third Report of the Law Reform Committee 'Occupiers' Liability to Invitees, Licensees and Trespassers' (Cmd 9305), which led to the passing of the 1957 Act.
[3]   Cf *Greenhalgh v British Railways Board [1969] 2 QB 286, [1969] 1 All ER 114, CA*.
[4]   See *Stone v Taffe [1974] 3 All ER 1016, [1974] 1 WLR 1575, CA* (person staying on licensed premises after hours).

Degree of simplification

[10.06]   While arguments based on the absence of reported cases can never be conclusive, since they discount the possibility of an inconvenient level of uncertainty when cases are decided on their own facts,[1] it is perhaps not unreasonable to infer that the legislation has been successful in achieving a useful degree of simplification of the law in this area. The Act also clarified the position of persons who enter premises under a right conferred by law, whose precise status had apparently been uncertain while the invitee and licensee distinction prevailed. Such persons now enjoy at least the same rights as 'visitors'.[2]

[1]   Cf the minority report of one member of the Law Reform Committee (the then Mr Kenneth Diplock QC) in Cmd 9305 at pp 43–44.
[2]   See the *Occupiers' Liability Act 1957, s 2(6)*.

The 'common duty of care'

[10.07]   The *Occupiers' Liability Act 1957, s 2(2)* provides as follows:

> 'The common duty of care is a duty to take such care as in all the circumstances of the case is reasonable to see that the visitor will be reasonably safe in using the premises for the purposes for which he is invited or permitted by the occupier to be there.'

It will be apparent that this formulation, guidance for the application of which is given in succeeding subsections, is virtually indistinguishable from the common law duty of care to 'neighbours' expounded in *Donoghue v Stevenson*.[1] In *McGivney v Golderslea*[2], Swinton Thomas LJ said that it was 'important to stress' that only *reasonable* care is required by the section. In that case the plaintiff slipped and fell against a glass door, which broke causing him injury. The strength of the glass did not comply with current building regulations but had complied with those in force when it was fitted. The Court of Appeal held that the defendant had not behaved unreasonably by failing to replace the original glass so as to comply with more modern practice.

[21]   *[1932] AC 562.*
[22]   *(2001) 17 Const LJ 454* (decided in 1997).

Activities on the land

[10.08] The similarity of the statutory formula to ordinary negligence, combined with the abolition of the elaborate distinction between the duties owed to invitees and licensees, has rendered less important a question which was sometimes significant at common law; namely, whether the rules relating to occupiers' liability were confined to injuries suffered due to the state of the premises or extended also to activities conducted by the occupier on them[1]. There was some authority for the proposition that, in the latter type of case, the duty owed was the general one laid down in *Donoghue*'s case, and that the entrants' status was irrelevant.[2] The reduction in the importance of this question, in the light of the formulation of occupiers' liability in the Act, is illustrated by the fact that no reported case since the Act has decided authoritatively whether that formulation does itself extend to the so-called 'activity' duty or is confined to the 'occupancy' duty.[3] The Act itself states that it is intended to regulate 'the duty which an occupier of premises owes to his visitors in respect of dangers due to the state of the premises *or to things done or omitted to be done on them*'.[4] But this wording does not itself settle the question since, having regard to the general background and context of the legislation, the phrase 'things done or omitted to be done' could not implausibly be confined to the erection of dangerous structures, or failure to repair, which would be within the scope of the 'occupancy' duty itself.

[1] 'The question whether the common law duty of care is subsumed in the common duty of care created by the *Occupiers Liability Act* or survives as an independent basis of claim in respect of activities carried out on premises is of no practical importance save possibly as a pleading point': *per* Mantell LJ in *Makepeace v Evans Brothers (Reading) [2001] ICR 241, CA* at para 7.

[2] See *Dunster v Abbott [1953] 2 All ER 1572, [1954] 1 WLR 58, CA; Slater v Clay Cross Co Ltd [1956] 2 QB 264, [1956] 2 All ER 625, CA*. See also *Slade v Battersea and Putney Hospital Management Committee [1955] 1 All ER 429, [1955] 1 WLR 207*.

[3] But cf *Videan v British Transport Commission [1963] 2 QB 650, [1963] 2 All ER 860, CA*.

[4] *Section 1(1)* (italics supplied).

Better view

[10.09] Indeed, the majority of commentators do take the view that the Act is confined to situations in which the condition of the premises themselves is dangerous,[1] albeit perhaps as a *result* of some activity, and does not cover dangerous activities unrelated to the premises as such but which just happen to be carried on there.[2] It is submitted that this is in fact the better view.[3] To expand the law relating to occupiers' liability to cover everything which happened to occur on a defendant's land would be illogical, and would also be apt to introduce unnecessary vagueness into the law.

[1] But cf dictum *per* Lord Keith in *Ferguson v Welsh [1987] 3 All ER 777* at 783, *[1987] 1 WLR 1553* at 1560, HL (dealing with the position under s *2(4)(b)* of the Act).

[2] See generally the discussion in P North *Occupiers' Liability* (1971) pp 71–87.

[3] Cf *Railway Comr v McDermott [1967] AC 169, [1966] 2 All ER 162, PC*.

Children[1]

[10.10] According to *section 2(3)* of the *Occupiers' Liability Act 1957*, the 'circumstances relevant' to establishing the content of the common duty of care in particular circumstances include 'the degree of care, and want of care, which would ordinarily be looked for in such a visitor'. The subsection then provides, by way of 'example', that 'an occupier must be prepared for children to be less careful than adults'. Whether an occupier has discharged his duty in a case in which a child visitor has been injured on his land will obviously be a question of fact in each case. Nevertheless, it is noteworthy that the courts have apparently been sensitive to the possible danger of imposing excessive burdens upon occupiers merely because they do not forbid children from playing on their land.[2] In *Simkiss v Rhondda Borough Council*[3] a seven-year-old child, accompanied by a friend aged ten, suffered serious injury when she fell down a steep grassy slope, which was a natural feature of the locality, while playing on land owned by the defendant council. The trial judge held the council liable for not having fenced off the area, but his decision was reversed by the Court of Appeal. Dunn LJ observed that:[4]

> 'It is almost as if it were suggested that an occupier should fence off a climbable tree in case a child climbed too high up it and fell out of it, and as far as I know a climbable tree has never been held to be dangerous to children ... There are many parts of the country with open spaces adjacent to houses where children play unattended, and this is to be encouraged.'

[1] See R Kidner 'The Duty of Occupiers Towards Children' (1988) 39 NILQ 150.
[2] See *Simonds v Isle of Wight Council [2003] EWHC 2303* (QB), (2003) Times, October 9, at para 30 *per* Gross J.
[3] *(1982) 81 LGR 460, CA.*
[4] *(1982) 81 LGR 460* at 470–471.

Parents' responsibility

[10.11] The primary responsibility for protecting small children from danger rests with their parents, and unless an area is so dangerous as to necessitate entry being forbidden in any event,[1] occupiers are entitled to assume, unless the known customs in the locality suggest the contrary, that parents will either warn their children of the existence of such dangers as are to be found there[2] or will prevent them from wandering on to the land in question unaccompanied.[3]

[1] In which case the children would be trespassers, on which see the *Occupiers' Liability Act 1984*, discussed below. But it should, perhaps, still be noted that a child attracted on to the defendant's land by an 'allurement' may, in consequence thereof, be classified in effect as a lawful visitor: see *Cooke v Midland Great Western Rly of Ireland [1909] AC 229, HL*. The importance of this doctrine is now, however, much reduced by virtue of the 1984 Act and the decision of the House of Lords in *British Railways Board v Herrington [1972] AC 877, [1972] 1 All ER 749, HL*.
[2] See *Simkiss v Rhondda Borough Council (1982) 81 LGR 460* at 471, *per* Dunn LJ.
[3] See *Phipps v Rochester Corpn [1955] 1 QB 450, [1955] 1 All ER 129*.

Removable hazards

[10.12] An occupier will be liable for any failing to take action with respect to removable hazards which foreseeably cause a risk to children. In *Jolley v Sutton London BC*[1] the defendants failed to remove an abandoned boat which had been left on their land. Children played on the boat, and one of them suffered serious injury when it fell on top of him. The House of Lords, reversing the Court of Appeal, held the defendants liable under the Act. Lord Steyn, referring to the words of the trial judge whose decision the House endorsed, said[2]:

> ' ... it has long been established that children are or may be attracted to meddle with objects on premises or property which constitute a danger when meddled

with …the occupier is under a duty to protect a child from danger caused by meddling with such an object by taking reasonable steps in the circumstances including, where appropriate, removing the object altogether so as to avoid the prospect of injury'.

1   *[2000] 3 All ER 409, HL.*
2   See *[2000] 3 All ER 409* at 412.

Risks incident to claimant's calling

[10.13] A further 'example' of the circumstances relevant to a determination of whether a defendant has discharged his duty of care is given by *section 2(3)(b)* of the *Occupiers' Liability Act 1957* which provides as follows: 'an occupier may expect that a person, in the exercise of his calling, will appreciate and guard against any special risks ordinarily incident to it, so far as the occupier leaves him free to do so.' In *Roles v Nathan*[1] the Court of Appeal applied the principle in the subsection to deny liability to the widows of two chimney-sweeps who had been killed by dangerous fumes while working on a defective boiler.[2] They had, in fact, deliberately chosen to ignore the risk which they incurred by needlessly choosing to work in the manner which they did. On the other hand, if the particular risk is one which all the skills of the claimant's calling do not enable him to avoid, then the defendant, whose negligence created the dangerous situation, will be liable even if the claimant's calling is actually to deal with situations of the kind in question[3]. Thus, in the important case of *Ogwo v Taylor*[4] the House of Lords confirmed[5] that firemen foreseeably injured while fighting a fire, caused by the defendant's negligence, have a right to damages.

1   *[1963] 2 All ER 908, [1963] 1 WLR 1117, CA.* Cf *Epp v Ridgetop Builders Ltd (1978) 94 DLR (3d) 505.*
2   'These chimney sweeps ought to have known that there might be dangerous fumes about and ought to have taken steps to guard against them': *[1963] 2 All ER 908* at 913, *[1963] 1 WLR 1117* at 1123, *per* Lord Denning MR.
3   See *Eden v West & Co [2003] PIQR Q2, 16 CA.*
4   *[1987] 3 All ER 961, [1987] 3 WLR 1145, HL.*
5   The House approved the earlier decision of Woolf J, on the same point, in *Salmon v Seafarer Restaurants [1983] 3 All ER 729, [1983] 1 WLR 1264.*

Entry pursuant to a contract

[10.14] The *Occupiers' Liability Act 1957, s 3(1)* provides that where an occupier is obliged by contract to allow people who are not parties to it to have access to his premises, such as workpeople who enter pursuant to a contract between himself and their employer, the common duty of care which the occupier owes to the entrants 'cannot be restricted or excluded by that contract'.[1] But the Act also provides that such persons can actually take the benefit of any provisions in the contract which have the effect of imposing on the occupier safety obligations more onerous than those required by the common duty of care.[2] If an entrant is entitled to access by virtue of a direct contract between himself and the occupier, but that contract contains no express term as to the latter's duty of care, the Act provides that a requirement for the common duty of care shall be implied into it.[3] If such an entrant is injured by breach of the duty, however, he is not obliged to sue in contract but can if he wishes elect to sue instead for breach of the duty in tort, as an ordinary visitor under the Act. In *Solle v W J Hallt Ltd*[4] Swanwick J held that the plaintiff's own contributory negligence would have had the effect of breaking the chain of causation if the defendant's breach of duty were treated as a breach of contract, and he would therefore have recovered nothing.[5] By suing in tort he was able to recover the appropriate proportion of his damages after allowance had been made for his contributory negligence.

1   See also *s 3(4)* (entry pursuant to the terms or conditions of a tenancy).
2   See *s 3(2)*. See now also the *Contracts (Rights of Third Parties) Act 1999, s 1.*
3   See *s 5(1)*.
4   *[1973] QB 574, [1973] 1 All ER 1032.*
5   Cf *Quinn v Burch Bros (Builders) Ltd [1966] 2 QB 370, [1965] 3 All ER 801.*

Warnings, volenti, and contributory negligence

Warning

[10.15]   The *Occupiers' Liability Act 1957, s 2(4)* provides, in limb (a), as follows:

> 'Where damage is caused to a visitor by a danger of which he had been warned by the occupier, the warning is not to be treated without more as absolving the occupier from liability, unless in all the circumstances it was enough to enable the visitor to be reasonably safe.'

The effect of this provision is to bring occupiers' liability into line with the law of negligence generally by ensuring that a defendant who has created a dangerous situation cannot absolve himself merely by giving a warning that is in reality inadequate. It reverses a majority decision of the House of Lords that had held that an occupier would be absolved from liability if the plaintiff entrant had known of the relevant hazard even if, in the circumstances, he could not be said to have been in a position freely to act on that knowledge so as to avoid danger.[1]

1   See *London Graving Dock Co Ltd v Horton [1951] AC 737, [1951] 2 All ER 1.*

Question of fact

[10.16]   Whether the warning will 'enable the visitor to be reasonably safe' will clearly be a question of fact in each case.[1] Thus, insufficient detail in the warning,[2] or a significant alteration in the factual circumstances against the background of which it was given,[3] might result in its being held ineffective. Moreover, inadequacy might be due to the claimant's having little real option, despite the warning, but to negotiate the hazard.[4]

1   See *Roles v Nathan [1963] 2 All ER 908, [1963] 1 WLR 1117, CA.*
2   Cf *per* Lord Denning MR (dissenting) in *White v Blackmore [1972] 2 QB 651, [1972] 3 All ER 158, CA.*
3   Cf *Smith v Austin Lifts [1959] 1 All ER 81, [1959] 1 WLR 100, HL; Roles v Nathan [1963] 2 All ER 908* at 915ff, *[1963] 1 WLR 1117* at 1128ff, CA (per Pearson LJ dissenting).
4   Cf *A C Billings & Sons v Riden [1958] AC 240, [1957] 3 All ER 1, HL.*

Obvious danger

[10.17]   On the other hand, it is clear that an occupier is under no duty to warn of a danger that should be obvious to the entrant. In one case a plaintiff slipped on the Cobb at Lyme Regis,[1] and in another a plaintiff fell while walking along cliffs in the Peak District.[2] In both cases the Court of Appeal rejected the contention that warning notices should have been provided, and the claims failed[3].

[10.18] *Liability of occupiers*

1   See *Staples v West Dorset District Council (1995) 93 LGR 536, CA.* See also *Darby v National Trust [2001] PIQR P27.*
2   See *Cotton v Derbyshire Dales District Council* (1994) Times, 20 June.
3   See also the 'trespasser' cases of *Tomlinson v Congleton BC* [2003] 3 All ER 1122 and *Donoghue v Folkestone Properties [2003] 3 All ER 1101, CA*, discussed below at paras [10.33] and [10.36].

Warning by third party

[10.18] It is to be noted that, although *subsection (4)* refers to a warning given 'by the occupier', it will be sufficient if it is given by someone who is clearly acting on his behalf.[1]

1   See *Roles v Nathan [1963] 2 All ER 908, [1963] 1 WLR 1117, CA.*

Assumption of risk

[10.19] The *Occupiers' Liability Act 1957, s 2(5)* provides as follows:

> 'The common duty of care does not impose on an occupier any obligation to a visitor in respect of risks willingly accepted as his by the visitor (the question whether a risk was so accepted to be decided on the same principles as in other cases in which one person owes a duty of care to another).'

The purpose of this provision is, of course, to confirm that the maxim *volenti non fit injuria* is applicable in the sphere of occupiers' liability. It is argued in a later chapter that *volenti* is best seen as a specific *defence* to a negligence action rather than as a denial that the defendant was in breach of duty.[1] By contrast, a defendant who avoids liability on the ground that he gave a warning, which is held to have been adequate within *section 2(4)(a)* of the 1957 Act, will in truth have *discharged* his duty rather than have contravened it but been able to rely on a 'defence'.

1   See CHAPTER 21 below.

Separate concepts

[10.20] There is thus no illogicality in the co-existence of 'warning' and *volenti* as separate concepts under the 1957 Act. In practice, however, there will of course often be a degree of overlap in the application of the two devices, since knowledge of the risk is a necessary, albeit not a sufficient, condition of the applicability of the *volenti* defence. On the other hand, a warning might be adequate to discharge the common duty of care even though, had it not done so, the defendant could not have succeeded in showing the requisite degree of consent to defeat the claimant on *volenti* grounds.[1] Conversely, a defendant who gave an inadequate warning, or no warning at all, might still succeed in proving that the claimant had been *volens* if, for example, he had acquired sufficient knowledge of the hazard from some source other than the occupier and could also be shown to have impliedly agreed to release the defendant from potential liability.

1   Cf *White v Blackmore [1972] 2 QB 651, [1972] 3 All ER 158, CA.*

Contributory negligence

[10.21] Although the defence of contributory negligence is not expressly referred to in the *Occupiers' Liability Act 1957*, there is in practice no doubt that the defence is applicable to a claim based on breach of the common duty of care under the Act. There are several reported examples[1] of damages being reduced in such cases pursuant to the apportionment provisions of the *Law Reform (Contributory Negligence) Act 1945*.

[1]   See *Stone v Taffe [1974] 3 All ER 1016, [1974] 1 WLR 1575, CA; Sole v Hallt Ltd [1973] QB 574, [1973] 1 All ER 1032*.

Employment of independent contractors

[10.22]   The *Occupiers' Liability Act 1957, s 2(4)* provides, in limb (b), as follows:

> 'where damage is caused to a visitor by a danger due to the faulty execution of any work of construction, maintenance or repair by an independent contractor employed by the occupier, the occupier is not to be treated without more as answerable for the danger if in all the circumstances he had acted reasonably in entrusting the work to an independent contractor and had taken such steps (if any) as he reasonably ought in order to satisfy himself that the contractor was competent and that the work had been properly done.'

This provision brings occupiers' liability broadly into line with vicarious liability in the law of negligence generally,[1] in which the employer of an independent contractor is not liable for damage caused by the latter's negligence except in special cases. The subsection removes doubts created by a case in which the House of Lords had held that an occupier had not discharged his duty of care by entrusting the performance of work on his premises to a reputable and competent independent contractor.[2] On the other hand, even apart from the restriction in the scope of the subsection itself to 'work of construction, maintenance or repair',[3] there is a limit to the extent to which the law relating to the vicarious liability of an occupier of premises for his independent contractors can be fully assimilated into the law governing employers of negligent contractors in other situations. Occupiers will often in practice have a higher degree of control over, and detailed awareness of, the activities of their independent contractors than is usual in other circumstances, particularly if the activity involved is a conspicuous one which lasts for a lengthy period of time. In *Bottomley v Todmorden Cricket Club*[4] the defendant occupiers appointed independent contractors to put on a fireworks display at one of their fund-raising events. The defendants were held liable when the claimant suffered severe burns due to the negligence of the contractors. The latter's competence and safety precautions had not been adequately checked by the defendants. It would, moreover, be wrong for an occupier to suppose that, simply by appointing a competent independent contractor, he will effectively have divested himself of responsibility for the safety of his visitors with respect to dangers emanating from the work to be undertaken.[5] In one controversial decision, *Gwilliam v West Hertfordshire Hospitals NHS Trust*,[6] a majority of the Court of Appeal held that an employer could in some circumstances even be under a duty to check that that its independent contractor carried adequate insurance against injury to third parties. In the case itself, which concerned a trampolining activity at a fund-raising event, the duty was nevertheless held to have been discharged by a mere inquiry of the contractor as to whether insurance existed: it was not considered necessary for the employer to insist on seeing the actual policy. *Gwilliam's* case has, however, been narrowly distinguished[7], and the proposition that there is any duty, except in exceptional circumstances, to check that an independent contractor has insurance, cannot be regarded as established[8].

[1]   See CHAPTER 18 below.
[2]   See *Thomson v Cremin [1953] 2 All ER 1185, [1956] 1 WLR 103n, HL.*
[3]   On the meaning to be attached to these words see P North *Occupiers' Liability* (1971) pp 142–144.
[4]   *[2003] EWCA Civ 1575*, (2003) Times, November 13.
[5]   Cf *Bloomstein v Railway Executive [1952] 2 All ER 418.*
[6]   *[2003] QB 443.* See Keith Stanton 'A Duty to Provide Insurance?' (2003) 11 Tort L Rev 65.
[7]   See *Payling v Naylor [2004] EWCA Civ 560*, (2004) Times, 2 June.
[8]   See the forceful dissenting judgment of Sedley LJ in *Gwilliam's* case.

Obligation must be taken seriously

[10.23]   There are indications that the court will be scrupulous to ensure that the occupier has taken seriously his own obligation, under the wording of *subsection (4)*, 'to satisfy himself ... that the work had been properly done'. In *A M F International Ltd v Magnet Bowling Ltd*,[1] which arose out of flood damage occurring during a major building operation, an attempt by the defendant occupiers to invoke *section 2(4)(b)* to avoid liability was unsuccessful. Mocatta J observed:[2]

> 'In the case of the construction of a substantial building I should have thought that the building owner, if he is to escape tortious liability for faulty construction, should not only take care to contract with a competent contractor ... but also to cause that work to be supervised by a properly qualified professional man such as an architect or surveyor'.

Moreover, his Lordship emphasised that this obligation applied not only to 'completed work' but also 'to precautions during the course of construction'. On the other hand, if the injury is suffered by one of the independent contractor's *own employees*, due to the contractor's using an unsafe system of work, the House of Lords has held that the subsection will not normally provide a basis for the imposition of liability on the occupier, even if the latter is aware of the dangerousness of the system.[3]

[1]   *[1968] 2 All ER 789, [1968] 1 WLR 1028.*
[2]   *[1968] 2 All ER 789 at 803, [1968] 1 WLR 1028 at 1044.*
[3]   See *Ferguson v Welsh [1987] 3 All ER 777, [1987] 1 WLR 1553, HL.* See also *Makepeace v Evans Brothers (Reading) [2001] ICR 241, CA.* In special circumstances the occupier may, however, be liable at *common law* along with the independent contractor, as a joint tortfeasor: see *Ferguson v Welsh [1987] 3 All ER 777 at 785, 786, [1987] 1 WLR 1553* at 1562, 1564 *per* Lord Oliver and Lord Goff.

Property

[10.24]   The question whether occupiers can be liable under the 1957 Act for damage to, or loss of, property, as distinct from personal injury, cannot be answered as unequivocally as might be wished. This is due to a lack of clarity in the Act's own provisions combined with a degree of uncertainty in the common law background to them.[1] There is, however, no real doubt that the common duty of care may in appropriate circumstances extend to the protection of a *visitor's* property from *damage* while he is on the defendant's premises in person.[2] The wording of the Act also clearly implies that property belonging to third parties will similarly be protected,[3] but probably only if it is brought on to the defendant's premises by a visitor[4] (to whom, for example, the property is on loan).

1   For discussion see, generally, P North *Occupiers' Liability* (1971) pp 94–114.
2   See *A M F International Ltd v Magnet Bowling Ltd [1968] 2 All ER 789, [1968] 1 WLR 1028.*
3   See the *Occupiers' Liability Act 1957, s 1(3)(b)* ('property of persons who are not themselves his visitors').
4   See North (above) p 101. Cf *Drive-Yourself Lessey's Pty Ltd v Burnside* [1959] SRNSW 390.

Theft by third party

[10.25] It is far less clear is whether the Act can apply to situations in which the visitor's goods are not damaged, but *stolen* by a third party while on the defendant's premises. At common law the authorities seemed to lean against the imposition of liability on an occupier in such circumstances.[1] In practice it will often be difficult to prove that a defendant occupier was actually careless in failing to prevent the theft, so the question will not arise all that frequently.[2] It is submitted, however, that if thefts from the defendant's premises had been frequent, he might be in breach of the common duty of care if he failed even to *warn* his visitors of this fact; and that in such circumstances theft of goods could come within the Act.[3]

1   See *Tinsley v Dudley [1951] 2 KB 18, [1951] 1 All ER 252, CA; Edwards v West Herts Group Hospital Management Committee [1957] 1 All ER 541, [1957] 1 WLR 415, CA.*
2   Of course, the defendant may be liable on some basis other than the 1957 Act: see the strict liability of innkeepers now governed by the *Hotel Proprietors Act 1956.*
3   See D Bowett 'Law Reform and Occupiers' Liability' (1956) 19 MLR 172 at 173: ' ... where the occupier of a store allows that store to become a hive of pickpockets, remaining negligently indifferent to their activities, he ought to be liable for the pecuniary loss of his lawful visitors resulting from the acts of these third persons on the same basis as he would be liable for bodily injury caused by a trap on his stairway.' Cf A Goodhart (1957) 73 LQR 313.

Economic loss

[10.26] If a visitor's property is damaged, and he suffers additional financial loss which is foreseeably consequential on that damage, that loss is, consistently with the general law of negligence, recoverable under the 1957 Act. This was expressly decided by Mocatta J in *A M F International Ltd v Magnet Bowling Ltd,*[1] where his Lordship expressed himself as follows:

> ' ... if the duty extends to the prevention of damage to property, I can see no reason in principle why the damages flowing from a breach of such duty should be limited or restricted (in the absence of express contractual provisions to that effect) other than by the ordinary rules as to the measure and remoteness of damage ... (F)inancial loss consequent upon personal injury is recovered every day in the courts and the same is frequently recovered in cases of damage to property.'

1   *[1968] 2 All ER 789* at 808, *[1968] 1 WLR 1028* at 1050–1051.

Applicability of general negligence principles

[10.27] In *Tomlinson v Congleton BC*[1], which was decided primarily under the *Occupiers' Liability Act 1984,* and is discussed below at para [10.36], Lord Hoffman took the opportunity to consider also the nature of an occupiers' responsibility under the 1957 Act. He emphasised that the statutory basis of the duty did not obviate the need to apply the fundamental principles of the common law of negligence[2]. These principles require the risk of harm to be balanced against other factors which include not only the cost of precautions but also the social utility of the activities in question[3]. It followed that merely because an occupier could foresee danger from a particular activity, such as swimming or mountain-climbing on his land, this did not necessarily oblige him to discourage those activities, or even to warn of the dangers if they were inherent in the activities themselves and not exacerbated by any special features on the land. Lord Hoffman therefore observed that[4]:

'... the balance between risk on the one hand and individual autonomy on the other ... is a judgment which the courts must make and which in England reflects the individualist values of the common law'.

[1]   *[2003] 3 All ER 1122.*
[2]   See above at para 39–50.
[3]   See PART ONE above.
[4]   See *[2003] 3 All ER 1122* at para 47.

C Liability to persons other than visitors

Persons covered by the Occupiers' Liability Act 1984

[10.28]   The *Occupiers' Liability Act 1984*[1] is complementary to the 1957 Act, since it deals with the relationship between an occupier and 'persons other than his visitors'. The most important category of such persons is that of trespassers, but the width of the formulation ensures that the benefit of the statutory duty under the Act is not confined to trespassers alone. The significance of this is that it also includes persons who enter pursuant to access agreements as well as users of private rights of way.

[1]   For discussion of the Act see, generally, M Jones (1984) 47 MLR 713; R A Buckley [1984] Conv 413. (Permission granted by Sweet & Maxwell Ltd, to reproduce here material which formerly appeared in the latter article, is gratefully acknowledged.)

Trespassers

[10.29]   The background to the 1984 Act was a belief that the law relating to liability towards trespassers needed to be clarified following the decision of the House of Lords in *British Railways Board v Herrington*.[1] In this case liability was imposed for injuries suffered by a six-year-old child trespasser when he was able to crawl through a fence, due to its dilapidated condition, on to an electrified railway line. Although the decision marked a major change in the approach of the law towards trespassers, and one significantly more favourable to them,[2] it was felt that the duty of 'common humanity' which it enunciated, under which the occupier's duty would 'vary according to his knowledge, ability and resources',[3] was excessively vague and liable to lead to uncertainty. The matter was therefore referred to the Law Commission and their report,[4] which was published in 1976, formed the basis, eight years later, for the *Occupiers' Liability Act 1984*.

[1]   *[1972] AC 877, [1972] 1 All ER 749, HL.* See also *Pannett v P McGuiness & Co Ltd [1972] 2 QB 599, [1972] 3 All ER 137, CA*; *Harris v Birkenhead Corpn [1976] 1 All ER 341, [1976] 1 WLR 279, CA.*
[2]   For the harsher approach formerly adopted see *Robert Addie & Sons (Collieries) v Dumbreck [1929] AC 358, HL.*
[3]   *[1972] AC 877 at 899, [1972] 1 All ER 749 at 758, per* Lord Reid.
[4]   Report on 'Liability for Damage or Injury to Trespassers and Related Questions of Occupiers' Liability' (Law Com no 75, Cmnd 6428).

Access agreements and the right to roam

[10.30] Although persons entering land pursuant to an access agreement or order made under the *National Parks and Access to the Countryside Act 1949, s 60* are not trespassers,[1] they were excluded from the protection of the *Occupiers' Liability Act 1957*, since that Act expressly provided that they were not 'visitors' either.[2] The Law Commission recommended that the new statutory duty which it proposed should apply for their benefit,[3] and they are now clearly covered by the *Occupiers' Liability Act 1984*. Persons entering land under the new rights of public access to private land conferred by the *Countryside and Rights of Way Act 2000*, known colloquially as the 'right to roam', are also 'persons other than visitors' for the purposes of the 1984 Act, but the duty owed to them is a specially restricted one[4].

[1]   See the 1949 Act, *s 60(1)*.
[2]   See the 1957 Act, *s 1(4)*.
[3]   See the Law Commission's Report, paras 37–41.
[4]   See below at para [10.42].

Users of private rights of way

[10.31] In *Holden v White*[1] the Court of Appeal held that users of private rights of way were not 'visitors', and were therefore not owed the common duty of care laid down by the *Occupiers' Liability Act 1957*. The background to the decision was the doctrine of the law of easements that positive obligations are not imposed on the owner of the servient tenement.[2] But it was not easy to see why this rule of property law should adversely affect the existence of liability in tort for carelessness,[3] and the effect of the formula adopted by the *Occupiers' Liability Act 1984* is clearly to bring users of private rights of way within the protection of the new statutory duty.[4]

[1]   *[1982] QB 679, [1982] 2 All ER 328, CA.*
[2]   See *[1982] QB 679* at 683, *[1982] 2 All ER 328* at 331, *per* Oliver LJ.
[3]   See K Stanton 'Occupiers' Liability and Rights of Way' (1982) 98 LQR 541. Cf R Griffith 'Easements and Occupiers' Liability' [1983] Conv 58. See also J R Spencer in [1983] CLJ 48, who argued that the *Holden v White* was decided *per* incuriam because the right of way cases of *Thomas v British Railways Board [1976] QB 912, [1976] 3 All ER 15, CA* and *Skeen v British Railways Board [1976] RTR 281* (in both of which the plaintiffs recovered damages) were not considered.
[4]   See *Vodden v Gayton [2001] PIQR P4* (claim failed on the facts). It should be noted that the 1984 Act does *not* apply to users of *public* rights of way since 'persons using the highway' are expressly excluded: see *s 1(7)*. For discussion of the position of such persons, see below at para [10.57].

The nature of the duty imposed by the 1984 Act

[10.32] The heart of the 1984 Act is to be found in *section 1(3)* and *(4)*, which provide as follows:

'(3)   An occupier of premises owes a duty to another (not being his visitor) in respect of any such risk as is referred to in subsection (1)[1] above if—

(a)   he is aware of the danger or has reasonable grounds to believe that it exists;

(b)   he knows or has reasonable grounds to believe that the other is in the vicinity of the danger concerned or that he may come into the vicinity of the danger (in either case, whether the other has lawful authority for being in that vicinity or not); and

    (c)   the risk is one against which, in all the circumstances of the case, he may reasonably be expected to offer the other some protection.

(4)   Where, by virtue of this section, an occupier of premises owes a duty to another in respect of such a risk, the duty is to take such care as is reasonable in all the circumstances of the case to see that he does not suffer injury on the premises by reason of the danger concerned.'

It is possible to criticise the wording of these provisions on the ground that the generalised approach adopted in them does not represent a significant advance upon the supposedly uncertain and unpredictable principles which *Herrington v British Railways Board* introduced into the common law.[2] On the other hand, the insertion of specific guidelines into the legislation, referring expressly to categories such as child trespassers[3] or criminal entrants,[4] might well have produced excessive complication in an area where a degree of uncertainty is unavoidable due to the extent that each case must depend heavily on its own facts.

[1]   Ie 'any risk of their suffering injury on the premises by reason of any danger due to the state of the premises or to things done or omitted to be done on them'. This wording is almost identical to that in s 1(1) of the *Occupiers' Liability Act 1957* discussed above at para [10.08].

[2]   See the criticism of the then Occupiers' Liability Bill by Lord Foot on Second Reading in the House of Lords: HL Deb, vol 443, series 5, col 724.

[3]   Cf the American Law Institute's *Restatement of the Law of Torts* (2nd) para 339.

[4]   Cf *Revill v Newbery [1996] 1 All ER 291*, in which the Court of Appeal held that a burglar who had been injured when the defendant occupier recklessly discharged a shotgun in his direction could obtain damages (reduced by two-thirds for contributory negligence) under *s 1* of the 1984 Act. The court rejected the contention that the claim could be defeated totally by the maxim *ex turpi causa non oritur actio*. When the then Occupiers' Liability Bill was before the House of Lords for Second Reading, Lord Mishcon felt that that maxim *could* apply to the criminal trespasser: HL Deb, vol 443, series 5, col 724. Lord Hailsham LC, however, in reply, doubted whether the maxim could apply in the law of tort at all, and suggested that criminal trespassers would fare badly in any claim simply by virtue of the application of the Act's general reasonableness test to them on the facts: HL Deb, vol 443, series 5, col 743.

Awareness of the danger

[10.33]   The requirement in *section 1(3)(a)* of the 1984 Act that the defendant should be 'aware' of the danger, or have 'reasonable grounds' upon which he should have been aware of it, is perhaps the most straightforward of the provisions in *section 1*. It is necessarily a question of fact in each case. In *Donoghue v Folkestone Properties*[1], Lord Phillips MR said:

'The obvious situation where a duty under the 1984 Act is likely to arise is where the occupier knows that a trespasser may come upon a danger that is latent. In such a case the trespasser may be exposed to the risk of injury without realising that the danger exists'.

Although the claim failed on other grounds, the facts of *Donoghue's* case provide an illustration of a situation falling within this particular provision. The defendants' owned and occupied a harbour which contained horizontal beams, set in concrete, upon which boats could be placed so that their hulls could easily be reached, presumably for repair and similar purposes. While these beams were visible at low tide, they became submerged at high tide and thereby provided a concealed hazard or trap for swimmers.

[1]   See *[2003] 3 All ER 1101* at para. 33.

Knowledge of trespass

[10.34]   The requirement in *section 1(3)(b)* of the 1984 Act that the defendant should know or have 'reasonable grounds to believe' that trespassers 'may come into the vicinity of the danger' enabled an occupier to defeat a claim in *Swain v Puri*[1]. In this case a nine-year-old boy climbed on to the roof of the defendants' empty industrial premises and sustained serious injury when he fell through a skylight. The premises were surrounded by a barbed wire fence, but the plaintiff had entered through a gap in it. The Court of Appeal held that the defendants had owed no duty to the plaintiff within the subsection, since they had no actual knowledge that children were in the habit of trespassing on the roof and no knowledge of facts from which a reasonable person would have inferred that such trespassing was likely to take place.

[1]   *[1996] PIQR P442, CA.*

Knowledge must be related to particular trespasser

[10.35]   *Section 1(3)(b)* of the 1984 Act was subjected to detailed consideration by the Court of Appeal in *Donoghue v Folkestone Properties*[1]. In this case the defendants conceded that they owed a duty to prevent trespassers, especially children, from swimming in their harbour, with its dangerous and often submerged beams, during the summer; and security guards would attempt to discourage such activity. Unfortunately, the claimant, a thirty-year-old adult, broke his neck as a result of hitting one of the beams while diving into the harbour at midnight in December. He contended that warning notices should have been provided at the point from which trespassers were known to enter the water. The trial judge found in favour of the claimant under the 1984 Act, but his judgment was reversed by the Court of Appeal. The subsection was held to require, as a condition of liability, reasonable grounds to believe that trespass would take place at a time, and in circumstances, similar to the claimant's *own* trespass. The defendants could not reasonably have been expected to anticipate midnight swims by trespassing adults in December, and no duty could arise in favour of such a trespasser merely because of summertime swimming by children.

[1]   *[2003] 3 All ER 1101.*

Reasonableness of offering protection

[10.36]   The circumstances in which an occupier 'may reasonably be expected to offer ... some protection' were, in effect, comprehensively considered by the House of Lords in the major case of *Tomlinson v Congleton Borough Council*[1]. Their Lordships approached the issue from a broad perspective of principle, and one of them[2] considered that the claimant had been a visitor rather than a trespasser, but the House was unanimous in holding that the claim would fail irrespective of whether the 1957 Act or the 1984 Act was applied. The claimant broke his neck while swimming in a lake, made from a disused sand quarry, in a public park. Although the park was for public recreation, and the lake was used for activities such as yachting, swimming was prohibited and there were notices to that effect, which rendered the claimant a trespasser on entering the water. There were not, however, any concealed obstructions in the lake and the claimant's accident appeared to have resulted from a badly executed shallow dive, rather than from any specific threat presented by the lake itself[3]. Nevertheless, a majority of the Court of Appeal, reversing the trial judge who had dismissed the claim, found in favour of the claimant under the 1984 Act. The view of the Court of Appeal was based on the fact that the notices prohibiting swimming were known to have been ineffective, and that the defendant Council should therefore have taken specific measures such as removing the artificial beaches, and planting reeds, in order to inhibit swimming. The House of Lords reversed the Court of Appeal, and denounced the reasoning of the majority as fundamentally flawed.

1   *[2003] 3 All ER 1122.*
2   Lord Scott of Foscote.
3   It should be noted that *s 1(1)(a)* of the 1984 Act refers to 'danger due to the *state of the premises*' (italics supplied). Lord Hoffman and Lord Hobhouse considered that the claim in *Tomlinson's* case should fail in any event on the ground that the defendants' premises were not in themselves dangerous, but cf *per* Lord Hutton at para. 53.

No duty

[10.37] Occupiers are under no duty to discourage trespassers or visitors from indulging in activities which themselves involve intrinsic and obvious dangers, and which are neither safer nor more dangerous when carried out on the defendant's land than they are when carried out elsewhere. Lord Hoffman said[1]:

'I think it will be extremely rare for an occupier of land to be under a duty to prevent people from taking risks which are inherent in the activities they freely choose to undertake upon the land. If people want to climb mountains, go hang gliding or swim or dive in ponds or lakes, that is their affair. Of course the landowner may for his own reasons wish to prohibit such activities. He may think that they are a danger or inconvenience to himself or others. Or he may take a paternalist view and prefer people not to undertake risky activities on his land. He is entitled to impose such conditions, as the council did by prohibiting swimming. *But the law does not require him to do so.*'[2]

Lord Hobhouse similarly protested against any suggestion that the law requires 'coastline and other beauty spots to be lined with warning notices' or 'attractive water-side picnic spots' to be removed merely because some individuals 'ignore warning notices and indulge in activities dangerous only to themselves'[3].

1   See *[2003] 3 All ER 1122* at para. 45.
2   See also *per* Lord Phillips MR in *Donoghue v Folkestone Properties [2002] 3 All ER 1101,* at para. 33: 'Where the state of the premises constitutes a danger that is perfectly obvious, and there is no reason for a person observing it to go near it, a duty under the 1984 Act is unlikely to arise'.
3   See *[2003] 3 All ER 1122* at para. 81.

'Such care as is reasonable'

[10.38] In practice, the general 'reasonableness' based approach adopted by the courts to cases involving personal injury will often not differ substantially whether the claim is made by a 'visitor' under the *Occupiers' Liability Act 1957*, someone 'other than a visitor' relying on *section 1(4)* the Act of 1984, or someone relying on general *Donoghue v Stevenson* negligence at common law.[1] In particular, the duty owed to trespassers will no longer depend upon the actual occupier's individual resources, as was apparently the case under the subjective *Herrington* test.

1   Cf *Pannett v P McGuinness & Co Ltd [1972] 2 QB 599, [1972] 3 All ER 137, CA.*

Precautions

[10.39] This does not imply, however, that the *precautions* which an occupier will need to take to avoid liability will be the same regardless of the nature of the potential claimant. The *content* of the duty may well differ not only according to the status of the entrant but also as between different types of trespasser[1]. Criminal activity in particular is unlikely to be looked upon with favour. It would seem to be very doubtful that a householder in an area notoriously prone to burglary should have to take special measures to protect burglars from injuries which might be caused, for example, by a missing staircase removed during renovations. Where a duty to protect trespassers does arise, however, it is likely to require such things as fences, warnings, or the removal of needless hazards such as abandoned cars[2]. But even defendants in breach of duty to fence under *section 1(4)* of the 1984 Act may avoid liability if it is established that the trespasser claimants would in any event have breached it[3].

1   See *per* Stuart-Smith LJ in *Ratcliffe v McConnell [1999] 1 WLR 670, CA* at p 683' ... the nature of what it is reasonable to expect of the occupier varies greatly depending on whether the trespasser is very young or very old and so may not appreciate the nature of the danger which is or ought to be apparent to an adult'.
2   Cf *Jolley v Sutton [2000] 3 All ER 409, HL.*
3   See *Scott v Associated British Ports (2000) WL 1741511, CA (LEXIS).*

Warnings and assumption of risk

[10.40] The *Occupiers' Liability Act 1984* provides that an occupier may discharge his duty 'by taking such steps as are reasonable in all the circumstances of the case to give *warning* of the danger concerned or to discourage persons from incurring the risk'.[1] The immediately following subsection provides for the applicability of the doctrine of assumption of risk (ie *volenti non fit injuria*).[2] In making separate provision for the two related, but nevertheless distinct, concepts of warning and assumption of risk, the Act does, of course, parallel the *Occupiers' Liability Act 1957*.[3]

1   *Section 1(5)* (emphasis added).
2   'No duty is owed by virtue of this section to any person in respect of risks willingly accepted as his by that person (the question whether a risk was so accepted to be decided on the same principles as in other cases in which one person owes a duty of care to another)': *s 1(6)*. See *Ratcliffe v McConnell* [1999] 1 WLR 670, CA (adult suffering serious injuries as a result of diving into a shallow swimming pool with full knowledge of the risk: no liability).
3   See the 1957 Act, *s 2(4)(a)* and (5), discussed above at paras [10.15] and [10.19].

No liability for damage to property

[10.41] A significant respect in which the scope of the duty owed to 'persons other than visitors' under the 1984 Act is narrower than that owed to 'visitors' under the *Occupiers' Liability Act 1957*, or that owed generally under the ordinary common law of negligence, is that claims under the 1984 Act are confined to personal injury or death; so that property damage is not recoverable.[1] Of course, claims for lost earnings immediately consequential upon death or personal injury, in addition to pain and suffering, loss of amenities etc, will be recoverable in a claim under the Act in the usual way.

1   See *s 1(9)* (defining 'injury'). The Law Commission considered recommending the making of a specific exception, so as to allow a trespasser to recover for damage to his clothes, but ultimately decided against it: see their Report (Law Com no 75, Cmnd 6428) para 30.

D Access under the Countryside and Rights of Way Act 2000

'Right to roam'

[10.42]   Under the *Countryside and Rights of Way Act 2000*[1] landowners will become obliged to grant members of the public access to specified areas of their land, typically open countryside or moorland, for recreational purposes. Formerly such access would have required the landowner's permission or the existence of a public right of way. The right has been colloquially categorised by user organisations, such as the Ramblers' Association, as 'the right to roam'. The 2000 Act makes clear that members of the public enjoying the right are not 'visitors' of the occupier for the purposes of the 1957 Act[2]. They are therefore 'persons other than visitors' and fall within the general purview of the 1984 Act.

[1]   See *section 2*.
[2]   See *section 13(1)* inserting a new provision to this effect into *section 1(4)* of the *Occupiers' Liability Act 1957*.

New provisions in the 1984 Act

[10.43]   *Section 13(2)* of the *Countryside and Rights of Way Act 2000* does, however, insert two additional provisions into the 1984 Act in order to minimise any conceivable burden which the new right of access might otherwise impose upon landowners. Thus three new subsections in *section 1 ((6A)-(6C))* of the 1984 Act now provide that persons enjoying the right of access under the 2000 Act will not be owed any duty by the occupier in respect of 'a risk resulting from the existence of any natural feature of the landscape'. The term 'natural feature' is defined widely. It includes ditches and ponds 'whether or not a natural feature' and 'any plant, shrub or tree, of whatever origin'. Nor is any duty owed in respect of a risk resulting in injury to a person 'when passing over, under or through any wall, fence or gate, except by proper use of the gate or of a stile'. The occupier would only forfeit his immunity if he intentionally created the risk, or was reckless as to whether or not it was created.

Minimising the burden

[10.44]   The effect of these provisions would seem effectively to confine potential areas of liability, towards those exercising the new right of access, to hazards arising from such things as ruined buildings and archaeological sites. But even here the 2000 Act is anxious to minimise any obligation which may fall upon the landowner, and also to minimise any alterations for safety or warning purposes to features which may be of significant interest from a heritage perspective. Thus a new section, *section 1A*, has been added to the 1984 Act providing that 'in determining whether any, and if so what, duty is owed' by the occupier to persons entering his land pursuant to the 1984 Act, 'regard is to be had' to 'the fact that the existence of that right ought not to place an undue burden (whether financial or otherwise) on the occupier', and also to 'the importance of maintaining the character of the countryside, including features of historic, traditional or archaeological interest'.

E Exclusion of liability

Visitors and non-business occupiers

Possibility of excluding liability

[10.45] The *Occupiers' Liability Act 1957, s 2(1)* provides that an occupier owes the common duty of care to his visitors 'except in so far as he is free to and does extend, restrict, modify or exclude his duty to any visitor or visitors by agreement or otherwise'. It is therefore clear that unless death or personal injury suffered on business premises is involved,[1] or the situation is one in which the occupier is for some other reason not 'free to' do so, unilateral action by him, without the express agreement of the visitor in question,[2] can achieve exclusion of the liability which would otherwise be imposed upon him. By analogy with the learning on exemption clauses in the law of contract, the test of whether reasonable steps have been taken to inform visitors of the exclusion is an objective, and not a subjective, one. The cases show that a suitably prominent notice, displayed so as to impose the relevant condition upon entry, will suffice.[3] Indeed, in one case such a notice was successfully relied upon even by an occupier who also gave a warning of the danger but one which was held to have been inadequate, a situation which Lord Denning MR, who dissented, considered anomalous.[4]

[1] See the *Unfair Contract Terms Act 1977, ss 1(1)(c), 1(3)(b)* and *2(1)*. But see also the *Occupiers' Liability Act 1984, s 2*. Both provisions are discussed below.

[2] Cf the *Occupiers' Liability (Scotland) Act 1960, s 2(1)*, in which only exclusion by agreement is contemplated (the words 'or otherwise' not appearing).

[3] See *Ashdown v Samuel Williams & Sons Ltd [1957] 1 QB 409, [1957] 1 All ER 35, CA*; *White v Blackmore [1972] 2 QB 651, [1972] 3 All ER 158, CA*. For criticisms of the *Ashdown* decision (and, by implication, the post-Act position) see L Gower (1956) 19 MLR 532; (1957) 20 MLR 181. Cf F Odgers [1957] CLJ 39, 42ff.

[4] See *White v Blackmore [1972] 2 QB 651, [1972] 3 All ER 158, CA* (Lord Denning attempted to remove the anomaly by denying that a disclaimer of liability could be effective unless it simultaneously satisfied the requirements relating to adequacy of warning: see *[1972] 2 QB 651* at 665–666.

Where the occupier is not 'free' to exclude liability[1]

[10.46] Although actual agreement with his visitors may not be necessary to achieve exclusion of an occupiers' liability, it appears that a visitor who is not in the circumstances able to exercise any real *choice* in the matter, since he is in reality inescapably committed to entering the occupier's premises, will not be bound by an exclusion clause even if he is actually aware of it.[2]

[124] See C Symmons 'How Free is the Freedom of the Occupier to Restrict or Exclude his Liability in Tort?' (1974) 38 Conv (NS) 253.

[125] See *Burnett v British Waterways Board [1973] 2 All ER 631, [1973] 1 WLR 700, CA*.

Right conferred by law

[10.47] There are two provisions of the *Occupiers' Liability Act 1957* itself which, although the matter is not entirely free from doubt, probably amount to implicit restrictions on the freedom of occupiers to exclude their liability. *Section 1(6)* of the 1957 Act provides that 'persons who enter premises for any purpose in the exercise of a right conferred by law are to be treated as permitted by the occupier to be there for that purpose, whether they in fact have his permission or not'. Although this wording could be construed narrowly so as merely to confirm, for the avoidance of doubt, that persons exercising a right of entry cannot be forcibly removed or sued for trespass, it is submitted that the better view is that it also prevents exclusion by notice of the common duty of care owed to them.[1]

[1]   Cf P North *Occupiers' Liability* (1971) pp 130–131.

Strangers to contract

[10.48]   Similarly, *section 3(1)* of the 1957 Act provides that 'where an occupier of premises is bound by contract to permit persons who are strangers to the contract to enter or use the premises, the duty of care which he owes to them as his visitors cannot be restricted or excluded by that contract'. If emphasis were placed upon the last three words quoted, the subsection could be taken to strike merely at the potential mischief of enabling liability to be restricted by a contractual provision which the visitor in question may never even have seen; but still leaving the occupier free to exclude liability by a notice which the visitor would see at the point of entry. Again, however, it is submitted that the better view is that such a notice would in fact be ineffective in this situation.[1] The visitors in question will often be employees of the contractor and will have no effective choice but to enter the occupier's premises if they are not to put their jobs in jeopardy.

[1]   Cf North (above) pp 148–152.

Persons other than visitors

[10.49]   The *Occupiers' Liability Act 1984* does not, unlike its 1957 predecessor, include any provision contemplating exclusion of liability. Moreover, its wording clearly requires the court to consider cases of injury to trespassers, and of others covered by it, on a broad basis of reasonableness. Any warning given, and its adequacy, will be taken into account along with such measures, if any, as were taken to try to prevent or discourage trespass.[1] Thus, if there is any kind of concealed or unusual hazard on the premises in question, a notice containing merely the time-honoured and inaccurate words 'trespassers will be prosecuted' is most unlikely to be enough. To this extent, it may be taken that the occupier does not enjoy the same freedom to exclude his liability to trespassers as he does to exclude his common duty of care to lawful visitors. It would also appear that the approach adopted by the later Act avoids the possibility of an occupier being able to rely upon a disclaimer to avoid the consequences of having given an inadequate warning.[2]

[1]   See *s 1(5)* of the 1984 Act.
[2]   Cf *White v Blackmore [1972] 2 QB 651, [1972] 3 All ER 158, CA.*

Visitors and business occupiers

[10.50]   Provided the case concerns 'the occupation of premises used for business purposes of the occupier',[1] the *Unfair Contract Terms Act 1977* expressly prevents the exclusion of liability 'for death or personal injury'[2] arising out of breach 'of the common duty of care imposed by the *Occupiers' Liability Act 1957'*.[3] Moreover, even 'in the case of other loss or damage' exclusion of liability is not permitted 'except in so far as the ... notice satisfies the requirement of reasonableness'.⁴ Unfortunately, the Act does not attempt a definition of a 'business' for its purposes, except to stipulate that it 'includes a profession and the activities of any government department or local or public authority'.⁵ While this omission will perhaps rarely be a source of serious difficulty, since it will probably usually be obvious whether or not the occupier's purposes bring him within the concept, there could still be difficult borderline cases involving prominent non-profit making institutions such as universities or private schools.

¹   *Unfair Contract Terms Act 1977* (hereafter referred to as '*UCTA*'), *s 1(3)(b)*.
²   *UCTA, s 2(1)*.
³   *UCTA, s 1(1)(c)*.
⁴   *UCTA, s 2(2)*. On the 'requirement of reasonableness' see, further, *s 11(3)*.
⁵   *UCTA, s 14*.

Entry for recreational or educational purposes

[10.51] In one specific area the freedom of business occupiers to exclude their liability, which was limited by the *Unfair Contract Terms Act 1977*, has subsequently been restored to them. The relevant provision is the *Occupiers' Liability Act 1984, s 2* which, unlike the main body of that Act, is concerned with visitors as distinct from persons other than visitors. The section inserts additional words into the Unfair Contract Terms Act, which have the effect of providing that an occupier who allows visitors access to his premises for recreational or educational purposes shall not be subject to the limitations on exclusion of liability towards such visitors otherwise imposed by that Act.¹ The new provision, which does not apply if the occupier is actually in the business of providing recreational or educational facilities, reflects a policy decision designed to ensure that farmers, or others in similar circumstances, to whose land access for recreational or educational purposes might be desirable, should not be unduly discouraged from permitting such access by fear of potential legal liability.²

¹   The *Occupiers' Liability Act 1984, s 2* provides as follows:
    'At the end of section 1(3) of the Unfair Contract Terms Act 1977 (which defines the liability, called "business liability", the exclusion or restriction of which is controlled by virtue of that Act) there is added–
    "but liability of an occupier of premises for breach of an obligation or duty towards a person obtaining access to the premises for recreational or educational purposes, being liability for loss or damage suffered by reason of the dangerous state of the premises, is not a business liability of the occupier unless granting that person such access for the purposes concerned falls within the business purposes of the occupier".'
²   See HL Deb, vol 443, series 5, col 721 (Lord Hailsham LC).

F When the Acts do not apply

Relationship with ordinary negligence

[10.52] If the narrower interpretation of the scope of the *Occupiers' Liability Act 1957*, which was contended for earlier in this chapter, is correct the 'common duty of care' embodied in that Act will be confined to the static condition of the defendant's premises and will not apply to activities carried out on his land which are unrelated to the condition or safety of the land itself or any buildings upon it. Liability for such activities will therefore be regulated by the ordinary common law of negligence. The clearest statement of this view, since the passing of the *Occupiers' Liability Act 1957*, was by Lord Denning MR in *Videan v British Transport Commission*,[1] which concerned a fatal accident caused by the negligent driving, by one of the defendant's employees, of a powered trolley on a railway track. His Lordship stated that the general law of negligence applied and continued:

> 'The principle that I have stated applies only where an occupier or a contractor or anyone else conducts activities on land. It does not apply where an occupier has done no work on the land: for then his liability is as an occupier and nothing else. I am not disturbed by the suggestion that it is difficult to distinguish between a man's activities on land and the static condition of premises. I should have thought that whenever an occupier does things on land, whether he runs a moving staircase, or puts a bull into a field, or drives a railway engine, or uses land as a cinder tip, or even digs a hole, he is conducting activities on the land and he is under a duty of care, even to trespassers, if he ought to foresee their presence: and he is nonetheless under that duty because he is an occupier.'

[1]   *[1963] 2 QB 650* at 667–668, *[1963] 2 All ER 860* at 867, CA. See also *per* Harman LJ *[1963] 2 QB 650* at 672–673, *[1963] 2 All ER 860* at 870. But cf Pearson LJ *[1963] 2 QB 650* at 678, *[1963] 2 All ER 860* at 873–874.

Lawful visitors

[10.53]   As far as lawful visitors are concerned, it would not appear to make any difference in practice whether their claims are based upon the *Occupiers' Liability Act 1957*, alleging that the premises themselves were in a dangerous condition, or upon an allegation of ordinary *Donoghue v Stevenson* negligence in the conduct of an activity. Indeed, the common duty of care is essentially a statutory exposition of negligence liability in the occupation context. It even seems clear that one respect in which a difference might possibly have been expected to exist, that of exclusion of liability, it does not in fact do so. It appears that an occupier can exclude by notice liability for negligent activities on the land, and that the possibility of such exclusion is not confined to the occupancy duty in the narrow sense.[1]

[1]   Both the leading cases of *Ashdown v Samuel Williams & Sons [1957] 1 QB 409, [1957] 1 All ER 35, CA*, and *White v Blackmore [1972] 2 QB 651, [1972] 3 All ER 158, CA*, concerned activities.

Persons other than visitors

[10.54]   Since the material provisions of the two statutes use identical phraseology,[1] it would appear reasonable to suppose that if the scope of the *Occupiers' Liability Act 1957* is limited to the state of the land or premises then that of the *Occupiers' Liability Act 1984* is similarly so limited. This means that the liability of occupiers to persons other than visitors, for the conduct of dangerous activities on the land, is still governed by the common law. If Lord Denning's contention is correct that the status of the entrant is wholly irrelevant where the activity duty is concerned, even if he is a trespasser, then the applicable common law will be the ordinary principles of negligence.[2] A somewhat surprising alternative possibility, however, would be to hold that a trespasser's status affects the nature of the duty owed to him, irrespective of whether it is an activity or the static condition of the premises which is in issue.[3] This reasoning would lead to the conclusion that the supposedly undesirably vague principles of 'common humanity', developed in *British Railways Board v Herrington*[4] still apply if the claim is based upon a dangerous activity. It is submitted that Lord Denning's view that *Donoghue v Stevenson* applies is to be preferred. Nevertheless, one paradoxical reason that a trespasser himself might have for supporting the opposite view is that it is at least arguable that, unlike ordinary negligence liability in this context, the doctrine of 'common humanity' represents an irreducible minimum of liability which it is impossible for an occupier to exclude by disclaimer.[5]

[1]   Ie danger due to ' ... the state of the premises or to things done or omitted to be done on them': *Occupiers' Liability Act 1957, s 1(1)* and *Occupiers' Liability Act 1984, s 1(1)(a)*.
[2]   Of course the fact of trespass could still be relevant on the issue of foreseeability.
[3]   Cf *per* Lord Pearson in *British Railways Board v Herrington [1972] AC 877* at 929, *[1972] 1 All ER 749* at 785. See also *Robert Addie & Sons (Collieries) Ltd v Dumbreck [1929] AC 358, HL*, which laid down the old law on liability to trespassers, and concerned an activity on the land.
[4]   *[1972] AC 877, [1972] 1 All ER 749, HL*.
[5]   See para [10.62] above.

Liability of non-occupiers

[10.55]   If injury is caused to a trespasser, not by the occupier of the land in question but by the carelessness of someone else such as a non-occupying independent contractor, the authorities on balance favour the view that the defendant cannot rely on the fact that the claimant is a trespasser, but owes to him the ordinary *Donoghue v Stevenson* duty in negligence. In *Buckland v Guildford Gas, Light and Coke Co*[1] a 12-year-old girl was electrocuted when she climbed a tree within the foliage of which the defendants had negligently allowed electric wires to be concealed. Morris J held that even if the deceased had been a trespasser on the tree, that fact could not be relied upon by the defendants, who were not the occupiers, to reduce their ordinary foreseeability duty, and liability was imposed.[2]

[1]   *[1949] 1 KB 410, [1948] 2 All ER 1086*.
[2]   See also *Davis v St Mary's Demolition and Excavation Co Ltd [1954] 1 All ER 578, [1954] 1 WLR 592; Creed v McGeoch & Sons Ltd [1955] 3 All ER 123, [1955] 1 WLR 1005*. But cf *per* Lord Pearson in *British Railways Board v Herrington [1972] AC 877* at 929, *[1972] 1 All ER 749* at 785; *Perry v Thomas Wrigley Ltd [1955] 3 All ER 243n, [1955] 1 WLR 1164*.

Cannot exclude by notice

[10.56]   Since a non-occupier does not have the power to determine who enters the land and who does not, it is submitted that, unlike the occupier, he does not enjoy the latter's privilege of excluding his liability to visitors on the land by mere notice.[1] The justification for that privilege is arguably that the occupier confers a benefit on the visitor to which conditions can be attached,[2] but if no privilege is conferred there is no reason why the general duty of care imposed by the law should not apply. Although not directly in point, it is suggested that support for this reasoning can be found by analogy in the speech of Lord Reid in *A C Billings & Sons Ltd v Riden*,[3] in which the appellant independent contractors were held liable for injuries suffered by an entrant. His Lordship said:

'The only reasonable justification I know of for the rights of a licensee being limited as they are is that a licensee generally gives no consideration for the rights which the occupier has given him and must not be allowed to look a gift horse in the mouth. That cannot apply to the appellants, who gave no concession to the respondent.'

1   Of course, in practice the question will seldom now arise since a non-occupier carrying out an activity on the land will usually be an independent contractor who will be acting 'in the course of a business' and hence caught by the ban on the exclusion of liability for death or personal injury contained in the *Unfair Contract Terms Act 1977*.
2   See also CHAPTER 4 above (negligent misstatement).
3   *[1958] AC 240* at 249, *[1957] 3 All ER 1* at 5, HL.

Users of the highway[1]

[10.57]   In *McGeown v Northern Ireland Housing Executive*[2] the House of Lords confirmed the continued validity of a long-standing rule[3] that users of public rights of way not maintainable at public expense are not 'visitors' of the occupier of the land in question, and so are not owed the common duty of care under the *Occupiers' Liability Act 1957*. Lord Keith of Kinkel expressed the reason for the rule as follows:[4]

> 'Rights of way pass over many different types of terrain, and it would place an impossible burden upon landowners if they not only had to submit to the passage over them of anyone who might choose to exercise them but also were under a duty to maintain them in a safe condition.'

The Law Commission, in their report which preceded the *Occupiers' Liability Act 1984*, had similarly taken the view that the abrogation of this rule might impose undue burdens upon those whose land happened to be subject to public rights of way theoretically usable by unlimited numbers of people, and they were therefore not prepared to recommend it.[5] As far as users of public rights of way maintainable at public expense are concerned, existing statutory provisions[6] place such persons, if they happen to suffer injury, in at least as favourable a position as plaintiffs in an ordinary negligence action, and the Law Commission accordingly took the view that no further legislative action was needed.[7] As a result, the *Occupiers' Liability Act 1984* includes a general provision, relating to users of both types of public right of way, which leaves the status quo, including the old common rule, unaffected. *Section 1(7)* of the 1984 Act reads as follows: 'No duty is owed by virtue of this section to persons using the highway, and this section does not affect any duty owed to such persons.'[8]

1   See F R Barker and N D M Parry 'Private Property, Public Access and Occupiers' Liability' (1995) 15 LS 335.
2   *[1995] 1 AC 233, [1994] 3 All ER 53, HL*.
3   See *Greenhalgh v British Railways Board [1969] 2 QB 286, [1969] 2 All ER 114, CA*. See also *Gautret v Egerton (1867) LR 2 CP 371*.
4   See *[1995] 1 AC 233* at 243, *[1994] 3 All ER 53* at 59.
5   See *Report on* 'Liability for Damage or Injury to Trespassers and Related Questions of Occupiers' Liability' (Law Com no 75, Cmnd 6428) paras 48–51. The *Royal Commission on Civil Liability and Compensation for Personal Injury* (Pearson), while acknowledging the apparent gap in the law, also felt unable to recommend any change: see Cmnd 7054–I, paras 1558–1562.
6   See the *Highways Act 1980*, especially *section 58*.
7   See their Report, paras 42–47.
8   It should be noted that users of *private* rights of way *are* brought within the umbrella of the 1984 Act, reversing *Holden v White [1982] QB 679, [1982] 2 All ER 328, CA*; see above at para [10.31].

Former duty merges in public right

[10.58]   In *McGeown v Northern Ireland Housing Executive*[1] the plaintiff had tripped into a hole, and broken her leg, while using a path which led to her home. Although her claim failed, on the ground explained in para [10.57], the case was complicated by the fact that, *prior* to the acquisition by the public of a right of way over the path in question, the defendants *would* have owed her a duty of care while using it, since at *that* time she *was* a visitor under the *Occupiers' Liability Act 1957*. This was because the path formed part of an estate, owned by the defendants, on which the plaintiff lived. 'The question', said Lord Keith,[2] 'is whether the licence to use the pathway which the defendants would have been held to have granted to the plaintiff before it became subject to the public right of way is to be held to have become merged in that right of way and so been extinguished, or whether it can be treated as having a continued existence'. His Lordship, with whom his brethren[3] concurred, concluded that the licence had been extinguished.

[1]   *[1995] 1 AC 233, [1994] 3 All ER 53.*
[2]   See *[1995] 1 AC 233* at 244, *[1994] 3 All ER 53* at 60.
[3]   Lord Goff, Lord Mustill and Lord Lloyd.

Invitees protected?

[10.59]   It is to be noted, however, that Lord Browne-Wilkinson expressly reserved his opinion on whether invitees, as distinct from licensees, could have their pre-existing rights extinguished in this way. 'To my mind', he said, 'it would be unfortunate if, as a result of the decision in this case, the owner of a railway bridge or shopping centre could, by expressly dedicating the land as a public highway or submitting to long public user, free himself from all liability to users whose presence he had encouraged'. Lord Browne-Wilkinson's suggestion, that entrants encouraged to use the highway 'for purposes linked to the business of the owners of the soil'[2] should not lose their protection, is not an unattractive one. It is at least questionable, however, whether the resuscitation of the distinction between invitees and licensees, upon which the suggestion depends, is consistent with their merger into the new category of 'visitor' in the *Occupiers' Liability Act 1957* itself. Moreover, Lord Browne-Wilkinson's suggestion has subsequently been rejected by the Court of Appeal in Northern Ireland.[3]

[1]   See *[1995] 1 AC 233* at 247, *[1994] 3 All ER 53* at 63.
[2]   See *[1995] 1 AC 233* at 248, *[1994] 3 All ER 53* at 64.
[3]   See *Campbell v Northern Ireland Housing Executive [1996] 1 BNIL 99.*

Possible relevance of the duty of common humanity?

[10.60]   Since it is therefore clear that users of public rights of way are afforded no protection by the *Occupiers' Liability Acts 1957* and *1984*, the question arises whether *any* duty at all *is* owed to users of non-maintainable public highways. Although, in the light of *McGeown v Northern Ireland Housing Executive*, they are not to be treated as 'visitors' it surely cannot be the case that they are owed no duty *at all* at common law. If, for example, the owner or occupier of land subject to a public right of way, which he knows is constantly used by children on their journey to and from school, discovers an unexploded bomb just below the surface of the path in question, he surely cannot just sit back and do nothing at all. Although users of the right of way are not trespassers it would, prior to the 1984 Act, have been logical to expect that the duty of common humanity enunciated in *British Railways Board v Herrington*[1] would have applied to them. Indeed, it can be argued that the decision of the Court of Appeal in *Thomas v British Railways Board,*[2] in which disrepair of a stile along a right of way enabled a small child to gain access to a railway line and thereby suffer injuries for which she was awarded damages, provides express authority for such a proposition.[3] If so, it would seem to follow from the preservation of the status quo by the 1984 Act that this is still the position.[4]

1   *[1972] AC 877, [1972] 1 All ER 749, HL.*
2   *[1976] QB 912, [1976] 3 All ER 15, CA.*
3   See, especially, *per* Scarman LJ (*[1976] QB 912* at 927, *[1976] 3 All ER 15* at 23): 'I think that the existence of a duty so to operate a railway that reasonable care is taken to reduce or avert danger to those who may reasonably be expected to be physically on the line, whether they be trespassers, visitors, or persons exercising their right to use a public highway, is to be deduced from the decision of the House of Lords in *Herrington v British Railways Board.*' See also F R Barker and N D M Parry 'Private Property, Public Access and Occupiers' Liability' (1995) 15 LS 335 at 347–352.
4   Although no support for the proposition in the text can be found in *McGeown v Northern Ireland Housing Executive* itself this is not, it is submitted, a fatal objection. Since the case involved a mere failure to repair a hole in the path, it could hardly be said to have resulted in a breach of the duty of common humanity and, in any event, the point was evidently not argued.

Convenient but ironical

[10.61]   This result is not unattractive. Any fears of an unduly burdensome liability upon the occupier, which underlies the rule confirmed in *McGeown*, are met by the emphasis in *Herrington* upon a subjective test related to the defendant's capacity, resources, and all the surrounding circumstances.[1] Thus, in the hypothetical case of the unexploded bomb, the occupier would not be expected to remove the bomb himself (any more than he would be, presumably, in a situation to which the common duty of care imposed by the *Occupiers' Liability Act 1957* applied) but he could reasonably be expected to go to the trouble of issuing a warning and alerting the police. Despite its convenience, the position thus revealed is not without irony since one of the main reasons for the Law Commission's disapproval of *Herrington*, which led eventually to the passing of the *Occupiers' Liability Act 1984*, was dislike of a duty subjectively related to the occupier's resources.[2]

1   See *[1972] AC 877* at 899, 920, 942, *[1972] 1 All ER 749* at 758, 777, 796, *per* Lord Reid, Lord Wilberforce and Lord Diplock.
2   See the Law Commission's Report (Law Com no 75, Cmnd 6428), para 12.

Where liability has been excluded

[10.62]   A similar question to that concerning the duty, if any, owed to persons using non-maintained public rights of way, concerns the position of visitors where the common duty of care which would normally have been owed under the *Occupiers' Liability Act 1957* has been validly excluded by notice of disclaimer.[1] In this context, as in the other one, it is difficult to believe that such persons are owed no duty *at all*. Since, moreover, the duty owed to trespassers under the *Occupiers' Liability Act 1984* apparently cannot be excluded by disclaimer,[2] it would be remarkable if this meant that lawful visitors might be worse off than trespassers. The Law Commission itself noted that it would be 'extraordinary' if, in order to avoid being affected by an exclusion notice, a lawful visitor sought to argue that he was in truth a trespasser.[3] The Commission also observed, however, that:

> 'since the decision of the House of Lords in *Herrington*'s case it has been suggested to us that the duty laid down in that case is incapable of exclusion, on the basis that the duty of humanity represents a minimum standard of conduct below which an occupier will not be permitted to go.'[4]

The Commission thought the argument an interesting one but their own recommendation for dealing with the problem,[5] which was, however, not implemented in the 1984 Act, made it unnecessary for them to express any view upon its validity. It is nevertheless submitted that the argument is indeed correct. The new statutory duty created by the *Occupiers' Liability Act 1984* is expressly confined to 'persons other than visitors', so that obviously cannot provide the basis for a minimum duty to be owed to visitors who are subject to a disclaimer. Accordingly, as in the rights of way situation, the unexcludable minimum is presumably once again the common law doctrine of common humanity[6] laid down in *Herrington v British Railways Board.*

[1] See above.
[2] But cf M Jones 'The Occupiers' Liability Act 1984' (1984) 47 MLR 713 at 723–725.
[3] See the Law Commission's Report (Law Com no 75, Cmnd 6428), para 66.
[4] Se the Report, para 60. The argument was apparently put to the Law Commission by Professor Jolowicz: see Symmons 'How Free is the Freedom of the Occupier to Restrict or Exclude his Liability in Tort' (1974) 38 Conv (NS) 253 at 268, n 70.
[5] Ie that *all* attempts to exclude liability should be subjected to a 'reasonableness' test, irrespective of whether the entrant was lawful or unlawful, invited or uninvited: see the Report, paras 67–75. See also cl 3 of the Draft Bill annexed to the Report.
[6] See J Mesher 'Occupiers, Trespassers and the Unfair Contract Terms Act' [1979] Conv 58 at 64; B Coote 'Exception Clauses and Common Humanity' (1975) 125 NLJ 752. See also P M North *Occupiers' Liability* (1971) p 132.

G The Defective Premises Act 1972, s 4

Landlords' liability

[10.63] Although the *Occupiers' Liability Act 1957* was obviously mainly concerned with the liability of occupiers it did contain one provision, *section 4*, which in certain circumstances put the landlord of premises out of occupation in the same position as if he had actually been an occupier, and imposed the common duty of care upon him. *Section 4* of the 1957 Act was in fact repealed by the *Defective Premises Act 1972* and replaced by *section 4* of *that* Act. The new provision is wider in scope than its predecessor. It also differs significantly from it, in that it does itself define the duty that it imposes upon the landlord, and does not adopt the technique of the earlier provision of treating him as if he were an occupier. Another respect in which the new provision moves beyond the original analogy of occupiers' liability, in the sense defined by the 1957 Act, is that it can apply in favour of persons who suffer damage while off the premises and is not confined to persons actually *on* the land or premises in question. In view of its legislative history, however, and since it can be relevant to claims for injury or damage suffered by persons who have entered upon the premises in question, it is convenient to set out *section 4* of the *Defective Premises Act 1972* here. The heart of the provision is to be found in the first two subsections and the first part of *subsection (3)* as follows:

'(1) Where premises are let under a tenancy which puts on the landlord an obligation to the tenant for the maintenance or repair of the premises, the landlord owes to all persons who might reasonably be expected to be affected by defects in the state of the premises a duty to take such care as is reasonable in all the circumstances to see that they are reasonably safe from personal injury or from damage to their property caused by a relevant defect.

(2) The said duty is owed if the landlord knows (whether as the result of being

notified by the tenant or otherwise) or if he ought in all the circumstances to have known of the relevant defect.

(3)   In this section 'relevant defect' means a defect in the state of the premises existing at or after the material time and arising from, or continuing because of, an act or omission by the landlord which constitutes or would if he had had notice of the defect, have constituted a failure by him to carry out his obligation to the tenant for the maintenance or repair of the premises … '

Subsection (4) puts a landlord who has a *right* to enter the premises in the same position for the purpose of *subsection (1)* as if the tenancy imposed an actual obligation on him to carry out those repairs.[1]

1   For a case in which the Court of Appeal *implied* the existence of a right of entry, thereby enabling the plaintiff tenant to benefit from the effect of *subsection (4)* in activating *subsection (1)*, see *McAuley v Bristol City Council [1992] QB 134, [1992] 1 All ER 749, CA.*

Non-excludable duty

[10.64]   It will be apparent that *section 4* of the 1972 Act imposes a negligence-type liability upon landlords, if they are under an obligation to their tenants to repair the premises in question, in favour of anyone who suffers loss or damage as a result of the landlord's failure to keep the premises in repair.[1] No doubt the duty, in terms of the actual degree of care required, will be very similar in practice to that owed by occupiers to their visitors under the *Occupiers' Liability Act 1957.* It should be noted, however, that in contrast with the position relating to the common duty of care as defined in the 1957 Act, exclusion of liability under the 1972 Act is prohibited.[2] But the fact that the duty is based upon a failure to *maintain or repair* necessarily entails that any act or omission which does not constitute such a failure cannot give rise to liability under the provision[3].

1   The use of the phrase 'all persons' in *subsection (1)* means that tenants themselves can take advantage of the provision: see *Barrett v Lounova (1982) Ltd [1990] 1 QB 348, [1989] 1 All ER 351* at 357–358, *per* Kerr LJ, following *Smith v Bradford Metropolitan Council (1982) 44 P&CR 171, CA.* See also *McAuley v Bristol City Council [1992] QB 134, [1992] 1 All ER 749, CA.*
2   *Section 6(3)* provides as follows: 'Any term of an agreement which purports to exclude or restrict, or has the effect of excluding or restricting, the operation of any of the provisions of this Act, or any liability arising by virtue of any such provision shall be void.'
3   See *Boldack v East Lindsey DC (1999) 31 HLR 41, CA.*

Chapter 11

Duties to neighbouring occupiers

A Negligence and private nuisance

Spread of negligence

[11.01]   In recent times the influence of negligence concepts has extended into other areas of the law which have traditionally been regarded, often for historical reasons, as being distinct. This is particularly true in the case of private nuisance[1], the unifying feature of which is usually perceived to be its focus upon the particular *interest* of the claimant which it protects: namely the use or enjoyment of land[2]. In this it may be said to differ from negligence where the focus is primarily upon the defendant's conduct[3]. Nevertheless, an increasingly persuasive argument can be advanced to the effect that nuisance should be regarded as assimilated within the law of negligence, on the ground that in both torts the notion of 'reasonableness' is adopted as the standard by which a defendant's behaviour is tested[4].

[1]   For public, as distinct from private, nuisance, see CHAPTER 14 below.
[2]   See *Clerk and Lindsell on Torts* (18th edn) p 973. See also Maria Lee 'What is Private Nuisance' (2003) 119 LQR 298.
[3]   '… the proper angle of approach to a case of alleged nuisance is rather from the standpoint of the victim of the loss or inconvenience than from the standpoint of the alleged offender' *per* Lord Cooper in *Watt v Jamieson (1954) SC 56* at 57–58. See also *Gertsen v Municipality of Metropolitan Toronto (1973) 41 DLR (3d) 646* at 669
[4]   See Glanville Williams and Hepple *Foundations of the Law of Tort* (2nd edn) p 123 onwards.

Close resemblance

[11.02]   No doubt a degree of caution is appropriate in responding to the assimilation argument; the term 'reasonableness' is used in such a variety of differing legal concepts, often with differing shades of meaning, that attempts at unification may simply mislead. Thus, resolving continuing disputes between neighbouring occupiers of land as to the legitimacy of their conflicting activities is a function which differs in important respects from that of allocating losses which occur as a result of momentary carelessness on the highway or elsewhere[1]. Nevertheless, many nuisance claims are based upon lack of foresight rather than upon the deliberate pursuit of intentional activities, so that they closely resemble negligence claims in any event. Moreover, the need across the broad range of nuisance cases to make fact-sensitive evaluations of human conduct on an intuitive or common-sense basis means that the language and general approach adopted in such cases is inevitably similar to that of the tort of negligence. In *Delaware Mansions v Westminster City Council*[2], a decision of the House of Lords in 2001 dealing with damage caused by encroaching tree-roots,

Lord Cooke of Thorndon referred to 'the concepts of reasonableness between neighbours (real or figurative) and reasonable foreseeability which underlie much modern tort law and, more particularly, the law of nuisance'. Insistence upon treating nuisance as a wholly discrete area would therefore be both artificial and unhelpful, and would leave a considerable gap in any attempt at a comprehensive and up to date exposition of the law of negligence[3].

1   Cf *Russell Transport v Ontario Malleable Iron Co [1952] 4 DLR 719* at 731, *per* McRuer CJHC.
2   *[2001] 4 All ER 737* at para 29.
3   See also *per* Lord Cooke in *Delaware Mansions v Westminster City Council [2001] 4 All ER 737* at para 31: 'The label nuisance or negligence is treated as of no real significance. In this field, I think, the concern of the common law lies in working out the fair and just content and incidents of a neighbour's duty rather than affixing a label and inferring the extent of the duty from it'.

Conventional vocabulary

[11.03]   It is nevertheless obviously convenient to retain the term 'nuisance' as an umbrella expression to denote those situations in which duties relating to the use and enjoyment of land are involved. It will therefore be used for that purpose in this chapter, and in subsequent chapters of this book in which similar issues arise[1].

1   See, especially, CHAPTERS 12, 13, 14, 23, 29 and 30.

B The test of reasonableness in land use cases

Balancing the interests of the parties

[11.04]   In *Cambridge Water Co Ltd v Eastern Counties Leather plc*[1] Lord Goff said[2]:

'… if the user is reasonable, the defendant will not be liable for consequent harm to his neighbour's enjoyment of his land; but if the user is not reasonable, the defendant will be liable, even though he may have used reasonable care and skill to avoid it'.

It follows that in determining 'reasonableness' the court will not examine the defendant's activity in isolation. On the contrary, in balancing the interests of the two parties the court will concern itself primarily, although not exclusively, with the *impact* of the defendant's activity upon the *claimant*[3]. If that impact verges on the oppressive it is unlikely to avail the defendant that he is conducting his business according to the best modern methods and taking all the usual precautions[4]. Moreover, in determining the question of reasonableness the court will consider one or more of a number of specific factors which require separate treatment. Among the most important of these are locality, duration, any hypersensitivity on the part of the claimant and any spiteful or malicious motive on the part of the defendant.

1   *[1994] 2 AC 264; [1994] 1 All ER 53.*
2   See above at 299 and 71.
3   Cf *Reinhardt v Mentasti (1889) 42 Ch D 685; A-G v Cole & Son [1901] 1 Ch 205.*
4   See *Bamford v Turnley (1860) 3 B&S 62; West v White (1877) 4 Ch D 631; Stockport Waterworks Co v Potter (1861) 7 H&N 160; Russell Transport Ltd v Ontario Malleable Iron Co Ltd [1952] 4 DLR 719 (Can).*

Locality

[11.05] In *St Helen's Smelting Co v Tipping*[1] the plaintiff purchased an estate in an area which contained many factories including the defendants' copper smelting works. Gases from the works spread on to the plaintiff's land damaging his trees and shrubs and rendering his cattle unhealthy. The value of his land was also reduced. In finding for the plaintiff the House of Lords drew a distinction between nuisances which, in the words of Lord Westbury LC, cause 'material injury to property' and those which merely occasion 'personal discomfort'. Whether a plaintiff complaining of the latter could succeed would 'depend greatly on the circumstances of the place where the thing complained of actually occurs' since it was desirable that those living in industrial areas should subject themselves 'to the consequences of those operations of trade which may be carried on in [their] immediate locality'[2]. This principle would not apply, however, 'to circumstances the immediate result of which is sensible injury to the value of the property'. Since the plaintiff in the *St Helen's* case itself was able to prove such injury he was able to succeed despite the fact that the defendants' activity was one common in the area.

1 *(1865) 11 HL Cas 642.*
2 See *(1865) 11 HL Cas* at 650–651. A formerly residential locality may become 'industrial', for this purpose, as a result of large-scale installations being constructed under statutory authority. See *Allen v Gulf Oil Refining Ltd [1981] AC 1001* at 1014A, *[1981] 1 All ER 353* at 357j, *per* Lord Wilberforce, and *per* Cumming-Bruce LJ in the Court of Appeal in the same case *[1980] QB 156* at 172, *[1979] 3 All ER 1008* at 1018. On the possible effect of planning permission on a locality's status for this purpose see CHAPTER 23 below.

Tactical nature of the principle

[11.06] The way in which the 'locality' principle emerged in *Tipping's* case suggests that it was developed partly in order to resolve a conflict between two previous cases. In *Hole v Barlow*[1] the Court of Common Pleas held that a defendant would be immune from liability in nuisance whenever his activity was carried on in a place which was 'convenient and proper' for it. This approach was, however, disapproved by the Court of Exchequer Chamber in *Bamford v Turnley*[2] as being far too favourable to defendants. In the latter case it was held[3] that a plaintiff would normally succeed in nuisance whenever he had suffered 'a sensible diminution of the comfortable enjoyment'[4] of his land. By holding that locality was a relevant factor, but only in situations involving discomfort as distinct from property damage, the House of Lords appears to have been seeking a *via media* between these two extremes.

1 *(1858) 4 CBNS 334, 27 LJ CP 207.*
2 *(1860) 3 B&S 62.*
3 Pollock CB dissenting.
4 *Per* Bramwell B, see above at 82. In his Lordship's view the only exception to this liability would be 'those acts necessary for the common and ordinary use and occupation of land and houses' (p 83).

Rarely applied

[11.07] The essentially tactical nature of the locality principle is also illustrated by the fact that it is rare to find it actually *applied* against a claimant. On the contrary it has invariably seemed to judges to be appropriate for cases *other* than the one they actually had to decide[1]. It is most commonly used, as in *St Helen's Smelting Co v Tipping* itself, merely in order to answer the argument *ab inconvenienti* put forward by defence counsel, that a decision favourable to the claimant would enable persons who built residential property in industrial areas to put a stop to the industrial activities being carried on there[2].

1   See *Rushmer v Polsue and Alfieri Ltd [1906] 1 Ch 234, 76 LJ Ch 79*; affd *[1907] AC 121, 76 LJ Ch 365* discussed post, CHAPTER 12. See also *Halsey v Esso Petroleum Co Ltd [1961] 2 All ER 145, [1961] 1 WLR 683*.
2   See *Sturges v Bridgman (1879) 11 Ch D 852* at 860, *per* counsel, *arguendo*, and *per* Thesiger LJ in reply at 865: '… what would be a nuisance in Belgrave Square would not necessarily be so in Bermondsey'. See also *per* Lord Wensleydale in *St Helen's Smelting Co v Tipping (1865) 11 HL Cas 642* at 653 and *per* Cozens-Hardy LJ in *Rushmer v Polsue and Alfieri Ltd [1906] 1 Ch 234* at 251.

Criticisms of the principle

Pollution

[11.08]   As a doctrine of substantive law the 'locality' principle has been subjected to criticism on two counts. From the point of view of control and improvement of the environment it has been pointed out by a Canadian writer that the principle is paradoxical in that it involves the courts' 'accepting the fact that those who suffer most from the ravages of pollution are the least worthy of protection'[1]. Nowadays, however, this criticism is of little relevance as far as England is concerned since improvement of the environment is effected mainly by public bodies acting under statutory powers[2]. Unlike the situation in the last century nuisance actions will only exceptionally be of general environmental significance[3]. Most cases arise out of ad hoc disputes between neighbours and in such situations it seems appropriate that locality should be a relevant, albeit marginal, factor so that a claimant in an urban area cannot complain of, eg noise to the same extent as a claimant in the countryside. The principle might operate the other way round with respect to, say, farmyard stenches caused by the activities of town-dwelling self-sufficiency enthusiasts.

1   Professor J P S McLaren in 'Nuisance Actions and the Environmental Battle' (1972) 10 Osgoode Hall Law Journal 505 at 534.
2   Eg the *Town and Country Planning Act 1990* and the *Environmental Protection Act 1990*. See, generally post, CHAPTER 12.
3   On the role of the tort of nuisance in the nineteenth century, see Professor J P S McLaren, 'Nuisance Law and the Industrial Revolution – Some Lessons from Social History' (1983) 3 OJLS 155.

Arbitrariness

[11.09]   A more fundamental criticism of the locality principle is that the distinction between property damage and mere discomfort is difficult to draw and will often be arbitrary[1]. Residential premises exposed, eg to nuisances interfering with comfort and enjoyment, will frequently depreciate in value. Conversely, not all sufferers from 'property' damage will have an equally strong case for recovery. There is force in this criticism, and it is submitted that that it would be wrong to rule out the application of the 'locality' principle against all claimants who could plausibly claim that their loss should be classified as damage to property.

1   See Ogus and Richardson, 'Economics and the Environment: A Study of Private Nuisance' (1977) 36 CLJ 284 at 299.

Presumption in property cases

[11.10]   The better view would seem to be that there is merely a presumption, albeit one difficult to rebut, against the locality principle operating in cases involving damage to property¹. Thus a claimant who lives in an exposed and mountainous region should not be entitled to complain merely because his neighbour fails to prevent the deposit by natural forces of damaging detritus from his higher land on to that of the claimant, if such deposits are characteristic of the particular environment. The mere fact that natural forces are involved will not exonerate a defendant in such a case², but it is submitted that in exceptional circumstances the 'locality' principle might do so. Moreover, it needs to be remembered that the principle is but one aspect of the overall test of 'reasonableness', and that a claimant who has suffered property damage might still be defeated by other principles encapsulated within that test, eg that he is hypersensitive³. In practice, however, cases in which defendants who have caused what is unquestionably property damage will rarely succeed on this ground.

¹ In *Kent v Dominion Steel and Coal Corpn (1964) 49 DLR (2d) 241* at 248 Furlong CJ said of *St Helen's Smelting Co v Tipping* that it was 'as though the Westbury proposition had imparted into the law of nuisance a doctrine akin to *res ipsa loquitur* in the law of negligence'.
² See *Leakey v National Trust for Places of Historic Interest or Natural Beauty [1980] QB 485, [1980] 1 All ER 17*, discussed in CHAPTER 13 below.
³ See below at para [11.14].

Duration

The rule in Harrison v Southwark and Vauxhall Water Co

[11.11] An annoyance which would otherwise amount to an actionable nuisance may be excused on the ground that it is a temporary consequence of the carrying out of certain works such as building or reconstruction. In *Harrison v Southwark and Vauxhall Water Co*¹ the defendant statutory undertakers sank a shaft on land adjacent to the plaintiff's house. The noise from the pumps used to sink the shaft seriously interfered with the plaintiff's comfort and he brought an action for nuisance. The pumps used were, however, the ones ordinarily used for the purpose in question, and although quieter pumps of a different type could have been used they would have been less convenient and more dangerous to the men working down the shaft. To render the quieter pumps safe would have been very expensive. In these circumstances Vaughan Williams J held that the defendants were not liable and stated the relevant principle as follows:

'It frequently happens that the owners or occupiers of land cause, in the execution of lawful works in the ordinary user of land, a considerable amount of temporary annoyance to their neighbours; but they are not necessarily on that account held to be guilty of causing an unlawful nuisance. The business of life could not be carried on if it were so. For instance, a man who pulls down his house for the purpose of building a new one no doubt causes considerable inconvenience to his next door neighbour during the process of demolition; but he is not responsible as for a nuisance if he uses all reasonable skill and care to avoid annoyance to his neighbour by the works of demolition. Nor is he liable to an action, even though the noise and dust and the consequent annoyance be such as would constitute a nuisance if the same had been created in sheer wantonness, or in the execution of works for a purpose involving a permanent continuance of the noise and dust'².

¹ *[1891] 2 Ch 409, 60 LJ Ch 630.*
² *[1891] 2 Ch 409* at 413–414. See also *Andreae v Selfridge & Co Ltd [1938] Ch 1, [1937] 3 All ER 255; Gosnell v Aerated Bread Co Ltd (1894) 10 TLR 661; Phelps v City of London Corpn [1916] 2 Ch 255, 85 LJ Ch 535.*

Potential cessation of interference

[11.12] A defendant whose continuing activity causes a nuisance will not, however, be able to excuse himself under the rule in *Harrison*'s case merely by proving that he is working on improvements to his machinery which he *hopes*, when perfected, will put an end to the annoyance. But the court might be persuaded to suspend the application of an injunction in such a case. Thus in *Colwell v St Pancras Borough Council*[1] the defendant Borough Council erected an electric generating station in proximity to the plaintiffs' houses. Vibration from the machinery caused a nuisance but the defendants alleged that this would be removed in time by alterations and improvements to the machinery. They contended that until the machinery was perfected the construction of their works was not complete, and that an action would therefore not lie against them because the annoyance was merely temporary. This argument failed. The court held that the defendants were not entitled to operate their generating station unless they could do so without creating a nuisance. An injunction was granted but suspended for six months. Similarly in *Metropolitan Properties v Jones*[2] noise from an electric motor which operated a central heating system was held to be an actionable nuisance, giving rise to an action for damages, even though modifications to the motor had put an end to the nuisance after only three weeks[3].

---

[1] *[1904] 1 Ch 707, 73 LJ Ch 275, per* Joyce J.
[2] *[1939] 2 All ER 202*, Goddard LJ sitting as an additional judge of the King's Bench Division.
[3] Cf *Kinney v Hove Corpn (1950) 49 LGR 696*: the fact that a circus would last only ten days was not in itself a ground for refusing an application for an injunction on the ground of nuisance (application ultimately failed but on other grounds).

Need for 'reasonableness'

[11.13] The principle in *Harrison's* case will not usually protect temporary nuisances which inflict actual damage to property[1] or cause the claimant to suffer economic loss[2]. Moreover it is essential, as Vaughan Williams J emphasised in the case itself, that the works should be carried out in a reasonable manner. In determining what is reasonable, methods of, eg building and demolition, must not be taken as stabilised, but new inventions and new methods may be reasonable in the altered circumstances and developments of the day even if their greater speed and efficiency causes more noise or interference than older methods[3]. Nevertheless it is most unlikely that a temporary nuisance which takes place *at night* and interferes with sleep will be regarded as reasonable[4]. Nor will the principle apply if the doing of the work which causes the nuisance is wrongful in itself, eg because it constitutes a breach of covenant[5].

---

[1] See *Clift v Welsh Office [1998] 4 All ER 852, CA per* Sir Christopher Slade at p 861: 'Where there is physical damage, the loss should in our judgment fall on the doer of the works rather than his unfortunate neighbour'. See also *Harris v Carnegie's Pty Ltd [1917] VLR 95 (Aus)*. Cf *Wildtree Hotels v Harrow London Borough Council [2000] 3 All ER 289, HL* (noise, dust and vibration falling short of physical damage).
[2] *Fritz v Hobson (1880) 14 Ch D 542, 49 LJ Ch 321; Matania v National Provincial Bank Ltd and Elevenist Syndicate Ltd [1936] 2 All ER 633, 106 LJKB 113.*
[3] See *Andreae v Selfridge [1938] Ch 1* at 6, *[1937] 3 All ER 255* at 264, *per* Sir Wilfred Greene MR.
[4] See *per* Sir Wilfred Greene MR in *Andreae v Selfridge* as reported in *[1937] 3 All ER 255* at 261: 'I certainly protest against the idea that, if persons, for their own profit and convenience, choose to destroy even one night's rest of their neighbours, they are doing something which is excusable'. See also *Webb v Barker [1881] WN 158; De Keyser's Royal Hotel Ltd v Spicer Bros Ltd and Minter (1914) 30 TLR 257* (injunction to restrain pile driving between 10 pm and 6.30 am). Cf *Clark v Lloyd's Bank Ltd (1910) 79 LJ Ch 645, 103 LT 211.*

5   *Newman v Real Estate Debenture Corpn Ltd and Flower Decorations Ltd [1940] 1 All ER 131, 162 LT 183.*

Hypersensitivity

The rule in Robinson v Kilvert

[11.14]   A claimant whose own activity is abnormally sensitive to interference may be unable to complain of any loss or damage inflicted by the defendant's activities, if those activities would not have affected a claimant whose use of his own land was not unusual or extraordinary. In the well-known case of *Robinson v Kilvert*[1] the defendant let the upper floor of a building to the plaintiff in order that the latter could use it as a paper warehouse. The defendant himself used the floor below, which he had retained, for a manufacturing process which required the air to be hot and dry. The heating apparatus used for this purpose raised the temperature on the floor of the room above to 80°F. The result of this heat was to damage the brown paper which the plaintiff stored in his warehouse and make it less valuable. Unfortunately for the plaintiff, however, the heat would not have damaged paper generally and the temperature in the warehouse itself never rose to a level at which the plaintiff's workforce would have been inconvenienced. The defendant was not aware that the plaintiff intended to use the premises for storing any particular kind of paper, and in these circumstances the Court of Appeal held that his action would fail. Lopes LJ said[2]:

> 'A man who carries on an exceptionally delicate trade cannot complain because it is injured by his neighbour doing something which would not injure anything but an exceptionally delicate trade'.

1   *(1889) 41 Ch D 88, 58 LJ Ch 392. See also Whycer v Urry [1955] CLY 1939.*
2   *(1889) 41 Ch D 88 at 97.*

Is the rule outdated?

[11.15]   In *Morris v Network Rail Infrastructure*[1], decided in 2004, the Court of Appeal doubted whether the principle in *Robinson v Kilvert* had any role in the modern law of nuisance, contending that the concepts of 'foreseeability' and 'reasonableness' suffice to cover the ground[2]. In the *Network Rail* case itself the claimant complained of interference with the operation of electronic guitars in his recording studios, allegedly caused by magnetic radiation emanating from the defendants' rail signalling system. The claim ultimately failed on the factual ground that the interference could not have been foreseen by the defendants, although the court rejected the submission that the latter could succeed simply on the ground that the claimant's activity had been 'abnormally sensitive'. The Court of Appeal emphasised the extent to which both nuisance and negligence are now governed by common principles, and to that extent the court's analysis is to be welcomed. Nevertheless, it is submitted that the concept of hypersensitivity can still be helpful, in cases of continuous interference, in order to provide a degree of *structure* to the application of the 'reasonableness' criterion. It serves to highlight that 'foreseeability' is merely a necessary, and not a sufficient, condition of liability; and that the extent to which the claimant's activity is less robust than those commonly encountered in the area in question can still form a significant part of the overall 'reasonableness' inquiry.

1   *[2004] EWCA Civ 172.*

² See, especially, *per* Buxton LJ at para 29 onwards.

Limited application of the principle

[11.16] The rule in *Robinson v Kilvert* is, however, in any event of limited application. Provided a claimant can make out a cause of action in nuisance independently of his special sensitivity, eg on the ground of emission of noxious or offensive gases, he may be able to recover in respect of damage suffered even if the particular head of damage would not have occurred but for the sensitivity. Thus in *Mckinnon Industries Ltd v Walker*¹ a plaintiff who grew flowers for sale was able to succeed in respect of all the damage caused by the emission of sulphur dioxide from the defendants' motor car plant. The argument that the growing of orchids should be excluded from the protection given, on the ground that orchid growing was a particularly difficult and delicate type of horticultural activity, was unsuccessful. The plaintiff's legal rights had been infringed and damage to the orchids was not too remote².

¹ *[1951] 3 DLR 577.*
² Cf *Cooke v Forbes (1867) LR 5 Eq 166, 37 LJ Ch 178; Spruzen v Dossett (1896) 12 TLR 246.*

Nature of hypersensitivity

Buildings

[11.17] The question of what is to be regarded as especially sensitive for the purpose of the rule clearly leaves the court with scope for the exercise of considerable discretion on the facts of each case. It is unlikely, however, that a dwelling-house would be normally so regarded even though old and less firm than when it was first built. Attempts by defendants, whose building operations have caused damage to older properties situated nearby, to rely upon *Robinson v Kilvert* have not met with success¹.

¹ See *Hoare & Co v McAlpine [1923] 1 Ch 167, 92 LJ Ch 81; Anger v Northern Construction Co [1938] 4 DLR 738; Barrette v Franki Compressed Pile Co of Canada Ltd [1955] 2 DLR 665.*

Electrical devices

[11.18] The courts have been more prepared, at least in years gone by, to regard electrical devices as hypersensitive for the purposes of the rule. Thus in *Bridlington Relay Ltd v Yorkshire Electricity Board*¹ the plaintiffs, who carried on a business of relaying sound and television broadcasts, sought a *quia timet* injunction to restrain the defendants from so operating a newly-erected power line as to interfere with their transmissions. Buckley J refused relief on the ground that the particular remedy sought would be inappropriate in circumstances in which the defendants had acted in good faith and undertaken to take every possible precaution to prevent the interference which the plaintiffs feared. Nevertheless his Lordship also indicated, obiter, that he was not satisfied that ability to receive television free from occasional, even if recurrent and severe, electrical interference was so important a part of an ordinary householder's enjoyment of his property that such interference should be regarded as an actionable nuisance. In the case itself, however, the aerial which the plaintiffs used for their transmissions was much larger than an ordinary domestic aerial and more prone to interference. Nowadays, the enormous increase in electronic-based activities means that the courts are reluctant to decide cases involving such activities merely by invoking the concept of hypersensitivity[2].

1   *[1965] Ch 436, [1965] 1 All ER 264.*
2   See *Morris v Network Rail Infrastructure [2004] EWCA Civ 172*, discussed above at para [11.15].

Domestic television reception

[11.19] With respect to the particular aerial in the *Bridlington* case itself, the doubts of Buckley J as to liability may have been justified[1], but in so far as they applied to ordinary domestic television reception it is submitted that his observations are open to question in modern circumstances. In the Canadian case of *Nor-Video Services Ltd v Ontario Hydro*[2], decided on facts which closely resembled those in the *Bridlington* case, it was held that the plaintiffs could recover in nuisance for interference with their television apparatus, whose sensitivity was equivalent to that of ordinary domestic receivers. The judge, Robins J, in differing from the approach of Buckley J, stated that 'television viewing is an important incident of ordinary enjoyment of property and should be protected as such'[3].

1   See also *Eastern and South African Telegraph Co Ltd v Cape Town Tramways Companies Ltd [1902] AC 381.* Cf *National Telephone Co v Baker [1893] 2 Ch 186, 62 LJ Ch 699.* The extent to which cases of this antiquity can still be regarded as authoritative on technological issues is, however, inevitably very limited: see, generally, *Morris v Network Rail Infrastructure [2004] EWCA Civ 172.*
2   *(1978) 84 DLR (3d) 221.*
3   *(1978) 84 DLR (3d) 221 at 231.*

Blocked signal

[11.20] In both the *Bridlington* and *Nor-Video* cases the interference with television reception had been caused by other electrical equipment. Even if the approach in the latter case is to be preferred, however, poor reception will still not be actionable if it arises not through the use of electrical devices but merely as a result of a large new building blocking the path of the signal. In *Hunter v Canary Wharf Ltd and London Docklands Development Corpn*[1] the House of Lords held that interference caused in this way was not actionable since it was equivalent to the loss of a view, which has never given rise to a cause of action in nuisance[2]. The House left open the question whether interference by other electrical equipment with television reception could be actionable, but several of their Lordships appeared to look favourably upon the possibility that it could be.[3]

1   *[1997] 2 All ER 426.*
2   'The analogy between a building which interferes with a view and a building which interferes with television reception seems to me ... to be very close': *per* Lord Lloyd in *[1997] 2 All ER 426* at 445. On loss of a view, or 'prospect', see CHAPTER 12 of the handbook.
3   See *[1997] 2 All ER 426* at 431 (Lord Goff); 453 (Lord Hoffman); 463 (Lord Cooke).

Malice

Relevance of the defendant's motive

[11.21] Since the notion of 'reasonable user' of land lies at the heart of the law of nuisance it would appear to be impossible for a defendant's motive to be regarded as being in all circumstances irrelevant, notwithstanding statements apparently to the contrary in some authorities. A defendant who is acting maliciously can hardly be regarded as acting 'reasonably', and it would be highly artificial to attempt to determine the liability of such a defendant by reference to some kind of objectively tolerable level of interference arrived at in cases in which the motive of the defendants had been unobjectionable.

Noise cases

[11.22] In *Christie v Davey*[1] the plaintiffs were a musical family and the sounds coming from their musical activities greatly annoyed the defendant who was their next-door neighbour. In order to retaliate the defendant adopted the practice of blowing whistles, banging tin trays and hammering on the party-wall. In giving the plaintiffs an injunction to restrain him North J took into account the fact that the defendant's noise had been made 'deliberately and maliciously' and said that he would have taken an entirely different view of the case if what had taken place 'had occurred between two sets of persons both perfectly innocent'. He continued[2]:

'But I am persuaded that what was done by the defendant was done only for the purpose of annoyance, and in my opinion it was not a legitimate use of the defendant's house to use it for the purpose of vexing and annoying his neighbours'.

In *Hollywood Silver Fox Farm Ltd v Emmett*[3] the defendant discharged a shotgun on his own land as near as possible to his boundary with the plaintiff who ran a silver fox farm. The defendant, who was a builder, feared that the proximity of the silver foxes would deter potential purchasers of the houses which he proposed to build on his land. The noise from the shotgun was intended to frighten the silver foxes into miscarrying or refusing to mate during the breeding season. The defendant argued in vain that he was merely shooting rabbits, something which he was surely entitled to do on his own land, and that, in any event, his motive was irrelevant. Macnaghten J relied upon *Christie v Davey* and granted the plaintiff an injunction[4].

[1]   *[1893] 1 Ch 316, 62 LJ Ch 439.*
[2]   *[1893] 1 Ch 316 at 327, 62 LJ Ch 439.*
[3]   *[1936] 2 KB 468, [1936] 1 All ER 825.*
[4]   See also *Ibbotson v Peat (1865) 3 H&C 644.* In the absence of malice the plaintiff in the *Hollywood* case would probably have failed on the ground of hypersensitivity: *Rattray v Daniels (1959) 17 DLR (2d) 134.* Contra if he could have proved negligence: *Western Silver Fox Ranch v Ross and Cromarty County Council (1940) SC 601.* Cf *MacGibbon v Robinson [1953] 2 DLR (2d) 689.*

Bradford Corpn v Pickles

[11.23] The case of *Bradford Corpn v Pickles*[1] is often regarded as House of Lords authority for the proposition that the defendant's motive is irrelevant in a nuisance action. The defendant owned land through which underground water percolated. The water eventually entered the plaintiffs' land and formed a spring which was used to supply water to the population of Bradford. The defendant abstracted the water, as it flowed through his land, and caused the spring to dry up. His motive was to make Bradford pay for the water. The plaintiffs brought an action and sought to distinguish the earlier case of *Chasemore v Richards*[2], in which it had been held that a landowner is entitled to abstract subterranean water irrespective of the effect upon his neighbour, by pointing to the defendant's avaricious motive in the present case. The action failed. In finding for the defendant, Lord Halsbury LC expressed in broad terms the view that motive is irrelevant to legality[3]. Significantly, however, Lord Macnaghten doubted whether the defendant's motive could be regarded as malicious. He merely wanted to sell his land to the Corporation and was anxious to compel a sale at a price advantageous to himself[4]. It is therefore submitted that *Bradford Corpn v Pickles* is not necessarily to be regarded as an authority for the wide proposition enunciated by Lord Halsbury LC[5].

[1]   *[1895] AC 587, 64 LJ Ch 759.*
[2]   *(1859) 7 HL Cas 349, 29 LJ Ex 81.* See also *Langbrook Properties Ltd v Surrey County Council [1969] 3 All ER 1424, [1970] 1 WLR 161.* But cf *Pugliese v National Capital Commission (1977) 79 DLR (3d) 592 (Can).*
[3]   See *[1895] AC 587* at 594.
[4]   '[The defendant] prefers his own interests to the public good. He may be churlish, selfish, and grasping. His conduct may seem shocking to a moral philosopher. But where is the malice? Mr Pickles has no spite against the people of Bradford. He bears no ill-will to the Corporation. They are welcome to the water and to his land too, if they will pay the price for it' *[1895] AC* at 601. See also Fridman, 'Motive in the English Law of Nuisance' (1954) 40 Virginia LR 583.
[5]   In *Hunter v Canary Wharf [1997] 2 All ER 426* at 465 Lord Cooke of Thorndon suggested that 'the malicious erection of a structure for the purpose of interfering with television reception should be actionable in nuisance'.

Pragmatism and the proof of malice

[11.24]   Moreover it is not without interest, as far as the particular fact situation which arose in *Pickles'* case is concerned, that there was judicial disagreement in *Chasemore v Richards* itself. The effect of that decision was to draw a sharp distinction between surface water, which at common law cannot be abstracted in such a way as unreasonably to interfere with the enjoyment of it by other riparian owners[1], and subterranean water which, it was held, may be abstracted at will. In the Court of Exchequer Chamber Coleridge J considered this distinction untenable[2], and in the House of Lords Lord Wensleydale almost dissented on the same ground[3]. They would have preferred to apply the reasonable user test applied to riparian owners in surface water cases[4]. The reason why the distinction was insisted upon by the majority was the pragmatic one that since underground water flows in undefined channels it would be impracticable to impose liability on defendants whose abstractions might potentially affect a very large number of neighbouring landowners[5]. It may be suggested, however, that this consideration has less weight in a case where the claimant is able to overcome the presumably onerous burden of proving an improper motive, than it might have otherwise. The obstacle provided by the burden of proof in such a case should act as a deterrent to potential claimants and thereby itself help to prevent the oppressiveness and uncertainty which the argument *ab inconvenienti* was concerned to avoid.

[1]   See *Embrey v Owen (1851) 6 Exch 353, 20 LJ Ex 212*; *Rugby Joint Water Board v Walters [1967] Ch 397, [1966] 3 All ER 497.* See also Brett, 'The Right to take Flowing Water' (1950) Conv (NS) 154. In practice the abstraction of both surface and underground water is now controlled by a statutory licensing scheme: see the *Water Resources Act 1991.* Cf *Cargill v Gotts [1981] 1 All ER 682.* A riparian owner does not enjoy any special right with respect to navigation over and above that enjoyed by the public: *Tate & Lyle Industries Ltd v Greater London Council [1983] 2 AC 509, [1983] 1 All ER 1159, HL.* See, generally, *Wisdom's Law of Watercourses* (5th edn, Howarth ed).
[2]   See *(1857) 2 H&N 168* at 186 onwards.
[3]   See *(1859) 7 HL Cas 349* at 380 onwards. See also the earlier case of *Dickinson v Grand Junction Canal Co (1852) 7 Exch 282, 21 LJ Ex 241* in which a plaintiff who complained of the abstraction of underground percolating water was held to have a good cause of action.

4   The reasonable user test has been applied in Canada, after an extensive review of the authorities, in preference to the rule in *Chasemore v Richards: Pugliese v National Capital Commission (1977) 79 DLR (3d) 592 (Ont CA)*. For further discussion, see Clayberg, 'The Law of Percolating Waters' (1915) 14 Mich LR 119. Cf Gutteridge, 'Abuse of Rights' (1935) 5 CLJ 22.
5   Cf *Palmer v Bowman [2000] 1 All ER 22, CA* (no easement can exist permitting the drainage of undefined and percolating rainwater).

C Fault and foreseeability

Intentional activities

[11.25]   A high proportion of nuisance cases require the court to determine the rights and duties of the parties in situations where the intentional activities of one or both of them have produced complaints of intolerable interference or inconvenience from the other. In such situations knowledge by the defendant of the claimant's grievance can usually be taken for granted from the date of the first complaint, and foreseeability of interference will therefore usually be self-evident. In cases of this type, where the main remedy sought will invariably be an injunction rather than damages, the real issue is the need to strike a reasonable balance between the interests of conflicting users of land[1].

1   'It is, of course, axiomatic that in this field we must be on our guard, when considering liability for damages in nuisance, not to draw inapposite conclusions from cases concerned only with a claim for an injunction. This is because, where an injunction is claimed, its purpose is to restrain further action by the defendant which may interfere with the plaintiff's enjoyment of his land, and ex hypothesi the defendant must be aware, if and when an injunction is granted, that such interference may be caused by the act which he is restrained from committing. It follows that these cases provide no guidance on the question whether foreseeability ... is a prerequisite of the recovery of damages ...' *per* Lord Goff in *Cambridge Water Co Ltd v Eastern Counties Leather plc [1994] 2 AC 264* at 300.

Damages cases

[11.26]   In cases involving actions for damages arising out of isolated occurrences which have inflicted loss on the claimant, however, the similarity to situations dealt with by the 'ordinary' law of negligence is obviously much greater. In the major case of *Cambridge Water Co Ltd v Eastern Counties Leather plc*[1] an underground supply of natural water, used for public consumption, was contaminated by solvent spilt on to the floor of the defendants' manufacturing premises. Although the defendants were aware that the spillages were occurring they had no reason to believe that they were anything other than harmless. The House of Lords exonerated the defendants from liability under the rule in *Rylands v Fletcher*[2], but also indicated that the same result would be reached by the application of nuisance principles[3]. The well known decision of the Judicial Committee of the Privy Council in *Overseas Tankship (UK) Ltd v Miller SS Co Pty (The Wagon Mound) (No 2)*[4], to the effect that the test for remoteness of damage in nuisance will normally be that of foreseeability, had, in the words of Lord Goff in *Cambridge Water*[5] 'settled the law to the effect that foreseeability of harm is indeed a prerequisite of the recovery of damages in private nuisance'.

1   *[1994] 2 AC 264.*
2   See post, CHAPTER 14.
3   See also *Savage v Fairclough [2000] Env LR 183, CA* in which *Cambridge Water* was applied.
4   *[1967] 1 AC 617, [1966] 2 All ER 709.*
5   *[1994] 2 AC 264 at 301.*

Need for actual or presumed knowledge

[11.27] The foreseeability principle is also seen in operation in the much earlier case of *Ilford UDC v Beal*[1]. Here the defendant bought land under which, unknown to her, the plaintiff local authority had previously placed a sewer. A retaining wall situated between the defendant's house and a nearby river was undermined by the river so that it moved and pressed against the plaintiffs' sewer, causing damage. In an action by the plaintiffs claiming damages for nuisance Branson J found for the defendant. Since she had not been aware, and could not reasonably have been expected to be aware, of the existence of the sewer she could not be held liable for the damage caused to it by her retaining wall[2]. The decision went the other way on the facts in the leading case of *Sedleigh-Denfield v O'Callaghan*[3]. A protective grating over a drainage pipe which flowed through the defendants' land had been incorrectly fitted causing the pipe to become blocked and to overflow. The plaintiffs' land was flooded as a result. In imposing liability on the defendants the House of Lords emphasised, however, that although the test for liability might not be identical with that in negligence[4], nevertheless, in the words of Lord Wright[5], 'Liability for nuisance is not, at least in modern law, a strict or absolute liability'[6]. The defendants were only liable because of their presumed knowledge of the existence of the defect[7].

[1] *[1925] 1 KB 671, 94 LJ KB 402.*
[2] The earlier case of *Humphries v Cousins (1877) 2 CPD 239*, decided on similar facts but in which strict liability was imposed, would no longer be followed: cf *per* Lord Goff in *Cambridge Water Co Ltd v Eastern Counties Leather plc [1994] 2 AC 264* at 302.
[3] *[1940] AC 880, [1940] 3 All ER 349.*
[4] See the discussion of the *Sedleigh-Denfield* case by R J Buxton in 'The Negligent Nuisance' (1966) 8 Malaya LR 1 at 12–16.
[5] *[1940] AC 880* at 904, *[1940] 3 All ER 349* at 365E.
[6] See also the decision of the Judicial Committee of the Privy Council in *Montana Hotels v Fasson (1986) 69 ALR 258.*
[7] See also *Leakey v National Trust for Places of Historic Interest or Natural Beauty [1980] QB 485, [1980] 1 All ER 17, C*; *Bybrook Barn Garden Centre v Kent County Council (2001) 3 LGLR 27, CA*; *Rees v Skerrett [2001] 1 WLR 1541.*

Scope

[11.28] The scope of the notion of presumed knowledge for present purposes was considered by the Court of Appeal in *Holbeck Hall Hotel v Scarborough Borough Council*[1]. Natural erosion had caused the defendants' land to collapse, thereby withdrawing support from the claimants' adjoining land. The likelihood of this collapse would have been apparent from a full geological investigation, but the Court held that the defendants were not liable for failing to carry out such an investigation. Stuart-Smith LJ said[2]:

> ' ... the defect must be patent and not latent; that is to say that it is a defect which can be observed; it is no answer for the landowner to say that he did not observe it, if a reasonable servant did so; or if as a responsible landowner he, or the person to whom he entrusted the responsibility of looking after the land, should have seen it. But if the defect is latent, the landowner or occupier is not to be held liable simply because, if he had made further investigation, he would have discovered it ... in my judgment that is what is meant by the expression "knowledge or presumed knowledge" '.

[1] *[2000] 2 All ER 705.*

2 See above at para 42. The expression 'knowledge or presumed knowledge' in this passage is taken from the speech of Viscount Maugham in *Sedleigh-Denfield v O'Callaghan [1940] AC 880* at 893, *[1940] 3 All ER 349* at 357.

Greater degree of liability

[11.29] Although the liability in damages is therefore clearly fault-based, the fact of landownership or occupation can involve a defendant in a potentially *greater* degree of liability for damage caused by the acts of third parties (by 'adoption' thereof) or for omissions to act, than is commonly found in areas of negligence where this factor is not present[1]. Thus in *Sedleigh-Denfield v O'Callaghan*[2] the drainage pipe and grating had been improperly inserted on the defendants' land by trespassing third parties, but this did not prevent the defendants themselves from being held liable for the damage caused by their failure to avert the harm which ensued[3].

1 For valuable discussion of this point see Gerry Cross 'Does Only the Careless Polluter Pay?' (1995) 111 LQR 445.
2 *[1940] AC 880, [1940] 3 All ER 349.*
3 See also *Page Motors Ltd v Epsom and Ewell Borough Council (1980) 78 LGR 505.* Cf the decision of the Court of Appeal in *Job Edwards Ltd v Birmingham Navigations [1924] 1 KB 341, 93 LJ KB 261* which was overruled by the House of Lords in *Sedleigh-Denfield v O'Callaghan.*

Subjective approach

[11.30] The liability of occupiers in 'nuisance' cases also differs from ordinary negligence by being, in certain circumstances, more *subjective*. In *Goldman v Hargrave*[1] the Judicial Committee of the Privy Council held a defendant liable for his failure to prevent a fire, which had been started by lightning, from spreading to his neighbour's land. Although Lord Wilberforce, in delivering the judgment of the Board, said that liability in the case rested 'upon negligence and nothing else'[2] he went on to define the scope of the defendant's duty in terms rather different from those normally associated with negligence. In particular the court, in deciding whether to impose liability for failure adequately to deal with a hazard of nature, would take into account the relative financial position of the parties. It was not enough to say that the defendant must act 'reasonably' since 'what is reasonable to one man may be very unreasonable, and indeed ruinous, to another'. The duty would therefore vary with the defendant's resources which 'whether physical or material, may be of a very modest character either in relation to the magnitude of the hazard, or as compared with those of his threatened neighbour'[3]. His Lordship continued:

> 'Thus, less must be expected of the infirm than of the able-bodied: the owner of a small property where a hazard arises which threatens a neighbour with substantial interests should not have to do as much as one with larger interests of his own at stake and greater resources to protect them: if the small owner does what he can and promptly calls on his neighbour to provide additional resources, he may be held to have done his duty: he should not be liable unless it is clearly proved that he could, and reasonably in his individual circumstances should, have done more'[4].

1 *[1967] 1 AC 645, [1966] 2 All ER 989.*
2 *[1967] 1 AC 645* at 657A, *[1966] 2 All ER 989* at 992B.
3 *[1967] 1 AC 645* at 663A–B, *[1966] 2 All ER 989* at 996A–B.
4 *[1967] 1 AC 645* at 663E–F, *[1966] 2 All ER 989* at 996D–E.

Negligence concepts

[11.31] It has also been suggested, in the Court of Appeal, that the now familiar negligence concepts of 'fairness, justice and reasonableness' can also be invoked in the context of adoption of nuisance, so as to prevent the imposition of liability considered by the court to be oppressive.[1]

---

[1] See *Holbeck Hall Hotel v Scarborough Borough Council [2000] 2 All ER 705, CA* at para 51.

Flexibility not confined to natural hazards

[11.32] The approach in *Goldman v Hargrave,* which was emphatically reaffirmed by the Court of Appeal in *Leakey v National Trust for Places of Historic Interest or Natural Beauty*[1], shows an awareness of the special sensitivity of the relationship between neighbouring landowners[2]. It is also in contrast with the usually objective approach of negligence in which impecuniosity or other lack of capacity will seldom provide defences[3]. It is not altogether clear whether the subjective approach is confined to natural hazards, or extends to all situations in which the nuisance has been caused by someone other than the defendant himself but for whose acts he is responsible. Although there is no mention of the subjective approach in *Sedleigh-Denfield v O'Callaghan*[4], it is submitted that the better view is that the approach is applicable in such cases. There would seem to be no justification for limiting the more flexible approach to only one type of situation in which the defendant did not himself cause the nuisance and for refusing to extend it to others. In *Holbeck Hall Hotel v Scarborough Council* Stuart-Smith LJ said[5]:

> 'There seems no reason why, where the defendant does not create the nuisance, but the question is whether he had adopted or continued it, different principles should apply to one kind of nuisance rather than another. In each case liability only arises if there is negligence, the duty to abate the nuisance arises from the defendant's knowledge of the hazard that will affect his neighbour'.

---

[1] *[1980] QB 485, [1980] 1 All ER 17.*

[2] Cf *British Railways Board v Herrington [1972] AC 877, [1972] 1 All ER 749* in which the House of Lords adopted a similar subjective approach towards the problem of the liability of an occupier of land for injury to trespassers.

[3] Cf *Nettleship v Weston [1971] 2 QB 691, [1971] 3 All ER 581* (no defence to claim arising out of a motor accident that the defendant was an 'L' driver insufficiently skilled to have been capable of avoiding the accident).

[4] *[1940] AC 880, [1940] 3 All ER 349.*

[5] See *[2000] 2 All ER 705* at para 35.

D Who can claim?

Interests capable of sustaining an action

[11.33] Since a private nuisance is an interference with the enjoyment of *land* the claimant must have *some* connection with the land affected in order to be able to sue. A freehold owner legally in occupation can obviously sue. The rights of an owner who has leased the property are, however, limited to nuisances likely to prove adverse to his reversionary interest[1] since the tort is concerned primarily to protect existing enjoyment. A tenant can sue if he is in occupation and he can proceed against his own landlord if necessary[2]. In the case of land in joint-ownership the co-owners can sue each other[3]. But mere occupation without any kind of proprietary or possessory interest in the land is not sufficient[4].

[1] See below at para [11.37].
[2] *Alston v Grant (1854) 3 E&B 128, 2 CLR 933.* See below at para [11.37].
[3] See *Hooper v Rogers [1975] Ch 43* at 51, *[1974] 3 All ER 417* at 422, *per* Scarman LJ.
[4] See *Butcher Robinson & Staples v London Regional Transport (1999) 79 P&CR 523.*

Hunter v Canary Wharf

[11.34] Although this conventional understanding of the law was challenged by a majority decision of the Court of Appeal in 1993, on the ground that interference with the enjoyment of a person's *home* should be sufficient to confer a cause of action[1], this view was emphatically rejected shortly afterwards by the House of Lords in *Hunter v Canary Wharf*[2]. By a majority of four to one[3] the House asserted that the traditional view was correct, and that 'an action in private nuisance will lie only at the suit of a person who has a right to the land affected'[4]. The House expressly upheld the authority of a 1907 decision of the Court of Appeal in which a wife who lived with her husband, in a house of which he alone was lessee, was unable to sue[5]. The suggestion that modern matrimonial legislation may have conferred a sufficient interest upon the wife of the owner or tenant to sue in nuisance was also rejected[6]. In an early case a husband was similarly unable to sue when his wife's garden, in which he had no right or interest beyond being allowed to cultivate it, was flooded as a result of the defendant's stopping up certain ditches on adjoining property[7]. *Hunter v Canary Wharf* can be criticised as outdated for its insistence upon property rights as the basis for claims in private nuisance. But the thesis has recently been advanced that protection of such rights could form the basis of a reformed, and more effective, law of nuisance, particularly in relation to the issues raised by genetically modified crops[8].

[1] See *Khorasandjian v Bush [1993] QB 727, [1993] 3 All ER 669.*
[2] *[1997] 2 All ER 426.*
[3] There was a powerfully argued dissent from Lord Cooke of Thorndon.
[4] See *[1997] 2 All ER 426* at 438 *per* Lord Goff. See Letitia Crabb 'The Property Torts?' (2003) 11 Tort LR 104.
[5] See *Malone v Laskey [1907] 2 KB 141.*
[6] 'I do not see how a spouse who has no interest in the matrimonial home has, simply by virtue of his or her cohabiting in the matrimonial home with his or her wife or husband whose freehold or leasehold property it is, a right to sue. No distinction can sensibly be drawn between such spouses and other cohabitees in the home, such as children, or grandparents': *per* Lord Goff in *[1997] 2 All ER 426* at 440. See also *per* Lord Hoffman at 453.
[7] See *Nunn v Parkes & Co (1924) 59 L Jo 806.* See also *Oldham v Lawson [1976] VR 654 (Aus).*
[8] See David Campbell 'Of Coase and Corn: A (Sort of) Defence of Private Nuisance' (2000) 63 MLR 197; Christopher P. Rodgers 'Liability for the Release of GMOS into the Environment: Exploring the Boundaries of Nuisance' [2003] 62 CLJ 371.

Exceptional cases

[11.35] In one case, which was referred to with approval in *Hunter v Canary Wharf*[1], Evershed J held that statutory undertakers legally in possession of land as licensees could sue[2], observing that 'though the cause of action may consist in an unlawful interference with land or with property in land, prima facie possession is sufficient to maintain the action'[3]. Moreover it was held in a New Zealand case[4] that even unlawful possession is sufficient on the ground that, as in trespass[5], the defence of *ius tertii* is not open to the defendant. This principle also appears to have been approved in

Hunter's case[6]. In addition Lord Hoffman indicated in that case that an earlier decision, in which a lessee had been unable to sue when he had assigned the whole of his legal estate in the land but re-entered when his sub-lessee absconded[7], was too restrictive and that the lessee *should* have been able to sue[8]. A flexible approach towards the question of who can sue in private nuisance is further indicated by the decision of the House of Lords in *Delaware Mansions v Westminster City Council*[9]. In this case it was held that, where there is a continuing nuisance, a person with an interest in the land can sue for loss which he has suffered as a result of the nuisance even though the cause of the loss originated before he acquired his interest[10].

[1] See *per* Lord Goff in *[1997] 2 All ER 426* at 435.
[2] See *Newcastle-under-Lyme Corpn v Wolstanton [1947] Ch 92, [1946] 2 All ER 447*; revsd, but not on this point, in *[1947] Ch 427, [1947] 1 All ER 218.*
[3] *[1947] Ch 92* at 107, *[1946] 2 All ER 447* at 455G. Cf *Charing Cross West End and City Electricity Supply Co v London Hydraulic Power Co [1914] 3 KB 772, 83 LJKB 1352.*
[4] See *Paxhaven Holdings Ltd v A-G [1974] 2 NZLR 185.*
[5] Cf *Foster v Warblington UDC [1906] 1 KB 648.*
[6] See *per* Lord Goff in *[1997] 2 All ER 426* at 435–436, see also *per* Lord Hoffman at 448–449.
[7] See *Metropolitan Properties Ltd v Jones [1939] 2 All ER 202.*
[8] See *[1997] 2 All ER 426* at 449–450.
[9] *[2001] 4 All ER 737.*
[10] See also *Masters v Brent London Borough Council [1978] QB 841, [1978] 2 All ER 664.*

'Tolerated trespassers'

[11.36] In *Pemberton v Southwark London Borough Council*[1] the claimant was a tenant of the defendant authority who had failed to pay her rent and had therefore become liable to eviction. The authority had not taken the final steps necessary to secure her removal, however, and she remained in occupation. She brought an action for nuisance arising out of alleged infestation of the premises by cockroaches. The defendants contended that the claimant did not have an interest in land entitling her to sue, but the Court of Appeal rejected this contention holding that she was a 'tolerated trespasser': a status deemed to have been produced by virtue of the provisions of the *Housing Act 1985*[2]. The court held that that status was sufficient to enable her to bring a nuisance claim notwithstanding the decision of the House of Lords in *Hunter v Canary Wharf* in which, as Sir Christopher Slade observed in *Pemberton's* case[3], the House had not been required to consider the concept of tolerated trespass.

[1] *[2000] 3 All ER 924, CA.*
[2] The expression was first used by Lord Browne-Wilkinson in *Burrows v Brent London Borough Council [1996] 4 All ER 577* at 584, *[1996] 1 WLR 1448* at 1455. See Susan Bright 'The Concept of the Tolerated Trespasser: an Analysis' (2003) 119 LQR 495.
[3] See *[2000] 3 All ER 924* at 937.

Reversioners

[11.37] The general rule is that to entitle a reversioner to sue on the ground of injury to his reversionary interest the injury must be of a permanent character[1]. The obvious example is violation of a right of support for the claimant's building[2]. In one case a lessee who had granted a sub-lease for the remainder of his term less the last three days was held entitled to sue for vibrations caused by the defendant's machinery, since the vibration 'was calculated to destroy the houses'[3]. It has been held that building a roof with eaves which discharge rainwater by a spout into adjoining premises is capable of constituting an injury to the reversion so as to enable the reversioner to sue[4]. In certain circumstances obstruction of a right of way can also constitute such injury[5]. On the other hand, according to the older authorities, nuisances which merely annoy, such as noise and smell, will not normally entitle a reversioner to sue since the acts complained of might be discontinued at any time before the end of the lessee's term[6]. This rule has been applied even in cases involving properties let to weekly tenants[7]. Evidence that the market value of the property will depreciate if the nuisance is continued is not sufficient to enable the reversioner to sue since the depreciation 'results from the presumed intention to continue' the nuisance and not from 'any thing that has been actually done'[8]. A more generous view of the reversioner's right to sue appears, however, to have been taken in *Hampstead and Suburban Properties v Diomedous*[9]. In this case Megarry J granted landlords an interlocutory injunction to restrain a noise nuisance which prevented their tenants from sleeping. The contention that the plaintiffs had no standing in the matter was dismissed as 'wholly lacking in substance'[10].

[1]   *Jackson v Pesked (1813) 1 M&S 234; Simpson v Savage (1856) 1 CBNS 347.*
[2]   See *Jeffries v Williams (1850) 5 Exch 792, 20 LJ Ex 14.*
[3]   *Colwell v St Pancras Borough Council [1904] 1 Ch 707* at 713, *per* Joyce J. See also *Meux's Brewery v City of London Electric Lighting Co [1895] 1 Ch 287.*
[4]   See *Tucker v Newman (1839) 11 Ad&El 40*. Cf *Jones v Llanrwst UDC [1911] 1 Ch 393, 80 LJ Ch 145.*
[5]   See *Kidgill v Moor (1850) 9 CB 364, 1 LM&P 131; Bell v Midland Rly Co (1861) 10 CBNS 287, 30 LJCP 273*. Cf *Dobson v Blackmore (1847) 9 QB 991, 16 LJ QB 233.*
[6]   See *Simpson v Savage (1856) 1 CBNS 347, 26 LJCP 50; Mumford v Oxford, Worcester and Wolver-hampton Rly Co (1856) 1 H&N 34, 25 LJ Ex 265; Mott v Shoolbred (1875) LR 20 Eq 22, 44 LJ Ch 380.*
[7]   See *Jones v Chappell (1875) LR 20 Eq 539, 44 LJ Ch 658; Cooper v Crabtree (1881) 19 Ch D 193;* affd *(1882) 20 Ch D 589, 51 LJ Ch 544.*
[8]   *Per* Bramwell B in *Mumford v Oxford, Worcester and Wolverhampton Rly Co (1856) 1 H&N 34 at 37.*
[9]   *[1969] 1 Ch 248, [1968] 3 All ER 545.*
[10]   See *[1969] 1 Ch 248 at 258G, [1968] 3 All ER 545 at 550E.*

Mortgagees

[11.38] It is uncertain whether a mortgagee out of possession can sue in nuisance but, by analogy with the rules governing reversioners, there would appear to be no reason why such a mortgagee should not be able to bring an action providing he can show clearly that his security is threatened[1].

[1]   See *Preston v Hilton (1920) 55 DLR 647 (Can).*

Personal injuries

[11.39] Although evidence of ill-health is clearly admissible in order to prove the gravity of an annoyance in private nuisance,[1] it is now clear that damages for personal injury as such cannot be recovered in private nuisance. In *Hunter v Canary Wharf* three members of the House of Lords were emphatic that this is the law[2]. Moreover, there appears to be no reported English case in which a plaintiff ever succeeded in recovering damages for personal injury as such in this tort, at any rate in circumstances where a negligence action would not have succeeded[3]. In one case in which such a claim was made the action failed on other grounds[4]. While it is true in a sense that a person who suffers personal injury while on his own land, as a result of an interference from that of his neighbour, is injured *qua* landowner,[5] the capacity of the land or property itself to provide enjoyment is not thereby diminished. Moreover, it would be anomalous to have a special class of claimants who might be able, merely by virtue of landownership, to escape the common law rule that 'an allegation of negligence is in general essential to the relevancy of an action of reparation for personal injuries'[6]. Damage to property can, however, be recovered in private nuisance,[7] and it seems to be clear that this extends to foreseeable damage to chattels on the claimant's land[8].

[1] Cf *Spruzen v Dossett (1896) 12 TLR 246.*
[2] See *per* Lord Hoffman at 453 ('So far as the claim is for personal injury, it seems to me that the only appropriate cause of action is negligence'); see also Lord Goff at 438 and Lord Lloyd at 442.
[3] Cf *Cunard v Antifyre Ltd [1933] 1 KB 551, 103 LJKB 321.*
[4] See *Malone v Laskey [1907] 2 KB 141, 76 LJKB 1134.*
[5] Cf Tylor, 'The Restriction of Strict Liability' (1947) 10 MLR 396.
[6] Per Lord Macmillan in *Read v J Lyons & Co Ltd [1947] AC 156* at 170–171, *[1946] 2 All ER 471* at 476A.
[7] See below CHAPTER 13.
[8] See *Howard Electric Ltd v A J Mooney Ltd [1974] 2 NZLR 762.* Damage to chattels is also recoverable under the rule in *Rylands v Fletcher*: see *Halsey v Esso Petroleum Co Ltd [1961] 2 All ER 145, [1961] 1 WLR 683.*

Rylands v Fletcher and public nuisance

[11.40] Consistently with the position as confirmed in *Hunter v Canary Wharf*, dicta in an even more recent decision of the House of Lords, *Transco v Stockport Metropolitan Borough Council*,[1] have held that damages for personal injury are not recoverable in actions based on the rule in *Rylands v Fletcher*, notwithstanding a slender line of authority to the contrary effect[2]. Damages for personal injury have occasionally been recovered in public nuisance[3], but it must now be very doubtful whether these decisions still represent the law[4].

[1] *[2004] 1 All ER 589,* see *per* Lord Hoffman at para 35 (' … damages for personal injuries are not recoverable under the rule'). See also Lord Hobhouse at para 52. See also *Read v J Lyons & Co Ltd [1947] AC 156, [1946] 2 All ER 471, HL.*
[2] See *Miles v Forest Rock Granite Co (Leicestershire) Ltd (1918) 34 TLR 500; Hale v Jennings Bros [1938] 1 All ER 579; Aldridge and O'Brien v Van Patter [1952] 4 DLR 93 (Can).* See also *Shiffman v Grand Priory in British Realm of Venerable Order of the Hospital of St John of Jerusalem [1936] 1 All ER 557.* Cf *Federic v Perpetual Investments Ltd (1969) 2 DLR (3d) 50 (Can).*
[3] See *Harrold v Watney [1898] 2 QB 320, 67 LJQB 771; Castle v St Augustine's Links (1922) 38 TLR 615; Mint v Good [1951] 1 KB 517, [1950] 2 All ER 1159.* It is essential that the plaintiff is injured while exercising a public right: *Bromley v Mercer [1922] 2 KB 126, 91 LJKB 577.* Cf *Jacobs v LCC [1950] AC 361, [1950] 1 All ER 737.*
[4] See *Hunter v Canary Wharf [1997] 2 All ER 426* at 438 *per* Lord Goff. On public nuisance see, generally, CHAPTER 14 below.

E Defendants and the extent of liability

Who can be sued?

Occupiers and creators

[11.41] The most appropriate defendant in a private nuisance action will normally be the occupier of the land from which the nuisance emanates[1]. Even if he did not himself create it he will usually be liable on the ground of having 'continued' or 'adopted' the nuisance[2]. The person who actually created it, if someone other than the occupier, will be liable in addition and it is no defence to an action for damages that the creator is no longer in a position to abate the nuisance[3], eg because he has since alienated the land from which it emanates and cannot re-enter without committing a trespass[4].

1   See *Russell v Shenton (1842) 3 QB 449, 2 Gal & Dav 573; A-G (ex rel Strand District Board of Works) v Kirk (1896) 12 TLR 514.*
2   See *Brent v Haddon (1619) Cro Jac 555; Broder v Saillard (1876) 2 Ch D 692; Sedleigh-Denfield v O'Callaghan [1940] AC 880, [1940] 3 All ER 349; Pemberton v Bright [1960] 1 All ER 792, [1960] 1 WLR 436; Page Motors Ltd v Epsom and Ewell Borough Council (1980) 78 LGR 505;* affd *(1981) 125 Sol Jo 590.* See also below.
3   *Thompson v Gibson (1841) 7 M&W 456, 10 LJ Ex 330.*
4   *Roswell v Prior (1701) Holt KB 500, 12 Mod Rep 635.* An injunction would clearly not be awarded against the creator of the nuisance in such a case.

Where the nuisance does not emanate from other land

[11.42]   The creator will clearly be the usual defendant in a case in which the nuisance does not emanate from other land[1]. The question whether such emanations can constitute private nuisance at all led to a difference of judicial opinion in the case of *Southport Corpn v Esso Petroleum Co Ltd*[2]. In order to refloat an oil-tanker which had run aground the captain discharged his cargo of oil with the result that it was washed up on the plaintiffs' beaches. At first instance Devlin J was of the opinion that the resultant fouling could be regarded as coming within the rubric of private nuisance. He said[3]:

> 'It is clear that to give a cause of action for private nuisance the matter complained of must affect the property of the plaintiffs ... and it is true that in the vast majority of cases it is likely to emanate from the neighbouring property of the defendant. But no statement of principle has been cited to me to show that the latter is a prerequisite to a cause of action, and I can see no reason why, if land or water belonging to the public or waste land is misused by the defendant ... he should not be liable for a nuisance in the same way as an adjoining occupier would be'.

In the Court of Appeal, however, Denning LJ took the view that the case could only be regarded as one of public nuisance[4] (which does not have any necessary connection with the enjoyment of land). In the House of Lords, Lord Radcliffe agreed with Denning LJ on this point[5]. It is submitted that the view of Devlin J is nevertheless to be preferred[6]. it would seem to be unduly restrictive and illogical to limit the scope of the tort to such cases, especially since the creator of a nuisance will be liable, as such, even if he is not the occupier of the land from which it emanates.

1   Ie interference with the claimant's land which does not emanate from other privately owned land, but from for example, the highway or the sea, can constitute a private nuisance *Esso Petroleum Co Ltd v Southport Corpn [1956] AC 218, [1955] 3 All ER 864.*
2   See *[1953] 2 All ER 1204, [1953] 3 WLR 773* (Devlin J), *[1954] 2 QB 182, [1954] 2 All ER 561, CA, [1956] AC 218, [1955] 3 All ER 864* (House of Lords sub nom. *Esso Petroleum Co Ltd v Southport Corpn*).
3   *[1953] 2 All ER 1204 at 1207, [1953] 3 WLR 773 at 776.*
4   See *[1954] 2 QB 182 at 196–197, [1954] 2 All ER 561 at 570–571.*
5   See *[1956] AC 218 at 242, [1955] 3 All ER 864 at 871.* The case was ultimately decided by the House of Lords on a pleading point which is not material here.
6   See also *Hubbard v Pitt [1976] QB 142, [1975] 3 All ER 1,* Stamp and Orr LJJ, Lord Denning MR dissenting (actionable private nuisance to picket premises from the highway). Cf *Barber v Penley [1893] 2 Ch 447; Lyons, Sons & Co v Gulliver [1914] 1 Ch 631.*

Liability for the acts of others

[11.43]   An occupier cannot escape liability for a nuisance which emanates from his land merely by showing that it was caused by the acts of third parties without his consent. In *A-G v Tod Heatley*[1] the defendants owned land, in a densely populated part of London, which was not in use but was surrounded by a hoarding. Unfortunately, however, people threw 'dead dogs and cats, vegetable refuse, fish, offal, rubbish, and all kinds of filth' over the hoarding and as a result the condition of the land became a continuing public nuisance. The Court of Appeal held that it was no defence that it was not the defendants themselves, but members of the public, who had deposited the rubbish. As Lindley LJ observed[2]:

'It is no defence to say: "I did not put the filth on, but somebody else did" '.

The Court of Appeal held by a majority in *Job Edwards Ltd v Birmingham Navigations Proprietors Co*[3] that the principle in the *Tod-Heatley* case was confined to public nuisances, but their decision was overruled by the House of Lords in *Sedleigh-Denfield v O'Callaghan*[4] and the rule is therefore now applicable to both public and private nuisance. It was held in a recent case to be applicable in a case against a local authority for failing to take effective measures against the presence, on land owned by the authority, of a group of travellers who were causing a nuisance to nearby farmers[5].

[1]   *[1897] 1 Ch 560, 66 LJ Ch 275.* Cf *R v Moore (1832) 3 B&Ad 184.*
[2]   *[1897] 1 Ch 550 at 566.*
[3]   [1924] 1 KB 341, Bankes LJ and Astbury J, Scrutton LJ dissenting. Cf *Saxby v Manchester, Sheffield and Lincolnshire Rly Co (1869) LR 4 CP 198, 38 LJCP 153.*
[4]   *[1940] AC 880, [1940] 3 All ER 349.* For discussion of this case see ante CHAPTER 1 of the handbook.
[5]   See *Lippiatt v South Gloucestershire Council [1999] 4 All ER 149, CA.* See also *Page Motors Ltd v Epsom and Ewell Borough Council (1980) 78 LGR 505*; affd *(1981) 125 Sol Jo 590.*

Need for effective measures

[11.44]   The liability is not, however, strict or absolute[1]. An occupier will only be liable for nuisances not caused by him if he can be said to have 'continued or adopted' them[2]. He will be regarded as having done so if he allows the nuisance to continue with knowledge or means of knowledge of its existence or of the state of affairs likely to give rise to it[3]. He will not be liable if, once he discovers the existence of the nuisance caused by a third party, he takes reasonable steps to stop it[4]. He will escape liability if it can be shown that no practical method of abating the nuisance exists[5] As in the case of nuisances caused by natural occurrences[6], the extent of liability is likely to be determined on a subjective basis and the defendant's resources will therefore normally be relevant[7].

[1]   See *Sedleigh-Denfield v O'Callaghan [1940] AC 880 at 904, [1940] 3 All ER 349 at 365, per* Lord Wright. See also *per* Lord Atkin *[1940] AC 880 at 897, [1940] 3 All ER 349 at 360.*
[2]   *Sedleigh-Denfield v O'Callaghan,* see above.
[3]   *Sedleigh-Denfield v O'Callaghan [1940] AC 880, [1940] 3 All ER 349; Pemberton v Bright [1960] 1 All ER 792, [1960] 1 WLR 436; Page Motors Ltd v Epsom and Ewell Borough Council (1980) 78 LGR 505*; affd *(1981) 125 Sol Jo 590.* Cf *R v Shorrock [1993] 3 All ER 917.*
[4]   See *Smith v Great Western Rly Co (1926) 135 LT 112.* Decisions to the contrary such as *Bell v Twentyman (1841) 1 QB 766, 1 Gal & Dav 223,* which was followed in *Humphries v Cousins (1877) 2 CPD 239, 46 LJQB 438,* cannot be regarded as good law after *Sedleigh-Denfield v O'Callaghan* (see para [11.27] above.
[5]   See *Regal v African Superslate (Pty) Ltd (1961) (4) SA 727.*
[6]   See *Goldman v Hargrave [1967] 1 AC 645, [1966] 2 All ER 989* and *Leakey v National Trust for Places of Historic Interest or Natural Beauty [1980] QB 485, [1980] 1 All ER 17* discussed above. See also CHAPTER 13 below.
[7]   See *Page Motors Ltd v Epsom and Ewell Borough Council (1980) 78 LGR 505* at pp 516–519, *per* Balcombe J.

Independent contractors

[11.45] The principles governing vicarious liability for independent contractors in nuisance cases are dealt with in a later chapter.[1]

¹ See below CHAPTER 18.

Landlords[1]

[11.46] An owner who has leased the land will not normally be liable for nuisances emanating therefrom and created by his tenant[2]. He will, however, be liable along with the tenant if he authorised the commission of the act which causes the nuisance[3]. In *Tetley v Chitty*[4] a local authority leased land for the purpose of developing a go-kart track. The activities of the lessees, a go-kart club, subsequently caused a nuisance for which McNeill J held the authority liable on the ground that the nuisance was 'a natural and necessary consequence'[5] of the purpose for which the lease had been granted[6]. While authorisation is, perhaps inevitably, a somewhat vague expression it does require something more than mere foreseeability, although in one Common-wealth case foreseeability of the tenant's conduct appears to have been regarded as sufficient.[7] The concept of authorisation cannot apply if the acts of the tenants were unrelated to their occupation of the landlord's premises. Thus in *Hussain v Lancaster City Council*[8] the defendant Council was not liable for acts of racial harassment carried out by their tenants on a shopkeeper who lived nearby.

¹ See Jonathan Morgan 'Nuisance and the Unruly Tenant' [2001] 60 CLJ 382.
² See *Russell v Shenton (1842) 3 QB 449, 2 Gal & Dav 573; Rich v Basterfield (1847) 4 CB 783, 16 LJCP 273.*
³ *Harris v James (1876) 45 LJQB 545, 35 LT 240; Winter v Baker (1887) 3 TLR 569.*
⁴ *[1986] 1 All ER 663.*
⁵ *[1986] 1 All ER 663* at 671, applying *Harris v James (1876) 45 LJQB 545, 35 LT 240.*
⁶ See also *De Jager v Payneham & Magill Lodges (1984) 36 SASR 498.*
⁷ See *Aussie Traveller Pty v Marklea Pty [1998] 1 Qd R 1 (Qld CA)*, referred to in *Mowan v Wandsworth London Borough Council (2001) 33 HLR 56, CA* at para 34.
⁸ *[1999] 4 All ER 125, CA:* ' ... the acts complained of unquestionably interfered persistently and intolerably with the plaintiffs' enjoyment of the plaintiffs' land, but they did not involve the tenants' use of the tenants' land and therefore fell outside the scope of the tort' *per* Hirst LJ at 144.

Ordinary user cannot constitute nuisance

[11.47] The ordinary user of premises cannot amount to a nuisance, and a landlord cannot be liable for letting premises for such user. If ordinary user by a tenant does in fact interfere with the enjoyment of neighbouring property, the occupier of the latter will therefore have no redress in nuisance, for the interference suffered, against either the tenant or his landlord. Moreover, a tenant cannot complain of defects in the property demised, which are neither dangerous nor in themselves a nuisance[1], unless he can point to a specific covenant in the lease. In the absence of such a covenant, or a pre-existing nuisance, the general rule of property law applies that a tenant must take the premises as he finds them. These principles were confirmed and applied by the House of Lords in *Southwark London Borough Council v Mills*[2]. Inadequate sound-proofing in a block of flats let by the defendant local authority meant that the sounds of ordinary living could readily be heard in adjacent flats, rendering the occupiers' lives intolerable. But the flats complied with the relevant building regulations then in force, and the House of Lords held that if higher standards were to be insisted upon that was a matter for the legislature and not the courts.

¹ Cf *Todd v Flight (1860) 9 CBNS 377, 30 LJCP 21*; *Spicer v Smee [1946] 1 All ER 489.*
² *[1999] 4 All ER 449.* Cf *Sampson v Hodson-Pressinger [1981] 3 All ER 710, CA* (distinguished and explained on other grounds in *Mills'* case).

Attempts to allocate liability by covenant

[11.48] In the nineteenth-century case of *Pretty v Bickmore*¹ it was held that if a landlord took a covenant to repair from his tenant he would not be liable to third parties for nuisances caused through disrepair, and that this would be so even if the premises were out of repair before they were demised. This case has, however, been criticised² and a majority of the Court of Appeal refused to follow it in a case involving premises out of repair before they were demised, even though the lease in question was one of fourteen years' duration³. On the other hand in *Smith v Scott*⁴, which did not concern disrepair but a nuisance caused by the unruly behaviour of tenants, the defendant landlords, a local authority, were held not liable where they had let the tenants into possession on conditions which expressly prohibited them from committing a nuisance. Pennycuick V-C held that the covenant enabled the landlords to escape liability even though they knew that the tenants were likely to disregard the prohibition⁵.

¹ (1873) LR 8 CP 401.
² See *Mint v Good [1951] 1 KB 517* at 528, *[1950] 2 All ER 1159* at 1166F, *per* Denning LJ.
³ See *Brew Bros Ltd v Snax (Ross) Ltd [1970] 1 QB 612, [1970] 1 All ER 587,* Sachs and Phillimore LJJ, Harman LJ dissenting.
⁴ *[1973] Ch 314, [1972] 3 All ER 645.* See also *Mowan v Wandsworth London Borough Council (2001) 33 HLR 56, CA*; *Hussain v Lancaster City Council [1999] 4 All ER 125, CA.*
⁵ Sed quaere. See criticism by Merritt, 'The Liability of Landlords for Nuisances Committed by Tenants' [1973] JPL 154. Cf *Tetley v Chitty [1986] 1 All ER 663* in which a local authority conceded that a clause in a lease obliging the lessees not to cause a nuisance would not in itself exonerate the authority from liability as lessors.

Right to repair

[11.49] A landlord who himself covenants to repair will be liable to third parties if he allows the premises to fall into disrepair and thereby cause a nuisance¹. Moreover a landlord who has reserved the right to enter and carry out repairs will be so liable even if he has not actually covenanted to repair². In the case of weekly tenancies which are silent as to liability for repairs the court will hold the landlord liable to third parties by, if necessary, implying terms into the agreement to the effect that the landlord will keep the premises in repair and is entitled to enter in order to do so³. Even if the lessor habitually carries out the repairs the tenant will normally be liable, *qua* occupier, along with his landlord, if the premises fall into disrepair and cause a nuisance⁴.

¹ See *Wringe v Cohen [1940] 1 KB 229, [1939] 4 All ER 241, CA.*
² *Wilchick v Marks and Silverstone [1934] 2 KB 56, 103 LJKB 372*; *Heap v Ind, Coope and Allsopp [1940] 2 KB 476, [1940] 3 All ER 634.*
³ *Mint v Good [1951] 1 KB 517, [1950] 2 All ER 1159.* See also the repairing obligations in short leases imposed upon landlords by the *Landlord and Tenant Act 1985, s 11.*
⁴ *Wilchick v Marks and Silverstone [1934] 2 KB 56, 103 LJKB 372.* Cf *Metropolitan Properties Ltd v Jones [1939] 2 All ER 202.*

Fire

[**11.50**] A landlord can be liable to third parties if his failure to exercise control over his tenants results in one of them causing a fire to begin which spreads to adjoining properties.[1]

1   See *Ribbee v Norrie [2001] PIQR P8, CA.*

Chapter 12

Interference with comfort and enjoyment

A The establishing of liability

Reasonableness

[12.01] The majority of disputes concerning the use and enjoyment of land involve complaints of discomfort or inconvenience caused by noise or smell. In resolving such disputes the court attempts to balance the conflicting interests of the parties by using, as far as possible, external gauges of the *reasonableness* or otherwise of the defendant's conduct and the complainant's complaint. The concept of reasonableness lies, albeit in different ways and with different methods of application, at the heart of so much of the common law. It is more important to work out how it applies in any given context than to debate whether the context in question should be formally classified as 'nuisance' or 'negligence'. Nevertheless, it remains appropriate to follow the language of the cases in using the terminology of nuisance when dealing with the situations with which the present chapter is concerned.

Robust approach

[12.02] The approach implied by the test of reasonableness in the context of disputes about interference with the enjoyment of land is a robust one. In *Walter v Selfe*[1] Knight Bruce V-C said[2]:

'... both on principle and authority the important point next for decision may properly, I conceive, be thus put: ought this inconvenience to be considered in fact as more than fanciful, more than one of mere delicacy or fastidiousness, as an inconvenience materially interfering with the ordinary comfort physically of human existence, not merely according to elegant or dainty modes of living, but according to plain and sober and simple notions among the English people'.

The application of this principle necessarily depends on the facts of each case. Conflicts of evidence as to the extent of the alleged interference are common and the value in this context, as elsewhere, of positive evidence over negative has often been emphasised. Sargant J once remarked, in a case which concerned the alleged emanation of offensive smells from a sewage farm, that 'one person who gives accurate evidence that he observed something is worth more than that of four or five persons who simply say that they never did observe that thing'[3].

---

[1]   (1851) 4 De G & Sm 315, 20 LJ Ch 433.
[2]   See above at 322. See also *Vanderpant v Mayfair Hotel Co Ltd [1930] 1 Ch 138* at 165, *per* Luxmoore J.

3   *Bainbridge v Chertsey Urban Council (1914) 84 LJ Ch 626* at 628. See also *Bareham v Hall (1870) 22 LT 116* at 117–118, *per* Stuart V-C; *Bosworth-Smith v Gwynnes Ltd (1919) 89 LJ Ch 368, 122 LT 15.*

Liability imposed

[12.03]   A typical example of a nuisance causing interference with comfort and enjoyment is provided by the case of *A-G v Gastonia Coaches Ltd*[4]. The defendant company owned a fleet of thirty-two coaches which they operated from their premises situated in an enclosed residential area. Eighteen of the vehicles were parked overnight on or near the premises but the remainder also visited them for refuelling and repairs. Several neighbouring householders brought an action alleging both private and public nuisance. Whitford J found the case proved in respect of smell caused by the emission of diesel fumes from the coaches and noise from the 'revving' of their engines. On the other hand, noises caused by the carrying out of repairs and cleaning were held not sufficiently serious to warrant relief. The plaintiffs were ultimately awarded both damages and an injunction, the latter suspended for one year, and four-fifths of their costs.

1   *[1977] RTR 219.*

Extent to which 'locality' is important

[12.04]   The nature of the area in which the parties live is, at least in theory, a relevant factor in cases of nuisance by discomfort or annoyance. But as has already been explained[1], the principle is one which judges are reluctant in practice to apply. Indeed, even in cases which might seem to call for the application of the principle the judges are meticulous in examining the precise extent of the interference to see whether it exceeds that to be expected in an area in which that general type of interference has to be tolerated. Thus in *Rushmer v Polsue and Alfieri*[2] a unanimous Court of Appeal and House of Lords upheld the grant of an injunction to restrain the defendants from using their printing presses at night, despite the fact that their premises were situated adjacent to Fleet Street in London and surrounded by other printing establishments some of which also ran at night. In a dictum which was subsequently quoted with approval in the House of Lords[3] Cozens-Hardy LJ said[4]:

> 'It does not follow that because I live, say, in the manufacturing part of Sheffield I cannot complain if a steam hammer is introduced next door, and so worked as to render sleep at night almost impossible, although previously to its introduction my house was a reasonably comfortable abode, having regard to the local standard, and it would be no answer to say that the steam hammer is of the most modern approved pattern and is reasonably worked. In short, if a substantial addition is found as a fact in any particular case, it is no answer to say that the neighbourhood is noisy, and that the defendants' machinery is of first class character'[5].

1   See above CHAPTER 11.
2   *[1906] 1 Ch 234, 75 LJ Ch 79*; affd *[1907] AC 121, 76 LJ Ch 365.*
3   *[1907] AC 121* at 123, *per* Lord Loreburn LC.
4   *[1906] 1 Ch 234* at 250–251.
5   See also *Crump v Lambert (1867) LR 3 Eq 409, 15 LT 600; Roskell v Whitworth (1871) 19 WR 804.*

An exceptional case

[12.05]   There are, however, occasionally decisions in which the nature of the area is treated as material. Thus in one case the 'locality' principle was applied in the defendants' favour in a situation in which the passage of heavy dockyard traffic was considered to have converted an area from a residential to a commercial one, thereby depriving the plaintiffs of any right to complain of what would formerly have been a public nuisance[1]. It is significant, however, that the correctness of the approach adopted in the case has been questioned in the Court of Appeal[2]. In any event the converse obviously does not apply, ie a defendant cannot avail himself of the 'locality' principle merely because an area, which is quiet and residential at the time of the complaint, can be shown to have been noisy and industrial at some former time[3].

---

[1] See *Gillingham Borough Council v Medway (Chatham) Dock Co Ltd [1993] QB 343, [1992] 3 All ER 923*.
[2] See *Wheeler v JJ Saunders Ltd [1995] 2 All ER 697, [1995] 3 WLR 466*.
[3] *Bosworth-Smith v Gwynnes Ltd (1919) 89 LJ Ch 368, 122 LT 15*.

B Noise and vibration[1]

Limitless possibilities

[12.06] The number of possible sources of nuisance by noise is infinite. The cases show that the following have all been held to give rise to good causes of action at common law: church bells[2], building[3] and demolition[4] operations, speedway[5] and go-kart[6] races, singing lessons[7], background music in a restaurant audible in the flat above[8], fun fairs[9], circuses[10], cockerels[11], cattle[12] and horses[13], printing presses[14], steam hammers[15], locomotives[16], circular saws[17], power stations[18], milk churns[19], boiler-houses[20], coaches[21], lorries[22], aero engines[23], children's playgrounds[24], 'problem families'[25] and caravan-dwellers[26]. As far as nuisance by vibration is concerned its effects are not necessarily confined to discomfort and interference with enjoyment. In particular, activities such as pile driving can easily give rise to actual structural damage[27].

---

[1] See generally, Kerse *The Law Relating to Noise* (London, 1975).
[2] *Soltau v De Held (1851) 2 Sim NS 133, 21 LJ Ch 153* (for an interesting historical account of this case, see Thomas Glyn Watkin 'Ring Happy Bells' (1994) NLJ 1775); *Haddon v Lynch* [1911] VLR 230 (Aus). Cf *Hardman v Holberton* [1866] WN 379.
[3] *Andreae v Selfridge & Co Ltd [1938] Ch 1, [1937] 3 All ER 255; Matania v National Provincial Bank Ltd and Elevenist Syndicate Ltd [1936] 2 All ER 633, 106 LJ KB 113; Webb v Barker [1881] WN 158*.
[4] *Clark v Lloyd's Bank Ltd (1910) 79 LJ Ch 645, 103 LT 211*.
[5] *Stretch v Romford Football Club Ltd (1971) 115 Sol Jo 741; Field v South Australian Soccer Association [1953] SASR 224*.
[6] *Tetley v Chitty [1986] 1 All ER 663*: 'The most common comparisons of the noise were to either a chain saw or a bee inside a jar: a persistent buzzing which penetrated closed windows and doors into living rooms': *per* McNeill J at 665.
[7] *Motion v Mills (1897) 13 TLR 427*.
[8] *Hampstead and Suburban Properties Ltd v Diomedous [1969] 1 Ch 248, [1968] 3 All ER 545*.
[9] *Winter v Baker (1887) 3 TLR 569; Bedford v Leeds Corpn (1913) 77 JP 430*.
[10] *Inchbald v Robinson (1869) 20 LT 259*. Cf *Kinney v Hove Corpn (1950) 49 LGR 696*.
[11] *Leeman v Montagu [1936] 2 All ER 1677*.
[12] See *London, Brighton and South Coast Rly Co v Truman (1885) 11 App Cas 45, 55 LJ Ch 354*.
[13] *Ball v Ray (1873) 8 Ch App 467, 30 LT 1*.
[14] *Rushmer v Polsue and Alfieri Ltd [1906] 1 Ch 234;* affd *[1907] AC 121, 76 LJ Ch 365; Heather v Pardon (1877) 37 LT 393*. Cf *Smith v Jaffray (1886) 2 TLR 480*.
[15] *Roskell v Whitworth (1871) 19 WR 804; Goose v Bedford (1873) 21 WR 449*.
[16] See *Hammersmith and City Rly Co v Brand (1869) LR 4 HL 171, 38 LJ QB 265*.
[17] *Husey v Bailey (1895) 11 TLR 221*.
[18] *Colwell v St Pancras Borough Council [1904] 1 Ch 707, 73 LJ Ch 275; Knight v Isle of Wight Electric Light and Power Co (1904) 73 LJ Ch 299, 90 LT 410*. Cf *Heath v Brighton Corpn (1908) 98 LT 718, 24 TLR 414*.

19   *Tinkler v Aylesbury Dairy Co Ltd (1888) 5 TLR 52*. Cf *Fanshawe v London and Provincial Dairy Co (1888) 4 TLR 694*.
20   *Halsey v Esso Petroleum Co Ltd [1961] 2 All ER 145, [1961] 1 WLR 683*.
21   *A-G v Gastonia Coaches Ltd [1977] RTR 219*.
22   *Halsey v Esso Petroleum Co Ltd [1961] 2 All ER 145, [1961] 1 WLR 683*. See also *Gillingham Borough Council v Medway (Chatham) Dock Co Ltd [1993] QB 343, [1992] 3 All ER 923*.
23   *Bosworth-Smith v Gwynnes Ltd (1919) 89 LJ Ch 368, 122 LT 15*.
24   *Dunton v Dover District Council (1978) 76 LGR 87*; cf *Moy v Stoop (1909) 25 TLR 262*.
25   *Smith v Scott [1973] Ch 314, [1972] 3 All ER 645*.
26   *A-G v Corke [1933] Ch 89, 148 LT 95* (decided under the rule in *Rylands v Fletcher*).
27   See *Hoare & Co v McAlpine [1923] 1 Ch 167, 92 LJ Ch 81*.

Principles applied

Playground noise

[12.07]   The approach of the court is well illustrated by *Dunton v Dover District Council*[1]. The plaintiff owned a small hotel with a garden which was surrounded by grazing land. In 1975 the local council, which owned the grazing land, built a housing estate upon it. A playground, which unfortunately adjoined the plaintiff's garden, was provided for the children of the estate. The playground was used from dawn to dusk by children of all ages causing noise which the plaintiff and his wife found intolerable. The trial judge, Griffiths J, emphasising that he had 'to hold the balance between the young and the old', awarded the plaintiff £200 damages for his past suffering. He also granted an injunction which restricted the opening of the playground to the hours between 10 am and 6.30 pm and limited its use to children aged twelve years and under. He did not, however, agree to order the closure of the playground for a period during the afternoon 'when more elderly people sometimes want to have a sleep'.

1   *(1977) 76 LGR 87*.

Aircraft

[12.08]   In *Dennis v Ministry of Defence*[1] the claimants lived close to an RAF base which was in constant use for the training of Harrier Jump Jet pilots. The claimant had written that 'the noise was so deafening that I could feel the juddering vibration in the house ... It is virtually impossible to talk and I'm concerned that the noise could affect the children's eardrums'[2]. Buckley J concluded that 'in respect of the nature and extent of the noise disturbance, it seems plain to me that the noise is ... a nuisance'[3]. His lordship awarded the claimants £950,000 in damages, but he declined to issue a declaration on the ground that it was not in the public interest to do so: the training of the pilots was essential to national security and it was not practicable to do it elsewhere without causing a similar nuisance[4].

1   *[2003] Env LR 34*. See Roderick Bagshaw 'Private Nuisance and the Defence of the Realm' (2004) 120 LQR 37.
2   See above at para 26.
3   See *[2003] Env LR 34* at para 34. The claimants also had a valid claim under the *Human Rights Act 1998* (under Article 1 and Article 8 of the Convention): see *[2003] Env LR 34* at 61.
4   On public interest as a defence, see below CHAPTER 23.

Disturbing sleep

[12.09]   The courts have shown a particular willingness to restrain noise at night-time and have indicated that defendants cannot expect to deprive complainants of sleep then, even if only for one night, without incurring liability[1]. There is, however, no inflexible rule of law relating to sleep. In *Murdoch v Glacier Metal Co*[2] the claimants lived near to a factory which operated at night, and the noise level was found to be just above that at which a report of the World Health Organisation had indicated that sleep could be affected. Nevertheless the Court of Appeal upheld a decision of the trial judge who, finding for the defendants, had said that 'taking into account the neighbourhood and the lack of complaint from the immediate neighbours' it had not been proved to him that the interference 'was sufficiently serious to constitute a nuisance'.

---

[1] See above CHAPTER 11. See also *Halsey v Esso Petroleum Co Ltd [1961] 2 All ER 145, [1961] 1 WLR 683*.

[2] *[1998] Env LR 732.*

Claimants who are peculiarly susceptible to noise

[12.10] In *Gaunt v Fynney*[1] Lord Selborne LC stressed that the court should exercise particular care in noise cases not to allow a hypersensitive plaintiff to impose excessive restraints on the defendant. He said[2]:

'... a nervous, or anxious, or prepossessed listener hears sounds which would otherwise have passed unnoticed, and magnifies and exaggerates into some new significance, originating within himself, sounds which at other times would have been passively heard and not regarded'.

In that case the plaintiffs complained in 1870 of noise and vibration caused by the working of a steam engine in the defendant's mill. The engine had, however, been in operation since 1865 and the plaintiffs conceded that it had caused them no annoyance until five years later. The defendant called evidence to show that there had been no change in the operation of the engine and that it had been worked at the same level throughout. The Lord Chancellor accepted that the plaintiffs honestly thought that the noise had become worse in 1870, but felt that this was because of an extraneous factor which had suddenly made them hypersensitive in that year to a noise which had always existed and yet had previously been regarded by them as unobjectionable[3].

---

[1] *(1872) 8 Ch App 8, 42 LJ Ch 122.*

[2] See above at 13.

[3] Cf *Dunton v Dover District Council (1977) 76 LGR 87* at 92.

Effect upon invalid

[12.11] On the other hand, a claimant who is able to prove that his ordinary comfort in the use of his home has been interfered with, will not fail merely because he has only been prompted into taking action by the effect of the noise upon an invalid who lives with him. In *Spruzen v Dossett*[1] the plaintiff complained of noise from a steam organ operated at 'Dossett's Forest Retreat' in Epping Forest. He relied particularly upon the distress which the noise caused to his invalid wife and the difficulty which it caused to the vicar when he visited her and tried to read to her. In granting the plaintiff an injunction Stirling J treated this evidence as relevant. He pointed out that although allegations of nuisance could not be considered solely from the point of view of a person in bad health[2], nevertheless, the fact that one of its inmates was an invalid gave a houseowner a good reason for insisting to the full on the enjoyment of such rights as the law allowed him.

Measurement

[12.12]   Nowadays the judicial process in noise cases may be facilitated by taking decibel readings with a sound-level meter in order to introduce a degree of objectivity into the collection and assessment of evidence[1]. In *Halsey v Esso Petroleum Co Ltd* Veale J sai[2].

> 'Scientific evidence is helpful in that it may tend to confirm or disprove the evidence of other witnesses. The scale of decibels from nought to 120 can be divided into colloquial descriptions of noise by the use of words: faint, moderate, loud, and so on. Between 40 and 60 decibels the noise is moderate, and between 60 and 80 it is loud. Between 80 and 100 it is very loud, and from 100 to 120 it is deafening'[3].

In that case readings taken outside the plaintiff's house indicated noise from the defendants' oil-storage plant of up to 68 decibels, rising to 83 decibels when one of the defendants' oil-tankers passed along the road. The plaintiff was awarded an injunction restraining the defendants from so operating their plant, and so driving their vehicles, as to cause a nuisance by noise to the plaintiff between the hours of 10 pm and 6 am Measurement of noise levels was also considered at length in the much more recent case of *Dennis v Ministry of Defence*. Buckley J quoted from a report put before him which pointed out that noise is now normally measured in 'A' weighted decibels or dB(A), explaining that '"A" weighting reflects the ear's frequency response to sound and therefore provides values which have some relation to subjective reactio[4]. His lordship continued:

> 'For example, a heavy lorry at 3m is 90 dB(A); the kerbside of a busy street is 80 dB(A); a high speed train at 2m is 105–110 dB(A)'.

Readings taken in the *Dennis* case itself 'recorded and gave a range for each day which typically was from the upper 70s to well over 100'[5].

1   On the measurement of noise see Penn *Noise Control* (2nd edn, 1995).
2   *[1961] 2 All ER 145* at 156A–B, *[1961] 1 WLR 683* at 697.
3   See also *Gillingham Borough Council v Medway (Chatham) Dock Co Ltd [1993] QB 343* at 356, *[1992] 3 All ER 923* at 931 *per* Buckley J: 'It is interesting to note that a quiet bedroom is about 35 on the scale, at 55 communication starts to become difficult, a car travelling at a steady 60 kph at 7 metres is just over 70, a heavy diesel lorry at 40 kph at 7 metres is 85, a pneumatic drill at 7 metres is 95 and 120 is the threshold of pain'.
4   *See [2003] Env LR 34* at para 14. Apparently there are also 'B' and 'C' weighting networks but these are not often used: see Taylor *Noise* (2nd edn, 1975) pp 59–60.
5   See *[2003] Env LR 34* at paras 15–16. See also para 21: 'It is helpful when seeking to compare the noise with the everyday examples given, to bear in mind the agreed expert evidence that a 10dB(A) increase equates to a doubling of loudness'.

Limits of expert evidence

[12.13]   Expert evidence does, however, have its limits. In the final analysis the court has to form an impression of the volume of noise in terms of day to day experience. In *Dunton v Dover District Council* Griffiths J said[1]:

'... it is a fact of life that when one gathers together a considerable number of small children, they are likely from time to time to make a great deal of noise. I have had it all turned into decibels by various experts. I am bound to say that I do not find such evidence very helpful because unless I am looking at a machine and at the same time listening to a child scream so that I can correlate the number of decibels with the noise I hear, I am unable to appreciate just how loud a sound is by being told that it is 60 or 50 decibels. It means nothing to the uninstructed, but I am satisfied on all the evidence that I have heard that from time to time there was a fearful racket coming from the playground, which is to be expected'.

1 *(1977) 76 LGR 87* at 89–90.

C Fumes, dust and smell

Modern cases

[12.14] In recent times legislation such as the Public Health and Clean Air Acts[1] has largely put an end to the situation that gave rise to many of the classic nineteenth-century nuisance cases[2]. Foul smoke pouring from factory chimneys is now a relatively rare occurrence, and most litigation in this area concerns the spread of dust by such activities as quarrying[3] or demolition[4], and the emission of powerful smells as a result of agricultural or industrial processes. It would, however, be wrong to suppose that the emission of noxious fumes or gases has ceased completely to be a source of litigation in modern times. In *Halsey v Esso Petroleum Co Ltd*[5], decided in 1961, the plaintiff recovered damages as a result of the emission of smuts containing sulphuric acid from the chimneys of the defendants' boiler-houses. The smuts had burnt holes in the plaintiff's laundry when it was hung out to dry, and had also damaged the paintwork of his car[6]. In the 1954 Scottish case of *Watt v Jamieson*[7] the Court of Session gave a pursuer leave to seek reparation for damage allegedly caused to his flat by the discharge of sulphur-impregnated water vapour from a defective gas water heater installed in the flat below[8].

1 See, generally, *Garner's Environmental Law*, Div V.
2 See *St Helen's Smelting Co v Tipping (1865) 11 HL Cas 642, 35 LJQB 66*. The emission of fumes from the burning processes used in the manufacture of bricks was a particularly fertile source of litigation in the last century, see *Walter v Selfe (1851) 4 De G&Sm 315, 20 LJ Ch 433*; *Pollock v Lester (1853) 11 Hare 266*; *Hole v Barlow (1858) 4 CBNS 334, 27 LJCP 207*. *Bamford v Turnley (1860) 3 B&S 62*; *Cleeve v Mahany (1861) 25 JP 819*; *Cavey v Ledbitter (1863) 13 CBNS 470, 32 LJCP 104*.
3 See *A-G v PYA Quarries Ltd [1957] 2 QB 169, [1957] 1 All ER 894*. Cf *Pwllbach Colliery Co Ltd v Woodman [1915] AC 634, 84 LJKB 874*.
4 See *Andreae v Selfridge & Co Ltd [1938] Ch 1, [1937] 3 All ER 255*. See also *Matania v National Provincial Bank [1936] 2 All ER 633, 106 LJKB 113*. Cf *Hunter v Canary Wharf Ltd and London Docklands Development Corpn [1995] NLJR 1645, CA* (deposit of dust held capable of giving rise to a cause of action in negligence).
5 *[1961] 2 All ER 145, [1961] 1 WLR 683*.
6 See also *McKinnon Industries Ltd v Walker [1951] 3 DLR 577*; *Russell Transport Ltd v Ontario Malleable Iron Co [1952] 4 DLR 719*.
7 *(1954) SC 56*.
8 See also *Federic v Perpetual Investments Ltd (1969) 2 DLR (3d) 50*.

Smell

[12.15] It is nevertheless true that offensive smells now provide the most frequent instances of this type of nuisance to come before the courts. It is not necessary to prove injury to health in order to succeed in an action for nuisance by smell[1], but further generalisation as to the types of smell which will create liability is probably impossible. As Lindley LJ said in *Rapier v London Tramways Co*[2]:

> 'The fact that somebody with a sensitive nose smells some ammonia and does not like it will not prove a nuisance; it is a question of degree. You can only appeal to the common sense of ordinary people. The test is whether the smell is so bad and continuous as to seriously interfere with comfort and enjoyment'.

The reports provide several relatively recent examples of successful actions under this head. In addition to all the other mischiefs to which it gave rise the defendants' depot in *Halsey v Esso Petroleum* occasionally emitted a pungent and nauseating smell, against which the plaintiff was awarded an injunction[3]. Similarly in *A-G v Gastonia Coaches*[4] the plaintiffs obtained relief in respect of smells caused by diesel fumes.

[1]   See *Crump v Lambert (1867) LR 3 Eq 409, 15 LT 600.*
[2]   *[1893] 2 Ch 588* at 600.
[3]   See *[1961] 2 All ER 145* at 154A–155D, *[1961] 1 WLR 683* at 694–696.
[4]   *[1977] RTR 219.*

'Nausea-making'

[12.16]   In *Shoreham-By-Sea UDC v Dolphin Canadian Proteins Ltd*[1] Donaldson J granted the plaintiff council an injunction to restrain the defendants from emitting an odour, described by his Lordship as 'all-pervasive' and 'nausea-making', from their factory at which they manufactured by-products out of chicken residues produced by the broiler chicken industry. Pig-farming figures prominently in the reported cases as a recurrent source of complaint. In *Wheeler v JJ Saunders Ltd*[2] the plaintiffs were awarded damages and an injunction after being subjected to 'constant malodorous air which frequently caused nausea' and often forced them to leave their property in order to eat; and relief was granted in *Bone v Seale*[3] in similar circumstances.

[1]   *(1972) 71 LGR 261.*
[2]   *[1995] 2 All ER 697, [1995] 3 WLR 466, CA.*
[3]   *[1975] 1 All ER 787, [1975] 1 WLR 797, CA.* See also *Milner v Spencer (1976) 239 EG 573.* Cf *Bainbridge v Chertsey Urban Council (1914) 84 LJ Ch 626; Lord Chesham v Chesham UDC (1935) 79 Sol Jo 453.*

D Further situations

Precise definition impossible

[12.17]   In *Thompson-Schwab v Costaki*[1] Lord Evershed MR observed that 'the forms which activities constituting actionable nuisance may take are exceedingly varied' and therefore 'not capable of precise or close definition'[2]. In that case the plaintiffs complained that the defendants used their own neighbouring premises for the purposes of prostitution. It was alleged that the sight of prostitutes and their clients entering and leaving premises, in what had hitherto been a good class residential street, diminished the enjoyment by the plaintiffs and their families of their own houses and reduced the value of those houses. The defendants were restrained by injunction from using their premises for the purposes of prostitution so as to cause a nuisance, despite a strenuous argument advanced on their behalf that matters of this kind, which did not interfere in any physical way with the use and enjoyment of their houses by the plaintiffs, were outside the scope of the tort. This argument was emphatically rejected by the Court of Appeal. A defendant's activities are not free from the risk of being categorised as an actionable nuisance 'merely because they do not impinge upon the senses, for example, the nose or the ear, as would the emanation of smells or fumes or noises'[3]. Another apparently novel situation for which liability was imposed, in a New Zealand case, concerned dazzling glare caused by reflected sunlight.[4]

¹ *[1956] 1 All ER 652, [1956] 1 WLR 335.*
² *[1956] 1 All ER 652* at 653–654, *[1956] 1 WLR 335* at 338.
³ *Thompson-Schwab v Costaki per* Lord Evershed MR. The decision in *Thompson-Schwab v Costaki* was applied in *Laws v Florinplace [1981] 1 All ER 659* (sex shop). See also *Poirier v Turkewich (1964) 42 DLR (2d) 259.*
⁴ See *Bank of New Zealand v Greenwood [1984] 1 NZLR 525*: 'The dearth of authority should ... present no great obstacle, for nuisance is one of those areas of the law where the courts have long been engaged in the application of certain legal concepts to a never-ending variety of circumstances; and that will continue to be so, for by its very nature the law of nuisance is intimately involved with the developing use of the environment, both natural and manmade, in which we all live': *per* Hardie Boys J at 530.

Games and protests

[12.18] Even normally harmless pastimes such as the playing of golf[1] or cricket[2] may be a legitimate source of complaint. Holding a protest meeting adjacent to the claimant's premises may also constitute a private nuisance. In *Hubbard v Pitt*[3] a majority of the Court of Appeal treated a protest demonstration on the highway outside the plaintiff's business premises as an actionable private nuisance, and in the earlier case of *J Lyons & Sons v Wilkins*[4] the picketing of a man's house from the highway during an industrial dispute was similarly treated.

¹ *Lester-Travers v City of Frankston [1970] VR 2 (Aus).*
² *Miller v Jackson [1977] QB 966, [1977] 3 All ER 338.* Cf *Bolton v Stone [1951] AC 850, [1951] 1 All ER 1078.*
³ *[1976] QB 142, [1975] 3 All ER 1,* Stamp and Orr LJJ, Lord Denning MR dissenting.
⁴ *[1899] 1 Ch 255, 68 LJ Ch 146.*

E Light

The easement of light

[12.19] Although the freedom to enjoy a reasonable measure of natural light might seem to belong to the same category of a landowner's legitimate expectations as freedom from noise or smell, the protection given to enjoyment of light has not been put by the law on the same footing as other areas of nuisance. At common law a landowner has no inherent right to the passage of natural light over his land[1]. The right can only exist as an *easement* and has to be thus acquired[2]. In practice, however, once the claimant is able to prove the existence of such an easement the approach nowadays adopted by the court to situations involving interference with it closely resembles that followed in other cases of interference with comfort or enjoyment.

¹ He does, however, have the right to restrain trespassers into his air-space (see *Kelsen v Imperial Tobacco Co Ltd [1957] 2 QB 334, [1957] 2 All ER 343*) and may thereby acquire a degree of protection indirectly.
² On easements and their acquisition see, generally, *Gale on Easements,* 17th edn, 2002 (Gaunt and Morgan eds), Jackson, *Law of Easements and Profits,* London, 1978.

Strict approach in former times

[12.20]   It was not always the case that the conventional tests used in other interference situations were used in disputes about light. In former times the theoretical basis of the enjoyment of light as a species of property led some judges to regard litigation in this area 'as an action to prevent the infringement of a right rather than an action to redress a wrong'[1]. Accordingly, a strict approach was often adopted towards defendants, and a plaintiff who was able to prove the existence of an easement was given a greater degree of protection than would have been possible had the more flexible tests used elsewhere in the law of nuisance been applied also to cases involving light[2]. Thus 'for many years the tendency of the courts [was] to measure the nuisance by the amount taken from the light acquired, and not to consider whether the amount left was sufficient for the reasonable comfort of the house according to ordinary requirement. If a man had a house with unusually excellent lights, it was treated as a nuisance if he was deprived of a substantial part of it, even although a fair amount for ordinary purposes was left'[3].

[1]   *Per* Lord Macnaghten in *Colls v Home and Colonial Stores Ltd [1904] AC 179* at 186.
[2]   See *Parker v Smith (1832) 5 C&P 438*; *Scott v Pape (1886) 31 Ch D 554, 55 LJ Ch 426.*
[3]   *Per* Farwell J in *Higgins v Betts [1905] 2 Ch 210* at 215 cited in *Gale on Easements*, p 267.

Nuisance tests now applied

[12.21]   The decision of the House of Lords in *Colls v Home and Colonial Stores Ltd*[1] marked a turning point in this branch of the law. In this case it was held that a plaintiff who is able to rely on a right to light will not succeed in proving infringement merely by showing that, as a result of the construction of the defendant's building, he receives less light than he did before[2]. There has to be a substantial deprivation of light such as to render the occupation of the house uncomfortable according to the ordinary notions of mankind[3]. In the words of Lord Lindley[4]:

> '... the right to light is in truth no more than a right to be protected against a particular form of nuisance, and ... an action for the obstruction of light which has in fact been used and enjoyed for twenty years without interruption or written consent cannot be sustained unless the obstruction amounts to an actionable nuisance; and this often depends upon considerations wider than the facts applicable to the complainant himself'.

[1]   *[1904] AC 179, 73 LJ Ch 484.*
[2]   In the Court of Appeal the plaintiff had been awarded a mandatory injunction for the demolition of the defendant's building (see *[1902] 1 Ch 302, 71 LJ Ch 146*), but the House of Lords, reversing the Court of Appeal, held that the plaintiff had no cause of action at all.
[3]   The difficulty of applying this test to the facts is, however, illustrated by the case of *Kine v Jolly [1905] 1 Ch 480, 74 LJ Ch 174*; affd sub nom *Jolly v Kine [1907] AC 1, 76 LJ Ch 1.* In this case Kekewich J held that there had been a nuisance by obstruction of light and his judgment was upheld by a majority in the Court of Appeal. In the House of Lords the four law lords who heard the appeal were equally divided and the judgment in the Court of Appeal therefore stood. Lords Robertson and Atkinson, who would have decided the case differently, however, considered that the decision of the Court of Appeal was impossible to reconcile with *Colls'* case.
[4]   *[1904] AC 179* at 212–213.

Flexible principles

[12.22]   Thus it would appear that a defendant is now entitled to insist upon the relevance of such flexible nuisance principles as that concerning the nature of the claimant's locality[1] if, eg the inhabitants customarily enjoy less light than is usually found elsewhere[2]. Nor does a claimant have any proprietary right to particular 'cones' or 'pencils' of light coming from any particular direction[3]. On the contrary, a defendant whose activities actually increase the amount of light flowing to the claimant's building from one direction is entitled to have that taken into account to his credit when the overall amount of light left to the claimant is being assessed[4]. In making this assessment a judge is 'entitled to have regard to the higher standards expected for comfort as the years go by'[5] and, although expert evidence as to the degree of diminution is useful[6], the Court of Appeal has emphasised that the decision is ultimately one of fact, in the making of which the trial judge might find a view to be helpful[7].

[1]   See above CHAPTER 11.
[2]   See *Ough v King [1967] 3 All ER 859* at 861G–H, *[1967] 1 WLR 1547* at 1552G–H, *per* Lord Denning MR. In practice, however, questions of locality will rarely be of importance in cases of nuisance by obstruction of light since 'the human eye requires as much light for comfortable reading or sewing in Darlington Street, Wolverhampton, as in Mayfair', *per* Russell J in *Hortons' Estate Ltd v James Beattie Ltd [1927] 1 Ch 75* at 78. Cf *Fishenden v Higgs and Hill Ltd (1935) 153 LT 128* at 140, *per* Romer LJ and 142–143, *per* Maugham LJ.
[3]   See *Davis v Marrable [1913] 2 Ch 421, 82 LJ Ch 510*.
[4]   *Davis v Marrable [1913] 2 Ch 421*. The claimant is, however, entitled to have disregarded light which he at present enjoys but of which he could at any moment be deprived by a third party: see *Gale on Easements*, p 274.
[5]   *Per* Lord Denning MR in *Ough v King [1967] 3 All ER 859* at 861H, *[1967] 1 WLR 1547* at 1553A.
[6]   On the methods of assessing diminution, including the well known test associated with the name of Mr P J Waldram, see Anstey and Chavasse, *The Right to Light* (London, 1963) (published by Estates Gazette).
[7]   *Ough v King [1967] 3 All ER 859, [1967] 1 WLR 1547*. A principle was at one time thought to exist that the right was not infringed if the plaintiff still had 45° of unobstructed light left, but this has since been repudiated and the figure of 45° is not conclusive for or against establishment of infringement of the right: see *Colls v Home and Colonial Stores [1904] AC 179, 73 LJ Ch 484* and Anstey and Chavasse, *The Right to Light*, Ch 7.

Internal arrangement of rooms

[12.23]   The internal arrangement of the rooms behind the windows, which may be changed by internal reconstruction of the building, cannot in itself be decisive in the assessment. In *Carr-Saunders v Dick McNeil Associates*[1] Millett J observed that the owner of the dominant tenement:

> ' ... is entitled to such access of light as will leave his premises adequately lit for all purposes for which they may reasonably be expected to be used. The court must, therefore, take account not only of the present use, but also of other potential uses to which the dominant owner may reasonably be expected to put the premises in the future'.

[1]   *[1986] 2 All ER 888* at 894.

Not confined to illumination

[12.24]   The protection accorded to a claimant by the easement of light is not limited to the enjoyment of the rays of the sun for the purposes of illumination. In *Allen v Greenwood*[1] the plaintiffs had an ordinary domestic greenhouse on their land which they had used in the normal way for over twenty years. The defendants erected an obstruction which limited the amount of light reaching the greenhouse and thereby rendered it useless for the purpose for which it existed, ie the cultivation of plants and flowers. There was still sufficient light reaching the greenhouse, however, to enable it to be used for other purposes such as reading a book or a newspaper. The plaintiffs sought an injunction to compel the removal of the obstruction but the defendants argued that the scope of the right to light did not extend to the use of the sun's rays for the purpose of providing heat, or other beneficial properties. This argument failed. The Court of Appeal held that the easement protected the normal use of the sun's rays for all purposes for which the type of building in question was ordinarily used. In the case of a greenhouse[2] this necessarily involved the provision of heat as well as light. Buckley LJ said[3] that even in the case of a dwelling-house it might well be argued that 'adequate light was important not only for illumination but also for health and hygiene'[4]. Their Lordships did, however, reserve their position on questions which might arise in the future in relation to special uses of the sun's rays for such purposes as solar heating.

[1]   *[1980] Ch 119, [1979] 1 All ER 819.*
[2]   A greenhouse is a 'building' for the purposes of the *Prescription Act 1832*: *Clifford v Holt [1899] Ch 698, 68 LJ Ch 332.*
[3]   *[1980] Ch 119 at 135G, [1979] 1 All ER 819 at 829c.*
[4]   Moreover even if keeping a greenhouse were to be regarded as an unusual use of land, and so not protected by the notion of ordinary user, the Court of Appeal held, as an alternative ground of decision, that a right to the additional protection required was capable of being acquired by prescription: *[1980] Ch 119 at 131F–132E, [1979] 1 All ER 819 at 825h–826e, per* Goff LJ; *[1980] Ch 119 at 137F–138B, [1979] 1 All ER 819 at 830g–831c, per* Buckley LJ.

No right of prospect

[12.25] It has long been clear that the law of nuisance does not confer protection upon enjoyment by an occupier of an attractive view or 'prospect', since that is 'a matter only of delight, and not of necessity'[1]. In *Hunter v Canary Wharf Ltd and London Docklands Development Corpn*[2] the House of Lords applied this principle in a novel context by holding that it prevented interference with television reception, caused by a large new building blocking the signal, from being actionable[3].

[1]   See *Aldred's case (1610) 9 Co Rep 57b.* Cf *Victoria Park Racing and Recreation Grounds Co Ltd v Taylor (1937) 58 CLR 479.*
[2]   *[1997] 2 All ER 426.*
[3]   For interference with television reception, see above CHAPTER 11.

F Air

Need for defined channels

[12.26] In the case of air, as distinct from that of light, a right to the free access of air flowing from the land of one's neighbour is unknown to the law and cannot be acquired even by prescription[1]. Although the right to air is therefore more limited than the right to light it is not altogether non-existent. A right to air can be acquired by prescription provided that the air flows through defined and limited channels or apertures. In *Bass v Gregory*[2] the cellar of the plaintiffs' public-house was ventilated by a subterranean shaft which had been cut through the ground so as to lead into a disused well, which was situated in an adjoining yard owned and occupied by the defendant. The air from the cellar passed through the shaft and out at the top of the well. The cellar had, with the knowledge of the defendant, been ventilated in this way for at least forty years. In these circumstances Pollock B held that the plaintiffs had acquired by prescription a right to the free passage of air from the cellar through the well, and granted an injunction to prevent the defendant from blocking up the mouth of the well[3].

1   See *Gale on Easements,* 17th edn, 2002 (Gaunt and Morgan eds).
2   *(1890) 25 QBD 481, 59 LJQB 574.*
3   See also *Hall v Lichfield Brewery Co (1880) 49 LJ Ch 655; Cable v Bryant [1908] 1 Ch 259.*

A possible exception?

[12.27]   It is possible that, as an exception to the general rule, a claimant who has acquired a cause of action against a defendant for infringement of his right to light might be able to claim additional redress for interference with the flow of air to his property, even if that flow was not through a defined channel. The argument for this exception is based on the interesting case of *Chastey v Ackland*[1]. The plaintiff and defendant lived in adjoining terraced houses in a row of such houses. To the rear of the houses were conveniences for the use of the occupants and a urinal attached to a nearby drill hall. The defendant erected a large building in the yard at the back of his house which slightly interfered with the plaintiff's right to light, and also cut down the free flow of air which had previously ventilated the yard at the back of the plaintiff's house. As a result the air stagnated and the smells from the various conveniences and from the urinal became oppressive. The plaintiff was awarded £10 damages for the interference with his right to light and this award was accepted by the defendant. However, the plaintiff also sought an injunction to restrain the defendant from maintaining the new building so as to obstruct the free passage of air. At first instance Cave J granted an injunction but the Court of Appeal, applying the orthodox rule, held that the defendant had committed no legal wrong in obstructing the air and discharged the injunction. The plaintiff's loss was *damnum absque injuria*. The plaintiff then appealed to the House of Lords. According to the brief report in the appeal cases, 'during the argument several of their Lordships expressed dissent from the reasoning and the decision of the Court of Appeal'[2]. The observations thus made were enough to persuade the respondent to settle the appeal on terms favourable to the appellant. Although the respondent kept his building the appellant received £300 by way of damages, ie £290 in excess of the sum which he had been awarded for infringement of the right to light. The appellant also received all his costs in the House of Lords and the courts below.

1   *[1895] 2 Ch 389, 64 LJQB 523, CA; [1897] AC 155, 76 LT 430, HL.*
2   See *[1897] AC 155.* A rather more extensive report, from which an impression of the nature of the views expressed in the House can be obtained, is to be found in *(1896–7) 13 TLR 237.* The report in *(1897) 76 LT 430* is as brief as that in the appeal cases.

Dependent upon infringement of right to light

[12.28]   Since the settlement precluded the House from reaching a decision in the case, the extent to which in such a decision they would have expressed their dissent from the reasoning of the Court of Appeal is a matter of speculation. One possible solution, however, is to be found in an observation of Lindley LJ in the Court of Appeal itself. His Lordship appears to have suggested, in the course of argument, that the fact that the building was unlawful, by virtue of its infringement of the right to light, might enable other damage it did to be taken into account even if that damage

261

would not have been actionable independently[1]. This proposition is not unattractive[2]. Since all the adjoining owners were in the same position with respect to the location of their conveniences it was inherently unreasonable for one owner to shut off the ventilation enjoyed by his neighbours.

1   See *[1895] 2 Ch 389 at 393*. This point is not mentioned in his Lordship's judgment.
2   Cf *McKinnon Industries v Walker [1951] 3 DLR 577* (damage otherwise irrecoverable on grounds of hypersensitivity not too remote a consequence of an actionable nuisance), see further CHAPTER 11 above.

Chapter 13

Physical damage to land and buildings

A Introduction

Negligence and nuisance again

[13.01] It is a view increasingly widely held that there is little to be gained, in situations involving actual damage to land and buildings, in continuing to distinguish formally between 'negligence' and 'nuisance'[1]. This is due to the increasing use by the courts of the concept of 'foreseeability', as well as that of reasonableness, in determining the existence, or otherwise, of liability in such cases. Nevertheless, even in this context it remains convenient to follow the courts in their reluctance formally to abandon usage of the term 'nuisance' itself. In some areas, notably that of 'nuisances' caused by the forces of nature, the extent of the duty is assessed using a rather more subjective approach to the position of the defendant than is usual in the rest of negligence. Moreover, in one area, that concerning the rule in *Rylands v Fletcher*, the House of Lords has recently confirmed the continued existence of the rule as a discrete principle, notwithstanding the considerable erosion of the 'strict' liability as a result of the influence of negligence.

[1]   See Christian Witting 'Physical Damage in Negligence' [2002] 61 CLJ 189, especially at p 206: 'The widening of the legal conception of damage emphasises the close (and closing) relationship between negligence and nuisance'.

Range of circumstances

[13.02] From a traditional 'nuisance' perspective, a sharp distinction between discomfort on the one hand and physical damage to property on the other is difficult to support[1]. Nevertheless, it is clear that in practice there are broad differences between the two types of situation[2]. Thus 'locality' is very rarely of relevance in 'damage' cases, and the fact that the primary remedy sought in such cases will invariably be compensation rather than an injunction also calls for differences of approach. The circumstances in which liability has been imposed for nuisances causing actual damage to property are, however, almost as varied as those involving the infliction of personal discomfort. Encroaching tree roots[3], flooding[4], fire caused by lightning[5], contamination by sewage[6], damage caused by the deposit of acid smuts[7] and damage to buildings caused by vibrations from machinery used nearby[8] are but examples.

[1]   See above CHAPTER 11. For discussion of what qualifies as 'damage' in property cases see below.
[2]   Cf *Clift v Welsh Office [1998] 4 All ER 852, CA.*
[3]   *Butler v Standard Telephones and Cables Ltd [1940] 1 KB 399, [1940] 1 All ER 121; Davey v Harrow Corpn [1958] 1 QB 60, [1957] 2 All ER 305; Morgan v Khyatt [1964] 1 WLR 475; Masters v Brent*

London Borough Council [1978] QB 841, [1978] 2 All ER 664; Russell v London Borough of Barnet [1984] 2 EGLR 44. Cf Solloway v Hampshire County Council (1981) 79 LGR 449.
4   See Bybrook Barn Garden Centre v Kent County Council (2001) 3 LGLR 27, CA. See also Fletcher v Smith (1877) 2 App Cas 781, 47 LJ QB 4; Whalley v Lancashire and Yorkshire Rly Co (1884) 13 QBD 131, 53 LJQB 285; Sedleigh-Denfield v O'Callaghan [1940] AC 880, [1940] 3 All ER 349.
5   Goldman v Hargrave [1967] 1 AC 645, [1966] 2 All ER 989.
6   See Marcic v Thames Water Utilities [2004] 1 All ER 135. See also Humphries v Cousins (1877) 2 CPD 239, 46 LJQB 438; Foster v Warblington UDC [1906] 1 KB 648, 75 LJKB 514; Jones v Llanrwst UDC [1911] 1 Ch 393, 80 LJ Ch 145; Haigh v Deudraeth RDC [1945] 2 All ER 661, 174 LT 243; Pride of Derby and Derbyshire Angling Association Ltd v British Celanese Ltd [1953] Ch 149, [1953] 1 All ER 179. Cf Smeaton v Ilford Corpn [1954] Ch 450, [1954] 1 All ER 923.
7   McKinnon Industries Ltd v Walker [1951] 3 DLR 577 (JCPC); Russell Transport Ltd v Ontario Malleable Iron Co [1952] 4 DLR 719; Halsey v Esso Petroleum Co Ltd [1961] 2 All ER 145, [1961] 1 WLR 683.
8   Roskell v Whitworth (1871) 19 WR 804; Grosvenor Hotel Co v Hamilton [1894] 2 QB 836; Shelfer v City of London Electric Lighting Co [1895] 1 Ch 287; Barrette v Franki Compressed Pile Co of Canada [1955] 2 DLR 665. Cf Hoare & Co v McAlpine [1923] 1 Ch 167, 92 LJ Ch 81.

Cases where proof of damage is not required

[13.03]   In a small number of situations, most of which involve interference with easements or similar rights of property, nuisance is actionable per se without proof of damage. In *Nicholls v Ely Beet Sugar Factory*[1] the plaintiff, who owned two several and exclusive fisheries in the River Ouse, complained that the defendants had discharged large quantities of refuse and effluent into the river, and sought an injunction and damages. The Court of Appeal held that it was not necessary for the plaintiff in such a case to show that he had sustained pecuniary loss since the mere invasion of his legal right, which was in the nature of an incorporeal hereditament, carried with it the right to damages[2]. Although the action was in nuisance the situation was analogous to one of trespass[3].

1   [1936] Ch 343, 105 LJ Ch 279.
2   The plaintiff's action ultimately failed, but on grounds of fact which do not affect the point in the text.
3   See also Holland v Lazarus (1897) 66 LJQB 285; Fay v Prentice (1845) 1 CB 828, 14 LJCP 298.

Vindicating rights

[13.04]   Similarly, in cases of interference with rights of light, or excessive diversion of water from a stream by one riparian owner to the detriment of others, it is unnecessary for a claimant to prove actual damage. In *Harrop v Hirst*[1] the plaintiffs, in common with other inhabitants of the district, enjoyed a customary right to take water for domestic purposes from a certain spout on the highway. The defendant, a riparian owner on the stream from which the spout was supplied with water, on various occasions diverted water from the stream in such quantities as to render what remained insufficient for the needs of the inhabitants. Although the plaintiffs had not themselves suffered any personal damage or inconvenience, it was held that they had a cause of action. An action for diverting the water was maintainable without proof of damage since the act of the defendant might, if repeated often enough without interruption, furnish evidence in derogation of the plaintiff's legal rights[2]. Since easements and analogous rights may be lost by cessation of user[3] it is desirable that a dominant owner should not be prevented, by insistence upon proof of actual loss, from vindicating the existence of his right before it is too late[4].

1   (1868) LR 4 Exch 43, 38 LJ Ex 1.

2   Of course an action for the diversion of water will fail if the extent of the defendant's user is not in itself unreasonable, and the presence or absence of damage can be relevant to *this* question: *Embrey v Owen (1851) 6 Exch 353, 20 LJ Ex 212.* See also *Smith v Thackerah (1866) LR 1 CP 564, Har & Ruth 615.*
3   See *Gale on Easements,* 15th edn, 2002 (Gaunt and Morgan eds).
4   See *Bower v Hill (1835) 1 Bing NC 549* at 555, *per* Tindal CJ.

Situations which have led to difficulty

[13.05] If the defendant's intentional activities foreseeably cause damage to the claimant's property, liability can usually be taken for granted[1]. The defendant will normally be liable in both negligence and nuisance, subject only to the rules governing remoteness of damage[2]. The main situations which have led to difficulty, in the area of property damage overall, have been those in which the concept of 'damage' itself has been in dispute; and those involving attempts to impose liability upon defendants for damage which was caused or exacerbated by the forces of nature, or for damage which the defendant otherwise claims occurred without 'fault' on his part. The rule in *Rylands v Fletcher* may still apply to some cases in the final category, while damage to which natural forces contributed has been the subject of two significant decisions relatively recently. The role of 'foreseeability' generally, in those cases which may be said to straddle the artificial borderline between negligence and nuisance, also requires attention. Finally, the law concerning rights of support for land and buildings falls to be dealt with in the present chapter.

1   See *St Helen's Smelting Co v Tipping (1865) 11 HL Cas 642, 35 LJQB 66* discussed in CHAPTER 11 above. Liability will extend to foreseeable damage to *chattels* on the land: see *Howard Electric Ltd v A J Mooney Ltd [1974] 2 NZLR 762.*
2   For remoteness of damage in nuisance and *Rylands v Fletcher* see below at para [13.49], for negligence see CHAPTER 3 above.

B Nature of damage

Depreciation unnecessary

[13.06] In the majority of cases a claimant will not succeed in a 'nuisance' action, any more than in negligence, unless he can prove damage. This must not be trivial or fleeting but need not result in actual depreciation of the claimant's property. Indeed although such depreciation, if it can be shown, is a convenient way of proving that the claimant has suffered damage[1], it is clearly not in itself conclusive proof of the existence of a nuisance; the situation might be one of *damnum absque injuria*[2]. Proof of damage required to give rise to a cause of action should not be confused with proof of quantifiable loss readily measurable in 'damages'[3].

1   See *Soltau v De Held (1851) 2 Sim NS 133* at 158–159, *per* Kindersley V-C; *Tinkler v Aylesbury Dairy Co Ltd (1888) 5 TLR 52, per* Kekewich J. See also *Dunton v Dover District Council (1977) 76 LGR 87* at 93, *per* Griffiths J. Cf *per* Pill LJ in *Hunter v Canary Wharf and London Docklands Development Corpn [1996] 1 All ER 482* at 499 (dust causing physical change, eg to a fabric, actionable in negligence).
2   See *Shuttleworth v Vancouver General Hospital [1927] 2 DLR 573 (Can):* no remedy for depreciation caused by fear of infection from a nearby smallpox hospital unless it can be shown that there is *actual* danger of infection. See also *A-G v Rathmines and Pembroke Hospital Board [1904] 1 IR 161* at 171–2, *per* Fitzgibbon LJ; *Metropolitan Asylum District Managers v Hill (Appeal No 1) (1882) 47 LT 29* at 32, *per* Lord Blackburn. Cf *Merlin v British Nuclear Fuels [1990] 2 QB 557.*
3   See *Lyons, Sons & Co v Gulliver [1914] 1 Ch 631* at 641, *per* Cozens-Hardy MR; *Vanderpant v Mayfair Hotel Co Ltd [1930] 1 Ch 138* at 154, *per* Luxmoore J.

Deposits and contamination

[13.07] The concept of 'damage' is wide enough to include the deposit of silt on a riverbed, even though the riverbed *itself* is not adversely affected[1]. In a case decided under the *Nuclear Installations Act 1965* the deposit of radioactive material on land, requiring removal of the contaminated topsoil, was held to constitute 'property damage' for the purposes of the Act[2].

1 See *Jan De Nul (UK) Ltd v Axa Royale Belge SA [2002] 1 Lloyd's Rep 583, CA.*
2 See *Blue Circle Industries v Ministry of Defence [1998] 3 All ER 385, CA.*

Need for 'visibility'?

[13.08] In the nineteenth-century case of *Salvin v North Brancepeth Coal Co*[1] it was held that a plaintiff who relies on damage to property is unlikely to succeed unless the damage is clearly ascertainable by the senses, unassisted by sophisticated techniques. The plaintiff in this case, who owned a valuable estate in County Durham, alleged that smoke and fumes from coke ovens operated by the defendants were causing damage to his trees. The damage was not, however, apparent to the naked eye and the plaintiff called expert botanical witnesses in an attempt to prove his case, which nevertheless failed. The plaintiff appealed and sought to criticise a passage in the judgment of Jessel MR, at first instance, in which his Lordship had referred to a need for the damage to be 'visible'. Counsel for the plaintiff sought to contrast this expression, unfavourably, with the adjective 'sensible', which had been used by Lord Westbury LC in *St Helen's Smelting Co v Tipping*[2]. The criticism was rejected. The Court of Appeal held that the distinction was one without a difference. James LJ said[3]:

> '... although when you once establish the fact of actual substantial damage it is quite right and legitimate to have recourse to scientific evidence as to the causes of that damage, still if you are obliged to start with scientific evidence, such as the microscope of the naturalist, or the tests of the chemist, for the purposes of establishing the damage itself, that evidence will not suffice. The damage must be such as can be shown by a plain witness to a plain common juryman'.

The emphasis of Mellish LJ, in his judgment, differed from that of James LJ but only slightly. He was prepared to concede that 'as a strict proposition of law' it was not correct to hold that damage need be 'visible' but 'as a matter of fact' it was 'impossible to be certain that ... substantial damage had actually been sustained' unless it was apparent to the eye'[4].

1 *(1874) 9 Ch App 705, 44 LJ Ch 149.*
2 See *(1865) 11 HL Cas 642 at 650–651.*
3 *(1874) 9 Ch App 705 at 709.*
4 *(1874) 9 Ch App 705 at 713.*

Subtle forms of harm

[13.09] In similar vein it has been held that an action for damages under the rule in *Rylands v Fletcher* requires tangible physical damage, so that a telegraph company which had suffered interference with signals passing through a submarine cable was unable to recover damages from a tramway company whose electrical discharges had caused the interference[1]. It must be doubtful whether the approach embodied in these cases is still appropriate in modern conditions, and the courts might now be less unwilling than formerly to afford protection against subtle forms of harm such as radiation damage. Loss or damage caused by radioactive substances is, however, governed by statute[2]; and although the Court of Appeal recently imposed liability under the legislation[3], in an earlier case the High Court held that there would be no liability for a reduction in the value of a house due to increased radioactivity levels. In the absence of evidence of any risk of injury to health the loss was due to stigma and not recoverable[4].

[1]   *Eastern and South African Telegraph Co v Cape Town Tramways Companies Ltd [1902] AC 381, 71 LJPC 122.* But cf *National Telephone Co v Baker [1893] 2 Ch 186, 62 LJ Ch 699.* Cf *Morris v Network Rail Infrastructure [2004] EWCA Civ 172.*
[2]   See the *Nuclear Installations Acts 1965* and *1969.* See also Street and Frame *Law Relating to Nuclear Energy* (London, 1966), and the *Radioactive Substances Act 1993.*
[3]   See *Blue Circle Industries v Ministry of Defence [1998] 3 All ER 385.*
[4]   See *Merlin v British Nuclear Fuels [1990] 2 QB 557.*

Apprehended injury

[13.10]   A claimant does not necessarily have to prove that damage has already actually occurred in order to bring an action since in certain circumstances a *quia timet* injunction may be obtainable to prevent injury which is merely apprehended[1].

[1]   See CHAPTER 29 below.

C Natural agencies

Development of the law

[13.11]   Despite long-standing criticism of the position it appeared until quite recently to be the law that a defendant would not be liable in nuisance if the damage suffered by his neighbour resulted primarily from the operation upon the defendant's land of the forces of nature, as distinct from any activities carried out on the land by him. In *Giles v Walker*[1] the defendant farmer neglected to mow thistles which appeared on his land. As a result thistle seeds were blown in large quantities on to the plaintiff's land where they took root and caused damage. The plaintiff brought an action for damages which was dismissed. In a very short judgment in the Divisional Court, Lord Coleridge CJ said[2]:

> 'I have never heard of such an action as this – there can be no duty as between adjoining occupiers to cut the thistles, which are the natural growth of the soil'.

This decision was cited in *Pontardawe RDC v Moore-Gwyn*[3] in which Eve J held a defendant not liable to obviate a dangerous situation caused by rocks on his land which threatened to fall and damage the plaintiffs' houses, on the ground that the rocks and their position were the product of the forces of nature[4].

[1]   *(1890) 24 QBD 656, 59 LJQB 416.* See also *Seligman v Docker [1949] Ch 53, [1948] 2 All ER 887; Sparke v Osborne (1908) 7 CLR 51.* But cf *French v Auckland City Corpn [1974] 1 NZLR 340.*
[2]   *(1890) 24 QBD 656* at 657.
[3]   *[1929] 1 Ch 656, 98 LJ Ch 242.*
[4]   'The action is … an attempt to impose on an owner … liability for damage sustained by the property of another through natural agencies. Such an action cannot in my opinion be maintained', *per* Eve J, as above, at 660. See also *Stearn v Prentice Bros Ltd [1919] 1 KB 394, 88 LJKB 422; Neath RDC v*

Williams [1951] 1 KB 115, [1950] 2 All ER 625. Cf *Radstock Co-operative and Industrial Society Ltd v Norton Radstock UDC [1968] Ch 605, [1968] 2 All ER 59, CA* (doubted in *Bybrook Barn Garden Centre v Kent CC (2001) 3 LGLR 27, CA*).

Liability established

[13.12]   The reasoning in these cases was, however, criticised by Professor Goodhart in an influential article[1], which was subsequently cited with approval by Lord Goddard CJ in the Court of Appeal[2] and by Lord Wilberforce delivering the judgment of the Judicial Committee of the Privy Council in *Goldman v Hargrave*[3]. In this case it was held to be no defence to an action for damage caused by the spread of fire that the fire had been started by lightning. On the contrary, their Lordships asserted the existence of a 'general duty upon occupiers in relation to hazards occurring on their land, whether natural or man-made[4]. This principle was applied in *Leakey v National Trust for Places of Historic Interest or Natural Beauty*[5]. The plaintiffs in this case owned houses in the village of Burrowbridge, Somerset, which were adjacent to a distinctive geological feature of the locality known as Burrow Mump. The land, of which the mound formed a part, was owned by the defendants, the National Trust, and over a number of years erosion of the mound by natural processes had caused large quantities of earth and rubble to become displaced from it in such a way as to present a threat to the plaintiffs' houses. At first instance O'Connor J held that the situation amounted to an actionable nuisance and ordered the National Trust to meet the cost of measures to prevent further collapse of the mound. His decision was upheld by the Court of Appeal, which overruled *Giles v Walker*[6] and disapproved of the reasoning in *Pontardawe RDC v Moore-Gwyn*[7], and held, despite a strenuous argument to the contrary by counsel for the defendant, that the broad duty asserted by the Privy Council in *Goldman v Hargrave*[8] correctly represented English law. Megaw LJ said[9]:

> 'If, as a result of the working of the forces of nature, there is, poised above my land, or above my house, a boulder or a rotten tree, which is liable to fall at any moment of the day or night, perhaps destroying my house ... am I without remedy? ... I believe that few people would regard it as anything other than a grievous blot on the law if the law recognises the existence of no duty on the part of the owner or occupier'.

[1]   'Liability for Things Naturally on the Land' (1930) 4 CLJ 13: 'The correct principle seems to be that an occupier of land is liable for a nuisance of which he knows, or ought to know, whether that nuisance is caused by himself, his predecessor in title, a third person or by nature' (as above, at 30). See also Noel, 'Nuisances from Land in its Natural Condition' (1942–3) 56 Harv LR 772.
[2]   See *Davey v Harrow Corpn [1958] 1 QB 60, [1957] 2 All ER 305.*
[3]   *[1967] 1 AC 645, [1966] 2 All ER 989.*
[4]   *[1967] 1 AC 645 at 661G–662A, [1966] 2 All ER 989 at 995D.*
[5]   *[1978] QB 849, [1978] 3 All ER 234*; affd *[1980] QB 485, [1980] 1 All ER 17.* On the decision at first instance, see Wedderburn (1978) 41 MLR 589. The case is noted by the present writer at *(1978) 94 LQR 338* and *(1980) 96 LQR 185.*
[6]   See above.
[7]   See above. It is possible that the actual decision in the *Pontardarwe* case was correct on the ground that the cost of maintaining the rocks in a state of safety, £300 (in 1929), would have been too heavy a burden to have imposed on the defendant: see *per* Lord Wilberforce in *Goldman v Hargrave [1967] 1 AC 645 at 663G, [1966] 2 All ER 989 at 996F.*
[8]   *[1967] 1 AC 645, [1966] 2 All ER 989.*
[9]   *[1980] QB 485 at 523F–524A, [1980] 1 All ER 17 at 34e–35a.*

Scope of liability for natural occurrences

[13.13]   The area of liability opened up by the *Goldman* and *Leakey* cases gave rise to a number of questions. These concerned the precise level and extent of the duty imposed upon defendants and the status of several earlier decisions, involving widely different types of natural phenomena, which were not pronounced upon either by the Privy Council or by the Court of Appeal.

Extent of the duty

Subjectivity

[13.14] The Court of Appeal in *Leakey v National Trust for Places of Historic Interest or Natural Beauty* emphasised that the extent of the defendant's duty, in cases of natural conditions on his land threatening that of his neighbour, was to be assessed on a subjective and relative basis. In so holding the Court followed *Goldman v Hargrave*[1]. In the words of Megaw LJ in *Leakey*[2]:

'The defendant's duty is to do that which it is reasonable for him to do. The criteria of reasonableness include, in respect of a duty of this nature, the factor of what the particular man, not the average man, can be expected to do, having regard, amongst other things, where a serious expenditure of money is required to eliminate or reduce the danger, to his means. Just as, where physical effort is required to avert an immediate danger, the defendant's age and physical condition may be relevant in deciding what is reasonable, so also logic and good sense require that, where the expenditure of money is required, the defendant's capacity to find the money is relevant. But this can only be in the way of a broad, and not a detailed, assessment; and, in arriving at a judgment on reasonableness, a similar broad assessment may be relevant in some cases as to the neighbour's capacity to protect himself from damage, whether by way of some form of barrier on his own land or by way of providing funds for expenditure for agreed works on the land of the defendant'.

Counsel for the National Trust had suggested that this approach would cause great uncertainty, perhaps even requiring discovery of the parties' bank accounts before an action involving damage caused by natural agencies could be settled, but this argument was dismissed as being 'more theoretical than practical'[3]. The court did not consider that so detailed an examination of the parties' financial resources would be necessary.

[1]   See the discussion of *Goldman's* case in CHAPTER 11 above.
[2]   *[1980] QB 485* at 526E–F, *[1980] 1 All ER 17* at 37b–d.
[3]   *Per* Megaw LJ in *[1980] QB at 527B, [1980] 1 All ER at 37g*.

Limits to subjective approach

[13.15] In some cases examination of the parties' relative financial resources will be considered by the court to be inappropriate in any event. In *Abbahall Ltd v Smee*[1] the defendant, who owned the upper floors of a building, allowed the roof to decay until it caused a nuisance to the occupier of the lower part of the building. The defendant's property, which she had acquired by adverse possession, was a 'flying freehold' and no covenants availed the lower occupiers to compel maintenance of the roof; it followed that their relationship with the claimant 'was regulated ... by the law of nuisance and negligence'[2]. The defendant argued that she was of limited means, dependent upon state benefits for support, and that in accordance with the observations in *Goldman v Hargrave* and *Leakey v National Trust for Places of Historic*

Interest or Natural Beauty, her liability should be limited to a small proportion of the cost of the repairs; with the greater portion being borne by the lower occupier, which was a commercial organisation. The Court of Appeal accepted that the defendant's duty was to do that which was 'reasonable in all the circumstances', but rejected the suggestion that her lack of means should be taken into account. Munby J, delivering the leading judgment in the Court of Appeal said:[3]

> 'Reasonableness between neighbours who choose to live together in the same building, sharing the same roof, requires that all share – and share equally – the cost of repairing and maintaining the roof … In a case such as this there is, in my judgment, no room for adjustment, on the grounds of relative poverty or wealth, to the respective shares of the liability which would otherwise attach to the claimant and the defendant'.

[1]   *[2003] 1 All ER 465.*
[2]   Per Munby J in *[2003] 1 All ER 465* at para 2.
[3]   See *[2003] 1 All ER 465* at paras 60–66.

Locality

[13.16]   The principle that the type of 'locality' in question is relevant to the resolution of nuisance cases will rarely, if ever, avail a defendant whose own activities have caused physical damage to his neighbour's property[1]. Where what is at issue is a mere omission to control or limit the operation of the forces of nature, however, it is submitted that in extreme cases the principle should be applicable. Where the situation involved is one which has been produced by natural forces operating in a natural environment, and which is *characteristic* of that particular type of natural environment, the justification for imposing any liability on the defendant is not obvious. Rugged or mountainous areas in remote parts of the country inevitably give rise to hazards which bodies, such as the National Trust, who happen to own land within them cannot either in practice or in principle be expected to eliminate or even to alleviate. There is some judicial support for this view. In the New Zealand case of *French v Auckland City Corpn*[2], which was approved by the Court of Appeal in *Leakey v National Trust for Places of Historic Interest or Natural Beauty*, a defendant was held liable for failing to prevent the spread of weeds through natural agencies on to his neighbour's property. Towards the conclusion of his judgment, however, the judge, McMullin J, expressed himself as follows[3]:

> 'I think it … proper to point out the limit of this decision. It is not to be thought that I am intending to lay down as a rule of law the proposition that an occupier of land will always be liable for the escape from it of weeds or weed seeds onto the property of another. Circumstances must always be relevant. The occupier of a weed-infested area in an urban or intensely farmed area may be liable, but the occupier of a property in a more remote area may be under no liability at all'.

[1]   For the 'locality' principle see CHAPTER 11 above.
[2]   *[1974] 1 NZLR 340.*
[3]   *[1974] 1 NZLR at 351.*

Sewage disposal

[13.17]   The principles developed in *Goldman v Hargrave* and *Leakey v National Trust for Places of Historic Interest or Natural Beauty*, relating to the liability of occupiers for nuisances originating on their land without initial fault on their part, do not apply without qualification in cases where the occupier is a statutory undertaker. In particular the law relating to sewage disposal has long been subject to special principles. Since water companies are obliged by statute to permit all households in their area to connect to the sewers, overloading causing flooding will sometimes be inevitable in the absence of the allocation of substantial resources to expand or improve the sewers themselves. In a long line of cases the courts have held that pressure for such allocation should be imposed via the political process, or such statutory machinery as the relevant legislation provides, rather than by imposing liability upon the water companies in nuisance actions[1]. The authority of these cases was reaffirmed by the House of Lords in *Marcic v Thames Water Utilities*[2], reversing a decision of the Court of Appeal which had imposed liability upon the defendants by invoking the *Goldman* and *Leakey* principles in preference to the special line of cases involving overloaded sewers. This issue is dealt with at greater length in a subsequent chapter[3].

[1]   See *Glossop v Heston and Isleworth Local Board (1879) 12 ChD 102*; *Smeaton v Ilford Corporation [1954] Ch 450.*
[2]   *[2004] 1 All ER 135* reversing *[2001] 4 All ER 426, [2002] QB 1003, CA.*
[3]   See below CHAPTER 23.

Types of natural phenomena

The land itself

[13.18]   It is clear from the actual decision in *Leakey v National Trust for Places of Historic Interest or Natural Beauty*[1] that movements of the land or soil itself can give rise to liability. Megaw LJ said in that case[2]:

> 'There is no valid distinction, to my mind, between an encroachment which consists, on the one hand, of the spread of fire from a tree on fire on the land, and, on the other hand, of a slip of soil or rock resulting from the instability of the land itself, in each case, the danger of encroachment, being brought about by the forces of nature'.

It is submitted, however, that this observation needs to be read in the context in which it was made. Although the area in question in the *Leakey* case, near to Bridgwater in Somerset, is a rural one it is in no sense remote or thinly populated. It is with respect to regions of the latter type that the apparent generality of the principle expressed in the case might in future require qualification. As Professor Newark once wrote[3]:

> 'It is sufficient confirmation of the fact that there is no liability ... to refer to the hundreds of thousands of acres of low-lying land in Britain which are bogged or barren because they suffer the descent of water or detritus from the adjacent hillsides. It is inconceivable that the law supplies a remedy in such cases'.

[1]   *[1980] QB 485, [1980] 1 All ER 17.*
[2]   *[1980] QB 485 at 514B–C, [1980] 1 All ER 17 at 25e.*
[3]   See 'Non-Natural User and *Rylands v Fletcher*' (1961) 24 MLR 557 at 558–559.

Trees

[13.19]   Even before *Goldman v Hargrave*[1] it was clear that liability could exist for damage caused to a neighbour's property by encroaching tree-roots or branches, regardless of whether the trees were the result of natural growth or had been planted[2]. In *Davey v Harrow Corpn*[3] the plaintiff's house was damaged by the penetration of roots which came from trees on the defendant's adjoining land. The defendant argued that on the evidence the trees were likely to have grown naturally and contended that this prevented liability. The Court of Appeal rejected this contention and held the defendant liable. No distinction was to be drawn between planted trees and those self-sown[4]. In either case, if roots or branches encroached and did damage an action for nuisance would lie[5]. This decision was followed with approval, on similar facts, by the Judicial Committee of the Privy Council in *Morgan v Khyatt*[6]. The liability for damage caused by encroaching tree roots is, however, dependent upon proof that the damage was reasonably foreseeable[7]. Accordingly in *Solloway v Hampshire County Council*[8] the Court of Appeal, applying the approach in *Leakey v National Trust for Places of Historic Interest or Natural Beauty*, refused to impose liability upon the defendant Council for serious subsidence which the roots of a tree owned by them had caused to the plaintiff's house, on the ground that the Council had not been at fault[9]. The approach in *Solloway*'s case was applied in a similar situation in *Russell v London Borough of Barnet,* although Tudor Evans J was able to impose liability on the facts[10].

1   *[1967] 1 AC 645, [1966] 2 All ER 989.*
2   One commentator implied that since *Goldman v Hargrave* itself concerned damage caused by a tree, albeit through fire rather than encroachment, this might limit the apparent generality of the ratio in that case: see Wedderburn, 'Natural Nuisances Again' (1978) 41 MLR 589 at 591. See also *per* Shaw LJ in *Leakey v National Trust for Places of Historic Interest or Natural Beauty [1980] QB 485* at 527H–528A, *[1980] 2 All ER 17* at 38d.
3   *[1958] 1 QB 60, [1957] 2 All ER 305.*
4   See also *Noble v Harrison [1926] 2 KB 332, 95 LJ KB 813.*
5   See also *Smith v Giddy [1904] 2 KB 448, 73 LJ KB 894; Butler v Standard Telephones and Cables Ltd [1940] 1 KB 399, [1940] 1 All ER 121; Masters v Brent London Borough Council [1978] 1 QB 841, [1978] 2 All ER 664.* Cf *Crowhurst v Amersham Burial Board (1878) 4 Ex D 5, 48 LJ QB 109.*
6   *[1964] 1 WLR 475.* See also George, 'Liability for Damage caused by Tree Roots' (1963) 27 Conv (NS) 179. For a case containing a lengthy analysis of causation, based on expert evidence, where the extraction of moisture from the soil by tree roots had damaged a building see *Bunclark v Hertfordshire County Council (1977) 234 EG 381,* 455. See also *Solloway v Hampshire County Council (1981) 79 LGR 449, CA* and *Russell v London Borough of Barnet [1984] 2 EGLR 44* ('… the hot summer of 1976 had the result of teaching people a lot about tree roots': *[1984] 2 EGLR 44* at 51).
7   '… there are two questions to be considered: (1) was there a foreseeable risk that the encroachment of these tree roots would cause damage to the plaintiff's house, and (2) were there any reasonable precautions which the defendants could have taken to prevent or minimise that risk?': *per* Stephenson LJ in *Solloway v Hampshire County Council (1981) 79 LGR 449* at 461.
8   *(1981) 79 LGR 449 CA.* Stephenson and Dunn LJJ and Sir David Cairns. See *per* Lord Cooke in *Delaware Mansions v Westminster City Council [2001] 4 All ER 737* at para 34: 'I see *Solloway v Hampshire County Council* as important as a salutary warning against imposing unreasonable and unacceptable burdens on local authorities or other tree owners'.
9   For two reported Australian cases, in which the same approach was adopted but liability was imposed on the facts, see *City of Richmond v Scantelbury [1991] 2 VR 38* and *Proprietors of Strata Plan No 14198 v Cowell (1989) 24 NSWLR 478.* See also *Paterson v Humberside County Council* [1995] NPC 37, Roger Toulson QC (Deputy High Court Judge); *Low v R J Haddock Ltd [1985] 2 EGLR 247,* Judge Newey QC (Official Referee).
10 *[1984] 2 EGLR 44.* Tudor Evans J also held that technical ownership of the roots of trees on the highway by the householder *plaintiffs* themselves, by virtue of the presumption *usque ad medium filum viae,* was no bar to the imposition of liability upon the defendant local authority whose statutory powers enabled them actually to *control* the offending trees.

Delaware Mansions v Westminster City Council

[13.20]   The leading case on damage caused by encroaching tree-roots is now the 2001 decision of the House of Lords in *Delaware Mansions v Westminster City Council*[1]. The owners of a block of flats damaged by encroachment were able to recover damages for the cost of underpinning, even though the encroachment had started before they had acquired their interest in the property[2]. The House of Lords was at pains to emphasise, however, in the words of Lord Cooke of Thorndon who gave the only judgment, that 'the answer to the issue falls to be found by applying the concepts of reasonableness between neighbours (real or figurative) and reasonable foreseeability which underlie much modern tort law'[3]. It followed that the defendant tree-owner must be given reasonable notice to enable it to take measures of its own, such as removal of the offending tree, before expensive measures such as underpinning are undertaken by the claimant. Lord Cooke said:[4]

> 'If reasonableness between neighbours is the key to the solution of problems in this field, it cannot be right to visit the authority or owner responsible for a tree with a large bill for underpinning without giving them notice of the damage and the opportunity of avoiding further damage by removal of the tree. Should they elect to preserve the tree for environmental reasons, they may fairly be expected to bear the cost of underpinning or other reasonably necessary remedial works; and the party on whom the cost has fallen may recover it, even though there may be elements of hitherto unsatisfied pre-proprietorship damage or protection for the future. But, as a general proposition, I think that the defendant is entitled to notice and a reasonable opportunity of abatement before liability for remedial expenditure can arise. In this case Westminster had ample notice and time before the underpinning and piling, and is in my opinion liable'.

[1]   *[2001] 4 All ER 737.*
[2]   See also *Masters v London Borough of Brent [1978] 2 All ER 664, [1978] QB 841.*
[3]   *[2001] 4 All ER 737* at para 29. For recent cases applying the principles confirmed in *Delaware Mansions* to subsidence allegedly caused by tree roots, see *Siddiqui v Hillingdon LBC [2003] EWHC 726, 89 Con LR 13* (claim failed) and *Malewski v Ealing LBC [2003] EWHC 763, 89 Con LR 1* (claim succeeded).
[4]   *[2001] 4 All ER 737* at para 34.

Weeds

[13.21]   Since the overruling of *Giles v Walker*[1] by the Court of Appeal in *Leakey v National Trust for Places of Historic Interest or Natural Beauty*[2], and the approval in the latter case of the New Zealand decision in *French v Auckland City Corpn*[3], which has already been cited, it is clear that the spread of weeds can create liability[4]. Indeed in one nineteenth-century case, decided before *Giles v Walker*, liability was imposed for a nuisance caused by the natural accumulation of seaweed in a harbour[5]. It should be noted, however, that in order to qualify as a nuisance there has to be a degree of interference with the claimant's property which the latter cannot reasonably be expected to tolerate. Many situations involving the spread of weeds are likely to be trivial and, in consequence, will not give rise to liability[6].

[1]   *(1890) 24 QBD 656, 59 LJQB 416* discussed above at para [13.12].
[2]   *[1980] QB 485, [1980] 1 All ER 17.*
[3]   *[1974] 1 NZLR 340.*
[4]   For a statutory liability for failing to prevent the spreading of certain types of injurious weeds, see the *Weeds Act 1959.*
[5]   See *Margate Pier and Harbour Co v Margate Town Council (1869) 20 LT 564.*
[6]   Goodhart thought that the actual decision in *Giles v Walker* might be supported on this ground: see 'Liability for Things Naturally on the Land' (1930) 4 CLJ 13 at 17.

Animals, birds, etc

[13.22]   In *Seligman v Docker*[1] the plaintiff farmer claimed that his crops had been damaged by wild pheasants which had congregated in very large numbers on the defendant's neighbouring land. It was alleged that the defendant, who owned the shooting rights over the plaintiff's land as well as his own, should have kept the number of pheasants down by shooting. Romer J refused to impose liability holding that, since the pheasants were *ferae naturae*, the defendant was under no legal duty to keep their numbers down[2]. The same result was reached, with respect to damage caused by rats, in the earlier case of *Stearn v Prentice Bros*[3]. In both of these cases *Giles v Walker*[4] was relied upon and applied. But unfortunately neither of them was discussed or cited in either *Goldman v Hargrave*[5] or *Leakey v National Trust for Places of Historic Interest or Natural Beauty*[6]. Nevertheless the better view is that, as a result of the development in the law established by these cases, there is no longer any general principle of immunity from liability in nuisance for damage caused by wild birds or animals[7]. The precise level of duty owed will reflect, however, the considerable degree of difficulty which might will be involved in controlling such rapidly moving natural phenomena, as well as the particular type of locality in which the mischief arises.

[1] *[1949] Ch 53, [1948] 2 All ER 887.*

[2] The earlier case of *Farrer v Nelson (1885) 15 QBD 258, 54 LJQB 385*, which had been decided the other way on similar facts, was distinguished on the ground that it had concerned pheasants which had been reared and stocked by the defendant.

[3] *[1919] 1 KB 394, 88 LJKB 422*. See also *Brady v Warren [1900] 2 IR 632* (rabbits).

[4] *(1890) 24 QBD 656, 59 LJQB 416* discussed ante, overruled in *Leakey v National Trust for Places of Historic Interest or Natural Beauty [1980] QB 485, [1980] 1 All ER 17.*

[5] *[1967] 1 AC 645, [1966] 2 All ER 989.*

[6] *[1980] QB 485, [1980] 1 All ER 17.*

[7] For statutory provisions relating to damage caused by rats and mice, see *Pt 1* of the *Prevention of Damage by Pests Act 1949*. See also the *Public Health Act 1961, s 74* (birds).

Water

Older cases

[13.23] There is a long line of cases in which it was held that a landowner was not liable for the escape of water from his land if the presence of the water occurred naturally as a result of rain or percolation[1]. This immunity was even extended to situations in which injuring his neighbour was the result of the carrying out of some legitimate and recognised activity by the defendant such as excavating, mining or quarrying[2]. A landowner was also entitled to take reasonable measures to protect his land from flooding by water of natural origin, even if in so doing he increased the flow of water on to the land of his neighbour[3]. Nor was a plaintiff entitled to complain if, having enjoyed protection from flood water as a result of an erection or outlet provided by the defendant, the latter removed the barrier with the result that the plaintiff's land became liable to flooding once more[4].

[1] For discussion see, generally, Derham, 'Interference with Surface Waters by Lower Landholders' (1958) 74 LQR 361. For statutory provisions regarding administrative matters related to the drainage of land, see the *Land Drainage Act 1991.*

[2] See *Rouse v Gravelworks Ltd [1940] 1 KB 489, [1940] 1 All ER 26*. See also *Smith v Kenrick (1849) 7 CB 515, 18 LJCP 172; Wilson v Waddell (1876) 2 App Cas 95, 35 LT 639*. Cf *Scots Mines Co v Leadhills Mines Co (1859) 34 LTOS 34.*

[3] *R v Pagham, Sussex etc, Sewers Comrs (1828) 8 B & C 355, 2 Man & Ry KB 468; Ridge v Midland Rly Co (1888) 53 JP 55; Maxey Drainage Board v Great Northern Rly Co (1912) 106 LT 429; Gerrard v Crowe [1921] 1 AC 395, 90 LJPC 42*. Cf *Greyvensteyn v Hattingh [1911] AC 355, 80 LJPC 158*. In a narrow form the so-called 'common enemy' rule is still good law: see *Arscott v The Coal Authority [2004] EWCA Civ 892* referred to below at para [13.27].

4   *Thomas and Evans Ltd v Mid-Rhondda Co-operative Society Ltd [1941] 1 KB 381, [1940] 4 All ER 357.*
See also *West Cumberland Iron and Steel Co v Kenyon (1879) 11 Ch D 782, 48 LJ Ch 793.* Cf *Nield v London and North Western Rly Co (1874) LR 10 Exch 4, 44 LJ Ex 15*; *Gartner v Kidman (1962) 108 CLR 12, [1962] ALR 620.*

Interference with natural flow

[13.24] On the other hand a defendant incurred liability if he removed a natural barrier against flooding, such as shingle from the sea-shore[1], and in one unusual case the defendant was held liable under the *Public Health Act 1875* for flooding caused by his failure to repair a flood barrier on his land[2]. Liability would also be incurred if the defendant took positive steps to increase the flow of natural water on to his neighbour's land by intervening with pumping engines[3] or taking unusual measures such as cutting holes in a railway embankment[4].

1   *A-G v Tomline (1880) 14 Ch D 58, 49 LJ Ch 377*; *Canvey Island Comrs v Preedy [1922] 1 Ch 179, 91 LJ Ch 203.*
2   *Clayton v Sale UDC [1926] 1 KB 415, 95 LJKB 178.*
3   *Baird v Williamson (1863) 15 CBNS 376, 3 New Rep 86*; *Snow v Whitehead (1884) 27 Ch D 588, 53 LJ Ch 885.*
4   *Whalley v Lancashire and Yorkshire Rly Co (1884) 13 QBD 131, 53 LJQB 285.* See also *Hurdman v North Eastern Rly Co (1878) 3 CPD 168, 47 LJQB 368.* Cf *Slater v Worthington's Cash Stores (1930) Ltd [1941] 1 KB 488, [1941] 3 All ER 28.*

End of immunity

[13.25] After the judgment of the Privy Council in *Goldman v Hargrave*[1] in which the 'water' cases were not discussed, it was held in Canada[2] that the decision in that case had not altered 'the principle exempting owners from liability for natural flow of surface water' which was regarded as 'too well-entrenched in our law to be dislodged or affected by general statements ... laid down in quite different circumstances[3]. According to the reasoning of the Court of Appeal in *Leakey v National Trust for Places of Historic Interest or Natural Beauty*[4], however, there is no longer an absolute immunity in England as far as large and dangerous quantities of naturally occurring water are concerned, since the new generalised liability for harm caused by natural agencies will apply instead. The argument that this could have the effect of imposing an oppressive burden on small landowners faced with a duty to prevent flood-water from inundating the land of their neighbours, was met by the court with the reply that the flexible, subjective form of the duty would prevent harshness or injustice from occurring. Megaw LJ said[5]:

> 'Take, by way of example ... the landowner through whose land a stream flows. In rainy weather, it is known, the stream may flood and the flood may spread to the land of neighbours. If the risk is one which can readily be overcome or lessened, for example by reasonable steps on the part of the landowner to keep the stream free from blockage by flotsam or silt carried down, he will be in breach of duty if he does nothing or does too little. But if the only remedy is substantial and expensive works, then it might well be that the landowner would have discharged his duty by saying to his neighbours, who also know of the risk and who have asked him to do something about it, "You have my permission to come onto my land and to do agreed works at your expense", or it may be, "on the basis of a fair sharing of expense" '.

1   *[1967] 1 AC 645, [1966] 2 All ER 989.*

2   See *Loring v Brightwood Golf and Country Club Ltd (1974) 44 DLR (3d) 161.*
3   Per MacKeigan CJNS in *(1974) 44 DLR (3d) 161* at 178–179.
4   *[1980] QB 485, [1980] 1 All ER 17.*
5   *[1980] QB 485* at 526G–527A, *[1980] 1 All ER 17* at 37d–e.

Bybrook Barn Garden Centre v Kent County Council

[13.26] *Leakey's* case was applied to a situation actually involving flooding in *Bybrook Barn Garden Centre v Kent County Council.*[1] In this case the claimants' property was damaged when a natural stream burst its banks. The defendants had been aware of the risk posed by the stream, which had increased over the years rendering a culvert inserted by the their predecessors in title inadequate. Observing that, 'in this area, perhaps more than any other, the law has developed over the years'[2], the Court of Appeal reversed the decision of the trial judge in favour of the defendants, and imposed liability.

1   *(2001) 3 LGLR 27, CA.*
2   See above at para 22, *per* Waller LJ.

'Common enemy' rule survives

[13.27] Notwithstanding the absence of immunity from liability for the escape of water of natural origin from the defendant's land to that of the claimant, the Court of Appeal confirmed in the 2004 case of *Arscott v The Coal Authority*[1], that in a narrow form the so-called 'common enemy' rule remains part of the common law. Thus a landowner is still entitled to take measures to protect floodwater from *entering* his land in the first place, even if an inevitable consequence is that it will enter someone else's land instead.

1   *[2004] EWCA Civ 892.*

Flow of unconcentrated natural water

[13.28] The principle that a landowner may now in certain circumstances be liable for failing to prevent flood-water from flowing from his land on to that of his neighbour does not entail that the owner of higher land is obliged to prevent the percolation of unconcentrated water, by natural drainage, to lower land. In *Palmer v Bowman*[1] the Court of Appeal held that no easement was necessary, or could exist, to provide for such drainage. Rattee J, delivering the leading judgment of the Court of Appeal, said 'it is nature, not the law, that imposes the burden of receiving on the lower land'[2].

1   *[2000] 1 All ER 22.*
2   See *[2000] 1 All ER 22* at 35.

Uncertainty as to rights of lower landowner

[13.29] In reaching its conclusion the Court of Appeal in *Palmer's* case approved much of the reasoning of Piers Ashworth QC, sitting as a Deputy High Court Judge, in the case of *Home Brewery plc v Davis & Co*[1]. In that case the plaintiffs, who owned higher land from which unconcentrated naturally occurring water had always, without interference, drained off on to the defendants' lower land, complained when the defendants in effect erected a barrier which *returned* the water to the plaintiffs' land and caused flooding. The judge concluded that although the unconcentrated natural flow from the higher to the lower land was *not* such as to subject the *plaintiffs* to a duty derived from *Leakey* to prevent it, it did not follow that the defendants were under an absolute duty actually to *receive* the water. Although the defendants would have been liable if they had returned the water maliciously[2] they were under no liability if, as in the case itself, in which they were simply developing their land for housing[3], the flow was foreseeably reversed by the ordinary and reasonable use of the lower land[4]. It is important to note, however, that the Court of Appeal in *Palmer v Bowman* stated that it expressed no view as to the correctness of the 'conclusion of the court in the *Home Brewery plc* case that the lower landowner has a right to take reasonable physical action on his land … without being liable in nuisance or negligence for any resultant damage to the higher land', since the point did not arise for decision in *Palmer's* case and it was unnecessary to express a view upon it[5].

1   *[1987] 1 All ER 637.*
2   See above at 646 *per* Piers Ashworth QC, distinguishing *Bradford Corpn v Pickles [1895] AC 587, 64 LJ Ch 759* (discussed in CHAPTER 11 above).
3   See also *Ellison v Ministry of Defence (1996) 81 BLR 101.*
4   See also *Gartner v Kidman (1962) 108 CLR 12* at 49 *per* Windeyer J (quoted in *Ryeford Homes Ltd v Sevenoaks District Council [1989] 2 EGLR 281* at 285 by Judge Newey QC, Official Referee, who said: 'The decision of the Australian High Court is not strictly binding on me, but it is by a very distinguished court and, if I may say so, it exhibits what is usually the main characteristic of the common law, namely common sense, and, therefore, like Mr Piers Ashworth, I respectfully follow it'). Although successful on the main point, the defendants in the *Home Brewery* case were held liable to the plaintiffs for a trivial sum in respect of a separate issue relating to *other* water, which had actually *accumulated* on the defendants' land and which they had 'squeezed out' to the detriment of the plaintiffs.
5   See *[2000] 1 All ER 22* at 35.

D Strict liability and the rule in Rylands v Fletcher

Origins and scope of the rule

[13.30]   It seems to be clear that the immediate cause of the formulation of the rule in *Rylands v Fletcher*[1] was a judicial desire to distinguish the immunity from liability for the escape of water accumulated by nature in a case which involved an artificial reservoir[2]. A mine owned by the plaintiff was flooded when independent contractors, employed by the defendant, negligently failed to block off underground shafts leading to the mine before filling the reservoir with water. The flooding had occurred without any fault on the part of the defendant employer, but he was held liable on the ground that anyone 'who for his own purposes brings on his lands and collects and keeps there anything likely to do mischief if it escapes, must keep it in at his peril, and, if he does not do so, is prima facie answerable for all the damage which is the natural consequence of its escape'[3].

1   *(1866) LR 1 Exch 265, 4 H&C 263*; affd sub nom *Rylands v Fletcher (1868) LR 3 HL 330, 37 LJ Ex 161.* For the background to the case see Simpson 'Legal Liability for Bursting Reservoirs: The Historical Context of *Rylands v Fletcher*' (1984) 13 JLS 209.
2   See Newark 'Non-Natural User and *Rylands v Fletcher*' (1961) 24 MLR 557.
3   *(1866) LR 1 Exch* at 279, *per* Blackburn J. On what constitutes a dangerous 'thing' within the rule see *Street on Torts* (9th edn) pp 381–383 and Stallybrass 'Dangerous Things and the Non-natural User of Land' (1929) 3 CLJ 379. The 'escape' need not necessarily be of the 'thing' itself: *A-G v Cory Bros & Co Ltd [1921] 1 AC 521, 90 LJ Ch 221* (pressure from accumulated colliery waste causing landslide).

Special type of nuisance

[13.31] Although the decision in *Rylands v Fletcher* became famous as an example of 'strict liability' it is significant that Blackburn J, who delivered the judgment of the Court of Exchequer Chamber, regarded as analogous to the case before him situations of continuing nuisance involving the escape of poisonous fumes from factory chimneys[1]. This suggests that the court imposed liability upon the defendant mainly because he had deliberately created a continuing situation, the presence of the reservoir, which constituted a threat to his neighbour and therefore an interference with the latter's enjoyment of his land[2]. The view that the rule in *Rylands v Fletcher* is a special category of the law of nuisance was confirmed by the House of Lords in two major recent cases, in which the House examined the rule in depth. In the first of the two, *Cambridge Water Co Ltd v Eastern Counties Leather plc*[3], which was decided in 1993[4], Lord Goff said that the rule should now 'be regarded essentially as an extension of the law of nuisance to cases of isolated escapes from land, even though the rule as established is not limited to escapes which are in fact isolated'[5].

[1]   See *(1866) LR 1 Exch* 265 at 285–6.
[2]   See Newark 'The Boundaries of Nuisance' (1949) 65 LQR 480 at 488: 'What was novel in *Rylands v Fletcher*, or at least clearly decided for the first time, was that as between adjacent occupiers an isolated escape is actionable'.
[3]   *[1994] 2 AC 264, [1994] 1 All ER 53*. See R F V Heuston 'The Return of *Rylands v Fletcher*' (1994) 110 LQR 185; P R Ghandhi 'Requiem for *Rylands v Fletcher*' [1994] Conv 309; Anthony Ogus, 'Water Rights Diluted' (1994) J Env L 137.
[4]   The case was the first time the House of Lords had considered the rule since *Read v J Lyons & Co Ltd [1947] AC 156, [1946] 2 All ER 471*, half a century earlier.
[5]   *[1994] 2 AC 264* at 306, *[1994] 1 All ER 53* at 76. His Lordship went on to point out that the *Cambridge Water* case itself involved not an 'isolated escape, but a continuing escape resulting from a state of affairs' as a substance used in the defendants' manufacturing process caused gradual contamination of the public water supply over a long period, and he observed that: 'Classically, this would have been regarded as a case of nuisance … '.

Transco v Stockport Metropolitan Borough Council

[13.32] In 2003 the House of Lords reviewed the functioning of the rule in *Rylands v Fletcher* in the definitive case of *Transco v Stockport Metropolitan BC*[1]. The House was invited by the defendants to hold that the rule was obsolete, and should be regarded as having been absorbed by the law of negligence. Their Lordships did, however, reject the invitation and instead confirmed that the rule remains part of English law. In the *Stockport* case water leaked, without negligence, from a pipe used by the defendant Council to supply water to a block of 66 flats. The water seeped undetected into the embankment of a nearby disused railway until the quantity was such that the embankment suddenly collapsed. As it happened, the embankment supported a gas main owned by the claimants and immediate measures were necessary to protect and support the newly exposed main. The claimants sought to place the cost of these measures upon the defendants, relying on the rule in *Rylands v Fletcher*. The claim ultimately failed, for reasons which are outlined below, but the House of Lords took the opportunity to conduct a widespread review of the rule, and all earlier cases now have to be read in the light of the decision which resolves a number of important issues which had previously been a matter of controversy.

[1]   *[2004] 1 All ER 589*.

Need for escape

[13.33] Lord Goff's reference, in the passage quoted above from *Cambridge Water Co Ltd v Eastern Counties Leather plc*, to the escapes being 'from land' reflects that the underlying principles of the rule are those of nuisance: applicable to occupiers of land in their capacity as such. For liability to be imposed there does have to have been an escape from the defendant's *land*, mere escape from his *control* is not sufficient. For this reason, in *Read v J Lyons & Co Ltd*[1] the House of Lords denied recovery to a plaintiff who claimed damages for injuries suffered as a result of an explosion while she was on the defendants' premises. This fundamental requirement of the rule was emphasised by the House of Lords in *Transco v Stockport Metropolitan BC*. 'No claim', said Lord Bingham, 'can arise if the events complained of take place wholly on the land of a single occupier. There must ... be an escape from one tenement to another'[2].

[1]   *[1947] AC 156, [1946] 2 All ER 471.*
[2]   See *[2004] 1 All ER 589* at para 9. See also *per* Lord Scott of Foscote at para 77 (who based his decision on this ground contending that the requirement was not satisfied on the facts of the *Transco* case itself), and *per* Lord Hoffman at para 34; although Lord Hoffman refers to the need for an escape 'from the defendant's land *or control*' (italics supplied) it is clear from the context that he was not intending to cast doubt on the decision in *Read's* case to the effect that escape from control is not in itself enough.

Personal injuries

[13.34]   More than half a century ago several members of the House of Lords in *Read v J Lyons & Co Ltd* also took the opportunity provided by the facts of that case to express doubt as to whether, in any event, an action for personal injuries is possible under *Rylands v Fletcher*. Lord Macmillan said[1]:

> 'Whatever may have been the law of England in early times I am of opinion that as the law now stands an allegation of negligence is in general essential to the relevancy of an action of reparation for personal injuries'[2].

On the other hand, the rule had been assumed to cover personal injuries in several cases[3] decided before *Read v J Lyons & Co Ltd* and Parker LJ subsequently expressed the view, obiter, that it was not open to the Court of Appeal to deny that the rule extended to such injuries[4]. Personal injuries have also been regarded as being within the rule in Canada[5] and Australia[6]. Nevertheless, it is now clear from the speeches of the House of Lords in *Transco v Stockport Metropolitan BC* that the observations in *Read v J Lyons & Co Ltd* accurately represent the present state of the law in England. Lord Bingham said, in the *Transco* case, that 'the claim cannot include a claim for death or personal injury, since such a claim does not relate to any right in or enjoyment of land'[7]. In fact no plaintiff since the war appears actually to have been awarded damages for personal injury on the basis of *Rylands v Fletcher,* and since the speeches of the House of Lords in *Hunter v Canary Wharf Ltd*[8] it has been clear that such damages are not recoverable in private (as distinct from public) nuisance. Indeed to permit such recovery on the basis of a supposed 'strict' liability in one branch of the law when the overwhelming majority of personal injury cases fall outside it, and require proof of negligence, would lead to serious anomaly[9]. Coherent reform of the law of damages for personal injury can now only be achieved by legislation. Damage to chattels is, however, recoverable under the rule[10].

[1]   *[1947] AC 156* at 170–171, *[1946] 2 All ER 471* at 476A.
[2]   See also *per* Lord Simonds, *[1947] AC 156* at 180–181, *[1946] 2 All ER 471* at 481C–D, and *per* Lord Porter, *[1947] AC 156* at 178 *[1946] 2 All ER 471* at 480A–D. Cf *per* Lord Uthwatt, *[1947] AC 156* at 186, *[1946] 2 All ER 471* at 494E–F.
[3]   See *Miles v Forest Rock Granite Co (1918) 34 TLR 500*; *Shiffman v Grand Priory in British Realm of Venerable Order of the Hospital of St John of Jerusalem [1936] 1 All ER 557*; *Hale v Jennings Bros [1938] 1 All ER 579*.

⁴   See *Perry v Kendrick's Transport [1956] 1 All ER 154* at 160I–161A, *[1956] 1 WLR 85* at 92.
⁵   See *Aldridge and O'Brien v Van Patter [1952] 4 DLR 93*.
⁶   See *Benning v Wong (1969) 43 ALJR 467*. But cf now *Burnie Port Authority v General Jones Pty Ltd (1994) 120 ALR 42*, discussed below at para [13.41].
⁷   See *[2004] 1 All ER 589* at para 9. See also *per* Lord Hoffman at para 35: ' ... damages for personal injuries are not recoverable under the rule'; and *per* Lord Hobhouse at para 52: 'It is not concerned with liability for personal injuries which is covered by other parts of the law of torts'.
⁸   *[1997] 2 All ER 426, [1997] AC 655*, discussed in CHAPTER 11 above.
⁹   But cf Tylor 'The Restriction of Strict Liability' (1947) 10 MLR 396 at 400: 'The suggestion that I can recover for an explosion wrecking my conservatory ... but not for an explosion blowing me out of my deck chair in my own garden ... has little to commend it'.
¹⁰ See *Halsey v Esso Petroleum Co Ltd [1961] 2 All ER 145, [1961] 1 WLR 683*.

'Act of God' and 'Act of a stranger'?¹

[13.35] In a number of cases, some dating back to the years soon after *Rylands v Fletcher* was decided, the courts showed a reluctance, notwithstanding the nominal status of the doctrine as one of 'strict liability', to impose liability under *Rylands v Fletcher* on defendants who had not been at all negligent. In particular, plaintiffs could not succeed if the 'escape' which took place was caused by what was termed an 'act of God', or by the act of a third party over whom the defendant had no control. In *Perry v Kendrick's Transport Ltd*² a group of boys trespassed on to the defendant's coach park, and threw a lighted match into the petrol tank of a coach. The plaintiff, who was standing on adjacent ground, suffered injury in the resulting explosion and brought an action under *Rylands v Fletcher*. In refusing to impose liability the Court of Appeal chose to base their decision on the ground that 'it has for a long time been an exception to the rule if the defendants can show that the act which brought about the escape was the act of a stranger'³. In these circumstances a situation was reached in which, according to Jenkins LJ, 'the claim based on *Rylands v Fletcher* merges into the claim in negligence'⁴. *Perry v Kendrick's Transport Ltd* was complicated by the fact that it concerned a claim for personal injuries. Nevertheless it is possible that the ratio of the case, in so far as it turned upon the absence of negligence, might need to be reconsidered in the light of the decisions of the House of Lords in the *Cambridge Water* and *Transco* cases. In as much as those decisions have confirmed that there is a role, albeit a limited one, for the rule in English law, they have served to highlight the anomaly of defences based, in effect, on the absence of fault in the context of liability intended, at least nominally, to be 'strict'. In *Cambridge Water* Lord Goff asserted that, where the rule applied, 'the defendant will be liable ... notwithstanding that he has taken all reasonable care and skill to prevent the escape from occurring'⁵. In the *Transco* case Lord Hoffman appeared sceptical of the correctness of the cases on the 'act of God' and 'act of a stranger', and expressed himself as follows:⁶

> 'Escapes of water and the like are often the result of natural events – heavy rain or drains blocked by falling leaves – or the acts of third parties, like vandals who open taps or sluices. This form of causation does not usually make the damage any the less a consequence of the risk created by the water or other escaping substance. No serious principle of allocating risk to the enterprise would leave the injured third party to pursue his remedy against the vandal'.

On the other hand, Lord Hoffman concluded his speech by observing that the liability 'is not particularly strict because it excludes liability when the escape is for the most common of reasons, namely vandalism or unusual natural events'⁷. So it may be premature to conclude that the 'defences' to the rule have been abrogated, even though the recognition of their illogicality at the highest judicial level has at least raised the possibility of their eventual removal.

1   See further, CHAPTER 23 below.
2   *[1956] 1 All ER 154, [1956] 1 WLR 85.*
3   *[1956] 1 All ER 154* at 161B, *[1956] 1 WLR 85* at 92. See also *Box v Jubb (1879) 4 Ex D 76, 48 LJQB 417*; *Rickards v Lothian [1913] AC 263, 82 LJPC 42*; *Northwestern Utilities Ltd v London Guarantee and Accident Co Ltd [1936] AC 108, 105 LJPC 18.*
4   *[1956] 1 All ER 154* at 160F, *[1956] 1 WLR 85* at 91. For a case in which the defence of act of stranger failed on the facts and negligence was proved see *A Prosser & Son Ltd v Levy [1955] 3 All ER 577, [1955] 1 WLR 1224.* See also *Abelson v Brockman (1889) 54 JP 119*; *Hale v Jennings Bros [1938] 1 All ER 579.*
5   See *[1994] 1 All ER 53* at 71.
6   See *[2004] 1 All ER 589* at para 32.
7   See *[2004] 1 All ER 589* at para 39.

Requirement of 'non-natural user'

[13.36]   When the decision of the Court of Exchequer Chamber in *Rylands v Fletcher* was upheld by the House of Lords, Lord Cairns LC used the phrase 'non-natural' to denote the kind of user of land which would give rise to liability under the principle involved in the case[1]. It seems probable that these words were intended simply to allow for the 'natural accumulation' cases[2] and not to lay down a different test for liability from that envisaged by Blackburn J. Nevertheless Lord Cairns' speech was subsequently regarded as having introduced a modified test for liability[3]. It was therefore held that liability would not be imposed if the defendant's activity was not 'unnatural', in the sense of abnormal or unusual in the particular circumstances. Thus there is no liability under the rule for the escape of water which has been introduced artificially but for the purpose of providing a domestic water system which 'has become, in accordance with modern sanitary views, an almost necessary feature of town life'[4]. Despite its somewhat doubtful historicity[5] the notion of non-natural user is well-established as a fundamental component of the rule. It is closely linked to the concept of 'anything likely to do mischief if it escapes', to which Blackburn J referred in the original judgment. The flexibility which the doctrine of non-natural use conferred on judges, enabling them to give effect to changes in social conditions and habits of living, was undoubtedly purchased at some cost in terms of consistency and predictability[6]. In *Read v J Lyons & Co Ltd* the House of Lords even suggested that operating a munitions factory in wartime might not be a non-natural use of land[7]. But the House has itself indicated subsequently that this was to stretch the concept of natural use of land too far, and in the *Cambridge Water* and *Transco* cases an attempt has been made to adopt a rather more structured approach to the question of what does, and what does not, constitute natural user.

1   See *(1868) LR 3 HL 330* at 339.
2   Especially *Smith v Kenrick (1849) 7 CB 515, 18 LJCP 172* which had been heavily relied on by the defendants and was referred to by Lord Cairns in his speech: see Newark 'Non-Natural User and *Rylands v Fletcher*' (1961) 24 MLR 557.
3   See the Canadian case of *J P Porter Co v Bell [1955] 1 DLR 62.* See also Williams 'Non-Natural Use of Land' (1979) 32 CLJ 310.
4   Per Lord Moulton in *Rickards v Lothian [1913] AC 263* at 281. See also *Collingwood v Home and Colonial Stores Ltd [1936] 3 All ER 200*; *Torette House Pty Ltd v Berkman (1940) 62 CLR 637*; *British Celanese Ltd v A H Hunt (Capacitors) Ltd [1969] 2 All ER 1252, [1969] 1 WLR 959.* The position is different if (as in *Rylands v Fletcher* itself) water is stored in bulk: *Western Engraving Co v Film Laboratories Ltd [1936] 1 All ER 106.* Cf *Smeaton v Ilford Corpn* [1954] Ch 450, [1954] 1 All ER 923. For discussion see Kadirgamar 'The Escape of Water from Domestic Premises' (1973) 37 Conv (NS) 179.
5   '... the result as applied in the modern cases is ... one which would have surprised Lord Cairns and astounded Blackburn J': Newark in (1961) 24 MLR 557 at 571.

6   See the comment of Upjohn J in *Smeaton v Ilford Corpn [1954] Ch 450* at 471, *[1954] 1 All ER 923* at 932H–933.
7   See *Read v J Lyons & Co Ltd [1947] AC 156, [1946] 2 All ER 471.* Sed quaere and cf *Rainham Chemical Works Ltd v Belvedere Fish Guano Co [1921] 2 AC 465, 90 LJKB 1252.*

Narrower interpretation

[13.37] In *Cambridge Water Co Ltd v Eastern Counties Leather plc*[1] the matter was reviewed, albeit obiter, by the House of Lords and a somewhat narrower interpretation of the defence of 'natural user' was contemplated than heretofore. At first instance in *Cambridge Water* Ian Kennedy J found for the defendants on the ground that the defendants' manufacturing activity was a natural use of land in the 'industrial village' in which it took place and in which its creation of employment was beneficial for the local community. Although the House of Lords restored[2] the decision of Ian Kennedy J in favour of Eastern Counties Leather (ECL), it did so on very different grounds. Lord Goff specifically disapproved the suggestion that the creation of employment was 'sufficient of itself to establish a particular use as constituting a natural or ordinary use of land'.[3] His Lordship found it unnecessary 'to attempt any redefinition of the concept of natural or ordinary use', and further clarification of the scope of the defence must await future cases. But his approach provides welcome confirmation that the views in some of the earlier cases, favouring a wide interpretation of the defence, will no longer be followed. He had no doubt that the defence was not available to ECL on the facts, and pointed out that in view of the emphasis upon the need for foreseeability of harm, which was the *ratio decidendi* of the House in the instant case[4], an expansive approach to the defence would no longer be necessary or appropriate. He concluded as follows[5]:

' ... I feel bound to say that the storage of substantial quantities of chemicals on industrial premises should be regarded as an almost classic case of non-natural use; and I find it very difficult to think that it should be thought objectionable to impose strict liability for damage caused in the event of their escape. It may well be that, now that it is recognised that foreseeability of harm of the relevant type is a prerequisite of liability in damages under the rule, the courts may feel less pressure to extend the concept of natural use to circumstances such as those in the present case; and in due course it may become easier to control this exception, and to ensure that it has a more recognisable basis of principle'.

1   *[1994] 2 AC 264, [1994] 1 All ER 53.*
2   It had been reversed by the Court of Appeal.
3   *[1994] 2 AC 264* at 309, *[1994] 1 All ER 53* at 79.
4   See below.
5   *[1994] 2 AC 264* at 309, *[1994] 1 All ER 53* at 79.

The decision in Transco

[13.38] The concepts of 'non-natural use' and 'mischievousness' were at the heart of the actual decision of the House of Lords in *Transco v Stockport Metropolitan BC* itself. Lord Bingham said in that case[1]:

'I do not think the mischief or danger test should be at all easily satisfied. It must be shown that the defendant has done something which he recognised, or judged by the standards appropriate at the relevant place and time, he ought reasonably to have recognised, as giving rise to an exceptionally high risk of danger or mischief if there should be an escape ... I think it clear that ordinary user is a preferable test to natural user, making it clear that the rule in *Rylands v Fletcher* is engaged only where the defendant's use is shown to be extraordinary and unusual'.

In the result the House concluded that in installing the water-pipe in the *Transco* case had not brought on to its land 'something likely to cause danger or mischief if it escaped' and was only making 'an ordinary user of its land'[2]. Lord Hoffman said[3]:

'The casualty was caused by the escape of water from the council's land. But the source was a perfectly normal item of plumbing. The pipe was, it is true, considerably larger than the ordinary domestic size. But it was smaller than a water main ... it was not a 'non-natural' user of land ... I agree with my noble and learned friend Lord Bingham of Cornhill that the criterion of exceptional risk must be taken seriously and creates a high threshold for a claimant to surmount'.

[1]   See *[2004] 1 All ER 589* at paras 10–11.
[2]   See *[2004] 1 All ER 589* at para 12 *per* Lord Bingham.
[3]   See *[2004] 1 All ER 589* at paras 48–49.

Non-natural user and 'consent'

[13.39]   The cases show that where the claimant and the defendant live in different parts of the same building, and share common facilities for such services as water and drainage, an action based upon *Rylands v Fletcher* is unlikely to succeed in the event of an escape or overflow[1]. Proof of negligence will normally be essential[2]. Although the decisions on this point have proceeded on the basis of 'common benefit', or the plaintiff's 'consent', it is clear from the decision in the *Transco* case that most of them could probably have been decided the same way on the basis of absence of non-natural user, notwithstanding the narrower scope of that defence after *Cambridge Water*. It is submitted that this would have been preferable[3]. Cases in which a defendant might succeed on 'consent', where he could not also have shown 'natural' user in situations of the kind in question, are unlikely to be numerous[4]. Such cases are likely to be limited to circumstances in which, although the arrangements are unusual, the claimant benefits from them[5]. Wide development of a defence of 'consent' in this context would conflict with the important principle that it is no defence that a claimant 'came to the nuisance'[6]. The claimant may normally only be taken to accept the existing arrangements because they are usual[7] and, in part, for his benefit[8]. Undue emphasis upon 'consent' as a separate defence is therefore misleading.

[1]   See *Carstairs v Taylor (1871) LR 6 Exch 217, 40 LJ Ex 129; Anderson v Oppenheimer (1880) 5 QBD 602, 149 LJQB 708; Blake v Woolf [1898] 2 QB 426, 67 LJQB 813; Kiddle v City Business Properties Ltd [1942] 1 KB 269, [1942] 2 All ER 216; Sachdeva v Sandhu [1989] 2 EGLR 273.*
[2]   As in *Abelson v Brockman (1889) 54 JP 119* and *A Prosser & Son Ltd v Levy [1955] 3 All ER 577, [1955] 1 WLR 1224.* See also *Sachdeva v Sandhu [1989] 2 EGLR 273.* Cf *Liverpool City Council v Irwin [1977] AC 239, [1976] 2 All ER 39.* See also the *Defective Premises Act 1972, s 4.*
[3]   But cf *per* Lord Hobhouse in *Transco v Stockport Metropolitan BC [2004] 1 All ER 589* at paras 61–62.
[4]   For a case in which the defence of consent succeeded in the Court of Appeal, although at first instance liability had been imposed on the basis of non-natural user: see *Peters v Prince of Wales Theatre (Birmingham) Ltd [1943] KB 73, [1942] 2 All ER 533* (sprinkler system in a factory).
[5]   Cf *Western Engraving Co v Film Laboratories Ltd [1936] 1 All ER 106.*
[6]   See CHAPTER 23 below. Cf Law Commission Report no 32, 'Civil Liability for Dangerous Things and Activities' p 20.
[7]   Cf *A Prosser & Son Ltd v Levy [1955] 3 All ER 577, [1955] 1 WLR 1224.*
[8]   See *Western Engraving Co v Film Laboratories Ltd [1936] 1 All ER 106.*

'For his own purposes'

[13.40] It was sometimes suggested that statutory undertakers, such as nationalised industries, were outside the scope of *Rylands v Fletcher* in that they did not collect substances such as water, gas or electricity for their 'own purposes', within the words of the judgment of Blackburn J[1], but for the general benefit of the community[2]. It was never easy to see the justification for this limitation. Although public bodies may in some circumstances be able to take advantage of the defence of statutory authorisation[3] it is not clear why they should have been put in a privileged position at common law on this ground[4]. In any event, since most of the relevant services are now provided by 'privatised' commercial organisations it is submitted that any conceivable justification for the alleged exception has wholly disappeared. The better view is therefore that statutory undertakers cannot now claim immunity from the rule in *Rylands v Fletcher* simply by denying that they act for their 'own purposes'[5]. This conclusion is reinforced by an important passage in the speech of Lord Walker of Gestingthorpe in *Transco v Stockport Metropolitan BC*[6]. His Lordship expressed himself as follows:

> 'It is understandable that any court might be inclined to deal more strictly with a defendant who has profited from a dangerous activity conducted on his own land, and less strictly with persons conducting similar activities for the general public good. But in this area (which is some way removed from the 'give and take' of minor nuisances) the court cannot sensibly determine what is an ordinary or special (that is, specially dangerous) use of land by undertaking some utilitarian balancing of general good against individual risk'.

[1]   See *(1866) LR 1 Exch 265* at 279.
[2]   See *per* Denning LJ in *Pride of Derby and Derbyshire Angling Association v British Celanese [1953] Ch 149* at 189, *[1953] 1 All ER 179* at 202H–203, and *per* Sellers LJ (delivering the judgment of the court) in *Dunne v North-Western Gas Board [1964] 2 QB 806* at 832, [1963] 3 All ER 916 at 921A–C.
[3]   See CHAPTER 23 below.
[4]   For forceful criticism of the alleged exception see *Smeaton v Ilford Corpn [1954] Ch 450* at 467–471, *[1954] 1 All ER 923* at 930G–932F, *per* Upjohn J; *Benning v Wong (1969) 43 ALJR 467* at 486, *per* Windeyer J.
[5]   They might, however, benefit from protection implicit in their statutory scheme: see *Marcic v Thames Water Utilities [2004] 1 All ER 135* discussed above at para [13.17].
[6]   See *[2004] 1 All ER 589* at para 105.

Rejection of Rylands v Fletcher in Australia

[13.41] In 1994 the High Court of Australia undertook a general examination of the rule in *Rylands v Fletcher* in *Burnie Port Authority v General Jones Pty Ltd*[1]. Although *Burnie* coincidentally took place almost contemporaneously with the deliberations by the House of Lords in *Cambridge Water Co v Eastern Counties Leather plc*,[2] the High Court reached a markedly different conclusion about the status of the rule from that favoured in England. In *Burnie* the negligence of the defendants' independent contractors caused a fire which spread to adjoining premises and destroyed a large quantity of frozen vegetables owned by the plaintiff. By a majority of five to two the court held the defendants liable. In so holding, however, the majority relied upon the law of negligence and concluded that the rule in *Rylands v Fletcher* had been subsumed in Australia by that tort. Liability was imposed on the basis that the circumstances were such as to give rise to a 'non-delegable duty' upon the defendants in negligence for the carelessness of their independent contractors. The two dissentients disagreed not only with the imposition of liability but also, and in a sense paradoxically, with the proposition that *Rylands v Fletcher* no longer enjoyed a separate existence from negligence in the law of Australia. Although robustly in favour of the retention of the rule and its strict liability, they concluded that the rule's requirements, that of non-natural user in particular, were not satisfied on the facts of the case. They also rejected the view of their colleagues that the circumstances gave rise to a 'non-delegable duty' in negligence.

¹ (1994) 120 ALR 42, Mason CJ, Deane, Dawson, Toohey and Gaudron JJ. Brennan and McHugh JJ dissenting. See (1994) 110 LQR 506 (R F V Heuston and R A Buckley).
² [1994] 2 AC 264, [1994] 1 All ER 53.

Rylands v Fletcher survives in England

[13.42] In *Transco v Stockport Metropolitan BC*¹ Lord Walker of Gestingthorpe reviewed the criticisms of the rule in *Rylands v Fletcher,* by the majority of the High Court of Australia in *Burnie Port Authority v General Jones Pty Ltd*, and concluded that 'they do not in my opinion make out the case for writing off *Rylands v Fletcher* as a dead letter'². In so far as the criticism was based on the degree of uncertainty surrounding the concept of 'non-natural use', and the related notion of 'dangerousness', Lord Walker considered that it could be met by clarification along the lines provided by his brethren in the *Transco* case itself. Moreover, the Australian decision is open to the objection that by invoking, without clearly defining, the vague and question-begging concept of 'non-delegable duty', it is likely to increase uncertainty in an area where more rather than less structure would seem to be desirable³. Overall, perhaps the most powerful objection to the proposition that developments in negligence have rendered the rule in *Rylands v Fletcher* redundant concerns the *burden of proof*. Lord Walker put it as follows⁴:

> 'The last observation that I wish to make about *Burnie* is on its implicit assumption that the imposition of strict liability is unnecessary and undesirable if a claim based solely in negligence would lead to the same outcome. That assumption seems to me, with respect, to overlook the practical implications, in a case of this sort, of bringing a claim in negligence, perhaps against a powerful corporate opponent. In such circumstances fairness may require that, instead of the claimant having to prove his case, the law casts on the defendant the burden of proving act of God, or some other defence to strict liability'.

¹ [2004] 1 All ER 589.
² See [2004] 1 All ER 589 at para 99.
³ See per Lord Walker in [2004] 1 All ER 589 at para 109.
⁴ See [2004] 1 All ER 589 at para 110.

Fire¹

[13.43] In *Johnson v BJW Property Developments²*, in which vicarious liability was imposed upon the defendant for a fire caused by the negligence of his independent contractor, Judge Thornton QC said³:

> 'Fire is an obvious "dangerous thing" so that any escape of fire gives rise to the potential of *Rylands v Fletcher* liability if the escape was caused by, or arose out of, a dangerous or non-natural user of land'.

In *Mason v Levy Auto Parts of England Ltd⁴* the defendants stored large quantities of combustible material on their land which caught fire for a reason that was never discovered. The resulting conflagration spread to the plaintiff's land and caused damage. Mackenna J found for the plaintiff, and sought to reformulate the rule so as to facilitate its application in cases involving fire. He said that a defendant would be liable if the following conditions were satisfied[5]:

'(1) he brought onto his land things likely to catch fire, and kept them there in such conditions that if they did ignite the fire would be likely to spread to the plaintiff's land;

(2) he did so in the course of some non-natural use; and

(3) the things ignited and the fire spread'[6].

In the earlier case of *Sochacki v Sas*[7] a claim based on *Rylands v Fletcher* for damage caused by a fire which had spread from the fireplace in the defendant's room, without negligence on his part, failed on the ground of absence of non-natural user. There had been merely, in the words of Lord Goddard CJ, 'an ordinary, natural, proper, everyday use of a fireplace in a room'[8]. On the other hand, use of a blow-lamp to unblock frozen pipes in a house has been held to be a non-natural use of land, and hence to give rise to liability under the rule in the event of a fire being caused as a result[9].

[1] See generally, Ogus 'Vagaries in Liability for the Escape of Fire' [1969] CLJ 104.
[2] *[2002] 3 All ER 574*. For further discussion see CHAPTER 18 below.
[3] See *[2002] 3 All ER 574* at para 31. See also the same judge in *Re-source America International v Platt Site Services [2003] EWHC 1142, 90 Con LR 139* at paras 170–171.
[4] *[1967] 2 QB 530, [1967] 2 All ER 62.*
[5] See *[1967] 2 QB 530* at 542C–D, *[1967] 2 All ER 62* at 70A–B.
[6] A fire which is within the rule in *Rylands v Fletcher* does not 'accidentally begin' for the purposes of the *Fires Prevention (Metropolis) Act 1774, s 86* so that a person from whose land such a fire 'escapes' is not able to take advantage of the special defence provided by the Act: *Musgrove v Pandelis [1919] 2 KB 43, 88 LJKB 915.*
[7] *[1947] 1 All ER 344.* See also *J Doltis Ltd v Isaac Braithwaite & Sons (Engineers) Ltd [1957] 1 Lloyd's Rep 522.*
[8] *[1947] 1 All ER* at 345A.
[9] See *Balfour v Barty-King [1956] 2 All ER 555, [1956] 1 WLR 779*; affd on other grounds *[1957] 1 QB 496, [1957] 1 All ER 156.* Cf *H & N Emanuel Ltd v Greater London Council [1971] 2 All ER 835.*

Act of stranger narrowly construed

[13.44] Although the defence of act of stranger will be available, even a slight degree of possible control over the third party will suffice to negate the defence in fire cases. In *Ribbee v Norrie*[1] a fire which spread to adjoining premises was started in a hostel of which the defendant was landlord; probably as a result of a cigarette being discarded by a resident. The trial judge found for the defendant, on the ground that he could not in practice have prevented the fire. His decision was, however, reversed by the Court of Appeal; which took the view that the defendant should have taken steps to regulate smoking by residents, or to display prominent warning notices.

[1] *[2001] PIQR P8.*

Statutory strict liability for certain escapes

Water Industry Act 1991

[13.45] The Water Industry Act 1991, section 209(1) provides that[1]:

'Where an escape of water, *however caused*, from a pipe vested in a water undertaker causes loss or damage, the undertaker shall be liable … for the loss or damage'.

The section imposes strict liability upon water undertakers where their own burst pipes cause damage, which includes personal injury[2]. The liability does not, however, arise if the escape was wholly due to the fault of the sufferer of the damage[3] and, notwithstanding that the liability is strict, the provisions of the *Law Reform (Contributory Negligence) Act 1945* can apply in favour of the water undertaker to secure an apportionment of the loss where appropriate[4]. A 'public gas supplier' cannot invoke the section[5].

[1]   Italics supplied.
[2]   '"Damage", in relation to individuals, includes death and any personal injury, including any disease or impairment of physical or mental condition': *Water Industry Act 1991, s 219(1)*. See also *Anglian Water Services Ltd v Crawshaw Robins & Co Ltd [2001] BLR 173* (interruption with domestic gas supply not 'loss or damage').
[3]   *Section 209(2)*.
[4]   *Section 209(4)*.
[5]   See *section 209(3)(b)*; see also *per* Lord Hoffman in *Transco v Stockport MBC [2004] 1 All ER 589* at para 42, pointing out that in consequence it would have been ironic if the claimant in that case had been permitted to succeed under the rule in *Rylands v Fletcher*.

New Roads and Street Works Act 1991

[13.46]   Another provision which gives rise to strict liability for escapes, but only in favour of a specially defined class of plaintiffs, is *section 82* of the *New Roads and Street Works Act 1991*. Highway authorities, and those in whom streets, bridges and sewers are vested[1], are entitled to compensation from the undertakers responsible when they suffer damage to their roads, bridges or drains due, in the words of *section 82(2)*, to:

'any explosion, ignition, discharge or other event occurring to gas, electricity, water or any other thing required for the purposes of a supply or service … '

Section 82(3) provides that the liability of the undertaker responsible for the supply or service arises:

'(a)   whether or not the damage or loss is attributable to negligence on his part or on the part of any person for whom he is responsible, and

(b)   notwithstanding that he is acting in pursuance of a statutory duty'.

The undertaker will, however, escape liability if the damage was caused by the negligence of a third party for which it was not responsible[2].

[1]   See the *New Roads and Street Works Act 1991, ss 49(6)* and *89(3)*.
[2]   *Section 82(4)*.

Relationship between the provisions

[13.47]   Although liability under *section 82* of the *New Roads and Street Works Act 1991* does not exonerate the undertaker from any other liability to which it may be subject[1], it does operate, as far as *water* undertakers are concerned, to preclude liability under *section 209* of the *Water Industry Act 1991*: since those entitled to compensation under *section 82* are excluded from the scope of *section 209*[2].

¹   *Section 82(6).*
²   See the *Water Industry Act 1991, s 209(3)(d)*.

Animals Act 1971

[13.48] In certain circumstances strict liability is imposed for damage caused by animals. The ancient common law in this area was superseded by the *Animals Act 1971*. Unfortunately the drafting of the Act has given rise to considerable difficulty in determining the precise scope of the liability. One sub-section in particular has given rise to a series of conflicting decisions and a recent bare majority decision of the House of Lords[1]. The whole topic is one upon which specialist works should be consulted[2].

¹   See *Mirvahedy v Henley [2003] 2 All ER 401*, construing the *Animals Act 1971 s 2(2)*.
²   See North *The Modern Law of Animals* (1972).

E Role of foreseeability

Remoteness of damage in 'nuisance'

[13.49] In a familiar passage from the judgment of the Judicial Committee of the Privy Council in *Overseas Tankship (UK) Ltd v Miller SS Co Pty, The Wagon Mound (No 2)*[1], delivered by Lord Reid and quoted in a later chapter[2], it was said of liability in nuisance that 'although negligence may not be necessary, fault of some kind is almost always necessary and fault generally involves foreseeability'. It will be recalled that in this case the defendants were held liable in negligence and nuisance[3] for damage caused when oil, carelessly discharged from their ship into Sydney Harbour, was foreseeably ignited by hot metal from oxy-acetylene welding taking place nearby[4]. In the fire which ensued, ships belonging to the plaintiffs were extensively damaged. The branch of nuisance upon which the plaintiffs relied was public nuisance since the case was, in the words once more of Lord Reid, 'one of creating a danger to persons or property in navigable waters (equivalent to the highway)'.

¹   *[1967] 1 AC 617 at 639E–F, [1966] 2 All ER 709 at 716F.*
²   See CHAPTER 14 below.
³   Somewhat confusingly the actual order of the Board *allowed* the appeal of the defendants against a judgment in the court below which had held them liable for nuisance; but this merely reflected an agreement between opposing counsel as to how the various points arising on the appeal should be argued, and does not affect the proposition that liability in nuisance against the defendants had been established: see a helpful note by L H Hoffman (subsequently Lord Hoffman) in (1967) 83 LQR 13.
⁴   In earlier litigation against the same defendants the same fire had been held to have been unforeseeable: see *Overseas Tankship (UK) v Morts Dock and Engineering Co, The Wagon Mound [1961] AC 388, [1961] 1 All ER 404*, discussed in CHAPTER 3 above. But the plaintiffs in that case had been different and 'the evidence led was substantially different': see *per* Lord Reid in *[1967] 1 AC 617 at 640, [1966] 2 All ER 709 at 717.*

Public nuisance

[13.50] Most of the cases cited by the Board in their judgment therefore concerned public nuisance[1], and the Board's assertion that liability in *this* area is similar to that in negligence is appropriate. Where no overlap with private nuisance is involved, public nuisance represents little more than an anomalous intrusion into a field more appropriately governed by negligence[2].

¹   The cases were: *Benjamin v Storr (1874) LR 9 CP 400, 43 LJCP 162*; *Sharp v Powell (1872) LR 7 CP 253, 41 LJCP 95*; *Pearson v Cox (1877) 2 CPD 369, 36 LT 495*; *Clark v Chambers (1878) 3 QBD 327, 47 LJQB 427*; *Harrold v Watney [1898] 2 QB 320, 67 LJQB 771*; *Dollman v A & S Hillman Ltd [1941] 1 All ER 355*; *Bolton v Stone [1951] AC 850, [1951] 1 All ER 1078*.
²   Cf Newark 'The Boundaries of Nuisance' (1949) 65 LQR 480. The burden of proof in public nuisance does, however, appear to differ from that in negligence. See, generally, CHAPTER 14 below.

Private nuisance and intentional activities

[13.51]   Although *The Wagon Mound (No 2)* was a case of public nuisance it has been treated, not least by the House of Lords in *Cambridge Water Co Ltd v Eastern Counties Leather plc*[1], as laying down general propositions regarding the relevance of foreseeability in the tort of nuisance as a whole. This is notwithstanding that only one private nuisance case is referred to, briefly and without discussion, in the judgment[2]. Moreover, in the most common type of private nuisance case, a dispute surrounding the pursuit by the defendant on his land of an intentional activity, foreseeability will rarely be an issue. The claimant will usually be seeking an injunction rather than damages and the problem will be one of balancing the conflicting interests of the neighbours[3]. This point is indeed made in the judgment of the Board itself in *The Wagon Mound (No 2)* as follows[4]:

> 'Nuisance is a term used to cover a wide variety of tortious acts or omissions and in many negligence in the narrow sense is not essential. An occupier may incur liability for the emission of noxious fumes or noise although he has used the utmost care in building and using his premises. The amount of fumes or noise which he can lawfully emit is a question of degree and he or his advisors may have miscalculated what can be justified'.

In a similar vein Lord Goff himself observed in *Cambridge Water Co Ltd v Eastern Counties Leather plc* that 'we must be on our guard, when considering liability for damages in nuisance, not to draw inapposite conclusions from cases concerned only with a claim for an injunction'[5].

¹   *[1994] 2 AC 264, [1994] 1 All ER 53*.
²   See the reference to *Sedleigh-Denfield v O'Callaghan [1940] AC 880, [1940] 3 All ER 349* in *[1967] 1 AC 617* at 639F, *[1966] 2 All ER 709* at 716G.
³   See CHAPTER 11 above.
⁴   *[1967] 1 AC 617* at 639C–D, *[1966] 2 All ER 709* at 716D–E.
⁵   *[1994] 2 AC 264* at 300, *[1994] 1 All ER 53* at 71.

Claims for compensation

[13.52]   Where the claimant has suffered quantifiable loss, however, for which he seeks compensation, *The Wagon Mound (No 2)*, as interpreted and affirmed by the House of Lords in *Cambridge Water Co Ltd v Eastern Counties Leather plc*[1], decides that a defendant will not be liable in nuisance where an unforeseeable occurrence causes damage to result from an otherwise unobjectionable activity from which harm could not normally have been anticipated[2]. This principle was applied by the Court of Appeal in *Savage v Fairclough*[3]. The defendants' pig-farming activities, despite being properly conducted by the standards of the time, contaminated a nearby spring from which the claimants drew their drinking water[4]. The defendants were held not to be liable for the pollution since it had not been foreseeable. Nevertheless the limitation on liability will only apply where the relevant *kind* of interference is unforeseeable. The defendant will still be liable for an unforeseeable increase in the *extent* of a foreseeable type of interference[5].

1   See below.
2   In this respect *The Wagon Mound (No 2)* may be regarded as resolving an ambiguity in the speeches of the House of Lords in *Sedleigh-Denfield v O'Callaghan* which might be interpreted as favouring a wider liability: see Buxton 'The Negligent Nuisance' (1966) 8 Malaya LR 1 at 12–15, and the same writer's 'Nuisance and Negligence Again' (1966) 29 MLR 676 at 679. Cf *Humphries v Cousins (1877) 2 CPD 239, 46 LJQB 438.*
3   *[2000] Env LR 183.*
4   See also *Arscott v The Coal Authority [2004] EWCA Civ 892* (harm not foreseeable if predictable only with sophisticated computer technology not available at the relevant time).
5   Cf *Hughes v Lord Advocate [1963] AC 837, [1963] 1 All ER 705.* See also Dias 'Trouble on Oiled Waters' (1967) CLJ 62 at 81.

Remoteness under Rylands v Fletcher

[13.53]   Despite its similarity to cases of continuing or intentional nuisance the situation in *Rylands v Fletcher* differed from the majority of such cases in that it concerned an action for damages rather than an injunction. In the law of nuisance itself notions of fault become more prominent where a claimant seeks compensation rather than merely the cessation of an offensive activity[1], and the role of fault in *Rylands v Fletcher* cases was authoritatively expounded by the House of Lords in *Cambridge Water Co Ltd v Eastern Counties Leather plc*[2]. The defendants repeatedly allowed solvent from their manufacturing process to drip on to the concrete floor of their premises. They assumed that the spillage was harmless and had no reason to believe otherwise. Unfortunately, many years later, it became apparent that the solvent was able to seep through the concrete into the floor below and thereby contaminate underground percolating water, which was used by the plaintiffs to provide part of the public water supply. The House of Lords held that the defendants were not liable.

1   See above CHAPTER 11.
2   *[1994] 2 AC 264, [1994] 1 All ER 53.* See also *Ellison v Ministry of Defence (1996) 81 BLR 101*; *Savage v Fairclough [2000] Env LR 183, CA.*

Need for foreseeability

[13.54]   Lord Goff, with whose speech the other members of the House simply agreed, having observed that 'the recovery of damages in private nuisance depends on foreseeability by the defendant of the relevant type of damage'[1], concluded that 'it would appear logical to extend the same requirement to liability under the rule in *Rylands v Fletcher*'[2]. Their Lordships took the view that if anomaly is to be avoided any generalised extension of the rule, based on concepts such as liability for 'ultra-hazardous operations', could only be achieved by the legislature[3], if at all[4].

1   *[1994] 2 AC 264* at 304. Lord Goff cited *The Wagon Mound (No 2) [1967] 1 AC 617* in support of this proposition, see further CHAPTER 14 below.
2   Earlier cases which appeared to be inconsistent with the foreseeability requirement were disapproved or distinguished: in particular *Humphries v Cousins (1877) 2 CPD 239, [1874–80] All ER Rep 313*; *West v Bristol Tramways Co [1908] 2 KB 14, [1908–10] All ER Rep 215*; *Rainham Chemical Works Ltd v Belvedere Fish Guano Co Ltd [1921] 2 AC 465, [1921] All ER Rep 48.*

³ 'If such liability is imposed by statute, the relevant activities can be identified, and those concerned can know where they stand. Furthermore, statute can where appropriate lay down precise criteria establishing the incidence and scope of such liability' *per* Lord Goff *[1994] 2 AC 264 at 305, [1994] 1 All ER* 53 at 76. See also *per* Lord Bingham in *Transco v Stockport Metropolitan BC [2004] 1 All ER 589* at para 7. Cf the American Law Institute's *Restatement of Torts* (2d) vol 3 (1977) para 519.

⁴ Cf Law Commission Report no 32, 'Civil Liability for Dangerous Things and Activities' paras 14–16. A much more radical approach has been adopted in India where the Bhopal disaster prompted the Supreme Court to embrace a doctrine of generalised liability for hazardous activities, free from the limitations on the scope of *Rylands v Fletcher*. See *Mehta v Union of India (1987) 1 SCC 395*: 'We are of the view that an enterprise which is engaged in a hazardous or inherently dangerous industry which poses a potential threat to the health and safety of the persons working in the factory and residing in the surrounding areas owes an absolute and non-delegable duty to the community to ensure that no harm results to anyone on account of [the] hazardous or inherently dangerous nature of the activity which it has undertaken', *per* Bhagwati CJ at 421.

Absence of fault

[13.55] The House also considered, however, that the rule, as it stands, still differs from liability in negligence, in so far as absence of fault with respect to the occurrence of the actual escape should not *ipso facto* constitute a defence. Lord Goff supported his reasoning with an analysis of the judgment of Blackburn J in *Rylands v Fletcher* itself, from which he concluded that[1]:

> 'The general tenor … is … that knowledge, or at least foreseeability of the risk, is a prerequisite of the recovery of damages under the principle; but … the principle is one of strict liability in the sense that the defendant may be held liable notwithstanding that he has exercised all due care to prevent the escape from occurring'.

¹ *[1994] 2 AC 264 at 302, [1994] 1 All ER 53 at 73.*

Confirmation in Transco

[13.56] The approach adopted by the House of Lords in *Cambridge Water Co Ltd v Eastern Counties Leather plc,* towards the relationship between any escape and the resulting damage, was confirmed by the House itself in its subsequent examination of the rule in *Transco v Stockport Metropolitan BC*[1]. Lord Hobhouse of Woodborough said[2]:

> 'It is … the creation of a recognisable risk to other landowners which is an essential constituent of the tort and the liability of the defendant. But, once such a risk has been created, the liability for the foreseeable consequences of failure to control and confine it is strict'.

¹ *[2004] 1 All ER 589.*
² See *[2004] 1 All ER 589* at para 64. See also *per* Lord Hoffman at para 33, commenting that Lord Goff's speech in *Cambridge Water* 'repays close attention'.

F Nuisance and rights of support

Land

[13.57] At common law a landowner is entitled to have his land supported by the land of his neighbour; he is therefore entitled to complain if positive steps, on the part of the latter, result in his land being let down. There is, however, no right of action unless and *until* appreciable damage is caused[1]. It was formerly the law that a landowner could not complain if the loss of support resulted not from anything positive *done* by the defendant, but from the latter's mere failure to protect his neighbour's land. There was therefore no cause of action if the subsidence was caused by natural forces operating on the defendant's land[2]. The law was, however, changed by the important decision of the Court of Appeal in *Holbeck Hall Hotel v Scarborough Borough Council*[3]. In this case the defendants' land subsided, thereby withdrawing support from the claimant's neighbouring land and causing his hotel to collapse. The Court of Appeal held, applying the principles developed in the 'natural' nuisance cases of *Goldman v Hargrave*[4] and *Leakey v National Trust for Places of Historic Interest or Natural Beauty*[5], that a landowner *could* be liable for *omitting* to take measures which would have prevented subsidence occurring to his own land, with consequent loss of support to that of his neighbour. Stuart-Smith LJ said[6]:

> ' ... it is difficult to see what difference there is in principle between a danger caused by loss of support on the defendant's land and any other hazard or nuisance there which affects the claimant's use and enjoyment of land. Encroachment is simply one form of nuisance; interference causing physical damage to the neighbour's land and building as a result of activities on the defendant's land is another form of nuisance. There seems no reason why, where the defendant does not create the nuisance, but the question is whether he had adopted or continued it, different principles should apply to one kind of nuisance rather than another'.

1   See *Midland Bank v Bardgrove Property Services [1991] 2 EGLR 283* in which the authorities are fully reviewed by the Court of Appeal.
2   Cf *Phipps v Pears [1965] 1 QB 76, [1964] 2 All ER 35*. See also *Rouse v Gravelworks [1940] 1 KB 489, [1940] 1 All ER 26*.
3   *[2000] 2 All ER 705*. See also *Rees v Skerrett [2001] 1 WLR 1541* (buildings), discussed below at para [13.61].
4   *[1967] 1 AC 645, [1966] 2 All ER 989, PC.*
5   *[1980] QB 485, [1980] 1 All ER 17*. See earlier in this chapter, and also CHAPTER 11 above.
6   See *[2000] 2 All ER 705* at para 35.

Negligence

[13.58]   Since the *Goldman* and *Leakey* principles are based on a modified form of negligence, however, it follows that there will be no liability if the possibility of subsidence was not reasonably detectable by the defendant. On this ground the actual claim in the *Holbeck Hall Hotel* case failed on the facts: 'liability only arises', observed Stuart-Smith LJ[1], 'if there is negligence, the duty to abate the nuisance arises from the knowledge of the hazard that will affect his neighbour'.

1   See *[2000] 2 All ER 705* at para 35

Minerals

[13.59]   The right of support itself is both lateral and vertical, so that relief may be obtained both against the owner of adjoining land and against the owner of minerals beneath the surface of the claimant's land if his land is caused to subside by their removal[1]. It needs to be remembered, however, that according to principles confirmed as recently as 1987, a landowner has no right to prevent the removal of subterranean water which flows beneath his land in undefined channels, and therefore has no cause of action if its removal by a neighbouring landowner causes subsidence². Nevertheless, in the light of *Holbeck Hall Hotel v Scarborough Borough Council* it is open to argument whether landowners will continue to enjoy immunity from liability for clearly foreseeable harm even in subterranean water cases. But assuming that the immunity has survived, difficult questions of fact may arise as to whether what has been removed is liquid, and therefore governed by the rule negating liability for the removal of water, or solid in which case the plaintiff is entitled to protection. In *Jordeson v Sutton, Southcoates and Drypool Gas Co*³ the defendants drained a bed of running silt which ran underneath the plaintiff's land as well as their own. The plaintiff's land collapsed as a result. By a majority the Court of Appeal held that the plaintiff had a good cause of action for loss of support. Vaughan Williams LJ dissented on the facts holding that the silt was really muddy water and that the plaintiff should therefore fail⁴.

¹ *Humphries v Brogden (1850) 12 QB 739*. On subsidence caused by coal mining, see the *Coal Mining Subsidence Act 1991*.
² See *Stephens v Anglian Water Authority [1987] 3 All ER 379, [1987] 1 WLR 1381*; *Chasemore v Richards (1859) 7 HL Cas 349, 29 LJ Ex 81*; *Langbrook Properties v Surrey County Council [1969] 3 All ER 1424, [1970] 1 WLR 161*; *Thomas v Gulf Oil Refining Ltd (1979) 123 Sol Jo 787*. See also *Popplewell v Hodkinson (1869) LR 4 Exch 248, 38 LJ Ex 126*; *Salt Union Ltd v Brunner, Mond & Co [1906] 2 KB 822, 76 LJKB 55*.
³ *[1899] 2 Ch 217, 68 LJ Ch 457*.
⁴ The majority decision was applied in *Lotus Ltd v British Soda Co Ltd [1972] Ch 123, [1971] 1 All ER 265*. See also *Trinidad Asphalt Co v Ambard [1899] AC 594, 68 LJ PC 114*. The *Brine Pumping (Compensation for Subsidence) Act 1891*, provides for the payment of compensation to owners whose property suffers as a result of subsidence caused by the pumping of brine.

Buildings

[13.60] There is no right of support at common law for *buildings*, as distinct from the land itself. Such a right can, however, be acquired as an *easement*¹. This was settled, after some uncertainty, by the House of Lords in the leading case of *Dalton v Angus*². The easement can be for support by adjoining land or by another building³. As far as the law of easements is concerned in isolation, in accordance with general principles the owner of the dominant tenement is only protected against the taking of positive measures by the servient owner which cause the loss of support; it follows that protection against mere neglect, such as failure to repair, is not available on that basis⁴.

¹ For full treatment see *Gale on Easements*, 17th edn, 2002 (Gaunt and Morgan eds); Jackson, *The Law of Easements and Profits* (London, 1978) Ch 10.
² *(1881) 6 App Cas 740, 50 LJQB 689*.
³ See Bodkin 'Rights of Support for Buildings and Flats' (1962) 26 Conv (NS) 210.
⁴ See *Jones v Pritchard [1908] 1 Ch 630, 77 LJ Ch 405*; *Sack v Jones [1925] Ch 235, 94 LJ Ch 229*; *Macpherson v London Passenger Transport Board (1946) 175 LT 279*. Cf *Saint v Jenner [1973] Ch 275, [1973] 1 All ER 127*.

Liability extended

[13.61] Recent developments in the law of nuisance and negligence have, however, significantly extended the rights and duties of landowners in this area beyond those conferred and imposed by the law of easements. In *Rees v Skerrett*¹ the claimant's house adjoined that of the defendant, which was demolished. The claimant suffered some damage as a result of the loss of support, but claimed *in addition* for damage caused by exposure to the weather; he contended that the defendant had been under an obligation to take measures to protect the claimant's property against this foreseeable consequence of the demolition, even though it was not a consequence of the loss of *support*[2]. The Court of Appeal held that this claim would succeed[3]. The law of easements now had to be seen in the context of broader common law developments. Waller LJ referred to *Leakey v National Trust for Places of Historic Interest or Natural Beauty* and said[4]:

> 'If someone can owe a duty to take reasonable steps to prevent damage to his neighbour's property from something naturally on his land ... it would seem strange that he should not owe some duty when he pulls down the house which he appreciates protect the wall of the neighbouring house'.

[1]   *[2001] 1 WLR 1541.*
[2]   Cf *Phipps v Pears [1965] 1 QB 76, [1964] 2 All ER 35.*
[3]   See also *Bradburn v Lindsay [1983] 2 All ER 408.*
[4]   See *[2001] 1 WLR 1541* at para 42. See also *per* Lloyd J at paras 33 and 36.

Chapter 14

Negligence and public nuisance

A Nature and scope of public nuisance

Introduction

[14.01] In one respect the relationship between negligence and 'public' nuisance is particularly close and sensitive. This is because, in contrast with private nuisance[1], it appears to have been long accepted that damages for personal injury are recoverable in public nuisance. In so far as 'fault' may not need to be proved in nuisance cases, at any rate to precisely the same extent as in negligence, the question arises as to whether it is still legitimate to permit claimants fortuitously able to rely upon public nuisance to escape the requirements of the law of negligence, when those requirements have to be satisfied by the great majority of those seeking compensation for personal injury. In *Hunter v Canary Wharf* Lord Goff of Chieveley said[2]:

> 'I wish to draw attention to the fact that although, in the past, damages for personal injury have been recovered at least in actions of public nuisance, there is now developing a school of thought that the appropriate remedy for such claims as these should lie in our fully developed law of negligence, and that personal injury claims should be altogether excluded from the domain of nuisance'.

Nevertheless, the authorities which favour the recovery of such compensation in public nuisance have yet to be overruled, and it remains necessary to examine the law on public nuisance generally, albeit with its relationship with the modern law of negligence very much in mind.

---

[1] See *Hunter v Canary Wharf [1997] AC 655, [1996] 1 All ER 482, HL*, and CHAPTER 11 above.
[2] See *[1996] 1 All ER 482* at 438. See also the observations of the same law lord in *Cambridge Water v Eastern Counties Leather [1994] 1 All ER 53* at 72, HL.

Civil actions and criminal proceedings

[14.02] A public nuisance is a criminal offence[1] at common law[2] and, as such, may be made the subject of a civil action for an injunction, brought by the Attorney-General, in addition to criminal proceedings[3]. A private nuisance, on the other hand, is merely a tort. A private individual can, however, bring an action in tort for damages or an injunction, in respect of a public nuisance, if he can show that he has suffered 'special damage' over and above that suffered by other members of the public affected by the nuisance. In the absence of such damage he is powerless to intervene unless he can persuade the Attorney-General to bring a relator action[4].

1   See *R v Goldstein* [2004] 2 All ER 589. See, generally, J R Spencer 'Public Nuisance – A Critical Examination' [1989] 48 CLJ 55.
2   If it is sought to hold a landowner criminally liable, on the ground that he permitted a third party to use the land for an activity amounting to a nuisance, the degree of knowledge which has to be shown on the defendant's part is the same as that in tort for private nuisance, ie it is sufficient that he *ought* to have known of what was likely to occur, *actual* knowledge is *not* required notwithstanding that the liability is criminal: *R v Shorrock* [1993] 3 All ER 917, CA applying *Sedleigh-Denfield v O'Callaghan* [1940] AC 880, [1940] 3 All ER 349, HL.
3   Cf *Gouriet v Union of Post Office Workers* [1978] AC 435, [1977] 3 All ER 70.
4   Local authorities were formerly in the same position as private individuals in this respect but see now the *Local Government Act 1972, s 221(1)(a)* discussed in CHAPTER 29 below.

Two categories

[14.03]   Public nuisances may be divided into two categories. The first category overlaps with private nuisance and consists of those cases which satisfy the require-ments of that tort, but affect a much larger number of people than is usual in a private nuisance situation. The second category consists of cases which involve interference with the safety or convenience of members of the public generally, but do not satisfy the basic requirement for an action in private nuisance of interference with an individual's enjoyment of his own *land*[1]. The majority of cases in the second category concern use of the highway, but the concept has also proved from criminal cases to be wide enough to include such varied situations as exposing unfit food for sale[2] and making bomb-hoaxes[3]. A recent, and somewhat unusual, example of a highway case is *Wandsworth LBC v Railtrack plc*[4], in which the defendant railway company was held liable in public nuisance for failing to prevent the fouling of a public footpath, underneath one of its railway bridges, caused by droppings from roosting pigeons.

1   See CHAPTER 11 above.
2   See *Shillito v Thompson (1875) 1 QBD 12, 45 LJMC 18*.
3   See *R v Madden [1975] 3 All ER 155* at 157h. See also *R v Goldstein [2004] 2 All ER 589* (sending salt through the post intending that the recipient should believe it was anthrax).
4   *[2002] QB 756*.

Crime and negligence

[14.04]   The existence of the second category, enabling a tort action for nuisance to be added to criminal sanctions for harming the public and, where one exists, to an existing civil action for negligence, is probably best seen as the anomalous result of an historical accident[1].

1   See Newark 'The Boundaries of Nuisance' (1949) 65 LQR 480. See also J R Spencer 'Public Nuisance – A Critical Examination' [1989] 48 CLJ 55.

Private nuisance situations affecting large numbers

[14.05]   The leading case on public nuisances falling within this category is *A-G v PYA Quarries*[1]. Blasting from the defendant's quarry caused vibration, dust, splinters and noise to affect a wide area. At the instance of the local authority the Attorney-General sought an injunction, which was granted. On appeal the defendants argued that public nuisance proceedings brought by the Attorney-General had been inappropriate on the ground that the nuisance was only a private nuisance, and one in which those living nearby should have been confined to the remedy of damages at common law. This argument failed. Denning LJ said[2]:

'... I decline to answer the question how many people are necessary to make up Her Majesty's subjects generally. I prefer to look to the reason of the thing and to say that a public nuisance is a nuisance which is so widespread in its range or so indiscriminate in its effect that it would not be reasonable to expect one person to take proceedings on his own responsibility to put a stop to it, but that it should be taken on the responsibility of the community at large'.

On the other hand in the old case of *R v Lloyd*[3] an indictment for public nuisance failed when the inhabitants of three chambers in Clifford's Inn complained that noise made by the defendant in his trade disturbed them at their work. It was held that an indictment will not lie for that which is a nuisance only to a few inhabitants of a particular place; if what had occurred was a nuisance at all it was a private nuisance only[4].

1 *[1957] 2 QB 169, [1957] 1 All ER 894.*
2 *[1957] 2 QB 169 at 190–191, [1957] 1 All ER 894 at 908D–E.*
3 *(1802) 4 Esp 200.*
4 Cf *R v Webb (1848) 2 Car & Kir 933; R v Madden [1975] 3 All ER 155, [1975] 1 WLR 1379.*

Successful claims

[14.06] Cases in which proceedings for public nuisances in this category have succeeded include, in addition to quarry blasting[1], the emission of noxious smells from a chicken-processing factory[2], the holding of a pop-festival[3], the storage of large quantities of inflammable material[4], and allowing the deposit of refuse and filth in a densely populated part of London[5]. In a number of cases in which plaintiffs have recovered for interference with the enjoyment of their land caused by the defendant's use of the highway, the court has indicated that the cause of action could be regarded as being in either public or private nuisance[6]. It is clear that normal use of the highway which would otherwise be perfectly lawful is capable of giving rise to a public nuisance, eg where heavy lorries make frequent use throughout the night of streets adjoined by houses[7].

1 See *A-G v PYA Quarries*, above at para [14.05].
2 *Shoreham-By-Sea UDC v Dolphin Canadian Proteins (1972) 71 LGR 261.* See also *A-G v Cole & Son [1901] 1 Ch 205, 70 LJ Ch 148.*
3 *A-G for Ontario v Orange Productions Ltd (1971) 21 DLR (3d) 257.* See also *A-G v Stone (1895) 60 JP 168, 12 TLR 76; R v Moore (1832) 3 B & Ad 184.* The holding of 'acid house parties' has resulted in a number of criminal convictions for public nuisance: see eg *R v Shorrock [1993] 3 All ER 917; R v Ruffell (1992) 13 Cr App R(S) 204; R v Taylor (1991) 13 Cr App R(S) 466.*
4 *R v Lister and Biggs (1857) Dears & B 209, 26 LJMC 196.* See also *R v Taylor (1742) 2 Stra 1167; R v Chilworth Gunpowder Co Ltd (1888) 4 TLR 557.*
5 *A-G v Tod Heatley [1897] 1 Ch 560, 66 LJ Ch 275.*
6 *Fritz v Hobson (1880) 14 Ch D 542, 49 LJ Ch 321; Barber v Penley [1893] 2 Ch 447, 62 LJ Ch 623; Campbell v Paddington Corpn [1911] 1 KB 869,* per Avory J at 874; *Halsey v Esso Petroleum Co Ltd [1961] 2 All ER 145* at 157C–159A, *[1961] 1 WLR 683* at 699–701. See also *Dwyer v Mansfield [1946] 2 All ER 247,* per Atkinson J at 249: 'It really does not matter for the purposes of this case whether you regard it as a public nuisance or a private nuisance'. Cf the judgment of Devlin J in *Southport Corpn v Esso Petroleum Co Ltd [1954] 2 QB 182, [1954] 2 All ER 561,* discussed in CHAPTER 11 above.
7 See *Gillingam Borough Council v Medway (Chatham) Dock Co Ltd [1993] QB 343, [1992] 3 All ER 923* (action failed on other grounds). See also *Halsey v Esso Petroleum Co Ltd [1961] 1 WLR 683.*

Nuisances affecting the highway[1]

Origins

[14.07] 'The Law of England', said Denning LJ in *Mint v Good*, 'has always taken particular care to protect those who use a highway'. For several centuries part of this protection has been accorded by the law of nuisance, which deals both with obstructions to the highway and the creation of dangerous situations upon it[3]. Indeed it will be evident that these two types of case will often overlap[4]. A confusion between *easements* entitling one landowner to cross another's land, and the right of everyone to use the public highway, seems to have been responsible for this extension into a wider field of a kind of tortious liability really appropriate only for interference with the enjoyment of land[5]. As Professor Newark wrote:

> 'Interference with a private right of way over another's tenement was undoubtedly nuisance. Interference with the public's right of way along a highway was something different: it was a purpresture, an unlawful encroachment against the king, and enquirable of by the king's justices. But men were satisfied by the superficial resemblance between the blocking of a private way and the blocking of a public highway to term the latter a nuisance as well, and thus was born the public nuisance, that wide term which came to include obstructed highways, lotteries, unlicensed stage-plays, common scolds and a host of other rag ends of the law'[6].

As already observed at the beginning of this chapter, the expansive nature of public nuisance is also reflected in the readiness in the older cases to provide damages for personal injury; in contrast to the position in private nuisance where has been clear since the decision of the House of Lords in *Hunter v Canary Wharf*[7] that such damages cannot be awarded[8].

[1] For statutory provisions relating to interference with the highway see, generally, the *Highways Act 1980, Pt IX*, especially *section 149* (nuisances to the highway).
[2] *[1951] 1 KB 517* at 526, *[1950] 2 All ER 1159* at 1165A.
[3] On the difference between obstruction and danger, see *Trevett v Lee [1955] 1 All ER 406* at 409C–E, *[1955] 1 WLR 113* at 117, *per* Evershed MR (citing *Salmond on Torts*).
[4] Cf *Dymond v Pearce [1972] 1 QB 496* at 505E, *[1972] 1 All ER 1142* at 1149e, *per* Edmund Davies LJ: ' … it is by no means always possible to allocate the facts of a particular case to only one or other of these two categories'.
[5] See Newark 'The Boundaries of Nuisance' (1949) 65 LQR 480.
[6] Newark, above, at p 482.
[7] *[1997] AC 655, [1996] 1 All ER 482, HL*.
[8] See Newark, above, who traces the anomalous recovery of damages for personal injury in public nuisance back to an 'incautious obiter dictum' in a case decided in 1535, at pp 482–486.

Danger

[14.08] The majority of highway cases in public nuisance have concerned claims for personal injury caused by dangerous situations on the highway. Since most of them were decided at a time when the question whether fault, in the sense of negligence, should be a necessary condition for the recovery of damages for personal injury was not as controversial an issue as it is today, it is often unclear whether a negligence-based claim would have succeeded on the facts in any event. In *Dollman v A and S Hillman*[1] the plaintiff was awarded damages for injuries suffered when she slipped on a piece of fat which had escaped on to the highway from a butcher's shop owned by the defendants. A long line of cases involves collapse on to the highway from adjoining premises of such things as windows[2] and shutters[3], walls[4] and fences[5], and even snow[6]. In *Castle v St Augustine's Links Ltd*[7] a plaintiff who lost an eye when a golf-ball smashed the window of his car as he was driving along the road, was awarded damages in public nuisance. This case was distinguished on the facts in *Stone v Bolton*[8], where a passer-by was hit by a cricket ball, on the ground that an isolated occurrence did not constitute a 'state of affairs' such as was thought necessary to ground liability in public nuisance[9]. Balls had escaped from the golf course in the earlier case relatively frequently, whereas escapes from the cricket ground in question were rare. It has been judicially asserted, however, that 'an isolated act may amount to a public nuisance if it is done under such circumstances that the public right to condemn it should be vindicated'[10].

[1]   *[1941] 1 All ER 355.* See also *Almeroth v W E Chivers & Sons Ltd [1948] 1 All ER 53.*
[2]   *Leanse v Lord Egerton [1943] KB 323, [1943] 1 All ER 489.*
[3]   *Wilchick v Marks and Silverstone [1934] 2 KB 56, 103 LJKB 372.*
[4]   *Mint v Good [1951] 1 KB 517, [1950] 2 All ER 1159.* Cf *Bromley v Mercer [1922] 2 KB 126, 91 LJKB 577.*
[5]   *Harrold v Watney [1898] 2 QB 320, 67 LJQB 771.*
[6]   *Slater v Worthington's Cash Stores (1930) Ltd [1941] 1 KB 488, [1941] 3 All ER 28.*
[7]   *(1922) 38 TLR 615.*
[8]   *[1950] 1 KB 201, [1949] 2 All ER 851.*
[9]   This point was not considered in *[1951] AC 850, [1951] 1 All ER 1078.*
[10]   See *A-G v PYA Quarries [1957] 2 QB 169* at 192, *[1957] 1 All ER 894* at 909B, *per* Denning LJ. See also the same judge in *Southport Corpn v Esso Petroleum Co Ltd [1954] 2 QB 182* at 196, *[1954] 2 All ER 561* at 571A (not considered in *[1956] AC 218, [1955] 3 All ER 864*).

Obstruction

[14.09] Apart from operations such as road-works, carried out by a local authority, most cases of obstruction of the highway fall into one of two classes. Obstruction may occur as the result of an activity, either on the part of a landowner whose premises adjoin the highway or on the part of someone passing along it[1]. In either case it is a question of fact whether the obstruction amounts to a public nuisance[2]. Nevertheless situations involving obstruction by adjoining owners are approached on grounds more analogous to those in private nuisance cases, and such defendants are apt to be regarded in a more favourable light than those in situations involving the other type of obstruction. In *Harper v G N Haden & Sons*[3] the defendants erected scaffolding on the highway in order to make alterations to their upper floor premises. A temporary pavement and hand-rail were constructed for pedestrians but the plaintiff tradesman, whose customers had to negotiate the course thus created, claimed that his business had suffered as a result of the erection and sought damages on the ground of public nuisance. His claim failed. The obstruction was temporary and, in the circumstances, reasonable. Romer LJ said[4]:

'The law relating to the user of highways is in truth the law of give and take. Those who use them must in doing so have reasonable regard to the convenience and comfort of others, and must not themselves expect a degree of convenience and comfort only obtainable by disregarding that of other people. They must expect to be obstructed occasionally. It is the price they pay for the privilege of obstructing others'.

[1]   Siltation of a river causing interference with the right of navigation can constitute a public nuisance: see *Tate & Lyle Industries Ltd v Greater London Council [1983] 2 AC 509, [1983] 1 All ER 1159; Jan De Nul (UK) Ltd v AxA Royale Belge SA [2002] 1 All ER (Comm) 767* (reduced ferry service).

2   See *East Hertfordshire District Council v Isabel Hospice Trading Ltd [2001] JPL 597*, in which the authorities are reviewed by Jack Beatson QC (sitting as a Deputy High Court Judge).
3   *[1933] Ch 298, 102 LJ Ch 6. Cf Amalgamated Theatres Ltd v Charles S Luney Ltd [1962] NZLR 226.*
4   *[1933] Ch 298* at 320.

Reasonable use of the highway

[14.10]   This principle was applied in *Trevett v Lee*[1]. In this case the defendants, whose house was not connected to the mains water supply, laid a small garden hosepipe across the adjoining country road, which carried little traffic, in order to obtain water from a nearby source when the rain water upon which they normally relied ran out. The defendants endeavoured to maintain a lookout while the pipe was in place but, the plaintiff pedestrian nevertheless tripped over it and suffered injury. The defendants were not liable. The Court of Appeal held that, in the circumstances, the obstruction was a reasonable use of the highway by the defendants and did not constitute a public nuisance[2].

1   *[1955] 1 All ER 406, [1955] 1 WLR 113.* But cf the 'note of warning' sounded by Parker LJ at *[1955] 1 All ER 406* at 413E, *[1955] 1 WLR 113* at 123.
2   See also *Dwyer v Mansfield [1946] KB 437, [1946] 2 All ER 247,* cf *Farrell v John Mowlem & Co Ltd [1954] 1 Lloyd's Rep 437.*

Imposition of liability

[14.11]   If, however, an obstruction does amount to a nuisance, an order for its removal cannot be resisted on the ground that it was trivial[1]. Road users who allowed motor vehicles to be parked for long periods in such a way as to cause obstruction of the highway have incurred liability, and such an obstruction does not fail to qualify as a nuisance merely because it is partial and only narrows the road without blocking it altogether. In *Dymond v Pearce*[2] a majority of the Court of Appeal held that a lorry parked on a road which reduced the width of the carriageway from 24ft to 16ft, but did not stop traffic, was a public nuisance[3]. In *A-G v Gastonia Coaches Ltd*[4] an injunction was granted to restrain a public nuisance caused by the parking of the defendants' coaches. The carriageway was never completely blocked, and the nuisance occurred only at certain periods of the day, but it was enough that drivers were sometimes forced up on to the grass verge or obliged to wait while other vehicles reversed[5].

1   See *East Hertfordshire District Council v Isabel Hospice Trading Ltd [2001] JPL 597* (wheeled rubbish bin outside charity shop).
2   *[1972] 1 QB 496, [1972] 1 All ER 1142.* Cf *Ellwand v Fitzgerald [1999] CLY 4070.*
3   The plaintiff's action in fact failed but on other grounds.
4   *[1977] RTR 219.* See also *A-G v Brighton and Hove Co-op Supply Association [1900] 1 Ch 276, 69 LJ Ch 204.*
5   Cf *A-G v WH Smith & Sons (1910) 103 LT 96, 26 TLR 482.*

B Damages and liability

Special damage

Nature of special damage[1]

[14.12]   In *Benjamin v Storr*[2] Brett J said[3] that 'in order to entitle a person to maintain an action for damage caused by that which is a public nuisance, the damage must be particular, direct, and substantial'. The plaintiff kept a coffee-house in a narrow street near Covent Garden. The defendants carried on an extensive business as auctioneers in the same neighbourhood and their vans, which were being continually loaded and unloaded nearby, affected the flow of light to the plaintiff's shop so as to render the use of artificial light necessary throughout the day. Access to the shop was also obstructed by the defendants' horses and their smell made the plaintiff's premises uncomfortable. A verdict for the plaintiff, and an award of damages, was upheld. The situation in this case could have been regarded as one of private nuisance, since the plaintiff was complaining of an interference with the enjoyment of his land[4].

[1]   The meaning of this term in public nuisance is not to be confused with 'special damages' in for example negligence actions for personal injury. Some writers prefer to use the expression 'particular' damage in nuisance to avoid confusion: see *Fleming on Torts* (8th edn) pp 412 onwards. See also *Rose v Groves (1843) 5 Man & G 613* at 616; *Walsh v Ervin [1952] VLR 361* at 369. For general discussion of the principles underlying the recovery of damages in this area see Gilbert Kodilinye 'Public Nuisance and Particular Damage in the Modern Law' (1986) 6 L S 182.

[2]   *(1874) LR 9 CP 400, 43 LJCP 162.*

[3]   *(1874) LR 9 CP 400* at 407.

[4]   See above CHAPTER 11 of the handbook. On the nature of the relationship between the public right of passage along the highway and the private right of an adjacent owner to access to and from his premises see: *A-G v Thames Conservators (1862) 1 Hem & M 1, 1 New Rep 121*; *W H Chaplin & Co Ltd v Westminster Corpn [1901] 2 Ch 329.*

Danger of inconsistency

[14.13]   In cases which do not involve overlap of this kind with private nuisance, the courts are more reluctant to uphold claims of special damage. The possibility of such claims creates a danger that, by invoking for his benefit a breach of the criminal law, a claimant may recover damages in what is essentially a private matter, and in an unprincipled fashion inconsistent with limitations developed in the law of tort by negligence or private nuisance. It is therefore clear that in obstruction cases it is not enough for the claimant 'to show that he suffers the same inconvenience in the use of the highway as other people do'[1].

[1]   *Per* Brett J in *Benjamin v Storr (1874) LR 9 CP 400* at 406.

Special damage held to exist

[14.14]   A highway case in which a claim for special damage succeeded, however, is *Rose v Miles*[1]. The defendant wrongfully obstructed a public navigable creek. The plaintiff, who was navigating his barges along the creek, was obliged as a result to unload the barges and convey his goods overland. He was allowed to recover the considerable expense this caused him. Dampier J said[2] 'If this be not a particular damage, I scarcely know what is'. The same principle was applied much more recently in *Tate & Lyle Industries Ltd v Greater London Council*[3] by the House of Lords. In this case the defendants caused siltation to occur at a point on the River Thames where it obstructed the public right of navigation. As a result the plaintiffs were put to great expense in themselves dredging the river to prevent certain jetties, which they owned and operated for the purposes of their business, from becoming unusable. The plaintiffs contended successfully that the dredging costs constituted special damage in public nuisance[4].

[1]   *(1815) 4 M & S 101*. See also *Boyd v Great Northern Rly Co [1895] 2 IR 555; Smith v Wilson [1903] 2 IR 45.*

² *(1815) 4 M & S 101* at 103.
³ *[1983] 2 AC 509, [1983] 1 All ER 1159.*
⁴ See also *Jan De Nul (UK) Ltd v AxA Royale Belge SA [2002] 1 All ER (Comm) 767.*

Recovery denied

[14.15] On the other hand in *Winterbottom v Lord Derby*⁶¹ the plaintiff found a path in his neighbourhood, which he frequently used, obstructed. He claimed that he had suffered special damage by virtue of the delay involved in having to use another route and by removing the obstruction, which he had done himself. His claim failed. He had merely 'suffered an inconvenience common to all who happened to pass that way². Moreover in this case it was held that he could not create a valid claim by deliberately incurring expense in removing the obstruction³. If the highway has been closed by statutory order no action for nuisance will lie until the validity of the order has been successfully challenged by way of judicial review⁴.

¹ *(1867) LR 2 Exch 316, 36 LJ Ex 194.*
² *(1867) LR 2 Exch 316* at 322, *per* Kelly CB.
³ Cf *per* Lord Diplock (dissenting) in *Tate & Lyle Industries Ltd v Greater London Council [1983] 2 AC 509* at 547, *[1983] 1 All ER 1159* at 1178.
⁴ See *Great House at Sonning v Berkshire CC [1996] RTR 407, CA.*

Pecuniary loss

[14.16] Claims for special damage are often based on loss of profit in a trade or business¹. Of course in the law of negligence itself claims for economic loss, suffered in isolation from physical damage, are in general disallowed through fear of excessive and uncontrollable liability on defendants². It is significant that it was at one time doubted whether such claims could be maintained in public nuisance, at any rate if the nuisance involved was merely obstruction of the highway³. But it does now seem to be clear that economic loss can constitute special damage for this purpose⁴. Nevertheless, the requirement of 'particularity', intended to protect the defendant against a multiplicity of actions, may well be interpreted very literally in such cases to a claimant's detriment. In *Martin v LCC*⁵ a shopkeeper sued the defendant local authority for damages caused by loss of business at his shop when the road which gave access to it was obstructed by them. It so happened, however, that all the other shopkeepers in the vicinity were similarly affected by the obstruction and, although the claim failed on other grounds, Smith LJ doubted, obiter, whether the plaintiff could in any event have succeeded. He said⁶:

> 'I am strongly inclined to think that the damage alleged to have been suffered by the plaintiff, which is damage of the same nature and kind as everyone else in the street suffered through the road being blocked, is not of such a character as to give a cause of action. In the present case the same damage is suffered by all, though the consequences to each individual may be small or great according to the way in which the different owners and occupiers in the street happen to be carrying on business. Whether they be greengrocers, or fishmongers, or jewellers, or householders, the same kind of damage has been occasioned to them all'⁷.

¹ See *Iveson v Moore (1699) 1 Ld Raym 486, Carth 451; Wilkes v Hungerford Market (1835) 2 Bing NC 281, 2 Scott 446; Fritz v Hobson (1880) 14 Ch D 542, 49 LJ Ch 321; Martin v LCC (1899) 80 LT 866;*

Harper v G N Haden & Sons [1933] Ch 298, 102 LJ Ch 6; Smith v Warringah Shire Council [1962] NSWR 944. Cf *Tate & Lyle Industries Ltd v Greater London Council [1983] 2 AC 509, [1983] 1 All ER 1159.*
2 See above CHAPTER 5.
3 See *Ricket v Metropolitan Rly Co (1867) LR 2 HL 175* at 188 (Lord Chelmsford LC) and 199 (Lord Cranworth). See also *Wildtree Hotels v Harrow London BC [2000] 3 All ER 289, HL* (on the limited scope of compensation for injurious affection under *section 10* of the *Compulsory Purchase Act 1965*).
4 See *Blundy, Clark & Co Ltd v London and North Eastern Rly Co [1931] 2 KB 334, 100 LJKB 401.* See also *Amalgamated Theatres Ltd v Charles S Luney Ltd [1962] NZLR 226.* Cf *Gravesham Borough Council v British Railways Board [1978] Ch 379, [1978] 3 All ER 853.*
5 *(1899) 80 LT 866.*
6 *(1899) 80 LT* at 867.
7 Cf *Hickey v Electric Reduction Co of Canada Ltd (1970) 21 DLR (2d) 368 (Can).*

Preventing evasion of negligence rule

[14.17] Even in cases not involving use of the highway, a rigorous application of the concept of 'particularity' may commend itself to the court as a means of preventing evasion of the non-recovery rule in negligence[1]. If the situation is one in which a claim based on expense or loss of profit can be accepted, however, it is apparently not necessary for the claimant to prove actual figures providing he can show that it is inevitable that he will have suffered such damage[2].

1 See *Ball v Consolidated Rutile [1991] Qd 524*: 'It would be a quite unsatisfactory state of affairs if upon the same facts by pursuing an action for damages for public nuisance the plaintiffs were able to avoid satisfying the test of proximity and recover in nuisance damages for economic loss caused to them in their prawn fishing endeavours which would not be recoverable in negligence', *per* Ambrose J, at 546.
2 See *Smith v Wilson [1903] 2 IR 45.*

General inconvenience to the public

[14.18] Where the claimant is unable even to show that his suffering was pecuniary in character, or that he suffered damage measurable in pecuniary terms[1], it is very doubtful whether a claim for special damage in public nuisance can be maintained. Inconvenience to members of the public generally is the reason for holding something to be a public nuisance in the first place and it is therefore difficult to see how the suffering of such inconvenience by a particular individual, even if it is unusual in degree, can satisfy the requirement of special and particular damage[2]. Nevertheless in the Australian case of *Walsh v Ervin*[3], which concerned obstruction of the highway, it was held that 'delay and inconvenience of a substantial character ... so long as not merely similar in nature and extent to that in fact suffered by the rest of the public, may amount to sufficient damage, particular to the individual plaintiff'[4], notwithstanding the absence of any actual pecuniary loss. But the reasoning in this case is open to criticism[5], and probably does not represent English law[6].

1 Eg personal injury.
2 See Fridman 'The Definition of Particular Damage in Nuisance' (1951–53) 2 Annual Law Review (University of Western Australia) 490.
3 *[1952] VLR 361* (Sholl J).
4 *[1952] VLR* at 369.
5 The learned judge relied, inter alia, upon the two Irish cases of *Boyd v Great Northern Rly Co [1895] 2 IR 555* and *Smith v Wilson [1903] 2 IR 45*, but in both of these a degree of pecuniary loss appears to have been present even though no specific figures were proved. See, further, Fridman, cited above.
6 For academic advocacy of a wider scope for recoverable damage in public nuisance see Estey 'Public Nuisance and Standing to Sue' (1972) 10 Osgoode Hall LJ 563.

Injunction

[14.19] A claimant who is able to establish a valid claim on the ground of special damage in public nuisance is not necessarily limited to an action for damages as his remedy. In an appropriate case he can obtain an injunction, just as in private nuisance, without any need to invoke the assistance of the Attorney-General[1].

[1] *Spencer v London and Birmingham Rly Co (1836) 8 Sim 193, 1 Ry & Can Cas 159; Soltau v De Held (1851) 2 Sim NS 133, 21 LJ Ch 153*. In *Halsey v Esso Petroleum Co Ltd [1961] 2 All ER 145, [1961] 1 WLR 683*, Veale J was prepared to assume that noise created by lorries on the highway was a public nuisance for the purpose of awarding an injunction to the plaintiff who lived nearby. On injunctions see, generally, CHAPTER 29 below.

No exemplary damages

[14.20] In *AB v South West Water Services*[1] the Court of Appeal held that exemplary damages cannot be awarded for public nuisance[2]. The case arose out of a very serious pollution incident when a large quantity of aluminium sulphate was accidentally poured into the public water supply at Camelford in Cornwall, causing widespread anxiety among members of the local population as to the long-term effects upon their health. Reversing the judge below, who had held that an award of exemplary damages was possible in respect of the allegedly high-handed and inadequate response of the defendants after the initial accident, the court held that the situation did not fall within a recognised category of such damages[3]. The court also took the view that public nuisance was peculiarly inappropriate for such an award in view of the large number of potential claimants. Sir Thomas Bingham MR said[4]:

'... a public nuisance may lead to numerous complaints, which a private nuisance will not ... in the case of a public nuisance affecting hundreds or even thousands of plaintiffs, how can the court assess the sum of exemplary damages to be awarded to any one of them to punish or deter the defendant without knowing at the outset the number of successful plaintiffs and the approximate size of the total bill for exemplary damages which the defendant must meet?'.

[1] *[1993] QB 507, [1993] 1 All ER 609*; reversing *[1992] 4 All ER 574*.
[2] Such damages can apparently be awarded in *private* nuisance: see *Guppys (Bridport) Ltd v Brookling and James (1983) 14 HLR 1, [1984] 1 EGLR 29, CA*.
[3] See *Rookes v Barnard [1964] AC 1129* at 1221 onwards, *[1964] 1 All ER 367* at 407 onwards, *per* Lord Devlin. See also *Cassell & Co Ltd v Broome [1972] AC 1027, [1972] 1 All ER 801*. The Law Commission has put forward proposals for reform of this area of the law, see *Aggravated, Exemplary and Restitutionary Damages* (Law Com no 247) (1997).
[4] *[1993] QB 507* at 531, *[1993] 1 All ER 609* at 627.

C Relevance of fault

Standard of liability

[14.21] The question of whether a defendant has to be in some sense at fault, or even negligent, in order to be liable in public nuisance is surrounded with difficulty. In cases in which an injunction is sought it may be assumed that the position is as in private nuisance; the activity will normally be a continuing one and an inquiry narrowly focused upon mere carelessness is unlikely to be helpful[1]. In highway cases, and analogous situations giving rise to claims for personal injury or damage, the position is less clear. In *Farrell v John Mowlem & Co*[2], decided in 1954, the plaintiff sustained personal injuries when he tripped over a pipe which had been laid across the pavement by the defendants, who were undertaking certain works to a sewer under contract with the London County Council[3]. Devlin J held the defendants liable in public nuisance, and expressly rejected the suggestion that it was necessary for the plaintiff to prove negligence. He said[4]:

> 'I think the law still is that any person who actually creates a nuisance is liable for it and for the consequences which flow from it, whether he is negligent or not'[5].

In the half century or so since Devlin J decided this case, however, negligence concepts have become much more pervasive throughout the law of tort.

[1] See above CHAPTER 11.
[2] *[1954] 1 Lloyd's Rep 437.*
[3] Statutory authority was not pleaded: see *per* Devlin J in *[1954] 1 Lloyd's Rep 437.*
[4] *[1954] 1 Lloyd's Rep* 437 at 440.
[5] In *The Wagon Mound (No 2)* (see para [14.22] below) Lord Reid said of this passage that it was 'quite true' (*[1967] 1 AC* 617 at 638, *[1966] 2 All ER* 709 at 715), but went on to question, as being unsupported by the citation of any authority, the succeeding passage in the judgment of Devlin J which is as follows: ',... it is no answer to say, "I laid the pipe across the pavement but I did it quite carefully and I did not foresee and perhaps a reasonable man would not have foreseen that anybody would be likely to trip over it" '.

Wagon Mound (No 2)

[14.22] Thus a different approach was adopted in the well known case of *Overseas Tankship (UK) Ltd v Miller SS Co Pty, The Wagon Mound (No 2)*[1]. The chief engineer of the defendants' ship carelessly allowed oil to be discharged into navigable waters and thereby helped to cause a fire which extensively damaged the plaintiffs' ships. The case was treated as being analogous to one involving the creation of danger to persons or property on a highway,[2] and in holding the defendants liable in public nuisance the Judicial Committee of the Privy Council based its decision squarely upon the finding that the defendants' employees had been at fault. They should have foreseen the danger they were creating and taken steps to eliminate it. Lord Reid said[3] that although 'negligence is not an essential element in nuisance' nevertheless 'fault of some kind is almost always necessary and fault generally involves foreseeability'.

[1] *[1967] 1 AC 617, [1966] 2 All ER 709.*
[2] See *per* Lord Reid *[1967] 1 AC 617* at 639G, *[1966] 2 All ER 709* at 716G–H.
[3] *[1967] 1 AC* 617 at 639, *[1966] 2 All ER* 709 at 716.

Collision cases

[14.23] Similar remarks to those of Lord Reid were made in the earlier case of *Maitland v Raisbeck*[1]. The plaintiff in this case had collided with the rear of the defendants' lorry. The rear light of the lorry had gone out but it was assumed that this was for some reason not referable to any negligence on the part of the defendants. The Court of Appeal held the defendants not liable, and Lord Greene MR said that if a person in fact causes an obstruction to the highway but one which 'is in no way referable to his fault, it is wrong to suppose that *ipso facto* and immediately a nuisance is created'[2]. In the more recent case of *Dymond v Pearce*[3], however, which also concerned a collision on the highway, and which was decided since *The Wagon*

Mound (No 2), two members of the Court of Appeal were still prepared to contemplate a wider liability in public nuisance, for road accidents resulting from obstruction, than that in negligence. The matter did not arise for decision because the plaintiff's case failed on the ground of causation. His own carelessness in colliding with the defendants' stationary vehicle was held to be the sole cause of the accident[4]. Nevertheless Sachs LJ expressed himself as follows[5]:

> 'What would be the position if, even though the lorry driver had not been negligent in leaving the lorry as it was in fact left, yet there had occurred some unexpected supervening happening – such as an onset of heavy weather, sea mist or fog or, for instance, a sudden rear light failure (potent cause of fatalities) – which had so affected the situation that the lorry became the cause of an accident? Should the risk fall entirely on those using the highway properly? Or should some liability attach to the person at fault in creating a nuisance? It may well be that, as I am inclined to think, he who created the nuisance would be under a liability ... If he was thus liable, this might be the only class of case in which an action in nuisance by obstruction of the highway could succeed where one in negligence would fail'.

Stephenson LJ expressly agreed with these observations and said[6] that 'there may still be rare cases when an injured plaintiff's claim in nuisance may succeed although his claim in negligence fails.'

[1]   *[1944] KB 689, [1944] 2 All ER 272. Cf Ware v Garston Haulage Co Ltd [1944] 1 KB 30, [1943] 2 All ER 558.*
[2]   *[1944] KB 689 at 691–692, [1944] 2 All ER 272 at 273A–B. Applied in Parish v Judd [1960] 3 All ER 33, [1960] 1 WLR 867.*
[3]   *[1972] 1 QB 496, [1972] 1 All ER 1142.*
[4]   See also *Ellwand v Fitzgerald [1999] CLY 4070.*
[5]   *[1972] 1 QB 496 at 503D–G, [1972] 1 All ER 1142 at 1147f–h.*
[6]   *[1972] 1 QB 496 at 508F, [1972] 1 All ER 1142 at 1152b.*

Onus of proof

[14.24] It seems unlikely that the conflicting approaches apparently revealed by these dicta reflect any fundamental differences of opinion as to the substantive law. One possible solution to the problem of reconciling the cases is to be found in a dictum of Denning LJ in *Southport Corpn v Esso Petroleum Co Ltd*[1]. His Lordship said[2]:

> 'One of the principal differences between an action for a public nuisance and an action for negligence is the burden of proof. In an action for a public nuisance, once the nuisance is proved and the defendant is shown to have caused it, then the legal burden is shifted on to the defendant to justify or excuse himself'[3].

On this view, once an obstruction or dangerous situation has been created on the highway the person who caused it will be liable unless he can prove that what occurred did so without his fault. Thus in the case of a broken-down vehicle blocking the carriageway and causing an accident, the defendant would have to show that he had taken normal and prudent care of the vehicle, prior to the breakdown, so as to render the event which had occurred one for which he could not reasonably be regarded as blameworthy[4]. It can perhaps be argued that since by committing a *public* nuisance the defendant has committed not merely a tort, but also a crime jeopardising the convenience or safety of large numbers of people, a different burden of proof from ordinary negligence is legitimate. This argument is not without its attractions, even if the preservation of such a difference in one isolated area of civil liability is not easy to justify in principle.

1   *[1954] 2 QB 182, [1954] 2 All ER 561.*
2   *[1954] 2 QB 182* at 197, *[1954] 2 All ER 561* at 571F–G.
3   Cf *per* Sachs LJ in *Radstock Co-operative and Industrial Society v Norton- Radstock UDC [1968] Ch 605* at 633–634, *[1968] 2 All ER 59* at 71C–D (private nuisance). See also *Kraemers v A-G for Tasmania [1966] Tas SR 113.*
4   In *Parish v Judd [1960] 3 All ER 33, [1960] 1 WLR 867*, Edmund Davies J held that 'the unlit condition of a vehicle on a road raises a presumption of negligence against the car owner' but having heard evidence from the defendant's mechanic, who had serviced the vehicle shortly before the accident, held that this presumption was displaced on the facts of the case.

Liability for dangerous property adjoining the highway

[14.25]   The authorities on liability in public nuisance for premises or other property adjoining the highway are unclear as to the standard of liability which should be imposed. In the well-known nineteenth-century case of *Tarry v Ashton*[1], a gas lamp which was attached to the defendant's house, and overhung the pavement, fell off and injured the plaintiff as she was walking underneath. The defendant had employed a competent gas-fitter to repair the lamp some months before, but the Divisional Court held that this was no defence; the lamp was a 'nuisance to the highway', and the defendant was under a non-delegable duty to keep it in a safe condition. It seems to be clear from the judgments, however, that the state of the lamp was such that its dangerous condition would have been evident to the defendant if he had inspected it. Indeed Blackburn J expressly left open, as a 'point of considerable doubt', what the position would have been if the defect had been latent so that the defendant could not have known of it.

1   *(1876) 1 QBD 314.*

Wringe v Cohen

[14.26]   *Tarry v Ashton* was nevertheless treated in the difficult case of *Wringe v Cohen*[1] as authority for the proposition that structures abutting the highway, which become dangerous through disrepair, attract strict liability. In this case part of the defendant's premises, which were let to a tenant, collapsed and caused damage to the plaintiff's adjoining premises[2]. The case did not, therefore, directly concern the highway at all, and would really seem to have been a private nuisance case. Nevertheless the Court of Appeal, in holding the defendant liable, decided the case on the basis that when 'owing to want of repair, premises on a highway become dangerous and, therefore, a nuisance ... the occupier, or the owner if he has undertaken the duty of repair, is answerable whether he knew or ought to have known of the danger or not'[3]. The judgment of the Court of Appeal appears to have been influenced, at least in part, by a degree of confusion in the argument of counsel for the plaintiff[4] between the defendant landlord's contractual duty to his tenant to keep the premises in repair and his duty in tort, owed to third parties, to ensure that the premises did not constitute a danger[5]. Moreover, it is noteworthy, that according to the evidence in the case, the defendant's house had been visibly in defective repair for three years[6]. The appeal, which was from a county court decision in favour of the plaintiff, was therefore unattractive on the merits and was based solely on the ground that it had not been *proved* that the defendant *knew* of the state of disrepair. But if, as has been suggested above, the law puts the onus of *disproving* fault upon the *defendant* in public nuisance cases[7], in accordance with the view later expressed by Denning LJ in the *Southport Corpn* case, the appeal could have been disposed of on this ground.

1   *[1940] 1 KB 229, [1939] 4 All ER 241.*
2   Cf *St Anne's Well Brewery Co v Roberts (1928) 140 LT 1.*
3   *[1940] 1 KB 229 at 233, [1939] 4 All ER 241 at 243F–G, per* Atkinson J delivering the judgment of the court.
4   See *[1940] 1 KB 229 at 232.*
5   See Buxton 'Nuisance and Negligence Again' (1966) 29 MLR 676 at 679, note 28. Liability to all persons likely to be affected by defects is now imposed by statute upon landlords whose tenancies require them to repair: see the *Defective Premises Act 1972, s 4.* But this liability is based on fault and is not strict: *s 4(2).*
6   See *[1940] 1 KB 229.*
7   The Court of Appeal regarded *Wringe v Cohen* as a case of public nuisance, sed quaere. Cf *Bromley v Mercer [1922] 2 KB 126, 91 LJKB 577; Jacobs v LCC [1950] AC 361, [1950] 1 All ER 737.*

Authorities favouring fault based liability.

[14.27] Other cases have based liability for property in a dangerous condition adjoining the highway upon negligence. In *Barker v Herbert*[1] a three-year-old boy suffered an injury when he fell through a gap in the railings which were in front of the plaintiff's house. The gap had been made shortly before by boys playing football in the street. The Court of Appeal held that the owner, who did not live on the premises, could not reasonably have been expected to know of the defect in the short time that had elapsed, and the plaintiff's action failed[2]. Vaughan Williams LJ said:

> 'In my opinion there is no such absolute responsibility as that contended for imposed upon a person who has property adjoining a highway ... In my judgment there can be no liability upon the part of the possessor of land in such a case, unless it is shown that he himself, or some person for whose action he is responsible, created that danger which constitutes a nuisance to the highway, or that he has neglected for an undue time after he became, or, if he had used reasonable care, ought to have become, aware of it, to abate or prevent the danger or nuisance'[3].

1   *[1911] 2 KB 633, 80 LJKB 1329.*
2   The case was distinguished in *Wringe v Cohen* on the ground that strict liability did not apply where the defect was caused by the act of a trespasser, or by a latent defect, as distinct from want of repair: see *[1940] 1 KB 229 at 242–246, [1939] 4 All ER 241 at 249–252.* But this distinction seems hard to support in relation to a liability in tort.
3   *[1911] 2 KB 633 at 636–637.* See also *Cushing v Peter Walker & Son (Warrington and Burton) Ltd [1941] 2 All ER 693.*

Trees

[14.28] Similarly in *Noble v Harrison*[1] a landowner was held not liable when a branch from one of his beech trees, which overhung the highway, broke off and damaged the plaintiff's motor coach which was passing underneath. The fracture of the branch was due to a latent defect not discoverable by any reasonably careful inspection, and neither the defendant nor his servants knew that the branch was dangerous. The same approach has been adopted in a number of similar cases involving trees[2], including one decided by the House of Lords[3]. In the light of these authorities, which are difficult in principle to reconcile with the reasoning in *Wringe v Cohen*, it is submitted that the judgment in that case does not represent the law[4].

1   *[1926] 2 KB 332.*
2   See *Cunliffe v Bankes [1945] 1 All ER 459; Caminer v Northern and London Investment Trust [1951] AC 88, [1950] 2 All ER 486; British Road Services Ltd v Slater [1964] 1 All ER 816, [1964] 1 WLR 498.* For a case in which a victim of a falling tree succeeded in proving that the defendant had been at fault, see *Chapman v Barking and Dagenham LBC [1998] CLY 4053, CA;* see also *Brown v Harrison (1947) 177 LT 281.*
3   *Caminer v Northern and London Investment Trust [1951] AC 88, [1950] 2 All ER 486.*
4   *Wringe v Cohen* was followed in *Heap v Ind, Coope and Allsopp Ltd [1940] 2 KB 476, [1940] 3 All ER 634* and *Mint v Good [1951] 1 KB 517, [1950] 2 All ER 1159,* but in both cases negligence was present. In *The Wagon Mound (No 2)* the Judicial Committee of the Privy Council expressed 'no opinion' on *Wringe v Cohen* but the underlying approach of the Board is clearly hostile to strict liability in nuisance: see above. Cf Friedmann 'Incidence of Liability in Nuisance' (1943) 59 LQR 63.

Nature of the duty of care

[14.29]   It is probable that the duty of care imposed by the fault-based liability in public nuisance, at any rate where no overlap with private nuisance is concerned, is objective, as in negligence itself, rather than subjective as has been laid down for application in certain types of private nuisance case[1]. The relationship of owners or occupiers of premises to those who suffer injury while using the highway nearby is more akin to that of road users to each other, which is governed by the tort of negligence, than to the kinds of situation dealt with by 'private nuisance'.

1   See *Goldman v Hargrave [1967] 1 AC 645, [1966] 2 All ER 989* and *Leakey v National Trust for Places of Historic Interest or Natural Beauty [1980] QB 485, [1980] 1 All ER 17,* discussed in CHAPTER 13 above.

Contributory negligence

[14.30]   It seems to be clear that contributory negligence can be a defence to claims for damages in public nuisance[1].

1   See *Farrell v John Mowlem & Co Ltd [1954] 1 Lloyd's Rep 437; Dymond v Pearce [1972] 1 QB 496* at 507D–E, *[1972] 1 All ER 1142* at 1151b–c, *per* Edmund Davies LJ. Cf *Trevett v Lee [1955] 1 All ER 406, [1955] 1 WLR 113.*

Public benefit as a defence?

[14.31]   In one old criminal case it was suggested that an obstruction which interfered with the public right of passage, such that it would normally constitute a nuisance, could be justified if it operated, on balance, to the benefit of the public. In *R v Russell*[1] staiths were erected in a navigable river to enable ships to be loaded with coal. The staiths did not block the river entirely and their presence would enable coal to be supplied to the public cheaper, and in a better condition, than otherwise. Bayley J, speaking of the obstruction, said that in such circumstances it was possible that 'the interests of trade and commerce give it a protection, and it is a justifiable erection, not a nuisance'[2]. Lord Tenterden CJ dissented, however, and in a later case it was held that it is no defence to an indictment for public nuisance that an obstruction produces a counter-balancing public benefit[3]. The reasoning in *R v Russell* was doubted. It is submitted that these doubts were well-founded. The view of Bayley J would involve the courts in the making of broad decisions of policy for which they are not equipped and which would not, in any event, be appropriate in determining the incidence of liability.

¹   (1827) 6 B & C 566, 9 Dow & Ry KB 566. Cf *Tate & Lyle Industries Ltd v Greater London Council* [1983] 2 AC 509, [1983] 1 All ER 1159.
²   (1827) 6 B & C 566 at 595. Aliter if the erection was made 'for pleasure, for whim, for caprice'.
³   See *R v Ward (1836) 4 Ad & El 384, 1 Har & W 703*. Cf *R v Train (1862) 2 B & S 640*.

Can affect the remedy

[14.32]   In certain circumstances, however, considerations of public interest may be relevant to the exercise of the court's discretion in granting injunctive relief in nuisance cases once liability has been established[1]. Although the relevant authorities concern private nuisance, it would seem desirable that the principle should be applicable to public nuisance in an appropriate case, notwithstanding that a criminal offence will, in theory, have been committed. In *Dennis v Ministry of Defence*[2] Buckley J held that noise created by the training of RAF jet aircraft pilots constituted a nuisance, but that the national interest in allowing the training to continue meant that the claimant would be confined to damages and denied specific relief. Although the claim was brought in private nuisance, the volume of noise alleged would seem to have been capable of constituting a public nuisance.

¹   See below CHAPTER 29.
²   *[2003] EWHC 793 (QB)*, (2003) Times, 6 May. See further CHAPTER 12 above.

Part five

Negligence against a statutory background

Chapter 15

Negligence and the exercise of statutory powers

A The problem of discretion

Introduction

[15.01] In *Barrett v Enfield London BC* Lord Hutton said:[1]

' ... the fact that the decision which is challenged was made within the ambit of a statutory discretion and is capable of being described as a policy decision is not in itself a reason why it should be held that no claim in negligence can be brought in respect of it ...It is only where the decision involves the weighing of competing public interests or is dictated by considerations which the courts are not fitted to assess that the courts will hold that the issue is non-justiciable on the ground that the decision was made in the exercise of a statutory discretion'.

Barrett's case is one of a number of recent decisions of the House of Lords dealing with negligence claims brought against a statutory background. These decisions tend to reflect, albeit in differing factual situations, contrasting approaches to the broad question of how such claims should be handled by the courts. In *Barrett* itself the House of Lords refused to strike out a negligence claim against a local authority in respect of the exercise of its statutory powers towards the claimant, who had been in the care of the authority throughout his childhood. In so holding the House of Lords reversed the Court of Appeal which had relied upon a recent decision of the House itself, in a somewhat similar context, to reach the opposite conclusion. That decision, *X v Bedfordshire County Council*[2], was distinguished by the House in speeches which were noticeably more favourable in tone towards the bringing of negligence claims against public bodies, arising out of the exercise of their statutory powers, than those in the earlier case had been. But in yet another decision of the House, *Stovin v Wise*[3], which was concerned with the powers of highway authorities, a bare majority favoured the adoption of a strikingly narrow approach towards the imposition of liability, seemingly urging a return to a rigid restrictive principle fashioned half a century earlier. In this chapter an attempt will be made to examine this overall area, and the difficult issues surrounding it[4].

---

[1] *[1999] 3 All ER 193* at 222.
[2] *X v Bedfordshire County Council [1995] 2 AC 633, [1995] 3 All ER 353.*
[3] *[1996] AC 923, [1996] 3 All ER 801.*
[4] I have explored some of the issues examined in this chapter at greater length in 'Negligence in the Public Sphere: Is Clarity Possible?' (2000) 51 NILQ 25.

Liability possible

[15.02] Notwithstanding current uncertainties relating to the application of the principle, it was established nearly 150 years ago that bodies which owe their existence and functions to Acts of Parliament can, in appropriate cases, be liable in tort for negligence. The mere fact that a body is wholly a creation of statute does not put it outside the province of the private law of tort. In *Mersey Docks and Harbour Board Trustees v Gibbs*[1] the trustees, a statutory body, were held liable for carelessly allowing an accumulation of mud to occur at their dock. Damage was caused to the cargo of a ship when a collision took place between the ship and the bank of mud. The trustees' argument that as a non-profit-making statutory body, which raised money solely for the purpose of operating the dock, their funds should not be called upon to pay damages, was rejected. Subject to any contrary indication in the statute creating the particular body in question, the legislature was presumed to have 'intended that the liability of corporations thus substituted for individuals should, to the extent of their corporate funds, be co-extensive with that imposed by the general law on the owners of similar works'.[2] If necessary, they would have to use their statutory fund-raising powers to acquire the additional finance necessary to meet any claims.

1   *(1866) LR 1 HL 93, HL.*
2   *Per* Blackburn J in *(1866) LR 1 HL 93* at 107 (delivering the opinion of the judges requested by the House of Lords).

Range and complexity of statutory powers

[15.03] If the claimant has been the victim of straightforward negligence, such as a carelessly caused traffic accident, the status of the defendant, whether it be a statutory body, a limited company, or a private individual, will usually be irrelevant.[1] Nevertheless, as the range and complexity of statutory powers became greater, with the increased outpouring of legislation in recent times, the courts gradually became aware that not all cases involving alleged carelessness in the exercise of statutory powers could be treated as indistinguishable from ordinary negligence claims against individuals or commercial organisations. In some situations the body in question may have been endowed with a very wide discretion, the nature of which implies that reconsideration of its decisions, within the limited framework of a private law claim for damages in negligence, is unlikely to be appropriate.

1   In theory, and depending upon the construction of the statute, the defence of statutory authority may be available to bodies exercising statutory powers. In practice, however, this defence is unlikely ever to avail against a negligence claim. Parliament is presumed to intend that statutory powers be exercised without carelessness (see *Geddis v Proprietors of Bann Reservoir (1878) 3 App Cas 430* at 455, HL, *per* Lord Blackburn). But in any event, the infinite variety of forms which carelessness may take would make it impossible for Parliament to authorise it in advance by the use of normal drafting techniques.

Choosing not to exercise discretion

[15.04] In the cases in which this problem was first perceived, the effect was to produce decisions which, whether or not they were correct on their facts, were based on reasoning and distinctions which now seem somewhat clumsy and difficult to support. In *Sheppard v Glossop Corpn*[1] the defendants had a statutory power to provide street lighting. They exercised it, but from 'motives of economy'[2] switched off the lamps every evening at 9 pm. The plaintiff met with an accident at 11.30 pm, which lighting would probably have prevented. The Court of Appeal dismissed the claim on the short ground that the Act itself, the Public Health Act 1875, s 161, did not impose any actual duty on the defendants to light, and that it followed that the plaintiff should fail as there would have been nothing wrongful if the defendants had simply chosen not to exercise their discretion and had provided no lighting at all. The court observed that the result might have been different if the defendants had themselves created the source of danger which had become hazardous due to lack of illumination,[3] but that was not the case.

1 *[1921] 3 KB 132, CA.*
2 *[1921] 3 KB 132* at 144, *per* Scrutton LJ.
3 See *[1921] 3 KB 132* at 140 (Bankes LJ); 143–144 (Scrutton LJ) and 151 (Atkin LJ). Cf *Fisher v Ruislip-Northwood UDC [1945] KB 584, [1945] 2 All ER 458, CA.*

East Suffolk

[15.05] Similarly, in *East Suffolk Rivers Catchment Board v Kent*[1] a board entrusted with statutory powers to deal with flood damage was held not liable when, in exercising its powers, it adopted very inefficient methods and in consequence allowed flooding to continue for much longer than it otherwise would have done. The board had to strike 'a just balance between the rival claims of efficiency and thrift'[2], and could have chosen not to exercise their powers at all. The House of Lords indicated that liability could have been imposed if the board's activities had actually made matters worse and *added* to the damage which the flooding had caused to the plaintiff,[3] but on the facts they had merely failed to remedy loss caused essentially by natural agencies as swiftly as they might otherwise have done.

1 *[1941] AC 74, [1940] 4 All ER 527, HL.*
2 *Per* du Parcq LJ, dissenting, in the Court of Appeal (the decision of which was reversed by the House of Lords), and quoted with approval by Viscount Simon LC, *[1941] AC 74* at 86, *[1940] 4 All ER 527* at 532 and by Lord Romer, *[1941] AC 74* at 103, *[1940] 4 All ER 527* at 544.
3 See *[1941] AC 74* at 102, 104, *[1940] 4 All ER 527* at 542, 545 *per* Lord Romer and Lord Porter.

B Justiciability

The policy and operational distinction

[15.06] In two decisions of the House of Lords in the 1970s an approach, more sophisticated than that previously adopted, was fashioned to deal with the problem of carelessness in the exercise of statutory powers. In *Home Office v Dorset Yacht Co*[1] the property of the plaintiff yacht company was damaged by borstal boys in the course of their escape from an open borstal, an escape which had allegedly been facilitated by carelessness on the part of prison officers. The House of Lords held that, in principle, the Home Office could be liable for negligence on such facts. The defendants contended that the possibility of such liability would unduly fetter the exercise of statutory powers to run open prisons and borstals, which inevitably involve a greater degree of risk of escapes than other types of prison regime. The House accepted that it would certainly not be appropriate for the courts to seek to evaluate the merits of penal policies as such, but denied that imposition of liability for specific acts of carelessness by prison officers *in carrying out* whatever policy was chosen by the Home Office would have that effect.

1 *[1970] AC 1004, [1970] 2 All ER 294, HL.*

[15.07] *Negligence and the exercise of statutory powers*

Ultra vires doctrine

[15.07] Lord Diplock, in his speech in *Dorset Yacht*, drew attention to the role of the ultra vires doctrine in limiting the scope and effectiveness of challenges in the courts to administrative decisions. In his Lordship's view it was a condition precedent to a successful negligence action arising out of the exercise of a statutory power that the acts or decisions impugned should have been ultra vires the power in question.[1] Once this was established, the court could proceed to consider whether the carelessness allegedly involved did in truth amount to actionable negligence. Although this analysis was beneficial in identifying explicitly the underlying problem involved in cases of negligence against the background of statutory discretion, it did not itself constitute a solution to that problem. In particular, the precise relationship which had to exist, if liability was to be imposed, between the exercise of the discretion and the act of carelessness remained unclear. The latter may have been far removed from the former, both in time and space. In the *Dorset Yacht* case itself, penal policy was decided in the Home Office, but the immediate cause of the escape was alleged to have been prison officers sleeping on duty on an island off the south coast. To require that this carelessness should be measured against the administrative law criteria used to determine the validity of discretionary decisions, even if only as a preliminary to applying the ordinary tests of the tort of negligence, seemed rather artificial.

[1] See *[1970] AC 1004* at 1064–1069, *[1970] 2 All ER 294* at 331–335.

Anns case

[15.08] Some degree of clarification was provided by the decision of the House of Lords in *Anns v Merton London Borough Council*,[1] which still appears to retain a measure of influence in this area despite being subsequently overruled on another point.[2] In this case the plaintiffs' flats developed structural damage as a result of having been built on inadequate foundations. They sought to sue, inter alia, the local authority for the area in question, which possessed statutory powers, under the *Public Health Act 1936* and byelaws made thereunder, to inspect and approve the foundations of new buildings.[3] It was unclear on the facts whether the foundations had been inspected carelessly or not inspected at all. The defendant local authority contended that, since it had a statutory discretion, it was free to choose not to exercise its powers at all, and that it should be immune from liability for negligence lest that discretion be subverted by its being turned into a *duty* to inspect in all cases. The matter was tried as a preliminary issue and the House of Lords in effect conceded the premise, but denied that the conclusion followed from it. The authority was free to choose to make no inspections, or to adopt a limited system of inspection, provided that in choosing to exercise its discretion in that way, perhaps for reasons of economy, it acted intra vires. This requirement would necessarily include the giving, in reaching its decision, of due and proper consideration to all the relevant factors. But once a system of making inspections had in fact been adopted, liability for negligence could be imposed if, due to carelessness in its implementation, the task itself was carried out negligently, or inspections which ought to have been made under the system were inadvertently omitted. Lord Wilberforce drew a distinction which was intended both to protect discretions from being improperly fettered, and to delineate the area within which negligence claims could nevertheless be entertained. He said:[4]

'Most, indeed probably all, statutes relating to public authorities or public bodies, contain in them a large area of policy. The courts call this "discretion" meaning that the decision is one for the authority or body to make, and not for the courts. Many statutes also prescribe or at least presuppose the practical execution of policy decisions: a convenient description of this is to say that in addition to the area of policy or discretion, there is an operational area. Although this distinction between the policy area and the operational area is convenient, and illuminating, it is probably a distinction of degree; many "operational" powers or duties have in them some element of "discretion". It can safely be said that the more "operational" a power or duty may be, the easier it is to superimpose upon it a common law duty of care.'

---

[1] *[1978] AC 728, [1977] 2 All ER 492, HL.*

[2] Ie the recoverability of economic loss in the circumstances of the case: see *Murphy v Brentwood District Council [1991] 1 AC 398, [1990] 2 All ER 908, HL.* For discussion see generally CHAPTER 6 above; see also CHAPTER 1.

[3] See also *Dutton v Bognor Regis UDC [1972] 1 QB 373, [1972] 1 All ER 462* (a decision of the Court of Appeal approved by the House of Lords in *Anns* case, but on different grounds). For more recent legislation on building control see the *Building Act 1984.*

[4] *[1978] AC 728 at 754, [1977] 2 All ER 492 at 500.*

Two fundamental problems

[15.09] The distinction thus drawn between the policy and operational spheres represented an ambitious attempt to reconcile the need to protect discretionary powers from being unduly restricted, with the perceived need to provide a remedy in tort for losses suffered through carelessness.[1] Unfortunately, however, the attempted reconciliation has not proved to be wholly successful, and at least two fundamental problems have continued to exercise the courts. The first is the contention, rejected in *Anns* itself, that the difficulty of drawing the distinction would in practice threaten substantially to fetter the exercise of any given discretion and thereby limit the freedom of those charged with it to focus exclusively upon the general public interest. The second problem, which will often be related to the first, reflects concern about the impact of the imposition of negligence liability upon the *resources* of the authorities concerned. With increasing recognition of the fact that the public finances are not limitless, and that hard choices are sometimes inevitable, it has begun to seem less self-evident that the occurrence of loss or damage, which the exercise of a statutory power would probably have prevented, should result automatically in the payment of compensation to the victim from public funds: even when the exercise of a statutory power would probably have prevented the loss, and the action or inaction in question could be deemed to have been 'operationally' negligent.

---

[1] The distinction originated in American case law: see P Craig 'Negligence in the Exercise of a Statutory Power' (1978) 94 LQR 428 at 442–447.

Loose presumption

[15.10] The tendency in later cases has therefore been to treat the distinction between policy and operational matters as being, at best, a somewhat loose presumption rather than a firmly established doctrine.[1] In *Barrett v Enfield London BC* Lord Slynn referred to the policy/operational distinction as a 'guide' in determining 'whether the particular issue is justiciable or whether the court should accept that it has no role to play'. He concluded that[2]:

'The greater the element of policy involved, the wider the area of discretion accorded, the more likely it is that the matter is not justiciable so that no action in negligence can be brought'.

¹   See especially *Rowling v Takaro Properties Ltd [1988] AC 473, [1988] 1 All ER 163* and *Lonrho plc v Tebbit [1992] 4 All ER 280*, CA; affg [1991] 4 All ER 973, discussed below.
²   See *[1999] 3 All ER 193* at 211.

The policy 'immunity'

Applicability

[15.11] In what might be termed 'ordinary' cases of negligence which nevertheless involve some statutory element in the background, such as a road accident caused by the careless driving of an employee of a statutory body on that body's business, the distinction between policy and operational areas of activity would seem to be neither helpful nor relevant.¹ The case should be decided on the same basis as negligence cases generally, without the added complication of that distinction. A difficulty at the outset, however, is to know precisely which cases fall within the 'ordinary' category, and which do not. In *Home Office v Dorset Yacht Co*² Lord Diplock suggested that the test is whether 'the act or omission complained of is not of a kind which would itself give rise to a cause of action at common law if it were not authorised by the statute'. Thus, in the *Dorset Yacht* case itself the statutory power to detain the borstal boys was the foundation of the negligence claim in the sense that, without that power, it would have been wrongful to have detained the boys at all; and a complaint about premature release would therefore have been meaningless. Similarly, in *Anns v Merton London Borough Council*³ the complaint about careless inspection of the building would have been meaningless without the statutory power to inspect. In the road accident cases, by contrast, the obvious analogy with ordinary litigation between private individuals would place such cases clearly on the other side of the line, even if the accident was caused by someone driving a vehicle in pursuance of a purpose ultimately referable to a statute.

¹   Cf *Woolfall v Knowsley Borough Council* (1992) Times, 26 June, CA (no excuse that a local authority failed to remove rubbish which constituted a hazard merely because it wished to avoid aggravating an industrial dispute with its employees).
²   *[1970] AC 1004* at 1066, *[1970] 2 All ER 294* at 331, HL.
³   *[1978] AC 728, [1977] 2 All ER 492, HL*.

Circularity

[15.12] The Diplock test does, therefore, have a certain utility as a rough and ready guide to the applicability of the policy and operational dichotomy. Nevertheless, as Harlow pointed out,¹ in strict logic the test is circular and hence cannot ultimately provide a sound basis for distinguishing between cases in which the dichotomy will be relevant and cases in which it will not.² This is because carelessness may take an infinite variety of forms, and it is therefore impossible to predicate of a certain act that it could never 'give rise to a cause of action at common law'. Even the fact situations in *Dorset Yacht* and *Anns*, which give the Diplock test an appearance of plausibility, have analogies with other tort cases not involving statutory powers.³ Thus, a private school may release a small child prematurely and hence cause an accident,⁴ or a solicitor's carelessness committed against the background of his contractual relationship with his client may cause loss to a third party.[5] In both situations ordinary common law claims for negligence may exist, and yet they are not wholly dissimilar from the situations in *Dorset Yacht* and *Anns* respectively. This does not, of course, in itself indicate that the policy and operational dichotomy was irrelevant, even in the cases in which it was developed, but simply that the Diplock test for the applicability of the dichotomy is flawed.

[1]   See C Harlow 'Fault Liability in French and English Public Law' (1976) 39 MLR 516 at 531.
[2]   See also S Bailey and M Bowman 'The Policy/Operational Dichotomy – A Cuckoo in the Nest' (1986) 45 CLJ 430 at 432.
[3]   See D Brodie 'Public Authorities: Negligence Actions – Control Devices' (1998) 18 LS 1 at 4–5.
[4]   Cf *Carmarthenshire County Council v Lewis [1955] AC 549, [1955] 1 All ER 565, HL*.
[5]   Eg as in *White v Jones [1995] 2 AC 207, [1995] 1 All ER 691, HL*.

Presumption that claims are justiciable

[15.13] To assume that every case involving an allegation of negligence against the background of a statutory power had to be subjected at the outset to some test to determine whether it was one to which the policy and operational dichotomy applied and, if so, whether the alleged carelessness fell within one category or the other, would be to adopt an approach both unnecessarily cumbersome and dubious in principle. From a constitutional standpoint the objection in principle is that the approach would notionally place all negligence claims against public bodies in a special category, and hence conflict with the ideal of equality before the law. The approach is unduly cumbersome in that a great many of the cases involving statutory powers which would be 'tested' for the applicability of the dichotomy would result in its being held irrelevant on their facts: the motor accident cases being the prime example. This is not to say, however, that the need to protect bodies exercising statutory discretions from being unduly fettered does not justify some negligence actions against public bodies being treated differently from ordinary tort claims against private individuals.

Public policy

[15.14] The right approach would appear to be to *presume* that all negligence claims against bodies exercising statutory powers are to be regarded as justiciable, *unless* the body in question succeeds in satisfying the court that the facts bring the case within the scope of a 'defence', or objection to judicial scrutiny, based upon public policy.[1] This concept would be intended to ensure that matters not appropriate to determination by the court, at least in the context of a negligence action, are properly kept non-justiciable. Thus, in *Rowling v Takaro Properties*[2] Lord Keith, delivering the judgment of the Judicial Committee of the Privy Council, said[3] that the distinction between policy and operational areas 'does not provide a touchstone of liability, but rather is expressive of the need to exclude altogether those cases in which the decision under attack is of such a kind that a question whether it has been made negligently is unsuitable for judicial resolution'.

[1]   Cf the 'public interest immunity' relating to the withholding of documents.
[2]   *[1988] AC 473, [1988] 1 All ER 163*.
[3]   *[1988] AC 473* at 501, *[1988] 1 All ER 163* at 172.

Unsuitable for judicial resolution

[15.15] In *Barrett v Enfield London BC*[1] Lord Hutton observed that:

' ... the courts will not permit a claim for negligence to be brought where a decision on the existence of negligence would involve the courts in considering matters of policy raising issues which they are ill-equipped and ill-suited to assess and on which Parliament could not have intended that the courts would substitute their views for the views of ministers or officials'.

Since so much depends on the circumstances of the particular case, specific criteria are unlikely ever to emerge. The best that can be done is to provide examples. The reasoning in *Home Office v Dorset Yacht Co*[2] itself indicates that if the escapes in that case had been brought about by the decision to allocate the borstal boys to the particular institution in question, with the relaxed regime the existence of which itself reflected a high-level decision on penal policy, the Home Office would enjoy an immunity from suit which would not apply if prison officers had simply fallen asleep on duty.[3] Similarly if, in *Anns v Merton London Borough Council*,[4] the building site had not been inspected because of a policy decision, perhaps reflecting economic constraints, to reduce inspections generally or to adopt a random system of inspection, the public policy objection to liability would have applied.[5]

[1] *[1999] 3 All ER 193* at 220. See also *per* Sir Nicolas Browne-Wilkinson V-C in *Lonrho plc v Tebbitt [1991] 4 All ER 973* at 981.
[2] *[1970] AC 1004, [1970] 2 All ER 294, HL.* Cf *Evangelical United Brethren v State 407 P 2d 440 (1965).*
[3] See *[1970] AC 1004* at 1068–1069, *[1970] 2 All ER 294* at 332–333, *per* Lord Diplock.
[4] *[1978] AC 728, [1977] 2 All ER 492, HL.*
[5] See P Craig 'Negligence in the Exercise of a Statutory Power' (1978) 94 LQR 428 at 440.

Immunity granted

[15.16] In two cases reported in the 1980s, decisions taken in the exercise of statutory discretions to determine the placing of road hazard markings on highways,[1] and the extent to which measures should be adopted by a highway authority to control the hazard to road users posed by stray dogs,[2] were unsuccessfully challenged, with the court in each case emphasising the degree of policy content in the decisions[3]. In *Department of Health and Social Security v Kinnear*[4] the Department succeeded in getting struck out certain allegations in a negligence action arising out of the use of whooping cough vaccine. The policy of promoting immunisation had been taken in pursuance of statutory powers conferred by the *National Health Service Act 1946*.

[1] *West v Buckinghamshire County Council* (1984) 83 LGR 449. See also *Weiss v Fote 167 NE 2d 63 (1960)* (timing of traffic lights). But cf *Bird v Pearce [1978] RTR 290*; affd *[1979] RTR 369, CA*.
[2] *Allison v Corby District Council [1980] RTR 111.*
[3] More recent highway cases show the same reluctance to impose liability in situations involving discretionary powers, even against a conceptual background which is more reluctant to recognise blanket immunities as such: see *Stovin v Wise [1996] AC 923, [1996] 3 All ER 801, HL; Larner v Solihull MBC* (2001) 3 LGLR 31, CA; *Gorringe v Calderdale MBC [2004] 2 All ER 326, HL*. These cases are discussed below.
[4] *(1984) 134 NLJ 886.*

Immunity denied

[15.17] If the decision taken pursuant to the statutory power involves the making of broad choices it is clearly unlikely, especially if resource allocation is involved, that the court will entertain a negligence claim. Even in *Anns v Merton London Borough Council*, Lord Wilberforce, while casting doubt on the overall reasoning in *East Suffolk Rivers Catchment Board v Kent*,[1] referred with approval to one familiar phrase from that case observing that 'public authorities have to strike a balance between the claims of efficiency and thrift: whether they get the balance right can only be decided through the ballot box, not in the courts'.[2] Nevertheless, it is important to bear in mind that the 'resources' point is only one factor that may be relevant in determining where the public interest lies in a particular case. Many decisions which would unquestionably be regarded as justiciable will have resource implications: the level of expenditure necessary to achieve a safe system of work in, for example, a government factory.

[1] *[1941] AC 74, [1940] 4 All ER 527, HL* and see above at para [15.05].
[2] *[1978] AC 728* at 754, *[1977] 2 All ER 492* at 501, HL.

Liability imposed

[15.18] Thus, in *Indian Towing Co v United States*[1] the defendant coast guard authority, in the exercise of a statutory discretion, erected a lighthouse. Due to carelessness in maintaining it, however, the light was not illuminated when the plaintiff's vessel ran aground in circumstances in which it would probably not have done if the lighthouse had been functioning properly. 'The Coast Guard', said Mr Justice Frankfurter in the US Supreme Court, 'need not undertake the lighthouse service. But once it exercised its discretion to operate a light ... it was obligated to use due care to make certain that the light was kept in good working order'. Similarly, attempts by local authorities in England to avoid liability for negligence against the background of statutory discretion by seeking to invoke public policy do not always succeed. The defence was rejected in *Bird v Pearce,*[2] in which the claim arose out of an accident partly caused by the defendant local authority's failure to take advantage of its powers to erect a temporary traffic sign at a dangerous road junction, when the permanent markings were obliterated during maintenance work. In *Vicar of Writtle v Essex County Council*[3] liability was imposed in circumstances which recalled *Home Office v Dorset Yacht Co*[4] itself. Inadequate supervision by social workers of a boy with fire-raising propensities, who had been remanded into the care of the defendant local authority, left him with sufficient freedom to enable him to set fire to the plaintiff's church.

[1] *350 US 61, 76 S Ct 122 (1955).*
[2] *[1979] RTR 369, CA*; affg *[1978] RTR 290.*
[3] *(1979) 77 LGR 656.* See also *Johnson v State of California 447 P 2d 352 (1968).*
[4] *[1970] AC 1004, [1970] 2 All ER 294, HL.*

No rigid criteria

[15.19] It is evident that there can be no rigid criteria for the application of the concept of immunity based upon public policy. It is certainly not the case that the defence applies automatically whenever some element of discretion can be identified in the conduct impugned.[1] But, equally, it is important that mechanistic application of ordinary negligence concepts should not result in the immunity being outflanked or indirectly subverted.

[1] Cf *per* Sloane J in *Ham v Los Angeles County 189 P 462* at *468 (1920)*: ' ... it would be difficult to conceive of any official act ... that did not admit of some discretion, even if it involved only the driving in of a nail' (quoted in *Johnson v State of California 447 P 2d 352* (1968) at 357).

C Applying negligence principles

Negating liability despite justiciability

[15.20] In *Rowling v Takaro Properties*[1] the plaintiff was refused consent by the Government of New Zealand for a proposed enterprise in that country. This refusal was subsequently held by the courts to have been ultra vires, as having been based upon irrelevant considerations. But by the time the legality of the enterprise had been determined, it was too late to proceed with it and the plaintiff brought a negligence action against the government for economic loss alleging, inter alia, that the minister in question had been careless in failing to take adequate legal advice before improperly refusing the consent. On appeal to the Privy Council it was held that the claim would fail. Significantly, however, that the board expressly declined to decide that the issue was non-justiciable. Instead their Lordships held that, on the assumption that it *was* justiciable, the situation was one in which (even if carelessness had been established which it had not) the imposition of a duty of care would be inappropriate for pragmatic reasons. Lord Keith said:[2]

> '[Their Lordships] recognise that the decision of the minister is capable of being described as having been of a policy rather than an operational character; but, if the function of the policy/operational dichotomy is as they have already described it, the allegation of negligence in the present case is not, they consider, of itself of such a character as to render the case unsuitable for judicial decision. *Be that as it may*, there are certain considerations which militate against imposition of liability in a case such as the present.'

In somewhat similar vein Lord Hutton expressed himself as follows in *Barrett v Enfield London BC*[3]:

> 'I consider that where a plaintiff claims damages for personal injuries which he alleges have been caused by decisions negligently taken in the exercise of a statutory discretion, and provided that the decisions do not involve issues of policy which the courts are ill-equipped to adjudicate upon, it is preferable for the courts to decide the validity of the plaintiff's claim by applying directly the common law concept of negligence than by applying as a preliminary test the public law concept of *Wednesbury* unreasonableness to determine if the decision fell outside the ambit of the statutory discretion'.[4]

[1] *[1988] AC 473, [1988] 1 All ER 163.*
[2] *[1988] AC 473 at 501, [1988] 1 All ER 163 at 172* (italics supplied).
[3] See *[1999] 3 All ER 193* at 225. See also *per* Lord Browne-Wilkinson in *X v Bedfordshire CC [1995] 3 All ER 353 at 369, [1995] 2 AC 633 at 736*: 'For myself, I do not believe that it is either helpful or necessary to introduce public law concepts as to the validity of a decision into the question of liability at common law for negligence'.
[4] See also S H Bailey and M J Bowman 'Public Authority Negligence Revisited' [2000] 59 CLJ 85.

Pragmatism favoured

[15.21] The preferred approach therefore does now appear to be to confine blanket immunity to those cases which, consistent with the presumption suggested above, are clearly political or macroeconomic in nature; but nevertheless to deploy a wide range of policy considerations under the umbrella of negligence concepts in order to determine pragmatically whether or not liability should be imposed in other cases.[1]

1   The need to avoid blanket immunities wherever possible is reinforced by the danger that such immunities might be held to contravene Article 6 of the European Convention for the Protection of Human Rights and Fundamental Freedoms: see *per* Lord Browne-Wilkinson in *Barrett v Enfield London BC [1999] 3 All ER 193* at 198–200.

Operational failures and decisions

[15.22] Thus, it is clear that even if the case *is* considered to be justiciable, it does not follow that negligence liability will be imposed for any alleged carelessness. Even at the 'operational' end of the spectrum the court may decline to impose liability. The reasons which have been put forward for so declining have included concern about the resource implications of imposing liability, and even concern about imposing undue pressure upon those charged with exercising the statutory discretion. Both factors can be seen at work in the cases, and must now be considered. But as far as the second factor is concerned, pressure on those carrying out statutory functions, the most recent authorities in one such field, that of social welfare, reveal a somewhat greater readiness to contemplate the imposition of liability than was previously the case.

Discretion and welfare

Child protection and education

[15.23] In the *X v Bedfordshire County Council*[1] case, which was decided by the House of Lords in 1995, it was contended that carelessness by local authorities and their servants when exercising, or failing to exercise, the powers conferred on them by statute to protect children from abuse, and promote their welfare, could constitute actionable negligence leading to the payment of damages to any children affected. The point had arisen in a number of different cases which were considered together on appeal to the House of Lords. In one case a child had been separated from her mother when, as a result of confusion over names, a psychiatrist wrongly identified her mother's boyfriend as an abuser of the child; in another case an authority had failed to take a child into care despite persistent evidence of serious abuse. A yet further set of cases concerned failure to take appropriate action with respect to the education of children in the context of special educational needs.[2] In so far as these claims were based directly upon alleged common law negligence by the local authorities concerned, against the background of their statutory powers, the House of Lords was unanimous in striking out all of them. Lord Browne-Wilkinson, who delivered the leading speech, said in reference to the abuse cases:[3]

> 'Here, for the first time, the plaintiffs are seeking to erect a common law duty in relation to the administration of a statutory social welfare scheme. Such a scheme is designed to protect weaker members of society (children) from harm done to them by others. The scheme involves the administrators in exercising discretions and powers which could not exist in the private sector and which in many cases bring them into conflict with those who, under the general law, are responsible for the child's welfare.'

1   *[1995] 2 AC 633, [1995] 3 All ER 353.*
2   For subsequent proceedings in one of the cases which was allowed to proceed on the basis of alleged professional negligence see *Keating v Bromley LBC [2003] EWHC 1070, [2003] ELR 590.*
3   *[1995] 2 AC 633* at 751, *[1995] 3 All ER 353* at 382.

'Extraordinary delicacy'

[15.24] In relation to both the abuse and the education cases, Lord Browne-Wilkinson considered that 'the courts should hesitate long before imposing a common law duty of care in the exercise of discretionary powers or duties conferred by Parliament for social welfare purposes';[1] and he concluded that it would not be 'just and reasonable' to superimpose a common law duty of care on local authorities in relation to the performance of their statutory responsibilities in the context of the cases under consideration. The reasons which led to this conclusion included the fact that the situations involved in such cases would often be 'extraordinarily delicate', and that the existence of administrative machinery to deal with complaints made it appropriate for the court to discourage 'often hopeless' litigation which would divert 'both money and human resources' from 'the performance of the social service for which they were provided'.[2]

1   *[1995] 2 AC 633* at 762, *[1995] 3 All ER 353* at 392. But for a case in which the Court of Appeal imposed liability, under the *Hedley Byrne* principle, upon a local authority for negligence by an environmental health officer see *Welton v North Cornwall District Council [1997] 1 WLR 570, CA*, discussed by Richard Mullender in 'Negligent Misstatement, Threats and the Scope of the *Hedley Byrne* Principle' (1999)62 MLR 425. Cf *Harris v Evans [1998] 3 All ER 522.*
2   *[1995] 2 AC 633* at 750, *[1995] 3 All ER 353* at 381.

Bedfordshire distinguished

[15.25] *X v Bedfordshire County Council* was distinguished by the House of Lords itself in *Barrett v Enfield London BC*[1]. The plaintiff had been in the care of the defendant authority from the age of ten months until he was 17. He alleged that the authority had negligently failed to provide him with proper social workers, had made placements for him with inappropriate foster parents, and had moved him too frequently between different residential homes. He claimed that, as a result, he had reached adulthood with profound difficulties of a psychological and psychiatric nature which constituted actionable personal injury[2]. The Court of Appeal struck out the claim[3], relying on *X v Bedfordshire County Council.* But the House of Lords distinguished *Bedfordshire* and reinstated it. While the decision considered in *Bedfordshire* actually to take, or not to take, a person into care may not be justiciable, it did not follow that 'having taken a child into care, an authority cannot be liable for what it or its employees do in relation to the child without it being shown that they have acted in excess of power'[4].

1   *[1999] 3 All ER 193.*
2   Despite some initial uncertainty it is now clear that psychological difficulties (including those resulting from untreated dyslexia) can constitute 'personal injuries' for the purpose of negligence claims: see *Adams v Bracknell Forest BC [2004] 3 All ER 897.*
3   See *[1997] 3 All ER 171.*
4   See *[1999] 3 All ER 193* at 211.

'Maintaining standards'

[15.26] Once justiciability had been established the House in *Barrett* did go on to consider, in accordance with conventional negligence doctrine, whether the possible imposition of liability would be 'just and reasonable'. Nevertheless, it is striking how the various factors grouped under this umbrella in the *Bedfordshire* case were considered *not* to 'have the same force separately or cumulatively'[1] in *Barrett* so as to outweigh the plaintiff's right to have his case substantively determined. In particular, both Lord Slynn and Lord Hutton expressly rejected the argument, to which the House had attached importance in *Bedford*, that a decision against the local authority would be objectionable on the ground that it might lead such authorities to 'adopt a more cautious and defensive approach to their duties'[2]. On the contrary, observed Lord Slynn, quoting from the dissenting judgment of Sir Thomas Bingham MR (as he then was) in the Court of Appeal in *X v Bedfordshire County Council*, 'the imposition of a duty of care' could contribute 'to the maintenance of high standards'[3].

[1] See *[1999] 3 All ER* 193 at 208 *per* Lord Slynn.
[2] See *[1999] 3 All ER* 193 at 228 (Lord Hutton) and 208 (Lord Slynn).
[3] See *[1999] 3 All ER* 193 at 208.

Liability despite reasoning in Bedfordshire

[15.27] The decision in *Barrett* therefore clearly demonstrated that, notwithstanding a background which involved the exercise of a discretionary power, a common law duty of care may be imposed in respect of negligence by social workers[1]. Moreover, the House of Lords has also held, in *Phelps v London Borough of Hillingdon*[2], that a local educational authority can incur vicarious liability at common law for the negligence of teachers and other educational professionals employed by it, notwithstanding the statutory context in which educational services are provided. In that case Lord Clyde observed that the imposition of liability 'may have the healthy effect of securing that high standards are sought and secured'[3]. In *D v East Berkshire NHS Trust*[4] the Court of Appeal reviewed the recent authorities, and expressed itself as follows:

'These decisions significantly restrict the effect of *Bedfordshire*. So far as the education authority cases are concerned, doubt was cast in *Phelps'* case on the proposition that an education authority owes no duty of care to children when exercising powers and discretions under the 1981 Act. So far as child abuse cases are concerned, much of the reasoning advanced by Lord Browne-Wilkinson to justify holding that there was no duty of care was called into question.'

Overall, it is now clear that, as a result of later decisions of the House of Lords itself, the reasoning in *X v Bedfordshire County Council* was too wide, even if the actual decisions reached by the House of Lords in that case may have been correct on their own facts[5].

[1] See also *W v Essex CC [2000] 2 All ER 237, HL.*
[2] *[2000] 4 All ER 504.*
[3] See *[2000] 4 All ER 504* at 535.
[4] *[2003] 4 All ER 796* at para 49 *per* Lord Phillips MR delivering the judgment of the court.
[5] It is still the law that no duty is owed to the *parents* of children taken into care as a result of abuse allegations: *D v East Berkshire NHS Trust.* For further discussion, see CHAPTER 1 above.

Resource implications

Stovin v Wise

[15.28] Concern about the resource implications of imposing liability was at the forefront of the reasoning of the House of Lords in *Stovin v Wise*[1]. The plaintiff motor-cyclist suffered serious personal injuries in a collision with a car, the driver of which had had her view obscured by a large bank of earth on land adjoining the highway. An attempt to hold the local highway authority jointly liable for the plaintiff's injuries, on the ground that the accident might have been prevented if it had exercised its statutory powers to compel removal of the bank of earth, was unsuccessful. A bare majority of the House of Lords, reversing the Court of Appeal, held that the claim against the authority would fail. Lord Hoffmann, giving the leading speech of the majority, said:[2]

> 'It is one thing to provide a service at the public expense. It is another to require the public to pay compensation when a failure to provide the service has resulted in loss ... To require payment of compensation increases the burden on public funds. Before imposing such an additional burden, the courts should be satisfied that this is what Parliament intended.'

His Lordship emphasised that liability in damages for breach of statutory *duty* is far from automatic, depending upon 'an examination of the policy of the statute to decide whether it was intended to confer a right to compensation for breach'; and while the question of whether a statute 'can be relied upon to support the existence of a common law duty of care' is not an identical one, 'the policy of the statute is nevertheless a crucial factor in the decision'. Moreover, in cases involving powers as distinct from duties 'the fact that Parliament has conferred a discretion must be some indication that the policy of the Act conferring the power was not to create a right to compensation'.[3]

[1] *[1996] AC 923.*
[2] *[1996] AC 923* at 952, *[1996] 3 All ER 801* at 827.
[3] *[1996] AC 923* at 953, *[1996] 3 All ER 801* at 829.

No obligation to compensate

[15.29] Lord Hoffmann said that he preferred to leave open the question whether the *Anns* case had been right to create *any* exception to the principle in the *East Suffolk* case that exercise, or non-exercise, of a statutory power could only give rise to liability if it actually made matters *worse*. He did, however, conclude significantly that 'the need to have regard to the policy of the statute' meant that 'exceptions will be rare'.[1] Thus, on the facts of *Stovin v Wise* itself, he considered that there were no grounds for supposing that, even if the defendant authority had been in breach of a public law duty to secure removal of the obstruction to visibility, it could not be said 'that the public law duty should give rise to an obligation to compensate persons who have suffered loss because it was not performed'.[2]

[1] *[1996] AC 923* at 953, *[1996] 3 All ER 801* at 829.
[2] *[1996] AC 923* at 957, *[1996] 3 All ER 801* at 832.

Restrictive approach in highway cases

[15.30] Although the reasoning of Lord Hoffman in *Stovin's* case is not free from difficulty, the decision itself has been followed in cases falling within the same area ie highway law[1]. Claims by road accident victims, based on allegations that a highway authority had *omitted* to take steps which could have been taken under statutory powers to improve safety at the scene of the accident, are not regarded with favour.[2] Thus *Stovin v Wise* was applied by the House of Lords itself in *Gorringe v Calderdale MBC*[3]. In this case the claimant contended that a general statutory provision requiring local authorities 'to promote road safety'[4] gave rise to a common law duty of care requiring the installation of road markings to alert motorists to hazards liable to cause accidents to those driving at excessive speed. The House of Lords was unanimous in robustly rejecting the claim. Lord Brown of Eaton-Under-Heywood said:[5]

> 'In the highway context ... the claimant (or some other road user involved in the accident) will almost inevitably himself have been at fault. In these circumstances it seems to me entirely reasonable that the policy of the law should be to leave the liability for the accident on the road user who negligently caused it rather than look to the highway authority to protect him against his own wrong'.

If, however, the highway authority was responsible for *creating* the danger, the situation is very different[6].

---

[1]   See *Larner v Solihull MBC (2001) 3 LGLR 31, CA*.
[2]   Cf *Goodes v East Sussex County Council [2000] 1 WLR 1356, HL* (but on the situation in this case, ie removing ice, see now the *Railways and Transport Safety Act 2003, s 111*).
[3]   *[2004] 2 All ER 326*.
[4]   See the *Road Traffic Act 1988, s 39(2)*.
[5]   See *[2004] 2 All ER 326* at para 100.
[6]   See *Kane v New Forest DC [2001] 3 All ER 914, CA*.

Liability established in some areas

[15.31]   The chances of success in a common law claim for damages for negligence, based upon the existence of a statutory power, would be reduced if the approach favoured by the majority in *Stovin's* case were to be applied generally. In practice, however, the less restrictive approach adopted by the House of Lords itself in subsequent cases[1], albeit in rather different contexts, makes widespread application of the *Stovin* decision outside the highway field somewhat unlikely. Moreover, in certain situations the existence of liability is too well established to be open to question. It could not now be seriously contended, for example, that the National Health Service should enjoy a blanket immunity from all claims for medical negligence on the ground that Parliament had intended to provide resources for treatment but not for damages. Nevertheless, such a conclusion might seem to be a possibility if the approach of Lord Hoffmann in *Stovin v Wise* were to be carried to its logical conclusion[2]. The doctrine of 'general reliance' probably provides the most satisfactory foundation for liability in cases involving the National Health Service.

---

[1]   Ie see *Barrett v Enfield London BC [1999] 3 All ER 193*; *Phelps v London Borough of Hillingdon [2000] 4 All ER 504*; *W v Essex CC [2000] 2 All ER 237*.
[2]   It should be noted that in *Gorringe v Calderdale MBC* Lord Hoffman himself accepted that public sector medical negligence claims rest 'upon a solid, orthodox common law foundation': see *[2004] 2 All ER 326, HL* at para 38.

'General reliance'

[15.32]   It is sometimes contended that if a statutory power is routinely exercised to such an extent as to create a general expectation in the community that a particular service will be provided, a failure to exercise it may ground liability under a so-called doctrine of 'general reliance'. In one Australian case 'the control of air traffic, the safety inspection of aircraft and the fighting of a fire in a building' were suggested as possible examples[1]. The situation in *Indian Towing Co v United States*[2] is also often cited in this context: the existence of the lighthouse created an expectation that it would warn sailors of danger. Since the doctrine was not considered to be relevant in *Stovin v Wise*, any observations upon it in that case are necessarily obiter. Nevertheless, the speech of Lord Hoffmann, for the majority, is notable for its scepticism on the point. His Lordship said that application of the doctrine 'may require some very careful analysis of the role which the expected exercise of the statutory power plays in community behaviour'.[3] The doctrine of 'general reliance' has also been subjected to criticism by the High Court of Australia in *Pyrenees Shire Council v Day*.[4] In that case a local authority failed to exercise its power to take follow-up action after an inspection revealed that certain premises presented a fire-risk. The High Court held the council liable to pay compensation for the damage caused when a fire occurred, but preferred to do so on the basis of a perceived legislative intention in favour of such compensation rather than upon any notion of 'personal reliance' by the community on the exercise of the council's powers. Gummow J could see 'no sound doctrinal footing for a doctrine of general reliance',[5] and Brennan CJ said:[6]

'If the "general expectations in the community" were to be the touchstone of liability, the proof of that fact would present considerable difficulty. The test seems to invite consideration of a general expectation of the exercise of a statutory power rather than an expectation referable to particular circumstances which might invite consideration of an exercise of the power. If community expectation that a statutory power will be exercised were to be adopted as a criterion of a duty to exercise the power, it would displace the criterion of legislative intention. In my respectful opinion, if the public law duty of a public authority is relevant to its liability in damages for a failure to exercise that power, the appropriate criterion is legislative intention. I am respectfully unable to accept "general reliance" as the basis of such liability.'[7]

[1]   See *Sutherland Shire Council v Heyman (1985) 157 CLR 424* at 464 *per* Mason J.
[2]   See above.
[3]   *[1996] AC 923* at 954–955, *[1996] 3 All ER 801* at 829. But cf *per* Lord Nicholls (dissenting): 'Reliance is a useful aid here, as in the field of negligent misstatement, because it leads easily to the conclusion that the authority can fairly be taken to have assumed responsibility to act in a particular way. Reliance may be actual, in the case of a particular plaintiff, or more general, in the sense that persons in the position of the plaintiff may be expected to act in reliance on the authority exercising its powers': *[1996] AC 923* at 937, *[1996] 3 All ER 801* at 813.
[4]   *(1997–1998) 151 ALR 147.*
[5]   See *(1997–1998) 151 ALR 147* at 190.
[6]   See *(1997–1998) 151 ALR 147* at 155.
[7]   See also *per* Kirby J in *(1997–1998) 151 ALR 147* at 155: 'In my opinion the criticisms of the notion to "rule" of "general reliance" are unanswerable.'

Intuitive notions of responsibility

[15.33]   While doubts such as these, expressed at a high judicial level, are significant, it is submitted that the preference for perceived legislative intention over the concept of 'general reliance' is not entirely convincing. As the cases on breach of statutory duty vividly illustrate, searching for unexpressed legislative intentions has strong overtones of fiction.[1] 'General reliance', on the other hand, has a firmer grounding in intuitive notions of responsibility and the experience of day-to-day life.[2] Thus, most people assume that the health and fire services will come to their aid if needed, whereas motorists do not proceed on the basis that every road upon which they travel will be configured at a uniformly high level of safety.[3]

[1]   See generally CHAPTER 16 below.

2   Cf *per* McHugh J, striking a rather different note from his brethren, in *Pyrenees Shire Council v Day* *(1997–1998) 151 ALR 147* at 177: 'I do not think that it is correct to say that the doctrine of general reliance is a fiction or that it gives rise to common law duties that are inconsistent with the conferment of discretionary powers and functions.'
3   Cf *Stovin v Wise [1996] AC 923, [1996] 3 All ER 801.*

Form and substance

[15.34]   In so far as the doctrine of 'general reliance' has a place within the conceptual structure of the negligence liability of public authorities, it will operate to constrain the discretionary freedom of an authority at the policy level. This makes it easier to understand why that doctrine is to be regarded with caution. Its capacity to convert a power directly into a duty, and thereby subvert the distinction between policy and operations, means inevitably that the opportunities for its sucessful invocation will be few in number. It is likely to have its greatest utility in situations in which the statutory power has been in existence for many years and has been so regularly exercised that, although in form a power, it has come to be regarded by authorities, as well as by the public at large, as being in substance a duty.

Regulatory functions

[15.35]   In *Davis v Radcliffe*[1] the plaintiffs lost money when a bank, which had been operated under a licence issued by an agency of the government of the Isle of Man, collapsed. The plaintiffs sued the defendant agency for negligence in not revoking the licence. But the Privy Council held that the defendants owed no duty of care to the plaintiff and, applying an earlier decision of its own in an appeal from Hong Kong involving similar facts,[2] struck the claim out. Lord Goff said:[3]

> '... it must have been the statutory intention that the licensing system should be operated in the interests of the public as a whole; and, when those charged with its operation are faced with making decisions with regard, for example, to refusing to renew licences or to revoking licences, such decisions can well involve the exercise of judgment of a delicate nature affecting the whole future of the relevant bank in the Isle of Man, and the impact of any consequent cessation of the bank's business in the Isle of Man, not merely on the customers and creditors of the bank, but indeed on the future of financial services in the island. In circumstances such as these, competing interests have to be carefully weighed and balanced in the public interest, and, in some circumstances ... it may for example be more in the public interest to attempt to nurse an ailing bank back to health than to hasten its collapse. The making of decisions such as these is a characteristic task of modern regulatory agencies; and the very nature of the task, with its emphasis on the broader public interest, is one which militates strongly against the imposition of a duty of care being imposed on such an agency in favour of any particular section of the public.'[4]

1   *[1990] 2 All ER 536, [1990] 1 WLR 821.*
2   See *Yuen Kun Yeu v A-G of Hong Kong [1988] AC 175, [1987] 2 All ER 705.*
3   *[1990] 2 All ER 536* at 541, *[1990] 1 WLR 821* at 827.
4   See also *Minories Finance Ltd v Arthur Young (a firm) [1989] 2 All ER 105.*

Absence of countervailing considerations

[15.36]   Thus, bodies entrusted with regulatory functions in the public interest are unlikely to be subject to negligence liability in so far as the discharge of wide discretionary functions is concerned. But if the exercise of discretion is not involved, it appears that liability may be imposed even if the overall context is one of regulatory governmental activity in the public interest. In *Lonrho plc v Tebbit*[1] the plaintiff company had given an undertaking to the Secretary of State for Trade and Industry that it would not acquire more than 30% of the shares in a certain company, following a report by the Monopolies and Mergers Commission that it would be against the public interest for it to do so. A subsequent report by the Commission concluded that acquisition of the company by the plaintiffs would not, after all, be against the public interest and the Secretary of State eventually released them from their undertaking. That release did, however, come too late for the plaintiffs to launch a takeover bid for the company in question, which they would otherwise have done, and they alleged that this delay had been avoidable and negligent and had caused them economic loss. The defendant (ie the government) sought to have the claim struck out on the ground that it disclosed no cause of action. Sir Nicolas Browne-Wilkinson V-C, in a judgment upheld by the Court of Appeal, held that the striking out application would fail. Notwithstanding the statutory and governmental context of the negligence action, and the fact that the claim was for economic loss, it was arguable that there were no countervailing considerations of public interest which would necessarily preclude the imposition upon the defendant of a private law duty of care in favour of the defendant.[2]

1   *[1991] 4 All ER 973*; affd *[1992] 4 All ER 280*.
2   'For all I know, the reason for the delay in releasing the undertaking was a purely administrative blunder (eg the papers being wrongly filed), involving no considerations of policy at all': *[1991] 4 All ER 973* at 985, *per* Sir Nicolas Browne-Wilkinson V-C. See also *R (on the application of A) v Secretary for the Home Department [2004] EWHC 1585 (Admin) [2004] NLJR 1411* (Home Secretary liable for administrative error by immigration officials which caused economic loss to claimant).

Relevance of the statute

[15.37]   In *X (minors) v Bedfordshire County Council* Lord Browne-Wilkinson said:[1]

' … the question whether there is …a common law duty and if so its ambit, must be profoundly influenced by the statutory framework within which the acts complained of were done … a common law duty of care cannot be imposed … if the observance of such common law duty of care would be inconsistent with, or have a tendency to discourage, the due performance by the local authority of its statutory duties'.

The inevitability of using the statute in this way as a starting point must not be confused with implausibly ascribing the outcome entirely to the statute itself[2]. Lord Browne-Wilkinson's insistence that the duty is a *common law* one is important. The court should seek to ascertain, in general terms, the broad purpose of the legislation as a preliminary to itself determining whether the imposition of a tortious duty of care in negligence would be appropriate. But the need to have regard to the statute *does* mean that distinctions which the common law draws elsewhere might be disregarded and, conversely, that other constraints may be imposed which would normally be irrelevant.

1   See *[1995] 2 AC 633* at 739. Subsequent criticism, and narrow distinguishing of the Bedfordshire case (see earlier in this chapter and in CHAPTER 1 above) have not affected the point in the text.
2   Cf *Stovin v Wise [1996] AC 923, [1996] 3 All ER 801*.

Health and safety

[15.38]   If the claimant has suffered personal injury, and if the statute was concerned, albeit not necessarily exclusively, with risks to health and safety[1], the courts appear more ready to impose liability than if the claim was for financial loss or damage to property[2]. In one case Morland J refused to strike out a claim against the Health and Safety Executive itself for alleged negligence in the discharge of routine inspection responsibilities[3]. The unquestioned assumption that the National Health Service is rightly held liable routinely in medical negligence cases is also in point here. Conversely, in *Reeman v Department of Transport*[4] the Court of Appeal rejected a negligent misstatement claim for substantial financial losses which resulted from the allegedly negligent certification as safe of a dangerous, and hence unsellable, fishing vessel. 'The purpose of the certificate', observed Lord Bingham CJ, 'was to safeguard the physical safety of the vessel and her crew; it was not directed in any way to the market value of the vessel'[5]. On the other hand, if the statutory power is expressly concerned with financial matters it is possible that it may facilitate a finding in favour of liability for pure economic loss, which the ordinary law of negligence would not countenance[6].

[1]   See *Kent v Griffiths [2000] 2 All ER 474, CA.* See also *Perrett v Collins [1998] 2 Lloyd's Rep 255, CA.*
[2]   This parallels the situation in the context of the action for breach of statutory duty where safety legislation, particularly in the employment field, is pre-eminent as a source of actionability: see Keith Stanton and others *Statutory Torts* (2003) Ch 10.
[3]   See *Thames Trains v Health and Safety Executive [2003] PIQR P202.* See also *Sutradhar v Natural Environment Research Council [2003] PIQR P34.*
[4]   *[1997] 2 Lloyd's Rep 648.*
[5]   See *[1997] 2 Lloyd's Rep 648* at 685.
[6]   See *per* Browne-Wilkinson V-C in *Lonrho plc v Tebbit [1991] 4 All ER 973* at 985–986.

D Liability at policy level

Carelessness relating to the discretion itself

[15.39]   At least in theory it seems to be clear that a body upon which a statutory power has been conferred may lose the protection of the public policy 'defence', and hence become subject to liability in negligence, even if the alleged carelessness related to the exercise or non-exercise of the discretion itself.[1] That is to say a claim in negligence is not a weapon which is inherently limited to the so-called 'operational' sphere.[2] A condition precedent to the establishment of such liability at the 'planning' or 'policy' level is that the body in question should have acted ultra vires the statutory power. This lies at the heart of the reasoning both of Lord Diplock in *Home Office v Dorset Yacht Co*[3] and of Lord Wilberforce in *Anns v Merton London Borough Council.*[4] Even if this condition is satisfied, however, it will be far from easy to make out a valid claim in negligence.

[1]   See *per* Lord Wilberforce in *Anns v Merton London Borough Council [1978] AC 728* at 755, *[1977] 2 All ER 492* at 501 ('Their immunity from attack ... though great is not absolute'). See also *Kane v New Forest DC [2002] 3 All ER 9141* rejecting the 'submission that a planning authority has blanket immunity from claims for negligence' (per May LJ at para 33).
[2]   But cf *per* Lord Browne-Wilkinson in *X v Bedfordshire County Council [1995] 3 All ER 353* at 371: ' ... a common law duty of care in relation to the taking of decisions involving policy matters cannot exist.'
[3]   *[1970] AC 1004, [1970] 2 All ER 294, HL.*
[4]   *[1978] AC 728, [1977] 2 All ER 492, HL.*

Ultra vires and negligence

[15.40]   The mere fact that a decision was ultra vires does not mean that it was necessarily taken negligently. In *Dunlop v Woollahra Municipal Council*[1] the plaintiff complained that he had suffered loss as a result of certain resolutions of a local planning authority, which had subsequently been judicially determined to have been ultra vires. The authority had, however, passed the resolutions in good faith and after taking competent legal advice. Moreover, until the resolutions were formally pronounced invalid, the arguments relating to their invalidity had been 'evenly balanced'.[2] The Judicial Committee of the Privy Council held that the plaintiff's allegation that the authority had been negligent in passing the resolutions failed.

[1]   *[1982] AC 158, [1981] 1 All ER 1202.*
[2]   *[1982] AC 158* at 172, *[1981] 1 All ER 1202* at 1209, *per* Lord Diplock, delivering the judgment of the Board.

Overkill

[15.41]   Indeed, situations in which plaintiffs will succeed in proving that ultra vires decisions were reached negligently are likely to be extremely rare. The formidable difficulties facing those who seek to establish cases on these lines were emphasised by the Judicial Committee of the Privy Council in *Rowling v Takaro Properties,*[1] in which such a claim was unsuccessfully advanced. The Board identified what it described as 'overkill' as one of the arguments *ab inconvenienti* against the imposition of liability. 'Once it became known', said Lord Keith delivering the judgment of the Board,[2] 'that liability in negligence may be imposed on the ground that a minister has misconstrued a statute and so acted ultra vires, the cautious civil servant may go to extreme lengths in ensuring that legal advice, or even the opinion of the court, is obtained before decisions are taken, thereby leading to unnecessary delay in a considerable number of cases'.

[1]   *[1988] AC 473, [1988] 1 All ER 163.*
[2]   *[1988] AC 473* at 502, *[1988] 1 All ER 163* at 173.

Very difficult to prove

[15.42]   If a statutory body *deliberately* misuses its powers it may be liable to damages for the tort of misfeasance in public office.[1] But falling short of instances of that kind, wrongdoing capable of constituting actionable carelessness will be very difficult to prove. Political compromises and trade-offs, not to mention clashes of personality between individuals involved, are characteristic, and quite legitimately so, of the ways in which committees and similar bodies function when charged with deciding broad policy questions. To attempt to dissect their deliberations, using the delicate apparatus of the law of negligence, will seldom be anything other than a thoroughly unsatisfactory exercise.

[1]   See *Three Rivers DC v Bank of England (No 3) [2000] 3 All ER 1, [2000] 2 WLR 79, HL; Akenzua v Home Secretary [2003] 1 All ER 35.*

Causation

[15.43]   If a claimant does succeed in proving that an ultra vires decision was reached carelessly, he may still experience difficulty in showing that any losses which he suffered were, in the legal sense, caused by the defendant.[1] It has even been suggested that, since everyone is entitled to ignore an invalid act, someone who relies on one to his detriment is the source of his own loss![2] But this is quite unrealistic. Until a decision has actually been pronounced invalid by a competent court it will seldom be prudent simply to ignore it.[3] It is submitted that this particular causation argument should therefore not constitute an effective obstacle to a claimant.

---

[1]   See generally C Harlow *Compensation and Government Torts* (1982) pp 92–97.
[2]   See *per* Lord Diplock, delivering the judgment of the Privy Council in *Dunlop v Woollahra Municipal Council [1982] AC 158* at 172, *[1981] 1 All ER 1202* at 1209.
[3]   In any event, ignoring it may not be possible: see *Hoffmann-La Roche & Co Ltd v Secretary of State for Trade [1975] AC 295, [1974] 2 All ER 1128, HL.*

Reaching the same decision

[15.44]   A more formidable objection to liability is that merely because a particular decision is held to have been, in the particular circumstances, ultra vires, it does not follow that the body in question could not have reached exactly the same decision and yet have stayed intra vires.[1] This will obviously be particularly so if the basis of invalidity is simply procedural irregularity, such as breach of the rules of natural justice. It will often be perfectly possible for the administrative body to correct the defect and act *validly* against the claimant's interest, for example by revoking his licence or whatever. In such circumstances there will clearly be considerable force in the contention that the claimant suffered no actionable loss.

---

[1]   Cf *per* Lord Keith, delivering the judgment of the Judicial Committee of the Privy Council, in *Rowling v Takaro Properties [1988] AC 473, [1988] 1 All ER 163.*

City of Kamloops v Nielsen

[15.45]   In view of all the attendant difficulties, it is not surprising that there appears to be no reported case decided in England in which an allegation of negligence has succeeded, in circumstances in which the decision in question could plausibly be regarded as having been one of discretion or policy with no 'operational' content. In *City of Kamloops v Nielsen,*[1] however, the Supreme Court of Canada, by a bare majority,[2] held a local authority liable in just such a case. The situation was one in which, following an inspection revealing a clear breach of building regulations[3], the authority took no follow-up action having instead, in the words of the majority judgment, 'dropped the matter because one of its aldermen was involved'.[4] The interest of this case is increased by the fact that two members of the court dissented precisely on the ground that the decision had been one of policy upon which a private law duty of care in negligence should not be superimposed.

---

[1]   *(1984) 10 DLR (4th) 641.* This case is among those discussed by Stephen Todd in 'The Negligence Liability of Public Authorities: Divergence in the Common Law' (1986) 102 LQR 370.
[2]   Wilson, Ritchie and Dickson JJ; McIntyre and Estey JJ dissenting.
[3]   Cf *Anns v Merton London Borough Council [1978] AC 728, [1977] 2 All ER 492.*
[4]   *(1984) 10 DLR (4th) 641* at 673.

E Protecting from harm inflicted by third parties

Omissions

[15.46]   In many of the situations in which attempts are made to impose liability upon statutory bodies the complaint is essentially that the body in question omitted to act promptly or decisively enough to prevent a third party, such as an insolvent bank, an abusing parent or a careless motorist, from inflicting loss on the claimant. In such circumstances the imposition of liability may potentially be in conflict with common law principles relating to the absence of liability for omissions as distinct from positive acts.[1] On the other hand, there are established common law exceptions to the fundamental principle of non-liability for omissions,[2] and it is evident that at least some statutory situations can be brought within the scope of these exceptions on fairly orthodox grounds. Thus, the existence of statutory powers might be regarded as creating a 'special relationship',[3] between public bodies and potential claimants, enabling concepts such as those of 'undertaking' or 'reliance' to be invoked. In *Stovin v Wise*[4] it was contended that the 'existence of the statutory powers' created 'a 'proximity' between the highway authority and the highway user which would not otherwise exist.[5] In response to this argument, Lord Hoffmann accepted that some of the factors which may negate liability for omissions in cases against private individuals do not apply to public bodies, in particular the need to respect the freedom and autonomy of individual human beings,[6] but his Lordship nevertheless concluded that 'this does not mean that the distinctions between acts and omissions is irrelevant to the duties of a public body'.[7]

[1] See M Bowman and S Bailey 'Negligence in the Realms of Public Law – A Positive Obligation to Rescue?' [1984] PL 277. See also *Davis v Radcliffe* [1990] 2 All ER 536 at 541, PC.
[2] For discussion of liability for omissions see generally P Atiyah *Accidents, Compensation and the Law* (6th edn, 1999, Cane ed) pp 60–69. See also CHAPTER 1 above.
[3] Cf *Hedley Byrne & Co Ltd v Heller & Partners Ltd [1964] AC 465, [1963] 2 All ER 575, HL.*
[4] *[1996] AC 923, [1996] 3 All ER 801.*
[5] *[1996] AC 923 at 947, [1996] 3 All ER 801 at 822.*
[6] 'It is one thing for the law to say that a person who undertakes some activity shall take reasonable care not to cause damage to others. It is another thing for the law to require that a person who is doing nothing in particular shall take steps to prevent another from suffering harm from the acts of third parties … or natural causes … In political terms it is less of an invasion of an individual's freedom for the law to require him to consider the safety of others in his actions than to impose upon him a duty to rescue or protect. A moral version of this point may be called the "Why pick on me?" argument. A duty to prevent harm to others or to render assistance to a person in danger or distress may apply to a large and indeterminate class of people who happen to be able to do something. Why should one be liable rather than another?' *per* Lord Hoffmann in *Stovin v Wise [1996] AC 923 at 943–944, [1996] 3 All ER 801 at 819.*
[7] *[1996] AC 923 at 946, [1996] 3 All ER 801 at 821.* But cf *per* Lord Nicholls (dissenting): 'Unlike an individual, a public authority is not an indifferent onlooker. An authority is entrusted and charged with responsibilities for the public good. The powers are intended to be exercised in a suitable case. Compelling a public authority to act does not represent an intrusion into private affairs in the same way as when a private individual is compelled to act': *[1996] AC 923 at 935, [1996] 3 All ER 801 at 811.*

Unsatisfactory distinctions

[15.47] It would be unfortunate, however, if emphasis upon the omissions question had the effect of resuscitating some of the unsatisfactory distinctions drawn in earlier cases involving negligence claims based upon statutory powers. It is therefore submitted that the insistence of Robert Goff J (as he then was) in *Fellowes v Rother District Council*[1] that there is now 'no rule that, *merely because* the defendant was acting under a statutory power as opposed to a statutory duty, liability is contingent on the defendant causing the plaintiff fresh or additional damage'[2] is still good law.[3]

[1] *[1983] 1 All ER 513 at 522.*
[2] Cf *East Suffolk Rivers Catchment Board v Kent [1941] AC 74, [1940] 4 All ER 527, HL.*
[3] See also *per* Lord Nicholls (dissenting) in *Stovin v Wise [1996] AC 923 at 931, [1996] 3 All ER 801 at 807.*

F Summary

[15.48] In the uncertain state of the authorities it may be a helpful, if hazardous, exercise to attempt to summarise the present state of the law in relation to negligence in the exercise of statutory powers in a series of numbered propositions:

(1)   All cases are presumed to be justiciable until the contrary is shown.

(2)   Decisions involving major decisions of policy may be non-justiciable, especially where the general allocation of resources is involved.

(3)   The court may be prepared to assume jurisdiction even in the 'policy' field if the decision which was reached was not merely 'ultra vires,' but had also been reached in a careless fashion. The fact that the decision-making processes involved in the taking of such decisions are, however, in a general sense, political in nature will make actionable carelessness exceedingly difficult to prove, and the chances of a claim succeeding are remote.

(4)   The more 'operational' the situation in which the damage occurred, in the sense of having involved the implementation of policy rather than policy itself, the more likely is any carelessness to be held to constitute actionable negligence. The distinction between 'policy' and 'operational' decisions will, however, often be a matter of degree rather than clear cut.

(5)   Once the court is satisfied that the carelessness in question did occur in the 'operational', rather than the policy, sphere the distinction between 'ultra vires' and 'intra vires' decisions is of no relevance.

(6)   Even if the 'operational' requirement in (4) above is satisfied, and carelessness was present, a claim will still fail if the loss which occurred as the result of the carelessness was not of a type which the statutory discretion was conferred to prevent.

(7)   Even if the loss *was* of a type which the statutory discretion was conferred to prevent, a claim *might* still fail on the ground that the overall statutory purpose is perceived to be hostile to funds being expended upon monetary compensation.

(8)   A broad statutory purpose in *favour* of compensation is more likely to be perceived to exist if the situation is one in which the claimant in particular, or members of society in general, can plausibly be said to have been entitled to *rely* on the discretion being exercised in order to prevent harm from occurring.

(9)   If a claimant *is* able to satisfy the foregoing requirements for liability in the context of operational negligence, he might nevertheless fail if the court does not consider it to be 'just and reasonable' to impose liability. This may occur if, for example, liability would tend to make public servants over-cautious or defensive.

(10)   If a claimant *has* succeeded in satisfying all the above requirements for the imposition of liability, including that of 'justice and reasonableness', he *cannot* be defeated on the ground that the carelessness in question merely failed to make matters worse and/or that the defendant merely failed to prevent a third party from inflicting harm on the plaintiff.

(11) If a claimant is unable to satisfy *any* of the above requirements, save only the threshold requirement of justiciability, he may still succeed in obtaining damages for negligence from the public authority for damage inflicted while exercising a statutory power if, *but only if*, the authority did actually intervene in the situation in question and, in so doing, caused additional harm which would not otherwise have occurred.

Chapter 16

The action for breach of statutory duty[1]

A The nature of liability

Introduction

[16.01] 'The basic proposition', said Lord Browne-Wilkinson in *X v Bedfordshire County Council*,[2] 'is that in the ordinary case a breach of statutory duty does not, by itself, give rise to any private law cause of action'. It is certainly now clear that, apart from the well-established exception of an employer's responsibility for the welfare of his employees,[3] tortious liability for contravention of a statute will rarely be imposed if the statute does not expressly provide for it. Nevertheless, although it is rare, such liability is far from being non-existent; and yet the law governing the recovery of damages for breach of statutory duty is notoriously uncertain. Some aspects of the topic concern the extent to which *intentional* activities of the defendant, which have adversely affected the claimant, should attract a legal remedy. Thus, much litigation has involved the relationship between statutory duties and the law of economic torts concerned with unfair trade competition.[4] Although such issues fall outside the scope of this book, the reasoning in some of the cases, on the scope of the action for breach of statutory duty in general, does have some relevance. Moreover, it is important to note that recent decisions of the European Court of Justice, concerning liability in damages for breach of European Community law,[5] may eventually have an impact upon the development of the municipal English law relating to breach of statutory duty, and that impact might not be confined to the competition field.[6]

---

[1]   Keith Stanton and others *Statutory Torts* (London, 2003); K M Stanton 'New Forms of the Tort of Breach of Statutory Duty' (2004) 120 LQR 324; R A Buckley 'Liability in Tort for Breach of Statutory Duty' (1984) 100 LQR 204. (The permission of Stevens & Sons Ltd to reproduce below material which formerly appeared in this article in the Law Quarterly Review is gratefully acknowledged.) See also F Bennion 'Codifying the Tort of Breach of Statutory Duty' (1996) 17 Statute LR 192.

[2]   See *[1995] 2 AC 633* at 731, *[1995] 3 All ER 353* at 364.

[3]   See the numerous cases arising out of accidents at work, some of which are considered in greater detail in CHAPTER 17 below.

[4]   See *Ex p Island Records [1978] Ch 122, [1978] 3 All ER 824, CA*; *Lonrho Ltd v Shell Petroleum Co Ltd (No 2) [1982] AC 173, [1981] 2 All ER 456, HL*; *RCA Corpn v Pollard [1983] Ch 135, [1982] 3 All ER 771, CA*; *Rickless v United Artists Corpn [1988] QB 40, [1987] 1 All ER 679*; *CBS Songs Ltd v Amstrad Consumer Electronics plc [1988] Ch 61, [1987] 3 All ER 151, CA*. Cf *O'Rourke v Camden London Borough Council [1998] AC 188, [1997] 3 All ER 23, HL*.

[5]   See especially *Brasserie du Pêcheur SA v Germany, R v Secretary of State for Transport, ex p Factortame Ltd [1996] 1 ECR 1029, [1996] 1 All ER (EC) 301*. See also *R v HM Treasury, ex p British Telecommunications plc [1996] 2 CMLR 217*. For a ruling of the Divisional Court resulting from the decision of the ECJ in the *Factortame* litigation, see *R v Secretary of State for Transport, ex p Factortame Ltd [1998] 1 All ER 736n*.

[16.02] *The action for breach of statutory duty[1]*

6   For discussion see P P Craig 'Once More Unto the Breach: the Community, The State and Damages Liability' (1997) 113 LQR 67, especially at p 87 onwards; T A Downes 'Trawling for a Remedy: State Liability Under Community Law' (1997) 17 LS 286, especially at p 299 onwards.

The issues

[16.02] For present purposes, however, we are concerned with situations in which claims for damages for breach of statutory duty are made in the context of careless, rather than deliberate, conduct, where the relationship with negligence is closer. Allied to, or specific aspects of, the broad question of the relationship between negligence and breach of statutory duty are issues such as the following. Just when will liability for the latter arise? Is such liability 'strict' or fault-based? What defences are available?

Background

[16.03] The *Statute 7 & 8 Vict c 112* (re merchant seamen, 1844), *s 18* required ships sailing from the UK to carry medicines on board as prescribed in a list published by the Board of Trade. In *Couch v Steel*[1] the plaintiff sailor became ill while at sea, and suffered damage as a result of the defendant shipowner having failed to comply with this requirement. His claim for damages was successful. Lord Campbell CJ spoke in broad terms of the 'right, by the common law, to maintain an action on the case for special damage sustained by the breach of a public duty'.[2] The correctness of this wide approach was subsequently doubted, however, in *Atkinson v Newcastle and Gateshead Waterworks*.[3] In this case the Court of Appeal held the defendant statutory undertakers not liable for damages arising out of their failure to maintain the water-pressure in a 'fire-plug', used for fighting fires, at the level required by statute.[4] Lord Cairns LC stated that the availability of a civil action, where a statute had been breached, 'must ... depend on the purview of the legislature in the particular statute, and the language which they have there employed'.[5] Although *Couch v Steel* has never been overruled, and in one twentieth-century case was relied on with approval by a strong Court of Appeal,[6] *Atkinson*'s case is generally regarded as having marked a sharp change in approach, whereby a narrower 'construction' technique replaced the earlier, wider, view as to the scope of tortious liability.[7]

1   *(1854) 3 E & B 402.*
2   *(1854) 3 Ex B 402* at 415.
3   *(1877) 2 Ex D 441.*
4   See also the recent case of *Church of Jesus Christ of Latter Day Saints (Great Britain) v West Yorkshire Fire and Civil Defence Authority,* sub nom *Capital and Counties plc v Hampshire County Council [1997] QB 1004, [1997] 2 All ER 865, CA,* in which liability was again denied in a somewhat similar situation. Cf *Dawson & Co v Bingley UDC [1911] 2 KB 149, CA* (which was distinguished in the *West Yorkshire* case).
5   *(1877) 2 Ex D 441* at 448. See also *Cowley v Newmarket Local Board [1892] AC 345 at 352, HL, per* Lord Herschell; *Saunders v Holborn District Board of Works [1895] 1 QB 64 at 68, per* Mathew J.
6   See *Simmonds v Newport Abercarn Black Vein Steam Coal Co [1921] 1 KB 616, CA* (Bankes, Scrutton and Atkin LJJ).
7   See *Winfield and Jolowicz on Tort* (16th edn, 2002), p 265; *Street on Torts* (11th edn, 2003) p 457, n 3.

'Construction' approach

[16.04] Thus, in *Phillips v Britannia Hygienic Laundry Co*[1] the Court of Appeal emphatically adopted the restrictive 'construction' approach when refusing to allow a claim for losses suffered by the plaintiff in a road accident, which had occurred in circumstances in which the *Motor Cars (Use and Construction) Order 1904* had been contravened by the defendant.² In a later case in the House of Lords,³ Lord Simonds stated expressly that the 'only rule which in all circumstances is valid is that the answer must depend on a consideration of the whole Act and the circumstances, including the pre-existing law, in which it was enacted'.

¹ *[1923] 2 KB 832, CA.*
² See also *Exel Logistics v Curran [2004] EWCA Civ 1249; Tan Chye Choo v Chong Kew Moi [1970] 1 All ER 266, [1970] 1 WLR 147*, PC. Cf *Badham v Lambs Ltd [1946] KB 45, [1945] 2 All ER 295.*
³ *Cutler v Wandsworth Stadium Ltd [1949] AC 398* at 407, *[1949] 1 All ER 544* at 548.

'Special damage'

[16.05] Nevertheless, traces of the older, wider, attitude can still be found in relatively recent judgments. These are apt to reflect the terminology and concepts familiar in the anomalous tort of public nuisance,¹ and to assert that an individual who can show that a criminal act has caused him 'special damage over and above the generality of the public'² can bring a civil action. It is possible that this approach may still occasionally be of relevance to claims for injunctive relief in cases involving the intentional carrying on of unlawful activities.³ As far as claims in tort for damages are concerned, however, it is submitted that, with the exception of isolated historical survivals, such as public nuisance highway cases,⁴ this wider view was finally swept away by the decision of the House of Lords in *Lonrho v Shell Petroleum.*⁵ Lord Diplock, with whom the other members of the House agreed, echoed the words of Lord Simonds in *Cutler v Wandsworth Stadium,* and observed that:

'the question whether legislation which makes the doing or omitting to do a particular act a criminal offence renders the person guilty of such offence liable also in a civil action for damages at the suit of any person who thereby suffers loss or damage is a question of construction of the legislation.'⁶

¹ See above CHAPTER 14.
² *Per* Lord Denning in *Ex p Island Records [1978] Ch 122* at 135, *[1978] 3 All ER 824* at 829, CA. See also *per* Lord Fraser in *Gouriet v Union of Post Office Workers [1978] AC 435* at 518, *[1977] 3 All ER 70* at 114, HL: 'The general rule is that a private person is only entitled to sue in respect of interference with a public right if *either* there is also interference with a private right of his *or the interference with the public right will inflict special damage on him*' (italics supplied).
³ Cf *CBS Songs Ltd v Amstrad Consumer Electronics plc [1988] Ch 61, [1987] 3 All ER 151, CA.*
⁴ See *Lonrho Ltd v Shell Petroleum Co Ltd (No 2) [1982] AC 173* at 185, *[1981] 2 All ER 456* at 461, *per* Lord Diplock.
⁵ *[1982] AC 173, [1981] 2 All ER 456, HL.*
⁶ *[1982] AC 173* at 183, *[1981] 2 All ER 456* at 460. See also *West Wiltshire District Council v Garland [1995] Ch 297, [1995] 2 All ER 17, CA.*

Tort and crime

[16.06] The demise of the 'special damage' approach in this area is to be welcomed. It would have made all crimes potentially torts as well. But the reasons for the imposition of criminal liability in a given situation might be quite different from those which normally underlie civil liability for damages,¹ and such an unprincipled extension of the law of tort would be quite inappropriate.

¹ A good example is provided by the now repealed statutes against forcible entry, which could subject a person to criminal liability for re-entering his own property following an illegal dispossession. The

courts understandably always refused to allow illegal possessors to recover damages for breach of statutory duty after a forcible re-entry had taken place: see *Beddall v Maitland (1881) 17 Ch D 174*; *Hemmings v Stoke Poges Golf Club [1920] 1 KB 720, CA.*

Fiction of legislative intention as to civil liability

[16.07]   Rejection of the 'special damage' approach to the imposition of civil liability for damages in this context should not be confused with approval of the proposition that the task of the courts is to determine whether or not the legislature, in passing the Act in question, impliedly *intended* to create a right of action in tort. On the contrary, the notion that liability in this area depends exclusively upon legislative intention, an intention *ex hypothesi* wholly unexpressed, is a patent fiction.[1] It is high time that it was finally abandoned.[2] The *general* purpose of the statute undoubtedly lies at the heart of the determination of the question, and to that extent the matter is rightly regarded as one of construction, but whether it is appropriate to seek to further that purpose by the addition of civil liability is ultimately a question for the common law itself.[3] As Lord Diplock observed in a case decided by the House of Lords on the *Factories Act 1961*: 'The statutes say nothing about civil remedies for breaches of their provisions. The judgments of the courts say all.'[4]

[1]   A misleading comparison is sometimes drawn between the action in tort for breach of statutory duty and certain specific aspects of the law relating to illegality in contract: see eg *Shaw v Groom [1970] 2 QB 504* at 523, *[1970] 1 All ER 702* at 711, CA, *per* Sachs LJ. In the latter context, however, the concept of legislative intent may be meaningful: see R A Buckley 'Implied Statutory Prohibition of Contracts' (1975) 38 MLR 535.

[2]   See *O'Connor v SP Bray (1937) 56 CLR 464* at 477–478, *per* Dixon J.

[3]   See E Thayer 'Public Wrong and Private Action' (1914) 27 Harv LR 317; Alexander 'Legislation and the Standard of Care in Negligence' (1964) 42 Can B Rev 243.

[4]   *Boyle v Kodak Ltd [1969] 2 All 439* at 446, *[1969] 1 WLR 661* at 672, HL.

Not confined to existing law of negligence

[16.08]   It is sometimes suggested that civil claims for damages arising out of breaches of statutes should be confined to situations in which the existing common law of negligence already imposes liability for carelessness.[1] The statutory provision is then regarded as determining, either conclusively or persuasively, that failure to take the measures required by it constitutes carelessness, thereby rendering it difficult or impossible for the defendant to argue that failure to take the relevant steps was not unreasonable in the circumstances. This approach may be unexceptionable in situations in which the statutory provision does in fact overlap with existing common law liability, but it would have an undesirable limiting effect on the imposition of liability in other types of case. It would, for example, imply that statutes which created positive duties to act could never give rise to civil liability unless the situation was one of those in which the existing common law, atypically, also imposed such a duty. A refusal to countenance liability outside the existing tort framework could lead to paradox: it will often be on account of defects or lacunae in the existing law that the statute will have been enacted.

[1]   See G Williams 'The Effect of Penal Legislation in the Law of Tort' (1960) 23 MLR 223. See also E Thayer 'Public Wrong and Private Action' (1914) 27 Harv LR 317.

Statutory negligence doctrine rejected

[16.09]   Fortunately, although the 'statutory negligence' doctrine has enjoyed some degree of support in the USA[1] and Canada,[2] English courts have never accepted the invitation to decline to use statutes to develop the law, in favour of the preservation of an existing conceptual straitjacket. In *London Passenger Transport Board v Upson*[3] Lord Wright expressed himself as follows:

> '… a claim for damages for breach of statutory duty intended to protect a person in the position of the particular plaintiff is a specific common law right which is not to be confused in essence with a claim for negligence. The statutory right has its origin in the statute, but the particular remedy of an action for damages is given by the common law in order to make effective, for the benefit of the injured plaintiff, his right to the performance by the defendant of the defendant's statutory duty. It is an effective sanction. It is not a claim in negligence in the strict or ordinary sense … it is essential to keep in mind the fundamental differences of the two classes of claim.'

[1]   See E Thayer, (1914) 27 Harv LR 317. For discussion of current American approaches, see generally Harper, James and Gray *The Law of Torts* (2nd edn, 1986) vol 3 pp 613–648; *Prosser and Keeton on Torts* (5th edn, 1984) pp 220–234.
[2]   See *The Queen in Right of Canada v Saskatchewan Wheat Pool (1983) 143 DLR (3d) 9*, noted by M H Mathews in (1984) 4 OJLS 429.
[3]   *[1949] AC 155* at 168, *[1949] 1 All ER 60* at 67, HL.

'Statutory negligence' and the nature of the loss

[16.10]   Perhaps the most famous example of implicit rejection of the constraints of the 'statutory negligence' doctrine is the decision of the Court of Appeal in *Monk v Warbey*.[1] In this case a defendant who, in breach of statute, permitted an uninsured driver to use his car, was held liable to a victim injured by the driver's negligence when the latter had insufficient funds to satisfy the claim himself. Despite being criticised as an 'improper type of judicial invention,'[2] this decision has been followed in subsequent cases[3] and its correctness assumed in the House of Lords.[4]

[1]   *[1935] 1 KB 75, CA.*
[2]   See G Williams in 'The Effect of Penal Legislation in the Law of Tort' (1960) 23 MLR 233 at 259.
[3]   See *Martin v Dean [1971] 2 QB 208, [1971] 3 All ER 279*. Cf *Daniels v Vaux [1938] 2 KB 203, [1938] 2 All ER 271; Fleming v M'Gillivray 1945 SLT 301.*
[4]   See *Houston v Buchanan [1940] 2 All ER 179, 1940 SC (HL) 17.*

Monk v Warbey distinguished

[16.11]   *Monk v Warbey* was, however, distinguished very narrowly by a majority of the Court of Appeal in *Richardson v Pitt-Stanley*.[1] In this case a company failed to maintain insurance for injuries sustained by its employees contrary to the *Employers' Liability (Compulsory Insurance) Act 1969*. The company went into liquidation before the plaintiff had been able to recover the damages to which he was entitled in respect of an industrial injury. He therefore sought to recover what was, in effect, economic loss by bringing an action for breach of statutory duty against the directors of the company who could, under *section 5* of the Act, personally be criminally liable if they had facilitated the company's failure to take out appropriate insurance. The claim failed: Russell and Stuart-Smith LJJ perceived fine differences to exist between this case and *Monk v Warbey* with respect both to the factual situations involved in the two cases and the precise wording of their respective enactments. It is submitted, however, that the dissenting judgment of Sir John Megaw in favour of liability is to be preferred.

[1]   *[1995] QB 123, [1995] 1 All ER 460, CA.*

Economic loss

[16.12]   Although Stuart-Smith LJ suggested in *Richardson v Pitt-Stanley*[1] that 'the court will more readily construe a statutory provision so as to provide a civil cause of action where the provision relates to the safety and health of a class of persons rather than where they have merely suffered economic loss', his Lordship also conceded that 'this point clearly cannot be taken too far because *Monk v Warbey* itself is a case of protecting the injured claimant against economic loss'. Indeed, long before the decision in *Hedley Byrne v Heller,* and independently of *Monk v Warbey*, it seems to have been clear that pure financial loss could be recovered in the action for breach of statutory duty.[2] There are also other situations in which liability for breach of statutory duty has been imposed in circumstances in which no common law duty existed.[3] In the final analysis, the 'statutory negligence' doctrine, with its appeal to conceptual neatness, is inconsistent with the deeply pragmatic nature of the common law.

[1]   See *[1995] QB 123* at 132, *[1995] 1 All ER 460* at 468.
[2]   Such a claim succeeded in *Woods v Winskill [1913] 2 Ch 303*. See also *Simmonds v Newport Abercarn Black Vein Steam Coal Co [1921] 1 KB 616, CA; Moore v Canadian Pacific SS Co [1945] 1 All ER 128.* But cf *Wentworth v Wiltshire County Council [1993] QB 654, [1993] 2 All ER 256, CA.*
[3]   See *Sephton v Lancashire River Board [1962] 1 All ER 183, [1962] 1 WLR 623.*

B The scope of the Act

Protection of a 'class'

[16.13]   In *X v Bedfordshire County Council*[1] Lord Browne-Wilkinson observed that a question often asked is whether 'the statutory duty was imposed for the protection of a limited class of the public'. The origins of this notion can perhaps be found in *Clegg, Parkinson & Co v Earby Gas Co.*[2] In this case a consumer was refused an action when the defendant company failed to provide him with a supply of gas in the quantity, and of the purity, required by the *Gasworks Clauses Act 1871*. Wills J observed that 'where there is an obligation created by statute to do something for the benefit of the public generally ... there is no separate right of action to every person injured, by breach of the obligation, in no other manner than the rest of the public'.[3] His Lordship felt that were the law otherwise 'the undertakers might speedily be ruined'. Emphasis specifically upon a 'class' of persons as such, however, probably dates from the famous case of *Groves v Lord Wimborne*,[4] which established that an action would lie in favour of workpeople injured through failure to fence dangerous machinery as required by the Factories Acts. Rigby LJ observed that the legislation was 'intended for the protection from injury of a particular class of persons, who come within the mischief of the Act'.[5] A L Smith and Vaughan Williams LJJ also both used very similar language.[6] Statements to the same effect have often been made in subsequent cases.[7] The notion has, however, also been forcefully criticised, most notably by Atkin LJ in *Phillips v Britannia Hygienic Laundry Co.*[8]

[1]   *[1995] 2 AC 633* at 731, *[1995] 3 All ER 353* at 364.
[2]   *[1896] 1 QB 592.*
[3]   *[1896] 1 QB 592* at 594–595.
[4]   *[1898] 2 QB 402, CA.* For a recent application of the principle in *Groves'* case see *Ziemniak v ETPM Deep Sea [2003] 2 All ER (Comm) 283.* Cf *Todd v Adams [2002] 2 Lloyd's Rep 293.*
[5]   *[1898] 2 QB 402* at 414.

6   *[1898] 2 QB 402* at 407, 415, *per* A L Smith LJ and Vaughan Williams LJ.

7   See *Read v Croydon Corpn [1938] 4 All ER 631* at 652, *per* Stable J; *Hartley v Mayoh & Co [1954] 1 QB 383* at 391, *[1954] 1 All ER 375* at 379, CA, *per* Singleton LJ; *Solomons v R Gertzenstein Ltd [1954] 2 QB 243* at 261, 256, *[1954] 2 All ER 625* at 634–635, 637, CA, *per* Birkett LJ and Romer LJ; *Canadian Pacific Steamships Ltd v Bryers [1958] AC 485* at 505, *[1957] 3 All ER 572* at 581, HL, *per* Lord Tucker; *A-G v St Ives RDC [1960] 1 QB 312* at 324, *[1959] 3 All ER 371* at 377, *per* Salmon J.

8   'It would be strange if a less important duty which is owed to a section of the public may be enforced by an action, while a more important duty which is owed to the public at large cannot': *[1923] 2 KB 832* at 841. See also *Monk v Warbey [1935] 1 KB 75* at 82, 85, CA, *per* Greer LJ and Maugham LJ; *Solomons v Gertzenstein Ltd [1954] 2 QB 243* at 255, *[1954] 2 All ER 625* at 630–631, CA, *per* Somervell LJ (dissenting on this point); *McCall v Abelesz [1976] QB 585* at 596, *[1976] 1 All ER 727* at 732, CA, *per* Ormrod LJ; *Commerford v Board of School Comrs of Halifax [1950] 2 DLR 207* at 212, *per* Ilsey J.

Separate objectives

[16.14]   As a control device to limit liability for breach of statutory duty, the concept of class benefit appears to represent a muddled and inappropriate attempt to achieve two separate objectives. The first of these, which concerns the mischief at which the Act in question was directed, is already effectively covered by a different device; and to this extent the notion simply produces a confusing and unnecessary duplication of tests to embarrass the court. The second objective, which relates mainly to the special position of public authorities and statutory undertakers, would be better dealt with by explicit examination of the issues involved. These issues tend to be obscured rather than illuminated by the concept of 'benefit of a class'; this criticism of the concept will be amplified in the next two paragraphs.

Need for harm to be within the risk

[16.15]   The first apparent purpose of the concept of 'benefit of a class' is to ensure that, before damages for breach of statutory duty can be recovered, the claimant is obliged to demonstrate that the harm which he has suffered is of a kind which the legislation was intended to prevent[1]. A good example of its use for this purpose is to be found in *Knapp v Railway Executive*.[2] In this case a car collided with the closed gates of a level-crossing. Pursuant to a provision of the relevant private Act,[3] the gates should have been firm enough to stay closed despite the collision, but they were not. As a result they swung open into the path of an oncoming train. The driver of the train was injured and the question arose whether he had a right of action for breach of statutory duty. The Court of Appeal held that he did not.[4] Jenkins LJ[5] stated that the legislation 'define[d] the class of person to whom the company owe[d] a duty', and concluded that the particular duty to provide secure level-crossings was owed only to users of the highway and not to persons travelling on the railway itself.[6]

1   See *Fytche v Wincanton Logistics [2004] UKHL 31*, discussed in CHAPTER 17 below.
2   *[1949] 2 All ER 508*, CA.
3   The *Brighton and Chichester Railway Act 1844, s 274*.
4   Cf *Buxton v North Eastern Rly Co (1868) LR 3 QB 549*.
5   *[1949] 2 All ER 508* at 515. See also *per* Rigby LJ in *Groves v Lord Wimborne* (quoted in the text above) who expressly linked the notions of 'class' and 'mischief'.
6   Even if a passenger on the train had been injured he or she could not have recovered. Cf dictum, *per* Kelly CB in *Gorris v Scott (1874) LR 9 Exch 125* at 128, explained in *Knapp's case [1949] 2 All ER 508* at 516, *per* Jenkins LJ.

Gorris v Scott

[16.16]   The issue in *Knapp*'s case was similar in principle to that in the well-known case of *Gorris v Scott*.[1] In this case the plaintiff's sheep were washed overboard from the defendant's ship. This would not have occurred if the defendant had not neglected the precaution, required by a statutory order, to keep the animals in pens. An action for breach of statutory duty nevertheless failed on the ground that the purpose of the relevant legislation[2] had been to prevent the spread of disease and not to prevent what had happened in the case in question, even though the precaution would incidentally have had that effect if it had been taken. Similarly, in *Knapp's* case the legislature obviously contemplated injury occurring to road users rather than train drivers if the statutory precautions were neglected; but, had they been taken, the train driver would not have been injured.

1   *(1874) LR 9 Exch 125.*
3   The *Contagious Diseases (Animals) Act 1869.*

Duplication

[16.17]   The rule in *Gorris v Scott* operates to delineate the scope of the risk in a statutory duty case in a manner somewhat similar to that of the rules relating to remoteness of damage in other situations.[1] This being so, the rule furnishes a useful encapsulation of a principle which the notion of 'benefit of a class' appears to duplicate. Clarity would be served if this overlap were recognised, and the number of concepts with which the courts have to grapple in these cases reduced accordingly.[2]

1   Cf *Overseas Tankship (UK) Ltd v Morts Dock and Engineering Co, The Wagon Mound [1961] AC 388, [1961] 1 All ER 404, PC.* See also J Fleming *Law of Torts* (7th edn, 1987) p 122, n 15. See generally G Williams 'The Risk Principle' (1961) 77 LQR 179.
2   Unfortunately, the overlap is embodied in the American Law Institute's *Restatement of The Law of Torts* (2nd edn) para 286 as follows:
    '*When Standard of Conduct Defined by Legislation or Regulation Will be Adopted.*
    The court may adopt as the standard of conduct of a reasonable man the requirements of a legislative enactment or an administrative regulation whose purpose is found to be exclusively or in part
    (a) to protect a class of persons which includes the one whose interest is invaded, and
    (b) to protect the particular interest which is invaded, and
    (c) to protect that interest against the kind of harm which has resulted, and
    (d) to protect that interest against the particular hazard from which the harm results.'

Categories (b), (c) and (d) would seem to make category (a) largely redundant. Indeed the fact-situations involved in the cases in which the *Restatement* has been judicially cited could be seen as supporting the contention that the concepts of 'class benefit' and 'risk' are usually interchangeable: see *Mangan v F C Pilgram NE 2d 374 & Co 336, (1975) 381; Misterek v Washington Mineral Products 531 P 2d 805, (1975) 807.*

Protection of statutory undertakers

[16.18]   The other purpose for which the idea underlying the concept of benefit of a particular class is invoked is rather different from that of remoteness of damage. It is clear from *Clegg, Parkinson & Co v Earby Gas Co*[1] that the denial in that case of a right of action in favour of any member of the general public, who had suffered as a result of breach of statutory duty by the defendant undertakers, was to protect the undertakers from a burden potentially so great as to be capable of overwhelming them or even driving them out of existence. The same idea can be seen at work in the background in other cases, including *Atkinson v Newcastle and Gateshead Water-works Co*[2] itself. It is also reflected in a series of decisions in the law of nuisance in which private law remedies, such as damages and injunctions, were refused in situations where sewerage systems had overflowed due to failure on the part of the drainage authorities to expand and improve their plant and equipment.³

1 *[1896] 1 QB 592.*
2 *(1877) 2 Ex D 441, CA.*
3 See *Glossop v Heston and Isleworth Local Board (1879) 12 Ch D 102, CA*. Cf *Robinson v Workington Corpn [1897] 1 QB 619, CA*; *Pasmore v Oswaldtwistle UDC [1898] AC 387, HL*; *Smeaton v Ilford Corpn [1954] Ch 450, [1954] 1 All ER 923*. In 2003 the House of Lords affirmed the continued validity of this line of authority: see *Marcic v Thames Water Utilities [2004] 1 All ER 135*, Cf *Pride of Derby and Derbyshire Angling Association Ltd v British Celanese Ltd [1953] Ch 149, [1953] 1 All ER 179, CA*.

Policy factors

[16.19] The argument *ab inconvenienti* based on the large number of potential claimants,¹ which is evidently one aspect of the judicial anxiety in these cases, is one which is often criticised. But it is not the only aspect of the problem. Statutory duty cases often arise out of situations involving some major objective which the legislature wishes to promote. It might still be perfectly possible to argue in a modern case, depending on the particular facts, that the legislative strategy could be excessively hindered if individual plaintiffs were permitted to polarise debate around their specific grievances.² Alternatively, a decision in favour of liability might provide a desirable stimulus to action, as well as meet a just claim for compensation. Whether an action for breach of statutory duty should be permitted will often call for sophisticated evaluation of these and other policy factors.³

1 Ie the fear of 'opening the floodgates'.
2 Cf *Watt v Kesteven County Council [1955] 1 QB 408, [1955] 1 All ER 473, CA* (education).
3 It is interesting to note that the Robens Committee on Safety and Health at Work suggested that the availability of the action for breach of statutory duty in factory accident cases had hindered rather than helped accident prevention: (Cmnd 5034) pp 144–147; 185–187. See also G Williams in (1960) 23 MLR 233 at 239, who questioned the need for the action in this context, given the existence of the social security industrial injuries scheme. Cf *Haigh v Charles W Ireland Ltd [1973] 3 All ER 1137* at 1147, *[1974] 1 WLR 43* at 54–55, HL, *per* Lord Diplock.

Reasoning not explicit

[16.20] In practice, the courts often seem to invoke the concept of a distinction between legislation intended to benefit the 'public', and legislation intended to benefit a 'class', in order to give effect to a decision reached in reliance on factors of this kind even if the reasoning is not always made explicit. An example is provided by *Church of Jesus Christ of Latter Day Saints (Great Britain) v West Yorkshire Fire and Civil Defence Authority*, sub nom *Capital and Counties plc v Hampshire County Council*.¹ In this case the plaintiffs' chapel was destroyed by a fire which the defendants had been unable to fight adequately due to defects in the fire hydrants in the vicinity. The plaintiffs claimed damages for breach of statutory duty under *section 13* of the *Fire Services Act 1947*, which requires a fire authority to 'take all reasonable measures for ensuring the provision of an adequate supply of water'. The Court of Appeal rejected the claim. Stuart-Smith LJ, delivering the judgment of the court, observed² that the Act contained no reference 'to any class of person short of the public as a whole' being concerned instead with the 'function of procurement placed on the fire authority in relation to supply of water for fire fighting generally'.

1 *[1997] QB 1004, [1997] 2 All ER 865, CA*, distinguishing *Dawson & Co v Bingley UDC [1911] 2 KB 149, CA*.
2 *[1997] QB 1004* at 1050, *[1997] 2 All ER 465* at 896.

[16.21] *The action for breach of statutory duty[1]*

Relevance of provision in the Act for a penalty

[16.21] One of the most confusing questions in this area concerns the relevance of the presence or absence of provision in the statute itself for a sanction, be it a criminal penalty or some other kind of remedy. In *Doe d Bishop of Rochester v Bridges*[1] Lord Tenterden CJ said that:

> 'where an Act creates an obligation, and enforces the performance in a specified manner, we take it to be a general rule that performance cannot be enforced in any other manner. If an obligation is created, but no mode of enforcing its performance is ordained, the common law may, in general, find a mode suited to the particular nature of the case.'[2]

This dictum, which has frequently been cited in later cases, and can probably be said to represent the orthodox view, thus favoured a presumption *against* liability for breach of statutory duty where the Act provides for a sanction,[3] and a presumption *in favour* of liability where it does not do so. It is submitted, however, that both aspects of the proposition are open to serious criticism, and that a different and preferable interpretation of the authorities is tenable.

---

[1]   *(1831) 1 B & Ad 847* at 859.
[2]   Cf *Wolverhampton New Waterworks Co v Hawkesford (1859) 6 CBNS 336* at 356, *per* Willes J.
[3]   See *Issa v Hackney London Borough Council [1997] 1 WLR 956, [1997] 1 All ER 999, CA.*

Criminal sanctions

[16.22] Despite the supposed presumption *against* liability, it has long been clear that provision for the imposition of a *fine* is not in itself conclusive against the availability of a civil action.[1] This point was occasionally obscured in the older cases by provision for recovery by a common informer[2] (who might himself be the sufferer of the mishap) of all or part of any penalty imposed, or even for payment of it direct to the victim in his capacity as such. Even in these situations, however, the courts would not hesitate to impose liability if they considered it appropriate. This was particularly apparent in the industrial injuries field, where one of the attractions of the action for breach of statutory duty was that it provided an avenue of escape from the consequences of the defence of common employment. The leading example is *Groves v Lord Wimborne*,[3] in which Rigby LJ observed[4] that even if the maximum fine which could have been imposed under the provision in question, £100, were eventually to reach the plaintiff, it would nevertheless seem 'monstrous to suppose that it was intended that in the case of death or severe mutilation arising through a breach of the statutory duty, the compensation to the workman or his family should never exceed' that figure.[5] The level at which a fine is imposed will usually reflect the defendant's culpability (which may be relatively small) as distinct from the claimant's loss (which may well be much larger).[6]

---

[1]   See the numerous cases decided under the Factories Acts, referred to by Lord Browne-Wilkinson in *X v Bedfordshire County Council [1995] 2 AC 633* at 731, *[1995] 3 All ER 353* at 364 when he said that 'the existence of some other statutory remedy is not necessarily decisive. It is still possible to show that on the true construction of the statute the protected class was intended by Parliament to have a private remedy'.
[2]   See *Couch v Steel (1854) 3 E & B 402.*
[3]   *[1898] 2 QB 402, CA.* See also *Black v Fife Coal Co [1912] AC 149, HL.* Cf *Caswell v Worth (1856) 5 E & B 849.*
[4]   *[1898] 2 QB 402* at 414.

⁵ Vaughan Williams LJ was more cautious than Rigby LJ. He reserved his opinion on what the position might have been if the victim had been statutorily *entitled* to the money; as it was the Secretary of State who had a *discretion* whether to make it over to him: see *[1898] 2 QB 402* at 417.

⁶ See *per* A L Smith LJ in *[1898] 2 QB 402* at 408. Professor Glanville Williams invoked this point as an argument *against* imposing liability for breach of statutory duty where no pre-existing tort exists. He argued that such liability is unprincipled as not providing the defendant with the protection which the careful limitations on the extent of criminal liability afford him: see (1960) 23 MLR 233 at 256. This argument does, however, prove too much. The courts not infrequently reinforce the criminal law, most prominently in the sphere of illegality in contract where forfeiture of contractual rights can constitute a substantial additional sanction for wrong-doing. Of course, it can be argued that the courts sometimes go too far, but denial *a priori* of any legitimacy in their adoption of this role would be difficult to support.

Action should be unaffected

[16.23] Even in cases in which the plaintiff was unsuccessful, and one of the reasons given was that the statutorily provided penalty excluded any other remedy, it is likely that the real reason for denying liability was different. Concern to minimise the liability of public utilities, was probably a predominant factor in a number of the relevant decisions.¹ Moreover, although most of the cases on the point in fact concerned fines, since they happened to involve provisions supported by that sanction, similar reasoning would seem to be applicable to other criminal penalties. It is therefore submitted that a provision in the statute for the imposition of a fine, or any other criminal sanction on the defendant, should not lean at all against the availability of an action for breach of statutory duty.²

¹ See *Atkinson v Newcastle and Gateshead Waterworks (1877) 2 Ex D 441*, CA.

² Cf the American Law Institute's Second *Restatement of Torts*, para 287: '*Effect of Provision for Penalty:* A provision for a penalty in a legislative enactment or administrative regulation has no effect upon liability ... unless the penalty is found to be intended to exclude it.'

Where the Act makes no provision for a remedy

[16.24] The second limb of Lord Tenterden's dictum from *Bishop of Rochester v Bridges,* quoted above, apparently pointing in favour of liability where no sanction is stipulated by the statute, was echoed in a much more recent obiter dictum by Lord Simonds in his influential speech in *Cutler v Wandsworth Stadium Ltd.*¹ His Lordship stated that 'if a statutory duty is prescribed but no remedy by way of penalty or otherwise for its breach is imposed, it can be assumed that a right of action accrues to the person who is damnified by the breach'. One of the difficulties which has arisen in this context is that it is unclear exactly what counts as a 'remedy' for the purpose of the presumption. Confusion has occurred in situations where the Act provides for alternative machinery, such as mandamus or intervention by a minister after complaint to him, but no criminal sanction. Sometimes provisions of this type have been treated as being equivalent to a criminal penalty for the purposes of the supposed presumption against a civil action,² and sometimes as being equivalent to no penalty at all and hence within Lord Simonds' statement in favour of liability.³ The dilemma was highlighted in one case⁴ involving an Act⁵ which did provide for criminal proceedings but only with the consent of the Attorney General. Ungoed-Thomas J, observed that:

'this might be relied on the one hand as a factor tending to indicate that persons injured were to have a remedy otherwise than by criminal proceedings, and on the other hand as a factor tending to indicate that there was to be no remedy except with the sanction of the Attorney-General.'⁶

[1]   *[1949] AC 398* at 407, *[1949] 1 All ER 544* at 548, HL.
[2]   See *Pasmore v Oswaldtwistle UDC [1898] AC 387, HL; Watt v Kesteven County Council [1955] 1 QB 408* at 415, CA; affg *[1954] 3 All ER 441* at 444, *per* Ormerod J at first instance; *Southwark London Borough Council v Williams [1971] Ch 734, [1971] 2 All ER 175, CA.*
[3]   See *Reffell v Surrey County Council [1964] 1 All ER 743* at 746, *[1964] 1 WLR 358* at 362, *per* Veale J; *Sephton v Lancashire River Board [1962] 1 All ER 183, [1962] 1 WLR 623.*
[4]   *Argyll v Argyll [1967] Ch 302, [1965] 1 All ER 611.*
[5]   The *Judicial Proceedings (Regulation of Reports) Act 1926.*
[6]   *[1967] Ch 302* at 341, *[1965] 1 All ER 611* at 632.

Administrative provisions

[16.25]   If the situation is one in which no formal legal sanction at all, not even an order of mandamus, is available to support the statutory 'duty', Lord Simonds' view that civil liability can be 'assumed' to exist seems highly questionable. Notwithstanding the understandable feeling that an Act of Parliament should be something more than a 'pious aspiration',[1] there is something of a paradox in the notion that such a provision should be capable of giving rise to a tort action. Where mandamus is available,[2] but no criminal sanction, there is, perhaps, less of a paradox in a presumption in favour of civil liability. Nevertheless, the basic objection remains. Prescriptions unsupported by penalties are usually instructions of an essentially administrative nature, often addressed to public bodies[3]. The grafting of civil liability in tort upon such provisions is likely to give rise to considerable practical difficulties and may also involve defiance of the policy factors relating to public utilities, and similar bodies, which have been referred to above.[4]

[1]   *[1949] AC 398* at 407.
[2]   Of course this itself may be a matter of dispute: see *Pasmore v Oswaldtwistle UDC [1898] AC 387, HL.*
[3]   See the *Road Traffic Act 1988, s 39(2)*:' Each local authority must prepare and carry out a programme of measures designed to promote road safety … '. (considered in *Gorringe v Calderdale MBC [2004] 2 All ER 326*).
[4]   In *K A & SBM Feakins Ltd v Dover Harbour Board [1998] 36 LS Gaz R 31* Tucker J declined to hold that the *Harbours Docks, and Piers Clauses Act 1847*, which relates to the keeping open of harbours for all who wish to use them, gives rise to a claim for breach of statutory duty.

Welfare provisions

[16.26]   Thus, in *O'Rourke v Camden London Borough Council*[1] the House of Lords held that a duty imposed upon local authorities by the *Housing Act 1985*, to provide accommodation for the homeless, was enforceable only by judicial review. Lord Hoffmann observed[2] that:

'   … the 1985 Act makes the existence of the duty to provide accommodation dependent upon a good deal of judgment on the part of the housing authority … The existence of all these discretions makes it unlikely that Parliament intended errors of judgment to give rise to an obligation to make financial reparation. Control by public law remedies would appear much more appropriate.'[3]

Similarly, in *X v Bedfordshire County Council*,[4] in which the House of Lords declined to impose liability in respect of the statutory obligations of local authorities relating to the welfare of children, Lord Browne-Wilkinson considered it significant[5] that the House had not been 'referred to any case where it had been held that statutory provisions establishing a regulatory system or a scheme of social welfare … had been held to give rise to a right of action for damages'. In *Phelps v London Borough of Hillingdon*[6], which was concerned with claims allegedly arising out of the *1944* and *1981 Education Acts*, Lord Slynn said:

'The general nature of the duties imposed on local authorities in the context of a national system of education and the remedies available by way of appeal and judicial review indicate that Parliament did not intend to create a statutory remedy by way of damages. Much of the 1981 Act is concerned with conferring discretionary powers or administrative duties in an area of social welfare where normally damages have not been awarded where there has been a failure to perform a statutory duty. The situation is quite different from that concerning the maintenance of factory premises as in *Groves v Wimborne (Lord)*'.

[1]   *[1998] AC 188, [1997] 3 All ER 23, HL.*
[2]   *[1998] AC 188* at 194, *[1997] 3 All ER 23* at 26–27.
[3]   In so holding, the House of Lords in *O'Rourke* overruled the decision of the Court of Appeal in *Thornton v Kirklees Metropolitan Borough Council [1979] QB 626, [1979] 2 All ER 349*. The *Kirklees* case had earlier been criticised by the present writer (in (1984) 100 LQR 204 at 217–220) and by K M Stanton in his *Liability in Tort for Breach of Statutory Duty* (1986) pp 80–81. Cf *per* Lord Bridge in *Cocks v Thanet District Council [1983] 2 AC 286* at 293, *[1982] 3 All ER 1135* at 1138, HL.
[4]   *[1995] 2 AC 633, [1995] 3 All ER 353, HL.*
[5]   See *[1995] 2 AC 633* at 731, *[1995] 3 All ER 353* at 364.
[6]   See *[2000] 4 All ER 504, HL* at pp 516–517.

Implication against an action for damages

[16.27]   It is accordingly submitted, contrary to the dictum of Lord Simonds in *Cutler v Wandsworth Stadium,* that the absence of any specific penalty in the statute is in fact a powerful indication *against* the imposition of an action for damages for breach of statutory duty, rather than a pointer in its favour. This submission derives further support from the decision of the House of Lords in *Hague v Deputy Governor of Parkhurst Prison*,[1] in which the House held that breach of a statutory rule dealing with the segregation of inmates in prison was not actionable by a prisoner who was improperly segregated.[2] No specific penalty was provided for breach of the rule, and Lord Jauncey expressed himself as follows:[3]

'The Prison Act is designed to deal with the administration of prisons and the management and control of prisoners. It covers such wide-ranging matters as central administration, prison officers, confinement and treatment of prisoners, release of prisoners on licence, provision and maintenance of prisons and offences. Its objects are far removed from those of legislation such as the Factories and Coal Mines Acts whose prime concern is to protect the health and safety of persons who work therein ... I find nothing in ... the Act to suggest that Parliament intended thereby to confer on prisoners a cause of action sounding in damages in respect of a breach of those provisions.'

[1]   *[1991] 3 All ER 733, HL.*
[2]   See also *Olutu v Home Office [1997] 1 All ER 385, [1997] 1 WLR 328, CA.*
[3]   *[1991] 3 All ER 733* at 750–751.

Specificity

[16.28]   If it is correct that provisions unsupported by remedies will not normally provide an appropriate basis for imposition of an action for damages for breach of statutory duty, because they will normally be administrative or discretionary in nature, the *converse* of the proposition does shed some light on the more general problem of identifying the situations in which such liability *will* properly be imposed. It is submitted that the correct approach is the adoption of a *presumption* to the effect that an action for breach of statutory duty is more likely to lie the more *specific* is the nature of the statutory obligation.¹ Similarly, the less specific the obligation, the less likely is it that the action will arise.² The present writer contended for a presumption along these lines in 1984.³ Since that time the law appears to have moved in the same direction. Thus, in *X v Bedfordshire County Council*⁴ Lord Browne-Wilkinson said:

> 'The cases where a private right of action for breach of statutory duty have been held to arise are all cases in which the statutory duty has been very limited and specific as opposed to general administrative functions imposed on public bodies and involving the exercise of administrative discretions.'

Of course, some element of judgment is often left to the persons subject to the duty even by quite specific provisions; for example, an obligation to fence dangerous machinery pursuant to the factories legislation may involve the making of choices as to the most appropriate protection in the particular circumstances. Moreover, the proposed test is subordinate both to the general question of the desirability of an action in the particular context, which, it has already been suggested above, the court should consider overtly as a matter of policy, and to determination that the harm suffered was 'within the risk' for the purposes of the rule in *Gorris v Scott*.⁵

¹   Cf *per* Shaw LJ in *McCall v Abelesz [1976] QB 585* at 600, *[1976] 1 All ER 727* at 735, CA: 'the offence must consist of a failure to perform a *defined duty* which the statute imposes on the potential offender' (italics supplied).
²   Cf *per* Lord Reid in *Cutler v Wandsworth Stadium Ltd [1949] AC 398* at 417, *[1949] 1 All ER 544* at 554, HL: 'If the legislature had intended to create ... rights I would expect to find them capable of reasonably precise definition.'
³   See R A Buckley 'Liability in Tort for Breach of Statutory Duty' (1984) 100 LQR 204.
⁴   See *[1995] 2 AC 633* at 732, *[1995] 3 All ER 353* at 365.
⁵   *(1874) LR 9 Exch 125*, discussed above at para [16.16].

Older cases explained

[16.29]   The apparent readiness of the courts, in relatively recent years¹, to move towards a presumption of the kind suggested should help to remove some of the confusion from this branch of the law. The proposition embodied by the presumption also explains most of the older authorities. Thus, the actual decision in *Couch v Steel²* can be supported on the ground that a specific list of medicaments had been laid down which the defendant failed to supply.³ Similarly, in *Monk v Warbey⁴* the duty was simply to refuse to allow an uninsured person to use a motor car. In *Phillips v Britannia Hygienic Laundry Co*,⁵ on the other hand, the relevant article of the statutory order simply imposed criminal liability for use of a defective motor vehicle, it did not specify particular measures or precautions to be taken with respect to the maintenance of such vehicles.⁶

¹   See *X v Bedfordshire County Council [1995] 2 AC 633, [1995] 3 All ER 353, HL; O'Rourke v Camden London Borough Council [1998] AC 188, [1997] 3 All ER 23 HL; R v Deputy Governor of Parkhurst Prison, exp Hague [1992] 1 AC 58, [1991] 3 All ER 733, HL.*
²   *(1854) 3 E & B 402.*
³   See also *Simmonds v Newport Abercarn Black Vein Steam Coal Co [1921] 1 KB 616, CA* (statutory obligation to provide written statement showing how wages payment was arrived at).
⁴   *[1935] 1 KB 75, CA.*
⁵   *[1923] 2 KB 832, CA.*

⁶ See also *Barkway v South Wales Transport Co [1950] AC 185, [1950] 1 All ER 392, HL*. See also below for discussion of the position under such general statutory provisions where fault can be proved against the defendant.

The relevance of fault

[16.30] Focus upon the specific nature of the statutory duty as a factor favouring the imposition of civil liability also casts light upon the question whether a defendant can avoid such liability by showing that he had not been careless, or otherwise blameworthy, in allowing the breach to occur. As Lord Atkin said in *Smith v Cammell Laird & Co Ltd*:¹ 'It is precisely in the absolute obligation imposed by statute to perform or forbear from performing a *specified activity* that a breach of statutory duty differs from the obligation imposed by common law, which is to take reasonable care to avoid injuring another.'

If the legislation sets out in detail what the defendant is meant to do, it will rarely be plausible for him to argue that he was not blameworthy in not doing what was required.² In effect, therefore, the position in most cases will be one of strict liability.

¹   *[1940] AC 242* at 258, *[1939] 4 All ER 381* at 390, HL (italics supplied).
²   The mere fact that the taking of the precautions would render the operation not viable economically is no defence: see *John Summers & Sons Ltd v Frost [1955] AC 740, [1955] 1 All ER 870, HL*. The general principle that ignorance of the law is no defence will presumably also apply.

Two types of provision

[16.31] There will, however, occasionally be situations in which the imposition of liability will be appropriate even though the statute is *not* specific in laying down exactly what has to be done. In such cases the degree of discretion left to the defendant will not be so great as to attract the presumption against civil liability but will simply reflect the impracticability, in the particular context, of laying down very precise requirements in advance. It seems to be clear that, in situations of this type, liability for breach of statutory duty will normally be fault-based. In consequence, there will usually be an overlap in such cases with ordinary negligence liability, especially in view of the tendency of that tort to expand.¹ But the existence of the action may still prove valuable in cases for which there is no liability at common law (such as most of those involving omissions), or in which the existence of liability at common law is doubtful.

¹   There are a number of cases in which civil liability for breach of general statutory provisions has been imposed, and in which the court has indicated that liability in ordinary common law negligence had also been established: see *Ching v Surrey County Council [1910] 1 KB 736, CA; Abbott v Isham (1920) 90 LJKB 309; Reffell v Surrey County Council [1964] 1 All ER 743, [1964] 1 WLR 358* (all decided under enactments relating to the safety of premises used for educational purposes). See also *Ministry of Housing and Local Government v Sharp [1970] 2 QB 223, [1970] 1 All ER 1009, CA*. Cf *Phillips v Britannia Hygienic Laundry Co [1923] 2 KB 832, CA*.

Read v Croydon Corporation

[16.32] The distinction between the strict and fault-based types of liability for breach of statutory duty was well brought out in the judgment of Stable J in *Read v Croydon Corpn*.¹ In this case the defendant corporation had allowed their water supply to become polluted with typhoid. They were held liable in tort both for negligence, and

[16.33] *The action for breach of statutory duty[1]*

for breach of their duty under the *Waterworks Clauses Act 1847* to provide 'a supply of pure and wholesome water'.[2] Even their liability for breach of statutory duty, however, was based upon a finding that they had been at fault as having failed to take reasonable care. The judge drew a distinction between statutory provisions whereby 'certain means are directed to serve a particular end' and those 'where the statute enjoins the end but not the means'. Examples of the former class, which attracted strict liability, were to be found in the detailed provisions of the Factories Acts. In the case before him, however, the legislation did not indicate how the provision of a pure water supply was to be maintained, but only that that was the end to be achieved. Indeed, his Lordship envisaged situations, such as prolonged drought, in which the maintenance of such a supply might become impossible without there being any question of the corporation's having been at fault. It followed that the obligation on the corporation was 'limited to the exercise of all reasonable care and skill to ensure that the water provided accord[ed] with the provisions of the Act'.[3]

---

[1]   *[1938] 4 All ER 631.*
[2]   The infant plaintiff, who had actually contracted typhoid, succeeded in negligence. Her father succeeded for breach of statutory duty, which was held to have been owed to him *qua* payer of water rates, for the expenses he had incurred in consequence of his daughter's illness.
[3]   See *[1938] 4 All ER 631* at 650–651.

C Defences and relationship with criminal liability

Contributory negligence and assumption of risk

[16.33] Even where the defendant's liability is strict, because the statutory duty is specific in nature, it is well established that contributory negligence[1] and even, in very rare cases, assumption of risk,[2] may be available as defences. In particular circumstances it may also be possible to avoid liability on the basis that, as between claimant and defendant, responsibility for the actual discharge of a statutory duty which was imposed upon both of them rested wholly with the claimant, and that he alone had been at fault.[3]

---

[1]   See *Caswell v Powell Duffryn Associated Collieries Ltd [1940] AC 152, [1939] 3 All ER 722, HL*. The apportionment provisions of the *Law Reform (Contributory Negligence) Act 1945* apply: *Cakebread v Hopping Bros (Whetstone) Ltd [1947] KB 641, [1947] 1 All ER 389, CA*. Such apportionment is, of course, a common occurrence in cases decided under the Factories Acts or similar legislation.
[2]   See *ICI Ltd v Shatwell [1965] AC 656, [1964] 2 All ER 999, HL*. The general rule is probably still that the defence is inapplicable in such cases, at least where employer and employee are concerned: *Wheeler v New Merton Board Mills [1933] 2 KB 669, CA*. On assumption of risk generally see CHAPTER 21 below.
[3]   See *Manwaring v Billington [1952] 2 All ER 747, CA*; *Ginty v Belmont Building Supplies Ltd [1959] 1 All ER 414*. See also *Ross v Associated Portland Cement Manufacturers Ltd [1964] 2 All ER 452* at 455, *[1964] 1 WLR 768* at 776, HL, *per* Lord Reid. For discussion generally of employers' liability to their employees, see CHAPTER 17 below.

Underlying purposes of the legislation

[16.34] The availability of these defences should not be regarded, however, as amounting to the introduction into this area of general negligence principles. There is not necessarily anything inappropriate in taking the claimant's conduct into account, even in circumstances in which the liability of the defendant is not itself fault-based.[1] The defences are best seen as a legitimate exercise of the function of the court in coming to its own policy decision as to how best to give effect to the underlying purposes of the legislation in question. Thus, the promotion of safety standards would hardly be enhanced if those whom they were intended to protect could be certain that their own disregard of elementary precautions would have no effect on their recovery of damages, if they had the misfortune to suffer an accident.²

¹ See G Williams *Joint Torts and Contributory Negligence* (1950) pp 207–210. See also D Payne 'Reduction of Damages for Contributory Negligence' (1955) 18 MLR 344.
² Cf *per* Lord Diplock in *Boyle v Kodak Ltd* [1969] 2 All ER 439 at 446, [1969] 1 WLR 661 at 673, HL: 'To say "You are liable to me for my own wrongdoing" is neither good morals nor good law.'

Where no offence has been committed

[16.35] The question may sometimes arise whether civil liability for breach of statutory duty can be imposed even though, in the particular circumstances, the defendant would not have incurred criminal liability. There may have been an absence of mens rea where the relevant provision is not, for the purposes of the criminal law, one of strict liability; or there may be a special defence to criminal proceedings, of 'due diligence' or the like, expressly provided for in the Act.¹ Judicial views have differed on the relationship between civil and criminal liability in such circumstances. Some have favoured giving the defendant the benefit of defences to criminal liability in civil proceedings,² while others have taken the opposite view.³ It is submitted that the proposition that such defences will not normally be available to a defendant in a civil action is to be preferred. The policy issues underlying civil and criminal liability are usually different (and the former does not attract the stigma of the latter). Of course, if the statute itself makes the position clear by dealing expressly and separately with both types of liability there is no room for argument. And it is noteworthy that while some statutes do provide that criminal defences are to be available in a civil action,⁴ others emphatically provide the opposite.⁵

¹ See the *Mineral Workings (Offshore Installations) Act 1971*, s 9(3).
² See the references to earlier cases collected by Tucker LJ in *Harrison v National Coal Board [1950] 1 KB 466 at 476, [1950] 1 All ER 171* at 178, CA. See also Glanville Williams in (1960) 23 MLR 233 at 243, n 34, arguing that to extend such defences to civil liability would represent 'sounder juristic principle', sed quaere.
³ 'Criminal and civil liability are two separate things ... The legislature might well be unwilling to convict an owner who failed to carry out an absolute statutory duty of a crime with which he was not himself directly concerned, but still be ready to leave the civil liability untouched ... The duty is broken though no crime has been committed': *per* Lord Porter in *Potts v Reid [1943] AC 1* at 31, *[1942] 2 All ER 161* at 176, HL. See also *Harrison v National Coal Board [1950] 1 KB 466* at 477, *[1950] 1 All ER 171* at 178, CA, *per* Tucker LJ and *[1951] AC 639* at 664, HL, *per* Lord Normand.
⁴ See the *Control of Pollution Act 1974*, s 88(2).
⁵ See the *Mineral Workings (Offshore Installations) Act 1971*, s 11(4). Cf the *Health and Safety at Work etc. Act 1974*, s 47(3).

D Reform?

An express provision?

[16.36] The suggestion is often made that Parliament should state expressly, either in each individual Act or by means of a general statutory presumption, whether or not contravention will give rise to a civil action.¹ The matter was considered in the 1960s by the Law Commission, which recommended the enactment of a general presumption to the effect that such an action would lie unless the particular Act expressly provided to the contrary.² The Commission put forward a draft Bill, which was subsequently introduced into Parliament as the Interpretation of Legislation Bill 1980. The relevant provision was cl 4, which provided as follows:

'Where any Act passed after this Act imposes or authorises the imposition of a duty, whether positive or negative and whether with or without a special remedy for its enforcement, it shall be presumed, unless express provision to the contrary is made, that a breach of the duty is intended to be actionable (subject to the defences and other incidents applying to actions for breach of statutory duty) at the suit of any person who sustains damage in consequence of the breach.'

The Bill was subsequently withdrawn.[3] Nevertheless, it is in practice increasingly common for individual statutes to provide expressly for the presence[4] or absence[5] of civil liability. On balance, however, it would be over-optimistic, for the reasons given in the next paragraph, to believe that a general presumption along the lines proposed by the Law Commission would effect a significant improvement in the quality of the law relating to damages for breach of statutory duty.

[1] The best-known expression of this view is by Lord du Parcq in *Cutler v Wandsworth Stadium Ltd [1949] AC 398* at 410, *[1949] 1 All ER 544* at 549, HL: 'To a person unversed in the science or art of legislation it may well seem strange that Parliament has not by now made it a rule to state explicitly what its intention is in a matter which is often of no little importance, instead of leaving it to the courts to discover, by a careful examination and analysis of what is expressly said, what that intention may be supposed probably to be. There are no doubt reasons which inhibit the legislature from revealing its intention in plain words. I do not know, and must not speculate, what those reasons may be. I trust, however, that it will not be thought impertinent, in any sense of that word, to suggest respectfully that those who are responsible for framing legislation might consider whether the traditional practice, which obscures, if it does not conceal, the intention which Parliament has, or must be presumed to have, might not safely be abandoned.' See also *McCall v Abelesz [1976] QB 585* at 597G, *[1976] 1 All ER 727* at 733, CA, *per* Ormrod LJ; R Cross *Statutory Interpretation* (1976) pp 162–163; A Samuels 'The Interpretation of Statutes' [1980] Stat LR 86 at 104–105.

[2] See Law Com no 21 (1969), para 38. The Commission favoured a presumption in *favour* of liability, rather than the other way round, in order to 'avoid any danger of the civil action being restricted in practice by a failure to provide for it in express terms'.

[3] For a recent suggestion that a statutory presumption to the *opposite* effect should be created, see Keith Stanton and others *Statutory Torts* (2003) p 54: 'A less dramatic statutory presumption would be one which stipulated non-actionability unless the statute in question expressly stipulated the contrary … It is suggested that this would be the best way of removing the existing difficulties whilst allowing the tort to evolve on a principled basis'.

[4] See the *Building Act 1984, s 38; Consumer Protection Act 1987, s 41*.

[5] See the *Guard Dogs Act 1975, s 5(1); Safety of Sports Grounds Act 1975, s 13*.

Difficulties with the Law Commission's proposal

[16.37] Whether the granting of a civil action would further the purposes of the particular legislation is a question to which the answer may sometimes vary according to the circumstances of the breach.[1] And it will often be quite unrealistic to expect the legislature (or the parliamentary draftsman) to foresee all such circumstances in advance. It may therefore be perfectly rational for Parliament to wish to leave the matter, in some contexts at least, to the courts. Accordingly, in this context, as elsewhere in the law, total predictability will not be possible. Moreover, if a statutory presumption along the lines proposed had been introduced, there might have been a danger that Parliament would 'play safe' in subsequent enactments by expressly excluding it virtually as a matter of routine. Since the Commission was apparently anxious not to see the scope of the action for breach of statutory duty unduly narrowed, this would mean that their proposal would have turned out to be counter-productive.

[1] Cf *Gorris v Scott (1874) LR 9 Exch 125*, discussed above at para [16.16].

Part six

Employers' liability

Chapter 17

Employers' liability to their employees

A Nature of the common law duty

Introduction

[17.01] The common law relating to the duty which an employer owes to his employees consists largely of the application of the ordinary principles of negligence in a special context. These principles include, where a claimant has been injured by the carelessness of a fellow-employee, the normal operation of an employer's vicarious liability for the negligence of one of his employees.[1] This is in practice often the route by which persons injured at work obtain damages from their employer: a route which only became available in relatively recent times when the old doctrine of common employment was finally abolished by statute.[2] Ordinary negligence and straightforward vicarious liability are not, however, the whole of the story. There is still an area of uncertain ambit within which an employer will be held liable to an employee for injuries carelessly inflicted, even though the employer was not himself personally at fault, and the person who inflicted the injuries was not one of his employees for the purposes of vicarious liability as generally understood. This area of so-called 'non-delegable duty', in which the employer is under a primary duty not merely to take reasonable care but to see that reasonable care is taken, was limited but not eradicated by the decision of the House of Lords in *Davie v New Merton Board Mills Ltd*.[3] It was at least hinted in that case that the concept was largely a historical relic of attempts to circumvent the doctrine of common employment.[4] Nevertheless its survival appears to be due at least in part to valid contemporary considerations of convenience: the employer being an appropriate and easily identifiable defendant on whom to shift losses suffered by the claimant at his place of work.[5]

[1] See CHAPTER 18 below.
[2] See the *Law Reform (Personal Injuries) Act, 1948, s 1(1)*.
[3] *[1959] AC 604, [1959] 1 All ER 346, HL.*
[4] See *[1959] AC 604* at 618, *[1959] 1 All ER 346* at 350, *per* Lord Simonds.
[5] Cf the *Employers' Liability (Defective Equipment) Act 1969*, discussed below at para [17.21].

Tort and contract

[17.02] It has been held that the basis of the application of negligence principles in employment cases is an implied term in the contract of employment that the employer will provide a safe working enviroment[1]. The question can arise as to possible inconsistencies between the implied term and the express provisions of the agreement. In *Johnstone v Bloomsbury Health Authority*[2] the plaintiff, a junior hospital doctor, contended that he had been required by his employers to work such long hours as foreseeably to damage his health. His employers argued that his claim, even if true, was unsustainable, since his contract expressly required him to work long hours and that this express provision took priority over any duty in tort, or implied term of the contract, to protect his health. The Court of Appeal accepted that the express terms of the contract took priority over any tortious or implied contractual duty but, by a majority,[3] refused to strike out the claim holding that, on the proper construction of the contract of employment, the express and implied duties were not inherently in conflict. The defendants had therefore not established beyond argument that they had in fact acquired a contractual right to work the plaintiff so hard as to damage his health. The implication, however, that if the contract unambiguously so provides an employer can at common law[4] acquire the right foreseeably to injure the health of his employees, seems, to say the least, unattractive.[5] Nevertheless *Johnstone's* case was referred to with approval by Lord Rodger of Earlsferry in the House of Lords in *Barber v Somerset County Council*[6], in which his Lordship observed that a tort-based duty of reasonable care to protect employees from stress may 'not sit easily with … contractual arrangements'.

[1] See *Bernadone v Pall Mall Services Group [1999] IRLR 617.*
[2] *[1992] QB 333, [1991] 2 All ER 293, CA.*
[3] Sir Nicolas Browne-Wilkinson V-C and Stuart-Smith LJ. Leggatt LJ dissented on the ground that 'those who cannot stand the heat should stay out of the kitchen': *[1991] 2 All ER 293* at 303.
[4] But cf *s 2(1)* of the *Unfair Contract Terms Act 1977*: 'A person cannot by reference to any contract term or to a notice given to persons generally or to particular persons exclude or restrict his liability for death or personal injury resulting from negligence.' The plaintiff in *Johnstone's* case was held also to have an arguable case on the basis of this provision (the Court of Appeal being unanimous on this point).
[5] It is submitted that the reasoning of Stuart-Smith LJ, who appeared in effect to dissent on this point, is to be preferred. Cf the 48-hour week introduced by the *Working Time Regulations 1998*.
[6] See *[2004] 2 All ER 385* at para 34.

Economic loss

[17.03] In *Reid v Rush & Tompkins Group plc*[1] the plaintiff was sent by his employers to work abroad in a country in which third-party motor insurance was not compulsory. He was seriously injured in a road accident for which the other driver, who was uninsured and unable to pay damages, was to blame. The plaintiff sought, in effect, to recover compensation for his injuries from his employers, arguing that the duty of care in the master-servant relationship extended, in the circumstances, either to insuring the plaintiff against accident themselves or to advising him of the desirability of taking out his own insurance. His claim failed. The Court of Appeal held that an employer's duty at common law extended only to protection of his servant against physical injury and not to protection against the incurring of economic loss. In the absence of a specific legislative enactment, only an express term in the contract would extend the liability of the employer in this way.

[1] *[1989] 3 All ER 228, [1990] 1 WLR 212, CA.*

Pensions

[17.04] A similar approach was adopted, in rather different circumstances, in *Outram v Academy Plastics*[1]. In this case the Court of Appeal held that an employer did not owe a duty to advise its employees about their membership, or otherwise, of the company's pension scheme, even though the employer was trustee of the scheme[2]. An employee left the defendant company but later rejoined; when he did so the defendants omitted to draw his attention to the need to rejoin the scheme if his benefits were not to be adversely affected. The Court of Appeal held that the defendants were in breach of no duty to the employee, and therefore could not be liable for their omission. Financial advice was a 'specialist subject' and a company 'which manufactures plastics' could not be expected 'to tender advice of its own volition'[3]. On the other hand an employer owes a duty of care to an employee when providing a reference[4], and the law relating to liability for financial loss is still developing[5]. It is therefore submitted that a rigid refusal to countenance the possibility of a duty to give at least some general warning to employees, about the dangers of giving insufficient attention to such matters as pensions and insurance in the context of their employment, would be undesirable. In *Lennon v Metropolitan Police Commissioner*[6] the Court of Appeal held, distinguishing *Outram's* case, that the defendant was vicariously liable to the claimant for failing to ensure that his conditions of service were protected when he moved to a different police force; one of the defendant's employees having expressly assumed responsibility for the task of making appropriate arrangements for the claimant's move.

1   *[2001] ICR 367.*
2   Cf *Scally v Southern Health and Social Services Board [1992] 1 AC 294, HL.* See also *University of Nottingham v Eyett [1999] PLR 17.*
3   See *[2001] ICR 367* at para 22 *per* Tuckey LJ.
4   See *Spring v Guardian Assurance [1995] 2 AC 296, HL.* Cf *Bartholomew v Hackney LBC [1999] IRLR 246, CA.*
5   See *per* Chadwick LJ in *Outram v Academy Plastics [2001] ICR 367* at para 32.
6   *[2004] 2 All ER 266, CA.*

B Stress

[17.05]   In *Walker v Northumberland County Council*[1] the plaintiff suffered a nervous breakdown due to the pressures resulting from his heavy workload as social worker. The breakdown had rendered him permanently unfit for work, and his claim for damages against his employers succeeded. Colman J emphasised, however, the need for the plaintiff to establish that his illness had been foreseeable and that his employers had failed to act reasonably. He said:[2]

> '... the question is whether it ought to have been foreseen that Mr Walker was exposed to a risk of mental illness materially higher than that which would ordinarily affect a social services middle manager in his position with a really heavy workload. For if the foreseeable risk were not materially greater than that there would not, as a matter of reasonable conduct, be any basis upon which the council's duty to act arose.'

On the facts of the case, however, it was established that the defendants had been in breach of their duty: the plaintiff had had an earlier nervous breakdown and, henceforth, the plaintiff was not afforded the 'measure of additional assistance'[3] with his work which he should have been given to avoid a repetition of the illness.[4]

1   *[1995] 1 All ER 737.*
2   See *[1995] 1 All ER 737* at 752.
3   See *[1995] 1 All ER 737* at 760.
4   See also *Petch v Customs and Excise Comrs [1993] ICR 789, CA* and *Gillespie v Commonwealth of Australia (1991) 104 ACTR 1*, in which claims similar to that in *Walker v Northumberland County Council* were advanced but failed on their facts.

Hatton v Sutherland

[17.06] In 2002 the Court of Appeal sought, in four conjoined appeals[1], to provide guidelines for the resolution of the increasing number of claims being made in relation to illness allegedly caused by stress at work. The court emphasised that the question at the outset of each case should be 'whether this kind of harm to this particular employee was reasonably foreseeable'[2]. Hale LJ, delivering the judgment of the court, said[3]:

> 'The question is not whether psychiatric injury is foreseeable in a person of 'ordinary fortitude'. The employer's duty is owed to each individual employee, not to some as yet unidentified outsider ... All of this points to there being a single test: *whether a harmful reaction to the pressures of the workplace is reasonably foreseeable in the individual employee concerned. Such a reaction will have two components: (1) an injury to health; which (2) is attributable to stress at work.* The answer to the foreseeability question will therefore depend upon the interrelationship between the particular characteristics of the employee concerned and the particular demands which the employer casts upon him'.

[1]   Sub nom *Hatton v Sutherland [2002] 2 All ER 1*.
[2]   See *[2002] 2 All ER 1* at para 23. (Italics are in the original.)
[3]   See above.

Establishing breach

[17.07] In order to determine, in the circumstances of a particular case, whether the defendant employer had acted reasonably, or had instead been in breach of duty, the court should consider the size of its operation and resources, and the interests of other employees[1]. An employer who offers 'confidential help to employees who fear that they may be suffering harmful levels of stress is unlikely to be found in breach of duty'[2], but the absence of such a facility is certainly not to be regarded as an indicator in favour of liability. The key question in each case is whether the employer should have been on notice that the claimant was an individual who was, or had become, particularly vulnerable to stress-induced illness[3]. Claims are therefore much more likely to succeed if an employee who has already been off work with such illness falls victim to a subsequent attack, in circumstances in which the employer took no measures with a view to protecting the employee from a recurrence[4]. Finally, the Court of Appeal noted that since 'many stress-related illnesses are likely to have a complex aetiology with several different causes'[5], care needs to be taken by courts dealing with such cases to apportion liability so as to ensure that the employers are not held liable for harm for which they were not responsible.

[1]   'It may not be reasonable to expect the employer to rearrange the work for the sake of one employee in a way which prejudices the others': *per* Hale LJ *[2002] 2 All ER 1* at para 33.
[2]   See *[2002] 2 All ER 1* at para 33.
[3]   See *Pratley v Surrey CC [2004] ICR 159, CA* (claim failed).
[4]   See *Barber v Somerset County Council* (below), and *Walker v Northumberland County Council* (above). See also *Young v Post Office [2002] IRLR 660*.
[5]   See *[2002] 2 All ER 1* at para 36.

Heightened scrutiny

[17.08] The four appeals considered by the Court of Appeal in *Hatton v Sutherland* were by employers who had been held liable to their employees. It is significant that all but one of the appeals succeeded. Subsequently, however, the House of Lords reversed the decision of the Court of Appeal in one of the three cases in which that court had decided in favour of the employer, and restored the decision at first instance in favour of the employee. Nevertheless, the House of Lords considered the case, *Barber v Somerset County Council*[1], to be 'fairly close to the borderline'[2]; and its own decision was not unanimous[3]. Moreover, even in the one case in which the Court of Appeal itself decided in favour of the employee, it stated that it had reached its conclusion 'not without some hesitation'[4]. While claimants should not be discouraged from pursuing clear cases, it is therefore likely that the overall effect of *Hatton v Sutherland* will have been to heighten the scrutiny to which the courts will subject claims for work-related illness based on stress.

[1] *[2004] 2 All ER 385.*
[2] See above at para 67 *per* Lord Walker of Gestingthorpe
[3] Lord Scott of Foscote dissented, and Lord Rodger of Earlsferry expressed reservations.
[4] See *[2002] 2 All ER 1* at para 66.

Barber v Somerset County Council

[17.09] Despite the heightened scrutiny towards stress cases likely to be adopted as a result of *Hatton v Sutherland*, appellate courts should still hesitate before disturbing the findings of the judge who heard and saw the witnesses. In *Barber v Somerset County Council*[1] the House of Lords held that the Court of Appeal had not been justified in overturning a decision in favour of the employee in a case in which the factual evidence had been critical. In *Barber* a teacher suffered a nervous beakdown. He had previously been off sick with anxiety and depression and the House, differing from the Court of Appeal, held that this should have put his employers on notice that steps to reduce his burden should have been considered when he returned to work. Lord Walker of Gestingthorpe said[2]:

> 'At the very least the senior management team should have taken the initiative in making sympathetic inquiries about Mr Barber when he returned to work, and making some reduction in his workload to ease his return. Even a small reduction in his duties, coupled with the feeling that the senior management team was on his side, might by itself have made a real difference. In any event Mr Barber's condition should have been monitored, and if it did not improve, some more drastic action would have had to be taken. Supply teachers cost money, but not as much as the cost of the permanent loss through psychiatric illness of a valued member of the school staff'.

[1] *[2004] 2 All ER 385.*
[2] See above at para 68.

C Safe system of work

[17.10] It was at one time usual to subdivide the employer's own common law duty to his employees into a three-fold classification relating to the need for competent fellow-employees, safe equipment, and appropriate methods of work.[1] More recently, however, the tendency has been to adopt a unified approach, since 'all three are ultimately only manifestations of the same duty of the master to take reasonable care so to carry out his operations as not to subject those employed by him to unnecessary risk'.[2] In *Parker v PFC Flooring Supplies*[3], decided in 2001, Potter LJ put it as follows:

'The over-all duty of the employer is to take reasonable steps for the safety of his employees against those types of risks which are reasonably foreseeable as likely to occur in the course of the employee's employment, which in turn depends upon the nature, functions, restrictions and general parameters of the employee's job and the broad areas of activity in which he is likely to be engaged or to engage himself in furtherance of his employer's interests'.

The House of Lords has emphasised that the question of the scope of the duty is essentially one of fact in each case, and that care should be taken not to convert reasons given by judges when deciding such questions into propositions of law capable of general application.[4]

[1]   See *Wilsons & Clyde Coal Co Ltd v English [1938] AC 57* at 78, *[1937] 3 All ER 628* at 640, *per* Lord Wright.
[2]   *Per* Pearce LJ in *Wilson v Tyneside Window Cleaning Co [1958] 2 QB 110* at 121, *[1958] 2 All ER 265* at 271, CA; see also *Wingfield v Ellerman's Wilson Line [1960] 2 Lloyd's Rep 16* at 22, CA, *per* Devlin LJ; *McDermid v Nash Dredging and Reclamation Co Ltd [1986] QB 965* at 974, *[1986] 2 All ER 676* at 681, CA, *per* Neill LJ (see also *McDermid's* case in the House of Lords *[1987] AC 906, [1987] 2 All ER 878*, discussed below).
[3]   See *[2001] EWCA Civ 1533* at para 22.
[4]   See *Qualcast (Wolverhampton) Ltd v Haynes [1959] AC 743, [1959] 2 All ER 38, HL.*

Equipment and supervision

[17.11] If the work which an employee is required to do involves a known risk, the employer is obliged to devise a method of working which, as far as possible, minimises the risk, and also to provide appropriate safety equipment or facilities. Thus, in *General Cleaning Contractors v Christmas*[1] the House of Lords held the defendant employers liable for failing to take suitable precautions which could have prevented their employee from falling and suffering serious injuries, while cleaning the windows of a building from the outside. Lord Reid expressed himself as follows:[2]

'Where the problem varies from job to job it may be reasonable to leave a great deal to the man in charge, but the danger in this case is one which is constantly found and it calls for a system to meet it. Where a practice of ignoring an obvious danger has grown up I do not think that it is reasonable to expect an individual workman to take the initiative in devising and using precautions. It is the duty of the employer to consider the situation, to devise a suitable system, to instruct his men what they must do, and to supply any implements that may be required ... '

The safety equipment or facilities should also be reasonably accessible where the employees who need them are actually working. In *Clifford v Charles H Challen & Sons Ltd*[3] the defendants kept barrier cream, to protect against the risk of their employees contracting dermatitis from the substance with which they worked, in the factory store but not in the workshop itself. Cohen LJ said:[4]

'Where an employer is making use of a dangerous process, it is not enough for him to have available somewhere in the factory the appliances necessary to minimise the danger. The system of working must be one in which the appliances are available at the place where they are needed ... '

1   *[1953] AC 180, [1952] 2 All ER 1110.* See also *Drummond v British Building Cleaners Ltd [1954] 3 All ER 507, [1954] 1 WLR 1434, CA.* Cf *Wilson v Tyneside Window Cleaning Co [1958] 2 QB 110, [1958] 2 All ER 265, CA.*

2   *[1953] AC 180* at 194, *[1952] 2 All ER 1110* at 1117.

3   *[1951] 1 KB 495, [1951] 1 All ER 72, CA.* Cf *Woods v Durable Suites Ltd [1953] 2 All ER 391, [1953] 1 WLR 857, CA.*

4   *[1951] 1 KB 495* at 500, *[1951] 1 All ER 72* at 76.

Equipment provided but unused

[17.12] If, however, the appropriate facilities *were* properly made available, to the knowledge of the workforce, a claimant employee who argues that insufficient pressure was put upon him actually to make use of those facilities will understandably find it much harder to succeed than claimants in cases where the defendants failed to provide safety equipment at all. In *Qualcast (Wolverhampton) Ltd v Haynes*[1] the plaintiff was an experienced foundry worker who was injured when molten metal splashed on to one of his feet. He was aware that spats and boots were available to protect against this risk but failed to wear them. He nevertheless claimed that the defendants had failed to provide him with a safe system of work in that he had not actually been ordered or advised to wear spats. His claim failed. Lord Radcliffe said:[2]

> ' ... though, indeed, there may be cases in which an employer does not discharge his duty of care towards his workmen merely by providing an article of safety equipment, the courts should be circumspect in filling out that duty with the much vaguer obligation of encouraging, exhorting and instructing workmen, or a particular workman, to make regular use of what is provided.'

In one case a plaintiff who had failed to use safety equipment which was available was unsuccessful in his claim even though, being unable to read, he had not understood a notice in the factory drawing attention to the equipment and urging that it should be used.[3]

1   *[1959] AC 743, [1959] 2 All ER 38, HL.*

2   *[1959] AC 743* at 753, *[1959] 2 All ER 38* at 40.

3   See *James v Hepworth & Grandage Ltd [1968] 1 QB 94, [1967] 2 All ER 829, CA.*

Need for proactivity

[17.13] On the other hand, it would be wrong to suppose that it will always be sufficient for an employer to do no more than merely provide proper safety equipment and make known its availability to the workforce. Particularly if disregard for the safety measures becomes widespread, the employer may be held liable if he acquiesces passively in this disregard and takes no steps at all to pressurise his employees into protecting themselves.[1] Thus, in *Bux v Slough Metals Ltd*[2] the defendants were held liable when one of their employees suffered serious eye injuries. Goggles, which would have prevented the accident, were available, but members of the workforce generally were notoriously reluctant to wear them as they considered that they impeded their work. Stephenson LJ said:[3]

> 'There was evidence which justified the judge's finding that the employers acquiesced in the universal rejection of goggles in the die-casting foundry ... That acquiescence came too early and too easily for the employers to rely on Lord Radcliffe's warning in *Qualcast* ... and I agree with the judge that there

was a clear breach of their duty to take reasonable precautions in relation to their employees, including the plaintiff, about the wearing of goggles by making it a rule and trying to enforce it by supervision.'

1   Cf *Pape v Cumbria County Council [1991] IRLR 463.*
2   *[1974] 1 All ER 262, [1973] 1 WLR 1358, CA.*
3   *[1974] 1 All ER 262 at 274, [1973] 1 WLR 1358 at 1371.*

Standard of care

[17.14] In *Stokes v Guest, Keen & Nettlefold (Bolts and Nuts) Ltd*[1] Swanwick J 'perused some of the standard line of authorities dealing with the duties of employers towards their workmen' and expressed his conclusions as follows:[2]

> 'From these authorities I deduce the principles, that the overall test is still the conduct of the reasonable and prudent employer, taking positive thought for the safety of his workers in the light of what he knows or ought to know; where there is a recognised and general practice which has been followed for a substantial period in similar circumstances without mishap, he is entitled to follow it, unless in the light of common sense or newer knowledge, it is clearly bad; but, where there is developing knowledge, he must keep reasonably abreast of it and not be too slow to apply it; and where he has in fact greater than average knowledge of the risks, he may be thereby obliged to take more than the average or standard precautions. He must weigh up the risk in terms of the likelihood of injury occurring and the potential consequences if it does; and he must balance against this the probable effectiveness of the precautions that can be taken to meet it and the expense and inconvenience they involve. If he is found to have fallen below the standard to be properly expected of a reasonable and prudent employer in these respects, he is negligent.'[3]

1   *[1968] 1 WLR 1776.*
2   *[1968] 1 WLR 1776 at 1783.*
3   In *Thompson v Smith's Shiprepairers (North Shields) Ltd [1984] QB 405* at 415, *[1984] 1 All ER 881* at 889 Mustill J described this as a 'succinct and helpful statement of the law'.

General practice

[17.15] That reliance upon 'general practice' will not absolve defendants if that practice involves an obvious risk, is illustrated by the leading case of *Morris v West Hartlepool Steam Navigation Co Ltd*,[1] in which the plaintiff seaman fell into the hold of a ship and suffered serious injuries. The House of Lords, by a majority, effectively condemned as negligent a general practice of not guarding or covering access to the hold from the inside of a vessel while the ship was at sea. Although the practice was long established, the patent nature of the risk, and the ease with which precautions could have been taken, meant that it failed to come 'up to the standard required from a reasonably prudent employer whose duty it is to take reasonable steps to avoid exposing his servants to unnecessary risks'.[2] *Morris'* case was distinguished in *Gray v Stead*[3], in which a fisherman fell overboard and was drowned. The Court of Appeal, reversing the trial judge, held that it had not been negligent of his employer to follow a common practice in the industry of not providing life jackets suitable for use by fishermen when working on deck.

1   *[1956] AC 552, [1956] 1 All ER 385, HL.* See also *Cavanagh v Ulster Weaving Co Ltd [1960] AC 145, [1959] 2 All ER 745, HL.*

2   *Per* Lord Tucker, *[1965] AC 552* at 576, *[1956] 1 All ER 385* at 400.
3   *[1999] 2 Lloyd's Rep 559.*

Developing knowledge

[17.16] Difficult questions may arise where negligence is alleged in a situation involving, in the words of Swanwick J in the *Stokes* case, 'developing knowledge'. In *Thompson v Smith's Shiprepairers (North Shields) Ltd*[1] the plaintiffs' hearing had been adversely affected by excessive noise over the course of 30 years' employment in the shipbuilding and shiprepairing trades. Some appreciation of the undesirability of continuous subjection to noise had existed throughout the plaintiffs' working lives, but it was only during the later years that research established the full seriousness of the risk and effective protective devices began to be developed. Mustill J expressed himself as follows:[2]

> '[There] is a type of risk which is regarded at any given time (although not necessarily later) as an inescapable feature of the industry. The employer is not liable for the consequences of such risks, although subsequent changes in social awareness, or improvements in knowledge and technology, may transfer the risk into the category of those against which the employer can and should take care.'

His Lordship awarded damages to the plaintiffs, not for their whole loss, but only for the extent to which they had suffered injury after the date at which 'a reasonable employer, with proper but not extraordinary solicitude for the welfare of his workers, [would] have identified the problem of excessive noise in his yard'.[3] The difficulties of proof in cases where medical knowledge is in a state of uncertainty, particularly where one school of thought perceives a complaint to have a psychological component, are vividly illustrated by *Pickford v Imperial Chemical Industries plc*.[4] This case produced sharp differences of judicial opinion as to whether causation had been proved in a claim for damages by a secretary for repetitive strain injury, allegedly resulting from an excessive typing load. Her claim failed at first instance, was allowed by a majority of the Court of Appeal, but was ultimately rejected by a majority decision of the House of Lords. In the somewhat similar case of *Alexander v Midland Bank*[5], however, the Court of Appeal held that the claimants' case had been established. Stuart-Smith LJ said this[6]:

> 'In my judgment the fallacy of the defendants' position is to assume that because the precise physical, pathological and anatomical explanation cannot as yet be explained, the condition must be all in the mind. I can see no basis for such a presumption, if all the other evidence is taken into account'.

1   [1984] QB 405, [1984] 1 All ER 881.
2   [1984] QB 405 at 415–416, [1984] 1 All ER 881 at 889.
3   [1984] QB 405 at 423, [1984] 1 All ER 881 at 894. See also *McSherry v British Telecommunications plc* [1992] 3 Med LR 129 (repetitive strain injury).
4   [1998] 3 All ER 462, [1998] 1 WLR 1189, HL.
5   [2000] ICR 464.
6   See above at para 44.

Weighing up the risk

[17.17] The process of weighing up a risk in terms of its likelihood, seriousness and the cost and effectiveness of possible precautions, is as relevant in this area as in the rest of the law of negligence. In *Latimer v AEC Ltd*[1] the House of Lords refused to hold the defendants liable for failing to take the 'drastic step'[2] of closing down their factory rather than allow their employees to run the risk of slipping on a floor across which oil had spread. Lord Tucker considered that it had not been proved 'that the floor was so slippery that, remedial steps not being possible, a reasonably prudent employer would have closed down the factory rather than allow his employees to run the risks involved in continuing work'. The plaintiff, who incurred injuries when he fell on the slippery floor, therefore failed in his claim for damages. In the case of the emergency services there is also a possibility that an employee's claim may be adversely affected by the need to take a deliberate risk in order to deal with a perceived greater threat[3].

1 *[1953] AC 643, [1953] 2 All ER 449, HL.*
2 *[1953] AC 643 at 643, 659, [1953] 2 All ER 449* at 451, 455, *per* Lord Porter and Lord Tucker.
3 See *Watt v Herfordshire County Council [1954] 1 WLR 835, [1954] 2 All ER 368, CA.* See also *King v Sussex Ambulance NHS Trust [2002] ICR 1413,* but note the doubts as to the correctness of the principle in *Watt's* case expressed by Buxton LJ in *King* at para 48.

Duty owed to each employee individually

[17.18] The employer's duty is one 'which is owed to each employee individually', observed Neill LJ in one case,[1] 'and accordingly account has to be taken of the ... [particular] employee whose safety may be at risk'. In the well-known case of *Paris v Stepney Borough Council*[2] the plaintiff, who was already blind in one eye, became totally blind when a piece of metal entered his other eye. The wearing of goggles would have prevented the accident, and the House of Lords held the defendant employers liable in negligence for failing to provide them for the plaintiff. This was notwithstanding the fact that the risk of any such injury occurring in the occupation in question was so low that it was neither usual nor necessary to provide goggles for two-eyed employees. But the gravity of the injury, if the risk should materialise, required that special steps should have been taken to protect a one-eyed employee.[3] Similarly, the level of skill and experience of the individual employee will often be relevant in determining the precise extent to which safety measures, and supervision with respect to such matters, may be necessary.[4]

1 See *McDermid v Nash Dredging and Reclamation Co Ltd* in the Court of Appeal: *[1986] QB 965* at 974, *[1986] 2 All ER 676* at 681, CA (*McDermid's* case itself, in which the decision of the Court of Appeal was subsequently affirmed by the House of Lords, is discussed below at para [17.24]).
2 *[1951] AC 367, [1951] 1 All ER 42, HL.* See also *Hatton v Sutherland [2002] 2 All ER 1* at para 23 *per* Hale LJ; *Walker v Northumberland County Council [1995] 1 All ER 737.*
3 See also *per* Stuart-Smith LJ in *Johnstone v Bloomsbury Health Authority [1992] QB 333* at 344, *[1991] 2 All ER 293* at 299–300.
4 'An experienced workman dealing with a familiar and obvious risk may not reasonably need the same attention or the same precautions as an inexperienced man who is likely to be more receptive of advice or admonition': *per* Lord Radcliffe in *Qualcast (Wolverhampton) Ltd v Haynes [1959] AC 743* at 754, *[1959] 2 All ER 38* at 40, HL. See also *per* Lord Keith of Avonholme *[1959] AC 743* at 755, *[1959] 2 All ER 38* at 42).

Duty does not extend to paternalism

[17.19] The proposition, illustrated by *Paris v Stepney Borough Council*, that an employer must take an employee's individual susceptibilities into account, does not imply that the employer must refuse to employ someone who is anxious to work for him even though the existence of special susceptibilities, combined with the nature of the job, will put the employee at some risk even if all proper care is taken. As Edmund Davies LJ put it in one case:[1]

> 'It requires no authority to illustrate the cogency of the proposition that the duty of reasonable care does not impose upon an employer the necessity of saying to an employee: "You are not fit for this properly-planned and entirely safe work because of your own physical condition, and therefore, despite your own desire to continue at it, we must dismiss you".'[2]

Thus, in *Withers v Perry Chain Co Ltd*[3] a plaintiff who willingly and deliberately continued to do work which unavoidably involved some risk of dermatitis, even though she knew that she was susceptible to the disease, completely failed in her claim against her employers when it materialised. Of course, the rule in this case presupposes that the employee is fully apprised of all the relevant circumstances. There might, as Devlin LJ observed, be liability 'if the employer were to conceal the risk or fail to give the employee information which he had and which might help her to evaluate it properly'.[4]

[1] *Kossinski v Chrysler United Kingdom Ltd (1973) 15 KIR 225*. See also *Bailey v Rolls-Royce (1971) Ltd [1984] ICR 688, CA*.
[2] See also *Hatton v Sutherland [2002] 2 All ER 1* at para 34 *per* Hale LJ.
[3] *[1961] 3 All ER 676, [1961] 1 WLR 1314, CA*. See also *Jones v Lionite Specialities (Cardiff) Ltd (1961) 105 Sol Jo 1082, CA*.
[4] *[1961] 3 All ER 676* at 680, *[1961] 1 WLR 1314* at 1320. But cf *White v Holbrook Precision Castings [1985] IRLR 215, CA* (no duty to warn of possibility of developing trivial condition causing minor discomfort).

Dangerous fellow-employees negligently left in post

[17.20] Since the abolition of the doctrine of common employment a claimant injured by a fellow-employee will, of course, be able to hold the employer liable vicariously if the fellow-employee was acting in the course of his employment. Cases occasionally arise, however, in which that employee caused injury while playing a practical joke which misfired, with serious consequences. In one case of this type the 'joke' was so closely connected with the tortfeasor's actual work that it was held to come just within the course of his employment, for the purposes of vicarious liability.[1] More usually, however, it will be difficult plausibly to contend that activities of this kind were within the course of employment.[2] It might then be alleged by the claimant victim that, by allowing a state of affairs to occur in which practical jokes could take place, the employer was himself negligent as being in breach of his own primary duty to provide a safe system of work. Such a claim succeeded in *Hudson v Ridge Manufacturing Co Ltd*.[3] In this case the plaintiff was tripped up by a fellow-worker who had persistently engaged, for several years, 'in horse-play and skylarking', and who had an 'almost incurable habit of tripping people up'. The defendants had frequently reprimanded him but to no effect; and they continued to employ him notwithstanding his behaviour. Streatfeild J observed that 'there existed ... in the system of work, a source of danger' for which the defendants should be held liable. His Lordship emphasised, however, that if the incident had been an isolated one or had, perhaps, occurred once before and been followed by a reprimand giving reasonable grounds for supposing that there would be no recurrence, liability could not be imposed on the employer.[4]

[1] See *Harrison v Michelin Tyre Co Ltd [1985] 1 All ER 918, [1985] ICR 696*.

2   See *Coddington v International Harvesters of Great Britain Ltd (1969) 6 KIR 146*. But cf *Lister v Hesley Hall [2001] 2 All ER 769*. On vicarious liability, see below CHAPTER 18.
3   *[1957] 2 QB 348, [1957] 2 All ER 229.*
4   See *[1957] 2 QB 348* at 350, *[1957] 2 All ER 229* at 230. See also *Smith v Crossley Bros Ltd (1951) 95 Sol Jo 655, CA* ('a wicked act which the defendants had no reason to foresee').

Employer's Liability (Defective Equipment) Act

[17.21]   The *Employer's Liability (Defective Equipment) Act 1969, s 1(1)* provides as follows:

'Where after the commencement of this Act—

(a)   an employee suffers personal injury in the course of his employment in consequence of a defect in equipment provided by his employer for the purposes of the employer's business; and

(b)   the defect is attributable wholly or partly to the fault of a third party (whether identified or not),

the injury shall be deemed to be also attributable to negligence on the part of the employer (whether or not he is liable in respect of the injury apart from this subsection), but without prejudice to the law relating to contributory negligence and to any remedy by way of contribution or in contract or otherwise which is available to the employer in respect of the injury.'

The purpose of this provision was to reverse the decision of the House of Lords in *Davie v New Merton Board Mills Ltd*.[1] In this case apparently sound equipment, obtained from a reputable source, turned out to be defective, due to negligence in its manufacture, and injured an employee of the defendants. The latter were held not liable on the ground that the employer had discharged his duty by taking reasonable care when acquiring the equipment: the employee's remedy was to proceed against the manufacturer under *Donoghue v Stevenson*. This decision was felt to be inconvenient, since the employee might in practice have difficulty in pursuing the third party supplier or manufacturer. Accordingly, providing the employee can show that the defect which caused him injury was due to carelessness, the Act enables him to recover against his employer regardless of whether or not he is able even to identify the negligent third party. Of course, if the employer has himself been negligent with respect to the equipment, for example by failing to inspect it or to remove it from use when he knew, or should have known, of the defect, then he will be liable to his injured employee at common law.[2]

1   *[1959] AC 604, [1959] 1 All ER 346, HL.*
2   See *Pearce v Round Oak Steel Works [1969] 3 All ER 680, [1965] 1 WLR 595, CA*; *Taylor v Rover Co Ltd [1966] 2 All ER 181, [1966] 1 WLR 1491*; *Condo v South Australia (1987) 47 SASR 584.*

Broad construction

[17.22]   The word 'equipment' is construed broadly. In *Knowles v Liverpool City Council*[1] the House of Lords rejected a contention that the scope of the Act was confined to tools and machinery and did not extend to materials upon which work was being done. In that case a flagstone which broke while it was being manhandled was held to come within the definition. In an earlier case the House of Lords held that an entire ship could be 'equipment' for the purposes of the Act.[2]

¹   *[1993] 4 All ER 321, [1993] 1 WLR 1428, HL.*

²   See *Coltman v Bibby Tankers Ltd, The Derbyshire [1988] AC 276, [1987] 3 All ER 1068, HL* ('The purpose of the Act was manifestly to saddle the employer with liability for defective plant of every sort with which the employee is compelled to work in the course of his employment and I can see no ground for excluding particular types of chattel merely on the ground of their size or the element upon which they are designed to operate', *per* Lord Oliver).

Insurance

[17.23]   It should be noted that an employer is required by statute to be insured 'against liability for bodily injury or disease sustained by his employees ... arising out of and in the course of their employment'. This provision is to be found in the *Employers' Liability (Compulsory Insurance) Act 1969, s 1(1)*. It obviously includes in its scope an employer's liability under the *Employers' Liability (Defective Equipment) Act 1969*, as well as his common law liability for failure to provide a safe system of work. Accordingly, an injured employee should now be able to recover compensation even if the defect in the equipment had been due to the negligence of a third party who subsequently turned out to be insolvent: a situation in which *Davie v New Merton Board Mills* would in practice have left him remediless.¹

¹   But cf *Richardson v Pitt-Stanley [1995] QB 123, [1995] 1 All ER 460, CA*, discussed in CHAPTER 16 above.

Non-delegable duty

[17.24]   The approach reflected by the legislature, in the *Employer's Liability (Defective Equipment) Act 1969*, to the problem of employer's liability for injuries suffered by their employees, is similar to that adopted by the common law, as it was perceived to be,¹ prior to the decision in *Davie v New Merton Board Mills Ltd*.² In that case, however, the House of Lords was apparently of the opinion that there should be some narrowing in the scope of an employer's liability for injuries with respect to which neither he, nor other employees of his, had been negligent. But the considerations of policy and convenience underlying the imposition of so-called 'non-delegable duties' upon employers continue to exercise influence, even at common law, notwithstanding the decision in *Davie*'s case. Accordingly, an employer might still find himself liable, beyond the normal confines of vicarious liability, for the fault of someone else. That this is so was strikingly demonstrated by another, more recent, unanimous decision of the House of Lords. In *McDermid v Nash Dredging and Reclamation Co Ltd*³ the defendants were held liable for injuries suffered by one of their employees as a result of the negligence of a tugboat captain, who was not their employee. The plaintiff had, however, been instructed by the defendants to work on a project in which both they and the tugboat captain were involved; and this had the effect of putting the plaintiff under the supervision of the captain, whose method of working was found to be unsafe and which caused the injury. Lord Brandon spoke as follows:⁴

> '... an employer owes to his employee a duty to exercise reasonable care to ensure that the system of work provided for him is a safe one ... The essential characteristic of the duty is that, if it is not performed, it is no defence for the employer to show that he delegated its performance to a person, whether his servant or not his servant, whom he reasonably believed to be competent to perform it. Despite such delegation the employer is liable for the non-performance of the duty.'⁵

1   See *Wilsons & Clyde Coal Co Ltd v English [1938] AC 57, [1937] 3 All ER 628, HL.*
2   *[1959] AC 604, [1959] 1 All ER 346, HL.*
3   *[1987] AC 906, [1987] 2 All ER 878, HL.* See also *Sumner v William Henderson & Sons Ltd [1964] 1 QB 450, [1963] 1 All ER 408.*
4   *[1987] AC 906 at 919, [1987] 2 All ER 878 at 887.*
5   See also *Wingfield v Ellerman's Wilson Line [1960] 2 Lloyd's Rep 16* at 22, CA, *per* Devlin LJ.

Australian authority

[17.25]   Lord Brandon's speech also included a reference to a 1984 decision of the High Court of Australia, *Kondis v State Transport Authority*,[1] in which a similar decision had been reached and which had been heavily relied on by the Court of Appeal in *McDermid*'s case.[2] Mason J, in that case, stated what he understood to be the reason for the imposition of liability upon employers in these circumstances, and also put the scope of that liability on a wide basis. He said:[3]

> 'The employer has the exclusive responsibility for the safety of the appliances, the premises and the system of work to which he subjects his employee and the employee has no choice but to accept and rely on the employer's provision and judgment in relation to these matters. The consequence is that in these relevant aspects the employee's safety is in the hands of the employer; it is his responsibility. The employee can reasonably expect therefore that reasonable care and skill will be taken. In the case of the employer there is no unfairness in imposing on him a non-delegable duty; it is reasonable that he should bear liability for the negligence of his independent contractors in devising a safe system of work. If he requires his employee to work according to an unsafe system he should bear the consequences.'[4]

1   *(1984) 55 ALR 225.*
2   See *[1986] QB 965, [1986] 2 All ER 676, CA.*
3   *(1984) 55 ALR 225* at 235.
4   See also *Morris v Breaveglen Ltd [1993] ICR 766, CA.* Cf *Nelhams v Sandells Maintenance Ltd* (1995) Times, 15 June, CA.

Duty discharged

[17.26]   *McDermid v Nash Dredging and Reclamation Co Ltd* was distinguished on the facts in *Cook v Square D Ltd*.[1] In this case the plaintiff was sent by his employers in the UK to work in Saudi Arabia at premises occupied by another firm, where he suffered injury due to a hazard on those premises. The Court of Appeal accepted that the duty owed by the UK employers could not be delegated but held that that duty, which was only to do what was reasonable in all the circumstances, had not been breached merely by the presence of a hazard on a site abroad occupied by supposedly competent international contractors. 'The suggestion that the home-based employer', observed Farquaharson LJ,[2] 'has any responsibility for the daily events of a site in Saudi Arabia has an air of unreality'. In *McDermid*'s case the relationship between the tugboat captain and the main employers had been much closer. Although the plaintiff in *Cook's* case therefore failed, Farquaharson LJ emphasised that, as the contrast with *McDermid* indeed illustrated, decisions in other cases could well be different even where the facts were superficially similar. He said:[3]

> 'Circumstances will, of course, vary, and it may be that in some cases where, for example, a number of employees are going to work on a foreign site or where one or two employees are called upon to work there for a very considerable

period of time that an employer may be required to inspect the site and satisfy himself that the occupiers were conscious of their obligations concerning the safety of people working there.'

1   *[1992] IRLR 34, CA*. See also *A (A Child) v Ministry of Defence [2003] PIQR P33*.
2   *[1992] IRLR 34* at 38.
3   *[1992] IRLR 34* at 38.

D Statutory duties

Introduction

[17.27]   It has long been established that an action for damages for breach of statutory duty can subsist in favour of an employee injured due to contravention by his employer of the statutory provisions or regulations relating to safety at places of work. Since 1997, provisions formerly contained in legislation such as the *Factories Act 1961*, and the *Offices, Shops and Railway Premises Act 1963*, have largely been replaced by regulations and approved codes of practice gradually promulgated, over a number of years, under the *Health and Safety at Work etc. Act 1974*. This has been done in order to improve the law in this area, by giving it a more unified and coherent structure, and in order to comply with EC directives relating to health and safety. The replacement regulations, made under powers conferred by the *Health and Safety at Work etc Act*[1] itself, continue to give rise to the action for damages for breach of statutory duty, except in so far as they themselves provide otherwise.[2] In at least one instance regulations which did originally provide otherwise have been subsequently amended so as to provide that such actions *can* be brought[3].

1   See *section 15*.
2   *SI 1992/3004. Health and Safety at Work etc Act, s 47(2)*.
3   See *Regulation 6* of the *Management of Health and Safety at Work and Fire Precautions (Workplace) (Amendment) Regulations 2003 (SI 2003/2457)* amending *Regulation 22* of the *Management of Health and Safety at Work Regulations 1999 (SI 1999/3242)*. For discussion, see Victoria Howes 'New Civil Action Against Employers' [2003] NLJR 1794.

New regulations

[17.28]   The gradual process of replacement was carried significantly forward in the year 1992. New regulations that year included the *Workplace (Health, Safety and Welfare) Regulations*,[1] the *Provision and Use of Work Equipment Regulations*,[2] the *Manual Handling Operations Regulations*[3] and the *Personal Protective Equipment at Work Regulations*.[4] Although these sets of Regulations only came into force, for existing workplaces, on 1 January 1996, they came into effect for new workplaces on 1 January 1993. Of necessity, comprehensive treatment of the detailed provisions relating to health and safety at work cannot be attempted in a work of this kind, and reference should be made to original sources and relevant specialist works.[5] Some highlighting of those regulations which replace legislative provisions which had formerly proved particularly conspicuous, as the source of reported case law relating to actions for breach of statutory duty brought by employees, is nevertheless appropriate.

1   *SI 1992/3004*.
2   *SI 1992/2932*. See now the *Provision and Use of Work Equipment Regulations 1998 (SI 1998/2306)*. For a case in which the Court of Appeal construed an obligation arising under the 1992 Regulations to be absolute in nature, see *Stark v Post Office [2000] ICR 1013*.

3   *SI 1992/2793.*
4   *SI 1992/2966.*
5   See J Hendy and M Ford *Munkman on Employer's Liability* (13th edn, 2001).

Dangerous machinery

'Practicable'

[17.29] *Regulation 11* of the *Provision and Use of Work Equipment Regulations 1998* provides, inter alia, that:

'(1)   Every employer shall ensure that measures are taken in accordance with paragraph (2) which are effective—

(a)   to prevent access to any dangerous part of machinery ...; or

(b)   to stop the movement of any dangerous part of machinery ... before any part of a person enters a danger zone.

(2) The measures required by paragraph (1) shall consist of—

(a)   the provision of fixed guards enclosing every dangerous part ... where and to the extent that it is practicable to do so ...'

The duty to 'fence' dangerous machinery was formerly to be found in *sections 12–16* of the *Factories Act 1961* and was the subject of many reported decisions.[1] The wording of the new Regulation differs significantly from the provisions in the 1961 Act, and much of the former case law will now be obsolete. *Regulation 11(2)(a)*, quoted above, is followed by a series of defined precautionary measures which are to be taken if 'the provision of fixed guards' is not 'practicable'. It is notable that, despite differences between the earlier legislation and the Regulation, the word 'practicable' has been retained in the latter; this was a familiar expression in the earlier legislation and the relevant decisions are, on the whole, notable for their interpretation of it in a manner favourable to the employee, so that alleged lack of 'practicability' seems seldom to have afforded a defence.[2] On the other hand, the expression appeared in a variety of different contexts in various provisions of the Factories Act, and observations at least potentially favourable to employers were occasionally made. In *Brooks v J & P Coates (UK) Ltd*,[3] decided under *section 63(1)* of the Act,[4] Boreham J said that he took ''practicable' in this context to mean a precaution which could be undertaken without practical difficulty'. The expression should, however, be contrasted with one found elsewhere in the Act: 'so far as is *reasonably* practicable.'[5] This expression seems to import a lower duty.[6] In *Wallhead v Ruston and Hornsby Ltd*[7] Bagnall J suggested that 'one difference ... between the two ... expressions is that questions of cost may be taken into account in deciding what is reasonably practicable but not in deciding what is practicable'.[8]

1   Cases decided by the House of Lords alone include the following: *F E Callow (Engineers) v Johnson [1971] AC 335, [1970] 3 All ER 639, HL; Mailer v Austin Rover Group plc [1989] 2 All ER 1087* at 1089 HL; *Midland and Low Moor Iron & Steel Co Ltd v Cross [1965] AC 343, [1964] 3 All ER 752, HL; Sparrow v Fairey Aviation Co Ltd [1964] AC 1019, [1962] 3 All ER 706, HL; Close v Steel Co of Wales Ltd [1962] AC 367, [1961] 2 All ER 953, HL; John Summers & Sons Ltd v Frost [1955] AC 740* at 766, *[1955] 1 All ER 870* at 883, HL; *Carroll v Andrew Barclay & Sons Ltd [1948] AC 477, [1948] 2 All ER 386, HL; Nicholls v F Austin (Leyton) Ltd [1946] AC 493, [1946] 2 All ER 92, HL.*
2   See *Sanders v F H Lloyd & Co Ltd [1982] ICR 360* at 365, *per* Drake J. See also *Boyton v Willment Bros [1971] 3 All ER 624, [1971] 1 WLR 1625, CA.*
3   *[1984] 1 All ER 702* at 718.

4   '... all practicable measures shall be taken to protect the persons employed against inhalation [of dust etc].'
5   Italics supplied. See also below.
6   See *Gregson v Hick Hargreaves & Co Ltd [1955] 3 All ER 507* at 516, *[1955] 1 WLR 1252* at 1267, CA, *per* Parker LJ.
7   *(1973) 14 KIR 285* at 292.
8   Cf *per* Edmund Davies LJ in *Cartwright v G K N Sankey Ltd (1973) 14 KIR 349* at 363, CA.

State of knowledge

[17.30]   It is clear, however, that even the higher level of duty requires reference 'to the state of knowledge at the time, and particularly to the knowledge of scientific people'.[1] In *Adsett v K & L Steelfounders and Engineers*[2] the defendants themselves were the first in the field in the development of a particular protective device which would have been effective in the case in question. The plaintiff suffered injury, however, before this development took place, but argued that he should nevertheless recover on the ground that the subsequent advances had shown that it would have been 'practicable' to provide protection at the time. The Court of Appeal rejected this argument and the plaintiff's claim failed. In the later case of *Richards v Highway Ironfounders (West Bromwich) Ltd,*[3] Evershed MR expressed himself as follows:

'The nature of the obligation has been epigrammatically expressed as being that the measures taken must be possible in the light of current knowledge and according to known means and resources. It is clear then, in my judgment, that the matter must be judged in the light of the state of the relevant knowledge at the time of the alleged breach. Thus, the fact that at some later date some method of protection has been discovered which was not dreamed of at the date of the alleged breach, even though all the individual materials therefor were known and available, will not suffice. On the other hand, I must not be taken to be saying that the state of knowledge, or absence of knowledge, within the limited scope of a particular industry, or branch of an industry, is by any means necessarily conclusive. It must be a question of fact and of the weight of all the material evidence in any particular case to assess what was in truth known, or what ought to have been known, by the employers charged at the relevant dates.'

1   *Adsett v K & L Steelfounders and Engineers Ltd [1953] 2 All ER 320* at 323, *[1953] 1 WLR 773* at 780, CA, *per* Singleton LJ.
2   *[1953] 2 All ER 320, [1953] 1 WLR 773, CA.*
3   *[1955] 3 All ER 205* at 210, *[1955] 1 WLR 1049* at 1054, CA. See also *Dugmore v Swansea NHS Trust [2003] 1 All ER 333* at para 17 *per* Hale LJ.

Claimant's conduct

[17.31]   The fact that the claimant acted carelessly, indolently, or even frivolously in coming into contact with the machine will not absolve his employer from liability for any failure to comply with *Regulation 11*: such actions by employees are reasonably foreseeable and safety precautions should guard against them.[1] The Factories Act decisions on this aspect of the matter presumably remain valid. It does not matter that the employee was not actually acting in the course of his employment at the time when he was injured. The expression 'a frolic of his own', which is relevant to an employer's vicarious liability for the torts of his servants, is not relevant here.[2] In *Uddin v Associated Portland Cement Manufacturers Ltd*[3] the plaintiff left his allotted place of work, entered a part of the factory where he was not authorised to be, and only came into contact with the unfenced machine which caused him injury when he leaned over it in order to catch a pigeon. He was nevertheless held able to sue his employers for breach of their statutory duty. Moreover, provided that the accident would not have happened had not the defendant employers failed to fence, it is irrelevant that the way in which the accident actually happened was unforeseeable or unexplained.[4]

1   *Smith v Chesterfield and District Co-operative Society Ltd [1953] 1 All ER 447, [1953] 1 WLR 370, CA.* Of course, the plaintiff's damages may be reduced for contributory negligence in such a case.
2   See *per* Diplock LJ in *Allen v Aeroplane and Motor Aluminium Castings [1965] 3 All ER 377* at 379, *[1965] 1 WLR 1244* at 1248, CA.
3   *[1965] 2 QB 582, [1965] 2 All ER 213, CA.*
4   See *Millard v Serck Tubes Ltd [1969] 1 All ER 598, [1969] 1 WLR 211.* See also *F E Callow (Engineers) Ltd v Johnson [1971] AC 335* at 347, *[1970] 3 All ER 639* at 645, HL, *per* Lord Hailsham LC.

Floors and access

'Reasonably practicable'

[17.32] *Regulation 12(3)* of the *Workplace (Health, Safety and Welfare) Regulations 1992* provides that:

> 'So far as is reasonably practicable, every floor in a workplace and the surface of every traffic route in a workplace shall be kept free from obstructions and from any article or substance which may cause a person to slip, trip or fall.'

Like a similar provision in the *Factories Act 1961*,[1] the Regulation uses the phrase 'reasonably practicable'. Cases on the earlier provision indicate that the onus of proving that the taking of precautions was *not* reasonably practicable lies upon the defendant: it is not necessary for the claimant to prove that such precautions *were* reasonably practicable.[2] A defendant who seeks to rely on the excuse must raise it specifically in his pleading.[3] In *Jenkins v Allied Ironfounders Ltd*[4] Lord Reid said that, in order to determine reasonable practicability, it was necessary to balance 'any expense, delays or other disadvantages involved in adopting the preventive system' against 'the nature and extent of the risks involved if that system was not adopted'.[5] In the case itself, precautions which 'would certainly have been possible'[6] were held nevertheless not to have been 'reasonably practicable'.

1   Cf *Latimer v AEC Ltd [1953] AC 643, [1953] 2 All 449, HL* (decided under the *Factories Act 1937, s 25*). See also the *Factories Act 1961, s 29(1)*, and the *Offices, Shops and Railway Premises Act 1963, s 16*.
2   See *Nimmo v Alexander Cowan & Sons [1968] AC 107, [1967] 3 All ER 187, HL.*
3   See *Bowes v Sedgefield District Council [1981] 1 C R 234, CA.* See also *Johnstone v Caddies Wainwright [1983] 1 CR 407, CA; Larner v British Steel plc [1993] 4 All ER 102, [1993] ICR 551, CA.*
4   *[1969] 3 All ER 1609, [1970] 1 WLR 304, HL.*
5   *[1969] 3 All ER 1609* at 1612, *[1970] 1 WLR 304* at 307. See also *per* Lord Goff in *Mailer v Austin Rover Group plc [1989] 2 All ER 1087* at 1090: 'If, for example, the defendant establishes that the risk is small, but that the measures necessary to eliminate it are great, he may be held to be exonerated from taking steps to eliminate the risk on the ground that it was not reasonably practicable for him to do so.'
6   *Per* Lord Reid in *Jenkins v Allied Ironfounders Ltd [1969] 3 All ER 1609* at 1612, *[1970] 1 WLR 304* at 307, HL.

Higher than common law duty

[17.33] It would be wrong to suppose, however, that the availability of the defence has the effect of reducing the level of the duty which the sections impose upon defendants so as to make it no higher than the ordinary common law duty of care imposed by the tort of negligence[1]. In particular, the degree of probability of the hazard manifesting itself, which if it is very low can sometimes exonerate a defendant from negligence liability, does not appear to be relevant. In *Bennett v Rylands Whitecross Ltd*[2] Kilner Brown J said that the fact that a danger 'was unwittingly created, or was a fluke, or a million to one chance, does not absolve the defendants from an obligation which is absolute unless they can show that it was not reasonably practicable for them to have prevented or removed it'. It also appears to be the case that a defendant who proves that he had established a reasonable system for the taking of precautions will nevertheless incur liability if that system broke down due to a non-negligent momentary lapse on the part of one of his employees in operating it. 'If it is reasonably practicable for steps to be taken by anyone', said Denning LJ in one case,[3] 'they must be taken'.[4]

[1] See *Dugmore v Swansea NHS Trust [2003] 1 All ER 333* at para 24 *per* Hale LJ.
[2] *[1978] ICR 1031* at 1034.
[3] *Braham v J Lyons & Co Ltd [1962] 3 All ER 281* at 283, *[1962] 1 WLR 1048* at 1051. See also *[1962] 3 All ER 281* at 284, *[1962] WLR 1048* at 1053, 1052–1053, *per* Pearson LJ and *per* Donovan LJ, dubitante.
[4] See also *Williams v Painter Bros Ltd (1968) 5 KIR 487* at 490, CA, *per* Winn LJ.

Injury caused by lifting heavy loads

[17.34] *Regulation 4(1)* of the *Manual Handling Operations Regulations 1992* provides as follows:

'Each employer shall—

(a)   so far as is reasonably practicable, avoid the need for his employees to undertake any manual handling operations at work which involve a risk of their being injured … '

The forerunner of this Regulation is *section 72(1)* of the *Factories Act 1961*, which provided that: 'A person shall not be employed to lift, carry or move any load so heavy as to be likely to cause injury to him.'[1] Some of the case law on this provision may remain relevant to the construction of the new Regulation. The section was considered and applied by the House of Lords in *Brown v Allied Ironfounders Ltd.*[2] In this case the plaintiff suffered injury when lifting a heavy load by herself. It was the normal practice for two employees to lift such loads together, but the defendant employers knew that some workers attempted to do it by themselves. Nevertheless, no express instruction was given to the plaintiff that she should seek help with the lifting, even though such help would have been available had she sought it. In these circumstances, the House of Lords held that the plaintiff had been 'employed' to move a load likely to injure her, for the purposes of the section, and she recovered damages.[3] The House emphasised, however, that the question whether the section had been contravened was one of fact which would turn upon 'the particular circumstances of each particular case'.[4] In the later case of *Black v Carricks (Caterers),*[5] a manageress, who found herself alone in the defendant's shop due to the illness of her assistants, complained over the telephone to her supervisor that certain trays of bread were too heavy for her to lift by herself. In reply she was told to do the best she could, and to obtain the assistance of a customer if she needed it. Her claim for damages for breach of statutory duty[6] in respect of a back injury, suffered when she in fact lifted one of the trays, was unsuccessful. The Court of Appeal held that the telephone instructions were only 'in the nature of guidance rather than directive', and that 'in trying to do better than was called for, [the plaintiff] became the victim of her own conscientiousness'.[7]

1   Cf the *Offices, Shops and Railway Premises Act 1963, s 23(1)*: 'No person shall, in the course of his work in premises to which this Act applies, be required to lift, carry or move a load so heavy as to be likely to cause injury to him.'
2   *[1974] 2 All ER 135, [1974] 1 WLR 527, HL.*
3   *Cf Peat v N J Muschamp & Co Ltd (1969) 7 KIR 469, CA.*
4   *[1974] 2 All ER 135* at 137, *[1974] 1 WLR 527* at 529, *per* Lord Morris. See also *per* Lord Kilbrandon (*[1974] 2 All ER 135* at 141, *[1974] 1 WLR 527* at 534): ' ... this is not the class of case in which the multiplication of citations is profitable.'
5   *[1980] IRLR 448, CA.*
6   The case was decided under the *Offices, Shops and Railway Premises Act 1963, s 23(1)*. Although the wording of this section is slightly different from that of *section 72(1)*, Megaw LJ did not think this implied any difference in meaning: see *[1980] IRLR 448* at 454. But cf *per* Shaw LJ (at 452).
7   *[1980] IRLR 448* at 452, *per* Shaw LJ.

Cases on the regulation

[17.35] The cases so far decided on *Regulation 4(1)* itself, as distinct from the previous Factories Act provision, do not indicate that the approach of the courts is significantly different. Even though one contrast between the old formulation of the duty and the new is that the latter refers to a 'risk' of injury, whereas the former used the word 'likely', it is doubtful whether this change has increased the extent of the employer's obligation.[1] In *Koonjul v Thameslink Healthcare Services*[2] the claimant, who was a care assistant in a residential home, injured her back while moving a bed away from the wall. Her claim under *Regulation 4(1)* was unsuccessful. Hale LJ observed that 'the level of risk which is required to bring a case within the obligations of Regulation 4 ... must be a real risk, a foreseeable possibility of injury, certainly nothing approaching a probability'[3]. She also stated that 'the employer is not entitled to assume that all his employees will on all occasions behave with full and proper concern for their own safety'. Nevertheless, there had to be 'an element of realism' in assessing the need for specific precautions. Even assuming that the carrying out of everyday tasks in a small residential home had involved a 'risk', for the purposes of the regulation, there had been no breach in the instant case since the employer had been entitled to rely on the fact that the claimant had had several years experience, and had also attended a course on 'Moving and Handling'. The same result was reached in *King v Sussex Ambulance NHS Trust*[4], in which an ambulance technician suffered serious back injuries while helping to carry a heavy patient down a staircase. It had not been demonstrated that greater training would have prevented the injury, and it would not have been appropriate to instruct employees to adopt in such circumstances the theoretically available course of summoning assistance from the fire brigade. There was therefore no 'reasonably practicable' alternative method of carrying out the task of moving the patient[5]. On the other hand, in *Swain v Denso Marston*[6] the Court of Appeal imposed liability under the regulation in favour of an employee whose hand had been crushed by a newly-delivered piece of equipment which had turned out to be unexpectedly heavy: the risk had not been appropriately assessed by the defendant employer.

1   On the meaning of 'likely' in *section 72(1)*, see *Bailey v Rolls Royce (1971) Ltd [1984] ICR 688, CA*. Cf *Whitfield v H & R Johnson (Tiles) Ltd [1990] 3 All ER 426, CA.*
2   *[2000] PIQR P123, CA.*
3   See above at P126.
4   *[2002] ICR 1413.*
5   For a case in which the Court of Appeal imposed liability under the Regulation because the defendant employer had not sought to establish that it had not been 'reasonably practicable' to avoid the risk, see *King v RCO Support Services [2001] ICR 608.*

⁶ *[2000] ICR 1079.*

Provision of safety equipment

[17.36] Various sections of the *Factories Act 1961* required the provision of safety equipment in particular circumstances. The *Personal Protective Equipment at Work Regulations 1992* now provide, inter alia, as follows:

'4(1) Every employer shall ensure that suitable personal protective equipment is provided to his employees who may be exposed to a risk to their health or safety while at work except where and to the extent that such risk has been adequately controlled by other means which are equally or more effective.

...

10(1) Every employer shall take all reasonable steps to ensure that any personal protective equipment provided to his employees by virtue of regulation 4(1) is properly used.'

Although each case will depend upon its own circumstances,[1] decisions on the earlier legislation indicate that a statutory duty to provide safety devices is unlikely to be fulfilled if the equipment is not immediately and readily available at the place where it is needed. In one case it was held that to have a pair of goggles hanging in the foreman's office, from where they could be fetched if desired, was not sufficient.[2] If the appropriate equipment was *not* provided, however, it was held that a plaintiff employee would still fail if the evidence suggested that the plaintiff would probably not have worn or used the devices even if they had been provided: in such a case it was considered that the breach of duty was not a cause of the plaintiff's loss.[3]

---

[1] Cf *per* Pearson J in *Ginty v Belmont Building Supplies Ltd [1959] 1 All ER 414* at 422: 'I do not think that there is any hard and fast meaning of the word "provided"; it must depend on the circumstances of the case as to what is "provided" and how what is "provided" is going to be used.'

[2] *Finch v Telegraph Construction and Maintenance Co Ltd [1949] 1 All ER 452.* See also *Nolan v Dental Manufacturing Co Ltd [1958] 2 All ER 449, [1958] 1 WLR 936.*

[3] See *Cummings or (McWilliams) v Sir William Arrol & Co Ltd [1962] 1 All ER 623, [1962] 1 WLR 295, HL.* See also *Wigley v British Vinegars [1964] AC 307, [1962] 3 All ER 161.*

Nature of risk

[17.37] For liability to be imposed under the Regulations the alleged breach must have related to the risk against which the protective equipment was provided. In one case steel-capped safety boots were provided to protect against the dropping of heavy objects on the wearer's feet[1]. Unfortunately an undetectable small hole in one of the boots resulted in the claimant suffering frostbite through walking in snow and ice in the course of his duties. He claimed that the boots were not 'in good repair', contrary to *Regulation 7(1)* of the 1992 Regulations. A bare majority of the House of Lords, affirming a majority decision of the Court of Appeal, held that the claimant's attempt to obtain damages for breach of statutory duty would fail. The risk which had materialised was not one in respect of which the special boots had been provided.

---

[1] See *Fytche v Wincanton Logistics [2004] UKHL 31.*

Causation and contributory negligence

[17.38] In *Westwood v Post Office*[1] Lord Kilbrandon expressed himself as follows:

'My Lords, the defence of contributory negligence as an answer, even as nowadays only a partial answer, to a claim arising out of breach of statutory duty is one which it must always be difficult to establish. The very existence of statutory safety provisions must be relevant to the consequences which a man may reasonably be expected to foresee as arising from his own conduct; his foresight as to that will be to some extent governed by what he may reasonably be expected to foresee as arising from his master's statutory obligations.'

Nevertheless, if the circumstances so warrant, the courts will not shrink from holding that a workman claiming for breach of statutory duty was contributorily negligent. Cases of this type, in which an apportionment is made under the *Law Reform (Contributory Negligence) Act 1945*, are an everyday occurrence in the courts[2]. But the well-known warning of Lord Tucker in *Staveley Iron & Chemical Co Ltd v Jones*[3] is often quoted in cases[4] in which contributory negligence by a workman is in issue. His Lordship said:

' … in cases under the Factories Acts, the purpose of imposing the absolute obligation is to protect the workmen against those very acts of inattention which are sometimes relied on as constituting contributory negligence, so that too strict a standard would defeat the object of the statute.'[5]

[1]   *[1974] AC 1 at 16, [1973] 3 All ER 184 at 193, HL.*
[2]   For recent reported Court of Appeal examples, see *Tasci v Pekalp of London [2001] ICR 633* and *King v RCO Support Services [2001] ICR 608.*
[3]   *[1956] AC 627 at 648, [1956] 1 All ER 403 at 414, HL.*
[4]   See *Mullard v Ben Line Steamers Ltd [1971] 2 All ER 424 at 428*, CA; *Westwood v Post Office [1974] AC 1 at 17, [1973] 3 All ER 184 at 193*, HL.
[5]   See also *Toole v Bolton MBC [2002] EWCA Civ 588* in which this passage was quoted by Buxton LJ (at para 14), and a finding by the trial judge of 75% contributory negligence was reversed in favour of the imposition of full liability upon the defendant employer.

Accident entirely claimant's fault

[17.39] The question of contributory negligence cannot arise until the claimant has discharged the burden of showing that the defendant's breach of statutory duty was a cause of his loss. 'In my judgment', said Lord Reid in *Bonnington Castings Ltd v Wardlaw*,[1] 'the employee must in all cases prove his case by the ordinary standard of proof in civil actions: he must make it appear at least that on a balance of probabilities the breach of duty caused or materially contributed to his injury'.[2] It follows that a claimant whose employers have been in breach of statutory duty may nevertheless, in an extreme case, be wholly defeated on causal grounds due to his own negligence, and fail even to achieve an apportionment under the 1945 Act. In *Rushton v Turner Bros Asbestos Co Ltd*[3] the plaintiff's fingers were crushed when he attempted, in defiance of a clear instruction never to do so, to clean an unfenced machine while it was working. Ashworth J held that the claim would fail completely and expressed himself as follows:[4]

'I have been pressed, and rightly pressed, by counsel for the plaintiff, with the submission that this accident does not differ in kind from many other accidents reported in the books in which the defendant employers have been found guilty of a breach of the Factories Act, and none the less the plaintiff has succeeded in spite of considerable contributory negligence on his own part. It seems to me that in each case it is a question of degree, looking at the whole of the circumstances, fairly and broadly, to see whether a breach of the Factories Act is of itself an operative cause of the accident or is more truly in a sense the circumstances in which the accident happened.'[5]

1   *[1956] AC 613* at 620, *[1956] 1 All ER 615* at 618, HL.
2   The earlier case of *Vyner v Waldenberg Bros Ltd [1946] KB 50, [1945] 2 All ER 547*, which appeared to suggest that the onus of disproving causation would be on the employer once breach of statutory duty was established, was disapproved by the House of Lords in *Bonnington Castings v Wardlaw*. For an exceptional type of case in which justice requires that full proof of causation should not be insisted upon see *Fairchild v Glenhaven Funeral Services [2002] 3 All ER 305* discussed in CHAPTER 3 above.
3   *[1959] 3 All ER 517, [1960] 1 WLR 96.*
4   *[1959] 3 All ER 517* at 521, *[1960] 1 WLR 96* at 101.
5   See also *Jayes v IMI (Kynoch) Ltd [1985] ICR 155, CA*, in which the Court of Appeal reached the same result by making a finding of 100% contributory negligence against the employee (see *per* Goff LJ, *[1985] ICR 155* at 159). See also *Koonjul v Thameslink Healthcare Services [2000] PIQR P123, CA*. On the question whether findings of 100% contributory negligence are ever legitimate, see below CHAPTER 22.

Assumption of risk

[17.40]   It is also possible, in exceptional circumstances, for the defence of assumption of risk to defeat a claim by a servant against his employer involving breach of statutory duty. In addition to the need to satisfy all the normal requirements of the defence,[1] however, it is possible that the scope of the defence will in practice be confined in this context to situations in which the employer was not personally at fault, and was only responsible vicariously for the breach of duty.[2]

1   See CHAPTER 21 below.
2   See generally *ICI v Shatwell [1965] AC 656, [1964] 2 All ER 999, HL*.

Third party acts

[17.41]   The deliberate, and unforeseeable, act of a fellow-employee calculated to injure the claimant may also break the chain of causation so as to negate an employer's liability for breach of statutory duty[1].

1   See *Horton v Taplin Contracts [2003] ICR 179*.

Coterminous fault

[17.42]   In one type of case the employee injured as the result of a breach of a statutory duty may himself have been the person properly entrusted by his employer with the task of seeing that the particular provision was complied with. It is well established that a defendant employer can defeat a claim by the claimant in such circumstances, even though the former may have been technically in breach of the statute due to the latter's failure to discharge the task which had been allotted to him.[1] At one time the question sometimes asked in these cases was whether the employer had 'delegated' the performance of the statutory duty to his employee.[2] In *Ginty v Belmont Building Supplies Ltd*,[3] however, Pearson J adopted a supposedly more straightforward test, which has since been generally accepted as the better approach. In finding against the plaintiff in the case before him, his Lordship expressed himself as follows:[4]

'There has been a number of cases ... in which it has been considered whether or not the employer delegated to the employee the performance of the statutory duty. In my view, the law which is applicable here is clear and comprehensible if one does not confuse it by seeking to investigate this very difficult and complicated question whether or not there was a delegation. In my view, the important and fundamental question in a case like this is not whether there was a delegation, but simply the usual question: Whose fault was it?'[5]

1. 'I would deem it incongruous and irrational if ... the plaintiff could, in effect, say to his employer: "Because of my disregard of your reasonable instructions I have brought about the position that you are in breach of your statutory obligations, and so I claim damages from you because of such breach" ': *per* Morris LJ in *Manwaring v Billington [1952] 2 All ER 747* at 750, CA.
2. See *Smith v Baveystock & Co Ltd [1945] 1 All ER 531*, CA.
3. *[1959] 1 All ER 414*. Cf *Nicol v Allyacht Spars Pty Ltd (1987) 163 CLR 611 (Aust HC)*.
4. *[1959] 1 All ER 414* at 423–424.
5. In *Ross v Associated Portland Cement Manufacturers Ltd [1964] 2 All ER 452* at 455, *[1964] 1 WLR 768* at 777, Lord Reid quoted this passage and added: 'If the question is put in that way one must remember that fault is not necessarily equivalent in this context to blameworthiness. The question really is whose conduct caused the accident.'

Additional illegality

[17.43] The principle of 'coterminous fault', as it is sometimes called,[1] will not enable a defendant totally to defeat the claimant's claim if the latter can show that there was additional illegality on the defendant's part, in which the claimant was not implicated, and which was also a factor in causing the accident.[2] In particular, an employer who fails to provide proper safety equipment cannot avoid all liability merely because his employee makes the most of a bad job, and goes ahead knowing that in so doing he is acting improperly. 'The respondents cannot escape liability by saying', observed Lord Guest in *Ross v Associated Portland Cement Manufacturers*,[3] '"You worked in a place which was obviously unsafe. You cannot therefore recover" '. Fault will also clearly not be 'coterminous' if the claimant was not sufficiently experienced or senior to have been properly entrusted with the performance of the statutory duty in the first place.[4]

1. See *Ross v Associated Portland Cement Manufacturers Ltd [1964] 2 All ER 452*, *[1964] 1 WLR 768, HL*; *Leach v Standard Telephones and Cables Ltd [1966] 2 All ER 523*, *[1966] 1 WLR 1392*.
2. See *Jenner v Allen West & Co Ltd [1959] 2 All ER 115*, *[1959] 1 WLR 554, CA*; *Leach v Standard Telephones and Cables Ltd [1966] 2 All ER 523*, *[1966] 1 WLR 1392*.
3. *[1964] 2 All ER 452* at 458, *[1964] 1 WLR 768* at 781.
4. See *Ross v Associated Portland Cement Manufacturers Ltd [1964] 2 All ER 452*, *[1964] 1 WLR 768, HL*.

E Relationship between statutory and common law duties

Separation

[17.44] The courts have, in general, been anxious to keep separate from each other the questions of whether an employer has been in breach of his statutory duty and whether he has been negligent at common law. In *Bux v Slough Metals Ltd*[1] defendants who had been exonerated from breach of statutory duty, but held liable for negligence at common law, unsuccessfully contended on appeal that, in the circumstances, these findings were inconsistent, and that compliance with their statutory duty constituted fulfilment of their common law duty also. In rejecting this argument, Stephenson LJ expressed himself as follows:[2]

'There is, in my judgment, no presumption that a statutory obligation abrogates or supersedes the employer's common law duty or that it defines or measures his common law duty either by clarifying it or by cutting it down – or indeed by extending it. It is not necessarily exhaustive of that duty or co-extensive with it and I do not, with all due respect to counsel for the defendants' argument, think it possible to lay down conditions in which it is exhaustive or to conclude that it is so in this case. The statutory obligation may exceed the duty at common law or it may fall short of it or it may equal it. The court has always to construe the statute or statutory instrument which imposes the obligation, consider the facts of the particular case and the allegations of negligence in fact made by the particular workman and then decide whether, if the statutory obligation has been performed, any negligence has been proved.'

[1]   *[1974] 1 All ER 262, [1973] 1 WLR 1358, CA.*
[2]   *[1974] 1 All ER 262 at 272, [1973] 1 WLR 1358 at 1369–1370.*

Chapter 18

Vicarious liability

A Introduction

Background

[18.01] 'It is a rule of law', observed Lord Reid in *Staveley Iron & Chemical Co Ltd v Jones*,[1] 'that an employer, though guilty of no fault himself, is liable for damage done by the fault or negligence of his servant acting in the course of his employment'. Similarly, in *Lister v Hesley Hall Ltd*, Lord Millett said:

> 'Vicarious liability is a species of strict liability. It is not premised on any culpable act or omission on the part of the employer; an employer who is not personally at fault is made legally answerable for the fault of the employee. It is best understood as a loss-distribution device'[2].

It is thus apparent that what may be termed 'true' vicarious liability constitutes a major exception, as far as the employer is concerned, to the principle of no liability without fault.

---

[1]   *[1956] AC 627* at 643, *[1956] 1 All ER 403* at 409, HL.
[2]   See *[2001] 2 All ER 769, HL* at para 65.

Repudiation of 'masters' tort' theory

[18.02] At one time a so-called 'master's tort' theory had its adherents.[1] This attempted to explain the cases seemingly based on vicarious liability by postulating that the employer had in some sense been in breach of a duty imposed by the law upon him. This approach was sometimes useful, particularly in enabling the unfortunate doctrine of common employment, which until 1948 prevented fellow-workers from suing each other for negligence at the workplace, to be circumvented.[2] In situations not involving such complications a superficial attraction of the 'master's tort' theory was that it purported to obviate the need to admit the existence of a major exception to the fault principle.[3] Nevertheless, this implausible doctrine, manifestly based on legal fiction, could not be counted a success. Accordingly, in the case from which Lord Reid's quotation is taken, the House of Lords explicitly rejected the theory and it can safely be regarded as having been buried.[4]

---

[1]   See *per* Uthwatt J at first instance in *Twine v Bean's Express Ltd [1946] 1 All ER 202*, criticised by F Newark in (1954) 17 MLR 102 (the decision of the Court of Appeal, reported in 175 LT 131, proceeded on different grounds).
[2]   See *Wilsons & Clyde Coal Co Ltd v English [1938] AC 57, [1937] 3 All ER 628, HL*. The doctrine of common employment was abolished by the *Law Reform (Personal Injuries) Act 1948*.

3   For a suggestion of another supposed attraction of the theory, in a certain type of defamation case, see *per* Lord Denning MR in *Riddick v Thames Board Mills Ltd [1977] QB 881 at 893, [1977] 3 All ER 677* at 685, CA.

4   But cf G Williams 'Vicarious Liability: Tort of the Master or of the Servant' (1956) 72 LQR 522. See also A Barak 'Mixed and Vicarious Liability – A Suggested Distinction' (1966) 29 MLR 160.

Policy

[18.03]   It is therefore now generally accepted that a straight exception to the fault principle is here being made for reasons of policy. In *ICI Ltd v Shatwell*[1] Lord Pearce put it as follows:

> 'The doctrine of vicarious liability has not grown from any very clear, logical or legal principle but from social convenience and rough justice. The master having (presumably for his own benefit) employed the servant, and being (presumably) better able to make good any damage which may occasionally result from the arrangement, is answerable to the world at large for all the torts committed by his servant within the scope of it.'

1   *[1965] AC 656 at 685, [1964] 2 All ER 999 at 1011–1012, HL.*

Employers' duties still important

[18.04]   The concept of duties which cannot be delegated by an employer still remains important – and more so in several areas of vicarious liability, in particular, that concerned with liability for independent contractors[1]. It has also been invoked in situations in which an employee's tortious behaviour was intentional, and for his own benefit or gratification, in order to overcome the employer's objection that such conduct was necessarily outside the course of employment[2]. Thus in *Lister v Hesley Hall Ltd*[3], in which the owners of a children's home were held to be vicariously liable for sexual abuse of the children in their care by the warden of the home, Lord Hobhouse said:

> 'The classes of persons or institutions that are in [a] type of special relationship to another human being include schools, prisons, hospitals and even, in relation to their visitors, occupiers of land. They are liable if they themselves fail to perform the duty which they consequently owe. If they entrust the performance of that duty to an employee and that employee fails to perform the duty, they are still liable. The employee, because he has, through his obligations to his employers, adopted the same relationship towards and come under the same duties to the plaintiff, is also liable to the plaintiff for his own breach of duty. The liability of the employers is a *vicarious* liability because the actual breach of duty is that of the employee. The employee is a tortfeasor. The employers are liable for the employee's tortious act or omission because it is to him that the employers have entrusted the performance of their duty. The employers' liability to the plaintiff is also that of a tortfeasor'.

1   See below at para [18.27].
2   See *Morris v C W Martin & Sons Ltd [1966] 1 QB 716, [1965] 2 All ER 725, CA; Lloyd v Grace Smith & Co [1912] AC 716, HL.*
3   See *[2001] 2 All ER 769* at para 65 (italics are those of Lord Hobhouse). See below at para [18.23] for further discussion of this case.

Where the employee has a defence

[18.05] It is implicit in rejection of the 'master's tort' theory that, for the employer to be liable, there must have been carelessness on the part of the employee which would normally constitute actionable negligence. This was the basis of the actual decision of the House of Lords in *Staveley Iron & Chemical Co Ltd v Jones*.[1] Similarly, in *ICI Ltd v Shatwell*[2] the House of Lords held that an employer not in breach of any duty of his own could not incur vicarious liability for the negligence of one of his employees where that employee would have had a complete defence of assumption of risk to any claim made against him personally by the claimant.

[1] *[1956] AC 627, [1956] 1 All ER 403, HL.*
[2] *[1965] AC 656, [1964] 2 All ER 999, HL.*

Substance

[18.06] There may, however, occasionally be situations where the employee enjoys some specific procedural defence which protects him from liability.[1] Although the employer may nevertheless incur liability in such cases, the better view is that they do not constitute genuine exceptions to the proposition that the employer's liability is vicarious rather than personal. The technical defence enjoyed by the employee does not detract from the proposition that his conduct has been in substance tortious, and the 'social convenience and rough justice', to which Lord Pearce referred,[2] make it appropriate that the employer should be liable on the same basis as if the technical defence did not exist.

[1] See *Broom v Morgan [1953] 1 QB 597, [1953] 1 All ER 849, CA* (the facts of this case, involving the inability at one time of husband and wife to sue each other in tort, can no longer recur in view of the *Law Reform (Husband and Wife) Act 1962*).
[2] See above, para [18.03].

B Who is an 'employee'?[1]

Control no longer conclusive

[18.07] Over the years the approach adopted by the courts in determining whether one person was the 'employee' of another, whether in relation to the imposition of vicarious liability in tort or for some other purpose, has inevitably undergone modification as the world of work has become more complex and sophisticated. It is necessary to distinguish someone employed under a contract *of service* from someone employed under a contract *for services* whose carelessness, as an independent contractor of his employer, will not result in the imposition of liability on the latter save in exceptional circumstances. The traditional test for the existence of a contract of service was whether the alleged employee was under the 'control' of his employer. But if this had been insisted upon in an age of increasing professionalism and technical skill, the result would have been greatly to diminish the scope of vicarious liability. In *Stevenson, Jordan and Harrison Ltd v MacDonald and Evans*[2] Denning LJ put it thus:

> 'There are many contracts of service where the master cannot control the manner in which the work is to be done, as in the case of a captain of a ship ... It is often easy to recognize a contract of service when you see it, but difficult to say

wherein the difference lies. A ship's master, a chauffeur, and a reporter on the staff of a newspaper are all employed under a contract of service; but a ship's pilot, a taxi-man, and a newspaper contributor are employed under a contract for services. One feature which seems to run through the instances is that, under a contract of service, a man is employed as part of the business, and his work is done as an integral part of the business; whereas, under a contract for services, his work, although done for the business, is not integrated into it but is only accessory to it.'

1   The terminology of 'employer' and 'employee' is now usually adopted in place of that of 'master' and 'servant' traditionally used in the cases until recently.
2   *[1952] 1 TLR 101* at 111, CA.

Individual skill

[18.08]   Recognition that the control test must be modified in modern circumstances has enabled vicarious liability to be imposed on hospital authorities for the negligence of doctors and other skilled medical staff,[1] whereas the literal application of that test would obviously have made the imposition of such liability impossible.[2] Moreover, it is apparent that, as was judicially observed in a case in which a market research interviewer was held to be an employee, the 'opportunity to deploy individual skill and personality is frequently present in what is undoubtedly a contract of service'.[3]

1   See *Cassidy v Ministry of Health [1951] 2 KB 343, [1951] 1 All ER 574, CA* and the note by O Kahn-Freund 'Servants and Independent Contractors' (1951) 14 MLR 504. The liability of hospital authorities is discussed more fully below at para [18.34].
2   Cf *Hillyer v St Bartholomew's Hospital (Governors) [1909] 2 KB 820, CA.*
3   *Market Investigations Ltd v Minister of Social Security [1969] 2 QB 173* at 188, *[1968] 3 All ER 732* at 740, *per* Cooke J.

Relevance of commercial risk

[18.09]   In the important case of *Ready Mixed Concrete (South East) Ltd v Minister of Pensions and National Insurance*[1] MacKenna J decided that a lorry driver who was required to wear the uniform of the Ready Mixed Concrete company, and to be available whenever that company required, was nevertheless a self-employed haulage contractor rather than an employee of the company. The fact that his contract declared his status to be that of an independent contractor was not conclusive in itself.[2] But the fact that he owned his own lorry, was responsible for its maintenance, and depended for his overall profitability on the use which he made of this asset and the extent to which he safeguarded it, led to the conclusion that he was indeed such a contractor and not an employee. The judge quoted[3] an important passage from the judgment of Lord Wright in a 1947 Privy Council case, reported only in Canada,[4] in which his Lordship observed that in the 'complex conditions of modern industry' determination of the master-servant relationship had to take into account 'ownership of the tools ... chance of profit' and 'risk of loss'. Although each case will depend upon its own facts, these considerations of commercial risk will clearly often be of central importance in modern cases.

1   *[1968] 2 QB 497, [1968] 1 All ER 433.*
2   ' ... whether the relation between the parties to the contract is that of master and servant or otherwise is a conclusion of law dependent upon the duties imposed by the contract. If these are such that the relation is that of master and servant, it is irrelevant that the parties have declared it to be something else': *[1969] 2 QB 497* at 513, *[1968] 1 All ER 433* at 439.

3   *[1969] 2 QB 497* at 520, *[1968] 1 All ER 433* at 443.
4   *Montreal v Montreal Locomotive Works [1947] 1 DLR 161* at 169. (The case was exhumed by P Atiyah in his *Vicarious Liability in the Law of Torts* (1967).

Relevance of nature of the claim

[18.10]   A number of the more recent authorities on determination of the existence of a contract of service, including the *Ready Mixed Concrete* case itself, have not in fact involved tort claims at all. They have more often been concerned with attempts to gain the taxation advantages of self-employed status.[1] In one case the Court of Appeal took the view that the appellant could not seek to have himself classified as self-employed for that purpose and yet seek to be re-classified as an employee when *that* would be to his advantage because he wished to bring a claim for unfair dismissal.[2] On the other hand, in a later unfair dismissal case, this decision was distinguished on its facts and re-classification was achieved.[3] Moreover, it is significant that in one case which *did* involve a tort claim, for injuries suffered at the plaintiff's place of work, the Court of Appeal held, albeit by a majority, that an employer-employee relationship *had* existed in substance despite the plaintiff's original agreement to function as a self-employed building worker.[4] Accordingly, if a situation were to arise involving a vicarious liability tort claim by a *third party* it would seem *a fortiori* that the court would be prepared to resolve any doubts which existed, about the presence of an employer-employee relationship, in favour of the claimant. It is submitted that such flexibility of approach would certainly be desirable.[5]

1   See *Hall (Inspector of Taxes) v Lorimer [1994] 1 All ER 250, [1994] 1 WLR 209, CA*. Cf *McMeechan v Secretary of State for Employment [1997] IRLR 353, CA*.
2   See *Massey v Crown Life Insurance Co [1978] 2 All ER 576, [1978] 1 WLR 676, CA*.
3   See *Young and Woods Ltd v West [1980] IRLR 201, CA*.
4   See *Ferguson v Dawson & Partners (Contractors) Ltd [1976] 3 All ER 817, [1976] 1 WLR 1213, CA*. See also *Lane v Shire Roofing Co (Oxford) Ltd [1995] IRLR 493, CA*.
5   Cf E McKendrick 'Vicarious Liability and Independent Contractors – A Re-examination' (1990) 53 MLR 770. See also R Kidner 'Vicarious Liability: For Whom Should the Employer be Liable' (1995) 15 LS 47.

Borrowed servants

[18.11]   An employer may sometimes lend one of his employees to another organisation, for which that person will work temporarily. Such an arrangement often arises in situations in which a piece of heavy machinery, such as a crane, is hired out along with its operator.[1] But it is not confined to such situations.[2] If a third party is injured as a result of the negligence of the 'borrowed' employee the original, or 'general', employer may in theory seek to show that, instead of himself, the *other* organisation is vicariously liable to the victim. In modern law, however, the possibility appears to be academic. It is clear from the leading case of *Mersey Docks and Harbour Board v Coggins and Griffith (Liverpool) Ltd*[3] that the burden of proving that the negligent person has become, *pro hac vice*,[4] the employee of the hirer is on the general employer, and that it is a heavy one to discharge. It would be necessary to prove, inter alia, that the employee had consented to the change of employer and that, in so far as *control* still has some relevance to the establishment of an employer-employee relationship, this rested with the temporary 'employer'. In practice, the burden is so heavy that there appears to be no reported English case since 1893 in which it has been successfully discharged.[5] Considerations of policy, such as convenience and certainty, clearly favour the imposition of vicarious liability upon the general employer, who is responsible for the administration of the relevant employer-employee relationship including such matters as payment of social security contributions.

¹ See *Mersey Docks and Harbour Board v Coggins and Griffith (Liverpool) Ltd [1947] AC 1, [1946] 2 All ER 345, HL.*

² See *Bhoomidas v Port of Singapore Authority [1978] 1 All ER 956, [1978] 1 WLR 189.*

³ *[1947] AC 1, [1946] 2 All ER 345, HL.*

⁴ '[W]hich I would translate *for the time being*': *per* Lord Denning MR in *Savory v Holland & Hannen & Cubitts (Southern) Ltd [1964] 3 All ER 18* at 20, *[1964] 1 WLR 1158* at 1162, CA.

⁵ *Per* Lord Salmon in *Bhoomidas v Port of Singapore Authority [1978] 1 All ER 956* at 959, *[1978] 1 WLR 189* at 191–192. The 1893 case is *Donovan v Laing, Wharton and Down Construction Syndicate [1893] 1 QB 629, CA,* which has been heavily criticised: see *per* Lord Macmillan in *Mersey Docks and Harbour Board v Coggins and Griffith [1947] AC 1* at 14, *[1946] 2 All ER 345* at 350. In *Denham v Midland Employers' Mutual Assurance Ltd [1955] 2 QB 437* at 444, *[1955] 2 All ER 561* at 564–565, CA Denning LJ apparently indicated obiter that the facts supported discharge of the burden in the case before him: sed quaere. For a relatively recent *Scottish* case in which liability was imposed upon the temporary employer see: *Sime v Sutcliffe Catering Scotland Ltd [1990] IRLR 228.*

Need to distinguish hirer's duty to the employee

[18.12] The hirer may, of course, himself incur liability in tort *to* the borrowed employee, and this may even include liability for breach of certain aspects of an employer's duty to provide a safe system of work.¹ But, in general, the courts are reluctant to hold that the general employer has effectively transferred legal responsibility for the safety of his employees to another party.² The fact that they are occasionally prepared so to hold, however, means that particular care is needed in reading some of the cases in which *Mersey Docks and Harbour Board v Coggins and Griffith* has been cited and discussed. The principles enunciated in that case have sometimes been relied on to justify decisions in which the hirer has been held to owe some of the duties of employers' liability to the borrowed employee,³ but these decisions are not authorities on the separate question of vicarious liability to third parties for carelessness *by* the employee.

¹ See *Garrard v A E Southey & Co and Standard Telephone and Cables Ltd [1952] 2 QB 174, [1952] 1 All ER 597; Gibb v United Steel Companies Ltd [1957] 2 All ER 110, [1957] 1 WLR 668.* For Employers' Liability see generally CHAPTER 17 above.

² See *O'Reilly v ICI Ltd [1955] 3 All ER 382, [1955] 1 WLR 1155.* Cf *Savory v Holland & Hannen Cubitts (Southern) Ltd [1964] 3 All ER 18, [1964] 1 WLR 1158, CA.* See also *McDermid v Nash Dredging and Reclamation Co Ltd [1987] AC 906, [1987] 2 All ER 878, HL* and *Morris v Breaveglen Ltd (trading as Anzac Construction Co) [1993] ICR 766, [1993] IRLR 350, CA.* See generally CHAPTER 17 above.

³ See *Garrard v A E Southey & Co and Standard Telephone Cables Ltd [1952] 2 QB 174, [1952] 1 All ER 597* and *Gibb v United Steel Companies Ltd [1957] 2 All ER 110, [1957] 1 WLR 668.*

General employer may be entitled to contractual indemnity

[18.13] 'As between himself and the public', observed Lord Pearce in *Arthur White (Contractors) Ltd v Tarmac Civil Engineering Ltd,*¹ 'the general master cannot divest himself of responsibility for the servant ... But the parties to the hiring contract may determine liability inter se'. Thus, it is perfectly possible for the general employer to stipulate in the contract of hiring that he is to be indemnified against the consequences of any carelessness on the part of the employee who is loaned. Such a provision obviously leaves the rights of the victim unaffected, but can clearly be of value to the general employer once he has settled the victim's claim. In the *Tarmac* case a point on the construction of such a contract was fought up to the House of Lords, and ended in the general employers securing a full indemnity from the hirers.²

1   *[1967] 3 All ER 586, [1967] 1 WLR 1508* at 1520, HL.
2   See also *Herdman v Walker (Tooting) Ltd [1956] 1 All ER 429, [1956] 1 WLR 209.*

C The course of employment

Wrongful method of performance

[18.14] In *Kooragang Investments Pty Ltd v Richardson and Wrench Ltd*[1]
Lord Wilberforce said of the authorities on the course of employment:

> 'These cases have given rise to a number of fine distinctions, the courts in some
> cases struggling to find liability, in others to avoid it … It remains true to say
> that, whatever exceptions or qualifications may be introduced, the underlying
> principle remains that a servant, even while performing acts of the class which he
> was authorised, or employed, to do, may so clearly depart from the scope of his
> employment that his master will not be liable for his wrongful acts.'

Situations in which employees, employed to drive their employers' vehicles, took
those vehicles off on journeys for purposes of their own, on routes wholly different
from those required by the business of the employers in question, provided early
examples of departure from the scope of employment such as negated the imposition
of vicarious liability.[2] A clear but remarkable recent example of employees acting
outside the course of employment is provided by *General Engineering Services Ltd v
Kingston and St Andrew Corpn.*[3] In this case a fire brigade, which was operating a 'go
slow' policy as part of industrial action, drove literally on a 'stop and go' basis
(ie constantly stopping and starting to prolong their journey), so as to reach a fire at the
plaintiffs' premises only after they had burned down. The Privy Council had no
hesitation in affirming the decision of the Court of Appeal of Jamaica that this conduct
was outside the course of employment of members of the fire brigade. On the other
hand, even deliberate criminal acts have sometimes been treated, in particular circumstances, as coming within the course of employment, as improper modes of performance of the employees' duties.[4] If, however, an employee's acts inside the course of
employment are not in themselves tortious, and only become so when combined with
other acts *outside* the course of employment, the employer will not be vicariously
liable[5].

1   *[1982] AC 462* at 473, *[1981] 3 All ER 65* at 70, PC.
2   See *Storey v Ashton (1869) LR 4 QB 476.* Cf *Aitchison v Page Motors Ltd (1935) 154 LT 128.*
3   *[1988] 3 All ER 867, [1989] 1 WLR 69, PC.*
4   See below at para [18.22].
5   See *Credit Lyonnais Bank v Export Credits Guarantee Department [1999] 1 All ER 929, HL.*

Milton as authority

[18.15] As far as acts of pure negligence on the part of employees are concerned,
perhaps the most striking example of a case in which the court may be said to have
'struggled to find liability' is the well-known decision of the House of Lords in
Century Insurance Co Ltd v Northern Ireland Road Transport Board.[1] The driver of a
petrol tanker, while watching the process of discharging his cargo at a garage, lit a
cigarette and threw the match on the floor. For the purposes of a liability insurance
policy taken out by the Board, the driver's carelessness, which not surprisingly

produced an explosion and a conflagration, was held to come within the course of his employment. Viscount Simon LC invoked Milton as an authority on the course of employment: 'In circumstances like these, "they also serve who only stand and wait".'[2]

¹ *[1942] AC 509, [1942] 1 All ER 491, HL.*
² *[1942] AC 509* at 514, *[1942] 1 All ER 491* at 494, quoting the last line of Milton's *Sonnet On His Blindness.*

Facts

[18.16] Although the question of whether a particular act was or was not in the course of employment is one of law, its solution will obviously depend very much on the facts of each individual case. Accordingly, the creation of the 'fine distinctions' to which Lord Wilberforce referred was perhaps inevitable. For the purposes of exposition it is convenient to group the decisions in certain broad categories of similar fact-situations. But it is not suggested that these categories reflect significant differences in the underlying principles involved.

The moving of vehicles

[18.17] A number of cases have concerned accidents caused by employees not qualified or permitted to drive vehicles in the course of their duties nevertheless doing so. In *Iqbal v London Transport Executive*[1] the Court of Appeal held the defendants not vicariously liable when one of their conductors, despite being expressly forbidden from doing so,[2] drove a bus in an attempt to move it so as to allow another bus to secure egress from the depot.[3] 'The driving of a bus', said Megaw LJ,[4] 'was not within the sphere of employment'. On the other hand, in *Kay v ITW Ltd*[5] the defendants' employee, who was employed to drive a fork lift truck, found a five-ton diesel lorry blocking the path of his truck. He promptly climbed into the empty cab of the lorry and, in attempting to drive it, caused it to reverse into the plaintiff causing him severe injuries. The Court of Appeal held the defendant employers vicariously liable.[6] The case was, in the words of Sellers LJ, 'near the borderline' but the employee's 'exceptional and excessive conduct' was not 'so gross and extreme as to take his act outside what he was employed to do'.[7] Sachs LJ perhaps came closest to formulating a working presumption that could be of use in cases of this kind and similar situations:[8]

> 'Once … it is conceded that [the employee] was doing something in his working hours, on his employers' premises, and when seeking to act in his employers' interests, and that, moreover, his act had a close connection with the work which he was employed to do, it seems to me that the onus shifts to the employers to show that the act was one for which they were not responsible.'

¹ *(1973) 16 KIR 329.*
² On prohibited acts generally, see below at para [18.20].
³ See also *Beard v London General Omnibus Co [1900] 2 QB 530, CA.*
⁴ *(1973) 16 KIR 329* at 336.
⁵ *[1968] 1 QB 140, [1967] 3 All ER 22, CA.*
⁶ See also *LCC v Cattermoles (Garages) Ltd [1953] 2 All ER 582, [1953] 1 WLR 997.*
⁷ *[1968] 1 QB 140* at 154, *[1967] 3 All ER 22* at 27.
⁸ *[1968] 1 QB 140* at 156, *[1967] 3 All ER 22* at 28.

Work, rest and play

[**18.18**] It is a long-established principle that accidents which occur on the highway, when the employee is merely travelling to or from work, do not come within the course of employment for the purposes of vicarious liability.[1]

> 'So a bank clerk who commutes to the City of London every day from Sevenoaks is not acting in the course of his employment when he walks across London Bridge from the station to his bank in the City. This is because he is not employed to travel from his home to the bank: he is employed to work at the bank, his place of work, and so his duty is to arrive there in time for his working day.'[2]

The correctness of this principle was affirmed, but its applicability distinguished on the facts, in the leading case of *Smith v Stages*.[3] Two employees working in the Midlands were sent by their employer to do an urgent job in Wales. They were paid for their journey time and also given the equivalent of the rail fare, although there was no stipulation that they should travel by train. The plaintiff was injured in a road accident caused by the negligence of his fellow employee when the two of them were returning from Wales in the latter's car. The House of Lords held that the accident had occurred in the course of employment. Lord Goff said:[4]

> 'In my opinion [the plaintiff] was required by the employers to make this journey, so as to make himself available to do his work … and it would be proper to describe him as having been employed to do so. The fact that he was not required by his employer to make the journey by any particular means, nor even required to make it on the particular working day made available to him, does not detract from the proposition that he was employed to make the journey.'[5]

[1] See *Vandyke v Fender [1970] 2 QB 292, [1970] 2 All ER 335, CA.*
[2] *Per* Lord Goff in *Smith v Stages [1989] AC 928 at 936, [1989] 1 All ER 833 at 836, HL.*
[3] *[1989] AC 928, [1989] 1 All ER 833, HL.*
[4] *[1989] AC 928 at 938, [1989] 1 All ER 833 at 838.*
[5] See also *per* Lord Lowry, *[1989] AC 928 at 955–956, [1989] 1 All ER 833* at 851 for a valuable summary of the general principles applicable in these cases.

During the working day

[**18.19**] Similarly, accidents on the highway which occur *during* the working day, when employees are travelling to or from particular sites, have been held to come within the course of employment, even if the particular journey in question was undertaken simply in order to procure lunch.[1] But a journey to a cafe for tea undertaken when the employees concerned, having 'taken the view that they had done enough work to pass muster, were filling in the rest of their time until their hours of work had come to an end' was held to be outside the course of employment.[2] Even a lorry driver who had, perfectly properly, stopped for lunch in the course of the working day, but carelessly caused an accident while crossing the road as a pedestrian, having just climbed down from his cab, was held to have been 'a stranger to his master from the moment when he left the lorry'.[3] Again, an employee who overstayed his ten-minute tea break by 50% was held to be outside the course of employment when injured during the extra five minutes.[4] Nevertheless, an employee on his employer's premises purely to collect his wages, and after his work has ceased, can still be within the course of employment.[5] Moreover, an employee who carelessly and improperly delegated his own duties to someone else was held to have been acting in the course of his employment in so doing, so as to lead to the imposition of vicarious liability on his employers when a third party was injured as a result.[6] Even a practical joke may be in the course of employment if it takes the form merely of an eccentric manner of discharging prescribed duties,[7] but not if it is a quite unrelated act of isolated misbehaviour.[8]

[1] See *Harvey v R G O'Dell [1958] 2 QB 78, [1958] 1 All ER 657.*
[2] *Hilton v Thomas Burton (Rhodes) Ltd [1961] 1 All ER 74* at 77, *[1961] 1 WLR 705* at 708–709, *per* Diplock J.
[3] *Crook v Derbyshire Stone Ltd [1956] 2 All ER 447* at 450, *[1956] 1 WLR 432* at 436, *per* Pilcher J.
[4] See *R v Industrial Injuries Comr, ex p Amalgamated Engineering Union (No 2) [1966] 2 QB 31, [1966] 1 All ER 97, CA.*
[5] *Staton v National Coal Board [1957] 2 All ER 667, [1957] 1 WLR 893.*
[6] *Ilkiw v Samuels [1963] 2 All ER 879, [1963] 1 WLR 991.*
[7] See *Harrison v Michelin Tyre Co [1985] 1 All ER 918, [1985] ICR 696.*
[8] See *O'Reilly v National Rail and Tramway Appliances Ltd [1966] 1 All ER 499.*

Prohibited acts

[18.20] It seems to be established that, as Stephenson LJ put it in *Stone v Taffe:*[1]

'a prohibition by an employer of what his servant may do is not by itself conclusive of the scope of his employment against third parties injured by the servant, but that the injured person cannot make the employer liable where he himself knows of the prohibition, and has the opportunity to avoid the danger of injury from the prohibited act, before he exposes himself to the danger.'[2]

On the other hand, even where the injured person does *not* know of the prohibition, the overall situation may still be analysed as one in which the employee acted outside the course of his employment, and the existence of the prohibition, while not conclusive by itself, could be highly relevant to the determination of that issue.[3]

[1] *[1974] 3 All ER 1016* at 1022, *[1974] 1 WLR 1575* at 1581, CA (certain passages in parenthesis in the original are omitted from the quotation in the text).
[2] In strict logic it is not easy to see why knowledge of the prohibition on the part of the claimant should be relevant, if the act of the employee would otherwise have been in the course of his employment. But the presence or absence of such knowledge does seem to help to explain the actual decisions (although not the reasoning) in some of the earlier cases. See, especially, F Newark in (1954) 17 MLR 102, discussing *Twine v Bean's Express Ltd [1946] 1 All ER 202*; affd on other grounds *(1946) 62 TLR 458*. But it should be noted that, on the facts of *Twine*'s case (which involved a notice to passengers in the cab of the defendants' vehicle in which their servant gave a lift to the plaintiff), the particular argument which Newark put forward would no longer be valid in view of the *Road Traffic Act 1988, s 149(2)*.
[3] See *Conway v George Wimpey & Co Ltd [1951] 2 KB 266, [1951] 1 All ER 363, CA.*

Purpose

[18.21] Another factor to which the court will attach importance, in deciding whether the employee's act took him outside the course of his employment, is the *purpose* for which it was done. This is certainly not a conclusive factor, however, and there are decided cases which indicate that the mere fact that the employee perceived himself as acting for his employer's purposes is neither a necessary[1] nor a sufficient[2] condition for the imposition of vicarious liability. But in a case which might otherwise be regarded as marginal, purpose can be the factor which ultimately tips the scales.[3] This was emphasised in *Rose v Plenty*,[4] in which the Court of Appeal, by a majority,[5] held the employers of a milk roundsman vicariously liable when the latter's carelessness caused injury to a boy whom he had taken on his van to help him in his deliveries, despite being explicitly forbidden by his employers from so doing. 'In considering whether a prohibited act was within the course of the employment', said Lord Denning MR, 'it depends very much on the purpose for which it is done. If it is done for his employers' business, it is usually done in the course of his employment, even though it is a prohibited act'.[6]

---

1   See *Lloyd v Grace Smith & Co [1912] AC 716, HL.*
2   See *Iqbal v London Transport Executive (1973) 16 KIR 329.*
3   See *Canadian Pacific Rly Co v Lockhart [1942] AC 591, [1942] 2 All ER 464*; *LCC v Cattermoles (Garages) Ltd [1953] 2 All ER 582, [1953] 1 WLR 997, CA.*
4   *[1976] 1 All ER 97, [1976] 1 WLR 141, CA.*
5   Lord Denning MR and Scarman LJ. Lawton LJ dissented.
6   *[1976] 1 All ER 97* at 100–101, *[1976] 1 WLR 141* at 144. Quaere, however, whether Lord Denning's formulation is not too wide. Cf *per* Scarman LJ *[1976] 1 All ER 97* at 103ff, *[1976] 1 WLR 141* at 146ff. (Lord Denning's approach is incidentally, as he acknowledges in his judgment, not really consistent with *Iqbal v London Transport Executive*, discussed above at para [18.17].)

Assaults and criminal acts[1]

[18.22] In *Lloyd v Grace Smith & Co*[2] the House of Lords imposed vicarious liability upon an employer for loss caused by a deliberate fraud which had been perpetrated by his employee purely for the latter's own benefit[3]. The employer was in effect held to owe the plaintiff a non-delegable duty as a result of his having clothed the dishonest employee with apparent authority[4]. A similar principle would appear to underlie cases in which liability has been imposed upon bailees for theft by their employees.[5]

---

1   See Robert Weekes 'Vicarious Liability for Violent Employees' [2004] 63 CLJ 53; F Rose 'Liability for an Employee's Assaults' (1977) 40 MLR 420.
2   [1912] AC 716, HL.
3   See also *Dubai Aluminium v Salaam [2003] 1 All ER 97.* Cf *Credit Lyonnais Bank Nederland NV v Export Credits Guarantee Department [1999] 1 All ER 929, HL.*
4   Cf *Armagas v Mundogas SA, The Ocean Frost [1986] AC 717, [1986] 2 All ER 385*, HL. See also *Kooragang Investments Ltd v Richardson & Wrench Ltd [1982] AC 462, [1981] 3 All ER 65* and comment by A Tettenborn 'Authority, Vicarious Liability and Negligent Misstatement' [1982] 41 CLJ 36.
5   See *Generale Bank Nederland NV v Export Credits Guarantee Department [1998] 1 Lloyd's Rep 19, CA*; *Morris v C W Martin & Sons Ltd [1966] 1 QB 716, [1965] 2 All ER 725, CA.* Cf *United Africa Co Ltd v Saka Owoade [1955] AC 130, [1957] 3 All ER 216.*

Lister v Hesley Hall

[18.23] The leading case on this aspect of vicarious liability is now the decision of the House of Lords in *Lister v Hesley Hall Ltd*[1]. The claimants were victims of sexual abuse perpetrated by the warden of a children's home. The House of Lords, reversing the Court of Appeal and overruling another recent decision of that Court[2], held that the owners of the home were vicariously liable for the warden's abuse. The House criticised an influential proposition in *Salmond on Torts*[3] which referred to an 'unauthorised mode of doing some act authorised' by the employer. This test was apt to be too narrow where *intentional* acts were concerned. In the instant case it was preferable 'to consider the question of vicarious liability on the basis that the employer undertook to care for the boys through the warden' and that the abuse was 'committed in the time and on the premises of [the] employers while the warden was also busy caring for the children'.[4] On the other hand, an employer will not be liable *merely* because the fact of his employment happened to give the employee the *opportunity* to commit those acts.[5] Thus if, in *Lister's* case, the acts of abuse had been committed not by the warden but by the groundsman, vicarious liability for the abuse itself would probably not have been imposed[6].

¹ *[2001] 2 All ER 769.* See also *Balfron Trustees v Petersen [2002] Lloyd's Rep PN 1.*
² See *Trotman v North Yorkshire CC [1999] LGR 584.*
³ See 1st edn (1907), p 83. See also *Salmond and Heuston on Torts* (21st edn, 1996) p 443.
⁴ See *per* Lord Steyn in *[2001] 2 All ER 769* at para 20.
⁵ See *per* Lord Clyde in *Lister v Hesley Hall Ltd [2001] 2 All ER 769* at para 45.
⁶ See *per* Lord Hobhouse in *[2001] 2 All ER 769* at para 62: but the owners might still be vicariously liable for the failure of the warden to prevent the abuse.

Outbursts of temper

[18.24] In situations in which the employee's act resembles negligence more closely than it does in the cases of deliberate dishonesty, namely physical assaults committed in a perceived emergency or the heat of the moment, the question whether the employee believed himself to be acting for the benefit of his employer, or on his own account, appears to be highly material in determining whether or not vicarious liability will be imposed upon the employer for the injuries suffered by the victim. Thus, in *Poland v John Parr & Sons*[1] an assault by an employee upon someone he thought was stealing his employer's property gave rise to the imposition of vicarious liability, when the assault had unexpectedly serious physical consequences for the victim.[2] Similarly, in *Racz v Home Office*[3] the House of Lords held that the Home Office could be vicariously liable for ill-treatment of prisoners by prison officers if the officers 'were engaged in a misguided and unauthorised method of performing their authorised duties'.[4] On the other hand, assaults by garage hands[5] and bus conductors,[6] not as a result of misconceived attempts to promote their employers' interests but due simply to their having been overcome by sudden outbursts of loss of temper in their dealings with members of the public, have been held to fall outside the course of employment. In the recent case of *Fennelly v Connex South Eastern*[7], however, the Court of Appeal imposed vicarious liability for an assault by a ticket-collector on a passenger. The court reversed the decision of the court below in favour of the employer, and warned against placing 'too narrow an emphasis on the concept of authorisation' in cases of this type, indicating that a 'broader approach' is appropriate[8]. The most recent cases suggest that such an approach is being adopted, and that the courts are now more prepared than formerly to impose vicarious liability in cases of this type. In *Mattis v Pollock*[9], decided in 2003, the Court of Appeal, reversing the trial judge, held a nightclub owner liable for serious stabbing injuries inflicted by one of his doormen, following an earlier violent incident in which the doorman had been involved. The assault took place outside the Club, some minutes after the doormen had initially been chased away from it by several customers, and after he had even had time to return to his own nearby flat to collect a knife. In another recent case vicarious liability was imposed upon a Chief Constable for an assault committed by an off-duty police officer.[10]

¹ *[1927] 1 KB 236, CA.*
² See also *Vasey v Surrey Free Inns [1996] PIQR P373, CA.*
³ *[1994] 2 AC 45, [1994] 1 All ER 97, HL.*
⁴ *[1994] 2 AC 45 at 53, [1994] 1 All ER 97* at 102, *per* Lord Jauncey of Tullichettle.
⁵ *Warren v Henleys Ltd [1948] 2 All ER 935.*
⁶ *Keppel Bus Co Ltd v Sa'ad Bin Ahmad [1974] 2 All ER 700, [1974] 1 WLR 1082.*
⁷ *[2001] IRLR 390.*
⁸ See *[2001] IRLR 390* at para 17, *per* Buxton LJ.
⁹ *[2003] 1 WLR 2158, [2004] 4 All ER 85.*

¹⁰ See *Weir v Chief Constable of Merseyside [2003] ICR 708*. Cf *Attorney-General of the British Virgin Islands v Hartwell [2004] 1 WLR 1273*.

The master's indemnity

[18.25]   In *Lister v Romford Ice & Coal Storage Co Ltd*¹ the House of Lords, by a bare majority, established that an employer who has been held vicariously liable to a third party for the negligence of his employee can obtain an indemnity from the employee by virtue of an implied contractual obligation that the latter will use due care in the performance of his duties on the employer's behalf.² The same result can be reached by awarding the employer 100% contribution under the *Civil Liability (Contribution) Act 1978*, employer and employee being joint tortfeasors.³ In *Lister v Romford Ice & Coal Storage Co Ltd* the House of Lords refused to countenance the implication into contracts of service of a term in favour of the *employee* that he would be indemnified by his employer against the consequences of his own negligence, even though the employer could be expected to carry insurance against the risk of liability to third parties brought about by carelessness on the part of his employees.

¹ *[1957] AC 555, [1957] 1 All ER 125, HL.*
² For dicta suggesting that a relatively narrow interpretation be placed upon the precise scope of this implied contractual obligation, see *Harvey v R G O'Dell Ltd [1958] 2 QB 78* at 106, *[1958] 1 All ER 657* at 667, *per* McNair J.
³ See *Semtex Ltd v Gladstone [1954] 2 All ER 206, [1954] 1 WLR 945; Harvey v R G O'Dell Ltd [1958] 2 QB 78, [1958] 1 All ER 657* (both decided under the earlier *Law Reform (Married Women and Tortfeasors) Act 1935*).

Industrial relations

[18.26]   The potentially disastrous consequences, for employees in particular, and for industrial relations in general if employers, or in practice their insurers exercising the right of subrogation, were to invoke the principle in *Lister v Romford Ice & Coal Storage Co Ltd* – led to legislation being considered to change the law as laid down by the House of Lords. In the event this was averted by a 'gentlemen's agreement',¹ whereby employers' liability insurers agreed that they would not seek to claim against employees under *Lister*. Interestingly, the existence of this agreement, and the industrial realities which it reflected, has had repercussions on the *law itself* outside the immediate area of insurance with which it deals; and, as a result, it has had an impact upon subrogation claims by persons who were not themselves insurers and were therefore not parties to the agreement. In *Morris v Ford Motor Co*² it enabled the Court of Appeal, in a situation to which *Lister v Romford Ice & Cold Storage* did not directly apply, to avoid extending that decision and instead to imply a term into a contract between a negligent employee's employers, and another company. The indirect effect of that implication was, in the particular circumstances of the *Morris* case, to confer a degree of actual *legal* protection upon the employee from his being called upon to pay the damages which his carelessness had caused.

¹ See *Morris v Ford Motor Co Ltd [1973] QB 792, [1973] 2 All ER 1084, CA.*
² *[1973] QB 792, [1973] 2 All ER 1084, CA.*

D Independent contractors

The concept of non-delegable duty

[18.27]   In *Salsbury v Woodland*¹ Widgery LJ said:

'It is trite law that an employer who employs an independent contractor is not vicariously responsible for the negligence of that contractor. He is not able to control the way in which the independent contractor does the work, and the vicarious obligation of a master for the negligence of his servant does not arise under the relationship of employer and independent contractor. I think that it is entirely accepted that those cases – and there are some – in which an employer has been held liable for injury done by the negligence of an independent contractor are in truth cases where the employer owes a direct duty to the person injured, a duty which he cannot delegate to the contractor on his behalf.'

Although this statement, including its assertion that the general rule is one of non-liability for independent contractors, accurately represents the broad approach of the law in this area,[2] an unresolved problem is the precise delineation of the situations in which non-delegable duties are in fact owed by the employers of independent contractors[3]. To hold the employer liable is effectively to make an exception to the general principle of no liability without fault.[4] One might therefore have expected that the situations in which non-delegable duties would be held to exist would simply be the same as those in which the law imposes strict liability even where independent contractors are not involved.[5]

1   *[1970] 1 QB 324* at 336–337, *[1969] 3 All ER 863* at 867, CA.
2   See also *per* Potter J in *Aiken v Stewart Wrighton Members' Agency Ltd [1995] 3 All ER 449* at 463, *[1995] 1 WLR 1281* at 1295.
3   There does not, however, appear to be a duty upon an employer to check whether an independent contractor carries adequate insurance against liability to third parties, except in special circumstances: see *Payling v Naylor [2004] EWCA Civ 560*, (2004) Times, 2 June. Cf *Gwilliam v West Hertfordshire Hospitals NHS Trust [2003] QB 443*.
4   Obviously, if the employer has been careless in choosing to employ a contractor whom he should have known was incompetent he will be personally liable for his own negligence in so choosing.
5   It is sometimes forgotten that *Rylands v Fletcher (1868) LR 3 HL 330* itself involved carelessness on the part of the defendant's independent contractor. But the case was rightly treated as turning solely upon the presence or absence of strict liability, since the defendant had not himself been at fault.

Complexity

[18.28]   There are three reasons, however, why the 'strict liability' test does not in fact provide a straightforward indication of the state of the law. First, the scope of strict liability itself is the subject of considerable uncertainty and lack of clarity. Secondly, the courts have not, in fact, limited liability for independent contractors to established strict liability situations but have sometimes been prepared to extend it, so as to give the claimant a further defendant,[1] in a manner which is apt to seem arbitrary from the standpoint of principle.[2] Thirdly, the concept of non-delegable duty has sometimes been invoked by the courts in cases turning mainly upon 'true' vicarious liability for actual employees[3]. The aim has been to overcome difficulties of various kinds within the law of vicarious liability itself; but the resulting overlap with, and use of concepts more familiar in, the independent contractor field has inevitably been a source of added complexity. As a result of the overall lack of clarity in the law relating to liability for independent contractors, it is necessary to consider separately the main types of situation within which the courts have invoked the concept of non-delegable duty.

1   Clearly, the independent contractor will be liable for his own negligence; the temptation to hold the employer liable as well arises where the contractor is not worth suing or is already actually insolvent.
2   See G Williams 'Liability for Independent Contractors' (1956) CLJ 180. Cf *Northern Sandblasting Pty Ltd v Harris (1997) 71 ALJR 1428* (High Court of Australia: noted by *Tan Keng Feng* in *(1998) 114 LQR 193*).

3   See *Lister v Hesley Hall Ltd [2001] 2 All ER 769 HL*, discussed above at para [18.23].

(i) Highways

[18.29] This is an area in which the general law relating to the imposition of strict liability is itself uncertain. In one much-criticised decision of the Court of Appeal it was held that where 'premises on a highway become dangerous', the owner, if he is contractually obliged or entitled to repair, will be responsible for any resulting loss or injury 'whether he knew or ought to have known of the danger or not'.[1] In fact, however, most of the better known 'highway' cases have themselves involved independent contractor situations,[2] so that attempting to ascertain the scope of strict liability from them becomes a circular exercise. But given that, for good or ill, it is established beyond doubt at common law that there is no liability without proof of fault for accidents actually occurring in the course of *travel* on the highway, it is unclear why other activities on or near the highway should warrant the imposition of a non-delegable duty upon the employers of independent contractors.

1   *Wringe v Cohen [1940] 1 KB 229* at 233, *[1939] 4 All ER 241* at 243, CA.
2   See *Tarry v Ashton (1876) 1 QBD 314*; *Holliday v National Telephone Co [1899] 2 QB 392, CA*.

Restrictive approach

[18.30] Indeed, when the matter was considered by the Court of Appeal in *Salsbury v Woodland*,[1] a restrictive approach to the scope of liability was adopted. The defendants employed an independent contractor to fell a tree in their garden. Due to the contractors' carelessness, the tree fell against some telephone wires, which in turn fell on to the nearby road and caused an accident. The court refused to hold the defendants liable for the negligence of the contractors.[2] Their Lordships indicated that only work undertaken actually on the highway itself or, work of an inherently dangerous nature, should lead to the imposition of liability.

1   *[1970] 1 QB 324*, *[1969] 3 All ER 863, CA*.
2   See also *Rowe v Herman [1997] 1 WLR 1390, CA*.

(ii) Dangerous activities

[18.31] The concept of 'extra-hazardous' activity has been used to impose liability upon the employers of independent contractors. In the 1934 case of *Honeywill & Stein Ltd v Larkin Bros*[1] independent contractors were employed to photograph the interior of a cinema; a procedure which in those days required the ignition of magnesium powder on a metal tray. Owing to the contractors' negligence, a fire was caused which damaged the cinema. The Court of Appeal held that the employers of the independent contractors would be liable to the cinema owners.[2] The Court accepted that it was 'well established as a general rule of English law that an employer is not liable for the acts of his independent contractors', but asserted the existence of 'special rules which apply to extra-hazardous or dangerous operations'.[3] Of course, if a situation which is perceived as one of special hazard happens to fit into a recognised category of strict liability, such as the rule in *Rylands v Fletcher*, then the imposition of liability for the negligence of independent contractors will be unexceptionable. Thus, in *Balfour v Barty-King*[4] the Court of Appeal imposed such liability upon an occupier, from whose premises independent contractors had caused fire to escape resulting in damage to a neighbouring property.

¹   *[1934] 1 KB 191, CA.*
²   See also *The Pass of Ballater [1942] P 112.* Cf *Brooke v Bool [1928] 2 KB 578.*
³   *[1934] 1 KB 191* at 196 and 200, *per* Slesser LJ delivering the judgment of the court.
⁴   *[1957] 1 QB 496, [1957] 1 All ER 156, CA.*

Fire and other hazards

[18.32]   It is notable that both *Honeywill & Stein Ltd v Larkin Bros* and *Balfour v Barty-King* were concerned with *fire*. Although the latter case could be brought within the *Rylands v Fletcher* principle¹, the former could not. Nevertheless, the common law has for centuries imposed vicarious liability upon occupiers 'for a fire spreading and escaping onto adjoining premises due to the non-accidental acts of anyone who is not a stranger'², and it is possible that this doctrine has survived largely unaffected by modern developments such as the principle that vicarious liability is rarely imposed for the acts of independent contractors³. But in the well-known case of *Read v J Lyons & Co*,⁴ the House of Lords expressly decided that the mere fact that an activity could be described as 'ultra hazardous' was not *by itself* sufficient to justify the imposition of strict liability. The elaborate factors which operate to limit the scope of such liability, such as the requirement of 'escape' under the rule in *Rylands v Fletcher*, also had to be satisfied. Since hazard depends upon context it would in any event, in the words of Lord Macmillan,⁵ 'be impracticable to frame a legal classification of things dangerous and things not dangerous'. The proposition that employers should be liable for the negligence of their independent contractors, merely because the context is one of particular danger, therefore seems difficult to support.⁶ No doubt powerful arguments can be advanced for the extension of strict liability, but such extension can only be achieved with a degree of certainty (which is particularly desirable so that potential defendants can know their insurance position) by some statutory mechanism.⁷ Covert extension of what amounts to strict liability, by fastening on to the fortuitous employment of an independent contractor in the particular case, will seldom be desirable. The existence of a separate category of 'danger' for the purposes of liability for independent contractors, with the possible exception of situations involving fire, is therefore doubtful.⁸

¹   Cf *Mason v Levy Auto Parts of England [1967] QB 530, [1967] 2 All ER 62.*
²   See *Johnson v BJW Property Developments Ltd [2002] 3 All ER 574* at para 39 *per* Judge Thornton QC.
³   See the judgment of Judge Thornton QC in *Johnson v BJW Property Developments Ltd*, passim.
⁴   *[1947] AC 156, [1946] 2 All ER 471, HL.*
⁵   *[1947] AC 156* at 172, *[1946] 2 All ER 471* at 477. See also W Stallybrass 'Dangerous Things and the Non-Natural User of Land' (1929) CLJ 376.
⁶   The proposition has been rejected by a majority of the High Court of Australia: *Stevens v Brodribb Sawmilling Co (1986) 160 CLR 16.* But cf the later decision of the same court in *Burnie Port Authority v General Jones Pty Ltd (1994) 120 ALR 42*, in which the majority held the Port Authority liable for a fire caused by the negligence of its independent contractor on the ground that the Authority had taken 'advantage of its occupation and control of the premises to allow its independent contractor to ... engage in a dangerous activity on the premises': see *(1994) 120 ALR 42* at 68. See also *Northern Sandblasting Pty Ltd v Harris (1997) 71 ALJR 1428*, another decision of the High Court of Australia (noted by Tan Keng Feng in (1998) 114 LQR 193), in which two members of the court (Toohey and McHugh JJ) were prepared to hold a landlord liable for a dangerous electrical repair carried out by an apparently competent, and properly selected, independent contractor.
⁷   See the recommendations of the *Royal Commission on Liability for Personal Injury and Accident Compensation* (Pearson) (Cmnd 7054) vol I ch 31.
⁸   Cf *Bottomley v Todmorden Cricket Club [2003] EWCA Civ 1575*, (2003) Times, 13 November 13, at para 50 *per* Brooke LJ.

(iii) Nuisance

[18.33] In reviewing the authorities on vicarious liability for independent contractors in *Johnson v BJW Property Developments Ltd*[1], Judge Thornton QC referred to the 'assimilation of negligence and nuisance in escape cases' resulting in 'the development of a general liability imposed on an owner or occupier of land that is based on a duty to take reasonable steps to prevent or remove a risk of damaging neighbouring property'. In *Matania v National Provincial Bank*[2] the defendants, who employed independent contractors to make alterations to their flat, were held liable by the Court of Appeal when dust and noise caused a nuisance to a neighbour. Recent cases have also imposed vicarious liability for contractors' negligence with respect to withdrawal of support[3], and work on a party-wall resulting in damage to adjoining premises[4]. The true principle is probably that the employer will be liable either if damage is inevitable from the nature of the work which his contractor is employed to do, or if he fails to restrain the contractor when obvious and continuing interference is being caused. The making, in such circumstances, of an exception to the general rule of no liability for the acts of independent contractors is not necessarily anomalous. Such situations typically involve, as did *Matania* itself, a continuing activity as distinct from sudden accidental damage. Since the defendant would be liable in nuisance if he did the work in the same objectionable way himself, the imposition of liability for his contractor would seem to accord with principle.

1. See *[2002] 3 All ER 574* at para 48.
2. *[1936] 2 All ER 633, CA.*
3. See *Rees v Skerrett [2001] 1 WLR 1541, CA.* See also *Bower v Peate (1876) 1 QBD 321.*
4. See *Alcock v Wraith (1991) 59 BLR 20, CA; Johnson v BJW Property Developments Ltd [2002] 3 All ER 574.*

(iv) Hospitals[1]

[18.34] In *Cassidy v Ministry of Health*[2] Denning LJ expressed the view that a hospital owes a non-delegable duty of care to its patients. He was anxious to establish that hospital authorities would be liable when negligence occurred, especially in situations in which *teams* of medical staff had been involved: some members of which had been employed under contracts of service while others had been outside consultants acting, in effect, as independent contractors. Lord Denning's objective was to circumvent the possibility of hospitals avoiding vicarious liability either by invoking the 'control' test, so as to deny that such liability was capable of arising at all out of the carelessness of skilled professional people such as doctors,[3] or by exploiting the difficulty which claimants in such cases will often have of identifying which individual member of the medical staff had actually been negligent; and hence of showing that the person concerned had been an 'employee' as distinct from an 'independent contractor'. Although the other members of the Court of Appeal, Somervell and Singleton LJJ, agreed with Denning LJ in finding for the plaintiff in *Cassidy's* case, they actually based their decision on the narrower ground of orthodox vicarious liability. Nevertheless, it seems likely that Lord Denning's concept of a non-delegable duty does now represent the law where treatment in National Health Service hospitals[4] is concerned.[5]

1. See generally, Newdick 'Who Should We Treat', 2nd edn, 2005 (OUP). See also Bettle 'Suing Hospitals Direct: Whose Tort was it Anyhow' (1987) 137 NLJ 573.
2. *[1951] 2 KB 343* at 359–365, *[1951] 1 All ER 574* at 584–588. See also *Roe v Minister of Health [1954] 2 QB 66* at 82, *[1954] 2 All ER 131* at 137, CA.
3. Cf *Hillyer v St Bartholomew's Hospital (Governors) [1909] 2 KB 820, CA.*

4   Different issues may arise where private hospitals are involved: cf *Yepremian v Scarborough General Hospital (1980) 110 DLR (3d) 513.*
5   The *Cassidy* approach has been followed in Australia: see *Albrighton v Royal Prince Alfred Hospital [1980] 2 NSWLR 542, CA.*

Resources

[18.35]   Related to, but not identical with, the question of whether hospitals should be subjected to a non-delegable duty giving rise to liability when normally competent doctors perform negligently, is the question whether hospital authorities can also be directly liable for inadequate treatment resulting from the underfunding and under-staffing of their institutions. As has already been indicated in an earlier chapter,[1] in *Wilsher v Essex Area Health Authority*[2] two members of the Court of Appeal expressed the view, albeit obiter, 'that there seems to be no reason in principle why ... a hospital management committee should not be held directly liable in negligence for failing to provide sufficient qualified and competent medical staff'.[3] If, however, the alleged failure simply reflected overall financial difficulties any such claim would appear to face formidable problems relating to the justiciability of resource allocation decisions.[4]

1   CHAPTER 7 above.
2   *[1987] QB 730, [1986] 3 All ER 801, CA.*
3   *[1987] QB 730* at 775, *[1986] 3 All ER 801* at 831, *per* Glidewell LJ. His Lordship was agreeing expressly on the point with Sir Nicholas Browne-Wilkinson V-C. Mustill LJ found it unnecessary to express an opinion (see *[1987] QB 730* at 748, *[1986] 3 All ER 831* at 811). The point was not considered when *Wilsher*'s case went to the House of Lords (see *[1988] 1 All ER 871).*
4   See generally CHAPTER 15 above.

(v) Injuries at work

[18.36]   In certain circumstances an employer's duty with respect to the safety of his employees at their place of work may be non-delegable. This was authoritatively reaffirmed by the House of Lords relatively recently,[1] and has been discussed in an earlier chapter.[2]

1   See *McDermid v Nash Dredging and Reclamation Co Ltd [1987] AC 906, [1987] 2 All ER 878, HL.*
2   CHAPTER 17 above.

(vi) Bailees

[18.37]   It is sometimes said that the responsibility of bailees for reward towards the owners of the property bailed is capable of amounting to a non-delegable duty of care.[1] Thus, garages entrusted with plaintiffs' motor cars have been held liable for damage caused by their employees in circumstances in which the employees in question were at least arguably acting outside the course of their employment, so that ordinary vicarious liability could not have been imposed.[2] The fact that bailment will often involve a contractual relationship between bailor and bailee, and that bailment is a concept of some antiquity in the law,[3] might account for what in terms of contemporary principle could appear anomalous. On the other hand, it has been forcefully argued that the concept of non-delegable duty is not in fact necessary to explain the relevant decisions. An employee wrongfully making use, on a journey of his own, of a car bailed to his employer, may legitimately be regarded as acting *inside* the course of his employment with respect to the care of the vehicle itself, even if he would be acting *outside* it with respect to any damage caused to a third party in a road accident.[4]

1   See *Morris v C W Martin & Sons Ltd [1966] 1 QB 716* at 722ff, *[1965] 2 All ER 725* at 730ff, CA, *per* Lord Denning MR.
2   See *Aitchison v Page Motors Ltd (1935) 154 LT 128*, as explained by Lord Denning MR in *Morris v C W Martin & Sons Ltd [1966] 1 QB 716* at 724–725, *[1965] 2 All ER 725* at 730, CA. Cf *Chowdhary v Gillot [1947] 2 All ER 541*.
3   See generally, N Palmer *Bailment* (2nd edn, 1991).
4   See *Clerk and Lindsell on Torts* (18th edn, 2000) pp 242–243.

'Collateral negligence'

[18.38]   In *Penny v Wimbledon UDC and Iles*[1] the Court of Appeal imposed liability upon the employers of independent contractors in a case which involved the creation of a dangerous situation on the highway. Romer LJ said, obiter, however, that he wished 'to point out that accidents arising from what is called casual or collateral negligence cannot be guarded against beforehand'[2] and that employers would not be liable for such negligence even in non-delegable duty situations. This 'principle' was apparently made the basis of the decision of the Court of Appeal in the difficult case of *Padbury v Holliday and Greenwood Ltd*.[3] The defendant builders employed sub-contractors to put in window-frames. One of the sub-contractors' servants carelessly left a tool on a window sill, from which it was blown by the wind on to the unfortunate plaintiff who was a pedestrian in the street below. The defendants were held not liable on the ground that:

> 'before a superior employer could be held liable for the negligent act of a servant of a sub-contractor it must be shown that the work which the sub-contractor was employed to do was work the nature of which, and not merely the performance of which, cast on the superior employer the duty of taking precautions.'[4]

1   *[1899] 2 QB 72, CA.*
2   *[1899] 2 QB 72* at 78.
3   *(1912) 28 TLR 494, CA.*
4   *Per* Fletcher Moulton LJ (as reported in the indirect speech of the Times Law Reports).

Incoherent concept

[18.39]   This reasoning in *Padbury's* case is difficult to follow.[1] If it be assumed, as it appears to have been in the case itself, that potentially dangerous activities on or very close to the highway are capable of giving rise to non-delegable duties, it is not easy to see why the employer should be exonerated from liability in the circumstances which arose. Providing that the person whose carelessness caused injury was acting in the course of his employment as an employee of the independent contractor, as he presumably was in the situation in *Padbury*, it should surely follow that the employers of the independent contractor will be liable. To hold otherwise is effectively to define the non-delegable duty out of existence in negligence cases. This is because independent contractors will normally be firms rather than individuals and hence will only be capable of negligence through the acts of their employees.[2] Significantly, in *Salsbury v Woodland*[3] Sachs LJ observed that he 'derived no assistance at all from any distinction between "collateral and casual" negligence and other negligence' and that 'such a distinction provide[d] too many difficulties for [him] to accept without question'. It is indeed submitted that the concept of 'collateral negligence' in this context is incoherent and that its use should be abandoned.[4]

1   But cf *Street on Torts* (11th edn, 2003) p 563.
2   In *Padbury v Holliday and Greenwood Ltd* itself an action against the sub-contractors themselves, to which it is difficult to see that there could have been any defence, was discontinued (perhaps on grounds of insolvency).
3   *[1970] 1 QB 324* at 348, *[1969] 3 All ER 863* at 878, CA.
4   But cf *Walsh v Holst & Co Ltd [1958] 3 All ER 33* at 42, *[1958] 1 WLR 800* at 814, CA, *per* Sellers LJ (sed quaere).

E 'Agents'

Car-owners

Terminology

[18.40]   Vicarious liability for the negligence of others is not confined to situations involving employees acting in the course of their employment, and those involving independent contractors in the exceptional situations which have been outlined above. In a special line of cases liability has been imposed upon the owners of motor cars for the carelessness of persons whom they have permitted to drive their vehicles, in circumstances in which that driving was undertaken at least in part for the benefit of the owner and at his request.[1] Somewhat confusingly, the careless drivers have sometimes been termed the 'agents' of the owners for the purposes of this principle.[2] The cases typically involve social or domestic situations so that the drivers could not appropriately be labelled as employees or as independent contractors of the owner, but it is not obvious that the term 'agent' is any more appropriate. It is true that there is some overlap between the concept of agency as used in the law of contract, and that of vicarious liability in the law of tort. Thus, an employer cannot be vicariously liable for his servant's deceit under the rule in *Lloyd v Grace Smith Ltd*[3], unless the servant's act fell within his actual or ostensible authority as defined by the law of agency.[4] Nevertheless, the two concepts are essentially different. As Eveleigh J observed in one case:[5]

> 'There is no general rule that a principal is liable for the acts of an agent performed for his benefit even though the acts are performed solely in the course of carrying out the project which the principal has commissioned. If that were the case, an independent contractor would involve his employer in liability as a general rule rather than exceptionally.'

Lord Denning MR put it in this way in *Launchbury v Morgans*:[6]

> 'The words "principal" and "agent" are not used here in the connotation which they have in the law of contract (which is one thing), or the connotation which they have in the business community (which is another thing). They are used as shorthand to denote the circumstances in which vicarious liability is imposed.'

1   Two of the earliest examples are *Samson v Aitchison [1912] AC 844* and *Pratt v Patrick [1924] 1 KB 488*.
2   See *Samson v Aitchison [1912] AC 844*.
3   [1912] AC 716, discussed above at para [18.22].
4   *Armagas Ltd v Mundogas SA, The Ocean Frost [1986] AC 717, [1986] 2 All ER 385, HL*.
5   *Nottingham v Aldridge [1971] 2 QB 739* at 749, *[1971] 2 All ER 751* at 757.
6   *[1971] 2 QB 245* at 255, CA (the later reversal of the Court of Appeal in this case by the House of Lords does not affect the terminology).

Scope

[18.41] Until the leading case of *Launchbury v Morgans*, decided by the House of Lords in 1971, the best-known post-war decision concerning the 'agency' liability of motor car owners was probably the decision of the Court of Appeal in *Ormrod v Crosville Motor Services Ltd.*[1] The defendant car owner, who was in Monte Carlo, arranged for a friend to drive the car to Monte Carlo to meet him. The driver was to visit friends of his own en route, but after he reached Monte Carlo the plan was for him and the defendant to go off on holiday together using the car. The driver was involved in an accident at the outset of his journey to Monte Carlo, before he had even left England, which was caused partly by his negligence. The defendant was held vicariously liable. Denning LJ said:[2]

> 'The law puts an especial responsibility on the owner of a vehicle who allows it out on to the road in charge of someone else, no matter whether it is his servant, his friend, or anyone else. If it is being used wholly or partly on the owner's business or for the owner's purposes, then the owner is liable for any negligence on the part of the driver.'

1   *[1953] 2 All ER 753, [1953] 1 WLR 1120.*
2   *[1953] 2 All ER 753* at *755, [1953] 1 WLR 1120* at *1123.*

Borderline cases

[18.42] The *Ormrod* case was subsequently applied by the Court of Appeal in *Carberry v Davies*,[1] in which a father anxious that his son, who was too young to drive, should gain some enjoyment from the family car, arranged for a friend to act as chauffeur. The father was held liable for the driving of the 'chauffeur' when the car was being used to take the son on a trip with his girlfriend. On the facts of the case, the interest and involvement of the father in the particular expedition was not very immediate, to say the least, and Harman LJ was indeed moved to remark that the case was 'very near the line'.[2] More typical are cases in which the scope of this particular doctrine of vicarious liability has received a narrower interpretation. The mere fact that the driver is using the car with the owner's permission is certainly not enough in itself to make the latter liable.[3] In *Hewitt v Bonvin*[4] the Court of Appeal refused to hold a car-owner liable for his son's negligent driving in circumstances in which the father had consented to the use of the car to take home two of the son's girlfriends.[5]

1   *[1968] 2 All ER 817, [1968] 1 WLR 1103, CA.*
2   *[1968] 2 All ER 817* at *819, [1968] 1 WLR 1103* at *1108.*
3   *A fortiori* if the owner's permission was not obtained: see *Klein v Caluori [1971] 2 All ER 701, [1971] 1 WLR 619.*
4   *[1940] 1 KB 188, CA.*
5   See also *Rambarran v Gurrucharran [1970] 1 All ER 749, [1970] 1 WLR 556.*

Launchbury v Morgans

[18.43] The line of cases extending vicarious liability to the owners of motor cars, albeit in limited circumstances, was prompted by the fact that the owner was more likely than the driver to be insured. In *Launchbury v Morgans*[1] Lord Denning MR,[2] in the Court of Appeal, attempted to take this underlying rationale nearer to its logical conclusion. He sought to extend the scope of liability to cases in which the car was merely being driven with the owner's permission; thereby effectively eliminating the restrictive conditions relating to the owner's involvement in, and request that, the car be used for the particular purpose. The defendant wife permitted her husband to use her car. On one occasion it was involved in a serious accident while the wife was at home, and the car had been taken by her husband on a 'pub crawl'. When the crash actually occurred, the driving had been taken over by a friend of the husband, the latter having become too intoxicated. Imposition by the Court of Appeal of liability on the wife was unanimously overturned by the House of Lords.

1 *[1973] AC 127, [1972] 2 All ER 606, HL*; revsg *[1971] 2 QB 245, [1971] 1 All ER 642, CA.*
2 Edmund Davies LJ agreed with Lord Denning as to the result, but adopted somewhat narrower reasoning. Megaw LJ dissented.

Rejection of radical extension

[18.44] The House refused to sanction what would have amounted to a radical extension, on policy grounds, of vicarious liability. The potentially far-reaching implications, in terms of insurance and resources, meant that such a change in the law could only appropriately be made by the legislature, not by the courts.[1] On the other hand, none of the earlier cases, including *Ormrod v Crosville Motor Services Ltd*[2] itself, was actually overruled, so it must be taken that they are still good law; especially as the House undertook a thorough review of the authorities in this area. Nevertheless, it is clear that the principle in the earlier cases is unlikely to be extended. Thus, in the 1981 case of *Norwood v Navan*,[3] the Court of Appeal refused to hold the owner liable for his wife's driving when she had taken the car out on a shopping expedition, notwithstanding that the purpose of the trip was partly to buy food for the family.

1 See *[1973] AC 127* at 137, 142–143, 151, *[1972] 2 All ER 606* at 610, 615–616, 622, *per* Lord Wilberforce, Lord Pearson and Lord Salmon.
2 *[1953] 2 All ER 753, [1953] 1 WLR 1120, CA.*
3 *[1981] RTR 457, CA.*

Other situations?

[18.45] In so far as the 'agency' cases can be said to be based upon any coherent principle, that principle would in theory appear to be capable of extending beyond situations involving the ownership of motor cars.[1] Indeed, the principle was used to impose liability in one case in which, although it involved a motor car, the defendant was not the vehicle's owner but merely a willing passenger and contributor to the cost of petrol, the car having been stolen.[2] In another case, albeit one in which the claim failed on the facts, the application of the principle to careless driving of a luggage trolly was considered.[3] But given the hostility of the House of Lords to the creation of new categories of vicarious liability[4] application of the principle in fresh contexts is likely to be rare[5]. The whole area was recently subjected to extensive review by the High Court of Australia in *Scott v Davis*[6], in which the court declined to extend the doctrine to private aircraft. The defendant was held not liable for permitting the use of his aeroplane for a pleasure flight, in which the defendant himself was not involved, which ended in disaster.

1 'The law … is the same whether the chattel being used with the permission of its owner is a car or, for example, a gun or a tennis racquet': *per* Edmund Davies LJ in *Launchbury v Morgans [1971] 2 QB 245* at 260, *[1971] 1 All ER 642* at 651. See also *per* Eveleigh J in *Nottingham v Aldridge [1971] 2 QB 739* at 750, *[1971] 2 All ER 751* at 758: ' … the motor vehicle is not in … a special category.'
2 See *Scarsbrook v Mason [1961] 3 All ER 767.*

3   See *Norton v Canadian Pacific Steamships Ltd [1961] 2 All ER 785, [1961] 1 WLR 1057, CA.*
4   Ie in *Morgans v Launchbury [1973] AC 127, [1972] 2 All ER 606, HL.*
5   Cf *Credit Lyonnais Bank v Export Credits Guarantee Department [1999] 1 All ER 929, HL.*
6   *(2000) 74 ALJR 1410.* See discussion by F M B Reynolds in 'Casual Delegation' (2001) 117 LQR 180.

Part seven

Defective products

Chapter 19

The common law

A Background

Development of liability

[19.01] The common law of negligence relating to defective products is less impor-tant than it formerly was. This is due to the introduction, by the *Consumer Protection Act 1987, Pt I*, of a strict liability regime for harm caused by defective products.[1] This regime, which is discussed in CHAPTER 20, applies not only to personal injuries but also, in certain circumstances, to property damage.[2] The Act does, however, expressly preserve existing remedies so the common law of negligence is not superseded.

[1] For a theoretical and comparative analysis of the entire field, see J Stapleton *Product Liability* (1994). See also Howells (ed) *The Law of Product Liability* (2000); M Mildred (ed) *Product liability – Law and Insurance* (2001). See, generally, Miller *Product Liability and Safety Encyclopaedia;* Miller and Goldberg *Product Liability* (2nd edn, 2004).

[2] The property must have been of a kind ordinarily used, and intended by the plaintiff to be used, for private consumption; and the damage must have amounted to at least £275 in value. See *section 5* of the Act.

'Dangerous things'

[19.02] Until the celebrated landmark decision in *Donogue v Stevenson*,[1] the falla-cious assumption, exploded by that case, that it would violate the doctrine of privity of contract to allow anyone, other than the person who had given value for it, to sue in respect of harm caused by a defective chattel, greatly obstructed the development of the law of tort in this context. Exceptions to the general rule of no liability outside contract tended to be confined, in an unsatisfactory manner, to specific categories. The concept of things 'dangerous in themselves' thus achieved prominence.[2] Although inherently artificial, since few things can be predicated in the abstract as being either always dangerous or completely safe, the concept even survived for some years after *Donoghue v Stevenson* should have rendered it redundant.

[1] *[1932] AC 562.*
[2] Cf *Longmeid v Holliday (1851) 6 Exch 761.*

Application post-Donoghue

[19.03] Thus, in the 1939 case of *Burfitt v A and E Kille*[1] the old terminology was used in imposing liability in tort upon a shopkeeper who sold a pistol to a 12-year-old boy, with which the latter shot and injured the plaintiff. The decision went the other way in the later case of *Ricketts v Erith Borough Council*,[2] which involved a claim against a shopkeeper in similar circumstances, except that the harm was caused by a bow and arrow: an object which was held not to be in itself dangerous. As late as 1949 the Court of Appeal, in the very doubtful case of *Ball v LCC*,[3] refused to impose liability for injuries caused by a negligently installed boiler because the boiler was not in the category of things regarded as dangerous per se.

[1]   *[1939] 2 KB 743, [1939] 2 All ER 372.*
[2]   *[1943] 2 All ER 629.*
[3]   *[1949] 2 KB 159, [1949] 1 All ER 1056, CA.*

Donoghue v Stevenson

[19.04] Notwithstanding the apparent durability of the 'dangerous things' concept, the true starting point of the modern common law of tort relating to dangerous or defective chattels is the speech of Lord Atkin in *Donoghue v Stevenson*. The importance of this case for the development of negligence liability in general clearly transcends its specific subject matter. Nevertheless, the actual context was a claim for personal injuries caused by a dangerous product: a bottle of ginger beer alleged to have contained a snail. Lord Atkin expressed the ratio decidendi of the decision in its narrower aspect in the following classic passage:[1]

> ' ... a manufacturer of products, which he sells in such a form as to show that he intends them to reach the ultimate consumer in the form in which they left him with no reasonable possibility of intermediate inspection, and with the knowledge that the absence of reasonable care in the preparation or putting up of the products will result in an injury to the consumer's life or property, owes a duty to the consumer to take that reasonable care.'

[1]   *[1932] AC 562* at 599.

Enormous range

[19.05] The years since *Donoghue v Stevenson* was decided have seen the principle of liability in negligence for defective products applied to an enormous range of differing fact-situations. Major early decisions which confirmed the significance of the newly forged principle involved items such as underwear,[1] and substances such as hair dyes.[2] A particularly important development was recognition that Lord Atkin's use of the word 'manufacturer' was not to be taken literally. Thus, the doctrine was extended to *distributors*[3] and, even more significantly, negligent *repairers* of chattels, such as motor vehicles[4] and lifts,[5] also began to be subjected to liability.

[1]   See *Grant v Australian Knitting Mills Ltd [1936] AC 85.*
[2]   See *Watson v Buckley, Osborne, Garrett & Co [1940] 1 All ER 174.*
[3]   See *Watson v Buckley, Osborne, Garrett & Co [1940] 1 All ER 174.*
[4]   See *Stennett v Hancock and Peters [1939] 2 All ER 578.*
[5]   See *Haseldine v Daw & Son Ltd [1941] 2 KB 343, [1941] 3 All ER 156, CA.*

B The duty

Negligence principles

[19.06] The duty of care owed at common law in respect of products is governed by the general principles of the law of negligence, and could be said to provide a paradigm instance of the applicability of those principles. Nevertheless, the cases show that some issues occur regularly in the application of the basic concepts to products claims, and it is appropriate to highlight these.

Warning

[19.07] Where substances such as potentially hazardous chemicals are concerned, a manufacturer may be under a duty to *warn* of his product's properties if he is not to be held liable in negligence. Thus, in *Vacwell Engineering Co Ltd v BDH Chemicals Ltd*[1] liability was imposed upon defendants who, because of their own inadequate research, failed to provide notification of the capacity of one of their substances to cause an explosion; such an explosion having occurred with fatal consequences.

[1]   *[1971] 1 QB 88, [1969] 3 All ER 1681* (subsequently varied in *[1971] 1 QB 111, [1970] 3 All ER 553, CA*).

Indirect communication

[19.08] On the other hand, if a warning *is* given, it may be effective, depending upon the particular circumstances, to discharge the manufacturer's duty of care even though not communicated to the injured claimant himself.[1] In *Holmes v Ashford*[2] the defendant manufacturers marketed hair dye with a warning to hairdressers that it might be harmful to certain skins, and recommending that a test should be carried out before it was used. The plaintiff contracted dermatitis when her hairdresser disregarded this warning. Her claim against the manufacturers failed, even though no warning had reached her as ultimate recipient of the product; the Court of Appeal held that the warning to hairdressers had constituted sufficient compliance with the duty.[3]

[1]   See P R Ferguson 'Liability for Pharmaceutical Products: A Critique of the "Learned Intermediary" Rule' (1992) 12 OJLS 59.
[2]   *[1950] 2 All ER 76, CA.*
[3]   See also *Kubach v Hollands [1937] 3 All ER 907.*

Products already in use

[19.09] The duty to warn is not confined to potentially dangerous substances or individual objects; indeed, it can be of great importance with respect to complex pieces of machinery such as cranes[1], or motor cars. If information about a particular hazard comes to light subsequently, the manufacturer can even be under a duty to issue warnings, and perhaps take further steps, with respect to products already distributed and in use.[2] The practice of motor car manufacturers of 'recalling' vehicles for examination or repair in certain circumstances undoubtedly reflects, not merely a moral obligation and concern for public relations, but an actual legal duty as well.[3]

[1]   See *Rivtow Marine Ltd v Washington Iron Works [1974] SCR 1189 (Can).*
[2]   See *Hobbs (Farms) Ltd v Baxenden Chemical Co Ltd [1992] 1 Lloyd's Rep 54.* See also the decision of the Canadian Supreme Court in *Dow Corning Corpn v Hollis (1995) 129 DLR (4th) 609* (medical products), and the earlier decision of the same court in *Rivtow Marine Ltd v Washington Iron Works [1974] SCR 1189.*
[3]   See *Walton v British Leyland UK Ltd (2 July 1978, unreported)* Willis J, noted in C J Miller *Product Liability and Safety Encyclopaedia* Div III, para 43. Cf *Carroll v Fearon* [1999] PIQR P416, in which the Court of Appeal was critical of the defendant manufacturers for limiting the disclosure of defects found in their car tyres in order to 'avoid the problems connected with a ... recall of all tyres' (per Judge LJ).

Exemption clauses

[19.10] Finally, a *warning* adequate to *discharge* the duty must be carefully distinguished from an *exemption* clause intended to *exclude* it; the enforceability of the latter may depend, subject to the particular circumstances, upon the provisions of the *Unfair Contract Terms Act 1977*.[1]

[1] See generally CHAPTER 22 below.

Testing

[19.11] In some circumstances, even persons in the chain of distribution other than the original manufacturer may owe to the ultimate recipient a duty to test the product for safety. In *Andrews v Hopkinson*[1] a second-hand car dealer was held liable for a collision caused by a dangerous steering defect in a vehicle which he had sold; the defect being one which could have been discovered by the defendant with the exercise of reasonable diligence. On the other hand, in *Sellars v Best*[2] Pearson J held that it would be taking *Donoghue v Stevenson* too far to hold an electricity board liable for failing to test the safety of electrical appliances, newly installed by a third party, before supplying electricity to a house; and thereby enabling a defect in one of the appliances to cause a fatal electric shock.[3] If the situation is one in which a test by someone other than the original manufacturer is appropriate, a failure to carry out the test may, depending upon the precise circumstances, exonerate the manufacturer provided he has taken all necessary steps to draw attention to the need for it. The hair dye case of *Holmes v Ashford*,[4] referred to in para [19.08], provides an example.[5]

[1] *[1957] 1 QB 229, [1956] 3 All ER 422.*
[2] *[1954] 2 All ER 389, [1954] 1 WLR 913.*
[3] Cf *Hartley v Mayoh & Co [1954] 1 QB 383, [1954] 1 All ER 375, CA.*
[4] *[1950] 2 All ER 76, CA.*
[5] See also *Kubach v Hollands [1937] 3 All ER 907.*

C Intermediate inspection

'Reasonable possibility'

[19.12] In the years following the decision in *Donoghue v Stevenson*, Lord Atkin's statement in his speech that liability for defective products was dependent, inter alia, upon the absence of any 'reasonable possibility of intermediate examination'[1] was often given special emphasis. It was described by Goddard LJ in one case as an 'all-important qualification';[2] and in two early reported cases at first instance, negligent manufacturers of electrical equipment succeeded in avoiding liability precisely on the ground that there had been clear opportunities for intermediate inspection by the users of the equipment which, if taken advantage of, would have revealed the defects.[3] The principle was recently applied in the context of real property in *Baxall Securities v Sheard Walshaw*[4]. In this case an action in tort against architects in respect of a defect in a building failed on the ground that the defect should have been discovered by the claimants' own surveyors. David Steel J, in the Court of Appeal, said[5]:

> 'Where, in the normal course of events, a surveyor would be engaged in a survey of a building for a purchaser, and, with the exercise of due diligence, that

surveyor would have discovered a defect, that defect is patent whether or not a surveyor is in fact engaged and, if engaged, whether or not the surveyor performs his task competently ... Actual knowledge of the defect, or alternatively a reasonable opportunity for inspection that would unearth the defect, will usually negative the duty of care or at least break the chain of causation'.

[1]   *[1932] AC 562* at 599.
[2]   *Haseldine v C A Daw & Son Ltd [1941] 2 KB 343* at 376, *[1941] 3 All ER 156* at 183, CA.
[3]   See *Dransfield v British Insulated Cables Ltd [1937] 4 All ER 382* and *Paine v Colne Valley Electricity Supply Co Ltd [1938] 4 All ER 803.*
[4]   *[2002] Lloyd's Rep PN 231*, CA.
[5]   See above at paras 53 and 54.

Limits to the concept

[19.13]   On the other hand, it is clear that, as a weapon for defendants, the concept of intermediate examination has its limits. Thus, an initial suggestion that the *Donoghue v Stevenson* principle should be confined to situations closely analogous to the facts of that case, in which the bottle of ginger beer had been 'stoppered and sealed' by the manufacturer so as to remain in that state until opened by the consumer, was rejected by the Privy Council in *Grant v Australian Knitting Mills Ltd.*[1] In that case liability was imposed upon negligent manufacturers of underwear who had allowed their product to be contaminated by a chemical which caused dermatitis. '... the essential point', said Lord Wright delivering the judgment of the Board,[2] 'was that the article should reach the consumer or user subject to the same defect as it had when it left the manufacturer'. It was accordingly irrelevant that the underwear had not been distributed in sealed packaging, nor was it an obstacle to liability that the plaintiff user had not considered it necessary to wash the garment before the first wearing.

[1]   *[1936] AC 85.*
[2]   *[1936] AC 85* at 106–107.

Defendant not protected

[19.14]   Similarly, even where there might have appeared to be ample opportunity for intermediate inspection, a claimant will still succeed if it becomes clear on the facts that the harm was suffered before that opportunity really existed.[1] Even if the opportunity did exist, the defendants will not be protected if they in truth never anticipated that there would be any intermediate inspection.[2] Finally, in *Haseldine v C A Daw & Son Ltd,*[3] Goddard LJ went so far as to suggest that the word 'probability' could be substituted for the phrase 'reasonable possibility' in Lord Atkin's dictum, and it is submitted that this proposition is correct. The careless creator of a source of danger should not escape liability at common law, except where he is entitled virtually to take it for granted that scrutiny by others of his work will take place before any harm can be expected to occur.

[1]   See *Barnett v H and J Packer & Co Ltd [1940] 3 All ER 575.*
[2]   See *Herschtal v Stewart & Ardern Ltd [1940] 1 KB 155, [1939] 4 All ER 123.*
[3]   *[1941] 2 KB 343* at 376, *[1941] 3 All ER 156* at 183, CA.

Relationship to causation and contributory negligence

[19.15]   Ultimately, the notion of intermediate inspection appears merely to represent the application, in the particular context of defective products, of the general principles of the law of negligence relating to causation.[1] It follows that, in practice, since the broader approach to causal questions which has resulted from the passing of the Law Reform (Contributory Negligence) Act 1945,[2] some decisions which before that Act ended in total defeat for the plaintiff might now be regarded as appropriate situations for apportionment if similar facts were to recur.[3] Of course, this would not be the case directly if the intermediate inspection should have been carried out not by the claimant himself but by a third party. But in such cases the claimant will normally have a cause of action against the third party. Moreover, the broader modern approach to causation will still be relevant in such cases in so far as it might enable the third party to make a claim for contribution, on the ground that he was not alone in being liable to the claimant.[4]

[1] See *The Diamantis Pateras [1966] 1 Lloyd's Rep 179* at 188, per Lawrence J.
[2] See generally CHAPTER 22 below.
[3] *Farr v Butters Bros & Co [1932] 2 KB 606, CA* is perhaps an example.
[4] See the *Civil Liability (Contribution) Act 1978*. It is to be noted that this Act, unlike its predecessor the *Law Reform (Married Women and Tortfeasors) Act 1935*, enables contribution to be sought between a defendant liable to the claimant in contract and one liable to him in tort and vice versa. This can obviously be of value in products liability cases where both retailer and manufacturer happen to be liable to the claimant. See generally CHAPTER 22 below.

Claimants' own safety

[19.16] If the case is one in which the allegation of contributory negligence is made against the claimant himself, it follows from the application of general principles that he must have failed to take reasonable care for his own safety before his damages can be reduced. Accordingly, even a claimant who inspected and discovered the defect might in some circumstances still recover in full, if the court is persuaded that he had no reasonable alternative but to take the risk.[1]

[1] Cf *Denny v Supplies and Transport Co Ltd [1950] 2 KB 374, CA*. See also *Targett v Torfaen Borough Council [1992] 3 All ER 27, CA*; *Rimmer v Liverpool City Council [1985] QB 1* at 14, *[1984] 1 All ER 930* at 938, CA.

D Proof of negligence

Two difficulties

[19.17] Victims who claim to have suffered harm due to a defective product, in circumstances in which causation is not entirely clear, are apt to come up against either or both of two contrasting difficulties in discharging the onus of proof necessary to succeed in negligence.

Lapse of time

[19.18] The first problem is that the longer the lapse of time since the product left the manufacturer, the more difficult it will be to show that the probabilities point to the attribution of fault to him rather than to subsequent interference with the product, or damage to it. Thus, in *Evans v Triplex Safety Glass Co Ltd*[1] a car windscreen suddenly shattered for no apparent reason, about a year after the date of manufacture. A claim for personal injuries suffered as a result was unsuccessful. Porter J observed that the question was one of degree rather than of law, but emphasised that he had 'to consider the question of time' and the possibility 'that the disintegration was due rather to the fitting of the windscreen than to faulty manufacture having regard to its use on the road and the damage done to a windscreen in the course of use'.

¹ *[1936] 1 All ER 283.*

Manufacturing process under the defendant's control

[19.19] The other main problem which can arise in product liability cases is that the manufacturing process will normally be under the defendant's control. He will therefore be the only party able in practice to furnish evidence as to the nature of that process, on the strength of which he may seek to contend that the best system reasonably possible had been operated and all proper precautions taken. In such cases, however, the claimant may benefit from a principle closely related to, if not identical with, that of *res ipsa loquitur.*[1] Thus, in *Grant v Australian Knitting Mills*, the facts of which have already been given, Lord Wright said:[2]

> 'According to the evidence the method of manufacture was correct; the danger of excess sulphites being left was recognised and was guarded against; the process was intended to be foolproof. If excess sulphites were left in the garment, that could only be because someone was at fault. The appellant is not required to lay his finger on the exact person in all the chain who was responsible or to specify what he did wrong. Negligence is found as a matter of inference from the existence of the defects taken in connection with all the known circumstances ...
> '

[1] See generally CHAPTER 2 above. But cf per Lord Macmillan in *Donoghue v Stevenson [1932] AC 562* at 622: 'There is no presumption of negligence in such a case as the present, nor is there any justification for applying the maxim *res ipsa loquitur.*' Sed quaere.
[2] *[1936] AC 85* at 101.

Traceable to manufacturer

[19.20] This passage was applied by the Court of Appeal in *Carroll v Fearon.*[1] In this case a car tyre burst, causing a head-on collision with fatal consequences. The manufacturers argued that the plaintiffs had failed to prove actual *negligence*, despite the fact that a defect had been found in the tyre which was traceable to its manufacture seven years earlier. The Court of Appeal unanimously held the manufacturers solely to blame for the accident. Judge LJ observed:

> ' ... once it was established that the tyre disintegrated because of an identified fault in the course of its manufacture the judge had to decide whether this fault was the result of negligence at Dunlop's factory. He did not have to identify any individual or group of employees or the acts or omissions which resulted in inadequate rubber penetration of the cords. If the manufacturing process had worked as intended this defect should not have been present.'[2]

[1] [1999] PIQR P416 (the case was decided under the common law since the product in question was manufactured before the passing of the *Consumer Protection Act 1987*).
[2] Quoted by Dr Gary Slapper in his discussion of *Carroll v Fearon* in 'Dangerous Product Litigation' (1998) NLJ 345.

Vicarious liability

[19.21] It is clear from both the *Grant* and *Carroll* cases that direct negligence by the manufacturer himself is not the only route to the imposition of liability. This was also emphasised by Mackenna J in the 1978 case of *Hill v James Crowe (Cases) Ltd*.[1] In finding for the plaintiff, his Lordship responded as follows to defence evidence of the high standard of operation in their factory:[2]

'The manufacturer's liability in negligence [does] not depend on proof that he had either a bad system of work or that his supervision was inadequate. He might also be *vicariously* liable for the negligence of his workmen in the course of their employment. If the plaintiff's injuries were a reasonably foreseeable consequence of *such* negligence, the manufacturer's liability [is] established ... '[3]

[1] *[1978] 1 All ER 812, [1978] ICR 298.*
[2] *[1978] 1 All ER 812* at 816, *[1978] ICR 298* at 303.
[3] Italics supplied. The relevance of vicarious liability appears wrongly to have been overlooked in the earlier case of *Daniels v R White & Sons Ltd [1938] 4 All ER 258*, which Makenna J chose not to follow in *Hill's* case: the passage quoted is a direct criticism of the reasoning in *Daniels*.

Danger of calling no evidence

[19.22] The readiness of the court in effect to apply the *res ipsa loquitur* approach in products liability negligence cases means that it is rarely safe, even for defendants who could not themselves be held responsible for the manufacturing process, to call no evidence when sued by someone harmed by the product, claiming that the claimant has not discharged the burden of proof. Reported cases in both the Court of Appeal,[1] and the House of Lords,[2] have vividly illustrated the perilous nature of this course for defendants.

[1] See *Pearce v Round Oak Steel Works Ltd [1969] 3 All ER 680, [1969] 1 WLR 595, CA*.
[2] See *Henderson v H E Jenkins & Sons [1970] AC 282, [1969] 3 All ER 756*. Cf *Tan Chye Choo v Chong Kew Moi [1970] 1 All ER 266, [1970] 1 WLR 147*.

E Economic loss

General rule of irrecoverability

[19.23] The general rule at common law is that, where defective products are concerned, the tort of negligence only provides redress in respect of personal injuries caused by the product, or in respect of damage to property *other* than the defective product itself.[1] That is to say, the owner or user of a defective chattel cannot normally sue in *tort* merely because the chattel turns out to be less valuable or less useful than he had supposed it to be. Thus, he cannot by claiming in negligence seek redress for his having incurred loss in repairing the product, in paying more for it than it had been worth, or in suffering a loss of profit in whatever activity he had sought to use it.

[1] For the difficulties which the application of this principle can create by making it necessary to consider whether, for example, a package or container is to be considered a separate entity from its contents, see *Aswan Engineering Establishment Co v Lupdine Ltd [1987] 1 All ER 135, [1987] 1 WLR 1, CA*. See also *Bacardi Martini Beverages v Thomas Hardy Packaging [2002] 2 All ER (Comm) 335, CA; The Orjula [1995] 2 Lloyd's Rep 395*. See, generally, CHAPTER 5 above.

Contract needed

[19.24] This limitation on the scope of liability is an application of the conventional doctrine that losses purely financial in nature, unconnected with damage to person or property, should not usually be recoverable in negligence.[1] Redress for such losses has to be sought in *contract*: the owner or user of a defective chattel should look to the person with whom he was in a contractual relationship with respect to the chattel, and the outcome will be governed by the terms of that contract.[2]

[1]   It is possible that a limited exception to this general rule, which may be relevant in some defective product cases, exists where the situation did originally involve a claim for actual physical damage: the success of which causes financial loss to be suffered by someone in the chain of distribution of the defective product. See *Lambert v Lewis [1982] AC 225* at 278, *[1981] 1 All ER 1185* at 1192, per Lord Diplock, and *Virgo Steamship Co SA v Skaarup Shipping Corpn [1988] 1 Lloyd's Rep 352.* But quaere whether this notion survived the decision of the House of Lords in *Murphy v Brentwood District Council [1991] 1 AC 398, [1990] 2 All ER 908.*

[2]   See, generally, P Atiyah *Sale of Goods* (10th edn, 2001, J N Adams ed).

Traditional view reasserted

[19.25] In 1982 the well-known decision of the House of Lords in *Junior Books Ltd v Veitchi Co Ltd*[1] appeared to cast doubt upon the correctness of the traditional view and to indicate that there was an exception to it, albeit of uncertain scope, whereby financial losses caused by a defective product *could* be recovered in tort. Subsequent cases, however, saw a vigorous reassertion of the narrow conventional view. In the particular context of defective products, the decision of the Court of Appeal in *Muirhead v Industrial Tank Specialities Ltd*[2] made it clear that *Junior Books v Veitchi* would be interpreted very narrowly. As a result, liability in negligence for financial losses flowing from a defect in the product appears to be confined to situations in which a close relationship, very similar to a contractual one, existed between claimant and defendant. The debate about the recovery of pure economic loss in negligence is considered at length elsewhere in this book.[3]

[1]   *[1983] 1 AC 520, [1982] 3 All ER 201, HL.*
[2]   *[1986] QB 507, [1985] 3 All ER 705, CA.*
[3]   See generally CHAPTER 5 above.

Limited scope of the duty to warn

Hamble Fisheries

[19.26] Consistently with the general rule that pure economic loss is irrecoverable, the Court of Appeal held in *Hamble Fisheries v L Gardner & Sons*[1] that the duty to warn about defects in products already in use[2], and to recall them if necessary, will normally be confined to situations in which the defect threatens to endanger people or, possibly, to damage other property. Unless the defendant can plausibly be said to have assumed responsibility to the claimant to protect him against pure economic loss arising out of the defect, such loss will not recoverable. This means that a defendant who is in breach of the duty to warn of danger will nevertheless escape liability if only economic loss results. Thus, in the *Hamble Fisheries* case itself, in which those responsible for the manufacture of marine engines did not warn of defects of which they were aware, the plaintiffs were unable to recover for pure economic losses resulting from their vessel's engine failing while at sea; but the Court of Appeal observed that claims for personal injury or property damage could well have succeeded if such injury or damage had occurred. Mummery LJ said[3]:

' ... the duty to warn against the foreseeable risk of physical damage, which never in fact materialised, does not by itself constitute the requisite degree of proximity to give rise to a voluntary assumption of responsibility either (a) for the cost of repair to or replacement of the defective product itself or (b) for loss of profit or for any other kind of pure financial loss flowing from the failure of the defective product'[4].

1   *[1999] 2 Lloyd's Rep 1, CA.*
2   See above.
3   See *[1999] 2 Lloyd's Rep 1, CA* at p 9.
4   See also *per* Nourse LJ at p 10: 'The respondents were very fortunate that [economic loss] was the only loss caused. For myself, I am in little doubt that had there been loss of or injury to the vessel itself or to those on board, the respondents would have been liable for such loss or injury, together, it would follow, with any economic loss that was consequent thereon'.

Chapter 20

Strict liability by statute

A European background

Consumer Protection Act 1987

[20.01] The *Consumer Protection Act 1987*[1] was passed in order to give effect to a Directive of the Council of the European Communities dated 25 July 1985.[2] The Directive was intended to bring about a regime of strict liability for defective products within the legal systems of the various member states of the EC.[3] Some knowledge of the content and wording of the Directive, as well as of the Act itself, is therefore necessary for a satisfactory appreciation of the scope of the law.[4]

[1]   For comment, see A Clark (1987) 50 MLR 614.
[2]   85/374/EEC:L 210/29.
[3]   *Section 1(1)* of the Act provides that: 'This Part shall have effect for the making of such provision as is necessary in order to comply with the product liability Directive and shall be construed accordingly.'
[4]   While the Bill was going through Parliament, the Government rejected a suggestion that the Directive should be set out in a Schedule.

B Strict liability

Scope

[20.02] Article 1 of the Directive states simply: 'The producer shall be liable for damage caused by a defect in his product.' Article 3 makes clear that the liability imposed upon producers is not limited to actual manufacturers and provides also for the imposition of liability, on the same basis as for producers, of *importers* of goods. The strict liability provided for by the Directive is set out in the 1987 Act, albeit by means of a rather different drafting technique, in the first two subsections of *section 2*, as follows:

'(1)... where any damage is caused wholly or partly by a defect in a product, every person to whom subsection (2) below applies shall be liable for the damage.

(2) This subsection applies to—

    (a)   the producer of the product;

    (b)   any person who, by putting his name on the product or using a trade mark or other distinguishing mark in relation to the product, has held himself out to be the producer of the product;

(c)   any person who has imported the product into a member State from a place outside the member States in order, in the course of any business of his, to supply it to another.'

The section thus makes clear that, in addition to manufacturers, the strict liability regime will also apply to those who sell goods within EC countries which they themselves have acquired from outside the community; and to retailers who put their own brand name on the goods which they sell even though those goods were in fact manufactured by others. In view of the widespread nature of this latter practice in the retail trade, this provision is of particular importance. Even within a strict liability regime for defective goods the claimant still has to prove *causation*,[1] and in some cases, particularly where drugs have been taken for a pre-existing condition,[2] this may not be an easy task.[3]

1   Article 4 of the Directive emphasises the point: 'The injured person shall be required to prove the damage, the defect and the causal relationship between defect and damage.' In a controversial recommendation the European Parliament's Committee on the Environment, Public Health and Consumer Protection once suggested that the burden of proving causation should be reversed, so that proof of damage would be sufficient to give rise to an inference of causation which the producer would have to disprove.
2   See C Newdick 'Strict Liability for Defective Drugs in the Pharmaceutical Industry' (1985) 101 LQR 405 at 420ff.
3   For an exceptional case in which a plaintiff succeeded in proving causation in a common law negligence claim for brain damage allegedly caused by the pertussis vaccine, which is routinely administered to children, see *Best v Wellcome Foundation [1994] 5 Med LR 81 (Supreme Court of Ireland)*.

Liability of suppliers

[20.03]   The *Consumer Protection Act 1987* contains an important provision protecting consumers who are unable themselves to *identify* the relevant defendant potentially liable to them under *section 2(1)*. They are able to call upon the person who *supplied* them with the goods to provide them with the identity of the producer, or other person to whom *section 2(2)* applies in relation to the product. If the supplier fails to comply with a request for that information within a reasonable time the Act provides that the supplier himself will be liable for the damage.[1]

1   See *section 2(3)*, giving effect to article 3.3 of the Directive.

Joint and several liability

[20.04]   It will be apparent that, by virtue of *section 2* of the *Consumer Protection Act 1987*, there may be a number of defendants against whom a claimant may be able to seek redress for damage caused to him by a defective product. *Subsection (5)* of the section therefore makes clear that their liability is joint and several.

'Products' and 'producers'[1]

[20.05]   *Section 1(2)* of the 1987 Act provides, inter alia, that: '"product" means any goods or electricity and … includes a product which is comprised in another product, whether by virtue of being a component part or raw material or otherwise.' Thus, the manufacturer of a defective component cannot escape products liability merely because he did not manufacture the finished article.[2] By virtue of *section 2*, however, the 'producer' of a product rendered defective by a defective component will be liable along with the manufacturer of that component. On the other hand, mere suppliers of assembled goods are given a measure of protection by *section 1(3)*, which provides as follows: ' ... a person who supplies any product in which products are comprised, whether by virtue of being component parts or raw materials or otherwise, shall not be treated by reason only of his supply of that product as supplying any of the products so comprised.'[3]

[1] See articles 2 and 3 of the Directive. See also S Whittaker 'European Product Liability and Intellectual Products' (1989) 105 LQR 125.
[2] Conversely, a component's manufacturer is not liable simply because the finished article itself is defective: see *section 4(1)(f)*.
[3] But note that a product will be defective, for the purpose of the imposition of liability upon its actual producer, and the other persons to whom *section 2(2)* applies, even if the defect arises out of a defect in a component part: see *section 3(1)*.

'Producers'

[20.06] It will be apparent from the foregoing provisions that, where assembled goods are concerned, the precise definition of 'producer' may well be crucial. On this point, *section 1(2)(c)* of the 1987 Act enacts the following:

> '"producer", in relation to a product, means-in the case of a product which has not been manufactured, won or abstracted but essential characteristics of which are attributable to an industrial or other process having been carried out ... the person who carried out that process.'

A person who merely provides a container within which a defective item is housed may, for example, be able to invoke this definition of 'producer', so as to avoid liability on the ground that his activity did not confer 'essential characteristics' on the finished product.

Agricultural products

[20.07] The Directive originally provided that member states should be free to exclude 'primary agricultural products' from the strict liability regime if they so chose, or free to include them.[1] According to art 2 of the Directive, '"primary agricultural products" meant the products of the soil, of stock-farming and of fisheries, excluding products which have undergone initial processing'.[2] The UK opted for exclusion,[3] but after the BSE crisis, the European Commission decided to seek to extend the Directive so as to include primary agricultural products and game.[4] This was achieved by EU Directive 99/34 which removed the exemption by extending the 1985 Directive to include agricultural produce[5].

[1] See articles 2 and 15(a).
[2] The definition in *section 1(2)* of the Act uses almost identical wording.
[3] See *section 2(4)* of the Act: 'Neither subsection (2) nor subsection (3) above [ie the sub-sections imposing the strict liability] shall apply to a person in respect of any defect in any game or agricultural produce if the only supply of the game or produce by that person to another was at a time when it had not undergone an industrial process.' The scope of 'industrial process' is not entirely clear: presumably frozen, and genetically modified, foods are 'processed', but is crop-spraying a 'process'?
[4] See Commission Proposal 97/C337/12.
[5] See the *Consumer Protection Act 1987 (Product Liability) Modification Order 2000*.

[20.08] *Strict liability by statute*

'Defect'[1]

[20.08] 'Defect' is defined in *section 3* of the Act.[2] A product is defective if its safety 'is not such as persons generally are entitled to expect'.[3] Inevitably, there will often be scope for debate over questions of fact and degree in deciding whether or not a particular product was defective[4]. Whether that adjective would be appropriate to describe a useful drug, which gives rise to dangerous side-effects, is but one example of the kind of context in which such issues might arise. *Section 3(2)* provides that 'all the circumstances are to be taken into account' in assessing safety and refers, inter alia, to the following[5]: 'the manner in which, and purposes for which, the product has been marketed, its get-up, … and any instructions for, or warnings with respect to, doing or refraining from doing anything with or in relation to the product.' 'Get-up' refers to the general presentation and packaging of the product.

[1]   See A Stoppa 'The Concept of Defectiveness in the Consumer Protection Act 1987: A Critical Analysis' (1992) 12 LS 210.
[2]   See also article 6 of the Directive.
[3]   *Section 3(1)*. The concept of safety is not confined to the context of death or personal injury but includes risks of damage to property: *s 3(1)*.
[4]   See *Abouzaid v Mothercare* (UK) *Ltd (2001) Times, 20 December, CA* (liability imposed in a case close to the borderline': *per* Pill LJ at para 27).
[5]   This list is not exclusive: see *A v National Blood Authority [2001] 3 All ER 289* at para 34.

Unknowability irrelevant

[20.09] In *A v National Blood Authority*[1] the claimants were infected with Hepatitis C during blood transfusions. It emerged that out of every 100 batches 1 would be contaminated, but at the relevant time the medical profession had no means of knowing which batches were contaminated and no way of preventing contamination. Burton J held that the contaminated batches were nevertheless 'defective' for the purposes of the 1987 Act[3].

[1]   *[2001] 3 All ER 289*. See Geraint Howells and Mark Mildred 'Infected Blood: Defect and Discoverability. A First Exposition of the EC Product Liability Directive' (2002) 65 MLR 95.
[2]   See above, especially at para 63.

Expectations

[20.10] *Section 3(1)* of the *Consumer Protection Act 1987* refers to what ' … persons generally are entitled to expect'. Accordingly, although unavoidability will not constitute a defence, the fact of public knowledge of the risk may do so 'if it could be shown that, because the risk is known, it was accepted, and lowered public expectations – like poison and alcohol'[1].

[1]   Per Burton J in *A v National Blood Authority* [2001] 3 All ER 289 at para 50.

Warnings

[20.11] Where *warnings* are concerned, their scope and effectiveness in any particular situation may give rise to difficult questions of fact. A warning given to a doctor by a drug company might not, for example, be passed on to the patient. If there is no possibility of direct communication between patient and drug company it is submitted that, other things being equal, the warning given to the doctor should be effective to exonerate the drug company. The patient would be left to seek a remedy against the doctor.

'Comprised in'

[20.12] *Section 3(1)* of the 1987 Act states that '"safety" in relation to a product, shall include safety with respect to products comprised in that product'. In the case of composite pieces of equipment, the notion of 'comprised in' is presumably a potential source of dispute. Are the tyres supplied with a new car 'comprised in' the car so as to render the manufacturer of the car liable in addition to the manufacturers of the tyres themselves?[1] It is submitted that an affirmative answer should be given to this particular question, but difficult borderline cases are almost bound to arise in other situations.

¹ Cf *Aswan Engineering Establishment Co v Lupdine Ltd [1987] 1 All ER 135* at 152, *[1987] 1 WLR 1* at 21, per Lloyd LJ, and see also *section 5(2)* of the Act (no liability for damage to the whole or any part of the product in question itself).

C Defences

'State of the art'¹

[20.13] The scope of any defences available under a supposed 'strict liability' regime are crucial in determining how strict the liability really is, or to what extent it in truth approximates to a fault based system. By far the most significant defence under *Part I* of the *Consumer Protection Act 1987* in this respect, is that sometimes referred to as the 'state of the art' defence. *Section 4(1)(e)* of the Act provides as follows:

> ' … it shall be a defence … to show that the state of scientific and technical knowledge at the relevant time was not such that a producer of products of the same description as the product in question might be expected to have discovered the defect if it had existed in his products while they were under his control.'

The wording of this provision differs somewhat from that of the Directive, which was thought in some quarters to be less favourable to producers than the Act. Instead of exonerating a producer who could not have been *'expected'* to discover the defect, article 7(e) of the Directive uses a formula based upon whether the state of knowledge was in fact such as to have *'enabled'* the existence of the defect to have been discovered.[2] As a result, the European Commission brought an action against the United Kingdom in the European Court of Justice contending that the 1987 Act had failed fully to comply with the obligation to implement the Directive.[3] On 29 May 1997, however, the court dismissed the action. When *section 1(1)* of the Act,[4] which expressly refers to the Directive for the purpose of the construction of the Act itself, was considered alongside the wording of *section 4(1)(e)*, the court concluded that the courts of the United Kingdom would be able to construe the Act so as fully to achieve the result intended by the Directive.

¹ See C Newdick 'The Development Risk Defence of the Consumer Protection Act 1987' [1988] 47 CLJ 455.
² See article 7(e).

3   *EC Commission v United Kingdom Case C-300/95 [1997] ECR I-2649, [1997] All ER (EC) 481, ECJ.*
    For comment on the decision see C Hodges 'Development Risks: Unanswered Questions' (1998) 61
    MLR 560 and a response to that note by M Mildred and G Howells in (1998) 61 MLR 570. See also P
    Milne 'Hope for manufacturers of defective products' (1997) NLJ 1437.
4   See above.

Accessibility and the Manchuria exception

[20.14] In *European Commission v UK* the European Court of Justice also indicated that 'for the relevant scientific and technical knowledge to be successfully pleaded as against the producer, that knowledge must have been *accessible* at the time when the product in question was put into circulation'.[1] Moreover, in his opinion in the same case, the Advocate General referred to the hypothetical example of 'research carried out by an academic in Machuria published in a local scientific journal in Chinese, which does not go outside the boundaries of the region'[2]. The Advocate General concluded as follows[3]:

> 'In such a situation, it would be unrealistic and, I would say, unreasonable to take the view that the study published in Chinese has the same chances as [studies in eg the US] of being known to a European product manufacturer. So, I do not consider that in such a case a producer could be held liable on the ground that at the time at which he put the product into circulation the brilliant Asian researcher had discovered the defect in it'.

This passage was not disapproved by the Court of Justice and therefore presumably reflects the law. The phrase 'might be expected to have discovered the defect' in *section 4(1)(e)* of the 1987 Act is thus to be construed 'on the basis reasonableness test' with respect to 'the actual opportunities for the information to circulate'.[4] Liability under the Act is therefore not absolute[5]. Nevertheless, the narrowness of the 'Manchuria exception' indicates that a producer's research will have to have been extensive if he is to succeed in contending that research which actually existed was not 'accessible'[6]. The Court of Justice indicated that the expression 'the state of scientific and technical knowledge' (in the Directive and in *section 4(1)(e)* of the Act) meant to include 'the most advanced level of such knowledge'.

1   Italics supplied. The passage is quoted by P Milne in 'Hope for Manufacturers of Defective Products'
    (1997) NLJ 1437.
2   Cf Professor Stapleton's question whether the defence could be negated on the basis of suggestions
    'only aired by a junior scientist at an informal, obscure and unpublicised seminar in Siberia': see J
    Stapleton 'Products Liability Reform-Real or Illusory?' (1986) 6 OJLS 392 at 418.
3   The passage is quoted in the judgment of Burton J in *A v National Blood Authority [2001] 3 All ER 289*
    at para 49.
4   The opinion of the Advocate General, in the above.
5   The European Parliament's Committee on the Environment, Public Health and Consumer Protection
    has recommended that the 'state of the art' defence should be abolished altogether, so as to put the risks
    of developing new products on the producers who stand to benefit from the profits they might generate.
6   It is noteworthy that even negligence cases have taken quite a severe view against defendants of what
    they ought to have discovered, which might be thought to approach strict liability: see *Vacwell
    Engineering Co Ltd v BDH Chemicals [1971] 1 QB 88, [1969] 3 All ER 1681* (failure to consult
    forgotten literature published at the turn of the century).

Absence of reporting of obvious dangers

[20.15] The mere fact that no previous incidents had ever been reported will not of itself mean that the producer can rely on the 'state of scientific and technical knowledge' defence if the defect should have been evident from the outset, had proper consideration been given to the construction of the product[1].

[1] See *Abouzaid v Mothercare (UK) Ltd* (2001) The Times, 20 December, CA (eye injury caused by a metal fastener attached to an elasticated strap).

Unavoidability irrelevant

[20.16] In *A v National Blood Authority* Burton J held that '*known risks* do not qualify' for the 'state of the art' defence 'even if unavoidable in the particular product'[1]. His Lordship said[2]:

> 'If there is a known risk, ie the existence of the defect is known or should have been known in the light of non-Manchurianly accessible information, then the producer continues to produce and supply at his own risk. It would, in my judgment, be inconsistent with the purpose of the directive if a producer, in the case of a known risk, continues to supply products simply because, and despite the fact that, he is unable to identify in which if any of his products the defect will occur or recur, or, more relevantly in a case such as this, where the producer is obliged to supply, continues to supply without accepting the responsibility for any injuries resulting, by insurance or otherwise'.

[1] See *[2001] 3 All ER 289* at para 78.
[2] See *[2001] 3 All ER 289* at para 74.

Other defences

[20.17] *Section 4* of the 1987 Act also provides that it shall be a defence to show that the supposed defect was attributable to compliance by the defendant with a statutory requirement imposed upon him,[1] or in the case of a component, wholly attributable to the design of the product of which the component formed a part, or to constraints which the specification of that product necessarily imposed.[2] An important limitation on the scope of the liability is that liability is not to be imposed if the supply of the product by the defendant 'was otherwise than in the course of a business'[3], or 'otherwise than with a view to profit'.[4] Presumably, trading companies operated by charitable organisations would not be able to invoke these provisions in their defence, but borderline cases in which the applicability of the provisions is uncertain could no doubt arise. In *Veedfald v Arhus Amtskommune*[5] a donor kidney, intended for transplant, was irretrievably damaged in the pre-operative process. The Court of Justice of the European Communities rejected a submission that article 7 of the Directive, on which this provision of the English statute is based, did not apply because the situation involved non-commercial national hospitals.

[1] See *section 4(1)(a)*.
[2] See *section 4(1)(f)*.
[3] See *section 4(1)(c)(i)*.
[4] See *section 4(1)(c)(ii)*.
[5] *[2003] 1 CMLR 1217*.

D Remedies

Contributory negligence, exclusion and limitation of liability

[20.18] The 1987 Act provides that the provisions of the *Law Reform (Contributory Negligence) Act 1945* will apply, where appropriate, to products' liability claims.[1]

Section 7 of the 1987 Act makes clear that liability cannot 'be limited or excluded by any contract term, by any notice or by any other provision'.[2] The normal three-year limitation period applies to claims under the Act,[3] but there is also an important special provision which extinguishes liability ten years after the putting into circulation of the product which caused the damage.[4]

[1]   See *section 6(4)* and article 8(2).
[2]   See also article 12.
[3]   See *Schedule 1*, adding an additional section, *section 11A*, to the *Limitation Act 1980*. See also article 10.1 of the directive.
[4]   See the *Limitation Act 1980, s 11A(3)*, inserted by the *Consumer Protection Act 1987, Sch 1*. See also article 11 of the Directive.

Damage

[20.19]   It is important to note that the *Consumer Protection Act 1987* is not confined to death or personal injury but extends to 'any loss of or damage to any property (including land)'.[1] But loss or damage to the product *itself*,[2] in whole or in part[3] cannot be made the basis of a claim.[4] The Act imposes a threshold on all claims relating to loss of or damage to property of £275.[5] This means that plaintiffs whose loss is below that figure can recover nothing, but those whose loss exceeds it can recover the full amount including the first £275. The intention is to discourage excessive litigation over small sums. In the case of damage to property, liability will not be imposed if the object lost or damaged was not of a kind 'ordinarily intended for private use, occupation or consumption' and was not 'intended by the person suffering the loss or damage mainly for his own private use, occupation or consumption'. The introduction of the concept of 'intention' here would appear to be a potential cause of uncertainty. What of damage to a sophisticated computer system which is used by the claimant partly in the operation of his business, which he runs from home, and partly used by him for playing games?

[1]   See *section 5(1)*, giving effect to article 9 of the Directive.
[2]   Cf *Murphy v Brentwood District Council [1991] 1 AC 398, [1990] 2 All ER 908 HL.*
[3]   Cf *D & F Estates Ltd v Church Comrs [1989] AC 177, [1988] 2 All ER 992, HL.*
[4]   See *section 5(2)*.
[5]   See *section 5(4)* and article 9(b) of the Directive.

Consequential losses

[20.20]   It is unclear whether financial losses consequential upon loss of or damage to any property will be recoverable under the 1987 Act. Such losses are, of course, recoverable in negligence (unlike pure economic loss), subject to the operation of the normal rules relating to remoteness of damage. But since the basic objective of the Act and the Directive is consumer protection, it might be appropriate to conclude that such losses are excluded since they are typically, although not exclusively, commercial in nature. If this is correct it means that, as Paul Dobson suggested:

'if … a toaster catches fire and the fire badly damages the plaintiff's house, the plaintiff will be entitled to claim the cost of repairing the house and replacing the burnt contents but will not be able to claim the cost of alternative accommodation rendered necessary because the house was uninhabitable until repaired.'[1]

In the case of death or personal injury, however, consequential losses such as loss of income will be recoverable just as in negligence.[2]

¹ Annotation to the *Consumer Protection Act 1987, s 5* (*Current Law Statutes Annotated*).
² Fatal Accidents Act claims can be based on the new liability: see the *Consumer Protection Act 1987, s 6*.

E Evaluation

[20.21] In the years immediately following the passing of the *Consumer Protection Act 1987* a number of commentators were sceptical about the extent to which the Act would succeed in practice in introducing strict liability. It was contended that the Act, and indeed the Directive itself, was vulnerable to criticism on the ground that, while purporting to introduce such liability, it used concepts which reflected the influence of negligence criteria.[1] But whatever the validity of these arguments on a theoretical level, it now appears that the courts are applying the Act in such a way as to impose liability in circumstances in which no negligence claim could have succeeded. In one case in which both the Act and the common law of negligence were relied upon, the Court of Appeal expressly decided that the claim under the Act would succeed and the common law claim would fail[2]. Of seminal importance is the decision of Burton J in *A v National Blood Authority*[3], imposing liability for undetectable and unpreventable contamination of blood used in transfusions. In the course of a judgment notable for its comprehensive scholarly analysis of the field, Burton J said[4]:

> 'It is quite plain to me that ... the directive was intended to eliminate proof of fault or negligence. I am satisfied that this was not simply a legal consequence, but that it was also intended to make it easier for claimants to prove their case, such that not only would a consumer not have to prove that the producer did not take reasonable steps, or all reasonable steps, to comply with his duty of care, but also that the producer did not take all legitimately expectable steps either'.

¹ See especially J Stapleton 'Products Liability Reform – Real or Illusory?' (1986) 6 OJLS 392, who argued that the concept of 'defect' itself introduced the kind of cost-benefit considerations which underly negligence irrespective of specific defences such as 'state of the art'. Cf C Newdick 'The Future of Negligence in Product Liability' (1987) 104 LQR 288.
² See *Abouzaid v Mothercare (UK) Ltd* (2001) Times, 20 December, CA.
³ *[2001] 3 All ER 289*.
⁴ See above at para 57.

Part eight

Defences

Chapter 21

Assumption of risk

A Scope of the concept

Extinguishes claims

[21.01] A defendant who succeeds in establishing that the claimant assumed the risk will defeat the claim in its entirety. The concept therefore differs in its effect from that of contributory negligence[1]; which enables an award of damages to be reduced to reflect the claimant's failure to take care for his own safety without extinguishing the claim completely. In the older cases, and often still in more recent ones, assumption of risk is referred to using the Latin maxim *volenti non fir injuria*.

[1]   See below CHAPTER 22.

Knowledge not enough

[21.02] In *Morris v Murray*[1] Stocker LJ said:

'... in order to defeat an otherwise valid claim on the basis that the plaintiff was volens the defendant must establish that the plaintiff at the material time knew the nature and extent of the risk and voluntarily agreed to absolve the defendant from the consequences of it by consenting to the lack of reasonable care that might produce the risk. It is common ground and long established that knowledge of the risk is not sufficient but there must also be consent to bear the consequences of it.'[2]

Thus, merely taking a risk, with full knowledge of the hazards involved, will not in itself be enough to bring the maxim into effect so as to absolve the defendant from all liability.[3] There must also be evidence of some understanding, even if only tacit and falling short of an actual contract,[4] that the claimant was prepared to abandon any right of legal redress against the defendant. In extreme cases, however, the very deliberate taking of a known risk can, if the claimant had a free choice and was not constrained,[5] be enough to constitute the necessary evidence.[6]

[1]   *[1991] 2 QB 6* at 18, *[1990] 3 All ER 801* at 809, CA.
[2]   See also *Nettleship v Weston [1971] 2 QB 691* at 701, *[1971] 3 All ER 581* at 587, CA, *per* Lord Denning MR: 'Knowledge of the risk of injury is not enough. Nor is a willingness to take the risk of injury. Nothing will suffice short of an agreement to waive any claim for negligence. The plaintiff must agree, expressly or impliedly, to waive any claim for any injury that may befall him due to the lack of reasonable care by the defendant.'
[3]   Cf *per* Diplock LJ in *Wooldridge v Sumner [1963] 2 QB 43* at 69, *[1962] 2 All ER 978* at 990, CA.

4   'The defendant must prove on the balance of probabilities that the plaintiff did assent ... to exempt the defendant from liability for the negligence which caused this accident. There is no requirement for a contract': *per* Ackner J in *Bennett v Tugwell [1971] 2 QB 267* at 274, *[1971] 2 All ER 248* at 253. See also *ICI v Shatwell [1965] AC 656* at 681, *[1964] 2 All ER 999* at 1009, HL, *per* Lord Hodson.
5   Cf *Burnett v British Waterways Board [1973] 2 All ER 631, [1973] 1 WLR 700, CA.*
6   Cf *Arthur v Anker [1997] QB 564* at 572, *[1996] 3 All ER 783* at 788, CA (driver held to have consented to his parked car being wheel-clamped until he paid to have the clamp removed).

Rare example

[21.03] The decision of the Court of Appeal in *Morris v Murray*[1] provides a rare example. The plaintiff went for a joyride in a light aircraft piloted by the deceased after he and the deceased had engaged in a heavy drinking session, during which the latter consumed the equivalent of 17 whiskies. In a crash, caused by the pilot's inability properly to control the aircraft, he was killed and the plaintiff was seriously injured. An action by the plaintiff against the deceased's estate was, however, defeated by the defence of volenti. Sir George Waller said:[2]

> 'To fly with a pilot who has consumed a large quantity of alcohol is very dangerous indeed. In this case ... the plaintiff was taking a very active part in the arrangements. He drove to the airfield; he had flown twice before with Mr Murray; he helped to start the aircraft; he helped to fill it with petrol; and he had been drinking with the pilot all the afternoon. In my judgment, having engaged himself to take part from the beginning, he not only knew the risks but the only implication is that he agreed to take them.'

It is submitted that the decision in *Morris v Murray* was correct; but it is important that its exceptional nature is borne in mind to avoid blurring the distinction between the defence of assumption of risk on the one hand, and the concepts of contributory negligence and of supervening events breaking the chain of causation on the other.[3] Since a finding of contributory negligence enables a flexible apportionment technique to be applied as between claimant and defendant its application is preferable, in most cases, to that of the 'all or nothing' concept of assumption of risk.[4] Most academic opinion supports this view.[5] On balance, most of the modern case law also does so.[6]

1   *[1991] 2 QB 6, [1990] 3 All ER 801, CA.* Cf *Dann v Hamilton [1939] 1 KB 509, [1939] 1 All ER 59.*
2   *[1991] 2 QB 6* at 32, *[1990] 3 All ER 801* at 820.
3   See A Jaffey 'Volenti Non Fit Injuria' [1985] CLJ 87.
4   See *Owens v Brimmell [1977] QB 859, [1976] 3 All ER 765.*
5   See Jaffey [1985] CLJ 87; G Williams *Joint Torts and Contributory Negligence* (1951) p 308ff. For the contrary view see D Gordon 'Drunken Drivers and Willing Passengers' (1966) 82 LQR 62.
6   But cf the decision of the House of Lords in *Titchener v British Railways Board [1983] 3 All ER 770, [1983] 1 WLR 1427* where, however, *volenti* only represented a subordinate ground of decision and the question of the nature of the defence was not really addressed by the House.

Need for tacit agreement

[21.04] Support for the proposition that something in the nature of a tacit understanding is necessary, to support a contention that the claimant had assumed the risk, can also be found in the decision of the House of Lords in *ICI v Shatwelll,*[1] in which the contention succeeded. In this case two shot-firers in a quarry together decided quite deliberately to test an electrical shot-firing circuit in a manner which they knew to be dangerous and contrary to safety regulations. An explosion resulted in which both were injured. One of them subsequently attempted to recover damages from their employer for his injuries, claiming that the company was vicariously liable for the negligence of each of them in their disastrous joint enterprise. The House of Lords held that the maxim *volenti non fit injuria* would have prevented the men from suing each other, and that there was therefore no basis for the imposition of vicarious liability on their employer. Lord Pearce even invoked the concept of the implied term, from the law of contract, in support of the applicability of *volenti*, contending that both men would have ridiculed the idea that they would be able to sue each other if the 'officious bystander' had raised it before the accident.[2] Lord Hodson, similarly, stated that 'the maxim is based on agreement'.[3]

[1]   *[1965] AC 656, [1964] 2 All ER 999, HL.*
[2]   See *[1965] AC 656* at 688, *[1964] 2 All ER 999* at 1013.
[3]   *[1965] AC 656* at 681, *[1964] 2 All ER 999* at 1009.

Employer and employee

[21.05]   The decision in *ICI v Shatwell* was striking, not least because it applied the defence in the employer and employee situation; a context in which it had long been thought obsolete. But the special facts of the case made it unusually easy to imply the existence of an agreement not to sue.[1] The workmen had deliberately and consciously embarked together on the dangerous act which led to the disaster.

[1]   See P Atiyah 'Causation, Contributory Negligence and Volenti Non Fit Injuria' (1965) 43 Can Bar Rev 609 at 630–631.

Inferring agreements

[21.06]   It is difficult to infer an agreement in a situation where the claimant has suffered as the result of a continuing activity, carelessly carried out by the defendant across a period of time.[1]

[1]   See *Dann v Hamilton [1939] 1 KB 509, [1939] 1 All ER 59.* But cf *Morris v Murray [1991] 2 QB 6, [1990] 3 All ER 801, CA.*

Road Traffic Act 1988, s 149(2)

[21.07]   It did prove possible to make such an implication in a number of cases in which passengers in motor cars were confronted with explicit disclaimers of liability for accidents;[1] but these are no longer applicable in their own context, since such disclaimers were nullified by the legislation which made it compulsory for drivers to carry insurance against the risk of injury to passengers.[2] Regardless of whether assumption of risk is perceived as based on implied agreement or not, the effect of *section 149(2)* of the *Road Traffic Act 1988*, is to strike generally at the applicability of the defence in the context with which it deals, ie it is not confined to explicit disclaimers.[3] The words of the section –

'clearly mean that it is no longer open to the driver of a motor vehicle to say that the fact of his passenger travelling in a vehicle in circumstances in which for one reason or another it could be said that he had willingly accepted a risk of negligence on the driver's part relieves him of liability for such negligence'.[4]

[1]   See *Buckpitt v Oates [1968] 1 All ER 1145*; *Bennett v Tugwell [1971] 2 QB 267, [1971] 2 All ER 248.*
[2]   See the *Road Traffic Act 1988, ss 143* and *149(2).*

3   See *Pitts v Hunt [1991] 1 QB 24, [1990] 3 All ER 344, CA.* See also K Williams 'Defences for Drunken Drivers: Public Policy on the Roads and in the Air' (1991) 54 MLR 745.
4   *Per* Beldam LJ in *Pitts v Hunt [1991] 1 QB 24* at 48, *[1990] 3 All ER 344* at 356. See also, *per* Balcombe LJ (*[1991] 1 QB 24* at 51, *[1990] 3 All ER 344* at 359): ' … the effect of [the section] is to exclude any defence of volenti which might otherwise be available.'

Objective test

[21.08]   It is not necessary, in order to prove the existence of an 'agreement', to show that there was a complete meeting of minds between the parties in a subjective sense. In one of the motoring cases, *Bennett v Tugwell*,[1] Ackner J put it as follows: 'What is required is an objective approach. Legal inquiry into a person being *volens* is not into what he feels or inwardly consents to, but into what his conduct or words evidence that he is consenting to.' Nevertheless, given the difficulties which, even on this basis, defendants in most situations will have in proving the existence of an agreement, the number of cases in which assumption of risk can be successfully invoked is likely to be small.

1   *[1971] 2 QB 267* at 273, *[1971] 2 All ER 248* at 252.

B Relationship with the duty of care[1]

[21.09]   A question sometimes debated is whether assumption of risk is not really a 'defence' as such, but rather a denial that a duty of care was owed, or had been broken; the claimant having in the circumstances absolved the defendant from the need to take the usual precautions as far as he was concerned.[2] In fact the issue would appear to be semantic, since nothing of substance seems to turn on it,[3] even as far as pleading is concerned.[4]

1   See R Kidner 'The Variable Standard of Care, Contributory Negligence and Volenti' (1991) 11 LS 1.
2   For discussion of this issue, see A Jaffey 'Volenti Non Fit Injuria' [1985] CLJ 87 at 104–109.
3   See *Condon v Basi [1985] 2 All ER 453* at 454, *[1985] 1 WLR 866* at 868, *per* Sir John Donaldson MR: 'I do not think it makes the slightest difference.'
4   ' … it seems improbable that a court would refuse to allow a defendant who had clearly pleaded the maxim to raise the defence notwithstanding that he may have admitted negligence': P Atiyah 'Causation, Contributory Negligence and Volenti non Fit Injuria' (1965) 43 Can Bar Rev 609 at 628.

Specific defence

[21.10]   It is nevertheless submitted that clarity is likely to be better served by treating assumption of risk as a defence in its own right.[1] This approach is less likely to cause confusion in cases in which differing claimants are all adversely affected by the same act of the defendant; but some of them are unable to recover damages by virtue of their having earlier agreed with the defendant that they would not be able to do so. The concept of a defence seems more straightforward in these situations than the notion of differing duties, or standards, of care.[2]

1   Cf *per* Fox LJ in *Morris v Murray [1991] 2 QB 6* at 15, *[1990] 3 All ER 801* at 807: 'You may say that [a plaintiff] is volens, or that he has impliedly waived the right to claim or that the [defendant] is impliedly discharged from the normal duty of care. In general, I think that the volenti doctrine can apply to the tort of negligence.'

2   See *Nettleship v Weston [1971] 2 QB 691, [1971] 3 All ER 581, CA*. In *Cook v Cook (1986) 162 CLR 376* the High Court of Australia adopted the opposite approach and chose not to follow *Nettleship's* case: sed quaere. For criticism of *Cook v Cook* see S Todd 'The Reasonable Incompetent Driver' (1989) 105 LQR 24.

Duty questions

[21.11]   Conversely, in situations where questions about the nature of the duty, and standard, of care are properly to be regarded as the central issue, analysis in terms of assumption of risk may be unhelpful and misleading. Thus, in situations in which participants, or spectators, have been injured at sporting events, what will sometimes be called for is an attempt to fashion criteria enabling conduct and behaviour in these rather special circumstances to be appropriately evaluated.[1] The question-begging dismissal of claims on the basis of assumption of risk is hardly likely to be conducive to this.[2]

1   See *Condon v Basi [1985] 2 All ER 453, [1985] 1 WLR 866, CA; Wooldridge v Sumner [1963] 2 QB 43, [1962] 2 All ER 978, CA*. See also *Rootes v Shelton [1968] ALR 33*.
2   Cf *Simms v Leigh Rugby Football Club [1969] 2 All ER 923; Murray v Harringay Arena Ltd [1951] 2 KB 529, [1951] 2 All ER 320n, CA*.

Not available where inconsistent with the duty

[22.12]   Assumption of risk cannot be invoked if the act relied upon in support of it is the very act which the defendant was under a duty of care to prevent. Thus, in *Reeves v Metropolitan Police Comr*[1] a majority of the Court of Appeal refused to allow the defence in respect of a prisoner, known to be a suicide risk, who took his own life while in the defendant's custody. The defendant's officers had been in breach of a duty to take reasonable care to prevent such an occurrence, and Lord Bingham CJ said:[2] 'If the defendant owed the deceased a duty of care despite the fact that the deceased was of sound mind, then it ... seems to me to empty that duty of meaningful content if any claim based on breach of that duty is inevitably defeated by a defence of volenti'.[3] When *Reeves'* case reached the House of Lords the Court of Appeal's rejection of the defence of assumption of risk was not challenged by the defendant, but Lord Hoffman, Lord Jauncey and Lord Hope did emphasise that they considered that the decision of the Court of Appeal had been correct on this point[4]. Lord Jauncey said[5] that 'if the defence were available in circumstances ... where a deceased was known to have suicidal tendencies it would effectively negative the effect of any duty of care in respect of such suicide'.

1   *[1998] 2 All ER 381, CA*, revsd in part in *[1999] 3 All ER 897, HL*.
2   See *[1998] 2 All ER 381* at 404.
3   See also *per* Buxton LJ in *[1998] 2 All ER 381* at 384–388. But cf *per* Morritt LJ, dissenting, in *[1998] 2 All ER 381* at 399–401.
4   See *[1999] 3 All ER 897, HL*. At 901 (Lord Hoffman), 909 (Lord Jauncey), 914 (Lord Hope). But cf *per* Lord Hobhouse dissenting at 918 et seq.
5   See above.

Chapter 22

Contribution and exclusion

A Scope of the chapter

[22.01] This chapter deals with contributory negligence and contribution between wrongdoers. The issue of apportionment makes for a degree of resemblance between these two topics. The third topic, which it is convenient to deal with alongside the first two, is that of exclusion of liability.

B Contributory negligence

Background

[22.02] The *Law Reform (Contributory Negligence) Act 1945, s 1(1)* provides:

> 'Where any person suffers damage as the result partly of his own fault and partly of the fault of any other person or persons, a claim in respect of that damage shall not be defeated by reason of the fault of the person suffering the damage, but the damages recoverable in respect thereof shall be reduced to such extent as the court thinks just and equitable having regard to the claimant's share in the responsibility for the damage.'

This provision replaced the old common law rule that contributory negligence was a complete defence. Prior to its abolition, that rule led to the development of an elaborate body of doctrine relating to causation; the objective of much of it being to circumvent the rule and enable plaintiffs to succeed, notwithstanding that they had themselves been careless. The possibility of apportionment introduced by the Act rendered the more far-fetched of these refinements obsolete. The court cannot raise the question of contributory negligence by its own motion: the defence has to be specifically pleaded.[1]

---

[1]   See *Fookes v Slaytor [1979] 1 All ER 137, [1978] 1 WLR 1293, CA.*

Failure on causal grounds

[22.03] It is nevertheless true that a claimant may still wholly fail, and do so on causal grounds, if the court is satisfied that antecedent carelessness by the defendant had lost all its causative potency by the time of the accident; so that the claimant was in reality the author of his own misfortune.[1] But in practice the availability of apportionment means that the court will normally lean against such a result except in extreme cases. However, in practice the same result has occasionally been reached indirectly by making a finding of 100% contributory negligence.[2] But whether such findings are legitimate has been the subject of conflicting decisions in the Court of Appeal. In *Jayes v IMI (Kynoch) Ltd*[3] Goff LJ considered that 'there is no principle of law which requires ... that there cannot be 100 per cent contributory negligence', but in the later case of *Pitts v Hunt*[4] Beldam LJ expressed a strong view to the opposite effect[5]. Most recently, in *Anderson v Newham College of Further Education*[6], the Court of Appeal subjected the reasoning in *Jayes'* case to penetrating analysis and concluded, in effect, that the decision had been made *per incuriam*. Sedley LJ expressed himself as follows[7]:

'In sum, *Jayes* should, in my respectful view, not be followed by judges of first instance and should not be relied upon by advocates in argument. The relevant principles are straightforward. Whether the claim is in negligence or for breach of statutory duty, if the evidence, once it has been appraised as the law requires, shows the entire fault to lie with the claimant there is no liability on the defendant. If not, then the court will consider to what extent, if any, the claimant's share in the responsibility for the damage makes it just and equitable to reduce the damages. The phrase "100 per cent contributory negligence", while expressive is unhelpful, because it invites the court to treat a statutory qualification of the measure of damages as if it were a secondary or surrogate approach to liability, which it is not. If there is liability, contributory negligence can reduce its monetary quantification, but it cannot legally or logically nullfy it'.

Although the conflicting Court of Appeal decisions mean that theoretically the matter awaits conclusive resolution by the House of Lords[8], it is submitted that the analysis of Sedley LJ is correct and that it has, in practice, put the question beyond doubt. A finding of 100 per cent contributory negligence would seem, in effect, either to be a finding that the defendant's negligence had lost all causative potency or that the defendant owed no duty of care[9]. It is submitted that it would be preferable for decisions to proceed on one of those substantive grounds as being more likely to focus the attention of the court on close scrutiny of the facts and the issues; than would the perhaps more casual dismissal of the claim on contributory negligence grounds.

1   See *McKew v Holland and Hannen and Cubitts (Scotland) Ltd [1969] 3 All ER 1621, HL*.
2   See *Jayes v IMI (Kynoch) Ltd [1985] ICR 155, CA*.
3   See above. See also *per* Morritt LJ, dissenting, in the Court of Appeal in *Reeves v Metropolitan Police Comr [1998] 2 All ER 381* at 402.
4   *[1991] 1 QB 24* at 48, *[1990] 3 All ER 344, CA*.
5   See *[1991] 1 QB 24* at 48, *[1990] 3 All ER 344* at 357. See also *per* Balcombe LJ in *[1991] 1 QB 24* at 51, *[1990] 3 All ER 344* at 359 and Dillon LJ *[1991] 1 QB 24* at 52, *[1990] 3 All ER 344* at 359.
6   *[2003] ICR 212*.
7   See *[2003] ICR 212* at para 1.18.
8   In the Court of Appeal in *Reeves v Metropolitan Police Comr [1998] 2 All ER 381* it was noted that the court in *Pitts v Hunt* had not been referred to *Jayes v IMI (Kynoch) Ltd*. The House of Lords did not express a view on the point in *Reeves'* case.
9   Cf *per* Lord Hoffman in *Reeves v Metropolitan Police Comr [1999] 3 All ER 897* at p 906, HL.

Intentional acts

[22.04] In *Reeves v Commissioner of Police of the Metropolis*[1] the House of Lords held that the fact that a claimant had acted intentionally did not preclude a finding of contributory negligence. In *Reeves'* case a prisoner committed suicide while in police custody. The House rejected the extreme views that an action for negligence against the police in respect of the death should either fail completely or succeed in full. Instead, the House apportioned responsibility equally between the deceased and the defendants, and awarded 50% of the value of the claim. 'It seems to me', said Lord Hope, 'that the definition of "fault" in s 4 is wide enough, when examined as a whole in its context, to extend to a plaintiff's deliberate acts as well as to his negligent acts'[2]. The position is not identical as far as the *defendant's* deliberate acts are concerned[3]: contributory negligence is not a defence to cases of fraudulent misrepresentation, for example, and fraudulent defendants therefore cannot invoke the apportionment provisions of the Act[4].

[1]   *[1999] 3 All ER 897.*
[2]   See *[1999] 3 All ER 897* at p 916. See also *per* Lord Jauncey at p 910.
[3]   See *Reeves v Commissioner of Police of the Metropolis [1999] 3 All ER 897* at 915 *per* Lord Hope. See also *Standard Chartered Bank v PNSC (No2) [2003] 1 All ER 173* at paras 11–12 *per* Lord Hoffman.
[4]   See *Standard Chartered Bank v PNSC (No2) [2003] 1 All ER 173.*

Not based on 'duty'

[22.05]   A defendant who alleges contributory negligence does not have to show that the claimant owed him a duty of care, in the sense in which that expression is used in the context of negligence as a cause of action. In *Froom v Butcher*[1] Lord Denning MR put it as follows:

> 'Negligence depends on a breach of duty, whereas contributory negligence does not. Negligence is a man's carelessness in breach of duty to *others*. Contributory negligence is a man's carelessness in looking after *his own* safety. He is guilty of *contributory* negligence if he ought reasonably to have foreseen that, if he did not act as a reasonable prudent man, he might hurt himself.'

[1]   *[1976] QB 286* at 291, *[1975] 3 All ER 520* at 524 (the emphasis is Lord Denning's).

Circumstances

[22.06]   Whether the claimant failed to take such care is to be judged in the light of all the circumstances. The court will, for example, be reluctant to hold contributorily negligent a claimant who is criticised merely for his actions in the heat of the moment, following an emergency created solely by the defendant's carelessness.[1] Similarly, although in clear cases people injured at their places of work may be held to have been contributorily negligent, the court will rarely be prepared to scrutinise in every last detail, in order to detect contributory negligence at the behest of a negligent employer, the conduct of conscientious employees.[2] In two cases it was even suggested that the phrase 'just and equitable' in section 1(1) of the 1945 Act enabled the court to refuse to make any reduction in the damages even where contributory negligence had been made out.[3] But in the subsequent case of *Boothman v British Northrop*[4] a unanimous Court of Appeal rejected this view. The special problems which can sometimes arise when making deductions for contributory negligence in actions brought against valuers by mortgage lenders were considered by the House of Lords in *Platform Home Loans v Oyston Shipways*[5]. This case is dealt with in another chapter[6].

[1]   Cf *British School of Motoring Ltd v Simms [1971] 1 All ER 317* at 320–321.
[2]   See *Machray v Stewarts and Lloyds [1964] 3 All ER 716*, *[1965] 1 WLR 602*. See also *Railways Comr v Halley (1978) 20 ALR 409 (Aust HC)*. Cf *Mullard v Ben Line Steamers Ltd [1971] 2 All ER 424*, *[1970] 1 WLR 1414, CA.*

3   See *Hawkins v Ian Ross (Castings) Ltd [1970] 1 All ER 180* at 188 (Fisher J) and *Stocker v Norprint Ltd (1970) 10 KIR 10* at 14, CA (Phillimore LJ).

4   (1972) 13 KIR 112: see especially *per* Stephenson LJ at 121–122. See also I Fagelson 'The Last Bastion of Fault? Contributory Negligence in Actions for Employers' Liability' (1979) 42 MLR 646 at 662–663.

5   *[1999] 1 All ER 833.*

6   See CHAPTER 9 above.

Causation and blameworthiness

[22.07] Lord Pearce, in a case decided by the House of Lords in 1967, said the following in relation to contributory negligence:[1]

' ... the investigation is concerned with "fault" which includes blameworthiness as well as causation. And no true apportionment can be reached unless both those factors are borne in mind.'[2]

Causation and blameworthiness are distinct, if sometimes interrelated,[3] concepts. A person may, for example, have been grossly careless and yet his carelessness may have been irrelevant, in the causal sense, to the injuries which he received. A hypothetical instance was given by Singleton LJ in *Jones v Livox Quarries:*[4]

' ... someone ... negligently and improperly sits upon an unsafe wall, and the driver of a motor-car not keeping a proper look-out runs into the wall and knocks it down; is the person sitting on the wall, who is injured, guilty of negligence which contributed to the accident? In those circumstances it might well be said he would not be ... '

Clearly, the need for the defendant to show that the claimant's conduct contributed causally to the accident is logically prior to consideration of the latter's blameworthiness. But causal arguments designed to show that the claimant's act had no causal potency at all, or alternatively that the claimant was the sole author of his own misfortune, will in practice now seldom find favour with the courts in borderline cases given the existence of the *Law Reform (Contributory Negligence) Act 1945*. In *Craven v Riches*[5] a participant seriously injured in a motorcycle event had his claim against the organisers dismissed at trial, essentially on the ground that the accident in which he had been injured had been his own fault. But the Court of Appeal reversed that decision and held that the organisers had been careless; damages were, however, only awarded to the extent of one-third of the claimant's loss, due to his substantial contributory negligence. Similarly, in two recent cases arising out of road traffic accidents which reached the Court of Appeal[6], that Court reversed trial judges who had held one of the parties wholly responsible; substituting findings of 50% contributory negligence in both cases.

1   *Miraflores (owners) v George Livanos (owners) [1967] 1 AC 826* at 845. Criticism of Lord Pearce's speech in this case on other grounds by Lord Ackner in *Fitzgerald v Lane [1989] AC 328* at 343–344, *[1988] 2 All ER 961* at 969 does not affect this point.

2   See also *Davies v Swan Motor Co (Swansea) Ltd [1949] 2 KB 291* at 326, *[1949] 1 All ER 620* at 632, CA, *per* Denning LJ. Cf The American Law Institute's *Restatement of the Law of Torts* (2nd edn) para 463: 'Contributory negligence is conduct on the part of the plaintiff which falls below the standard to which he should conform for his own protection, and which is a legally contributing cause co-operating with the negligence of the defendant in bringing about the plaintiff's harm.'

3   See H Hart and T Honoré *Causation in the Law* (2nd edn, 1985) p 234.

4   *[1952] 2 QB 608* at 612.

5   *[2002] PIQR P23.*

6   See *Hatton v Cooper [2001] RTR 544* and *Jenkins v Holt [1999] RTR 411.*

Complexity discouraged

[22.08] Broadly speaking, if causal arguments need to be at all complex or elaborate they will usually be out of place. In *Rouse v Squires*[1] the defendant negligently caused his lorry to jack-knife and block a motorway. Five to ten minutes later, and after several other vehicles had successfully navigated round the obstruction, a collision occurred when another vehicle came on to the scene at excessive speed and failed to stop in time. Despite strenuous attempts to persuade the Court of Appeal that the original jack-knifing had become causally irrelevant by the time of the collision, that court reversed the trial judge, before whom the attempts had been successful, and found the defendant 25% responsible for the accident.[2] If, however, the situation is broadly similar to that which occurred in *Rouse v Squires* except that the later driver who crashed into the wreckage of the earlier accident had actually been driving *recklessly*, and would have avoided causing the second collision if he had *merely* been negligent, then the later driver may be held solely responsible for the second collision.[3]

[1] *[1973] QB 889, [1973] 2 All ER 903, CA.*
[2] See also *March v E & M H Stramare Pty Ltd (1991) 171 CLR 506 (Aust HC).*
[3] See *Wright v Lodge and Shepherd [1993] 4 All ER 299, CA.* But cf the decision of the High Court of Australia in *March v E & M H Stramare Pty Ltd (1991) 171 CLR 506.*

Basis of apportionment

[22.09] In reaching their figures for apportionment in individual cases the courts rarely separate out causation from blameworthiness. The concepts are interwoven in the largely intuitive process which is involved. It has sometimes been contended by commentators that, once the initial causation requirement is satisfied, blameworthiness should be the only factor used to determine apportionment;[1] on the ground that attempts to evaluate in percentage terms the relative strengths of causal factors which had contributed to an accident would be both artificial and hopelessly complicated.[2] But the better view appears to be that it is possible, on a commonsense basis, coherently to assess degrees of causation.[3] In truth the extent to which causation or blameworthiness predominate in the judicial assessment will vary depending on the facts of each case. If several defendants are involved, for example, the insistence by the House of Lords on a rigid separation between the issues of the claimant's own contributory negligence on the one hand, and the apportionment of the damages as between the defendants themselves on the other,[4] could in practice increase the emphasis upon the claimant's blameworthiness in such cases. In less complicated situations, however, it is suggested that causation will often take pride of place where the activities of claimant and defendant are very similar, drivers of moving vehicles which collide on the road being the most obvious example. Assuming that both drivers have been careless (without which the question of contributory negligence obviously does not arise), an analysis of the accident in terms of causative potency will more often be fruitful than one which attempts precisely to categorise on a scale of iniquity the lack of driving skill shown by each party. This will certainly be true if, as in the majority of such cases[5], both drivers were guilty merely of momentary inattention.[6]

[1] See G Williams *Joint Torts and Contributory Negligence* (1951) para 98. Cf I Fagelson 'The Last Bastion of Fault?' (1979) 42 MLR 646.
[2] 'Causation Itself is Difficult Enough; Degrees of Causation Really Would be a Nightmare': S Chapman in (1948) 64 LQR 26 at 28. See also O Payne 'Reduction of Damages for Contributory Negligence' (1955) 18 MLR 344 at 353–354.

[3]   See H Hart and T Honoré *Causation in the Law* (2nd edn, 1985) p 233. See also N Gravells 'Three Heads of Contributory Negligence' (1977) 93 LQR 581 at 595–596.
[4]   See *Fitzgerald v Lane [1989] AC 328, [1988] 2 All ER 961, HL*, discussed below at para [22.11].
[5]   See *Jenkins v Holt [1999] RTR 411, CA*.
[6]   Clearly, if one of them were drunk, for example, the position would be different.

Differing roles

[22.10]   On the other hand, blameworthiness is more likely to prove appropriate as the major factor in situations where the activities carried on by claimant and defendant were markedly different in nature[1]. In *Brannan v Airtours plc*[2] the claimant consumed considerable quantities of alcohol at a party organised by the defendant travel company. He suffered injury when struck by a low electric fan after climbing on to the table. The trial judge found that the defendants had been negligent with respect to the positioning of the table in relation to the fan, but held that the claimant had been 75% contributorily negligent. The Court of Appeal altered this apportionment, however, and reduced the deduction to 50%; this was to reflect the culpability of the defendants in exposing party-goers to a situation in which injury could be anticipated, as a result of the lack of inhibition likely in such circumstances. Another example of the significance of differing roles in this context is provided by the functions of employer and employee in a factory. The desirability of treating blameworthiness as the primary criterion in situations of that kind was once clearly expressed by Lord Pearce, who said:[3]

> 'A dangerous machine is unfenced and a workman gets his hand caught in it. So far as causation alone is concerned it may be fair to say that at least half the cause of the accident is the fact that the workman put his hand into the danger. But so far as "fault" (and therefore liability) is concerned the answer may be very different. Suppose that the workman was a normally careful person who, by a pardonable but foolish reaction, wanted to save an obstruction from blocking the machine and so put his hand within the danger area. Suppose further that the factory owner had known that the machine was dangerous and ought to be fenced, that he had been previously warned on several occasions but through dilatoriness or on the grounds of economy failed to rectify the fault and preferred to take a chance. In such a case the judge, weighing the fault of one party against the other, the deliberate negligence against the foolish reaction, would not assess the workman's fault at anything approaching the proportion which causation alone would indicate.'

[1]   Eg in collisions between pedestrians and motorists: see *Eagle v Chambers [2004] RTR 115*: 'It is rare indeed for a pedestrian to be found more responsible than a driver unless the pedestrian has suddenly moved into the path of an oncoming vehicle', *per* Hale LJ at para 16. Cf *Goddard v Greenwood [2003] RTR 10, CA*.
[2]   (1999) Times, February 1, CA.
[3]   See *Miraflores (owners) v George Livanos (owners) [1967] 1 AC 826 at 845, [1967] 1 All ER 672 at 678, HL*.

If there is more than one defendant

[22.11]   In *Fitzgerald v Lane*[1] the plaintiff was seriously injured when struck by two cars, while attempting to cross a pelican pedestrian crossing when the lights were red for pedestrians. The trial judge, having held that the plaintiff was equally to blame with the two motorists, proceeded to award the plaintiff two-thirds of his damages.

The Court of Appeal allowed an appeal against his decision, and the House of Lords confirmed the result reached by the Court of Appeal. The judge had confused the extent of the plaintiff's contribution to his own loss with the separate issue of the apportionment of the damages between the defendants. Given his finding that the plaintiff had been equally to blame with the motorists for the accident the judge should only have awarded the plaintiff one-half of his loss, and not two-thirds of it. Lord Ackner said:[2]

'Apportionment of liability in a case of contributory negligence between plaintiff and defendants must be kept separate from *apportionment of contribution between the defendants inter se*. Although the defendants are each liable to the plaintiff for the whole amount for which he has obtained judgment, the proportions in which, as between themselves, the defendants must meet the plaintiff's claim do not have any direct relationship to the extent to which the total damages have been reduced by the contributory negligence.'

The judge in the present case had erred in –

'allowing his judgment on the issue of contributory negligence to be coloured by his decision as to the proper apportionment of blame between the defendants. While stating in substance on the one hand that the plaintiff's responsibility was no more and no less than that of either of the defendants, his ultimate conclusion, as mirrored in his order, was that each of the defendants was twice as much to blame as the plaintiff. This could not be right on the facts.'[3]

In effect, therefore:

'where the plaintiff successfully sues more than one defendant for damages for personal injuries and there is a claim between co-defendants for contribution, there are two distinct and different stages in the decision-making process, the one in the main action and the other in the contribution proceedings.'[4]

[1]   *[1989] AC 328, [1988] 2 All ER 961, HL*; affg (on other grounds) *[1987] QB 781, [1987] 2 All ER 455, CA.*
[2]   *[1989] AC 328* at 339, *[1988] 2 All ER 961* at 965 (emphasis in original).
[3]   *[1989] AC 328* at 341, *[1988] 2 All ER 961* at 966, *per* Lord Ackner.
[4]   *[1989] AC 328* at 341, *[1988] 2 All ER 961* at 966, *per* Lord Ackner.

Where the claimant contributes to the severity of his damage

[22.12]   In certain circumstances the damages awarded to a claimant may be reduced for contributory negligence even though his carelessness did not contribute to the causing of the accident itself, which would have occurred anyway. The situations in which some reduction will nevertheless be made include those in which the claimant's failure to take reasonable safety precautions had the effect of causing him to suffer injuries in an accident from which he would otherwise have escaped without injury, or to suffer injuries more severe than he need have done. The most common instances are failure by motor-cyclists to wear crash-helmets, and failure by drivers and passengers in motor cars to wear seat-belts. After some initial judicial disagreement in the lower courts, it was established by the Court of Appeal, even before Parliament made the wearing of crash-helmets and seat-belts compulsory, that it was appropriate to reduce damages on the ground of failure in these respects. In *O'Connell v Jackson*[1] the Court of Appeal reduced by 15% the damages awarded to a motor cyclist who had suffered head injuries in an accident, caused solely by the defendant's negligence, which would have been less severe if he had worn a crash-helmet. In *Froom v Butcher*,[2] the Court of Appeal reduced by 20% the damages awarded to the driver of a motor-car in circumstances in which his injuries would have been less severe had he worn his seat-belt.

1   *[1972] 1 QB 270, [1971] 3 All ER 129, CA. Cf Hilder v Associated Portland Cement Manufacturers Ltd [1961] 3 All ER 709, [1961] 1 WLR 1434.*
2   *[1976] QB 286, [1975] 3 All ER 520, CA.*

Guidelines in seat-belt cases

[22.13]   The Court of Appeal in *Froom v Butcher* also took the opportunity to issue guidelines to promote uniformity in future decisions. Thus, if the injuries would have been prevented altogether if a seat-belt had been worn the reduction will be 25%. If the claimant would probably have suffered considerable injuries in any event, but their severity would have been reduced, the appropriate reduction will usually be in the region of 15%. In *J (A Child) v Wilkins*[1] the Court of Appeal applied *Froom v Butcher* to a case decided under the *Civil Liability (Contribution) Act 1977,* holding that a mother was 25% responsible for the injuries suffered by her two year old child in a road accident. The child had been sitting on her mother's knee, in the front seat of the car, restrained only by her mother's lap-belt, and might have avoided injury if carried in a proper child-seat. This case was decided twenty-three years after *Froom v Butcher,* and the Court of Appeal observed that the guidelines may be said to have stood the test of time in as much as there appeared to be no reported seat-belt case in the intervening years in which a deduction greater than 25% had been made[2].

1   *[2001] RTR 283.*
2   See above at para 15 *per* Keene LJ.

Special circumstances

[22.14]   In *Capps v Miller*[1] the Court of Appeal had to consider a case in which a motor-cyclist had been wearing his crash helmet but had carelessly omitted to secure it correctly so that, when he was involved in an accident, it came off before his head hit the ground. 'It seems to me', said Glidewell LJ, 'that in the altered circumstances where a crash helmet is worn but not properly fastened, the whole scale of reduction, because of the lesser blameworthiness, should to an extent be less'.[2] By a majority[3] the court reduced the damages by 10%. Exceptions may also be made to the general rule of deduction itself in special circumstances. Thus, as Lord Denning MR put it in *Froom v Butcher,* 'a man who is unduly fat or a woman who is pregnant may rightly be excused because, if there is an accident, the strap across the abdomen may do more harm than good.'[4] It should also be noted that claims by passengers that their drivers had been at fault in failing to encourage the wearing of seat-belts will rarely succeed.[5] '[A]dult passengers possessed of their faculties', observed Lord Denning MR in *Froom v Butcher,*[6] 'should not need telling what to do'. Of course, if the evidence shows that the wearing of a seat-belt would have made no difference at all, and that the same injuries would have occurred anyway, the defendant will not have made out a case of contributory negligence of the relevant type and no reduction at all will be made.[7]

1   *[1989] 2 All ER 333, [1989] 1 WLR 839, CA.*
2   *[1989] 2 All ER 333 at 343, [1989] 1 WLR 839 at 852.*
3   Ie Glidewell and May LJJ. Croom-Johnson LJ, dissenting, would have made a 15% reduction.

4   *[1976] QB 286 at 295, [1975] 3 All ER 520 at 527. See also MacKay v Borthwick (1982) SLT 265.*
5   See *Eastman v South West Thames Area Health Authority [1991] RTR 389, CA.*
6   *[1976] QB 286 at 296, [1975] 3 All ER 520 at 528.* See also *Madden v Quirk [1989] 1 WLR 702 at 708, per* Simon Brown J.
7   See *Owens v Brimmell [1977] QB 859, [1976] 3 All ER 765.*

General exposure to risk by the claimant

[22.15]   Another type of case in which a claimant may have his damages reduced for contributory negligence, despite his not having contributed in an immediate sense to the causing of the accident itself, occurs where he has knowingly placed himself in an avoidable situation of potential danger.[1] The most typical situation of this kind again involves passengers in motor vehicles.[2] In *Owens v Brimmell*[3] the plaintiff passenger accompanied the defendant driver on a visit to a series of public houses during which they each consumed at least eight pints of beer. The car subsequently hit a lamp-post due to the defendant's greatly impaired driving, and the plaintiff suffered serious injuries. Tasker Watkins J reduced the damages awarded by 20% for contributory negligence. Following a review of the relevant Commonwealth authorities, his Lordship set out the relevant principles as follows:[4]

> '... a passenger may be guilty of contributory negligence if he rides with the driver of a car whom he knows has consumed alcohol in such quantity as is likely to impair to a dangerous degree that driver's capacity to drive properly and safely. So, also, may a passenger be guilty of contributory negligence if he, knowing that he is going to be driven in a car by his companion later, accompanies him on a bout of drinking which has the effect, eventually, of robbing the passenger of clear thought and perception and diminishes the driver's capacity to drive properly and carefully.'

It is to be noted that, as the first part of the quotation makes clear, the principle can apply where the passenger himself, unlike the plaintiff in *Owens v Brimmell*, is in fact sober, and only the driver is drunk, as well as to situations in which both have been drinking. The principle has also been applied in a situation in which the plaintiff passenger knew that the vehicle in which she was travelling was mechanically defective. In *Dawrant v Nutt*[5] the plaintiff rode in the side-car attached to her husband's motor-cycle when she knew that the lights had failed. The damages for the injuries she received in an accident were reduced by 25% for contributory negligence.

1   For valuable discussion of this topic, and of contributory negligence generally, see N Gravells 'Three Heads of Contributory Negligence' (1977) 93 LQR 581.
2   For a different type of case, see *Slater v Clay Cross Co Ltd [1956] 2 QB 264, [1956] 2 All ER 625, CA.*
3   *[1977] QB 859, [1976] 3 All ER 765.* Cf *Morris v Murray [1991] 2 QB 6, [1990] 3 All ER 801, CA.* See also *Pitts v Hunt [1991] 1 QB 24, [1990] 3 All ER 344, CA.*
4   *[1977] QB 859 at 866–867, [1976] 3 All ER 765 at 771.*
5   *[1960] 3 All ER 681, [1961] 1 WLR 253* (Stable J).

Contributory negligence by children

[22.16]   In *Gough v Thorne*[1] Lord Denning MR said:

> 'A very young child cannot be guilty of contributory negligence. An older child may be; but it depends on the circumstances. A judge should only find a child guilty of contributory negligence if he or she is of such an age as reasonably to

be expected to take precautions for his or her own safety: and then he or she is only to be found guilty if blame should be attached to him or her.'

In the case from which this quotation is taken the Court of Appeal, reversing the trial judge, acquitted a thirteen and a half-year-old girl from contributory negligence for crossing a busy road in reliance on an indication from a lorry driver, who had waved her across in front of him and signalled following traffic to stop. The plaintiff was hit by an overtaking vehicle, being negligently driven by the defendant, which failed to stop in time. The court rejected as unreasonable the trial judge's view that the plaintiff had been contributorily negligent in relying wholly on the lorry driver's signal, and not making an independent check of her own that the following traffic had stopped. While such prudence and caution 'might reasonably be expected of a grown-up person with a fully developed road sense',[2] it was not to be expected of someone the plaintiff's age.

[1]   *[1966] 3 All ER 398* at 399, *[1966] 1 WLR 1387* at 1390.
[2]   *[1966] 3 All ER 398* at 399, *[1966] 1 WLR 1387* at 1391, *per* Lord Denning MR. See also *Jones v Lawrence [1969] 3 All ER 267.*

Age

[22.17]   Obviously, the older the child is the more ready the court is likely to be, depending upon the circumstances, to make a finding of contributory negligence. The Canadian Supreme Court upheld a finding that a 15-year-old-boy had been 20% contributorily negligent in an accident in a school gymnasium in which he had been seriously injured.[1] In a road accident case involving a sixteen and a half-year-old plaintiff the Court of Appeal, while holding that the trial judge had been wrong to equate the plaintiff with an adult and dismiss his claim altogether, nevertheless assessed damages on the basis of 75% contributory negligence.[2] Findings of contributory negligence towards the lower end of the age range are not unknown. In *Minter v D & H Contractors*[3] Tudor Evans J, emphasising that such cases depended purely on their own facts, held that a nine-year-old boy, who had suffered injuries while riding his bicycle, was contributorily negligent to the extent of 20%. No other vehicle had been involved in the accident, in which the child had ridden his bicycle into a pile of hardcore left on the road. And in one case a judge suggested, obiter, that had he not rejected the claim altogether he 'would have found a substantial percentage of contributory negligence' against an eight-year-old claimant who had been injured while sliding down the banisters at school[4]. In *Morales v Eccleston*[5] an 11-year-old boy was held by the Court of Appeal to have been 80% contributorily negligent when he ran into the road without looking while chasing a ball. In the light of this case it is of interest to note that the *Royal Commission on Civil Liability and Compensation for Personal Injury* (Pearson)[6] recommended that a statutory change in the law should be made. This would be in order to provide 'that the defence of contributory negligence should not be available in cases of motor vehicle injury where the plaintiff was, at the time of the injury, under the age of 12'. No action has been taken on this recommendation.

[1]   See *Myers v Peel County Board of Education (1981) 123 DLR (3d) 1.*
[2]   See *Foskett v Mistry [1984] RTR 1.*
[3]   (1983) Times, 30 June. See also *Speirs v Gorman [1966] NZLR 897.*
[4]   See *Gough v Upshire Primary School [2002] ELR 169* at para 25.
[5]   *[1991] RTR 151.*
[6]   Cmnd 7054–I, para 1077.

Fire

[22.18] The notorious fascination of fire to children has more than once engaged the courts in consideration of contributory negligence. In one case[1] a boy of nine told a deliberate lie to buy petrol, with which he subsequently caused serious burns to himself while playing 'Red Indians'. He was acquitted of all contributory negligence, by the Judicial Committee of the Privy Council, in a negligence action against the petrol station for having allowed him to have the petrol. The Board considered that the boy's behaviour was only such as could have been expected from a nine year old; but there is some indication in the judgment that a subjective test is appropriate in such cases. Their Lordships indicated that they might have taken a different view if it had been shown, which it had not, that the boy had been specially instructed by his parents about the dangers of petrol.[2] In the recent case of C *(A Child) v Imperial Design*[3] a thirteen-year-old boy was severely burned in an explosion which occurred when he deliberately set light to a drum containing chemical residues, which had been carelessly discarded outside the defendants' factory. On the question of apportionment, Hale LJ, in the Court of Appeal, said[4]:

> 'The question therefore is, has the claimant taken such care for his own safety as it is reasonable to expect of a 13-year-old child? In this case the answer is obviously that he has not. It cannot be the law that, because some 13-year-old boys are naughty or irresponsible, all such boys are absolved from a duty to take care for their own safety. The only question is, what is reasonable?'

The trial judge had assessed the claimant's responsibility at 75% but the Court of Appeal, despite its reluctance to interfere with apportionment decisions, considered this to be too severe in the circumstances, and reduced the deduction to 50%.

1 *Yachuk v Oliver Blais Co Ltd [1949] AC 386, [1949] 2 All ER 150, PC.*
2 See *[1949] AC 386* at 396, *per* Lord Du Parcq delivering the judgment of the Board ('A careful examination of the evidence has satisfied their Lordships that the boy had no knowledge of the peculiarly dangerous quality of gasoline').
3 *[2001] Env LR 33.*
4 See above at para 39.

Contributory negligence and contract[1]

[22.19] The decision of the Court of Appeal in *Forsikringsaktieselskapet Vesta v Butcher*[2] removed much of the uncertainty which had earlier surrounded the question of whether a defendant sued for breach of contract could seek apportionment under the provisions of the *Law Reform (Contributory Negligence) Act 1945*. Prior to the *Butcher* case, differing approaches to the problem had been adopted. Some judges of first instance considered that the Act could apply to contract cases,[3] a view which had academic support.[4] Other judges took the opposite view.[5] But the need to consider various *types* of contract claim, as well as the statutory wording itself, militated against the emergence of a general solution.[6] Indeed, in a previous case the Court of Appeal treated the question as an open one,[7] notwithstanding that in an earlier decision, albeit one in which the point had not really been argued, that court had itself actually applied the Act in a contractual context.[8] But it can now be taken as settled, as a result of the *Butcher* case, that if the defendant's liability in contract depended on his having failed to take reasonable care, and that failure also constituted negligence actionable as such in tort, then the Act will apply and apportionment can be sought.[9] This result appears to be sensible. A rigid demarcation between tort and contract would seem mechanistic and outdated today, not least in the expanding field of professional negligence where allegations, amounting in substance to claims that defendants failed to take reasonable care, are often advanced in a contractual context. Thus, in *Gran Gelato Ltd v Richcliff (Group) Ltd*[10] Sir Donald Nicholls V-C held that the *Law Reform (Contributory Negligence) Act 1945* and its apportionment provisions apply to a claim under *section 2(1)* of the *Misrepresentation Act 1967*, which is predicated upon the misrepresentor's failure to show that he took reasonable care.[11]

[1] See the Law Commission Report *Contributory Negligence in Contract Law* (Law Com no 219, 1993).
[2] *[1989] AC 852, [1988] 2 All ER 43, CA*; affg *[1986] 2 All ER 488* (Hobhouse J).
[3] See *Quinn v Burch Bros (Builders) Ltd [1966] 2 QB 370, [1965] 3 All ER 283* (Paull J) and *De Meza and Stuart v Apple, van Straten, Shena and Stone [1974] 1 Lloyd's Rep 508* (Brabin J).
[4] See G Williams *Joint Torts and Contributory Negligence* (1951) pp 328–329. Cf J Swanton 'Contributory Negligence as a Defence to Actions for Breach of Contract' (1981) 55 ALJ 278.
[5] See especially *AB Marintrans v Comet Shipping Co Ltd [1985] 3 All ER 442, [1985] 1 WLR 1270* (Neill LJ sitting as a judge of first instance).
[6] See *Basildon District Council v J E Lesser (Properties) Ltd [1985] QB 839, [1985] 1 All ER 20; Rowe v Turner, Hopkins & Partners [1980] 2 NZLR 550; James Pty Ltd v Duncan [1970] VR 705.*
[7] See *De Meza v Apple [1975] 1 Lloyd's Rep 498, CA.*
[8] See *Sayers v Harlow UDC [1958] 2 All ER 342, [1958] 1 WLR 623, CA.*
[9] See *Barclays Bank v Fairclough Building (No 2) [1995] IRLR 605, CA; UCB Bank v Hepherd Winstanley & Pugh [1999] Lloyd's Rep PN 963, CA.* But cf the different view taken by a majority of the High Court of Australia in *Astley v Austrust [1999] Lloyd's Rep PN 758.*
[10] *[1992] Ch 650, [1992] 1 All ER 865.*
[11] For comment, see P Cane 'Negligent Solicitor Escapes Liability' (1992) 108 LQR 539 at 544.

Where the liability is strict

[22.20] If, however, the liability in contract is *strict*, so that negligence is *not* a prerequisite, it is equally clear that the 1945 Act will be inapplicable. This was confirmed by the Court of Appeal in *Barclays Bank plc v Fairclough Building Ltd*,[1] in which the court also emphasised that a defendant in such a case cannot seek to make the Act relevant by arguing that he had not merely been in breach of his strict contractual duty but also negligent as well![2]

[1] *[1995] QB 214, [1995] 1 All ER 289, CA.* For other claims arising out of the same proceedings, but between different parties, see *Barclays Bank v Fairclough Building (No 2) [1995] IRLR 605, CA.*
[2] See especially *per* Simon Brown LJ in *[1995] 1 All ER 289* at 306: 'Are we to have trials at which the defendant calls an expert to implicate him in tortious liability, whilst the plaintiffs' expert seeks paradoxically to exonerate him? The answer to all these questions is surely No.'

Non-tortious carelessness

[22.21] Some uncertainty still remains with respect to an intermediate type of case, in which the contractual liability is fault-based but where the situation would, for some reason or other, fall outside the scope of the tort of negligence itself. The balance of existing authority is probably against applicability in such circumstances. But except in situations involving the non-recoverability of pure economic loss,[1] the expansion of the tort in recent times combined with confirmation of the possibility of concurrent liability in contract and tort,[2] is likely to render the size of the intermediate category relatively small.

[1] See CHAPTER 5 above.
[2] See *Henderson v Merrett Syndicates Ltd [1995] 2 AC 145, [1994] 3 All ER 506, HL.* See also *Holt v Payne Skillington [1996] PNLR 179, CA.* The defence of contributory negligence was upheld in a situation involving concurrent liability in *Barclays Bank v Fairclough Building (No 2) [1995] IRLR 605, CA.*

C Contribution between wrongdoers

Where more than one is liable

[22.22] Situations sometimes arise in which more than one person is liable to the claimant for the loss which he has suffered[1]. Special rules exist to govern the liability of such persons among themselves. In former times it was sometimes important to distinguish 'joint' tortfeasors, strictly so-called, from 'concurrent' (or 'several') tortfeasors. The former inflicted damage on the claimant in pursuit of a common design, co-conspirators for example, whereas the latter acted separately even though the combined effect of their actions was to inflict on the claimant the loss of which he complained.[2] It will be apparent that in negligence cases the latter type of situation is much more common than the former, such as where a passenger is injured in a collision between two careless motorists. In cases of vicarious liability, however, employer and employee are regarded as joint tortfeasors. But although this distinction between joint and concurrent tortfeasors had certain consequences at common law,[3] these have largely ceased, mainly through statutory intervention, to be of practical significance in negligence cases. In *either* type of situation, every individual tortfeasor is potentially liable in full to the claimant for the loss incurred, and they can also all be joined in one action. The statutory rules now to be considered provide for the recovery of contribution towards that liability as between the persons responsible for infliction of the loss.

1   See *Fitzgerald v Lane [1989] AC 328, [1988] 2 All ER 961, HL*, discussed above at para [22.11].
2   Clearly, if the loss inflicted by one defendant is itself separate from that inflicted by another, the tortfeasors will be neither joint nor several and each one will simply be liable for the loss which he inflicted: see *Performance Cars Ltd v Abraham [1962] 1 QB 33, [1961] 3 All ER 413, CA.*
3   For a concise account see *Winfield on Tort* (16th edn, 2002) pp 738–740.

When contribution can be claimed

[22.23] The *Civil Liability (Contribution) Act 1978* now governs the circumstances in which a defendant who is liable to a claimant, whether in negligence or otherwise, can recover contribution from someone else whom he claims is also responsible for the loss which the claimant has suffered. The statute law on this subject was previously to be found in the *Law Reform (Married Women and Tortfeasors) Act 1935, s 6*, which originally abrogated the old common law rule whereby contribution between tortfeasors was, in general, forbidden on the ground that a person should not be able to make a cause of action out of his own wrong. The 1978 Act, which followed an investigation of the subject by the Law Commission,[1] replaced the 1935 Act in this regard; and also significantly increased the scope of the relevant provisions. The most important change is that contribution can now be sought from someone else who is responsible for the same damage even though the legal basis of that other person's liability is different.[2] The 1935 Act only provided that tortfeasors could claim contribution from other tortfeasors, but it can now be sought as between, eg a tortfeasor and someone liable to the claimant in contract.[3] A right to contribution which would otherwise have existed may, however, be precluded by the terms of the contractual arrangements to which the various parties had committed themselves.[4]

1   See Law Commission Report no 79 (1977).
2   The 1978 Act has no retrospective effect: see *section 7(2)*. This section fell to be construed by the Court of Appeal in *Lampitt v Poole Borough Council [1991] 2 QB 545, [1990] 2 All ER 887*, where the court was able to reject an ingenious argument that it had inadvertently had a further and unintended consequence of *removing* rights to contribution which would otherwise have existed.

³ See *sections 1(1)* and *6(1)* of the 1978 Act. See also *Friends' Provident Life Office v Hillier Parker May & Rowden (a firm) (Estates and General plc, third parties) [1997] QB 85, [1995] 4 All ER 260, CA* (restitution).
⁴ See *Cooperative Retail Services v Taylor Young [2002] 1 WLR 1419.*

'Same damage'

[22.24] Under the 1978 Act the person claiming contribution, and the person from whom contribution is claimed, must still be liable in respect of 'the same damage'[1] to the same person: it is not enough that the liabilities of the various parties arose out of the same general incident.[2] The meaning of this phrase was considered by the House of Lords in *Royal Brompton Hospital NHS Trust v Hammond*[3], in which an architect unsuccessfully attempted to seek contribution from a contractor towards his liability to their employer. The attempt failed because the harm caused by the contractor had been *delay*, whereas the architect had caused *prejudice* to the employer's position under the contract by wrongfully issuing certificates[4]. They were therefore not liable in respect of 'the same damage'. Counsel for the architect had contended that the statutory phrase should be given a broad interpretation. Lord Steyn responded to this submission as follows[5]:

> 'The legislative technique of limiting the contribution principle under the 1978 Act to the same damage was a considered policy decision. The context does not therefore justify an expansive interpretation of the words "the same damage" so as to mean substantially or materially similar damage. Such solutions could have been adopted but considerations of unfairness to parties who did not in truth cause or contribute to the same damage would have militated against them. Moreover, the adoption of such solutions would have led to uncertainty in the application of the law. That is the context of s1(1) and the phrase "the same damage". It must be interpreted and applied on a correct evaluation and comparison of claims alleged to qualify for contribution under s1(1). No glosses, extensive or restrictive, are warranted. The natural and ordinary meaning of "the *same* damage" is controlling'.

The House approved, and applied by analogy, a Canadian case decided under similar legislation in which a lawyer, sued by a motor-accident victim for negligently allowing her claim to become time-barred, was not permitted to seek contribution from the negligent motorist in the original accident[6]. Nevertheless, a personal injury action against one defendant by the deceased before his death, and a subsequent Fatal Accidents Act claim against a different defendant, are in respect of 'the same damage' for the purpose of the Act.[7]

¹ See *section 1(1)* of the 1978 Act.
² See *Birse Construction Ltd v Haiste Ltd (Watson, third parties) [1996] 2 All ER 1, [1996] 1 WLR 675, CA* in which a claim to contribution failed even though it shared a common factual background with the original claim (construction of a defective reservoir).
³ *[2002] 2 All ER 801.*
⁴ See above at para 48 *per* Lord Hope.
⁵ See *[2002] 2 All ER 801* at para 27.
⁶ See *Wallace v Litwiniuk (2001) 92 Alta LR (3d) 249 (Alta CA).*
⁷ See *Jameson v Central Electricity Generating Board (Babcock Energy Ltd, third party) [1998] QB 323, [1997] 4 All ER 38, CA* (revsd on other grounds *[1999] 1 All ER 193, HL*).

Removal of bar to recovery

[22.25] In addition to providing for contribution between tortfeasors and others liable to the claimant but on a different basis, the 1978 Act also makes of general application the removal of the old common law doctrine whereby even an unsatisfied judgment was a bar to recovery against another person jointly liable for the same loss. This change was originally made by the 1935 Act itself, but confined to situations involving joint tortfeasors, In thus broadening the scope of the abrogation of that harsh rule, the new Act also took the opportunity to make clear that the removal of the bar extended to situations in which judgment is obtained against one of a number of defendants sued in a single action, as well as to those in which the claimant brought successive actions:[1] a point which the wording of the 1935 Act had left somewhat unclear.[2]

1   'Judgment recovered against any person liable in respect of any debt or damage shall not be a bar to an action, or to the continuance of an action, against any other person who is (apart from any such bar) jointly liable with him in respect of the same debt or damage': *section 3*.
2   Cf *Bryanston Finance v de Vries [1975] QB 703* at 722, *[1975] 2 All ER 609* at 618, *per* Lord Denning MR; *Wah Tat Bank v Chan Cheng Kum [1975] AC 507, [1975] 2 All ER 257*, PC.

Release by claimant

[22.26] On the other hand, if the claimant actually reaches an agreement with one joint tortfeasor, and that agreement is construed as a 'release' of the claimant's cause of action as distinct from a mere covenant not to sue the particular defendant, then the common law rule that such an agreement releases all the tortfeasors jointly liable remains intact, and is unaffected by the Act. The Law Commission decided against recommending the abolition of this rule, even though the technical distinction to which it gives rise, between releases[1] and covenants not to sue,[2] can lead to decisions being reached which turn on fine points of construction, and which may have unintended consequences.[3] Since, however, a release of one 'concurrent', as distinct from 'joint', tortfeasor does not, even at common law, release the other concurrent tortfeasors,[4] the point will rarely be material in negligence cases apart from those involving vicarious liability.[5]

1   See *Cutler v McPhail [1962] 2 QB 292*.
2   See *Jameson v Central Electricity Generating Board (Babcock Energy Ltd, third party) [1998] QB 323* at 336, *[1997] 4 All ER 38* at 47, CA, *per* Auld LJ: 'Because of the hardship that the rule can cause, the inclination of the courts has been to confine it narrowly.' See *Gardiner v Moore [1969] 1 QB 55, [1966] 1 All ER 365*.
3   See Law Commission Report no 79 (1977), paras 42–43. See also D Morgan 'Civil Liability (Contribution) Act 1978' (1978) NLJ 1042.
4   See *Jameson v Central Electricity Generating Board (Babcock Energy Ltd, third party) [1998] QB 323, [1997] 4 All ER 38*, CA (revsd on other grounds [1999] 1 All ER 193, HL). The reason for this is that there is a separate cause of action against each 'concurrent' tortfeasor, but only one cause of action against joint tortfeasors.
5   Full 'satisfaction' of the claimant's claim will, however, necessarily prevent the claimant from claiming against other tortfeasors, since he cannot recover more than his total loss. Moreover, a negotiated settlement will constitute 'satisfaction' for this purpose (unless its express terms are clearly to the contrary) even if it was for a lesser sum than might have been obtained if the matter had been successfully pursued to judgment: see *Jameson v Central Electricity Generating Board (Babcock Energy Ltd, third party) [1999] 1 All ER 193, HL*; reversing *[1998] QB 323, [1997] 4 All ER 38, CA*.

Where claim is compromised

[22.27] If the claimant's claim against one concurrent tortfeasor is compromised this *may* have the effect of preventing the claimant from proceeding against the other tortfeasors. It will only do so, however, if the compromise agreement was entered into on the basis that it constituted full satisfaction of the claimant's whole claim. In

Jameson v Central Electricity Generating Board (Babcock Energy Ltd, third party)[1] a majority of the House of Lords, reversing a unanimous Court of Appeal and the trial judge, held that a negotiated settlement which clearly represented less than the claimant's total loss had had that effect. Before his death the deceased had settled a claim in respect of his mesothelioma against one defendant, and this was held to preclude his executors from subsequently pursuing a Fatal Accidents Act claim on behalf of his widow against another defendant who was also responsible for causing the deceased's illness. This case was apparently considered in some quarters to have laid down a rule to the effect that full and final settlement of his claim against one tortfeasor would automatically prevent any claim against another tortfeasor, if that claim overlapped the claim which had been settled. In the later case of *Heaton v Axa Equity and Law Life Assurance Society1*[2], however, the House of Lords held that *Jameson's* case had *not* had such a draconian effect; it was to be interpreted merely as a decision on its own facts. In *Heaton's* case Lord Mackay of Clashfern, in relation to *Jameson*, said:

> 'I read the majority decision as authority for the proposition that where an action is founded on specified damage suffered by the claimant and the existence of that damage is essential to the success of the action, if the claimant has entered into an agreement under which he accepts a sum as full compensation for that damage, the action cannot proceed. *Whether a particular agreement has that effect is a question of construction of the words, in the light of all the relevant facts surrounding it*'[3].

Moreover, the absence of any express reservation of his right to sue other tortfeasors will not be fatal to the claimant since it is unnecessary for him to reserve a right to do that which he is, in the words of Lord Bingham, 'in the ordinary way fully entitled to do without any such reservation'[4].

[1]   *[1999] 1 All ER 193.*
[2]   *[2002] 2 All ER 961.* See also *Cape & Dalgleish v Fitzgerald [2002] UKHL 16, [2002] All ER (D) 231 (Apr).*
[3]   See *[2002] 2 All ER 961* at para 41. Italics supplied.
[4]   See *[2002] 2 All ER 961* at para 9. See also *per* Lord Rodger at para 81.

Claim for contribution against a defendant no longer liable to the claimant

[22.28]   *Section 1(3)* of the 1978 Act provides that a wrongdoer who has ceased to be liable to the claimant himself, eg because of the expiry of the limitation period[1] or dismissal of an action for want of prosecution,[2] can nevertheless be called upon to make contribution by another wrongdoer who is actually liable to the claimant.[3] The other wrongdoer's claim for contribution will only fail in such circumstances if that claim is itself barred by limitation.[4] It follows that a defendant who has previously reached a settlement (but not a 'release'[5]) with the claimant whereby the latter promised not to sue him, may nevertheless be called upon to make contribution by another defendant against whom the claimant *has* proceeded.[6]

[1]   Cf *George Wimpey & Co Ltd v BOAC [1955] AC 169, [1954] 3 All ER 661, HL; Nottingham Health Authority v Nottingham City Council [1988] 1 WLR 903, CA.*
[2]   Cf *Hart v Hall and Pickles Ltd [1969] 1 QB 405, [1968] 3 All ER 291, CA.*
[3]   'A person shall be liable to make contribution ... notwithstanding that he has ceased to be liable in respect of the damage in question since the time when the damage occurred ... ' On the interpretation of this provision see *Cooperative Retail Services v Taylor Young [2002] 1 WLR 1419* at paras 52–60 *per* Lord Hope.
[4]   The relevant period is two years: see the *Limitation Act, 1980, s 10.*

5   See para [22.26] above.
6   See *Jameson v Central Electricity Generating Board (Babcock Energy Ltd, third party) [1998] QB 323, [1997] 4 All ER 38, CA* revsd on other grounds *[1999] 1 All ER 193*, HL. See also *Logan v Uttlesford District Council [1986] NLJ Rep 541, CA*. Of course if the settlement had constituted full 'satisfaction' of the claimant's claim the point will not arise: see para [22.26] above.

Claim for contribution by a defendant who has settled

[22.29]   *Section 1(4)* of the 1978 Act provides as follows:

'A person who has made or agreed to make any payment in bona fide settlement or compromise of any claim made against him in respect of any damage (including a payment into court which has been accepted) shall be entitled to recover contribution … without regard to whether or not he himself is or ever was liable in respect of the damage, provided, however, that he would have been liable assuming that the factual basis of the claim against him could be established.'

This subsection encourages settlements by making it unnecessary for one defendant to fight a claim against him to the finish in order to ensure that his rights to contribution against other wrongdoers are not prejudiced. The position as between joint tortfeasors before the passing of the 1978 Act was that a defendant who had compromised the plaintiff's claim could seek contribution from another party, but would fail in his attempt unless he was able, in the contribution proceedings, to achieve the paradoxical task of proving that he had indeed himself been a tortfeasor who could have been sued to judgment.[1] Such proof is no longer required. The reference in the subsection to the need for the settlement to be bona fide should, however, be noted. Collusive or fraudulent agreements between claimant and defendant, whereby the latter deliberately settles the claim for more than it is worth in the hope of passing on a major share of the burden to someone else, will obviously not be effective for contribution purposes.[2]

[1]   See *Stott v West Yorkshire Road Car Ltd [1971] 2 QB 651, [1971] 3 All ER 534, CA*.
[2]   Cf *Corvi v Ellis (1969) SLT 350*.

Conclusiveness of judgments

[22.30]   If the claimant himself had earlier brought an action against the defendant from whom contribution is subsequently sought by another party, and that action had proceeded to judgment, then the judgment thus given will be conclusive on any question determined by it in favour of the defendant. Thus, someone who has, for example, been acquitted of negligence after trial on the merits cannot be subjected to having that finding reopened in contribution proceedings. This is achieved by *section 1(5)* of the 1978 Act, which provides as follows:

'A judgment given in any action brought in any part of the United Kingdom by or on behalf of the person who suffered the damage in question against any person from whom contribution is sought … shall be conclusive in the proceedings for contribution as to any issue determined by that judgment in favour of the person from whom the contribution is sought.'

Procedural dismissal

[22.31] If the 'judgment' is merely a dismissal on procedural grounds, *subsection (5)* will presumably not apply and *section 1(3)*, which preserves rights to contribution, will apply instead. It has been suggested,[1] however, that this is far from self-evident and that there could in fact be a conflict between *subsections (3)* and *(5)*, particularly with respect to limitation. The wide words 'any issue' in the latter subsection could, taken literally, prevent a defendant who secured dismissal of the claimant's claim against him on the ground that it was statute-barred, from being held liable in contribution proceedings. Whereas *subsection (3)* provides, as explained above, that limitation as against the claimant, at any rate where no actual judgment was involved, should not be a bar in such proceedings. But the solution is probably that *subsection (5)* should be read subject to *subsection (3)*, so that a judgment based solely on limitation will not constitute determination of an issue within *subsection (5)*.

[1] See *Clerk and Lindsell on Torts* (18th edn, 2000) pp 209–210.

Abolition of the 'sanction in damages'

[22.32] Under the provisions of the 1935 Act, a plaintiff who chose to bring more than one action in respect of the damage he had suffered (for example because not all the tortfeasors had been traced when he first commenced proceedings so that it was not possible to sue them together) was unable to recover by execution a higher sum than the damages awarded in the first action, even though the amounts actually awarded in the subsequent actions might have been higher. This 'sanction in damages' reflected a fear that multiplicity of proceedings might otherwise be encouraged, particularly at a time when juries normally assessed damages in civil actions so that plaintiffs might have been encouraged to 'shop around' for higher awards. But the rule could operate unfairly if, for example, the first defendant to be sued enjoyed some special limitation on his liability which those sued later did not. The Law Commission concluded that this sanction is no longer appropriate in modern circumstances, and it was accordingly abolished by the 1978 Act.[1]

[1] This is the effect of the wording of *section 4*, quoted below in para [22.33], being narrower than the wording of the equivalent provision in the 1935 Act which it replaced.

Sanction in costs

[22.33] The 1978 Act does retain a 'sanction in costs', which was also included in the 1935 Act. The Law Commission considered that this was an adequate deterrent against the avoidable bringing of a series of actions. *Section 4* accordingly provides as follows:

> 'If more than one action is brought in respect of any damage by or on behalf of the person by whom it was suffered against persons liable in respect of the damage (whether jointly or otherwise) the plaintiff shall not be entitled to costs in any of those actions, other than that in which judgment is first given, unless the court is of the opinion that there was reasonable ground for bringing the action.'

It should be noted that the abolition of the 'sanction in damages' obviously 'does not ... mean that the plaintiff should be allowed to enforce judgments twice over for the same damages but simply that the amount for which one defendant may be adjudged liable should not set a limit on the sum for which judgment may be enforced against another'.[1]

[1] Law Commission Report no 79 (1977), para 41.

Assessment of contribution

[22.34] *Subsections (1)* and *(2)* of *section 2* of the 1978 Act in substance reproduce an equivalent provision in the 1935 Act. *Subsection (1)* provides that the amount recoverable in contribution proceedings 'shall be such as may be found by the court to be just and equitable having regard to the extent of that person's responsibility for the damage in question'. *Subsection (2)* gives the court power 'to exempt any person from liability to make contribution, or to direct that the contribution to be recovered shall amount to a complete indemnity'.[1] The 'just and equitable' formula is, of course, the same as that used in the *Law Reform (Contributory Negligence) Act 1945.* The theoretical questions concerning the relationship between causation and blameworthiness, for the purposes of apportionment, are the same in both contexts.[2] At the practical level, however, the Law Commission felt able to conclude that the existing formula 'had given rise to no difficulties or injustices in contribution proceedings between tortfeasors'[3], and it was therefore retained in the new legislation. Persons whose liability is vicarious are liable to contribution on the same basis as the person for whom they are vicariously liable, their absence of personal fault does not affect their liability to contribution[4].

[1] See *Semtex Ltd v Gladstone [1954] 2 All ER 206, [1954] 1 WLR 945.* See also *Lister v Romford Ice and Cold Storage [1957] AC 555* at 579–80, *[1957] 1 All ER 125, HL, per* Lord Simonds.
[2] See *Madden v Quirk [1989] 1 WLR 702,* especially at 707 (Simon Brown J).
[3] Law Commission Report no 79 (1977) para 69. But cf T Hervey '"Responsibility" under the Civil Liability (Contribution) Act 1978' (1979) 129 NLJ 509 at 510: 'If the courts are presented with a case requiring an apportionment, they will respond by providing a set of percentages. But the process by which these percentages are achieved has never been adequately elucidated.'
[4] See *Dubai Aluminuim v Salaam [2003] 1 All ER 97.*

Where a contributor's liability to the claimant is limited

[22.35] Situations may arise in which some of those who have contributed to the claimant's damage enjoy a limitation on their liability to him which the other contributors do not.[1] For example, since the 1978 Act enables contribution to be sought as between tortfeasors and contract-breakers, the contract-breaker may point to some special clause in his contract which limits his liability to the claimant to a certain sum: and that sum may be less than he would otherwise be required, if the limiting clause were to be disregarded, to contribute on apportionment. Conversely, a defendant who was a contract-breaker could sometimes be at a *disadvantage* as against a defendant who was a tortfeasor. This would happen if the claimant himself had been contributorily negligent, but the defendant's contractual liability happened to be strict, in which event contributory negligence is probably not a defence.[2] The tortfeasor will then be able to rely on the contributory negligence to limit the extent of his liability to the claimant, but the contract-breaker will not.

[127] See Law Commission Report no 79 (1977) paras 70–79.
[128] See above.

The Act

[22.36] The 1978 Act does, indeed, provide that any such advantages which a defendant could rely on as against the claimant will also apply as between himself and the other contributors. A defendant cannot, therefore, be required to contribute on apportionment a greater sum than that for which he could have been held liable to the clamant directly. This may seem unfair to the other contributors, who will as a result shoulder a greater share of the overall burden of the liability to the claimant than they otherwise would have done. On the other hand, it might also have seemed unfair to deny in contribution proceedings the benefits of limitations on liability which otherwise existed; and the Act refuses to do so. *Section 2(3)* of the Act, which is a new provision, accordingly provides as follows:

'Where the amount of the damages which have or might have been awarded in respect of the damage in question in any action brought in England and Wales by or on behalf of the person who suffered it against the person from whom the contribution is sought was or would have been subject to—

(a)   any limit imposed by or under any enactment or by any agreement made before the damage occurred;

(b)   any reduction by virtue of section 1 of the Law Reform (Contributory Negligence) Act 1945 or section 5 of the Fatal Accidents Act 1976; or

(c)   any corresponding limit or reduction under the law of a country outside England and Wales;

the person from whom the contribution is sought shall not by virtue of any contribution awarded ... be required to pay in respect of the damage a greater amount than the amount of those damages as so limited or reduced.'

D Exclusion of liability

Exclusion by contract

[22.37] The freedom of contracting parties to limit their liability to each other in tort for negligence was, over the years, gradually restricted by legislative intervention in various fields. Widespread restrictions are now imposed by the *Unfair Contract Terms Act 1977*. The provisions of this Act severely limit the extent to which 'business' defendants can rely on exemption clauses in their contracts to exclude liability. Such defendants cannot exclude liability for 'death or personal injury resulting from negligence'[1] at all, and attempts by them to exclude liability for negligence in other cases are subject to a test of 'reasonableness'.[2] Of course, a claimant will not even need to rely on the provisions of the Act if the defendant is unable to show that the clause was incorporated into the contract at all;[3] or if the strict rules of construction applied to exemption clauses by the common law prevent the wording of the clause from being effective to exclude negligence liability in the first place.[4] Moreover, the common law learning on exemption clauses remains of general importance in cases which fall outside the terms of the Unfair Contract Terms Act because the defendant relying on the clause is not a 'business'.[5]

[1]   See *section 2(1)*.
[2]   See *sections 2(2)* and *11(1)*.
[3]   Cf *Olley v Marlborough Court Ltd [1949] 1 KB 532, [1949] 1 All ER 127, CA.*

⁴   See *White v John Warrick & Co Ltd [1953] 2 All ER 1021, [1953] 1 WLR 1285, CA.* Cf *Photo Production v Securicor Transport [1980] AC 827, [1980] 1 All ER 556, HL.*
⁵   See *sections 1* and *14.*

Non-contractual disclaimers

[**22.38**]   It is well established at common law that, in certain situations, a defendant can exclude his liability in tort for negligence by a mere notice or disclaimer to that effect, even though it does not form part of an actual contract. The best-known situations are those involving the liability for negligent misstatement established by *Hedley Byrne v Heller,*¹ and the liability of an occupier to his visitors.² No general principle underlying these instances, capable of application throughout the law of negligence, has ever been clearly enunciated. They do, however, possess a strong 'contractual flavour', even if the technical requirements such as offer and acceptance are not satisfied. Thus, if a defendant attempts gratuitously to assist the claimant by making a statement intended for the latter's benefit, or by permitting him to enter the defendant's property when he could be kept out, it is perhaps not unreasonable that the generosity should be accompanied by conditions limiting the defendant's liability for misfortune. Such situations represent an area on the borderline between contract and tort, in which the distinction between these two concepts is itself under strain.³ It is therefore submitted that a mere exclusion notice should not be effective to exclude liability for negligence unless the situation is, in fact, closely analogous to contract in that the disclaimer is accompanied by some benefit conferred upon the claimant which the latter has a choice whether or not to accept.⁴ To hold otherwise would be contrary to principle: the law of tort exists for the benefit of society in general, and it cannot be right to allow defendants of their own motion unilaterally to declare themselves independent of it.⁵

¹   [1964] AC 465, [1963] 2 All ER 575, HL. See also CHAPTER 4 above for further discussion of disclaimers in the context of negligent misstatement.
²   See CHAPTER 10 above.
³   Cf *Junior Books Ltd v Veitchi Co Ltd [1983] 1 AC 520, [1982] 3 All ER 201, HL* (especially *[1983] 1 AC 520* at 546, *[1982] 3 All ER 201* at 214, *per* Lord Roskill).
⁴   See *Wilkie v London Passenger Transport Board [1947] 1 All ER 258, CA.* Cf *Gore v Van der Lann [1967] 2 QB 31, [1967] 1 All ER 360, CA.*
⁵   Cf L C B Gower 'A Tortfeasor's Charter?' (1956) 19 MLR 532 and 'Tortfeasor's Charter Upheld' (1957) 20 MLR 181.

Disclaimers and privity of contract

[**22.39**]   The fact that issues involving disclaimers frequently arise in territory surrounding the border between tort and contract is also illustrated by two decisions of the Court of Appeal in which plaintiffs who had suffered damage, while engaged in activities arising out of their contractual relationships, sought unsuccessfully to sue in tort defendants who were not parties to the contracts in question. In *Norwich City Council v Harvey*¹ the Court of Appeal in effect permitted a defendant subcontractor, whose negligence had caused a fire, to invoke an exemption clause in the plaintiff's agreement with the main contractor which would have protected the latter if the damage had been caused by him. May LJ said² that the question had to be approached 'on the basis of what [was] just and reasonable' and he did 'not think that the mere fact that there [was] no strict privity between the employer and the sub-contractor should prevent the latter from relying on the clear basis on which all the parties contracted in relation to damage to the employer's building caused by fire, even when due to the negligence of the contractors or sub-contractors'.[3] Similarly, in *Pacific Associates v Baxter*[4] the question whether the defendant owed a duty of care to the plaintiff in a claim for negligent misstatement was said only to be answerable 'in the context of the factual matrix, including especially the contractual structure against which such duty [was] said to arise'.[5] The fact that that structure included a disclaimer intended to protect the defendant was one of the reasons which led the Court of Appeal to find in his favour, even though he was not himself a party to the contract.

[1] *[1989] 1 All ER 1180, [1989] 1 WLR 828, CA.*
[2] *[1989] 1 All ER 1180* at 1187, *[1989] 1 WLR 828* at 837.
[3] Cf *British Telecommunications plc v James Thomson [1999] 1 WLR 9, HL*, in which the House of Lords held in a not dissimilar factual situation from that in *Harvey*'s case, that it *was* appropriate to impose liability upon a subcontractor. *Harvey*'s case was distinguished on the ground that the contractual provisions differed substantially from those in the instant case.
[4] *[1990] 1 QB 993, [1989] 2 All ER 159, CA.*
[5] *[1990] 1 QB 993* at 1011, *[1989] 2 All ER 159* at 171, *per* Purchas LJ.

Contracts (Rights of Third Parties) Act 1999

[22.40] Depending upon the precise terms of the contracts involved, the law applicable to situations resembling those in *Norwich City Council v Harvey* and *Pacific Associates v Baxter* may now be more straightforward in so far as the third parties seeking to rely on an exemption from liability may be in a position to benefit from the *Contracts (Rights of Third Parties) Act 1999*. This Act was passed to remove the difficulties associated with the doctrine of privity of contract. For present purposes, the relevant provisions are *sections 1(1)* and *1(6)*. These are as follows:

'1.

(1)   … a person who is not a party to a contract (a "third party") may in his own right enforce a term of the contract if-

(a)   the contract expressly provides that he may, or

(b)   the term purports to confer a benefit on him.

(6)   Where a term of a contract excludes or limits liability in relation to any matter references in this Act to the third party enforcing the term shall be construed as references to his availing himself of the exclusion or limitation'.

If, therefore, there has been an express agreement in advance to confer the benefit of an exemption from liability upon a third party, the Act itself will now enable that party to enforce the agreement. Nevertheless, the common law is not abrogated, so the approach reflected in such cases as those considered above may still come to the aid of third parties unable to point to specific contractual provisions as required by the Act.

Relationship with assumption of risk

[22.41] It was suggested in the previous chapter[1] that the concept of assumption of risk will only take effect when there was at least a tacit or implied agreement between claimant and defendant, whereby the former agreed to release the latter from liability. If this contention is correct, it will be apparent that there is a close connection between that defence and exclusion of liability by disclaimer, particularly if the analysis of the latter suggested above[2] is also correct. Indeed, it may well be that in many cases in which the defendant is treated as having succeeded specifically by virtue of a disclaimer, the same result could have been reached by analysing the situation, including the disclaimer, as one in which the claimant had assumed the risk.

¹ See above CHAPTER 21.
² Ie in para [22.38].

Conceptually distinct defences

[22.42] Nevertheless, it is still appropriate to regard the two defences as conceptually distinct, for two reasons. First, if the disclaimer merely took the form of a notice issued to persons generally the court may be reluctant to give effect to it unless its position had been very prominent and its wording had been clear and precise. By contrast, if the claimant and defendant dealt personally with each other the court may be prepared, as some of the decisions on assumption of risk show,¹ to infer the existence of an agreement which was never even made explicit. In this sense the paradigm assumption of risk case involves that defence being easier to establish than disclaimer, when the latter defence is based merely on a general notice. Secondly, and more importantly, however, if it is true that some element of 'benefit to the claimant' is necessary to make a disclaimer as such effective, then this also constitutes a distinguishing factor. Perhaps, indeed, the relationship between these two factors, and in truth the defences themselves, is a reciprocal one. The more general the disclaimer, the more specific and tangible the benefit to the claimant will need to be before it can be effective. Conversely, as the degree of specific (even if implied) agreement between claimant and defendant increases, so the need for any 'benefit' to the former is reduced until, in what might be termed 'pure' assumption of risk cases such as *ICI v Shatwell*,² it reaches vanishing point.

¹ See *ICI Ltd v Shatwell* [1965] AC 656, [1964] 2 All ER 999, HL. See also *Bennett v Tugwell* [1971] 2 QB 267, [1971] 2 All ER 248.
² See above. For discussion of *ICI v Shatwell* see CHAPTER 21, above.

Non-contractual disclaimers and the Unfair Contract Terms Act

[22.43] It is submitted that the analysis in the previous paragraph, of the relationship between disclaimers and the defence of assumption of risk, helps to explain a somewhat obscure subsection of the Unfair Contract Terms Act 1977. *Section 2(3)* of that Act provides, where relevant, as follows:

'Where a ... notice purports to exclude or restrict liability for negligence a person's agreement to or awareness of it is not of itself to be taken as indicating his voluntary acceptance of any risk.'

The provision may be taken to mean that if the disclaimer is merely a general notice, then it will not be effective to exclude liability for negligence (if the defendant is a 'business') unless specifically accompanied by some recognisable quid pro quo to the claimant.¹

¹ An admitted difficulty with this interpretation is that the subsection also refers to 'contract terms', whereas a case in which the requirements of the doctrine of consideration are fulfilled, would seem of necessity to come within the proposed 'benefit to claimant' doctrine. But perhaps in the contract field the legislature was simply concerned to prevent a defendant from invoking the concept of assumption of risk merely by pointing to some obscure exclusion clause buried in a standard form contract.

Applicability of the UCTA

[22.44] More generally, as *section 2(3)* itself illustrates, it is important to remember that the provisions of the *Unfair Contract Terms Act 1977* are not confined to the law of contract. Non-contractual disclaimers also fall within its scope. Thus, businesses cannot by 'a notice given to persons generally or to particular persons exclude or restrict' their 'liability for death or personal injury resulting from negligence'.[1] In the case of 'other loss or damage'[2] the non-contractual notice has to satisfy the reasonableness test if the defendant is a 'business'. It is in effect left to the courts themselves to fashion the criteria for the application of that test in this context. The relevant provision of the Act, section 11(3), merely provides as follows:

> 'In relation to a notice (not being a notice having contractual effect), the requirement of reasonableness under this Act is that it should be fair and reasonable to allow reliance on it, having regard to all the circumstances obtaining when the liability arose or (but for the notice) would have arisen.'

In *Smith v Eric S Bush*[3] the House of Lords applied the Unfair Contract Terms Act and invalidated a disclaimer contained in a survey report which had been produced by a building society's surveyor and relied upon by the claimant house purchaser.[4]

[1]   See *section 2(1)*.
[2]   *Section 2(2)*. But see also the *Contract (Rights of Third Parties) Act 1999, s 7(2)*.
[3]   *[1990] 1 AC 831, [1989] 2 All ER 514*.
[4]   See further CHAPTER 4 above.

Chapter 23

Land use cases

A Introduction

Ordinary negligence principles modified

[23.01] Although situations traditionally regarded as falling under the 'nuisance' umbrella are increasingly perceived as being governed in effect by negligence principles, it remains the case that some disputes arising out of land use still require a degree of modification to ordinary negligence doctrine if they are to be successfully resolved. This is particularly so where the issue concerns the legitimacy of a continuing, deliberate, activity rather than an isolated act of carelessness resulting in sudden injury or damage. Thus, whereas statutory authority will rarely, if ever, provide a defence against an ordinary common law negligence claim, the issue is more problematic if a particular activity has been authorised; and it is contended that the statute has justified what would otherwise be an actionable nuisance. The question of when the action of a third party can be invoked as a defence to a claim has also given rise to particular difficulty in land use cases. Furthermore, the need to ensure that one occupier cannot adversely affect the utility and value of neighbouring land means that 'negligence' defences such as assumption of risk cannot be applied without significant qualification against neighbouring occupiers, merely because the latter were aware of the defendant's objectionable activities before they acquired their interest. On the contrary, it is usually no defence that the claimant 'came to the nuisance'. In addition, concepts such as prescription, which are hardly likely to be relevant to a negligence claim not involving land use, may conceivably be applicable very occasionally in the context of 'nuisance'. In this Chapter the various possible defences in land use cases, effective or otherwise, will be examined.

B Statutory authorisation[1]

Duties and powers

[23.02] It is evident that there can be no liability for doing what would otherwise be tortious if the legislature by statute has required it to be done. The effect of the authorities was summarised in *Department of Transport v North West Water Authority*[2] in which the House of Lords reaffirmed that there can be no liability, in the absence of negligence, for a nuisance wholly attributable to the performance of a statutory duty. In *Department of Transport v North West Water Authority* itself this principle was applied in favour of the defendant water authority, to exonerate it from liability for damage caused to the highway by a burst water main. The principle will apply even if the statute includes a clause expressly preserving liability for nuisance[3]. If the statute confers merely a *power* to act, however, as distinct from a *duty* such a clause may encourage the court to be more ready than it otherwise might have been to impose liability for nuisance upon a non-negligent defendant[4]. But in view of the tendency to construe clauses preserving nuisance liability narrowly[5], their importance is still likely to be marginal.

[1]   See generally Kodilinye (1990) 19 An-Am LR 72; see also Linden, 'Strict Liability, Nuisance and Legislative Authorization' (1966) 4 Osgoode Hall LJ 196.
[2]   *[1984] AC 336, [1983] 3 All ER 273*. Cf *New Road and Street Works Act 1991, s 82*.
[3]   *[1984] AC 336* at 359, *[1983] 3 All ER 273* at 276 *per* Lord Fraser.
[4]   *Department of Transport v North West Water Authority [1984] AC 336* at 359, *[1983] 3 All ER 273* at 276 *per* Lord Fraser.
[5]   See below.

Feasibility of avoiding interference

[23.03]   The general approach of the court to cases involving statutory powers, whether or not the statute contains a clause expressly preserving liability for nuisance, is to examine the extent to which any feasible exercise of the power would be likely in practice to lead to some degree of interference of the type in question. In *London, Brighton and South Coast Rly Co v Truman*[1] a railway company was empowered by statute to carry cattle, and was also empowered to purchase land in order to provide station yards for the accommodation of cattle and for other purposes. The company accordingly purchased a piece of land adjoining one of their stations and used it for unloading cattle. The noise of the cattle and drovers led to an action for nuisance being brought by the occupiers of certain houses near to the station. The House of Lords held that the company was not liable. The fact that the yard had to be near to a railway station necessarily limited the company in its choice of possible sites, and since such stations are of necessity close to centres of population the yard would be likely to constitute an actual or potential nuisance wherever it was put.

[1]   *(1885) 11 App Cas 45, 55 LJ Ch 354*. Followed in *Buley v British Railways Board [1975] CLY 2458*.

Avoidable consequences

[23.04]   Discussion of the position where it is alleged that what has occurred was not an avoidable consequence of the exercise of a statutory power, but could have been avoided, has long been overshadowed by the famous statement of Lord Blackburn in *Geddis v Proprietors of Bann Reservoir*[1] that 'no action will lie for doing that which the legislature has authorised, if it be done without negligence'. It is true that the *converse* of this proposition will usually be valid, so that the court will be reluctant to construe a statute as conferring authorisation if negligence is present[2]. Nevertheless, Lord Blackburn's statement is liable to mislead with respect to land use cases involving continuing activities. In such cases the question is rather: could the activity authorised by statute realistically have been carried on without committing a nuisance? And it would be quite wrong to suppose that actual negligence has to be present before a defendant can be held liable for causing an avoidable nuisance[3]. An error of judgment as to the environmental consequences of a particular course of action, which might be sufficient to nullify a defence of statutory authority, will not necessarily denote carelessness.

¹   *(1878) 3 App Cas 430* at 455–456. See also *Vaughan v Taff Vale Rly Co (1860) 5 H & N 679, 29 LJ Ex 247*.

²   See *Tate & Lyle Industries Ltd v Greater London Council [1983] 2 AC 509, [1983] 1 All ER 1159*, especially *per* Lord Templeman in *[1983] 2 AC 509* at 538, *[1983] 1 All ER 1159* at 1171: 'I would be reluctant to find that the 1962 Act had the effect of enabling the GLC negligently to inflict unnecessary damage on the public or on any individual … ' But cf Lord Diplock, *dubitante* on the particular point of construction involved in the *Tate & Lyle* case in *[1983] 2 AC 509* at 544–545, *[1983] 1 All ER 1159* at 1176.

³   Cf *Tock v St John's Metropolitan Area Board (1989) 64 DLR (4th) 620* in which the authorities relating to statutory authorisation as a defence to nuisance were reviewed by the Supreme Court of Canada. The Justices gave differing reasons for their decision and, apart from Sopinka J who was broadly in favour of the English approach, took a much narrower view of the defence than has been adopted in England. Even Sopinka J, however, agreed with his colleagues that: 'It is insufficient for the defendant to negative negligence' (at 651). See also the decision of the Ontario Court of Appeal in *A-G of Canada v Regional Municipality of Ottawa-Carleton (1991) 83 DLR (4th) 725*.

Degree of discretion

[23.05]   Indeed the question whether a particular authorised activity could have been carried on without causing a nuisance is apt to prove difficult to answer in practice, since it usually turns on the degree of discretion implicit in the statutory scheme[1]. Although nuisance may be difficult to avoid in the case of a new railway if steam locomotives are authorised to be run along a prescribed route[2], the same may not necessarily be true of a new hospital if the body empowered to build it has a wide discretion in the choice of possible sites[3]. But it is important that the court does not attach so high a priority to the prevention of nuisance as effectively to deprive the statutorily conferred discretion of all content[4].

¹   See, generally, Arrowsmith, *Civil Liability and Public Authorities*, (1992) Ch 8.

²   See *Hammersmith and City Rly Co v Brand (1869) LR 4 HL 171, 38 LJQB 265*. Cf *Allen v Gulf Oil Refining Ltd [1981] AC 1001, [1981] 1 All ER 353, HL*.

³   See *Metropolitan Asylum District Managers v Hill (1881) 6 App Cas 193, 50 LJQB 353*. See also *Canadian Pacific Rly Co v Parke [1899] AC 535, 68 LJPC 89*. Cf *London, Brighton and South Coast Rly Co v Truman (1886) 11 App Cas 45*.

⁴   See Arrowsmith, *Civil Liability and Public Authorities* (1992), p 216: 'The test should be whether the apparent discretion would be *substantially* stultified if private rights could not be interfered with'. (The italics are in the original).

Compensation provisions

[23.06]   Where the statute provides its own compensation scheme for those affected by the exercise of the power this may be taken to afford some indication that nuisance was regarded as inevitable, so that common law rights will be abrogated[1]. The absence of such a scheme is not, however, conclusive in favour of there having been no intention to authorise interference with private rights[2].

¹   See *Marriage v East Norfolk Rivers Catchment Board [1950] 1 KB 284, [1949] 2 All ER 1021*. Cf *Hammersmith and City Rly Co v Brand (1869) LR 4 HL 171*.

²   See *Edgington v Swindon Corpn [1939] 1 KB 86, [1938] 4 All ER 57*. A general right to compensation is now provided by the *Land Compensation Act 1973, s 1* to those adversely affected by public works when their rights of action in nuisance have been nullified by statutory authorisation. For discussion of the Act see Davies (1974) 90 LQR 361

Authorisation by necessary implication

[23.07]   The intention of Parliament to authorise a particular activity, and so give rise to the defence, may appear by necessary implication from the Act as well as by express words. In *Allen v Gulf Oil Refining Ltd*[1] the defendants operated an oil refinery, near Milford Haven, which had been built after a private Act of Parliament had authorised the compulsory acquisition of land for its construction. Local residents brought an action for nuisance based on the emission from the refinery of smell, noise and vibration. They sought to overcome a defence of statutory authorisation by arguing that, taken literally, all that the relevant provision, *section 5* of the *Gulf Oil Refining Act 1965*, had done, was to authorise the *acquisition of land* for the purpose of building a refinery. It had not expressly authorised the *operation* of a refinery, nor referred to any particular method of construction. As a private Act the statute should be construed strictly *contra proferentem*[2]. This question was tried as a preliminary point of law and the plaintiffs' arguments found favour with the Court of Appeal[3]. The House of Lords, however, by a majority[4], found the suggested interpretation artificial. The general purpose of the Act was clearly to facilitate the provision of refining oil and, as Lord Diplock observed[5], 'Parliament can hardly be supposed to have intended the refinery to be nothing more than a visual adornment to the landscape in an area of natural beauty'. The case was therefore sent for trial on the facts to determine whether or not the alleged nuisance would have been an inevitable consequence of operating *any* refinery, in which case the defendants would ultimately avoid liability by virtue of the authorisation implicit in the Act; or whether it would be possible to operate a refinery on the site in question without causing a nuisance, in which case the plaintiffs would succeed if the appropriate degree of interference was proved.

[1]   *[1981] AC 1001, [1981] 1 All ER 353.*
[2]   Cf *Altrincham Union Assessment Committee v Cheshire Lines Committee (1885)* 15 QBD 597 at 603, *per* Lord Esher MR.
[3]   See *[1980] QB 156, [1979] 3 All ER 1008* (Lord Denning MR and Cumming-Bruce LJ). Noted by the present writer in (1980) 43 MLR 219.
[4]   Lord Keith of Kinkel dissenting.
[5]   *[1981] AC 1001* at 1014, *[1981] 1 All ER 353* at 358d.

Cost of precautions

[23.08] Whether or not the nuisance is unavoidable is decided not on absolute grounds, but on whether it could have been avoided by taking such precautions as would be reasonable in all the circumstances. In *Manchester Corpn v Farnworth*[1] Lord Dunedin said[2]:

> 'The onus of proving that the result is inevitable is on those who wish to escape liability for nuisance[3], but the criterion of inevitability is not what is theoretically possible but what is possible, according to the state of scientific knowledge at the time, having also in view a certain commonsense appreciation which cannot be rigidly defined, of practical feasibility in view of situation and of expense'[4].

[1]   *[1930] AC 171, 99 LJKB 83.*
[2]   *[1930] AC 171* at 183.
[3]   See also *Allen v Gulf Oil Refining Ltd [1981] AC 1001* at 1013, *[1981] 1 All ER 353* at 357h, *per* Lord Wilberforce.
[4]   A contrary view appears to have been expressed by Lord Edmund Davies in *Allen v Gulf Oil Refining Ltd*: '… it would be for the defendant to establish that any proved nuisance was wholly unavoidable, *and this is quite regardless of the expense which might necessarily be involved in its avoidance*' (italics supplied): *[1981] AC 1001* at 1015, *[1981] 1 All ER 353* at 359a, sed quaere.

Reasonableness

[23.09] In *Farnworth*'s case the plaintiff complained that noxious fumes were emitted from the chimneys of an electricity generating station, which had been erected

463

pursuant to statutory powers by the defendant Corporation. The defendants sought to persuade the House of Lords that the nuisance was an unavoidable consequence of operating the station in the manner authorised by statute. It appeared that greater precautions to prevent interference were possible, but the Corporation objected that these would make their electricity much more expensive. Viscount Sumner accepted that 'the cost, trouble and inconvenience' to the Corporation of preventing the interference was a relevant factor, but it was not a conclusive one[1]. His Lordship emphasised that 'great powers often involve great responsibilities', and said[2]:

> 'It must be remembered that, in making reasonableness the measure of what must be done before the production of a nuisance can be excused the law, as it always does, means reasonable according to all the circumstances, and reasonable not only in the interests of the undertakers, but also in that of the sufferers. The legislature, in authorising a very big concern, must not be taken to be chary of requiring that much care is to be taken'.

In the result the defence failed and the Corporation was held liable[3].

1   *[1930] AC 171* at 194.
2   *[1930] AC 171* at 201.
3   See also *Shelfer v City of London Electric Lighting Co [1895] 1 Ch 287, 64 LJ Ch 216*; *Wise v Metropolitan Electric Supply Co (1894) 10 TLR 446*.

Where cost excessive

[23.10]   The decision went the other way on the facts in *Harrison v Southwark and Vauxhall Water Co*[1]. The defendant statutory undertakers were able to show that they had taken reasonable precautions to minimise noise when sinking certain shafts, and were not deprived of the defence of statutory authorisation merely because additional steps to limit the noise still further, which would have been possible, had not been adopted. The additional measures would have been very expensive and in the circumstances, which involved a mere temporary operation, it was not reasonable to expect the defendants to take them.

1   *[1891] 2 Ch 409, 60 LJ Ch 630.*

Rylands v Fletcher and statutory powers

[23.11]   The courts are reluctant to impose liability under the rule in *Rylands v Fletcher* upon bodies acting under statutory powers which have not been negligent. The High Court of Australia refused to do so, although a dissentient minority would have put the burden of disproving negligence on the defendant in such a case[1]. On the other hand, in *Midwood & Co v Manchester Corpn*[2] the Court of Appeal held that a clause in the relevant statute which expressly preserved liability for nuisance would be taken to include liability under the rule in *Rylands v Fletcher*, and in *Department of Transport v North West Water Authority*[3] the House of Lords apparently accepted that such clauses could still lead to the imposition of liability upon non-negligent defendants. In other cases, however, such clauses have been narrowly construed even as regards nuisance itself[4], and in *Smeaton v Ilford Corpn*[5] Upjohn J refused to impose liability under the rule in a situation involving such a clause[6].

1   See *Benning v Wong (1970) 43 ALJR 467*. McTiernan, Menzies and Owen JJ, Barwick CJ and Windeyer
    J dissenting. The High Court has since held that *Rylands v Fletcher* has been wholly absorbed within
    negligence in Australia: see *Burnie Port Authority v General Jones Pty Ltd (1994) 120 ALR 42*,
    discussed in CHAPTER 13 above.
2   *[1905] 2 KB 597, 74 LJKB 884.*
3   *[1984] AC 336* at 359, *[1983] 3 All ER 273* at 276 *per* Lord Fraser.
4   See *Hammond v St Pancras Vestry (1874) LR 9 CP 316, 43 LJCP 157*; *Stretton's Derby Brewery Co Ltd
    v Derby Corpn [1894] 1 Ch 431, 63 LJ Ch 135.*
5   *[1954] Ch 450, [1954] 1 All ER 923.* See also *Benning v Wong (1970) 43 ALJR 467* (in which the statute
    included a 'nuisance' clause).
6   Ie *section 31* of the *Public Health Act 1936*: 'A local authority shall so discharge their functions under
    the … provisions of this … Act as not to create a nuisance'.

When nuisance liability not preserved

[23.12]   Where there was no clause in the Act preserving liability for nuisance the
Court of Appeal, in *Dunne v North Western Gas Board*[1], held that a body exercising a
statutory power was immune from liability in the absence of negligence, with the
result that the rule in *Rylands v Fletcher* was not applicable. The House of Lords
reached the same result in a public nuisance case involving injury on the highway[2], a
situation sometimes said to attract strict liability at common law[3]. On the other hand,
in the earlier case of *West v Bristol Tramways*[4] the Court of Appeal imposed liability
under the rule in *Rylands v Fletcher* on a tramway company, acting under statutory
authority, which had caused avoidable damage. The company had been exonerated
from negligence on the ground that they could not reasonably have been expected to
have been aware, in the state of knowledge at the relevant time, of an alternative
method of acting which in fact existed and would have avoided the loss. The decision
in *West v Bristol Tramways* was, however, doubted by the House of Lords in
Cambridge Water Co Ltd v Eastern Counties Leather plc[5], which emphasised the need
for 'foreseeability by the defendant of the relevant type of damage' under *Rylands v
Fletcher* as well as in nuisance[6]. It is therefore likely that the decision in *Dunne v
North Western Gas Board* will be followed in future cases and not that in *West v Bristol
Tramways*.

1   *[1964] 2 QB 806, [1963] 3 All ER 916.*
2   See *Longhurst v Metropolitan Water Board [1948] 2 All ER 834.*
3   See above CHAPTER 14.
4   *[1908] 2 KB 14, 77 LJKB 684.*
5   *[1994] 2 AC 264, [1994] 1 All ER 53.*
6   *Per* Lord Goff, above at 304 and 75. See, generally, CHAPTERS 11 and 13 above.

Transco on private and public interests

[23.13]   Although the law therefore appears to be clear that bodies exercising statutory powers non-negligently will not incur *Rylands v Fletcher* liability, it is not
obvious as a matter of principle why individual victims should have to bear the burden
of harm inflicted in the pursuit of public objectives. Traces of concern on this point
can be detected in the speeches in the House of Lords in *Transco v Stockport
Metropolitan Borough Council*. Thus Lord Hoffman observed[1]:

> 'If the principle of *Rylands v Fletcher* is that costs should be internalised, the
> undertakers should be liable in the same way as private entrepreneurs. The fact
> that Parliament considered the construction and operation of the works to be in
> the public interest should make no difference'.

Similarly, Lord Walker of Gestingthorpe cautioned against an 'inclination', which he detected in *Dunne v North Western Gas Board*, for the court to attempt 'some utilitarian balancing of general good against individual risk'[2]. On the other hand Lord Scott of Foscote, in the same case, was apparently content that 'members of the public are expected to put up with any adverse effects ... provided always that it is carried out with due care', on the ground that 'use of the land for carrying on the activity cannot be characterised as unreasonable if it has been authorised or required by statute'[3].

[1]   See *[2004] 1 All ER 589* at para 30.
[2]   See *[2004] 1 All ER 589* at para 105.
[3]   See *[2004] 1 All ER 589* at para 89, sed quaere.

Statutory authorisation and planning permission

[23.14]   'In my opinion', said Sir John May in *Wheeler v JJ Saunders Ltd*[1], 'the effect of the grant of planning permission cannot be treated, even in a limited sense, as the equivalent of statutory authority'. In *Wheeler's* case the defendants attempted to avoid liability for a nuisance caused by pig-farming by pointing to the fact that they had been granted planning permission for their operations. They relied upon *Gillingham Borough Council v Medway (Chatham) Dock Co Ltd*[2], decided a few years earlier, in which Buckley J had held that activities which would otherwise have constituted a public nuisance did not do so. His Lordship considered that a grant of planning permission, which had given rise to the activities, had had the effect of negating liability by changing the nature of the area in question, for the purposes of the law of nuisance, from a residential locality into a commercial one[3]. The Court of Appeal distinguished the *Gillingham* decision in *Wheeler v JJ Saunders Ltd*, on the ground that the planning permission had not had so far-reaching an effect as that in the earlier case, and rejected the defendants' argument[4]. The court therefore applied what had previously been 'the general assumption', in the words of Peter Gibson LJ, 'that private rights to claim in nuisance were unaffected by the permissive grant of planning permission, the developer going ahead with the development at his own risk if his activities were to cause a nuisance'[5].

[1]   *[1995] 2 All ER 697* at 713, *[1996] Ch 19* at 37C. See also *per* Staughton LJ, at 28A and 704.
[2]   *[1993] QB 343*, *[1992] 3 All ER 923*. See Steele and Jewell 'Nuisance and Planning' (1993) 56 MLR 568.
[3]   'In short, where planning consent is given for a development or change of use, the question of nuisance will thereafter fall to be decided by reference to a neighbourhood with that development or use and not as it was previously': *[1993] QB 343* at 361, *[1992] 3 All ER 923* at 935 *per* Buckley J.
[4]   See *per* Staughton LJ in *[1995] 2 All ER 697* at 706, *[1996] Ch 19* at D–E: 'It would in my opinion be a misuse of language to describe what has happened in the present case as a change in the character of a neighbourhood. It is a change of use of a very small piece of land ... '
[5]   *[1995] 2 All ER 697* at 711g, *[1996] Ch 19* at 35E

Individual interests not to be readily overridden

[23.15]   Although it was unnecessary for the Court of Appeal in *Wheeler* to determine whether *Gillingham Borough Council v Medway (Chatham) Dock Co Ltd* had been correctly decided, it is clear that the court was uneasy with the implied exception to the previously understood position which it represented. Thus Peter Gibson LJ considered that the court 'should be slow to acquiesce in the extinction of private rights without compensation as a result of administrative decisions'[1], and Sir John

May thought that 'if a planning authority were with notice to grant a planning permission, the inevitable consequence of which would be the creation of a nuisance, then it is well arguable that that grant would be subject to judicial review on the ground of irrationality'[2]. It is submitted that these doubts are justified. The powers of planning authorities should not be confused with those of the legislature to override the interests of individuals by statute. The approach in *Wheeler v JJ Saunders Ltd* was followed by the Court of Appeal itself in *Hunter v Canary Wharf Ltd and London Docklands Development Corpn*[3], in which it was unsuccessfully contended that the unusually wide planning powers given by Parliament in relation to 'enterprise zones' impliedly authorised what might otherwise have been actionable at common law[4] When *Hunter's* case reached the House of Lords, the view expressed in the Court of Appeal on this particular point was not challenged; although Lord Hoffman indicated his agreement with it, stating that he thought it would 'be wrong to allow the private rights of third parties to be taken away by a permission granted by the planning authority to the developer'[5].

[1]   *[1995] 2 All ER 697* at 711j, *[1996] Ch 19* at 35g.
[2]   *[1995] 2 All ER 697* at 713g, *[1996] Ch 19* at 37H–38E.
[3]   *[1996] 1 All ER 482.*
[4]   'I reject the submission that the powers and duties conferred on planning authorities, even those such as the LDDC, are such that in granting planning permissions under their delegated powers they are conferring an immunity in nuisance upon works pursuant to the permissions': *per* Pill J *[1996] 1 All ER 482* at 493d.
[5]   See *[1997] 2 All ER 426* at 455. Cf *per* Lord Cooke of Thorndon at 465–466.

C Act of a third party

Continuation and adoption

[23.16] It is not, in itself, a defence to an action in nuisance against an occupier of land that the nuisance emanating from his land was caused not by him but by the act of a third party such as a trespasser[1]. Liability in such cases does, however, depend upon proof that the defendant has 'continued' or 'adopted' the nuisance which in practice usually means simply that he or his servants can be shown to have had some knowledge of the existence of the nuisance or of the likelihood of its occurring[2].

[1]   See *Lippiatt v South Gloucestershire Council [1999] 4 All ER 149, CA.*
[2]   *Sedleigh-Denfield v O'Callaghan [1940] AC 880, [1940] 3 All ER 349.* But cf *Regal v African Superslate (Pty) Ltd 1961 (4) SA 727* (no liability if no practical method of abating the nuisance exists).

Nuisances from overloaded sewers

[23.17]   The general rule imposing liability upon defendants for nuisances emanating from their land, even though caused by strangers, does not apply if the defendant is obliged by statute to receive offensive matter on to his land and has no control over the amount. In *Marcic v Thames Water Utilities*[1] the claimant sought damages from the defendant water company, and an order to compel improvements to their sewers. These had become overloaded as the number of houses they served had increased. As a result the claimant's property had suffered from flooding for many years. There was nothing inherently wrong with the sewers themselves, which had been adequate when laid. The company had no control over the extent of new building in the area which it served, and the overloading had resulted from the exercise by new house-owners of their statutory right to connect their houses to the defendant's sewers. The House of Lords held that the claim would fail. Unanimously reversing the Court of Appeal[2], which had held that the defendants could be liable under the principles relating to 'adoption' of nuisance, the House chose to uphold and apply a well-known line of cases, going back to the nineteenth century, holding that plaintiffs who suffered flooding as a result of overloaded sewers could not sue in nuisance[3]. Such plaintiffs could seek orders of mandamus if the defendants had been in neglect of an existing statutory duty to provide better facilities; but even that was unavailable if the duty had been one only enforceable in a special manner provided by the Act itself, eg by the Minister responsible after complaint to him[4].

[1] *[2004] 1 All ER 135.*
[2] See *[2002] 2 All ER 55.*
[3] See *Smeaton v Ilford Corpn [1954] Ch 450, [1954] 1 All ER 923* (Upjohn J). See also *Glossop v Heston and Isleworth Local Board (1879) 12 Ch D 102, 49 LJ Ch 89; A-G v Guardians of Poor of Union of Dorking (1882) 20 Ch D 595, 51 LJ Ch 585.* Prior to *Marcic's* case the authorities were extensively reviewed in *Dear v Thames Water (1992) 33 Con LR 43* (Judge Peter Bowsher QC, Official Referee).
[4] See *Pasmore v Oswaldtwistle UDC [1898] AC 387, 67 LJQB 635.*

Principle reasserted

[23.18] Notwithstanding the privatisation of the water industry, which on one view might have justified a greater readiness to impose liability on profit-making organisations in contrast to the public corporations formerly responsible, the House of Lords held that the statutory framework to which the industry was subject rendered the principles established in the older cases still fully apposite[1]. 'Since sewerage undertakers have no control over the volume of water entering their sewerage systems', observed Lord Nicholls[2], 'it would be surprising if Parliament intended that whenever sewer flooding occurs, every householder whose property has been affected can sue the appointed sewerage undertaker for an order that the company build more sewers or pay damages. The *Water Industry Act 1991* provides for a Director General of Water Services to whom customers can complain, and whose decisions are subject to judicial review. In those circumstances a common law action was held not to be an appropriate remedy for the flooding suffered in *Marcic's* case, since it would be inconsistent with the statutory scheme[3]. The claimant should instead have complained to the Director General. The vast capital expenditure to finance new sewers raises major questions of public interest 'which courts', in the words of Lord Hoffman[4], 'are not equipped to make in ordinary litigation'; and it is therefore 'not surprising that for more than a century the question of whether more or better sewers should be constructed has been entrusted by Parliament to administrators rather than judges'.

[1] See also *Norweb plc v Dixon [1995] 3 All ER 952* (relationship between a private electricity company and its customers held to remain primarily statutory rather than contractual).
[2] See *[2004] 1 All ER 135* at para 35.
[3] A contention that the claimant could rely upon the *Human Rights Act 1998*, on the basis that his rights to respect for his home and peaceful enjoyment of his possessions had been contravened, was also rejected: the *Water Industry Act 1991* had struck an appropriate balance between public and private interest which was held to comply with the requirements of the law relating to human rights.
[4] See *[2004] 1 All ER 135* at para 64.

Treatment before discharge

[23.19] On the other hand, if a water company takes positive steps to treat the sewage before discharging it, the company may be regarded as having itself adopted or continued the nuisance, thereby incurring liability. In *Pride of Derby and Derbyshire Angling Association v British Celanese Ltd*[1] a water authority was held liable for polluting the river Derwent by the discharge into it of untreated sewage. The Court of Appeal distinguished the well-established principle, subsequently applied in the *Marcic* case, on the ground that the defendants had attempted to treat the sewage and had taken it into their sewage works for that purpose. This was sufficient to render them liable when they subsequently discharged it into the Derwent, despite having failed to render it completely harmless[2]. The *Pride of Derby* case was referred to by the House of Lords in *Marcic v Thames Water Utilities*, with apparent approval[3]. The distinction between the two types of situation will, however, sometimes be a fine one if the failure adequately to treat the sewage simply reflects a lack of capacity requiring substantial investment to remedy it.

1   *[1953] Ch 149, [1953] 1 All ER 179.*
2   See also *A-G and Dommes v Basingstoke Corpn (1876) 45 LJ Ch 726.*
3   See *per* Lord Hoffman in *[2004] 1 All ER 135* at paras 58–59.

Act of stranger as a defence to Rylands v Fletcher

[23.20]   Apart from the exceptional sewerage cases, the general position in nuisance is therefore that the actions of a third party, such as a trespasser, will not constitute a defence if the defendant 'adopted' or 'continued' the nuisance. In several cases dealing with the rule in *Rylands v Fletcher,* on the other hand, 'act of a stranger' has been treated as a well-established defence. This can perhaps be explained on the ground that the often instantaneous nature of the escape in such cases makes it difficult to apply the criteria of 'adoption' or 'continuance' used to impose liability in 'nuisance' proper. Nevertheless this explanation does not fit easily alongside the notion, to which the House of Lords committed itself in *Cambridge Water Co Ltd v Eastern Counties Leather plc*[1], that *Rylands v Fletcher* is best seen as a special type of continuing nuisance[2].

1   *[1994] 2 AC 264, [1994] 1 All ER 53.*
2   See, generally, CHAPTER 13 above. See also *per* Lord Hoffman in *Transco v Stockport Metropolitan Borough Council [2004] 1 All ER 589* at para 33.

Eroding strict liability

[23.21]   Moreover, the defence clearly had the effect of eroding the nominally strict liability under the rule[1]. In *Box v Jubb*[2], the defendant's reservoir overflowed and flooded the plaintiff's land. The overflow resulted from the defendant's reservoir being itself flooded when a higher reservoir was emptied. This emptying would not have had any adverse consequences but for the fact that certain sluice or lock-gates in a watercourse which connected the two reservoirs, and over which the defendant had no control, was blocked causing the water from the higher reservoir to flow into the lower. The blockage was presumed to have been caused by some trespassing third party, and the Court of Exchequer held the defendant not liable[3]. Kelly CB said[4]:

> 'The matters complained of took place through no default or breach of duty by the defendants, but were caused by a stranger over whom and at a spot where they had no control. It seems to me to be immaterial whether this is called vis major or the unlawful act of a stranger: it is sufficient to say that the defendants had no means of preventing the occurrence'.

It follows that if the judgment of Kelly CB is still good law, liability will only be imposed if the defendant can be shown to have been negligent in failing to take steps which would have prevented the third party from precipitating the damage.

1   See Goodhart, 'The Third Man' (1951) 4 CLP 177. See also *per* Lord Hoffman in *Transco v Stockport Metropolitan Borough Council* [2004] 1 All ER 589 at para 39.
2   *(1879) 4 Ex D 76, 48 LJQB 417.*
3   See also *Rickards v Lothian [1913] AC 263, 82 LJPC 42*; *Perry v Kendrick's Transport Ltd [1956] 1 All ER 154, [1956] 1 WLR 85.* Cf *Ribee v Norrie [2001] PIQR P8, CA.*
4   *(1879) 4 Ex D 76 at 79.*

Limiting the defence

[23.22] In *Cambridge Water Co Ltd v Eastern Counties Leather plc*[1], however, the House of Lords appeared to draw a distinction between the presence of foreseeability of the relevant type of harm, and of carelessness in allowing the escape to occur. Although the former would be a prerequisite of liability in *Rylands v Fletcher* cases, the latter would *not* be[2]. To that extent the rule has been reasserted as one of strict liability and the correctness of the reasoning[3] in *Box v Jubb*, and a number of other cases[4], is perhaps now open to question[5]. Moreover, there is some indication that, especially in borderline cases, the court will scrutinise defence submissions that a particular individual was indeed a 'stranger' to the occupier with a degree of scepticism: a recent decision of the Court of Appeal involved reversal, in the claimant's favour, of the view of the trial judge that the defence had been made out on this ground[6].

1   *[1994] 2 AC 264, [1994] 1 All ER 53.* See, especially, *per* Lord Goff at 302 and 73.
2   See, generally, CHAPTER 13 above.
3   The actual decision in *Box v Jubb* can perhaps be supported on the ground that the watercourse connecting the two reservoirs was for the mutual benefit of both plaintiff and defendant and that, in the circumstances, the defence of 'consent' was available to the latter.
4   See *Hale v Jennings Bros [1938] 1 All ER 579*; *A Prosser & Son Ltd v Levy [1955] 3 All ER 577, [1955] 1 WLR 1224*; *Northwestern Utilities Ltd v London Guarantee and Accident Co Ltd [1936] AC 108, 105 LJPC 18.*
5   Cf *per* Lord Hoffman in *Transco v Stockport Metropolitan Borough Council [2004] 1 All ER 589* at para 32: 'No serious principle of allocating risk to the enterprise would leave the injured party to pursue his remedy against the vandal'.
6   See *Ribee v Norrie [2001] PIQR P8.*

D Act of God

[23.23] In most 'nuisance' cases the defence of act of God[1] will be irrelevant since the imposition of liability will presuppose either an intentional activity, or awareness of the situation giving rise to complaint, on the part of the defendant. Nevertheless it is possible that the surrounding circumstances may change due to unpredictable factors over which the defendant has no control. But the cases are few and the scope of the defence, even where it might be relevant, is likely to be extremely limited. In *Lord Chesham v Chesham UDC*[2] a water authority sought to rely on it by arguing that an exceptional drought had so diminished a river as to make normal dilution of the sewage discharged therein impossible. The authority was nevertheless held liable for polluting the river and an injunction was granted.

1   See Hall 'An Unsearchable Providence: The Lawyer's Concept of Act of God' (1993) 13 OJLS 227.
2   *(1935) 79 Sol Jo 453.*

Overflowing lakes

[23.24] In *Fletcher v Rylands*[1] Blackburn J said that a defendant might 'perhaps', in a future case, avoid liability under the rule he laid down by showing 'that the escape was the consequence of *vis major*, or the act of God'. The defence succeeded in *Nichols v Marsland*[2] when three artificial lakes constructed by the defendant for ornamental purposes overflowed, and destroyed four bridges belonging to the plaintiff. The flooding had been caused by rainfall which was found by the jury to have been so severe that it could not reasonably have been anticipated. This decision was, however, distinguished very sharply by the House of Lords in *Greenock Corpn v Caledonian Rly Co*[3] which was decided on almost identical facts. Lord Shaw expressly said that the defendants would not escape liability even if the rainfall had been 'extraordinary or even unprecedented in quantity'[4]. Moreover, the affirmation by Lord Goff in the House of Lords in *Cambridge Water Co Ltd v Eastern Counties Leather plc*, that the *Rylands v Fletcher* principle 'is one of strict liability' in that the exercise of 'all due care to prevent the escape from occurring'[5] will not necessarily negate liability, also supports the proposition that successful recourse to the defence of act of God will be rare[6]. Nevertheless *Nichols v Marsland* has not been overruled, and the possibility of raising the defence to a *Rylands v Fletcher* action remains, but quite exceptional circumstances will be required for it to succeed[7].

[1] *(1866) LR 1 Exch 265* at 280.
[2] *(1876) 2 Ex D 1, 46 LJQB 174.*
[3] *[1917] AC 556, 86 LJPC 185.*
[4] *[1917] AC 556* at 579.
[5] *[1994] 2 AC 264* at p 302, *[1994] 1 All ER 53* at 73. See, further, CHAPTER 13 above.
[6] In exceptional circumstances the defence of 'necessity' might be available: see *Rigby v Chief Constable of Northamptonshire [1985] 2 All ER 985* at 996, *[1985] 1 WLR 1242* at 1255, *per* Taylor J.
[7] Cf *per* Lord Hobhouse in *Transco v Stockport Metropolitan Borough Council [2004] 1 All ER 589* at para 59: 'Act of God is not, and never was, the same as inevitable accident or the absence of negligence'.

E 'Coming to the nuisance'

No defence

[23.25] It is no defence that the claimant 'came to the nuisance'. In *Bliss v Hall*[1] the defendant attempted to rely on the fact that the establishment of his business as a tallow-chandler, from which noxious fumes were emitted over the plaintiff's land, had pre-dated the latter's arrival by some three years. The defence failed. Tindal CJ said[2]:

> '... the Plaintiff came to the house he occupies with all the rights which the common law affords, and one of them is a right to wholesome air. Unless the Defendant shows a prescriptive right to carry on his business in the particular place the Plaintiff is entitled to judgment'.

[1] *(1838) 4 Bing NC 183, 1 Arn 19.* See also *Elliotson v Feetham (1835) 2 Bing NC 134, 1 Hodg 259.*
[2] *(1838) 4 Bing NC 183* at 186.

Sound principle

[23.26] Moreover, since time does not begin to run in a defendant's favour until an actionable nuisance has arisen, even a defendant whose activity pre-dates that of the claimant by more than twenty years may incur liability[1]. The principle underlying the denial of a defence of this is sound. It is not for one landowner, merely because he happens to be first in the field, to determine unilaterally the character of his surrounding neighbourhood and the viability of using land nearby, which does not belong to him, for purposes which may conflict with his own.

1   See *Sturges v Bridgman (1879) 11 Ch D 852, 48 LJ Ch 785.*

Miller v Jackson

[23.27]   In the well-known case of *Miller v Jackson*[1] the Court of Appeal, by a majority[2], affirmed the validity of the rule that it is no defence that the plaintiff came to the nuisance. But Lord Denning, who dissented on this point, criticised the rule regarding it as unsuited to modern conditions and policy considerations[3]. Even the affirmation of the rule by the majority was not without reluctance[4]. It is submitted that these doubts were unjustified. In the words of one writer, the principle 'is based on sound sense, for if the rule were otherwise land could become burdened with diverse and sterilising incidents'[5]. In *Miller's* case the plaintiffs were the owners of one of several semi-detached houses which had recently been built, on previously unoccupied ground, overlooking a cricket pitch. The pitch had been in use for over seventy years without complaint, but owing to the unusually short distance between the wicket and the new houses[6], cricket balls not infrequently fell into the gardens of the houses. On average eight or nine did so every summer, and the plaintiff's brickwork and roof tiles were often damaged[7]. On a number of occasions, occupants of the houses narrowly escaped personal injury. At first instance the plaintiffs were awarded an injunction to close the cricket ground. Although the Court of Appeal upheld the finding of liability in favour of the plaintiffs it also, by a majority[8], deprived them of the injunction and awarded only damages. Alone of the three judges, Geoffrey Lane LJ, who dissented on the remedies point, would have maintained the injunction[9]. It is submitted that his view, which is more in keeping with the spirit of the denial of a defence based on a plaintiff's having come to the nuisance, is to be preferred.

1   *[1977] QB 966, [1977] 3 All ER 338.*
2   Geoffrey Lane and Cumming-Bruce LJJ.
3   See *[1977] QB 966* at 980H–982A, *[1977] 3 All ER 338* at 344d–345c.
4   'If the matter were *res integra*, I confess I should be inclined to find for the defendants. It does not seem just that a long-established activity – in itself innocuous – should be brought to an end because someone chooses to build a house nearby and so turn an innocent pastime into an actionable nuisance': *per* Geoffrey Lane LJ in *[1977] QB 966* at 986E–F, *[1977] 3 All ER 338* at 384j–349a.
5   'Injunctions Against Hits for Six' (1977) 93 LQR 481 at 482 (editorial case-note). See also *Fleming on Torts* (8th edn) p 442.
6   Only 102 feet separated the centre of the pitch from the plaintiffs' garden.
7   The situation was therefore very different from that in the well known case of *Bolton v Stone [1951] AC 850, [1951] 1 All ER 1078,* in which the escape of balls from the ground was extremely rare and had occurred only about six times in thirty years.
8   Lord Denning MR and Cumming-Bruce LJ.
9   Cf *Kennaway v Thompson [1981] QB 88, [1980] 3 All ER 329.*

F Assumption of risk and contributory negligence

[23.28]   It follows from the rule that it is no defence that the claimant 'came to the nuisance' that there can be little scope in land use cases for the operation of the defence of assumption of risk, or that of contributory negligence[1]. Defences based upon a claimant's having chosen to enter or remain within range of the defendant's activities despite awareness of their consequences, which may be crucial in negligence cases, will rarely assist in resolving disputes over conflicting uses of land. In *Leakey v National Trust for Places of Historic Interest or Natural Beauty*[2], however, Megaw LJ expressed himself, obiter, as follows[3]:

'... while it is no defence to a claim in nuisance that the plaintiff has "come to the nuisance", it would have been a properly pleadable defence to this statement of claim that the plaintiffs, knowing of the danger to their property, by word or deed, had shown their willingness to accept that danger. Moreover, I find it hard to imagine circumstances in which the facts which would provide a defence of *volenti non fit injuria* would not also provide a defence in a case such as the present'.

In this case the defendants were held liable in nuisance in consequence of natural erosion on their land which, as they were aware, was threatening the nearby property of the plaintiffs. Megaw LJ did not give examples of the kinds of situation in which he envisaged the defence of *volenti* being applicable. A possible interpretation of his remarks, however, might be that the decision would have been different if, for example, the plaintiffs had only acquired their property after the effects of the erosion had already become visible. But unless the defendant in such a case could show that the entire locality was one in which erosion was characteristic and widespread[4], it is at least arguable that failure to take such steps as are reasonably within his ability to remedy the situation should result in liability even to a new householder who takes property nearby with full knowledge of the circumstances[15]. Similarly, most of the cases holding that the rule in *Rylands v Fletcher* will not normally apply as between parties in one building sharing common water or drainage facilities, and in which the language of 'consent' is often found[6], are probably better regarded as having been decided on the nuisance-based ground of absence of non-natural user[7].

[1] Winfield in his 'Nuisance as a Tort' (1931) 4 CLJ 189 at 200 considered that contributory negligence was not a defence in nuisance cases. For a different view see Williams, *Joint Torts and Contributory Negligence* p 205.
[2] *[1980] QB 485, [1980] 1 All ER 17.*
[3] *[1980] QB 485 at 515A–B, [1980] 1 All ER 17 at 26b–c.*
[4] For discussion of the 'locality' principle see CHAPTER 11 above.
[5] Cf *Masters v Brent London Borough Council [1978] QB 841, [1978] 2 All ER 664.* See also *Morley v Dubinsky (1966) 59 DLR (2d) 217 (Can).*
[6] See *Blake v Woolf [1898] 2 QB 426* at 428, *per* Wright J; *Kiddle v City Business Properties Ltd [1942] 1 KB 269* at 274, *[1942] 2 All ER 216* at 217H–218A, *per* Goddard LJ (referred to by Lord Millett in *Southwark London BC v Mills [1999] 4 All ER 449* at 461, HL).
[7] See above CHAPTER 13.

Agreement and acquiescence

[23.29] Nevertheless, it is clear that in appropriate cases a private nuisance may be legalised by an actual *contract* between the parties, even if the relevant term is not express but merely implied. In *Thomas v Lewis*[1] the defendant, who operated a quarry, granted grazing rights over land nearby to the plaintiff. The plaintiff subsequently alleged that interference with the grazing rights, emanating from the quarry, constituted a nuisance. His claim failed. Farwell J said that it was 'an implied term of the agreement that he took the rights over the land subject to the rights of the defendant to continue the quarry as he had worked it before'[2]. There will also be no cause of action in the rare event of a claimant actually *encouraging* the creation of the nuisance[3]. A plaintiff who seeks an injunction may also find his position adversely affected by any delay or acquiescence on his part[4].

¹   *[1937] 1 All ER 137.*
²   *[1937] 1 All ER 137* at 140G. See also *Lyttelton Times Co Ltd v Warners Ltd [1907] AC 476, 76 LJPC 100*; *Southwark London BC v Mills [1999] 4 All ER 449, HL.*
³   See *Williams v Jersey (1841) Cr & Ph 91, 10 LJ Ch 149.*
⁴   See *Gaunt v Fynney (1872) 8 Ch App 8, 42 LJ Ch 122*; *Rogers v Great Northern Rly Co (1889) 53 JP 484*. But cf *Savile v Kilner (1872) 26 LT 277* at 280, *per* Bacon V-C. On injunctions see, generally, CHAPTER 29 below.

Mitigation

[23.30] It is important to note that the proposition that assumption of risk and contributory negligence will not readily afford defences in private nuisance cases, does not mean that a claimants in such cases are not subject to the normal duty to mitigate their loss[1].

¹   See, generally, *The Law of Tort* (Grubb ed) pp 192–194. *Clerk and Lindsell on Torts* (18th edn, 2000) pp 1561–1562.

Public nuisance

[23.31] One sphere in which it appears that the two defences *can* operate is that of claims for compensation based on special damage in that area of *public* nuisance which is unrelated to private nuisance, and is mainly concerned with incidents on the highway[1].

¹   See above CHAPTER 14.

G Prescription[1]

Difficult to establish

[23.32] In theory the right to commit what would otherwise be a private nuisance can be acquired by prescription as an easement. The obstacles in the way of establishing the defence are, however, formidable and according to *Gale on Easements* 'it does not seem that a contested claim to a prescriptive right to commit a nuisance by noise, smell or the like has ever, in fact, succeeded'. A public nuisance can never be legalised by prescription[2].

¹   On prescription see, generally, *Gale on Easements*, 17th edn, 2002, (Gaunt and Morgan eds), Ch 4; Jackson *The Law of Easements and Profits* (1978) Ch 7.
²   *R v Cross (1812) 3 Camp 224*; *A-G v Barnsley Corpn [1874] WN 37.*

Actionability throughout the prescriptive period

[23.33] It is not enough for the party seeking to establish the right to show merely that he has carried out the activity which is now complained of throughout the prescriptive period. He must also show that it amounted to an actionable *nuisance* throughout that time. In *Sturges v Bridgman*[1] a confectioner had, for more than twenty years, used a pestle and mortar in an area at the back of his premises which adjoined the garden of his neighbour, a physician. The noise and vibration were not treated as a nuisance, however, and not complained of by the physician, until shortly before action brought when he erected a consulting-room at the end of his garden, whereupon the noise and vibration became a nuisance. The Court of Appeal held that, since it was no defence that the plaintiff had 'come to the nuisance'[2], time did not begin to run in favour of the confectioner until the consulting-room was erected, and the physician was therefore entitled to an injunction[3].

[1] *(1879) 11 Ch D 852, 48 LJ Ch 785.*
[2] See above.
[3] See also *Ball v Ray (1873) 8 Ch App 467, 30 LT 1*; *Russell Transport Ltd v Ontario Malleable Iron Co [1952] 4 DLR 719 (Can).*

Character of prescriptive rights

[23.34] For the defence to succeed the defendant must show that his activity is capable of satisfying the requirements relating to prescriptive rights generally. In *Liverpool Corpn v H Coghill & Son*[1] the defendants had for more than twenty years discharged waste liquors from their borax works into the plaintiffs' sewers. There was, however, evidence that the discharges had been made intermittently and at night. Moreover the resultant damage to the crops on the plaintiffs' sewage farm, of which they now complained, had only been visible for a much shorter period than twenty years. Eve J held that as the enjoyment of the alleged easement had been secret and unknown, and unsuspected by the plaintiffs, it was not of such a character as would establish a prescriptive right.

[1] *[1918] 1 Ch 307, 87 LJ Ch 186.*

Subject matter of a grant

[23.35] Probably the greatest difficulty in the way of a claim that a nuisance has been legalised by prescription lies in the requirement that, in order to qualify as an easement, a right must admit of being defined with sufficient certainty and precision to be capable of forming the subject matter of a grant. In *Hulley v Silversprings Bleaching and Dyeing Co*[1] the defendants claimed a prescriptive right to pollute a stream. The claim failed, inter alia[2], because the progressive increase in the size of the defendants' mill, and in the volume of the water polluted, was destructive of the certainty and uniformity essential for the measurement of the user by which the extent of a prescriptive right was to be ascertained[3]. In *Woodman v Pwllbach Colliery Co Ltd*[4] the Court of Appeal doubted, obiter, whether a right to deposit coal-dust over a wide area, as a result of the defendant mine-owners' screening and breaking operations, was capable of existing as an easement. In the same case in the House of Lords, Lord Sumner was similarly inclined to the view that 'a claim to spread ... coal dust in injurious quantities anywhere over the plaintiff's land, in any direction and to any distance, just as the wind, blowing where it listeth, may chance to carry it' was 'too indeterminate to be an easement proper'[5]. Rights too indefinite to qualify as easements may nevertheless be validly created by agreement so as to bind the parties to the contract. In one case a nuisance by noise was held to have been legalised by necessary implication from an agreement between the parties[6].

[1] *[1922] 2 Ch 268, 91 LJ Ch 207.*
[2] An alternative ground of decision was that the alleged easement would have contravened the *Rivers Pollution Prevention Act 1876: [1922] 2 Ch* at 281–282. See now the *Water Resources Act 1991, Pt III, Ch II.*
[3] See also *Scott-Whitehead v National Coal Board [1987] 2 EGLR 227* (Stuart-Smith J).

Need to meet contemporary standards

[23.36] Even a defendant who succeeded in establishing a prescriptive right would not necessarily thereby acquire an indefeasible right to carry on his trade for ever afterwards in the precise manner in which he had done during the prescriptive period. He would still be obliged to take account of modern developments which might enable the interference with his neighbours to be limited. In *Shoreham-By-Sea UDC v Dolphin Canadian Proteins Ltd*[1], in which the defendants were held liable for a nuisance emanating from their chicken-processing factory, Donaldson J said[2]:

> '... if and in so far as one can have a prescriptive right to create what would otherwise be a nuisance in an area, that prescriptive right can go no further than to entitle the person concerned to carry on the business to which the prescriptive right attaches in the best practicable way, that is to say, the way that causes the least practicable nuisance applying reasonable standards, not being the standards which have existed throughout the prescriptive period, but being the standards which apply in the light of the state of the art at the time when the nuisance is alleged to have been created'.

1   *(1972) 71 LGR 261.*
2   *(1972) 71 LGR 261* at 267.

H Others contribute'

Not a defence in itself

[23.37] It is no defence that others contribute to the nuisance[1]. Thus where several manufacturers, whose works were adjacent to a stream, caused a nuisance to a riparian owner lower down, by discharging offensive matter into the stream, it was held to be no answer to an action brought against one of them that his particular contribution to the nuisance was infinitesimal and inappreciable. The lower riparian owner was entitled to have the water of the stream sent down in its original pure condition and to proceed against each manufacturer to prevent him from making his contribution to what was in aggregate a serious nuisance[2].

1   *Crossley & Sons Ltd v Lightowler (1867) 2 Ch App 478, 36 LJ Ch 584; Thorpe v Brumfitt (1873) 8 Ch App 650.*
2   See *Blair and Sumner v Deakin, Eden and Thwaites v Deakin (1887) 57 LT 522.*

When the locality is polluted

[23.38] Of course, if the case is one of interference with comfort or enjoyment, a claimant might still fail on the ground that the nature of the particular locality is such that the defendant's activity within it is unexceptionable[1]. The distinction between the locality doctrine, and the rule that contribution by others to the nuisance is no defence, appears to rest upon causation. If the area in question is so polluted that it is impossible to trace any meaningful contribution to the harm to the defendant, then the case may be treated as being within the locality principle so that no cause of action will arise[2].

¹ See above CHAPTER 11.
² See the judgment of Page-Wood V-C at first instance in *Crossley & Sons Ltd v Lightowler (1866) 3 Eq 279* at 289. See also *per* Kay J in *Blair and Sumner v Deakin, Eden and Thwaites v Deakin (1887) 57 LT 522* at 526.

Possible safeguard

[23.39] The rule against contribution as a defence is potentially harsh, in that it is capable of rendering actionable activities which, taken in isolation, are neither actionable nor unlawful[1]. One possible safeguard, however, is that although there is no requirement that the contributors should be acting in concert for the rule to apply, it is probably necessary that each of them should at least be aware of the existence of the others and their contributions[2]. Even though the causes of action against the individual contributors to the nuisance are distinct[3], it should usually prove possible for them to be joined as parties to one action on the ground that the complaints against the various defendants raise a common question of law or fact[4].

¹ See *Lambton v Mellish [1894] 3 Ch 163, 63 LJ Ch 929*. But cf *per* Buckley J in *Gillingham Borough Council v Medway (Chatham) Dock Co Ltd [1993] QB 343* at 365, *[1992] 3 All ER 923* at 938: 'Even assuming that A's excessive use of a particular highway could amount to a public nuisance, that could not mean that B, C or D could not use the highway, however reasonably, for fear of committing public nuisance'.
² Cf *per* Chitty J in *Lambton v Mellish [1894] 3 Ch 163* at 166: 'If the acts of two persons, *each being aware of what the other is doing*, amount in the aggregate to what is an actionable wrong … '.
³ Cf *Sadler v Great Western Rly Co [1896] AC 450, 65 LJQB 462*.
⁴ The House of Lords refused to allow joinder in a case of joint nuisance in *Sadler v Great Western Rly Co [1896] AC 450*, but shortly thereafter the rules of court were changed to facilitate joinder in situations in which it had previously been refused and, as a result, *Sadler v Great Western Rly Co* would probably now be decided differently: see *per* Scrutton LJ in *Payne v British Time Recorder Co Ltd and W W Curtis Ltd [1921] 2 KB 1* at 15.

I 'Defendant unable to remedy'

Continuing liability in damages

[23.40] If the defendant is the original wrongdoer it is no defence that he is not in a position to abate the nuisance. Although an injunction would not be awarded[1], such a defendant remains liable to pay damages even if he has alienated the land since creating the nuisance and cannot re-enter to put a stop to it[2]. On the other hand, where the nuisance was created by a stranger over whom the defendant had no control, such as a predecessor in title, there will be no liability upon the innocent occupier if abatement of the nuisance is not a practical possibility[3].

¹ See *London and South Western Rly Co v Webb (1863) 15 CBNS 450, 9 LT 291*.
² See *Thompson v Gibson (1841) 7 M & W 456, 10 LJ Ex 330; Roswell v Prior (1701) Holt KB 500, 12 Mod Rep 635*.
³ See *Regal v African Superslate (Pty) Ltd (1961) (4) SA 727*.

Part nine

Damages and their assessment

Chapter 24

The making of awards in personal injury cases

A Heads of damage

Established practice

[24.01] 'The practice is now established', said Lord Denning MR in 1979 when the case of *Lim Poh Choo v Camden and Islington Area Health Authority* was in the Court of Appeal,[1] 'that, in personal injury cases, the award of damages is assessed under four main heads. First, special damages in the shape of money actually expended. Second, cost of future nursing and attendance and medical expenses. Third, pain and suffering and loss of amenities. Fourth, loss of future earnings'. The latter three headings are collectively referred to as 'general damages'.

[1]   *[1979] QB 196* at 217–218, *[1979] 1 All ER 332* at 342.

Special damages

[24.02] These consist of 'accrued and ascertained financial loss'[1] which the claimant has incurred by the date of the trial. They have to be expressly pleaded and, in practice, are usually agreed by the parties prior to the hearing. Although they relate to specific pecuniary losses which the claimant says have already been incurred, they are governed by the same principles which apply to damages generally and, in particular, future probabilities can be taken into account in calculating them.

[1]   *Per* Edmund Davies LJ in *Cutler v Vauxhall Motors [1971] 1 QB 418* at 426, *[1970] 2 All ER 56* at 61. See also *Coates v Curry* (1997) Times, 22 August, in which the Court of Appeal emphasised the importance of maintaining the distinction between special and general damages.

Where treatment inevitable

[24.03] In *Cutler v Vauxhall Motors Ltd*[1] the plaintiff grazed one of his ankles at work due to his employers' negligence. Shortly afterwards, he was discovered to have a varicose condition in both legs, which must have existed before the accident. The effect of the injury, against the background of that condition, was to cause an ulcer to develop at the site of the graze. This necessitated surgery for the varicose condition itself. The operation was properly carried out, but in consequence the plaintiff lost £173 in wages due to time off work. The Court of Appeal held by a majority,[2] however, that this sum was not recoverable as special damages since the probability was that, because of the pre-existing condition, he would have had to have had the same operation in a few years anyway.

1   *[1971] 1 QB 418, [1970] 2 All ER 56. Cf Salih v Enfield Health Authority [1991] 3 All ER 400, CA.*
2   Edmund Davies and Karminski LJJ; Russell LJ dissenting.

Delaying trial

[24.04] It has been held that special damages for pre-trial lost earnings may also be reduced if a claimant disabled by a neurotic condition, which can be expected to clear up after the trial, prolongs his disability by unjustifiably delaying the trial.[1]

1   *James v Woodhall Duckham Construction Co Ltd [1969] 2 All ER 794, [1969] 1 WLR 903, CA.*

General damages

Categorisation not exclusive

[24.05] General damages consist of all post-trial pecuniary losses along with all non-pecuniary loss. They familiarly include the three items listed in the above quotation by Lord Denning, but those headings, although often convenient, are not exclusive in the sense that losses which cannot easily be categorised within them are thereby excluded. For example, the *distress* caused by estrangement[1] or divorce,[2] if a foreseeable consequence of the claimant's injuries, can be taken into account in calculating general damages. Distress caused by potential difficulties in starting or completing a family has been the subject of awards in medical negligence cases.[3] Successful claims have also included awards for inability to carry out unpaid services, such as housework,[4] and even loss of enjoyment of a holiday.[5] Although general damages as such do not have to be pleaded, a claimant who alleges that he will sustain losses in the future of a kind not normally to be expected must nevertheless ensure that the basis for such a claim appears on the pleadings, and that appropriate evidence is adduced in support.[6]

1   See *Lampert v Eastern National Omnibus Co [1954] 2 All ER 719n, [1954] 1 WLR 1047.*
2   The *financial* consequences of divorce, however, apparently *cannot* be taken into account: see *Pritchard v J H Cobden [1988] Fam 22, [1987] 1 All ER 300,* CA, not following *Jones v Jones [1985] QB 704, [1984] 3 All ER 1003,* CA.
3   See *Kralj v MacGrath [1986] 1 All ER 54.*
4   *Daly v General Steam Navigation Co Ltd, The Dragon [1980] 3 All ER 696, [1981] 1 WLR 120, CA.*
5   *Ichard v Frangoulis [1977] 2 All ER 461, [1977] 1 WLR 556.*
6   See *Domsalla v Barr (t/a AB Construction) [1969] 3 All ER 487, [1969] 1 WLR 630, CA.*

Fresh evidence

[24.06] Particular items of loss might, of course, be too remote,[1] or irrecoverable on grounds of public policy.[2] If a claimant's situation changes dramatically between the date of the trial and the hearing of an appeal, the otherwise rarely exercised discretion to admit fresh evidence may be exercised in relation to the assessment of general damages.[3] Even the House of Lords may be prepared in such a case to take into account events which have occurred since the hearing in the Court of Appeal.[4]

1   See CHAPTER 3 above.
2   Cf *Burns v Edman [1970] 2 QB 541, [1970] 1 All ER 886.*

³   *Mulholland v Mitchell [1971] AC 666, [1971] 1 All ER 307, HL; McCann v Sheppard [1973] 2 All ER 881, [1973] 1 WLR 540, CA.*
⁴   *Murphy v Stone-Wallwork (Charlton) Ltd [1969] 2 All ER 949, [1969] 1 WLR 1023, HL.*

Itemisation and the overall sum

[24.07]   The practice of assessing the various components of general damages separately, referred to by Lord Denning MR in the *Lim* case, originated in relatively recent times. Lord Denning himself once apparently favoured the view that one global sum should be awarded comprising both the pecuniary and non-pecuniary losses, and that trial judges should not perceive themselves as being under a duty expressly to itemise in their judgments the sums awarded under the various heads.[1] The main justification advanced in support of this view was the belief that itemisation would tend to produce larger awards, and that this would be undesirable.[2]

¹   See *Watson v Powles [1968] 1 QB 596, [1967] 3 All ER 721, CA.*
²   See *Fletcher v Autocar & Transporters Ltd [1968] 2 QB 322* at 335–336, *[1968] 1 All ER 726* at 733–734, *per* Lord Denning MR.

Introduction of itemisation

[24.08]   The adoption of itemisation fortuitously became necessary, however, as a result of a change in the statute law quite unrelated to the underlying issues of principle or policy involved. In 1969 the *Administration of Justice Act, s 22* made it obligatory for the courts to award interest on damages in personal injury cases.[1] In *Jefford v Gee*[2] the Court of Appeal held that it would be appropriate for the different components of an award to carry interest at differing rates, and for differing periods, and that in consequence itemisation of awards would henceforth become necessary. Since 1970 the practice of itemisation has accordingly become general.[3] As a result, it is now possible for awards to be appealed on the basis that individual components thereof have been wrongly assessed;[4] and if an error of principle is disclosed which would make a substantial difference to the total figure, the appeal will succeed.[5] Nevertheless, the appellate courts have tended to insist until very recently that it is the total figure 'which must be fair and reasonable'[6] and to discourage highly detailed calculations of each component when the size of the 'single capital sum ... is the figure that matters to the plaintiff'.[7]

¹   See now the *Supreme Court Act 1981, s 35A* (inserted by the *Administration of Justice Act 1982, s 15* and *Sch 1*).
²   *[1970] 2 QB 130, [1970] 1 All ER 1202, CA.*
³   Cf *Jamil bin Harun v Yang Kamsiah Bte Meor Rasdi [1984] AC 529, [1984] 2 WLR 668*, PC; see also *Lai Wee Lian v Singapore Bus Service (1978) Ltd [1984] AC 729, [1984] 3 WLR 63*, PC.
⁴   See *George v Pinnock [1973] 1 All ER 926, [1973] 1 WLR 118, CA.*
⁵   See *Lai Wee Lian v Singapore Bus Service (1978) Ltd [1984] AC 729, [1984] 3 WLR 63, PC.*
⁶   See *per* Lord Scarman in *Lim Poh Choo v Camden and Islington Area Health Authority [1980] AC 174* at 191, *[1979] 2 All ER 910* at 921.
⁷   See *per* Lord Diplock in *Paul v Rendell (1981) 34 ALR 569* at 580, PC. The *Royal Commission on Civil Liability and Compensation for Personal Injury* (Pearson) recommended that 'an award of damages, however itemised, should not be interfered with on appeal unless it is inordinately high or inordinately low as a whole' (Cmnd 7054–I, para 763).

Change in approach

[24.09]   A significant change in approach would, however, appear to have been brought about by the decision of the House of Lords in *Wells v Wells*.[1] In that case the

House favoured the use of actuarial tables and the adoption of a more precise, and less impressionistic, approach to the calculation of future losses in personal injury cases. Lord Clyde, in particular, expressed himself as follows:[2]

> 'The lump sum award which has to be made is in most cases a composition of several distinct elements. Each requires to be assessed as a single sum and the total represents the compensation. But while in the course of the exercise the judge's task may involve an exercise of a discretion based on his experience coloured by the particular facts of the case, the totality of the elements should not be a matter open to increase or modification merely on account of a feeling that the total seems unduly large or small. If each of the elements has individually achieved the best approximation possible to the proper compensation for each particular aspect of the claim, then the total figure should correspondingly represent the best assessment possible for the total claim. If at the conclusion of the exercise the judge is uneasy at the total result he should not seek to make any overall adjustment in either direction to the total award to meet his unease; he should return to reconsider each element in the calculation and secure that there is no need for revision at that level.'

[1]   *[1998] 3 All ER 481, HL.* See further CHAPTER 25 below.
[2]   See *[1998] 3 All ER 481* at 512.

Overlap

[24.10]   In most cases', said Lord Scarman in *Lim Poh Choo v Camden and Islington Area Health Authority,* 'the risk of overlap is not great, nor, where it occurs, is it substantial'.[1] Nevertheless, the danger of 'over-compensation', by duplication of losses under different heads, is one to which the courts have been alive.[2] Clearly, the expenses involved in earning the income which has been lost have to be taken into account in calculating the award for lost earnings. Similarly, where a claimant is totally incapacitated, and requires permanent care, the damages awarded under this head must not overlap with the award for lost earnings in so far as the actual expenses of living itself are concerned.[3] In addition, however, it has sometimes been judicially suggested that the courts should also take into account a supposed possible overlap between damages for lost earnings on the one hand, and damages for pain and suffering and loss of amenities on the other. One basis for the suggestion was that enjoyment of the amenities, if the claimant had not been injured, would have involved expenditure of part of the earnings.[4] Another was simply that, particularly where the figure for lost earnings is very substantial, this in itself should to some extent reduce the claimant's distress and could therefore be allowed to count towards compensation for pain and suffering and loss of amenities.[5]

[1]   *[1980] AC 174* at 191, *[1979] 2 All ER 910* at 921.
[2]   See *Taylor v Bristol Omnibus Co Ltd [1975] 2 All ER 1107* at 1113, *[1975] 1 WLR 1054* at 1057, *per* Lord Denning MR.
[3]   See *Lim Poh Choo v Camden Health Authority [1980] AC 174* at 191, *[1979] 2 All ER 910* at 921.
[4]   See *Fletcher v Autocar & Transporters [1968] 2 QB 322* at 351, *[1968] 1 All ER 726* at 743, *per* Diplock LJ.
[5]   See *Smith v Central Asbestos [1972] 1 QB 244* at 262, *[1971] 3 All ER 204* at 213, *per* Lord Denning MR (not considered in *[1973] AC 518*).

Proposition invalid

[24.11]   On the other hand, both the Law Commission[1] and the Pearson Commission[2] were opposed to any alteration in the size of awards, for pecuniary and non-pecuniary loss respectively, by reference to the size of the other. In *Lim Poh Choo v Camden Health Authority* Lord Scarman expressed no final opinion on the point, but he noted the view of the Pearson Commission and stated that he, too, doubted the possibility of overlap between these two heads.[3] Moreover, the proposition that any such alleged overlap should be taken into account would now seem to be inconsistent with the more precise approach to the assessment of damages for personal injury favoured by the House of Lords in *Wells v Wells*.[4] It is submitted that the proposition can therefore be regarded as invalid.

[1] See Law Commission Report no 56 (1973) (*Report on Personal Injury Litigation-Assessment of Damages*). The Commission took the same view when it looked at the matter again a quarter of a century later: see *Damages for Personal Injury: Non-Pecuniary Loss* (Law Com no 257, 1999) paras 2.65–2.68.

[2] See the Report of the *Royal Commission on Civil Liability and Compensation for Personal Injury* (Pearson) (Cmnd 7054–I) para 759.

[3] *[1980] AC 174* at 192, *[1974] 2 All ER 910* at 922.

[4] *[1998] 3 All ER 481, HL.*

B Mitigation

Claimant's state of knowledge

[24.12] The general law relating to a claimant's duty to mitigate his loss applies to damages for personal injury. In one case[1] it was unsuccessfully contended that the plaintiff had failed in this duty by omitting to claim, until it was too late to do so, certain social security benefits which, had they been obtained, would have been partially deducted from the damages under the *Law Reform (Personal Injuries) Act 1948, s 2(1)*.[2] The reason for the plaintiff's failure to claim was ignorance on her part of her entitlement to do so. In resolving the point in the plaintiff's favour, MacKenna J observed that:

'a plaintiff must always do what is reasonable to mitigate his loss, but in deciding what was reasonable for him to do, one must have regard to his actual knowledge whether of law or of fact. A plaintiff who does not know that he has a right does not act unreasonably in failing to exercise it.'[3]

[1] *Eley v Bedford [1972] 1 QB 155, [1971] 3 All ER 285.*

[2] A provision repealed by the *Social Security (Recovery of Benefits) Act 1997.*

[3] *[1972] 1 QB 155* at 158, *[1971] 3 All ER 285* at 288. On the deductability of social security benefits generally, and the effect of the *Social Security (Recovery of Benefits) Act 1997*, see below CHAPTER 25.

Refusal of medical treatment

[24.13] Questions involving the duty to mitigate often arise where the claimant refuses to undergo surgery, or other medical treatment, which the defendant claims would remove or ameliorate the condition brought about by the latter's negligence.[1] Here also the matter is to be resolved in the light of the claimant's state of knowledge having regard to the medical or other advice actually received by him. A claimant may therefore be reasonable, for the purposes of the rule, in refusing treatment even if it can be shown that if better informed, or better presented, advice had been given to him, the same decision would have been unreasonable.[2] The question of reasonableness itself, however, is usually resolved objectively: 'would a reasonable man in all the circumstances, receiving the advice which the plaintiff did receive, have refused the operation.'[3] Thus, overwhelming fear of surgical treatment, however bona fide and deep-seated, will not apparently be enough in itself to justify refusal.[4] This objective approach has been adopted by the Supreme Court of Canada.[5]

[1]   See A H Hudson 'Refusal of Medical Treatment' (1983) 3 LS 50.
[2]   See *Fazlic v Milingimbi Community Inc (1981) 38 ALR 424 (Aust Full Ct HC)*, referred to with approval by the Privy Council in *Selvanayagam v University of the West Indies [1983] 1 All ER 824, [1983] 1 WLR 585, PC*. See also *Karabotsos v Plastex Industries Pty Ltd [1981] VR 675*.
[3]   *Morgan v T Wallis Ltd [1974] 1 Lloyd's Rep 165* at 170, *per* Browne J.
[4]   *Morgan v T Wallis [1974] 1 Lloyd's Rep 165*. See also *Marcroft v Scruttons [1954] 1 Lloyd's Rep 395, CA*.
[5]   See *Janiak v Ippolito (1985) 16 DLR (4th) 1*. For a valuable note on the various issues in this case, see A H Hudson 'Mitigation and Refusal of Medical Treatment Again' (1986) 49 MLR 381.

Sympathetic treatment of claimant

[24.14]   On the other hand, there are also indications in the authorities that the objective approach should not be applied with excessive rigour.[1] In a case on the point decided under the old Workmen's Compensation Acts, which reached the House of Lords,[2] Lord Wright observed that 'the workman's own physical or mental idiosyncrasy cannot in general be excluded'. His Lordship favoured the adoption of 'a humane and liberal spirit, realising that the question cannot be decided save on a sympathetic estimate of the workman's personality and the special circumstances of the particular case'.[3] A similar approach is, perhaps, reflected in the recent decision of the Judicial Committee of the Privy Council in *Geest v Lansiquot*[4], in which the Board held that the medical evidence relied on by the defendants was insufficient to establish that the plaintiff's refusal to undergo surgery on her back had been unreasonable. Where the relevant medical opinions given to the claimant are at all conflicting it is very unlikely that his decision to refuse treatment will be regarded as unreasonable.[5] If, however, the claimant *is* found to have been unreasonable in refusing treatment, the Supreme Court of Canada has held that he may nevertheless be entitled to damages to reflect the chance that even if the treatment had been administered it might not in fact have been successful.[6]

[1]   See *Karabotsos v Plastex Industries Pty Ltd [1981] VR 675*, in which the cases are reviewed.
[2]   *Steele v Robert George & Co (1937) Ltd [1942] AC 497, [1942] 1 All ER 447, HL*.
[3]   *[1942] AC 497* at 503–504, *[1942] 1 All ER 447* at 450.
[4]   *[2002] 1 WLR 3111*.
[5]   See *Steele v Robert George & Co (1937) Ltd [1942] AC 497, [1942] 1 All ER 447, HL*. See also *McAuley v London Transport Executive [1957] 2 Lloyd's Rep 500* at 505, *per* Jenkins LJ.
[6]   See *Janiak v Ippolito (1985) 16 DLR (4th) 1*.

Onus of proof

[24.15]   The burden of proving that the plaintiff is in breach of his duty to mitigate is in general on the defendant.[1] In *Selvanayagam v University of West Indies*,[2] however, the Judicial Committee of the Privy Council held that, on the particular question of refusal of medical treatment, the onus was on the plaintiff to show that his refusal was reasonable, and not on the defendant to show that it was unreasonable.[3] This view was, however, inconsistent with a long line of authorities to the contrary which do not appear to have been cited to the Board[4]. Moreover, in *Janiak v Ippolito* the Canadian Supreme Court refused to follow it. Fortunately, the decision in *Selvanayagam's* case would now appear, in effect, to have been overruled by the much more recent decision of the Privy Council itself in *Geest v Lansiquot*[6]. In this case the Board referred to the heavy criticism to which *Selvanayagam's* case had been subjected by commentators, and accepted as 'soundly based' the proposition that 'the decision cannot be relied on as an accurate statement of the law on this point'[7]. The Board in *Geest v Lansiquot* also emphasised that a defendant who proposes to contend that a plaintiff failed to mitigate should clear notice to the latter in advance, by pleading or otherwise[8].

[1] *McGregor on Damages* (17th edn, 2003) p 223, para 7–019.
[2] *[1983] 1 All ER 824, [1983] 1 WLR 585.*
[3] *[1983] 1 All ER 824* at 827, *[1983] 1 WLR 585* at 589, *per* Lord Scarman delivering the judgment of the Board (burden discharged on the facts).
[4] See *Steele v Robert George & Co (1937) Ltd [1942] AC 497, [1942] 1 All ER 447, HL; Watts v Rake (1960) 108 CLR 158* at 159, *per* Dixon CJ; *Morgan v T Wallis [1974] 1 Lloyd's Rep 165* at 170, *per* Browne J.
[5] *(1985) 16 DLR (4th) 1.*
[6] *[2002] 1 WLR 3111.*
[7] See above at para 14 of the judgment of the Board.
[8] See *[2002] 1 WLR 3111* at para 16.

C Subsequent events

Allowance for contingencies

[24.16] In assessing damages for future lost earnings in personal injury cases it was long 'accepted doctrine', in the words of Lord Wilberforce in *Jobling v Associated Dairies Ltd*,[1] that 'allowance, if necessary some discount, has to be made ... for the normal contingencies of life'. It was felt that the plaintiff would be over-compensated if the possibility of contingencies such as unemployment, which might have struck him at some time in the future irrespective of the injury inflicted by the defendant, were to be ignored in assessing the lump sum awarded at the conclusion of the trial.

[1] *[1982] AC 794* at 802, *[1981] 2 All ER 752* at 754, HL.

Multiplier and actuarial tables

[24.17] The need to allow for the 'contingencies of life' was conventionally reflected in the choice of 'multiplier' used to calculate the damages for lost earnings in the particular case.[1] In *Wells v Wells*,[2] however, the House of Lords held that, as far as the cost of future *care* is concerned, the court should attempt to arrive at the multiplier by using actuarial tables, and should only take into account additionally any medical evidence relating to the effect of the particular plaintiff's condition on his or her life expectancy. Lord Lloyd said:[3]

'[Counsel for the plaintiff] conceded that there is room for a judicial discount when calculating the loss of future earnings, when contingencies may affect the result. But there is no room for any discount in the case of a whole life multiplier with an agreed expectation of life. In the case of loss of earnings, the contingencies can work only in one direction – in favour of the defendant. But in the case of life expectancy, the contingency can work in either direction. The plaintiff may exceed his normal expectation of life, or he may fall short of it. There is no purpose in the courts making as accurate a prediction as they can of the plaintiff's future needs if the resulting sum is arbitrarily reduced for no better reason than that the prediction might be wrong'.

[1] See CHAPTER 25 below.

²   *[1998] 3 All ER 481, HL.*
³   See *[1998] 3 All ER 481* at 497.

General discounting discouraged

[24.18] Although the focus of their Lordships in *Wells v Wells* was primarily upon the assessment of the cost of future care, it is clear that the general emphasis in the speeches was opposed to substantial general discounting of multipliers on vague grounds not closely related to the specific case[1]. This welcome new approach will therefore have an effect upon the assessment of damages for lost earnings as well as upon those for the cost of future care. Moreover, the 'Ogden Tables'[2] seek to take contingencies such as the risk of unemployment into account, so that their use should also limit the scope for judicial discounting for risks of that kind except on grounds peculiar to the particular case. An increase in multipliers was therefore anticipated in *Wells v Wells*.[3]

¹   See also *Royal Victoria Infirmary v B [2002] PIQR Q10.*
²   Ie the *Actuarial Tables with explanatory notes for use in Personal Injury and Fatal Accident cases*, produced by a working party chaired by Sir Michael Ogden QC and published by the Government Actuary.
³   See *per* Lord Clyde and Lord Hutton in *Wells v Wells [1998] 3 All ER 481* at 515, 521.

Occurrence of events before trial

[24.19] It is paradoxical that, in the case law, greater uncertainty has been generated by situations in which the need for speculation has been removed. This occurs where a subsequent and unrelated event, which substantially affects the claimant, actually materialises before the trial of his claim against the defendant. Where the subsequent event is illness, however, it is now established that the principle that 'the court must not speculate when it knows'[1] will apply. The illness will therefore be taken into account and, if appropriate, the award of damages will be reduced. In *Jobling v Associated Dairies*[2] the plaintiff suffered a back injury, due to the negligence of the defendants, which halved his former earning capacity. But before the case came on for trial the plaintiff developed a disease, unrelated to the accident, which rendered him wholly unfit for work. Although the trial judge held that the illness should neverthe-less be ignored in calculating the plaintiff's damages for lost earnings, his decision was unanimously reversed by the Court of Appeal and the House of Lords, which held that the plaintiff was not entitled from the date of the onset of the illness.[3]

¹   *Per* Lord Edmund-Davies in *Jobling v Associated Dairies [1982] AC 794* at 807, *[1981] 2 All ER 752* at 758. Cf *Curwen v James [1963] 2 All ER 619, [1963] 1 WLR 748, CA.*
²   *[1982] AC 794, [1981] 2 All ER 752, HL.*
³   See also *Hodgson v General Electricity Co Ltd [1978] 2 Lloyd's Rep 210; Penner v Mitchell [1978] 5 WWR 328.*

Where subsequent event is tortious

[24.20] The position is less certain, however, if the subsequent event is itself a tort. In *Baker v Willoughby*[1] the plaintiff suffered an injury to his left leg in a road accident. But before his claim, for the injuries which he incurred, was tried he was unfortunately the victim of an attack by armed robbers. He was shot in the left leg and the leg had to be amputated. In these circumstances the House of Lords held that the defendant, the negligent motorist, was liable for all the plaintiff's losses, calculated on the assumption that the disability caused by the motor accident had not been superseded by the robbery. Their Lordships were concerned to avoid a situation in which the first defendant in such circumstances could claim that his damages should be reduced by the second incident, while the second defendant could claim that, since his victim had already been disabled, the extent of his liability should on that account be reduced. If this were to be allowed the plaintiff would obviously be under-compensated even if he succeeded in obtaining judgment against both defendants.[2] In order to avoid the injustice of such a result, it is possible that, in its own facts, the decision in *Baker v Willoughby* remains correct.[3]

[1] *[1970] AC 467.* Cf *Performance Cars Ltd v Abraham [1962] 1 QB 33, [1961] 3 All ER 413, CA.*
[2] See *[1970] AC 467* at 495, *per* Lord Pearson.
[3] See *Jobling v Associated Dairies [1982] AC 794* at 810, 815, *[1981] 2 All ER 752* at 760, 764, *per* Lord Russell and Lord Keith. Cf Borrowdale 'Vicissitudes in the Assessment of Damages' (1983) 32 ICLQ 651.

Difficult distinction

[24.21] Nevertheless, a sharp distinction between tortious and non-tortious supervening events does not in principle seem easy to support in the present context.[1] Moreover, although the case was not overruled, the reasoning in *Baker v Willoughby* was heavily criticised by the House of Lords itself in *Jobling v Associated Dairies*,[2] and is unlikely to be extended.[3] It is also somewhat surprising that, as Lord Edmund-Davies pointed out in the latter case,[4] no mention was made in *Baker v Willoughby* of the possibility of the plaintiff's claiming under the Criminal Injuries Scheme in respect of the injuries inflicted by the robbers.

[1] Cf *per* Lord Keith in *Jobling v Associated Dairies [1982] AC 752* at 816, *[1981] 2 All ER 752* at 764. See also A Davies in (1982) 45 MLR 329 at 332.
[2] *[1982] AC 794, [1981] 2 All ER 752.* But for a forceful defence of *Baker v Willoughby*, see M A Jones *Textbook on Torts* (8th edn, 2002) pp 2534–2554.
[3] See especially *per* Lord Edmund-Davies and Lord Bridge, *[1982] AC 794* at 804ff, 816ff, *[1981] 2 All ER 752* at 757ff, 765ff.
[4] See *[1982] AC 794* at 807, *[1981] 2 All ER 752* at 758.

Assessing damages for second tort

[24.22] In *Murrell v Healy*[1] the claimant was involved in two road accidents, six months apart, and received compensation in respect of both of them. The first accident left him able only to undertake light work, whereas the second accident rendered him unable to work at all. When the award for the second accident was considered by the Court of Appeal, however, the claimant contended that he should be compensated in full in respect of his inability to work, and that the compensation which he had already received in respect of the first accident should be ignored. The court rejected this contention. Waller LJ said[2]:

' … it would seem to be accepted even in *Baker v Willoughby* that the second tortfeasor is only responsible for the additional damage that the second tortfeasor has caused'.

[1] *[2001] 4 All ER 345.*
[2] See *[2001] 4 All ER 345* at para 19.

Contingencies principle unaffected

[24.23] In *Heil v Rankin (Appeal against Damages)*[1] the claimant, a police officer, was involved in two serious tortious events, twelve years apart. The first one had left him prone to attacks of post-traumatic stress disorder, but still able to work. The second triggered a major attack of post-traumatic stress disorder and effectively left him unable to work. In assessing the claimant's damages for loss of future earnings in respect of the second tort, the judge discounted the award to reflect the chance that, even if that incident had not occurred, some other tortious event might have triggered a serious attack of the claimant's disorder leaving him incapacitated. The claimant contended, by analogy with *Baker v Wllloughby*, that the judge's approach had been incorrect. He argued that, since an actual subsequent tort had been ignored in that case, hypothetical future torts should also be ignored. The Court of Appeal rejected this submission. The judge had done 'no more than apply what has become known as the "vicissitudes' principle" '[2]. Unlike *Baker v Willoughby* itself, where the House of Lords had been anxious to avoid under-compensation, the claimant would be over-compensated 'if future vicissitudes [were] not taken into account under the normal principle'[3]. Otton LJ said[4]:

> 'If future tortious acts had to be ignored, even though they were, as they were found to be in this case, a foreseeable, indeed likely, source of early termination of the plaintiff's employment, but the plaintiff had nonetheless to be compensated on the basis of full employment to retiring age, then it seems self-evident that he would be compensated for sums that the tort had not caused him to lose'[5].

[1] *[2001] PIQR Q3, CA.*
[2] See above at para 12, *per* Otton LJ.
[3] See *[2001] PIQR Q3, CA* at para 19.
[4] See above at the same paragraph.
[5] Cf a dictum of the High Court of Australia, apparently to the opposite effect, in *Wynn v NSW Insurance Corporation (1995) 184 CLR 405* at 498–499. This passage is considered, but rejected, in the judgment of the Court of Appeal in *Heil v Rankin*.

D Allowing for deterioration

Provisional damages

[24.24] In certain cases a complicating factor in the assessment of damages is that the full nature and extent of the claimant's injuries may not reveal themselves until long after the trial, perhaps not until years have elapsed. The chance that epilepsy[1] may subsequently develop as a result of a blow on the head is a well-known example.[2] The best that the court could formerly do in such a case was to award a sum greater than would have been appropriate if development of the disability had not been a possibility, but smaller than would have been appropriate had it been a certainty. Depending upon the eventual outcome, the level of compensation received would of necessity be unfair to either the plaintiff or the defendant. The *Administration of Justice Act 1982, s 6*, however, sought to tackle this problem by making possible awards of 'provisional damages' in such cases. The section added a new provision, *section 32A*, to the *Supreme Court Act 1981* which, where material, reads as follows:

> 'provision may be made by rules of court, in such circumstances as may be prescribed, to award the injured person—

(a) damages assessed on the assumption that the injured person will not develop the disease or suffer the deterioration in his condition; and

(b) further damages at a future date if he develops the disease or suffers the deterioration.'

[1] See M Weller 'The Statute of Time Limitation in Post-Traumatic Epilepsy' (1986) NLJ 409.
[2] See *Hawkins v New Mendip Engineering Ltd [1966] 3 All ER 228, [1966] 1 WLR 1341*, CA; *Jones v Griffith [1969] 2 All ER 1015, [1969] 1 WLR 795, CA.*

More accurate awards

[24.25] The provision came into force in 1985 when the relevant rules of court were promulgated. The court therefore now has the power to achieve, in theory at least, accurate awards in situations of the kind in question by certifying that the award at the trial is to be provisional only and that the claimant can apply for further damages if the situation so warrants. It should be noted that a claim for provisional damages has to be included in the statement of claim and the court has to be satisfied, if the defendant objects, that the action is of a kind within the scope of *section 32A*.[1] The section was considered by Scott Baker J in *Willson v Ministry of Defence*,[2] who held, inter alia, that 'serious deterioration' had to be distinguished from the ordinary deterioration to be expected as part of the progression of the particular condition in question.

[1] The court has a discretion: *Willson v Ministry of Defence [1991] 1 All ER 638.*
[2] *[1991] 1 All ER 638.*

Fatal Accidents Act awards unaffected

[24.26] The *Damages Act 1996, s 3* further enhanced the attractiveness of provisional damages by ensuring that such an award does not operate, in the event of the victim's death, totally to exclude a claim by his dependants under the *Fatal Accidents Act 1976.*[1]

[1] See CHAPTER 26 below.

Other procedures for postponing assessment

[24.27] Other, longer-established, procedures will sometimes be relevant in situations in which the assessment of damages either will, or ought to be, delayed for any reason. One of these is the power, if liability is admitted (or established by interlocutory judgment), to compel certain categories of defendant to make interim payments of damages to the claimant prior to the full hearing on quantum. Another is the power of the court to order that the issues of liability and quantum be tried separately.[1] The court will not, however, issue declarations that claimants should be indemnified by defendants, in the event of speculative future events occurring, when such declarations would circumvent the limitations on the scope of *section 32A* of the *Supreme Court Act 1981* itself[2].

[1] See *Coenen v Payne [1974] 2 All ER 1109, [1974] 1 WLR 984, CA.* Awards in such cases only carry interest from the date of the final judgment on quantum and not from that of the earlier judgment on liability: *Thomas v Bunn [1991] 1 AC 362, [1991] 1 All ER 193, HL.*
[2] See *Firth v Geo Ackroyd Junior Ltd [2001] PIQR Q4.*

E Interest

Special damages

[24.28] Since 1969 the courts have been obliged to award interest on damages in cases of personal injury.[1] Special damages normally carry interest at half the 'appropriate rate' from the date of service of the writ to the date of the trial.[2] The 'appropriate rate' is the rate payable on money paid into court which is placed on special investment account.[3] The rate is halved in order to allow, in a rough and ready way, for the fact that not all of the recoverable expenditure will have been incurred at the same time, so that the claimant will not have been out of pocket with respect to the whole sum throughout the relevant period.

[1] See now the *Supreme Court Act 1981, s 35A* and the *County Courts Act 1959, s 97A*: provisions inserted by the *Administration of Justice Act 1982, s 15* to supersede the *Administration of Justice Act 1969, s 22*.

[2] *Jefford v Gee [1970] 2 QB 130, [1970] 1 All ER 1202, CA*. A claimant who wishes to claim interest on his special damages at a different rate must make clear the special circumstances on which he relies in so claiming: *Dexter v Courtaulds [1984] 1 All ER 70, [1984] 1 WLR 372, CA*.

[3] The relevant rates since 1965 are set out in the *Supreme Court Practice*.

General damages

[24.29] Damages for loss of future earnings, or for loss of earning capacity, do not carry interest, since *ex hypothesi* they compensate for losses which have not yet been incurred.[1] For a time there was considerable judicial uncertainty as to the position regarding damages for non-economic loss, ie pain and suffering and loss of amenities. In one case the Court of Appeal suggested that no interest at all should be awarded under this head,[2] but this was overruled by the House of Lords in *Pickett v British Rail Engineering Ltd*.[3] The House did not indicate, however, in *Pickett*'s case what rate of interest should be applied. Subsequently the Court of Appeal, in *Birkett v Hayes*,[4] held that normally 2% would be appropriate, and this was confirmed by the House of Lords in *Wright v British Railways Board*.[5] The underlying reasoning was that in a period of high inflation, such as appertained until relatively recently, it is extremely difficult to increase in real terms the value of sums invested, and the effect of inflation upon the value of money generally should be reflected by appropriate increases in the figures awarded for the non-economic loss itself.[6] Their Lordships accepted that, in the event of greater stabilisation in the value of money, an increase in the 2% figure would be appropriate. But they also emphasised the desirability of having a fixed figure that will remain constant for long periods, in order to facilitate settlement of the great majority of personal injury cases which never come to trial.[7]

[1] *Jefford v Gee [1970] 2 QB 130, [1970] 1 All ER 1202, CA*; *Cookson v Knowles [1979] AC 556, [1978] 2 All ER 604, HL*.

[2] See *Cookson v Knowles [1977] QB 913, [1977] 2 All ER 820, CA*; not considered in *[1979] AC 556, [1978] 2 All ER 604, HL*.

[3] *[1980] AC 136, [1979] 1 All ER 774, HL*.

[4] *[1982] 2 All ER 710, [1982] 1 WLR 816*.

[5] *[1983] 2 AC 773, [1983] 2 All ER 698*.

[6] See *Wright v British Rlys Board [1983] 2 AC 773* at 785, *[1983] 2 All ER 698* at 706, *per* Lord Diplock.

[7] See *[1983] 2 AC 773* at 784, *[1983] 2 All ER 698* at 705, *per* Lord Diplock. The rate remained at 2% in 2003. But see D Kemp QC in 'Damages for Personal Injuries: A Sea Change' (1998) 114 LQR 570 at 571, contending that the logic of the decision of the House of Lords in *Wells v Wells [1998] 3 All ER 481* is that 3% (the current Index Linked Government Stock figure) should now be adopted.

Chapter 25

Damages recoverable for personal injury

A Non-pecuniary loss

Pain and suffering

[25.01] In *Wells v Wells*[1] Lord Hope of Craighead observed that:

> 'The amount of the award to be made for pain, suffering and loss of amenity cannot be precisely calculated. All that can be done is to award such sum, within the broad criterion of what is reasonable and in line with similar awards in comparable cases, as represents the court's best estimate of the plaintiff's general damages.'[2]

Awards for pain and suffering on the one hand, and those for loss of amenities on the other, are usually lumped together and rarely itemised separately. Nevertheless, it is clear from cases involving unconscious accident victims that pain and suffering is a conceptually distinct head of damage, since such victims are awarded damages for loss of amenity[3] but not for pain and suffering. The latter is necessarily a subjective matter and a person who, due to unconsciousness, is unaware of his condition and cannot feel pain, will not receive any award under this head.[4] By contrast, a person in the position of the plaintiff in one case, who was described as having 'painful and prolonged awareness of how much she has lost and what little she has left',[5] will warrant a substantial award.

---

[1] *[1998] 3 All ER 481* at 507, HL.

[2] See also *per* Diplock LJ in *Wise v Kaye [1962] 1 QB 638* at 664, *[1962] 1 All ER 257* at 271, CA: '"Pain and suffering", which ... I take as comprising both physical and mental anguish, if there be any scientific distinction between the two, cannot be measured in pounds, shillings and pence. Looked at in isolation, there is no logical reason why for one week of pain the right award should be £20 rather than £200. All that can be said is that, once you accept as a premise or convention that £20 is the right award for one week of pain, the right award for two weeks of similar pain is in the region of £40 and not in the region of £400, and that a figure in the same region is the right award for each of two sufferers with similar thresholds of pain.'

[3] See below.

[4] *See H West & Son v Shephard [1964] AC 326, [1963] 2 All ER 625, HL.* See also *Wise v Kaye [1962] 1 QB 638, [1962] 1 All ER 257, CA.*

[5] *Powell v Phillips [1972] 3 All ER 864* at 871, *per* Stephenson LJ.

Some degree of awareness

[25.02] The presence or absence of awareness can, however, in some cases of seriously injured victims, itself be a matter of uncertainty. In practice, however, it appears that if the claimant is not actually comatose he will usually be taken to have some degree of awareness of his condition, and assumed thereby to 'suffer' in consequence of it, even if not in actual physical pain. The plaintiff in *Lim Poh Choo v Camden Health Authority*[6] suffered very extensive brain damage in an anaesthetic accident. In the words of the trial judge, a doctor who examined her 'found her emotional state to be blank and she was completely lacking in volition and spontaneity. Her powers of reasoning were impossible to test'.[7] Nevertheless, in the Court of Appeal Lawton LJ said that he did 'not accept that the plaintiff was in such an insensitive condition that it can be assumed that she does not appreciate what her condition is ... The fact that she cannot express what she feels does not mean she does not feel at all'.[8]

1   *[1980] AC 174, [1979] 2 All ER 910, HL*; affg *[1979] QB 196, [1979] 1 All ER 332, CA.*
2   *[1979] QB 196* at 201, *[1979] 1 All ER 332* at 335 (Bristow J).
3   *[1979] QB 196* at 224, *[1979] 1 All ER 332* at 347, CA; see also, *per* Browne LJ *[1979] QB 196* at 227, *[1979] 1 All ER 332* at 349–350. Cf, *per* Lord Scarman in the House of Lords *[1980] AC 174* at 189, *[1979] 2 All ER 910* at 919.

Duration

[25.03]   Although compensation for pain and suffering necessarily involves quantifying the unquantifiable, actual or probable *duration* of the pain is in principle measurable. As a part of general damages the sum awarded for pain and suffering notionally covers both pre-trial and future 'loss'. But if the claimant dies before the trial, the finite duration of any pain and suffering will necessarily produce a lower award than would otherwise have been the case.[1]

1   See *McCann v Sheppard [1973] 2 All ER 881, [1973] 1 WLR 540, CA.*

Reduced life expectancy

[25.04]   Prior to 1982, plaintiffs whose lives had been shortened as a result of negligence were able to recover a fixed conventional sum[1] (by 1981 it was usually a little over £1,000[2]) in respect of this loss. If they died before trial their estate could similarly recover the same sum under the *Law Reform (Miscellaneous Provisions) Act 1934*.[3] This award was always distinct from the much more substantial amount payable to living plaintiffs, as part of their damages for pain and suffering, to compensate them for their distress in *knowing* that their expectation of life had been reduced. The conventional award for loss of expectation of life was abolished by the *Administration of Justice Act 1982, s 1(1)(a)*, but the same Act also made clear that the recovery as appropriate under the head of pain and suffering is not affected by the abolition. *Section 1(1)(b)* of the 1982 Act provides as follows:

'If the injured person's expectation of life has been reduced by the injuries, the court, in assessing damages in respect of pain and suffering caused by the injuries, shall take account of any suffering caused or likely to be caused to him by awareness that his expectation of life has been so reduced.'

1   See *Benham v Gambling [1941] AC 157, [1941] 1 All ER 7, HL.*
2   In *Gammell v Wilson [1982] AC 27, [1981] 1 All ER 578, HL*, £1,250 was awarded under this head.
3   See *Rose v Ford [1937] AC 826, [1937] 3 All ER 359, HL.*

Loss of amenity

[25.05] The general principles underlying the award of damages for loss of amenity were set out by Lord Morris in *West & Son v Shephard*[1] as follows:

'... money cannot renew a physical frame that has been battered and shattered. All that judges and courts can do is to award sums which must be recognised as giving reasonable compensation. In the process there must be the endeavour to secure some uniformity in the general method of approach. By common assent awards must be reasonable and must be assessed with moderation. Furthermore, it is eminently desirable that so far as possible comparable injuries should be compensated by comparable awards. When all this is said it still must be said that amounts which are awarded are to a considerable extent conventional.'

In trying to decide upon 'reasonable compensation' for personal injury the courts adopt a broadly objective approach. It has sometimes been argued that the extent to which the injury interfered, or must be taken to have interfered, with the plaintiff's 'happiness' should be the basis of the assessment.[2] But this view has been rejected,[3] largely because it is felt that the subjectivity inherent in it would undermine the principle that, in the words of Lord Morris, 'comparable injuries should be compensated by comparable awards'.

[1] *[1964] AC 326* at 346, *[1963] 2 All ER 625* at 631, HL.
[2] See *Wise v Kaye [1962] 1 QB 638* at 665–666, *[1962] 1 All ER 257* at 271, CA, *per* Diplock LJ. Cf A Ogus 'Damages for Lost Amenities: For a Foot, a Feeling or a Function?' (1972) 35 MLR 1.
[3] Ie by the majorities in *Wise v Kaye [1962] 1 QB 638*, *[1962] 1 All ER 257, CA* and *H West & Son v Shephard [1964] AC 326*, *[1963] 2 All ER 625, HL*.

Certainty

[25.06] The objective approach is desirable in the interests of certainty and the promotion of settlements. It is submitted that it also accords with intuitive notions of justice. As Lord Pearce put it in *West v Shephard*: 'It would be lamentable if the trial of a personal injury claim put a premium on protestations of misery and if a long face was the safe passport to a large award.'[1] This is not to say that subjective factors are wholly ignored; a keen sportsman will, for example, be awarded more for the loss of a leg than someone whose work and leisure pursuits are largely sedentary.[2] It is a corollary of the objective approach, however, that it is no concern of the court how the money awarded to the claimant will ultimately be used.[3]

[1] *[1964] AC 326* at 368–369, *[1963] 2 All ER 625* at 645, Lord Pearce continued as follows: 'Under the present practice there is no call for a parade of personal unhappiness. A plaintiff who cheerfully admits that he is as happy as he was, may yet receive a large award as reasonable compensation for the grave injury and loss of amenity over which he has managed to triumph.'
[2] See *H West & Son v Shephard [1964] AC 326* at 365, *[1963] 2 All ER 625* at 643, *per* Lord Pearce.
[3] 'He can spend it well or stupidly; he can enjoy it by gambling or giving it away; he can invest it and accumulate the income and give it by will to his relations or to charity; it is under his entire dominion in every way, and he can deal with it as he pleases ... ': *per* Upjohn LJ in *Wise v Kaye [1962] 1 QB 638* at 658, *[1962] 1 All ER 257* at 267, CA.

Relevance of awards in other cases

[25.07] The pursuit of consistency in awards is facilitated by the fact that for many years personal injury cases have been tried by judge alone; a practice in effect made general by the decision of a five member Court of Appeal in 1965 in *Ward v James*,[1] and further reinforced by the decision of the Court of Appeal in *H v Ministry of Defence*.[2] This makes possible the citation in argument of awards in other cases, which had not been permitted when trial was by jury. Such awards are collected systematically in various publications,[3] and since 1992 the Judicial Studies Board has produced *Guidelines for the Assessment of Damages in Personal Injury Cases*.[4] These facilitate the achievement of as high a degree of predictability as can reasonably be expected in this sphere. In *Heil v Rankin*[23], Lord Woolf MR said:

'Consistency is important, because it assists in achieving justice between one claimant and another and one defendant and another. It also assists to achieve justice by facilitating settlements. The courts have become increasingly aware that this is in the interests of the litigants and society as a whole, particularly in the personal injury field. Delay in resolving claims can be a source of great injustice as well as the cause of expense to the parties and the judicial system. It is for this reason that the introduction of the guidelines by the Judicial Studies Board (JSB) in 1992 was such a welcome development'.

1   *[1966] 1 QB 273, [1965] 1 All ER 563, CA.* Since this case was decided there has apparently been only one reported instance of an order for trial by jury of a personal injury case (being *Hodges v Harland & Wolff Ltd [1965] 1 All ER 1086, [1965] 1 WLR 523, CA).*
2   *[1991] 2 QB 103, [1991] 2 All ER 834, CA.* See also the *Supreme Court Act 1981, s 69(3),* which was construed in H's case as 'indicating that, other things being equal, jury trial was to be considered as less preferable than hitherto': *per* Lord Donaldson MR, delivering the judgment of the court, *[1991] 2 QB 103 at 110, [1991] 2 All ER 834 at 838.*
3   See *Kemp & Kemp The Quantum of Damages*; *Butterworths Personal Injury Litigation Service.*
4   Published by Blackstone Press.
5   See *[2000] 3 All ER 138* at para 25.

Not binding precedents

[25.08]   The House of Lords held, in *Wright v British Railways Board*,[1] that the Court of Appeal is, in the words of Lord Diplock, 'the tribunal best qualified to set the guidelines' for non-pecuniary loss in personal injury cases and that the House of Lords itself 'should hesitate before deciding to depart from them, particularly if the departure [would] make the guideline less general in its applicability or less simple to apply'. The guidelines thus established are not binding precedents, and can be varied as circumstances require, but 'too frequent alteration deprives them of their usefulness in providing a reasonable degree of predictability in the litigious process and so facilitating settlement of claims without going to trial'.

1   *[1983] 2 AC 773, [1983] 2 All ER 698.*

Unconscious claimants

[25.09]   In *H West & Son v Shepherd*[1] the House of Lords upheld the award of substantial damages for loss of amenity in respect of a plaintiff who was permanently unconscious. 'The fact of unconsciousness', said Lord Morris, 'does not … eliminate the actuality of the deprivations of the ordinary experiences and amenities of life'.[2] Cases of this kind are unique in that the claimant will be unaware that he has been awarded the damages and, since the cost of nursing and care is compensated separately, it will not be possible for them to be put to any use on his behalf. Not surprisingly, the issue has revealed a high degree of judicial disagreement. The decision of the House in *West* was by a bare majority,[3] and upheld an earlier decision of the Court of Appeal, on the same point, which had also been reached by a majority.[4] A subsequent decision of the Court of Appeal, again by a majority, awarded substantial damages under this head in respect of a child aged eight, who lived in an unconscious state for 12 months after a road accident but who had actually died by the date of the trial.[5] On the other hand, the High Court of Australia,[6] also by a majority, refused to follow *West v Shepherd*.

---

[1] *[1964] AC 326, [1963] 2 All ER 625, HL.*
[2] *[1964] AC 326* at 349, *[1963] 2 All ER 625* at 633.
[3] Lord Tucker, Lord Morris and Lord Pearce; Lord Reid and Lord Devlin dissenting.
[4] See *Wise v Kaye [1962] 1 QB 638, [1962] 1 All ER 257, CA* (Sellers and Upjohn LJJ; Diplock LJ dissenting).
[5] *Andrews v Freebourgh [1967] 1 QB 1, [1966] 2 All ER 721, CA* (Willmer and Davies LJJ; Winn LJ dissenting).
[6] See *Skelton v Collins [1966] ALR 449.*

Two considerations

[25.10] The view that substantial damages for loss of amenity should be awarded in these cases appears to be based upon two considerations. One is the belief that they are necessary in order to maintain the integrity of the 'objective' approach to such damages generally, and hence the system of 'guidelines' which facilitates predictability in the case of awards to conscious claimants.[1] The other is the belief that it would be undesirable, as a matter of public policy, for courts of law to be perceived as treating unconscious people as being, for practical purposes, already dead.[2] Nevertheless, the Pearson Commission[3] recommended 'that non-pecuniary damages should no longer be recoverable for permanent unconsciousness', but this recommendation has not been implemented.

---

[1] See especially the speech of Lord Pearce in *H West & Son v Shephard [1964] AC 326* at 369, *[1963] 2 All ER 625* at 645.
[2] See *Wise v Kaye [1962] 1 QB 638* at 654, *[1962] 1 All ER 257* at 265, CA, *per* Sellers LJ. Cf P Skegg 'Irreversibly Comatose Individuals: "Alive" or "Dead" ' [1974] CLJ 130.
[3] *Royal Commission on Civil Liability and Compensation for Personal Injury* (Cmnd 7054–I) paras 393–398. Cf *Lim Poh Choo v Camden and Islington Area Health Authority [1980] AC 174* at 188–189, *[1979] 2 All ER 910* at 918–919, HL, *per* Lord Scarman.

Raising award levels

[25.11] Damages for non-pecuniary loss are assessed by reference to the value of money at the date of the trial.[1] In theory, awards should therefore broadly keep pace with inflation.[2] Nevertheless, towards the end of the twentieth century concern began to develop that awards for the most serious injuries had in practice failed to maintain their value compared with those of a generation or so earlier. Moreover, other factors including an increase in wealth in society generally, and the greater life-expectancy of seriously injured people due to medical advances, led many to advocate substantial increases in real terms. Against this background the Law Commission undertook a general review of the law of the law relating to damages for non-pecuniary loss. The Commission reported in 1999, and its recommendations included a suggestion that awards in excess of £3,000 'should be increased by a factor of at least 1.5'.[3] The Commission hoped that the courts would themselves act upon its report by revising the guideline figures, rather than waiting for legislative intervention. In response a five-member Court of Appeal in *Heil v Rankin*[4] considered, in the year 2000, eight conjoined cases in order to provide a comprehensive judicial consideration of the issues. Lord Woolf MR, delivering the judgment of the court, said[5]:

> 'Care must be exercised not to freeze the compensation for non-pecuniary loss at a level which the passage of time and changes in circumstances make inadequate. The compensation must remain fair, reasonable and just. Fair compensation for the injured person. The level must also not result in injustice to the defendant, and it must not be out of accord with what society as a whole would perceive as being reasonable'.

[1] See *Walker v John McLean & Sons [1979] 2 All ER 965* at 970, *[1979] 1 WLR 760* at 765, *per* Cumming-Bruce LJ.
[2] See *per* Lord Diplock in *Wright v British Railways Board [1983] 2 AC 773* at 785, *[1983] 2 All ER 698* at 706, HL, quoted above.
[3] See *Damages for Personal Injury: Non-Pecuniary Loss* (Law Com no 257) para 3.40.
[4] *[2000] 3 All ER 138*. See Richard Lewis 'Increasing the Price of Pain: Damages, The Law Commission and *Heil v Rankin*' (2001) 64 MLR 100.
[5] See above at para 27.

Modest increase

[25.12] The court considered economic evidence, and submissions as to the likely impact of any increases in the general level of awards on the insurance industry and the National Health Service. In the result the court decided upon increases, but of a considerably lower order than those recommended by the Law Commission, which the court considered to be inappropriate. The decision would therefore 'not radically alter the courts present approach to the assessment of damages', but implement a 'modest increase' instead[1]. Awards would remain unchanged where existing levels were below £10,000. At the other extreme, awards for the most catastrophic injuries would be increased by about a third, with lower awards being increased by proportionately less on a sliding scale.

[1] See *[2000] 3 All ER 138* at para 82.

Catastrophic injuries

[25.13] In recent times increasing numbers of serious accident victims have survived, due to advances in treatment, where formerly many of them might not have done so.[1] The courts have therefore been obliged to assess damages for pain, suffering and loss of amenity in respect of claimants who, though conscious, may be brain-damaged and may also be totally or partially paralysed. The inherent difficulty of placing a money value upon personal injuries is particularly conspicuous in such cases, while at the same time their place at an extreme of the spectrum makes them especially sensitive for the system of 'guidelines' generally. In *Heil v Rankin* The court held that awards for quadriplegia should be in the range (at 2000 values) of £150,000 to £200,000, whereas the previous existing guideline had suggested a bracket of £120,000 to £150,00 with the latter representing an effective maximum for all cases[2].

[1] See *Lim Poh Choo v Camden and Islington Area Health Authority [1979] QB 196* at 216, *[1979] 1 All ER 332* at 340, CA, *per* Lord Denning MR.
[2] The court considered that the judgment of O'Connor LJ in *Housecroft v Burnett [1986] 1 All ER 332, CA* may have 'had an unduly depressing effect on awards in the highest category': *per* Lord Woolf MR in *Heil v Rankin [2000] 3 All ER 138* at para 94.

B Financial loss

Calculation of future lost earnings

[25.14] The existing method of calculating damages for lost earnings as well as for future financial expenditure was summarised in the House of Lords by Lord Clyde, in *Wells v Wells*,[1] as follows:

> 'The present appeals are concerned with the calculation of lump sums in respect of future recurring expenses and losses which have been brought about as a result of the injuries which the respective plaintiffs have sustained. It is common ground that that lump sum in each case may be seen as funding a notional annuity from which both capital and income may be derived sufficient to secure the appropriate annual amounts over the likely future period or periods to which they relate. In practice the sum is calculated as the product of a multiplier representing an appropriate number of years' purchase and a multiplicand representing the amount of the annual loss or expense. The assessment of the latter will necessarily depend significantly on the facts of the particular case.'

As far as claims for lost earnings are concerned, the 'multiplicand' will normally be equivalent to the claimant's net annual pay; ie his earned income after deduction of tax and social security contributions. In practice, the greater difficulty, and an issue which has caused significant controversy in recent years, is the choice of the 'multiplier'.[2]

[1] See *[1998] 3 All ER 481* at 512.
[2] See R Nelson-Jones *Multipliers* (1998). Multipliers used in actual cases are also listed in Kemp & Kemp *The Quantum of Damages* vol 1. The appropriate date for determining the multiplier is that of the trial. In *Pritchard v J H Cobden [1988] Fam 22, [1987] 1 All ER 300, CA* the Court of Appeal rejected a defendant's contention that the date of the accident (by analogy with Fatal Accidents Act cases in which the date of death is taken) would be more appropriate.

Actuarial tables now normally used

[25.15] The submission of actuarial evidence by plaintiffs in support of claims for future lost earnings was formerly discouraged by the courts.[1] The prevailing judicial view was that to rely closely on actuarial calculations would lend a false aura of certainty to an essentially speculative exercise, and would tend to over-compensate plaintiffs by giving insufficient allowance for the contingencies of life and their possible impact upon the future of the individual claimant.[2] This position was, however, forcefully criticised,[3] and in 1984 a working party, with the assistance of the Government Actuary, compiled *Actuarial Tables with Explanatory Notes for Use in Personal Injury and Fatal Accident Cases*. Successive editions of what are known as the Ogden Tables, after the Chairman of the Working Party,[4] have been published by the Stationery Office and are now in frequent use in the courts.[5] Thus, in *Wells v Wells*,[6] Lord Lloyd indicated that 'hesitation to embrace the actuarial tables' was no longer appropriate, and he continued:

> 'I do not suggest that the judge should be a slave to the tables. There may well be special factors in particular cases. But the tables should now be regarded as the starting point, rather than a check. A judge should be slow to depart from the relevant actuarial multiplier on impressionistic grounds, or by reference to "a spread of multipliers in comparable cases" especially when the multipliers were fixed before actuarial tables were widely used.'

1   See *Hunt v Severs [1994] 2 AC 350* at 365–366, *[1994] 2 All ER 385* at 396–397, *per* Lord Bridge. See also *Watson v Powles [1968] 1 QB 596, [1967] 3 All ER 721, CA; Mitchell v Mulholland (No 2) [1972] 1 QB 65, [1971] 2 All ER 1205, CA; Auty v National Coal Board [1985] 1 All ER 930, [1985] 1 WLR 784, CA.*
2   See *per* Edmund Davies LJ in *Mitchell v Mulholland (No 2) [1972] 1 QB 65* at 77, *[1971] 2 All ER 1205* at 1212–1213. Cf *per* Oliver LJ in *Auty v National Coal Board [1985] 1 All ER 930* at 939, *[1985] 1 WLR 784* at 800–801: ' … as a means of providing a reliable guide to individual behaviour patterns, or to future economic and political events, the predictions of an actuary can be only a little more likely to be accurate (and will almost certainly be less entertaining) than those of an astrologer.'
3   See D Kemp 'The Assessment of Damages for Future Pecuniary Loss in Personal Injury Claims' (1984) 3 CJQ 120.
4   Sir Michael Ogden QC.
5   See *section 10* of the *Civil Evidence Act 1995*, which was passed to overcome doubts as to the admissibility of the tables.
6   See *[1998] 3 All ER 481* at 498.

Significant change

[25.16]   Lord Lloyd's insistence that departure on 'impressionistic grounds' from the actuarial multiplier should be discouraged represented a welcome and significant change from the previous approach of the courts, which usually involved *general* reduction of multipliers on the rather vague basis of allowing for 'life's manifold contingencies'.[1] In practice, 18 was regarded as the maximum multiplier, even for young adults at the commencement of their working lives.[2] In *Wells v Wells* this approach was decisively repudiated. In the words, again, of Lord Lloyd:[3]

> 'The purpose of the award is to put the plaintiff in the same position, financially, as if he had not been injured. The sum should be calculated as accurately as possible, making just allowance, where this is appropriate, for contingencies. But once the calculation is done, there is no justification for imposing an artificial cap on the multiplier. There is no room for judicial scaling down.'[4]

1   See *Hunt v Severs [1994] 2 AC 350* at 365, *[1994] 2 All ER 385* at 397b, *per* Lord Bridge: criticised by Lord Lloyd in *Wells v Wells [1998] 3 All ER 481* at 498.
2   See *Wells v Wells [1998] 3 All ER 481* at 501, *per* Lord Steyn.
3   *[1998] 3 All ER 481* at 484.
4   See also *per* Lord Clyde in *[1998] 3 All ER 481* at 512.

Scope for variables limited

[25.17]   In *Wells v Wells* the House of Lords was primarily concerned with whole-life multipliers to calculate compensation for the cost of future care. Thus, when Lord Lloyd refers to 'making … just allowance for contingencies', the only justification for reducing the multiplier from that indicated by the actuarial tables will now normally only be medical evidence relating to the particular claimant's prognosis. Although contingencies such as the employment prospects of the particular claimant may continue to play a part in assessing damages for future lost earnings, the use of the Ogden Tables should limit the scope for the introduction of such variables[1]. The rejection in *Wells v Wells* of 'judicial scaling down' of multipliers, on unexpressed criteria, is relevant to lost earnings as well as to the cost of care. One may therefore expect multipliers for lost earnings to be more precisely reasoned than was the case prior to the decision in *Wells v Wells*.

1   See *Herring v Ministry of Defence [2004] 1 All ER 44* (' … the justification for a discount for contingencies substantially in excess of the figure to be obtained from the notes to the Ogden Tables is not apparent': *per* Potter LJ at para 38*).*

Inflation and the multiplier

[25.18] Since the lump sum is assessed on the basis that income as well as capital will be used to provide the compensation, it is necessary to assume a rate of return when selecting the multiplier. Clearly, the higher the projected rate, the lower the award, and vice versa. For many years the courts adopted a discount rate of 4–5%, despite criticism that this had the effect of producing awards at levels which, in view of the effect of inflation, left victims, particularly those with permanent disabilities, seriously undercompensated.[55] Nevertheless, the courts declined to take inflation into account, insisting, albeit unrealistically, that it was up to victims to try and protect the value of their awards by prudent investment in equities.[56] This view was maintained even after the introduction, in 1981, of index-linked government stock (ILGS), which provide full protection against inflation.

[1] See especially the articles by D Kemp QC 'Discounting Compensation for Future Loss' and 'Discounting Damages for Future Loss' in (1985) 101 LQR 556 and (1997) 113 LQR 195 respectively. ('I have derived much assistance from Mr Kemp's commentary, for which I am grateful': *per* Lord Lloyd in *Wells v Wells [1998] 3 All ER 481* at 490.) See also *Structured Settlements and Provisional Damages* (Law Com Report no 224, 1994).

[2] See *per* Lord Scarman in *Lim Poh Choo v Camden and Islington Area Health Authority [1980] AC 174* at 193, *[1979] 2 All ER 910* at 923 HL: 'The correct approach should be ... to assess damages without regard to the risk of future inflation ... the victims of tort who receive a lump sum award are entitled to no better protection against inflation than others who have to rely on capital for their future support.' See also *Hodgson v Trapp [1989] AC 807, [1988] 3 All ER 870, HL*. Cf *Taylor v O'Connor [1971] AC 115, [1970] 1 All ER 365, HL; Young v Percival [1974] 3 All ER 677, [1975] 1 WLR 17, CA*.

Investment in ILGS

[25.19] In *Wells v Wells*,[1] which was decided in the summer of 1998, the House of Lords unanimously held, in a striking and far-reaching reversal of previous orthodoxy,[2] that lump sums should henceforth be calculated on the assumption that plaintiffs would invest in ILGS. '[T]he plaintiff', stated Lord Lloyd, 'is entitled to be protected against future inflation at the expense of the tortfeasor; otherwise he does not receive full compensation'.[3] In *Wells v Wells* itself the court reduced the discount rate to 3%, with a corresponding increase in the level of multipliers and of the sums awarded.[4] In explaining the repudiation of the former approach, Lord Steyn expressed himself as follows:[5]

> 'Typically, by investing in equities an ordinary investor takes a calculated risk which he can bear in order to improve his financial position. On the other hand, the typical plaintiff requires the return from an award of damages to provide the necessities of life. For such a plaintiff it is not possible to cut back on medical and nursing care as well as other essential services. His objective must be to ensure that the damages awarded do not run out. It is money that he cannot afford to lose. The ordinary investor does not have the same concerns. It is therefore unrealistic to treat such a plaintiff as an ordinary investor. It seems to me entirely reasonable for such a plaintiff to be cautious and conservative ... [I]t is reasonable for such a plaintiff to take the safe course of investing in index-linked government stock. From this it follows that the discount rate ought to be fixed on this assumption.'

[1] *[1998] 3 All ER 481, HL*; revsg *[1997] 1 All ER 673, CA*. See D Kemp QC 'Damages for Personal Injuries: A Sea Change' (1998) 114 LQR 570.

[2] ' ... one of the most important decisions in personal injury litigation since the Second World War': D Kemp QC (1998) 114 LQR 570 at 571.

Statutory prescription of the discount rate

[25.20] *Section 1* of the *Damages Act 1996* contains the following provision:

'(1) In determining the return to be expected from the investment of a sum awarded as damages for future pecuniary loss in an action for personal injury the court shall ... take into account such rate of return (if any) as may from time to time be prescribed by an order made by the Lord Chancellor.

(2) Subsection (1) above shall not however prevent the court taking a different rate of return into account if any party to the proceedings shows that it is more appropriate in the case in question.'

While the litigation in *Wells v Wells* was going through the courts, the Lord Chancellor indicated that he proposed to await the outcome of those proceedings before exercising this new statutory power. Eventually, in June 2001, the power was exercised; and the current rate of return as prescribed by the *Damages (Personal Injury) Order*[1] is 2.5%. Lord Irvine of Lairg LC published his reasons for setting this figure, which included the following[2]:

'Since it is in the context of larger awards, intended to cover longer periods, that there is the greatest risk of serious discrepancies between the level of compensation and the actual losses incurred if the discount rate set is not appropriate, I have had this type of award particularly in mind when considering the level at which the discount rate should be set'.

¹ SI 2000/2301, Art 2.
² See *Warriner v Warriner [2003] 3 All ER 447, CA* at para 13 (quoting Lord Irvine).

Exceptional cases?

[25.21] *Section 1(2)* of the *Damages Act 1996* makes clear that a different rate of return may be used if the court considers it to be more appropriate in the circumstances of a particular case. In *Warriner v Warriner*[1] the Court of Appeal gave guidance as to the circumstances in which that proviso might be successfully invoked. The claimant in this case, who had suffered brain damage in a road accident, still had a life expectancy of 46 years and her damages claim was for a sum in excess of £3million. She sought to introduce expert evidence justifying a discount rate of 2%. The 0.5% reduction on the prescribed rate could have added half a million pounds to her award. The Court of Appeal nevertheless refused to sanction the introduction of the evidence and held that there were no grounds for justifying any departure from the standard rate. Such departures would be rare, in order to preserve certainty, and would, in any event, only be considered in cases which fell outside the Lord Chancellor's published reasons for fixing the prescribed rate. Since those reasons had specifically referred to large awards covering long periods the claim in the instant case was not exceptional. Dyson LJ said[2]:

'We are told that this is the first time that this court has had to consider the 1996 Act, and that guidance is needed as to the meaning of "more appropriate in the case in question" in s 1(2). The phrase "more appropriate", if considered in isolation, is open-textured. It prompts the question: by what criteria is the court to judge whether a different rate of return is more appropriate in the case in question? But the phrase must be interpreted in its proper context, which is that Lord Irvine LC has prescribed a rate pursuant to s 1(1) and has given very detailed reasons explaining what factors he took into account in arriving at the rate that he has prescribed. I would hold that in deciding whether a different rate is more appropriate in the case in question, the court must have regard to those reasons. If the case in question falls into a category that Lord Irvine did not take into account and/or there are special features of the case which (a) are material to the choice of rate of return and (b) are shown from an examination of Lord Irvine's reasons not to have been taken into account, then a different rate of return may be "more appropriate" ... If s 1(2) is interpreted in this way, it is likely that it will be in comparatively few cases that s 1 (2) will be successfully invoked'.

[1] *[2003] 3 All ER 447.*
[2] See *[2000] 3 All ER 447* at paras 33 and 35. See also *Page v Plymouth Hospitals NHS Trust [2004] 3 All ER 367 per* Davis J at paras 61–63.

Before the order

[25.22] Reluctance to sanction departures from a settled rate was also apparent in cases decided before the 2001 order. In *Wells v Wells* itself the House of Lords took into account taxation at the standard rate, and rejected a submission that a lower rate, and therefore a higher multiplier, should be adopted in situations involving higher rates of tax[1]. Their Lordships did indicate, however, that in 'exceptional cases plaintiffs would be free to place their arguments for a lower rate before the court'.[2]

[1] See also *Van Oudenhaven v Griffin Inns [2000] 1 WLR 1413, CA.* Cf *Biesheuvel v Birrell (No 2) [1999] PIQR Q40.*
[2] See *per* Lord Steyn, Lord Hope and Lord Hutton, *[1998] 3 All ER 481* at 506, 510, 521. In adopting this approach their Lordships applied observations to the same effect of Lord Oliver on *Hodgson v Trapp [1989] 1 AC 807* at 835, *[1988] 3 All ER 870* at 885–886, HL.

Management costs not recoverable

[25.23] The costs of managing the fund awarded to the claimant, and of obtaining investment advice, are not recoverable as part of the damages[1].

[1] See *Eagle v Chambers (No 2) [2004] EWCA Civ 1033*; *Page v Plymouth Hospitals NHS Trust [2004] 3 All ER 367.*

Risk of future unemployment due to injury

[25.24] An accident victim may incur a permanent degree of disability which is not so severe as to deprive him immediately of his present employment, but which would have an adverse effect upon his chances of obtaining another job should his present employment cease for any reason at some future date.[1] It is clear that this handicap, although in a sense only potential, in that its financial consequences have yet to materialise, represents an *existing* loss for which, if negligence is proved, the claimant is entitled to damages.[2] The calculation of such damages is necessarily highly speculative, however, and the multiplier system, used where the claimant is already suffering an immediate loss of earnings, has not generally been considered appropriate by the courts for adoption in this context.[3] In *Moeliker v Reyrolle & Co*[4] Browne LJ observed that 'any guidance can only be on very broad lines, because the facts may vary almost infinitely'.[5] His Lordship subsequently continued as follows:[6]

'I do not think one can say more by way of principle than this. The consideration of this head of damages should be made in two stages. 1. Is there a "substantial" or "real" risk that a plaintiff will lose his present job at some time before the estimate end of his working life? 2. If there is (but not otherwise), the court must assess and quantify the present value of the risk of the financial damage which the plaintiff will suffer if that risk materialises, having regard to the degree of the risk, the time when it may materialise, and the factors, both favourable and unfavourable, which in a particular case will, or may, affect the plaintiff's chances of getting a job at all, or an equally well paid job.'

[1]   See *Smith v Manchester Corpn (1974) 17 KIR 1, CA*. In certain circumstances a claim may arise under this head even if the claimant is not actually employed at the time of the trial: *Cook v Consolidated Fisheries [1977] ICR 635, CA*. See also *Herring v Ministry of Defence [2004] 1 All ER 44, CA*.
[2]   See *Smith v Manchester Corpn (1974) 17 KIR 1 at 8, CA, per* Scarman LJ.
[3]   See *Smith v Manchester Corpn (1974) 17 KIR 1* at 6, 8, *per* Edmund Davies and Scarman LJJ. Cf Bankes 'Quantifying Loss of Earning Capacity' (1983) 80 LS Gaz 1150.
[4]   *[1976] ICR 253*. See also *Nicholls v National Coal Board [1976] ICR 266*.
[5]   *[1977] 1 All ER 9* at 15, *[1976] ICR 253* at 261, CA.
[6]   *[1977] 1 All ER 9* at 17, *[1976] ICR 253* at 263.

Evidence

[25.25] The claimant will therefore normally be required to adduce evidence to establish both the existence of a risk of loss of his present employment, and the extent to which his earning capacity would be adversely affected by the disability were he to do so.[1] There was formerly a dispute as to whether the sums thus awarded for loss of earning capacity represent a head of damage distinct from that for loss of future earnings.[2] The better view, however, is that they do not do so.[3] It follows that they are liable to the same deductions as are required to be made from awards for loss of future earnings.[4]

[1]   See *Chan Wai Tong v Li Ping Sum [1985] AC 446 at 460, [1985] 2 WLR 396 at 404, per* Lord Fraser, delivering the judgment of the Privy Council.
[2]   See *Foster v Tyne and Wear County Council [1986] 1 All ER 567* at 571–572, CA, and the references there given.
[3]   See the Report of the *Royal Commission on Civil Liability and Compensation for Personal Injury* (Pearson) (Cmnd 7054–I) para 338.
[4]   See *Foster v Tyne and Wear County Council [1986] 1 All ER 567, CA*. For the deductions, see below.

Multiplier approach may be applicable

[25.26] In some cases of this general type the evidence may be just sufficient to justify the use of the multiplier system. In *Stefanovic v Carter*[1] the claimant felt, on reasonable grounds, that he was unable to continue training as an accountant due to a severe facial disfigurement resulting from an accident for which the defendant was responsible. He worked instead in the building trade, in which his earnings in the short term were not significantly different from those as a trainee accountant. In future years, however, such evidence as was available indicated that his income would be substantially lower than it would have been if he had been able to pursue a career in accountancy. The judge used the multiplier system and awarded the claimant a very substantial sum for future lost earnings. This award was, however, challenged by the defendant who contended that the matter was too speculative to justify use of the multiplicand and multiplier system, and that the claimant was not entitled to anything other than a single award for loss of earning capacity. The Court of Appeal rejected the appeal and confirmed the judge's approach. Although it had been a 'speculative and difficult' task for him the judge had been provided with objective statistical evidence of average earnings in the accountancy profession, which entitled him 'to take the multiplier/multiplicand approach'[2].

1   *[2001] PIQR Q6, CA.*
2   See above at paras 12 and 13 *per* Hale LJ.

Children

[25.27]   Children who, through disablement caused by the defendant's negligence, have had their eventual adult employment prospects reduced or destroyed, are also entitled to compensation.[1] The calculation will inevitably vary with the facts of each case. In two such cases, in each of which the plaintiff was totally disabled, the Court of Appeal used the multiplier system, apparently taking a figure approximating to the national average wage as the starting point.[2] In two other cases, however, where the plaintiffs were only partially disabled and could be expected to find employment of some kind, the Court of Appeal preferred to approach the matter more broadly and simply stated what it considered to be an appropriate sum.[3]

1   See *S v Distillers Co (Biochemicals) Ltd [1969] 3 All ER 1412, [1970] 1 WLR 114.* See also *Jamil Bin Harun v Yang Kamsiah Bte Meor Rasdi [1984] AC 529, [1984] 2 WLR 668,* PC.
2   See *Taylor v Bristol Omnibus Co [1975] 2 All ER 1107, [1975] 1 WLR 1054,* CA; *Croke v Wiseman [1981] 3 All ER 852, [1982] 1 WLR 71* (Lord Denning MR, dissenting, would have allowed no damages for lost future earnings).
3   See *Joyce v Yeomans [1981] 2 All ER 21, [1981] 1 WLR 549* (but cf *per* Brandon LJ, *[1981] 2 All ER 21 at 27, [1981] 1 WLR 549* at 557); *Mitchell v Liverpool Area Health Authority* (1985) Times, 17 June, CA.

Loss of marriage prospects

[25.28]   Where young female plaintiffs lost marriage prospects as a result of their injuries it was formerly held that, in the calculation of future lost earnings, some discount should be made for the probability that, if uninjured, they would in any event have taken some years out of employment for marriage and child-bearing.[1] It is, however, no longer the practice to do this in most cases, not least in recognition of the forceful argument that the services of a wife and mother represent an economic contribution normally at least as great as that made by persons in paid employment.[2] Some deduction might still be considered appropriate, however, if the woman's earnings and income expectation had, prior to the accident, been at so exceptionally high a level that they could not reasonably be regarded as the economic equivalent of the services of a wife and mother.[3] It must also be remembered that loss of marriage prospects is a recognised factor in awarding damages for pain and suffering and loss of amenity. In assessing the correctness of the overall sum, and in order to avoid overlap, courts have sometimes allowed high sums under this head of non-pecuniary loss to offset awards for loss of future earnings which, taken in isolation, might have been too low because the erroneous concept of marriage and child-bearing as economically negative had reduced them.[4]

1   See *Harris v Harris [1973] 1 Lloyd's Rep 445, CA; Moriarty v McCarthy [1978] 2 All ER 213, [1978] 1 WLR 155.*
2   See *Hughes v McKeown [1985] 3 All ER 284, [1985] 1 WLR 963.*
3   See *Housecroft v Burnett [1986] 1 All ER 332* at 345, CA, *per* O'Connor LJ.
4   See *Harris v Harris [1973] 1 Lloyd's Rep 445, CA;* and *Moriarty v McCarthy [1978] 2 All ER 213, [1978] 1 WLR 155,* as explained in *Hughes v McKeown [1985] 3 All ER 284, [1985] 1 WLR 963.* See also *Housecroft v Burnett [1986] 1 All ER 332* at 345, CA, *per* O'Connor LJ.

Damages for the 'lost years'

[25.29]   In *Pickett v British Rail Engineering Ltd*[1] the House of Lords held that a plaintiff whose life expectancy has been reduced as a result of the accident can recover damages to compensate for the earnings which would be lost to him as a result of his premature death. In so holding, their Lordships overruled the much criticised decision of the Court of Appeal in *Oliver v Ashman,*[2] which had held that lost earnings could only be recovered on the basis of the post-accident expectation of life. A central reason for the decision of the House of Lords was the injustice which occurred where a plaintiff whose life expectancy had been reduced, but who had dependants to support, brought an action during his own lifetime. Since this debars the dependants from bringing their own action under the Fatal Accidents Act after his death, the rule in *Oliver v Ashman* meant that the dependants would go uncompensated.

1   *[1980] AC 136, [1979] 1 All ER 774, HL.*
2   *[1962] 2 QB 210, [1961] 3 All ER 323, CA.*

Estate not to benefit

[25.30]   Although it remedied one anomaly, one effect of the *Pickett* decision was to create another, but this was swiftly corrected by statute. The *Administration of Justice Act 1982, s 4(2)* modified the *Law Reform (Miscellaneous Provisions) Act 1934, s 1(2)(a)* so as to provide that 'any damages for loss of income in respect of any period after [a] person's death' will not survive for the benefit of his estate. This was to prevent defendants being liable to the deceased's estate under the 1934 Act, as well as to his dependants under the Fatal Accidents Act, for future economic loss caused by the death of the victim.[1]

1   Cf *Gammell v Wilson [1982] AC 27, [1981] 1 All ER 578, HL.*

Amount of damages

[25.31]   In *Pickett v British Rail Engineering* itself the House of Lords apparently contemplated that damages for lost earnings during the lost years would be calculated in a manner broadly similar to that used in Fatal Accident Act cases. This, indeed, was consistent with the underlying *raison d'être* of the decision in *Pickett.* But this method, which while deducting the deceased's own living expenses normally still credits his dependants with a substantial proportion of his earnings, might be considered less appropriate where no dependants are actually involved.[1] The general principles governing the calculation of deductions must, however, presumably be the same regardless of the claimants actual family commitments.[2] Nevertheless, it does appear that a method which reduces awards in this category generally, by taking a more limited view of the amount which the claimant would be likely to have had available to him after a realistic proportion of his income had been expended, is favoured by the courts.[3]

[1]   See generally Evans and Stanton 'Valuing the Lost Years' (1984) 134 NLJ 515 at 553.
[2]   See *Harris v Empress Motors [1983] 3 All ER 561, [1984] 1 WLR 212, CA.*
[3]   See *Harris v Empress Motors [1983] 3 All ER 561, [1984] 1 WLR 212, CA.* Although the facts in this case arose before the passing of the *Administration of Justice Act 1982, s 4(2)* and concerned a deceased plaintiff, the general problem of assessing damages remains relevant after the Act in relation to living plaintiffs. In *Phipps v Brooks Dry Cleaning Services Ltd* [1996] PIQR Q100 the Court of Appeal applied *Harris'* case and held expressly that the method of assessment would be less generous to plaintiffs than that adopted in assessing dependency under the Fatal Accidents Acts.

Children unlikely to recover under the Pickett principle

[25.32]   Although even small children can theoretically claim for lost earnings during the lost years,[1] in practice such an award would be so speculative that usually none is made.[2] Children can, however, claim for prospective lost earnings during their post-accident life-expectancy.

[1]   See *Connolly v Camden and Islington Area Health Authority [1981] 3 All ER 250.*
[2]   See *[1981] 3 All ER 250.* Cf *per* Lord Scarman in *Gammell v Wilson [1982] AC 27* at 78, *[1981] 1 All ER 578* at 593, HL.

Gains obtained by the claimant[1]

Gifts and charitable payments

[25.33]   Notwithstanding that damages for personal injury are intended to compensate the claimant, and should therefore not render him better off financially than he was before the accident, it has long been established that, in calculating them, no account is to be taken of gifts or of charitable payments made to the claimant because of the misfortune which has befallen him.[2]

[1]   See *Damages for Personal Injury: Medical, Nursing and other Expenses; Collateral Benefits* (Law Com no 262, 1999). See also R Lewis 'Deducting Collateral Benefits from Damages: Principle and Policy' (1998) 18 LS 15.
[2]   See *Cunningham v Harrison [1973] QB 942* at 950–951, *[1973] 3 All ER 463* at 468, *per* Lord Denning MR. See also *Redpath v Belfast and County Down Rly [1947] NI 167.*

Insurance and analogous arrangements

[25.34]   Similarly, benefits accruing, albeit in consequence of the accident, to the claimant as a result of private insurance policies are not to be taken into account.[1] It is generally considered to be inconsistent with intuitive notions of justice that advantages gained by the claimant by virtue of his own thrift should be deducted from damages. In *Parry v Cleaver[2]* the House of Lords held that this principle extended to include disablement pensions paid by virtue of the plaintiff's former employment, and to do so regardless of whether the pension scheme had been contributory or non-contributory. Participation in such a scheme should, it was held, be regarded as analogous in principle to a private insurance policy; in choosing a job which had such a scheme the plaintiff had presumably voluntarily accepted lower levels of remuneration while working in order to pay for it.

¹   *Bradburn v Great Western Rly Co (1874) LR 10 Exch 1.*
²   *[1970] AC 1, [1969] 1 All ER 555, HL.* See also *Wood v British Coal Corpn [1991] IRLR 22, CA.*

Parry's case confirmed

[25.35] *Parry v Cleaver* was decided by a bare majority,¹ and overruled an earlier majority decision of the Court of Appeal.² Nevertheless, that it continues to represent the law is now beyond doubt. In the 1991 case of *Smoker v London Fire and Civil Defence Authority*³ the House of Lords was invited to invoke the 1966 Practice Statement to depart from it, but chose instead expressly and unanimously to affirm its authority. The point was again revisited by the House in 1998 in *Longden v British Coal Corp.*⁴ In that case the defendants conceded that a disablement pension could not be taken into account in assessing lost *earnings*, but argued that payments made under the disability pension scheme even *before* normal retirement age should be taken into account in assessing the plaintiff's loss of pension *after* that age:⁵ a contention which, if it had been accepted, would have extinguished the claim for loss of pension on the facts of the case itself. The House of Lords unanimously rejected the argument as inconsistent with the logic of *Parry v Cleaver*, but also considered it to be inherently unfair.⁶

¹   Lord Reid, Lord Pearce and Lord Wilberforce (Lord Morris and Lord Pearson dissenting).
²   See *Browning v War Office [1963] 1 QB 750, [1962] 3 All ER 1089, per* Lord Denning MR and Diplock LJ. Donovan LJ dissented.
³   *[1991] 2 AC 502, [1991] 2 All ER 449, HL.*
⁴   *[1998] AC 653, [1998] 1 All ER 289, HL.*
⁵   It was, of course, accepted by the plaintiff that, in accordance with *Parry v Cleaver*, the disablement pension payments to be received *after* normal retirement age could be taken into account in assessing the actual *pension* loss in those years, since that involves comparing 'like with like'. Similarly, if a claimant receives a lump sum as part of his disablement pension, such portion of that sum as is attributable to the post-retirement period will also be deducted: see *Longden v British Coal Corpn [1998] 1 All ER 289* at 302–303, HL.
⁶   'I think that it would … strike the ordinary man as unjust if the plaintiff's claim for loss of pension after his normal retirement age were to be extinguished by capitalising sums paid to him before that age as an incapacity pension to assist him during his disability': *per* Lord Hope in *Longden v British Coal Corpn [1998] 1 All ER 289* at 300–301.

Payments by the tortfeasor

'Benevolence'

[25.36] The rule that 'gift' payments received by the claimant as a result of the accident are not to be deducted from his damages does *not* apply if the payment was made by the tortfeasor himself. In *Gaca v Pirelli General*¹ the claimant was dismissed after suffering an injury at work which rendered him unfit for continued employment with the defendants. The latter made a payment to him, before any claim was made against them. When a damages award was eventually made to the claimant the defendants sought to set off the earlier payment. The Court of Appeal held that they could do so. Dyson³ LJ said²:

'I would hold that ex gratia payments made to victims by tortfeasors do not normally fall within the benevolence exception, even if it can be shown that they are made from motives of benevolence.'[3]

In so holding the Court of Appeal effectively overruled the controversial, and much criticised, 1990 decision of the same court in *McCamley v Cammell Laird Shipbuilders Ltd*[4].

[1]   *[2004] 3 All ER 348.*
[2]   See above at para 31.
[3]   See also *Williams v BOC Gases [2000] ICR 1181, CA*, especially *per* Brooke LJ at para 32: 'Deductibility will encourage [defendants] to make benevolent payments in future to injured employees, rather than the reverse'.
[4]   *[1990] 1 All ER 854, [1990] 1 WLR 963.*

'Insurance'

[25.37]   In *Hussain v New Taplow Paper Mills*[1] a disablement income, which the plaintiff became contractually entitled to receive as a result of an accident at his place of work, was deducted in a negligence action from his damages for loss of earnings.[2] The defendant employers had in fact insured against their liability to pay the sums in question; and it was contended that the payments forthcoming represented in essence the fruits of insurance, *in effect* paid for by the plaintiff himself, through the services he had given to his employer prior to the accident. This contention was rejected. The House of Lords held that the disablement income was indistinguishable in principle from the wages he would have received if uninjured. Lord Bridge said:[3]

'It positively offends my sense of justice that a plaintiff, who has certainly paid no insurance premiums *as such*, should receive full wages during a period of incapacity to work from two separate sources, his employer and the tortfeasor. It would seem to me still more unjust and anomalous where, as here, the employer and the tortfeasor are one and the same.'

[1]   *[1988] AC 514, [1988] 1 All ER 541.*
[2]   For comment on the decision of the Court of Appeal, reported in *[1987] ICR 28* and upheld by the House of Lords, see L J Anderson 'Assessment of Loss in Personal Injury Cases' (1987) 50 MLR 963.
[3]   *[1988] AC 514* at 532, *[1988] 1 All ER 541* at 548 (emphasis supplied).

Who paid?

[25.38]   The converse of the decision in *Hussain's* case is that a payment made by the employer will not be deducted if, in substance, it was in fact paid for by the employee. Indeed this is the basis upon which non-contributory pensions are non-deductible under the *Parry v Cleaver* principle. Difficult borderline decisions may sometimes arise in which it is arguable how the background to a payment made to the claimant, at least nominally by his employer, is to be interpreted. It is clear, however, that an employee seeking to cross the borderline will face a hard task. In *Gaca v Pirelli General*[1] Dyson LJ said:

' ... an employee is not to be treated as having paid for, or contributed to the cost of, insurance merely because the insurance has been arranged by his employer for the benefit of his employees. The insurance moneys must be deducted unless it is shown that the claimant paid or contributed to the insurance premium directly or indirectly. Payment or contribution will not be inferred simply from the fact that the claimant is an employee for whose benefit the insurance has been arranged'.[2]

1 See *[2004] 3 All ER 348,* at para 56.
2 See also the decision of the Supreme Court of Canada in *Cunningham v Wheeler, Cooper v Miller, Shanks v McNee [1994] 1 SCR 359* (referred to in *Gaca v Pirelli General*).

Law Commission

[25.39] At the end of the twentieth century the Law Commission conducted a major review of deductibility of collateral benefits in personal injury cases.[1] It concluded against recommending any statutory change in the law. Both the Commission itself, a generation earlier, and the Royal Commission on Civil Liability and Compensation for Personal Injury, had previously recommended against any change.[2]

1 See *Damages for Personal Injury: Medical, Nursing and other Expenses; Collateral Benefits* (Law Com no 262, 1999).
2 See *Report on Personal Injury Litigation – Assessment of Damages* (Law Com Report no 56, 1973) p 34 onwards, and the Report of the *Royal Commission on Civil Liability and Compensation for Personal Injury* (Cmnd 7054–I, 1978) paras 517–520.

Relationship with state benefits

[25.40] The *Social Security Act 1989* originally introduced a new regime regulating the relationship between tort damages and state benefits. This replaced an earlier, more limited, provision in the *Law Reform (Personal Injuries) Act 1948*. The new regime is now to be found in the *Social Security (Recovery of Benefits) Act 1997*.

Deductibility under the 1997 Act

[25.41] In a series of decisions, culminating in the decision of the House of Lords in *Hodgson v Trapp*,[1] which dealt with attendance and mobility allowances, the courts had moved in the direction of favouring the deductibility of most of the state benefits not expressly covered by the 1948 Act.[2] This policy was originally put into statutory form by the *Social Security Act 1989, s 22* and *Sch 4*,[3] and subsequently incorporated in *Pt IV* of the *Social Security Administration Act 1992*. The statutory regime does, however, include elaborate machinery to ensure that tortfeasors themselves do not benefit, at the taxpayer's expense, from the deductions so made. The relevant provisions are now to be found in the *Social Security (Recovery of Benefits) Act 1997*, which has significantly modified the earlier legislation[4]. Social security benefits paid or to be paid to the victim for five years from the date of the accident are to be deducted from the damages award (or out-of-court settlement), in order to avoid over-compensation. But in order simultaneously to ensure that the state does not thereby subsidise tortfeasors, the latter are obliged to reimburse to the Department of Social Security the value of the benefits so paid or to be paid[5]. The tortfeasor is required to obtain a certificate from the department's Compensation Recovery Unit of the relevant sums and to make the deduction, and reimbursement to the department, accordingly.

1 *[1989] AC 807, [1988] 3 All ER 870, HL.*

2 See *Nabi v British Leyland (UK) Ltd [1980] 1 All ER 667, [1980] 1 WLR 529, CA* (unemployment benefit); *Lincoln v Hayman [1982] 2 All ER 819, [1982] 1 WLR 488, CA* (supplementary benefit); *Gaskill v Preston [1981] 3 All ER 427* (family income supplement).

3 See now the *Social Security (Recovery of Benefits) Act 1997.*

4 For a helpful exposition of the scheme of the Act see the (dissenting) judgment of Hale LJ in *Lowther v Chatwin [2003] PIQR Q5.*

5 Persons making compensation payments are also liable to reimburse the NHS for expenditure incurred in treating the victim: see the *Health and Social Care (Community Health and Standards) Act 2003, Pt 3.*

Deductions only against comparable heads

[25.42] A major difference made by the 1997 Act, as compared with the legislation which dated from 1989, is that the deduction was formerly made from the total amount of damages, ie both pecuniary and non-pecuniary loss. The much criticised consequence was that damages for pain and suffering and loss of amenity could be diminished on account of receipt of benefits concerned with financial losses. In order to fine-tune the system so as to avoid this result, the deductions are now to be made only against comparable heads of compensation[1]. The following table (which is reproduced from *Schedule 2* of the 1997 Act), sets out the nature of the scheme. It will be noted that the arrangements now have the effect of protecting compensation for non-pecuniary loss from any deductions.[2]

1 In *McCarthy v Reticel [2000] PIQR Q74* a claim was struck out for want of prosecution on the ground that the plaintiff's delay had prejudiced the defendants because the passing of the new Act in the meantime had resulted in their losing the benefit of the earlier regime.

2 *Defendants*, however, remain liable to repay the *total* amount of recoverable benefits to the Secretary of State even where they are not deductible from the award to the plaintiff: see *section 6(1)* of the Act.

Schedule 2
Calculation of compensation payment

(1)	(2)
Head of compensation	*Benefit*
1. Compensation for earnings lost during the relevant period	
	Disablement pension payable under *section 103* of the 1992 Act
	Incapacity benefit
	Income support
	Invalidity pension and allowance
	Jobseeker's allowance
	Reduced earnings allowance
	Severe disablement allowance
	Sickness benefit
	Statutory sick pay
	Unemployability supplement
	Unemployment benefit
2. Compensation for cost of care incurred during the relevant period	Attendance allowance
	Care component of disability living allowance

(1)	(2)
	Disablement pension increase payable under *section 104* or *105* of the 1992 Act
3. Compensation for loss of mobility during the relevant period	Mobility allowance
	Mobility component of disability living allowance

Interest

[25.43] The way in which the 1997 Act operates is by separating the reimbursement process, which is treated as a matter between the tortfeasor and the State, from the resolution of the dispute between the tortfeasor and the claimant. The reimbursement process therefore has its own distinct machinery and appeal provisions. The separation is clearly stated in *section 17* of the Act as follows:

'In assessing damages in respect of any accident, injury or disease, the amount of any listed benefits paid or likely to be paid is to be disregarded'.

In *Wisely v John Fulton (Plumbers) Ltd*[1] the question arose whether this provision applied to *interest* on the special damages in respect of which the claimant had received deductible state benefits. The consequence of applying the wording of the section literally would be that the claimant would receive interest just as if he had not, in fact, received compensation for his special damage when, in reality, he had been in receipt of benefits covering the same loss. The House of Lords nevertheless held that the provision *is* to be applied in precisely that way: the tortfeasor is therefore liable to the claimant for interest regardless of the fact that the claimant has not been out of pocket in respect of the sum for which the interest is awarded. The principle in *Wisely's* case does, however, apparently cease to be applicable if the benefits to be reimbursed to the State by the tortfeasor exceed the amount for which the defendant was liable to the claimant, thereby extinguishing the latter's claim altogether in respect of the head of damage in question. The defendant is not required to pay 'interest' to the claimant in those circumstances[2].

[1]   *[2000] 2 All ER 545, HL*. See also *Eagle v Chambers (No 2) [2004] EWCA Civ 1033*.
[2]   See *Griffiths v British Coal Corporation [2001] WLR 1493*.

Where the statutory scheme does not apply

[25.44] As far as benefits not coming within the statutory regime are concerned, it should be noted that state retirement pensions have been held not to be deductible.[1] But redundancy payments may constitute a contribution to earnings which will be lost due to injury, and in such cases they will be deducted from damages.[2] It has also been held that payments made under the *Pneumoconiosis etc (Workers' Compensation) Act 1979* should be deducted from any damages award against a defendant responsible for the claimant's contraction of the disease for which the payment was made[3].

[1]   See *Hewson v Downs [1970] 1 QB 73, [1969] 3 All ER 193*.
[2]   See *Wilson v National Coal Board (1981) SLT 67, HL*, applied in *Colledge v Bass Mitchells & Butlers [1988] 1 All ER 536, CA*.
[3]   See *Ballantine v Newalls Insulation Co Ltd [2001] ICR 25, CA*.

Tax

[25.45] It was established by the well-known decision of the House of Lords in *British Transport Commission v Gourley*,[1] itself a personal injuries case, that the likely incidence of taxation must be taken into account in assessing damages for lost earnings. The claimant will therefore only be awarded a sum representing his probable net loss after tax, rather than one representing his gross pre-tax income. It follows from *Gourley* that the claimant must give credit, in his claim for special damages, for any tax rebate received by him as a result of his absence from work due to the injury.[2] In *Cooper v Firth Brown*[3] it was held that the *Gourley* principle also applied in respect of the plaintiff's social security contributions, and that a sum representing these too should be taken into account. If it can be proved to the satisfaction of the court, however, that the claimant was in the habit of making certain dispositions, such as covenanted gifts, in order to *reduce* his tax liability, then this factor will also be taken into account in calculating the damages.[4]

[1] *[1956] AC 185, [1955] 3 All ER 796.* See W Bishop and J Kay 'Taxation and Damages: The Rule in Gourley's Case' (1987) 103 LQR 211.
[2] See *Hartley v Sandholme Iron Co [1975] QB 600, [1974] 3 All ER 475.*
[3] *[1963] 2 All ER 31, [1963] 1 WLR 418.*
[4] See *Beach v Reed Corrugated Cases [1956] 2 All ER 652, [1956] 1 WLR 807, HL.* For comment see L J Anderson 'Assessment of Loss in Personal Injury Cases' (1987) 50 MLR 963.

Pension contributions not recoverable

[25.46] In *Dews v National Coal Board*[1] the plaintiff was injured in an accident for which the defendants were liable. He contended that his award for lost earnings should not be reduced to take account of pension scheme contributions which would have been deducted from his wages if he had not been injured. The House of Lords rejected his contention. The plaintiff had sought to invoke the principle that it is, in general, no concern of the defendant how the plaintiff chooses to spend his own disposable income. Their Lordships held, however, that an exception had to be made to that principle where part of the income is used to provide a pension for retirement. This is because loss of pension rights is itself a recoverable head of loss for which damages can be awarded. Therefore, to allow a plaintiff to recover both a sum in respect of such lost rights, if any,[2] *and* the contributions which would have been necessary to secure them had they not been lost, would be to permit double recovery. It is important to note that the House did *not* decide *Dews'* case on the ground that the mere fact that the deduction of the pension contributions from the plaintiff's wages would have been *compulsory* was itself sufficient to defeat his contention. This reasoning had been adopted by Sir John Donaldson MR in the Court of Appeal,[3] which had decided the case the same way as the House of Lords. The other two members of the Court of Appeal, however, Parker and Woolf LJJ, had pointed out that this approach could be a source of anomaly in other situations – for example, those in which a plaintiff contractually agrees with his employer that the latter may deduct trade union dues, or charitable donations, at source.

[1] *[1988] AC 1, [1987] 2 All ER 545, HL.* For comment see L J Anderson 'Assessment of Loss in Personal Injury Cases' (1987) 50 MLR 963.
[2] On the facts of *Dews v National Coal Board* itself, the plaintiff had not, in fact, suffered any diminution in his pension entitlement.
[3] See *[1987] QB 81, [1986] 2 All ER 759, CA.*

C Cost of care

General calculation

[25.47] Claimants who are seriously and permanently disabled often require constant nursing attendance and medical care for the rest of their lives. The cost of this is recoverable as a recognised head of general damages. The award, as in the case of loss of future earnings, is calculated by working out the likely annual cost and then multiplying it to yield the appropriate lump sum. Indeed, it was the approach to choosing the multiplier for the *cost of care* which was at the heart of the far-reaching decision of the House of Lords in *Wells v Wells*,[1] which has been discussed above in the context of the recovery of future financial loss. In accepting the argument that previous practice had artificially reduced the level of multipliers, and left victims seriously under-compensated, the House in *Wells* emphasised that this under-compensation was, if anything, a greater source of concern where compensation for the cost of future care is concerned than where financial losses fall to be assessed.[2] Accordingly, as established in *Wells v Wells*, the multiplier should now be chosen with the aid of actuarial tables using a discount rate of 2.5% as provided in the *Damages (Personal Injury) Order 2001*[3]. Since the fixing of this statutory figure the Court of Appeal has firmly resisted any attempt to allow for the higher rate of inflation, which tends to occur in relation to health care costs, by increasing the multiplicand. In *Cooke v United Bristol Healthcare NHS Trust*[4] such an attempt was dismissed as being 'in the end nothing but smoke and mirrors' and an 'illegitimate assault' on the discount rate itself[5].

[1] *[1998] 3 All ER 481.*
[2] See *per* Lord Hope, *[1998] 3 All ER 481* at 508: 'Whatever policy reasons there might have been for regarding it as acceptable that there may be less than a full recovery in regard to wage loss – and I should make it clear that I do not subscribe to that policy – *there can be no good reason for a shortfall in the amount required for future care* or to meet all the other outlays which have been rendered necessary by the disability' (italics supplied). See also, *per* Lord Hutton *[1998] 3 All ER 481* at 519 'it is vital for the plaintiffs that they receive constant and costly nursing care for the remainder of their lives and that they should be able to pay for it' and *per* Lord Steyn, *[1998] 3 All ER 481* at 502.
[3] See above.
[4] *[2004] 1 All ER 797.*
[5] See above at para 30 *per* Laws LJ.

Accommodation

[25.48] In addition to the cost of care, adaptations to the claimant's house or even, in some cases, the purchase of new accommodation may be necessary,[1] and an appropriate figure will be recoverable as damages as a result.[2]

[1] See *George v Pinnock [1973] 1 All ER 926, [1973] 1 WLR 118, CA* (purchase of bungalow); cf *Cunningham v Harrison [1973] QB 942, [1973] 3 All ER 463, CA.*
[2] On the approach to be adopted in calculating the appropriate sum to be awarded in respect of the purchase of special accommodation, see *per* Lord Lloyd in *Thomas v Brighton Health Authority*, sub nom *Wells v Wells [1998] 3 All ER 481* at 498–499, approving and discussing the approach of the Court of Appeal in *Roberts v Johnstone [1989] QB 878.* See also *Snowden v Lodge [2005] 1 All ER 581.*

Use of National Health Service facilities

[25.49] The *Law Reform (Personal Injuries) Act 1948, s 2(4)* provides as follows:

'In an action for damages for personal injuries ... there shall be disregarded, in determining the reasonableness of any expenses, the possibility of avoiding those expenses or part of them by taking advantage of facilities available under the National Health Service ...'

Accordingly, if the claimant chooses to be treated within the private medical sector, the defendant cannot argue that the expenditure incurred should be disallowed as unreasonable merely because the equivalent facilities could have been obtained free of charge in the state sector. Although this provision has been much criticised,[1] the Law Commission has recently recommended, it is submitted correctly, that the subsection should be retained and in its present form.[2] But if the expenditure incurred in caring for the claimant at his own home is substantially greater than that of caring for him in an institution, the burden of proving that it is reasonable for him to remain at home lies on the claimant.[3]

[1]   The Pearson Commission considered that the provision should be repealed: see Report of the *Royal Commission of Civil Liability and Compensation for Personal Injury* (Cmnd 7054–I, 1978) para 341.
[2]   See *Damages for Personal Injury: Medical, Nursing and other Expenses; Collateral Benefits* (Law Com no 262, 1999) para 3.18.
[3]   See *Rialas v Mitchell (1984) 128 Sol Jo 704, CA* (burden discharged on the facts). For the approach to be adopted in resolving this issue see the important discussion by the Court of Appeal in *Snowden v Lodge [2005] 1 All ER 581.*

When expenditure will not be incurred

[25.50] It is important to note that the 1948 Act does not require that a claimant should be allowed to recover expenses which he will never, in fact, incur.[1] It is, of course, true that a claimant who obtains damages assessed on the basis of private medical care can subsequently use National Health Service facilities and spend the award on something else, since the court cannot interfere with the use to which the claimant ultimately puts his own money. Nevertheless, if it is clear that the claimant will in fact be treated under the National Health Service, he cannot claim damages assessed on the basis of private treatment. Moreover, in some situations the claimant is regarded as having no real choice, because it is shown that suitable accommodation or treatment, for his condition or disability, can only be found within the state sector.[2] In such cases, however, the court must not assume that all the services which the claimant will receive from the state will necessarily be completely free of charge to him. Although medical treatment under the National Health Service is (except for prescriptions) free of charge to the user, local authorities are entitled to charge disabled people for certain welfare services which they may provide for them.[3]

[1]   See *Harris v Brights Asphalt Contractors [1953] 1 QB 617* at 635, *[1953] 1 All ER 395* at 402.
[2]   See *Cunningham v Harrison [1973] QB 942, [1973] 3 All ER 463, CA.* See also *Lim Poh Choo v Camden and Islington Health Authority [1980] AC 174* at 188, *[1979] 2 All ER 910* at 918, HL, *per* Lord Scarman.
[3]   See the *Health and Social Services and Social Security Adjudications Act 1983, s 17.* See also *Taylor v Bristol Omnibus Co [1975] 2 All ER 1107* at 1112, 1116, *[1975] 1 WLR 1054* at 1058, 1063, CA. Cf *Wipfli v Britten (1983) 145 DLR (3d) 80.*

Living expenses sometimes deductible

[25.51] A claimant who is disabled both from working and from looking after himself will normally recover damages both for the cost of care and for lost earnings. If the care is residential in, for example, a hospital or nursing home, it will usually be appropriate to make a deduction from the award for the cost of care to allow for the 'domestic element' of board and lodging etc.[1] Since the claimant would have used part of his earnings to feed and house himself, if he had not been injured, there would be an element of over-compensation in such a case if the claimant recovered all his lost earnings along with the full cost of care, where the latter includes food and basic necessities.[2] Similarly, when the claimant obtains board and lodging either subsidised, or free of charge, in a state institution, it is now the law that a reduction may be made in any award for lost earnings to allow for this. The Court of Appeal had held in *Daish v Wauton*[3] that no such reduction should be made, but the Pearson Commission recommended that this decision should be reversed,[4] and *section 5* of the *Administration of Justice Act 1982* accordingly provides as follows:

> 'In an action … for personal injuries … any saving to the injured person which is attributable to his maintenance wholly or partly at public expense in a hospital, nursing home or other institution shall be set off against any income lost by him as a result of his injuries.'

[1]   See *Lim Poh Choo v Camden and Islington Area Health Authority [1980] AC 174* at *191, [1979] 2 All ER 910* at 921, *per* Lord Scarman. The deduction should not be reflected in the choice of multiplier but should, instead, be made from the starting-point (or 'multiplicand'): see *per* Lord Scarman, *[1980] AC 174* at 196, *[1979] 2 All ER 910* at 925. See also *per* Browne LJ in the Court of Appeal *[1979] QB 196* at 234–235, *[1979] 1 All ER 332* at 853–854.

[2]   Cf *Shearman v Folland [1950] 2 KB 43, [1950] 1 All ER 976, CA.*

[3]   *[1972] 2 QB 262, [1972] 1 All ER 25, CA.*

[4]   See the Report of the *Royal Commission on Civil Liability and Compensation for Personal Injury* (Cmnd 7054–I, 1978) paras 508–512.

Care by relatives

[25.52]   Often an injured claimant will be cared for at home by a parent or spouse in circumstances in which, had this help not been forthcoming, professional nursing assistance, or an increase in the existing level of such assistance, would have been necessary. It has been clear since the decision of the Court of Appeal in *Donnelly v Joyce*,[1] which resolved earlier uncertainty, that the claimant can recover in his damages a sum enabling him to pay for the services so provided. It is not necessary for any formal agreement to be drawn up obliging the claimant to pay for the care he receives.[2] In *Donnelly v Joyce* it was held that the claimant claims in his own right and, in theory at least, not on behalf of the relative or relatives in question.[3] This aspect of the reasoning in *Donnelly's* case was, however, disapproved by the House of Lords in *Hunt v Severs*.[4] In that case the House held that 'the injured plaintiff who recovers damages under this head should hold them on trust for the voluntary carer'.[5]

[1]   *[1974] QB 454, [1973] 3 All ER 475, CA.*

[2]   Cf *Haggar v de Placido [1972] 2 All ER 1029, [1972] 1 WLR 716.* Any such agreement drawn up, for the purpose of increasing the award, will now be regarded as a sham: see *Housecroft v Burnett [1986] 1 All ER 332* at 343, CA, *per* O'Connor LJ. It is possible, however, that formal agreements may again become necessary, as a result of the much criticised decision of the House of Lords in *Hunt v Severs [1994] 2 AC 350, [1994] 2 All ER 385*, if the plaintiff's carer is also the tortfeasor: see below.

[3]   See *per* Megaw LJ, *[1974] QB 454* at 462, *[1973] 3 All ER 475* at 480 (judgment of the court).

[4]   *[1994] 2 AC 350, [1994] 2 All ER 385, HL.* Cf *Kars v Kars (1996) 71 ALJR 107*, in which the High Court of Australia preferred *Donnelly v Joyce* to *Hunt v Severs*.

[5]   *Per* Lord Bridge, *[1994] 2 AC 350* at 363, *[1994] 2 All ER 385* at 394, HL.

Not confined to the most serious cases

[25.53]   The principle that damages may be awarded to reflect the services of family carers is not confined to cases of serious and permanent illness. In *Giambrone v JMC*

Holidays (No 2)[1] the Court of Appeal upheld awards made in respect of the care of young children who had suffered from temporary, but severe, gastro-enteritis for several weeks after their return from a holiday during which they had been infected due to the defendants' negligence. The 'governing principle' is that 'an award for the value of gratuitous care might be allowed if the claimant's illness or injury [is] sufficiently serious to give rise to a need for care and attendance significantly over and above that which would be given anyway in the ordinary course of family life'[2].

1   *[2004] 2 All ER 891.*
2   See above at para 8, *per* Brooke LJ.

Where defendant is the carer

[25.54]   In *Hunt*'s case itself the plaintiff's husband, who supplied the care, was also the defendant tortfeasor. The effect of the reasoning of the House was therefore to prevent the plaintiff from including in her claim a sum representing the value of her husband's care since, in the words of Lord Bridge, 'there can be no ground ... for requiring the tortfeasor to pay to the plaintiff, in respect of the services which he himself has rendered, a sum of money which the plaintiff must then repay to him'.[1] Although this is a logical result, it is also a socially unfortunate one.[2] *Hunt v Severs* arose out of a road accident, and the plaintiff was in reality seeking legitimately to ensure that the family was fully compensated out of the proceeds of their compulsory insurance policy.[3] The Law Commission has recommended that the decision in *Hunt v Severs* should be reversed by legislation; and its Report included a draft bill which, if enacted, would have this effect[4].

1   *Per* Lord Bridge, *[1994] 2 AC 350* at 363, *[1994] 2 All ER 385* at 394, HL.
2   The Court of Appeal (and the trial judge) had managed to allow the plaintiff's claim: see *[1993] QB 815, [1993] 4 All ER 180, CA.*
3   The House was not prepared to take this into account: 'At common law the circumstance that a defendant is contractually indemnified against a particular legal liability can have no relevance whatever to the measure of that liability': *per* Lord Bridge, *[1994] 2 AC 350* at 363, *[1994] 2 All ER 385* at 395.
4   See *Damages for Personal Injury: Medical, Nursing and other Expenses; Collateral Benefits* (Law Com no 262, 1999).

Calculation

[25.55]   It is clear that an award can be made under this head even though the relative in question has not given up paid employment to look after the claimant.[1] If such employment has been given up, the value of the income lost will be relevant in calculating the award; provided that it does not exceed the full commercial rate for the services received by the claimant, which is the ceiling for such an award.[2] This ceiling figure will not necessarily be awarded in every case since, as it was put in an Australian case:

> '[the] calculation of compensation with reference to charges made for the supply of services on a commercial basis may not always be appropriate ... Services provided by relatives and friends may not be exactly the same as those provided by commercial agencies. The latter will also necessarily have an element of profit in their charges.'[3]

In *Donnelly v Joyce* the damages were calculated by reference to the wages in fact lost by the plaintiff's mother, it being clear that the cost of professional help, if she had been unavailable, would have been greater.[4] In *Croke v Wiseman*[5] the plaintiff's mother gave up her job as a teacher to look after him, and the claim for nursing care included a sum in respect of the pension rights which she had thereby forfeited. By a majority,[6] the Court of Appeal allowed this claim on the ground that the overall sum thereby awarded for care was not excessive given the high quality of the nursing care which the mother provided and that the 'parents [would] in fact be on duty for longer hours every week than … professional nurses, and they [would] have the whole of the weekends to cope with'.[7] In cases at the opposite end of the spectrum, where the illness has been unpleasant but temporary, such as gastro-enteritis in young children, the Court of Appeal has indicated that £50 per week (at 2004) values represents a suitable guideline figure which should only be exceeded in cases of proportionately greater severity[8].

[1]   See *Cunningham v Harrison [1973] QB 942, [1973] 3 All ER 463, CA; Taylor v Bristol Omnibus Co [1975] 2 All ER 1107, [1975] 1 WLR 1054, CA.*
[2]   *Housecroft v Burnett [1986] 1 All ER 332* at 343, CA. On the calculation of compensation under this head, see generally *Hodges v Frost (1983) 53 ALR 373 (Aust).*
[3]   *Per* Kirby J in *Hodges v Frost (1983) 53 ALR 373* at 381.
[4]   See *[1974] QB 454* at 459–460, *[1973] 3 All ER 475* at 478, CA, *per* Megaw LJ, delivering the judgment of the court.
[5]   *[1981] 3 All ER 852, [1982] 1 WLR 71, CA.*
[6]   Griffiths and Shaw LJJ; Lord Denning MR dissenting.
[7]   *[1981] 3 All ER 852* at 860, *[1982] 1 WLR 71* at 81, *per* Griffiths LJ.
[8]   See *Giambrone v JMC Holidays (No2) [2004] 2 All ER 891, CA per* Brooke LJ at para 33.

Where claimant is a carer

[25.56]   If the claimant was a carer for a disabled relative, but because of his injuries can no longer fulfil that role, he can include in his claim the value of the services which will now have to be provided by someone else[1].

[1]   See *Lowe v Guise [2002] 3 All ER 454, CA.* In Scotland such a claim is expressly provided for by statute: see the *Administration of Justice Act 1982, s 9* (which does not apply in England).

Principle not applicable to commercial services

[25.57]   In *Hardwick v Hudson*[1] the plaintiff sought to recover damages to reflect the value of services of a managerial nature which, as a result of his injuries, the plaintiff's wife had performed for his business. The Court of Appeal disallowed the claim. The principle relating to personal care such as nursing would not be extended by analogy to cover services normally the subject of a contract of employment.

[1]   *[1999] 3 All ER 426.*

D Structured settlements[1]

Periodical payments

[25.58]   One of the most significant developments relating to personal injuries compensation towards the end of the twentieth century was the development of 'structured settlements'. The effect of these is to provide a claimant with periodic payments, instead of a lump sum, for the remainder of his or her life. The payments are usually funded by the purchase of a series of annuities enabling the achievement, inter alia, of indexation. This fact, coupled with a favourable tax regime,[2] can make such settlements very attractive to claimants.[3] Following an examination by the Law Commission[4], *section 2* of the *Damages Act 1996* was enacted to promote the use of such settlements by enhancing the protection afforded to claimants.[5] As the law stood until a new version of *section 2* was substituted by the *Courts Act 2003*, however, such settlements required agreement between the parties, usually before the case reached court. They could not be imposed by judicial decision. Although the court now had the power to make an order for periodic payments,[6] where formerly all actual awards of damages had to be in the form of lump sums, the power could only be exercised with the consent of the parties.[7] In March 2002 the Lord Chancellor's Department published a Consultation Paper, 'Damages for Future Loss', on the desirability of the courts' making awards in the form of periodical payments without the consent of the parties. The paper concluded 'that in most circumstances periodical payments are, in principle, the most appropriate means for paying compensation for future financial loss'[8]; and proposed that the courts should be given a discretionary power to order periodical payments, in place of lump sums, for large awards. As a result, the new version of *section 2* was substituted, and the provision now reads as follows:

'A court awarding damages for future pecuniary loss in respect of personal injury-may order that the damages are wholly or partly to take the form of periodical payments, and shall consider whether to make that order.

(2) A court awarding other damages in respect of personal injury may, if the parties consent, order that the damages are wholly or partly to take the form of periodical payments'.

The new provisions were brought into force in November 2004, along with detailed machinery of financial protection[9].

[1]   See I S Goldrein QC and M de Haas (eds) *Structured Settlements – A Practical Guide* (2nd edn, 1998); R Lewis *Structured Settlements: The Law and Practice* (1993).
[2]   See the *Finance Act 1996, s 150* and *Sch 26.*
[3]   See D Allen 'Structured Settlements' (1988) 104 LQR 448.
[4]   See *Structured Settlements and Interim and Provisional Damages* (Law Com Report no 224, 1994).
[5]   See also *sections 4, 5* and *6.*
[6]   See the *Damages Act 1996, s 2.*
[7]   *Damages Act 1996, s 2.* 'Such agreement is never, or virtually never, forthcoming. The present power to order periodic payments is a dead letter': *per* Lord Steyn in *Wells v Wells [1998] 3 All ER 481* at 502.
[8]   See the Executive Summary. See also *per* Lord Steyn in *Wells v Wells [1998] 3 All ER 481* at 502: The court ought to be given the power of its own motion to make an award for periodic payments rather than a lump sum in appropriate cases. Such a power is perfectly consistent with the principle of full compensation for pecuniary loss. Except perhaps for the distaste of personal injury lawyers for change to a familiar system, I can think of no substantial argument to the contrary. But the judges cannot make the change. Only Parliament can solve the problem.'
[9]   See the *Courts Act 2003, s.101* substituting *sections 4* and *5* of the *Damages Act 1996*. The new scheme is outlined by Nicholas Bevan and Hugh Gregory in 'Structured Settlements' (2004) NLJ 1280, 1388 and 1658.

Chapter 26

Cases involving death

A Survival of causes of action

Law Reform (Miscellaneous Provisions) Act 1934

[26.01] At common law the death of a person automatically terminated all causes of action against or in favour of that person. This inconvenient rule was largely abrogated by the *Law Reform (Miscellaneous Provisions) Act 1934, s 1(1)*, which provides that, with the exception of claims for defamation, 'on the death of any person ... all causes of action subsisting against or vested in him shall survive against, or, as the case may be, for the benefit of, his estate'. Thus, if the claimant is seriously injured by the negligence of the defendant, and subsequently dies from his injuries, his estate can bring or continue an action for the losses, both pecuniary or non-pecuniary, incurred by him up to the date of his death. In *Hicks v Chief Constable of South Yorkshire*,[1] which was the second case arising out of the 1989 Hillsborough football stadium disaster to reach the House of Lords,[2] an attempt by the estates of victims to recover damages on this basis failed on the facts: it being found that the deaths had, in effect, been instantaneous so that no actionable pre-death pain and suffering had occurred. An example of a successful claim is *Thomas v Kwik Save Stores*[3]. The deceased had survived for three weeks after her accident, had been in pain and had undergone an operation. The Court of Appeal, halving the figure awarded by the trial judge, made an award of £2,500 under this head.

[1]   *[1992] 2 All ER 65, HL.*
[2]   For the first and third ones see CHAPTER 1 above.
[3]   Times, June 27, 2000.

'Lost years' loss of income does not survive

[26.02] An important provision was added to the *Law Reform (Miscellaneous Provisions) Act 1934* by the *Administration of Justice Act 1982, s 4*. As a result, *section 1(2)* of the 1934 Act now reads, where relevant, as follows:

'Where a cause of action survives ... for the benefit of the estate of a deceased person, the damages recoverable for the benefit of the estate of that person shall not include ... any damages for loss of income in respect of any period after that person's death.'

This provision became necessary as a consequence of the decision of the House of Lords in *Pickett v British Rail Engineering*,[1] which was reflected in the later decision of the House in *Gammell v Wilson*.[2] In the former case the House of Lords held that a living plaintiff whose life had been shortened by the negligence of the defendant could recover damages for the lost earnings which he would never receive due to his likely premature death.[3] This decision enabled justice to be achieved in the case of a living plaintiff, not least because it enabled such a person, if he wished, to ensure that any dependants of his would be appropriately catered for after his death; his own action during his lifetime in respect of his injury having destroyed any claims they might themselves have subsequently brought under the Fatal Accidents Act.[4] The decision of the House in *Gammell v Wilson* made clear, however, that the effect of the *Law Reform (Miscellaneous Provisions) Act 1934, s 1*, when combined with the *Pickett* decision, was to enable the estates of already deceased persons to claim lost earnings for the 'lost years'. Such claims would necessarily be irrespective of whether or not the deceased had left any dependants and, if he had done so, would be additional to any claim by those dependants under the Fatal Accidents Act. Defendants could thus even have found themselves liable twice over for the same economic loss: once to the deceased's estate under the 1934 Act and once to his dependants under the Fatal Accidents Act. The 1982 provision rectified this situation by preventing claims for lost income during the lost years from surviving for the benefit of the estate.

[1]   *[1980] AC 136, [1979] 1 All ER 774.*
[2]   *[1982] AC 27, [1981] 1 All ER 578.*
[3]   This overruled the decision of the Court of Appeal in *Oliver v Ashman [1962] 2 QB 210, [1961] 3 All ER 323*. For further discussion, see CHAPTER 25 above.
[4]   See below.

Where injured person dies from another cause

[26.03]   It is to be noted that the wording of the provision which prevents the deceased's estate from claiming for future lost earnings does not distinguish between victims who die from their injuries and injured persons who die from other causes. A person's life expectancy may be shortened by an accident caused by the defendant's negligence, but he may die from some unrelated non-tortious cause before he has brought an action in respect of his injuries. In such an eventuality his dependants will necessarily have no claim under the Fatal Accidents Act, and yet the blanket wording of the new provision will prevent his estate from recovering the lost earnings which, in the majority of cases, would actually have passed to the dependants and so protected them indirectly. Dependants in such circumstances will therefore be in the same position in which they would have been before *Pickett v British Rail Engineering* was decided, when lost earnings during the 'lost years' could not be recovered at all. It has been suggested that this result is anomalous.[1] But the criticism seems misplaced, since the dependants are only in the same position as persons generally who die from causes, such as disease, for which there is no legal redress.[2]

[1]   See P Cane and D Harris 'Administration of Justice Act 1982, s 4(2): A Lesson in How Not to Reform the Law.' (1983) 46 MLR 478.
[2]   Cf *Jobling v Associated Dairies Ltd [1982] AC 794, [1981] 2 All ER 752*. See also A Burrows *Remedies for Torts and Breach of Contract* (2nd edn, 1994) p 207, n 9.

B Claims by dependants[1]

Background

[26.04]   The long-standing hostility of the common law to the recovery of pure economic loss meant that a family whose breadwinner was killed by the defendant's negligence was remediless. Statutory intervention to ameliorate this situation came as early as 1846 with the passing in that year of the *Fatal Accidents Act*. The relevant statute law is now contained in the consolidating *Fatal Accidents Act 1976*. It is important to note, however, that the first four sections of this Act are now to be found in the *Administration of Justice Act 1982, s 3*, which substituted new provisions for those originally contained in the 1976 Act when it was passed.

[1]   See *Claims for Wrongful Death* (Law Commission Report no 263, 1999).

Who can claim

[26.05]   The *Fatal Accidents Act 1976* only applies if the victim of the accident would himself have been able to obtain judgment, usually for negligence, in respect of it had he lived.[1] If, however, he does obtain judgment in his lifetime, or settles the claim, then the dependants cannot subsequently sue the defendant under the Fatal Accidents Act.[2] Consistent with its general approach, the Act provides that the damages recoverable under it may be reduced by virtue of the *Law Reform (Contributory Negligence) Act 1945* if the victim of the accident had himself been contributorily negligent.[3] If the person whose negligence caused the death of the deceased was himself one of the dependants, he obviously cannot bring a Fatal Accidents Act claim but will, on the contrary, be himself liable under the Act to the other dependants.[4] Any claim under the Act has to be brought by the executor or administrator of the deceased; but may be brought by the dependants themselves six months after the death, if no action has been brought by then.[5]

[1]   'If death is caused by any wrongful act, neglect or default which is such as would (if death had not ensued) have entitled the person injured to maintain an action and recover damages in respect thereof, the person who would have been liable if death had not ensued shall be liable to an action for damages, notwithstanding the death of the person injured': *Fatal Accidents Act 1976, s 1(1)*.
[2]   Cf *Pickett v British Rail Engineering [1980] AC 136, [1979] 1 All ER 774*.
[3]   See *Fatal Accidents Act 1976, s 5*.
[4]   See *Dodds v Dodds [1978] QB 543, [1978] 2 All ER 539* (husband killed by wife's driving; action on behalf of children). A dependant whose negligence *contributed* to the death will be able to recover but the damages will be reduced proportionately: *Mulholland v McCrea [1961] NI 135*.
[5]   *Fatal Accidents Act 1976, s 2*.

Provisional damages

[26.06]   The general principle, that a judgment obtained against the defendant by the deceased during his lifetime precludes a subsequent action after his death by his dependants under the *Fatal Accidents Act 1976*, gave rise to uncertainty when 'provisional damages' awards were introduced.[1] It was uncertain whether such an award, which enables a claimant to seek further damages in the event of a deterioration in his condition, operated to prevent his dependants from claiming under the Fatal Accidents Act in the event of his death. In order to ensure that provisional damages awards do not have this effect, the following provision, in accordance with a recommendation by the Law Commission,[2] was enacted in the *Damages Act 1996, s 3*:

'3.—(1) This section applies where a person—

(a)   is awarded provisional damages; and

(b)   subsequently dies as a result of the act or omission which gave rise to the cause of action for which the damages were awarded,

(2) The award of the provisional damages shall not operate as a bar to an action in respect of that person's death under the Fatal Accidents Act 1976.'

In order to prevent a defendant being liable twice in respect of the same loss the section goes on to provide as follows:

'(3) Such part (if any) of—

(a)   the provisional damages; and

(b)   any further damages awarded to the person in question before his death,

as was intended to compensate him for pecuniary loss in a period which in the event falls after his death shall be taken into account in assessing the amount of any loss of support suffered by the person or persons for whose benefit the action under the Fatal Accidents Act 1976 is brought.'

---

¹   For provisional damages, see the *Supreme Court Act 1981, s 32A* (added by the *Administration of Justice Act 1982, s 6*). See generally Chapter 7 of the handbook.

²   See *Structured Settlements and Interim and Provisional Damages* (Law Com Report no 224, 1994).

Discharge of concurrent tortfeasor by settlement

[26.07]   In *Jameson v Central Electricity Generating Board*¹ a plaintiff, who was dying as a result of contact with asbestos while at work, settled a negligence claim against his former employers. After his death his widow brought a claim under the *Fatal Accidents Act 1976* against a different defendant which, as occupier of the premises upon which the exposure to asbestos had taken place, was a concurrent tortfeasor² in respect of her husband's death along with his former employer. The House of Lords, reversing the Court of Appeal,³ held that the deceased's settlement had constituted full satisfaction of his claim against his employer, and that it had therefore released the concurrent tortfeasor from liability. It followed that the widow could not sue the latter in respect of her lost dependency even though the money due under the settlement was not actually paid until several days *after* the death of the deceased. The agreement itself 'discharged the deceased's claim of damages, subject [only] to an implied resolutive condition which would render it void *ab initio* if the debt which was due under it was not satisfied'.⁴

---

¹   *[1999] 1 All ER 193, HL*.

²   See CHAPTER 22 above for the distinction between joint and concurrent tortfeasors.

³   *[1998] QB 323, [1997] 4 All ER 38, CA*. The Court of Appeal had held that the settlement had fallen short of full satisfaction.

⁴   See *[1999] 1 All ER 193* at 207, *per* Lord Hope.

The dependants

[26.08]   The dependants of the deceased, who are entitled to claim under the *Fatal Accidents Act, 1976* are listed in *section 1* of the Act. The relevant subsections read as follows:

'(3) In this Act 'dependant' means—

(a)   the wife or husband or former wife or husband of the deceased;

(b)   any person who—

> (i) was living with the deceased in the same household immediately before the date of the death; and
>
> (ii) had been living with the deceased in the same household for at least two years before that date; and

(c) any parent or other ascendant of the deceased;

(d) any person who was treated by the deceased as his parent;

(e) any child or other ascendant of the deceased;

(f) any person (not being a child of the deceased) who, in the case of any marriage to which the deceased was at any time a party, was treated by the deceased as a child of the family in relation to that marriage;

(g) any person who is, or is the issue of, a brother, sister, uncle or aunt of the deceased.

(4) The reference to the former wife or husband of the deceased in subsection (3)(a) above includes a reference to a person whose marriage to the deceased has been annulled or declared void as well as a person whose marriage to the deceased has been dissolved.

(5) In deducing any relationship for the purposes of subsection (3) above—

(a) any relationship by affinity shall be treated as a relationship by consanguinity, any relationship of the half blood as a relationship of the whole blood, and the stepchild of any person as his child, and

an illegitimate person shall be treated as the legitimate child of his mother and reputed father.'

Expanded list

[26.09] In its new form this provision considerably expands the list of possible dependants beyond that originally contained in the 1976 Act itself and earlier legislation. For example, divorced spouses can now claim for the first time,[1] as can persons unrelated to the deceased but who were treated by him, in respect of his marriage, as children of the family. Perhaps the most significant change, however, is the addition to the list of unmarried cohabitees[2] of deceased persons, provided that the partners had been living together for at least two years.[3]

[1]   Cf *Payne-Collins v Taylor Woodrow Construction Ltd [1975] QB 300, [1975] 1 All ER 898.*
[2]   Cf *K v JMP Co Ltd [1976] QB 85, [1975] 1 All ER 1030.*
[3]   See the *Fatal Accidents Act*, s 1(3)(b). See also *Kotke v Saffarini [2005] EWCA Civ 221* (claim failed on the facts).

Loss must flow from the defined relationship

[26.10] In *Burgess v Florence Nightingale Hospital*[1] the plaintiff and his wife had been professional dancing partners. After his wife had been killed by the negligence of the defendants, the plaintiff claimed under the Fatal Accidents Act for earnings lost due to his inability to perform professionally without his partner. His claim failed. It was clear on the evidence that not all professional dancing partners were married, and Devlin J held that the earnings lost had not been derived from the marital relationship itself as such.[2] This decision was applied by the Court of Appeal in *Cox v Hockenhull*[3]. In this case the deceased's husband had been in receipt of invalid care allowance in respect of his wife, who had been disabled. Although that allowance necessarily ceased with the death it could not be included in the Fatal Accidents Act claim: it had not been derived from the marriage relationship, since it is payable to carers irrespective of whether or not they are related to the disabled person.

[1]   *[1955] 1 QB 349, [1955] 1 All ER 511.*
[2]   Cf *Behrens v Bertram Mills Circus Ltd [1957] 2 QB 1, [1957] 1 All ER 583*, in which Devlin J distinguished his own earlier decision in *Burgess v Florence Nightingale Hospital* and reached a different conclusion on very special facts.
[3]   *[1999] 3 All ER 577.*

Reality of the situation

[26.11]   Nevertheless, in determining whether losses did in truth flow from the relationship within the Act the court will look at the reality of the situation rather than its form. In *Malyon v Plummer*[1] the plaintiff and her deceased husband had been co-directors of a family company. The plaintiff had been paid a salary by the company which was considerably in excess of the market value of her services. This had apparently been for tax reasons and was accepted by the court as having been legitimate. The defendants claimed, however, that the full value of the salary actually paid to the plaintiff should be taken into account in calculating the extent of her dependancy on her husband. This argument failed. The Court of Appeal held that only a sum representing the market value of her services should be taken into account. In reality, the plaintiff was substantially dependant upon her husband, whose activity in running an essentially one-man company generated the family income. The book-keeping transaction whereby the wife was nominally a well-paid employee of the company would not be allowed to obscure the true situation.

[1]   *[1964] 1 QB 330, [1963] 3 All ER 344.*

Lost tax advantages

[26.12]   Another defence attempt to claim that losses incurred should be treated as outside the scope of the relationship defined by the Act failed in *Davies v Whiteways Cyder Co.*[1] During his lifetime the deceased had made substantial capital payments to his wife and son in order to avoid the fiscal disadvantages of disposing of the sums in his will. Since he was, however, killed by the negligence of the defendants less than seven years after making the gifts the tax advantages were lost. The deceased's widow successfully claimed under the Fatal Accidents Act a sum representing the amount which had had to be paid to the Revenue to discharge the tax liability. A suggestion that the loss flowed from the relationship of donor to donee, as distinct from the family relationship within the Act, was rejected.

[1]   *[1975] QB 262, [1974] 3 All ER 168* (O'Connor J).

Shared expenses

[26.13]   If the person claiming under the Act, and the deceased, had in fact both been earners, and had shared the expenses of the household, a sum reflecting the increased expense to the claimant of living alone can properly be awarded as damages. In *Burgess v Florence Nightingale Hospital* Devlin J said:[1]

> 'It seems to me that when a husband and wife, either with separate incomes or with a joint income to which they are both beneficially entitled, are living together and sharing their expenses, and in consequence of that fact their joint living expenses are less than twice the expenses of each one living separately, then each, by the fact of the sharing, is conferring a benefit on the other, and I think that mutual benefits clearly arise from the relationship by virtue of which they are living together, namely, the relationship of husband and wife, and, accordingly, that comes within the Fatal Accidents Act.'

[1]   *[1955] 1 QB 349* at 362, *[1955] 1 All ER 511* at 519.

Joint operations

[26.14]   A somewhat unusual situation was considered in *Cookson v Knowles*.[1] The deceased husband and wife had separate jobs, but the former's help was partly necessary for the full discharge of the latter's duties. The wife worked as a cleaner at a school but attending to certain high windows, and dealing with the boiler, was not physically possible for her unaided. Accordingly, she lost her own job when her husband was killed due to the negligence of the defendants. On the other hand, her earning capacity as such had not been lost, as she would be able to do other work in the future. On the facts of the case the Court of Appeal held that, for the purpose of calculating the Fatal Accidents Act award, the lost earnings of the deceased husband would be regarded as his own income plus one third of his wife's.

[1]   *[1977] QB 913, [1977] 2 All ER 820* (not considered in *[1979] AC 556, [1978] 2 All ER 604*).

How damages are assessed

[26.15]   It is the practice to divide awards made under the *Fatal Accidents Act 1976* into two parts: the first consisting of the actual loss between the date of the death and the date of the trial, and the second the future pecuniary loss.[1] In *Taylor v O'Connor*[2] Lord Pearson described the process followed in making the award under the second head as follows:

> 'There are three stages in the normal calculation, namely: (i) to estimate the lost earnings, ie the sums which the deceased probably would have earned but for the fatal accident; (ii) to estimate the lost benefit, ie the pecuniary benefit which the dependants probably would have derived from the lost earnings, and to express the lost benefit as an annual sum over the period of the lost earnings; and (iii) to choose the appropriate multiplier which, when applied to the lost benefit expressed as an annual sum, gives the amount of the damages which is a lump sum.'

[1]   *Cookson v Knowles [1979] AC 556, [1978] 2 All ER 604.*
[2]   *[1971] AC 115* at 140, *[1970] 1 All ER 365* at 377.

Lost earnings

[26.16]   The starting point for the estimation of future pecuniary loss is the deceased's net income as it would have been at the date of the trial.[1] Difficult questions may sometimes arise in assessing 'the value in monies worth of the loss of a husband and father when the family's financial affairs are not straight forward'[2]. The dependants are entitled to have taken into account possible future real increases in his earnings which the defendant might have received had he lived. Where the likelihood of some such real increase due, say, to promotion is sufficient to justify its being reflected in the final award, but the evidence is imprecise as to what the increase might have been, the court may simply choose a higher multiplier than it would otherwise have done. If, however, there is a clear promotion ladder[3], or evidence of a similarly specific kind is available, the approach which is apparently preferred by the courts is to take this factor into account at the initial stage of the calculation by reaching a figure for the deceased's likely average future earnings over the dependancy period.[4]

[1] See *Cookson v Knowles [1979] AC 556* at 575, *[1978] 2 All ER 604* at 614, *per* Lord Fraser.
[2] *Per* Latham LJ in *O'Loughlin v Cape Distribution Ltd [2001] PIQR Q8,* at para 2 (deceased had been a property developer with strong entrepreneurial skills).
[3] See *D v Donald [2001] PIQR Q5* (likelihood of promotion to NCO in the army).
[4] See *Young v Percival [1974] 3 All ER 677, [1975] 1 WLR 17, CA*; *Robertson v Lestrange [1985] 1 All ER 950.*

Lost benefit: the 'dependency'

[26.17] Obviously, not all the deceased's net income would have been spent on his dependants; apart from anything else, part of it would have been necessary for his own food and clothing. The pecuniary benefit which the dependants have lost must therefore be calculated by subtracting from the deceased's earnings his own keep and any other relevant disbursements such as, for example, the cost of any expensive hobbies of his or regular payments to his favourite charities. Although the calculation has necessarily to be made on the facts of each case, the task is usually simplified by the adoption of a standardised approach, unless the context otherwise requires. In *Harris v Empress Motors Ltd* O'Connor LJ said:[1]

'In the course of time the courts have worked out a simple solution to the ... problem of calculating the net dependency under the Fatal Accidents Acts in cases where the dependants are wife and children. In times past the calculation called for a tedious inquiry into how much housekeeping money was paid to the wife, who paid how much for the children's shoes, etc. This has all been swept away and the modern practice is to deduct a percentage from the net income figure to represent what the deceased would have spent exclusively on himself. The percentages have become conventional in the sense that they are used unless there is striking evidence to make the conventional figure inappropriate because there is no departure from the principle that each case must be decided upon its own facts. Where the family unit was husband and wife the conventional figure is 33 per cent and the rationale of this is that broadly speaking the net income was spent as to one-third for the benefit of each and one-third for their joint benefit ... No deduction is made in respect of the joint portion because one cannot buy or drive half a motor car ... Where there are children the deduction falls to 25 per cent.'

[1] *[1983] 3 All ER 561* at 565, *[1984] 1 WLR 212* at 216–217.

Where dependant was an earner

[26.18] The approach thus outlined by O'Connor LJ is modified if, as is increasingly common, the dependant herself or himself also had an income which contributed to the overall finances of the family. In *Cox v Hockenhull*[1] Stuart-Smith LJ quoted the above passage from *Harris v Empress Motors Ltd,* but then continued as follows[2]:

'That is a reasonable approach where the deceased is the sole source of income. Where both spouses contribute to the joint income the correct approach is to deduct the income of the surviving dependant from the appropriate portion of the joint income (be that proportion two-thirds or some other proportion) provided that there is a reasonable expectation that such income will continue'.

[1]   *[1999] 3 All ER 577, CA.*
[2]   See *[1999] 3 All ER 577* at 585.

The multiplier and the capital sum

[26.19]   A multiplier is applied to the figure representing the annual dependency in order to produce a lump sum which in principle is intended to provide, by the use of both capital and income, replacement for the financial support lost by the dependants until it becomes exhausted at the expiry of the likely period of dependency.[1] The date for the selection of the appropriate multiplier is the date of the death, not that of the trial.[2] The number of years which have elapsed since the death, for which a separate award of pre-trial loss is made, is then simply deducted from the multiplier.[3] The Law Commission has recommended that the existing rule for the selection of the multiplier should be changed, preferably by the courts themselves rather than by legislation, to make the date of the trial the one to be used[4]. Choosing the date of death leads to the selection of lower multipliers than would be the case if the date of trial were chosen, and adopting the latter would avoid the under-compensation which is a perceived consequence of the existing rule. The views of the Law Commission were pressed upon Nelson J in *White v ESAB Group (UK) Ltd*[5], who said that he agreed with them but that, as a judge of first instance, he felt obliged to apply the existing rule.

[1]   See *per* Lord Pearson in *Taylor v O'Connor [1971] AC 115* at 143, *[1970] 1 All ER 365* at 379.
[2]   See *Graham v Dodds [1983] 2 All ER 953, [1983] 1 WLR 809, HL.* Cf *Pritchard v J H Cobden [1988] Fam 22, [1987] 1 All ER 300, CA* (confirming that date of trial remains appropriate in personal injury cases).
[3]   See *Corbett v Barking Havering and Brentwood Health Authority [1991] 2 QB 408, [1991] 1 All ER 498, CA,* in which the majority of the Court of Appeal (Purchas and Farquaharson LJJ) did, however, adjust the multiplier upwards to avoid hardship which this rule would have caused to the plaintiff on the facts of the case. Ralph Gibson LJ dissented on the ground that the course adopted by the majority was 'in effect, to calculate the multiplier as at the date of trial' (*[1991] 2 QB 408* at 440, *[1991] 1 All ER 498* at 524) which was impermissible.
[4]   See *Claims for Wrongful Death* (Law Com no 263, 1999) paras 4.1–4.23.
[5]   *[2002] PIQR Q6.*

Actuarial tables

[26.20]   Since the decision of the House of Lords in *Wells v Wells*[1], actuarial tables provide the basis for the selection of multipliers in Fatal Accident Act cases just as they do in personal injury cases[2].

[1]   *[1998] 3 All ER 481.* See CHAPTERS 24 and 25 above.
[2]   Use of the tables should greatly limit general judicial discounting for 'contingencies', such as the possibility of the deceased's becoming unemployed had he lived (see eg *per* Lord Diplock in *Cookson v Knowles [1979] AC 556* at 568, *[1978] 2 All ER 604* at 608), since the 'Ogden Tables' produced by the Government Actuary (*Actuarial Tables with explanatory notes for use in Personal Injury and Fatal Accident cases*) seek to take such contingencies into account.

Possibilities and their effect on quantum

[26.21] In making its assessment of what the future might hold, or have held, in store for the purpose of calculating damages under the *Fatal Accidents Act 1976*, the court does not confine itself to probabilities. Mere possibilities may also be relevant. It is clear that a claimant can qualify for an award even in respect of a dependency which had not existed at the time of the death, but which might possibly have developed at some future time. Thus, if the circumstances warrant it, parents may recover under the Act in respect of a deceased son or daughter even though the deceased may still have been in education or training at the time of the death and had not yet begun to earn.[1] Especially if the parents are infirm or elderly they might have had a reasonable expectation that the deceased would eventually have provided them with some financial support.[2] In cases of this type, and those involving similar situations, the court should estimate the degree of likelihood that a dependency would have occurred, or that some change in the level of an existing dependency might have developed, and the damages awarded should be proportionate to that assessment[3] (even if in straightforward cases this process of reasoning is rarely made explicit).

[1]   See *Taff Vale Rly Co v Jenkins [1913] AC 1* (16-year-old-daughter). Cf *Barnett v Cohen [1921] 2 KB 461* (deceased a child aged 4: no award).
[2]   See *Kandalla v British Airways Board [1981] QB 158, [1980] 1 All ER 341*.
[3]   See *Davies v Taylor [1974] AC 207, [1972] 3 All ER 836*.

Davies v Taylor

[26.22] The leading case on the approach to be adopted in the face of uncertainties of this kind is the decision of the House of Lords in *Davies v Taylor*.[1] The plaintiff and her deceased husband had separated prior to his death but the plaintiff brought an action under the Fatal Accidents Act contending that, if he had lived, a reconciliation might have taken place resulting in her becoming dependent upon him. The trial judge, Bridge J, held that the plaintiff would fail because she had not established on the balance of probabilities that a reconciliation would have occurred. The House of Lords held, however, that this approach, based on the burden of proof used to determine questions of existing fact, was not correct where the issue turned upon the chances of possible events occurring in the future.[2] Lord Cross observed that 'so long as the chance of future support which the plaintiff has lost was substantial or fairly capable of valuation the court ought … to set a value on it even though it was less – and possibly much less – than a 50 per cent chance.'[3] If the balance of probabilities were the test the anomalous result would follow that where the chances of reconciliation were just below evens, the plaintiff would receive no damages at all, whereas full damages, with no discount, would be awarded if the chances were just above evens.[4] In neither case would the result be satisfactory. Instead, 'the damages would', in the words of Lord Simon, 'be scaled down from those payable to a dependant spouse of a stable union, according as the possibility [of reconciliation] became progressively more remote. But she would still be entitled to some damages up to the point where the possibility was so fanciful and remote as to be *de minimis*'.[5]

[1]   *[1974] AC 207, [1972] 3 All ER 836*.
[2]   See *[1974] AC 207 at 212–213, [1972] 3 All ER 836 at 838–839, per* Lord Reid.
[3]   *[1974] AC 207 at 223, [1972] 3 All ER 836 at 847*. See also *Corbett v Barking Havering and Brentwood Health Authority [1991] 2 QB 408, [1991] 1 All ER 498, CA* (dependant child entitled to have his chances of proceeding to higher education assessed and valued in percentage terms).
[4]   See *[1974] AC 207 at 213, [1972] 3 All ER 836 at 847, per* Lord Reid; see also *per* Lord Cross, *[1974] AC 207 at 223, [1972] 3 All ER 836 at 847*.

⁵   *[1974] AC 207 at 220, [1972] 3 All ER 836 at 845.*

Valuing the chance

[26.23]   On the facts of *Davies v Taylor* itself the House of Lords held that the possibility of reconciliation fell within the 'fanciful and remote' category, so that the actual decision rejecting the plaintiff's claim altogether was ultimately affirmed.[1] On the other hand, in a case in which the marriage was still subsisting at the time of the husband's death, but he had been having a secret affair, the possibility that the marriage might have failed at some stage was merely reflected in a discounted multiplier[2]. The Law Commission has, however, recommended that the possibility of divorce should be ignored 'unless the couple were no longer living together at the time of death, or one of the couple had petitioned for divorce, judicial separation or nullity'[3].

¹   See also *Burns v Edman [1970] 2 QB 541, [1970] 1 All ER 886*: possibility that deceased, who had been
    a criminal, would have reformed and earned an honest living described as 'entirely speculative and
    unproven to the point of impossibility' (Crichton J).
²   See *D v Donald [2001] PIQR Q5.*
³   See *Claims for Wrongful Death* (Law Com no 263, 1999) paras 4.54–4.66.

Allowance for possible discontinuance where existing support had not been legally enforceable

[26.24]   The general principle of calculating the damages for future loss with respect to the estimated degree of likelihood of particular events occurring is also applicable where the claimant was already enjoying financial support from the deceased at the time of his death, but not by virtue of any actual legal obligation. In *Dolbey v Goodwin*[1] the deceased was a 29-year-old bachelor who lived with, and helped to maintain, his widowed mother. The award by the trial judge, which had apparently been as high as might have been expected if the deceased had been the plaintiff's husband, was substantially reduced by the Court of Appeal. Not only had there been no legal liability on the deceased to maintain the plaintiff, but allowance also had to be made for the possibility that the deceased might have married at some point in the future, with a consequent reduction in his capacity to assist his mother. The possible discounting of damages to allow for the degree of likelihood of discontinuance, where support existing at the time of the death had not been legally enforceable, is also contemplated by the provision enabling unmarried cohabitees to establish dependencies. The *Fatal Accidents Act 1976, s 3(4)* (inserted by the *Administration of Justice Act 1982, s 3(1)*) reads as follows:

> 'In an action under this Act where there fall to be assessed damages payable to a person who is a dependant … in respect of the death of the person with whom the dependant was living as husband or wife there shall be taken into account (together with any other matter that appears to the court to be relevant to the action) the fact that the dependant had no enforceable right to financial support by the deceased as a result of their living together.'

¹   *[1955] 2 All ER 166, [1955] 1 WLR 553.*

No increase in dependency to allow for possibility that claimant and deceased might have started a family

[26.25]   Of course, some of the contingencies which might have occurred if the deceased had not been killed might have increased his financial support of the claimant rather than reduced it. Hence the well-established practice of taking into account the deceased's promotion prospects.[1] Nevertheless, one contingency which will not be allowed to increase the dependency is the possibility that, had he not been killed, a deceased husband and his widow might have started a family, causing the latter to give up work and become wholly supported by the former whose support had previously only been partial. This was affirmed by the decision of Russell J in *Malone v Rowan*,[2] following an unreported decision of the Court of Appeal[3] which had held that, since the death had deprived the plaintiff of the chance of starting a family, it had also negated the possibility of a consequent increase in the dependency. This decision has been criticised,[4] and Russell J followed it with reluctance. But the Court of Appeal appears to have based its decision, at least in part, on the proposition that to increase the dependency in such circumstances would indirectly constitute damages for the non-financial loss of 'the joys of motherhood',[5] which cannot be compensated for under the Act.

[1] See above at para [26.16].
[2] *[1984] 3 All ER 402.*
[3] *Higgs v Drinkwater [1956] CA Transcript 129A.*
[4] See *Kemp & Kemp The Quantum of Damages* vol 1, para 25–003. For a different view, supporting the outcome, see A Burrows *Remedies for Torts and Breach of Contract* (2nd edn, 1994) p 214.
[5] *Per* Denning LJ in *Higgs v Drinkwater* (quoted in *Malone v Rowan [1984] 3 All ER 402* at 405).

Re-marriage and prospects of re-marriage by widow ignored

[26.26]   The *Fatal Accidents Act 1976, s 3(3)* (as enacted in the *Administration of Justice Act 1982, s 3(1)*) provides as follows:

'In an action under this Act where there fall to be assessed damages payable to a widow in respect of the death of her husband there shall not be taken account the re-marriage of the widow or her prospects of re-marriage.'

This provision, which dates back to 1971,[1] had its origin in judicial distaste for the task of evaluating the marriage prospects, and hence attractiveness, of widows.[2] It constitutes an exception not only to the general principle that contingencies should be taken into account in assessing future loss, but also to the principle that facts existing at the date of the trial should not be ignored;[3] since it applies to actual re-marriage as well as to prospects of re-marriage.

[1] See the *Law Reform (Miscellaneous Provisions) Act 1971, s 4.*
[2] See *Buckley v John Allen & Ford (Oxford) Ltd [1967] 2 QB 637* at 644–645, *[1967] 1 All ER 539* at 542, *per* Phillimore J.
[3] Cf *Curwen v James [1963] 2 All ER 619, [1963] 1 WLR 748.*

Provision criticised

[26.27]   The provision has been heavily criticised,[1] particularly on the ground that it leads to over-compensation where re-marriage has actually taken place. The *Royal Commission on Civil Liability and Compensation for Personal Injury* recommended that such re-marriage before trial should be taken into account,[2] but the recommendation has not been implemented. Two other aspects of the provision have also rendered it vulnerable to criticism. First, it applies only to widows and not to widowers: an anomalous distinction which both the Law Commission (in 1973) and the Royal Commission considered should be removed to make the law the same for both sexes.[3]

Secondly, it follows from the wording, which confines the provision to damages 'payable to a widow', that re-marriage or the prospects thereof will still be relevant in the case of any children of the widow and her deceased husband. That this is so was confirmed by the decision of Boreham J in *Thompson v Price*.[4] Thus, if the children acquire, or are likely to acquire, a stepfather who becomes under a legal obligation to maintain them, their damages under the *Fatal Accidents Act 1976* will still fall to be reduced correspondingly.[5]

1   See P Atiyah *Accidents, Compensation and the Law* (6th edn, 1999 Cane ed) p 113 (' ... one of the most irrational pieces of law "reform" ever passed by Parliament').
2   See Cmnd 7054–1 (1978) paras 409–412 (referring to 'the manifest absurdity of awarding damages for a loss which is known to have ceased').
3   See Law Com no 56 (1973) para 252; Royal Commission para 414. Cf *Regan v Williamson [1976] 2 All ER 241* at 245, *[1976] 1 WLR 350* at 309–310, *per* Watkins J: ' ... widowers must still, by reason of a distinction which I am unable to comprehend, go through the embarrassing process of being asked questions in the witness box about the possibility of remarrying.' For the latest (provisional) views of the Law Commission, see *Claims for Wrongful Death* (Law Com Consultation Paper no 148, 1997) paras 3.56–3.68.
4   *[1973] QB 838, [1973] 2 All ER 846*.
5   See *Reincke v Gray [1964] 2 All ER 687, [1964] 1 WLR 832, CA*.

Law Commission's recommendation

[26.28] In its 1999 report, *Claims for Wrongful Death*[1], the Law Commission recommended that *section 3(3)* of the *Fatal Accidents Act 1976* should be repealed. The prospect of re-marriage should be ignored unless the claimant was engaged to be married, or actually married, at the time of the trial. The new provision would apply to widowers as well as to widows and would also operate to prevent remarriage prospects being taken into account in relation to the dependency of children.

1   See Law Com no 263, paras. 4.30–4.53.

Loss of services of mother

[26.29] Where a very young child is orphaned', said Croom-Johnson LJ in *Spittle v Bunney*,[1] 'there is a practice of valuing the lost services of the mother by having regard to the cost of hiring a nanny'. But his Lordship emphasised that the calculations thus made have to be on a flexible common-sense basis which takes into account 'that as children get older they may also get more independent of their parents and less in need of being looked after'. He continued:[2]

> 'In the early years the services rendered by her mother to her small child may be valued by the cost of a hired nanny. The requirements are to some degree comparable. As the child grows older, and reaches school age, the valuation by commercial standards becomes less and less appropriate, and to use them is ... not comparing like with like. Once the child has begun school, at least by the age of six, the extent of the services decreases in amount. She needs, for a time, to be taken to and from school. Later on, she may go there by herself. Not only is the yardstick of a nanny's wage less appropriate, but the services rendered by the mother change in nature'.[3]

The circumstances of the particular case, as Sir David Croom-Johnson himself observed on another occasion, may also serve to displace the cost of employing a nanny even as a starting point.[4] In *Mehmet v Perry*[5] the plaintiff widower was left with five young children, two of whom suffered from a rare disease which required treatment on a daily basis. The plaintiff gave up his own employment to look after the children. The court took the view that this was a reasonable thing for the father to have done, and held that damages for loss of his wife's housekeeping services should be assessed by reference to his own loss of wages rather than by reference to the cost of employing a housekeeper.[6] In the similar case of *Bailey v Barking and Havering Area Health Authority*[7] the same result was reached, even though the plaintiff widower there sought to have the calculation based on the cost of employing a housekeeper in preference to his own loss of wages, since the former would have produced a higher figure. Peter Pain J observed that it would be repugnant to allow a husband to make a profit from his wife's death, and confined the award to the value of the plaintiff's actual lost wages.

[1]   *[1988] 3 All ER 1031* at 1037, *[1988] 1 WLR 847* at 854, CA.
[2]   *[1988] 3 All ER 1031* at 1040, *[1988] 1 WLR 847* at 858.
[3]   But cf *per* Purchas LJ in *Corbett v Barking Havering and Brentwood Health Authority [1991] 2 QB 408* at 421, *[1991] 1 All ER 498* at 526, CA.
[4]   'On the facts of this case the whole concept of valuing the lost services by reference to a "notional nanny" is inappropriate. Whether this expedient is useful in other cases is another matter, but there is no room for using it when on the facts a nanny would never have been employed. Mr Hayden was not going to use one, and never did': *Hayden v Hayden [1992] 4 All ER 681* at 693, *[1992] 1 WLR 986* at 998, CA, *per* Sir David Croom-Johnson.
[5]   *[1977] 2 All ER 529.*
[6]   See also *Cresswell v Eaton [1991] 1 All ER 484, [1991] 1 WLR 1113.*
[7]   *[1979] LS Gaz R 793, QBD.*

Broader approach

[26.30]   In the more usual type of case, where the court has to evaluate the loss of the wife's housekeeping services as such, there is some authority for the adoption of a rather broader approach than one based narrowly on the cost of obtaining housekeeping assistance in the open market. In *Regan v Williamson*[1] Watkins J, in awarding a higher figure than this latter test would have provided, expressed himself as follows:

'I am ... of the view that the word "services" has been too narrowly construed. It should, at least, include an acknowledgement that a wife and mother does not work to set hours and, still less, to rule. She is in constant attendance, save for those hours when she is, if that is the fact, at work. During some of those hours she may well give the children instruction on essential matters to do with their upbringing and, possibly, with such things as their homework. This sort of attention seems to me to be as much of a service, and probably more valuable to them, than the other kinds of service conventionally so regarded.'[2]

Even in *Mehmet v Perry*, in which the children of the deceased had the full-time attention of their father, the judge awarded a 'modest' additional sum to reflect 'the fact that the children have lost the personal attention of their mother and that they now have only one parent to look after them instead of two'.[3] On the other hand, if the deceased had been a somewhat inadequate parent this will be reflected in the award of a lower sum.[4] And if the child is adopted after her mother's death, the adoptive mother becomes legally obliged to look after the child and the non-pecuniary dependency on the deceased mother is accordingly extinguished from the date of the adoption.[5]

[1]   *[1976] 2 All ER 241* at 244, *[1976] 1 WLR 305* at 309.
[2]   See also *Hay v Hughes [1975] QB 790* at 802–803, *[1975] 1 All ER 257* at 261, *per* Lord Edmund-Davies, and *McGregor on Damages* (17th edn, 2003) pp 1367–1370, para 36–090 et seq.

3   *[1977] 2 All ER 529* at 537. Cf *Hayden v Hayden [1992] All ER 681, [1992] 1 WLR 986, CA.*
4   See *Stanley v Saddique [1992] QB 1, [1991] 1 All ER 529, CA.*
5   *Watson v Willmott [1991] 1 QB 140, [1991] 1 All ER 473.*

Interest

[26.31]   In *Cookson v Knowles*[1] the House of Lords held, as mentioned above, that awards under the *Fatal Accidents Act 1976* should be divided into two parts: the first consisting of the loss actually sustained up to the date of the trial, and the second the sum in respect of future loss. Only the pre-trial loss would carry interest, and the rate would be one-half of that payable over the relevant period on money in court placed in a special investment account.[2] If the court considers the claimant to have been guilty of serious delay, some of the interest may be forfeited.[3]

1   *[1979] AC 556, [1978] 2 All ER 604.*
2   See *Jefford v Gee [1970] 2 QB 130, [1970] 1 All ER 1202, CA.* See also *Dodds v Dodds [1978] QB 543* at 553, *[1978] 2 All ER 539* at 548.
3   See *Spittle v Bunney [1988] 3 All ER 1031, [1988] 1 WLR 847, CA* and *Corbett v Barking Havering and Brentwood Health Authority [1991] 2 QB 408, [1991] 1 All ER 498, CA* ('The power to deprive a tardy litigant of interest when he is guilty of unjustifiable delay is an essential discipline': *per* Farquaharson LJ, *[1991] 2 QB 408* at 446, *[1991] 1 All ER 498* at 528).

Apportionment

[26.32]   The *Fatal Accidents Act 1976, s 3(1)* (as enacted by the *Administration of Justice Act 1982, s 3(1)*) provides that:

'In the action such damages ... may be awarded as are proportioned to the injury resulting from the death to the dependants respectively.'

In *K v JMP Co Ltd*[1] Stephenson LJ observed that 'what has to be ascertained is the net loss of the family and the apportionment between widow and children is comparatively unimportant, [and] is often a matter of agreement'. If, however, the defendant in fact disagrees with the apportionment made by the court, this will not give him any right to challenge the award on appeal if the overall sum is correct.[2] In the most common type of case, where the deceased breadwinner leaves a widow and children, the largest sum is usually apportioned to the widow. In *Rawlinson v Babcock & Wilcox*[3] Chapman J expressed himself as follows:

'Frequently in making an assessment under the Fatal Accidents Acts the courts have taken the total dependency figure for the whole family and, after fixing an appropriate multiplier by referring to the expectation of life of the deceased and his widow, have arrived at an equitable sum to cover all the claims, comparatively modest sums being then allocated to the children. The basis for this is that their support through infancy and school days and until able to earn their own living is the legal obligation of the widow and that she can be trusted to fulfil this obligation out of the money allocated to her.'

His Lordship went on to observe, however, that this method was not always 'appropriate or justifiable' and that a 'separate assessment should be made ... whenever doubts may arise as to the continued ability and willingness of the widow to safeguard the child adequately'.

1   *[1976] QB 85* at 95–96, *[1975] 1 All ER 1030* at 1037, CA.

² See *Eifert v Holt's Transport Co [1951] 2 All ER 655n, CA.*
³ *[1966] 3 All ER 882* at 884, *[1967] 1 WLR 481* at 483.

Protecting children

[26.33] Some judges are inclined to place even greater emphasis on the need to ensure as far as is possible that the interests of a dependant child cannot be adversely affected by future events. Thus, in *Benson v Biggs Wall & Co Ltd*[1] Peter Pain J said:

> 'Certainly it is my experience in a large number of these cases, both at the Bar and on the Bench, that one looked at the child's genuine dependancy and not merely at what I might call a "pocket money" dependency. That seems to be right in principle, because the function of the court is to safeguard the child. Even with a mother who is a model one could not effectively safeguard the child if one treated the child's dependency as being partly included in the mother's figure. The point being this, that if one leaves the cost of maintaining the child as being included in the mother's figure that money becomes hers; she may well spend it on the child, look after it beautifully, but decide after a short while that it would be to the child's advantage as well as to her own if she remarries, then unhappily in a year or two she meets with an accident or something and dies without having taken the precaution of making a will. Then so far as the Fatal Accidents Act money is concerned which has gone to her, if that has been saved it will pass to the stepfather so far as the first £25,000 is concerned plus a life interest in half the remainder. The stepfather, one would hope, would give effect to the moral claim of the child, but law is not content to rely on a moral claim.'

¹ *[1982] 3 All ER 300* at 303, *[1983] 1 WLR 72n* at 74.

Individual entitlement

[26.34] Moreover, the 'global sum' approach should in any event not be allowed to obscure the fact that, although only one Fatal Accidents Act action can be brought in respect of the death,[1] each dependant is nevertheless individually entitled to his own damages. Thus, if one dependant is himself the tortfeasor, and hence unable to claim, he will still be liable to the other dependants under the Act.[2] Time may also begin to run against different dependants at different times for limitation purposes.[3] If individual assessments are made where several children of differing ages are involved, separate multipliers will normally be chosen for each child according to when he or she could be expected to achieve independence.[4]

¹ 'One action alone can be brought, and the persons who stand out stand out for ever': *Avery v London and North Eastern Rly Co [1938] AC 606* at 613, *[1938] 2 All ER 592* at 595, HL, *per* Lord Atkin.
² See *Dodds v Dodds [1978] QB 543, [1978] 2 All ER 539.*
³ See the *Limitation Act 1980, s 13.*
⁴ See *K v JMP [1976] QB 85, [1975] 1 All ER 1030.*

Disregard of benefits

[26.35] The *Administration of Justice Act 1982* effected a radical simplification of the law by enacting a provision which replaced the previously existing version of the *Fatal Accidents Act 1976, s 4*. That section accordingly now reads as follows:

'In assessing damages in respect of a person's death in an action under this Act, benefits which have accrued or will or may accrue to any person from his estate or otherwise as a result of his death shall be disregarded.'

Although it had long been the case that the proceeds of insurance policies, gratuitous payments and the like, would not be deducted from a Fatal Accidents Act award, 'the general rule' was nevertheless that 'any benefit accruing to a dependant by reason of the relevant death must be taken into account'.[1] A complex body of law developed to determine whether particular benefits fell within the general rule,[2] or whether one of the established exceptions to it applied. The elaborate refinements thereby created were swept away by the 1982 version of *section 4* in response to a recommendation by the Law Commission in 1973 that the general rule, which gave rise to them, should itself be abrogated.[3] It is to be noted, however, that in its 1999 report, *Damages for Wrongful Death*, the Law Commission favoured the view that *section 4* should be replaced by a regime which would bring Fatal Accident Act claims more into line with personal injury claims, by facilitating deduction of benefits in circumstances in which failure to so would in effect lead to double compensation[4].

1 *Davies v Powell Duffryn Associated Collieries Ltd [1942] AC 601* at 606, *[1942] 1 All ER 657* at 658, HL, *per* Lord Russell of Killowen.
2 Cf *Hay v Hughes [1975] QB 790, [1975] 1 All ER 257.*
3 See *Personal Injury Litigation – Assessment of Damages* (Law Com no 56, 1973) paras 255 and 256.
4 See Law Com no 263 paras 5.1–5.73 (Part V).

Contrast with personal injury claims

[26.36] That the existing principle, that benefits are to be disregarded,[1] is in sharp contrast with the position applying to common law actions for personal injury[2] was emphasised by the Court of Appeal in *Pidduck v Eastern Scottish Omnibuses*.[3] In this case a defendant's attempt to circumvent the section, by arguing that the recipient of a widow's pension had not suffered any loss as a result of her husband's death since the same pension fund had indirectly supported her via her husband during his life, was rejected. Sir Roger Ormrod said:[4]

'This argument goes too far. If it is right, it would pre-empt the express provisions of s 4 of the 1976 Act and emasculate it in many cases because it would apply to all pension fund cases where the deceased was living on a pension and the scheme included a widow's benefit. In my judgment, the "injury" suffered by the widow is the loss of her dependency on her deceased husband. The value of this loss is to be quantified in accordance with the provisions of s 4. The widow's allowance is, therefore, to be disregarded in the calculation.'

1 See *Wood v Bentall Simplex [1992] PIQR P332, CA.*
2 See CHAPTER 25 above.
3 *[1990] 2 All ER 69, [1990] 1 WLR 993, CA.*
4 *[1990] 2 All ER 69* at 76–77, *[1990] 1 WLR 993* at 1001.

Gratuitous care

[26.37] In *Stanley v Saddique*[1] the court held that a child who lost his mother's services was not disentitled to recover damages when, as a result of her death, he benefited by acquiring a stepmother who in fact provided him with a much higher standard of care than the deceased, whose services would have been, according to the trial judge, 'of an indifferent quality and lacking in continuity'. This decision was, however, narrowly distinguished by the Court of Appeal itself in *Hayden v Hayden*,[2] where care provided in substitution for the services of the deceased mother by the plaintiff's father (who was also the tortfeasor, having caused his wife's death by his own negligent driving) was taken into account in reduction of the damages on the ground that such care was not a 'benefit' resulting from the death and could legitimately be taken into account at the earlier stage in calculating the level of the plaintiff's *loss*.

[1]   *[1992] QB 1, [1991] 1 All ER 529.*
[2]   *[1992] 4 All ER 681, [1992] 1 WLR 986,* Parker LJ and Sir David Croom-Johnson, McCowan LJ dissenting.

Care by formerly non-supporting parent

[26.38]   In *A (Children) v MS*[1] the children's parents had separated, and the surviving one had provided no support for his children until after the death; whereupon he did take care of his children and assume parental responsibility. The Court of Appeal held that the care provided would fall to be ignored pursuant to *section 4* of the 1976 Act Kennedy LJ said[2]:

> 'In my judgment, in the light of the authorities, the position is reasonably clear. Where, as here, infant children are living with and are dependant on one parent, with no support being provided by the other parent, in circumstances where the provision of such support in the future seems unlikely, and the parent with whom they are living is killed, in circumstances giving rise to liability under the Fatal Accidents Act 1976, after which the other parent (who is not the tortfeasor) houses and takes responsibility for the children, the support which they enjoy after the accident is a benefit which has accrued as a result of the death and, pursuant to s 4, it must be disregarded, both in the assessment of loss and in the calculation of damages'.

The damages awarded as a result would, however, be held on trust for the carer[3].

[1]   *[2003] QB 965.* See also *L (A Child) v Barry May Haulage [2002] PIQR Q3.*
[2]   See above at para 29.
[3]   See *[2003] QB 965* at para 30.

Public policy

[26.39]   In certain circumstances a claim under the *Fatal Accidents Act 1976* may fail on grounds of public policy. Although trivial illegalities will normally be ignored,[1] if the deceased met his death in the course of the commission of a serious criminal act his widow may well be found not to have a cause of action. Thus, in *Murphy v Culhane*[2] the Court of Appeal held that the defendant, who had himself been convicted of the manslaughter of the deceased, was nevertheless entitled to plead illegality as a defence to his widow's claim on the basis that her husband had died in a criminal affray in which he had been a deliberate participant. Lord Denning MR observed:[3]

> ' ... suppose that a burglar breaks into a house and the householder, finding him there, picks up a gun and shoots him, using more force maybe than is reasonably

necessary. The householder may be guilty of manslaughter and liable to be brought before the criminal courts. But I doubt very much whether the burglar's widow could have an action for damages. The householder might well have a defence ... of *ex turpi causa non oritur actio.*'

1   See *Le Bagge v Buses Ltd [1958] NZLR 630*. But cf *Hunter v Butler [1996] RTR 396, CA*.
2   *[1977] QB 94, [1976] 3 All ER 533*.
3   *[1977] QB 94* at 98, *[1976] 3 All ER 533* at 536. But cf *Revill v Newberry [1996] QB 567, [1996] 1 All ER 291, CA*, in which a burglar obtained damages for personal injury (subject to a substantial reduction for contributory negligence) from a householder who shot him. If this decision is correct it is difficult to see why the widow in Lord Denning's example should be denied all compensation (*unless* burglary had been the deceased's main occupation).

Damages disallowed

[26.40]   Even if the widow has a cause of action under the *Fatal Accidents Act 1976*, she may still fail to recover substantial damages if the earnings of the deceased, out of which she had been maintained during his lifetime, were to her knowledge themselves the proceeds of a life of crime.[1] In *Burns v Edman*[2] the claim of the widow of an apparently full-time professional criminal, whose record included a conviction for robbery with violence, failed on this ground despite the fact that he had been killed by the defendant's negligence in an ordinary motor accident. On the other hand, if the deceased had not earned his living unlawfully, the mere fact that his own criminal act was the immediate cause of his death will not defeat his widow's claim, if there remains an unbroken chain of causation back to the earlier tortious infliction of injuries upon him by the defendant. In *Pigney v Pointers Transport Services Ltd*[3] the deceased took his own life as a direct result of depression brought on by injuries for which the defendants were responsible. Although suicide was at that time still a crime,[4] his widow succeeded in obtaining damages under the Act.

1   Quaere what her position would be if she were ignorant of the facts. Cf *per* Crichton J in *Burns v Edman [1970] 2 QB 541* at 544, *[1970] 1 All ER 886* at 887: 'I have already found as a fact that she did know, or that she did not succeed in establishing that she did not know ... '
2   *[1970] 2 QB 541, [1970] 1 All ER 886*. Cf *Le Bagge v Buses Ltd [1958] NZLR 630*.
3   *[1957] 2 All ER 807, [1957] 1 WLR 1121*. Quaere whether the suicide was a foreseeable consequence of the defendant's negligence (cf *Meah v McCreamer (No 2) [1986] 1 All ER 943*). It should be noted that *Pigney*'s case was decided before *Overseas Tankship (UK) v Morts Dock and Engineering Co Ltd, The Wagon Mound [1961] AC 388, [1961] 1 All ER 404, PC*.
4   See now the *Suicide Act 1961, s 1*.

C Damages for bereavement

Fixed sum to be awarded to spouses or parents

[26.41]   The *Administration of Justice Act 1982, s 3* added an entirely new provision to the *Fatal Accidents Act 1976*, which took effect as *section 1A* of that Act. It reads as follows:

'(1) An action under this Act may consist of or include a claim for damages for bereavement.

(2) A claim for damages for bereavement shall only be for the benefit—

(a)   of the wife or husband of the deceased: and

(b)   where the deceased was a minor who was never married—

   (i)   of his parents, if he was legitimate; and

   (ii) of his mother, if he was illegitimate.

(3) Subject to subsection (5) below, the sum to be awarded as damages under this section shall be £3,500.

(4) Where there is a claim for damages under this section for the benefit of both of the parents of the deceased, the sum awarded shall be divided equally between them (subject to any deduction falling to be made in respect of costs not recovered from the defendant).

(5) The Lord Chancellor may by order made by statutory instrument, subject to annulment in pursuance of a resolution of either House of Parliament, amend this section by varying the sum for the time being specified in subsection (3) above.'

In introducing the concept of damages for bereavement, the section implemented a recommendation of the Law Commission,[1] which believed 'that an award of damages, albeit small, can have some slight consoling effect where parents lose an infant child or where a spouse loses husband or wife'. The Commission considered that 'if money can, even minimally, compensate for such bereavement ... it should be recoverable'.[2] Where an infant dies after attaining the age of 18 his parents will be unable to claim bereavement damages even if the injuries which led to his death were suffered before he was 18.[3]

[1]   See *Personal Injury Litigation – Assessment of Damages* (Law Com no 56, 1973) paras 172–180. For the Law Commission's latest views on bereavement damages see *Claims for Wrongful Death* (Law Com no 263, 1997) paras 6.1–6.65 (Part VI).
[2]   Law Com Consultation Paper no 148, para 174.
[3]   *Doleman v Deakin* (1990) Times, 30 January, CA.

The law prior to the 1982 Act

[26.42]   Until the head of damages for loss of expectation of life was abolished by the *Administration of Justice Act 1982* itself, it had been possible for the parents of children to recover what amounted to compensation for bereavement by an indirect and artificial route. As a result of the *Law Reform (Miscellaneous Provisions) Act 1934*, the estate of a deceased person could recover damages for loss of expectation of life even if death had been instantaneous, or had occurred soon after the accident.[1] By what was, in effect, judicial legislation,[2] this award became a conventional sum, which in 1979 was around £1,250.[3] If the estate passed to persons also able to claim for lost dependancy under the *Fatal Accidents Act 1976*, the conventional sum was simply deducted from their damages under that Act, so that if the bereaved parent or spouse had actually been dependent upon the deceased they did not benefit from damages under the 1934 Act. Moreover, the whole concept of damages for non-pecuniary loss in respect of shortened life expectancy (as distinct from damages for awareness of that shortening) was in any event much criticised.[4]

[1]   See *Rose v Ford [1937] AC 826, [1937] 3 All ER 359, HL*. Cf *Hicks v Chief Constable of South Yorkshire [1992] 2 All ER 65, HL*.
[2]   See *Benham v Gambling [1941] AC 157, [1941] 1 All ER 7, HL*.
[3]   See *Gammell v Wilson [1982] AC 27, [1981] 1 All ER 578, HL*.
[4]   See *per* Lord Diplock in *Gammell v Wilson [1982] AC 27 at 62–63, [1981] 1 All ER 578 at 581–582*.

[26.43] *Cases involving death*

Overt provision

[26.43] The 1982 Act replaced that anomalous head of damage based on the 1934 Act and provided overtly and more fully for compensation for bereavement, which the earlier law merely permitted covertly in a fortuitous and partial fashion. The *Royal Commission on Civil Liability and Compensation for Personal Injury* would have preferred an even more far-reaching proposal than that favoured by the Law Commission. The Royal Commission recommended that damages for non-pecuniary loss arising out of the death of a close relative should not be confined to parents and spouses, and that an unmarried minor child should also be able to recover such damages in respect of the loss of a parent.[1] This proposal was not, however, implemented.

[1] See Cmnd 7054–1 (1978) paras 418–431, pp 96–99.

Nature of award

[26.44] By providing for a fixed sum, currently of £10,000, which the court cannot vary, and which is subject only to alteration by statutory instrument,[1] the 1982 Act is intended to ensure that, in the words of the Law Commission,[2] there will 'be not judicial enquiry at all into the consequences of bereavement'. The fact that the new head of damage takes effect under the *Fatal Accidents Act 1976*, however, necessarily means that the award will only be recoverable if the deceased would have had a cause of action for negligence had he lived; and also that the sum will in fact fall to be reduced if the deceased had been contributorily negligent.[3]

[1] See the *Damages for Bereavement (Variation of Sum) (England and Wales) Order 2002 (SI 2002/644)*, which substituted £10,000 for the figure of £7,500 which had been laid down in 1990.
[2] Report no 56, para 175.
[3] Report no 56, para 175.

Funeral expenses

[26.45] Damages in respect of the funeral expenses of a person negligently killed may be recovered by his estate from the defendant.[1] Alternatively, such damages can be recovered under the Fatal Accidents Act by his dependants if they have incurred them.[2]

[1] See the *Law Reform (Miscellaneous Provisions) Act 1934, s 1(2)(c)*.
[2] See *Fatal Accidents Act 1976, s 3(5)* (as re-enacted by the *Administration of Justice Act 1982, s 3(1)*). Damages in respect of funeral expenses may be recovered by the dependents even if they are not able to recover any other damages under the Act: see *Burns v Edman [1970] 2 QB 541, [1970] 1 All ER 886*.

Scope

[26.46] Questions may sometimes arise as to what is properly included in funeral expenses.[1] In *Stanton v Ewart F Youlden Ltd*,[2] for example, McNair J said the following:

'The legal position is that a stone over a grave may properly be considered as part of the funeral expenses if it is a reasonable expenditure for the persons in the position of the deceased and of the relatives who are responsible for the actual ordering of the stone; but in so far as it is merely a memorial set up as a sign of love and affection, then it should not be included.'

In *Gammell v Wilson* the Court of Appeal[3] upheld, albeit with some hesitation, a trial judge's award of £595 for a headstone in respect of a funeral which had taken place in 1976. One member of the court observed that 'the tombstone ... in this case was very near the boundary between a headstone and a memorial'.[4]

1   Cf *Goldstein v Salvation Army Assurance Society [1917] 2 KB 291*. For an award of expenses in respect of a Buddhist funeral, see *St George v Turner [2003] CLY 936* (ChD, Laddie J).
2   *[1960] 1 All ER 429* at 432, *[1960] 1 WLR 543* at 545–546.
3   Reported in *[1982] AC 27, [1980] 2 All ER 557*. The point was not considered in the House of Lords.
4   *[1982] AC 27* at 55, *[1980] 2 All ER 557* at 578, *per* Sir David Cairns. See also *per* Megaw LJ, *[1982] AC 27* at 43, *[1980] 2 All ER 557* at 569.

Chapter 27

Property damage and other losses

A Damage to chattels

'Restitutio in integrum'

[27.01] A claimant whose chattel has been negligently damaged by the defendant is entitled to damages calculated according to 'the principle of *restitutio in integrum*'.[1] In the present context the application of this principle will normally involve the award of *either* the market value of the chattel in question, *or* the cost of repairing it. Determining which of these two approaches is appropriate on the facts of the particular case can sometimes be a source of difficulty. In addition, it may be possible to seek damages for loss of use.

[1] *Per* Hewson J in *The Fortunity [1960] 2 All ER 64* at 68, *[1961] 1 WLR 351* at 356.

Repair or difference in value?

[27.02] In *Darbishire v Warran*[1] Harman LJ said:

> 'It has come to be settled that in general the measure of damage is the cost of repairing the damaged article; but there is an exception if it can be proved that the cost of repairs greatly exceeds the value in the market of the damaged article ... In the latter cases the measure is the value of the article in the market and this, of course, supposes that there is a market in which the article can be bought. If there is none the cost of repairs may still be claimed.'

The question whether, in the particular circumstances, the appropriate course was to repair, or to seek the market value, is determined on the basis of reasonableness. In one Scottish case[2] the claimant's dilemma was put as follows:

> 'The owner of a damaged article must ... decide whether the article is capable of being economically repaired or is to be treated as a constructive total loss. If he makes a wrong decision, he may lay himself open to the charge by the wrongdoer that he has failed in his duty to minimise the damage. The test is: What would a prudent owner, who had himself to bear the loss, do in the circumstances?'

[1] *[1963] 3 All ER 310* at 312, *[1963] 1 WLR 1067* at 1071, CA.
[2] *Pomphrey v James A Cuthbertson (1951) SC 147* at 161, *per* Lord Jamieson.

Reasonableness

[27.03] The approach to be adopted in determining whether a claimant is entitled to the full cost of reinstatement was considered by the Court of Appeal in *Southampton Container Terminals v Hansa Schiffahrts (The Maersk Colombo)*[1]. The defendants' ship negligently collided with the claimants' dock when attempting to berth, and damaged a crane beyond repair. The claimants sought the cost of replacing the crane, which was approximately £2.4million, whereas the defendants contended that damages should be limited £0.6million, which was the resale value of the crane prior to the accident. The claimants had already ordered, before the accident, two new cranes as part of its development planning; and had never intended to replace the crane which was damaged. Moreover, the claimants had been able to operate without significant difficulty before the arrival of the new cranes, despite the loss of the damaged crane, because 'it was a relatively quiet time of year'[2]. The Court of Appeal summarised the law in six propositions as follows[3]:

'(1) On proof of the tortious destruction of a chattel, the owner is prima facie entitled to damages reflecting the market value of the chattel 'as is'.

(2) He is so entitled whether or not he intends to obtain a replacement.

(3) The market or resale value is to be assessed on the evidence, there being no standard measure applicable to all circumstances.

(4) If the claimant intends to replace the chattel, and if the market or resale value as assessed is inadequate for that purpose, then the higher replacement value may, in the event, be the appropriate measure of damages.

(5) When and if replacement value is claimed, the claimant can only succeed to the extent that the claim is reasonable; that is, that it reflects reasonable mitigation of its loss.

(6) The claim will ordinarily be reasonable if it is reasonable to replace the chattel and the cost of replacement is reasonable.'

On the facts of *The Maersk Colombo* itself, the Court of Appeal upheld the decision of the court below in favour of the defendants. Replacement was not reasonable in the circumstances, and damages awarded to the claimants were therefore confined to the resale value of the existing crane.

[1]   *[2001] 2 Lloyd's Rep 275.*
[2]   As above, *per* Clarke LJ at para 12 (quoting David Steel J in the court below).
[3]   See *[2001] 2 Lloyd's Rep 275* at para 71 (*per* Clarke LJ but attributed by him to Holland J, who was also a member of the Court). See also the subsequent decision of the Court of Appeal in *Ali-Reza Delta Transport Co v United Arab Shipping Co [2003] 2 All ER (Comm) 269*, in which the propositions were adopted and applied.

Damaged cars

[27.04] The application of the test of reasonableness to situations involving damaged motor-cars is illustrated by two contrasting cases. In *Darbishire v Warren* the plaintiff owned an 11-year-old second-hand car which was damaged in a collision caused by the defendant's negligence. He chose to have the car repaired, even though the cost of the repairs was more than twice the cost in the market of a second-hand car of the same age and make. The plaintiff sought to justify his decision on the ground that the vehicle was in an unusually good condition for its age since; being a mechanical engineer, he had maintained it himself with great care. The Court of Appeal rejected his contention, however, and limited the damages to the market value of the car before the accident.[1] In so doing the court distinguished the earlier case of *O'Grady v Westminster Scaffolding Ltd*,[2] which was decided the other way on the facts. The owner of an MG motor car, which was over 20 years old, had the car repaired after it had been negligently damaged. Defence evidence at the trial, however, estimated the cars pre-accident market value as lower than the cost of the repairs. But Edmund Davies J took into account the excellent condition of the vehicle prior to the accident: it had been impeccably maintained, and had recently had a new engine fitted and its coachwork renewed. His Lordship emphasised 'that the pre-accident market value of chattels affords a guide to the measure of compensation when, and only when, a similar chattel can be obtained on the open market'[3] and concluded that the plaintiff had 'acted reasonably'.

[1] But see dicta *per* Pearson LJ on the desirability of avoiding an excessively rigid approach to the assessment of the market value, and on the need for 'an element of flexibility in the assessment of damages to achieve a result which is fair and just as between the parties in the particular case': *[1963] 3 All ER 310* at 316, *[1963] 1 WLR 1067* at 1077.
[2] *[1962] 2 Lloyd's Rep 238.*
[3] *[1962] 2 Lloyd's Rep 238* at 240.

Assessment of value

[27.05] If the case is one of total, or constructive total, loss, the court, in estimating the value of the article before it was damaged, must reach its decision on the evidence before it and not on some kind of judicial intuition. This is reflected in the third of the Court of Appeal's propositions from *The Maersk Colombo* quoted above at para [27.03]. In *Thatcher v Littlejohn*[1] the plaintiff led expert evidence as to the pre-accident value of a motor car. Even though this evidence went unchallenged, the judge awarded a lower figure. The Court of Appeal allowed an appeal by the plaintiff. Sir David Cairns said of the judge's figure that there 'was no evidence to support that assessment at all'. His Lordship continued:[2]

'It is said ... that the valuation of second-hand motor cars is not an exact science and that the judge is entitled to take his own view of the probable value even if that does not accord with the evidence. I am afraid I do not accept that proposition where the whole of the evidence points in one direction. There is no indication that the judge regarded either of the two witnesses as being in any way untrustworthy, and it seems to me that it is upon that evidence that the assessment must be based.'[3]

[1] *[1978] RTR 369, CA.*
[2] *[1978] RTR 369* at 371–372.
[3] See also *Dominion Mosaics and Tile Co Ltd v Trafalgar Trucking Co Ltd [1990] 2 All ER 246* at 254–255, *per* Taylor LJ. In this case the Court of Appeal awarded the plaintiffs the reinstatement value of certain machines, reversing the trial judge who had awarded a lesser figure on an incorrect basis unsupported by evidence.

Damage constitutes immediate loss

[27.06] When a chattel is damaged the owner suffers an immediate loss, and is entitled to compensation for the damage. If, therefore, it is reasonable to repair the chattel, the full cost of repair will be recoverable by the owner even if he chooses in fact not to have the value repaired, or if the cost of those repairs is in fact met by a third party[1]. The position is different with regard to damages for loss of use[2], when principles of mitigation have effect

1   See *Burdis v Livsey [2003] QB 36* at paras 84–105. See also *Dimond v Lovell [2002] 1 AC 384* at p 406 *per* Lord Hobhouse.
2   See below at para [27.07].

B Loss of use

Methods of calculation

[27.07] If his chattel is damaged or destroyed due to the defendant's negligence, the claimant is entitled to damages for loss of its use until it is repaired or replaced.[1] These will be additional to the cost of repair or replacement itself.[2] If the chattel was used for trading purposes, the measure of damages will be such a sum as can reasonably be taken to reflect the profits which would have been earned during the relevant period.[3] Moreover, it has long been established that damages for loss of use can also be recovered even if the chattel was not used to earn profit,[4] and that such damages will be substantial and not nominal.[5] Broadly speaking, two methods of estimating the damages for lost use in such cases have been developed, mainly in a series of decisions reached in collision actions involving ships. The first method is to award a figure representing interest on the capital value of the chattel.[6] The second is to make a calculation based on the normal cost to the plaintiff of maintaining the chattel in service, on the assumption that this expenditure represents its value.[7] In *Birmingham Corpn v Sowsbery*[8] Geoffrey Lane J, in a judgment which helpfully outlines the basic principles involved, applied the latter method to a claim by a non-profit making municipal bus company for loss of the use of one of its vehicles. If the claimant in fact bases his claim on lost profits, he cannot seek to obtain additional damages for lost use based on one of the other methods of calculation.[9]

1   *The Argentino (1889) 14 App Cas 519, HL.*
2   See *The Racine [1906] P 273, CA* approving *The Kate [1899] P 165.*
3   See *The Fortunity [1960] 2 All ER 64, [1961] 1 WLR 351*; see also *Dixons (Scholar Green) Ltd v Cooper [1970] RTR 222, CA.*
4   *The Greta Holme [1897] AC 596, HL.*
5   See *The Mediana [1900] AC 113, HL.* See also *Berrill v Road Haulage Executive [1952] 2 Lloyd's Rep 490* (though quaere whether the £2 awarded in that case was consistent with the spirit of the principle that damages should not be nominal).
6   See *Admiralty Comrs v SS Chekiang [1926] AC 637, HL; The Hebridean Coast [1961] AC 545, [1961] 1 All ER 82, HL.*
7   See *The Marpessa [1907] AC 241, HL.*
8   *[1970] RTR 84.*
9   *The Pacific Concord [1961] 1 All ER 106, [1961] 1 WLR 873.*

During the period of deprivation

[27.08] A claimant clearly cannot claim damages for lost use if, for reasons uncon-nected with the defendant's negligence, he would not in fact have enjoyed the use of the chattel during the relevant period anyway.[1] But a claimant is not prevented from claiming merely because he takes advantage of an inevitable period of detention for repairs, caused by the defendant's negligence, to do other work on the damaged chattel in addition.[2] In deciding when and how to do repairs, the claimant must act reasonably and not, for example, needlessly prolong the period during which he is deprived of the use of his chattel.[3]

[1]   See *Carslogie SS Co Ltd v Royal Norwegian Government [1952] AC 292, [1952] 1 All ER 20, HL.* See also *The York [1929] P 178, CA.*
[2]   *Admiralty Comrs v SS Chekiang [1926] AC 637, HL.*
[3]   See *The Pacific Concord [1961] 1 All ER 106, [1960] 1 WLR 873; O'Grady v Westminster Scaffolding [1962] 2 Lloyd's Rep 238.* Cf *Jones v Port of London Authority [1954] 1 Lloyd's Rep 489.*

Hire of substitute

[27.09]   In certain circumstances, commonly where motor accidents are involved, the claimant may simply hire a substitute until the damaged chattel is repaired or replaced.[1] In such a case the damages for lost use will be the cost of the hire. The claimant must, however, act reasonably. Where hire of a motor car is involved, for example, the full cost may not be awarded if the court takes the view that the claimant could have obtained more cheaply a vehicle still broadly similar to, if less prestigious than, the one damaged.[2] But each case depends on its own facts, and in one case in which a defence attempt was made on these lines to reduce the award, it was judicially rejected as follows: 'I see no reason why the plaintiffs should have been required to shop around in order to hire for a lesser sum a car of a lower standard from some concern with whom they did not normally deal'.[3] In *Moore v DER Ltd*[4] the plaintiff was entitled to the pre-accident second-hand value of his car, after the defendant's negligence had caused it to become a constructive total loss, but chose to buy a new car instead, of course paying the difference himself. But this involved him in a wait of 18 weeks, whereas a second-hand model, comparable in age and make to the damaged one, could have been acquired in three weeks or less. The Court of Appeal nevertheless held that he was entitled to the full cost of the hire of a substitute until the arrival of the new car: he was a busy professional man and his insistence on the need for the reliability of a new car was considered to be not unreasonable.

[1]   See *Giles v Thompson [1994] 1 AC 142, [1993] 3 All ER 321, HL.*
[2]   See *Watson-Norie Ltd v Shaw [1967] 1 Lloyd's Rep 515, CA.*
[3]   *Daily Office Cleaning Contractors v Shefford [1977] RTR 361* at 364, *per* Judge William Stabb QC (sitting as a deputy judge of the Queen's Bench Division). See also *Berg v Loftus Road plc [2001] CLY 1519,* in which the hire of a prestige car was held to be justified by the nature of the claimant's business and his need to impress wealthy clients (Central London County Court).
[4]   *[1971] 3 All ER 517, [1971] 1 WLR 1476, CA.*

Bailee

[27.10]   It has been held that, if the claimant was only a bailee of the damaged car, it may be reasonable for him to reimburse the owner for the full cost of hiring an exactly equivalent vehicle during repairs, and to recover that full cost from the negligent defendants, even if such a course could possibly have been considered extravagant if taken directly by the owner himself.[1]

[1]   See *H L Motorworks (Willesden) Ltd v Alwahbi [1977] RTR 276, CA.*

Assessing the sum recoverable

[27.11]   In *Dimond v Lovell*[1] it was held by, a majority of the House of Lords[2], that the cost of hiring a substitute motor-car, while the one damaged by the defendant's negligence is being repaired, will be calculated by reference to the charges of ordinary car hire companies for a vehicle of equivalent type. In *Dimond v Lovell* itself the claimant accepted the offer of a vehicle from a company specialising in the supply of vehicles to innocent drivers after accidents. Such organisations seek reimbursement ultimately from the negligent driver's insurers. But the House held that the higher rates charged by such companies, to cover their expenses and profit, will not be recoverable, and the claimant will be confined to the ordinary hire figure[3].

1   *[2002] 1 AC 384.*
2   Lord Browne-Wilkinson, Lord Hoffman and Lord Hobhouse; Lord Nicholls dissenting (Lord Saville reserved his opinion).
3   Evidence will therefore be required in each case 'as to the rate charged by a car hire company in the relevant area'; defendants wishing to challenge that figure will then be obliged 'to show that it would not have been reasonable to use that particular car hire company' and that a cheaper one should have been chosen instead: see *Burdis v Livsey [2003] QB 36* at para 148 *per* Aldous LJ delivering the judgment of the court.

Impecunious claimants

[27.12]   In some cases, however, the impecuniosity of the claimant may be such as to make it impossible for him to hire a car in the market in the ordinary way. He will therefore be obliged to use the services of one of the specialist organisations in order to obtain a substitute vehicle. In *Lagden v O'Connor*[1] the House of Lords held, by a bare majority[2], that the higher rate of the specialist organisations would be fully recoverable in such circumstances[3]. Lord Nicholls of Birkenhead said[4]:

> 'Here, as elsewhere, a negligent driver must take his victim as he finds him. Common fairness requires that if an innocent plaintiff cannot afford to pay car hire charges, so that left to himself he would be unable to obtain a replacement car to meet the need created by the negligent driver, then the damages payable under this head of loss should include the reasonable costs of a credit hire company'[5].

1   *[2004] 1 All ER 277.*
2   Lord Nicholls of Birkenhead, Lord Slynn of Hadley and Lord Hope of Craighead.
3   Lord Scott of Foscote and Lord Walker of Gestingthorpe dissented contending that it would cause unacceptable uncertainty to make any exception to the general rule established in *Dimond v Lovell*.
4   See *[2004] 1 All ER 277* at para 6.
5   The decision in *Lagden's* case involved overruling the rule associated with *Liesbosch Dredger v SS Edison (Owners) [1933] AC 449 at 459, HL* that a plaintiff's impecuniosity should be ignored in assessing his loss. For further discussion see CHAPTER 3 above.

Other losses

[27.13]   The proposition that the claimant is entitled to recover the repair cost or pre-accident value of the chattel, combined with compensation for loss of use, is only a general guide appropriate in the majority of cases. Since the overriding principle is that of *restitutio in integrum*, all losses flowing from the defendant's negligence are recoverable, provided only that they are not too remote[1], and that the plaintiff acted reasonably in mitigating his damage. For example, in *Ironfield v Eastern Gas Board*[2] the plaintiff, who had been compensated by his own insurers after his car had been damaged by the defendants' negligence, was able to recover compensation for the loss of his 'no-claims' bonus. This decision was approved by the Court of Appeal in the later case of *Patel v London Transport Executive*,[3] in which a plaintiff in similar circumstances was able to recover from the defendants the unexpired premium on his motor insurance, since that was forfeited under the terms of the policy. Moreover, in *Payton v Brooks*[4] the Court of Appeal held that even where it had been appropriate to repair a damaged chattel the plaintiff might, providing adequate proof was forthcoming, recover compensation for diminution in its market value *in addition* to the cost of repairs. Roskill LJ put it as follows:[5]

> '... the cost of repairs is a prima facie method of ascertaining the diminution in value. But it is not the only method of measuring the loss. In a case where the evidence justifies a finding that there has been, on top of the cost of repairs, some diminution in market value – or, to put the point another way, justifies the conclusion that the loss to the plaintiff has not been fully compensated by the receipt of the cost of complete and adequate repairs, because of a resultant diminution in market value – I can see no reason why the plaintiff should be deprived of recovery under that head of damage also.'

[1]   On remoteness of damage see generally CHAPTER 3 above.
[2]   *[1964] 1 All ER 544n, [1964] 1 WLR 1125n.*
[3]   *[1981] RTR 29, CA.*
[4]   *[1974] RTR 169, [1974] 1 Lloyd's Rep 241, CA.*
[5]   *[1974] 2 Lloyd's Rep 241 at 245.*

Gains by the claimant

[27.14] The claimant may sometimes acquire a gain as a result of the defendant's negligence.[1] For example, the damage inflicted upon it may free a profit-earning chattel from a losing contract and its repairs may be completed, or its replacement become available, at a time when the claimant is fortuitously able to take advantage of better market conditions. In those circumstances, the claimant must give credit to the defendants for the value of the benefit thus obtained.[2] But where a chattel which has been repaired becomes more valuable than it was before it was damaged, because of the addition of new parts or materials, it is not normally considered appropriate to require the plaintiff to give credit for 'betterment'.[3] The claimant will usually have had no choice but to repair, and it would not be appropriate to assume that he would have chosen to invest his resources in improvement of his existing equipment had the damage not occurred.[4]

[1]   But ex gratia payments to the claimant from charitable and similar sources will be disregarded: see *Wollington v State Electricity Commission of Victoria (No 2) [1980] VR 91*; *Cusack v Heath [1950] QWN 16*.
[2]   See *The World Beauty [1969] P 12, [1968] 2 All ER 673* (varied in *[1970] P 144, [1968] 3 All ER 158, CA*).
[3]   See *The Pactolus (1856) Sw 173* at 174. See also *Bacon v Cooper (Metals) Ltd [1982] 1 All ER 397* at 401–402.
[4]   See *Harbutt's Plasticine Ltd v Wayne Tank and Pump Co Ltd [1970] 1 QB 447* at 472–473, *[1970] 1 All ER 225* at 240, *per* Widgery LJ (cited with approval by Lord Hope of Craighead in *Lagden v O'Connor [2004] 1 All ER 277* at para 32).

C Land and buildings

Reinstatement or difference in value

[27.15] In *Dominion Mosaics and Tile Co Ltd v Trafalgar Trucking Co Ltd*[1] Taylor LJ said:

'The basic principle governing the measure of damages where the defendant's tort has caused damage to the plaintiff's land or building is restitutio in integrum. The damages should be such as will, so far as money can, put the plaintiff in the same position as he would have held had the tort not occurred. In applying that principle to particular cases, the problem has been whether restitutio is to be achieved by assessing the diminution in value of the damaged premises or the cost of reinstatement or possibly on some other basis.'

The 'appropriateness' or 'reasonableness' of claiming the cost of restoration may be a source of dispute, since in the majority of cases involving buildings that cost is likely to exceed the diminution in value caused by the damage. In earlier times, the view adopted appears to have been that restoration cost would hardly ever be awarded, and that plaintiffs would have to be content with the difference in value.[2] More recently, however, there have been signs of greater flexibility. The usefulness of attempting to amplify, with more precise guidelines as to the measure of damages in postulated situations, the general principle that the defendant must make restitution subject only to the overriding requirement of reasonableness, has also been questioned.[3]

[1]   *[1990] 2 All ER 246* at 249, CA.
[2]   See *Jones v Gooday (1841) 8 M & W 146*. See also *Moss v Christchurch RDC [1925] 2 KB 750*.
[3]   See *per* May J in *C R Taylor (Wholesale) Ltd v Hepworths Ltd [1977] 2 All ER 784* at 791–793, *[1977] 1 WLR 659* at 667–669.

Facts

[27.16]   The issue is one to be determined on the facts of each case.[1] In the *Dominion Mosaics* case the plaintiffs' business premises were severely damaged by fire due to the negligence of the defendants. The plaintiffs decided that rebuilding would be too expensive and impracticable and that it would be cheaper to acquire new premises, which they did. They claimed the cost of so doing from the defendants who asserted that their liability should be limited to the mere diminution in value of the existing premises. The Court of Appeal found in favour of the plaintiffs. If they had not sought new premises quickly they would, as a commercial concern, have suffered heavy consequential loss of profits, which might have exceeded the cost of acquiring the new premises and which they could have looked to the defendants to reimburse. Awarding the cost of the new premises was therefore favourable, in a sense, to the defendants who might indeed have argued that the plaintiffs had been in breach of their duty to mitigate had they not swiftly sought the means to continue trading. Notwithstanding the admitted presumption in favour of the diminution in value approach,[2] its displacement in favour of 'reinstatement or its equivalent' would, in the words of Stocker LJ,[3] sometimes be appropriate in the case of commercial premises as 'the only reasonable method of compensating a plaintiff for future loss of profits derived from the asset destroyed'.

[1]   For an unusual case in which a plaintiff who lost a sale as a result of radioactive contamination was awarded diminution in value, calculated on a 75% chance that the sale would have gone through without the contamination, see *Blue Circle Industries plc v Ministry of Defence [1998] 3 All ER 385, CA* (decided under *section 12* of the *Nuclear Installations Act 1965*).
[2]   'The true principle is that the owner of a building is entitled to the diminution in value between the building as it was before the wrong and after it, unless he establishes that he intends to or has reasonably rebuilt the structure damaged or destroyed *and* that his is an exceptional case in which justice requires that he should be paid the cost of restoration': *per* Kenny J in *Munnelly v Calcon Ltd [1978] IR 387* at 407 (the emphasis is Kenny J's).
[3]   *[1990] 2 All ER 246* at 256.

[27.17] *Property damage and other losses*

Where diminution in value appropriate

[27.17] Nevertheless, there will often be cases in which the application of the presumption in favour of diminution in value will remain appropriate, notwithstanding the presence of a commercial element. In *C R Taylor v Hepworths*[1] the plaintiffs owned a disused billiard hall which they had continued to own only for the potential development value of the site. Their attempt to recover on the basis of restoration cost, when the building was destroyed by a fire for which the defendants were responsible, was understandably rejected. Reinstatement of the unwanted building would have cost some ten times the site value. 'In these circumstances', observed May J, 'it would in my opinion not only be totally unrealistic, but also unreasonable as between the plaintiffs and the defendants, to award the former the notional cost of reinstating the premises'.[2]

[1]   *[1977] 2 All ER 784, [1977] 1 WLR 659.*
[2]   *[1977] 2 All ER 784 at 794, [1977] 1 WLR 659 at 670.* See also *Munnelly v Calcon Ltd [1978] IR 387* and *Hole & Son (Sayers Common) Ltd v Harrisons of Thurnscoe Ltd [1973] 1 Lloyd's Rep 345.*

Restoration and betterment

[27.18] On the other hand, in *Hollebone v Midhurst and Fernhurst Builders Ltd*[1] the owner-occupier of a distinctive dwelling-house with unique characteristics was awarded restoration cost, rather than the lower figure for diminution in value, when it was damaged by fire due to the negligence of the defendants.[2] Nor did the judge consider it appropriate to make any allowance in favour of the defendants for 'betterment' as a result of the restoration. The reluctance of the court to make such an allowance, in cases where restoration cost is considered to be the appropriate award, is also illustrated by *Harbutts Plasticine v Wayne Tank and Pump Co Ltd*:[3] a case which shows in addition that reinstatement can be legitimate in a commercial context and is not confined to the residential. The plaintiff's factory was burnt down in circumstances for which the defendants were responsible.[4] Lord Denning MR expressed himself as follows:[5]

> '... when this mill was destroyed, the plasticine company had no choice. They were bound to replace it as soon as they could, not only to keep their business going, but also to mitigate the loss of profit (for which they would be able to charge the defendants). They replaced it in the only possible way, without adding any extras. I think they should be allowed the cost of replacement. True it is that they got new for old; but I do not think the wrongdoer can diminish the claim on that account. If they had added extra accommodation or made extra improvements, they would have to give credit. But that is not this case.'[6]

[1]   *[1968] 1 Lloyd's Rep 38.* See also *Jens v Mannix Co [1978] 5 WWR 486 (Can).*
[2]   See also *Ward v Cannock Chase District Council [1986] Ch 546 at 577, [1985] 3 All ER 537 at 558* (' ... an exceptional case in which justice requires ... the cost of reinstatement').
[3]   *[1970] 1 QB 447, [1970] 1 All ER 225, CA.* This was a case of breach of contract but on the facts the relevant principles as to measure of damages were the same as those in tort: see *per* May J (who had been counsel for the successful plaintiffs in the *Harbutt's Plasticine* case) in *C R Taylor (Wholesale) Ltd v Hepworths Ltd [1977] 2 All ER 784 at 791, [1977] 1 WLR 659 at 666.*
[4]   The overruling of the *Harbutt's Plasticine* case in *Photo Production Ltd v Securicor Transport Ltd [1980] AC 827, [1980] 1 All ER 556, HL,* does not affect the point in the text.
[5]   *[1970] 1 QB 447 at 468, [1970] 1 All ER 225 at 236.* See also *Lagden v O'Connor [2004] 1 All ER 277, HL* at para 32 in which Lord Denning's passage was quoted with approval by Lord Hope of Craighead.
[6]   See also *Dominion Mosaics and Tile Co Ltd v Trafalgar Trucking Co Ltd [1990] 2 All ER 246* at 252, CA, *per* Taylor LJ.

Gains

[27.19] In *Hussey v Eels*[1] the plaintiffs were induced to buy a bungalow from the defendants due to a negligent misrepresentation by the latter that it had not been subject to subsidence, when in fact it had. After living in the property for some time the plaintiffs decided that, in view of the subsidence, their best course was to demolish the bungalow and seek planning permission for the erection of two new bungalows on the same ground. Before the plaintiffs' action against the defendants for negligent misrepresentation came on for trial, the plaintiffs had in fact sold the property to a developer, with the benefit of the planning permission, for substantially more than they had paid for it. The defendants claimed that this profit extinguished the loss which the plaintiffs had suffered in paying, as a result of the misrepresentation, more for the bungalow than it had been worth. The Court of Appeal rejected this argument and allowed the plaintiffs to recover a sum representing the difference in value at the time of the original sale. It could not be said that the plaintiffs had been under any duty to mitigate their loss by taking the elaborate steps with respect to planning permission and eventual sale which they had in fact taken. Moreover, although circumstances can clearly occur to prevent a plaintiff from suffering any loss without these circumstances having arisen as a result of mitigation by him, that overriding principle did not avail the defendants in the present case. The plaintiffs were not property speculators; and their subsequent sale of the bungalow with planning permission could not plausibly be regarded as an event so intertwined with the original purchase, induced by the defendants' negligent misrepresentation, that the latter could rely upon it as having given rise to a gain inseparable from the loss which their wrong had caused.[2]

[1] *[1990] 2 QB 227, [1990] 1 All ER 449, CA*. See A J Oakley 'The Effect on the Availability of Damages for Misrepresentation of a Profitable Resale' (1990) 49 CLJ 394.
[2] 'Ultimately, as with so many disputes about damages, the issue is primarily one of fact. Did the negligence which caused the damage also cause the profit, if profit there was? I do not think so': *per* Mustill LJ in *[1990] 2 QB 227* at 241, *[1990] 1 All ER 449* at 459.

Hussey v Eels followed

[27.20] *Hussey v Eels* was followed by a majority of the Court of Appeal in *Gardner v Marsh & Parsons*.[1] As a result of a negligent survey, which had failed to discover structural defects, the plaintiff purchased a leasehold property for more than it was worth. The Court of Appeal held, by a majority, that the plaintiff was entitled to recover the difference in value at the date of the purchase even though the defects in the property had, by the time the action was brought, been rectified by his landlord without cost to the plaintiff, albeit only after the latter, having lost a sale, had threatened the landlord with legal action under the *Defective Premises Act 1972*. The majority[2] considered that the landlord's carrying out of the repairs was too remote from the defendant's negligence to affect the plaintiff's claim for damages.[3]

[1] *[1997] 3 All ER 871, [1997] 1 WLR 489, CA*. See also *Needler Financial Services v Taber [2002] 3 All ER 501*.
[2] Hirst and Pill LJJ.
[3] Peter Gibson LJ dissented on the ground that the plaintiff was in effect seeking double recovery, to which he was not entitled.

Negligent surveys

[27.21] By allowing the plaintiff to recover from the negligent surveyor the amount by which the purchase price had exceeded the true value at the time of the original purchase, the decision of the Court of Appeal in *Gardner v Marsh & Parsons* incidentally illustrated what is, in fact, the general rule in relation to contractual actions for professional negligence against surveyors. This rule had been clearly stated much earlier by Lord Denning MR in *Perry v Sidney Philips & Son*[1] when he said:

> '[where a] surveyor agrees to survey a house and make a report on it – and he makes it negligently – and the client buys the house on the faith of the report, then the damages are to be assessed … according to the difference in price which the buyer would have given if the report had been carefully made from that which he in fact gave owing to the negligence of the surveyor … The buyer is not entitled to remedy the defects and charge the cost to the surveyor.'

There is no doubt that these observations, although obiter on the facts of *Perry v Sidney Phillips & Son* itself, since the house which had been negligently surveyed in that case was actually sold by the plaintiff instead of repaired by him, accurately reflect the usual position adopted by the courts in the case of negligence by privately appointed surveyors[2]. Oliver LJ expressly agreed[3] with Lord Denning's view, which followed the earlier decision of the Court of Appeal in *Phillips v Ward*.[4]

[1] *[1982] 3 All ER 705* at 708, *[1982] 1 WLR 1297* at 1302, CA.
[2] See *Holder v Countrywide Surveyors [2003] PNLR 3*. See also *McKinnon v E Surv [2003] Lloyd's Rep PN 174*.
[3] See *[1982] 3 All ER 705* at 710, *[1982] 1 WLR 1297* at 1304.
[4] *[1956] 1 All ER 874, [1956] 1 WLR 471*, CA. See also *Treml v Ernest W Gibson & Partners [1984] 2 EGLR 162*. Cf *Bolton v Puley (1982) 2647 EG 1160*.

Extremely strong presumption

[27.22] The possibility that, if justice requires it in exceptional circumstances, a surveyor might be held liable for repair costs should perhaps not be entirely discounted.[1] In *Perry v Sidney Phillips & Son* the judge at first instance, who heard the case before the house was sold and when the possibility of repair was still a live issue, made his award of damages on this basis.[2] And in the Court of Appeal, the third judge, Kerr LJ, chose to reserve his view on the question[3] rather than associate himself with the explicit rejection, by Lord Denning MR and Oliver LJ, of the trial judge's approach. Nevertheless the proposition that difference in value, and not the cost of repairs, will be the applicable measure is, at the very least, an extremely strong presumption. It was reaffirmed by the Court of Appeal in 1991, after full consideration of the authorities, in *Watts v Morrow*[4]; and a more recent attempt to persuade the Court of Appeal that the facts of the case before it were sufficiently special to warrant the award of repair costs was emphatically rejected[5]. Of course the claimant may be able to recover damages for losses additional to the difference in value, such as compensation for general disruption and the need to obtain alternative accommodation[6], but this will not affect the basic rule that the difference in value test is to be applied to the surveyed property itself.

[1] See P A Chandler 'Negligent Surveys: An Expanding Liability?' (1990) 106 LQR 196. Cf *Patel v Hooper & Jackson [1999] 1 All ER 992*, CA.
[2] The case is reported at first instance in *[1982] 1 All ER 1005* (Patrick Bennett QC sitting as a deputy judge of the High Court).
[3] See *[1982] 3 All ER 705* at 711, *[1982] 1 WLR 1297* at 1306.
[4] *[1991] 4 All ER 937, [1991] 1 WLR 1421*.
[5] See *Smith v Peter North & Partners [2002] Lloyd's Rep PN 111*.
[6] See *Patel v Hooper & Jackson [1999] 1 All ER 992*, CA. See also 'Additional losses' at para [27.28] below.

Liability to lenders

[27.23] In *Swingcastle Ltd v Alastair Gibson (a firm)*[1] the House of Lords considered the liability of a surveyor for negligent valuation not to a purchaser but to a mortgagee. Due to the defendant's over-valuation, the plaintiff lenders advanced money, which they would not otherwise have done, at a high rate of interest. When the borrowers defaulted the plaintiffs sought to recover, as part of their damages, the outstanding interest which the borrowers had contracted to pay but which was now irrecoverable. The claim was rejected by the House, which reversed the Court of Appeal[2] and overruled an earlier decision of that court.[3] Lord Lowry said:[4]

'My Lords, it is clear that the lenders ought to have presented their claim on the basis that, if the valuer had advised properly, they would not have lent the money. Where they went wrong was to claim, not only correctly that they had to spend all the money which they did, but incorrectly that the valuer by his negligence deprived them of the interest which they would have received from the borrowers if the borrowers had paid up. The security for the loan was the property but the lenders did not have a further security consisting of a guarantee by the valuer that the borrowers would pay everything, or indeed anything, that was due from them to the lenders at the date, whenever it occurred, on which the loan transaction terminated. The fallacy of the lenders' case is that they have been trying to obtain from the valuer compensation for the borrowers' failure and not the proper damages for the valuer's negligence.'

[1]   *[1991] 2 AC 223, [1991] 2 All ER 353, HL.*
[2]   Reported at *[1990] 3 All ER 463, [1990] 1 WLR 1223.*
[3]   Ie *Baxter v F W Gapp & Co Ltd [1939] 2 KB 271, [1939] 2 All ER 752, CA.*
[4]   *[1991] 2 AC 223 at 238, [1991] 2 All ER 353 at 365.*

Market changes

[27.24]   A further important limitation on the scope of a negligent surveyor's liability to a lender was established by *South Australia Asset Management Corpn v York Montague Ltd,*[1] in which the House of Lords held that the surveyor will not be liable for losses suffered by the lender as the result of reduction in the value of the security brought about by a general fall in the property market rather than by the negligent valuation. Moreover, the negligent surveyor can take advantage of a *rise* in property values to extinguish the lender's loss.[2]

[1]   *[1997] AC 191, [1996] 3 All ER 365, HL.* For further discussion of this case, see CHAPTER 3 and CHAPTER 9.
[2]   'If the market moves upwards, it reduces or eliminates the loss which the lender would otherwise have suffered. If it moves downwards, it may result in more loss than is attributable to the valuer's error. There is no contradiction in the asymmetry. A plaintiff has to prove both that he has suffered loss and that the loss fell within the scope of the duty. The fact that he cannot recover for loss which he has not suffered does not entitle him to an award of damages for loss which he has suffered, but which does not fall within the scope of the valuer's duty of care': *per* Lord Hoffmann in *South Australia Asset Management Corpn v York Montague Ltd [1997] AC 191 at 218, [1996] 3 All ER 365 at 376.*

Date of assessment

[27.25] It is clear from *South Australia Asset Management Corp v York Montague Ltd* that the normal date for assessing the value of property in negligent valuation cases is the date of the valuation itself. In effect, this is also the general rule in property cases,[1] including those involving actual damage, ie the date on which the damage occurred is the relevant date for the assessment of damages, whether diminution in value or the cost of reinstatement is considered to be the appropriate measure. Notwithstanding the award of interest on the judgment, this will often leave the claimant out of pocket, particularly in times of high inflation such as occurred in the 1970s.[2] Accordingly, in *Dodd Properties (Kent) v Canterbury City Council*[3] the Court of Appeal emphasised that using the date on which the damage occurred is not an inflexible rule but one qualified by the general principle that, subject to overriding considerations of reasonableness, a claimant is entitled to full compensation for his loss. In this case the plaintiffs' building was damaged in 1968. The defendants denied liability until just before the trial, which did not occur until ten years later. The parties then agreed that repair costs, rather than difference in value, was the appropriate basis for the award of damages; but they disagreed as to the date for the making of the calculation. The building had not, in fact, been repaired by the time of the trial, and the plaintiffs claimed the cost of repair at 1978 values. The Court of Appeal held that it had been commercially reasonable for the plaintiffs to have postponed the repairs until liability was admitted and they could be sure of recouping the cost. The court then went on to hold that in consequence the plaintiff's claim as to the appropriate date would be upheld.[4] Megaw LJ said:[5]

> 'The true rule is that, where there is a material difference between the cost of repair at the date of the wrongful act and the cost of repair when the repairs can, having regard to all relevant circumstances, first reasonably be undertaken, it is the latter time by reference to which the cost of repair is to be taken in assessing damages.'

[1]   See *Philips v Ward [1956] 1 All ER 874* at 876, *[1956] 1 WLR 471* at 474, CA, *per* Lord Denning MR. See also *Clark v Woor [1965] 2 All ER 353, [1965] 1 WLR 650.*

[2]   See D Feldman and D Libling 'Inflation and the Duty to Mitigate' (1979) 95 LQR 270; D Wallace 'Cost of Repair and Inflation' (1980) 96 LQR 101, 341. In 'The Date for the Assessment of Damages' (1981) 97 LQR 445, S M Waddams argued that preservation of the traditional rule, combined with the award of interest, is to be preferred on grounds of efficiency to compensating for inflation by choosing a later date.

[3]   *[1980] 1 All ER 928, [1980] 1 WLR 433, CA.* See W Rogers 'Damages for Injury to a Building' (1980) 124 Sol Jo 383.

[4]   Cf *Birmingham Corpn v West Midland Baptist (Trust) Association Inc [1970] AC 874, [1969] 3 All ER 172, HL.*

[5]   *[1980] 1 All ER 928* at 933, *[1980] 1 WLR 433* at 451.

Postponement due to impecuniosity

[27.26]   In *Alcoa Minerals of Jamaica v Broderick*[1] the Judicial Committee of the Privy Council affirmed the authority of *Dodd Properties (Kent) v Canterbury City Council* and, moreover, took the plaintiff's impecuniosity into account in holding that a date later than that on which the damage occurred could be used to determine damages[2]. The plaintiff's house was damaged by emissions from the defendants' industrial plant, but he had insufficient funds to carry out repairs at the time. By the time of the trial inflation had caused the repair costs to increase substantially. The Privy Council held that repair costs could be recovered and, in order to avoid injustice to the plaintiff, they would be assessed as at the date of the trial.

[1]   *[2002] 1 AC 371.*

[2]   The Board distinguished *Liesbosch Dredger v SS Edison (Owners) [1933] AC 449* at 459, HL but the principle in *Liesbosch* was itself subsequently overruled unanimously by the House of Lords in *Lagden v O'Connor [2004] 1 All ER 277.*

Dependent on facts

[27.27] In *Dodd's* case the date applied was also the year of the trial, as that happened to be when liability was admitted.[1] Nevertheless, what is a reasonable date will necessarily depend upon the facts of each case. Moreover, in *Dodd's* case Donaldson LJ expressed the view that 'in normal circumstances' the date of the damage would remain the relevant one in cases where difference in value rather than reinstatement was the appropriate measure of damage.[2] Even in reinstatement cases the appropriate date would by no means necessarily be the date of the trial. Donaldson LJ put it as follows:[3]

'... in a case in which a plaintiff has reinstated his property before the hearing, the costs prevailing at the date of that operation which were reasonably incurred by him are prima facie those which are relevant. Equally in a case in which a plaintiff has *not* effected reinstatement by the time of the hearing, there is a prima facie presumption that the costs then prevailing are those which should be adopted in ascertaining the cost of reinstatement. There may indeed be cases in which the court has to estimate costs at some future time as being the reasonable time at which to reinstate ... This is, however, only a prima facie approach. It may appear on the evidence that the plaintiff, acting reasonably, should have undertaken the reinstatement at some date earlier than that in fact adopted or, as the case may be, earlier than the hearing. If so, the relevant costs are those ruling at that earlier date.'

1   See also *Marriott v Carson's Construction Ltd (1983) 146 DLR (3d) 126.*
2   See *[1980] 1 All ER 928* at 939, *[1980] 1 WLR 433* at 457. Cf *Ward v Cannock Chase District Council [1986] Ch 546* at 578, *[1985] 3 All ER 537* at 559, *per* Scott J (continuing wrong leading to eventual demolition: date of demolition appropriate).
3   *[1980] 1 All ER 928* at 939, *[1980] 1 WLR 433* at 458.

Additional losses

[27.28] If a building is damaged it is not unlikely that the claimant will suffer losses additional to the difference in the building's value or the cost of reinstating it. Thus, if the building is used for commercial purposes, a sum will frequently be claimable due to interruption of the business caused by the damage itself or by inability to trade normally while repairs are taking place.[1] Such losses must, however, be consequential upon the damage itself[2].

1   See *Dodd Properties (Kent) v Canterbury City Council [1980] 1 All ER 928, [1980] 1 WLR 433, CA.*
2   Cf *Spartan Steel & Alloys v Martin & Co [1973] QB 27, [1972] 3 All ER 557, CA.* See, generally, CHAPTER 5.

Non-pecuniary loss

[27.29] Damages in respect of non-pecuniary losses arising out of defects in property are often sought in contractual actions for professional negligence against surveyors. In *Perry v Sidney Phillips & Son*[1] the Court of Appeal upheld an award of damages to the plaintiff for all the 'vexation, distress and worry'[2] which he suffered due to his purchase, brought about by the negligence of his surveyor, of a house in a deplorable condition.[3] This principle was confirmed and applied by the Court of Appeal itself in *Watts v Morrow*[4]. In this case also a surveyor negligently reported that a house was sound when, in fact, substantial repairs were found to be necessary after its purchase.

Bingham LJ said that damages were 'recoverable for physical inconvenience and discomfort caused by the breach and mental suffering directly related to that inconvenience and discomfort'[5]. Moreover, if a surveyor undertakes to investigate a specific matter relating to a proposed purchase, and negligently fails to do so, damages for non-pecuniary loss may be awarded even if the claimant's distress is not immediately associated with the physical condition of the property itself. Thus in *Farley v Skinner*[6] the House of Lords upheld such an award in favour of a claimant who had been wrongly advised that the property in question would not be significantly affected by aircraft noise.

[1]   *[1982] 3 All ER 705, [1982] 1 WLR 1297, CA.*
[2]   *[1982] 3 All ER 705 at 709, [1982] 1 WLR 1297 at 1302, per* Lord Denning MR. Cf *Jarvis v Swan Tours [1973] QB 233, [1973] 1 All ER 71, CA*; *Jackson v Horizon Holidays [1975] 3 All ER 92, [1975] 1 WLR 1468 CA.*
[3]   See generally K Franklin 'Damages for Heartache: The Award of General Damages for Inconvenience and Distress in Building Cases' (1988) 4 Const LR 264. For a relatively recent example, see *Patel v Hooper & Jackson [1999] 1 All ER 992, CA.*
[4]   *[1991] 4 All ER 937.*
[5]   See above at p 960. See also analysis of Bingham LJ's judgment in this case by the House of Lords in *Farley v Skinner [2001] 4 All ER 801.*
[6]   *[2001] 4 All ER 801.*

Awards to be modest

[27.30]   Awards for non-pecuniary loss in cases relating to buildings damaged, or less valuable than reported, will not be large[1]. Moreover, they are likely, in practice, to be confined to owner-occupiers. In *Hutchinson v Harris*[2] the Court of Appeal refused to make an award under this head to a plaintiff who had purchased the property for letting purposes. Waller LJ emphasised that the plaintiff 'was not concerned with her own home' and therefore had to accept that she had 'to concern herself with this sort of problem as an inevitable incident of being a landlord'.[3] Moreover, to qualify for an award the distress and anxiety suffered by the claimant must not be due merely to the 'tension or frustration of a person who is involved in a legal dispute',[4] because this is obviously not a recoverable head of damage.

[1]   See *Perry v Sidney Phillips & Son [1982] 3 All ER 705* at 709, *[1982] 1 WLR 1297* at 1303, *per* Lord Denning MR. See also *Watts v Morrow [1991] 4 All ER 937* at 960 *per* Bingham LJ ('awards should be restrained') and *per* Lord Steyn in *Farley v Skinner [2001] 4 All ER 801* at para 28 ('restrained and modest').
[2]   *(1978) 10 BLR 19, CA.*
[3]   *(1978) 10 BLR 19* at 46. See also *per* Stephenson LJ at 37.
[4]   *Per* Kerr LJ in *Perry v Sidney Phillips & Son [1982] 3 All ER 705* at 712, *[1982] 1 WLR 1297* at 1307.

Nuisance

[27.31]   The question can arise in nuisance cases as to how damages should be assessed for forms of interference which cause discomfort, and thereby diminish the extent to which the property affected can be enjoyed, but without necessarily reducing its value. It is probably impossible to lay down any general principles applicable to this class of case, but in the 1974 case of *Bone v Seale* the Court of Appeal suggested that damages provided in personal injury cases might provider a loose analogy. The defendant owned a pig farm from which offensive smells emanated. These smells caused great annoyance to the plaintiffs, who lived nearby, but did not affect the value of their property. The nuisance lasted for over twelve years, and at first instance

Walton J calculated the damages at £500 per annum making a total of over £6,000 to be paid by the defendant to each plaintiff. The defendant appealed against this figure and Stephenson LJ observed, in the Court of Appeal, that the 'figure of over £6,000 for what is a nuisance and is offensive but no more – something which is rightly described as a nuisance – does seem at first blush to be a very high figure'. His Lordship continued[1]:

'It is difficult to find an analogy to damages for interference with the enjoyment of property ... The nearest analogy would seem to be the damages which are awarded almost daily for loss of amenity in personal injury cases; it does seem to me that there is perhaps a closer analogy than at first sight appears between losing the enjoyment of your property as a result of some interference by smell or by noise caused by a next door neighbour, and losing an amenity as a result of a personal injury. Is it possible to equate loss of sense of smell as a result of the negligence of a defendant motor driver with having to put up with positive smells as a result of a nuisance created by a negligent neighbour? There is, as it seems to me, some parallel between the loss of amenity which is caused by personal injury and the loss of amenity which is caused by a nuisance of this kind.'

Approaching the case on that basis it was apparent that the figure awarded by Walton J had been too high, similar to 'the kind of figure that would only be given for a serious and permanent loss of amenity as the result of a very serious injury'[2] In the result the order of Walton J was varied and the damages were reduced to £1,000 for each plaintiff.

1   See *[1975] 1 All ER 787* at 793e–h, *[1975] 1 WLR 797* at 803G–804A.
2   *Per* Stephenson LJ.

Analogy doubted

[27.32]   In *Hunter v Canary Wharf Ltd*[1], however, Lord Hoffman said the following:

'I cannot agree with Stephenson LJ in *Bone v Seale* that damages in an action for nuisance caused by smells from a pigsty should be fixed by analogy with damages for loss of amenity in an action for personal injury ...In the case of a transitory nuisance, the capital value of the property will seldom be reduced. But the owner or occupier is entitled to compensation for the diminution in the amenity value of the property during the period for which the nuisance persisted. To some extent this involves placing a value on intangibles. But estate agents do this all the time. The law of damages is sufficiently flexible to be able to do justice in such a case'.

In the light of these observations the use of personal injury awards as a *starting point* for the assessment of damages in nuisance is unlikely to be appropriate. Nevertheless, comparison with such awards may still assist in helping to check, as in *Bone v Seale* itself, that the figure ultimately arrived at is not too *high*[2].

1   See *[1997] 2 All ER 426* at 451.
2   See *per* Lord Lloyd in *Hunter v Canary Wharf Ltd [1997] 2 All ER 426* at 444.

D New areas of recovery

[27.33]   The expansion of the tort of negligence in recent times has led to successful claims being made in situations unrelated to the traditional fields of property damage and personal injury. The focus of concentration in these cases has inevitably been on the nature of the causes of action rather than specifically upon the measure of damages. Indeed, the widely differing nature of the circumstances involved has meant that little has emerged in these areas to provide more detailed amplification of the general principle that damages should, as far as possible, put the plaintiff in the position which he would have been in if the tort had not been committed.[1] But one which should be noted is that, particularly in professional negligence cases, losses themselves may be calculated in a fashion formerly more familiar in contract than in tort. Thus, if the defendant undertakes to provide a service intended for the benefit of the claimant,[2] the latter may be able to recover the losses he suffers in consequence of the task in question not being correctly performed due to negligence, and such losses could well include compensation for *gains* which the claimant has failed to realise.[3]

[1]   Cf *County Personnel (Employment Agency) Ltd v Alan R Pulver & Co [1987] 1 All ER 289* at 297, *[1987] 1 WLR 916* at 925, *per* Bingham J (need for a 'general assessment' rather than 'an invariable approach ... mechanically applied' in claims against solicitors for professional negligence).
[2]   See A Burrows *Remedies for Torts and Breach of Contract* (2nd edn, 1994) pp 184–186.
[3]   See especially *White v Jones [1995] 2 AC 207, [1995] 1 All ER 691, HL*. See also *Carr-Glyn v Frearsons [1998] 4 All ER 225, CA*. Cf *Murray v Lloyd [1990] 2 All ER 92, [1989] 1 WLR 1060*.

Striking innovation

[27.34]   Another type of damages award, and one strikingly innovatory in character[1], was created in 2003 by the 4–3 majority decision of a seven member House of Lords in *Rees v Darlington Memorial Hospital*[2]. The House held that, where a child is born following a negligently performed sterilisation operation, a conventional award of £15,000 should be made to the parent. The award would be made, and its level would remain the same, irrespective of whether the child was healthy or whether the parent or the child was disabled. Lord Bingham of Cornhill said[3]:

'The conventional award would not be, and would not be intended to be, compensatory. It would not be the product of calculation. But it would not be a nominal, let alone a derisory, award. It would afford some measure of recognition of the wrong done'.

[1]   In a dissenting speech, Lord Steyn, said: 'There are limits to permissible creativity for judges. In my view the majority have strayed into forbidden territory': *Rees v Darlington Memorial Hospital [2003] 4 All ER 987* at para 46.
[2]   *[2003] 4 All ER 987*.
[3]   See *[2003] 4 All ER 987* at para 8.

Chapter 28

Limitation of actions

A General principles

Time limits

[28.01] The law on limitation of actions is contained in the Limitation Act 1980, which consolidates earlier legislation.[1] With the major exception of cases involving personal injuries, negligence actions are governed by *section 2* of the Act which provides that: 'An action founded on tort shall not be brought after the expiration of six years from the date on which the cause of action accrued.'

[1] See generally, A McGhee *Limitation Periods* (4th edn, 2002). For criticism of the 1980 Act see P Davies 'Limitations on the Law of Limitation' (1982) 98 LQR 249. For a very concise history of the law down to 1978, see *Firman v Ellis [1978] QB 886* at 903–905, *[1978] 2 All ER 851* at 858–859, CA, *per* Lord Denning.

Different period for personal injury

[28.02] In personal injury and Fatal Accident Act cases, the basic limitation period is not six years but three.[1] But by virtue of a provision originally introduced to protect victims of insidious industrial diseases, where the existence of illness may not be immediately apparent, time in personal injury cases may be calculated from the date of knowledge of the person injured if that is later than the date on which the cause of action actually accrued[2]. Moreover, since 1975,[3] the courts have had a very wide discretion to override the three-year time limit in personal injury cases if 'it would be equitable'[4] to do so. The special provisions relating to personal injury, and Fatal Accidents Act, cases are dealt with separately below.

[1] See section 11(4) of the 1980 Act. The shortening of the period from six years to three in personal injury cases was originally introduced by the *Law Reform (Limitation of Actions) Act 1954*.
[2] The question of how far this provision may have retrospective effect has given rise to difficult questions of construction: see *McDonnell v Christian Brothers [2004] 1 All ER 641*, HL; *Arnold v Central Electricity Generating Board [1988] AC 228*, *[1987] 3 All ER 694*, HL.
[3] See the *Limitation Act 1975, s 2D*.
[4] See the *Limitation Act 1980, s 33(1)*.

Major changes expected

[28.03] In 2001 the Law Commission proposed far-reaching changes to the law on limitation of actions[1]. The Government has accepted the recommendations in principle, and it seems likely that legislation to replace the *Limitation Act 1980* will be introduced in the not too distant future. The Law Commission's recommendations, in so far as they affect the law of negligence, are very briefly outlined at the end of this chapter at para [28.46].

[1]   See *Limitation of Actions* (Law Com no 270, 2001).

Computation of dates

[28.04] For the purpose of calculating the limitation period, the day on which the cause of action accrued is not included.[1] Moreover, if the court offices were closed on the last available day, the period will not expire until the end of the next day on which the offices reopen.[2]

[1]   See *Marren v Dawson Bentley & Co Ltd [1961] 2 QB 135, [1961] 2 All ER 270.*
[2]   See *Pritam Kaur v S Russell & Sons Ltd [1973] QB 336, [1973] 1 All ER 617, CA.*

Persons under a disability

[28.05] If a person is under a disability on the date when a cause of action accrues to him, the limitation period is extended so that he is allowed the full period (whether it be six years or three) calculated from the date on which he ceased to be under the disability.[1] A person is under a disability if he is an infant or of unsound mind.[2] In the case of infants there was formerly a rule that time did begin to run against an infant if he was in the custody of a parent when the cause of action accrued.[3] This rule was considered too harsh,[4] however, and was abrogated by the *Limitation Act 1975.* In consequence, a defendant who injures a very young child may find himself sued more than 20 years after the event took place.[5]

[1]   See the *Limitation Act 1980*, s 28. It follows that if the plaintiff is under a *permanent* disability there is in effect no limitation period at all: *Turner v W H Malcolm Ltd (1992) 15 BMLR 40, CA.*
[2]   *Limitation Act 1980*, s 38(2). A person is of unsound mind if he 'by reason of mental disorder within the meaning of the *Mental Health Act 1983*, is incapable of managing and administering his property and affairs': s 38(3). Cf *Kirby v Leather [1965] 2 QB 367, [1965] 2 All ER 441, CA.* See also *Limitation Act 1980, s 38(4)*: (conclusive presumption as to unsoundness of mind in certain cases).
[3]   See *Todd v Davison [1972] AC 392, [1971] 1 All ER 994, HL.* The rule was introduced by the *Law Reform (Limitation of Actions) Act 1954.*
[4]   For criticism of the rule, see the Twentieth Report of the Law Reform Committee: *Interim Report on Limitation of Actions in Personal Injury Claims* (1974) (Cmnd 5630) pp 35–39.
[5]   Cf *Tolley v Morris [1979] 2 All ER 561, [1979] 1 WLR 592, HL.*

Procedure

[28.06] Limitation is technically a matter of procedure. The *Limitation Act 1980* does not extinguish the claimant's right but merely bars his remedy. It follows that a defendant who considers that he has a valid defence of limitation cannot have the claim struck out as disclosing no reasonable cause of action.[1] Striking out on the ground of abuse of process might, however, be possible in a clear case; otherwise, the defence has to be pleaded and the matter tried.[2]

[1]   See *Ronex Properties Ltd v John Laing Construction Ltd [1983] QB 398, [1982] 3 All ER 961, CA.*
[2]   See above.

Human Rights Act invoked

[28.07] Complicated procedural issues sometimes arise where an action is commenced within the limitation period, but permission is sought to amend the pleadings after the period has expired.[1] CPR 17.4(2) provides that:

'The court may allow an amendment whose effect will be to add or substitute a new claim, but only if the new claim arises out of the same facts or substantially the same facts as a claim in respect of which the party applying for permission has already claimed a remedy in the proceedings'.

This rule was considered by the Court of Appeal in *Goode v Martin*[2]. In that case the claimant sought to amend her claim after the expiry of the period in order to contend that, even if the facts pleaded by the defendant by way of defence were true, he had still been negligent. The defendant resisted the amendment on the ground that the amendment involved a different set of facts from those originally pleaded by the claimant. The Court of Appeal allowed the amendment but, in order to do so, found it necessary to resort to *section 3(1)* of the *Human Rights Act 1998*; so as to depart from a conventional interpretation of the rule and to read words into it. This was to prevent the rule from depriving the claimant of access to the court without good reason, contrary to article 6(1) of the European Convention for the Protection of Human Rights and Fundamental Freedoms. Accordingly, the rule was read as if the words *'are already in issue on'* were added immediately after the words 'same facts as'.

[1] For discussion, see I Scott 'Limitation of Actions and Amendments to Join Defendants' (1982) 1 CJQ 205. See also *Ketteman v Hansel Properties Ltd [1985] 1 All ER 352* at 360–362, *[1984] 1 WLR 1274* at 1285–1288, *per* Lawton LJ, and the same case in the House of Lords: *[1987] AC 189, [1988] 2 All ER 38*.
[2] *[2002] 1 All ER 620.*

Adding parties

[28.08] Difficulties can also arise when attempts are made to add an additional *party* by a late amendment. In general, the long-established rule of practice is that such an amendment will not be permitted if to allow it would deprive the new party of a limitation defence which he would otherwise have enjoyed.[1]

[1] See *Liff v Peasley [1980] 1 All ER 623, [1980] 1 WLR 781, CA*; *Marshall v Gradon Construction Services Ltd [1997] 4 All ER 880, CA*. See also the *Limitation Act 1980, s 35(3)* and *Welsh Development Agency v Redpath Dorman Long Ltd [1994] 4 All ER 10, [1994] 1 WLR 1409, CA* (overruling *Kennett v Brown [1988] 2 All ER 600, [1988] 1 WLR 582, CA*).

Accrual of the cause of action

[28.09] Since negligence is not actionable without proof of damage, the cause of action will not accrue until damage occurs.[1] Where a property which turns out to be defective is purchased as a result of a negligent survey report, damage occurs when the claimant is irrevocably committed to the purchase of the property, ie at the date of exchange of contracts and not at the later date of completion[2]. And a performer who enters into a recording contract on unfavourable terms, due to negligent advice from a solicitor, suffers loss immediately the agreement is entered into even if its significance does not become apparent to him until later[3]. Nevertheless not all negligence cases will involve readily apparent dates, however, and ascertaining the point at which damage occurred may be far from straightforward[4].

1 Cf *Darley Main Colliery Co v Mitchell (1886) 11 App Cas 127, HL.*
2 See *Byrne v Hall Pain & Foster [1999] 2 All ER 400, CA.*
3 See *McCarroll v Statham Gill Davies [2003] Lloyd's Rep PN 167.*
4 See *Havenledge v Graeme John & Partners [2001] Lloyd's Rep 223*, in which each member of the Court of Appeal favoured a different date as that on which loss occurred.

Loan transactions

[28.10] In *Nykredit Mortgage Bank plc v Edward Erdman Group Ltd (No 2)*[1] the House of Lords had to decide at what point a lender suffered damage as a result of negligent valuation of the security against which the loan, to an ultimately insolvent borrower, had been made. Lord Hoffmann expressed the dilemma, and their Lordships' approach to its solution, as follows:[2]

> 'There may be cases in which it is possible to demonstrate that ... loss is suffered immediately upon the loan being made. The lender may be able to show that the rights which he has acquired are worth less in the open market than they would if the security had not been overvalued. But I think that this would be difficult to prove in a case in which the lender's personal covenant still appears good and interest payments are being duly made. On the other hand, loss will easily be demonstrable if the borrower has defaulted, so that the lender's recovery has become dependent upon the realisation of his security and that security is inadequate. On the other hand, I do not accept [the] submission that no loss can be shown until the security has actually been realised. Relevant loss is suffered when the lender is financially worse off by reason of a breach of the duty of care than he would otherwise have been.'

1 *[1998] 1 All ER 305, [1997] 1 WLR 1627, HL.* The case actually concerned the date from interest should be paid on a judgment in favour of the plaintiffs in earlier proceedings, but the House held that the solution depended upon the same principles as those applicable to limitation: see *per* Lord Hoffmann, *[1998] 1 All ER 305* at 315.
2 See *[1998] 1 All ER 305* at 316–317. See also *First National Commercial Bank plc v Humberts (a firm) [1995] 2 All ER 673, CA.*

Individual circumstances

[28.11] Choosing as the relevant date the point at which the lender is 'financially worse of' will inevitably mean that accrual of the cause of action will depend upon the circumstances of the individual case, but the House considered that such difficulties as might arise as a result would, in the words of Lord Nicholls,[1] be 'evidential and practical difficulties, not difficulties in principle'. His Lordship added that:[2]

> 'It should be acknowledged at once that, to a greater or lesser extent, quantification of the lender's loss is bound to be less certain, and therefore less satisfactory, if the quantification exercise is carried out before, rather than after, the security is ultimately sold ... But the difficulties of assessment at the earlier stage do not seem to me to lead to the conclusion that at the earlier stage the lender has suffered *no* measurable loss and has no cause of action, and that it is only when the assessment becomes more straightforward or final that loss first arises and with it the cause of action.'

1 See *[1998] 1 All ER 305* at 310.

²   *[1998] 1 All ER 305* at 310 (the emphasis is Lord Nicholls').

Ignorance of damage

[28.12]   A general difficulty arising out of the principles governing accrual of the cause of action is that damage may occur before the party suffering it is conscious of the fact. In *Bell v Peter Browne & Co (a firm)*¹ the defendant solicitors acted for the plaintiff on the breakdown of his marriage. The plaintiff transferred ownership of the former matrimonial home to his wife in return for her agreement to provide him with a one-sixth share of the proceeds in the event of sale. Unfortunately, the defendants negligently failed to take the appropriate steps to protect and register the plaintiff's interest, but this only came to light eight years later when the wife sold the house and spent all the proceeds.² The Court of Appeal held that the plaintiff's claim against his solicitors ran from a date on or around the making of the agreement between the plaintiff and his wife, when the defendants failed to act as they should have done, and not from the later date when the house was sold. In consequence, the claim was statute-barred. Originally, this principle was applied even in personal injury cases, but the hardship which it could cause, especially where insidious industrial diseases were concerned,³ gave rise to substantial statutory changes in the law in that area. These were eventually followed by legislative reform in the area of latent damage in cases other than personal injury. As a result of these changes, cases such as *Bell v Peter Browne & Co* which, although decided in 1990 was in fact governed by the old law, would now be decided differently. The rules relating generally to limitation in personal injury cases will be considered below, followed by those relating to latent damage in other types of case.

¹   *[1990] 2 QB 495, [1990] 3 All ER 124, CA.* See also *Forster v Outred & Co [1982] 2 All ER 753, [1982] 1 WLR 86, CA; Knapp v Ecclesiastical Insurance Group [1998] PNLR 172, CA; Martin v Britannia Life [2000] Lloyd's Rep PN 412.*
²   'Once the solicitors closed their file, it was unlikely that [their] failure would come to the notice of Mr Bell, or the solicitors, until the house was sold and it was too late. That, on the pleaded facts, is exactly what happened': *[1990] 3 All ER 124* at 128, *per* Nicholls LJ.
³   See *Cartledge v E Jopling & Sons Ltd [1963] AC 758, [1963] 1 All ER 341, HL.*

B Personal injuries¹

Special time limit

[28.13]   In the case of personal injury claims the basic time limit is only three years.¹ However, not only is there a wide discretion to override this time limit,² but the limit itself can be calculated, if necessary, in a way more favourable to the claimant than if the date of accrual were the only one available.⁴ Thus, *section 11(4)* of the 1980 Act provides that the three years run from:

'(a)   the date on which the cause of action accrued; or

(b)   the date of knowledge (if later) of the person injured.'

This provision, expressly allowing calculation to be made from the date of the claimant's knowledge, dates back to the *Limitation Act 1975*. The original concept reflected by the provision first appeared in the *Limitation Act 1963*, which was passed in the wake of the decision of the House of Lords in *Cartledge v E Jopling &*

Sons Ltd;[5] a case involving pneumoconiosis which showed that, as the law then stood, a claim could become statute-barred before the victim even knew that he had the disease.

1   See *Limitation Act 1980, s 11.* In cases of unwanted pregnancy as a result of negligent sterilisation operations, the financial cost of rearing the child counts as 'personal injury' for limitation purposes and is therefore governed by the three-year and not the six-year period: *Walkin v South Manchester Health Authority [1995] 4 All ER 132, [1995] 1 WLR 1543, CA.*
2   See below.
3   Contractual claims in respect of personal injuries are within the scope of the provision, which is not confined to actions in tort: see *Howe v David Brown Tractors (Retail) Ltd [1991] 4 All ER 30, CA.* Cf *Ackbar v C F Green & Co Ltd [1975] QB 582, [1975] 2 All ER 65.*
4   *[1963] AC 758, [1963] 1 All ER 341, HL.*

Date of knowledge

[28.14]   *Section 14* of the 1980 Act contains elaborate provisions defining the 'date of knowledge'. *Section 14(1)* is as follows:

'... references to a person's date of knowledge are references to the date on which he first had knowledge of the following facts—

(a)   that the injury in question was significant; and

(b)   that the injury was attributable[1] in whole or in part to the act or omission which is alleged to constitute negligence, nuisance of breach of duty; and

(c)   the identity of the defendant; and

(d)   if it is alleged that the act or omission was that of a person other than the defendant, the identity of that person and the additional facts supporting the bringing of an action against the defendant;

and knowledge that any acts or omissions did or did not, as a matter of law, involve negligence, nuisance or breach of duty is irrelevant.'

1   On the meaning of 'attributable' in *section 14(1)(b),* see *Nash v Eli Lilly [1993] 4 All ER 383* at 396–399, CA, *per* Purchas LJ delivering the judgment of the court. Cf *Spargo v North Essex District Health Authority [1997] 8 Med LR 125, CA.* See also *Dobbie v Medway Health Authority [1994] 4 All ER 450* at 456, CA, *per* Sir Thomas Bingham MR: 'Time starts to run against the claimant when he knows that the personal injury on which he founds his action is capable of being attributed to something done or not done by the defendant whom he wishes to sue. This condition is not satisfied where a man knows that he has a disabling cough or shortness of breath but does not know that his injured condition has anything to do with his working conditions. It is satisfied when he knows that his injured condition is capable of being attributed to his working conditions, even though he has no inkling that his employer may have been at fault.'

Proviso

[28.15]   The proviso in the concluding words of the subsection, making knowledge of the law irrelevant, was passed in order to overcome uncertainty on the point reflected in the decision of the House of Lords in *Central Asbestos Co Ltd v Dodd,*[1] based on the construction of the earlier provision in the *Limitation Act 1963.* The proviso was applied, with the result that the plaintiff's claim was statute-barred, in *Broadley v Guy Clapham & Co*[2] in which Hoffmann LJ said[3] that the concluding words 'put beyond doubt' that the section 'rejects any need for the plaintiff to have known that he had a cause of action'.[4]

1 *[1973] AC 518, [1972] 2 All ER 1135, HL.*
2 *[1994] 4 All ER 439, CA*, overruling *Bentley v Bristol and Western Health Authority [1991] 2 Med LR 359.*
3 See *[1994] 4 All ER 439* at 448.
4 See also *Dobbie v Medway Health Authority [1994] 4 All ER 450* at 458, CA, *per* Sir Thomas Bingham MR: ' ... it is necessary to emphasise that knowledge of fault or negligence is not needed to start time running.' Cf *Saxby v Morgan [1997] 8 Med LR 293, CA.*

'Significant'

[28.16] The requirement in *section 14(1)(a)* of the 1980 Act 'that the injury in question was significant' is expanded by *section 14(2)*, which provides as follows:

'For the purposes of this section an injury is significant if the person whose date of knowledge is in question would reasonably have considered it sufficiently serious to justify his instituting proceedings for damages against a defendant who did not dispute liability and was able to satisfy a judgment.'

Although the case was decided under earlier and differently worded legislation, a passage in the judgment of Lord Denning MR in *Goodchild v Greatness Timber Co Ltd*[1] conveniently expresses the underlying purpose of this somewhat curiously worded provision:

' ... I would say this on those words: they are intended to apply to cases where a man has an injury which he reasonably believes is trifling (for example, a knock on the head) and it is not worthwhile to bring an action for it, but then after three years it is found to be far more serious than anyone realised (for instance, to cause a tumour) ... His time will be extended. But if the injury was from the beginning fairly serious, or at any rate sufficiently serious to make it worthwhile to bring an action, then he must bring it within the first three years. The time will not be extended simply because it turns out after three years to be more serious than he at first thought.'

1 *[1968] 2 QB 372* at 380, *[1968] 2 All ER 255* at 257. In *Miller v London Electrical Manufacturing Co Ltd [1976] 2 Lloyd's Rep 284* the Court of Appeal apparently took the view that, by the wording of what is now *section 14(2)*, 'Parliament has in effect given its imprimatur to [*Goodchild's*] case': *[1976] 2 Lloyd's Rep 284* at 288, *per* Bridge LJ.

Partly subjective

[28.17] The meaning of what is now *section 14(2)* of the *Limitation Act 1980* was also expounded by Geoffrey Lane LJ in *McCafferty v Metropolitan Police District Receiver*[1] as follows:

' ... it is clear that the test is partly a subjective test, namely: would this plaintiff have considered the injury sufficiently serious? And partly an objective test, namely: would he have been reasonable if he did *not* regard it as sufficiently serious? It seems to me that [s 14(2)] is directed at the nature of the injury as known to the plaintiff, with *that* plaintiff's intelligence, would he have been reasonable in considering the injury not sufficiently serious to justify instituting proceedings for damages?'

1 *[1977] ICR 799* at 807–808, CA (italics are those of Geoffrey Lane LJ). See also *Nash v Eli Lilly & Co [1993] 4 All ER 383, CA.*

[28.18] *Limitation of actions*

Where claim and initial damage are distinct.

[28.18] In *KR v Bryn Alyn Community*, Auld LJ said[1]:

'In any s 14 case, it is important to distinguish between the occurrence of initial damage that may itself amount to a significant injury in a s 14(2) sense and that which, although the claimant could have successfully sued for it, does not'.

This observation was made in the context of claims for psychiatric injury caused by sexual abuse. The defendants contended that time should run from when the abusive acts themselves were committed, of which the claimants necessarily had knowledge. But the Court of Appeal held that since the claims were for psychiatric injury caused by the abuse, and not for the actual acts of abuse themselves, the relevant date was the much later one when the claimants could have been expected to realise that they had suffered significant *psychiatric* injury.

[1]   *[2004] 2 All ER 716* at para 39.

Factors not counting towards 'significance'

[28.19]   An accident victim who refrains from bringing an action initially merely 'because of the regard he has for the defendants or ... because he is averse to litigation'[1] cannot claim subsequently that his injury was not 'significant' for the purposes of the subsection. Nor can one who failed to make a claim because he did not want to 'sponge',[2] or was simply afraid of losing his job,[3] do so. Such factors may, however, be taken into account when the court is considering the exercise of its general discretion to override the time limit.[4]

[1]   *Per* Salmon LJ in *Goodchild v Greatness Timber Co Ltd [1968] 2 QB 372* at 381, *[1968] 2 All ER 255* at 258, CA.
[2]   *Buck v English Electric Co Ltd [1977] ICR 629.*
[3]   *McCafferty v Metropolitan Police District Receiver [1977] 2 All ER 756, [1977] 1 WLR 1073, CA.* Cf *Driscoll-Varley v Parkside Health Authority [1991] 2 Med LR 346.*
[4]   See below at para [28.29].

'Attributable'

[28.20]   In *Dobbie v Medway Health Authority*[1], Sir Thomas Bingham MR provided the following illustration of how the word 'attributable' in *section 14(1)(b)* of the 1980 Act may apply in practice:

'Time starts to run against the claimant when he knows that the personal injury on which he founds his action is capable of being attributed to something done or not done by the defendant whom he wishes to sue. This condition is not satisfied where a man knows that he has a disabling cough or shortness of breath but does not know that his injured condition has anything to do with his working conditions. It is satisfied when he knows that his injured condition is capable of being attributed to his working conditions, even though he has no inkling that his employer may have been at fault.'[2]

[1]   *[1994] 4 All ER 450* at 456, CA
[2]   See also *Nash v Eli Lilly [1993] 4 All ER 383* at 396–399, CA, *per* Purchas LJ delivering the judgment of the court. Cf *Spargo v North Essex District Health Authority [1997] 8 Med LR 125, CA.*

'The identity of the defendant'

[28.21] The working of *section 14(1)(c)* of the *Limitation Act 1980* is illustrated by *Simpson v Norwest Holst Southern Ltd.*[1] The plaintiff injured his leg while working on a building site. He consulted solicitors within weeks of the accident, but confusion then ensued in determining precisely who the plaintiff's employers were. The documents which had been given to him ostensibly containing such particulars, pursuant to the employment legislation, identified them as the 'Norwest Holst Group', and a similar expression appeared on his pay slips. That expression did not, however, identify any legal entity, there being at least four companies forming the 'group', each with registered titles embodying different variations of the 'Norwest' theme. In consequence, some letters from the plaintiff's solicitors went unanswered, others met with long delays. By the time they were in a position to commence proceedings, more than three years had elapsed since the date of the accident. Nevertheless, the Court of Appeal held, applying the subsection, that the proceedings were within the time limit because, in the circumstances, it ran from the date on which the plaintiff discovered his employer's identity.

[1] *[1980] 2 All ER 471, [1980] 1 WLR 968, CA.*

Knowledge and advice

[28.22] *Section 14(3)* of the *Limitation Act 1980* provides as follows:

'For the purposes of this section a person's knowledge includes knowledge which he might reasonably have been expected to acquire —

(a) from facts observable or ascertainable by him; or

(b) from facts ascertainable by him with the help of medical or other appropriate expert advice which it is reasonable for him to seek;

but a person shall not be fixed under this subsection with knowledge of a fact ascertainable only with the help of expert advice so long as he has taken all reasonable steps to obtain (and, where appropriate, to act on) that advice.'

Thus, constructive, as well as actual, knowledge will be sufficient to start time running against the claimant if he unreasonably fails to obtain expert advice which could have been expected to reveal the true state of facts to him.[1]

[1] See *Adams v Bracknell Forest BC [2004] 3 All ER 897*, discussed below at para [28.25].

Where advice inadequate

[28.23] The proviso incorporated in the closing words of the subsection was applied in *Marston v British Railways Board.*[1] The plaintiff was injured at work in 1957 when a chip flew off a hammer he was using, and embedded itself in his neck. Shortly after the accident, expert advice was taken as to whether the hammer had been defective; but the expert's report was not comprehensive and it failed to indicate, as it could have done, that the hammer had in fact been defective in a material respect. In the light of the report, the plaintiff assumed that he had no cause of action against his employers, and the hammer was subsequently destroyed. It was not until 1969 that the chip itself was removed from the plaintiff's neck (it having been too dangerous to do so earlier), and expert testing of it finally revealed at that stage that the hammer had, in fact, been defective. Croom-Johnson J held, in the plaintiff's favour, that a claim brought after the discovery of the true facts was not time-barred. Since he had acted reasonably in obtaining expert advice initially, it followed from the wording of the proviso that the inadequacy of that advice did not adversely affect the plaintiff's position.[2]

---

1   *[1976] ICR 124.*
2   Cf *Pickles v National Coal Board (intended action) [1968] 2 All ER 598, [1968] 1 WLR 997.*

Failure to obtain advice

[28.24]   This case may be contrasted with *Forbes v Wandsworth Health Authority.*[1] The claim of a plaintiff whose leg had to be amputated in 1982, immediately following two unsuccessful by-pass operations, was held to be statute-barred by 1992 even though expert medical advice, to the effect that the amputation could have become necessary because of possible negligent delay in carrying out the second of the two by-pass operations, was only obtained in 1991. The plaintiff was affected by constructive knowledge, within *section 14(3)(b)* of the 1980 Act, by virtue of his failure to obtain expert medical advice shortly after the amputation itself rather than waiting nine years. Stuart-Smith LJ said:[2]

> 'One of the problems with the language of s 14(3)(b) is that two alternative courses of action may be perfectly reasonable. Thus it may be perfectly reasonable for a person who is not cured when he hoped to be to say "Oh well, it is just one of those things. I expect the doctors did their best"; alternatively the explanation for the lack of success may be due to want of care on the part of those in whose charge he was, in which case it would be perfectly reasonable to take a second opinion. And I do not think that the person who adopts the first alternative can necessarily be said to be acting unreasonably. But he is in effect making a choice, either consciously by deciding to do nothing, or unconsciously by in fact doing nothing. Can a person who has effectively made this choice many years later, and without any alteration of circumstances, change his mind and then seek advice which reveals that all along he had a claim? I think not.'

The plaintiff had therefore not, in the view of the majority of the Court of Appeal[3] 'taken all reasonable steps to obtain' expert advice within the proviso to *section 14(3).*[4]

---

1   *[1997] QB 402, [1996] 4 All ER 881, CA.*
2   See *[1997] QB 402* at 412, *[1996] 4 All ER 881* at 889.
3   Stuart-Smith and Evans LJJ. Roch LJ dissented.
4   See also *Broadley v Guy Clapham & Co [1994] 4 All ER 439, CA.*

Is the test subjective or objective?

[28.25]   The courts have experienced difficulty in determining to what extent the claimant's individual position and abilities may be taken into account in applying *section 14(3)* of the *Limitation Act 1980.* In *Nash v Eli Lilly & Co*[1] Purchas LJ, delivering the judgment of the court, said that it was appropriate 'to take into consideration the position, and circumstances and character of the plaintiff' in deciding whether he had acted unreasonably for the purposes of the provision. But in *Forbes v Wandsworth Health Authority*[2] all three members of the Court of Appeal criticised this proposition; Stuart-Smith LJ said that he had 'difficulty in seeing how the individual character and intelligence of the plaintiff can be relevant to an objective test'[3]. This conflict was considered by the House of Lords in *Adams v Bracknell Forest BC*,[4] which resolved the issue broadly in favour of the reasoning in the *Forbes* case and the adoption of an objective approach. At the same time, however, *Bracknell* illustrates the extent to which decisions in this area inevitably turn largely upon their own facts, and frequently involve the interaction of subjective and objective considerations. The claimant had experienced difficulty with reading and writing throughout his schooldays, but it was not until a chance social encounter, at the age of 30, with an educational psychologist that he was alerted to the possibility that he might be dyslexic. He then brought an action in respect of the defendants' failure to diagnose that condition when he was at school. The defendants contended that the action was time-barred, arguing that the claimant should have sought advice much earlier. They accepted that the fact that the claimant had reading and writing difficulties could be taken into account in determining how promptly he should have sought advice, but denied that the fact that he suffered from low self-esteem as a result of his difficulties, and was reluctant to do anything to highlight them, was relevant. Although the trial judge and Court of Appeal rejected the defence submission, and held that the action was not out of time, the House of Lords unanimously reversed their decision and upheld the defendants' appeal[5]. Lord Hoffman said[6]:

> 'It is true that the plaintiff must be assumed to be a person who has suffered the injury in question and not some other person ... In my opinion, s 14(3) requires one to assume that a person who is aware that he has suffered a personal injury, serious enough to be something about which he would go and see a solicitor if he knew he had a claim, will be sufficiently curious about the causes of the injury to seek whatever expert advice is appropriate ... In principle, I think the judge was right in applying the standard of reasonable behaviour to a person assumed to be suffering from untreated dyslexia. If the injury itself would reasonably inhibit him from seeking advice, then that is a factor which must be taken into account. My difficulty is with the basis for the finding that such a person could not reasonably be expected to reveal the source of his difficulties to his medical adviser ... Although one can easily understand someone wanting to avoid the social embarrassment of revealing his difficulties about reading and writing to colleagues at work and other acquaintances, I think it would need some evidential foundation before one could assume that such a person was likely to be unable to speak about the matter to his own doctor ... In my opinion, there is no reason why the normal expectation that a person suffering from significant injury will be curious about its origins should not also apply to dyslexics.'

1 See *[1993] 4 All ER 383* at 399, *[1993] 1 WLR 782* at 801, CA.
2 *[1997] QB 402, [1996] 4 All ER 881*, CA.
3 See *[1996] 4 All ER 881* at 891, CA.
4 *[2004] 3 All ER 897*.
5 The House also held that the discretion under *section 33* to override the time limit (see below at para [28.27]) would not be exercised in the claimant's favour.
6 See *[2004] 3 All ER 897* at paras 47–51.

Protection only for questions of fact

[28.26] It is important to note that the proviso to *section 14(3)* of the 1980 Act only protects the claimant with respect to defective advice on questions of *fact*. It follows from the proviso to *section 14(1)* that if a claimant believes that he has no cause of action merely on account of his having received incorrect advice as to the law, time will still run against him.[1] Moreover, even where 'facts' are concerned the proviso will not prevent a claimant from being affected by constructive knowledge, within *section 14(3)*, if the reason for his not having actual knowledge was failure by his solicitors to acquire it as promptly as they could or should have done. Such failure on factual matters by solicitors does not constitute 'expert advice' within the wording of the proviso. Thus, in *Henderson v Temple Pier Co Ltd*[2] the plaintiff was affected by constructive knowledge, resulting in her claim becoming statute-barred, when her solicitors failed to discover, as quickly as they could and should have done, the name of the correct person to sue. Appointing solicitors to handle her case did not prevent the plaintiff from being affected by constructive knowledge, since the relevant facts should have been 'observable or ascertainable' by the plaintiff herself under *section 14(3)(a)*. 'The proviso is not intended to give an extended period of limitation', said Bracewell J in the Court of Appeal,[3] 'to a person whose solicitor acts dilatorily in acquiring information which is obtainable without particular expertise'.

1   Cf P Davies 'Limitations of the Law of Limitation' (1982) 98 LQR 249 at 255–256. See also *Halford v Brookes [1991] 3 All ER 559, CA*.
2   *[1998] 1 WLR 1540, [1998] 3 All ER 324, CA*. See also *Copeland v Smith [2000] 1 All ER 457, CA*.
3   See *[1998] 1 WLR 1540* at 1545, *[1998] 3 All ER 324* at 329.

Discretion to override the time limit

[28.27]   *Section 33* of the *Limitation Act 1980* re-enacts a provision originally introduced by the *Limitation Act 1975*, in the light of a recommendation made by the Law Reform Committee in its Twentieth Report.[1] The section confers a general discretion upon the court, if 'it appears … that it would be equitable to allow an action to proceed', to direct that the three-year time limit imposed by *section 11* 'shall not apply'.[2] The court is enjoined, in deciding whether to exercise the discretion, to balance the 'prejudice [to] the plaintiff' which would occur if the time limit were to be insisted upon against the 'prejudice [to] the defendants' which would occur if it were to be overridden.[3] In *KR v Bryn Alyn Community*,[4] Auld LJ summarised the position as follows:

> 'The burden of showing that it would be equitable to disapply the limitation period lies on the claimant and it is a heavy burden. Another way of putting it is that it is an exceptional indulgence to a claimant, to be granted only where equity between the parties demands it'.

1   See *Interim Report on Limitation of Actions in Personal Injury Claims* (Cmnd 5630) (1974).
2   *Section 33(1)*.
3   *Section 33(1)*. For discussion see D Morgan 'Limitation and Discretion: Procedural Reform and Substantive Effect' (1982) 1 CJQ 109. See also P Davies 'Limitations of the Law of Limitation' (1982) 98 LQR 249 at 260–275.
4   See *[2004] 2 All ER 716* at para 74.

Factors of particular relevance

[28.28]   *Section 33(3)* of the 1980 Act provides a list of particular factors to which the court should have regard in coming to its decision. The list is not, however, exhaustive.[1] The factors enumerated are as follows: the length of the claimant's delay and the reasons for it,[2] the effect of the delay upon the cogency of the evidence,[3] the conduct of the defendant,[4] the duration of any disability affecting the claimant,[5] the degree to which the claimant in fact acted promptly once he knew the facts,[6] and the steps taken by the claimant to obtain expert advice along with the nature of any such advice.[7]

1 ' ... the court shall have regard to *all* the circumstances': *s 33(3)* (emphasis supplied).
2 *Section 33(3)(a)*. See *Coad v Cornwall and Scilly Isles Health Authority* [1997] 1 WLR 189, CA.
3 *Section 33(3)(b)*.
4 *Section 33(3)(c)*.
5 *Section 33(3)(d)*.
6 *Section 33(3)(e)*.
7 *Section 33(3)(f)*. See also *Jones v G D Searle & Co Ltd [1978] 3 All ER 654, [1979] 1 WLR 101, CA* (statutory wording means that plaintiff can be required to answer an interrogatory on the nature of legal advice received, professional privilege notwithstanding).

Width of discretion

Rule in Walkley's case

[28.29] In *Walkley v Precision Forgings Ltd*[1] the House of Lords held that a plaintiff who brought an action within the normal three-year period for a personal injuries claim, but either discontinued it or allowed it to become liable to dismissal for want of prosecution, ipso facto becomes disentitled to seek the exercise of the discretion to override the time limit in order to bring a new action.[2] The decision was based on a statutory condition precedent, for the existence of the discretion to override, that the plaintiff would be 'prejudiced' by the normal time limit if that limit were to be insisted upon.[3] Their Lordships held that a plaintiff who did manage to commence proceedings within the time limit could not be said to have been prejudiced by it, but rather by his own dilatoriness or that of his advisers, if that first action was not properly pursued. The rule in *Walkley's* case has not proved popular. The Law Commission has described it as 'artificial'[4]; and in *Shapland v Palmer*[5] Simon Brown LJ noted that the 'general tendency' of the cases suggested 'a marked unwillingness on the court's part to apply *Walkley's* case unless it is plainly indistinguishable'[6]. He continued as follows[7]:

> 'By the same token that the *Walkley* principle itself rests upon a narrow and somewhat technical construction of s 33, so too it is in my judgment possible to escape it on just such grounds. That, moreover, is particularly appropriate given the undoubted anomalies that in any event arise from the application of the principle – most notably ...its failure to impact on cases of perhaps greater negligence where no writ was ever issued in the first place. I would accordingly rule that the s 33 discretion arises in all cases save those which fall four-square within the *Walkley* principle'[8].

In *Shapland v Palmer* itself *Walkley's* case was narrowly distinguished on the basis that failure to pursue a vicarious liability claim against an employer did not preclude a new action arising out of the same incident against the employee personally, and the *section 33* discretion was held to be applicable[9].

1 *[1979] 2 All ER 548, [1979] 1 WLR 606, HL*.
2 See also *Deerness v John R Keeble & Sons (Brantham) Ltd [1983] 2 Lloyd's Rep 260*, HL; *Forward v Hendricks [1997] 2 All ER 395*, CA. Cf *White v Glass* (1989) Times, 18 February, CA (power to override time limit can survive if earlier proceedings invalid).
3 See the *Limitation Act 1980, s 33(1)*.
4 See *Limitation of Actions* (Law Com no 270, 2001), para 3.166.
5 *[1999] 3 All ER 50, CA*.
6 See *[1999] 3 All ER 50* at 55. See also *per* Clarke LJ at 59: ' ... the decision in *Walkley's* case should be confined to its own facts and not extended ... '
7 See above.
8 Cf *Thompson v Brown Construction (Ebbw Vale) Ltd [1981] 2 All ER 296* at 303, *[1981] 1 WLR 744* at 752, HL, *per* Lord Diplock.

⁹ See also *Piggott v Aulton (decd) [2003] PIQR P22, CA*. But cf *Young (decd) v Western Power Distribution [2003] 1 WLR 2868*, in which the Court of Appeal reluctantly felt compelled to apply the *Walkley* principle.

Onus on the claimant

[28.30] The rule in *Walkley's* case appears to be the only situation in which a claimant is actually precluded from seeking the exercise of the statutory discretion in his favour. The scope of what is now *section 33* of the 1980 Act was considered by the House of Lords in *Thompson v Brown Construction Ebbw Vale*.¹ In a speech with which his brethren agreed, Lord Diplock observed that the 'onus of showing that in the particular circumstances of the case it would be equitable' to override the limit 'lies on the plaintiff; but, subject to that, the court's discretion to make or refuse an order if it considers it equitable to do so is, in my view, unfettered'.² In *Donovan v Gwentoys Ltd*³ the plaintiff suffered an injury while below the age of majority. She brought an action less than six months after the expiry of the three-year limitation period which commenced with her eighteenth birthday. The House of Lords held, however, that in considering the prejudice to the defendants in the general exercise of its discretion the court was entitled to have regard to the fact that they were unaware of the claim until five years after the accident: ie it was not confined to considering only the delay which occurred *after* the expiry of the limitation period. The House upheld the limitation defence and Lord Oliver expressed himself as follows:⁴

'A defendant is always likely to be prejudiced by the dilatoriness of a plaintiff in pursuing his claim. Witnesses' memories may fade, records may be lost or destroyed, opportunities for inspection and report may be lost. The fact that the law permits a plaintiff within prescribed limits to disadvantage a defendant in this way does not mean that the defendant is not prejudiced. It merely means that he is not in a position to complain of whatever prejudice he suffers. Once a plaintiff allows the permitted time to elapse, the defendant is no longer subject to that disability, and in a situation in which the court is directed to consider all the circumstances of the case and, to balance the prejudice of the parties, the fact that the claim has, as a result of the plaintiff's failure to use the time allowed to him, become a thoroughly stale claim cannot, in my judgment, be irrelevant.'

¹ *[1981] 2 All ER 296, [1981] 1 WLR 744, HL.*
² *[1981] 2 All ER 296 at 303, [1981] 1 WLR 744 at 752* See also *Firman v Ellis [1978] QB 886, [1978] 2 All ER 851* (a decision of the Court of Appeal no longer correct on its facts, as earlier proceedings had already been commenced within the time limit, but correct on the otherwise unfettered nature of the discretion: see *Chappell v Cooper [1980] 2 All ER 463, [1980] 1 WLR 958, CA*).
³ *[1990] 1 All ER 1018, [1990] 1 WLR 472, HL.*
⁴ *[1990] 1 All ER 1018 at 1025, [1990] 1 WLR 472 at 479–480.*

Not to be fettered by guidelines

[28.31] An appellate court will therefore be very reluctant to interfere with the exercise by the trial judge of the discretion entrusted to him.¹ 'I do not consider', said Parker LJ in *Hartley v Birmingham City District Council*,² 'that it is either useful or desirable to attempt to lay down guidelines, for circumstances are infinitely variable. The task of the judge is to consider whether in all the circumstances it is equitable, or fair and just, that the action should be allowed to proceed'³. In *Ramsden v Lee*⁴ the Court of Appeal expressly declined an invitation to introduce a guideline which would, in effect, have constituted a presumption against exercise of the discretion in a plaintiff's favour if the delay had not been minimal and the defendant had not been at fault with respect to it.[5] It is important to note that the fact that the claimant may initially have sought unsuccessfully to bring himself within *section 11* of the 1980 Act, by relying on the 'date of knowledge' principle, is no bar to his succeeding under *section 33*.[6] Moreover, the same evidence which proved insufficient to establish an extended time limit under *section 11* may be influential in persuading the court to exercise its discretion in the claimant's favour.[7] In several of the cases in which the court has overridden the time limit, it had earlier ruled against the claimant on *section 11*.[8]

[1] *Conry v Simpson [1983] 3 All ER 369, CA*. See also *Burke v Ashe Construction [2004] PIQR P11, CA*.
[2] *[1992] 2 All ER 213* at 224–225, *[1992] 1 WLR 968* at 980, CA.
[3] Cf *KR v Bryn Alyn Community [2004] 2 All ER 716* at paras 80–82, CA.
[4] *[1992] 2 All ER 204, CA*.
[5] 'To my mind there is a considerable danger in laying down guidelines where the need for guidelines has not been made entirely apparent. The risk is that then more and more cases will come which are treated as matters of law on the application not of the statute but of the guidelines': *[1992] 2 All ER 204* at 209, CA, *per* Dillon LJ.
[6] *McCafferty v Metropolitan Police District Receiver [1977] 2 All ER 756, [1977] 1 WLR 1073, CA*.
[7] See *McCafferty v Metropolitan Police District Receiver [1977] 2 All ER 756, [1977] 1 WLR 1073, CA*.
[8] See *Sniezek v Bundy (Letchworth) Ltd [2000] PIQR P213, CA*; *McCafferty v Metropolitan Police District Receiver [1977] 2 All ER 756, [1977] 1 WLR 1073, CA*. See also *Halford v Brookes [1991] 3 All ER 559, [1991] 1 WLR 428, CA* and *Hendy v Milton Keynes Health Authority (No 2) [1992] 3 Med LR 119*. Cf *Marston v British Railways Board [1976] ICR 124*.

Dependent on facts

[28.32] Since every case will therefore depend on its own facts, the decisions in past cases are merely examples. Clearly, the longer the delay the heavier will be the burden on the claimant,[1] but his task will be eased if the availability of the evidence has not been substantially affected.[2] The overall potential strength of the claimant's case has also been held to be a relevant factor.[3] If the claimant is likely to have a remedy against his own solicitor for negligence if the normal time limit is insisted upon, this will be taken into account as a factor pointing against exercise of the discretion,[4] but it will by no means be decisive.[5] There is certainly no rule of law that a claimant will have the errors of his advisors attributed to him[6]. If the defendant is not fully insured, this will be relevant as an indication of the degree of prejudice which *he* will suffer if the time limit is overridden.[7] Conversely, 'it is legitimate to take into account that the defendant *is* insured. If he is deprived of his fortuitous defence he will have a claim on his insurers'.[8]

[1] See *Forbes v Wandsworth Health Authority [1997] QB 402, [1996] 4 All ER 881, CA*; *Dobbie v Medway Health Authority [1994] 4 All ER 450, [1994] 1 WLR 1234, CA*; *Dale v British Coal Corpn (No 2) (1992) 136 Sol Jo LB 199, CA*.
[2] See *Brooks v J & P Coates (UK) Ltd [1984] 1 All ER 702, [1984] ICR 158*.
[3] ' ... if it is shown that the claim is a poor case lacking in merit, there may be significant and relevant prejudice to the defendants if the limitation provisions are disapplied'; *per* Purchas LJ in *Nash v Eli Lilly & Co [1993] 4 All ER 383* at 403, *[1993] 1 WLR 782* at 804, CA. See also *per* Stuart-Smith LJ in *Forbes v Wandsworth Health Authority [1997] QB 402* at 415, *[1996] 4 All ER 881* at 894, CA, citing his own remarks in the earlier case of *Dale v British Coal Corp [1992] PIQR P373* at P380–P381, CA.
[4] See *Donovan v Gwentoys Ltd [1990] 1 All ER 1018, [1990] 1 WLR 472, HL*. Cf *Unitramp SA v Jenson & Nicholson (S) Pte Ltd [1992] 1 All ER 346, [1992] 1 WLR 862*.
[5] See *Thompson v Brown Construction (Ebbw Vale) Ltd [1981] 2 All ER 296, [1981] 1 WLR 744, HL*; *Ramsden v Lee [1992] 2 All ER 204, CA*. See also *Hartley v Birmingham City District Council [1992] 2 All ER 213*, especially *per* Parker LJ at 224, CA: ' ... if the plaintiff has to change from an action against a tortfeasor, who may know little or nothing of the weak points of his case, to an action against his solicitor, who will know a great deal about them, the prejudice may well be major rather than minor.'

6   See *Das v Ganju [1999] PIQR P260, CA*; *Corbin v Penfold Metallising Co [2000] Lloyd's Rep Med 247, CA*.
7   See *Davies v Soltenpur (1983) 133 NLJ 720*. Cf *Liff v Peasley [1980] 1 All ER 623* at 630, *[1980] 1 WLR 781* at 789, CA, *per* Stephenson LJ ('unrealistic and inequitable to disregard the insurance position').
8   *Per* Parker LJ in *Hartley v Birmingham City District Council [1992] 2 All ER 213* at 224, CA (italics supplied).

Where death results

[28.33]   If the victim dies from his injuries, but fails to bring an action himself within the normal three-year time limit (calculated, if appropriate, from his 'date of knowledge'), then it will not be possible for his dependants to bring an action under the *Fatal Accidents Act 1976*. Moreover, the possibility that, had he lived, the court might have exercised its discretion under *section 33* of the *Limitation Act 1980*, is to be discounted for this purpose.[1] If, however, a claim by the deceased would not have been statute-barred in this way, then his dependants have three years from the date of his death or from 'the date of knowledge of the person for whose benefit the action is brought', whichever is the later, in which to claim.[2] As a result, the time limit may expire at different times for different dependants, depending upon their respective 'dates of knowledge'.[3] In addition, the exercise of the discretion to override the time limit, under *section 33*, may also be sought by dependants in a Fatal Accidents Act claim.[4]

1   *Limitation Act 1980, s 12(1).*
2   *Limitation Act 1980, s 12(2).*
3   *Limitation Act 1980, s 13(1).*
4   *Limitation Act 1980, s 12(3).*

C Concealment of the cause of action

Start of period postponed

[28.34]   The *Limitation Act 1980, s 32* deals, inter alia, with situations in which the defendant has been guilty of fraud, or analogous misconduct, and provides for postponement of the start of the limitation period in such cases. It re-enacts, as subsequently amended, a similar provision in the *Limitation Act 1939*. The only provisions likely to be relevant in cases where the claimant's basic cause of action is merely for negligence are *section 32(1)(b)* and *section 32(2)*, which provide as follows:

> '(1)(b) [If] any fact relevant to the plaintiff's right to action has been deliberately concealed from him by the defendant … the period of limitation shall not begin to run until the plaintiff has discovered the … concealment … or could with reasonable diligence have discovered it.

> (2) For the purposes of subsection (1) above, deliberate commission of a breach of duty in circumstances in which it is unlikely to be discovered for some time amounts to deliberate concealment of the facts involved in that breach of duty'.

Not applicable where defendant unaware of negligence

[28.35]   In *Cave v Robinson Jarvis & Rolf*[1] the defendant solicitors acted for the claimant in a transaction whereby the latter was granted certain mooring rights intended to last for 100 years. Unfortunately the defendants failed to register the rights with the Land Registry so that they were merely of contractual effect, and were lost when the grantor company went into receivership. More than six years after the transaction was completed, but only four years after the claimant was notified that his mooring rights had been lost, the claimant started proceedings against the solicitors for negligence. In response to a defence of limitation the claimant sought to rely on *section 32(2)* of the *Limitation Act 1980*. Although it was not suggested that the defendants had deliberately sought to carry out the transaction wrongly, it was contended that the fact that carrying the transaction out was necessarily an intentional act was in itself enough to constitute 'deliberate commission of a breach of duty'. This rather surprising construction of *section 32(2)* was supported by an earlier decision of the Court of Appeal, *Brocklesby v Armitage & Guest*[2], which the same court felt obliged to follow in *Cave's* case itself. If upheld this would have had effect of giving the claimant six years from his discovery of the loss of the mooring rights in which to claim.

[1]   *[2002] 2 All ER 641.*
[2]   *[2001] 1 All ER 172, [2002] 1 WLR 598n, CA.* See also *Liverpool Roman Catholic Archdiocese Trustees v Goldberg [2001] 1 All ER 182.*

Inadvertent wrongdoing not within the subsection

[28.36]   The House of Lords, however, had no hesitation in reversing the Court of Appeal and in overruling *Brocklesby's* case. Lord Millett observed[1] that that decision would 'deprive a professional man, charged with having given negligent advice and who denies that his advice was wrong let alone negligent, of any effective limitation defence', and 'subverts the whole purpose of the Limitation Acts'. Instead, the correct construction of *section 32(2)* maintained the distinction 'between intentional wrong-doing on the one hand and negligence or inadvertent wrongdoing on the other'. Lord Millett concluded as follows[2]:

'In my opinion, s 32 of the 1980 Act deprives a defendant of a limitation defence in two situations: (i) where he takes active steps to conceal his own breach of duty after he has become aware of it; and (ii) where he is guilty of deliberate wrongdoing and conceals or fails to disclose it in circumstances where it is unlikely to be discovered for some time. But it does not deprive a defendant of a limitation defence where he is charged with negligence if, being unaware of his error or that he has failed to take proper care, there has been nothing for him to disclose'.

For *section 32(2)* to be relevant in a negligence action there must therefore be some factor, giving rise to the concealment, which is distinct from the defendant's initial act of carelessness itself.[3] It is now clear from *Cave's* case that the subsection does not deal with the problem which arises when it is in the nature of the defendant's activity itself that any negligence may not manifest itself for some time.[4]

[1]   See *[2002] 2 All ER 641* at paras 15–17.
[2]   See *[2002] 2 All ER 641* at paras 25. See also *per* Lord Scott of Foscote at para 31 onwards.
[3]   Cf *UBAF v European American Banking Corpn [1984] QB 713, [1984] 2 All ER 226, CA.*
[4]   For this, see 'Latent damage in cases other than personal injury', below at para [28.39]. The relevant provision (*section 14A of the Limitation Act 1980*) did not avail the claimant in *Cave's* case as the extended period of three years from discovery of his loss of the mooring rights which it accorded him had already been exhausted: see *[2002] 2 All ER 641* at para 55–56 *per* Lord Scott of Foscote.

Non-disclosure and concealment

[28.37] The defendant need not, however, have acted positively to conceal his carelessness for *section 32(1)(b)* of the *Limitation Act 1980* to apply.[1] Where he is in fact *aware* that he has been negligent (or even merely reckless as to whether he has been or not[2]), it may be enough that the defendant simply keeps it secret, if the relationship between the parties is such that non-disclosure would be unconscionable.[3] The equivalent provision in the *Limitation Act 1939* was applied in unusual circumstances in *Kitchen v Royal Air Forces Association*.[4] In 1946 the defendant solicitors negligently failed to bring an action on behalf of the plaintiff, against a tortfeasor, until it was impossible to do so. The tortfeasor, acting through the solicitors, subsequently made a modest ex gratia payment to the plaintiff on condition that the source of the payment was not disclosed to her. It was found as a fact that the defendants had accepted, and perhaps even themselves suggested, the secrecy requirement as a means of keeping from the plaintiff the fact of their earlier carelessness. The plaintiff did not discover what had happened until 1955, but the Court of Appeal held that the provision enabled her to sue the solicitors for their breach of duty nine years earlier. On the other hand, it has been held that merely requiring a person to sign a disclaimer, before the accident occurred, does not constitute concealment of a subsequent cause of action for negligence even if the disclaimer would have been invalid due to the provisions of the *Unfair Contracts Terms Act*[5].

[1]   It is to be noted that the expression 'deliberately concealed' is used in preference to the phrase 'concealed by fraud' in the equivalent provision (*section 26(b)*) of the *Limitation Act 1939*. This was in order to give effect to court decisions which had construed the earlier wording widely to extend to so-called 'equitable fraud': see the *Twenty-first Report of the Law Reform Committee (Final Report on Limitation of Actions)*, pp 6–16.
[2]   Cf *Beaman v ARTS Ltd [1949] 1 KB 550, [1949] 1 All ER 465, CA.*
[3]   See *King v Victor Parsons & Co [1973] 1 All ER 206, [1973] 1 WLR 29, CA.*
[4]   *[1958] 2 All ER 241, [1958] 1 WLR 563, CA.*
[5]   See *Skerratt v Linfax [2004] PIQR P10, CA.*

Not confined to contemporaneous concealment

[28.38] In *Sheldon v R H M Outhwaite (Underwriting Agencies)*[1] a cause of action accrued in 1982, but in 1984 the defendants took steps to conceal their breaches of duty from the plaintiffs, who did not issue their writ until 1990, ie more than six years after the original accrual of the cause of action. The defendants argued that the action was time-barred on the ground that *section 32(1)(b)* of the 1980 Act only applied to situations in which the concealment was contemporaneous with the accrual of the cause of action, since once time had actually started to run in a defendant's favour only an *express* statutory provision could actually *stop* it. The plaintiffs, however, contended that far from *stopping* the clock, the literal meaning of the subsection entailed that subsequent concealment would prevent time from running in the defendant's favour at all: in other words, the clock was 'turned back to zero even if the defendant had already acquired a limitation defence before the concealment took place'.[2] By a bare majority[3] the House of Lords accepted this argument and decided in favour of the plaintiffs: given that the choice[4] was either to treat the concealment as irrelevant or to deprive the defendant of the benefit of such time as had run in his favour prior to concealment, only the latter construction was felt to accord with the policy of the provision. If the defendants' contention had succeeded the effect would have been positively to encourage concealment.[5]

[1]   *[1996] AC 102, [1995] 2 All ER 558, HL.*

2   *[1996] AC 102* at 152, *[1995] 2 All ER 558* at 574, *per* Lord Nicholls.
3   Lord Keith, Lord Browne-Wilkinson and Lord Nicholls, Lord Mustill and Lord Lloyd dissenting. Their Lordships reversed a majority decision of the Court of Appeal.
4   The sensible course of stopping time from running when concealment occurred, but without depriving the defendant of the benefit of such time as had already run, was unfortunately considered to be precluded by the wording of the provision: see *[1996] AC 102* at 155, *[1995] 2 All ER 558* at 576, *per* Lord Nicholls.
5   See *[1995] 2 All ER 558* at 574, *per* Lord Nicholls. See also *per* Lord Browne-Wilkinson *[1995] 2 All ER 558* at 568.

D Latent damage in cases other than personal injury

Background

[28.39] The situation in which the limitation of actions is most likely to cause hardship is where 'damage' is deemed to have occurred, so as to create a cause of action, but nevertheless fails actually to manifest itself in a discoverable form until after the time limit has expired. Reform by statute to deal with the problem came first in the personal injuries field, in the form of the provisions already discussed. Legislative change to the basic rule outside that sphere came only with the passing of the *Latent Damage Act 1986*. The provisions of this Act are explained below. Nevertheless, ascertainment of the date on which damage occurred or is deemed to have occurred remains the starting point for the running of time in negligence cases, and may therefore necessarily still prove crucial in many situations in which limitation is in issue.

The *Pirelli* case

[28.40] Unfortunately, a degree of confusion crept into the law on the point at which damage occurred, largely as a result of a 1983 decision of the House of Lords in which questions relating to limitation became interwoven with the principles governing the recovery of economic loss in negligence, which were at that time in a state of flux. Although the economic loss issue has now been clarified, the precise effect of that clarification on the status of the case, *Pirelli General Cable Works Ltd v Oscar Faber & Partners*,[1] is not altogether clear. In *Pirelli* the defendant firm of consulting engineers negligently designed a chimney which was built for the plaintiffs. It was found as a fact that damage, in the form of cracks in the chimney, had actually occurred soon after it was built. Nevertheless, the cracks were at the very top of the chimney, and it was also found that they could not reasonably be regarded as having been actually discoverable until significantly later. The House of Lords held that time ran from the date at which the cracks first occurred, notwithstanding that they were then in practice undiscoverable, and in consequence the plaintiff's claim was statute-barred. At the time when *Pirelli* was decided it was a tenable view, which the case itself helped to reinforce, that economic loss caused by a building or chattel being merely defective, and not a source of damage to persons or *other* property, was recoverable in tort.[2] That assumption was, however, exploded by the decisions of the House of Lords itself in *D & F Estates Ltd v Church Comrs for England*[3] and *Murphy v Brentwood District Council*.[4]

1   *[1983] 2 AC 1*, *[1983] 1 All ER 65*. See E McKendrick '*Pirelli* re-examined' (1991) 11 LS 326.
2   Cf *Junior Books Ltd v Veitchi Co Ltd [1983] 1 AC 520, [1982] 3 All ER 201, HL*.
3   *[1989] AC 177, [1988] 2 All ER 992, HL*.

Negligent design

[28.41] The decision in *Pirelli General Cable Works Ltd v Oscar Faber & Partners*[1] has not actually been overruled.[2] It was referred to by Lord Keith in *Murphy v Brentwood District Council,*[3] who suggested that it could be considered as a *Hedley Byrne*-type of negligent misstatement case, rather than simply as one involving pure economic loss resulting from a defective product. On the other hand, if this is the correct interpretation, it is not altogether easy to see why time did not run from the *even earlier* date when the advice was acted upon by the commencement of the construction, rather than from the later date when cracks developed in the completed chimney.[4] Nevertheless, there is no actual presumption that damage occurs when advice is acted upon: it is a question of fact in each case.[5] Accordingly, the actual decision in *Pirelli* may still be correct if seen as one purely on limitation in a special type of negligent design case.[6] It was applied by Dyson J in *New Islington and Hackney Housing Association v Pollard Thomas and Edwards*[7] to hold that damage had occurred to the owners of a negligently designed building at the moment they had taken the building over, and not the later time when the defects became apparent. Dyson J observed that 'it is because a claimant can suffer loss without being aware of it that the Latent Damage Act 1986 was passed'[8].

¹   *[1983] 2 AC 1, [1983] 1 All ER 65, HL.*
²   The Privy Council has held, however, that 'it is not good law in New Zealand'. See *Invercargill City Council v Hamlin [1996] AC 624, [1996] 1 All ER 756*, in which the Judicial Committee held that tort claims for economic loss arising out of defective buildings are still possible in New Zealand (not following the *D & F Estates* and *Murphy* cases), and that the cause of action in a *Pirelli*-type situation only accrues 'when the cracks become so bad, or the defects so obvious, that any reasonable homeowner would call in an expert' rather than at the earlier date adopted by the House of Lords in the *Pirelli* case itself (see *per* Lord Lloyd delivering the judgment of the Board, *[1996] AC 624 at 648, [1996] 1 All ER 756 at 772–773*).
³   *[1991] 1 AC 398 at 466, [1990] 2 All ER 908 at 919, HL.*
⁴   Cf *Forster v Outred & Co [1982] 2 All ER 753, [1982] 1 WLR 86, CA.*
⁵   See *D W Moore & Co Ltd v Ferrier [1988] 1 All ER 400 at 410, [1988] 1 WLR 267 at 278, CA, per* Neill LJ.
⁶   Cf *Dove v Banhams Patent Locks Ltd [1983] 2 All ER 833, [1983] 1 WLR 1436*, in which a defective security system was installed in a house 13 years before its inadequacy became apparent when it was easily foiled by a burglar. Hodgson J held that time only ran from the date of the burglary. See also *Nitrigin Eireann Teoranta v Inco Alloys Ltd [1992] 1 All ER 854, [1992] 1 WLR 498.*
⁷   *[2001] Lloyd's Rep PN 243.*
⁸   See above at para 39.

Latent Damage Act 1986

[28.42] The limitation problem in cases of latent damage not involving personal injury was referred to the Law Reform Committee in 1980. The Committee reported in 1984,[1] and its recommendations formed the basis of the *Latent Damage Act 1986*[2]. The Act inserted two additional sections, *ss 14A* and *14B*, into the *Limitation Act 1980*. In addition, the 1986 Act made provision[3] to protect purchasers of property with latent defects who only acquire their interest after the cause of action has accrued but before the damage manifests itself. This was to overcome the difficulty that, not being owners at the time when the cause of action first accrued, such purchasers arguably had no cause of action at all.[4] Now they are given the same cause of action, *if any*, as if they had in fact had an interest in the property at the time when the original cause of action accrued in favour of their predecessor in title. Since, however, the scope for recovery in negligence of economic loss resulting from latent defects to property has been drastically curtailed by the common law since the Act was passed,[5] this particular provision is now unlikely to be invoked with any frequency.

[1]   Twenty-fourth Report (*Latent Damage*) (Cmnd 9390). For comment see M Jones, 'Latent Damage – Squaring the Circle?' (1985) 48 MLR 564. See also N J Mullany 'Reform of the Law of Latent Damage' (1991) 54 MLR 349, who compares the United Kingdom approach to the problem with that adopted in other Commonwealth jurisdictions.

[2]   The Act is applicable generally to latent damage claims in tort for negligence and is not confined, as some had apparently suggested when the reform was being considered, to the construction industry: see *Latent Damage*, Twenty-fourth Report of the Law Reform Committee (Cmnd 9390) para 4.22 (p 25).

[3]   In *section 3*.

[4]   See Professor G Robertson 'Defective Premises and Subsequent Purchasers' (1983) 99 LQR 599 and M Jones 'Defective Premises and Subsequent Purchasers – A Comment' (1984) 100 LQR 413.

[5]   Ie in *D & F Estates Ltd v Church Comrs for England [1989] AC 177, [1988] 2 All ER 992, HL* and *Murphy v Brentwood District Council [1991] 1 AC 398, [1990] 2 All ER 908, HL*. See generally CHAPTER 5 above.

Three-year extension

[28.43]   The new *section 14A* of the *Limitation Act 1980* provides that the basic principle continues to be that a six-year period runs from when damage occurs, but that this is subject to an *extension* of three years, in cases involving latent defects, from the date when the damage was actually discovered or reasonably could have been discovered.[1] Thus, a claimant in a case where damage only becomes discoverable at the end of the six-year period will be able to claim up to nine years after the damage actually occurred. A claimant in a case where the damage only became discoverable *after* the six-year period had already expired would have three years, from the date of discoverability, in which to claim. *Section 14A* also contains detailed provisions which, broadly speaking, are similar to those already in the 1980 Act for personal injury cases,[2] dealing with the meaning of 'knowledge' for the purposes of awareness of the existence of the damage[3]. It should be noted that the section is confined to actions in tort for negligence and does not extend to situations in which the claimant can claim only in contract.[4]

[1]   See *Hallam-Eames v Merrett [1996] 7 Med LR 122, CA*.

[2]   See above.

[3]   See *Oakes v Hopcraft [2000] Lloyd's Rep PN 946, CA*; *Mortgage Corp Plc v Lambert [2000] Lloyd's Rep PN 624, CA*; *Babicki v Rowlands [2002] Lloyd's Rep PN 121, CA*. See also *Graham v Entec Europe [2003] 4 All ER 1345, CA* (knowledge for the purposes of subrogation claims).

[4]   *Société Commerciale de Réassurance v ERAS Ltd [1992] 2 All ER 82n, CA*. See also *Iron Trade Mutual Insurance Co Ltd v J K Buckenham Ltd [1990] 1 All ER 808*. The point is less significant in view of the decision of the House of Lords in *Henderson v Merrett Syndicates Ltd [1995] 2 AC 145, [1994] 3 All ER 506* (see below at para [28.45]).

'Long stop'

[28.44]   The inserted *section 14B* of the *Limitation Act 1980* contains a very important 'long stop' provision to protect defendants in latent defect cases not involving personal injury. It provides that claims will in any event become statute-barred 15 years after the occurrence of the original act of negligence which gave rise to the damage, regardless of when that damage subsequently manifested itself and even if it only did so after the 15-year period itself had expired. Claims outside the 15-year period will only be possible in the event of fraud, concealment or mistake, or where the claimant had been under a disability.

Concurrent liability

[28.45] In *Henderson v Merrett Syndicates Ltd*[1] the House of Lords held that where the defendant's negligence also happens to constitute breach of a contract between himself and the claimant, the latter is free to choose to sue in either contract or tort. In contract time begins to run from the date of the breach, regardless of when damage occurred. Accordingly, a claimant able to sue either in tort or contract will potentially be in a more favourable position with respect to limitation than one able only to sue in contract, and in *Henderson*'s case itself the effect of their Lordships' decision was that the plaintiffs were able to take advantage of the later accrual of a cause of action in tort. In so holding, the House resolved uncertainty caused by earlier conflicting authorities: some cases favouring concurrent liability[2], and others apparently doubting it.[3] Those who opposed concurrent liability took the view that the contract between the parties should exclusively govern their relationship, including the applicability of the relevant limitation period. It is submitted, however, that the position established as a result of *Henderson v Merrett Syndicates Ltd* is to be welcomed as being consistent with the underlying pragmatism of the common law, given that differing limitation periods in fact exist for contract and tort. Thus, Lord Goff[4] characterised the rejection of concurrent liability as reflecting 'the temptation of elegance', and as leading 'to the startling possibility that a client who has had the benefit of gratuitous advice from his solicitor may in this respect be better off than a client who has paid a fee'.

[1] *[1995] 2 AC 145, [1994] 3 All ER 506.*
[2] See *Midland Bank Trust Co Ltd v Hett, Stubbs and Kemp [1979] Ch 384, [1978] 3 All ER 571*; *Batty v Metropolitan Property Realisations Ltd [1978] QB 554, [1978] 2 All ER 445, CA*. See also *Esso Petroleum Co Ltd v Mardon [1976] QB 801, [1976] 2 All ER 5, CA*.
[3] See *Tai Hing Cotton Mill Ltd v Liu Chong Hing Bank Ltd [1986] AC 80* at 107, *[1985] 2 All ER 947* at 957, *per* Lord Scarman. Cf *Bell v Peter Browne & Co [1990] 2 QB 495* at 511, *[1990] 3 All ER 124* at 134, CA, *per* Mustill LJ. See also *Bagot v Stevens Scanlan & Co Ltd [1966] 1 QB 197, [1964] 3 All ER 577*.
[4] See *[1995] 2 AC 145* at 186, *[1994] 3 All ER 506* at 525.

E Reform?

[28.46] The law relating to limitation of actions has been the subject of a thorough and wide-ranging review by the Law Commission.[1] The Commission's recommendations, in so far as they relate to the law of negligence, are in barest outline as follows. There should be a basic limitation period of three years running from the date of knowledge. But except in personal injury cases (in which there would be no long-stop at all), there should also be a long-stop period of ten years, which would run from the date of the accrual of the cause of action. The court would retain, in personal injury cases, the discretion currently contained in *section 33* of the *Limitation Act 1980* to disapply the limitation period.

[1] See *Limitation of Actions* (Law Com no 270, 2001).

Part ten

Redress for continuing interference

Chapter 29

Injunctions

A Introduction

[29.01] Claimants in 'negligence' cases will normally seek damages rather than an injunction. Nevertheless, the extent to which the underlying principles governing damages claims in negligence and nuisance have converged in recent times, and the fact that claimants in the latter will often seek both remedies, reinforces the artificiality of seeking to maintain any rigid distinction between the two torts. Moreover, even in cases not involving land use, claimants may sometimes seek *quia timet* injunctions as an interim remedy against conduct which they perceive to be dangerous. It is therefore both appropriate and necessary for injunctions to be dealt with in this book. Since the majority of injunction applications which fall within the subject-matter of the book relate to land use cases, however, it is convenient to retain the terminology of nuisance for the purposes of exposition.

Powerful weapon

[29.02] The injunction is the most powerful weapon in the armoury of the court in nuisance cases, and is a form of relief frequently awarded in such cases. It enables the court to order the immediate cessation of the activity giving rise to the nuisance but, as a discretionary remedy, it is highly flexible and can often enable the court to reach a balanced result which takes into account the interests of both parties and, where appropriate, those of the public. This is sometimes achieved by postponing the date of the effectiveness of the order, so as to give the defendant time to effect modifications and improvements and thereby obviate the source of complaint[1]. The remedy has proved useful in cases involving physical damage to property, such as subsidence caused by encroaching tree-roots[2], as well as in the more obvious situations of noise and smell giving rise to personal discomfort[3]. It proved particularly effective in cases arising out of the pollution of rivers[4]. In order to obtain an injunction to restrain a nuisance there must normally be a *threat* by the defendant to continue the nuisance. But the satisfaction of this requirement will usually be self-evident and will seldom give rise to difficulty[5]. An injunction may be awarded if the nuisance has ceased by the date of the trial, provided it existed at the time of action brought[6], but in such a case the court may well, in the exercise of its discretion, refuse to make an order[7]. The perpetual injunction enables a defendant to be restrained permanently from committing a nuisance[8], and may in certain circumstances be sought *quia timet* where interference is apprehended but has not yet occurred. Injunctions may take the form of both prohibitory and mandatory orders, the former being more common.

1   See *Pride of Derby and Derbyshire Angling Association Ltd v British Celanese Ltd [1953] Ch 149, [1953] 1 All ER 179*. For an interesting exercise of the discretion see *Great Central Rly Co v Doncaster Rural Council (1917) 87 LJ Ch 80, 118 LT 19* (injunction suspended until six months after the termination of the war).

2   See *McCombe v Read [1955] 2 QB 429, [1955] 2 All ER 458*.

3   See *Halsey v Esso Petroleum Co Ltd [1961] 2 All ER 145, [1961] 1 WLR 683*; *A-G v Gastonia Coaches Ltd [1977] RTR 219*.

4   See *per* Denning LJ in *Pride of Derby and Derbyshire Angling Association Ltd v British Celanese Ltd [1953] Ch 149* at 192, *[1953] 1 All ER 179* at 204. See also G H Newsom QC, 'River Pollution and the Law' (1969–72) 2 Otago LR 383 at 384–385: 'Over and over again I have seen cases in which the defendant … has asserted that the pollution is not curable, or not economically curable, right down to the moment when the injunction has been granted. Once that has occurred, the difficulties have vanished like the snow in springtime'.

5   But cf *Hawley v Steele (1877) 6 Ch D 521, 46 LJ Ch 782*.

6   See *Dean and Chapter of Chester v Smelting Corpn Ltd (1901) 85 LT 67*.

7   See *Barber v Penley [1893] 2 Ch 447, 62 LJ Ch 623*.

8   The practical effect of such an order may sometimes be not so much to stop the defendant as to enable the claimant to bargain for a high price as the cost of legitimising the activity: see Ogus and Richardson, 'Economics and the Environment' [1977] CLJ 284 at 293.

Interim injunctions

[29.03]   An injunction may be granted as an interim order to afford temporary relief to a claimant pending trial. A claimant who seeks an interim injunction must normally give an undertaking in damages to the defendant. The decision of the House of Lords in *American Cyanamid Co v Ethicon*[1] made it clear that the decision whether or not to award an interim injunction must be made on a broad basis of whether there is a serious issue to be tried, and where lies the balance of convenience between the parties. This case abrogated the previous rule requiring a plaintiff both to establish a prima facie case, and the threat of substantial and irreparable injury, before such an injunction could be awarded.

1   *[1975] AC 396, [1975] 1 All ER 504*.

B Exercise of the discretion

Degree of gravity

[29.04]   In general a claimant who proves a continuing violation of his common law rights, such that damages would be an inadequate remedy, will be granted a perpetual prohibitory injunction 'as a matter of course'[1]. This was established, in the context of nuisance, by the House of Lords in *Imperial Gas Light and Coke Co v Broadbent*[2]. It is not necessary for the claimant to prove that he has suffered loss quantifiable as damages[3]. An injunction may, however, be refused if the injury or inconvenience suffered by the claimant is regarded by the court as trivial or trifling[4].

1   *Per* Lord Campbell LC in *Imperial Gas Light and Coke Co v Broadbent (1859) 7 HL Cas 600* at 609. See also *per* Lord Evershed MR in *Pride of Derby and Derbyshire Angling Association v British Celanese Ltd [1953] Ch 149* at 181, *[1953] 1 All ER 179* at 197G–H.

2   *(1859) 7 HL Cas 600*.

3   See *Lyons, Sons & Co v Gulliver [1914] 1 Ch 631* at 641, *per* Cozens-Hardy MR; *Vanderpant v Mayfair Hotel Co Ltd [1930] 1 Ch 138* at 154, *per* Luxmoore J. See also *Bostock v North Staffordshire Rly Co (1852) 5 De G & Sm 584; A-G v Acton Local Board (1882) 22 Ch D 221; Mudge v Penge Urban Council (1916) 86 LJ Ch 126, 115 LT 679*.

4   See *Lillywhite v Trimmer (1867) 36 LJ Ch 525, 16 LT 318*. Cf *Llandudno UDC v Woods [1899] 2 Ch 705, 68 LJ Ch 623* and *Behrens v Richards [1905] 2 Ch 614, 74 LJ Ch 615* (trespass). See also

Wandsworth Board of Works v London and South Western Rly Co (1862) 31 LJ Ch 854; Swaine v Great Northern Rly Co (1864) 4 De G J & Sm 211, 3 New Rep 399; Cooke v Forbes (1867) LR 5 Eq 166, 37 LJ Ch 178.

Intermittent interference

[29.05] An injunction may also be refused on the ground that the interference is too intermittent to justify imposing what might amount to a total stoppage of his activities upon the defendant[1]. A claimant who has only suffered trifling and imperceptible injury may, however, be able to secure an injunction by showing that if relief is not granted the situation is likely to deteriorate, and might even enable the defendant to acquire a prescriptive right to commit substantial interference. In *Goldsmid v Tunbridge Wells Improvement Comrs*[2] the plaintiff was awarded an injunction to restrain the defendants from depositing sewage from their town into a stream which passed through his land. Although no substantial inconvenience had arisen it was pointed out that the size of the town was increasing, and that the potential nuisance was severe. Sir GJ Turner LJ said[3]:

> '... it is not in every case of nuisance that this court should interfere. I think that it ought not to do so in cases in which the injury is merely temporary and trifling; but I think it ought to do so in cases in which the injury is permanent and serious: and in determining whether the injury is serious or not, regard must be had to all the consequences which may flow from it'.

[1] See *Swaine v Great Northern Rly Co (1864) 4 De G J & Sm 211, 3 New Rep 399.*
[2] *(1866) 1 Ch App 349, 35 LJ Ch 382.*
[3] *(1866) 1 Ch App 349 at 354–355.*

Public interest

[29.06] In exercising its discretion the court will take into account the balance of convenience between the parties, and also the effect upon the public generally if an injunction is granted[1]. In the controversial 1977 decision of the Court of Appeal in *Miller v Jackson*[2] it was suggested that the court is now prepared to attach rather more weight than formerly to the public interest, and correspondingly less to the need to vindicate private rights, where the two factors seem to be in conflict. In *Miller's* case the Court, by a majority, refused an injunction to a plaintiff on to whose house and garden balls from an adjacent cricket-pitch were apt to fall on most summer weekends. Lord Denning MR said[3]:

> 'There is a contest here between the interest of the public at large; and the interest of a private individual. The *public* interest lies in protecting the environment by preserving our playing fields in the face of mounting development, and by enabling our youth to enjoy all the benefits of outdoor games, such as cricket and football. The *private* interest lies in securing the privacy of his home and garden without intrusion or interference by anyone ... As between their conflicting interests, I am of opinion that the public interest should prevail over the private interest'.

[1] See Spry *Equitable Remedies* (4th edn), pp 461–465.
[2] *[1977] QB 966, [1977] 3 All ER 338.* See ante, Chapter 23.
[3] *[1977] QB 966* at 981G–982B, *[1977] 3 All ER 338* at 345a–e (the italics are those of Lord Denning).

Rarely succeeded in earlier cases

[29.07] Although the public interest has always been a relevant factor in injunction cases, the earlier authorities tended to regard it as one which could tip the balance only if the inconvenience suffered by the plaintiff was relatively slight[1]. It rarely succeeded in preventing the grant of relief in situations involving serious nuisances. Pleas based on the argument *ab inconvenienti* in such cases normally met with the response that the defendants should take steps to secure legislative protection[2]. In *Manchester Corpn v Farnworth*[3] the House of Lords upheld the grant of an injunction against the appellant corporation, to restrain them from committing a nuisance by the emission of poisonous fumes from a power station. The argument that the effect of the order would be to impose an unconscionable burden on the people of Manchester was of no avail. Viscount Sumner said[4]:

> 'The nature and degree of the plaintiff's suffering and the cost, trouble and inconvenience to the defendant corporation of saving him from it are elements on the two sides of the case, which must be considered in deciding what is reasonable, but I cannot see that either on principle or on authority it is a sufficient answer to a criticism, otherwise sound, to say that, if so, Manchester's electricity would cost it more ... I do not know by what authority, short of the express direction of the legislature, the interests of the public are thus summarily to override the rights of the individual'[5].

1   See *Lillywhite v Trimmer (1867) 36 LJ Ch 525, 16 LT 318*; *Wandsworth Board of Works v London and South Western Rly Co (1862) 31 LJ Ch 854*. Cf *Swindon Waterworks Co v Wilts and Berks Canal Navigation Co (1875) LR 7 HL 697, 45 LJ Ch 638*.
2   See *A-G v Birmingham Borough Council (1858) 4 K & J 528* at 541 *per* Page-Wood V-C ('if the case be one of such magnitude as it is represented to be, Parliament ... will take measures accordingly'). See also *Prices Patent Candle Co Ltd v LCC [1908] 2 Ch 526* at 550.
3   *[1930] AC 171, 99 LJKB 83*. See also *Colwell v St Pancras Borough Council [1904] 1 Ch 707, 73 LJ Ch 275*; *Wood v Conway Corpn [1914] 2 Ch 47, 83 LJ Ch 498*.
4   *[1930] AC* at 194–195.
5   See *Bellew v Irish Cement Ltd [1948] IR 61* (interlocutory injunction granted to restrain blasting at a quarry for several months even though this would seriously interrupt Ireland's supply of cement, four-fifths of which came from the quarry).

Dicta in Miller v Jackson doubted

[29.08] Insistence upon the protection of private rights as rigorous as that favoured in some of the earlier authorities is unlikely to be considered appropriate today[1]. In *Dennis v Ministry of Defence*[2], decided in 2003, the court held that a serious noise nuisance caused by the training of jet pilots for the RAF would be allowed to continue in the national interest, and the claimants confined to damages. Buckley J said:

> 'As this case illustrates, the greater the public interest, the greater the interference. If public interest is considered at the remedy stage and since the court has a discretion, the nuisance may continue but the public, in one way or another, pays for its own benefit'[3].

It nevertheless seems to be clear that the factor of public interest has not attained as dominant a position, in applications for injunctions, as the majority in *Miller v Jackson* appeared to hold. The situation in that case could not be regarded as trifling since it involved the inevitability of continuing damage to property and a clear risk of personal injury[4]. Moreover one member of the court, Geoffrey Lane LJ, dissented, and would have granted an injunction, while another appears to have been under a misapprehension as to the state of the relevant authorities[5]. In the later case of *Kennaway v Thompson*[6] the activities of the defendants' motor boat racing club, on a lake near to the plaintiff's house, caused a nuisance by noise which the trial judge, Mais J, described as 'quite intolerable and wholly unreasonable'. Nevertheless his Lordship refused an injunction on the ground, inter alia, that there was 'considerable public interest' in the club and that the public attended its activities in large numbers. His Lordship awarded £15,000 damages for future interference in lieu of an injunction. The defendant accepted the finding on liability, but the plaintiff appealed successfully against denial of an injunction. The Court of Appeal, in a single judgment of the Court[7], disapproved Lord Denning's statement in *Miller v Jackson* that the public interest should prevail over the private interest, and granted an injunction[8]. It is submitted that the approach of adopted in *Kennaway's* case is to be preferred. The proposition that an injunction should be refused on grounds of public interest will rarely avail defendants fighting disputes of a commercial or similar nature, but it may occasionally assist those exercising governmental or related powers[9].

[1] For a striking Canadian decision turning on the public interest, see *Bottom v Ontario Leaf Tobacco Co [1935] 2 DLR 699* (injunction refused against a factory on the ground that its closure would increase unemployment).

[2] *[2003] EWHC 793 (QB)*.

[3] See above at para 46.

[4] See *[1977] QB 966* at 987C–E, *[1977] 3 All ER 338* at 349e–f, *per* Geoffrey Lane LJ.

[5] Cumming-Bruce LJ, refusing an injunction, relied upon a dictum of Lord Romilly MR in *Raphael v Thames Valley Rly Co (1866) LR 2 Eq 37* at 46 in which the Master of the Rolls refused a decree of specific performance in an action against a railway company on the ground that inconvenience would be caused to members of the public generally if it were granted. Lord Romilly's decision was, however, subsequently reversed and a decree was granted: see *(1867) 2 Ch App 147*. In his judgment on the appeal Lord Chelmsford LC expressly stated that on the facts of the case the element of public inconvenience should *not* have been taken into account: see *(1867) 2 Ch App 147* at 151. Cumming-Bruce LJ does not mention that Lord Romilly's decision was reversed.

[6] *[1981] QB 88, [1980] 3 All ER 329*. Noted by the present writer in (1981) 44 MLR 212.

[7] Lawton and Waller LJJ and Sir David Cairns.

[8] In *Elliott v London Borough of Islington [1991] 1 EGLR 167* at 169 Lord Donaldson MR said: ' ... it is not generally appropriate that specific private rights should be denied in order to give rise to indefinite advantages to the general public. Were it otherwise, the court would, as I see it, be legislating to deprive people of their rights'. See also *Tetley v Chitty [1986] 1 All ER 663* (go-kart racing) ' ... damages would be a wholly insufficient remedy here ... ': *per* McNeill J at 675.

[9] See *Dennis v Ministry of Defence [2003] EWHC 793 (QB)*. See also *Gillingham Borough Council v Medway (Chatham) Dock Co Ltd [1993] QB 343* at 364, *[1992] 3 All ER 923* at 937–938 (public interest in maintaining dock facility). Cf *Marcic v Thames Water Utilities [2004] 1 All ER 135*.

C Quia timet injunctions

Apprehended acts

[29.09] *Quia timet* injunctions exist to restrain the commission of apprehended acts which, if allowed to take place, would be likely to cause actionable damage or inconvenience. In *Hooper v Rogers*[1] the defendant, using a bulldozer, deepened a track on land surrounding the plaintiff's farmhouse. This had the effect of exposing the land to a process of soil erosion, which would lead eventually to support being withdrawn from the farmhouse causing it to collapse. The Court of Appeal held that in this situation a mandatory *quia timet* injunction could be awarded to compel the defendant to reinstate the ground[2]. The defendant argued, without success, that the danger was not sufficiently imminent to warrant an injunction.

[1] *[1975] Ch 43, [1974] 3 All ER 417*.

2   The plaintiff was in fact awarded damages in lieu of an injunction but this does not affect the point in the text.

Question of fact

[29.10]   The precise degree of likelihood of danger necessary to justify relief can, however, give rise to difficult questions of fact, and *Hooper v Rogers* should be contrasted with the earlier case of *Fletcher v Bealey*[1]. The plaintiff in this case was a riparian owner who used water from the river in his paper-manufacturing process. The defendants were alkali manufacturers and were in the habit of depositing heaps of refuse on to their land, which was close to the river about a mile and a half upstream from the plaintiff's mill. It was proved that within a few years a noxious liquid would begin to flow from the heap, and that if this should find its way into the river to any appreciable extent the water would be rendered unfit for use in the plaintiff's process; and his trade would be ruined. The plaintiff had not as yet suffered any actual injury, and the defendants said that they intended to take all proper precautions to prevent the liquid from getting into the river. Pearson J stated the law as follows[2]:

' ... there are at least two necessary ingredients for a *quia timet* action. There must, if no actual damage is proved, be proof of imminent danger, and there must also be proof that the apprehended danger will, if it comes, be very substantial. I should almost say it must be proved that it will be irreparable, because, if the damage is not proved to be so imminent that no one can doubt that, if the remedy is delayed, the damage will be suffered, I think it must be shewn that, if the damage does occur at any time, it will come in such a way and under such circumstances that it will be impossible for the plaintiff to protect himself against it if relief is denied to him in a *quia timet* action'[3].

Since it was possible by the use of due care to prevent the liquid from flowing into the river, and it was also conceivable that by the time it began to flow from the heap some method of rendering it innocuous might have been devised, the action was dismissed; but without prejudice to the plaintiff's right to bring fresh proceedings subsequently should the situation warrant it[4].

1   *(1885) 28 Ch D 688, 54 LJ Ch 424.*
2   *(1885) 28 Ch D 688 at 698.*
3   The notion of 'irreparable damage' in this context does *not* mean 'that there must be no physical possibility of repairing the damage' but merely that 'the damage must be substantial and one which would not be adequately remedied by a pecuniary payment': *per* PO Lawrence J in *Litchfield-Speer v Queen Anne's Gate Syndicate (No 2) Ltd [1919] 1 Ch 407* at 411.
4   See also *Haines v Taylor (1846) 10 Beav 75*; *Kinney v Hove Corpn (1950) 49 LGR 696* (remote risk of animals escaping not a legitimate ground to prevent the holding of a circus). Cf *Luscombe v Steer (1867) 17 LT 229.*

Need for rational basis

[29.11]   Even if the supposed danger is imminent a *quia timet* action will fail if the fear cannot be shown to have a secure scientific or rational basis. In refusing for this reason to grant a *quia timet* injunction to restrain the building of a smallpox hospital on grounds of fear of infection Chitty J said that 'the principle which I think may be properly and safely extracted from the *quia timet* authorities is, that the plaintiff must shew a strong case of probability that the apprehended mischief will, in fact, arise'[1].

1   *A-G v Manchester Corpn [1893] 2 Ch 87* at 92. See also *A-G v Nottingham Corpn [1904] 1 Ch 673*, *73 LJ Ch 512*.

D Mandatory injunctions

Cautious approach

[29.12] Since mandatory injunctions are much more drastic in their effect than prohibitory orders[1], requiring the taking of positive steps such as the demolition of property, the granting of them is 'attended with the greatest possible caution'[2]. Although both types of remedy are discretionary a claimant who makes out his case is normally entitled to a negative order 'as of course'. The position is different with respect to mandatory injunctions[3]. In *Durell v Pritchard*[4] Turner LJ said:

> ' ... this court will not interfere by way of mandatory injunction, except in cases in which extreme, or at all events very serious, damage will ensue from its interference being withheld'.

1   A negative order can in practice also prove very onerous on the defendant. For example, a prohibitory injunction in a case involving pollution of a river by sewage may put the defendant to great expense to prevent the nuisance. Cf *per* Lord Upjohn in *Redland Bricks Ltd v Morris [1970] AC 652* at 664E, *[1969] 2 All ER 576* at 578G.
2   *Per* Lord Westbury LC in *Isenberg v East India House Estate Co (1863) 3 De G J & Sm 263* at 272.
3   See *Redland Bricks Ltd v Morris [1970] AC 652* at 665F, *[1969] 2 All ER 576* at 579G, *per* Lord Upjohn.
4   *(1865) 1 Ch App 244* at 250.

Requirements

[29.13] It is, of course, a necessary condition for a mandatory order that damages will not be a sufficient or adequate remedy[1]. There is no actual rule preventing the award of a mandatory injunction on an interim application; but the court is inevitably far more reluctant to grant mandatory than prohibitory orders in such circumstances, and 'the case has to be unusually strong and clear before a mandatory injunction will be granted'[2] at the interlocutory stage. Nor is there any rule preventing a claimant who could have applied for interim relief before the defendants' work reached an advanced stage, but failed to do so, from securing a mandatory injunction to bring about, eg the demolition of completed buildings[3]. Nevertheless in accordance with ordinary equitable principles of laches and acquiescence any unnecessary delay will tell heavily against the claimant in such a case[4]. Moreover the court is, in practice, extremely reluctant to order the demolition of property[5] and has, in its discretion, refused to do so even in circumstances in which defendants have gone ahead deliberately and with full knowledge of the risks they were taking[6]. But such behaviour is clearly a relevant factor to be weighed in the balance against the defendant[7], and in one case Brightman J warned of a 'rude awakening' which may await developers who choose to build in deliberate disregard of restrictive convenants[8].

1   See *Redland Bricks Ltd v Morris [1970] AC 652* at 665H, *[1969] 2 All ER 576* at 579H, *per* Lord Upjohn.
2   *Per* Megarry J in *Shepherd Homes Ltd v Sandham [1971] Ch 340* at 349B, *[1970] 3 All ER 402* at 409h.
3   See *Wrotham Park Estate Co v Parkside Homes Ltd [1974] 2 All ER 321* at 337f, *[1974] 1 WLR 798* at 810H–811A, *per* Brightman J. See also *Durell v Pritchard (1865) 1 Ch App 244*, 35 L J Ch 223.
4   Cf *Shepherd Homes Ltd v Sandham [1971] Ch 340* at 349C–D, *[1970] 3 All ER 402* at 409h–410a, *per* Megarry J. See also *Wrotham Park Estate Co v Parkside Homes Ltd [1974] 2 All ER 321* at 337d–g, *[1974] 1 WLR 798* at 810G–811A, *per* Brightman J.

[5] See *per* Brightman J in *Wrotham Park Estate Co v Parkside Homes Ltd [1974] 2 All ER 321* at 337g, *[1974] 1 WLR 798* at 811B: 'an unpardonable waste of much needed houses'.

[6] See *Isenberg v East India House Estate Co (1863) 3 De G J & Sm 263*; *Wrotham Park Estate Co v Parkside Homes Ltd [1974] 2 All ER 321, [1974] 1 WLR 798.* Cf *Charrington v Simons & Co [1970] 2 All ER 257* at 261–262, *[1970] 1 WLR 725* at 730.

[7] See note 2 below in para [29.14], and references there given.

[8] See *Wrotham Park Estate Co v Parkside Homes Ltd [1974] 2 All ER 321* at 338a, *[1974] 1 WLR 798* at 811C. See also *Daniel v Ferguson [1891] 2 Ch 27* and *Von Joel v Hornsey [1895] 2 Ch 774, 65 LJ Ch 102* (interlocutory mandatory injunctions for the demolition of buildings awarded).

Where cost disproportionate

[29.14] If the cost of doing the work is very high relative to the value of the land affected this will be a factor against the award of a mandatory injunction if the defendant's conduct, albeit wrongful, had not been unreasonable[1]. But it will carry little weight if the defendant 'acted wantonly and quite unreasonably in relation to his neighbour'[2].

[1] See *Redland Bricks Ltd v Morris [1970] AC 652, [1969] 2 All ER 576.*

[2] See *per* Lord Upjohn in *Redland Bricks Ltd v Morris [1970] AC 652* at 666B, *[1969] 2 All ER 576* at 580A. Cf *Woodhouse v Newry Navigation Co [1898] 1 IR 161.*

Need for clarity

[29.15] It is important that a person against whom a mandatory order is granted knows exactly what is required[1]. In *Redland Bricks Ltd v Morris*[2] the defendant brick company excavated earth and clay on land which adjoined the plaintiffs' market garden. The plaintiffs' land lost support as a result and started to slip. The trial judge ordered the defendants to refill the excavated land in order to make good the damage, but the House of Lords reversed his decision. The judge's order had been in such general terms, imposing an unqualified obligation upon the defendants to restore support to the land, that it was impossible to tell exactly what works the defendants would have to carry out in order to comply with it. The *Redland* case therefore reaffirmed the familiar principle that the court will not make a vague order for a series of operations which it cannot supervise.

[1] See *per* Maugham LJ in *Fishenden v Higgs and Hill Ltd (1935) 153 LT 128* at 142 cited with approval in *Redland Bricks Ltd v Morris [1970] AC 652* at 667B, *[1969] 2 All ER 576* at 580H.

[2] *[1970] AC 652, [1969] 2 All ER 576.*

Plans in complicated cases

[29.16] Nevertheless there is no objection to making an order for remedial measures, where appropriate, in situations similar to that in the *Redland* case provided that 'the work to be done', as Sargant J emphasised when awarding a mandatory injunction against a colliery company whose tipping had caused a landslide, 'is quite specific and definite, and no real difficulty can be reasonably apprehended in ascertaining whether the defendants have complied with … the order or not'[1]. In complicated cases the court may make its order with reference to plans drawn up by an expert appointed for the purpose[2].

[1] See *Kennard v Cory Bros & Co Ltd [1922] 1 Ch 265* at 274; affd *[1922] 2 Ch 1, 91 LJ Ch 452* and cited with approval in *Redland Bricks Ltd v Morris [1970] AC 652* at 666E–F, *[1969] 2 All ER 576* at 580D–E, *Kennard v Cory Bros & Co Ltd* was the sequel to the decision of the House of Lords in *A-G v Cory Bros & Co Ltd [1921] AC 521, 90 LJ Ch 221.*

² See *Redland Bricks Ltd v Morris [1970] AC 652* at 667A, *[1969] 2 All ER 576* at 580G. See also *Kennard v Cory Bros & Co Ltd [1922] 1 Ch 265* at 274–275, *per* Sargant J.

E Damages in lieu of injunction[1]

Compensation for future annoyance

[29.17]   The common law regarded future annoyance, even where emanating from an existing nuisance which had already given rise to a cause of action, as necessitating the bringing of a series of actions for damages; rather than a single action in which compensation for future losses could be awarded. Until 1858 the only satisfactory remedy in such cases was therefore the award by the Court of Chancery of an injunction. The *Chancery Amendment Act* of that year (familiarly known as 'Lord Cairns' Act'), however, gave the Court of Chancery the power to award damages in lieu of an injunction[2]. One of the consequences of this Act is that damages for future losses, to which continuance of the nuisance is likely to give rise, can be awarded[3]. Moreover, since the jurisdiction extends to *quia timet* injunctions[4], it also enables compensation to be paid to a claimant who does not even enjoy an existing cause of action at common law. The effect of an award under the Act is that the defendant in practice acquires the right to commit the nuisance[5].

¹   See Tromans 'Nuisance-Prevention or Payment' [1982] CLJ 87; Jolowicz, 'Damages in Equity – A Study of Lord Cairns' Act' (1975) 38 CLJ 224.

²   See *section 2*. It has long been clear that the jurisdiction to which it gave rise survived the repeal of the Act itself: see *Leeds Industrial Co-operative Society Ltd v Slack [1924] AC 851, 93 LJ Ch 436*. The jurisdiction is now exercised under *section 50* of the *Supreme Court Act 1981*.

³   See, generally, *Jaggard v Sawyer [1995] 2 All ER 189, [1995] 1 WLR 269* in which the principles governing the exercise of the jurisdiction were reviewed by the Court of Appeal.

⁴   *Leeds Industrial Co-operative Society Ltd v Slack [1924] AC 851, 93 LJ Ch 436*.

⁵   While claimants often understandably express opposition to awards for this reason, disingenuous attempts by *defendants* to invoke it as an argument against being ordered to pay damages will receive less sympathy from the court: *Sampson v Hodson-Pressinger [1981] 3 All ER 710* at 715, CA *per* Eveleigh LJ.

Shelfer v City of London Electric Lighting Co

[29.18]   The manner in which the discretion conferred by Lord Cairns' Act should be exercised was considered by the Court of Appeal in the well-known case of *Shelfer v City of London Electric Lighting Co*[1]. The plaintiff complained of vibration and noise from works operated by the defendant company near to his house. Kekewich J, at first instance, held that the plaintiff had a good cause of action in nuisance, but exercised his jurisdiction under the Act and awarded damages only and refused an injunction. The Court of Appeal reversed his decision on the discretion point and awarded an injunction. Lindley LJ said[2] that in cases of 'continuing actionable nuisances' the jurisdiction to refuse an injunction and award damages instead 'ought not to be exercised ... except under very exceptional circumstances'[3]. He referred by way of example to 'trivial and occasional nuisances', and situations involving oppressive or vexatious behaviour on the plaintiff's part. A L Smith LJ expressed himself as follows[4]:

'In my opinion, it may be stated as a good working rule that –

(1)   If the injury to the plaintiff's legal rights is small[5],

(2)   And is one which is capable of being estimated in money,

(3)   And is one which can be adequately compensated by a small money payment,

(4)   And the case is one in which it would be oppressive to the defendant to grant an injunction[6]; then damages in substitution for an injunction may be given'.

His Lordship also pointed out that, even if the four conditions *were* satisfied, a defendant who had acted 'with a reckless disregard to the plaintiff's rights' might nevertheless still find himself subjected to an injunction[7].

[1]   *[1895] 1 Ch 287.*
[2]   *[1895] 1 Ch 287 at 316–317.*
[3]   For a striking illustration of the reluctance of the court to exercise the jurisdiction in a defendant's favour in a serious case of continuing nuisance, see *Wood v Conway Corpn [1914] 2 Ch 47, 83 LJ Ch 498, CA.* See also *Maberley v Peabody & Co of London Ltd [1946] 2 All ER 192.*
[4]   *[1895] 1 Ch 287 at 322–323.*
[5]   In *Elliott v London Borough of Islington [1991] 1 EGLR 167* in which the defendants' tree pressed against the plaintiffs' garden wall, the Court of Appeal rejected a submission that an injunction should be refused: 'I am very far from satisfied that the injury to the plaintiff's legal rights is small. I think it is very considerable. In inches, no doubt, his wall has only been moved a relatively small distance, but … I am very far from accepting that the injury to the plaintiff's legal rights is small in having this tree pushing his wall in the way in which it is common ground that it does' *per* Lord Donaldson MR at 168.
[6]   'It is important to bear in mind that the test is one of oppression, and the court should not slide into application of a general balance of convenience test': *per* Sir Thomas Bingham MR in *Jaggard v Sawyer [1995] 2 All ER 189* at 203, *[1995] 1 WLR 269* at 283.
[7]   Cf *Pugh v Howells (1984) 48 P & CR 298, CA.*

Shelfer principles not applicable in all cases

[**29.19**]   It would be wrong to suppose that, wherever the conditions laid down in *Shelfer v City of London Electric Lighting Co*[1] are *not* satisfied, the claimant may expect to be awarded an injunction virtually as of right. A claimant may still be deprived of an injunction in such a case on general discretionary grounds[2]. This point has sometimes been overlooked. In *Kennaway v Thompson*[3] failure by the defendant to bring the case within the conditions enunciated in the *Shelfer* case appears almost to have been treated as entitling the plaintiff to an injunction[4]. The question arises whether a claimant to whom an injunction probably would have been refused in any event can be awarded damages under the *Chancery Amendment Act 1858*. The answer seems to be that provided the court would have had *jurisdiction* to grant an injunction[5], at the date of the claim form, then the Act can be invoked notwithstanding that the actual grant of an injunction would have been unlikely[6]. But to satisfy the jurisdiction requirement the claimant must 'establish a case for equitable relief, not only by proving his legal right and an actual or threatened infringement by the defendant, but also by overcoming all equitable defences such as laches, acquiescence or estoppel'[7]. Once these established defences have been negatived, however, a broad interpretation of the court's powers under the Act seems to be adopted[8]. In *Miller v Jackson*[9] Cumming Bruce LJ appears to have assumed that this was the position since he favoured refusal of an injunction on grounds of public interest, and yet the award of damages in lieu[10].

[1]   See above at para [29.18].
[2]   See *Redland Bricks Ltd v Morris [1970] AC 652, [1969] 2 All ER 576.*
[3]   *[1981] QB 88, [1980] 3 All ER 329.* Cf the reversed decision of the Court of Appeal in *Morris v Redland Bricks Ltd [1967] 3 All ER 1, [1967] 1 WLR 967.*

4   See *[1981] QB 88* at 93B–H, *[1980] 3 All ER* at 332g–333c, sed quaere. The actual *decision* in *Kennaway's* case, to grant an injunction, was, however, almost certainly correct, see above at para [29.08].

5   Cf *Proctor v Bayley (1889) 42 Ch D 390* at 401, *per* Fry LJ. See also *Lavery v Pursell (1888) 39 Ch D 508* at 519, *per* Chitty J (damages refused).

6   See *Jaggard v Sawyer [1995] 2 All ER 189* at 205, *[1995] 1 WLR 269* at 285, *per* Millett LJ. See also *Hooper v Rogers [1975] Ch 43* at 48, *[1974] 3 All ER 417* at 419, *per* Russell LJ.

7   *Per* Millett LJ in *Jaggard v Sawyer [1995] 2 All ER 189* at 208, *[1995] 1 WLR 269* at 287.

8   See Spry, *Equitable Remedies* (4th edn), p 617 onwards. See also *Eastwood v Lever (1863) 4 De G J & Sm 114, 3 New Rep 232.* Cf *Elmore v Pirrie (1887) 57 LT 333* at 335–336, *per* Kay J. See also Jolowicz, 'Damages in Equity – A Study of Lord Cairns' Act' (1975) 34 CLJ 224 at 241 onwards.

9   *[1977] QB 966* at 988. Cf *Bottom v Ontario Leaf Tobacco Co [1935] 2 DLR 699 (Can).*

10 See also *per* Graham J in *Bracewell v Appleby [1975] Ch 408* at 419C, *[1975] 1 All ER 993* at 999j–1000a. Cf *Price v Strange [1978] Ch 337, [1977] 3 All ER 371.*

Scope of the jurisdiction

[29.20]   The limiting conditions laid down in the *Shelfer* case should therefore be confined to situations in which, but for the statutory jurisdiction, the claimant would have enjoyed a clear and legitimate expectation that equitable relief would be granted to him. The conditions are not a comprehensive statement of the situations in which the jurisdiction can be exercised[1]. It is submitted that damages in lieu may therefore be awarded to a claimant deprived by discretion of an injunction on, say, general public interest grounds in circumstances in which the injury was *not* small or capable of being adequately compensated by a small money payment etc[2]. The assessment of damages in such cases is, however, potentially a matter of some difficulty which has never been fully explored[3]. But in the more usual type of case, governed by the *Shelfer* principles, the correct approach to assessing damages under the Act is to consider what sum a reasonable claimant might have charged as the price of consenting to the defendant's activities[4].

1   See *per* Romer LJ in *Fishenden v Higgs and Hill Ltd (1935) 153 LT 128* at 141.

2   Cf Tromans 'Nuisance-Prevention or Payment' [1982] CLJ 87.

3   Cf the uncertainty surrounding the award of damages for loss of amenity in nuisance cases, considered in CHAPTER 27 above.

4   See *Jaggard v Sawyer [1995] 2 All ER 189* applying *Wrotham Park Estate Co v Parkside Homes Ltd [1974] 2 All ER 321, [1974] 1 WLR 798.* Although these were cases of trespass the same approach would seem to be applicable in nuisance cases; it was adopted in *Carr-Saunders v Dick McNeil Associates Ltd [1986] 2 All ER 888* to a case involving interference with a right to light.

F Procedure

Form of the order

[29.21]   It is usual for injunctions in nuisance cases to include a phrase enjoining the defendant 'not to cause a nuisance' or similar words equally general in effect[1]. Although this language will be qualified by the rest of the order, which will be as specific in its terms as circumstances allow[2], the fact that nuisance is invariably a question of degree will often make it impossible to define with precision the exact point at which interference becomes wrongful. Nevertheless the court will not readily sympathise with the argument that the unavoidable uncertainty this may sometimes cause would constitute such hardship to the defendant as should prevent an injunction from being granted[3]. The court may occasionally seek to assist the parties, when granting an injunction in general terms, by stating in advance that it would not consider the order to have been broken if the defendant were to carry out his activity in a certain way[4]. The main focus of the order, however, will normally be the external impact which the defendant's activity has upon the claimant. The court will rarely attempt to specify what modifications, if any, should be made to the defendant's process or activity to avoid commission of the nuisance. 'It is not for this court', said Donaldson J in *Shoreham-By-Sea UDC v Dolphin Canadian Proteins Ltd*[5], 'to adopt the role of technical adviser and say that particular measures have to be taken'[6].

[1]   See generally Atkin's Court Forms vol 22 (1) (2001 Issue) INJUNCTIONS. See also discussion by the Court of Appeal of the appropriate form of order in *Thompson-Schwab v Costaki [1956] 1 All ER 652, [1956] 1 WLR 335.*

[2]   For an example of a very specific order, see *Kennaway v Thompson [1981] QB 88, [1980] 3 All ER 329.* See also *Shotts Iron Co v Inglis (1882) 7 App Cas 518, 9 R (HL) 78.* It is not uncommon for orders to be made with respect to specific *hours*, especially when sleep has been disturbed at night-time: see *Halsey v Esso Petroleum Co Ltd [1961] 2 All ER 145, [1961] 1 WLR 683; Vanderpant v Mayfair Hotel Co Ltd [1930] 1 Ch 138, 99 LJ Ch 84.* See also *Dunton v Dover District Council (1977) 76 LGR 87.*

[3]   See *Hampstead and Suburban Properties v Diomedous [1969] 1 Ch 248 at 257, [1968] 3 All ER 545 at 549 per* Megarry J ('The court is always slow to repose on the easy pillow of uncertainty').

[4]   See *Leeman v Montagu [1936] 2 All ER 1677, per* Greaves-Lord J. But cf *Walker v Brewster (1867) LR 5 Eq 25 at 34.*

[5]   *(1972) 71 LGR 261 at 268.*

[6]   See *Tetley v Chitty [1986] 1 All ER 663 at 675 per* McNeill J: ' … it is not, I think, for this court to work out for defendants at fault the way in which they can continue an operation which, as … it has been continued, was an offending operation'. Cf *Fleming v Hislop (1886) 11 App Cas 686.*

Public nuisances

[29.22]   An individual who suffers special damage as a result of a public nuisance can seek an injunction, as well as damages, in his own right, ie without the need to bring a relator action with the aid of the Attorney-General[1]. In the absence of special damage, however, he cannot bring civil proceedings in respect of a public nuisance without the assistance of the Attorney-General to overcome his lack of locus standi[2].

[1]   See *Spencer v London and Birmingham Rly (1836) 8 Sim 193, 7 LJ Ch 281; Soltau v De Held (1851) 2 Sim NS 133, 21 LJ Ch 153.*

[2]   See *Gouriet v Union of Post Office Workers [1978] AC 435, [1977] 3 All ER 70.* See also *Vanderpant v Mayfair Hotel Co Ltd [1930] 1 Ch 138 at 153–154.*

Local authorities

[29.23]   Formerly the position of local authorities was no different from that of a private citizen. Except in special cases provided for by statute[1], a local authority had to show special damage, or join the Attorney-General in a relator action[2], unless it could maintain an action in *private* nuisance on the ground that the matters complained of affected land which was in the ownership of the authority. An authority did not, merely as such, have locus standi to enforce public rights for the protection of its inhabitants[3]. The position is now, however, governed by the *Local Government Act 1972, s 222(1)(a)* which enables such authorities to institute 'civil proceedings' in their own name to protect the interests of their inhabitants[4]. It seems to be clear that an injunction to restrain a public nuisance is a 'civil proceeding', even in the absence of special damage, notwithstanding that public nuisance is a crime[5].

[1]   Eg *Public Health Act 1936, s 100.* See now *the Environmental Protection Act 1990, s 80(4).*

[2]   See *A-G v PYA Quarries [1957] 2 QB 169, [1957] 1 All ER 894; A-G v Cory Bros & Co Ltd [1921] 1 AC 521, 90 LJ Ch 221; A-G v WH Smith & Sons (1910) 103 LT 96; A-G v Stone (1895) 60 JP 168.*

[3]   See *Stoke Parish Council v Price [1899] 2 Ch 277, 68 LJ Ch 447.*

⁴   The scope of *section 222* was considered by the House of Lords in *Stoke-on-Trent Council v B & Q Retail Ltd* [1984] AC 754, [1984] 2 All ER 332. See also the decision of the House in *Kirklees Borough Council v Wickes Building Supplies Ltd [1993] AC 227, [1992] 3 All ER 717*. For discussion of the section see, generally, Hough 'Local Authorities as Guardians of the Public Interest' (1992) PL 130.

⁵   See *City of London Corpn v Bovis Construction Ltd [1992] 3 All ER 697* at 713 *per* Bingham LJ, and at 716 *per* Taylor LJ (the case was decided in 1988). See also See also *Gillingham Borough Council v Medway (Chatham) Dock Co Ltd [1993] QB 343, [1992] 3 All ER 923* (action failed on the merits).

G Limitations on availability

[29.24]   A claimant who seeks an injunction must be able to satisfy the general doctrines of equity. He must come with clean hands[1]. The doctrines of laches and acquiescence may also provide pitfalls. In *Gaunt v Fynney*[2] plaintiffs who established obstruction of their ancient lights were refused an injunction, and left to seek damages at law, on the ground that they had allowed six years to elapse after the obstruction occurred before making a complaint[3]. On the other hand, it was noted in one case that the doctrine of acquiescence should not be used to enable a plaintiff who does not have a prescriptive right to be put in the same position as if he had one[4]. A limitation of a different kind is typified by the line of cases involving unsuccessful attempts to compel those responsible for public drainage to improve the facilities available[5]. Such disputes are apt to be perceived as falling outside the realm of private law; leaving claimants to invoke any complaints mechanism provided by the relevant legislation, or seek judicial review[6]. But in an appropriate case private law remedies, such as the injunction, can be sought in a judicial review application for civil wrongs arising out of alleged breaches of duty in the public sphere.

¹   See Spry *Equitable remedies* (4th edn) p 400 onwards.
²   *(1872) 8 Ch App 8, 42 LJ Ch 122.*
³   See also *Rogers v Great Northern Rly Co (1889) 53 JP 484.*
⁴   See *Savile v Kilner (1872) 26 LT 277* at 280, *per* Bacon V-C, cf *Ball v Ray (1873) 8 Ch App 467, 30 LT 1.*
⁵   *(1879) 12 Ch D 102, 49 LJ Ch 89.* See also *A-G v Dorking Union Guardians (1882) 20 Ch D 595, 51 LJ Ch 585.*
⁶   See, generally, *Marcic v Thames Water Utilities [2004] 1 All ER 135.*

Chapter 30

Abatement

A Introduction

Form of self-help

[30.01] Any attempt to expound negligence and nuisance on the basis that they are governed by common principles cannot entirely neglect the doctrine of abatement of nuisance, even though its subject-matter necessarily places it some way away from the paradigm of an action for damages arising out of harm carelessly inflicted by the defendant. The doctrine 'is an exception to the general law of England, that a man has no right to take the law into his own hands'[1]. As a form of self-help it has been referred to in the House of Lords as 'a remedy which the law does not favour and is not usually advisable'[2].

[1] *Per* Wilde B in *Jones v Jones (1862) 1 H & C 1* at 5–6.
[2] *Lagan Navigation Co v Lambeg Bleaching Dyeing and Finishing Co [1927] AC 226* at 244, *per* Lord Atkinson. See also *Sedleigh-Denfield v O'Callaghan [1940] AC 880* at 899–900, *[1940] 3 All ER 349* at 362B, *per* Lord Atkin; *Campbell Davys v Lloyd [1901] 2 Ch 518* at 524, *per* Collins LJ.

Examples

[30.02] The scope of the remedy is therefore subject to a number of important limitations, and its exercise prevents the victim of the nuisance from subsequently bringing an action in the courts[1]. Nevertheless it has been held that an injunction can be granted in a suitable case to *compel* a defendant to abate a nuisance caused by a third party[2] even though the taking of legal proceedings against a third party for the same purpose cannot be so ordered[3]. Moreover, even where the claimant's right to abate is open to question, the court may refuse to intervene by way of injunction to prevent abatement if the case of the party seeking the order is technical and without merit[4]. Examples of abatement include the stopping up of drains[5] and watercourses[6], the cutting of branches from overhanging trees[7] and even the demolition of buildings[8]. Abatement can be exercised not only against the original creator of the nuisance but also against his successor in title[9], but notice must normally be given in such a case before the right is exercised[10].

[1] *Baten's Case (1610) 9 Co Rep 53b*; *Lagan Navigation Co v Lambeg Bleaching Dyeing and Finishing Co [1927] AC 226* at 244, *per* Lord Atkinson.
[2] *Charles v Finchley Local Board (1883) 23 Ch D 767, 52 LJ Ch 554.*
[3] See *A-G v Dorking Union Guardians (1882) 20 Ch D 595, 51 LJ Ch 585.*
[4] See *Bagshaw v Buxton Local Board of Health (1875) 1 Ch D 220, 45 LJ Ch 260.*
[5] *Charles v Finchley Local Board (1883) 23 Ch D 767, 52 LJ Ch 554.*

6   *Roberts v Rose (1865) LR 1 Exch 82, 4 H & C 103.*
7   *Lemmon v Webb [1895] AC 1, 64 LJ Ch 205*; cf *Smith v Giddy [1904] 2 KB 448, 73 LJKB 894.* See also *Dayani v Bromley LBC (No2) [2001] BLR 503.*
8   See *Davies v Williams (1851) 16 QB 546, 20 LJQB 330; Lodie v Arnold (1697) 2 Salk 458*; cf *Lane v Capsey [1891] 3 Ch 411, 61 LJ Ch 55.*
9   *Penruddock's Case (1598) 5 Co Rep 100b, Jenk 260.*
10 See below at para [30.05].

Unsuitable where questions of degree are involved

[30.03] 'Ever since the assize of nuisance became available', observed Lloyd LJ in *Burton v Winters*[1], 'the courts have confined the remedy by way of self-redress to simple cases such as an overhanging branch, or an encroaching root, which would not justify the expense of legal proceedings, and urgent cases which require an immediate remedy'. It follows that abatement is not an appropriate remedy where the question whether the defendant has committed a nuisance at all raises difficult matters of degree. In the old case of *Kirby v Sadgrove*[2] the defendant had a right of common over the plaintiff's land. The plaintiff planted trees on the land which the defendant cut down. To an action brought by the plaintiff the defendant argued that he was merely abating a nuisance. The defence failed. Eyre CJ said that if the owner had totally destroyed the exercise of the right of common, eg by enclosure, the defendant could have abated but he observed[3] that 'if it is a question as to the excess of a legal use of the soil, the commoner is not to judge of this excess, but must bring his action'. His Lordship continued[4]:

> 'Abatement ought only to be allowed in clear cases of nuisance where the injury is apparent on the first view of the matter. The abater makes himself his own judge, and proceeds at his own hazard to destroy the thing which he considers as an infringement of his right; whereas in an action, the invasion of his property meets with a fair discussion, and obtains for him a proper recompence, without the previous destruction of the thing in dispute. We ought not to strain a point to let in this species of remedy, and the cases are clearly the other way'.

1   *[1993] 3 All ER 847* at 851, *[1993] 1 WLR 1077* at 1081.
2   *(1797) 3 Anst 892.* The case also appears in *(1797) 1 Bos & P 13* but the report of the judgment there differs slightly from that in Anstruther.
3   *(1797) 3 Anst 892* at 895.
4   *(1797) 3 Anst 892* at 896.

B Scope and requirements

May be wider than legal redress

[30.04] In *Campbell Davys v Lloyd*[1] Collins LJ said, obiter, that 'there may, in the case of positive nuisance, be a right to abate where there is no cause of action, there being insufficient special damage'. Thus a landowner can cut the branches from his neighbour's overhanging trees even though, since such encroachment is not a trespass, no action would lie unless damage had been suffered[2]. Similarly, the dominant owner in a situation involving an easement of, eg support, may enter upon the servient land in order to effect repairs[3], even though the servient owner is under no duty himself to maintain the servient property in repair but merely to refrain from actively withdrawing support[4]. It is clear that the victim of a potential nuisance may abate before he suffers actual damage[5]. At one time the mere existence of a right to abate seemed almost to be regarded as a justification for refusing to impose actual liability, even where damage had occurred, if the plaintiff chose to seek legal redress instead[6]. This argument was clearly unsound, however, and has since been discredited[7].

1   *[1901] 2 Ch 518* at 525.
2   See *Lemmon v Webb [1894] 3 Ch 1* at 11, *per* Lindley LJ. Cf *Smith v Giddy [1904] 2 KB 448, 73 LJKB 894.*
3   See *Jones v Pritchard [1908] 1 Ch 630* at 638 (Parker J). See also Jackson, *The Law of Easements and Profits* (1978) p 59. Cf *Access to Neighbouring Land Act 1992.*
4   See *Sack v Jones [1925] Ch 235, 94 LJ Ch 229; Macpherson v London Passenger Transport Board (1946) 175 LT 279.*
5   *Penruddock's Case (1598) 5 Co Rep 100b, Jenk 260.*
6   See *Job Edwards Properties Co Ltd v Birmingham Navigations [1924] 1 KB 341, 93 LJKB 261; Saxby v Manchester Sheffield and Lincolnshire Rly (1869) LR 4 CP 198, 38 LJCP 153.* But cf *Smith v Giddy [1904] 2 KB 448* at 451, *per* Wills and Kennedy JJ.
7   See *Sedleigh-Denfield v O'Callaghan [1940] AC 880, [1940] 3 All ER 349.*

Need for notice

[30.05] Unless the owner of the land from which the nuisance emanates himself created the nuisance, a person who intends to enter the land in order to abate must normally give notice, to the owner of that land, of his intention to act. Notice is therefore necessary where the land has been alienated by the original wrongdoer since the nuisance was created. On the other hand, where the nuisance has been created by a third party, such as a trespasser, which the owner has simply failed to remedy, it appears that the wrong will be treated as that of the owner himself so that notice will not, strictly speaking, be necessary.

Rules

[30.06] The rules relating to notice are clearly set out in *Jones v Williams*[1], in which a defendant who sued for trespass argued unsuccessfully that he had been lawfully abating a nuisance. He had entered the plaintiff's land to remove manure which he claimed was giving rise to an offensive smell. Parke B said[2]:

> 'It is clear, that if the plaintiff himself was the original wrongdoer, by placing the filth upon the *locus in quo*, it might be removed by the party injured, without any notice to the plaintiff; and so, possibly, if by his default in not performing some obligation incumbent on him, for that is his own wrong also; but if the nuisance was levied by another, and the defendant succeeded to the possession of the *locus in quo* afterwards, the authorities are in favour of the necessity of a notice being given to him to remove, before the party aggrieved can take the law into his own hands ... We think that a notice or request is necessary, upon these authorities, in the case of a nuisance continued by an alienee; and, therefore, the plea is bad, as it does not say that such a notice was given or request made, nor that the plaintiff was himself the wrongdoer, by having levied the nuisance, or neglected to perform some obligation, by the breach of which it was created[3].

1   *(1843) 11 M & W 176, 12 LJ Ex 249.* See also *Traian v Ware [1957] VR 200 (Aus).*
2   *(1843) 11 M & W 176* at 181–182.
3   Dicta in the House of Lords in *Lemmon v Webb [1895] AC 1, 64 LJ Ch 205* could be taken to imply that notice is necessary even to the creator of the nuisance if abatement requires entry upon his land (see *per* Lord Herschell in *[1895] AC 1* at 5; *per* Lord Davey at 8). The better view, however, is that these observations were not intended to displace the orthodox rule: see *Suttles v Cantin (1915) 8 WWR 1293, 24 DLR 1 (Can).*

Cases where notice is not required

[30.07] In addition to situations involving the original wrongdoer, an exception to the requirement of notice also exists where there is an 'emergency'. In *Earl of Lonsdale v Nelson*[1] Best J said:

> 'The security of lives and property may sometimes require so speedy a remedy as not to allow time to call on the person on whose property the mischief has arisen, to remedy it. In such cases an individual would be justified in abating a nuisance ... without notice'.

The criteria for the existence of an emergency for this purpose have not been the subject of much judicial examination, although in one Canadian case, in which the authorities on abatement were discussed, the principle was applied in favour of the defendant in a trespass action[2]. The requirement of notice is also inapplicable if abatement is possible without entry on to the neighbouring land. This was the actual ratio decidendi of the House of Lords in *Lemmon v Webb*[3] in which it was held that notice is unnecessary for the cutting of overhanging trees, provided the cutting can be done from the land of the person suffering the encroachment[4].

---

1 *(1823) 2 B & C 302* at 311–312. See also *Jones v Williams (1843) 11 M & W 176* at 182, *per* Lord Abinger CB.
2 See *Suttles v Cantin [1915] 8 WWR 1293, 24 DLR 1*.
3 *[1895] AC 1, 64 LJ Ch 205*.
4 The right to cut branches does not carry with it the right to pick and appropriate any fruit thereon. The person abating will be liable to the owner of the tree for such appropriation: *Mills v Brooker [1919] 1 KB 555, 88 LJKB 950*.

Abatement cannot be positive

[30.08] Abatement is generally confined to negative acts such as putting out fires and cutting branches from trees. It will not normally extend to positive acts such as, eg the construction of bridges. In *Campbell Davys v Lloyd*[1] there was a public right of way over the plaintiff's land and across a bridge which had formerly spanned a river adjacent to the land. The bridge had, however, long ago fallen into decay and disappeared. The defendants, at their own expense, took it upon themselves to build a new bridge which involved them in placing piles and other erections on the plaintiff's land. The plaintiff sought damages for trespass and an injunction, but the defendants claimed that they were merely abating a nuisance caused by the impedance of the right of way arising from the absence of the bridge. The plaintiff succeeded and the defence of abatement failed. Collins LJ said[2]:

> '... there is a broad difference between removing an obstruction, which has been wrongfully placed in the highway, and making good by a permanent structure the result of mere non-feasance on the part of those charged with the duty of repairing, and I doubt whether such an operation could properly fall under the term "abatement". Even if the right to "abate" can be said to exist at all in the case of a nuisance arising from mere non-feasance ... I do not think the cases which establish the right to abate by an individual for the purpose of passage would extend to protect such acts as were done by the defendant in this case. If this were the law, every individual who was obstructed in his desire to cross would be equally entitled to erect a permanent structure of his own design, although the obligation to repair and the incidental right to determine the method might be in other persons, who, moreover, might be reached by indictment'.

¹   *[1901] 2 Ch 518, 70 LJ Ch 714*. See also *Cooperative Wholesale Society v British Railways Board [1995] NPC 200, (1995) Times*, December 20, CA.
²   *[1901] 2 Ch 518* at 523–524.

Emergencies and minor repairs

[30.09]   Similarly, in the earlier case of *Earl of Lonsdale v Nelson*¹ several defendants entered the plaintiff's land in order to rebuild an ancient structure which had fallen into disrepair but which the defendants claimed was necessary for the safe navigation of the nearby river Derwent. The defendants were held liable in trespass although one of the judges appeared to suggest that in a genuine emergency, which had not been made out in the present case, positive acts *might* be justified by way of abatement². Moreover, it is clearly necessary to distinguish major acts of construction from the undertaking of minor repairs to e.g. the servient tenement by a dominant owner seeking to preserve an easement of support³. The right to enter the land of the servient owner to effect such repairs is well-established, and does not come within the scope of the rule against the taking of positive measures.

¹   *(1823) 2 B & C 302, 3 Dow & Ry KB 556*.
²   See *per* Best J in *(1823) 2 B & C 302* at 311–312.
³   See above at para [30.04].

Nuisances by omission

[30.10]   The passage from the judgment of Collins LJ in *Campbell Davys v Lloyd*, quoted above, illustrates that the rule that abatement cannot be positive is often linked to another supposed principle: that nuisances caused by mere omissions to act, or non-feasance, will rarely give rise to a right to abate¹. The two rules are obviously not identical, however, since it may be perfectly possible to abate a nuisance caused by omission without taking positive measures.

¹   See also *Earl of Lonsdale v Nelson (1823) 2 B & C 302* at 311, *per* Best J.

Justification not apparent

[30.11]   Moreover, the justification for the supposed rule against abating nuisances caused by non-feasance is far less apparent than that against the taking of major positive measures. It would clearly be inconvenient if structures of a novel and permanent nature could be erected at the whim of the victim of a nuisance, but this factor is not present where the act of abatement is merely negative. In addition, the judgment of Parke B in *Jones v Williams*¹, which assumed that abatement without notice could be justified even in cases where the owner of the land had merely been in 'default in not performing some obligation incumbent on him', would appear to be inconsistent with any principle restricting abatement to nuisances caused by misfeasance.

¹   See above at para [30.06].

Major exception

[30.12]   Furthermore, even if such a principle exists it is subject to a major exception in the form of the rule in *Lemmon v Webb*¹. The principle confirmed by the House of

Lords in that case has long been recognised even by judges hostile to the abatement of nuisances caused by omissions. Thus in *Earl of Lonsdale v Nelson* Best J said[2]:

> '... there is no decided case which sanctions the abatement, by an individual, of nuisances from omission, except that of cutting the branches of trees which overhang a public road, or the private property of the person who cuts them. The permitting these branches to extend so far beyond the soil of the owner of the trees, is a most unequivocal act of negligence which distinguishes this case from most of the other cases that have occurred'.

1   *[1895] AC 1, 64 LJ Ch 205.*
2   *(1823) 2 B & C 302* at 311.

C Loss or damage inflicted during abatement

No greater than necessary

[30.13]   The action taken by the victim must not be greater than is necessary to abate the nuisance[1]. Nevertheless it has been held that if a person who has a limited right abuses it so as to cause a nuisance the victim may, by way of abatement, render impossible even the permissible user[2]. It will then be up to the offender to insist upon his right provided he makes clear that his abuse of it will cease[3]. According to the oldest cases, the courts will not scrutinise too closely actions taken during abatement. In *Lodie v Arnold*[4] a person entitled to demolish a house, which was obstructing the highway, allowed the bricks to roll away into the sea even though this was unnecessary and could have been prevented. The owner of the house sued for trespass but the defence of abatement was upheld. It was not necessary for the defendant to show that he had abated with utmost care doing as little damage as possible[5]. But it would seem unlikely that this case would now be followed.

1   *Greenslade v Halliday (1830) 6 Bing 379, 4 Moo & P 71.*
2   See *Cockwell v Russell (1856) 28 LTOS 105*, but cf *Kirby v Sadgrove (1797) 3 Anst 892* at 895–896, *per* Eyre CJ, quoted above.
3   See *per* Pollock CB in *Cockwell v Russell (1856) 28 LT OS 105.*
4   *(1697) 2 Salk 458.*
5   See also *James v Hayward (1630) Cro Car 184.*

Reasonable care needed

[30.14]   The better view is that a person abating a nuisance must exercise reasonable care[1], and that failure to do so will involve his risking liability in negligence and trespass[2]. In the Canadian case of *Lorraine v Norrie*[3] a person abating a nuisance met with resistance from the landowner whose property he had entered. Although reasonable force to overcome this resistance would have been lawful[4], since entry for the purpose of abatement was justified, excessive force was used and the person who had entered to abate was held liable for assault. If, however, damage is inflicted during abatement which could have been avoided, but only by inflicting damage upon an innocent third party, the person responsible for the nuisance is not entitled to complain[5].

1   Cf *Wyatt v Great Western Rly Co (1865) 6 B & S 709, 6 New Rep 259.*
2   Ie trespass *ab initio*. On this doctrine see the *Six Carpenters' Case (1610) 8 Co Rep 146a* and *Clerk and Lindsell on Torts* (18th edn) para 18–42.

3 *(1912) 6 DLR 122.*
4 See *McCurdy v Norrie (1912) 6 DLR 134*, another case arising out of the same incident as that in *Lorraine v Norrie (1912) 6 DLR 122.*
5 See *Roberts v Rose (1865) LR 1 Exch 82, 4 H & C 103.*

D Abatement of public nuisances

Special damage

[30.15] An individual may abate a public nuisance[1] but, as in the case of legal redress, only a member of the public who suffers special damage is so entitled[2].

1 *James v Hayward (1630) Cro Car 184.*
2 *Colchester Corpn v Brooke (1845) 7 QB 339, 15 LJQB 59.* For public nuisance and the concept of special damage therein, see above CHAPTER 14. It is possible, however, that a broader view of what constitutes special damage is permissible in order to justify abatement than would be appropriate in cases where a claimant seeks monetary compensation for public nuisance.

Should obstruction be total?

[30.16] In the case of obstructions to the highway it is not altogether clear on the authorities whether there has to be total obstruction to justify abatement, or whether it is sufficient if the right of passage cannot be exercised with reasonable convenience. The point was expressly left open by Lord Campbell CJ in the nineteenth century case of *Dimes v Petley*[1], but in the later case of *Bateman v Bluck*[2] the same judge held that a defendant who had removed an obstruction to a right of passage had to show 'not only that he had such a right, but that there was no way in which he could exercise it without the removal'. On the other hand, in the old case of *James v Hayward*[3] it was held that a gate unlawfully erected across the highway could be cut down by any of the King's subjects passing that way, even if the gate was not fastened but on hinges so that it could be opened at will, 'for women and old men are more troubled with opening of gates than they should be if there were none'. Although it must be very doubtful whether the actual decision in this case is still good law it is submitted that, despite *Bateman v Bluck*, it remains enough to warrant abatement that a right of passage cannot be exercised without unreasonable risk or inconvenience.

1 *(1850) 15 QB 276, 19 LJQB 449.*
2 *(1852) 18 QB 870* at 876.
3 *(1630) Cro Car 184.*

Authorities

[30.17] Highway authorities may remove obstructions upon highways which are statutorily vested in them just as any owner can abate a private nuisance[1]. Moreover, it is possible that local authorities may be entitled to abate public nuisances in their areas at common law without showing special damage[2], even though they can only seek legal redress in such cases by virtue of specific statutory enactment[3].

1 See *Reynolds v Presteign UDC [1896] 1 QB 604, 65 LJQB 400.* For statutory powers relating to removal of obstructions on the highway see, generally, the *Highways Act 1980, Pt IX.*
2 See *Bagshaw v Buxton Local Board of Health (1875) 1 Ch D 220, 45 LJ Ch 260.*
3 See the *Local Government Act 1972*, s 222(1)(a) discussed in CHAPTER 29 above. Cf *Stoke Parish Council v Price [1899] 2 Ch 277, 68 LJ Ch 447.*

E Abatement after refusal of equitable relief

Negative answer given by Court of Appeal

[30.18] In *Burton v Winters*[1] the question arose whether a plaintiff who had a good cause of action, but had been refused equitable relief by way of injunction, could nevertheless avail herself of the common law right to abate. The question had been noted earlier, in a case at the close of the nineteenth century[2], and left undecided, although Chitty J had indicated that he was not satisfied that the right to abate would necessarily disappear in such circumstances[3]. It is submitted that, having regard to the variety of differing reasons which might lead to refusal of equitable relief, the doubts of Chitty J with respect to an automatic end to abatement were justified. These doubts were not, however, shared by the Court of Appeal in *Burton v Winters* which chose to give the question a clear answer in the negative. Lloyd LJ said[4]:

> 'Self-redress is a summary remedy, which is justified only in clear and simple cases, or in an emergency. Where a plaintiff has applied for a mandatory injunction and failed, the sole justification for a summary remedy is gone. The court has decided the very point in issue. This is so whether the complaint lies in trespass or nuisance. In the present case, the court has decided that the plaintiff is not entitled to have the wall on her side of the boundary removed. It follows that she has no right to remove it herself'.

[1]   *[1993] 3 All ER 847, [1993] 1 WLR 1077, CA.*
[2]   *See Lane v Capsey [1891] 3 Ch 411, 61 LJ Ch 55.*
[3]   See *[1891] 3 Ch 411* at 416.
[4]   *[1993] 3 All ER 847* at 852, *[1993] 1 WLR 1077* at 1082.

Non-compliance with injunction

[30.19] One question that remains unclear is whether a claimant who *is* granted an injunction can still abate if he wishes, in the event of non-compliance, instead of bringing proceedings for contempt. It is submitted that this should be allowed, provided that the case is one in which the right of abatement would have existed before the commencement of legal proceedings; and provided also that the claimant does nothing which would have been outside the scope of the injunction.

Part eleven

Tort, the state and the future

Chapter 31

Insurance and state provision

A Introduction

Broader context

[31.01] Although proof of negligence is usually a necessary condition, under the tort system, for the making of a monetary award to an accident victim, it is obvious that a wholly traditional account of the operation of the fault principle, in isolation from its broader social and financial context, would nowadays be seriously incomplete. There are two main reasons for this. First, even where a claimant is successful in his negligence claim, the damages, in the vast majority of cases, will not be paid by the defendant himself but by an insurance company. Indeed, uninsured defendants are seldom worth suing. A brief account of the impact of insurance in this area, with reference to the main statutory provisions in the road traffic and employment spheres, in which insurance is compulsory and which account for the great majority of tort claims, is therefore essential. The second reason for a broader account is that, looking at the problem of compensation for personal injury and disability as a whole, it is important to recognise that tort claims provide the background to only about one-quarter of the total amount of money paid out to accident victims. Apart from other sources (including victims' *own* insurance policies), which account for another quarter, the lion's share, *half* of the overall total, is provided by the state in various forms of welfare benefit.[1]

[1] See the Report of the *Royal Commission on Civil Liability and Compensation for Personal Injury* (*Pearson*) (Cmnd 7054–I) pp 12–13. It should be stressed that these proportions concern money actually paid out. As a percentage of all accident victims the figure for successful tort claimants is very much lower: about 6.5%. See the Report, vol 1, p 24.

Similarity with tort

[31.02] It is obviously beyond the scope of a work on the law of negligence to give a full account of our now highly developed and complex social security system.[1] Moreover, since, in the great majority of situations with which that system deals, the *manner* in which the injury or disability occurred is irrelevant, the very *basis* of the system is fundamentally different from that of negligence.[2] There are, however, a number of areas of state provision in which the manner in which an injury or disability was *caused*, or at least the context in which it occurred, is of relevance to the making of an award. Since these could therefore be perceived as having a degree of similarity with tort, and because they are likely to be particularly relevant to situations in which the making of tort claims may also be considered, they require at least outline mention in a work of this kind. Those to be looked at will be the industrial injuries scheme, the vaccine damage payments scheme, and the criminal injuries compensation scheme. But the first topic to be considered will be the relevance of insurance to negligence cases.

1   The leading work is A I Ogus, E M Barendt and N J Wikeley *The Law of Social Security* (4th edn, 1995).
2   Some critics argue that the social security approach is inherently preferable, and that it should be allowed to replace the tort of negligence altogether. This view is now held much less widely than in the relatively recent past, however, and even its remaining advocates would probably concede that it is unrealistic in contemporary circumstances. See, generally, CHAPTER 32 below.

B The role of insurance

Negligence: appearance and reality[1]

[31.03]   Until relatively recently, it was considered to be improper for the court even to be told whether the parties to a negligence action were insured. Although it is safe to assume that this is no longer the case, due at least in part to the insistence of Lord Denning upon considering overtly the relevance of insurance in such cases during his long and influential judicial career[2], it is worthy of note that the adoption of a more traditional reticence on the matter by leading counsel in one case received favourable judicial comment from the Court of Appeal as late as 1973.[3] On the other hand, it is almost certainly true that, even when the presence or absence of insurance was supposedly shrouded in secrecy, its existence influenced covertly the development of the law.[4] For example, the objective or 'reasonable man' test for the presence of negligence means that liability will not infrequently be imposed upon defendants who have merely been unlucky, rather than blameworthy in any real sense.[5] If motorists and doctors, for example, had to look to their own resources to pay the huge sums often awarded against them, the imposition of liability would be both impracticable and morally objectionable. Another reason why insurance can sometimes have the effect of causing the reality of negligence liability to differ markedly from its appearance is the exercise of the right of *subrogation*[6]. This enables a claimant's own indemnity insurers to use his name, even against his wishes[7], to sue the defendant who caused the damage, once they have recompensed him for his losses in accordance with the terms of his policy. The doctrine is capable of producing in some cases an unreal situation, in which neither of the nominal parties to the action is in truth conducting the litigation or is even interested in its outcome.[8]

1   See J Stapleton 'Tort, Insurance and Ideology' (1995) 58 MLR 820. Cf Jonathan Morgan 'Tort, Insurance and Incoherence' (2004) 67 MLR 384. See also M Davies 'The End of the Affair: Duty of Care and Liability Insurance' (1989) 9 LS 67.
2   See *Lamb v Camden London Borough Council [1981] QB 625* at 638, *[1981] 2 All ER 408* at 414–415, CA.
3   See *Launchbury v Morgans [1971] 2 QB 245* at 263, *[1971] 1 All ER 642* at 654, CA, *per* Megaw LJ.
4   See F James 'Accident Liability Reconsidered: The Impact of Liability Insurance' (1948) 57 Yale LJ 549.
5   See *Nettleship v Weston [1971] 2 QB 691, [1971] 3 All ER 581, CA* (learner driver) and *Roberts v Ramsbottom [1980] 1 All ER 7, [1980] 1 WLR 823* (stroke victim).
6   See Mitchell *The Law of Subrogation* (1994).
7   See *Lister v Romford Ice and Cold Storage [1957] AC 555, [1957] 1 All ER 125, HL.*
8   See *Mark Rowlands Ltd v Berni Inns Ltd [1986] QB 211, [1985] 3 All ER 473, CA.* Cf *Hobbs v Marlowe [1978] AC 16, [1977] 2 All ER 241.* For criticism of the availability of subrogation rights see T Weir 'Governmental Liability' [1989] PL 40.

Continuing influence of the traditional view

[31.04] Although it is no longer considered improper to disclose the incidence of insurance, the traditional view that it should not affect the imposition or otherwise of liability still remains strong. In the 1994 case of *Hunt v Severs*[1] the plaintiff sought to recover the cost of her care from the defendant who happened, however, to be her spouse and to be himself the provider of the care. The litigation arose out of a motor accident and, in reality, the claim represented an attempt by the family to recover its loss from the defendant's insurance policy. Indeed, before the House of Lords, the plaintiff attempted to make this the explicit basis of recovery in order to overcome the objection that such liability would, in theory, be unjust to the defendant by making him liable for the cost of care which he had himself provided. Thus, Lord Bridge observed that counsel for the plaintiff 'recognising the difficulty of formulating any principle of public policy which could justify recovery against the tortfeasor who has to pay out of his own pocket, advanced the bold proposition that such a policy could be founded on the liability of insurers to meet the claim'. His Lordship tersely responded that the 'short answer' to the contention was that 'at common law the circumstance that a defendant is contractually indemnified by a third party against a particular legal liability can have no relevance whatever to the measure of that liability'.[2] Similarly, in *Capital and Counties plc v Hampshire County Council*[3] the Court of Appeal rejected a submission that, because property owners are usually insured against fire damage, fire brigades should be immune from any liability for negligence. Stuart-Smith LJ re-iterated the 'general rule in English law ... that in determining the rights inter se of A and B, the fact that one of them is insured is to be disregarded'.[4]

[1]   *[1994] 2 AC 350, [1994] 2 All ER 385, HL.*
[2]   See *[1994] 2 AC 350* at 363, *[1994] 2 All ER 385* at 395. The Law Commission has recommended that the actual *decision* in *Hunt v Severs* should be reversed by a legislation provision whereby 'In an action for personal injury, no rule of law is to be treated as preventing damages from being recovered in respect of the gratuitous provision of services for the injured person by an individual merely because he is the defendant': *Damages for Personal Injury: Medical, Nursing and Other Expenses; Collateral Benefits* (Law Com No 262).
[3]   *[1997] QB 1004, [1997] 2 All ER 865, CA.* See CHAPTER 15 above.
[4]   See *[1997] QB 1004* at 1044, *[1997] 2 All ER 865* at 891.

Opposite extreme

[31.05] At the opposite extreme from this traditional judicial orthodoxy, some commentators have contended that an insurance-based approach to compensation, at least in personal injury cases, should largely *replace* the law of negligence itself. One version of this argument would favour encouraging or compelling greater use of *first party* insurance, whereby people would be encouraged primarily to insure themselves and their income *directly* against losses arising through injury[1]. Such insurance, whereby the premiums can be geared more precisely to the particular risk, is commonly supposed to be more efficient and less wasteful than *liability* insurance, the use of which underpins negligence; the latter being apt to give rise to high transaction costs, through settlement negotiations or litigation. Radical suggestions of this kind do not, however, enjoy only limited support among commentators. The importance of the deterrent and symbolic functions of the law of tort are rightly perceived by many to remain crucial. Professor Stapleton has also drawn attention to the ideralogical implications of a move towards first party insurance, which would often have the effect of shifting resources away from the relatively disadvantaged in favour of the wealthy.[2] Nor is liability insurance necessarily inefficient, given the right market circumstances.[3] And the possibility that increased premiums, imposed through the medium of liability insurance, may have a beneficial effect upon accident prevention and safety, should not be wholly discounted or ignored.[4] Moreover, insurers, whose expertise lies in developing products in response to demand, created by such factors as the incidence of legal liability, can sometimes appear unsure what is required of them when invited by legal reformers to use their experience to make suggestions as to how the law itself should be changed.[5] On the other hand, the legislature, as distinct from the common law, already intervenes substantially with insurance considerations as its objective. By far the most prominent sphere of existing legislative intervention is, of course, that of motor transport, to which we now turn.

[1]   See P S Atiyah *The Damages Lottery* (Oxford, 1997).
[2]   See J Stapleton 'Tort, Insurance and Ideology' (1995) 58 MLR 820.
[3]   See M Furmston (ed) *The Law of Tort* (1986) p 199 (E W Hitcham on 'Some Insurance Aspects'). See also 'The Law of Tort and Non-Physical Loss: Insurance Aspects' (1972) 12 JSPTL (NS) 119 at 174 (report of discussion of a paper presented to a Ford Foundation Workshop by A V Alexander).
[4]   See P J Sherman 'The Pearson Report and Insurance' in D Allen, C Bourn and J Holyoak (eds) *Accident Compensation after Pearson* (1979) pp 129–130.
[5]   See, generally, the papers of Hitcham and Alexander cited above. See also that by Sherman, noted above.

Road Traffic Act

[31.06]   The *Road Traffic Act 1988, s 143(1)* provides that:

'(a)   a person must not use a motor vehicle on a road unless there is in force in relation to the use of the vehicle such a policy of insurance … in respect of third party risks as complies with the requirements of this Part of this Act, and

(b)   a person must not cause or permit any other person to use a motor vehicle on a road unless there is in force in relation to the use of the vehicle by that other person such a policy of insurance … in respect of third party risks …
'

This well-known provision is intended to ensure that victims of negligence in motor accident cases do not go uncompensated, due to inability on the part of the driver responsible to meet the claim out of his own resources. Although the carrying of liability insurance by motorists has been compulsory for 70 years,[1] it was not until 1972 that it became obligatory for the cover to include *passengers* in the driver's own vehicle.[2] Since that year it has no longer been possible for drivers, and their insurance companies, to seek to exclude liability to passengers by causing a notice of disclaimer to be exhibited in the vehicle.[3]

[1]   It was originally introduced by the *Road Traffic Act 1930*.
[2]   See the *Road Traffic Act 1988, s 145* (the provision originated in the *Motor Vehicles (Passenger Insurance) Act 1971, s 1*).
[3]   See the *Road Traffic Act 1988, s 149*.

Liability of insurer to victim

[31.07]   If the situation is one to which the statutory obligation to insure applies, the *Road Traffic Act 1988, s 151* provides that the insurer will become directly liable to the victim to satisfy a judgment obtained against the policy-holder.[1] In certain circumstances this can apply even if the insurer would have had a valid defence if sued on the policy by the customer himself.[2] In such a case, however, the insurer is entitled to seek recoupment, of any damages which he has been compelled to pay, from the policy-holder. Accident victims are even protected, by virtue of an extra-statutory scheme, which must now be considered, if the driver was uninsured or even unidentified.

[1] It is important to note that the insurer has to be given notice of the claim by the victim, if this right is to arise, within seven days of proceedings being commenced against the policy-holder: *s 152(1)*.

[2] See *section 151(5)* of the 1988 Act, but note that *section 152(2)* does entitle the insurer to avoid liability to the victim if the policy is voidable for non-disclosure or false representation. In the event of such avoidance the victim would have to claim from the Motor Insurers' Bureau, see below at para [31.08].

The Motor Insurers' Bureau

[31.08] Making it a criminal offence for drivers to drive while uninsured, and also giving accident victims a direct statutory right against the driver's insurance company where he is insured, does not of itself assist the victims of drivers who, albeit in breach of the criminal law, in fact failed to take out insurance policies as required by the legislation. This gap is met by the extra-statutory device of an agreement between the Motor Insurers' Bureau, which is a body set up by insurers transacting motor vehicle business, and the Secretary of State for the Environment.[1] The agreement originally dates from 1946 but the version currently operative dates from 1999[2]. It provides that the Bureau will satisfy judgments against uninsured drivers in respect of the statutory obligation to insure under the *Road Traffic Act 1988*.

[1] The history of the agreement is set out in the speech of Lord Nicholls in *White v White [2001] 2 All ER 43*. See, generally, D B Williams *Hit and Run and Uninsured Driver Personal Injury Claims*.

[2] For criticism of the new agreement see Andrew Ritchie 'The Men in Black' (1999) NLJ 1447.

Privity

[31.09] Since the agreement is between the Bureau and the Secretary of State, the doctrine of privity could in theory have been invoked to prevent accident victims, who are necessarily third parties, from enforcing it. But the Bureau resolved never to take the point so that, notwithstanding occasional murmurs of judicial disquiet at being asked to give judgment in favour of parties who have no cause of action,[1] the agreement in practice provides effective protection for accident victims in the situation with which it deals.[2]

[1] See *per* Viscount Dilhorne in *Albert v Motor Insurers' Bureau [1972] AC 301* at 320, *[1971] 2 All ER 1345* at 1354, HL.

[2] But see *Stinton v Stinton [1995] RTR 167, CA* (passenger who uses a vehicle on a joint venture with the driver, knowing that there is no insurance, is outside the protection of the MIB Scheme). Cf *White v White [2001] 2 All ER 43* (passenger who was merely careless as to whether or not the driver was insured is protected).

Defences

[31.10] It is important to note that the Bureau can and does take *other* defences which would have been available to an insurer sued directly by the policy-holder's victim under the *Road Traffic Act 1988*.[1] In fact, the Bureau is able to get itself added as a defendant in appropriate cases to ensure that relevant points are taken.[2] Of course, the effect of a victim's direct rights, under the Road Traffic Acts, against insurers will sometimes prevent the Bureau, just as it prevents insurers, from taking certain defences against the victim which could have been taken against an attempt by an actual policy-holder to sue his insurer. Thus, in *Gardner v Moore*[3] the House of Lords confirmed that the Bureau would be liable where an uninsured driver *deliberately* injured his victim since, on the true construction of the Road Traffic Act, this risk was one against which drivers were obliged to be insured; even though the principle that no one can profit from his own wrong would have prevented an insured driver from himself enforcing his liability policy in such circumstances.[4] The decision of the House on this point confirmed the well-known decision of the Court of Appeal, reached 20 years earlier, in *Hardy v Motor Insurers' Bureau*.[5] Finally, it is important to note that, just as in claims against insurers under the Road Traffic Act, the Motor Insurers' Bureau must be given notice of proceedings arising out of an accident within fourteen days of their commencement.[6] In one case the Bureau actually took the point by way of defence that the appropriate notice had not been given.[7]

[1] See *Randall v Motor Insurers' Bureau [1969] 1 All ER 21, [1968] 1 WLR 1900*.
[2] See *Gurtner v Circuit [1968] 2 QB 587, [1968] 1 All ER 328, CA*. Cf *White v London Transport Executive [1971] 2 QB 721, [1971] 3 All ER 1, CA*.
[3] *[1984] AC 548, [1984] 1 All ER 1100, HL*.
[4] Cf *Gray v Barr [1971] 2 QB 554, [1970] 2 All ER 949, CA*; *Meah v Creamer (No 2) [1986] 1 All ER 943*.
[5] *[1964] 2 QB 745, [1962] 2 All ER 742, CA*.
[6] Under the 1988 agreement the period was only seven days.
[7] See *Cooper v Motor Insurers' Bureau [1985] QB 575, [1985] 1 All ER 449*, and see *per* Cumming-Bruce LJ *[1985] QB 575* at 581, *[1985] 1 All ER 449* at 452: 'I ventured in argument to describe that defence as meritorious but unattractive. But there is no answer to it.'

Hit and run drivers

[31.11] It is perhaps surprising that, although the Bureau sometimes made ex gratia payments to victims in such cases, it was not until 1969 that the agreement between the government and the Bureau covered the serious problem of 'hit and run' drivers who are untraced. Until that year, the contractual obligations of the Bureau were confined to situations in which an identified driver was either uninsured or in which his insurer had been able to deny liability. Now, however, a separate agreement, which in its currently operative form dates from from 1996, provides that the Bureau will also cover 'hit and run' situations.

Lack of consistency

[31.12] In addition to motor vehicle and employment, the legislature has intervened in a number of other situations to make the taking out of liability insurance compulsory[1]. It has, however, done so without much regard to consistency. Thus Professor Richard Lewis has written[2]:

'When viewed as a whole, the law can be seen as developing in an *ad hoc* fashion, responding to particular concerns at different points in time. Little thought seems to have been given to the overall picture. Why one group of victims – whether suffering personal injury, property damage or economic loss – should be better protected than others in similar circumstances is rarely discussed. Policy discussion of the role of the state in compelling its citizens to take out private insurance would be better informed if the areas where such protection is presently required were viewed as a whole'.

[1] See the examples collected in Lewis 'When You Must Insure' (2004) NLJ 1474 and 1537.

2   See (2004) NLJ at 1537.

Employers' liability

[31.13]   The *Employers' Liability (Compulsory Insurance) Act 1969, s 1(1)* provides as follows:

> 'Except as otherwise provided by this Act, every employer carrying on any business in Great Britain shall insure, and maintain insurance, under one or more approved policies with an authorised insurer or insurers against liability for bodily injury or disease sustained by his employees, and arising out of and in the course of their employment in Great Britain in that business ... '

With the passing of this Act of 1969 the principle of compulsory liability insurance was extended to include employers.[1] Unlike the case of motor-accident victims, however, the injured employees are not given a direct statutory right of action against the employer's insurer, nor is there any institution similar to the Motor Insurers' Bureau to protect the employees of uninsured employers.

1   For comment see Hassan (1974) 3 ILJ 79.

Where the holder of a liability policy is insolvent

[31.14]   If the holder of a liability insurance policy becomes bankrupt, or makes a composition order with his creditors, or if a company with such a policy is wound up or has a receiver appointed, 'his rights against the insurer in respect of the liability shall ... be transferred to and vest in the third party to whom the liability was ... incurred'. These words are contained in the *Third Parties (Rights Against Insurers) Act 1930, s 1*. This Act ensures that anyone who had a claim against an insolvent policy-holder, which comes within the terms of the liability policy, can claim directly from the insurance company. The object is to ensure that the proceeds go to the victim and do not simply become part of the general assets of the insured, and hence lost in the distribution to his creditors.[1] It is important to realise that this valuable provision is not confined to situations in which the taking out of liability insurance is compulsory, but extends to all situations in which such a policy has in fact been taken out by a tortfeasor who becomes insolvent. Unlike the road traffic situation, however, the victim can never be in a better position against the insurance company than the policy holder himself would have been, so that any defences which would have been available to the insurance company against him will also be available against his victim.[2] Moreover, in *Bradley v Eagle Star Insurance Co Ltd*[3] the House of Lords held, by a majority, that the victim did not acquire any rights under the section against the insurers until the existence and amount of the tortfeasor's liability had been established.[4] In the case itself, which concerned an industrial disease, this had not been done and could not now be done directly since the company in question had been wound up many years before.[5] The plaintiff's claim was therefore not allowed to proceed, even though trial of it would have been indistinguishable in practice from the great majority of such cases in which the effective defendant is an insurance company and the alleged tortfeasor is defendant in name only.[6] The Government has accepted a Law Commission recommendation that the decision in *Bradley's* case should be reversed, enabling third parties to commence proceedings against the insurance company before the establishing of liability on the part of the insured.

¹   In 2001 the Law Commission recommended changes to the Act to improve the protection which it provides to claimants: see *The Third Parties (Rights Against Insurers) Act 1930* (Law Com no 184).
²   *McCormick v National Motor and Accident Insurance Union (1934) 49 Ll L Rep 361; Post Office v Norwich Union Fire Insurance Society [1967] 2 QB 363, [1967] 1 All ER 577, CA.*
³   *[1989] AC 957, [1989] 1 All ER 961, HL.*
⁴   Ie in litigation or by agreement. See also *Woolwich Building Society v Taylor [1995] 1 BCLC 132; Cox v Bankside Members Agency Ltd [1995] 2 Lloyd's Rep 437* (discussed by A Quick (1995) NLJ, 23 June).
⁵   Since the decision of the House of Lords in *Bradley v Eagle Star Insurance Co*, the position of claimants in such cases has been assisted by a change in company law which enables companies to be revived for the purpose of personal injury claims if they were dissolved up to 20 years earlier: see the *Companies Act 1989, s 141*. This provision, which is retrospective in effect, amends the *Companies Act 1985, s 651*, which only permitted revival within two years of dissolution.
⁶   Cf *[1989] 1 All ER 961* at 968, *per* Lord Templeman dissenting: 'The dissolution of the … company has no significance in the present case save that it enables the [insurers] to argue that they are not bound to pay in respect of a liability which they accepted and for which they were paid premiums.'

C Injury at work¹

Background and structure

[31.15]   The *Workmen's Compensation Act* of 1897 introduced a special scheme of compensation for those injured at work. It was originally paid for by employers themselves and had the great advantage over the common law, whose deficiencies no doubt helped to account for its introduction, that it was not necessary to prove negligence. With the expansion of general welfare provision made by the 1945–51 Labour government, in the light of reforms recommended by the Beveridge Report, compensation for industrial injuries and diseases became part of what is now known as the Social Security system. The so-called 'industrial preference', whereby more generous treatment is accorded to work victims than to others, has been greatly eroded over the years, consistently with the criticism of those who consider it wrong in principle that a welfare system should distinguish between recipients according to the context in which their particular misfortunes arose. Nevertheless, it has not yet been found politically practicable wholly to abolish the preservation, as a separate category, of compensation for industrial accidents and diseases, and it still remains the case that certain work victims can enjoy a degree of preferential treatment within the social security system.

Accidents and diseases

[31.16]   The *Social Security Contributions and Benefits Act 1992, s 94(1)*, re-enacting earlier legislation, provides that entitlement to benefit is dependent upon the employee suffering 'personal injury caused … by accident arising out of and in the course of his employment'. Over the years a large body of case law was built up by decisions of National Insurance Commissioners as to which situations come within this phrase and which do not.¹ To establish that someone contracted a disease at work will usually be less straightforward than proving that he had an 'accident',² and diseases are therefore dealt with separately. A list of prescribed diseases and the occupations with which they are associated is provided. There is then a rebuttable presumption that a claimant thus employed, who has developed a prescribed disease, did so at work.

¹   For a recent example of a case which reached the House of Lords see *Chief Education Officer v Faulds [2000] 2 All ER 961, HL.*

2   But much difficulty has arisen in this field in distinguishing an 'accident' (or 'event') from a 'process': the latter not providing the basis for a claim unless it gives rise to a prescribed industrial disease. See A I Ogus and E M Barendt and N J Wikeley *The Law of Social Security* (4th edn, 1995), ch 7.

Disablement Benefit

[31.17] In recent years, significant changes have been made to the industrial injuries compensation scheme, which have had the effect of further eroding the 'industrial preference', and of promoting an even closer relationship between the scheme and the mainstream of social security. With the abolition in 1990 of reduced earnings allowance, which provided compensation for those whose earning capacity had been reduced by injury at work, the main benefit peculiar to the scheme which still survives is Disablement Benefit. This represents what is, for social security, an unusual concept since it provides financial compensation for what is, at least in the way in which it is calculated, non-pecuniary loss. It is a benefit payable to industrially disabled people to reflect the loss of faculty caused to them by their disability, and is therefore not dissimilar in principle from the damages for loss of amenity recoverable in negligence at common law.

Assesment

[31.18] An assessment is made on a percentage basis by comparing the claimant's condition with the position enjoyed by an able-bodied person,[1] and weekly payments are then made accordingly subject to a statutory maximum. Formerly, assessments could be made of disabilities as low as 1%, with the payments made for the lower degrees of disability usually being paid as lump sum gratuities rather than as weekly pensions. But the *Social Security Act 1986* provided that,[2] henceforth, there would be no entitlement to benefit for those injured in the future whose degree of disability is rated as being lower than 14%. Those whose disability is rated at between 14 and 20% will automatically receive the same level of benefit as those rated at 20%. The effect of this is that the making of lump sum payments will disappear.

1   See A I Ogus, E M Barendt and N J Wikeley *Law of Social Security* (4th edn, 1995) p 332 onwards.
2   See now the *Social Security Contributions and Benefits Act 1992, s 103*.

D Vaccine damage

[31.19] As a result of public concern over the plight of certain vaccination victims, on whose behalf it would be difficult if not impossible to prove negligence at common law, the *Vaccine Damage Payments Act 1979* introduced an ad hoc scheme whereby tax-free lump sums can be paid to those whom vaccination in respect of certain diseases has left with very serious brain damage.[1] The 1979 Act itself provided for a lump sum of £10,000, but the figure can be increased by delegated legislation, and it is currently £30,000.

1   It should be noted that claimants are still required to prove *causation*, on a balance of probabilities, before a vaccine damage tribunal; and the figures for successful claims suggest that there may be disturbing discrepancies in the criteria adopted on this point by different tribunals: see C Newdick 'Strict Liability for Dangerous Drugs in the Pharmaceutical Industry' (1985) 101 LQR 405 at 429, and references there given.

E Criminal injuries

Criminal Injuries Compensation Scheme

[31.20] In 1964 a body known as the Criminal Injuries Compensation Board was set up to administer an ad hoc scheme, not part of the social security system.[1] As originally created, the Criminal Injuries Compensation Scheme was non-statutory and provided what was described as ex gratia compensation, but which came out of government funds included in the Home Office Vote.[2] Since 1995, however, it has been governed by the *Criminal Injuries Compensation Act* of that year, and administered by a new Criminal Injury Compensation Authority. The Authority's claims officers entertain applications from victims, or the dependants of victims, of personal injury which is directly attributable to the commission, broadly speaking, of violent criminal activity. Compensation was formerly assessed in accordance with the principles applicable to the assessment of damages at common law. In view of government concern about the cost of the scheme,[3] however, the new scheme which accompanied the 1995 Act operates on a radically different basis. Awards are based on a tariff system, whereby several hundred different injuries are listed with specific sums ranging, according to gravity, from £1,000 to £250,000.[4] Provision is also made for loss of earnings to be recovered but the assessment is to be made on the basis that the rate is not to exceed one and a half times average industrial earnings.

[1]   See D Miers *State Compensation for Criminal Injuries* (1997).
[2]   Even as a non-statutory body, the Board was subject to the supervisory jurisdiction of the High Court exercised by judicial review: see *R v Criminal Injuries Compensation Board, ex p Lain [1967] 2 QB 864, [1967] 2 All ER 770.*
[3]   During the year 1991–92 the former Criminal Injuries Compensation Board paid out in total more than £144m in compensation.
[4]   The legislation was necessitated by the majority decision of the House of Lords in *R v Secretary of State for the Home Department, ex p Fire Brigades Union [1995] 2 All ER 244*, which held that an attempt, the previous year, to introduce a tariff on a non-statutory basis had been ultra vires, since it contravened provisions in the *Criminal Justice Act 1988*. Those provisions (*ss 108–117*) would have put the scheme on a statutory footing but without the limitations of a tariff, and although they were never brought into force their Lordships held that, as long as they remained on the statute book, they were effective to prevent the government from acting inconsistently with them.

Justification for the Scheme

[31.21] The existence of the Criminal Injuries Compensation Scheme has been criticised[1] as being characteristic of the piecemeal approach to provision for the victims of personal injury, which is sometimes considered to have undesirably impeded the development of a system capable of dealing with victims in a manner unrelated to how their injuries were caused. On this view it is irrational to single out the victims of criminal violence for especially generous treatment, distinct from that accorded by the welfare state to other victims of personal injury. In the absence, however, of greatly improved state provision for all sufferers, it is submitted that the existence of the Criminal Injuries Compensation Authority is justifiable. What is unusual about situations involving criminal violence is the particularly acute sense of grievance apt to be felt by the victim, combined with the exceptionally low degree of probability that compensation will in practice be recoverable from the criminal for what is obviously serious tortious conduct.[2] It is significant that a research study on the Scheme reported that 'victims saw compensation, whatever its source, as symbolic – a judgment about their offence and their suffering'.[3]

1   See P S Atiyah *Accidents, Compensation and the Law* (Cane ed) (6th edn, 1999) ch 12.
2   If the victim does succeed in obtaining common law damages any award from the Board has to be repaid.
3   See Appendix B (summarising research by J Shapland) to *Compensation and Support for Victims of Crime*, HC 43, Session 1984/85 (First Report of the House of Commons Home Affairs Select Committee: quoted at p 929 of the 4th edition of B Hepple and M Matthews *Tort Cases and Materials*).

Chapter 32

Reform?

A Criticisms of the existing system

Introduction

[32.01] Although the suggestion has been put forward, by the most radical proponents of reform of the law of tort, that the redress which it affords to those who suffer *property damage* should be abolished,[1] by far the greatest attention and criticism has been focused upon compensation through the tort of negligence for *personal injury*. While the various objections to the operation of the law of negligence in this area overlap, they can nevertheless be conveniently grouped under three main heads. The first is that tort is a very inefficient and wasteful system for compensating victims of personal injury. The second is that its operation, both in theory and in practice, is arbitrary and capricious. The third is that the spread of liability insurance, which shields tortfeasors in many situations from the financial consequences of their actions, has deprived the tort of negligence of any principled basis which it might once have had.[2]

[1]   See T Ison *The Forensic Lottery* (1987) ch 6. See also P Atiyah *Accidents Compensation and the Law* (Cane, ed) (6th edn, 1994) ch 19, pp 423–424.
[2]   Cf D Harris 'Evaluating the Goals of Personal Injury Law: Some Empirical Evidence' in P Cane and J Stapleton (eds) *Essays for Patrick Atiyah* (1991).

Inefficiency

[32.02] The administration costs of the law of negligence are astonishingly high. 1978 Lord Pearson's *Royal Commission on Civil Liability and Compensation for Personal Injury*[1] reported as follows:

'We estimate that the operating costs of the tort system amount to about 85 per cent of the value of tort compensation payments, or about 45 per cent of the combined total of compensation and operating costs. Of these operating costs, about 40 per cent is accounted for by the costs of insurers in handling claims and on general administration. The remaining elements are the commissions paid by insurers to brokers and agents, claimants' legal fees, and profit. Each represents about a fifth. On small claims, the expenses can be greater than the damages paid.'

Such evidence as there is indicates that the pattern has not changed significantly in the quarter of a century since Pearson reported[2]. The Commission also reported,[3] in contrast to the position in tort, that the 'cost of administering social security benefits for injured people is about 11 per cent of the value of compensation payments, or 10 per cent of the cost of payments and administration'.

1 Cmnd 7054–I, para 83.
2 Reports by the Department of Work and Pensions and the Office of Fair Trading, published in 2003, apparently indicated that 40p out of every £1 paid out by insurers in respect of accidents goes to lawyers: see (2003) New LJ 1813 (5 December).
3 See vol 1, para 121.

Arbitrariness

Great majority of accident and disease victims excluded

[32.03] The basic flaw in the law of negligence, *if it is evaluated purely as a compensation system and without regard to other considerations*, is the concentration, which by definition is central to it, upon the way in which a given injury or disability was *caused*. The overwhelming majority of disabled persons, possibly as high as 90%, are sufferers from disease and congenital handicap rather than victims of accidental injury.[1] Moreover, even among accident victims, 35 to 40% of the total have their mishaps in their own homes so that the making of negligence claims will rarely be feasible. The investigations of the Pearson Royal Commission in the 1970s revealed that at that time the proportion of accident victims (themselves only a very small proportion of the disabled) which actually succeeded in obtaining tort compensation was the remarkably low figure of 6.5%.[2]

1 See P Atiyah *Accidents Compensation and the Law* (Cane, ed) (6th edn, 1999) ch 1.
2 See the *Report of the Royal Commission* (Cmnd 7054–I), para 78, table 5. It possible that this figure might have increased somewhat in recent years, especially in view of the possibility of financing claims on a 'no win, no fee' basis.

Difficulties of proof

[32.04] In addition to the arbitrariness inherent in distinguishing between sufferers from disability on the ground of causation, the law of negligence can also operate capriciously, even within its accepted sphere of operation, due to the differing degrees of difficulty which discharging the onus of proof may provide for claimants. The difficulties are particularly acute where the accident happens very quickly; they can also be severe where the disability occurs very slowly.[1] The problems experienced where an accident takes place suddenly are, of course, typified by mishaps involving motor vehicles. The point was made vividly in para 991 of the Pearson Royal Commission,[2] which reads as follows:

'A retired county court judge told us that his "main difficulty in trying running down cases was the lack of certainty of the evidence. This uncertainty is largely attributable to the very nature of the accidents, the split second timing and the fallibility of the human brain in grasping accurate detail in a moment." Often the victim is in no position to look for witnesses himself. As one road accident victim, interviewed in a BBC television "Man Alive" report broadcast in May 1976, put it, "It's rather awkward if you're lying on the road with your leg sticking through your trousers".'

1   See J Stapleton *Disease and the Compensation Debate* (1986) chs 1–4. The latency of many industrial diseases, and the gradualness of their contraction, gives rise to particular difficulties for the tort system as far as causation and limitation of actions, are concerned. See above CHAPTER 3 (causation), and CHAPTER 28 (limitation).
2   Cmnd 7054–I, p 211.

Insurance and the moral basis of negligence

[32.05]   Were it not for the existence of liability insurance, the usefulness in practice of the tort of negligence would long ago have been reduced to vanishing point. There is little point in suing a defendant who would be unable to pay damages even if the litigation were successful. But once it is conceded that the defendant will not be obliged to pay the damages himself, the justification for predicating liability only upon fault becomes less apparent. Indeed, as was pointed out in the previous chapter, use of the notion of the 'reasonable man' so as to render the test for fault 'objective' would in many cases be unacceptable; were it not for recognition of the fact that the defendant will not have to pay the damages himself, and that little or no stigma of personal culpability will attach to him. Only on this basis is it acceptable that accidents caused by learner drivers,[1] or stroke victims,[2] which the defendants in question could not have avoided causing, can give rise to tortious liability. Thus, Professor J A Jolowicz once expressed the view that:[3]

> 'The essential justification for the principle of liability for fault and its apparent logical corollary that, special cases apart, there should be no liability without fault, is to be found in ... ideas ... which belong to a morality which, for better or worse, is no longer capable of being given practical effect in any but exceptional cases.'

1   See *Nettleship v Weston [1971] 2 QB 691, [1971] 3 All ER 581, CA.*
2   See *Roberts v Ramsbotham [1980] 1 All ER 7, [1980] 1 WLR 823.*
3   See J A Jolowicz 'Compensation for Personal Injury and Fault' in D Allen, C Bourn and J Holyoak (eds) *Accident Compensation after Pearson* (1979) p 40.

The search for coherence

[32.06]   In recent years a lively philosophical debate has arisen, particularly in North America, around the question whether the law of tort in fact possesses any underlying coherence, given its apparently conflicting aims and purposes[1]. In Aristotelian terms it is a branch of the law which appears to move uneasily between giving effect to the claims of corrective justice on one hand, and competing considerations of distributive justice on the other. The debate will go on, but any attempt to deduce radical prescriptive solutions from exchanges conducted at such a high level of abstraction must be regarded with caution. Reform should be driven by practical considerations, albeit with an internally consistent agenda, and the possibility that an institution which has developed pragmatically over time does possess a coherence, of a kind which has yet to be fully appreciated, should not be lightly dismissed[2]. As Lord Hoffman put it in *Reeves v Commissioner of Police*[3]:

> 'The law of torts is not just a matter of simple morality but contains many strands of policy, not all of them consistent with each other, which reflect the complexity of life'.

¹   The views of many of the leading protagonists down to 1995 are conveniently collected in *Philosophical Foundations of Tort Law* (Owen, ed) (Oxford). See also *Philosophy and the Law of Torts* (Postema, ed) (Cambridge, 2001).

²   For an intriguing suggestion that the notion of 'complementarity', as formulated by the physicist Niels Bohr in the context of quantum theory, could provide a basis for perceiving harmony in the coexistence of apparently conflicting values in tort see Izhak Englard *The Philosophy of Tort Law*, Dartmouth (Aldershot, 1992) ch 5, and the same author's 'Complementarity and Pluralism' in *Philosophical Foundations of Tort Law* (Owen, ed) (Oxford, 1995). See also David Howarth 'Three Forms of Responsibility: On the Relationship between Tort Law and the Welfare State' [2001] 60 CLJ 553 contending for the existence of a higher degree of consistency than is sometimes supposed between concepts of individual and collective responsibility.

³   See *[1999] 3 All ER 897* at 906.

B Various proposals for reform

The Pearson Commission

Terms of reference

[32.07]   The Royal Commission on Civil Liability and Compensation for Personal Injury, chaired by Lord Pearson, was set up in the 1970s, partly as a result of public concern over the Thalidomide tragedy, and reported in 1978. Although its main recommendations have never been implemented, the Commission's wide-ranging investigation still remains a necessary starting point for discussion of the possibility of change. Its terms of reference were as follows:

> 'To consider to what extent, in what circumstances and by what means compensation should be payable in respect of death or personal injury (including ante-natal injury) suffered by any person—
>
> a.   in the course of employment;
>
> b.   through the use of a motor vehicle or other means of transport;
>
> c.   through the manufacture, supply or use of goods or services;
>
> d.   on premises belonging to or occupied by another or
>
> e.   otherwise through the act or omission of another where compensation under the present law is recoverable only on proof of fault or under the rules of strict liability,
>
> having regard to the cost and other implications of the arrangements for the recovery of compensation, whether by way of compulsory insurance or otherwise.'

For the purposes of exposition in outline, the main recommendations of the Royal Commission can be divided into two parts: first, their proposal for a special statutory scheme to compensate road accident victims; and, secondly, their proposals for reform of the law of tort itself.

(i) Road accident scheme

[32.08]   The Commission recommended that a special scheme should be introduced, within the social security system, to provide compensation, without the necessity of proving fault required by the common law of tort, for victims of road accidents. The scheme would be modelled on the industrial injuries scheme, which already provided more generous earnings-related benefits for those injured at work than those obtainable under ordinary social security welfare provisions, and which included compensation for non-pecuniary loss in the form of payments for loss of faculty. The Commission proposed that the scheme should be paid for by all motorists through the medium of a levy on the cost of petrol. In 1991 the Lord Chancellor's Department outlined proposals for a limited scheme of no-fault compensation for victims of minor road accidents, in response to a suggestion made by the Civil Justice Review in 1988, but the proposals bore little resemblance to the Pearson recommendations. They would have been funded not by a levy on petrol, but through higher motor insurance premiums, and they would only have allowed victims to claim for personal injuries without proving fault up to a very modest limit of £2,500.[1] Neither these proposals, nor the earlier proposals of the Pearson Commission, have been implemented.

[1] See E Gilvarry (1991) LS Gaz, 22 May.

(ii) Reform of tort

[32.09] The Commission recommended that benefits received by plaintiffs from the social security system should henceforth be offset against any damages in tort which they subsequently recovered. In effect, the substance of this proposal has been implemented by legislation.[1] But his implementation was of course not combined with the introduction of a major scheme of greatly increased social security payments for victims of road accidents, which Pearson had recommended. If it had been, the result would have been a substantial disincentive to the mounting of litigation for negligence at common law in such cases.

[1] See now the *Social Security (Recovery of Benefits) Act 1997*; and CHAPTER 25 above.

Further recommendations

[32.10] Two further recommendations were intended to deal with the view that there the tort system tended to over-compensate the less seriously injured, and under-compensate the victims of serious injury. The Commission proposed that no damages for non-pecuniary loss (ie pain and suffering and loss of amenity) should be recoverable for the first three months after the injury. In the case of the seriously injured, changes should be made in the method of calculating their future pecuniary loss so as to ensure that the amounts which they were awarded would be more generous.[1] The Commission also recommended that, that unless he could satisfy the court that in his special circumstances a lump sum would be more appropriate, a plaintiff should be obliged to receive compensation for future pecuniary loss in the form of periodic payments. Since periodic payments made by way of 'structured settlements' are now a major feature of the resolution of serious personal injury claims[2], this proposal has, in a sense, begun to be implemented in practice. In addition, the Commission recommended that certain situations should be identified by statute as involving exceptional risk, and that provision should be made for the imposition in such cases of strict rather than fault-based liability. The Commission also proposed the introduction of a system of strict liability for defective products.[3]

[1] See now *Wells v Wells [1998] 3 All ER 481, HL*; and CHAPTER 25 above.
[2] See CHAPTER 25 above.

Criticism of the report

[32.11] The report of the Pearson Commission met with a hostile reception from critics of many differing persuasions.[1] Such critics found common ground in perceiving that the report was fundamentally flawed by the lack of a coherent overall strategy. Those opposed to the preservation of tort as a compensation system for personal injury at all regretted the fact that the Commission placed a narrow interpretation upon its terms of reference; thereby preventing itself from considering the possibility of implementing a comprehensive accident compensation scheme, along the lines of that in New Zealand,[2] involving the abolition of tort in this area. Others considered that the somewhat casually advanced proposals for the extension of strict liability in tort had not been thought through, and that they had profound implications for the whole structure and philosophy of civil liability. The Commission seemed to be unaware of these implications, and indeed of their doubtful consistency with the main body of the report, which contemplated the preservation of negligence as a necessary condition for the imposition of tort liability in the majority of cases. The singling out of road accident victims for a special compensation scheme, based on a generous regime of increased social security benefits, was criticised as an undesirably ad hoc proposal, unfair to those who suffer in other situations. It would have increased rather than simplified the complexity of the overall picture as regards compensation, and retarded rather than advanced progress towards comprehensive reform. The earnings-related benefits under the proposed scheme, to be paid for by a flat rate levy on petrol, would also have unduly favoured the better off at the expense of the less well off.[3] Although some of the less radical proposals have been put into effect,[4] albeit in modified forms, it is hardly surprising that, in view of the reception which the report received, the main thrust of the Commission's recommendations have not been implemented and the report is destined to gather dust.

¹ See, generally, the papers collected in D Allen, C Bourn and J Holyoak (eds) *Accident Compensation after Pearson* (1979), especially those by Professor J A Jolowicz and Professor P S Atiyah. See also J Fleming 'The Pearson Report: Its "Strategy" ' (1979) 42 MLR 249.
² See below at para [32.12].
³ See D R Harris 'An Appraisal of the Pearson Strategy' in D Allen, C Bourn and J Holyoak (eds) *Accident Compensation after Pearson* (1979).
⁴ See the *Administration of Justice Act 1982*, and CHAPTERS 24, 25, and 26 above. Of course a system of strict liability for defective products has now also been introduced: see CHAPTER 20 above.

The New Zealand scheme

[32.12] By far the most radical reform in this area, in any common law country, was introduced in New Zealand in 1972.[1] It took the form of a comprehensive state compensation system for those who suffer personal injury as a result of accidents, provided compensation for both pecuniary and non-pecuniary loss, and actually abolished the common law tort action for such accident victims. The relevant legislation is now to be found in the country's *Accident Rehabilitation and Compensation Insurance Act* of 1992. This Act makes substantial changes to the nature of the scheme, which in its relatively generous original form was proving difficult to fund, and reduces the benefits which it provides. The new scheme in practice resembles a compulsory insurance system. Premiums are paid by drivers, medical personnel, employers and earners. The scheme also derives income from a levy on the price of petrol and from general taxation. Claimants who suffer lost earnings as a result of their injuries are awarded 80% of their losses, on a periodic payments basis, up to a statutory maximum. But the lump sum payments for non-pecuniary loss such as pain and suffering, which the scheme originally provided, have been abolished and replaced by an 'independence allowance', where a claimant suffers a degree of disability of at least 10%. The scheme is administered by the Accident Rehabilitation and Compensation Insurance Corporation, and is relatively straightforward to oper-ate; the victim making his claim by seeing a doctor and filling out an official form, copies of which are readily available. It is possible to challenge, ultimately in the courts, rejection of a claim.

[1] See D Harris 'Accident Compensation in New Zealand: A Comprehensive Insurance System' (1974) 37 MLR 361. See also Report of the *Royal Commission on Civil Liability and Compensation for Personal Injury* (*Pearson*) (Cmnd 7054–III) vol 1, ch 10, and J Holyoak in D Allen, C Bourn and J Holyoak (eds) *Accident Compensation after Pearson* (1979) pp 180–196.

Bold experiment

[32.13] Even in its modified form, the New Zealand scheme represents a bold experiment,[1] but it is limited in its scope: being largely confined to 'accidents'[2] and 'medical misadventures'[3], and not extending to those who suffer disability as a result of disease, except through 'occupational disease'.[4] The cost implications of extending it to all disabled people proved prohibitive even for the scheme in its original form. Moreover, the funding difficulties which the scheme has experienced only serve to highlight the obvious point that providing compensation to everyone affected by injury or illness, on the same scale as tort provides for a 'lucky' few accident victims, is always likely to be beyond the capacity of any country's economy. But in so far as the New Zealand scheme preserves discrimination between the disabled, based on the *cause* of their disabilities, it necessarily falls short of the ideal of those who wish to see such discrimination disappear. On the other hand, the more conservatively minded will have doubts about the wisdom, or acceptability in this country, of outright abolition of the common law action for negligence in the majority of personal injury cases. It is to be noted that one member of the Pearson Commission observed that, even if it had not felt constrained by its terms of reference, it is doubtful whether the Commission would have recommended a scheme along the New Zealand lines for the United Kingdom.[5] Even in New Zealand itself, concern has been expressed about the 'moral hazard' effect upon those who would otherwise be defendants, of removing the right to sue for negligence, particularly in the area of medical mishaps.[6]

[1] For a review of the early years of the scheme's operation, see T Ison *Accident Compensation: A Commentary on the New Zealand Scheme* (1980).
[2] See the *Accident Rehabilitation and Compensation Insurance Act 1992, s 3*.
[3] See the *Accident Rehabilitation and Compensation Insurance Act 1992, s 5*.
[4] See the *Accident Rehabilitation and Compensation Insurance Act 1992, s 7*.
[5] See N Marsh 'The Pearson Report on Civil Liability and Compensation for Death or Personal Injury' (1979) 95 LQR 513 at 517.
[6] See citations in M A McGregor Vennell and J Manning 'Accident Compensation' [1992] NZULR 1, pp 6–7.

Proposals by members of the Oxford Centre for Socio-Legal Studies

[32.14] In the period 1976–79 the Centre for Socio-Legal Studies at Wolfson College, Oxford carried out a major survey of victims of illness and injury, involving several thousand such people. The results of the survey, and the recommendations of the research team, were published in 1984 in a volume entitled *Compensation and Support for Illness and Injury*. Unlike that of the Pearson Royal Commission, the Oxford inquiry was frankly intended from its inception to shift the focus of attention away from the causes of *accidents* and towards 'the *consequences* of mental and physical disabilities, whether temporary or permanent'.[1] Although it was already well known that those disabled by illness greatly outnumber those who suffer serious accidental injury, the inquiry produced results which highlighted the differing long-term effects of the two kinds of misfortune: victims of illness being overall more likely than accident victims to suffer long-term incapacity. It also produced striking evidence of the imbalance within the tort system itself as regards different categories of accident victim. It to some extent weakened the case for singling out road accident victims for generous treatment, as Pearson had recommended, by pointing out that they are already the most successful category of accident victims under tort. Thus, according to the Group's findings, between one quarter and one third of those injured in road accidents recovered tort damages. The equivalent proportion of those injured at work was around one fifth. But the proportion of victims of other types of accident who succeeded in tort, albeit including those who would presumably have had little or no chance of proving negligence, was less than one in fifty. As far as the relative consequences of accident and illness are concerned, it appeared that victims of illness, consistent with their greater tendency to suffer from long-term incapacity, used the 'benefits in kind' provided by social services, such as help in the home, nearly three times as much as did victims of accident; the elderly, inevitably, making particular use of these services. It also appeared that illness was responsible for twice as much absence from work as accident.

[1]   D Harris et al *Compensation and Support for Illness and Injury* (1984) p 3.

Group's recommendations

[32.15] On the basis of their findings, the Oxford group recommended that 'the future policy-maker should plan to phase out all existing compensation systems which favour accident victims (or any category of them) over illness victims',[1] and hence that the tort action should be abolished in this area. Thus, *cause* should cease to be a relevant factor in awarding compensation for illness and injury, and benefits should instead be based entirely on *need*. The *financing* of the compensation scheme should, however, 'incorporate some measure of risk relationship',[2] possibly by differential levies on employers with bad accident records, for example. The administration of the compensation system would inevitably be primarily a matter for the state, but there could still be scope for the private sector, both in financing parts of the scheme, particularly where relatively short-term losses were involved, and in providing top-up insurance for those who wanted it. In particular, the private market could have a role in insuring against non-pecuniary losses, such as pain and suffering; since the group assumed that public funds would not be available to compensate for such losses, at least for the foreseeable future. The essential strategy of the Oxford group was therefore to press for *income support*, for all victims of illness and accident, as the highest public priority in this area. Thus, benefits would be earnings-related for earners; particular importance being attached to restricting 'the extent to which disabled people are forced to rely on means-tested (supplementary) benefits'.[3] The new scheme should also be weighted to ensure a greater concentration of resources on the provision of benefits to the relatively few long-term disabled rather than those whose losses are short-term. The group thus concluded as follows: 'We believe that the damages system for death and personal injury should be abolished as soon as improvements in sick pay and social security provision produce a rational, coherent, and integrated system of compensation for illness and injury.'[4]

1   D Harris et al *Compensation and Support for Illness and Injury* (1984) p 327.
2   As above, p 341.
3   As above, p 338.
4   As above, p 328.

Changing the burden of proof?

[32.16] A change sometimes proposed, in order to streamline the operation of the law of tort, is to alter the burden of proving negligence in certain situations. The Pearson Commission noted[1] that, as early as 1932, a Bill was introduced into Parliament, with government support, to reverse the burden of proof in situations in which cyclists or pedestrians were killed or injured in accidents involving motor vehicles. The Bill did not, of course, become law, but some members of the Royal Commission were apparently impressed by the arguments in favour of such a measure. It is in the road accident field that the operation of the law of negligence is popularly supposed to be particularly unsatisfactory, despite the relatively high success rate of claimants. A considerable proportion of the notoriously high administration costs of tort are probably accounted for by the difficulty of proving negligence in such cases. Reversing of the burden of proof against drivers of motor vehicles, in cases involving collisions causing injury to other road users, would be likely to increase the number of claims settled without trial and on terms more favourable to the non-motorist accident victim.

1   See the *Royal Commission on Civil Liability and Compensation for Personal Injury* (Cmnd 7054–I) paras 1069–1075.

Merits further consideration

[32.17] The Pearson Commission was eventually against recommending a change in the burden of proof, on the ground that it would cut across their plan for introducing a comprehensive scheme of compensation for road accident victims outside tort. But the Commission noted that such 'a reversal of the burden of proof appears to operate satisfactorily in more than one European jurisdiction'.[1] Moreover, such a reversal also operates in the common law jurisdiction of Ontario. *Section 167* of *Ontario's Highway Traffic Act*[2] is worth setting out in full:

'(1) When loss or damage is sustained by any person by reason of a motor vehicle on a highway, the onus of proof that the loss or damage did not arise through the neglect or improper conduct of the owner or driver of the motor vehicle is upon the owner or driver.

(2) This section does not apply in case of a collision between motor vehicles ... nor to an action brought by a passenger in a motor vehicle in respect of any injuries sustained by him while a passenger.'

It is submitted that, notwithstanding the view of the Pearson Commission, the possibility of introducing a provision of this kind into English law merits further consideration.[3]

1   Cmnd 7054–I, para 1072.

² RSO 1980, ch 198.
³ See J Fleming 'The Pearson Report: Its "Strategy" ' (1979) 42 MLR 249 at 262.

Extending strict liability?

[32.18] A more radical method of preserving yet reforming the law of tort would be to extend and restructure the incidence of strict liability. This could reduce the amount of litigation caused in negligence by the need to prove fault, at least provided the fault issue was not allowed too readily to re-enter through the back door via defences such as contributory negligence.[1] But a badly structured regime of strict liability could lead to an increase in litigation, if too much scope existed for demarcation disputes as to which situations did, and which did not, attract the liability.[2] A rationale for the extension of strict liability has been put forward by a number of economic analysts, in particular Professor Calabresi[3] in America, who advocated it as a vehicle for helping to ensure that the full costs of risk-creating activities are 'internalised': that is to say, placed on the shoulders of those who benefit from the activities in question. In theory, it was argued, such an approach could help to deter the creation of avoidable danger through the operation of the price mechanism.

¹ See J A Jolowicz 'Compensation for Personal Injury and Fault' in D Allen, C Bourn, and J Holyoak (eds) *Accident Compensation after Pearson* (1979) pp 60–61.
² See P Atiyah 'What Now?' in D Allen, C Bourn and J Holyoak (eds) *Accident Compensation after Pearson* (1979) pp 234–238.
³ *The Cost of Accidents: A Legal and Economic Analysis* (1970).

Difficulties and attractions

[32.19] There are, however, considerable difficulties with this particular justification for the imposition of strict liability, not least the many other factors which can influence the operation of the market and thereby greatly diminish the significance of the imposition of legal liability for damage caused.[1] Moreover, any regime of strict liability based on presumed attribution of risk, or 'enterprise liability' as it is some-times called, could raise difficult questions of causation and of which risks should be attributed to which activities.[2] The Pearson Commission[3] put forward proposals for the introduction by statute of schemes of strict liability for activities and situations regarded as particularly hazardous, but these have not been implemented. Neverthe-less, the introduction by statute of a strict liability regime for defective products[4] constitutes, at least in theory, a major reform of the law away from negligence principles. Indeed, despite the potential difficulties involved, and without subscribing to the intricate economic theories advanced by some of its supporters, it is possible to see considerable attractions in the extension of strict liability as an appropriate strategy for reform of the law; in a manner fundamentally different from the abolition of tort and its replacement by state welfare provision. As Professor J A Jolowicz a quarter of a century ago:[5]

> 'Accidents will continue to happen despite the exercise of care by all concerned; it is essential that we learn to accept responsibility for the consequences of our decisions and our actions, not only of our faults, and that lesson a properly constructed system of civil liability, but not a system of social security, can help to teach us.'[6]

¹ See generally P Atiyah *Accidents, Compensation and the Law* (Cane, ed) (6th edn, 1999) ch 18.

2 See J Stapleton *Disease and the Compensation Debate,* Oxford, 1986 chs 5 and 6: 'Ironically ... the distinction between risks to be ascribed to the enterprise and those which are not, still falls to be decided in complex and costly case by case assessments of attribution/responsibility, etc. comparable to those which the shift to strict liability was designed to avoid' (p 95). See also T Ison *The Forensic Lottery* (1967) pp 37–41; Henderson 'The Boundary Problems of Enterprise Liability' (1982) 41 MdLR 659.

3 *Royal Commission on Civil Liability and Compensation for Personal Injury* (Cmnd 7054–I) ch 31.

4 See CHAPTER 20 above.

5 'Compensation for Personal Injury and Fault' in D Allen, C Bourn and J Holyoak (eds) *Accident Compensation after Pearson* (1979) p 78.

6 See also Professor Jolowicz' article 'Liability for Accidents' [1968] CLJ 50.

C Conclusions

Significance of intuition

[32.20] Two questions underly the debate about reform of the law of tort relating to personal injuries. First, is it ever legitimate to distinguish between victims of misfortune according to the manner in which their plight was *caused*? Secondly, is it desirable to *abolish* civil liability (whether fault-based or not) for personal injury? It is clear from the way in which public pressure has led to the creation of ad hoc compensation schemes in particular situations, and the response to charitable appeals following major disasters, that greater sympathy is felt for some sufferers from misfortune than for others. No doubt this is due in part to the publicity given by the media to particularly dramatic cases. Nevertheless, it seems not improbable that the trauma of disability through accident or work-induced illness is more likely to evoke feelings of anger and concern, on the part of the immediate victim and others, than the development of equivalent disabilities by natural causes. Part of this reaction may be due to a retributive instinct,[1] which some reformers are apt to regard as primitive, or even attempt unconvincingly to explain away by arguing that it is a response which reflects the concepts of the legal system rather than the other way round.[2] Obviously, the law should not give effect to all the prejudices which may be discernible in the popular will. But nor can it afford wholly to ignore public opinion on matters which arguably reflect fundamental intuitions[3].

1 Cf S Ehrenzweig 'A Psychoanalysis of Negligence' (1953) 40 Northwestern Univ LR 855.

2 See S Lloyd-Bostock 'Fault and Liability for Accidents: the Accident Victim's Perspective' in D Harris et al *Compensation and Support for Illness and Injury* (1984) ch 4.

3 The impossibility of wholly eliminating intuitive preferences in this area is intriguingly illustrated by the fact that the Oxford group, which otherwise favoured uniform treatment for all the disabled, was prepared to admit that *one* exception might be justified, namely 'battle casualties, that is, the provision of special pensions for those injured in actual armed hostilities, which is the exceptional situation where society may compel citizens to be the front-line of defence against large-scale, organized attack': D Harris et al *Compensation and Support for Illness and Injury* (1984) p 336.

Role of tort in a free society

[32.21] The fact that only a relatively small number negligence of cases reach trial, and that in many instances insurance companies can effectively choose which ones will do so,[1] does not detract from the fundamental importance of the preservation in a free society of the right of any citizen for his own purposes to sue, or even with appropriate attendant publicity merely to *threaten* to sue, in the independent courts of the country, the government itself; or any individual or organisation whose actions he believes have caused him harm.[2] Moreover, on specific issues such as the quantum of damages in personal injury cases, decisions reached by the courts can provide a valuable benchmark against which the levels of benefit provided by the welfare state can be judged, even though the impossibility of providing compensation at tort levels for all is admitted.[3]

1   See generally H Genn *Hard Bargaining* (1987).
2   Cf Linden 'Tort Law as Ombudsman' (1973) 51 Can Bar Rev 155.
3   The contrast is vividly, if ironically, illustrated by the deliberate reduction in compensation for criminal injuries below common law levels and the introduction instead of a tariff system: see CHAPTER 31 above.

Abolition opposed

[32.22]   It is noteworthy that the abolition of tort is usually opposed by trades unions. This is sometimes derided as simply reflecting a desire to preserve an inducement to membership by providing legal services. But this reaction seems too cynical; it has been dismissed as 'turning history on its head'.[1] The arguments were well put by in 1979 by the then Legal Officer of the General and Municipal Workers' Union as follows:[2]

> 'The practical advantages ... of retaining the right to make a common law claim alongside a satisfactory state system are at least three-fold. First, it is usually difficult to make breakthroughs in a state scheme to include illnesses not previously accepted as employment-caused, eg radiation cases. The advantage of a tort claim is that individuals backed by their unions can establish a causal link, get publicity and thus put pressure on the state scheme to keep it up-to-date. This may be particularly necessary when the state or a state corporation is the employer concerned. Secondly, a worker may want to establish that his employer was to blame for his illness or disability. Even a good state system of compensation with some degree of differential contributions is unlikely to apportion blame to an individual employer. Thirdly, in cases of unjust refusal of benefit a worker has another avenue through which he or she may obtain compensation.'

1   See T Gill 'Pearson: Implications for Victims of Industrial Accidents' in D Allen, C Bourn and J Holyoak (eds) *Accident Compensation after Pearson* (1979) p 158.
2   As above.

Pruned and healthy?

[32.23]   The climate in which any discussion of reform of the law of tort now takes place is very different from that of a generation ago, when the Pearson Commission reported, and continuing expansion of the welfare state was still widely taken for granted. Recognition of the consequences of such expansion for public finance, allied to increased emphasis upon individual responsibility, makes unlikely any reform which would require a significant increase in public expenditure. What then is to be done? A useful objective might be to bring about some reduction in the role of negligence by expanding the scope of strict liability. Attention might also be given to the possibility of reversing the burden of proving negligence in some situations. In a few special areas, of which that involving medical accidents is probably the most conspicuous, it could well be appropriate to develop compensation systems independ-

[32.23] *Reform?*

ent of legal process. It is possible that a pruned and healthier common law of negligence might then emerge, which would be seen to have a vital role in the legal system of a free society.

Index

C

T

U